THE FIFTH BOOK OF MOSES, CALLED

DEUTERONOMY

THE PREACHER'S OUTLINE & SERMON BIBLE®

THE FIFTH BOOK OF MOSES, CALLED

DEUTERONOMY

THE PREACHER'S OUTLINE & SERMON BIBLE®

OLD TESTAMENT

KING JAMES VERSION

Leadership Ministries Worldwide
Chattanooga, TN

**THE PREACHER'S OUTLINE & SERMON BIBLE® - DEUTERONOMY
KING JAMES VERSION**

Copyright © 1996 by ALPHA-OMEGA MINISTRIES, INC.

All Rights Reserved

All other Bible study aids, references, indexes, reference materials
Copyright © 1991 by Alpha-Omega Ministries, Inc.

**All rights reserved. No part of this publication may be reproduced, stored
in a retrieval system, or transmitted in any form or by any means—electronic,
mechanical, photo-copy, recording, or otherwise—without the prior
permission of the copyright owners.**

Previous Editions of **The Preacher's Outline & Sermon Bible®**,
New International Version NT   Copyright © 1998
King James Version NT   Copyright © 1991, 1996, 2000
by Alpha-Omega Ministries, Inc.

Please address all requests for information or permission to:
Leadership Ministries Worldwide
PO Box 21310
Chattanooga, TN 37424-0310
Ph.# (423) 855-2181   FAX (423) 855-8616   E-Mail info@outlinebible.org
http://www.outlinebible.org

Library of Congress Catalog Card Number: 96-75921
ISBN Softbound Edition: 978-1-57407-146-7
ISBN Deluxe 3-Ring Edition: 978-1-57407-147-4

**LEADERSHIP MINISTRIES WORLDWIDE
CHATTANOOGA, TN**

Printed in the United States of America

11   12   13   14   15   16   17   18   19   20

LEADERSHIP MINISTRIES WORLDWIDE

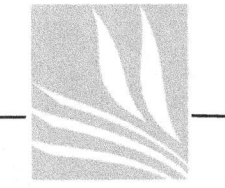

DEDICATED

To all the men and women of the world who preach and teach the Gospel of our Lord Jesus Christ and to the Mercy and Grace of God

- Demonstrated to us in Christ Jesus our Lord.

  "In whom we have redemption through His blood, the forgiveness of sins, according to the riches of His grace." (Ep.1:7)

- Out of the mercy and grace of God, His Word has flowed. Let every person know that God will have mercy upon him, forgiving and using him to fulfill His glorious plan of salvation.

  "For God so loved the world, that he gave His only begotten Son, that whosoever believeth in Him should not perish, but have everlasting life. For God sent not his son into the world to condemn the world, but that the world through him might be saved." (Jn.3:16-17)

  "For this is good and acceptable in the sight of God our Saviour; who will have all men to be saved, and to come unto the knowledge of the truth." (1 Ti.2:3-4)

The Preacher's Outline & Sermon Bible®

is written for God's servants to use in their study, teaching, and preaching of God's Holy Word...

- to share the Word of God with the world.
- to help believers, both ministers and laypersons, in their understanding, preaching, and teaching of God's Word.
- to do everything we possibly can to lead men, women, boys, and girls to give their hearts and lives to Jesus Christ and to secure the eternal life that He offers.
- to do all we can to minister to the needy of the world.
- to give Jesus Christ His proper place, the place the Word gives Him. Therefore, no work of Leadership Ministries Worldwide—no Outline Bible Resources—will ever be personalized.

ACKNOWLEDGMENTS AND BIBLIOGRAPHY

Every child of God is precious to the Lord and deeply loved. And every child as a servant of the Lord touches the lives of those who come in contact with him or his ministry. The writing ministries of the following servants have touched this work, and we are grateful that God brought their writings our way. We hereby acknowledge their ministry to us, being fully aware that there are many others down through the years whose writings have touched our lives and who deserve mention, but whose names have faded from our memory. May our wonderful Lord continue to bless the ministries of these dear servants—and the ministries of us all—as we diligently labor to reach the world for Christ and to meet the desperate needs of those who suffer so much.

THE REFERENCE WORKS

Archer, Gleason L. Jr. *A Survey of Old Testament Introduction.* Chicago, IL: Moody Bible Institute of Chicago, 1974.

Atlas of the World. Hammond Concise Edition. Maplewood, NJ: Hammond Incorporated, MCMXCIII.

Baker's Dictionary of Theology. Everett F. Harrison, Editor-in-Chief. Grand Rapids, MI: Baker Book House, 1960.

Barker, William P. *Everyone in the Bible.* Westwood, NJ: Fleming H. Revell Co., 1966.

Brown, Francis. *The New Brown-Driver-Briggs-Gesenius Hebrew-English Lexicon.* Peabody, MA: Hendrickson Publishers, 1979.

Cruden's Complete Concordance of the Old & New Testament. Philadelphia, PA: The John C. Winston Co., 1930.

Dake, Finis Jennings. *Dake's Annotated Reference Bible, The Holy Bible.* Lawrenceville, GA: Dake Bible Sales, Inc., 1963.

Funk & Wagnalls Standard Desk Dictionary. Lippincott & Crowell, Publishers, 1980, Vol.2.

Geisler, Norman. *A Popular Survey of the Old Testament.* Grand Rapids, MI: Baker Book House, 1977.

Good News Bible. Old Testament: © American Bible Society, 1976. New Testament: © American Bible Society, 1966, 1971, 1976. Collins World.

Good News for Modern Man, the New Testament. New York, NY: American Bible Society, 1971.

Good, Joseph. *Rosh HaShanah and the Messianic Kingdom to Come.* Pt. Arthur, TX: Hatikva Ministries, 1989.

Harrison, Roland Kenneth. *Introduction to the Old Testament.* Grand Rapids, MI: Eerdmans Publishing Company, 1969.

Josephus, Flavius. *Complete Works.* Grand Rapids, MI: Kregel Publications, 1981.

Kohlenberger, John R. III. *The Interlinear NIV Hebrew-English Old Testament.* Grand Rapids, MI: Zondervan Publishing House, 1987.

Kouffman, Donald T. *The Dictionary of Religious Terms.* Westwood, NJ: Fleming H. Revell Co., 1967.

Life Application® Bible. Wheaton, IL: Tyndale House Publishers, Inc., 1991.

Life Application® Study Bible. New International Version. Tyndale House Publishers, Inc.: Wheaton, IL 1991, and Zondervan Publishing House: Grand Rapids, MI, 1984.

Lindsell, Harold and Woodbridge, Charles J. *A Handbook of Christian Truth.* Westwood, NJ: Fleming H. Revell Company, A Division of Baker Book House, 1953.

Lipis, Joan R. *Celebrate Passover Haggadah.* San Francisco, CA: Purple Pomegranate Productions, 1993.

Living Quotations For Christians. Edited by Sherwood Eliot Wirt and Kersten Beckstrom. New York, NY: Harper & Row, Publishers, 1974.

Lockyer, Herbert. *All the Books and Chapters of the Bible.* Grand Rapids, MI: Zondervan Publishing House, 1966.

———. *All the Men of the Bible.* Grand Rapids, MI: Zondervan Publishing House, 1958.

———. *All the Miracles of the Bible.* Grand Rapids, MI: Zondervan Publishing House, 1961.

———. *All the Parables of the Bible.* Grand Rapids, MI: Zondervan Publishing House, 1963.

———. *The Women of the Bible.* Grand Rapids, MI: Zondervan Publishing House, 1967.

Martin, Alfred. *Survey of the Scriptures*, Part I, II, III. Chicago, IL: Moody Bible Institute of Chicago, 1961.

McDowell, Josh. *Evidence That Demands A Verdict*, Vol.1. San Bernardino, CA: Here's Life Publishers, Inc., 1979.

Miller, Madeleine S. & J. Lane. *Harper's Bible Dictionary.* New York, NY: Harper & Row Publishers, 1961.

Nave, Orville J. *Nave's Topical Bible.* Nashville, TN: The Southwestern Company. Copyright © by J.B. Henderson, 1921.

New American Standard Bible, Reference Edition. La Habra, CA: The Lockman Foundation, 1975.

New American Standard Bible, Updated Edition. La Habra, CA: The Lockman Foundation, 1995.

New Bible Dictionary, 3rd Edition. Leicester, England: Universities & Colleges Christian Fellowship, 1996.

New International Version Study Bible. Grand Rapids, MI: Zondervan Bible Publishers, 1985.

New Living Translation, Holy Bible. Wheaton, IL: Tyndale House Publishers, Inc., 1996.

NIV Exhaustive Concordance. Grand Rapids, MI: Zondervan Corporation, 1990.

Orr, William. *How We May Know That God Is.* Wheaton, IL: Van Kampen Press, n.d.

Owens, John Joseph. *Analytical Key to the Old Testament*, Vols.1, 2, 3. Grand Rapids, MI: Baker Book House, 1989.

Payne, J. Barton. *Encyclopedia of Biblical Prophecy.* New York, NY: Harper & Row, Publishers, 1973.

ACKNOWLEDGMENTS AND BIBLIOGRAPHY
THE REFERENCE WORKS
(CONTINUED)

Pilgrim Edition, Holy Bible. New York, NY: Oxford University Press, 1952.

Ridout, Samuel. *Lectures on the Tabernacle.* New York, NY: Loizeaux Brothers, Inc., 1914.

Roget's 21st Century Thesaurus, Edited by Barbara Ann Kipfer. New York, NY: Dell Publishing, 1992.

Rosen, Ceil and Moishe. *Christ In The Passover.* Chicago, IL: Moody Press, 1978.

Slemming, C.W. *Made According To Pattern.* Fort Washington, PA: Christian Literature Crusade, 1983.

Smith, William. *Smith's Bible Dictionary.* Peabody, MA: Hendrickson Publishers, n.d.

Soltau, Henry W. *The Holy Vessels And Furniture Of The Tabernacle.* Grand Rapids, MI: Kregel Publications, 1971.

———. *The Tabernacle The Priesthood And The Offerings.* Grand Rapids, MI: Kregel Publications, 1972.

Stone, Nathan J. *Names of God.* Chicago, IL: Moody Press, 1944.

Strong, James. *Strong's Exhaustive Concordance of the Bible.* Nashville, TN: Thomas Nelson, Inc., 1990.

———. *The Tabernacle Of Israel.* Grand Rapids, MI: Kregel Publications, 1987.

The Amplified Bible. Scripture taken from THE AMPLIFIED BIBLE, Old Testament copyright © 1965, 1987 by the Zondervan Corporation. The Amplified New Testament copyright © 1958, 1987 by The Lockman Foundation. Used by permission.

The Evangelical Dictionary of Theology. Elwell, Walter A., Editor. Grand Rapids, MI: Baker Book House, 1984.

The Hebrew-Greek Key Study Bible, New International Version. Spiros Zodhiates, Th.D., Executive Editor. Chattanooga, TN: AMG Publishers, 1996.

The Holy Bible in Four Translations. Minneapolis, MN: Worldwide Publications. Copyright © The Iversen-Norman Associates: New York, NY, 1972.

The Interlinear Bible, Vol.1, 2, & 3. Translated by Jay P. Green, Sr. Grand Rapids, MI: Baker Book House Company, 1976.

The International Standard Bible Encyclopaedia, Edited by James Orr. Grand Rapids, MI: Eerdmans Publishing Company, 1939.

The NASB Greek/Hebrew Dictionary and Concordance. La Habra, CA: The Lockman Foundation, 1988.

The Nelson Study Bible, New King James Version. Nashville, TN: Thomas Nelson Publishers, Inc., 1997.

The New Compact Bible Dictionary. Edited by T. Alton Bryant. Grand Rapids, MI: Zondervan Publishing House, 1967. Used by permission of Zondervan Publishing House.

The New Scofield Reference Bible. Edited by C.I. Scofield. New York, NY: Oxford University Press, 1967.

The New Thompson Chain Reference Bible. Indianapolis, IN: B.B. Kirkbride Bible Co., Inc., 1964.

The Open Bible. Nashville, TN: Thomas Nelson Publishers, 1975.

The Quest Study Bible. New International Version. Grand Rapids, MI: Zondervan Publishing House, 1994.

The Zondervan Pictorial Encyclopedia of the Bible, Vol.1. Merrill C. Tenney, Editor. Grand Rapids, MI: Zondervan Publishing House, 1982.

Theological Wordbook of the Old Testament. Edited by R. Laird Harris. Chicago, IL: Moody Bible Institute of Chicago, 1980.

Unger, Merrill F. & William White, Jr. *Nelson's Expository Dictionary of the Old Testament.* Nashville, TN: Thomas Nelson Publishers, 1980.

Vine, W.E., Merrill F. Unger, William White, Jr. *Vine's Complete Expository Dictionary of Old and New Testament Words.* Nashville, TN: Thomas Nelson Publishers, 1985.

Webster's Seventh New Collegiate Dictionary. Springfield, MA: G. & C. Merriam Company, Publishers, 1971.

Wilson, William. *Wilson's Old Testament Word Studies.* McLean, VA: MacDonald Publishing Company, n.d.

Wood, Leon. *A Survey of Israel's History.* Grand Rapids, MI: Zondervan Publishing House, 1982.

Young, Edward J. *An Introduction to the Old Testament.* Grand Rapids, MI: Eerdmans Publishing Company, 1964.

Young, Robert. *Young's Analytical Concordance to the Bible.* Grand Rapids, MI: Eerdmans Publishing Company, n.d.

Zehr, Paul M. *Glimpses of the Tabernacle.* Lancaster, PA: Mennonite Information Center, 1976.

THE COMMENTARIES

Ackland, Donald F. *Studies in Deuteronomy.* Nashville, TN: Convention Press, 1964.

Anderson, Norman. *Issues of Life and Death.* London, England: Hodder & Stoughton Limited, 1977.

Barclay, William. *The Old Law & The New Law.* Edinburgh, Scotland: The Saint Andrew Press, 1972.

Barnes' Notes, Exodus to Esther. F.C. Cook, Editor. Grand Rapids, MI: Baker Book House, n.d.

Blair, Edward P. *Deuteronomy, Joshua.* "The Layman's Bible Commentary," Volume 5. Atlanta, GA: John Knox Press. © M.E. Bratcher, 1964.

Briscoe, Stuart. *The Ten Commandments.* Wheaton, IL: Harold Shaw Publishers, 1986.

Burroughs, P.E., D.D. *Old Testament Studies.* Nashville, TN: Sunday School Board, Southern Baptist Convention, 1915.

Acknowledgments and Bibliography
The Commentaries
(CONTINUED)

Bush, George. *Exodus*. Minneapolis, MN: Klock & Klock Christian Publishers, Inc., 1981.
Craigie, Peter C. *The Book of Deuteronomy*. "The New International Commentary on the Old Testament." Grand Rapids, MI: William B. Eerdmans Publishing Company, 1976.
Cumming, The Rev. John. *Sabbath Morning Readings on the Book of Deuteronomy*. London: John Farquhar Shaw, 1856. USA Publication by Klock & Klock Christian Publishers, Inc., 1982.
Dunnam, Maxie. *Mastering the Old Testament, Vol.2: Exodus*. Dallas, TX: Word Publishing, 1987.
Francisco, Clyde T. *The Book of Deuteronomy*. "Shield Bible Study Series." Grand Rapids, MI: Baker Book House Company, 1964.
Gill, John. *Gill's Commentary*, Vol.1. Grand Rapids, MI: Baker Book House, 1980.
Henry, Matthew. *Matthew Henry's Commentary*, 6 Volumes. Old Tappan, NJ: Fleming H. Revell Co., n.d.
Huey, F.B. Jr. *A Study Guide Commentary, Exodus*. Grand Rapids, MI: Zondervan Publishing House, 1977.
Keil-Delitzsch. *Commentary on the Old Testament*, Vol.1. Grand Rapids, MI: Eerdmans Publishing Company, n.d.s
Maclaren, Alexander. *Expositions of Holy Scripture*, 11 Vols. Grand Rapids, MI: Eerdmans Publishing Company, 1952-59.
Maxwell, John. *Mastering the Old Testament, Vol.5: Deuteronomy*. Dallas, TX: Word Publishing, 1987.
Mayes, A.D.H. *Deuteronomy*. "The New Century Bible Commentary." England: Marshall, Morgan & Scott (Publications) Ltd., 1979. USA Rights by Wm B. Eerdmans Publishing Company: Grand Rapids, MI.
McGee, J. Vernon. *Thru The Bible*, Vol.1. Nashville, TN: Thomas Nelson Publishers, 1981.
Pink, Arthur W. *The Ten Commandments*. Grand Rapids, MI: Baker Books, 1994.
Poole, Matthew. *Matthew Poole's Commentary on the Holy Bible*. Peabody, MA: Hendrickson Publishers, n.d.
Rogers, Adrian. *Ten Secrets For A Successful Family*. Wheaton, IL: Crossway Books, 1996.
Saphir, Adolph. *Christ and Israel*. Grand Rapids, MI: Kregel Publications, n.d.
Schultz, Samuel J. *Deuteronomy*. "Everyman's Bible Commentary." Chicago, IL: Moody Press, 1971.
Spurgeon, C.H. *Spurgeon's Sermon Notes. Genesis to Malachi*. Westwood, NJ: Fleming H. Revell Co., n.d.
Strauss, Lehman. *Devotional Studies in Galatians & Ephesians*. Neptune, NJ: Loizeaux Brothers, 1957.
The Expositor's Bible Commentary, Vol.3. Frank E. Gaebelein, Editor. Grand Rapids, MI: Zondervan Publishing House, 1990.
The Interpreter's Bible, 12 Vols. New York, NY: Abingdon Press, 1956.
The Pulpit Commentary. 23 Volumes. Edited by H.D.M. Spence & Joseph S. Exell. Grand Rapids, MI: Eerdmans Publishing Company, 1950.
Thomas, W.H. Griffith. *Through the Pentateuch Chapter by Chapter*. Grand Rapids, MI: Eerdmans Publishing Company, 1957.
Thompson, J.A. *Deuteronomy*. Leicester, England: Inter-Varsity Press, 1974.
Von Rad, Gerhard. *Deuteronomy*. Germany: SCM Press Ltd, 1966. USA Rights by The Westminster Press: Philadelphia, PA.
Wiersbe, Warren W. *Be Obedient*. Wheaton, IL: Victor Books, 1991.
Wuest, Kenneth S. *Ephesians and Colossians*. "Word Studies in the Greek New Testament," Vol.1. Grand Rapids, MI: Eerdmans Publishing Co., 1966.
Youngblood, Ronald F. *Exodus*. Chicago, IL: Moody Press, 1983.

ABBREVIATIONS

&	=	and	O.T.	=	Old Testament
Bc.	=	because	p./pp.	=	page/pages
Concl.	=	conclusion	Pt.	=	point
Cp.	=	compare	Quest.	=	question
Ct.	=	contrast	Rel.	=	religion
e.g.	=	for example	Rgt.	=	righteousness
f.	=	following	Thru	=	through
Illust.	=	illustration	v./vv.	=	verse/verses
N.T.	=	New Testament	vs.	=	versus

THE BOOKS OF THE OLD TESTAMENT

Book	Abbreviation	Chapters	Book	Abbreviation	Chapters
GENESIS	Gen. or Ge.	50	Ecclesiastes	Eccl. or Ec.	12
Exodus	Ex.	40	The Song of Solomon	S. of Sol. or Song	8
Leviticus	Lev. or Le.	27	Isaiah	Is.	66
Numbers	Num. or Nu.	36	Jeremiah	Jer. or Je.	52
Deuteronomy	Dt. or De.	34	Lamentations	Lam.	5
Joshua	Josh. or Jos.	24	Ezekiel	Ezk. or Eze.	48
Judges	Judg. or Jud.	21	Daniel	Dan. or Da.	12
Ruth	Ruth or Ru.	4	Hosea	Hos. or Ho.	14
1 Samuel	1 Sam. or 1 S.	31	Joel	Joel	3
2 Samuel	2 Sam. or 2 S.	24	Amos	Amos or Am.	9
1 Kings	1 Ki. or 1 K.	22	Obadiah	Obad. or Ob.	1
2 Kings	2 Ki. or 2 K.	25	Jonah	Jon. or Jona.	4
1 Chronicles	1 Chron. or 1 Chr.	29	Micah	Mic. or Mi.	7
2 Chronicles	2 Chron. or 2 Chr.	36	Nahum	Nah. or Na.	3
Ezra	Ezra or Ezr.	10	Habakkuk	Hab.	3
Nehemiah	Neh. or Ne.	13	Zephaniah	Zeph. or Zep.	3
Esther	Est.	10	Haggai	Hag.	2
Job	Job or Jb.	42	Zechariah	Zech. or Zec.	14
Psalms	Ps.	150	Malachi	Mal.	4
Proverbs	Pr.	31			

THE BOOKS OF THE NEW TESTAMENT

Book	Abbreviation	Chapters	Book	Abbreviation	Chapters
MATTHEW	Mt.	28	1 Timothy	1 Tim. or 1 Ti.	6
Mark	Mk.	16	2 Timothy	2 Tim. or 2 Ti.	4
Luke	Lk. or Lu.	24	Titus	Tit.	3
John	Jn.	21	Philemon	Phile. or Phm.	1
The Acts	Acts or Ac.	28	Hebrews	Heb. or He.	13
Romans	Ro.	16	James	Jas. or Js.	5
1 Corinthians	1 Cor. or 1 Co.	16	1 Peter	1 Pt. or 1 Pe.	5
2 Corinthians	2 Cor. or 2 Co.	13	2 Peter	2 Pt. or 2 Pe.	3
Galatians	Gal. or Ga.	6	1 John	1 Jn.	5
Ephesians	Eph. or Ep.	6	2 John	2 Jn.	1
Philippians	Ph.	4	3 John	3 Jn.	1
Colossians	Col.	4	Jude	Jude	1
1 Thessalonians	1 Th.	5	Revelation	Rev. or Re.	22
2 Thessalonians	2 Th.	3			

HOW TO USE
The Preacher's Outline & Sermon Bible®
Follow these easy steps to gain maximum benefit from The POSB.

① SUBJECT HEADING

② MAJOR POINTS

③ SUBPOINTS & SCRIPTURE

④ COMMENTARY

---

1 CORINTHIANS 13:1-13

CHAPTER 13

D. The Most Excellent Quality of Life: Love, Not Gifts, 13:1-13[DS1]

1. The great importance of love
   a. Verdict 1: Tongues without love are meaningless

   b. Verdict 2: Gifts without love are nothing
      1) Prophecy is nothing
      2) Understanding all mysteries & knowledge are nothing
      3) Faith is nothing
   c. Verdict 3: Giving without love profits nothing
      1) Giving one's goods
      2) Giving one's life—martyrdom

2. The great acts of love

Though I speak with the tongues of men and of angels, and have not charity, I am become as sounding brass, or a tinkling cymbal. 2 And though I have the gift of prophecy, and understand all mysteries, and all knowledge; and though I have all faith, so that I could remove mountains, and have not charity, I am nothing. 3 And though I bestow all my goods to feed the poor, and though I give my body to be burned, and have not charity, it profiteth me nothing. 4 Charity suffereth long, and is kind; charity envieth not; charity vaunteth not itself, is not puffed up. 5 Doth not behave itself unseemly, seeketh not her own, is not easily provoked, thinketh no evil;

6 Rejoiceth not in iniquity, but rejoiceth in the truth; 7 Beareth all things, believeth all things, hopeth all things, endureth all things. 8 Charity never faileth: but whether *there* be prophecies, they shall fail; whether *there* be tongues, they shall cease; whether *there* be knowledge, it shall vanish away. 9 For we know in part, and we prophesy in part. 10 But when that which is perfect is come, then that which is in part shall be done away. 11 When I was a child, I spake as a child, I understood as a child, I thought as a child: but when I became a man, I put away childish things. 12 For now we see through a glass, darkly; but then face to face: now I know in part; but then shall I know even as also I am known. 13 And now abideth faith, hope, charity, these three; but the greatest of these *is* charity.

3. The great permanence of love
   a. It never fails, never ceases, never vanishes

   b. It is perfect & complete

   c. It is maturity—mature behavior

   d. It is the hope of being face-to-face with God—possessing perfect consciousness & knowledge

4. The great supremacy of love

DIVISION VII

THE QUESTIONS CONCERNING SPIRITUAL GIFTS, 12:1–14:40

D. The Most Excellent Quality of Life: Love, Not Gifts, 13:1-13

(13:1-13) **Introduction**: there is no question, what the world needs more than anything else is love. If people loved each other, really loved each other, there would be no more war, crime, abuse, injustice, poverty, hunger, starvation, homelessness, deprivation, or immorality. Love is the one ingredient that could revolutionize society. Love is the greatest quality of human life. Love is the supreme quality, the most excellent way for a man to live.
1. The great importance of love (vv.1-3).
2. The great acts of love (vv.4-7).
3. The great permanence of love (vv.8-12).
4. The great supremacy of love (v.13).

DEEPER STUDY # 1
(13:1-13) **Love**: throughout this passage, the word used for love or charity is the great word *agape*. (See DEEPER STUDY # 4, Love—Jn.21:15-17 for more discussion.) The meaning of *agape* love is more clearly seen by contrasting it with the various kinds of love. There are essentially four kinds of love. Whereas the English language has only the word *love* to describe all the affectionate experiences of men, the Greek language had a different word to describe each kind of love.
1. There is *passionate love* or *eros love*. This is the physical love between sexes; the patriotic love of a person for his nation; the ambition of a person for power, wealth, or fame. Briefly stated, *eros love* is the base love of a man that arises from his own inner passion. Sometimes *eros love* is focused upon good and other times it is focused upon bad. It should be noted that *eros love* is never used in the New Testament.
2. There is *affectionate love* or *storge love*. This is the kind of love that exists between parent and child and between loyal citizens and a trustworthy ruler. *Storge love* is also not used in the New Testament.
3. There is an *endearing love*, the love that cherishes. This is *phileo love*, the love of a husband and wife for each other, of a brother for a brother, of a friend for the dearest of friends. It is the love that cherishes, that holds someone or something ever so dear to one's heart.
4. There is *selfless and sacrificial love* or *agape love*. Agape love is the love of the mind, of the reason, of the will. It is the love that goes so far...
   • that it loves a person even if he does not deserve to be loved
   • that it actually loves the person who is utterly unworthy of being loved

---

① Glance at the **Subject Heading**. Think about it for a moment.

② Glance at the **Subject Heading** again, and then the **Major Points** (1, 2, 3, etc.). Do this several times, reviewing them together while quickly grasping the overall subject.

③ Glance at **both** the **Major Points** and **Subpoints** together while reading the **Scripture**. Do this slower than Step 2. Note how these points sit directly beside the related verse and simply restate what the Scripture is saying—in Outline form.

④ Next read the **Commentary**. Note that the *Major Point Numbers* in the Outline match those in the Commentary. A small raised number (**DS1, DS2**, etc.) at the end of a Subject Heading or Outline Point, directs you to a related **Deeper Study** in the Commentary.

Finally, read the **Thoughts** and **Support Scripture** (not shown).

As you read and re-read, pray that the Holy Spirit will bring to your attention exactly what you should preach and teach. May God bless you richly as you study and teach His Word.

The POSB contains everything you need for sermon preparation:

1. **The Subject Heading** describes the overall theme of the passage, and is located directly above the Scripture (keyed *alphabetically*).

2. **Major Points** are keyed with an outline *number* guiding you to related commentary. Note that the Commentary includes *"Thoughts"* (life application) and abundant Supporting Scriptures.

3. **Subpoints** explain and clarify the Scripture as needed.

4. **Commentary** is fully researched and developed for every point.

   • **Thoughts** (in bold) help apply the Scripture to real life.

   • **Deeper Studies** provide in-depth discussions of key words.

"Woe is unto me, if I preach not the gospel"
(1 Co.9:16)

TABLE OF CONTENTS
DEUTERONOMY

	PAGE
INTRODUCTION TO DEUTERONOMY	1
GENERAL OUTLINE OF DEUTERONOMY	5
DIVISION I. THE SCENE AND BACKGROUND OF THE GREAT BOOK OF DEUTERONOMY: MESSAGES FOR ALL BELIEVERS, 1:1-5	7
DIVISION II. THE FIRST GREAT THEME PREACHED BY GOD'S AGED SERVANT: REMEMBER THE LESSONS FROM HISTORY, 1:6–4:43	19
DIVISION III. THE SECOND GREAT THEME PREACHED BY GOD'S AGED SERVANT (PART 1): REMEMBER THE TEN COMMANDMENTS—THE FUNDAMENTAL LAWS TO GOVERN MAN AND SOCIETY, 4:44–11:32	67
DIVISION IV. THE SECOND GREAT THEME PREACHED BY GOD'S AGED SERVANT (PART 2): REMEMBER THE CIVIL AND RELIGIOUS LAWS OF ISRAEL—HELPFUL PRINCIPLES TO GOVERN MAN AND SOCIETY, 12:1–26:19	187
DIVISION V. THE THIRD GREAT THEME PREACHED BY GOD'S AGED SERVANT: THE CHARGE TO RENEW THE COVENANT WITH GOD, 27:1–30:20	333
DIVISION VI. THE FINAL ACTS AND DEATH OF MOSES, GOD'S AGED SERVANT: REMEMBER THE ENCOURAGEMENT AND THE WARNING OF GOD, 31:1–34:12	380
PRACTICAL BIBLE HELPS AND RESOURCES – DEUTERONOMY	435
MAP 1: Map of the Wilderness Wanderings of Israel	436
CHART 1: An Overview of the Life of Moses	437
CHART 2: The Blessings for Obedience to God and the Curses for Disobedience	450
TYPES IN DEUTERONOMY	
➢ Alphabetical Outline	464
➢ Chronological Outline	466
OUTLINE & SUBJECT INDEX – DEUTERONOMY	468

THE FIFTH BOOK OF MOSES, CALLED
DEUTERONOMY

AUTHOR: Moses, the aged servant of God.

Deuteronomy means "the second law" or "the repetition of the law." The law was first given to the Israelites at Mt. Sinai. But they—the first generation of believers—proved to be a sinful people, a people of unbelief and disobedience. They did not believe God, not enough to lay hold of the promised land. As a result, they wandered about for forty years and died in the desert wilderness. Now forty years later, this aged servant of God stands before the second generation of believers—the sons and daughters of the unbelieving generation—and repeats the law to them. For a second time he seeks to prepare a generation of believers to enter the promised land.

The great book of *Deuteronomy* is a series of messages preached by Moses as he seeks to prepare the second generation of Israelites to enter, conquer, and possess the promised land. The evidence that Moses wrote Deuteronomy is strong, very strong:

1. The book itself claims to be written by Moses.

> "These *be* the words which Moses spake unto all Israel on this side Jordan in the wilderness, in the plain over against the Red *sea,* between Paran, and Tophel, and Laban, and Hazeroth, and Dizahab" (De.1:1).
>
> "On this side Jordan, in the land of Moab, began Moses to declare this law, saying" (De.1:5).
>
> "And this is the law which Moses set before the children of Israel" (De.4:44).
>
> "These *are* the words of the covenant, which the LORD commanded Moses to make with the children of Israel in the land of Moab, beside the covenant which he made with them in Horeb" (De.29:1).
>
> "And Moses wrote this law, and delivered it unto the priests the sons of Levi, which bare the ark of the covenant of the LORD, and unto all the elders of Israel" (De.31:9).
>
> "Moses therefore wrote this song the same day, and taught it the children of Israel" (De.31:22).
>
> "And it came to pass, when Moses had made an end of writing the words of this law in a book, until they were finished" (De.31:24).

2. Other Old Testament books claim that Moses wrote *Deuteronomy*.

> "And they were to prove Israel by them, to know whether they would hearken unto the commandments of the LORD, which he commanded their fathers by the hand of Moses" (Jud.3:4).
>
> "For thou didst separate them from among all the people of the earth, *to be* thine inheritance, as thou spakest by the hand of Moses thy servant, when thou broughtest our fathers out of Egypt, O Lord GOD" (1 K.8:53).
>
> "But the children of the murderers he slew not: according unto that which is written in the book of the law of Moses, wherein the LORD commanded, saying, The fathers shall not be put to death for the children, nor the children be put to death for the fathers; but every man shall be put to death for his own sin" (2 K.14:6).
>
> "Because they obeyed not the voice of the LORD their God, but transgressed his covenant, *and* all that Moses the servant of the LORD commanded, and would not hear *them,* nor do *them*" (2 K.18:12).
>
> "Then stood up Jeshua the son of Jozadak, and his brethren the priests, and Zerubbabel the son of Shealtiel, and his brethren, and builded the altar of the God of Israel, to offer burnt offerings thereon, as *it is* written in the law of Moses the man of God" (Ezr.3:2).
>
> "We have dealt very corruptly against thee, and have not kept the commandments, nor the statutes, nor the judgments, which thou commandedst thy servant Moses" (Ne.1:7).
>
> "He made known his ways unto Moses, his acts unto the children of Israel" (Ps.103:7).
>
> "Yea, all Israel have transgressed thy law, even by departing, that they might not obey thy voice; therefore the curse is poured upon us, and the oath that *is* written in the law of Moses the servant of God, because we have sinned against him" (Da.9:11).
>
> "Remember ye the law of Moses my servant, which I commanded unto him in Horeb for all Israel, *with* the statutes and judgments" (Mal.4:4).

3. Jesus Christ Himself attributed the book of *Deuteronomy* to Moses and quoted *Deuteronomy* as the Word of God in resisting the temptation of Satan (Mt.4:4, 7, 10).

> "They say unto him, Why did Moses then command to give a writing of divorcement, and to put her away? He saith unto them, Moses because of the hardness of your hearts suffered you to put away your wives: but from the beginning it was not so" (Mt.19:7-8).
>
> "For Moses said, Honour thy father and thy mother; and, Whoso curseth father or mother, let him die the death" (Mk.7:10).
>
> "And he answered and said unto them, What did Moses command you? And they said, Moses suffered to write a bill of divorcement, and to put *her* away. And Jesus answered and said unto them, For the hardness of your heart he wrote you this precept" (Mk.10:3-5).
>
> "Saying, Master, Moses wrote unto us, If any man's brother die, having a wife, and he die without children, that his brother should take his wife, and raise up seed unto his brother" (Lu.20:28).
>
> "For had ye believed Moses, ye would have believed me: for he wrote of me. But if ye believe not his writings, how shall ye believe my words?" (Jn.5:46-47).

INTRODUCTION TO DEUTERONOMY

4. The New Testament quotes or alludes to Moses' authorship of *Deuteronomy* over one hundred times.

> "For Moses truly said unto the fathers, A prophet shall the Lord your God raise up unto you of your brethren, like unto me; him shall ye hear in all things whatsoever he shall say unto you" (Ac.3:22).
>
> "But I say, Did not Israel know? First Moses saith, I will provoke you to jealousy by *them that are no people, and* by a foolish nation I will anger you" (Ro.10:19).
>
> "For it is written in the law of Moses, Thou shalt not muzzle the mouth of the ox that treadeth out the corn. Doth God take care for oxen?" (1 Co.9:9).

5. Joshua, the immediate successor to Moses, stated that Moses was the author of *Deuteronomy*.

> "Only be thou strong and very courageous, that thou mayest observe to do according to all the law, which Moses my servant commanded thee: turn not from it *to* the right hand or *to* the left, that thou mayest prosper whithersoever thou goest" (Jos.1:7).

6. The external evidence strongly points to Moses as being the author of *Deuteronomy*.
   a. Tradition—both Jewish and Christian tradition—has been unanimous in holding that Moses is the author of Deuteronomy. In fact, tradition is strong in holding that Moses wrote the entire Pentateuch *(Genesis, Exodus, Leviticus, Numbers, Deuteronomy)*.
   b. Archaeology also points to Moses' writing *Deuteronomy*. The author certainly lived during the day when the events of *Deuteronomy* took place. What shows us this? The facts we find in the Pentateuch, facts describing such matters as…
   - customs
   - conduct
   - geography
   - history
   - events
   - places
   - names

(See Introduction, Author—*Genesis, Exodus, Leviticus, Numbers* for more discussion.)

DATE: About 1406 B.C. The great book of *Deuteronomy* was written at the end of the forty years wilderness wanderings right before the Israelites were to enter the promised land. (See Introduction, Date—*Genesis*, Vol.1, for more discussion.)

TO WHOM WRITTEN: Israel in particular and the human race in general.

1. *Deuteronomy* was written to the new or second generation of Israelites who were poised to enter the promised land. This review, this second giving of the law, was preached to the sons and daughters of the unbelieving generation who had wandered about and died during the forty years of wilderness wanderings. Moses, the aged servant of God, challenged the new generation of believers to rededicate their lives to God, to renew their covenant and obedience to God.

2. *Deuteronomy* was written to all people of all generations…
   - to give an example and warning to us.

> "Now all these things happened unto them for examples: and they are written for our admonition, upon whom the ends of the world are come" (1 Co.10:11).

   - to teach us how to live, that it is through Scripture that we learn endurance, obtain comfort, and receive great hope.

> "For whatsoever things were written aforetime were written for our learning, that we through patience and comfort of the scriptures might have hope" (Ro.15:4).

PURPOSE: there are at least three distinct purposes for the great book of *Deuteronomy*.

1. The *Historical Purpose*: to prepare the second generation of Israelites for their entrance into the promised land. Moses, the aged servant of God, prepared the second generation by challenging them to do five specific things:
   ⇒ To remember the great lessons from history (1:6-4:43)
   ⇒ To remember the fundamental laws of God—the Ten Commandments—that are to govern man and society (4:44-11:32)
   ⇒ To remember the civil and religious laws of Israel—the helpful principles that are to govern man and society (12:1-26:19).
   ⇒ To rededicate their lives to God, renew their commitment or covenant with Him (27:1-30:20).
   ⇒ To be encouraged, but to remember the warning of God as they entered the promised land (31:1-34:12).

2. The *Doctrinal or Spiritual Purpose*: a twofold doctrinal or spiritual purpose is clearly seen in the great book of *Deuteronomy*.
   ⇒ First, *Deuteronomy* was written to teach God's people how to live victorious lives. It teaches the believer how to conquer all the enemies, trials, and temptations that confront him day by day and that seek to keep him out of the land of blessing, the promised land of God.
   ⇒ Second, *Deuteronomy* was written to stir God's people to rededicate their lives to God, to renew their commitment to obey God and to keep the covenant made with Him.

INTRODUCTION TO DEUTERONOMY

3. The *Christological or Christ-Centered Purpose*:
   ⇒ To teach that God will send a greater Prophet than Moses to proclaim the Word of God to His people. That great Prophet is Christ the Messiah.

   "I will raise them up a Prophet from among their brethren, like unto thee, and will put my words in his mouth; and he shall speak unto them all that I shall command him. And it shall come to pass, *that* whosoever will not hearken unto my words which he shall speak in my name, I will require *it* of him" (De.18:18-19).
   "For Moses truly said unto the fathers, A prophet shall the Lord your God raise up unto you of your brethren, like unto me; him shall ye hear in all things whatsoever he shall say unto you. And it shall come to pass, *that* every soul, which will not hear that prophet, shall be destroyed from among the people. Yea, and all the prophets from Samuel and those that follow after, as many as have spoken, have likewise foretold of these days" (Ac.3:22-24).
   "This is that Moses, which said unto the children of Israel, A prophet shall the Lord your God raise up unto you of your brethren, like unto me; him shall ye hear" (Ac.7:37; see Jn.1:45; 5:46; 6:14; 7:40).

   ⇒ To teach the restoration of Israel that will take place sometime in the future through the Lord Jesus Christ.

   "That then the LORD thy God will turn thy captivity, and have compassion upon thee, and will return and gather thee from all the nations, whither the LORD thy God hath scattered thee" (De.30:3).
   "And so all Israel shall be saved: as it is written, There shall come out of Sion the Deliverer, and shall turn away ungodliness from Jacob" (Ro.11:26).

SPECIAL FEATURES:
1. *Deuteronomy* is "The Great Book of the Second Law or the Repetition of the Law." The very meaning of the word *Deuteronomy* is "second law" or the "repetition of the law." The law had first been given at Mt. Sinai to the older generation of Israelites, the generation who had died in the desert wilderness because of their sin and unbelief. Now, about forty years later, Moses covered the law for a second time with the sons and daughters of the unbelieving generation. Deuteronomy is the second giving of the law, the second series of messages preached by Moses on the law of God.

2. *Deuteronomy* is "The Great Book of Spiritual Preparation." The second generation of Israelite believers were camped in the plains of Moab close by the Jordan River, right across from the great city of Jericho. They were poised to enter, conquer, and take possession of the promised land. But before they launched their campaign to conquer the promised land, the people needed to be fully prepared. Deuteronomy is a *series of messages* preached by Moses to prepare the people for conquering the promised land.

3. *Deuteronomy* is "The Great Book Revealing How to Live a Victorious Life." Enemy after enemy was to be faced in the promised land, both physical enemies such as the Canaanites and spiritual enemies such as the temptation to commit idolatry and immorality. Conquest over all enemies was possible, but only through the power of God.

4. *Deuteronomy* is "The Great Book of Rededication and Renewal, the Renewal of One's Covenant with God." Deuteronomy stresses the utter necessity for a person to rededicate his life and renew his covenant with God occasionally, as the need arises. The first covenant made at Mt. Sinai was between God and the first generation of Israelite believers (Ex.19:5-6; see outlines and notes—Ex.19:1-25; 20:1-26; 21:1-24:18 for more discussion).

Now, it was time for the sons and daughters, the second generation, to renew the covenant for themselves. The renewal of the covenant—the call for God's people to rededicate their lives to God—is the message of this great book. *Deuteronomy* is a *series of messages* preached by Moses, messages that challenged God's people to renew their commitment, their covenant with God.

Note this fact: rededicating one's life and renewing one's commitment or covenant with God is periodically necessary. This is clearly demonstrated in the life of Israel. The Israelites rededicated themselves and renewed their covenant with God several times:
   ⇒ Under the leadership of Moses (De.27:1–30:20).
   ⇒ Under the leadership of Joshua (Jos.24).
   ⇒ Under the leadership of Ezr. (Ne.8).

5. *Deuteronomy* is "The Great Book That Spells Out the Pattern for Covenant Renewal." The outline of *Deuteronomy* actually follows the pattern of an ancient Middle East Treaty between two parties:
   a. The Preamble or Introduction to the covenant (1:1-5).
   b. The Historical Prologue: the review of history, of the relationship between the two parties and of the events that make a covenant necessary (1:6–4:43).
   c. The Basic Stipulations or laws of the agreement (4:44–26:19).
   d. The Ratification of the Covenant: the charge to keep the covenant and the results of obeying and disobeying the covenant (27:1–30:20).
   e. The Witnesses and Leadership Succession spelled out (31:1–34:12).

6. *Deuteronomy* is "The Great Book of Promise and Hope." Camped close by the Jordan River, the people were poised to cross over the Jordan and enter the promised land for the very first time. At long last, they were ready to receive their inheritance, the wonderful promise of God. Their hearts were filled with great hope and anticipation. All the blessings of the promised land were soon to be theirs. The great promise and hope that flooded their hearts can be sensed as one studies the great book of *Deuteronomy*.

INTRODUCTION TO DEUTERONOMY

7. *Deuteronomy* is "The Great Book That Stresses the Need for God's Presence and Guidance." To conquer the promised land, the presence and guidance of God were absolute essentials. Moses preached this fact time and again throughout *Deuteronomy*.

8. *Deuteronomy* is "The Great Book That Stresses the Covenant between God and His People."

9. *Deuteronomy* is "The Great Book That Is Often Quoted in the New Testament." There are around 100 quotations or references to the book in the New Testament.

10. *Deuteronomy* is "The Great Book That Stresses Theology."
    a. *Deuteronomy* stresses the Word of God, the wonderful fact that God spoke and gave His Word to Moses and His dear people. A quick glance at each chapter shows how often God spoke, instructing and guiding His people and giving them promise after promise (see 1:6; 2:2, 17, 31; 4:12f; etc.).
    b. *Deuteronomy* stresses the prophetic ministry of God's appointed servant, Moses (see 1:5-6; 1:9f 2:16f; 4:1f; etc.).
    c. *Deuteronomy* predicted the coming prophet that was to be more than a prophet, predicted the coming of the Lord Jesus Christ (De.18:18-19).
    d. *Deuteronomy* stresses the need to renew the old covenant with God, but points to the new covenant mediated by Jesus Christ (Jn.1:21-25; He.8:10; 10:16).
    e. *Deuteronomy* stresses the importance of personal devotions—face-to-face communion and fellowship with God—through the study of His Word, prayer, obedience, and maintaining an unbroken communion with God (34:10).
    f. *Deuteronomy* stresses the fact that history is the drama of redemption. *Deuteronomy* demonstrates how God's will and Word are being carried out in the events of history—all for the sake of saving those who believe and follow Him.
        ⇒ By studying the history of the past, a person sees the glorious salvation of God in the events of history, the fulfillment of His Word and promises (De.5:6).
        ⇒ By studying the history of the future—foreseen in the great promises of God—a person is stirred to commit his life to God.
    g. *Deuteronomy* stresses obedience to God and His commandments (5:7-21; 28:1-2).
    h. *Deuteronomy* stresses love for God (6:5).
    i. *Deuteronomy* stresses love for one's neighbor (22:1f; 23:15-16; 23:19-20; 23:24-25; 24:1-22; 25:1-19).
    j. *Deuteronomy* stresses the promises and blessings of God for obedience (28:1-14).
    k. *Deuteronomy* stresses the judgment and curses of God for disobedience (27:11-26; 28:15-68).
    l. *Deuteronomy* stresses the need to never forget God.
    m. *Deuteronomy* stresses the need to care for the needy of the world (22:1f; 23:15-16; 23:19-20; 23:24-25; 24:1-22; 25:1-19).
    n. *Deuteronomy* stresses the importance of God's presence and guidance as one walks day by day throughout life.
    o. *Deuteronomy* stresses the need to continually renew one's life to God, to renew one's covenant or commitment to follow God ever so diligently and faithfully.
    p. *Deuteronomy* predicts the restoration of Israel when the people return to the LORD (30:1-20).

11. *Deuteronomy* is "The Great Book That Presents Life As Sacred to God." Therefore, man is to be holy—totally set apart to God—and live a pure and holy life before God.

12. *Deuteronomy* is "The Great Book That Reviews the Birth of Israel As a Nation." Peter C. Craigie makes an excellent statement that stresses this fact:

> The Exodus marked the liberation of the Hebrews from a long period of servitude in Egypt. The end of servitude and the beginnings of liberation were in effect the birth of Israel as a nation whose king was God (Exod.15:18); yet the Israelites were a nation without a land and without a constitution. The constitution was formed at Sinai in the covenant sealed between the Lord and his people in which Moses acted as mediator. The covenant was in part a renewal of the older covenants made with the patriarchs; like the earlier covenants, the Sinai Covenant continued to hold forth the promise of God for the future, the promise that the Israelites would become God's special nation. In the covenant, the people were required to be obedient to God, the Lord of the covenant, who had liberated them from the Egyptian bondage. In summary, the covenant was the constitution of a theocracy. God was king and had claimed his people for himself out of Egypt; the people, who owed everything to God, were required to submit to him in a covenant which was based on love. Israel now had a constitution, but still it did not have a land to call its own.[1]

When Israel was liberated, freed from the slavery of Egypt, they were chosen by God to be His very special people. They were to be a nation of people who would be His witnesses to the immoral and unrighteous of the earth. Marching out of Egypt, the Israelites were a nation of people whose king was God Himself. But they had no constitution that legally formed them into a nation and no land to call their home. The constitution was drawn up at Mt. Sinai, a constitution (covenant) that was to govern the relationship between the people and their King. The form of government established by the constitution or covenant was a *theocracy*. God Himself was the King, the wonderful Ruler who had saved the Israelites from the terrible fate of slavery and death in Egypt (a symbol of the world). Therefore, the people owed their lives to God. They were to be the subjects of the Ruler who had so graciously saved them, the subjects of God Himself.

This was the history of Israel's birth, the formation of Israel as a theocratic nation ruled by God Himself. The Israelites had their King and their constitution. Now, they were soon to receive the inheritance of their land, the great promise of God.

---

[1] Peter C. Craigie. *The Book of Deuteronomy*. "The New International Commentary on the Old Testament." (Grand Rapids, MI: William B. Eerdmans Publishing Company, 1976), pp.18-19.

OUTLINE OF DEUTERONOMY

THE PREACHER'S OUTLINE AND SERMON BIBLE® is *unique*. It differs from all other Study Bibles and Sermon Resource Materials in that every Passage and Subject is outlined right beside the Scripture. When you choose any *Subject* below and turn to the reference, you have not only the Scripture but also an outline of the Scripture and Subject *already prepared for you—verse by verse*.

For a quick example, choose one of the subjects below and turn over to the Scripture; you will find this to be a marvelous help for more organized and streamlined study.

In addition, every point of the Scripture and Subject is *fully developed in a Commentary with supporting Scripture* at the end of each point. Again, this arrangement makes sermon preparation much simpler and more efficient.

Note something else: the Subjects of *Deuteronomy* have titles that are both Biblical and *practical*. The practical titles are often more appealing to people. This *benefit* is clearly seen for use on billboards, bulletins, church newsletters, etc.

A suggestion: for the *quickest* overview of *Deuteronomy*, first read *all the Division titles* (I, II, III, etc.), then come back and read the individual outline titles.

OUTLINE OF DEUTERONOMY

I. **THE SCENE AND BACKGROUND OF THE GREAT BOOK OF DEUTERONOMY: MESSAGES FOR ALL BELIEVERS, 1:1-5**

II. **THE FIRST GREAT THEME PREACHED BY GOD'S AGED SERVANT: REMEMBER THE LESSONS FROM HISTORY, 1:6–4:43**

   A. The Pilgrimage of the First Generation of Israelite Believers: A Picture of Great Hope and Tragic Failure, 1:6–2:15
   B. The Pilgrimage of the Second Generation of Israelite Believers: A Picture of Triumphant Victory and Warning, 2:16–3:29
   C. The Strong Exhortation to the Second Generation of Israelite Believers: Obey God's Laws and Acknowledge that the LORD—He and He Alone—Is God, 4:1-43

III. **THE SECOND GREAT THEME PREACHED BY GOD'S AGED SERVANT (PART 1): REMEMBER THE TEN COMMANDMENTS—THE FUNDAMENTAL LAWS TO GOVERN MAN AND SOCIETY, 4:44–11:32**

   A. The Introduction and Overall Look at the Law: The Importance of the Law, 4:44–5:6
   B. The Ten Commandments (Part 1): The Laws Governing Man's Duty to God, 5:7-15
   C. The Ten Commandments (Part 2): The Laws Governing Man's Duty to Others, 5:16-21
   D. The Purposes of the Law: Why God Gave the Ten Commandments and the Law, 5:22-33
   E. The Summary of the Commandments—the Greatest Commandment of All: Love the LORD, 6:1-25
   F. The Greatest Hindrance to Obeying the Commandments of God: The Enemies of the Promised Land, 7:1-26
   G. The Safeguards to Assure Obedience to the Commandments of God: How to Guard Against Forgetting God, 8:1-20
   H. The Warnings Against Self-righteousness and Disobedience: Warnings That Must Be Heeded to Inherit the Promised Land, 9:1–10:11
   I. The Nine Supreme Requirements of Obedience: What Is Demanded by God, 10:12–11:32

IV. **THE SECOND GREAT THEME PREACHED BY GOD'S AGED SERVANT (PART 2): REMEMBER THE CIVIL AND RELIGIOUS LAWS OF ISRAEL—HELPFUL PRINCIPLES TO GOVERN MAN AND SOCIETY, 12:1–26:19**

   A. Laws That Regulate the Worship of God: A Picture of True Worship, 12:1-32
   B. Laws That Protect a Person from Idolatry: The Dangers of Being Seduced into False Worship, 13:1-18
   C. Laws That Mark the Believer As a Child of God—As Holy, Different, Distinctive, 14:1-29
   D. Laws That Demand Generosity and Giving: The Believer Must Not Hoard, Be Hard-hearted Nor Tightfisted, 15:1-23
   E. Laws That Govern the Three Pilgrimage Festivals of Worship: Remember the Great Blessings, Salvation, and Guidance of God, 16:1-17
   F. Laws That Govern the Administration of Justice and the Appointment of Rulers: Four Major Concerns of Society, 16:18–17:20
   G. Laws That Govern the Administration of Religion: Some Concerns of Believers, 18:1-22

OUTLINE
continued

- H. Laws That Demand Justice for the Defenseless: A Deep Concern for Justice, 19:1-21
- I. Laws That Govern the Conduct of War: A Picture of the Believer's Spiritual Warfare Against the Enemies of This World, 20:1-20
- J. Laws That Govern Some Unique Issues within Families and Society: God's Concern for Human Rights, 21:1-23
- K. Laws That Govern Seven Important Social Issues: Being a Good Neighbor and a Strong Testimony for the LORD, 22:1-12
- L. Laws That Govern Sexual Behavior: Living a Moral and Pure Life, 22:13-30
- M. Laws That Govern Several Social and Religious Issues: God's Concern for Both the Major and Minor Details of Life, 23:1-25
- N. Laws That Protect Relationships within Society: How to Prevent Abuse, 24:1-22
- O. Laws That Prevent Wrong Behavior and That Demand Justice, 25:1-19
- P. Laws That Require Special Confession and Obedience, 26:1-19

V. THE THIRD GREAT THEME PREACHED BY GOD'S AGED SERVANT: THE CHARGE TO RENEW THE COVENANT WITH GOD, 27:1–30:20

- A. The Charge to Renew the Covenant: The Command to Obey God, and Those to Be Cursed for Disobeying God, 27:1-26
- B. The Results of Obeying the Covenant: The Blessings of God, 28:1-14
- C. The Results of Disobeying God: The Curses for Disobedience, 28:15-68
- D. The Terms of the Covenant: Obey God or Face His Judgment, 29:1-29
- E. The Strong Appeal and Hope of the Covenant: Restoration—Repentance and Forgiveness, 30:1-20

VI. THE FINAL ACTS AND DEATH OF MOSES, GOD'S AGED SERVANT: REMEMBER THE ENCOURAGEMENT AND THE WARNING OF GOD, 31:1–34:12

- A. The Final Preparations for Entering the Promised Land: Five Strong Charges of Encouragement and Warning, 31:1-29
- B. The Song of Moses: A Strong Warning and Witness to God's People and to Those Who Reject Him, 31:30–32:52
- C. The Prophetic Blessing of Moses: The Last Words Spoken by the Man of God—a Message of Great Assurance and Encouragement, 33:1-29
- D. The Death of Moses: The Joyful Yet Sorrowful Passing of God's Dear Servant, 34:1-12

THE FIFTH BOOK OF MOSES, CALLED
DEUTERONOMY

CHAPTER 1

I. THE SCENE & BACKGROUND OF THE GREAT BOOK OF DEUTERONOMY: MESSAGES FOR ALL BELIEVERS, 1:1-5

1. The messenger—Moses, the servant of God: A symbol of Christ & of the minister
2. The recipients—all Israel: A symbol of all believers
3. The strategic place, east of the Jordan—right at the entrance to the promised land:

These *be* the words which Moses spake unto all Israel on this side Jordan in the wilderness, in the plain over against the Red *sea*, between Paran, and Tophel, and Laban, and Hazeroth, and Dizahab.
2 (*There are* eleven days' journey from Horeb by the way of mount Seir unto Kadeshbarnea.)
3 And it came to pass in the fortieth year, in the eleventh month, on the first *day* of the month, *that* Moses spake unto the children of Israel, according unto all that the LORD had given him in commandment unto them;
4 After he had slain Sihon the king of the Amorites, which dwelt in Heshbon, and Og the king of Bashan, which dwelt at Astaroth in Edrei:
5 On this side Jordan, in the land of Moab, began Moses to declare this law, saying,

A symbol of heaven & of spiritual conquest & rest
4. The time—40 years after the Exodus: A symbol of God's great deliverance from this world & its enslavements
5. The message: The Word of God—all the commandments of God
6. The purpose
   a. To encourage God's people to continue their victorious march into the promised land
   b. To expound the law of God one last time before entering the promised land & to renew the covenant with God

DIVISION I

THE SCENE AND BACKGROUND OF THE GREAT BOOK OF DEUTERONOMY: MESSAGES FOR ALL BELIEVERS, 1:1-5

(1:1-5) Introduction—Nation, Foundation of—Society, Basis of—Victorious Life, Basis of: God had delivered the Israelites from the enslavement of Egypt (a symbol of the world), and He had led them through forty years of wilderness wanderings. This has been seen in the great books of *Exodus* and *Numbers*. The book of *Numbers* closed with the Israelites camped in the plains of Moab close by the Jordan River, right across from the great city of Jericho.

At last, they are poised to enter the promised land of God. But before they can cross the Jordan to lay claim to their promised inheritance, they must be prepared—spiritually prepared. Spiritual preparation is the thrust of the great book of *Deuteronomy*. To prepare the people, Moses preached a *series of messages* that were grouped under three basic subjects:

1. The need to remember the lessons from history (1:6–4:43). By learning from the past, the Israelites would know how to conquer the promised land and build a strong, orderly society within the promised land.
2. The need to remember the Ten Commandments and the laws that are to govern man and society (4:44–26:19). The Israelites had to know and obey the law to please God. They had to know the law in order to live victorious and fruitful lives and to build a just and righteous society.
3. The charge to rededicate their lives to God, to renew their covenant or commitment with God (27:1–30:20). Once the Israelites had been led to recommit their lives to God, then and only then would they be ready to inherit the promised land of God.

Note that while the first outline of *Deuteronomy* covers only five verses, it serves as an introduction to the entire book. This is: *The Scene and Background of the Great Book of Deuteronomy: Messages for All Believers,* 1:1-5.

1. The messenger—Moses, the servant of God: a symbol of Christ and of the minister (v.1).
2. The recipients—all Israel: a symbol of all believers (v.1).
3. The strategic place, east of the Jordan—right at the entrance to the promised land: a symbol of heaven and of spiritual conquest and rest (v.2).
4. The time—40 years after the Exodus: a symbol of God's great deliverance from this world and its enslavements (v.3).
5. The message: the Word of God—all the commandments of God (v.3).
6. The purpose (vv.4-5).

1 **(1:1) Messenger, of God—Servant, of God—Moses, Messenger of God—Symbol, of Christ:** there was the messenger, Moses, the servant of God. As the messenger of God, Moses was a symbol of both Christ and the minister of God. Moses was chosen by God...

- to be the *liberator* of Israel, freeing them from Egyptian slavery
- to be the great *leader* of Israel, leading them to the promised land
- to be the *founding father* of Israel as a nation
- to be the *intercessor* who stood between God and His people

But this was not all. God also chose Moses to be the *messenger* of God, the great *giver* and *communicator* of the law of God. It is this call, this function of Moses—to be the messenger of God—that is the focus of the great book of *Deuteronomy*. God had three sermons—three strong challenges—that He wanted declared to His people. In obedience to God, the messenger of God was to stand boldly before the people and preach the sermons. This is one of the great scenes of the book of *Deuteronomy*: Moses standing and preaching three sermons, three strong challenges to the people of God.

DEUTERONOMY 1:1-5

OUTLINE	SCRIPTURE
1. The messenger—Moses, the servant of God: A symbol of Christ & of the minister	These *be* the words which Moses spake unto all Israel on this side Jordan in the wilderness, in the plain over against the Red *sea*, between Paran, and Tophel, and Laban, and Hazeroth, and Dizahab.

Thought 1. The minister of God is chosen to proclaim the Word of God to the people of God. This is the very purpose for which he is called: to be the messenger of God, to proclaim the Word of God.

"And he said unto them, Go ye into all the world, and preach the gospel to every creature" (Mk.16:15).

"Ye have not chosen me, but I have chosen you, and ordained you, that ye should go and bring forth fruit, and *that* your fruit should remain: that whatsoever ye shall ask of the Father in my name, he may give it you" (Jn.15:16).

"He saith unto him the third time, Simon, *son* of Jonas, lovest thou me? Peter was grieved because he said unto him the third time, Lovest thou me? And he said unto him, Lord, thou knowest all things; thou knowest that I love thee. Jesus saith unto him, Feed my sheep" (Jn.21:17).

"And straightway he [Paul] preached Christ in the synagogues, that he is the Son of God" (Ac.9:20).

"Take heed therefore unto yourselves, and to all the flock, over the which the Holy Ghost hath made you overseers, to feed the church of God, which he hath purchased with his own blood" (Ac.20:28).

"Feed the flock of God which is among you, taking the oversight *thereof*, not by constraint, but willingly; not for filthy lucre, but of a ready mind" (1 Pe.5:2).

"I have set watchmen upon thy walls, O Jerusalem, *which* shall never hold their peace day nor night: ye that make mention of the Lord, keep not silence" (Is.62:6).

"And I will give you pastors according to mine heart, which shall feed you with knowledge and understanding" (Je.3:15).

"And I will set up shepherds over them which shall feed them: and they shall fear no more, nor be dismayed, neither shall they be lacking, saith the Lord" (Je.23:4).

"Son of man, I have made thee a watchman unto the house of Israel: therefore hear the word at my mouth, and give them warning from me" (Eze.3:17).

Thought 2. Moses stood between God and the people, stood as the messenger of God. As the messenger of God, Moses is a picture of Christ. Jesus Christ came to earth as the perfect Messenger of God, came to save man and to proclaim the way of salvation to man.

"For unto you is born this day in the city of David a Saviour, which is Christ the Lord" (Lu.2:11).

"For the Son of man is come to seek and to save that which was lost" (Lu.19:10).

"For God so loved the world, that he gave his only begotten Son, that whosoever believeth in him should not perish, but have everlasting life. For God sent not his Son into the world to condemn the world; but that the world through him might be saved" (Jn.3:16-17).

"Jesus saith unto him, I am the way, the truth, and the life: no man cometh unto the Father, but by me" (Jn.14:6).

"Him hath God exalted with his right hand *to be* a Prince and a Saviour, for to give repentance to Israel, and forgiveness of sins" (Ac.5:31).

"Wherefore he is able also to save them to the uttermost that come unto God by him, seeing he ever liveth to make intercession for them" (He.7:25).

2 **(1:1) Israel, Messages to—Symbol, of Israel, Believers—Believers, Symbolized by Israel—Deuteronomy, Recipients**: the recipients of the messages were the Israelites, the people chosen by God to be His witnesses upon earth. As the people of God, Israel was a symbol of believers, a symbol of all who would become true followers of the *Promised Seed*, the coming Messiah and Savior of the world, the Lord Jesus Christ, God's very own Son.

Note that Moses preached to *all* the Israelites, not just to a small number of them. These messages were important, so important that everyone needed to hear what was being preached.

DEUTERONOMY 1:1-5

OUTLINE	SCRIPTURE
2. The recipients—all Israel: A symbol of all believers	These *be* the words which Moses spake unto all Israel on this side Jordan in the wilderness, in the plain over against the Red *sea*, between Paran, and Tophel, and Laban, and Hazeroth, and Dizahab.

Thought 1. The message of God's Word is important, so important that every person needs to hear and heed what God has to say. People should be running to hear the Word of God preached and taught, seeking after the LORD while He may be found.

"Seek ye the LORD while he may be found, call ye upon him while he is near" (Is.55:6).

"Search the scriptures; for in them ye think ye have eternal life: and they are they which testify of me" (Jn.5:39).

"But these are written, that ye might believe that Jesus is the Christ, the Son of God; and that believing ye might have life through his name" (Jn.20:31).

"These were more noble than those in Thessalonica, in that they received the word with all readiness of mind, and searched the scriptures daily, whether those things were so" (Ac.17:11).

"For whatsoever things were written aforetime were written for our learning, that we through patience and comfort of the scriptures might have hope" (Ro.15:4).

"Now all these things happened unto them for ensamples: and they are written for our admonition, upon whom the ends of the world are come" (1 Co.10:11).

"Study to show thyself approved unto God, a workman that needeth not to be ashamed, rightly dividing the word of truth" (2 Ti.2:15).

"All scripture *is* given by inspiration of God, and *is* profitable for doctrine, for reproof, for correction, for instruction in righteousness" (2 Ti.3:16).

"As newborn babes, desire the sincere milk of the word, that ye may grow thereby: If so be ye have tasted that the LORD *is* gracious" (1 Pe.2:2-3).

"These things have I written unto you that believe on the name of the Son of God; that ye may know that ye have eternal life, and that ye may believe on the name of the Son of God" (1 Jn.5:13).

"But if from thence thou shalt seek the LORD thy God, thou shalt find *him,* if thou seek him with all thy heart and with all thy soul" (De.4:29).

Thought 2. The true Israelite believers were a type, a picture of all who would believe and become followers of the *Promised Seed*, the coming Messiah and Savior of the world, the Lord Jesus Christ.

"And he [Abraham] received the sign of circumcision, a seal of the righteousness of the faith which *he had yet* being uncircumcised: that he might be the father of all them that believe, though they be not circumcised; that righteousness might be imputed unto them also: And the father of circumcision to them who are not of the circumcision only, but who also walk in the steps of that faith of our father Abraham, which *he had* being *yet* uncircumcised" (Ro.4:11-12).

"He staggered not at the promise of God through unbelief; but was strong in faith, giving glory to God; And being fully persuaded that, what he had promised, he was able also to perform. And therefore it was imputed to him for righteousness. Now it was not written for his sake alone, that it was imputed to him; But for us also, to whom it shall be imputed, if we believe on him that raised up Jesus our LORD from the dead; Who was delivered for our offences, and was raised again for our justification" (Ro.4:20-25).

"Even as Abraham believed God, and it was accounted to him for righteousness. Know ye therefore that they which are of faith, the same are the children of Abraham. And the scripture, foreseeing that God would justify the heathen through faith, preached before the gospel unto Abraham, *saying,* In thee shall all nations be blessed. So then they which be of faith are blessed with faithful Abraham" (Ga.3:6-9).

"Now to Abraham and his seed were the promises made. He saith not, And to seeds, as of many; but as of one, And to thy seed, which is Christ" (Ga.3:16).

3 (1:2) **Promised Land—Israel, Second Generation of—Israel, Preparation to Enter the Promised Land:** the strategic place where the messages were preached was east of the Jordan River—right at the entrance to the promised land (see Map of the Wilderness Wanderings of Israel on page 436). Israel was camped by the river, right across from the great city of Jericho—poised to enter the promised land. The people were anxious, excited. For years they had longed for this day to come, the day they would enter the promised land and be able to settle down, build their homes and cities, plant their crops, start their businesses, establish their worship center, and live like God expected them to live—in spiritual conquest and rest. They had never known what it was to have a permanent roof over their heads, to live in freedom and security, nor to possess the spiritual peace and rest that God alone gives to those who walk obediently before Him.

DEUTERONOMY 1:1-5

But now the Israelites stood at the threshold of laying claim to the inheritance promised by God. There the land lay, right across the river from them. Obviously, as any of us would do, various groups of Israelite believers often gathered on the bank of the Jordan River, excitedly talking about what they were going to do when they inherited their place in the promised land of God.

This was the setting for the three great messages that are preached in the book of *Deuteronomy*, a strategic setting—by the Jordan River across from the great city of Jericho. The people were poised to enter the promised land of God.

OUTLINE	SCRIPTURE
3. The strategic place, east of the Jordan—right at the entrance to the promised land: A symbol of heaven & of spiritual conquest & rest	2 (*There are* eleven days' *journey* from Horeb by the way of mount Seir unto Kadeshbarnea.)

Thought 1. Two strong lessons are seen in this point.
(1) Some people stand on the threshold of receiving Christ and inheriting the promised land of God. But note: they have not yet crossed the threshold. They are still on the outside, still refusing to receive Christ as their Savior. The consequence is tragic: they continue to live in unbelief. They never receive the promised land of heaven, never know the spiritual conquest and rest of God, and never inherit eternal life.
(2) Other believers are on the threshold of entering the promised land of conquest, victory, and spiritual rest. But they have not yet crossed the threshold. After their conversion, they fail to study and grow in Christ, fail to learn how to walk and live for Christ. Some sin, some worldliness, some unbelief seeps into their lives. The consequence is tragic: they live defeated not victorious lives, restless not restful lives. They simply do not experience spiritual conquest and victory, do not possess the spiritual rest of soul that conquers all the trials and temptations of this life and that fills the soul with the deepest sense of fulfillment, purpose, and satisfaction.

"Take my yoke upon you, and learn of me; for I am meek and lowly in heart: and ye shall find rest unto your souls" (Mt.11:29).

"Who shall separate us from the love of Christ? *shall* tribulation, or distress, or persecution, or famine, or nakedness, or peril, or sword?...Nay, in all these things we are more than conquerors through him that loved us. For I am persuaded, that neither death, nor life, nor angels, nor principalities, nor powers, nor things present, nor things to come, Nor height, nor depth, nor any other creature, shall be able to separate us from the love of God, which is in Christ Jesus our LORD" (Ro.8:35, 37-39).

"There hath no temptation taken you but such as is common to man: but God *is* faithful, who will not suffer you to be tempted above that ye are able; but will with the temptation also make a way to escape, that ye may be able to bear *it*" (1 Co.10:13).

"Wherefore (as the Holy Ghost saith, To day if ye will hear his voice, Harden not your hearts, as in the provocation, in the day of temptation in the wilderness: When your fathers tempted me, proved me, and saw my works forty years. Wherefore I was grieved with that generation, and said, They do alway err in *their* heart; and they have not known my ways. So I sware in my wrath, They shall not enter into my rest)" (He.3:7-11).

"Take heed, brethren, lest there be in any of you an evil heart of unbelief, in departing from the living God" (He.3:12).

"But exhort one another daily, while it is called To day; lest any of you be hardened through the deceitfulness of sin. For we are made partakers of Christ, if we hold the beginning of our confidence stedfast unto the end" (He.3:13-14).

"Let us therefore fear, lest, a promise being left *us* of entering into his rest, any of you should seem to come short of it. For unto us was the gospel preached, as well as unto them: but the word preached did not profit them, not being mixed with faith in them that heard *it*" (He.4:1-2).

"Let us labour therefore to enter into that rest, lest any man fall after the same example of unbelief" (He.4:11).

"Submit yourselves therefore to God. Resist the devil, and he will flee from you" (Js.4:7).

"For whatsoever is born of God overcometh the world: and this is the victory that overcometh the world, *even* our faith. Who is he that overcometh the world, but he that believeth that Jesus is the Son of God?" (1 Jn.5:4-5).

"I will therefore put you in remembrance, though ye once knew this, how that the LORD, having saved the people out of the land of Egypt, afterward destroyed them that believed not" (Jude 5).

"And I heard a voice from heaven saying unto me, Write, Blessed *are* the dead which die in the LORD from henceforth: Yea, saith the Spirit, that they may rest from their labours; and their works do follow them" (Re.14:13).

"And he said, My presence shall go *with thee,* and I will give thee rest" (Ex.33:14).

"Return unto thy rest, O my soul; for the LORD hath dealt bountifully with thee" (Ps.116:7).

"And it shall come to pass in the day that the LORD shall give thee rest from thy sorrow, and from thy fear, and from the hard bondage wherein thou wast made to serve" (Is.14:3).

DEUTERONOMY 1:1-5

4 (1:3) **Deliverance, of Israel, from Egyptian Slavery—Israel, Second Generation—Preparation, to Enter the Promised Land—Promised Land, Preparation to Enter**: the messages of *Deuteronomy* were preached forty years after the Exodus of Israel from Egyptian slavery. Keep in mind that Egypt is a symbol of the world with all its enslavements and bondages. The Exodus is a picture of God's great deliverance from the enslavement of this world, from the sin and death of this world.

Standing there on the banks of the Jordan River, they must have thought about the great Exodus that had taken place forty years earlier; and remember, the forty years of wilderness wanderings had just ended. This is significant: it means that the people standing before Moses were the children of the Israelites who had experienced the great Exodus and the giving of the law at Mt. Sinai. All the adults of the first generation—20 years old and older—had died in the desert wilderness because of their terrible sin and unbelief, died under the judgment of God. Only the children 20 years old and younger had survived the ordeal of the wilderness wanderings and God's judgment. Many of the second generation had not yet been born or were too young to understand the law of God when it was first taught at Mt. Sinai. Consequently, there was great need for the present generation to be prepared before they could enter the promised land of God.

In fact, the second generation needed special preparation since they had not been eyewitnesses of the events of God's glorious power in delivering and guiding His people. There was a dire need for these events to be reviewed for one last time before the present generation of believers launched their campaign to claim the promised inheritance. A fresh grasp and consciousness of God's power and guidance were needed. The people needed a new work of God's Spirit in their hearts and lives. This was the setting for *Deuteronomy* when the messages of this great book were preached—forty years after the Exodus—at the very end of the forty-year wilderness journey.

OUTLINE	SCRIPTURE
4. The time—40 years after the Exodus: A symbol of God's great deliverance from this world & its enslavements	3 And it came to pass in the fortieth year, in the eleventh month, on the first *day* of the month, *that* Moses spake unto the children of Israel, according unto all that the LORD had given him in commandment unto them;

Thought 1. A person has to be prepared to enter the spiritual conquest and rest of the promised land of heaven. Preparation is essential.

> "Ye are all the children of light, and the children of the day: we are not of the night, nor of darkness. Therefore let us not sleep, as *do* others; but let us watch and be sober" (1 Th.5:5-6).
>
> "Teaching us that, denying ungodliness and worldly lusts, we should live soberly, righteously, and godly, in this present world; Looking for that blessed hope, and the glorious appearing of the great God and our Saviour Jesus Christ" (Tit.2:12-13).
>
> "Be sober, be vigilant; because your adversary the devil, as a roaring lion, walketh about, seeking whom he may devour" (1 Pe.5:8).
>
> "Nevertheless we, according to his promise, look for new heavens and a new earth, wherein dwelleth righteousness. Wherefore, beloved, seeing that ye look for such things, be diligent that ye may be found of him in peace, without spot, and blameless" (2 Pe.3:13-14).
>
> "Behold, I come quickly: hold that fast which thou hast, that no man take thy crown" (Re.3:11).
>
> "Behold, I come as a thief. Blessed *is* he that watcheth, and keepeth his garments, lest he walk naked, and they see his shame" (Re.16:15).

5 (1:3) **Word of God—Commandments, of God—Deuteronomy, Message of**: the message preached was the Word of God—all the commandments of God—all that God had commanded the people to do. The people needed to learn the Word of God, learn more and more about the commandments of God before they entered the promised land (v.3). Like all people of all generations, they needed to know exactly...

- what God demanded and expected
- how they were to live and where they could secure the power to live life to the fullest
- what God had promised and how they could claim His promises
- how they could secure the promised land of God and conquer the enemies who opposed them
- how they could be assured of God's continued presence and blessings

God's Word, His commandments, answered all this for the people. Once they learned the Word of God, they would know how to live life to the fullest, live life exactly as God commanded. The people would be ready to enter the promised land of God, ready to lay claim to the great inheritance promised by God.

DEUTERONOMY 1:1-5

OUTLINE	SCRIPTURE
5. The message: The Word of God—all the commandments of God	3 And it came to pass in the fortieth year, in the eleventh month, on the first *day* of the month, *that* Moses spake unto the children of Israel, according unto all that the LORD had given him in commandment unto them;

"But seek ye first the kingdom of God, and his righteousness; and all these things shall be added unto you" (Mt.6:33).

"The thief cometh not, but for to steal, and to kill, and to destroy: I am come that they might have life, and that they might have *it* more abundantly" (Jn.10:10).

"Jesus answered and said unto him, If a man love me, he will keep my words: and my Father will love him, and we will come unto him, and make our abode with him" (Jn.14:23).

"If ye keep my commandments, ye shall abide in my love; even as I have kept my Father's commandments, and abide in his love" (Jn.15:10).

"These things have I spoken unto you, that my joy might remain in you, and *that* your joy might be full" (Jn.15:11).

"But all these things will they do unto you for my name's sake, because they know not him that sent me" (Jn.15:21).

"And now, brethren, I commend you to God, and to the word of his grace, which is able to build you up, and to give you an inheritance among all them which are sanctified" (Ac.20:32).

"And I myself also am persuaded of you, my brethren, that ye also are full of goodness, filled with all knowledge, able also to admonish one another" (Ro.15:14).

"Now all these things happened unto them for ensamples: and they are written for our admonition, upon whom the ends of the world are come" (1 Co.10:11).

"Let the word of Christ dwell in you richly in all wisdom; teaching and admonishing one another in psalms and hymns and spiritual songs, singing with grace in your hearts to the LORD" (Col.3:16).

"Study to show thyself approved unto God, a workman that needeth not to be ashamed, rightly dividing the word of truth" (2 Ti.2:15).

"All scripture *is* given by inspiration of God, and *is* profitable for doctrine, for reproof, for correction, for instruction in righteousness" (2 Ti.3:16).

"As newborn babes, desire the sincere milk of the word, that ye may grow thereby: If so be ye have tasted that the LORD *is* gracious" (1 Pe.2:2-3).

"And this is his commandment, That we should believe on the name of his Son Jesus Christ, and love one another, as he gave us commandment" (1 Jn.3:23).

"Wherewithal shall a young man cleanse his way? by taking heed *thereto* according to thy word" (Ps.119:9).

"Thy word have I hid in mine heart, that I might not sin against thee" (Ps.119:11).

"Thy word *is* a lamp unto my feet, and a light unto my path" (Ps.119:105).

"For the commandment *is* a lamp; and the law *is* light; and reproofs of instruction *are* the way of life" (Pr.6:23).

"Thy words were found, and I did eat them; and thy word was unto me the joy and rejoicing of mine heart: for I am called by thy name, O LORD God of hosts" (Je.15:16).

6 (1:4-5) **Encouragement, to Live a Life of Victory—Victory, over Enemies—Promised Land, March to—Deuteronomy, Purpose of**: there were two major purposes for preaching the messages of *Deuteronomy*.

OUTLINE	SCRIPTURE
6. The purpose a. To encourage God's people to continue their victorious march into the promised land b. To expound the law of God one last time before entering the promised land & to renew the covenant with God	4 After he had slain Sihon the king of the Amorites, which dwelt in Heshbon, and Og the king of Bashan, which dwelt at Astaroth in Edrei: 5 On this side Jordan, in the land of Moab, began Moses to declare this law, saying,

a. The people needed encouragement, a strong encouragement, to continue their victorious march into the promised land (v.4). God had already given great victories over two mighty armies, the army of King Sihon of the Amorites and the army of King Og of Bashan (Nu.21:21-35).

They were going to face terrifying enemies as they sought to enter and secure the promised land of God. Enemy after enemy would assault the people of God. A spirit of doubt, fear, and cowardice could grip the people and lead to their defeat. They needed a strong spirit of faith, courage, and conquest. God had assured them of the promised land, that the land would

DEUTERONOMY 1:1-5

be theirs. Victory was assured if they marched forth in faith, believing and obeying God. They would triumph over all the enemies who tried to keep them out of the promised land of God. This was the purpose for the three messages of *Deuteronomy*: to encourage God's people—arouse them to continue their victorious march into the promised land.

Thought 1. As we march to the promised land of heaven, enemy after enemy will confront us, enemies such as...
- temptations
- trials
- greed
- lust
- immorality
- covetousness
- theft
- anger
- malice
- evil thoughts
- drugs
- alcohol
- gluttony
- bitterness
- ill will
- pride
- haughtiness
- selfishness

Such enemies stand opposed to the promised land of God. They are strong and mighty, able to enslave and defeat the believer. Such enemies will keep the believer out of the promised land, keep him from ever knowing the spiritual conquest and rest promised by God. But this is not the call of God. God calls the believer to victory. The believer can rest assured: the power of God is at his disposal. If he will just believe and obey God, he will conquer and triumph over all the enemies who oppose him. Victory is guaranteed. The conquering power of God in the life of the believer is assured.

"And ye shall be hated of all *men* for my name's sake. But there shall not an hair of your head perish. In your patience possess ye your souls" (Lu.21:17-19).

"Neither yield ye your members *as* instruments of unrighteousness unto sin: but yield yourselves unto God, as those that are alive from the dead, and your members *as* instruments of righteousness unto God" (Ro.6:13).

"Who shall separate us from the love of Christ? *shall* tribulation, or distress, or persecution, or famine, or nakedness, or peril, or sword?...Nay, in all these things we are more than conquerors through him that loved us....Nor height, nor depth, nor any other creature, shall be able to separate us from the love of God, which is in Christ Jesus our LORD" (Ro.8:35, 37, 39).

"There hath no temptation taken you but such as is common to man: but God *is* faithful, who will not suffer you to be tempted above that ye are able; but will with the temptation also make a way to escape, that ye may be able to bear *it*" (1 Co.10:13).

"For though we walk in the flesh, we do not war after the flesh: (For the weapons of our warfare *are* not carnal, but mighty through God to the pulling down of strong holds;) Casting down imaginations, and every high thing that exalteth itself against the knowledge of God, and bringing into captivity every thought to the obedience of Christ" (2 Co.10:3-5).

"Finally, my brethren, be strong in the LORD, and in the power of his might. Put on the whole armour of God, that ye may be able to stand against the wiles of the devil. For we wrestle not against flesh and blood, but against principalities, against powers, against the rulers of the darkness of this world, against spiritual wickedness in high *places*. Wherefore take unto you the whole armour of God, that ye may be able to withstand in the evil day, and having done all, to stand" (Ep.6:10-13).

"But thou, O man of God, flee these things; and follow after righteousness, godliness, faith, love, patience, meekness. Fight the good fight of faith, lay hold on eternal life, whereunto thou art also called, and hast professed a good profession before many witnesses" (1 Ti.6:11-12).

"Thou therefore endure hardness, as a good soldier of Jesus Christ. No man that warreth entangleth himself with the affairs of *this* life; that he may please him who hath chosen him to be a soldier" (2 Ti.2:3-4).

"Blessed *is* the man that endureth temptation: for when he is tried, he shall receive the crown of life, which the LORD hath promised to them that love him" (Js.1:12).

"Submit yourselves therefore to God. Resist the devil, and he will flee from you" (Js.4:7).

"For whatsoever is born of God overcometh the world: and this is the victory that overcometh the world, *even* our faith. Who is he that overcometh the world, but he that believeth that Jesus is the Son of God?" (1 Jn.5:4-5).

"For the eyes of the LORD run to and fro throughout the whole earth, to show himself strong in the behalf of *them* whose heart *is* perfect toward him. Herein thou hast done foolishly: therefore from henceforth thou shalt have wars" (2 Chr.16:9).

"The angel of the LORD encampeth round about them that fear him, and delivereth them" (Ps.34:7).

"Through thee will we push down our enemies: through thy name will we tread them under that rise up against us" (Ps.44:5).

"My son, if sinners entice thee, consent thou not" (Pr.1:10).

"Enter not into the path of the wicked, and go not in the way of evil *men*" (Pr.4:14).

b. The people needed the law of God explained one last time by God's aged servant, and they again needed to renew their covenant with God. They needed these two things before Moses died and before they set out to conquer the promised land of God (v.5).

DEUTERONOMY 1:1-5

The word *law* (Torah) means more than just dictates, commandments, and statutes. Basically, the law (Torah) means all the instructions and teachings of God.[1] It refers to the entire Pentateuch or Decalogue,[2] the first five books of the Bible. The law includes all that the LORD commanded (v.3): the Ten Commandments, the civil and religious laws, and all the other instructions given by God to His people. It is the wonderful law of God (Torah)—the full instruction and teaching of God—that tells people how to live life to the fullest. (See DEEPER STUDY # 1—Nu.4:1-2 for more discussion.) It was the law of God that the people needed to review right before entering the promised land. Once they were in the promised land, the law needed to be fresh upon their minds. It was the law of God—the full scope of His Word and teaching—that told the people what to do and how to live. But note this fact as well: the law of God is a covenant between God and man. The covenant of the law is conditional. God promised to bless man; but to receive the blessings of God's promises, a person must obey God. A person does not inherit the promised land unless he obeys God. The very purpose for explaining the law was to stir the people to obey God—to arouse them to renew their covenant or commitment to God. This was the purpose for the three messages being preached to the people of God, the very purpose for the great book of *Deuteronomy* being written.

Thought 1. Man desperately needs to learn the law of God—all the instructions and teachings of God. It is the law of God that tells us what to do and how to live life to the fullest. Keep in mind that Jesus Christ came to fulfill the law. (See note—Mt.5:17-18 for more discussion.) This simply means that He completed the law, fulfilled all its demands. By so doing, Jesus Christ stands before us as the Ideal, Perfect Man. We are no longer to focus upon the law but upon Jesus Christ. We are now to follow Him. But always remember: in following Christ, we obey the commandments of God. For Jesus Christ embraced the law *plus* so much more. We do not choose between Christ and the law. Christ fulfills the law: the commandments of God are fulfilled in Christ. Therefore, to follow Christ is to follow all that He is and represents: the law and so much more.

"All scripture *is* given by inspiration of God, and *is* profitable for doctrine, for reproof, for correction, for instruction in righteousness" (2 Ti.3:16).

"Not every one that saith unto me, Lord, Lord, shall enter into the kingdom of heaven; but he that doeth the will of my Father which is in heaven" (Mt.7:21).

"Therefore whosoever heareth these sayings of mine, and doeth them, I will liken him unto a wise man, which built his house upon a rock" (Mt.7:24).

"Jesus answered and said unto him, If a man love me, he will keep my words: and my Father will love him, and we will come unto him, and make our abode with him" (Jn.14:23).

"If ye keep my commandments, ye shall abide in my love; even as I have kept my Father's commandments, and abide in his love...Ye are my friends, if ye do whatsoever I command you" (Jn.15:10, 14).

"Study to show thyself approved unto God, a workman that needeth not to be ashamed, rightly dividing the word of truth" (2 Ti.2:15).

"Blessed *are* they that do his commandments, that they may have right to the tree of life, and may enter in through the gates into the city" (Re.22:14).

"Now therefore, if ye will obey my voice indeed, and keep my covenant, then ye shall be a peculiar treasure unto me above all people: for all the earth *is* mine: And ye shall be unto me a kingdom of priests, and an holy nation" (Ex.19:5-6).

"Now these *are* the commandments, the statutes, and the judgments, which the LORD your God commanded to teach you, that ye might do *them* in the land whither ye go to possess it: That thou mightest fear the LORD thy God, to keep all his statutes and his commandments, which I command thee, thou, and thy son, and thy son's son, all the days of thy life; and that thy days may be prolonged. Hear therefore, O Israel, and observe to do *it;* that it may be well with thee, and that ye may increase mightily, as the LORD God of thy fathers hath promised thee, in the land that floweth with milk and honey" (De.6:1-3).

"This day the LORD thy God hath commanded thee to do these statutes and judgments: thou shalt therefore keep and do them with all thine heart, and with all thy soul" (De.26:16).

"The law of the LORD *is* perfect, converting the soul: the testimony of the LORD *is* sure, making wise the simple. The statutes of the LORD *are* right, rejoicing the heart: the commandment of the LORD *is* pure, enlightening the eyes. The fear of the LORD *is* clean, enduring for ever: the judgments of the LORD *are* true *and* righteous altogether. More to be desired *are they* than gold, yea, than much fine gold: sweeter also than honey and the honeycomb. Moreover by them is thy servant warned: *and* in keeping of them *there is* great reward" (Ps.19:7-11).

---

[1] *The Nelson Study Bible, New King James Version.* (Nashville, TN: Thomas Nelson Publishers, Inc., 1997), notes on De.1:5.
[2] James Strong. *Strong's Exhaustive Concordance of the Bible.* (Nashville, TN: Thomas Nelson Publishers, Inc., 1990), #8451.

DEUTERONOMY 1:1-5

TYPES, SYMBOLS, AND PICTURES
(Deuteronomy 1:1-5)

Historical Term	Type or Picture (Scriptural Basis for Each)	Life Application for Today's Believer	Biblical Application
The Messenger—Moses, the Servant of God De.1:1	Moses is a symbol of Christ and of the minister. Moses was chosen by God... • *to be the liberator of Israel, freeing them from Egyptian slavery* • *to be the great leader of Israel, leading them to the promised land* • *to be the founding father of Israel as a nation* • *to be the intercessor who stood between God and His people* But this was not all. God also chose Moses to be the messenger of God, the great giver and communicator of the law of God. It is this call, this function of Moses—to be the messenger of God—that is the focus of the great Book of Deuteronomy. **"These *be* the words which Moses spake unto all Israel on this side Jordan in the wilderness, in the plain over against the Red sea, between Paran, and Tophel, and Laban, and Hazeroth, and Dizahab" (De.1:1).**	⇒ Moses stood between God and the people, stood as the messenger of God. As the messenger of God, Moses is a picture of Christ. Jesus Christ came to earth as the perfect Messenger of God, came to save man and to proclaim the way of salvation to man. ⇒ The minister of God is chosen to proclaim the Word of God to the people of God. This is the very purpose for which he is called: to be the messenger of God, to proclaim the Word of God.	"He that loveth me not keepeth not my sayings: and the word which ye hear is not mine, but the Father's which sent me" (Jn.14:24). "For unto you is born this day in the city of David a Saviour, which is Christ the LORD" (Lu.2:11). "For the Son of man is come to seek and to save that which was lost" (Lu. 19:10). "In the beginning was the Word, and the Word was with God, and the Word was God" (Jn.1:1). "God, who at sundry times and in divers manners spake in time past unto the fathers by the prophets, Hath in these last days spoken unto us by his Son, whom he hath appointed heir of all things, by whom also he made the worlds" (He.1:1-2). "And he said unto them, Go ye into all the world, and preach the gospel to every creature" (Mk.16:15). "Ye have not chosen me, but I have chosen you, and ordained you, that ye should go and bring forth fruit, and that your fruit should remain: that whatsoever ye shall ask of the Father in my name, he may give it you" (Jn.15:16; see Jn.21:17; see Ac. 9:20; Ac. 20:28; 1 Pe.5:2; Is.62:6; Je.3:15; Je.23:4; Eze.3:17).
All Israel De.1:1	The true Israelite believers were a type, a picture of all who would believe and become followers of the Promised Seed, the coming Messiah and Savior of the world, the Lord Jesus Christ. Note that Moses preached to "all" the Israelites, not just to a small number of them. These messages were important, so important that everyone needed to hear what was being preached. **"These *be* the words which Moses spake unto all Israel on this side Jordan in the wilderness, in the plain over against the Red**	⇒ The true Christian believer is the person who... • believes what God says and obeys Him • follows Christ into the promised land of heaven	"And he [Abraham] received the sign of circumcision, a seal of the righteousness of the faith which he had yet being uncircumcised: that he might be the father of all them that believe, though they be not circumcised; that righteousness might be imputed unto them also: And the father of circumcision to them who are not of the circumcision only, but who also walk in the steps of that faith of our father Abraham, which he had being yet uncircumcised" (Ro.4:11-12). "He staggered not at the

DEUTERONOMY 1:1-5

Historical Term	Type or Picture (Scriptural Basis for Each)	Life Application for Today's Believer	Biblical Application
	sea, between Paran, and Tophel, and Laban, and Hazeroth, and Dizahab" (De.1:1).		*promise of God through unbelief; but was strong in faith, giving glory to God; And being fully persuaded that, what he had promised, he was able also to perform. And therefore it was imputed to him for righteousness. Now it was not written for his sake alone, that it was imputed to him; But for us also, to whom it shall be imputed, if we believe on him that raised up Jesus our Lord from the dead; Who was delivered for our offences, and was raised again for our justification"* (Ro.4:20-25; See also Ga.3:16; see Ga.3:6-9).
The Promised Land De.1:1-5 (See also De.4:1-5; De.26:3)	*The promised land is a symbol of heaven and of spiritual conquest and rest.* *The promised land is a symbol of the new heavens and earth. God has set apart the obedient to be His people and to inherit the promised land, the land that flows with milk and honey, the land that did belong to the immoral and lawless of the world.* *"Now therefore hearken, O Israel, unto the statutes and unto the judgments, which I teach you, for to do them, that ye may live, and go in and possess the land which the LORD God of your fathers giveth you"* (De.4:1).	⇒ The obedient person will inherit the promised land of God. Who is the obedient person? The obedient person is the person who obeys God, who lives a life of separation, a life that is entirely different from the immoral and lawless people of the earth.	*"Wherefore come out from among them, and be ye separate, saith the LORD, and touch not the unclean thing; and I will receive you"* (2 Co.6:17). *"And take heed to yourselves, lest at any time your hearts be overcharged with surfeiting, and drunkenness, and cares of this life, and so that day come upon you unawares"* (Lu.21:34). *"And with many other words did he testify and exhort, saying, Save yourselves from this untoward generation"* (Ac.2:40). *"I beseech you therefore, brethren, by the mercies of God, that ye present your bodies a living sacrifice, holy, acceptable unto God, which is your reasonable service. And be not conformed to this world: but be ye transformed by the renewing of your mind, that ye may prove what is that good, and acceptable, and perfect, will of God"* (Ro.12:1-2). *"And have no fellowship with the unfruitful works of darkness, but rather reprove them"* (Ep.5:11).
The Exodus De.1:3 (See also De.20:1-20)	*The Exodus is a picture of God's great deliverance from the enslavement of this world, from the sin and death of this world.* *"And it came to pass in the fortieth year, in the eleventh month, on the first day of the month, that Mo-*	⇒ A person has to be prepared to enter the spiritual conquest and rest of the promised land of heaven. Preparation is essential if a person is to escape from the death grip of sin and the world.	*"There hath no temptation taken you but such as is common to man: but God is faithful, who will not suffer you to be tempted above that ye are able; but will with the temptation also make a way to escape, that ye may be able to bear it"* (1 Co.10:13).

DEUTERONOMY 1:1-5

Historical Term	Type or Picture (Scriptural Basis for Each)	Life Application for Today's Believer	Biblical Application
	...ses spake unto the children of Israel, according unto all that the LORD had given him in commandment unto them" (De.1:3).		"Now unto him that is able to do exceeding abundantly above all that we ask or think, according to the power that worketh in us" (Ep.3:20). "But I am poor and needy; yet the LORD thinketh upon me: thou art my help and my deliverer; make no tarrying, O my God" (Ps.40:17). "Fear thou not; for I am with thee: be not dismayed; for I am thy God: I will strengthen thee; yea, I will help thee; yea, I will uphold thee with the right hand of my righteousness" (Is.41:10). "When thou passest through the waters, I will be with thee; and through the rivers, they shall not overflow thee: when thou walkest through the fire, thou shalt not be burned; neither shall the flame kindle upon thee" (Is.43:2).
Egypt De.1:3 (See also Nu.3:5-13; 9:1-14; Le.11:44-47; Le.19:33-34)	*Egypt is a symbol of the world with all its enslavements and bondages.* *God had saved His people from the slavery of the world (Egypt), from the slavery of its sin and death. Note why:* *1. He saved them to be their God.* *2. He saved them to set them apart as His holy people.* "And it came to pass [after being freed from the enslavement of Egypt] in the fortieth year, in the eleventh month, on the first day of the month, that Moses spake unto the children of Israel, according unto all that the LORD had given him in commandment unto them" (De.1:3).	⇒ The application and lesson for us is clear: 1. We must declare that God is the Savior of the world, the Savior who delivered us from the world (Egypt). We must bear testimony, strong testimony, that God is building a new race of people, a people... • who will let Him be *their God* • who will be *set apart* and live as the holy people of God 2. We must be holy because God is holy. As believers, we have no choice: the command is direct and forceful. We must be like God: consecrated—set apart—holy. 3. We must learn to discern more and more between the clean and unclean, the holy and unholy. We must sharpen our power to discern, learn to distinguish between right and wrong, the just and unjust, the moral and immoral, the kind and	"That he would grant unto us, that we being delivered out of the hand of our enemies might serve him without fear, In holiness and righteousness before him, all the days of our life" (Lu.1:74-75). "Having therefore these promises, dearly beloved, let us cleanse ourselves from all filthiness of the flesh and spirit, perfecting holiness in the fear of God" (2 Co.7:1). "Follow peace with all men, and holiness, without which no man shall see the LORD" (He.12:14). "But sanctify [set apart as holy, pure] the LORD God in your hearts: and be ready always to give an answer to every man that asketh you a reason of the hope that is in you with meekness and fear" (1 Pe. 3:15). "But the natural man receiveth not the things of the Spirit of God: for they are foolishness unto him: neither can he know them, because they are spiritually discerned" (1 Co.2:14). "But strong meat belongeth to them that are of full age, even those who by reason of use have their senses

DEUTERONOMY 1:1-5

Historical Term	Type or Picture (Scriptural Basis for Each)	Life Application for Today's Believer	Biblical Application
		unkind, the selfish and unselfish.	*exercised to discern both good and evil" (He.5:14).* *"Give therefore thy servant an understanding heart to judge thy people, that I may discern between good and bad: for who is able to judge this thy so great a people?" (1 K.3:9).*

DIVISION II

THE FIRST GREAT THEME PREACHED BY GOD'S AGED SERVANT: REMEMBER THE LESSONS FROM HISTORY, 1:6–4:43

(1:6–4:43) **DIVISION OVERVIEW**: the wonderful promise of the promised land was first given by God to Abraham (Ge.12:1-3; 15:18). Down through the centuries, the promise was repeated time and again to God's people (De.1:8). Now, as the Israelites sat camped in the plains of Moab, Moses the aged servant of God was preparing the people to cross the Jordan and lay claim to the promised land. He was preparing them by preaching a *series of messages* that challenged them to rededicate their lives to God. They must renew their commitment, their covenant with God, before they entered the promised land. They must be spiritually prepared. How? First, they must learn the lessons of history. This is the subject of the First Division of the great book of *Deuteronomy*.

THE FIRST GREAT THEME PREACHED BY GOD'S AGED SERVANT: REMEMBER THE LESSONS FROM HISTORY, 1:6–4:43

A. The Pilgrimage of the First Generation of Israelite Believers: A Picture of Great Hope and Tragic Failure, 1:6–2:15
B. The Pilgrimage of the Second Generation of Israelite Believers: A Picture of Triumphant Victory and Warning, 2:16–3:29
C. The Strong Exhortation to the Second Generation of Israelite Believers: Obey God's Laws and Acknowledge That the LORD—He and He Alone—Is God, 4:1-43

DEUTERONOMY 1:6–2:15

II. THE FIRST GREAT THEME PREACHED BY GOD'S AGED SERVANT: REMEMBER THE LESSONS FROM HISTORY, 1:6–4:43

A. The Pilgrimage of the First Generation of Israelite Believers: A Picture of Great Hope & Tragic Failure, 1:6–2:15

1. Remember the call & charge of God to break camp—leave Sinai—move on—march & lay claim to the promised land: A picture of marching to heaven & of spiritual conquest & rest
   a. Was a great land
      1) Arabah: Jordan Valley
      2) The central mountains
      3) The western foothills
      4) South: The Negev
      5) West: The sea coast
      6) North: Canaanite land & Lebanon to the Euphrates
   b. Was promised to Abraham & all his descendants by a covenant, a contract: His descendants^{DS1} include all believers (Ge.12:1-3, 7; see Ro.4:11-13, 16; Ga.3:6-9)

2. Remember the provision of leaders & of justice
   a. The need for leaders
      1) The explosive population growth necessitated leaders
      2) The constant prayer for continued population growth necessitated leaders
      3) The weight of leadership was too heavy for Moses to bear alone (v.9, 12)
   b. The appointment & qualifications of the leaders
      1) To have wisdom & understanding & to be respected
      2) To represent each tribe
   c. The organizational structure
      1) The people were broken down into groups of thousands, hundreds, & tens
      2) Some leaders were to serve as commanders & tribal leaders
      3) Other leaders were to serve as judges
   d. The special charge to

6 The LORD our God spake unto us in Horeb, saying, Ye have dwelt long enough in this mount:
7 Turn you, and take your journey, and go to the mount of the Amorites, and unto all *the places* nigh thereunto, in the plain, in the hills, and in the vale, and in the south, and by the sea side, to the land of the Canaanites, and unto Lebanon, unto the great river, the river Euphrates.
8 Behold, I have set the land before you: go in and possess the land which the LORD sware unto your fathers, Abraham, Isaac, and Jacob, to give unto them and to their seed after them.
9 And I spake unto you at that time, saying, I am not able to bear you myself alone:
10 The LORD your God hath multiplied you, and, behold, ye *are* this day as the stars of heaven for multitude.
11 (The LORD God of your fathers make you a thousand times so many more as ye *are*, and bless you, as he hath promised you!)
12 How can I myself alone bear your cumbrance, and your burden, and your strife?
13 Take you wise men, and understanding, and known among your tribes, and I will make them rulers over you.
14 And ye answered me, and said, The thing which thou hast spoken *is* good *for us* to do.
15 So I took the chief of your tribes, wise men, and known, and made them heads over you, captains over thousands, and captains over hundreds, and captains over fifties, and captains over tens, and officers among your tribes.
16 And I charged your judges at that time, saying, Hear *the causes* between your brethren, and judge righteously between *every* man and his brother, and the stranger *that is* with him.
17 Ye shall not respect persons in judgment; *but* ye shall hear the small as well as the great; ye shall not be afraid of the face of man; for the judgment *is* God's: and the cause that is too hard for you, bring *it* unto me, and I will hear it.
18 And I commanded you at that time all the things which ye should do.
19 And when we departed from Horeb, we went through all that great and terrible wilderness, which ye saw by the way of the mountain of the Amorites, as the LORD our God commanded us; and we came to Kadeshbarnea.
20 And I said unto you, Ye are come unto the mountain of the Amorites, which the LORD our God doth give unto us.
21 Behold, the LORD thy God hath set the land before thee: go up *and* possess *it*, as the LORD God of thy fathers hath said unto thee; fear not, neither be discouraged.
22 And ye came near unto me every one of you, and said, We will send men before us, and they shall search us out the land, and bring us word again by what way we must go up, and into what cities we shall come.
23 And the saying pleased me well: and I took twelve men of you, one of a tribe:
24 And they turned and went up into the mountain, and came unto the valley of Eshcol, and searched it out.
25 And they took of the fruit of the land in their hands, and brought *it* down unto us, and brought us word again, and said, *It is* a good land which the LORD our God doth give us.
26 Notwithstanding ye would not go up, but rebelled against the commandment of the LORD your God:
27 And ye murmured in your tents, and said, Because the LORD hated us, he hath brought us forth out of the land of Egypt, to deliver us into the hand of the Amorites, to destroy us.

execute justice
   1) To judge fairly: Even between a brother & a foreigner
   2) To show impartiality: Equal justice for all
   3) To fear no person: One is accountable only to God
   4) To refer difficult cases to the chief judge, Moses himself

3. Remember the terrible sins that kept the first generation of Israelites out of the promised land: Fear, unbelief, grumbling, & rebellion
   a. The people started out obeying God: Marched through a *vast, terrible* desert or wilderness (150 miles) to Kadesh Barnea
   b. The people were given the privilege of seeing the promised land: Had reached the border, the hill country of the Amorites
   c. The people were challenged, exhorted
      1) To arise, go up & take possession of the land
      2) Not to fear nor be discouraged
   d. The people shut their ears to the exhortation—allowed fear & unbelief to take a foothold: Insisted that spies be sent to spy out the land
      1) Moses agreed to the idea: Sent 12 spies, one from each tribe
      2) The spies carried out their mission: Spied out the hill country & the Valley of Eshcol
      3) The spies returned with samples of fruit
         • Reported that the land was good
         • Reported that the enemies were too strong (v.28)
   e. The people became gripped with fear & unbelief, & they rebelled against God
      1) Grumbled in their tents: Blaming God for their circumstances
      2) Lost heart because of the spies' negative report

DEUTERONOMY 1:6–2:15

- The enemy was stronger & taller
- The cities were fortified
- The Anak (giants) were there

f. The people again were exhorted by Moses
  1) Not to be terrified nor fear
  2) To trust God
     - He would lead them & fight for them: Just as He had in Egypt & in the desert
     - He would carry them as a father carries his son

g. The people again rejected the exhortation: Were gripped by unbelief—did not trust God—did not trust His guidance, the guidance of the cloud by day nor the fiery cloud by night

h. The response of the LORD: Anger & judgment

  1) The people of the first generation were not allowed to enter the promised land

  2) Caleb, who believed & followed the LORD, was given an inheritance in the promised land

  3) Moses was barred from the promised land (Nu.20:1-13, esp. 12)

  4) Joshua was to enter the promised land: To be encouraged, for he was to replace Moses as leader

  5) The children of the disobedient parents—the second generation of believers—were to enter the promised land & possess it

4. **Remember the incomplete confession, the disobedience of the first generation**
  a. The charge to turn around

28 Whither shall we go up? our brethren have discouraged our heart, saying, The people is greater and taller than we; the cities are great and walled up to heaven; and moreover we have seen the sons of the Anakims there.
29 Then I said unto you, Dread not, neither be afraid of them.
30 The LORD your God which goeth before you, he shall fight for you, according to all that he did for you in Egypt before your eyes;
31 And in the wilderness, where thou hast seen how that the LORD thy God bare thee, as a man doth bear his son, in all the way that ye went, until ye came into this place.
32 Yet in this thing ye did not believe the LORD your God,
33 Who went in the way before you, to search you out a place to pitch your tents in, in fire by night, to show you by what way ye should go, and in a cloud by day.
34 And the LORD heard the voice of your words, and was wroth, and sware, saying,
35 Surely there shall not one of these men of this evil generation see that good land, which I sware to give unto your fathers,
36 Save Caleb the son of Jephunneh; he shall see it, and to him will I give the land that he hath trodden upon, and to his children, because he hath wholly followed the LORD.
37 Also the LORD was angry with me for your sakes, saying, Thou also shalt not go in thither.
38 But Joshua the son of Nun, which standeth before thee, he shall go in thither: encourage him: for he shall cause Israel to inherit it.
39 Moreover your little ones, which ye said should be a prey, and your children, which in that day had no knowledge between good and evil, they shall go in thither, and unto them will I give it, and they shall possess it.
40 But as for you, turn you, and take your journey into the wilderness by the way of the Red sea.

41 Then ye answered and said unto me, We have sinned against the LORD, we will go up and fight, according to all that the LORD our God commanded us. And when ye had girded on every man his weapons of war, ye were ready to go up into the hill.
42 And the LORD said unto me, Say unto them, Go not up, neither fight; for I am not among you; lest ye be smitten before your enemies.
43 So I spake unto you; and ye would not hear, but rebelled against the commandment of the LORD, and went presumptuously up into the hill.
44 And the Amorites, which dwelt in that mountain, came out against you, and chased you, as bees do, and destroyed you in Seir, even unto Hormah.
45 And ye returned and wept before the LORD; but the LORD would not hearken to your voice, nor give ear unto you.
46 So ye abode in Kadesh many days, according unto the days that ye abode there.

CHAPTER 2

Then we turned, and took our journey into the wilderness by the way of the Red sea, as the LORD spake unto me: and we compassed mount Seir many days.
2 And the LORD spake unto me, saying,
3 Ye have compassed this mountain long enough: turn you northward.
4 And command thou the people, saying, Ye are to pass through the coast of your brethren the children of Esau, which dwell in Seir; and they shall be afraid of you: take ye good heed unto yourselves therefore:
5 Meddle not with them; for I will not give you of their land, no, not so much as a foot breadth; because I have given mount Seir unto Esau for a possession.
6 Ye shall buy meat of them for money, that ye may eat; and ye shall also buy water of them for money, that ye may drink.

b. The incomplete & false confession: Confessed but did not repent
  1) Mobilized to fight in their own strength
  2) Mobilized without God's presence

c. The warning of God: Must not fight—without His presence they would be defeated

d. The refusal to listen
  1) Showed continued disobedience & rebellion
  2) Marched into the land of the Amorites

e. The result: Soundly defeated
  1) Were routed
  2) Were driven down to Hormah (about 50 miles)

f. The false confession again seen in the people: Wept because of their defeat not because of their disobedience

g. The wilderness wandering around Kadesh Barnea: For 38 years

5. **Remember the wilderness wanderings & the death of the first generation: A picture of God's faithfulness**
  a. God was faithful to guide His people
    1) The people wandered around for 38 years, until the 1st generation died
    2) God instructed the 2nd generation to march north to the promised land
  b. God was faithful to warn His people when necessary
    1) God warned the Israelites: They were soon to pass through Seir where the Edomites lived (were brothers to the Israelites through Esau)
       - Were not to provoke them: Israel would be defeated
       - Were to know that God had given Esau the land of Seir
    2) God gave a 2nd warning to the Israelites: They must pay for the food & water taken in Edom

c. God was faithful in blessing & meeting the needs of His people
  1) Blessed their work
  2) Watched over them through their wilderness wanderings (40 years)
 	
  3) Saw that they lacked for nothing
 	
d. God was faithful to honor His Word through all generations
  1) Instructed Israel not to harass the Moabites
  2) The reason: Because He had promised the land of Moab to Lot & his descendants
 	
e. God was faithful to encourage His people, assuring them that He would give them victory over their enemies
  1) The Moabites had defeated a strong &
	7 For the LORD thy God hath blessed thee in all the works of thy hand: he knoweth thy walking through this great wilderness: these forty years the LORD thy God *hath been* with thee; thou hast lacked nothing.
	8 And when we passed by from our brethren the children of Esau, which dwelt in Seir, through the way of the plain from Elath, and from Eziongaber, we turned and passed by the way of the wilderness of Moab.
	9 And the LORD said unto me, Distress not the Moabites, neither contend with them in battle: for I will not give thee of their land *for* a possession; because I have given Ar unto the children of Lot *for* a possession.
	10 The Emims dwelt therein in times past, a people great, and many, and tall, as the Anakims;
	11 Which also were accounted giants, as the Anakims;
		but the Moabites call them Emims.
		12 The Horims also dwelt in Seir beforetime; but the children of Esau succeeded them, when they had destroyed them from before them, and dwelt in their stead; as Israel did unto the land of his possession, which the LORD gave unto them.
		13 Now rise up, *said I*, and get you over the brook Zered. And we went over the brook Zered.
		14 And the space in which we came from Kadeshbarnea, until we were come over the brook Zered, *was* thirty and eight years; until all the generation of the men of war were wasted out from among the host, as the LORD sware unto them.
		15 For indeed the hand of the LORD was against them, to destroy them from among the host, until they were consumed.
			numerous race of giants, the Emim or Emites
			  2) The Edomites had defeated the Horites & settled in the land: A strong, powerful people
			  3) The lesson: God was encouraging His people, assuring them of victory over all enemies, even over the most powerful
			
			f. God was faithful to execute judgment & chastisement
			
			  1) The charge of God to cross the Zered Valley: Thirty-eight years after they had left Kadesh Barnea—marked a new beginning for God's people
			
			  2) The entire first generation perished in the wilderness wanderings: Under the hand of God's discipline & chastisement

DIVISION II

THE FIRST GREAT THEME PREACHED BY GOD'S AGED SERVANT: REMEMBER THE LESSONS FROM HISTORY, 1:6–4:43

A. The Pilgrimage of the First Generation of Israelite Believers: A Picture of Great Hope and Great Failure, 1:6–2:15

(1:6–2:15) **Introduction**: hope is one of the most powerful forces on earth. Hope is what keeps us going and what drives us to do more and more. Hope is the energy of life, the driving force that arouses a person to get up and march forth. Hope is the energy that drives us to achieve, accomplish, grow, develop, and progress.

Israel had hope—great hope—in the promised land of God. The great task that confronted Moses was how to keep this hope alive, how to keep it beating in the hearts of God's people. Keep this fact in mind: This passage is a sermon that Moses was preaching to the second generation of believers. Moses was doing all he could to arouse strong hope in the hearts of the people. If they were gripped by strong hope, they would courageously march into the promised land and lay claim to their inheritance. They would allow nothing to stop them.

Knowing this, Moses challenged the second generation to remember the experience of their parents: how they had started out with such great hope, but how miserably they had failed. This is the subject now preached by God's aged servant: *The Pilgrimage of the First Generation of Israelite Believers: A Picture of Great Hope and Great Failure,* 1:6–2:15.

1. Remember the call and charge of God to break camp—leave Sinai—move on—march and lay claim to the promised land: a picture of marching to heaven and of spiritual conquest and rest (1:6-8).
2. Remember the provision of leaders and of justice (1:9-17).
3. Remember the terrible sins that kept the first generation of Israelites out of the promised land: fear, unbelief, grumbling, and rebellion (1:18-39).
4. Remember the incomplete confession, the disobedience of the first generation (1:40-46).
5. Remember the wilderness wanderings and the death of the first generation: a picture of God's faithfulness (2:1-15).

1 (1:6-8) **Charge, Described, to March to the Promised Land—Promised Land, Duty to Possess—Conquest, Assured by God—Victory, Assured by God—Promised Land, Promised to Israel—Canaan, Promised to Israel—Canaan, Boundaries of—Promised Land, Boundaries of—Covenant, Abrahamic**: remember the call and charge of God to break camp, leave Sinai, march forth and lay claim to the promised land. The promised land is a picture of marching to heaven and of spiritual conquest and rest (see DEEPER STUDY # 1—De.1:8 for more discussion). Horeb was the mountain range in which Mt. Sinai was located. Because of this, Mt. Sinai is sometimes called Mt. Horeb (Ex.3:1; 17:6; 33:6; 1 K.19:8; Ps.106:19; Mal.4:4). The word *horeb* means desolate or desolation. The Israelites had been camped at Horeb or Mt. Sinai for

DEUTERONOMY 1:6–2:15

about a year when the charge of God to break camp was given. God charged His people to leave Sinai—to march and lay claim to the promised land of God. Note the Scripture and outline:

OUTLINE	SCRIPTURE	SCRIPTURE	OUTLINE

1. Remember the call & charge of God to break camp—leave Sinai—move on—march & lay claim to the promised land: A picture of marching to heaven & of spiritual conquest & rest
a. Was a great land
  1) Arabah: Jordan Valley
  2) The central mountains
  3) The western foothills
  4) South: The Negev
	6 The LORD our God spake unto us in Horeb, saying, Ye have dwelt long enough in this mount:
	7 Turn you, and take your journey, and go to the mount of the Amorites, and unto all *the places* nigh thereunto, in the plain, in the hills, and in the vale, and in the south, and by the sea side, to
		the land of the Canaanites, and unto Lebanon, unto the great river, the river Euphrates.
		8 Behold, I have set the land before you: go in and possess the land which the LORD sware unto your fathers, Abraham, Isaac, and Jacob, to give unto them and to their seed after them.
			5) West: The sea coast
			6) North: Canaanite land & Lebanon to the Euphrates
			
			b. Was promised to Abraham & all his descendants by a covenant, a contract: His descendants include all believers[DS1] (Ge.12:1-3, 7; see Ro.4:11-13, 16; Ga.3:6-9)

  a. The land promised to Israel was a great land that included some major localities that were well known in that day. Some of the localities are even identifiable today:
    1) The Arabah: this was the Jordan Valley that stretched from Lake Galilee to the area south of the Dead Sea.
    2) The central mountains: this included all the central hill country.
    3) The western foothills: this refers to a range of rolling hills that stretched from the Judean mountains toward the Mediterranean Sea.
    4) The southern boundary refers to the Negev: this was the dry wasteland that lay at the southern-most boundary of the promised land.
    5) The western boundary: this was the seacoast of the Mediterranean Sea.
    6) The northern boundary: this included the land of the Canaanites that reached all the way up to Lebanon and then stretched to the northeast reaching all the way to the Euphrates River.
  This was an enormous amount of land promised by God. The promised land would include most of modern Palestine and Syria.[1]
  b. The promised land was promised to Abraham and all his descendants by covenant, by a contract that was guaranteed by God Himself (v.8; see outline and notes—Ge.12:1-3; 15:7-21 for more discussion).

> "Now the LORD had said unto Abram, Get thee out of thy country, and from thy kindred, and from thy father's house, unto a land that I will show thee: And I will make of thee a great nation, and I will bless thee, and make thy name great; and thou shalt be a blessing: And I will bless them that bless thee, and curse him that curseth thee: and in thee shall all families of the earth be blessed" (Ge.12:1-3).
>
> "In the same day the LORD made a covenant with Abram, saying, Unto thy seed have I given this land, from the river of Egypt [the Nile] unto the great river, the river Euphrates" (Ge.15:18).

Thought 1. There are two pictures painted for us in this point:
(1) Abraham is the father, the symbol, of all believers. Every person who believes and follows God is a descendant of Abraham. This is the clear declaration of Scripture.

> "And he received the sign of circumcision, a seal of the righteousness of the faith which *he had yet* being uncircumcised: that he might be the father of all them that believe, though they be not circumcised; that righteousness might be imputed unto them also: And the father of circumcision to them who are not of the circumcision only, but who also walk in the steps of that faith of our father Abraham, which *he had* being *yet* uncircumcised. For the promise, that he should be the heir of the world, *was* not to Abraham, or to his seed, through the law, but through the righteousness of faith" (Ro.4:11-13).
>
> "Therefore *it is* of faith, that *it might be* by grace; to the end the promise might be sure to all the seed; not to that only which is of the law, but to that also which is of the faith of Abraham; who is the father of us all [believers]" (Ro.4:16).
>
> "Even as Abraham believed God, and it was accounted to him for righteousness. Know ye therefore that they which are of faith, the same are the children of Abraham. And the scripture, foreseeing that God would justify the heathen through faith, preached before the gospel unto Abraham, *saying,* In thee shall all nations be blessed. So then they which be of faith are blessed with faithful Abraham" (Ga.3:6-9).

(2) The promised land is a symbol of heaven and of the spiritual conquest and rest the believer is to experience as he marches to the promised land of heaven. (See DEEPER STUDY # 1—De.1:8 for more discussion.)

DEEPER STUDY # 1
(1:8) Land, Promised—Canaan—Covenant—Heaven—Inheritance—Rest, Spiritual—Conquest, Spiritual—Victory, Spiritual: because of the length of this Deeper Study, it is being placed at the end of this particular outline and Scripture, after major point 6.

---

[1] Peter Craigie. *The Book of Deuteronomy*, p.95.

DEUTERONOMY 1:6–2:15

2 (1:9-17) **Leadership, Duties of—Judges, Duties of—Israel, Organization of—Justice, Organization of—Israel, Leaders of—Israel, Judges of**: remember the provision of leaders and of justice. When God called Israel to leave Mt. Sinai and begin the march to the promised land, the people had to organize immediately. There were two to three million Israelites at this particular time, far too many people for one person (Moses) to lead and manage, much less control. Moreover, the journey was to be harsh and difficult—a march through a vast and terrifying desert wilderness. Moses needed help in leading and ruling the people, in executing justice among them.

OUTLINE	SCRIPTURE	SCRIPTURE	OUTLINE

2. Remember the provision of leaders & of justice
  a. The need for leaders
 	
    1) The explosive population growth necessitated leaders
 	
    2) The constant prayer for continued population growth necessitated leaders
 	
    3) The weight of leadership was too heavy for Moses to bear alone, vv.9, 12
  b. The appointment & qualifications of the leaders
    1) To have wisdom & understanding & to be respected
    2) To represent each tribe
 	
  c. The organizational structure
	9 And I spake unto you at that time, saying, I am not able to bear you myself alone:
	10 The LORD your God hath multiplied you, and, behold, ye *are* this day as the stars of heaven for multitude.
	11 (The LORD God of your fathers make you a thousand times so many more as ye *are*, and bless you, as he hath promised you!)
	12 How can I myself alone bear your cumbrance, and your burden, and your strife?
	13 Take you wise men, and understanding, and known among your tribes, and I will make them rulers over you.
	14 And ye answered me, and said, The thing which thou hast spoken *is* good *for us* to do.
	15 So I took the chief of
		your tribes, wise men, and known, and made them heads over you, captains over thousands, and captains over hundreds, and captains over fifties, and captains over tens, and officers among your tribes.
		16 And I charged your judges at that time, saying, Hear *the causes* between your brethren, and judge righteously between *every* man and his brother, and the stranger *that is* with him.
		17 Ye shall not respect persons in judgment; *but* ye shall hear the small as well as the great; ye shall not be afraid of the face of man; for the judgment *is* God's: and the cause that is too hard for you, bring *it* unto me, and I will hear it.
			1) The people were broken down into groups of thousands, hundreds, & tens
			2) Some leaders were to serve as commanders & tribal leaders
			3) Other leaders were to serve as judges
			d. The special charge to execute justice
			  1) To judge fairly: Even between a brother & a foreigner
			  2) To show impartiality: Equal justice for all
			  3) To fear no person: One is accountable only to God
			  4) To refer difficult cases to the chief judge, Moses himself

  a. There was the need for leaders to help Moses. Quite frankly, the people were too heavy a burden for Moses to lead by himself (vv.9-12). There were just too many people; the population had exploded. The people numbered as the stars in the sky (v.10; see Ge.15:5; 22:17). However, it was not only the explosive population that had already taken place, but Moses was constantly praying for continued population growth. In fact, standing there preaching and thinking about the ever-expanding population, Moses broke out in a prayer that God would increase their numbers a thousand times and bless them just as He had promised.

  Again, the weight of leadership was too heavy for Moses to bear all alone. Note how he remembered the very words he had cried out years ago to the first generation of believers: "How can I bear your problems, your burdens, and your complaints all by myself?"

  b. There was the appointment and qualification of the leaders (vv.13-14). In a democratic process, Moses had apparently charged the people to choose the leaders themselves. The leaders were to be wise and understanding and to be respected by the people.

    ⇒ The word *wise* (hakam) means to possess knowledge, intelligence, and wisdom; to have the knowledge and intelligence to know both what to do and how to do it.
    ⇒ The word *understanding* (biyn) means the ability to discern and to diligently consider; to have the ability to think, perceive, regard, ponder, comprehend, explain, instruct, and judge.

A wise and understanding person is a person who has gained great knowledge and experience throughout life. But note: these were not the only two qualities required. The leader chosen had to be a person who was held in high regard by the people, a person of unwavering integrity with a solid reputation. The leader of God's people was to be a strong example with a dynamic testimony for the LORD. Note that a leader was to be chosen from each tribe: each tribe was to be represented.

  c. There was a wise organizational structure devised for the people (v.15). The people were broken down into groups of thousands, hundreds, and tens. Some leaders were to serve as commanders and tribal leaders. As commanders they led the people into battle. As tribal leaders they governed the affairs of the tribe. Note that other leaders were apparently chosen to serve as judges of legal matters that arose between the people.

  d. There was the special charge to execute justice (vv.16-17). Without fair and equal justice, a people cannot long survive. This was the reason Moses gave special emphasis in his sermon to the execution of justice.

    1) Judges had to judge fairly in settling all disputes among the Israelites. But this was not all: the judges had to judge fairly between a citizen and a foreigner who might be in the land. Fair and equitable justice was to be carried out no matter who was involved.
    2) Judges were to show no partiality whatsoever in executing justice. There was to be no favoritism shown to any person. "Equal justice for all" was to be the foundation stone of justice throughout the land.

DEUTERONOMY 1:6–2:15

3) Judges were to fear no person, not the powerful nor the rich. Justice and judgment belonged to God, not to man. God cares for all people equally; therefore, all people are to be treated fairly and equally in the courts of law. Judges are accountable to God and God alone.
4) Judges were to refer difficult cases to the chief judge, Moses himself.

Thought 1. There are two strong lessons for us in this point:
(1) There is a desperate need for leaders in the church and leaders who will serve God's people. People will never reach the promised land of heaven without qualified leaders. The Israelites needed qualified leaders, and believers today need qualified leaders.

"And he said unto them, Go ye into all the world, and preach the gospel to every creature" (Mk.16:15).

"Ye have not chosen me, but I have chosen you, and ordained you, that ye should go and bring forth fruit, and *that* your fruit should remain: that whatsoever ye shall ask of the Father in my name, he may give it you" (Jn.15:16).

"So when they had dined, Jesus saith to Simon Peter, Simon, *son* of Jonas, lovest thou me more than these? He saith unto him, Yea, LORD; thou knowest that I love thee. He saith unto him, Feed my lambs. He saith to him again the second time, Simon, *son* of Jonas, lovest thou me? He saith unto him, Yea, LORD; thou knowest that I love thee. He saith unto him, Feed my sheep. He saith unto him the third time, Simon, *son* of Jonas, lovest thou me? Peter was grieved because he said unto him the third time, Lovest thou me? And he said unto him, LORD, thou knowest all things; thou knowest that I love thee. Jesus saith unto him, Feed my sheep" (Jn.21:15-17).

"But the LORD said unto him, Go thy way: for he is a chosen vessel unto me, to bear my name before the Gentiles, and kings, and the children of Israel" (Ac.9:15).

"Take heed therefore unto yourselves, and to all the flock, over the which the Holy Ghost hath made you overseers, to feed the church of God, which he hath purchased with his own blood" (Ac.20:28).

"But rise, and stand upon thy feet: for I have appeared unto thee for this purpose, to make thee a minister and a witness both of these things which thou hast seen, and of those things in the which I will appear unto thee" (Ac.26:16).

"Now then we are ambassadors for Christ, as though God did beseech *you* by us: we pray *you* in Christ's stead, be ye reconciled to God" (2 Co.5:20).

"Feed the flock of God which is among you, taking the oversight *thereof*, not by constraint, but willingly; not for filthy lucre, but of a ready mind" (1 Pe.5:2).

"Also I heard the voice of the LORD, saying, Whom shall I send, and who will go for us? Then said I, Here *am* I; send me" (Is.6:8).

"And I will give you pastors according to mine heart, which shall feed you with knowledge and understanding" (Je.3:15).

(2) Justice must be executed fairly. Every person must be treated equally under the law. Partiality and favoritism must never be shown in executing justice.

"I charge *thee* before God, and the Lord Jesus Christ, and the elect angels, that thou observe these things without preferring one before another, doing nothing by partiality" (1 Ti.5:21).

"Are ye not then partial in yourselves, and are become judges of evil thoughts" (Js.2:4).

"Ye shall do no unrighteousness in judgment: thou shalt not respect the person of the poor, nor honour the person of the mighty: *but* in righteousness shalt thou judge thy neighbour" (Le.19:15).

"Ye shall not respect persons in judgment; *but* ye shall hear the small as well as the great; ye shall not be afraid of the face of man; for the judgment *is* God's: and the cause that is too hard for you, bring *it* unto me, and I will hear it" (De.1:17).

"He will surely reprove you, if ye do secretly accept persons" (Jb.13:10).

"How long will ye judge unjustly, and accept the persons of the wicked?" (Ps.82:2).

"These *things* also *belong* to the wise. *It is* not good to have respect of persons in judgment" (Pr.24:23).

"An unjust man *is* an abomination to the just: and *he that is* upright in the way *is* abomination to the wicked" (Pr.29:27).

"Therefore have I also made you contemptible and base before all the people, according as ye have not kept my ways, but have been partial in the law" (Mal.2:9).

3 (1:18-39) **Fear, Results of—Unbelief, Results of—Grumbling, Results of—Rebellion, Results of—Israel, Twelve Spies of—Israel, Judgment upon—Israel, Unbelief of**: remember the terrible sins that kept the first generation of Israelites out of the promised land: fear, unbelief, grumbling, and rebellion. This was one of the major lessons from history that God's people needed to learn: sin would keep them out of the promised land, especially the sins of unbelief, grumbling, and rebellion (see Map of the Wilderness Wanderings of Israel on page 436). The Scripture and outline show exactly how Moses drove the point home to the hearts of the believers:

DEUTERONOMY 1:6–2:15

OUTLINE	SCRIPTURE	SCRIPTURE	OUTLINE
3. Remember the terrible sins that kept the first generation of Israelites out of the promised land: Fear, unbelief, grumbling, & rebellion a. The people started out obeying God: Marched through a "vast, terrible" desert or wilderness (150 miles) to Kadesh Barnea b. The people were given the privilege of seeing the promised land: Had reached the border, the hill country of the Amorites c. The people were challenged, exhorted 1) To arise, go up & take possession of the land 2) Not to fear nor be discouraged d. The people shut their ears to the exhortation—allowed fear & unbelief to take a foothold: Insisted that spies be sent to spy out the land 1) Moses agreed to the idea: Sent 12 spies, one from each tribe 2) The spies carried out their mission: Spied out the hill country & the Valley of Eshcol 3) The spies returned with samples of fruit • Reported that the land was good • Reported that the enemies were too strong (v.28) e. The people became gripped with fear & unbelief, & they rebelled against God 1) Grumbled in their tents: Blaming God for their circumstances 2) Lost heart because of the spies' negative report • The enemy was stronger & taller • The cities were fortified	18 And I commanded you at that time all the things which ye should do. 19 And when we departed from Horeb, we went through all that great and terrible wilderness, which ye saw by the way of the mountain of the Amorites, as the LORD our God commanded us; and we came to Kadeshbarnea. 20 And I said unto you, Ye are come unto the mountain of the Amorites, which the LORD our God doth give unto us. 21 Behold, the LORD thy God hath set the land before thee: go up *and* possess *it*, as the LORD God of thy fathers hath said unto thee; fear not, neither be discouraged. 22 And ye came near unto me every one of you, and said, We will send men before us, and they shall search us out the land, and bring us word again by what way we must go up, and into what cities we shall come. 23 And the saying pleased me well: and I took twelve men of you, one of a tribe: 24 And they turned and went up into the mountain, and came unto the valley of Eshcol, and searched it out. 25 And they took of the fruit of the land in their hands, and brought *it* down unto us, and brought us word again, and said, *It is* a good land which the LORD our God doth give us. 26 Notwithstanding ye would not go up, but rebelled against the commandment of the LORD your God: 27 And ye murmured in your tents, and said, Because the LORD hated us, he hath brought us forth out of the land of Egypt, to deliver us into the hand of the Amorites, to destroy us. 28 Whither shall we go up? our brethren have discouraged our heart, saying, The people *is* greater and taller	than we; the cities *are* great and walled up to heaven; and moreover we have seen the sons of the Anakims there. 29 Then I said unto you, Dread not, neither be afraid of them. 30 The LORD your God which goeth before you, he shall fight for you, according to all that he did for you in Egypt before your eyes; 31 And in the wilderness, where thou hast seen how that the LORD thy God bare thee, as a man doth bear his son, in all the way that ye went, until ye came into this place. 32 Yet in this thing ye did not believe the LORD your God, 33 Who went in the way before you, to search you out a place to pitch your tents *in*, in fire by night, to show you by what way ye should go, and in a cloud by day. 34 And the LORD heard the voice of your words, and was wroth, and sware, saying, 35 Surely there shall not one of these men of this evil generation see that good land, which I sware to give unto your fathers, 36 Save Caleb the son of Jephunneh; he shall see it, and to him will I give the land that he hath trodden upon, and to his children, because he hath wholly followed the LORD. 37 Also the LORD was angry with me for your sakes, saying, Thou also shalt not go in thither. 38 *But* Joshua the son of Nun, which standeth before thee, he shall go in thither: encourage him: for he shall cause Israel to inherit it. 39 Moreover your little ones, which ye said should be a prey, and your children, which in that day had no knowledge between good and evil, they shall go in thither, and unto them will I give it, and they shall possess it.	• The Anak (giants) were there f. The people again were exhorted by Moses 1) Not to be terrified nor fear 2) To trust God • He would lead them & fight for them: Just as He had in Egypt & in the desert • He would carry them as a father carries his son g. The people again rejected the exhortation: Were gripped by unbelief—did not trust God—did not trust His guidance, the guidance of the cloud by day nor the fiery cloud by night h. The response of the LORD: Anger & judgment 1) The people of the first generation were not allowed to enter the promised land 2) Caleb, who believed & followed the LORD, was given an inheritance in the promised land 3) Moses was barred from the promised land (Nu.20:1-13, esp. 12) 4) Joshua was to enter the promised land: To be encouraged, for he was to replace Moses as leader 5) The children of the disobedient parents—the second generation of believers—were to enter the promised land & possess it

a. The people—the first generation of Israelite believers—started out obeying God (v.19). They marched through a vast, terrible desert wilderness all the way to Kadesh Barnea. This wilderness was the desert of Paran—a dusty, dry, thirsty, most difficult journey that covered about one hundred and fifty miles.[2] The dry desert sat upon a waterless plateau of limestone.

---

[2] Frank E Gaebelein, Editor. *The Expositor's Bible Commentary*, Vol.2. (Grand Rapids, MI: Zondervan Publishing House, 1990), p.25.

DEUTERONOMY 1:6–2:15

One can just imagine how thirsty, dusty, and uncomfortable the people became as they marched along with perspiration dripping down their faces into their eyes and soaking their clothes.

    b. The people were given the privilege of seeing the promised land (v.20). Kadesh Barnea was in the hill country of the Amorites and, in fact, sat on the border of the promised land. This means that the Israelites had indeed reached the very border of the promised land itself. The people could actually stand on the hills and look out into the promised land.

    c. The people were challenged and exhorted by Moses to arise, go up and take possession of the land (v.21). They were not to fear nor be discouraged, for God had promised to give them victory over the enemies who stood against them. Conquest was assured. Possession of the land was guaranteed by God Himself. Consequently, there was no reason to fear nor to become discouraged. The people were to be courageous and march forth conquering all the enemies who opposed their entering the promised land.

    d. The people took the first step toward failure: they shut their ears to the exhortation. They allowed fear and unbelief to take a foothold. They insisted that spies be sent to gather information on the enemies before they launched their campaign to lay claim to the promised land (v.22).

        1) After seeking the LORD, Moses agreed to the idea (Nu.13:1-3). He sent twelve spies, one from each tribe.

        2) At Moses' command, the spies carried out their mission: they spied out the hill country and the valley of Eshcol (v.24). This was obviously a fruitful valley, so productive that it was almost unbelievable. A single cluster of grapes was so large that it had to be carried along with other fruit on a pole by two men. The word *eshcol* means "the valley of the cluster" (Nu.13:23-24).

        3) After forty days, the spies returned with the samples of fruit from the promised land. They reported that the land was good, but the enemies were too strong and fortified for a campaign to be launched against them (v.25, see v.28).

    e. The people became gripped with fear and unbelief, and they rebelled against God (vv.26-28).

        1) The people grumbled in their tents, blaming God for their circumstances (v.27).

        2) The people lost heart because of the spies' negative report (vv.27-28). Note how they continually stressed the negative and exposed the unbelief of their hearts.
- ⇒ The enemy was stronger and taller.
- ⇒ The cities were fortified.
- ⇒ The Anak or giants were there.

We know from the book of Numbers that the ten spies who opposed the campaign began to spread their bad, defeatist report among the people (Nu.13:32). They stressed, exaggerated, and distorted the negative factors.

    f. The people again were exhorted by Moses (v.29). Moses did all he could: he challenged the people not to fear their enemies but to trust God. He assured the people that God would lead them and fight for them just as He had led and fought for them in Egypt and in the desert wilderness. God would carry them along just as a father carries his son. Note that God's leadership and power on behalf of His people had been demonstrated before their very eyes (v.30). The first generation of believers had been *eyewitnesses* of God's presence, guidance, and power. But despite this wonderful and phenomenal experience, they tragically failed again.

    g. The people once more rejected the exhortation of God's servant. They were gripped by unbelief and refused to trust God. They did not trust His guidance, refused to trust the promise of His presence and leadership (vv.32-33). They refused to follow God who had so wonderfully proven His guidance through the movements of the cloud by day and the fiery cloud by night (Ex.40:34-38).

    h. The response of the LORD was inevitable, unpreventable: anger and judgment (vv.34-39).

        1) The people of the first generation were prohibited from ever entering the promised land (v.35). Not a single person twenty years old or older would ever enter the promised land, no person except Joshua and Caleb who had proven faithful (see outline and notes—Nu.14:10-25; 14:26-39 for more discussion). Note that the first generation of believers was called an "evil generation."

> **"And the LORD spake unto Moses and unto Aaron, saying, How long *shall I bear with* this evil congregation, which murmur against me? I have heard the murmurings of the children of Israel, which they murmur against me. Say unto them, *As truly as* I live, saith the LORD, as ye have spoken in mine ears, so will I do to you: Your carcases shall fall in this wilderness; and all that were numbered of you, according to your whole number, from twenty years old and upward, which have murmured against me, Doubtless ye shall not come into the land, *concerning* which I sware to make you dwell therein, save Caleb the son of Jephunneh, and Joshua the son of Nun. But your little ones, which ye said should be a prey, them will I bring in, and they shall know the land which ye have despised. But *as for* you, your carcases, they shall fall in this wilderness. And your children shall wander in the wilderness forty years, and bear your whoredoms, until your carcases be wasted in the wilderness. After the number of the days in which ye searched the land, *even* forty days, each day for a year, shall ye bear your iniquities, *even* forty years, and ye shall know my breach of promise. I the LORD have said, I will surely do it unto all this evil congregation, that are gathered together against me: in this wilderness they shall be consumed, and there they shall die. And the men, which Moses sent to search the land, who returned, and made all the congregation to murmur against him, by bringing up a slander upon the land, Even those men that did bring up the evil report upon the land, died by the plague before the LORD. But Joshua the son of Nun, and Caleb the son of Jephunneh, *which were* of the men that went to search the land, lived *still*" (Nu.14:26-38).**

        2) Caleb believed and followed the LORD; therefore, he was given an inheritance in the promised land (v.36). Caleb was one of the two spies who had challenged the people to launch the campaign to lay claim to the promised land. Note that he followed the LORD *wholly* (male), with his whole heart. The Hebrew actually says that "he completely filled himself with the LORD." The word means to be complete, full, wholly filled. The idea is that Caleb was so full of the LORD that he was totally dedicated and willing to follow the LORD anyplace, even against the strongest enemies.

3) Moses himself was barred from the promised land because of his terrible sin, the sin of disobedience and of failing to honor the LORD before the people (see outline and notes—Nu.20:7-13 for more discussion). The tragic disobedience of Moses had taken place at the waters of Meribah (Kadesh). The people had no water, so they began to grumble against the LORD and His dear servant. To solve the problem, God gave clear instructions to Moses. He was to walk up to a particular rock in the presence of all the people and charge the rock to gush out a stream of water. But Moses disobeyed God:

⇒ He did not speak to the rock but rather lashed out at the people.
⇒ He did not give God the full credit and honor for the miraculous gift of water. In lashing out against the people, he charged them with being "rebels" and asked them, "Must 'we' bring you water?" Note that he put himself on a level with God, suggesting that it was he and God who were going to provide water for the people. Standing there before the people, he failed to honor God as the only Person who can meet man's need, in particular man's need for living water. Moses exalted himself, accepting some of the credit for the miracle that was about to happen.
⇒ He struck the rock instead of just speaking to it as commanded by God. And note: he struck the rock not once but twice.

The response of the LORD was immediate. In justice and chastisement God made two charges against Moses: he had failed to trust God and he had disobeyed God; he had failed to honor God as holy before the people. Consequently, Moses was to be barred from ever entering the promised land. He would not have the privilege of leading the people in their conquest of the promised land.

4) Joshua was to replace Moses as leader of the people; he was to guide them into the promised land. Therefore, Joshua was to be encouraged by Moses and the people (v.38).

5) The children of the disobedient parents—the second generation of believers—were to be given the promised land (v.39). In their rebellion the parents had used the children as an excuse for not entering the promised land. They did not want their children to become captives, slaves of the enemies who would oppose them. Their excuse was a slap in the face of God, a total lack of trust in God. Because they used their children as the excuse for distrusting God, the children were saved from the judgment of God. All children twenty years old and younger would enter the promised land. The inheritance of the promised land would be given to the second generation of believers. Remember: the Israelites standing before Moses as he preached this sermon were the second generation.

Thought 1. We must remember the terrible sins that kept the first generation of Israelites out of the promised land: the sins of fear, unbelief, grumbling, and rebellion. We must remember the terrible failure of the Israelites for two reasons:

(1) God judges and chastises (disciplines) His people when they sin—when they fail to believe and follow Him.

"For the Son of man shall come in the glory of his Father with his angels; and then he shall reward every man according to his works" (Mt.16:27).

"Every branch in me that beareth not fruit he taketh away: and every *branch* that beareth fruit, he purgeth it, that it may bring forth more fruit" (Jn.15:2).

"But when we are judged, we are chastened of the LORD, that we should not be condemned with the world" (1 Co.11:32).

"For we must all appear before the judgment seat of Christ; that every one may receive the things *done* in *his* body, according to that he hath done, whether *it be* good or bad" (2 Co.5:10).

"And ye have forgotten the exhortation which speaketh unto you as unto children, My son, despise not thou the chastening of the LORD, nor faint when thou art rebuked of him: For whom the LORD loveth he chasteneth, and scourgeth every son whom he receiveth" (He.12:5-6).

"And if ye call on the Father, who without respect of persons judgeth according to every man's work, pass the time of your sojourning *here* in fear" (1 Pe.1:17).

"And, behold, I come quickly; and my reward *is* with me, to give every man according as his work shall be" (Re.22:12).

"Also unto thee, O LORD, *belongeth* mercy: for thou renderest to every man according to his work" (Ps.62:12).

"My son, despise not the chastening of the LORD; neither be weary of his correction: For whom the LORD loveth he correcteth; even as a father the son *in whom* he delighteth" (Pr.3:11-12).

"I the LORD search the heart, *I* try the reins, even to give every man according to his ways, *and* according to the fruit of his doings" (Je.17:10).

(2) There is to be a day of judgment out in the future, a day when God will judge every human being who has ever lived.

"And as it is appointed unto men once to die, but after this the judgment" (He.9:27).

"When the Son of man shall come in his glory, and all the holy angels with him, then shall he sit upon the throne of his glory: And before him shall be gathered all nations: and he shall separate them one from another, as a shepherd divideth *his* sheep from the goats: And he shall set the sheep on his right hand, but the goats on the left" (Mt.25:31-33).

"And to you who are troubled rest with us, when the LORD Jesus shall be revealed from heaven with his mighty angels, In flaming fire taking vengeance on them that know not God, and that obey not the gospel of our Lord Jesus Christ" (2 Th.1:7-8).

"The LORD knoweth how to deliver the godly out of temptations, and to reserve the unjust unto the day of judgment to be punished" (2 Pe.2:9).

"But the heavens and the earth, which are now, by the same word are kept in store, reserved unto fire against the day of judgment and perdition of ungodly men" (2 Pe.3:7).

"Behold, the LORD cometh with ten thousands of his saints, To execute judgment upon all, and to convince all that are ungodly among them of all their ungodly deeds which they have ungodly committed, and of all their hard *speeches* which ungodly sinners have spoken against him" (Jude 14-15).

DEUTERONOMY 1:6–2:15

"Behold, he cometh with clouds; and every eye shall see him, and they *also* which pierced him: and all kindreds of the earth shall wail because of him. Even so, Amen" (Re.1:7).

"Before the LORD: for he cometh, for he cometh to judge the earth: he shall judge the world with righteousness, and the people with his truth" (Ps.96:13).

"I said in mine heart, God shall judge the righteous and the wicked: for *there is* a time there for every purpose and for every work" (Ec.3:17).

4 (1:40-46) **Confession, False—Repentance, False—Rebellion, against God—Israel, Defeat of:** remember the incomplete confession, the disobedience of the first generation. What happened was tragic: the people acted without God, continuing in their unbelief and rebellion. They heard what Moses said about the judgment of God, that they were to die wandering about in the desert wilderness because of their refusal to follow God in conquering the promised land. They did not really believe that the judgment of God would fall upon them. The Scripture and outline clearly show what happened:

OUTLINE	SCRIPTURE	SCRIPTURE	OUTLINE

4. Remember the incomplete confession, the disobedience of the first generation
a. The charge to turn around
b. The incomplete & false confession: Confessed but did not repent
  1) Mobilized to fight in their own strength
  2) Mobilized without God's presence
 	
c. The warning of God: Must not fight—without His presence they would be defeated
 	
d. The refusal to listen
	40 But *as for* you, turn you, and take your journey into the wilderness by the way of the Red sea.
	41 Then ye answered and said unto me, We have sinned against the LORD, we will go up and fight, according to all that the LORD our God commanded us. And when ye had girded on every man his weapons of war, ye were ready to go up into the hill.
	42 And the LORD said unto me, Say unto them, Go not up, neither fight; for I *am* not among you; lest ye be smitten before your enemies.
	43 So I spake unto you; and
		ye would not hear, but rebelled against the commandment of the LORD, and went presumptuously up into the hill.
		44 And the Amorites, which dwelt in that mountain, came out against you, and chased you, as bees do, and destroyed you in Seir, *even* unto Hormah.
		45 And ye returned and wept before the LORD; but the LORD would not hearken to your voice, nor give ear unto you.
		46 So ye abode in Kadesh many days, according unto the days that ye abode *there*.
			1) Showed continued disobedience & rebellion
			2) Marched into the land of the Amorites
			
			e. The result: Soundly defeated
			  1) Were routed
			  2) Were driven down to Hormah (about 50 miles)
			
			f. The false confession again seen in the people: Wept because of their defeat not because of their disobedience
			
			g. The wilderness wandering around Kadesh Barnea: For 38 years

  a. The charge of God was clear: the people were to turn around and march into the wilderness toward the Red Sea (v.40).

  b. But note what the people did: they made an incomplete, partial, false confession. That is, they confessed their sin but they did not repent. They did not turn to God, accepting and trusting what He had said. They continued in their disobedience (v.41). Obviously, they were sensing deep sorrow for their sin, for refusing to follow God. But the sorrow the people felt was a worldly sorrow, not a godly sorrow that leads to repentance (2 Co.7:10). They were sorry that they were missing out on the promised land, not that they had sinned and cut the heart of God. Their sorrow was a selfish, self-centered sorrow, totally focused upon themselves and their own fleshly desires. They were not focused upon doing the will of God and pleasing Him. Therefore, the people mobilized to fight in their own strength, mobilized without God's presence.

  c. But note: God gave a strong warning through His servant Moses: the people must not fight without His presence or they would be defeated (v.42).

  d. The warning fell upon deaf ears: the people refused to listen (v.43). They showed continued disobedience and rebellion: they marched into the promised land against the Amorites.

  e. The result was tragic: the people were soundly defeated (v.44). They were routed and driven down to Hormah, a distance of about fifty miles. Imagine the terror, the fright of being hunted down by murderous enemies—pursued for about fifty miles.

  f. The false confession was again seen in the people: they wept before the LORD. But they wept because of their defeat not because of their disobedience (v.45).

  g. After this terrible experience, the first generation settled down around Kadesh Barnea and became desert wanderers. This was the major period of the wilderness wanderings that lasted about thirty-eight years (v.46).

Thought 1. An incomplete confession, a partial, false confession receives nothing from God. The only confession that receives anything from God is one that involves repentance. True confession always involves repentance, a turning away from sin to God. A person who repents and turns to God follows God. He obeys God. True confession does not disobey God. True confession always leads a person to repentance. A person listens to God's Word and does exactly what God says. The confession that leads to repentance is the only confession that receives the forgiveness of sins and leads to full restoration before God.

"Then Peter said unto them, Repent, and be baptized every one of you in the name of Jesus Christ for the remission of sins, and ye shall receive the gift of the Holy Ghost" (Ac.2:38).

"Repent ye therefore, and be converted, that your sins may be blotted out, when the times of refreshing shall come from the presence of the LORD" (Ac.3:19).

"Repent therefore of this thy wickedness, and pray God, if perhaps the thought of thine heart may be forgiven thee" (Ac.8:22).

"If we confess our sins, he is faithful and just to forgive us *our* sins, and to cleanse us from all unrighteousness" (1 Jn.1:9).

DEUTERONOMY 1:6–2:15

"If my people, which are called by my name, shall humble themselves, and pray, and seek my face, and turn from their wicked ways; then will I hear from heaven, and will forgive their sin, and will heal their land" (2 Chr.7:14).

"Let the wicked forsake his way, and the unrighteous man his thoughts: and let him return unto the LORD, and he will have mercy upon him; and to our God, for he will abundantly pardon" (Is.55:7).

"But if the wicked will turn from all his sins that he hath committed, and keep all my statutes, and do that which is lawful and right, he shall surely live, he shall not die" (Eze.18:21).

"Cast away from you all your transgressions, whereby ye have transgressed; and make you a new heart and a new spirit: for why will ye die, O house of Israel" (Eze.18:31).

5 (2:1-15) **Faithfulness, of God—Wilderness Wanderings, Deliverance through—Israel, Wilderness Wanderings of, God's Guidance—Guidance, of God**: remember the wilderness wanderings and the death of the first generation. The point of God's faithfulness is now being stressed. Keep in mind that Moses was standing before the second generation preaching, doing all he could to encourage them. The second generation was soon to launch a campaign against the enemies of the promised land. They were to lay claim to the inheritance promised by God. Courage—strong courage—was needed. The people needed a strong determination and conviction that God would be present with them, guiding them all the way. Moses knew this; for that reason, he stressed the faithfulness of God. He preached and reminded the people of God's faithfulness. This he did in six points:

OUTLINE	SCRIPTURE	SCRIPTURE	OUTLINE
	CHAPTER 2	Eziongaber, we turned and passed by the way of the wilderness of Moab.	d. God was faithful to honor His Word through all generations
5. Remember the wilderness wanderings & the death of the first generation: A picture of God's faithfulness	Then we turned, and took our journey into the wilderness by the way of the Red sea, as the LORD spake unto me: and we compassed mount Seir many days.	9 And the LORD said unto me, Distress not the Moabites, neither contend with them in battle: for I will not give thee of their land for a possession; because I have given Ar unto the children of Lot for a possession.	1) Instructed Israel not to harass the Moabites 2) The reason: Because He had promised the land of Moab to Lot & his descendants
a. God was faithful to guide His people 1) The people wandered around for 38 years, until the 1st generation died 2) God instructed the 2nd generation to march north to the promised land	2 And the LORD spake unto me, saying, 3 Ye have compassed this mountain long enough: turn you northward.	10 The Emims dwelt therein in times past, a people great, and many, and tall, as the Anakims;	e. God was faithful to encourage His people, assuring them that He would give them victory over their enemies
b. God was faithful to warn His people when necessary 1) God warned the Israelites: They were soon to pass thru Seir where the Edomites lived (were brothers to the Israelites thru Esau) • Were not to provoke them: Israel would be defeated • Were to know that God had given Esau the land of Seir 2) God gave a 2nd warning to the Israelites: They must pay for the food & water taken in Edom	4 And command thou the people, saying, Ye are to pass through the coast of your brethren the children of Esau, which dwell in Seir; and they shall be afraid of you: take ye good heed unto yourselves therefore: 5 Meddle not with them; for I will not give you of their land, no, not so much as a foot breadth; because I have given mount Seir unto Esau for a possession. 6 Ye shall buy meat of them for money, that ye may eat; and ye shall also buy water of them for money, that ye may drink.	11 Which also were accounted giants, as the Anakims; but the Moabites call them Emims. 12 The Horims also dwelt in Seir beforetime; but the children of Esau succeeded them, when they had destroyed them from before them, and dwelt in their stead; as Israel did unto the land of his possession, which the LORD gave unto them. 13 Now rise up, said I, and get you over the brook Zered. And we went over the brook Zered.	1) The Moabites had defeated a strong & numerous race of giants, the Emim or Emites 2) The Edomites had defeated the Horites & settled in the land: A strong, powerful people 3) The lesson: God was encouraging His people, assuring them of victory over all enemies, even over the most powerful
c. God was faithful in blessing & meeting the needs of His people 1) Blessed their work 2) Watched over them through their wilderness wanderings (40 years) 3) Saw that they lacked for nothing	7 For the LORD thy God hath blessed thee in all the works of thy hand: he knoweth thy walking through this great wilderness: these forty years the LORD thy God hath been with thee; thou hast lacked nothing. 8 And when we passed by from our brethren the children of Esau, which dwelt in Seir, through the way of the plain from Elath, and from	14 And the space in which we came from Kadeshbarnea, until we were come over the brook Zered, was thirty and eight years; until all the generation of the men of war were wasted out from among the host, as the LORD sware unto them. 15 For indeed the hand of the LORD was against them, to destroy them from among the host, until they were consumed.	f. God was faithful to execute judgment & chastisement 1) The charge of God to cross the Zered Valley: Thirty-eight years after they had left Kadesh Barnea—marked a new beginning for God's people 2) The entire first generation perished in the wilderness wanderings: Under the hand of God's discipline & chastisement

a. God was faithful to guide His people throughout their wilderness wanderings (vv.1-3). The judgment and chastisement of God had been pronounced upon the terrible sin of the first generation of believers: they were to wander around in the desert wilderness for forty years until the last adult had died. But God still proved faithful: just as He had promised, He instructed the second generation to march north and prepare to lay claim to the promised land. The second generation must always remember how God had led and guided His people throughout the wilderness wanderings and then charged them (the second generation) to march and prepare to receive their glorious inheritance in the promised land.

b. God was faithful to warn His people when a warning was necessary, necessary to prevent harm from coming to them (vv.4-6).

  1) God warned the Israelites: they were soon to pass through Seir where the Edomites lived. The Edomites were descendants of Esau; therefore, they were brothers to the Israelites. The Israelites were not to provoke the Edomites. If they did, Israel would be defeated, for God had given the land of Seir to Esau and his descendants. Edom was a descendant of Esau who was the brother of Jacob (Ge.27:30; 32:28; 36:1).

  2) God then gave a second warning to the Israelites: as they passed through the land of Edom, they must pay for the food and water taken along the way (v.6). (See outline and notes—Nu.20:14-22 for more discussion.)

c. God was faithful to bless and meet the needs of His people as the needs arose (vv.7-8). The second generation of believers needed to remember how God had blessed the work of their hands, blessed all their labor and employment. Throughout all the wilderness wanderings, God's presence had been with His people. God had watched over His dear people for forty years, making sure they lacked for nothing.

d. God was faithful to honor His Word through all generations (vv.8-9). Just as God had led the first generation, He would lead the second generation of believers. Moses reminded the second generation of God's presence and guidance. After the second generation had marched past Edom where the descendants of Esau lived, they approached the land of Moab. As they approached, God again proved faithful: He instructed Israel not to harass the Moabites. God had promised the land of Moab to Lot and his descendants (Ge.19:37). The land was not to be a part of the promised land of God.

The point to see is the faithfulness of God in leading and guiding His people step by step as they marched to the promised land.

e. God was faithful to encourage His people, assuring them that He would give them victory over their enemies (vv.10-12). Note that these verses cover a brief history of the area, showing how God fulfilled His promise to Abraham by using Lot and Esau (Ge.12:1-3). The point is striking: if God fulfilled His Word to Abraham by using Lot and Esau, He will fulfill it to all faithful believers—believers who obey and follow God with all their hearts.

  1) The Moabites, descendants of Lot, had defeated a strong and numerous race of giants, the Emim or Emites (vv.10-11). The reference to the other two races of people—the Anakites and the Rephaites—simply means that they were giants, a tall, big, large-framed people.

  2) The Edomites, descendants of Esau, had defeated the Horites and settled in the land. The Horites were a strong, powerful people who were scattered throughout Palestine, Syria, and Mesopotamia.

  3) The lesson is clear: God was encouraging His people through the sermon of Moses, assuring them of victory over all enemies—even over the most powerful enemies (v.12).

f. God was faithful to execute judgment and chastisement, even upon His own people who committed terrible sin (vv.13-15). This is seen in the charge of God to the second generation: they were to arise and cross over the Zered Valley. This charge was given 38 years after they had left Kadesh Barnea, and the charge marked a *new beginning* for God's people. The second generation was now the focus and attention of God. God's presence and guidance would lead His dear people into the promised land. The entire first generation had perished in the wilderness wanderings because of their terrible sin. They had perished under the hand of God's discipline and chastisement. Not a single person from the first generation was left: each person twenty years old and older had been eliminated from the camp of God's people. This one thing needed to be remembered by the second generation of believers: God does judge and chastise His people when they sin. No person escapes the judgment of God. God is faithful to execute judgment upon all sin.

> **Thought 1.** God is faithful, never failing to keep His promises. What God has promised, He will do. God will keep His Word. Once God has spoken, He will fulfill His promises to us just as He did to the first and second generations of Israelites believers. God is faithful, always faithful to His Word, always faithful to do exactly what He promises us.
>
>   "**God *is* faithful, by whom ye were called unto the fellowship of his Son Jesus Christ our LORD**" (1 Co.1:9).
>
>   "**But the LORD is faithful, who shall stablish you, and keep *you* from evil**" (2 Th.3:3).
>
>   "**If we believe not, *yet* he abideth faithful: he cannot deny himself**" (2 Ti.2:13).
>
>   "**Wherefore in all things it behooved him to be made like unto *his* brethren, that he might be a merciful and faithful high priest in things *pertaining* to God, to make reconciliation for the sins of the people**" (He.2:17).
>
>   "**Let us hold fast the profession of *our* faith without wavering; (for he is faithful that promised;)**" (He.10:23).
>
>   "**Know therefore that the LORD thy God, he *is* God, the faithful God, which keepeth covenant and mercy with them that love him and keep his commandments to a thousand generations**" (De.7:9).
>
>   "**Blessed *be* the LORD, that hath given rest unto his people Israel, according to all that he promised: there hath not failed one word of all his good promise, which he promised by the hand of Moses his servant**" (1 K.8:56).
>
>   "**Thy mercy, O LORD, *is* in the heavens; *and* thy faithfulness *reacheth* unto the clouds**" (Ps.36:5).
>
>   "**Maschil of Ethan the Ezrahite. I will sing of the mercies of the LORD for ever: with my mouth will I make known thy faithfulness to all generations**" (Ps.89:1).

DEUTERONOMY 1:6–2:15

DEEPER STUDY # 1
(1:8) Land, Promised—Canaan—Covenant—Heaven—Inheritance—Rest, Spiritual—Conquest, Spiritual—Victory, Spiritual: God promised that He would give Abraham *the promised land* of Canaan. Note the great promise:

> "Now the LORD had said unto Abram, Get thee out of thy country, and from thy kindred, and from thy father's house, unto a land that I will show thee: And I will make of thee a great nation, and I will bless thee, and make thy name great; and thou shalt be a blessing: And I will bless them that bless thee, and curse him that curseth thee: and in thee shall all families of the earth be blessed" (Ge.12:1-3).

God actually promised land to Abraham. But note: the land was only promised: it lay out in the future; it was not to be immediately possessed. The land was just what believers have called it for centuries, *the promised land*. It was to be the great hope of Abraham. This is the reason the land of Canaan is referred to as *the promised land*.

All Abraham had to go on was the promise of God, on what God had said. Abraham had to step out in faith and believe God's Word—His promise—about *the promised land*. Note several facts about this great promise to Abraham.

1. *The promised land* definitely refers to Palestine, the land of Israel. This is clearly stated by God time and again.

   a. Note God's promise to Abraham.

   > "And Abram passed through the land unto the place of Sichem, unto the plain of Moreh. And the Canaanite was then in the land. And the LORD appeared unto Abram, and said, Unto thy seed will I give this land: and there builded he an altar unto the LORD, who appeared unto him" (Ge.12:6-7).

   > "And the LORD said unto Abram, after that Lot was separated from him, Lift up now thine eyes, and look from the place where thou art northward, and southward, and eastward, and westward: for all the land which thou seest, to thee will I give it, and to thy seed for ever....Arise, walk through the land in the length of it and in the breadth of it: for I will give it unto thee" (Ge.13:14-15, 17).

   > "And he said unto him, I am the LORD that brought thee out of Ur of the Chaldees, to give thee this land to inherit it....In the same day the LORD made a covenant with Abram, saying, Unto thy seed have I given this land, from the river of Egypt unto the great river, the river Euphrates: the Kenites, and the Kenizzites, and the Kadmonites, and the Hittites, and the Periozzites, and the Rephaims, and the Amorites, and the Canaanites, and the Girgashites, and the Jebusites" (Ge.15:7, 18-21).

   > "And I will give unto thee, and to thy seed after thee, the land wherein thou art a stranger, all the land of Canaan, for an everlasting possession: and I will be their God" (Ge.17:8).

   b. Note God's promise to Abraham's son, Isaac.

   > "Sojourn in this land, and I will be with thee, and will bless thee; for unto thee, and unto thy seed, I will give all these countries, and I will perform the oath which I sware unto Abraham thy father" (Ge.26:3).

   c. Note God's promise to Abraham's grandson, Jacob.

   > "And, behold, the LORD stood above it, and said, I am the LORD God of Abraham thy father, and the God of Isaac: the land whereon thou liest, to thee will I give it, and to thy seed" (Ge.28:13).

   > "And the land which I gave Abraham and Isaac, to thee I will give it, and to thy seed after thee will I give the land" (Ge.35:12).

2. *The promised land* definitely refers to heaven. The promised land of Canaan is a symbol of heaven. It is a type, a picture, an illustration of heaven, of God's promise to the believer that he will inherit heaven, the new heavens and earth. Note two facts:

   a. God's promised land refers to *the whole world*. It is *the whole world* that Abraham and believers are to *inherit*.

   > "For the promise, that he should be the heir of the world, was not to Abraham, or to his seed, through the law, but through the righteousness of faith" (Ro.4:13).

   The inheritance of the whole world could only refer to the *new heavens and earth*—the new universe—that God is going to recreate in the end time. It could not refer to a corruptible universe that is deteriorating, wasting away, and running down, a universe that would eventually cease to exist millions of years from now—cease to exist just by the natural process of time. (See outlines and notes—2 Pe.3:1-18 for more discussion.)

   > "But the day of the LORD will come as a thief in the night; in the which the heavens shall pass away with a great noise, and the elements shall melt with fervent heat, the earth also and the works that are therein shall be burned up. Seeing then that all these things shall be dissolved, what manner of persons ought ye to be in all holy conversation and godliness. Looking for and hasting unto the coming of the day of God, wherein the heavens being on fire shall be dissolved, and the elements shall melt with fervent heat? Nevertheless we, according to his promise, look for new heavens and a new earth, wherein dwelleth righteousness" (2 Pe.3:10-13).

   > "And I saw a new heaven and a new earth: for the first heaven and the first earth were passed away; and there was no more sea. And I John saw the holy city, new Jerusalem [the capital of the new universe], coming down from God out of heaven, prepared as a bride adorned for her husband. And I heard a great

voice out of heaven saying, Behold, the tabernacle of God is with men, and he will dwell with them, and they shall be his people, and God himself shall be with them, and be their God. And God shall wipe away all tears from their eyes; and there shall be no more death, neither sorrow, nor crying, neither shall there be any more pain: for the former things are passed away" (Re.21:1-4).

"Of old hast thou laid the foundation of the earth: and the heavens are the work of thy hands. They shall perish, but thou shalt endure: yea, all of them shall wax old like a garment; as a vesture shalt thou change them, and they shall be changed: but thou art the same, and thy years shall have no end" (Ps.102:25-27).

"And all the host of heaven shall be dissolved, and the heavens shall be rolled together as a scroll: and all their host shall fall down, as the leaf falleth off from the vine, and as a falling fig from the fig tree" (Is.34:4).

"Lift up your eyes to the heavens, and look upon the earth beneath: for the heavens shall vanish away like smoke, and the earth shall wax old like a garment, and they that dwell therein shall die in like manner: but my salvation shall be for ever, and my righteousness shall not be abolished" (Is.51:6).

"For, behold, I create new heavens and a new earth: and the former shall not be remembered, nor come into mind" (Is.65:17).

"For as the new heavens and the new earth, which I will make, shall remain before me, saith the LORD, so shall your seed and your name remain" (Is.66:22).

b. God's promised land refers to *a heavenly country* and *a heavenly city*. It is a heavenly home—a heavenly country and city that are eternal—that Abraham and believers are to inherit. Note how clearly Scripture states this:

"By faith Abraham, when he was called to go out into a place which he should after receive for an inheritance, obeyed; and he went out, not knowing whither he went. By faith he sojourned in the land of promise, as in a strange country, dwelling in tabernacles with Isaac and Jacob, the heirs with him of the same promise: for he looked for a city which hath foundations, whose builder and maker is God....These all died in faith, not having received the promises, but having seen them afar off, and were persuaded of them, and embraced them, and confessed that they were strangers and pilgrims on the earth. For they that say such things declare plainly that they seek a country. And truly, if they had been mindful of that country from whence they came out, they might have had opportunity to have returned. But now they desire a better country, that is, an heavenly: wherefore God is not ashamed to be called their God: for he hath prepared for them a city" (He.11:8-10, 13-16).

"But ye are come unto mount Sion, and unto the city of the living God, the heavenly Jerusalem, and to an innumerable company of angels" (He.12:22).

"For here have we no continuing city [a perfect heavenly city], but we seek one to come" (He.13:14).

"And I John saw the holy city, new Jerusalem, coming down from God out of heaven, prepared as a bride adorned for her husband. And I heard a great voice out of heaven, saying, Behold, the tabernacle of God is with men, and he will dwell with them, and they shall be his people, and God himself shall be with them, and be their God. And God shall wipe away all tears from their eyes; and there shall be no more death, neither sorrow, nor crying, neither shall there be any more pain: for the former things are passed away" (Re.21:2-4).

"And he carried me away in the spirit to a great and high mountain, and showed me that great city, the holy Jerusalem, descending out of heaven from God" (Re.21:10).

3. *The promised land* represented many things to Abraham.
   a. The promised land was the assurance of *a personal inheritance*: the possession of a new country, of his own property with all its good land, wealth, and rights. Abraham believed that he would live in a new city within his own land and country—all given by God Himself. And the land was to be forever, for it was promised by the eternal God Himself.

   Note this, for it is important: Abraham's hope was for a permanent, eternal city and country. True, he was physically journeying all throughout the promised land of Canaan, believing that God was going to give him and his seed (descendants) the land of Canaan. But while he was journeying, his hope was for the permanent, eternal city and country of God. Abraham knew that God's promised land referred to the heavenly as well as to the earthly land. Note how clearly Scripture states this:

   ⇒ **"For all the land which thou seest, to thee will I give it, and to thy seed for ever" (Ge.13:15).**

   God's promise included the eternal, permanent possession of the promised land, and Abraham knew this.

   ⇒ **"By faith he sojourned in the land of promise, as in a strange country, dwelling in tabernacles with Isaac and Jacob, the heirs with him of the same promise: for he looked for a city which hath foundations, whose builder and maker is God" (He.11:9-10).**

   This refers to the heavenly Jerusalem, the capital of the new heavens and earth (see Heb.12:22; 13:14. See pt.2 above. Also see note—Re.21:2.)

   ⇒ **"These all died in faith, not having received the promises, but having seen them afar off, and were persuaded of them, and embraced them, and confessed that they were strangers and pilgrims on the earth. For they that say such things declare plainly that they seek a country. And truly, if they had been mindful of that country from whence they came out, they might have had opportunity to have returned. But now they desire a better country, that is, an heavenly: wherefore God is not ashamed to be called their God: for he hath prepared for them a city" (He.11:13-16).**

DEUTERONOMY 1:6–2:15

Note v.15: it clearly states that Abraham's mind was on the heavenly and eternal country. If it had not been, he would have returned to his former home. He would have never wandered about, suffering the hardships he bore.

Thought 1. Note how the promise given to Abraham parallels the promise given to the believer. Abraham was to inherit *the promised land* if he turned away from the world and followed God. We are to inherit *the promised land of heaven* if we turn away from the world and follow God. *The promised land* is a symbol, a type, a picture of heaven.

(1) The promise given to Abraham.

"And I will give unto thee, and to thy seed after thee, the land wherein thou art a stranger, all the land of Canaan, for an everlasting possession; and I will be their God" (Ge.17:8).

(2) The promise given to the believer.

"In my Father's house are many mansions: if it were not so, I would have told you. I go to prepare a place for you. And if I go and prepare a place for you, I will come again, and receive you unto myself; that where I am, there ye may be also" (Jn.14:2-3).

"For we know that if our earthly house of this tabernacle were dissolved, we have a building of God, an house not made with hands, eternal in the heavens" (2 Co.5:1).

"For our conversation [citizenship] is in heaven; from whence also we look for the Saviour, the Lord Jesus Christ: who shall change our vile body, that it may be fashioned like unto his glorious body, according to the working whereby he is able even to subdue all things unto himself" (Ph.3:20-21).

"By faith Abraham, when he was called to go out into a place which he should after receive for an inheritance, obeyed; and he went out, not knowing whither he went. By faith he sojourned in the land of promise, as in a strange country, dwelling in tabernacles with Isaac and Jacob, the heirs with him of the same promise: for he looked for a city which hath foundations, whose builder and maker is God" (He.11:8-10).

"These all died in faith, not having received the promises, but having seen them afar off, and were persuaded of them, and embraced them, and confessed that they were strangers and pilgrims on the earth. For they that say such things declare plainly that they seek a country. And truly, if they had been mindful of that country from whence they came out, they might have had opportunity to have returned. But now they desire a better country, that is, an heavenly: wherefore God is not ashamed to be called their God: for he hath prepared for them a city" (He.11:13-16).

"Blessed be the God and Father of our Lord Jesus Christ, which according to his abundant mercy hath begotten us again unto a lively hope by the resurrection of Jesus Christ from the dead, to an inheritance incorruptible, and undefiled, and that fadeth not away, reserved in heaven for you, who are kept by the power of God through faith unto salvation ready to be revealed in the last time" (1 Pe.1:3-5).

"Blessed are they that do his commandments, that they may have right to the tree of life, and may enter in through the gates into the city [New Jerusalem]" (Re.22:14).

b. The promised land was the assurance of *conquest and rest, of spiritual victory and spiritual rest*. The promised land was to bring a God-given peace and security, freedom and liberty, deliverance and salvation to Abraham. The promised land meant victory and rest to Abraham, a God-given victory and rest...
- from having to wander about
- from never being settled
- from restlessness
- from being exposed to all kinds of trials, dangers, threats, attacks, slavery, and bondage that comes from having no settled home within this world, from having no place that is given and protected by God Himself

To Abraham, the promised land was the assurance of victory and rest, the conquest and triumph over all enemies, a victory and rest that was to be given by God Himself.

Thought 1. Note how the spiritual victory and rest promised to Abraham represents the spiritual rest promised to the believer (see note—He.4:1 for more discussion).

(1) The promise given to Abraham.

"And I will make of thee a great nation, and I will bless thee, and make thy name great; and thou shalt be a blessing: and I will bless them that bless thee, and curse him that curseth thee: and in thee shall all families of the earth be blessed" (Ge.12:2-3).

"After these things the word of the LORD came unto Abram in a vision, saying, Fear not, Abram: I am thy shield, and thy exceeding great reward" (Ge.15:1).

"That in blessing I will bless thee, and in multiplying I will multiply thy seed as the stars of the heaven, and as the sand which is upon the sea shore; and thy seed shall possess the gate of his enemies; and in thy seed shall all the nations of the earth be blessed; because thou hast obeyed my voice" (Ge.22:17-18).

(2) The promise given to the believer.

"Take my yoke upon you, and learn of me; for I am meek and lowly in heart: and ye shall find rest unto your souls" (Mt.11:29).

"Let us therefore fear, lest, a promise being left us of entering into his rest, any of you should seem to come short of it. For unto us was the gospel preached, as well as unto them: but the word preached did not profit them, not being mixed with faith in them that heard it. For we which have believed do enter into rest" (He.4:1-3).

"Let us labour therefore to enter into that rest, lest any man fall after the same example of unbelief" (He.4:11).

"And I heard a voice from heaven saying unto me, Write, Blessed are the dead which die in the LORD from henceforth: yea, saith the Spirit, that they may rest from their labours; and their works do follow them" (Re.14:13).

"And he said, My presence shall go with thee, and I will give thee rest" (Ex.33:14).

"And I said, Oh that I had wings like a dove! for then would I fly away, and be at rest" (Ps.55:6).

"Return unto thy rest, O my soul; for the LORD hath dealt bountifully with thee" (Ps.116:7).

"To whom he said, This is the rest wherewith ye may cause the weary to rest; and this is the refreshing: yet they would not hear" (Is.28:12).

c. The promised land was the assurance of *God's own presence*, that is, of God's love, care, provision, and protection. Abraham was bound to know this: if God was going to give him the promised land, then God must love and care for him. God would therefore provide and protect him no matter what lay ahead. God—His strong presence—would be with him through all the trials and struggles of life.

Thought 1. Abraham's assurance of God's presence symbolizes the believer's experience. The believer can be assured of God's presence: of God's love, care, provision, and protection.

(1) The promise given to Abraham.

"And I will give unto thee, and to thy seed after thee, the land wherein thou art a stranger, all the land of Canaan, for an everlasting possession; and I will be their God" (Ge.17:8).

"And, behold, I am with thee, and will keep thee in all places whither thou goest, and will bring thee again into this land; for I will not leave thee, until I have done that which I have spoken to thee of" (Ge.28:15).

(2) The promise given to the believer.

"When thou goest out to battle against thine enemies, and seest horses, and chariots, and a people more than thou, be not afraid of them: for the LORD thy God is with thee, which brought thee up out of the land of Egypt" (De.20:1).

"When thou passest through the waters, I will be with thee; and through the rivers, they shall not overflow thee: when thou walkest through the fire, thou shalt not be burned; neither shall the flame kindle upon thee" (Is.43:2).

"But seek ye first the kingdom of God, and his righteousness; and all these things shall be added unto you" (Mt.6:33).

"Lo, I am with you alway, even unto the end of the world" (Mt.28:20).

"Let your conversation be without covetousness; and be content with such things as ye have: for he hath said, I will never leave thee, nor forsake thee" (He.13:5).

DEUTERONOMY 1:6–2:15

TYPES, SYMBOLS, AND PICTURES
(Deuteronomy 1:6–2:15)

Historical Term	Type or Picture (Scriptural Basis for Each)	Life Application for Today's Believer	Biblical Application
Abraham De.1:6-8	*Abraham is the father, the symbol of all believers.* "Behold, I have set the land before you: go in and possess the land which the LORD sware unto your fathers, Abraham, Isaac, and Jacob, to give unto them and to their seed after them" (De.1:8).	⇒ Every person who believes and follows God is a descendant of Abraham. Believers will inherit the world and reign with Christ through all eternity. Abraham was promised that he would be the father of many nations or of many descendants, and believers are those descendants. This is the clear declaration of Scripture.	*"And he received the sign of circumcision, a seal of the righteousness of the faith which he had yet being uncircumcised: that he might be the father of all them that believe, though they be not circumcised; that righteousness might be imputed unto them also: And the father of circumcision to them who are not of the circumcision only, but who also walk in the steps of that faith of our father Abraham, which he had being yet uncircumcised. For the promise, that he should be the heir of the world, was not to Abraham, or to his seed, through the law, but through the righteousness of faith" (Ro.4:11-13).* *"Therefore it is of faith, that it might be by grace; to the end the promise might be sure to all the seed; not to that only which is of the law, but to that also which is of the faith of Abraham; who is the father of us all [believers]" (Ro.4:16).* *"Even as Abraham believed God, and it was accounted to him for righteousness. Know ye therefore that they which are of faith, the same are the children of Abraham. And the scripture, foreseeing that God would justify the heathen through faith, preached before the gospel unto Abraham, saying, In thee shall all nations be blessed. So then they which be of faith are blessed with faithful Abraham" (Ga.3:6-9).*
The March to the Promised Land De.1:6-8	*The march to the promised land is a picture of marching to heaven and of spiritual conquest and rest.* "Behold, I have set the land before you: go in and possess the land which the LORD sware unto your fathers, Abraham, Isaac, and Jacob, to give unto them and to their seed after them" (De.1:8).	⇒ The promised land is a symbol of heaven and of the spiritual conquest and rest the believer is to experience as he marches to the promised land of heaven. (See DEEPER STUDY #1—De.1:8 for more discussion.)	*"In my Father's house are many mansions: if it were not so, I would have told you. I go to prepare a place for you. And if I go and prepare a place for you, I will come again, and receive you unto myself; that where I am, there ye may be also" (Jn.14:2-3).* *"For we know that if our earthly house of this tabernacle were dissolved, we have a building of God, an house not made with hands,*

DEUTERONOMY 1:6–2:15

Historical Term	Type or Picture (Scriptural Basis for Each)	Life Application for Today's Believer	Biblical Application
			eternal in the heavens" (2 Co.5:1). "For our conversation [citizenship] is in heaven; from whence also we look for the Saviour, the Lord Jesus Christ: who shall change our vile body, that it may be fashioned like unto his glorious body, according to the working whereby he is able even to subdue all things unto himself" (Ph.3:20-21). "By faith Abraham, when he was called to go out into a place which he should after receive for an inheritance, obeyed; and he went out, not knowing whither he went. By faith he sojourned in the land of promise, as in a strange country, dwelling in tabernacles with Isaac and Jacob, the heirs with him of the same promise: for he looked for a city which hath foundations, whose builder and maker is God" (He.11:8-10; see He.11:13-16; 1 Pe.1:3-5; Re.22:14).

DEUTERONOMY 2:16–3:29

	B. The Pilgrimage of the Second Generation of Israelite Believers: A Picture of Triumphant Victory & Warning, 2:16–3:29		
1. Remember the new beginning, the fresh start toward the promised land: Began only after the sinful rebels had died, been removed from the camp	16 So it came to pass, when all the men of war were consumed and dead from among the people,	Kedemoth unto Sihon king of Heshbon with words of peace, saying,	Israel for safe passage
2. Remember the supreme power of God: A picture that God has the power to fulfill His promises (Ge.12:1-3; 13:5-18)	17 That the LORD spake unto me, saying,	27 Let me pass through thy land: I will go along by the high way, I will neither turn unto the right hand nor to the left.	• The offer of peace • The assurance that Israel would stay on the main road, not ravaging the land or crops • The offer to pay for all food & water
a. God warned Israel not to harass the Ammonites	18 Thou art to pass over through Ar, the coast of Moab, this day:	28 Thou shalt sell me meat for money, that I may eat; and give me water for money, that I may drink: only I will pass through on my feet;	
1) They were the descendants of Lot, nephew of Abraham	19 And *when* thou comest nigh over against the children of Ammon, distress them not, nor meddle with them: for I will not give thee of the land of the children of Ammon *any* possession; because I have given it unto the children of Lot *for* a possession.	29 (As the children of Esau which dwell in Seir, and the Moabites which dwell in Ar, did unto me;) until I shall pass over Jordan into the land which the LORD our God giveth us.	• The reminder that Israel had been allowed to pass through Seir & Moabite territory • The only objective was the land across the Jordan
2) God had given the land to Lot			
b. Moses encouraged Israel by reminding them of God's great power in controlling the affairs of nations	20 (That also was accounted a land of giants: giants dwelt therein in old time; and the Ammonites call them Zamzummims;	30 But Sihon king of Heshbon would not let us pass by him: for the LORD thy God hardened his spirit, and made his heart obstinate, that he might deliver him into thy hand, as *appeareth* this day.	4) The refusal, rejection of the request • Because of his own stubborn, evil heart • Because God "gave him up" to his own stubborn, defiant heart (see Ro.1:24, 26, 28)
1) God had used the Ammonites to defeat & occupy the land of a strong & numerous people (the Rephaites or Zamzummites)	21 A people great, and many, and tall, as the Anakims; but the LORD destroyed them before them; and they succeeded them, and dwelt in their stead:	31 And the LORD said unto me, Behold, I have begun to give Sihon and his land before thee: begin to possess, that thou mayest inherit his land.	5) The assurance of victory given by God
2) God had used the descendants of Esau to defeat & occupy strong nations (Ge.27: 39-40; 36:1-43)	22 As he did to the children of Esau, which dwelt in Seir, when he destroyed the Horims from before them; and they succeeded them, and dwelt in their stead even unto this day:	32 Then Sihon came out against us, he and all his people, to fight at Jahaz.	6) The hostile attack against Israel
• God used those in Seir to destroy the Horites		33 And the LORD our God delivered him before us; and we smote him, and his sons, and all his people.	7) The great victory given by God • Defeated Sihon, his sons, & the entire army
• God used the Caphtorites to destroy the Avvites	23 And the Avims which dwelt in Hazerim, *even* unto Azzah, the Caphtorims, which came forth out of Caphtor, destroyed them, and dwelt in their stead.)	34 And we took all his cities at that time, and utterly destroyed the men, and the women, and the little ones, of every city, we left none to remain:	• Destroyed all the towns & people: Their "cup was full of sin," had "reached its full measure" (Nu.20:16-18; Ge.15:16)
3) The point: God has the power to fulfill His promise to His people		35 Only the cattle we took for a prey unto ourselves, and the spoil of the cities which we took.	• Confiscated the spoils of war: The livestock & things of value
3. Remember the victorious march over your enemies: A picture of the believer's spiritual victory	24 Rise ye up, take your journey, and pass over the river Arnon: behold, I have given into thine hand Sihon the Amorite, king of Heshbon, and his land: begin to possess *it*, and contend with him in battle.	36 From Aroer, which *is* by the brink of the river of Arnon, and *from* the city that *is* by the river, even unto Gilead, there was not one city too strong for us: the LORD our God delivered all unto us:	• Conquered all the Amorite cities & territory—through the presence & power of God
a. The great victory over the Amorite king Sihon			
1) The charge to conquer (Nu.21:21-32)			
2) The promise of God: He would strike fear in the hearts of all enemies, the fear of His people	25 This day will I begin to put the dread of thee and the fear of thee upon the nations *that are* under the whole heaven, who shall hear report of thee, and shall tremble, and be in anguish because of thee.	37 Only unto the land of the children of Ammon thou camest not, *nor* unto any place of the river Jabbok, nor unto the cities in the mountains, nor unto whatsoever the LORD our God forbad us.	• Stopped at the Ammonite border just as God had commanded (Nu.2:19)
3) The diplomatic, non-threatening request by	26 And I sent messengers out of the wilderness of		

38

DEUTERONOMY 2:16–3:29

b. The great victory over Og, king of Bashan (Nu.21:33-35)
  1) The attack of Og: Marched out against Israel
  2) The strong assurance of victory from the LORD
    - Were not to fear their enemy
    - Were to conquer—completely, totally

  3) The victory given by God
    - Struck down all the wicked: The king & his entire army

    - Conquered sixty heavily fortified cities, the entire territory of Bashan: Included all the surrounding villages

    - Destroyed all the cities & people: Their "cup was full of sin," had "reached its full measure" (Ge.15:16)
    - Confiscated all the livestock & valuables

c. The extensive territory of East Jordan that was conquered: A picture of victory given by God
  1) From the Arnon Gorge to Mt. Herman
  2) All the cities on the plateau & all Gilead
  3) All Bashan that was part of Og's kingdom
  4) King Og was the last of the Rephaites or giants: God led to his defeat
    - His bed was more than 13' long & 6' wide
    - It was on display in Rabbah

4. Remember the distribution of the conquered land of East Jordan: A picture that one must not settle down, be complacent, at ease before total conquest of the promised land

CHAPTER 3

Then we turned, and went up the way to Bashan: and Og the king of Bashan came out against us, he and all his people, to battle at Edrei.
2 And the LORD said unto me, Fear him not: for I will deliver him, and all his people, and his land, into thy hand; and thou shalt do unto him as thou didst unto Sihon king of the Amorites, which dwelt at Heshbon.
3 So the LORD our God delivered into our hands Og also, the king of Bashan, and all his people: and we smote him until none was left to him remaining.
4 And we took all his cities at that time, there was not a city which we took not from them, threescore cities, all the region of Argob, the kingdom of Og in Bashan.
5 All these cities were fenced with high walls, gates, and bars; beside unwalled towns a great many.
6 And we utterly destroyed them, as we did unto Sihon king of Heshbon, utterly destroying the men, women, and children, of every city.
7 But all the cattle, and the spoil of the cities, we took for a prey to ourselves.
8 And we took at that time out of the hand of the two kings of the Amorites the land that was on this side Jordan, from the river of Arnon unto mount Hermon;
9 (Which Hermon the Sidonians call Sirion; and the Amorites call it Shenir;)
10 All the cities of the plain, and all Gilead, and all Bashan, unto Salchah and Edrei, cities of the kingdom of Og in Bashan.
11 For only Og king of Bashan remained of the remnant of giants; behold, his bedstead was a bedstead of iron; is it not in Rabbath of the children of Ammon? nine cubits was the length thereof, and four cubits the breadth of it, after the cubit of a man.
12 And this land, which we possessed at that time, from Aroer, which is by the river Arnon, and half mount Gilead, and the cities thereof, gave I unto the Reubenites and to the Gadites.
13 And the rest of Gilead, and all Bashan, being the kingdom of Og, gave I unto the half tribe of Manasseh; all the region of Argob, with all Bashan, which was called the land of giants.
14 Jair the son of Manasseh took all the country of Argob unto the coasts of Geshuri and Maachathi; and called them after his own name, Bashan-havoth-jair, unto this day.
15 And I gave Gilead unto Machir.
16 And unto the Reubenites and unto the Gadites I gave from Gilead even unto the river Arnon half the valley, and the border even unto the river Jabbok, which is the border of the children of Ammon;
17 The plain also, and Jordan, and the coast thereof, from Chinnereth even unto the sea of the plain, even the salt sea, under Ashdoth-pisgah eastward.
18 And I commanded you at that time, saying, The LORD your God hath given you this land to possess it: ye shall pass over armed before your brethren the children of Israel, all that are meet for the war.
19 But your wives, and your little ones, and your cattle, (for I know that ye have much cattle,) shall abide in your cities which I have given you;
20 Until the LORD have given rest unto your brethren, as well as unto you, and until they also possess the land which the LORD your God hath given them beyond Jordan: and then shall ye return every man unto his possession, which I have given you.
21 And I commanded Joshua at that time, saying, Thine eyes have seen all that the LORD your God hath done unto these two kings: so shall the LORD do unto all the kingdoms whither thou passest.
22 Ye shall not fear them: for the LORD your God he shall fight for you.
23 And I besought the LORD at that time, saying,
24 O Lord GOD, thou hast

a. The territory given to the tribes of Reuben & Gad
b. The territory given to the half-tribe of Manasseh

c. The northern region of Argob was given to Jair, a descendant of Manasseh: Named the area after himself (Havvoth Jair)
d. The northern section of Gilead was given to the clan Makir
e. The area from the southern part of Gilead down to the middle of the Arnon Gorge & out to the Jabbok River border was given to the Reubenites & Gadites

f. The western border was the Jordan River, all the way from Kinnereth (the Sea of Galilee) to the Arabah (the Salt Sea)

g. The strong warning: Must not settle down before achieving total conquest of the promised land
  1) They must fight with their brothers: Actually take the lead until they secured their inheritance
  2) They could leave their families behind in the cities with their livestock

  3) They absolutely must fight until their brothers had achieved their rest in the promised land of God
  4) They could then return to their inheritance

5. Remember the strong assurance & charge given to Joshua
  a. The strong assurance: The LORD will give victory over all the enemies of the promised land—just as He has in the past

  b. The strong charge: Do not fear the enemy—the LORD will fight for you

6. Remember the warning: Moses himself—the dear servant of God—was not allowed to

39

DEUTERONOMY 2:16–3:29

Outline	Scripture	Outline

enter the promised land
  a. The touching prayer of Moses
    1) Acknowledged the greatness of God: God had only begun to work in Moses such mighty works
    2) Requested the privilege to cross over Jordan to see the promised land
 	
  b. The LORD's response:
    1) Anger: Denied the request—forbade Moses to speak about the matter
	begun to show thy servant thy greatness, and thy mighty hand: for what God *is there* in heaven or in earth, that can do according to thy works, and according to thy might?
	25 I pray thee, let me go over, and see the good land that *is* beyond Jordan, that goodly mountain, and Lebanon.
	26 But the LORD was wroth with me for your sakes, and would not hear me: and the LORD said unto me, Let it suffice thee; speak no more unto me of this matter.
	27 Get thee up into the top of Pisgah, and lift up thine eyes westward, and northward, and southward, and eastward, and behold *it* with thine eyes: for thou shalt not go over this Jordan.
	28 But charge Joshua, and encourage him, and strengthen him: for he shall go over before this people, and he shall cause them to inherit the land which thou shalt see.
	29 So we abode in the valley over against Bethpeor.
		2) Mercy: Granted Moses the privilege of seeing the land from the top of Mt. Pisgah
		
		  c. The LORD's charge
		    1) To commission Joshua as the new leader of Israel
		    2) To encourage & strengthen Joshua
		
		  d. The people remained in the valley near Beth Peor

DIVISION II

THE FIRST GREAT THEME PREACHED BY GOD'S AGED SERVANT: REMEMBER THE LESSONS FROM HISTORY, 1:6–4:43

B. The Pilgrimage of the Second Generation of Israelite Believers: A Picture of Triumphant Victory and Assurance, 2:16–3:29

(2:16-3:29) **Introduction—Life, Victorious—Victory, over Enemies**: a victorious life is the longing of every human heart. People ache for a victorious, triumphant life. They want a conquering spirit, a spirit of assurance, courage, fearlessness, and strong faith. People want to overcome the trials and tribulations, the pain and suffering of life, and they want to be freed from the fear of death. People want to be freed from marital and family conflict, job insecurity, and financial difficulties. People want to be freed from emptiness, purposelessness, loneliness, and desertion. People long to conquer all the trials and tribulations of life, long to be triumphant and victorious as they walk throughout life day by day.

This is the great subject that Moses now preached to the second generation of Israelite believers. They needed to be encouraged, aroused to march forth with a triumphant spirit. They needed to be fully convinced of God's power, that God would give victory over all the enemies who opposed them. Their duty was to march and enter the promised land. Once they began their march, God would empower them to conquer any and all enemies who stood against them. Victory was assured if they would just follow and obey God.

Keep in mind that Moses is preaching this passage in a sermon to the second generation of believers. He is doing all he can to arouse the people to march victoriously into the promised land. He is challenging the people to remember the great works of God among them in the past. This is the subject now preached by God's aged servant: *The Pilgrimage of the Second Generation of Israelite Believers: A Picture of Triumphant Victory and Assurance*, 2:16–3:29.

1. Remember the new beginning, the fresh start toward the promised land: began only after the sinful rebels had died, been removed from the camp (2:16).
2. Remember the supreme power of God: a picture that God has the power to fulfill His promises (2:17-23).
3. Remember the victorious march over your enemies: a picture of the believer's spiritual victory (2:24–3:11).
4. Remember the distribution of the conquered land of East Jordan: a picture that one must not settle down, be complacent, at ease before total conquest of the promised land (3:12-20).
5. Remember the strong assurance and charge given to Joshua (3:21-22).
6. Remember the warning: Moses himself—the dear servant of God—was not allowed to enter the promised land (3:23-29).

1 (2:16) **New Beginning—Land, Promised—Chastisement—Church, Growth—Pilgrimage, Believer's—March, to the Promised Land**: remember the new beginning, the fresh start toward the promised land (see Map of the Wilderness Wanderings of Israel on page 436). The march to the promised land was resumed only after the sinful rebels had died, been removed from the camp of God's people.

OUTLINE	SCRIPTURE
1. Remember the new beginning, the fresh start toward the promised land: Began only after the sinful rebels had died, been removed from the camp	16 So it came to pass, when all the men of war were consumed and dead from among the people,

There had been sin in the camp. Unbelief and rebellion had gripped the hearts of the first generation of believers. When the twelve spies had returned from their reconnaissance mission, ten of the spies gave a negative report. In their eyes the enemy was too strong and too well fortified to defeat. They sowed unbelief, a spirit of defeatism among the people. Despite the

DEUTERONOMY 2:16–3:29

encouragement of Moses and the assurance of victory from God, the people allowed fear and unbelief to grip their hearts. They rebelled against God and refused to march into the promised land. They refused to believe God, refused to trust the promise that God would empower them to conquer all opposition and lead them forth victoriously.

The result was inevitable: the chastisement and judgment of God fell. Time and again the first generation of believers had shown that they would never believe and follow God—not completely, not fully. They refused to enter the promised land; therefore, they would reap what they had sown. This would be their chastisement, their judgment: they would never be allowed to enter the promised land. They would all die in the desert wilderness, all die in a restless and unsettled state, die while wandering about in the wilderness. They would never live victoriously over the enemies of life and never know the spiritual rest of the promised land.

This is the stress of the present point: until all the people of fighting age (20 years old and older) had died, the march to the promised land could not be resumed. But once the judgment of God had been carried out—once the first generation had all died—a *new beginning* could take place. A new generation of believers could get a fresh start: they could resume the march to the promised land of God.

Thought 1. The warning is clear: sin disrupts our march to the promised land of heaven. Sin separates us from God, cuts us off from fellowship with God. Sin causes God to turn His face away from us and keeps Him from hearing and answering our prayers. This is true of both believers and the church. There is only one answer: sin has to be removed before we can be reconciled with God, removed before our march to the promised land can be resumed. Once sin has been removed, a *new beginning* can take place. We can get a fresh start in seeking the promised land of God.

(1) Sin separates us from God.

"If I regard iniquity in my heart, the LORD will not hear *me*" (Ps.66:18).

"But your iniquities have separated between you and your God, and your sins have hid *his* face from you, that he will not hear" (Is.59:2).

"And *there is* none that calleth upon thy name, that stirreth up himself to take hold of thee: for thou hast hid thy face from us, and hast consumed us, because of our iniquities" (Is.64:7).

(2) Sin must be removed from us.

"Let the wicked forsake his way, and the unrighteous man his thoughts: and let him return unto the LORD, and he will have mercy upon him; and to our God, for he will abundantly pardon" (Is.55:7).

"But if the wicked will turn from all his sins that he hath committed, and keep all my statutes, and do that which is lawful and right, he shall surely live, he shall not die" (Eze.18:21).

(3) Once sin has been removed, we can have a new beginning, a fresh start in seeking the promised land.

"Repent ye therefore, and be converted, that your sins may be blotted out, when the times of refreshing shall come from the presence of the LORD" (Ac.3:19).

"Therefore if any man *be* in Christ, *he is* a new creature: old things are passed away; behold, all things are become new" (2 Co.5:17).

"But God, who is rich in mercy, for his great love wherewith he loved us, Even when we were dead in sins, hath quickened us together with Christ, (by grace ye are saved;) And hath raised *us* up together, and made *us* sit together in heavenly *places* in Christ Jesus: That in the ages to come he might show the exceeding riches of his grace in *his* kindness toward us through Christ Jesus" (Ep.2:4-7).

"If ye then be risen with Christ, seek those things which are above, where Christ sitteth on the right hand of God" (Col.3:1).

"But the day of the LORD will come as a thief in the night; in the which the heavens shall pass away with a great noise, and the elements shall melt with fervent heat, the earth also and the works that are therein shall be burned up. *Seeing* then *that* all these things shall be dissolved, what manner *of persons* ought ye to be in *all* holy conversation and godliness, Looking for and hasting unto the coming of the day of God, wherein the heavens being on fire shall be dissolved, and the elements shall melt with fervent heat? Nevertheless we, according to his promise, look for new heavens and a new earth, wherein dwelleth righteousness" (2 Pe.3:10-13).

"If my people, which are called by my name, shall humble themselves, and pray, and seek my face, and turn from their wicked ways; then will I hear from heaven, and will forgive their sin, and will heal their land" (2 Chr.7:14).

"Cast away from you all your transgressions, whereby ye have transgressed; and make you a new heart and a new spirit: for why will ye die, O house of Israel?" (Eze.18:31).

2 (2:17-23) **Power, of God—Sovereignty, of God, in the Affairs of Nations—God, Sovereign Power of, over Nations—Promises, of God—Ammonites—Lot, Descendants of—Esau, Descendants of—Rephaites—Zamzummites—Horites**: remember the supreme power of God. God has the power to fulfill His promises to His people. This is clearly seen in the event that Moses now covers in his sermon.

DEUTERONOMY 2:16–3:29

OUTLINE	SCRIPTURE	SCRIPTURE	OUTLINE

2. Remember the supreme power of God: A picture that God has the power to fulfill His promises (Ge.12:1-3; 13:5-18)
 	
a. God warned Israel not to harass the Ammonites
  1) They were the descendants of Lot, nephew of Abraham
  2) God had given the land to Lot
 	
b. Moses encouraged Israel by reminding them of God's great power in controlling the affairs of nations
	17 That the LORD spake unto me, saying,
	18 Thou art to pass over through Ar, the coast of Moab, this day:
	19 And *when* thou comest nigh over against the children of Ammon, distress them not, nor meddle with them: for I will not give thee of the land of the children of Ammon *any* possession; because I have given it unto the children of Lot *for* a possession.
	20 (That also was accounted a land of giants: giants dwelt therein in old time; and the Ammonites call them Zamzummims;
		21 A people great, and many, and tall, as the Anakims; but the LORD destroyed them before them; and they succeeded them, and dwelt in their stead:
		22 As he did to the children of Esau, which dwelt in Seir, when he destroyed the Horims from before them; and they succeeded them, and dwelt in their stead even unto this day:
		23 And the Avims which dwelt in Hazerim, *even* unto Azzah, the Caphtorims, which came forth out of Caphtor, destroyed them, and dwelt in their stead.)
			1) God had used the Ammonites to defeat & occupy the land of a strong & numerous people (the Rephaites or Zamzummites)
			
			2) God had used the descendants of Esau to defeat & occupy strong nations (Ge.27:39-40; 36:1-43)
			  • God used those in Seir to destroy the Horites
			
			  • God used the Caphtorites to destroy the Avvites
			
			3) The point: God has the power to fulfill His promise to His people

a. As the second generation of believers were marching to the promised land, God warned them not to harass the Ammonites (v.19). The reason is clearly stated: they were the descendants of Lot, Abraham's nephew, and God had given the land to Lot and his descendants. Note that God clearly says that it was He, His power, that enabled Lot and his descendants to take possession of the land.

b. Moses also encouraged Israel by reminding them of God's great power in controlling the affairs of nations (vv.20-23). Moses declares that it was God who had used the Ammonites to defeat and occupy the land of a strong and numerous people, the Rephaites or Zamzummites (v.21). These were the giants of the land, a tall, physically large race of people. The point is clear: if God used His mighty power to destroy the giants of the land for Lot and his descendants, how much more would God use His power to destroy the giants who opposed His people?

But this was not the only demonstration of God's power to remember: God used the descendants of Esau to defeat and occupy the lands of other strong nations (Ge.27:38-40; 36:1-43). God used the descendants in Seir to destroy the Horites (v.22) and used the Caphtorites to destroy the Avvites (v.23).

Moses has driven the point home to the hearts of the people: God has the power to fulfill His promises to His people. If He exercised His power in behalf of Lot and Esau—two carnal believers of past history—how much more would He use His power to fulfill His promises to His dear people? He will lead them to the promised land and give them the inheritance He has promised to them. He will use His power to defeat the giants and strong enemies who stand against His dear people.

> **Thought 1**. God is Omnipotent. He has supreme power. God has the power to fulfill all His promises to His dear people.
>
> "But Jesus beheld *them,* and said unto them, With men this is impossible; but with God all things are possible" (Mt.19:26).
>
> "For with God nothing shall be impossible" (Lu.1:37).
>
> "Now to him that is of power to stablish you according to my gospel, and the preaching of Jesus Christ, according to the revelation of the mystery, which was kept secret since the world began, But now is made manifest, and by the scriptures of the prophets, according to the commandment of the everlasting God, made known to all nations for the obedience of faith: To God only wise, *be* glory through Jesus Christ for ever. Amen" (Ro.16:25-27).
>
> "Now unto him that is able to do exceeding abundantly above all that we ask or think, according to the power that worketh in us" (Ep.3:20).
>
> "For our conversation [citizenship] is in heaven; from whence also we look for the Saviour, the Lord Jesus Christ: Who shall change our vile body, that it may be fashioned like unto his glorious body, according to the working whereby he is able even to subdue all things unto himself" (Ph.3:20-21).
>
> "I know whom I have believed, and am persuaded that he is able to keep that which I have committed unto him against that day" (2 Ti.1:12).
>
> "Wherefore he is able also to save them to the uttermost that come unto God by him, seeing he ever liveth to make intercession for them" (He.7:25).
>
> "Now unto him that is able to keep you from falling, and to present *you* faultless before the presence of his glory with exceeding joy, To the only wise God our Saviour, *be* glory and majesty, dominion and power, both now and ever. Amen" (Jude 24-25).
>
> "I know that thou canst do every *thing,* and *that* no thought can be withholden from thee" (Jb.42:2).
>
> "But our God *is* in the heavens: he hath done whatsoever he hath pleased" (Ps.115:3).
>
> "Yea, before the day *was* I *am* he; and *there is* none that can deliver out of my hand: I will work, and who shall let [hinder] it?" (Is.43:13).

3 (2:24–3:11) **Victory, Spiritual—Victory, over Enemies—Israel, Conquest of Amorites—Amorites, Conquered by Israel—Sihon—Og—Triumph, over Enemies—March, Believer's**: remember the victorious march over your enemies. This is a clear picture of the believer's spiritual victory as he marches to the promised land. The second generation of

DEUTERONOMY 2:16–3:29

believers had already experienced two glorious victories over two great nations. In his sermon, Moses reminded the people of this fact. God had given them victory over the Amorite King Sihon and over King Og who ruled the land of Bashan. In these two great victories, God had already proven that He would help His dear people conquer all enemies who opposed them. But they had a responsibility: they must be faithful and obey God: continue their march to the promised land to lay claim to the promised inheritance. As Moses preached to the people, he drove the point home: they must remember the victorious march, the great victory God had given over these two mighty kings. Note the forcefulness of the point in the Scripture and outline:

OUTLINE	SCRIPTURE	SCRIPTURE	OUTLINE

3. Remember the victorious march over your enemies: A picture of the believer's spiritual victory
a. The great victory over the Amorite king Sihon
  1) The charge to conquer (Nu.21:21-32)
  2) The promise of God: He would strike fear in the hearts of all enemies, the fear of His people
 	
  3) The diplomatic, non-threatening request by Israel for safe passage
 	
    • The offer of peace
    • The assurance that Israel would stay on the main road, not ravaging the land or crops
 	
    • The offer to pay for all food & water
 	
    • The reminder that Israel had been allowed to pass thru Seir & Moabite territory
    • The only objective was the land across the Jordan
  4) The refusal, rejection of the request
    • Because of his own stubborn, evil heart
    • Because God "gave him up" to his own stubborn, defiant heart (see Ro.1:24, 26, 28)
  5) The assurance of victory given by God
 	
  6) The hostile attack against Israel
	24 Rise ye up, take your journey, and pass over the river Arnon: behold, I have given into thine hand Sihon the Amorite, king of Heshbon, and his land: begin to possess *it*, and contend with him in battle.
	25 This day will I begin to put the dread of thee and the fear of thee upon the nations *that are* under the whole heaven, who shall hear report of thee, and shall tremble, and be in anguish because of thee.
	26 And I sent messengers out of the wilderness of Kedemoth unto Sihon king of Heshbon with words of peace, saying,
	27 Let me pass through thy land: I will go along by the high way, I will neither turn unto the right hand nor to the left.
	28 Thou shalt sell me meat for money, that I may eat; and give me water for money, that I may drink: only I will pass through on my feet;
	29 (As the children of Esau which dwell in Seir, and the Moabites which dwell in Ar, did unto me;) until I shall pass over Jordan into the land which the LORD our God giveth us.
	30 But Sihon king of Heshbon would not let us pass by him: for the LORD thy God hardened his spirit, and made his heart obstinate, that he might deliver him into thy hand, as *appeareth* this day.
	31 And the LORD said unto me, Behold, I have begun to give Sihon and his land before thee: begin to possess, that thou mayest inherit his land.
	32 Then Sihon came out against us, he and all his people, to fight at Jahaz.
		33 And the LORD our God delivered him before us; and we smote him, and his sons, and all his people.
		34 And we took all his cities at that time, and utterly destroyed the men, and the women, and the little ones, of every city, we left none to remain:
		35 Only the cattle we took for a prey unto ourselves, and the spoil of the cities which we took.
		36 From Aroer, which *is* by the brink of the river of Arnon, and *from* the city that *is* by the river, even unto Gilead, there was not one city too strong for us: the LORD our God delivered all unto us:
		37 Only unto the land of the children of Ammon thou camest not, *nor* unto any place of the river Jabbok, nor unto the cities in the mountains, nor unto whatsoever the LORD our God forbad us.
		
		CHAPTER 3
		
		Then we turned, and went up the way to Bashan: and Og the king of Bashan came out against us, he and all his people, to battle at Edrei.
		2 And the LORD said unto me, Fear him not: for I will deliver him, and all his people, and his land, into thy hand; and thou shalt do unto him as thou didst unto Sihon king of the Amorites, which dwelt at Heshbon.
		3 So the LORD our God delivered into our hands Og also, the king of Bashan, and all his people: and we smote him until none was left to him remaining.
		4 And we took all his cities at that time, there was not a
			7) The great victory given by God
			    • Defeated Sihon, his sons, & the entire army
			    • Destroyed all the towns & people: Their "cup was full of sin," had "reached its full measure" (Nu. 20:16-18; Ge.15:16)
			    • Confiscated the spoils of war: The livestock & things of value
			
			    • Conquered all the Amorite cities & territory—thru the presence & power of God
			
			    • Stopped at the Ammonite border just as God had commanded (Nu.2:19)
			
			b. The great victory over Og, king of Bashan (Nu.21:33-35)
			  1) The attack of Og: Marched out against Israel
			  2) The strong assurance of victory from the LORD
			    • Were not to fear their enemy
			    • Were to conquer—completely, totally
			
			  3) The victory given by God
			    • Struck down all the wicked: The king & his entire army
			
			    • Conquered sixty heavily fortified cities, the entire

DEUTERONOMY 2:16–3:29

OUTLINE	SCRIPTURE	SCRIPTURE	OUTLINE
territory of Bashan: Included all the surrounding villages	city which we took not from them, threescore cities, all the region of Argob, the kingdom of Og in Bashan. 5 All these cities *were* fenced with high walls, gates, and bars; beside unwalled towns a great many. 6 And we utterly destroyed them, as we did unto Sihon king of Heshbon, utterly destroying the men, women, and children, of every city. 7 But all the cattle, and the spoil of the cities, we took for a prey to ourselves. 8 And we took at that time out of the hand of the two kings of the Amorites the	land that *was* on this side Jordan, from the river of Arnon unto mount Hermon; 9 (*Which* Hermon the Sidonians call Sirion; and the Amorites call it Shenir;) 10 All the cities of the plain, and all Gilead, and all Bashan, unto Salchah and Edrei, cities of the kingdom of Og in Bashan. 11 For only Og king of Bashan remained of the remnant of giants; behold, his bedstead *was* a bedstead of iron; *is* it not in Rabbath of the children of Ammon? nine cubits *was* the length thereof, and four cubits the breadth of it, after the cubit of a man.	given by God 1) From the Arnon Gorge to Mt. Herman 2) All the cities on the plateau & all Gilead 3) All Bashan that was part of Og's kingdom 4) King Og was the last of the Rephaites or giants: God led to his defeat • His bed was more than 13' long & 6' wide • It was on display in Rabbah
• Destroyed all the cities & people: Their "cup was full of sin," had "reached its full measure" (Ge.15:16) • Confiscated all the livestock & valuables c. The extensive territory of East Jordan that was conquered: A picture of victory			

Thought 1. The kings of the Amorites stood between the Israelites and the promised land. This is a picture of the world and the enemies of life standing between the believer and the promised land of heaven. As we march to the promised land of heaven, enemy after enemy will attack us, enemies such as...

- accidents
- disease
- death
- immorality
- greed
- covetousness
- pornography
- anger
- hostility
- discouragement
- depression
- loneliness
- emptiness
- purposelessness
- failure
- financial difficulty
- unemployment
- temptations
- trials

But no matter the enemy—no matter its strength or threat—God is stronger. And God will give victory to His people. God will empower His people to conquer and triumph over all the enemies of life. If we will only believe and obey God, we will march victoriously throughout life. We will experience victory after victory over our enemies. We will know what it is to live a victorious life as we march to the promised land of God. We will be victorious even as the Israelite believers were victorious over these two mighty kings. This is the clear declaration of Scripture.

> "These things I have spoken unto you, that in me ye might have peace. In the world ye shall have tribulation: but be of good cheer; I have overcome the world" (Jn.16:33).
>
> "Who shall separate us from the love of Christ? *shall* tribulation, or distress, or persecution, or famine, or nakedness, or peril, or sword?...Nay, in all these things we are more than conquerors through him that loved us. For I am persuaded, that neither death, nor life, nor angels, nor principalities, nor powers, nor things present, nor things to come, Nor height, nor depth, nor any other creature, shall be able to separate us from the love of God, which is in Christ Jesus our LORD" (Ro.8:35, 37-39).
>
> "There hath no temptation taken you but such as is common to man: but God *is* faithful, who will not suffer you to be tempted above that ye are able; but will with the temptation also make a way to escape, that ye may be able to bear *it*" (1 Co.10:13).
>
> "For we wrestle not against flesh and blood, but against principalities, against powers, against the rulers of the darkness of this world, against spiritual wickedness in high *places*. Wherefore take unto you the whole armour of God, that ye may be able to withstand in the evil day, and having done all, to stand" (Ep.6:12-13).
>
> "For whatsoever is born of God overcometh the world: and this is the victory that overcometh the world, *even* our faith" (1 Jn.5:4).
>
> "To him that overcometh will I grant to sit with me in my throne, even as I also overcame, and am set down with my Father in his throne" (Re.3:21).
>
> "Through thee will we push down our enemies: through thy name will we tread them under that rise up against us" (Ps.44:5).

Thought 2. Note the reference to the bed of King Og (v.11). He was a giant of a man. John Maxwell quotes an amusing poem written by a friend about Og and his bed:

DEUTERONOMY 2:16–3:29

Bed of Og

While browsing through the Bible once
I ran across the queerest thing:
A Bashanite of giant height
Upon his nation's throne was king.
His name was Og.

There is no record whether he
Was dull or smart or sour or gay.
He had a bedstead made of iron—
That's all the Bible has to say
About this Og.

He must have used a lot of room!
They laid a tapeline on his bed;
From side to side it was six feet wide
And fifteen feet from foot to head.
Some man, this Og!

I wonder, was he cruel or kind?
A gentleman or snooty cad?
And did he have a smile or frown?
A bedstead made of iron he had!
That's all we know.

I hope when I have lived my life
And gone the common way of man,
The folks will find I've left behind
Something for memory better than
Old Og's iron bed!

I'd rather be remembered by
One gentle, friendly word I've said,
One smile I've worn or song I've sung
Than by a fifteen-foot iron bed
Like poor old Og![1]

4 **(3:12-20) Complacency—Comfort, Seeking—Rest, Seeking—Ease, Seeking—Half-hearted Commitment—Selfishness—East Jordan, Distribution of Land—Land, Distribution of East Jordan—Distribution, of East Jordan Land**: remember the distribution of the conquered land of East Jordan. This is a clear picture that the believer must not settle down, be complacent, or at ease before conquering all of the promised land. The task was to be completed before settling down. (See outline and notes—Nu.32:1-42 for full discussion.) The Israelites were camped by the Jordan River right across from the great city of Jericho. They were poised, almost ready to cross the Jordan into the promised land. Once they crossed the river and conquered a large territory of land, a dangerous temptation would threaten them. A spirit of complacency, of seeking comfort, rest, and ease from battle would attack them—long before they completed the conquest of the land. Moses knew that he must prepare the people to face this dangerous spirit of complacency, of worldly comfort and ease. Preaching with fire in his heart, he reminded the people of the strong warning he had given when the conquered land of East Jordan was distributed among the tribes of Reuben, Gad, and the half-tribe of Manasseh. Reuben and Gad had requested the territory of East Jordan. After much negotiation, Moses compromised with the tribes and divided the territory among them and gave a portion to the half-tribe of Manasseh. Once the territory had been divided, Moses issued his strong warning against complacency and worldly comfort and rest. Note the Scripture and outline:

OUTLINE	SCRIPTURE	SCRIPTURE	OUTLINE
4. Remember the distribution of the conquered land of East Jordan: A picture that one must not settle down, be complacent, at ease before total conquest of the promised land a. The territory given to the tribes of Reuben & Gad b. The territory given to the	12 And this land, *which* we possessed at that time, from Aroer, which *is* by the river Arnon, and half mount Gilead, and the cities thereof, gave I unto the Reubenites and to the Gadites. 13 And the rest of Gilead,	and all Bashan, *being* the kingdom of Og, gave I unto the half tribe of Manasseh; all the region of Argob, with all Bashan, which was called the land of giants. 14 Jair the son of Manasseh took all the country of Argob unto the coasts of Geshuri	half-tribe of Manasseh c. The northern region of Argob was given to Jair, a descendant of Manasseh:

---

[1] John Maxwell. *The Preacher's Commentary on Deuteronomy.* (Nashville, TN: Thomas Nelson, 1987, 2003), pp.71-72. (The poem was written by Mr. Maxwell's friend, Lon Woodrum.)

DEUTERONOMY 2:16–3:29

OUTLINE	SCRIPTURE	SCRIPTURE	OUTLINE
Named the area after himself (Havvoth Jair)	and Maachathi; and called them after his own name, Bashan-havoth-jair, unto this day.	your God hath given you this land to possess it: ye shall pass over armed before your brethren the children of Israel, all *that are* meet for the war.	achieving total conquest of the promised land 1) They must fight with their brothers: Actually take the lead until they secured their inheritance
d. The northern section of Gilead was given to the clan Makir	15 And I gave Gilead unto Machir.		
e. The area from the southern part of Gilead down to the middle of the Arnon Gorge & out to the Jabbok River border was given to the Reubenites & Gadites	16 And unto the Reubenites and unto the Gadites I gave from Gilead even unto the river Arnon half the valley, and the border even unto the river Jabbok, *which is* the border of the children of Ammon;	19 But your wives, and your little ones, and your cattle, (*for* I know that ye have much cattle,) shall abide in your cities which I have given you;	2) They could leave their families behind in the cities with their livestock
		20 Until the LORD have given rest unto your brethren, as well as unto you, and *until* they also possess the land which the LORD your God hath given them beyond Jordan: and *then* shall ye return every man unto his possession, which I have given you.	3) They absolutely must fight until their brothers had achieved their rest in the promised land of God 4) They could then return to their inheritance
f. The western border was the Jordan River, all the way from Kinnereth (the Sea of Galilee) to the Arabah (the Salt Sea)	17 The plain also, and Jordan, and the coast *thereof*, from Chinnereth even unto the sea of the plain, *even* the salt sea, under Ashdoth-pisgah eastward.		
g. The strong warning: Must not settle down before	18 And I commanded you at that time, saying, The LORD		

Thought 1. God warns us against complacency, against seeking worldly comfort, rest, and ease. As we march to the promised land of heaven, God has called us to a life of total commitment to Him. We are engaged in a spiritual warfare, struggling against the enemies of this life, enemies that want to keep us out of the promised land:

⇒ compromise ⇒ unbelief ⇒ worldliness
⇒ covetousness ⇒ indifference ⇒ lust of the eyes
⇒ selfishness ⇒ neglect ⇒ worldly desires
⇒ half-hearted commitment ⇒ ignorance ⇒ indulgence
⇒ disunity ⇒ comfort and ease ⇒ self-gratification
⇒ disloyalty

We must press on and conquer these enemies of the promised land. God demands total conquest. We must never stop short. We must defeat the spirit of complacency, the spirit of worldly comfort, ease, and rest. We must never compromise with the lethargy of this world, never become self-satisfied, smug, and unconcerned. We must press on to secure the promised land of God, the great inheritance God has promised. We must press on until we have conquered all the enemies of the promised land, press on until we reach the spiritual rest of our glorious inheritance—the spiritual rest promised by God. During life upon this earth, there is no room for complacency or worldly comfort and ease.

"And every one that heareth these sayings of mine, and doeth them not, shall be likened unto a foolish man, which built his house upon the sand: And the rain descended, and the floods came, and the winds blew, and beat upon that house; and it fell: and great was the fall of it" (Mt.7:26-27).

"And because iniquity shall abound, the love of many shall wax cold. But he that shall endure unto the end, the same shall be saved" (Mt.24:12-13).

"Therefore, my beloved brethren, be ye stedfast, unmovable, always abounding in the work of the LORD, forasmuch as ye know that your labour is not in vain in the LORD" (1 Co.15:58).

"Therefore to him that knoweth to do good, and doeth *it* not, to him it is sin" (Js.4:17).

"And Joshua said unto the children of Israel, How long *are* ye slack to go to possess the land, which the LORD God of your fathers hath given you?" (Jos.18:3).

"Our soul is exceedingly filled with the scorning of those that are at ease, *and* with the contempt of the proud" (Ps.123:4).

"Woe to them *that are* at ease in Zion, and trust in the mountain of Samaria, *which are* named chief of the nations, to whom the house of Israel came!" (Am. 6:1).

5 (3:21-22) **Victory, Assurance of—Charge, to Joshua—Joshua, Charge to—Fear, How to Overcome**: remember the strong assurance and charge given to Joshua. Right after distributing the land of East Jordan, God's aged servant turned to the young man who was to replace him. Moses began to encourage Joshua.

OUTLINE	SCRIPTURE
5. Remember the strong assurance & charge given to Joshua a. The strong assurance: The LORD will give victory over all the enemies of the promised land—just as He has in the past b. The strong charge: Do not fear the enemy—the LORD will fight for you	21 And I commanded Joshua at that time, saying, Thine eyes have seen all that the LORD your God hath done unto these two kings: so shall the LORD do unto all the kingdoms whither thou passest. 22 Ye shall not fear them: for the LORD your God he shall fight for you.

a. Moses gave strong assurance to Joshua: the presence and victorious power of God would be with him as he led God's dear people to conquer the promised land (v.21). Note that Joshua had been an eyewitness of God's glorious victory over the two kings, Sihon and Og. He could, therefore, rest assured that God would give victory over all the enemies who opposed His people. God would do in the future just what He had done in the past: give victory to His people.

b. Moses issued a strong charge to Joshua: do not fear the enemy, for the LORD God Himself will fight for His precious people (v.22).

"But there shall not an hair of your head perish" (Lu.21:18).

"So that we may boldly say, The LORD *is* my helper, and I will not fear what man shall do unto me" (He.13:6).

"The LORD shall fight for you, and ye shall hold your peace" (Ex.14:14).

"And he said, My presence shall go *with thee,* and I will give thee rest" (Ex.33:14).

"When thou goest out to battle against thine enemies, and seest horses, and chariots, *and* a people more than thou, be not afraid of them: for the LORD thy God *is* with thee, which brought thee up out of the land of Egypt" (De.20:1).

"For the eyes of the LORD run to and fro throughout the whole earth, to show himself strong in the behalf of *them* whose heart *is* perfect toward him" (2 Chr.16:9).

"The LORD *is* my strength and my shield; my heart trusted in him, and I am helped: therefore my heart greatly rejoiceth; and with my song will I praise him" (Ps.28:7).

"The angel of the LORD encampeth round about them that fear him, and delivereth them" (Ps.34:7).

"But I *am* poor and needy; *yet* the LORD thinketh upon me: thou *art* my help and my deliverer; make no tarrying, O my God" (Ps.40:17).

"He shall cover thee with his feathers, and under his wings shalt thou trust: his truth *shall be thy* shield and buckler" (Ps.91:4).

"As the mountains *are* round about Jerusalem, so the LORD *is* round about his people from henceforth even for ever" (Ps.125:2).

"Fear thou not; for I *am* with thee: be not dismayed; for I *am* thy God: I will strengthen thee; yea, I will help thee; yea, I will uphold thee with the right hand of my righteousness" (Is.41:10).

"When thou passest through the waters, I *will be* with thee; and through the rivers, they shall not overflow thee: when thou walkest through the fire, thou shalt not be burned; neither shall the flame kindle upon thee" (Is.43:2).

6 (3:23-29) **Warning, Against Sin—Promised Land, Barred from—Moses, Chastisement of—Warning, of Judgment—Chastisement, Caused by:** remember the warning: that Moses himself—the dear servant of God—was not allowed to enter the promised land. Even this great servant of God was barred from the promised land because of sin. He had committed the terrible sin of disobedience and of dishonoring the LORD before the people (see note, pt.8, c—De.1:18-39; see outline and notes—Nu.20:7-13 for more discussion).

But note what happened: while Moses was encouraging Joshua, he himself was gripped with a deep, earnest desire to personally lead the people of God into the promised land. After all, it was this for which God had originally called him and for which he had labored so faithfully throughout the years. The hope that God would remove His hand of chastisement swelled up within the heart of Moses, so he sought the LORD in prayer, begging God to allow him to enter the promised land. The Scripture and outline show us exactly what happened:

OUTLINE	SCRIPTURE	SCRIPTURE	OUTLINE

6. Remember the warning: Moses himself—the dear servant of God—was not allowed to enter the promised land
a. The touching prayer of Moses
  1) Acknowledged the greatness of God: God had only begun to work in
	23 And I besought the LORD at that time, saying,
	24 O Lord GOD, thou hast begun to show thy servant thy greatness, and thy mighty hand: for what God *is there* in heaven or in earth, that can do according to thy
		works, and according to thy might?
		25 I pray thee, let me go over, and see the good land that *is* beyond Jordan, that goodly mountain, and Lebanon.
		26 But the LORD was wroth
			Moses such mighty works
			  2) Requested the privilege to cross over Jordan to see the promised land
			b. The LORD's response:

DEUTERONOMY 2:16–3:29

OUTLINE	SCRIPTURE	SCRIPTURE	OUTLINE
1) Anger: Denied the request—forbade Moses to speak about the matter	with me for your sakes, and would not hear me: and the LORD said unto me, Let it suffice thee; speak no more unto me of this matter.	for thou shalt not go over this Jordan. 28 But charge Joshua, and encourage him, and strengthen him: for he shall go over before this people, and he shall cause them to inherit the land which thou shalt see.	c. The LORD's charge 1) To commission Joshua as the new leader of Israel 2) To encourage & strengthen Joshua
2) Mercy: Granted Moses the privilege of seeing the land from the top of Mt. Pisgah	27 Get thee up into the top of Pisgah, and lift up thine eyes westward, and northward, and southward, and eastward, and behold *it* with thine eyes:	29 So we abode in the valley over against Bethpeor.	d. The people remained in the valley near Beth Peor

a. The prayer of Moses is touching, revealing his intense love and reverence for God (v.24). He acknowledged the greatness of God, addressing God as "O LORD God" ("O sovereign LORD.") Moses appealed to God, to the fact that God had only begun to work in his heart and life, that God had only begun to reveal His greatness and power to him. God and God alone could do the mighty works that had been done for him personally and for the nation as a whole. Courageously, Moses made his request: he asked for the privilege to cross over the Jordan to see the promised land (v.25).

b. The LORD's response was immediate. In anger, God denied the request of Moses. Moses should never have brought up the subject because he was responsible for terrible sin. He was to reap what he had sown, bear the chastisement of God against sin. Moreover, Moses was never again to speak about the matter (v.26). But note the mercy of God: God would grant Moses the privilege of seeing the land from the top of Mt. Pisgah (v.27). God loved His dear servant, and God knew that the beat of His servant's heart was to see the promised land. Furthermore, God knew that Moses had been faithful down through the years, that he had seriously slipped in a major way only this once. Therefore, in love and mercy, God was going to grant him the privilege of at least seeing the land with his own eyes.

c. The LORD gave a clear charge to Moses: he was to commission Joshua to be the new leader of Israel. In addition, he was to focus the rest of his time upon encouraging and strengthening Joshua to lead God's beloved people (v.28).

d. From this time forward, the people of Israel remained in the valley near Beth Peor (v.29). This area was just east of the Jordan River, right across from Jericho, where the people were poised to cross the river and enter the promised land.

Thought 1. God chastises the believer who sins, no matter who he is. No believer is ever too high or important for God to discipline if the believer sins. No doubt, Moses was one of the greatest and most faithful servants of all time, yet God chastised him. When he sinned, the judgment and chastisement of God fell upon him. He reaped what he had sown. So it is with every believer. If a believer sins, he reaps what he has sown. The chastisement of God falls upon him.

"Every branch in me that beareth not fruit he taketh away: and every *branch* that beareth fruit, he purgeth it, that it may bring forth more fruit" (Jn.15:2).

"And ye have forgotten the exhortation which speaketh unto you as unto children, My son, despise not thou the chastening of the LORD, nor faint when thou art rebuked of him: For whom the LORD loveth he chasteneth, and scourgeth every son whom he receiveth" (He.12:5-6).

"Now no chastening for the present seemeth to be joyous, but grievous: nevertheless afterward it yieldeth the peaceable fruit of righteousness unto them which are exercised thereby. Wherefore lift up the hands which hang down, and the feeble knees; And make straight paths for your feet, lest that which is lame be turned out of the way; but let it rather be healed. Follow peace with all *men*, and holiness, without which no man shall see the LORD: Looking diligently lest any man fail of the grace of God; lest any root of bitterness springing up trouble *you,* and thereby many be defiled" (He.12:11-15).

"Thou shalt also consider in thine heart, that, as a man chasteneth his son, *so* the LORD thy God chasteneth thee" (De.8:5).

"Blessed *is* the man whom thou chastenest, O LORD, and teachest him out of thy law" (Ps.94:12).

"My son, despise not the chastening of the LORD; neither be weary of his correction: For whom the LORD loveth he correcteth; even as a father the son *in whom* he delighteth" (Pr.3:11-12).

TYPES, SYMBOLS, AND PICTURES
(Deuteronomy 2:16–3:29)

Historical Term	Type or Picture (Scriptural Basis for Each)	Life Application for Today's Believer	Biblical Application
The Victorious March over the Canaanite Enemies De.2:24-3:11 (See also De.28:7)	*The victorious march over the Canaanite enemies is a picture of the believer's spiritual victory. The kings of the Amorites stood between the Israelites and the promised land.* "Rise ye up, take your journey, and pass over the river Arnon: behold, I	⇒ No matter the enemy—no matter its strength or threat—God is stronger. And God will give victory to His people. God will empower His people to conquer and triumph over all the enemies of life. If we will only believe and obey God, we will march victoriously throughout	*"These things I have spoken unto you, that in me ye might have peace. In the world ye shall have tribulation: but be of good cheer; I have overcome the world" (Jn.16:33).* *"Who shall separate us from the love of Christ? shall tribulation, or distress, or persecution, or famine,*

DEUTERONOMY 2:16–3:29

Historical Term	Type or Picture (Scriptural Basis for Each)	Life Application for Today's Believer	Biblical Application
	have given into thine hand Sihon the Amorite, king of Heshbon, and his land: begin to possess *it*, and contend with him in battle" (De.2:24).	life. We will experience victory after victory over our enemies. We will know what it is to live a victorious life as we march to the promised land of God. We will be victorious even as the Israelite believers were victorious over these two mighty kings.	or nakedness, or peril, or sword?...Nay, in all these things we are more than conquerors through him that loved us. For I am persuaded, that neither death, nor life, nor angels, nor principalities, nor powers, nor things present, nor things to come, Nor height, nor depth, nor any other creature, shall be able to separate us from the love of God, which is in Christ Jesus our Lord" (Ro.8:35, 37-39). "There hath no temptation taken you but such as is common to man: but God is faithful, who will not suffer you to be tempted above that ye are able; but will with the temptation also make a way to escape, that ye may be able to bear it" (1 Co.10:13).
The Distribution of the Conquered Land of East Jordan De.3:12-20	The distribution of the conquered land of East Jordan is a picture that one must not settle down, be complacent, at ease before total conquest of the promised land. "And I commanded you at that time, saying, The LORD your God hath given you this land to possess it: ye shall pass over armed before your brethren the children of Israel, all *that are* meet for the war" (De.3:18).	⇒ God warns us against complacency, against seeking worldly comfort, rest, and ease. As we march to the promised land of heaven, God has called us to a life of total commitment to Him. We are engaged in a spiritual warfare, struggling against the enemies of this life, enemies that want to keep us out of the promised land. ⇒ We must press on and conquer these enemies of the promised land. God demands total conquest. We must never stop short. We must defeat the spirit of complacency, the spirit of worldly comfort, ease, and rest. We must never compromise with the lethargy of this world, never become self-satisfied, smug, and unconcerned. We must press on to secure the promised land of God, the great inheritance God has promised. We must press on until we have conquered all the enemies of the promised land, press on	"And every one that heareth these sayings of mine, and doeth them not, shall be likened unto a foolish man, which built his house upon the sand: And the rain descended, and the floods came, and the winds blew, and beat upon that house; and it fell: and great was the fall of it" (Mt.7:26-27). "And because iniquity shall abound, the love of many shall wax cold. But he that shall endure unto the end, the same shall be saved" (Mt.24:12-13). "Therefore, my beloved brethren, be ye stedfast, unmovable, always abounding in the work of the Lord, forasmuch as ye know that your labour is not in vain in the Lord" (1 Co.15:58). "Therefore to him that knoweth to do good, and doeth it not, to him it is sin" (Js.4:17). "And Joshua said unto the children of Israel, How long are ye slack to go to possess the land, which the LORD God of your fathers hath given you?" (Jos.18:3). "Our soul is exceedingly filled with the scorning of those that are at ease, and

DEUTERONOMY 2:16–3:29

Historical Term	Type or Picture (Scriptural Basis for Each)	Life Application for Today's Believer	Biblical Application
		until we reach the spiritual rest of our glorious inheritance—the spiritual rest promised by God. During life upon this earth, there is no room for complacency or worldly comfort and ease.	*with the contempt of the proud"* (Ps.123:4). *"Woe to them that are at ease in Zion, and trust in the mountain of Samaria, which are named chief of the nations, to whom the house of Israel came!"* (Am.6:1).

DEUTERONOMY 4:1-43

1. **Listen to God's laws & obey His laws: That you may live & inherit the promised land of God (a symbol of heaven, of spiritual conquest & rest)**[DS1]

   a. You must not add to nor subtract from God's commandments: Simply obey them

   b. You must not commit the sins of Baal Peor: Immorality & false worship (Nu.25:1-18)
      1) The result: Judgment—death
      2) The escape: Must hold fast to the LORD to live & escape judgment

   c. You must obey God's law after reaching the promised land: Obey while seeking victory & rest over the enemies of the promised land

2. **Remember the results of obedience: What happens when you carefully obey God's law**
   a. You will bear a strong testimony & witness: Others will declare that you are wise & understanding

   b. You will have the presence & power of God when you pray

   c. You will learn to cherish the law of God—all because it is righteous (fair, just)

3. **Take heed! Be careful! Guard yourself closely! Do not forget your experience with the LORD nor the Ten Commandments (v.13)**
   a. Do not let them slip from your heart
   b. Teach them to your children
   c. Remember the wonderful experience of God's

C. **The Strong Exhortation to the Second Generation of Israelite Believers: Obey God's Laws & Acknowledge That the Lord—He & He Alone—Is God, 4:1-43**

Now therefore hearken, O Israel, unto the statutes and unto the judgments, which I teach you, for to do *them*, that ye may live, and go in and possess the land which the LORD God of your fathers giveth you.
2 Ye shall not add unto the word which I command you, neither shall ye diminish *ought* from it, that ye may keep the commandments of the LORD your God which I command you.
3 Your eyes have seen what the LORD did because of Baal-peor: for all the men that followed Baal-peor, the LORD thy God hath destroyed them from among you.
4 But ye that did cleave unto the LORD your God *are* alive every one of you this day.
5 Behold, I have taught you statutes and judgments, even as the LORD my God commanded me, that ye should do so in the land whither ye go to possess it.
6 Keep therefore and do *them*; for this *is* your wisdom and your understanding in the sight of the nations, which shall hear all these statutes, and say, Surely this great nation *is* a wise and understanding people.
7 For what nation *is there so* great, who *hath* God *so* nigh unto them, as the LORD our God *is* in all *things that* we call upon him *for*?
8 And what nation *is there so* great, that hath statutes and judgments *so* righteous as all this law, which I set before you this day?
9 Only take heed to thyself, and keep thy soul diligently, lest thou forget the things which thine eyes have seen, and lest they depart from thy heart all the days of thy life: but teach them thy sons, and thy sons' sons;
10 *Specially* the day that thou stoodest before the LORD thy God in Horeb, when the LORD said unto me, Gather me the people together, and I will make them hear my words, that they may learn to fear me all the days that they shall live upon the earth, and *that* they may teach their children.
11 And ye came near and stood under the mountain; and the mountain burned with fire unto the midst of heaven, with darkness, clouds, and thick darkness.
12 And the LORD spake unto you out of the midst of the fire: ye heard the voice of the words, but saw no similitude; only *ye heard* a voice.
13 And he declared unto you his covenant, which he commanded you to perform, *even* ten commandments; and he wrote them upon two tables of stone.
14 And the LORD commanded me at that time to teach you statutes and judgments, that ye might do them in the land whither ye go over to possess it.
15 Take ye therefore good heed unto yourselves; for ye saw no manner of similitude on the day *that* the LORD spake unto you in Horeb out of the midst of the fire:
16 Lest ye corrupt *yourselves*, and make you a graven image, the similitude of any figure, the likeness of male or female,
17 The likeness of any beast that *is* on the earth, the likeness of any winged fowl that flieth in the air,
18 The likeness of any thing that creepeth on the ground, the likeness of any fish that *is* in the waters beneath the earth:
19 And lest thou lift up thine eyes unto heaven, and when thou seest the sun, and the moon, and the stars, *even* all the host of heaven, shouldest be driven to worship them, and serve them, which the LORD thy God hath divided unto all nations under the whole heaven.
20 But the LORD hath taken you, and brought you forth out of the iron furnace, *even* out of Egypt, to be unto him a people of inheritance, as *ye*

presence at Mt. Horeb (Sinai)
   1) His purpose: To teach you to fear Him & stir you to teach His Word to your children

   2) His glorious, frightening appearance: In blazing fire, black clouds, & deep darkness

   3) His booming voice
      - Words were heard, but no form was seen
      - Only a voice was heard

   d. Remember & obey the covenant He proclaimed: The Ten Commandments
      1) You are to obey them
      2) He wrote them in permanent form for you
      3) You are to learn the commandments—all the laws & decrees of God: You are to obey them in the promised land of God

4. **Guard against all false gods & false worship**
   a. Reason 1: You have seen no form of God (God is Spirit, Jn.4:24)

   b. Reason 2: You will corrupt yourself
      1) Must not worship people, man or woman

      2) Must not worship animals or fish

      3) Must not worship nature: The heavenly bodies—the sun, moon, or stars
         - Must not be enticed to worship these
         - God gave these to serve man

   c. Reason 3: You were saved to be God's people, His special inheritance, saved out of the furnace of iron, out of Egypt (a symbol of the world)

51

DEUTERONOMY 4:1-43

d. Reason 4: God judges those who sin—bars them from the promised land of God
  1) The first generation had committed idolatry & were barred
  2) Moses was held accountable as their leader & was barred: Condemned to die in the wilderness
  3) The safeguard against judgment: Obedience
     - Must not forget the covenant of the LORD, the Ten Commandments
     - Must not make nor worship any idol (image, false god)
     - The reason: God is a consuming fire, a jealous God
e. Reason 5: You have the strong warning & prophecy of God—you will be removed from the promised land
  1) False worship will cause you to be judged even after you have lived in the promised land for a long time
  2) False worship will cause heaven & earth to witness against you
     - You will perish, be removed from the promised land
     - You will be scattered among the peoples of the world (a picture of returning to worldliness): Only a few will survive
     - You will worship manmade gods that are lifeless
f. Reason 6: You have the glorious promise of God
  1) The promise that if you diligently seek the LORD, you will find Him
  2) The promise that when you suffer the distress of the world, you will return & obey God (a prophecy concerning Israel but applicable to us all)
  3) The promise of God's mercy
     - God is merciful

are this day.
21 Furthermore the LORD was angry with me for your sakes, and sware that I should not go over Jordan, and that I should not go in unto that good land, which the LORD thy God giveth thee *for* an inheritance:
22 But I must die in this land, I must not go over Jordan: but ye shall go over, and possess that good land.
23 Take heed unto yourselves, lest ye forget the covenant of the LORD your God, which he made with you, and make you a graven image, *or* the likeness of any *thing*, which the LORD thy God hath forbidden thee.
24 For the LORD thy God *is* a consuming fire, *even* a jealous God.
25 When thou shalt beget children, and children's children, and ye shall have remained long in the land, and shall corrupt *yourselves*, and make a graven image, *or* the likeness of any *thing*, and shall do evil in the sight of the LORD thy God, to provoke him to anger:
26 I call heaven and earth to witness against you this day, that ye shall soon utterly perish from off the land whereunto ye go over Jordan to possess it; ye shall not prolong *your* days upon it, but shall utterly be destroyed.
27 And the LORD shall scatter you among the nations, and ye shall be left few in number among the heathen, whither the LORD shall lead you.
28 And there ye shall serve gods, the work of men's hands, wood and stone, which neither see, nor hear, nor eat, nor smell.
29 But if from thence thou shalt seek the LORD thy God, thou shalt find *him*, if thou seek him with all thy heart and with all thy soul.
30 When thou art in tribulation, and all these things are come upon thee, *even* in the latter days, if thou turn to the LORD thy God, and shalt be obedient unto his voice;
31 (For the LORD thy God *is* a merciful God;) he will not forsake thee, neither destroy thee, nor forget the covenant of thy fathers which he sware unto them.
32 For ask now of the days that are past, which were before thee, since the day that God created man upon the earth, and *ask* from the one side of heaven unto the other, whether there hath been *any such thing* as this great thing *is*, or hath been heard like it?
33 Did *ever* people hear the voice of God speaking out of the midst of the fire, as thou hast heard, and live?
34 Or hath God assayed to go *and* take him a nation from the midst of *another* nation, by temptations, by signs, and by wonders, and by war, and by a mighty hand, and by a stretched out arm, and by great terrors, according to all that the LORD your God did for you in Egypt before your eyes?
35 Unto thee it was showed, that thou mightest know that the LORD he *is* God; *there is* none else beside him.
36 Out of heaven he made thee to hear his voice, that he might instruct thee: and upon earth he showed thee his great fire; and thou heardest his words out of the midst of the fire.
37 And because he loved thy fathers, therefore he chose their seed after them, and brought thee out in his sight with his mighty power out of Egypt;
38 To drive out nations from before thee greater and mightier than thou *art*, to bring thee in, to give thee their land *for* an inheritance, as *it is* this day.
39 Know therefore this day, and consider *it* in thine heart, that the LORD he *is* God in heaven above, and upon the earth beneath: *there is* none else.
40 Thou shalt keep therefore his statutes, and his commandments, which I command thee this day, that it may go well with thee, and with thy children after thee, and that thou mayest prolong *thy* days upon the earth, which the LORD thy God giveth thee, for ever.
41 Then Moses severed three

- God will not forget His covenant with Israel's forefathers
5. Acknowledge that the LORD—He & He alone—is God
  a. The LORD is the great Creator of man, the Creator who has done marvelous things for His people: Things never before done or heard about
  b. The LORD is the God of revelation or communication: He reveals Himself, speaks with His people
  c. The LORD is the God of power & might & of miraculous works—all on behalf of His people: Demonstrated in His dealings with Egypt

  d. The LORD is God, the only living & true God, the Sovereign Majesty of the universe (Jehovah, Yahweh)
  e. The LORD is the God of discipline (correction) & holiness

  f. The LORD is the God of love & salvation: Proven by the deliverance of His people out of Egypt (a symbol of the world) by His Presence & power
  g. The LORD is the God who gives victory over all enemies & guides His people to the promised land

  h. The LORD is the Sovereign God over all in heaven & on earth: He & He alone is the only living & true God

  i. The LORD is the God who demands obedience
    1) Must keep His laws & commandments
    2) The result
       - Things will go well
       - A long life in the promised land

6. Remember God's command

DEUTERONOMY 4:1-43

to set up cities of refuge (Nu.35:13-14): A picture of Christ, our refuge from death & from the storms & threats of life a. The purpose: To be a place of safety for a person guilty	cities on this side Jordan toward the sunrising; 42 That the slayer might flee thither, which should kill his neighbour unawares, and hated him not in times past; and that fleeing unto one of these	cities he might live: 43 *Namely*, Bezer in the wilderness, in the plain country, of the Reubenites; and Ramoth in Gilead, of the Gadites; and Golan in Bashan, of the Manassites.	of accidental manslaughter b. The location: Three cities in east Jordan 1) In Bezer:^{DS2} For Reuben 2) In Ramoth:^{DS3} For Gad 3) In Golan:^{DS4} For the half-tribe of Manasseh

DIVISION II

THE FIRST GREAT THEME PREACHED BY GOD'S AGED SERVANT: REMEMBER THE LESSONS FROM HISTORY, 1:6–4:43

C. The Strong Exhortation to the Second Generation of Israelite Believers: Obey God's Laws and Acknowledge That the LORD—He and He Alone—Is God, 4:1-43

(4:1-43) **Introduction**: disrespect for authority is sweeping the earth today. People want few restrictions: they desire to do what they want, when they want, like they want. For years now there has been a continued deterioration of respect for such authority figures as...

- teachers
- policemen
- politicians
- lawyers
- judges
- ministers
- business persons
- physicians
- government employees

The slide of respect has slipped so far that even parents are dishonored and treated disrespectfully. Parental disrespect is serious, very serious, but there is a disrespect that supersedes all bad behavior toward others: the disrespect of God Himself. When a person shows dishonor to God, he does so to his own detriment. He is daring the judgment of God to fall upon him, and it will. Scripture declares this loudly and clearly.

God must be honored, and He is honored by being obeyed. To show respect for God is to show respect for His law, His commandments. This is the subject of this most important passage of Scripture: *The Strong Exhortation to the Second Generation of Israelite Believers: Obey God's Laws and Acknowledge That the* LORD—*He and He Alone—Is God*, 4:1-43.

1. Listen to God's laws and obey His laws: that you may live and inherit the promised land of God (a symbol of heaven, of spiritual conquest and rest) (vv.1-5).
2. Remember the results of obedience: what happens when you carefully obey God's law (vv.6-8).
3. Take heed! Be careful! Guard yourself closely! Do not forget your experience with the LORD nor the Ten Commandments (vv.9-14).
4. Guard against all false gods and false worship (vv.15-31).
5. Acknowledge that the LORD—He and He alone—is God (vv.32-40).
6. Remember God's command to set up cities of refuge (Nu.35:13-14): a picture of Christ, our refuge from death and from the storms and threats of life (vv.41-43).

1 (4:1-5) **Law, of God—Promised Land, How to Enter—Obedience, Charge to—Word of God, Adding to—Word of God, Abuse of—Baal Peor**: listen to God's laws and obey His laws. If a person listens and obeys, he will inherit the promised land of God.

OUTLINE	SCRIPTURE	SCRIPTURE	OUTLINE
1. Listen to God's laws & obey His laws: That you may live & inherit the promised land of God (a symbol of heaven, of spiritual conquest & rest)^{DS1} a. You must not add to nor subtract from God's commandments: Simply obey them b. You must not commit the sins	Now therefore hearken, O Israel, unto the statutes and unto the judgments, which I teach you, for to do *them*, that ye may live, and go in and possess the land which the LORD God of your fathers giveth you. 2 Ye shall not add unto the word which I command you, neither shall ye diminish *ought* from it, that ye may keep the commandments of the LORD your God which I command you. 3 Your eyes have seen	what the LORD did because of Baal-peor: for all the men that followed Baal-peor, the LORD thy God hath destroyed them from among you. 4 But ye that did cleave unto the LORD your God *are* alive every one of you this day. 5 Behold, I have taught you statutes and judgments, even as the LORD my God commanded me, that ye should do so in the land whither ye go to possess it.	of Baal Peor: Immorality & false worship (Nu.25:1-18) 1) The result: Judgment— death 2) The escape: Must hold fast to the LORD to live & escape judgment c. You must obey God's law after reaching the promised land: Obey while seeking victory & rest over the enemies of the promised land

DEUTERONOMY 4:1-43

Note the word "now" in verse 1. This refers back to what Moses had already preached:
⇒ The great hope but tragic failure that kept the first generation of Israelites out of the promised land—the sins of unbelief, grumbling, and rebellion (see outline and notes—De.1:6-2:15 for more discussion).
⇒ The triumphant victory and warning given by God to the second generation of Israelite believers (see outline and notes—De.2:16-3:29 for more discussion).

"Now"—in light of the lessons learned in the past—listen to God's laws and obey His laws. If you will listen and obey, you will not fall into sin and face the judgment of God as the first generation did. Rather, you will live a fruitful and productive life. Moreover, you will experience the power of God, conquering all the enemies who oppose you as you march into the promised land. You will be victorious and take possession of the promised land. You will know the spiritual conquest and rest of the inheritance promised by God. But note what Moses declared: to know such a fruitful and victorious life God's people must do three things.

a. They must not add to nor subtract from God's commandments, but simply obey them (v.2). God has spoken, stated exactly what He wants to say to man. Nothing more, nothing less is needed. Man is not to tamper with God's holy commandments, His Holy Word:
⇒ Man must not add his own ideas or thoughts to God's Word nor the ideas and thoughts of other people.
⇒ Man must not take away from God's Word, must not omit any statement or requirement of God's Word.
⇒ Man is to accept God's Holy Word just as it has been given by God. No person is to attempt to explain away God's clear commandment in order to justify his sinful behavior. The commandments of God are adequate, sufficient for life: they are exactly what man needs in order to live a fruitful and productive life, a victorious life conquering all of the enemies of life.

> "For this cause also thank we God without ceasing, because, when ye received the word of God which ye heard of us, ye received *it* not *as* the word of men, but as it is in truth, the word of God, which effectually worketh also in you that believe" (1 Th.2:13).
>
> "For I testify unto every man that heareth the words of the prophecy of this book, If any man shall add unto these things, God shall add unto him the plagues that are written in this book: And if any man shall take away from the words of the book of this prophecy, God shall take away his part out of the book of life, and out of the holy city, and *from* the things which are written in this book" (Re.22:18-19).
>
> "What thing soever I command you, observe to do it: thou shalt not add thereto, nor diminish from it" (De.12:32).

b. God's people must not commit the sins of Baal Peor, the sins of immorality and false worship (see outline and notes—Nu.25:1-18 for more discussion). This is a primary example of disobedience to God's commandments. The sins committed at Baal Peor stand as a strong warning against disobedience. While camped by the Jordan River, thousands had become involved with their pagan neighbors and indulged in sexual relationships. But this was not all: their pagan neighbors had eventually invited them to share in their worship services and socials. The result was inevitable: many of the Israelite believers began to participate in the false worship and commit the gross sin of idolatry. They became guilty not only of immorality but of idolatry as well. They broke the clear commandments of God against idolatry and adultery. They broke the heart of God. The result was the judgment, the chastisement of God's hand. Because of their disobedience, over twenty-four thousand Israelite believers died. It was in this particular rebellion that the last of the first generation died and passed off the scene of human history. Tragically, they had all died because of sin and the inevitable judgment of God against sin.

But this is not the whole story. Note that all who held fast to the LORD lived and escaped the judgment of God. In fact, note exactly what Scripture says: they were all—the obedient—still alive. They were all standing there listening to this sermon preached by Moses. The point is electrifying: the believer must obey the commandments of God. He must not commit the sins of Baal Peor, the sins of immorality and false worship. He must never follow in the footsteps of the disobedient. Disobedience arouses judgment. And judgment falls upon all the disobedient.

> "But I say unto you, That whosoever looketh on a woman to lust after her hath committed adultery with her already in his heart" (Mt.5:28).
>
> "For the wrath of God is revealed from heaven against all ungodliness and unrighteousness of men, who hold the truth in unrighteousness; Because that which may be known of God is manifest in them; for God hath showed *it* unto them. For the invisible things of him from the creation of the world are clearly seen, being understood by the things that are made, *even* his eternal power and Godhead; so that they are without excuse: Because that, when they knew God, they glorified *him* not as God, neither were thankful; but became vain in their imaginations, and their foolish heart was darkened. Professing themselves to be wise, they became fools, And changed the glory of the uncorruptible God into an image made like to corruptible man, and to birds, and fourfooted beasts, and creeping things" (Ro.1:18-23).
>
> "Know ye not that the unrighteous shall not inherit the kingdom of God? Be not deceived: neither fornicators, nor idolaters, nor adulterers, nor effeminate, nor abusers of themselves with mankind, Nor thieves, nor covetous, nor drunkards, nor revilers, nor extortioners, shall inherit the kingdom of God. And such were some of you: but ye are washed, but ye are sanctified, but ye are justified in the name of the LORD Jesus, and by the Spirit of our God" (1 Co.6:9-11).
>
> "Flee fornication [all forms of illicit sex]. Every sin that a man doeth is without the body; but he that committeth fornication sinneth against his own body" (1 Co.6:18).
>
> "For this is the will of God, *even* your sanctification, that ye should abstain from fornication: That every one of you should know how to possess his vessel in sanctification and honour; Not in the lust of concupiscence, even as the Gentiles which know not God" (1 Th.4:3-5).

DEUTERONOMY 4:1-43

"And to you who are troubled rest with us, when the LORD Jesus shall be revealed from heaven with his mighty angels, In flaming fire taking vengeance on them that know not God, and that obey not the gospel of our Lord Jesus Christ: Who shall be punished with everlasting destruction from the presence of the LORD, and from the glory of his power" (2 Th.1:7-9).

"But the fearful, and unbelieving, and the abominable, and murderers, and whoremongers, and sorcerers, and idolaters, and all liars, shall have their part in the lake which burneth with fire and brimstone: which is the second death" (Re.21:8).

"I *am* the LORD: that *is* my name: and my glory will I not give to another, neither my praise to graven images" (Is.42:8).

c. God's people must obey God's law even after reaching the promised land. Even after they achieve the spiritual victory and rest of the promised land, they must still continue to obey God's law. There was to be no room for complacency or worldly comfort and rest. So long as a believer was on the earth, he was to be diligent in his worship, in living a holy, distinctive life, and in bearing a strong testimony to his neighbors.

"Not every one that saith unto me, Lord, Lord, shall enter into the kingdom of heaven; but he that doeth the will of my Father which is in heaven" (Mt.7:21).

"Therefore whosoever heareth these sayings of mine, and doeth them, I will liken him unto a wise man, which built his house upon a rock: And the rain descended, and the floods came, and the winds blew, and beat upon that house; and it fell not: for it was founded upon a rock" (Mt.7:24-25).

"If ye keep my commandments, ye shall abide in my love; even as I have kept my Father's commandments, and abide in his love" (Jn.15:10).

"Ye are my friends, if ye do whatsoever I command you" (Jn.15:14).

"This day the LORD thy God hath commanded thee to do these statutes and judgments: thou shalt therefore keep and do them with all thine heart, and with all thy soul" (De.26:16).

"And Samuel said, Hath the LORD *as great* delight in burnt offerings and sacrifices, as in obeying the voice of the LORD? Behold, to obey *is* better than sacrifice, *and* to hearken than the fat of rams" (1 S.15:22).

DEEPER STUDY # 1
(4:1-2) Law—Judgments—Commandments—Testimonies—Torah: Several words are used in this chapter to describe the law of God. Each word is used to stress a different shade of meaning.

1. The word *statute* or *decree* (vv.1, 45, choq or hoq) means a rule, regulation, decree, statute, commandment, or law. The word has the force of being determined once for all, of being cut or chiseled in wood, metal, or stone. The statute or decree is fixed, set as a law forever, It has the force of being issued by a king or some legal authority. The *statutes* of God's Word are determined and established forever by the King of the universe, the supreme legal authority over all.

2. The word *judgments* or *laws* (vv.1, 45, mispal) means a judgment, a legal decision passed down by a judge (Wenham, Gordon J. *The Book of Leviticus,* p.253); a just decision that must be kept; a law or regulation of true justice; a law that has to be obeyed in order for justice to be done.

3. The word *commandment* or *command* (v.2, mitsvah or miswah) means a law, order, instruction, ordinance, rule, charge, commission, or command given by some authority, whether human or divine. When a commandment is given by God, it is to be done. The commandments of God are to be obeyed.

4. The word *testimonies* or *stipulations* (v.45, edah or edut) means a testimony or witness that is given; a stipulation, regulation, or requirement that is demanded. The idea is this: the laws and commandments of God are testimonies to His nature. They are stipulations or requirements of His righteousness.

5. The word *law* (v.44, Torah) means a precept, statute, regulation, or instruction. It includes the idea of teaching, pointing out, informing, instructing. The picture of the law is that of an arrow shot by an archer. The arrow flies straight to the target, straight to the goal, the objective. So it is with the *law* (Torah). The *law* points, directs a person straight to the goal of righteousness, to the objective of *right living.*

But note: the word *law* (Torah) means more than just statutes and regulations. Basically, the law (Torah) means all the instructions and teachings of God.[1] It refers to the entire Pentateuch or Decalogue,[2] the first five books of the Bible. The law includes all that the LORD commanded (v.3): the Ten Commandments, the civil and religious laws, and all the other instructions given by God to His people. It is the wonderful law of God (Torah)—the full instruction and teaching of God—that tells people how to live life to the fullest.

---

2 **(4:6-8) Obedience, Results of—Law of God, Results of Obedience—Testimony, a Strong—Prayer, How to Pray—Law, Nature of**: remember the results of obedience, what happens when you carefully obey God's law. This is a strong charge: obey—be careful to obey God's law. It is the law of God that sets God's people apart and makes them distinctive, a holy and righteous people. When you, as one of God's people, obey God's law, three significant things happen. Note the Scripture and outline:

---

[1] *The Nelson Study Bible, New King James Version,* p.292, notes on De.1:5.
[2] James Strong. *Strong's Exhaustive Concordance of the Bible,* #8451.

DEUTERONOMY 4:1-43

OUTLINE	SCRIPTURE	SCRIPTURE	OUTLINE
2. Remember the results of obedience: What happens when you carefully obey God's law a. You will bear a strong testimony & witness: Others will declare that you are wise & understanding b. You will have the presence	6 Keep therefore and do *them*; for this *is* your wisdom and your understanding in the sight of the nations, which shall hear all these statutes, and say, Surely this great nation *is* a wise and understanding people. 7 For what nation *is there*	so great, who *hath* God *so* nigh unto them, as the LORD our God *is* in all *things that* we call upon him *for*? 8 And what nation *is there* so great, that hath statutes and judgments *so* righteous as all this law, which I set before you this day?	& power of God when you pray c. You will learn to cherish the law of God—all because it is righteous (fair, just)

a. You will bear a strong testimony and witness to your neighbors (v.6). The law of God is full of wisdom and understanding. Any person who studies God's law clearly sees the wisdom lying behind the law, the impact the law would have upon human behavior. Any people who would adopt and obey the Ten Commandments would be declared a great nation, a wise and understanding people. This was exactly what God was declaring to the Israelites: if they obeyed His law, they would bear a strong testimony and witness before the world. The world would declare that they were a great nation, a wise and understanding people. Note that Israel's greatness was not to lie in military strength nor economic wealth; their greatness would lie in the great laws that governed their nation, even the law of God itself, in particular the Ten Commandments.

"The law of the LORD *is* perfect, converting the soul: the testimony of the LORD *is* sure, making wise the simple" (Ps.19:7).

"Whoso keepeth the law *is* a wise son" (Pr.28:7).

"The statutes of the LORD *are* right, rejoicing the heart: the commandment of the LORD *is* pure, enlightening the eyes" (Ps.19:8).

"O that my ways were directed to keep thy statutes!" (Ps.119:5).

"The entrance of thy words giveth light; it giveth understanding unto the simple" (Ps.119:130).

"Who *is* wise, and he shall understand these *things*? prudent, and he shall know them? for the ways of the LORD *are* right, and the just shall walk in them: but the transgressors shall fall therein" (Ho.14:9).

"Wherefore the law *is* holy, and the commandment holy, and just, and good" (Ro.7:12).

"O the depth of the riches both of the wisdom and knowledge of God! how unsearchable *are* his judgments, and his ways past finding out!" (Ro.11:33).

"Therefore whosoever heareth these sayings of mine, and doeth them, I will liken him unto a wise man, which built his house upon a rock: And the rain descended, and the floods came, and the winds blew, and beat upon that house; and it fell not: for it was founded upon a rock. And every one that heareth these sayings of mine, and doeth them not, shall be likened unto a foolish man, which built his house upon the sand: And the rain descended, and the floods came, and the winds blew, and beat upon that house; and it fell: and great was the fall of it" (Mt.7:24-27).

"For the word of God *is* quick, and powerful, and sharper than any twoedged sword, piercing even to the dividing asunder of soul and spirit, and of the joints and marrow, and *is* a discerner of the thoughts and intents of the heart" (He.4:12).

b. You will have the presence and the power of God when you pray (v.7). Obedience will result in answered prayer. A personal, intimate relationship will be established with God. If a person kept the Ten Commandments, the presence and power of God would be with him, looking after and taking care of him.

"If ye abide in me, and my words abide in you, ye shall ask what ye will, and it shall be done unto you" (Jn.15:7).

"And whatsoever we ask, we receive of him, because we keep his commandments, and do those things that are pleasing in his sight" (1 Jn.3:22).

"If my people, which are called by my name, shall humble themselves, and pray, and seek my face, and turn from their wicked ways; then will I hear from heaven, and will forgive their sin, and will heal their land" (2 Chr.7:14).

"If I regard iniquity in my heart [disobedience], the LORD will not hear *me*" (Ps.66:18).

"But your iniquities have separated between you and your God, and your sins [disobedience] have hid *his* face from you, that he will not hear" (Is.59:2 sins).

"And ye shall seek me, and find *me*, when ye shall search for me with all your heart" (Je.29:13).

c. You will learn to cherish the law of God—all because the law was righteous and fair and just (v.8). The law of God established fair and just treatment between neighbors. By obeying the law, every person will be treated fairly and justly. No partiality or favoritism will be shown; no lawlessness or violence will be tolerated; no unjust weight or treatment will be allowed.

"Wherefore the law *is* holy, and the commandment holy, and just, and good" (Ro.7:12).

"But we know that the law *is* good, if a man use it lawfully" (1 Ti.1:8).

"One law shall be to him that is homeborn, and unto the stranger that sojourneth among you" (Ex.12:49).

"Ye shall have one manner of law, as well for the stranger, as for one of your own country: for I *am* the LORD your God" (Le.24:22).

DEUTERONOMY 4:1-43

"One law and one manner shall be for you, and for the stranger that sojourneth with you" (Nu.15:16).

"The law of his God *is* in his heart; none of his steps shall slide" (Ps.37:31).

"I delight to do thy will, O my God: yea, thy law *is* within my heart" (Ps.40:8).

"And I will delight myself in thy commandments, which I have loved" (Ps.119:47).

"The law of thy mouth *is* better unto me than thousands of gold and silver" (Ps.119:72).

"O how love I thy law! it *is* my meditation all the day" (Ps.119:97).

"Thy word *is* very pure: therefore thy servant loveth it" (Ps.119:140).

"But this *shall be* the covenant that I will make with the house of Israel; After those days, saith the LORD, I will put my law in their inward parts, and write it in their hearts; and will be their God, and they shall be my people" (Je.31:33).

3 **(4:9-14) Believer, Experience with the LORD—Ten Commandments, Duty to Keep—Covenant, of the Ten Commandments—Obedience—Presence, of God—Backsliding, Caused by—Warning, Described as:** Take heed! Be careful! Guard yourself closely! Do not forget your experiences with the LORD nor the Ten Commandments. Note that this warning is repeated again in verse 15 and verse 23: *Take heed! Be careful! Watch, guard yourself closely!* Four instructions are given in this warning:

OUTLINE	SCRIPTURE	SCRIPTURE	OUTLINE

3. Take heed! Be careful! Guard yourself closely! Do not forget your experience with the LORD nor the Ten Commandments (v.13)
a. Do not let them slip from your heart
b. Teach them to your children
c. Remember the wonderful experience of God's presence at Mt. Horeb (Sinai)
  1) His purpose: To teach you to fear Him & stir you to teach His Word to your children
 	
  2) His glorious, frightening appearance: In blazing
	9 Only take heed to thyself, and keep thy soul diligently, lest thou forget the things which thine eyes have seen, and lest they depart from thy heart all the days of thy life: but teach them thy sons, and thy sons' sons;
	10 *Specially* the day that thou stoodest before the LORD thy God in Horeb, when the LORD said unto me, Gather me the people together, and I will make them hear my words, that they may learn to fear me all the days that they shall live upon the earth, and *that* they may teach their children.
	11 And ye came near and stood under the mountain;
		and the mountain burned with fire unto the midst of heaven, with darkness, clouds, and thick darkness.
		12 And the LORD spake unto you out of the midst of the fire: ye heard the voice of the words, but saw no similitude; only *ye heard* a voice.
		13 And he declared unto you his covenant, which he commanded you to perform, *even* ten commandments; and he wrote them upon two tables of stone.
		14 And the LORD commanded me at that time to teach you statutes and judgments, that ye might do them in the land whither ye go over to possess it.
			fire, black clouds, & deep darkness
			
			  3) His booming voice
			  • Words were heard, but no form was seen
			  • Only a voice was heard
			
			d. Remember & obey the covenant He proclaimed: The Ten Commandments
			  1) You are to obey them
			  2) He wrote them in permanent form for you
			  3) You are to learn the commandments—all the laws & decrees of God: You are to obey them in the promised land of God

    a. First, do not let your experiences with the LORD nor the Ten Commandments slip from your heart (v.9). The word for *slip* or *depart* (soor or surl) means to depart; to be removed; to be taken away, plucked away, cut off. The Israelite believers had been eyewitnesses of the miraculous salvation of God from Egypt and throughout the wilderness wanderings. They had never seen God with their eyes, but they had seen the works of God, such works as...

- God's salvation and deliverance
- God's guidance and direction
- God's provision and care
- God's protection and security

    God had saved them from Egyptian slavery and set them free. Moreover, He had led them day by day through the forty years of wilderness wanderings. They had experienced God's presence, guidance, and provision day by day. God had given them victory over the enemies who had opposed their march to the promised land. But more than all this, God had given them a deep sense and consciousness of His presence and guidance day by day. They had the very Tabernacle of God's holy presence in their midst and the pillar of cloud that symbolized His holy presence. Experience after experience with God had been given to the Israelite believers. Their very eyes had seen the mighty salvation and works of God. And God had given them His Holy Word and the Ten Commandments (see v.13). Because they had been given so much, they must take heed! Be careful! Guard themselves closely! Never forget their experiences with the LORD nor the Ten Commandments. They must never let them slip from their hearts.

    b. Second, teach God's Word and commandments to your children and share your spiritual experiences with them (v.9). Believers were responsible to teach and educate their children in the ways of the LORD. Note that each generation was to be taught, the children and then their children after them. Generation after generation was to be taught the Word of God, His saving power, provision, and guidance day by day. This would give continuity to the covenant, guaranteeing the continued obedience of God's people. Just as the parents did, the children would live holy and distinctive lives before the surrounding nations. They would be dynamic witnesses to the holy character and demands of the true God (Jehovah, Yahweh). They would be a living testimony to the truth of God's Holy Word and commandments, that they are the commandments from the only living God; therefore, they must be obeyed and taught to the children of all succeeding generations.

DEUTERONOMY 4:1-43

c. Third, remember the wonderful experience of God's presence at Mt. Sinai (vv.10-12). There were two major illustrious experiences in the history of Israel: the exodus from Egypt and the giving of the law at Mt. Sinai. These are the two cardinal experiences that are most remembered throughout Scripture. As Moses preached to the people, he challenged them to remember the day they stood before the LORD and experienced the wonderful presence of God Himself. God gave a visible manifestation of His presence for two primary purposes:

⇒ to teach them to fear and reverence Him
⇒ to stir them to teach His Holy Word and commandments to their children

God's presence descended upon Mt. Sinai in a most glorious, frightening appearance. The descent of God's presence upon Mt. Sinai was symbolized in blazing fire with flames reaching up into the dark, black clouds and with deep darkness surrounding the mountain (v.11). Then all of a sudden, God's booming voice spoke out of the fire (v.12). Words were heard, but no form was seen. There was only a voice speaking out of the fire.

d. Fourth, remember and obey the covenant God proclaimed, the Ten Commandments (v.13). The Ten Commandments were given by God Himself; therefore, God's people are to obey them. Note that they were written in permanent form upon two stone tablets. The permanence of the Ten Commandments stresses the importance of learning and obeying them. Also note that all the statutes and judgments or laws and decrees are mentioned; that is, the entire Word of God—all the commandments and laws of God—were to be obeyed by God's people as they entered and lived in the promised land.

Thought 1. There are three significant lessons for us in this point.

(1) We must not let our experiences with the LORD nor His Word slip from our hearts. We must never backslide, never slide away from God.

"And Jesus said unto him, No man, having put his hand to the plough, and looking back, is fit for the kingdom of God" (Lu.9:62).
"Wherefore let him that thinketh he standeth take heed lest he fall" (1 Co.10:12).
"I marvel that ye are so soon removed from him that called you into the grace of Christ unto another gospel: Which is not another; but there be some that trouble you, and would pervert the gospel of Christ. But though we, or an angel from heaven, preach any other gospel unto you than that which we have preached unto you, let him be accursed. As we said before, so say I now again, If any *man* preach any other gospel unto you than that ye have received, let him be accursed" (Ga.1:6-9).
"Now the just shall live by faith: but if *any man* draw back, my soul shall have no pleasure in him" (He.10:38).
"Nevertheless I have *somewhat* against thee, because thou hast left thy first love" (Re.2:4).
"The backslider in heart shall be filled with his own ways" (Pr.14:14).
"Ah sinful nation, a people laden with iniquity, a seed of evildoers, children that are corrupters: they have forsaken the LORD, they have provoked the Holy One of Israel unto anger, they are gone away backward" (Is.1:4).
"And my people are bent to backsliding from me: though they called them to the most High, none at all would exalt *him*" (Ho.11:7).

(2) We must teach the Word of God and the Ten Commandments to our children. We must teach them to walk in the ways of the LORD.

"Study to show thyself approved unto God, a workman that needeth not to be ashamed, rightly dividing the word of truth" (2 Ti.2:15).
"Only take heed to thyself, and keep thy soul diligently, lest thou forget the things which thine eyes have seen, and lest they depart from thy heart all the days of thy life: but teach them thy sons, and thy sons' sons" (De.4:9).
"And these words, which I command thee this day, shall be in thine heart: And thou shalt teach them diligently unto thy children, and shalt talk of them when thou sittest in thine house, and when thou walkest by the way, and when thou liest down, and when thou risest up" (De.6:6-7).
"Therefore shall ye lay up these my words in your heart and in your soul, and bind them for a sign upon your hand, that they may be as frontlets between your eyes. And ye shall teach them your children, speaking of them when thou sittest in thine house, and when thou walkest by the way, when thou liest down, and when thou risest up" (De.11:18-19).
"Train up a child in the way he should go: and when he is old, he will not depart from it" (Pr.22:6).

(3) We must obey the commandments of God. There is to be no exception: no person is exempt from any of the Ten Commandments.

"He that hath my commandments, and keepeth them, he it is that loveth me: and he that loveth me shall be loved of my Father, and I will love him, and will manifest myself to him" (Jn.14:21).
"Jesus answered and said unto him, If a man love me, he will keep my words: and my Father will love him, and we will come unto him, and make our abode with him" (Jn.14:23).
"If ye keep my commandments, ye shall abide in my love; even as I have kept my Father's commandments, and abide in his love" (Jn.15:10).
"Ye are my friends, if ye do whatsoever I command you" (Jn.15:14).
"Blessed *are* they that do his commandments, that they may have right to the tree of life, and may enter in through the gates into the city" (Re.22:14).
"Whoso keepeth the law *is* a wise son: but he that is a companion of riotous *men* shameth his father" (Pr.28:7).

DEUTERONOMY 4:1-43

4 **(4:15-31) Warning, Against Idolatry—Warning, Against False Worship—Idolatry, Warning Against—Worship, False, Warning Against—Judgment, Safeguards Against—Prophecy, Concerning Israel, Apostasy and Restoration**: guard against all false gods and false worship. This is a detailed warning against the dangers of idolatry and false worship. The warning was an absolute essential, for the Israelites had already corrupted themselves at the golden calf incident and at Baal Peor (see outline and notes—Ex.32:1-35; Nu.25:1-18 for more discussion). All forms of wickedness, idolatry, and false worship have swept the earth and influenced believers from the beginning of time. So it was to be with the Israelite believers: they were constantly going to be tempted by the false worship and customs of the surrounding nations. They must, therefore, take heed! Be careful! Watch themselves closely! Moses preached six reasons why the believer must guard against all false gods and false worship:

OUTLINE	SCRIPTURE	SCRIPTURE	OUTLINE
4. Guard against all false gods & false worship a. Reason 1: You have seen no form of God (God is Spirit, Jn.4:24) b. Reason 2: You will corrupt yourself 1) Must not worship people, man or woman 2) Must not worship animals or fish 3) Must not worship nature: The heavenly bodies—the sun, moon, or stars • Must not be enticed to worship these • God gave these to serve man c. Reason 3: You were saved to be God's people, His special inheritance, saved out of the furnace of iron, out of Egypt (a symbol of the world) d. Reason 4: God judges those who sin—bars them from the promised land of God 1) The first generation had committed idolatry & were barred 2) Moses was held accountable as their leader & was barred: Condemned to die in the wilderness 3) The safeguard against judgment: Obedience • Must not forget the covenant of the LORD, the Ten Commandments	15 Take ye therefore good heed unto yourselves; for ye saw no manner of similitude on the day *that* the LORD spake unto you in Horeb out of the midst of the fire: 16 Lest ye corrupt *yourselves*, and make you a graven image, the similitude of any figure, the likeness of male or female, 17 The likeness of any beast that *is* on the earth, the likeness of any winged fowl that flieth in the air, 18 The likeness of any thing that creepeth on the ground, the likeness of any fish that *is* in the waters beneath the earth: 19 And lest thou lift up thine eyes unto heaven, and when thou seest the sun, and the moon, and the stars, *even* all the host of heaven, shouldest be driven to worship them, and serve them, which the LORD thy God hath divided unto all nations under the whole heaven. 20 But the LORD hath taken you, and brought you forth out of the iron furnace, *even* out of Egypt, to be unto him a people of inheritance, as *ye are* this day. 21 Furthermore the LORD was angry with me for your sakes, and sware that I should not go over Jordan, and that I should not go in unto that good land, which the LORD thy God giveth thee *for* an inheritance: 22 But I must die in this land, I must not go over Jordan: but ye shall go over, and possess that good land. 23 Take heed unto yourselves, lest ye forget the covenant of the LORD your God, which he made with you, and make you a graven image, *or*	the likeness of any *thing*, which the LORD thy God hath forbidden thee. 24 For the LORD thy God *is* a consuming fire, *even* a jealous God. 25 When thou shalt beget children, and children's children, and ye shall have remained long in the land, and shall corrupt *yourselves*, and make a graven image, *or* the likeness of any *thing*, and shall do evil in the sight of the LORD thy God, to provoke him to anger: 26 I call heaven and earth to witness against you this day, that ye shall soon utterly perish from off the land whereunto ye go over Jordan to possess it; ye shall not prolong *your* days upon it, but shall utterly be destroyed. 27 And the LORD shall scatter you among the nations, and ye shall be left few in number among the heathen, whither the LORD shall lead you. 28 And there ye shall serve gods, the work of men's hands, wood and stone, which neither see, nor hear, nor eat, nor smell. 29 But if from thence thou shalt seek the LORD thy God, thou shalt find *him*, if thou seek him with all thy heart and with all thy soul. 30 When thou art in tribulation, and all these things are come upon thee, *even* in the latter days, if thou turn to the LORD thy God, and shalt be obedient unto his voice; 31 (For the LORD thy God *is* a merciful God;) he will not forsake thee, neither destroy thee, nor forget the covenant of thy fathers which he sware unto them.	• Must not make nor worship any idol (image, false god) • The reason: God is a consuming fire, a jealous God e. Reason 5: You have the strong warning & prophecy of God—you will be removed from the promised land 1) False worship will cause you to be judged even after you have lived in the promised land for a long time 2) False worship will cause heaven & earth to witness against you • You will perish, be removed from the promised land • You will be scattered among the peoples of the world (a picture of returning to worldliness): Only a few will survive • You will worship man-made gods that are lifeless f. Reason 6: You have the glorious promise of God 1) The promise that if you diligently seek the LORD, you will find Him 2) The promise that when you suffer the distress of the world, you will return & obey God (a prophecy concerning Israel but applicable to us all) 3) The promise of God's mercy • God is merciful • God will not forget His covenant with Israel's forefathers

a. You must guard against idolatry and false worship because you have seen no form of God (v.15). God did not appear in visible form at Mt. Sinai. In a spectacular display of majestic glory, God did speak to the people and they heard His voice. They even saw a blazing fire with flames reaching up into the very heavens—all in the midst of black clouds and deep darkness. But they saw no form, no image of God. Scripture declares that God is Spirit; therefore, no form, no image or idol, is ever to be made to represent God. God created man; man does not create God. Therefore, man must not devise false gods nor false worship.

DEUTERONOMY 4:1-43

"God *is* a Spirit: and they that worship him must worship *him* in spirit and in truth" (Jn.4:24).

"Whosoever believeth that Jesus is the Christ is born of God: and every one that loveth him that begat loveth him also that is begotten of him" (1 Jn.5:1).

"So God created man in his *own* image, in the image of God created he him; male and female created he them" (Ge.1:27).

b. You must guard against false gods and false worship because they will corrupt you (vv.16-19). The word *corrupt* (shachath or sahat) means destroyed, decayed, spoiled, utterly wasted, ruined, corrupted, devastated, laid wasted, struck down.

A strong warning is issued against the three specific forms of idolatry and false worship:

⇒ The worship of people (v.16). Far too often a person admires, loves, and becomes attached or devoted to another person more than to God. Hero worship is a common form of idolatry.

⇒ The worship of animals (vv.17-18). Down through the centuries some people have worshipped animals, such as serpents, crocodiles, and cows. Tragically, some people show more affection and attention to animals and pets than to other people and God.

⇒ The worship of nature (v.19). There are people who take something within creation and make it an object of worship. But there are others who worship nature as a whole, who show more affection and attention to nature and the enjoyment of it than to other people and God. Note what Scripture says: believers must not be enticed to worship nature or the things of nature. The heavenly bodies—all of nature—was given by God to serve man, not man to serve nature.

"Forasmuch then as we are the offspring of God, we ought not to think that the Godhead is like unto gold, or silver, or stone, graven by art and man's device" (Ac.17:29).

"For the invisible things of him from the creation of the world are clearly seen, being understood by the things that are made, *even* his eternal power and Godhead; so that they are without excuse: Because that, when they knew God, they glorified *him* not as God, neither were thankful; but became vain in their imaginations, and their foolish heart was darkened. Professing themselves to be wise, they became fools, And changed the glory of the uncorruptible God into an image made like to corruptible man, and to birds, and fourfooted beasts, and creeping things" (Ro.1:20-23).

"Little children, keep yourselves from idols. Amen" (1 Jn.5:21).

"Thou shalt not make unto thee any graven image, or any likeness *of any thing* that *is* in heaven above, or that *is* in the earth beneath, or that *is* in the water under the earth" (Ex.20:4).

"Ye shall make you no idols nor graven image, neither rear you up a standing image, neither shall ye set up *any* image of stone in your land, to bow down unto it: for I *am* the LORD your God" (Le.26:1).

"Take heed to yourselves, that your heart be not deceived, and ye turn aside, and serve other gods, and worship them" (De.11:16).

"I *am* the LORD: that *is* my name: and my glory will I not give to another, neither my praise to graven images" (Is.42:8).

c. You must guard against false gods and false worship because God saved you to be His people, His special inheritance. God saved you out of the furnace of iron, out of the enslavement of Egypt (v.20). Remember: Egypt is a symbol of the enslavement of the world. Being enslaved is a terrible experience: it is just like living in an iron furnace. But God had saved His people out of enslavement, saved them to be His very special people, His very special inheritance and possession.

"Ye have not chosen me, but I have chosen you, and ordained you, that ye should go and bring forth fruit, and *that* your fruit should remain: that whatsoever ye shall ask of the Father in my name, he may give it you" (Jn.15:16).

"But ye *are* a chosen generation, a royal priesthood, an holy nation, a peculiar people; that ye should show forth the praises of him who hath called you out of darkness into his marvellous light" (1 Pe.2:9).

"Now therefore, if ye will obey my voice indeed, and keep my covenant, then ye shall be a peculiar treasure unto me above all people: for all the earth *is* mine: And ye shall be unto me a kingdom of priests, and an holy nation. These *are* the words which thou shalt speak unto the children of Israel" (Ex.19:5-6).

"For thou *art* an holy people unto the LORD thy God: the LORD thy God hath chosen thee to be a special people unto himself, above all people that *are* upon the face of the earth" (De.7:6).

"For thou *art* an holy people unto the LORD thy God, and the LORD hath chosen thee to be a peculiar people unto himself, above all the nations that *are* upon the earth" (De.14:2).

"And the LORD hath avouched thee this day to be his peculiar people, as he hath promised thee, and that *thou* shouldest keep all his commandments; And to make thee high above all nations which he hath made, in praise, and in name, and in honour; and that thou mayest be an holy people unto the LORD thy God, as he hath spoken" (De.26:18-19).

"But know that the LORD hath set apart him that is godly for himself: the LORD will hear when I call unto him" (Ps.4:3).

"Save thy people, and bless thine inheritance: feed them also, and lift them up for ever" (Ps.28:9; see Ps.33:12; 68:9; 78:62-71; 79:1; 94:14; Joel 2:17; 3:2; Mi.7:14, 18).).

d. You must guard against idolatry and false worship because God judges those who sin. All who continue in sin will be barred from the promised land of God, never experiencing the spiritual conquest and rest promised by God. When the Israelite believers committed adultery and idolatry with their neighbors, they were barred from the promised land. Even Moses himself, the dear servant of God, was held accountable and was barred because of his terrible sin. (See outline and notes—Nu.20:1-13 for more discussion.) There is only one safeguard against judgment—that of obedience (vv.23-24).

DEUTERONOMY 4:1-43

⇒ The believer must not forget the covenant of the LORD, the Ten Commandments. He must obey them in order to escape the judgment of God (v.23).
⇒ The believer must not make any idol of God nor engage in any false worship. He must never worship a false god. False worship and idolatry will arouse the judgment of God (v.23).
⇒ The reason is clearly stated by Scripture: the LORD is a consuming fire, a jealous God. This is stern language, but idolatry and false worship are serious offenses against God. A person who commits idolatry and engages in false worship turns away from the very source of life, the Creator and Sovereign LORD of the universe. A person who rejects God—who denies and curses God—who rebels and raises his fist up in the face of God—who turns to the worship of false gods—that person dishonors God. That person is bound to arouse the jealousy of God and arouse the consuming fire of His judgment. Again, God judges those who sin. Therefore, if a person commits idolatry or false worship, he will face the judgment of God and be barred from the promised land of God. Note the judgment that is to fall upon idolaters and false worshippers:

"For the wrath of God is revealed from heaven against all ungodliness and unrighteousness of men, who hold the truth in unrighteousness....Being filled with all unrighteousness, fornication, wickedness, covetousness, maliciousness; full of envy, murder, debate, deceit, malignity; whisperers, Backbiters, haters of God, despiteful, proud, boasters, inventors of evil things, disobedient to parents, Without understanding, covenantbreakers, without natural affection, implacable, unmerciful" (Ro.1:18, 29-31).

"So then every one of us shall give account of himself to God" (Ro.14:12).

"Know ye not that the unrighteous shall not inherit the kingdom of God? Be not deceived: neither fornicators, nor idolaters, nor adulterers, nor effeminate, nor abusers of themselves with mankind, Nor thieves, nor covetous, nor drunkards, nor revilers, nor extortioners, shall inherit the kingdom of God" (1 Co.6:9-10).

"Now the works of the flesh are manifest, which are *these;* Adultery, fornication, uncleanness, lasciviousness, Idolatry, witchcraft, hatred, variance, emulations, wrath, strife, seditions, heresies, Envyings, murders, drunkenness, revellings, and such like: of the which I tell you before, as I have also told *you* in time past, that they which do such things shall not inherit the kingdom of God" (Ga.5:19-21).

"But the fearful, and unbelieving, and the abominable, and murderers, and whoremongers, and sorcerers, and idolaters, and all liars, shall have their part in the lake which burneth with fire and brimstone: which is the second death" (Re.21:8).

e. You must guard against false gods and false worship because of the strong warning and prophecy of God. If you commit these two terrible sins, you will be removed, barred from the promised land (vv.25-28). Remember, Moses is standing before the people preaching this *strong warning* to them.
  1) False worship will cause you to be judged even after you have lived in the promised land for a long time (v.25). The warning is clear: once the people had settled down in the promised land, there was the danger that they would become comfortable, at ease, and satisfied. The result? Complacency would creep into their lives and they would forget God.
  2) False worship will cause heaven and earth to witness against you (vv.26-28). All the beings within heaven and earth will be eyewitnesses of your idolatry and false worship, standing as witnesses against your terrible sins. Note the results:
     ⇒ The idolaters and false worshippers would perish, be removed from the promised land (v.26).
     ⇒ The idolaters and false worshippers would be scattered among the peoples of the world with only a few surviving. This is a picture of believers returning to worldliness (v.27).
     ⇒ The idolaters and false worshippers would worship man-made gods that were lifeless, unable to see or hear or eat or smell (v.28). In times of trouble and need, the false gods would be unable to help. The sinful and disobedient would be left to themselves: they would have only the limited, frail help that other people could give. The only living and true God would not be available to meet their needs, for they would be separated, alienated from Him.

"For the wages of sin *is* death; but the gift of God *is* eternal life through Jesus Christ our LORD" (Ro.6:23).

"How shall we escape, if we neglect so great salvation; which at the first began to be spoken by the LORD, and was confirmed unto us by them that heard *him*" (He.2:3).

"If I regard iniquity in my heart, the LORD will not hear *me*" (Ps.66:18).

"But your iniquities have separated between you and your God, and your sins have hid *his* face from you, that he will not hear" (Is.59:2).

"And *there is* none that calleth upon thy name, that stirreth up himself to take hold of thee: for thou hast hid thy face from us, and hast consumed us, because of our iniquities" (Is.64:7).

"The soul that sinneth, it shall die" (Eze.18:4).

f. You must guard against idolatry and false worship because of the glorious promise of God (vv.29-31). There is hope for the rebel, for any who rebel against God, turning to false idols and false worship. Keep in mind that this is a prophecy concerning Israel, but it is applicable to any generation of believers.
  1) God makes a wonderful promise to sinful rebels: if they will diligently seek Him with all of their hearts and souls, they will find Him (v.29). The word "find" (matsa or masa) means to acquire, meet, get a hold upon, take hold of, discover, reach, attain. The idea is that the person who diligently seeks the LORD—who seeks Him with all his heart and soul—will find God. He will be accepted by God and brought into the very presence of God, for communion and fellowship with Him.
  2) God makes another wonderful promise: when the sinful rebel suffers distress out in the world, he will repent and return to God. Repentance will give him a new beginning, a new start with God. The repentant sinner will worship God and worship Him alone. He will obey God.

DEUTERONOMY 4:1-43

3) God also gave the wonderful promise of His mercy (v.31). God is merciful and He will not forget His covenant with Israel's forefathers. He confirmed the covenant with an oath, swearing that He would fulfill His promise. Therefore, when any believer repents and turns to God, God will have mercy and save him. God saves all who truly repent and return to Him, worshipping Him and His dear Son, the Lord Jesus Christ. (See outline and notes—Ro.11:1-10; 11:11-16; 11:17-24; 11:25-36 for more discussion.)

"Then Peter said unto them, Repent, and be baptized every one of you in the name of Jesus Christ for the remission of sins, and ye shall receive the gift of the Holy Ghost" (Ac.2:38).

"Repent ye therefore, and be converted, that your sins may be blotted out, when the times of refreshing shall come from the presence of the LORD" (Ac.3:19).

"If we confess our sins, he is faithful and just to forgive us *our* sins, and to cleanse us from all unrighteousness" (1 Jn.1:9).

"If my people, which are called by my name, shall humble themselves, and pray, and seek my face, and turn from their wicked ways; then will I hear from heaven, and will forgive their sin, and will heal their land" (2 Chr.7:14).

"He that covereth his sins shall not prosper: but whoso confesseth and forsaketh *them* shall have mercy" (Pr.28:13).

"Let the wicked forsake his way, and the unrighteous man his thoughts: and let him return unto the LORD, and he will have mercy upon him; and to our God, for he will abundantly pardon" (Is.55:7).

"But if the wicked will turn from all his sins that he hath committed, and keep all my statutes, and do that which is lawful and right, he shall surely live, he shall not die" (Eze.18:21).

"Cast away from you all your transgressions, whereby ye have transgressed; and make you a new heart and a new spirit: for why will ye die, O house of Israel?" (Eze.18:31).

5 (4:32-40) **God, Proof of—God, Nature of—God, Works of—God, Facts About—Existence, of God**: acknowledge that the LORD—He and He alone—is God. All of a sudden, standing before the people and preaching with fire in his heart, Moses is gripped with a deep sense of God's presence. The very person of God—just who God is in all of His wonderful person and wonderful works—floods the heart of Moses. He begins to wax eloquent and describe just who God is. Using a series of questions and statements, he declares that the dramatic revelation of God's holy presence at Mt. Sinai was the greatest event in human history up to that time. Nowhere else has such an event ever taken place.

Note that this passage is poetic, one of the most beautiful passages in Scripture. The focus is on God, His wonderful nature and His works. Three eloquent questions are asked in the first three verses (vv.32-34). And then statement after statement is made—all to reveal the person and works of God Himself. A brief reading of the Scripture and outline will show the reader how Moses heaps word upon word in order to reveal that the LORD—He and He alone—is God.

OUTLINE	SCRIPTURE	SCRIPTURE	OUTLINE
5. Acknowledge that the LORD—He & He alone—is God a. The LORD is the great Creator of man, the Creator who has done marvelous things for His people: Things never before done or heard about b. The LORD is the God of revelation or communication: He reveals Himself, speaks with His people c. The LORD is the God of power & might & of miraculous works—all on behalf of His people: Demonstrated in His dealings with Egypt d. The LORD is God, the only living & true God, the Sovereign Majesty of the universe (Jehovah, Yahweh) e. The LORD is the God of discipline (correction) & holiness	32 For ask now of the days that are past, which were before thee, since the day that God created man upon the earth, and *ask* from the one side of heaven unto the other, whether there hath been *any such thing* as this great thing *is*, or hath been heard like it? 33 Did *ever* people hear the voice of God speaking out of the midst of the fire, as thou hast heard, and live? 34 Or hath God assayed to go *and* take him a nation from the midst of *another* nation, by temptations, by signs, and by wonders, and by war, and by a mighty hand, and by a stretched out arm, and by great terrors, according to all that the LORD your God did for you in Egypt before your eyes? 35 Unto thee it was showed, that thou mightest know that the LORD he *is* God; *there is* none else beside him. 36 Out of heaven he made thee to hear his voice, that he might instruct thee: and upon	earth he showed thee his great fire; and thou heardest his words out of the midst of the fire. 37 And because he loved thy fathers, therefore he chose their seed after them, and brought thee out in his sight with his mighty power out of Egypt; 38 To drive out nations from before thee greater and mightier than thou *art*, to bring thee in, to give thee their land *for* an inheritance, as *it is* this day. 39 Know therefore this day, and consider *it* in thine heart, that the LORD he *is* God in heaven above, and upon the earth beneath: *there is* none else. 40 Thou shalt keep therefore his statutes, and his commandments, which I command thee this day, that it may go well with thee, and with thy children after thee, and that thou mayest prolong *thy* days upon the earth, which the LORD thy God giveth thee, for ever.	f. The LORD is the God of love & salvation: Proven by the deliverance of His people out of Egypt (a symbol of the world) by His Presence & power g. The LORD is the God who gives victory over all enemies & guides His people to the promised land h. The LORD is the Sovereign God over all in heaven & on earth: He & He alone is the only living & true God i. The LORD is the God who demands obedience 1) Must keep His laws & commandments 2) The result • Things will go well • A long life in the promised land

DEUTERONOMY 4:1-43

a. The LORD is the great Creator of man, the Creator who has done marvelous things for His people. God has done things never before done or heard about (v.32). It is God who created man, and it is God who revealed Himself at Mt. Sinai and established His covenant, the Ten Commandments, with His people. Nothing like this event has ever happened before, not since the creation of man upon earth. In fact, a person could ask from one end of the heavens to the other whether such an important event had ever taken place, and the answer would be: "No!" God and God alone is the great Creator who has done marvelous things for His people, things never before done or heard about.

b. The LORD is the God of communication. God talks with man, reveals Himself by speaking with His people (v.33). At Mt. Sinai, God spoke with His people out of the fire. Note that they were not stricken dead, but they lived. The implication is striking: in an ordinary situation, the holiness of God would strike out and consume any person standing in the presence of God. But at Mt. Sinai, God's purpose was to give His commandments to His people in such a way that they would never forget the experience. Therefore, God allowed the people to see the revelation of His glory and majesty. The point is clear: God does reveal Himself and communicate with His people. He actually speaks, gives His Word to His people.

> "All scripture *is* given by inspiration of God, and *is* profitable for doctrine, for reproof, for correction, for instruction in righteousness" (2 Ti.3:16).
>
> "For the prophecy came not in old time by the will of man: but holy men of God spake *as they were* moved by the Holy Ghost" (2 Pe.1:21).

c. The LORD is the God of power and might and of miraculous works. God acts on behalf of His dear people: He works for them. These works were demonstrated in His dealings with Egypt when He delivered His people from slavery (v.34).

d. The LORD is the only living and true God (Jehovah, Yahweh, v.35). Note what Moses declared: the revelation of God was for one purpose and one purpose only—so that people might know that the LORD is God. There is no other God besides Him.

e. The LORD is the God of discipline and holiness (v.36). God gave His commandments in order to discipline His people. The covenant, the Ten Commandments, provided discipline by showing the people how to live and by correcting them when they disobeyed. The blazing fire on the mount was a symbol of God's holiness. When God's presence first descended in the blazing fire upon the mountain, the people became terrified and trembled before the LORD. They were in danger of being consumed by the holiness of God, and they were forced to keep a great distance between themselves and God's holy presence (Ex.19:16-21).

f. The LORD is the God of love and salvation (v.37). His love is proven by the deliverance of His people out of Egypt (a symbol of the world). God loves His dear people; therefore, He saves them from the enslavement of this world. And note how He saves them: by His presence and mighty power.

g. The LORD is the God who gives victory over all enemies and who guides His dear people to the promised land (v.38). God alone can give a victorious life to a person; God alone can guide a person to the promised land. No other being—on earth or in heaven, physical or spiritual—can empower man enough to conquer all the enemies of life, enemies such as...

- disease
- accident
- selfishness
- purposelessness
- sinful behavior
- death
- loneliness
- emptiness
- depression
- discouragement
- hopelessness
- helplessness

God alone has the power to conquer all the enemies of life. Therefore, a person must allow the Spirit of God to live in his heart. It is the power of God's Spirit—and His Spirit alone—that can empower us to conquer and be victorious as we march throughout life. It is God alone who holds the keys to the promised land, who can lead His people to the promised inheritance.

h. The LORD is Sovereign—He is God over all in heaven and on earth (v.39). He and He alone is the only living and true God. Note the strong challenge and appeal of Moses: Know this fact! Acknowledge it! Take it to heart! Keep it firmly in mind! It is the LORD Himself who is the Sovereign God, who rules and reigns over all that is in heaven above and on earth below. There is no other.

i. The LORD is the God who demands obedience (v.40). Therefore, the people of God must keep His laws and commandments. They must obey God. If they obey, the most wonderful result will take place:

⇒ Things will go well with them. They will live a fruitful and productive life, a life full of love, joy, and peace.

⇒ They will live a long life in the promised land of God. They will possess a victorious life, know what it is to triumph and conquer all the trials and temptations that oppose life. They will know what it is to experience spiritual rest and comfort, confidence and assurance, satisfaction and fulfillment—all throughout life. This is the fruit of obedience, the life that results from obeying God.

Thought 1. We must acknowledge that the LORD—He and He alone—is God. There is none other. There is only one living and true God.

> "Who *is* like unto thee, O LORD, among the gods? who *is* like thee, glorious in holiness, fearful *in* praises, doing wonders?" (Ex.15:11).
>
> "Wherefore thou art great, O LORD God: for *there is* none like thee, neither *is there any* God beside thee, according to all that we have heard with our ears" (2 S.7:22).
>
> "And he said, LORD God of Israel, *there is* no God like thee, in heaven above, or on earth beneath, who keepest covenant and mercy with thy servants that walk before thee with all their heart" (1 K.8:23).
>
> "O LORD, *there is* none like thee, neither *is there any* God beside thee, according to all that we have heard with our ears" (1 Chr.17:20).
>
> "For who in the heaven can be compared unto the LORD? *who* among the sons of the mighty can be likened unto the LORD?" (Ps.89:6).

DEUTERONOMY 4:1-43

"To whom then will ye liken God? or what likeness will ye compare unto him? The workman melteth a graven image, and the goldsmith spreadeth it over with gold, and casteth silver chains. He that *is* so impoverished that he hath no oblation chooseth a tree *that* will not rot; he seeketh unto him a cunning workman to prepare a graven image, *that* shall not be moved. Have ye not known? have ye not heard? hath it not been told you from the beginning? have ye not understood from the foundations of the earth? *It is* he that sitteth upon the circle of the earth, and the inhabitants thereof *are* as grasshoppers; that stretcheth out the heavens as a curtain, and spreadeth them out as a tent to dwell in: That bringeth the princes to nothing; he maketh the judges of the earth as vanity" (Is.40:18-23).

6 (4:41-43) **Life, Storms of—Refuge, from the Storms of Life—Cities, of Refuge—Refuge, Cities of—Symbol, of Christ—Christ, Symbol of—Storms, of Life**: remember God's command to set up cities of refuge. And remember, the cities of refuge are a picture of Christ, our refuge from death and from the storms and threats of life. (See outline and notes—Nu.35:9-34 for more discussion.)

OUTLINE	SCRIPTURE	SCRIPTURE	OUTLINE
6. Remember God's command to set up cities of refuge (Nu.35:13-14): A picture of Christ, our refuge from death & from the storms & threats of life a. The purpose: To be a place of safety for a person guilty	41 Then Moses severed three cities on this side Jordan toward the sunrising; 42 That the slayer might flee thither, which should kill his neighbour unawares, and hated him not in times past; and that fleeing unto	one of these cities he might live: 43 *Namely*, Bezer in the wilderness, in the plain country, of the Reubenites; and Ramoth in Gilead, of the Gadites; and Golan in Bashan, of the Manassites.	of accidental manslaughter b. The location: Three cities in east Jordan 1) In Bezer:^{DS2} For Reuben 2) In Ramoth:^{DS3} For Gad 3) In Golan:^{DS4} For the half-tribe of Manasseh

The cities of refuge were to be a place of safety for any person who was guilty of accidental manslaughter. The cities of refuge were off limits to any person who sought revenge (the avenger of blood). By law the guilty party was protected as long as he remained in the city. Six locations altogether were to be chosen, three in East Jordan and three in the promised land itself. Some time after Moses preached the message covered in this particular chapter, he set aside three cities of refuge in the land that had already been conquered, the territory of East Jordan. The cities of refuge in East Jordan were:

⇒ Bezer, which was to serve as a refuge for the tribe of Reuben
⇒ Gilead Ramoth, which was to serve as a refuge for the tribe of Gad
⇒ Golan, which was to serve as a refuge for the half-tribe of Manasseh

Thought 1. The LORD is our Refuge from the threats and storms of life. Scripture declares four wonderful truths about the protection the LORD gives us.
(1) The LORD is our Refuge.

"The eternal God *is* thy refuge, and underneath *are* the everlasting arms: and he shall thrust out the enemy from before thee; and shall say, Destroy *them*" (De.33:27).
"For in the time of trouble he shall hide me in his pavilion: in the secret of his tabernacle shall he hide me; he shall set me up upon a rock" (Ps.27:5).
"Thou shalt hide them in the secret of thy presence from the pride of man: thou shalt keep them secretly in a pavilion from the strife of tongues" (Ps.31:20).
"God *is* our refuge and strength, a very present help in trouble" (Ps.46:1).
"Be thou my strong habitation, whereunto I may continually resort: thou hast given commandment to save me; for thou *art* my rock and my fortress" (Ps.71:3).
"In the fear of the LORD *is* strong confidence: and his children shall have a place of refuge" (Pr.14:26).
"The name of the LORD *is* a strong tower: the righteous runneth into it, and is safe" (Pr.18:10).
"For thou hast been a strength to the poor, a strength to the needy in his distress, a refuge from the storm, a shadow from the heat, when the blast of the terrible ones *is* as a storm *against* the wall" (Is.25:4).

(2) The LORD is our Hiding Place.

"Keep me as the apple of the eye, hide me under the shadow of thy wings" (Ps.17:8).
"For in the time of trouble he shall hide me in his pavilion: in the secret of his tabernacle shall he hide me; he shall set me up upon a rock" (Ps.27:5).
"Thou shalt hide them in the secret of thy presence from the pride of man: thou shalt keep them secretly in a pavilion from the strife of tongues" (Ps.31:20).
"Thou *art* my hiding place; thou shalt preserve me from trouble; thou shalt compass me about with songs of deliverance. Selah" (Ps.32:7).
"Hide me from the secret counsel of the wicked; from the insurrection of the workers of iniquity" (Ps.64:2).
"Thou *art* my hiding place and my shield: I hope in thy word" (Ps.119:114).
"Deliver me, O LORD, from mine enemies: I flee unto thee to hide me" (Ps.143:9).

(3) The LORD is our Shield in protecting us.

"After these things the word of the LORD came unto Abram in a vision, saying, Fear not, Abram: I *am* thy shield, *and* thy exceeding great reward" (Ge.15:1).
"Our soul waiteth for the LORD: he *is* our help and our shield" (Ps.33:20).
"For the LORD God *is* a sun and shield: the LORD will give grace anwd glory: no good *thing* will he withhold from them that walk uprightly" (Ps.84:11).
"O Israel, trust thou in the LORD: he *is* their help and their shield" (Ps.115:9).
"Every word of God *is* pure: he *is* a shield unto them that put their trust in him" (Pr.30:5).

(4) The LORD is our Atoning Sacrifice who delivers us from the avenger of death.

"For God so loved the world, that he gave his only begotten Son, that whosoever believeth in him should not perish, but have everlasting life" (Jn.3:16).
"And whosoever liveth and believeth in me shall never die. Believest thou this" (Jn.11:26).
"To them who by patient continuance in well doing seek for glory and honour and immortality, eternal life" (Ro.2:7).
"The last enemy that shall be destroyed is death" (1 Co.15:26).
"For this corruptible must put on incorruption, and this mortal must put on immortality. So when this corruptible shall have put on incorruption, and this mortal shall have put on immortality, then shall be brought to pass the saying that is written, Death is swallowed up in victory" (1 Co.15:53-54).
"For we know that if our earthly house of this tabernacle were dissolved, we have a building of God, an house not made with hands, eternal in the heavens" (2 Co.5:1).
"Then we which are alive and remain shall be caught up together with them in the clouds, to meet the LORD in the air: and so shall we ever be with the LORD" (1 Th.4:17).
"But is now made manifest by the appearing of our Saviour Jesus Christ, who hath abolished death, and hath brought life and immortality to light through the gospel" (2 Ti.1:10).
"But we see Jesus, who was made a little lower than the angels for the suffering of death, crowned with glory and honour; that he by the grace of God should taste death for every man" (He.2:9).
"Forasmuch then as the children are partakers of flesh and blood, he also himself likewise took part of the same; that through death he might destroy him that had the power of death, that is, the devil; And deliver them who through fear of death were all their lifetime subject to bondage" (He.2:14-15).
"And God shall wipe away all tears from their eyes; and there shall be no more death, neither sorrow, nor crying, neither shall there be any more pain: for the former things are passed away" (Re.21:4).
"He will swallow up death in victory; and the LORD God will wipe away tears from off all faces; and the rebuke of his people shall he take away from off all the earth: for the LORD hath spoken it" (Is.25:8).

DEEPER STUDY # 2
(4:43) **Bezer, City Of**: a city of refuge established in the territory assigned to Reuben (De.4:43; Jos.20:8). Bezer, like the other cities of refuge, was established to be a place of safety for any person who was guilty of accidental manslaughter. Later on, it was given to the Levites as a city in which they could live (Jos.21:36).

DEEPER STUDY # 3
(4:43) **Gilead Ramoth, City Of**: a city of refuge established in the territory assigned to the tribe of Gad (De.4:43; Jos.20:8). Ramoth, like the other cities of refuge, was established to be a safe place for any person who was guilty of accidental manslaughter. It, too, was given to the Levites as a city in which they could live (Jos.21:29). Note that Ramoth is also known as Jarmuth.

DEEPER STUDY # 4
(4:43) **Golan, City Of**: a city of refuge established in the territory assigned to the half-tribe of Manasseh (De.4:43; Jos.20:8). Golan, like the other cities of refuge, was established as a place of shelter for any person who was guilty of accidental manslaughter. Later on, it became a Levitical city, a city in which the Levites lived (Jos.21:27).

DEUTERONOMY 4:1-43

TYPES, SYMBOLS, AND PICTURES
(Deuteronomy 4:1-43)

Historical Term	Type or Picture (Scriptural Basis for Each)	Life Application for Today's Believer	Biblical Application
Israel Being Scattered among the Peoples of the World De.4:27	*Being scattered among the peoples of the world is a picture of returning to worldliness: Only a few will survive.* "And the LORD shall scatter you among the nations, and ye shall be left few in number among the heathen, whither the LORD shall lead you" (De.4:27)	⇒ Note the forceful judgment upon those who commit false worship: 1. They will be removed from the promised land. 2. They will be judged even after they have lived in the promised land for a long time. 3. They will have heaven and earth to witness against them. 4. They will perish, be removed from the promised land.	*"For the wages of sin is death; but the gift of God is eternal life through Jesus Christ our Lord" (Ro.6:23).* *"How shall we escape, if we neglect so great salvation; which at the first began to be spoken by the Lord, and was confirmed unto us by them that heard him" (He.2:3).* *"If I regard iniquity in my heart, the Lord will not hear me" (Ps.66:18).* *"But your iniquities have separated between you and your God, and your sins have hid his face from you, that he will not hear" (Is.59:2).* *"And there is none that calleth upon thy name, that stirreth up himself to take hold of thee: for thou hast hid thy face from us, and hast consumed us, because of our iniquities" (Is.64:7).* *"The soul that sinneth, it shall die" (Eze.18:4).*

DIVISION III

THE SECOND GREAT THEME PREACHED BY GOD'S AGED SERVANT (PART 1): REMEMBER THE TEN COMMANDMENTS—THE FUNDAMENTAL LAWS TO GOVERN MAN AND SOCIETY, 4:44–11:32

(4:44–11:32) **DIVISION OVERVIEW—Obedience**: this second theme of Moses is the longest series of messages he preached (4:44–26:19). It falls very naturally into two parts or sections:
⇒ First, the present section that reviews the Ten Commandments (4:4–11:32).
⇒ Second, the next section that reviews the civil and religious laws of Israel (12:1–26:19).

Obedience is an absolute essential to inherit the promised land of God. God could not accept nor bless the Israelites unless they obeyed Him. He could not give them the promised land unless they dedicated their lives to Him, made a commitment to keep His commandments. What good would the promised land be if the Israelites lived immoral, sinful lives just like the Canaanites? If there was no difference between the Israelites and the idolaters and false worshippers of Canaan? The Israelites were to worship the true and living God, the LORD Himself (Yahweh, Jehovah), and they were to obey Him. Moses knew this was the demand of God. Therefore, the aged servant of God preached a series of messages on the Ten Commandments, challenging the people to obey God, the only living and true God. If they obeyed Him, God would give them the promised land, give them the power to conquer and live victorious and fruitful lives day by day.

THE SECOND GREAT THEME PREACHED BY GOD'S AGED SERVANT (PART 1): REMEMBER THE TEN COMMANDMENTS—THE FUNDAMENTAL LAWS TO GOVERN MAN AND SOCIETY, 4:44–11:32

A. The Introduction and Overall Look at the Law: The Importance of the Law, 4:44–5:6
B. The Ten Commandments (Part 1): The Laws Governing Man's Duty to God, 5:7-15
C. The Ten Commandments (Part 2): The Laws Governing Man's Duty to Others, 5:16-21
D. The Purposes of the Law: Why God Gave the Ten Commandments and the Law, 5:22-33
E. The Summary of the Commandments—the Greatest Commandment of All: Love the LORD, 6:1-25
F. The Greatest Hindrance to Obeying the Commandments of God: The Enemies of the Promised Land, 7:1-26
G. The Safeguards to Assure Obedience to the Commandments of God: How to Guard Against Forgetting God, 8:1-20
H. The Warnings Against Self-righteousness and Disobedience: Warnings That Must Be Heeded to Inherit the Promised Land, 9:1–10:11
I. The Nine Supreme Requirements of Obedience: What Is Demanded by God, 10:12–11:32

DEUTERONOMY 4:44–5:6

	III. THE SECOND GREAT THEME PREACHED BY GOD'S AGED SERVANT (PART 1): REMEMBER THE TEN COMMANDMENTS—THE FUNDAMENTAL LAWS TO GOVERN MAN & SOCIETY, 4:44–11:32	48 From Aroer, which *is* by the bank of the river Arnon, even unto mount Sion, which *is* Hermon, 49 And all the plain on this side Jordan eastward, even unto the sea of the plain, under the springs of Pisgah.	3) It was a vast land • It ran from Aroer at the edge of the Arnon Gorge to Mt. Hermon • It included all the Arabah of east Jordan as far south as the Dead Sea, below the slopes of Mt. Pisgah
	A. The Introduction & Overall Look at the Law: The Importance of the Law, 4:44–5:6	**CHAPTER 5** And Moses called all Israel, and said unto them, Hear, O Israel, the statutes and judgments which I speak in your ears this day, that ye may learn them, and keep, and do them.	2. The stress of the law—obedience: Must hear, learn, & obey the law
1. The subject of the message: The law of God	44 And this *is* the law which Moses set before the children of Israel: 45 These *are* the testimonies, and the statutes, and the judgments, which Moses spake unto the children of Israel, after they came forth out of Egypt,		
a. The strategic time: After they had been delivered from Egyptian slavery (a symbol of the world)		2 The LORD our God made a covenant with us in Horeb. 3 The LORD made not this covenant with our fathers, but with us, *even* us, who *are* all of us here alive this day. 4 The LORD talked with you face to face in the mount out of the midst of the fire, 5 (I stood between the LORD and you at that time, to show you the word of the LORD: for ye were afraid by reason of the fire, and went not up into the mount;) saying,	3. The heart of the law: The covenant—the Ten Commandments^{DS1} a. The parties to the covenant: God & man—all who are alive today b. The source of the covenant: God c. The mediator of the covenant: Moses 1) He stood between God & the people 2) The reason: They feared the fire of God's glory
b. The strategic place—east of Jordan, right at the entrance to the promised land: A symbol of heaven & of spiritual conquest & rest 1) It was near Beth Peor 2) It was the land conquered from the two Amorite kings, Sihon and Og	46 On this side Jordan, in the valley over against Bethpeor, in the land of Sihon king of the Amorites, who dwelt at Heshbon, whom Moses and the children of Israel smote, after they were come forth out of Egypt: 47 And they possessed his land, and the land of Og king of Bashan, two kings of the Amorites, which *were* on this side Jordan toward the sunrising;	6 I *am* the LORD thy God, which brought thee out of the land of Egypt, from the house of bondage.	4. The basis of the law a. God's name: The LORD b. God's relationship: Your God c. God's salvation, deliverance

DIVISION III

THE SECOND GREAT THEME PREACHED BY GOD'S AGED SERVANT (PART 1): REMEMBER THE TEN COMMANDMENTS—THE FUNDAMENTAL LAWS TO GOVERN MAN AND SOCIETY, 4:44–11:32

A. The Introduction and Overall Look at the Message: The Importance of the Law, 4:44–5:6

(4:44–5:6) **Introduction—Law, Importance of**: law is the foundation of society, the chain that holds people together. It is law that controls the behavior of people, telling them what to do and what not to do. The law enables people to relate together, work together, and build together. It is the laws of society that guarantee both personal and community services such as fire and police protection, health care, social services, roads and highways, property security, and military protection. The benefits that flow out from the law are almost innumerable. The law is an absolute essential for society; its importance cannot be overstressed.

Obedience to the law was needed when the Israelites entered and settled in the promised land. They were destined to become a great nation of people if they did just one thing: obey their laws, the laws established by God. Remember, there were over three million Israelites camped in the plains of Moab by the Jordan River, right across from the great city of Jericho. They were poised to enter and lay claim to the promised land of God. But before they entered, they needed to be focused upon the laws that were to govern their nation. They needed the laws embedded in their hearts so they could build a strong society and nation. The strength of their community would depend upon their laws, their obedience to the laws. This Moses knew. Therefore, he summoned all the people together to renew their commitment to the commandments of God. He sought to drive the law into their minds, stressing the importance of the laws time and again. The people needed to learn the commandments of God and renew their commitment to follow them. The present passage is an introduction to the law, preliminary facts that the people needed to know: *The Introduction and Overall Look at the Law: The Importance of the Law*, 4:44–5:6.

1. The subject of the message: The law of God—His testimonies (stipulations), statutes, and judgments (regulations, laws) (4:44-49).
2. The stress of the law—obedience: must hear, learn, and obey the law (5:1).
3. The heart of the law: the covenant of the Ten Commandments (5:2-5).
4. The basis of the law (5:6).

DEUTERONOMY 4:44–5:6

1 (4:44-49) **Message, Preached—Law, Declared by Moses—Preaching, of Moses—Law, Subject of Preaching—Israel, Recipients of the Law—East Jordan, Territory of**: the subject of the message preached by Moses was the law of God, His testimonies (stipulations), statutes, and judgments (regulations, laws). Matthew Henry says that these messages of Moses were probably preached on Sabbath days, the days when the people were resting and worshipping, not having to work. Whatever the case, this message includes so much material it was probably preached over a number of Sabbaths or days when no work was required.

These were days of excitement, unusual and stirring excitement—days of planning and activity. The people were about ready to enter the promised land and lay claim to their promised inheritance. Careful preparation had to be made; the law of God had to be reviewed.

OUTLINE	SCRIPTURE	SCRIPTURE	OUTLINE
1. The subject of the message: The law of God	44 And this *is* the law which Moses set before the children of Israel:	out of Egypt:	
a. The strategic time: After they had been delivered from Egyptian slavery (a symbol of the world)	45 These *are* the testimonies, and the statutes, and the judgments, which Moses spake unto the children of Israel, after they came forth out of Egypt,	47 And they possessed his land, and the land of Og king of Bashan, two kings of the Amorites, which *were* on this side Jordan toward the sunrising;	2) It was the land conquered from the two Amorite kings, Sihon and Og
b. The strategic place—east of Jordan, right at the entrance to the promised land: A symbol of heaven & of spiritual conquest & rest 1) It was near Beth Peor	46 On this side Jordan, in the valley over against Bethpeor, in the land of Sihon king of the Amorites, who dwelt at Heshbon, whom Moses and the children of Israel smote, after they were come forth	48 From Aroer, which *is* by the bank of the river Arnon, even unto mount Sion, which *is* Hermon, 49 And all the plain on this side Jordan eastward, even unto the sea of the plain, under the springs of Pisgah.	3) It was a vast land • It ran from Aroer at the edge of the Arnon Gorge to Mt. Hermon • It included all the Arabah of east Jordan as far south as the Dead Sea, below the slopes of Mt. Pisgah

a. Note the time of the message, when the message was preached to the people: after they had been delivered from Egyptian slavery (v.45). God saved the Israelites to be His people, a people of His law and Word. The Israelites were chosen to be a special, distinctive people—special and distinctive in that they were to follow God and obey His law explicitly. It was the law of God—the obedience to God's law—that was to distinguish and set apart God's people from their immoral and worldly neighbors. It was after their salvation experience, their deliverance from Egyptian slavery, that Moses stood there preaching to the people of God. Being freed from Egyptian slavery, they were formed into the people of God, a body of people who were to be distinguished, set apart by the law of God. Right before they were to enter the promised land, it was necessary to review the law, the very thing that held them together as a people.

b. Note the strategic place where the message was preached: in the plains of Moab near Beth Peor, east of the Jordan River. This great sermon was preached right at the entrance to the promised land (vv.46-49). This was the land that had been conquered and taken from the two Amorite kings, Sihon and Og. East Jordan was a vast land that extended from Aroer at the edge of the Arnon Gorge to Mt. Hermon (v.48). The territory included all the Arabah of East Jordan as far south as the Dead Sea, below the slopes of Mt. Pisgah (v.49).

The second great message of Moses was preached at a strategic time and in a strategic place. It was preached after the Israelites had been delivered from Egyptian slavery, preached when they were being formed into a people of the law, God's law. It was preached right at the entrance to the promised land, the last possible place they could review the law before claiming their inheritance. Simply stated, the people needed to review and make a renewed commitment to the law before they began conquering and settling down in the promised land of God.

> **Thought 1**. The Word of God—His law, His commandments—must be preached. It is God's Word that tells people how to live, how to live a fruitful and productive life that brings purpose, satisfaction, and fulfillment to the human heart.
>
> "Sanctify them through thy truth: thy word is truth" (Jn.17:17).
>
> "For whatsoever things were written aforetime were written for our learning, that we through patience and comfort of the scriptures might have hope" (Ro.15:4).
>
> "All scripture *is* given by inspiration of God, and *is* profitable for doctrine, for reproof, for correction, for instruction in righteousness" (2 Ti.3:16).
>
> "Preach the word; be instant in season, out of season; reprove, rebuke, exhort with all longsuffering and doctrine" (2 Ti.4:2).
>
> "For the word of God *is* quick, and powerful, and sharper than any twoedged sword, piercing even to the dividing asunder of soul and spirit, and of the joints and marrow, and *is* a discerner of the thoughts and intents of the heart" (He.4:12).
>
> "As newborn babes, desire the sincere milk of the word, that ye may grow thereby: If so be ye have tasted that the LORD *is* gracious" (1 Pe.2:2-3).
>
> "Be ye therefore very courageous to keep and to do all that is written in the book of the law of Moses, that ye turn not aside therefrom *to* the right hand or *to* the left" (Jos.23:6).
>
> "Wherewithal shall a young man cleanse his way? by taking heed *thereto* according to thy word" (Ps.119:9).
>
> "Whoso keepeth the law *is* a wise son: but he that is a companion of riotous *men* shameth his father" (Pr.28:7).

DEUTERONOMY 4:44–5:6

2 (5:1) **Law, Duty—Obedience, Duty—Word of God, Duty—Israel, Duty**: Moses preached the stress of the law—obedience. The believer must hear the law, learn the law, and obey the law. Note the Scripture and outline:

OUTLINE	SCRIPTURE
	CHAPTER 5
2. The stress of the law—obedience: Must hear, learn, & obey the law	And Moses called all Israel, and said unto them, Hear, O Israel, the statutes and judgments which I speak in your ears this day, that ye may learn them, and keep, and do them.

All the Israelites were called together to hear the sermon on the law. No person was too great or important to be above God's command; neither was any person too low or unimportant to be relieved from God's law. Every person was responsible to obey God's holy law; therefore, all the people were called together to review and renew their commitment. Note the challenge given:

⇒ The people were to *hear* (shama or sama) the law. The word means to hear intelligently; to carefully pay attention; to diligently give ear, discern, listen. The word has the sense of obeying: it is hearing that leads to obedience.

⇒ The people were to *learn* (lamad) the law. The word means to grasp the information and meaning of the law; to lay hold of the law, even to memorize it if necessary; to adopt, cultivate, and experience the law; to know and be well informed on the law.

⇒ The people were to be careful to *do, observe,* or *follow* (asah or asahl) the law. The word means to obey in the broadest sense: to obey fully, completely, thoroughly, wholly, and totally. It means to be strict in obedience: to do, observe, and follow in the broadest sense possible, accomplishing exactly what the law says. It means to carry out the law to the fullest extent possible.

Moses strikes the point home to the hearts of the people: they are to obey God. They must, therefore, hear the law: not be sleepy-eyed or drowsy while he is teaching the law. They must stay awake and hear exactly what the law says. Then they must learn the law and do, observe, and follow it. They must be careful, very careful, to obey the law wholeheartedly.

"Not every one that saith unto me, LORD, LORD, shall enter into the kingdom of heaven; but he that doeth the will of my Father which is in heaven" (Mt.7:21).

"Blessed *are* they that do his commandments, that they may have right to the tree of life, and may enter in through the gates into the city" (Re.22:14).

"This day the LORD thy God hath commanded thee to do these statutes and judgments: thou shalt therefore keep and do them with all thine heart, and with all thy soul" (De.26:16).

"This book of the law shall not depart out of thy mouth; but thou shalt meditate therein day and night, that thou mayest observe to do according to all that is written therein: for then thou shalt make thy way prosperous, and then thou shalt have good success" (Jos.1:8).

"And Samuel said, Hath the LORD *as great* delight in burnt offerings and sacrifices, as in obeying the voice of the LORD? Behold, to obey *is* better than sacrifice, *and* to hearken than the fat of rams" (1 S.15:22).

3 (5:2-5) **Law, Heart of—Covenant, Mosaic, Applicable to All—Ten Commandments, Fact, Is the Heart of the Law—Ten Commandments, Mediator of**: Moses preached the heart of the law, the covenant of the Ten Commandments. (See DEEPER STUDY # 1—De.5:2-5 for more discussion. Because of its length, this study is being placed at the end of this outline.) When the law of God is mentioned, most people picture the Ten Commandments. This is because the Ten Commandments are the very heart of God's law. They are the basis, the very foundation of life. It is the Ten Commandments that tell people exactly how God wants them to live. Moses is getting ready to review the commandments with God's people; therefore, he wants to drive the point home: above all else, these Ten Commandments must be learned and followed. But before he reviews the commandments, he covers a few preliminary facts about the covenant established by the commandments.

OUTLINE	SCRIPTURE	SCRIPTURE	OUTLINE
3. The heart of the law: The covenant—the Ten Commandments^{DS1}	2 The LORD our God made a covenant with us in Horeb.	you face to face in the mount out of the midst of the fire,	God
a. The parties to the covenant: God & man—all who are alive today	3 The LORD made not this covenant with our fathers, but with us, *even* us, who *are* all of us here alive this day.	5 (I stood between the LORD and you at that time, to show you the word of the LORD: for ye were afraid by reason of the fire, and went not up into	c. The mediator of the covenant: Moses 1) He stood between God & the people 2) The reason: They feared the fire of God's glory
b. The source of the covenant:	4 The LORD talked with	the mount;) saying,	

a. The parties to the covenant were God and man—all who were alive standing before Moses (v.3). God did not make the covenant with the fathers of Israel, that is, Abraham, Isaac, and Jacob. Rather, God made the covenant with the Israelite

DEUTERONOMY 4:44–5:6

believers who had been freed from Egyptian slavery and who were to follow God into the promised land. At Mt. Sinai, God had established His covenant with the following promise:

> "Now therefore, if ye will obey my voice indeed, and keep my covenant, then ye shall be a peculiar treasure unto me above all people: for all the earth *is* mine: And ye shall be unto me a kingdom of priests, and an holy nation. These *are* the words which thou shalt speak unto the children of Israel" (Ex.19:5-6).

In one word, God told His people what He expected of them: obedience. He had saved and delivered them; now He expected them to follow the law, to keep His covenant. If they obeyed, God made three great promises to His people:

⇒ God's people would be special *treasures* (sequallah) to Him (v.5). The Hebrew means select, choice, prized, precious, something held dear. They would become God's *personal possession*, *precious treasure*, and *choice property*.
⇒ God's people would be a *kingdom of priests* to Him (v.6). The idea is that of both *kings* and *priests*. The person who obeys God becomes both a king and a priest to God.
⇒ God's people would be a *holy nation* of people (v.6). The word *holy* (qadosh or qados) means to be sanctified, separate, different, pure, righteous within and without, totally consecrated to God and His mission upon earth.

b. The source of the covenant was God Himself (v.4). Man did not dream up the Ten Commandments nor the covenant of the law as a whole. The Ten Commandments were given by God to man—face to face, word by word. They were given openly and clearly to the thousands who stood at the foot of Mt. Sinai, given to thousands so there could never be any mistake: the commandments were the commandments of God Himself, the commandments given to show man how to live his life upon earth. No excuse could ever be given: man must obey the commandments of God. He must obey, for the commandments came from the very mouth of God Himself.

c. The mediator of the covenant was Moses (v.5). In this, Moses was a type of Christ. Remember, the presence of God had descended upon Mt. Sinai in a blazing fire that roared high up into the sky. The mountain was covered with black clouds and deep darkness (Ex.19:16-19; De.4:11-12). The people were gripped with an awesome sense of God's blazing holiness and were frightened. They were afraid to approach the mountain lest the holiness of God flash out and consume them because of their sinful, depraved nature. It was necessary—absolutely necessary—that Moses stand as the mediator between God and the people. As the mediator, Moses was a picture of the coming Savior and Messiah of the world, the Lord Jesus Christ. It is Jesus Christ who stands as the Mediator between God and man: it is He and He alone who reconciles man to God.

> "For *there is* one God, and one mediator between God and men, the man Christ Jesus; Who gave himself a ransom for all, to be testified in due time" (1 Ti.2:5-6; see He.8:6; 9:15; 24-28; 12:24; 1 Jn.2:1-2).

Thought 1. Think for a moment what has just been studied in this point: concentrate upon the great covenant and promises made by God. If we obey God and keep His commandments, we become...
- the *personal possession* of God
- the *choice property* of God
- a king to God
- a priest to God
- a holy—sanctified, pure, righteous, consecrated—people to God

> "What? know ye not that your body is the temple of the Holy Ghost *which is* in you, which ye have of God, and ye are not your own? For ye are bought with a price: therefore glorify God in your body, and in your spirit, which are God's" (1 Co.6:19-20).
>
> "For by grace are ye saved through faith; and that not of yourselves: *it is* the gift of God: Not of works, lest any man should boast" (Ep.2:8-9).
>
> "Ye also, as lively stones, are built up a spiritual house, an holy priesthood, to offer up spiritual sacrifices, acceptable to God by Jesus Christ" (1 Pe.2:5).
>
> "But ye *are* a chosen generation, a royal priesthood, an holy nation, a peculiar people; that ye should show forth the praises of him who hath called you out of darkness into his marvellous light" (1 Pe.2:9).
>
> "And this is his commandment, That we should believe on the name of his Son Jesus Christ, and love one another, as he gave us commandment" (1 Jn.3:23).
>
> "And [Christ] hath made us kings and priests unto God and his Father; to him *be* glory and dominion for ever and ever. Amen" (Re.1:6).
>
> "And hast [Christ] made us unto our God kings and priests: and we shall reign on the earth" (Re.5:10).
>
> "For thou *art* an holy people unto the LORD thy God: the LORD thy God hath chosen thee to be a special people unto himself, above all people that *are* upon the face of the earth" (De.7:6).
>
> "For thou *art* an holy people unto the LORD thy God, and the LORD hath chosen thee to be a peculiar people unto himself, above all the nations that *are* upon the earth" (De.14:2).

4 (5:6) **Law, Basis of—Ten Commandments, Basis of—God, Name of—Jehovah—Relationship, with God—Deliverance—Salvation:** the basis of the Ten Commandments and of the law is God Himself. This means a most wonderful thing: the Ten Commandments have been set in stone, in the Rock of Ages, in the One who is the Alpha and Omega, the Beginning and the End, the First and the Last. Therefore, the Ten Commandments work. They work because God knows man, knows exactly what man needs to live a fulfilled and orderly life. The Ten Commandments are based upon God Himself, upon His Person and work, upon His knowledge of what man needs, upon His understanding and wisdom. Right before discussing the Ten Commandments, Moses covers the basis, the very foundation of the law and its commandments. (See outline and notes—Ex.20:1-2 for a complete discussion of the basis of the law.)

OUTLINE	SCRIPTURE

4. The basis of the law
   a. God's name: The LORD
   b. God's relationship: Your God
   c. God's salvation, deliverance
	6 I *am* the LORD thy God, which brought thee out of the land of Egypt, from the house of bondage.

a. The first basis of the Ten Commandments is God's name. (See DEEPER STUDY # 1—Ex.20:2 for more discussion.) Note that the name of God is the LORD (Jehovah-Yahweh).
- The name of God means that He is the great I AM: "I AM THAT I AM." God is the Essence, Force, and Energy of Being, the Self-existent One (see DEEPER STUDY # 1—Ex.3:14-15 for more discussion).
- The name of God means that He is the God of salvation, deliverance, and redemption.
- The name of God means that He is the God of revelation. (See DEEPER STUDY # 1—Jn.6:20 for more discussion.)

God's very name means that He is the Source of all being; that He created man; that He loves man; that He saves, delivers, and redeems man; that He reveals and unveils the truth to man; that He reveals the truth of God and of the world to man. This is what the Ten Commandments (the law of God) are: the revelation of a loving God seeking to help man, showing man how to live. The very name of God tells us this. God's name is the basis, the very reason, the Ten Commandments are given to us. The name of God tells us that the LORD Himself loves us: He saves, delivers, and redeems us. He reveals the truth to us, showing us how to live and relate to Him and to one another. This He has done in the Ten Commandments. Simply stated, the LORD God loves us and wants us to know how to live; therefore, He gave us the Ten Commandments.

> **"And God said unto Moses, I AM THAT I AM: and he said, Thus shalt thou say unto the children of Israel, I AM hath sent me unto you. And God said moreover unto Moses, Thus shalt thou say unto the children of Israel, The LORD God of your fathers, the God of Abraham, the God of Isaac, and the God of Jacob, hath sent me unto you: this is my name for ever, and this is my memorial unto all generations" (Ex.3:14-15).**
>
> **"Hear, O Israel: The LORD our God is one LORD: And thou shalt love the LORD thy God with all thine heart, and with all thy soul, and with all thy might. And these words, which I command thee this day, shall be in thine heart: And thou shalt teach them diligently unto thy children, and shalt talk of them when thou sittest in thine house, and when thou walkest by the way, and when thou liest down, and when thou risest up" (De.6:4-7).**
>
> **"For the LORD is our judge, the LORD is our lawgiver, the LORD is our king; he will save us" (Is.33:22).**
>
> **"Hearken unto me, my people; and give ear unto me, O my nation: for a law shall proceed from me, and I will make my judgment to rest for a light of the people. My righteousness is near; my salvation is gone forth, and mine arms shall judge the people; the isles shall wait upon me, and on mine arm shall they trust" (Is.51:4-5).**

b. The second basis of the Ten Commandments is God's relationship with man. Note that God is said to be the LORD *your* God. God is not far off in outer space someplace, unreachable, unapproachable. God is near, near enough for us to speak to Him. In fact, God wants us to communicate with Him, for God wants to develop a relationship with us, a personal, loving relationship. This is the reason God gave us the Ten Commandments. He is the great Creator and Father of mankind. Therefore, He gave us the commandments to nourish the relationship between Him and the people He created. He gave us the Ten Commandments to guide us into a closer relationship with Him.

> **"Now therefore, if ye will obey my voice indeed, and keep my covenant, then ye shall be a peculiar treasure unto me above all people: for all the earth is mine: And ye shall be unto me a kingdom of priests, and an holy nation. These are the words which thou shalt speak unto the children of Israel" (Ex.19:5-6).**
>
> **"O that there were such an heart in them, that they would fear me, and keep all my commandments always, that it might be well with them, and with their children for ever!" (De.5:29).**
>
> **"He that hath my commandments, and keepeth them, he it is that loveth me: and he that loveth me shall be loved of my Father, and I will love him, and will manifest myself to him" (Jn.14:21).**
>
> **"Jesus answered and said unto him, If a man love me, he will keep my words: and my Father will love him, and we will come unto him, and make our abode with him" (Jn.14:23).**
>
> **"Wherefore come out from among them, and be ye separate, saith the LORD, and touch not the unclean thing [keep the commandments]; and I will receive you, And will be a Father unto you, and ye shall be my sons and daughters, saith the LORD Almighty" (2 Co.6:17-18).**

c. The third basis of the Ten Commandments is God's salvation, deliverance, and redemption. Note that God Himself rescued Israel from the evil place of bondage, the land of Egypt (a symbol of the world). God gave us the Ten Commandments to save us from the evil and lawlessness of this world, evil and lawlessness such as...

DEUTERONOMY 4:44–5:6

- covetousness and greed
- lying
- stealing
- adultery
- murder
- abuse
- violating the Sabbath, the day of rest and worship
- cursing God
- false worship
- unbelief, denial of God

Evil and lawlessness have always swept the world in places where the Ten Commandments were not followed. The commandments help us only if we keep them. This is the reason God demands one thing above all else: *obedience*. God is our Savior and Deliverer. He wants us out of harm's way, living like we should, living in peace and reconciliation, both with Him and with one another. Therefore, He gave us the Ten Commandments. God's salvation, deliverance, and redemption are the bases of the Ten Commandments.

"O that there were such an heart in them, that they would fear me, and keep all my commandments always, that it might be well with them, and with their children for ever!" (De.5:29).

"But the salvation of the righteous is of the LORD: he is their strength in the time of trouble" (Ps.37:39).

"Behold, God is my salvation; I will trust, and not be afraid: for the LORD JEHOVAH is my strength and my song; he also is become my salvation" (Is.12:2).

"And it shall be said in that day, Lo, this is our God; we have waited for him, and he will save us: this is the LORD; we have waited for him, we will be glad and rejoice in his salvation" (Is.25:9).

"The LORD thy God in the midst of thee is mighty; he will save, he will rejoice over thee with joy; he will rest in his love, he will joy over thee with singing" (Zep.3:17).

"This book of the law shall not depart out of thy mouth; but thou shalt meditate therein day and night, that thou mayest observe to do according to all that is written therein: for then thou shalt make thy way prosperous, and then thou shalt have good success" (Jos.1:8).

"For the grace of God that bringeth salvation hath appeared to all men, Teaching us that, denying ungodliness and worldly lusts, we should live soberly, righteously, and godly, in this present world; Looking for that blessed hope, and the glorious appearing of the great God and our Saviour Jesus Christ" (Tit.2:11-13).

DEEPER STUDY # 1

(5:2-5, 6) Mosaic Covenant—Abrahamic Covenant—Believer, Life and Walk: the Mosaic covenant is a continuation of God's covenant with His people, a continuation of the Abrahamic covenant. Remember, in ancient history the whole world had forsaken God. Few if any people were totally following God (see outlines and notes—Ge.11:10-32). Thus God had chosen one man and given him the great promises of God. That man was Abraham. God called Abraham to forsake the world, to believe God, and to seek the great promises of God. If Abraham forsook the world and believed God, diligently seeking God's promises, then God would fulfill the promises in the lives of Abraham's descendants. There were three great promises given to Abraham:

⇒ the promise of the promised land, the land of Canaan (a symbol of heaven).
⇒ the promise that Abraham would be a blessing to all the nations of the earth, meaning that the Savior and Messiah of the world would come through his descendants and bless the whole world.
⇒ the promise of the promised seed, meaning both a multitude of descendants who would become a great nation of people and the promised seed of the Messiah (see Ga.3:16).

This great nation of people was Israel. At Mt. Sinai, God was ready to expand and enlarge His covenant given to Abraham.
⇒ God called Abraham to believe Him and to seek the great promises of God.
⇒ God called Israel to obey Him and to become two things: the holy people of God and His witnesses to the world.

Simply stated, the Mosaic covenant was a continuation of the Abrahamic covenant. The following chart shows both the connection and the additional items of the Mosaic covenant.

The call/challenge	The promises
Abrahamic Covenant (Ge.12:1-3; Ac.3:12; Ga.3:6-8; 3:16)	⇒ God's people would inherit the promised land
	⇒ God's people would be a blessing to the entire world, meaning that the Messiah and Savior of the world would come through his descendants and bless the whole world
	⇒ God's people would bear the promised seed, both a great nation of people and the Savior and Messiah

The call/challenge	The promises
Mosaic Covenant (Ex.19:5-6)	⇒ God's people would become the special people of God
	⇒ God's people would become a holy nation, marked as the true followers of the only living and true God, a nation set apart to follow God in all righteousness and godliness
	⇒ God's people would become a kingdom of priests, the witnesses of God to the world

DEUTERONOMY 4:44–5:6

Note this significant fact: the Abrahamic covenant pictures *salvation* and the Mosaic covenant pictures the *believers' life and walk*.

1. The Abrahamic covenant pictures salvation: if a person forsakes the world, believes God, and diligently seeks the promises of God...
   - he inherits the promised land
   - he blesses the world by possessing Christ, by following Christ, and by offering Christ to the world
   - he *bears seed*, a number of spiritual descendants who become believers

2. The Mosaic covenant pictures the believer's life and walk: if a person obeys God...
   - he becomes a special person, a valuable treasure to the LORD, a person marked as a follower of the only living and true God
   - he becomes a holy person, a member of the holy nation of God
   - he becomes a king and a priest to God, a witness for God to the whole world

Another significant fact needs to be noted at this point: Scripture refers to the Mosaic Covenant as the *old* or *first* covenant. The *old covenant* is often contrasted with the *new covenant* established by Christ. Ronald Youngblood says this about the two covenants:

> *Our Bible is divided into two Testaments: Old and New. The word for "testament" can also be translated "covenant," a term that implies significant and intimate relationship between two parties (whether collective or individual). Many Scripture passages compare and contrast the "old" or "first" covenant with the "new covenant" (see, for example, Je.31:31-34; Heb.9:15-22). Although the Bible (particularly the Old Testament) describes many covenants in detail, the terms old covenant and first covenant always refer to the one we are about to study, the Mosaic (Sinaitic) covenant (see especially 2 Co.3:14-15; Heb.9:15-20), the most important of the older covenants. The Old Testament, then, is basically the story of redemption ratified by the "old covenant" (the Mosaic covenant), and the New Testament is basically the story of redemption ratified by the "new covenant" (instituted by Jesus during the Last Supper; see Luke 22:20). Both covenants become effective only through the shedding of blood (Exod.24:8; Matt.26:28).*[1]

TYPES, SYMBOLS, AND PICTURES
(Deuteronomy 4:44–5:6)

Historical Term	Type or Picture (Scriptural Basis for Each)	Life Application for Today's Believer	Biblical Application
Moses as the Mediator of the Covenant De.5:2-5 (See also De.29:1)	In this, Moses was a type of Christ who stands as the Mediator between God and man: it is He and He alone who reconciles man to God. Remember, the presence of God had descended upon Mt. Sinai in a blazing fire that roared high up into the sky. The mountain was covered with black clouds and deep darkness (Ex. 19:16-19; De.4:11-12). The people were gripped with an awesome sense of God's blazing holiness and were frightened. They were afraid to approach the mountain lest the holiness of God flash out and consume them because of their sinful, depraved nature. It was necessary—absolutely necessary—that Moses stand as the mediator between God and the people. As the mediator, Moses was a picture of the coming Savior and Messiah of the world, the Lord Jesus Christ. **"(I stood between the LORD and you at that time, to show you the word of**	⇒ The mediator is a negotiator, a middle person, an arbitrator, a go-between. This is Jesus Christ. However, there is one distinct and unique difference between Jesus Christ and human mediators. Jesus Christ is the *Perfect Mediator*. He is the Mediator chosen by God Himself to stand between God and man. Jesus Christ was chosen to be the Mediator because He is perfect. He presents the terms of the covenant perfectly. He does not lie, deceive, twist, change, add to, take away from, or misrepresent the terms of God's covenant. He spells out and proclaims the truth of the terms clearly and perfectly.	*"For there is one God, and one mediator between God and men, the man Christ Jesus; Who gave himself a ransom for all, to be testified in due time"* (1 Ti.2:5-6). *"But now hath he obtained a more excellent ministry, by how much also he is the mediator of a better covenant, which was established upon better promises"* (He.8:6). *"And for this cause he is the mediator of the new testament, that by means of death, for the redemption of the transgressions that were under the first testament, they which are called might receive the promise of eternal inheritance"* (He.9:15). *"And to Jesus the mediator of the new covenant, and to the blood of sprinkling, that speaketh better things than that of Abel"* (He.12:24). *"My little children, these things write I unto you, that ye sin not. And if any man sin, we have an advocate*

---

[1] Ronald F. Youngblood. *Exodus*. (Chicago, IL: Moody Press, 1983), pp.90-91.

Deuteronomy 4:44–5:6

Historical Term	Type or Picture (Scriptural Basis for Each)	Life Application for Today's Believer	Biblical Application
	the LORD: for ye were afraid by reason of the fire, and went not up into the mount;) saying," (De.5:5).		*with the Father, Jesus Christ the righteous: And he is the propitiation for our sins: and not for ours only, but also for the sins of the whole world"* *(1 Jn.2:1-2).*

DEUTERONOMY 5:7-15

	B. The Ten Commandments (Part 1): The Laws Governing Man's Duty to God, 5:7-15		
1. Commandment 1—*God's being*: Have no other gods *whatsoever*	7 Thou shalt have none other gods before me.	hold *him* guiltless that taketh his name in vain.	a. He is the LORD your God
2. Commandment 2—*God's worship*: Do not make, worship, or serve any idol whatsoever	8 Thou shalt not make thee *any* graven image, *or* any likeness *of any thing* that *is* in heaven above, or that *is* in the earth beneath, or that *is* in the waters beneath the earth:	12 Keep the sabbath day to sanctify it, as the LORD thy God hath commanded thee.	b. He will hold you accountable
a. Not an idol of anything in heaven, earth, or water		13 Six days thou shalt labour, and do all thy work:	4. Commandment 4—I *God's day*: Observe & keep the Sabbath day holy^{DS1}
b. The reasons	9 Thou shalt not bow down thyself unto them, nor serve them: for I the LORD thy God *am* a jealous God, visiting the iniquity of the fathers upon the children unto the third and fourth *generation* of them that hate me,	14 But the seventh day *is* the sabbath of the LORD thy God: *in* it thou shalt not do any work, thou, nor thy son, nor thy daughter, nor thy manservant, nor thy maidservant, nor thine ox, nor thine ass, nor any of thy cattle, nor thy stranger that *is* within thy gates; that thy manservant and thy maidservant may rest as well as thou.	a. The commandment:
1) God is a jealous God			1) Work for six days
2) The influence of idolatry is passed down from fathers to children			2) Set apart the Sabbath to the LORD for worship
			3) Do no work whatsoever on the Sabbath: No person & no animal
3) The influence of loving & obeying God lasts for a thousand generations	10 And showing mercy unto thousands of them that love me and keep my commandments.	15 And remember that thou wast a servant in the land of Egypt, and *that* the LORD thy God brought thee out thence through a mighty hand and by a stretched out arm: therefore the LORD thy God commanded thee to keep the sabbath day.	b. The reasons
3. Commandment 3—*God's name*: Never misuse the LORD'S name	11 Thou shalt not take the name of the LORD thy God in vain: for the LORD will not		1) Because you are to remember the redemption of God: His great deliverance from Egypt (a symbol of the world)
			2) Because the LORD your God commands you to keep the Sabbath day

DIVISION III

THE SECOND GREAT THEME PREACHED BY GOD'S AGED SERVANT (PART 1): REMEMBER THE TEN COMMANDMENTS—THE FUNDAMENTAL LAWS TO GOVERN MAN AND SOCIETY, 4:44–11:32

B. The Ten Commandments (Part 1): The Laws Governing Man's Duty to God, 5:7-15

(5:7-15) **Introduction—Morality—Society, Solution to Problems—Commandments, the Ten**: What is the basis of morality? Who can be absolutely sure what is right or wrong? The world offers various opinions. But is it left up to man to formulate his own values, his own system of morality and ethics? Unfortunately, there are many voices in the world today who believe anything goes, ideas that encourage...

- taking what a person wants
- saying what a person wants
- doing what a person wants
- believing what a person wants

The result has been tragic: man is losing control of society and the world; sin and evil are sweeping the world, running rampant, out of control, the sin and evil of...

- lawlessness
- drugs
- alcohol
- abuse
- violence
- murder
- war
- immorality

At times, the problems of sin and evil seem insurmountable. Humanly there seems to be no answer to the problems of society; the situation seems almost hopeless. But note: there is good news. The solution for a world that has gone berserk does not lie with man. Thousands of years ago, God gave man a plan for order within society, a plan that was to guide man down through the centuries, a plan that will work today as much as it would have worked in ancient history. What is that plan? The *Ten Commandments*. The Ten Commandments will work within any generation—if man will just institute and enforce them. God's Ten Commandments can bring order to the world. How can we say this? Because the Ten Commandments were given by God Himself. The Ten Commandments are not based upon...

- the prejudices and morality of men
- the latest popularity polls
- the worldly desires of people
- the purposes of government

The basis of the Ten Commandments has been set in stone, in the Rock of Ages, in the One who is the Alpha and the Omega, the Beginning and the End, the First and the Last. The basis of the Ten Commandments is God Himself. Therefore, the Ten Commandments work. They work because God knows man, knows exactly what man needs to live a fulfilled and orderly life. The Ten Commandments are based upon God Himself, upon His person and work, upon His knowledge of what man needs, upon His understanding and wisdom. This is now the great focus of our study: the Ten Commandments. Note that the commandments fall into two very natural studies:

DEUTERONOMY 5:7-15

Part 1: Man's duty to God (vv.7-15, commandments one to four).
Part 2: Man's duty to others (vv.16-21, commandments five to ten).

A thorough discussion on each of the Ten Commandments is given in Exodus. (See all outlines and notes—Ex.19:1–20:26 for more discussion.) The present study covers the first four commandments: *The Ten Commandments (Part 1): The Laws Governing Man's Duty to God*, 5:7-15.

1. Commandment 1 concerns God's being: have no other gods whatsoever (v.7).
2. Commandment 2 concerns God's worship: do not make, worship, or serve any idol whatsoever (vv.8-10).
3. Commandment 3 concerns God's name: never misuse the LORD's name (v.11).
4. Commandment 4 concerns God's day: observe and keep the Sabbath day holy (vv.12-15).

1 (5:7) **Obedience—Idolatry, Forbidden—God, Nature—Commandments, Ten—God, Existence**: commandment one concerns God's Being: "You are to have no other gods before me."

OUTLINE	SCRIPTURE
1. Commandment 1—*God's being*: Have no other gods *whatsoever*	7 Thou shalt have none other gods before me.

What is forbidden by this commandment? How is this commandment broken, violated?

God is declaring that He alone is the *Supreme Being*, the absolute authority of the universe. There is no other *supreme being*, no other god who created and who rules and reigns over the universe. He alone is the LORD, the only living and true God, the only living and true Creator. Note that God makes three stringent demands, three clear requirements in this commandment.

  a. Man is to have no other gods, none whatsoever (v.7).
    1) Man is not to set himself up as a god. Man is not to believe that he himself nor any other being or energy in the universe is the ultimate source of the universe.
       ⇒ Man is not to deny God, declaring there is no God (atheism).
       ⇒ Man is not to question God, saying God may exist but He also may not exist (agnosticism).
       ⇒ Man is not to declare that man himself is the supreme being, the ultimate authority of his world (humanism).
       ⇒ Man is not to look to science and technology as the ultimate power in life (secularism).
       ⇒ Man is not to hold that his own knowledge and reasoning ability are the ultimate control of the universe.
       ⇒ Man is not to believe that the spirit of man (the combined spirit of all men) is the ultimate energy of the universe.
       ⇒ Man is not to proclaim some impersonal mass, energy, or gas in the universe as *the force* behind all things.

    2) Man is not to believe that other beings, animals, or material things are God. Man is not to look in the sky above nor in the earth below nor in the sea and its depths and declare that something therein is God.
       ⇒ Man is not to look at the sky and declare the heavenly bodies and beings to be the supreme force of the universe: not the sun, moon, stars, angels, principalities, powers nor any other creature of any world or any dimension of being.
       ⇒ Man is not to look at the earth nor at some material substance of the earth and declare it to be God.
       ⇒ Man is not to look upon animals as some god, no matter what the animal is.
       ⇒ Man is not to consider the physical mass nor energy nor gases that comprise the basic substance of things as a god: not the atoms, protons, neutrons, nor whatever the most minute building-block of existence may be.

    3) Man is not to believe in many gods (polytheism). There is only one living and true God, only one true Creator, only one LORD and Majesty of the universe (monotheism). Therefore, man is to have no other gods whatsoever. All other so-called gods are nothing more than...
       • things created by the imaginations and thoughts of people
       • things called gods by people
       • things that are lifeless and powerless
       • things that are only images made out of metal, wood, stone, chemicals, or dirt

  b. God also makes a second demand of man: "You shall have no other gods *before me*" (v.7). The words *before me* (alpamaya) mean literally *before my face, against my face, in hostility toward me, in my presence, in my sight*. It means that man...
       • is to set no god *before* the LORD God
       • is to set no god *beside* the LORD God
       • is to set no god *in the presence* of the LORD God
       • is to set no god *in the face* of the LORD God

The great nineteenth century commentator George Bush makes several excellent statements that tell us exactly what the first commandment means:
       ⇒ [Creating idols] may be done mentally as well as manually. There may be idolatry without idols.
       ⇒ [This commandment] forbids the making of any other objects [as gods] whether persons or things, real or imaginary.
       ⇒ [Our] supreme regard, reverence, esteem, affection, and obedience [is due] God alone.

⇒ *God is the fountain of happiness, and no intelligent being can be happy but through him...[consequently] whoever seeks for supreme happiness in the creature instead of the Creator is guilty of a violation of this command.*[1]

If we set up anything that is a rival interest in our hearts and minds, anything that absorbs the love and service which belong only to the true God, then that thing becomes another god. Whatever the heart clings to, that becomes our god. Consequently...
- the proud man who idolizes himself makes himself a god.
- the ambitious man who pays homage to popular applause makes his ambition and the praise of men his god.
- the covetous person who craves money and things makes a god out of money and things.
- the greedy person who hoards possessions makes possessions his god.
- the immoral person who craves sex makes sex his god.
- the glutton who craves food makes eating his god.
- the doting lover—whether husband, wife, mother or father—who sets his supreme affection on the person loved instead of upon God makes that person his god.[2]

c. God also makes a third demand of us: man is to know and acknowledge the only true and living God—the LORD God Himself.
1) God declares that people who think there is no God (atheists) are wrong. I AM the LORD God, the true and living God. *Atheists* may deny God, and *agnostics* may question if God really exists, but God is forceful in His declaration.
⇒ "I AM—I AM the LORD Your God" (Ex.20:2).

"The fool hath said in his heart, There is no God" (Ps.14:1).

2) No other object and no other being are ever to be set up as so-called "gods." Taking ideas or objects and beings and calling them God is forbidden, absolutely forbidden.
⇒ The LORD Himself (Jehovah, Yahweh) emphatically declares:

"I am the LORD: that is my name: and my glory will I not give to another, neither my praise to graven images" (Is.42:8).

⇒ The great apostle Paul declared:

"For though there be [many] that are called gods, whether in heaven or in earth, (as there be gods many, and lords many,) But to us there is but one God, the Father, of whom are all things" (1 Co.8:5-6).

We make a god out of anything that we esteem or love, fear or serve more than God. Again, whatever the heart clings to, that is a person's god. It may be oneself. Frankly, many people focus upon pleasing and satisfying themselves. They live by their own values and are concerned primarily with their own feelings, comfort, desires, and pleasures. They simply live like they want and do their own thing. They have exalted themselves to be their own god. Other people make gods out of...

heavenly bodies	images	recognition	family	the latest style of clothing
science	money	fame	sex	cars, trucks
force, energy	property	career	food	sports
animals	position	power	pleasure	recreation

A god can be anything or any person. Man's first allegiance, first loyalty, first devotion is to be to the LORD God. The LORD God is to be first in a man's life; He is to be enthroned in the heart of man. Man is to know and acknowledge that there is one God and one God alone. The first commandment of the LORD is to be obeyed:

"You shall have no other gods before me" (v.7)

Thought 1. Note several points.
(1) The so-called gods of heaven and earth are nothing more than the creation of man's imagination and hands.

"Their idols are silver and gold, the work of men's hands. They have mouths, but they speak not: eyes have they, but they see not: They have ears, but they hear not: noses have they, but they smell not: They have hands, but they handle not: feet have they, but they walk not: neither speak they through their throat. They that make them are like unto them; so is every one that trusteth in them" (Ps.115:4-8).
"To whom then will ye liken God? or what likeness will ye compare unto him? The workman melteth a graven image, and the goldsmith spreadeth it over with gold, and casteth silver chains. He that is so impoverished that he hath no oblation chooseth a tree that will not rot; he seeketh unto him a cunning workman to prepare a graven image, that shall not be moved" (Is.40:18-20).

---
1 George Bush. *Exodus*. (Minneapolis, MN: Klock & Klock Christian Publishers, Inc., 1981), p.260. Points outlined by us for clarity.
2 The idea for this paragraph was also taken from George Bush, *Exodus*, p.260.

DEUTERONOMY 5:7-15

"Assemble yourselves and come; draw near together, ye that are escaped of the nations: they have no knowledge that set up the wood of their graven image, and pray unto a god that cannot save" (Is.45:20).

"Thus saith the LORD, Learn not the way of the heathen, and be not dismayed at the signs of heaven; for the heathen are dismayed at them. For the customs of the people are vain: for one cutteth a tree out of the forest, the work of the hands of the workman, with the axe. They deck it with silver and with gold; they fasten it with nails and with hammers, that it move not. They are upright as the palm tree, but speak not: they must needs be borne, because they cannot go. Be not afraid of them; for they cannot do evil, neither also is it in them to do good" (Je.10:2-5).

"Professing themselves to be wise, they became fools, And changed the glory of the uncorruptible God into an image made like to corruptible man, and to birds, and fourfooted beasts, and creeping things" (Ro.1:22-23).

"Ye know that ye were Gentiles, carried away unto these dumb idols, even as ye were led" (1 Co.12:2).

(2) There is only one true and living God, the LORD Himself (Jehovah, Yahweh).

"Unto thee it was showed, that thou mightest know that the LORD he is God; there is none else beside him" (De.4:35).

"Hear, O Israel: The LORD our God is one LORD: And thou shalt love the LORD thy God with all thine heart, and with all thy soul, and with all thy might" (De.6:4-5).

"Wherefore thou art great, O LORD God: for there is none like thee, neither is there any God beside thee, according to all that we have heard with our ears" (2 S.7:22).

"O LORD, there is none like thee, neither is there any God beside thee, according to all that we have heard with our ears" (1 Chr.17:20).

"That men may know that thou, whose name alone is JEHOVAH, art the most high over all the earth" (Ps.83:18).

"For thou art great, and doest wondrous things: thou art God alone" (Ps.86:10).

"Ye are my witnesses, saith the LORD, and my servant whom I have chosen: that ye may know and believe me, and understand that I am he: before me there was no God formed, neither shall there be after me. I, even I, am the LORD; and beside me there is no saviour" (Is.43:10-11).

"Thus saith the LORD the King of Israel, and his redeemer the LORD of hosts; I am the first, and I am the last; and beside me there is no God" (Is.44:6).

"For thus saith the LORD that created the heavens; God himself that formed the earth and made it; he hath established it, he created it not in vain, he formed it to be inhabited: I am the LORD; and there is none else" (Is.45:18).

"Look unto me, and be ye saved, all the ends of the earth: for I am God, and there is none else" (Is.45:22).

"And the scribe said unto him, Well, Master, thou hast said the truth: for there is one God; and there is none other but he" (Mk.12:32).

"And Jesus answered him, The first of all the commandments [is], Hear, O Israel; The LORD our God is one LORD" (Mk.12:29).

"As concerning therefore the eating of those things that are offered in sacrifice unto idols, we know that an idol is nothing in the world, and that there is none other God but one. For though there be that are called gods, whether in heaven or in earth, (as there be gods many, and lords many,) But to us there is but one God, the Father, of whom are all things, and we in him; and one Lord Jesus Christ, by whom are all things, and we by him" (1 Co.8:4-6).

"One God and Father of all, who is above all, and through all, and in you all" (Ep.4:6).

"For there is one God, and one mediator between God and men, the man Christ Jesus" (1 Ti.2:5).

(3) There is only one sovereign Creator who meets the needs of man.

"In the beginning God created the heaven and the earth" (Ge.1:1).

"Thou, even thou, art LORD alone; thou hast made heaven, the heaven of heavens, with all their host, the earth, and all things that are therein, the seas, and all that is therein, and thou preservest them all; and the host of heaven worshippeth thee" (Ne.9:6).

"He stretcheth out the north over the empty place, and hangeth the earth upon nothing" (Jb.26:7).

"By the word of the LORD were the heavens made; and all the host of them by the breath of his mouth" (Ps.33:6).

"Of old hast thou laid the foundation of the earth: and the heavens are the work of thy hands" (Ps.102:25).

"For as I passed by, and beheld your devotions, I found an altar with this inscription, TO THE UNKNOWN GOD. Whom therefore ye ignorantly worship, him declare I unto you. God that made the world and all things therein, seeing that he is LORD of heaven and earth, dwelleth not in temples made with hands; Neither is worshipped with men's hands, as though he needed any thing, seeing he giveth to all life, and breath, and all things; And hath made of one blood all nations of men for to dwell on all the face of the earth, and hath determined the times before appointed, and the bounds of their habitation; That they should seek the LORD, if haply they might feel after him, and find him, though he be not far from every one of us: For in him we live, and move, and have our being; as certain also of your own poets have said, For we are also his offspring. Forasmuch then as we are the offspring of God, we ought

DEUTERONOMY 5:7-15

not to think that the Godhead is like unto gold, or silver, or stone, graven by art and man's device. And the times of this ignorance God winked at; but now commandeth all men every where to repent: Because he hath appointed a day, in the which he will judge the world in righteousness by that man whom he hath ordained; whereof he hath given assurance unto all men, in that he hath raised him from the dead" (Ac.17:23-31).

"Through faith we understand that the worlds were framed by the word of God, so that things which are seen were not made of things which do appear" (He.11:3).

Thought 2. The very first commandment says, "You shall have no other gods *before me*" (v.7). Note the words *before me*. This suggests at least two facts:
(1) If we set some so-called god *before God*, He knows it. We cannot hide the fact from Him.
(2) If we set a god *before Him*, His anger is aroused.

"If we have forgotten the name of our God, or stretched out our hands to a strange god; Shall not God search this out? for he knoweth the secrets of the heart" (Ps.44:20-21).

"I am the LORD: that is my name: and my glory will I not give to another, neither my praise to graven images" (Is.42:8).

"For the wrath of God is revealed from heaven against all ungodliness and unrighteousness of men, who hold the truth in unrighteousness" (Ro.1:18).

2 (5:8-10) **Obedience—Idolatry—Worship, False—Images, of Worship—Worship, Images of—Covetousness—Forbidden—Gods, False**: commandment two concerns the worship of God: "You shall not make any idol nor worship or serve any false god—none whatsoever."

OUTLINE	SCRIPTURE	SCRIPTURE	OUTLINE
2. **Commandment 2—God's worship**: Do not make, worship, or serve any idol whatsoever a. Not an idol of anything in heaven, earth, or water b. The reasons 1) God is a jealous God	8 Thou shalt not make thee *any* graven image, *or* any likeness *of any thing* that *is* in heaven above, or that *is* in the earth beneath, or that *is* in the waters beneath the earth: 9 Thou shalt not bow down thyself unto them, nor serve them: for I the LORD thy God	*am* a jealous God, visiting the iniquity of the fathers upon the children unto the third and fourth *generation* of them that hate me, 10 And showing mercy unto thousands of them that love me and keep my commandments.	2) The influence of idolatry is passed down from fathers to children 3) The influence of loving & obeying God lasts for a thousand generations

a. How is this commandment broken? How is it violated? Scripture says that this commandment forbids at least three things. First, this commandment prohibits the *making* of any idol whatsoever; therefore, the commandment is broken and violated by making idols (v.8).
 1) To make an image of anything for worship is wrong. Note the verse: We must not build an image of anything for worship, not an image of anything in the sky above nor that is in the earth beneath, nor that is in the water upon the earth. Nothing in the universe is ever to have an image made of it, not for worship.
 Note that the entire universe is covered; even the unseen world of heaven is covered. No idol of anything is ever to be made for worship...
 - not heavenly creatures: angels, demons, devils, or imaginary gods
 - not heavenly bodies such as the sun, moon, or stars
 - not earthly creatures such as cows, elephants, or man
 - not water creatures such as fish, crocodiles, or sea animals

 The making of any idol whatsoever is forbidden—absolutely forbidden. God emphatically declares, "You shall never make an idol of anything, not ever—not of anything."
 2) This commandment also forbids the making of an image of God Himself, for He is a spiritual being (v.8). Note that "no image or form or likeness of anything in heaven is to be made" (v.8). God is in heaven, in the spiritual world or dimension of being; therefore, no image is to be made of God.
 3) A question needs to be asked at this point: What about images such as pictures, crucifixes, statues, and other symbols that are used to stir our memories to pray and worship? Is this commandment speaking against such images? There is a tendency within human nature to focus upon that which is seen instead of upon the unseen, a tendency to fix our attention upon the seen object (the picture, the crucifix, etc.) instead of upon God. Reason and honesty—especially *honesty*—demand that we acknowledge this fact. Consequently, if we use visible objects to arouse us to pray and worship, there is great danger...
 - that a pure and spiritual worship of God will fade, deteriorate, and be degraded.
 - that the physical object will become more valued and receive more of our attention than God. Why? Because God is spiritual and unseen, and the physical object is seen.

DEUTERONOMY 5:7-15

William Barclay has an excellent statement on idolatry. Note carefully what he says:

> [Idolatry] began because men found it difficult to worship a god they could not see. So they said to themselves, "We will make something which will represent the god and that will make it easier to think of the god." In the first instance the idol was never meant to be the god; it was meant only to stand for the god.
>
> We can perhaps understand it, if we think of it this way. Suppose we have a friend whom we have not seen for a very long time, and suppose we sit down to write a letter to that friend, and suppose we find the letter hard to write, because we have been separated for so long. In such a situation it might well help if we took a photograph of the friend and put it where we could see it, and wrote, as it were, looking at the photograph. The photograph would bring our friend nearer to our mind. At first that is what an idol was meant to do.
>
> The trouble was that men began to worship the idol instead of the god it stood for; men began to worship the symbol instead of the reality it was supposed to represent. It is not really difficult to see how idolatry began, and it is not really so silly as it looks. For all that, we may well be saying, "I am not likely to do a thing like that." But perhaps we are more likely to do it than we think.
>
> Take a very small thing first of all. Quite a lot of people carry some kind of lucky mascot, some kind of charm. Some carry a lucky penny or a lucky sign of the zodiac, or, for instance, if they go on a journey, they take a St. Christopher sign to avoid accidents. That is really idolatry, for it is believing that in some way the carrying of a little bit of metal or plastic can have an effect on their lives.
>
> But there is something much more serious than that. The real essence of idolatry is that a man worships a thing instead of God.
>
> There is no doubt at all that there is a great deal of that today. People assess their success in life by the number of things which they possess....
>
> This is obviously wrong.[3]

Arthur W. Pink gives a thought-provoking statement on idolatry that is well worth quoting:

> This commandment strikes against a desire, or should we say a disease, which is deeply rooted in the human heart, namely, to bring in some aids to the worship of God, beyond those which He has appointed—material aids, things which can be perceived by the senses. Nor is the reason for this difficult to find: God is incorporeal, invisible, and can be realized only by a spiritual principle, and since that principle is dead in fallen man, he naturally seeks that which accords with his carnality. But how different is it with those who have been quickened by the Holy Spirit. No one who truly knows God as a living reality needs any images to aid his devotions; none who enjoys daily communion with Christ requires any pictures of Him to help him to pray and adore, for he conceives of Him by faith and not by fancy.[4]

Now, having said this, the commandment does not forbid artistic talent, that is, the making of sculptures, pictures, statues, and crucifixes for the purpose of the fine arts. The commandment strikes against making and using images and idols...

- for the purpose of worship
- for the purpose of controlling our lives and looking after us

This steals our hearts away from the only living and true God.

Thought 1. Adrian Rogers has an excellent illustration dealing with making an image or likeness of God for the purpose of worship and prayer:

> Idolatry is wrong because it gives a distorted or false picture of God. An idol is a material thing, and no idol can represent the invisible, spiritual God. Jesus said in John 4:24, "God is a Spirit." I know the King James Version includes the indefinite article, but the literal translation is, God is spirit." That is, spirit is His very essence.
>
> No wonder, then, that Jesus went on to say, "They that worship him must worship him in spirit and in truth." What material thing could possibly represent spirit? God is a circle whose center is everywhere and whose circumference is nowhere. God is spirit. There is nowhere where God is not, and no material thing can represent Him.
>
> There's nothing you can compare God to or with. There's nothing that says, "This is what God is totally like." God Himself asked, "To whom then will ye liken me, or shall I be equal?" (Isaiah 40:25). We can say one man is like another man, one chair is like another chair, one piano like another piano, and so on. But there's only one God. You can't compare Him to anything or anyone....
>
> Suppose a woman walks into a room and finds her husband embracing another woman. He sees his wife out of the corner of his eye and says, "Now wait a minute, honey. Don't get the wrong idea here. Let me tell you what I was doing. This woman is so beautiful, she reminded me of you. I was really just thinking of you when I was embracing her."
>
> There's not a woman in America who would buy that, including my wife, Joyce! And God doesn't buy it either when we worship something else and say, "Now, LORD, wait a minute. Don't get the wrong idea here. I was only worshiping this thing because it reminds me of You. I'm really worshiping You."
>
> No, you really aren't. That's what the Second Commandment is all about.[5]

---

[3] William Barclay. *The Old Law and the New Law.* (Edinburgh, Scotland: The Saint Andrew Press, 1972), pp.11-13.
[4] Arthur W. Pink. *The Ten Commandments.* (Grand Rapids, MI: Baker Books, 1994), pp.21-22.
[5] Adrian Rogers. *Ten Secrets For A Successful Family.* (Wheaton, IL: Crossway Books, 1996), pp.44-45.

Thought 2. There is only one true image of God, only one *image* that is acceptable to God.[6]
(1) Jesus Christ is the visible image of the invisible God.

> "[God] who hath delivered us from the power of darkness, and hath translated us into the kingdom of his dear Son: In whom we have redemption through his blood, even the forgiveness of sins: Who is the image of the invisible God, the firstborn of every creature" (Col.1:13-15).

(2) Jesus Christ is the express image, the exact representation, of God's person.

> "God, who at sundry times and in divers manners spake in time past unto the fathers by the prophets, Hath in these last days spoken unto us by his Son, whom he hath appointed heir of all things, by whom also he made the worlds; Who being the brightness of his glory, and the express image of his person, and upholding all things by the word of his power, when he had by himself purged our sins, sat down on the right hand of the Majesty on high" (He.1:1-3).

(3) Jesus Christ is the very form, the very nature, of God.

> "Who, being in the form of God, Thought it not robbery to be equal with God" (Ph.2:6).

(4) Jesus Christ is the fullness of the Godhead bodily.

> "For in him dwelleth all the fulness of the Godhead bodily. And ye are complete in him, which is the head of all principality and power" (Col.2:9-10).

(5) Jesus Christ is the image to whom we are to be conformed.

> "For whom he did foreknow, he also did predestinate to be conformed to the image [likeness, NIV] of his Son, that he might be the firstborn among many brethren" (Ro.8:29).

(6) Jesus Christ is the image to which we shall be gloriously and eternally made (transformed).

> "Beloved, now are we the sons of God, and it doth not yet appear what we shall be: but we know that, when he shall appear, we shall be like him; for we shall see him as he is" (1 Jn.3:2).

(7) Jesus Christ is the very nature and revelation of God Himself.

> "If ye had known me, ye should have known my Father also: and from henceforth ye know him, and have seen him. Philip saith unto him, LORD, show us the Father, and it sufficeth us. Jesus saith unto him, Have I been so long time with you, and yet hast thou not known me, Philip? he that hath seen me hath seen the Father; and how sayest thou [then], Show us the Father? Believest thou not that I am in the Father, and the Father in me? the words that I speak unto you I speak not of myself: but the Father that dwelleth in me, he doeth the works" (Jn.14:7-10).

Second, this commandment prohibits the *worship* of any false god whatsoever, prohibits the worship of anything other than God Himself (v.9).
1) This strikes a death blow against one of the most common ideas and claims of people: that all religions worship the same god, that no matter what we may call god and no matter what religion we follow, we all worship the same *supreme being*.

Remember the first commandment: there are no other gods; there is only one true and living God (v.9). Therefore, if we create a god within our own minds—if we worship something else, some other so-called god, if we treat something else as a god—we misrepresent the truth. No matter how large our religion may become, even if billions of people followed, our worship would be a lie. It would be wrong; it would be sinful behavior. Our idea of God would be inaccurate, incomplete, and false. And false worship is a gross insult to the *only* living and true God, to the *only* Sovereign LORD and Majesty of the universe.

⇒ It is wrong to worship things in the sky such as the sun, moon, and stars; wrong to trust and use the zodiac and other so-called *fortune-tellers* to guide one's life.
⇒ It is wrong to worship things in the earth such as man, cows, elephants, and other animals.
⇒ It is wrong to worship things in the water such as fish, crocodiles, and so-called sea creatures.
⇒ It is wrong to worship false messiahs and saviors.
⇒ It is wrong to engage in the false worship of anything.

Simply stated, it is wrong to worship the image of God created by man's imagination, wrong to picture what we think God is like and wrong to worship our image of God. God has revealed Himself, revealed exactly who He is and what He is like, in the Lord Jesus Christ and in the Holy Scripture. It is the LORD God revealed by Jesus Christ and the Holy Scripture that we are to picture and worship. We are to worship the LORD *God of revelation*—the LORD

---

[6] These points are taken from the Sunday School material: *Ten Overlooked Principles in Building Successful Families* which is derived from Adrian Rogers' *Ten Secrets For A Successful Family*.

DEUTERONOMY 5:7-15

God *revealed by Jesus Christ*—worship Him and Him alone. (See note, pt.2—Ex.20:1; also see outline and note—Jn.14:4-7; 14:8-14.)

2) This commandment also strikes a death blow against what was mentioned earlier, that of using images of heavenly beings for worship and prayer (v.9). God does not accept any worship that comes to Him through an idol. God is Spirit, not physical and material. God is invisible, not visible to the naked eye. Therefore, to worship an image of God is to misrepresent God, and misrepresentation of God is a lie, is sinful behavior. It is a gross insult to the Sovereign LORD of the universe.

⇒ It is wrong to worship any physical or visible image of God, wrong to worship any idol or anything else upon earth, even wrong to worship an invisible image of God created within the imagination of man.

⇒ It is even wrong to worship religious rituals; our worship and passion should be only for God Himself.

"To whom then will ye liken me, or shall I be equal? saith the Holy One" (Is.40:25)

God is Spirit. He has no physical form that can be seen with the human eye. Therefore, God is not to be worshipped through physical, visible objects. When God is worshipped in some visible form, the glory of the invisible God is degraded. Why? Because God is Spirit, omnipotent and omnipresent Spirit, the all-powerful and all-knowing Sovereign of the Universe, the Creator of all things that are in heaven and earth, both visible and invisible. God cannot be bottled up; His glory cannot be formed and sculpted into any image whatsoever. No imagination of man can picture God. Man's thoughts, descriptions, and images of God are totally incomplete and inadequate. As Spirit, He is out beyond the universe, surrounding and embracing the universe. No planet or star—no heavenly body—extends out beyond God's presence and knowledge.

As stated, God is Spirit and they that worship Him must worship Him in Spirit and in truth. The Scripture emphatically declares:

"God [is] a Spirit: and they that worship him must worship [him] in spirit and in truth" (Jn.4:24).
"For the invisible things of him from the creation of the world are clearly seen, being understood by the things that are made, even his eternal power and Godhead; so that they are without excuse: Because that, when they knew God, they glorified him not as God, neither were thankful; but became vain in their imaginations, and their foolish heart was darkened. Professing themselves to be wise, they became fools, And changed the glory of the uncorruptible God into an image made like to corruptible man, and to birds, and fourfooted beasts, and creeping things. Wherefore God also gave them up to uncleanness through the lusts of their own hearts, to dishonour their own bodies between themselves: Who changed the truth of God into a lie, and worshipped and served the creature more than the Creator, who is blessed for ever. Amen" (Ro.1:20-25).
"Little children, keep yourselves from idols. Amen" (1 Jn.5:21).
"Ye shall make you no idols nor graven image, neither rear you up a standing image, neither shall ye set up any image of stone in your land, to bow down unto it: for I am the LORD your God" (Le.26:1).
"Take ye therefore good heed unto yourselves; for ye saw no manner of similitude [form] on the day that the LORD spake unto you in Horeb out of the midst of the fire: Lest ye corrupt yourselves, and make you a graven image, the similitude of any figure, the likeness of male or female, The likeness of any beast that is on the earth, the likeness of any winged fowl that flieth in the air, The likeness of any thing that creepeth on the ground, the likeness of any fish that is in the waters beneath the earth: And lest thou lift up thine eyes unto heaven, and when thou seest the sun, and the moon, and the stars, even all the host of heaven, shouldest be driven to worship them, and serve them, which the LORD thy God hath divided unto all nations under the whole heaven" (De.4:15-19).
"Take heed to yourselves, that your heart be not deceived, and ye turn aside, and serve other gods, and worship them" (De.11:16).

Third, this commandment prohibits *covetousness*, prohibits craving after and seeking anything more than one craves after and seeks God (v.9, see Col.3:5). Scripture emphatically declares...

- "Covetousness...is idolatry" (Col.3:5).

Covetousness is craving and desiring something so much that a person makes it the primary thing in his life. The object becomes the first thing in a person's life, the major craving, the longing desire of the person's heart and life. A person can covet and make an idol out of anything:

⇒	sex	⇒	girlfriend	⇒	money	⇒	position	⇒	ritual
⇒	drugs	⇒	boyfriend	⇒	fame	⇒	business	⇒	ceremony
⇒	alcohol	⇒	recreation	⇒	power	⇒	job	⇒	crucifix or cross
⇒	family	⇒	sports	⇒	pornography	⇒	country		

A person's god or idol is that which he puts first in his life, that which he desires and craves the most, that to which he gives his life: his primary thoughts, energy, time, and money. Note what God said about man during the last days of human history:

⇒ they would be lovers of self (2 Ti.3:2)
⇒ they would be lovers of pleasure (2 Ti.3:4)
⇒ their god would be their stomachs (Ph.3:19)

DEUTERONOMY 5:7-15

"(For many walk, of whom I have told you often, and now tell you even weeping, that they are the enemies of the cross of Christ: Whose end is destruction, whose God is their belly, and whose glory is in their shame, who mind earthly things)" (Ph.3:18-19).

"This know also, that in the last days perilous times shall come. For men shall be lovers of their own selves, covetous, boasters, proud, blasphemers, disobedient to parents, unthankful, unholy, Without natural affection, trucebreakers, false accusers, incontinent, fierce, despisers of those that are good, Traitors, heady, highminded, lovers of pleasures more than lovers of God; Having a form of godliness, but denying the power thereof: from such turn away" (2 Ti.3:1-5).

Thought 1. Maxie Dunnam has a practical comment on this commandment that is well worth quoting at length:

God is unseen, a Spirit and Power invisible to our eyes. So, we need settings, symbols, places of worship to be vivid reminders of God. The problem comes when the symbol, the reminder, becomes a substitute, when it becomes an idol and takes the place of God.

There's a dramatic story of this in Numbers 21. In their wandering through the wilderness, the people of Israel were attacked and tortured by fiery serpents. Moses, on the instruction of God, made a bronze serpent and set it up on a pole. Those who had been bitten looked at the bronze serpent and were healed. Not much is made of that story as it is found in Numbers 21:6-9, but centuries later we find that bronze serpent making another brief appearance. This time, we find King Hezekiah breaking the serpent in pieces, because the people had been burning incense to it (2 Kings 18:4). What had happened? What Moses had used as a reminder of God's power prevailing over the poison of the serpents, bit by bit, had become a god itself.

This has happened in Christian history in relation to the cross and the crucifix. That which is to be a reminder of the love of the cross, meant to help men and women in looking at it to fix their hearts and minds on the One who bled and died there, becomes regarded with superstitious reverence. The cross, or the crucifix, becomes a holy thing. The symbol is identified and confused with the reality for which it stands.

The core lesson is this: whenever anyone or anything usurps the place that God should have in our lives, we're guilty of idolatry.

For most of us, that would not be a graven image such as a cross or a crucifix. But how easily money becomes an idol. We allow money—how we get it and how we use it—to edge God out of the number one place in our lives.

I've seen love in marriage distorted to the point that it usurps God's place in our lives. I've certainly seen love of country distorted to the point that it blinds people to God's call to justice and righteousness.

The making of idols usually means making the means an end. This happens all the time in the church. I know some people who do that with the Bible. The Bible itself becomes an idol. Listen carefully to people who passionately crusade, in their words, to "save the Bible." Look at their lives. We can angrily wage a war to protect the inerrancy of the Bible, and appear to be righteous in the cause, and still lose our souls. That's the problem Jesus was addressing when He said, "Not everyone who says to Me, LORD, LORD, will enter the Kingdom of Heaven, but those who do the will of My heavenly Father."

In all sorts of ways, we have committed the sin of idolatry by making the means an end. Even in our worship, we turn the liturgy, our means of worshipping God, into an end itself, so that the means and methods of worship become more important than the worship itself. We need to even look at...our spiritual disciplines. Spiritual discipline is for the purpose of facilitating our relationship to God. We pray and worship and study Scripture, sometimes we fast, to be open to God, to cultivate Christ's presence. But to make these disciplines ends in themselves, to make them the measurement of how holy we are, is making discipline a fetish. Not only are we in danger of turning others off when we zealously exaggerate these disciplines, they become idols.[7]

Thought 2. J. Vernon McGee also has an excellent application on this commandment.

Some people may feel that this passage does not apply to us today. Colossians 3:5 tells us that "...covetousness...is idolatry." Anything that you give yourself to, especially in abandonment, becomes your "god." Many people do not worship Bacchus, the cloven-footed Greek and Roman god of wine and revelry of long ago, but they worship the bottle just the same. There are millions of alcoholics in our country right now. The liquor interests like to tell us about how much of the tax burden they carry, when actually they do not pay a fraction of the bill for the casualties they cause by their product. A lot of propaganda is being fed to this generation and large groups of people are being brainwashed. Whether or not folk recognize it, they worship the god Bacchus.

Other people worship Aphrodite, that is, the goddess of sex. Some people worship money. Anything to which you give your time, heart, and soul, becomes your God. God says that we are not to have any gods before Him.[8]

"Wherefore should the heathen say, Where is now their God? But our God is in the heavens: he hath done whatsoever he hath pleased. Their idols are silver and gold, the work of men's hands. They have mouths, but they speak not: eyes have they, but they see not: They have ears, but they hear not: noses have they, but they smell not: They have hands, but they handle not: feet have they, but they walk not: neither speak they through their throat. They that make them are like unto them; so is every one that trusteth in them" (Ps.115:2-8).

---

[7] Maxie Dunnam. *The Preacher's Commentary on Exodus.* (Nashville, TN: Thomas Nelson, 1987, 2003), pp.255-256.
[8] J. Vernon McGee. *Thru The Bible*, Vol.1. (Nashville, TN: Thomas Nelson Publishers, 1981), p.267.

DEUTERONOMY 5:7-15

"They [idols] are upright as the palm tree, but speak not: they must needs be borne, because they cannot go. Be not afraid of them; for they cannot do evil, neither also is it in them to do good" (Je.10:5).

b. Why did God give this commandment? God gave this commandment for at least three reasons. (See DEEPER STUDY # 1—Ex.20:4-6 for more discussion.)

1) First, God prohibits the worship of idols because He is a jealous God. The Hebrew word for *jealous* means to be red in the face. God loves and cares for man. God does not want people living in error and following false gods that can do absolutely nothing to help them throughout life. Therefore, God is jealous—hot in the face—against anything that turns people away from the truth and from God Himself.

Note this fact: Scripture declares that idolatry is *spiritual adultery*; therefore, the displeasure of God against idolatry is rightly called jealousy.[9] Jealousy means that God has a sensitive nature, a nature of love. God is jealous of anything or anyone who threatens to take away the honor, recognition, or reverence that is due Him. Therefore, if a person gives his primary devotion, his primary attention, honor, time, energy, effort, or money to anything other than God Himself, he commits spiritual adultery against God. He turns away from God to something else. The result: God becomes jealous, red-hot against any person who is unfaithful to Him. Man must never forget: God does not tolerate unfaithfulness; He will never allow a rival to replace Him. Note what Scripture says:

⇒ God's jealousy will not allow His glory and honor ever to be transferred to another.

"I am the LORD: that is my name: and my glory will I not give to another, neither my praise to graven images" (Is.42:8).

"For mine own sake, even for mine own sake, will I do it: for how should my name be polluted? and I will not give my glory unto another" (Is.48:11).

⇒ God declares that His very name is *Jealous*; therefore, He absolutely will not tolerate the worship of any other god.

"But ye shall destroy their altars, break their images, and cut down their groves: For thou shalt worship no other god: for the LORD, whose name is Jealous, is a jealous God" (Ex.34:13-14).

⇒ God's jealousy arouses His anger against those who deny and hate Him.

"(For the LORD thy God is a jealous God among you) lest the anger of the LORD thy God be kindled against thee, and destroy thee from off the face of the earth" (De.6:15).

⇒ God's jealousy will judge all those who oppose Him.

"The LORD will not spare him [the idolater], but then the anger of the LORD and his jealousy shall smoke against that man, and all the curses that are written in this book shall lie upon him, and the LORD shall blot out his name from under heaven" (De.29:20; see 1 K.14:22; Ps.79:5; Is.42:13; Is.59:17; Eze.5:13; 16:38; 23:25; 36:5).

"God is jealous, and the LORD revengeth; the LORD revengeth, and is furious; the LORD will take vengeance on his adversaries, and he reserveth wrath for his enemies" (Na.1:2).

"Neither their silver nor their gold shall be able to deliver them in the day of the LORD'S wrath; but the whole land shall be devoured by the fire of his jealousy: for he shall make even a speedy riddance of all them that dwell in the land" (Zep.1:18; see Zep.3:8).

"He that overcometh shall inherit all things; and I will be his God, and he shall be my son. But the fearful, and unbelieving, and the abominable, and murderers, and whoremongers, and sorcerers, and idolaters, and all liars, shall have their part in the lake which burneth with fire and brimstone: which is the second death" (Re.21:7-8).

⇒ God's jealousy, His zeal, will vindicate His true people, His true followers.

"For out of Jerusalem shall go forth a remnant, and they that escape out of mount Zion: the zeal of the Lord of hosts shall do this" (2 K.19:31).

"Of the increase of his government and peace there shall be no end, upon the throne of David, and upon his kingdom, to order it, and to establish it with judgment and with justice from henceforth even for ever. The zeal of the Lord of hosts will perform this" (Is.9:7; see Is.26:11).

"Therefore thus saith the Lord GOD; Now will I bring again the captivity of Jacob, and have mercy upon the whole house of Israel, and will be jealous for my holy name" (Eze.39:25).

"Then will the Lord be jealous for his land, and pity his people" (Joel 2:18; Zec.1:14).

"Thus saith the Lord of hosts; I was jealous for Zion with great jealousy, and I was jealous for her with great fury" (Zec.8:2).

⇒ God's jealousy demands total allegiance, loyalty, and devotion.

"For thou shalt worship no other god: for the Lord, whose name is Jealous, is a jealous God" (Ex.34:14).

---

[9] Matthew Henry. *Matthew Henry's Commentary*, Vol. 1. (Old Tappan, NJ: Fleming H. Revell Co., n.d.), p.359.

DEUTERONOMY 5:7-15

> "And Joshua said unto the people, Ye cannot serve the LORD: for he is an holy God; he is a jealous God; he will not forgive your transgressions nor your sins" (Jos.24:19).

2) Second, God prohibits the worship of idols because the influence of idolatry is passed down from the parents to their children. If a person's worship is false, he leads his children and grandchildren into false worship. What he does greatly influences and affects his family.

We must never forget this one fact: the human race is a living organism. What one person does affects other persons. This is clearly seen in acts of love, care, benevolence, war, lawlessness, drunkenness, drugs, immorality—in all the acts of behavior. The closer a person is to others, the more the person's actions affect them. People influence people, and the point of this verse is that parents influence children, greatly influence them. A mother who is a drug addict is likely to lead her children to use drugs. A father who loves and puts sports before God leads his children to love and put things before God.

Note that Scripture uses the word *hate* (v.9). If parents deny and *hate* God and worship idols, the children will be greatly influenced to deny and *hate* God and worship idols. Consequently, God's judgment falls upon the children for generations. The result and consequences of idolatry are terrible. The worship of idols, just like all other behavior, influences the children of a family. Children are conditioned, heavily influenced by the behavior of their parents and their surroundings. Therefore, if a parent worships idols, most likely the children will worship idols. And all idolaters shall be judged by God. Therefore, the sin of idolatry and the judgment upon idolatry are passed down from generation to generation. Terrible consequences! All due to the *sins of the fathers and mothers*, especially the evil sin of idolatry.

This is what is known as the *judicial judgment of God*, a judgment that is justly deserved. (See DEEPER STUDY # 1—Jn.12:39-41; note—Ro.1:24 for more discussion.) If a parent sows the seed of idolatry, he is usually going to bear children who will be greatly influenced by his behavior. The children will deny and hate God and worship the idols of man. But note: this does not mean that God holds a child guilty for the sins of his parents. God is not talking about the guilt of sin. He is talking about the results, the consequences of sin. Every person shall bear the judgment and punishment for his own sin. No person will ever be judged and punished for the sins of others.

> "The fathers shall not be put to death for the children, neither shall the children be put to death for the fathers: every man shall be put to death for his own sin" (De.24:16).

Thought 1. God punishes sin, the sins of all people for all generations. God executes justice upon the sins of the fathers and the sins of the children. No generation of sin ever escapes the judgment of God.

> "[God] now commandeth all men every where to repent: Because he hath appointed a day, in the which he will judge the world in righteousness by that man whom he hath ordained; whereof he hath given assurance unto all men, in that he hath raised him from the dead" (Ac.17:30-31).

> "And to you who are troubled rest with us, when the LORD Jesus shall be revealed from heav-en with his mighty angels, In flaming fire taking vengeance on them that know not God, and that obey not the gospel of our Lord Jesus Christ: Who shall be punished with everlasting destruction from the presence of the LORD, and from the glory of his power" (2 Th.1:7-9).

> "And Enoch also, the seventh from Adam, prophesied of these, saying, Behold, the LORD cometh with ten thousands of his saints, To execute judgment upon all, and to convince all that are ungodly among them of all their ungodly deeds which they have ungodly committed, and of all their hard speeches which ungodly sinners have spoken against him" (Jude 14-15).

> "Behold, it is written before me: I will not keep silence, but will recompense, even recompense into their bosom, Your iniquities, and the iniquities of your fathers together, saith the LORD, which have burned incense upon the mountains, and blasphemed me upon the hills: therefore will I measure their former work into their bosom" (Is.65:6-7).

> "Then shalt thou say unto them, Because your fathers have forsaken me, saith the LORD, and have walked after other gods, and have served them, and have worshipped them, and have forsaken me, and have not kept my law; And ye have done worse than your fathers; for, behold, ye walk every one after the imagination of his evil heart, that they may not hearken unto me: Therefore will I cast you out of this land into a land that ye know not, neither ye nor your fathers; and there shall ye serve other gods day and night; where I will not show you favour" (Je.16:11-13).

> "I the LORD search the heart, I try the reins, even to give every man according to his ways, and according to the fruit of his doings" (Je.17:10).

> "Behold, all souls are mine; as the soul of the father, so also the soul of the son is mine: the soul that sinneth, it shall die" (Eze.18:4).

3) Third, God prohibits the worship of idols because the influence of a loving and obedient parent lasts forever, for a thousand generations. Note that the sin and punishment of idolatry is passed down for three or four generations, but the love and obedience of parents is passed down to their children for *thousands of generations*. This is what is known as Hebrew parallelism: it does not mean thousands of people, but thousands of generations. Note exactly what the verse says: God's mercy is shown to thousands of those who love and obey Him, shown for thousands of generations. Parents who love God and keep God's commandments...
- will influence their children for thousands of generations
- will have the mercy of God showered upon thousands of their children for thousands of generations

DEUTERONOMY 5:7-15

This shows the awesome influence of parents upon their children and the absolute necessity for loving and obeying God. Judgment will fall upon those who disobey this commandment—fall upon both the parents and their children for three or four generations. But God's mercy will be showered upon those who obey this commandment, be showered upon thousands of children for thousands of generations.

However, note a most significant fact: God's mercy is showered only upon the obedient, only upon those who love God and keep His commandments, the very commandments He is spelling out in this passage.

> "And the LORD was with Jehoshaphat, because he walked in the first ways of his father David, and sought not unto Baalim" (2 Chr.17:3).
>
> "And he [Uzziah] did that which was right in the sight of the LORD, according to all that his father Amaziah did" (2 Chr.26:4).
>
> "Train up a child in the way he should go: and when he is old, he will not depart from it" (Pr.22:6).
>
> "When I call to remembrance the unfeigned faith that is in thee [Timothy], which dwelt first in thy grandmother Lois, and thy mother Eunice; and I am persuaded that in thee also" (2 Ti.1:5).

[3] **(5:11) Cursing—Profanity—Swearing—Vulgarity—Foul Language—Name, of God—Obedience—Commandment, the Ten—God, Name of:** What is forbidden by this commandment: "You shall never misuse, never take the name of the LORD God in vain"?

OUTLINE	SCRIPTURE
3. Commandment 3—*God's name*: Never misuse the LORD's name a. He is the LORD your God b. He will hold you accountable	11 Thou shalt not take the name of the LORD thy God in vain: for the LORD will not hold *him* guiltless that taketh his name in vain.

a. How is this Scripture broken or violated? The Hebrew word *vain* or *misuse* (lassaw) means empty, meaningless, thoughtless, senseless, frivolous, worthless, groundless. It means using God's name in a thoughtless and insincere way. The root of the word (shawu) has the idea of a vapor that fades and vanishes away, a vapor that is meaningless and worthless.[10] It also has the idea of a tempest, a storm, a tornado that is erratic, that jumps here and there, that causes destruction and devastation, that is totally senseless and destructive.[11]

b. Why did God give this commandment? Why does God forbid vulgarity? Why must we never misuse God's name, never swear, curse, nor damn anything upon earth, never damn anything in creation? Two reasons are given within the commandment itself.

1) First, you must not use vulgarity or misuse God's name for a very clear reason: because the LORD is *your* God (vv.11). If you have accepted Christ as your Savior, then the LORD has saved you from Egypt, from the enslavements and bondages of this earth. He has saved you from sin, shame, and death. He has saved you from the bondages of the flesh, from...

- adultery and immorality
- drunkenness and carousing
- false worship and idolatry
- hatred and strife
- jealousy and envy
- wild living and sensuality
- cursing and lying
- sorcery and witchcraft
- anger and division
- selfish ambition and greed

And on and on. God has saved you from all this to a life of love, joy, and peace. Moreover, He has saved you from death and the judgment to come. He has saved you from hell itself. You are going to live forever, eternally with Him. The LORD is now your God. How could you ever misuse His name?

Now note: if you have never accepted Christ, then all the above can be yours. God will save you from the enslavements and bondages of this earth and give you life eternal. The point is this: the drive and energy of your heart must be not to misuse the name of the LORD God, the Savior of the world. The drive and energy of your life must be to stand in awe of His name: to praise, worship, serve, and bear testimony to His name.

> "Enter into his gates with thanksgiving, and into his courts with praise: be thankful unto him, and bless his name" (Ps.100:4).
>
> "Sanctify the LORD of hosts himself; and let him be your fear, and let him be your dread" (Is.8:13).
>
> "For thus saith the high and lofty One that inhabiteth eternity, whose name is Holy; I dwell in the high and holy place, with him also that is of a contrite and humble spirit, to revive the spirit of the humble, and to revive the heart of the contrite ones" (Is.57:15).
>
> "And being found in fashion as a man, he humbled himself, and became obedient unto death, even the death of the cross. Wherefore God also hath highly exalted him, and given him a name which is above every name: That at the name of Jesus every knee should bow, of things in heaven, and things in earth, and things under the earth: And that every tongue should confess that Jesus Christ is LORD, to the glory of God the Father" (Ph.2:8-11).

---

10 William Wilson. *Wilson's Old Testament Word Studies*. (McLean, VA: MacDonald Publishing Company, n.d.), p.465.
11 James Strong. *Strong's Exhaustive Concordance of the Bible*, #7723.

DEUTERONOMY 5:7-15

"By him therefore let us offer the sacrifice of praise to God continually, that is, the fruit of our lips giving thanks to his name" (He.13:15).

"But ye are a chosen generation, a royal priesthood, an holy nation, a peculiar people; that ye should show forth the praises of him who hath called you out of darkness into his marvellous light" (1 Pe.2:9).

2) Second, you must not use vulgarity, must not misuse God's name for a terrifying reason: because the LORD holds you accountable if you misuse His name. The word *guiltless* (waqah) means that God will not count us clear or free from blame. He will not count us clean or pure, innocent or guiltless. God will not acquit us, not let us go unpunished.

A man may curse God or swear falsely to his wife or neighbor or even to some jury, and he may not be corrected or punished. But God knows that the man cursed His name or lied, and Scripture is clear: God will punish him. God will avenge the person who insulted His great and glorious name. In fact, note what Scripture says: the person who curses and misuses God's name stands as an *enemy of God*.

"Thine enemies take thy name in vain" (Ps.139:20).

⇒ The person who uses profanity openly declares that he is the sworn enemy of the high and holy God. This person is condemned; God will avenge His name and judge the *curser*.

⇒ The person who swears falsely deliberately declares that he is the sworn enemy of the true and righteous God. The person is condemned; God will avenge His name and judge the *false swearer*.

⇒ The person who uses God's name in an irreverent way, who is careless and thoughtless in the use of God's name, will not be guiltless. He will be condemned. God will avenge His name and judge the *irreverent person*.

⇒ The person who uses God's name hypocritically stands as the sworn enemy of God. The hypocrite is condemned. God will avenge His name and severely judge the *hypocrite*.

⇒ The person who misuses God's name—the bold sinner—must appear before God and give an account for his cursing and lying and for his irreverent use of God's holy name. If a person curses God, he curses the name of the high and lofty One, the name of the LORD God Himself, the only living and true God, the only holy name that could have saved him from death and judgment to come. God will avenge His name and judge the *bold sinner*.

"As he loved cursing, so let it come unto him: as he delighted not in blessing, so let it be far from him" (Ps.109:17).

"And I will come near to you to judgment; and I will be a swift witness against the sorcerers, and against the adulterers, and against false swearers, and against those that oppress the hireling [hired laborer] in his wages, the widow, and the fatherless, and that turn aside the stranger from his right, and fear not me, saith the LORD of hosts" (Mal.3:5).

"And to you who are troubled rest with us, when the LORD Jesus shall be revealed from heaven with his mighty angels, In flaming fire taking vengeance on them that know not God, and that obey not the gospel of our Lord Jesus Christ" (2 Th.1:7-8).

"And as it is appointed unto men once to die, but after this the judgment" (He.9:27).

"But the heavens and the earth, which are now, by the same word are kept in store, reserved unto fire against the day of judgment and perdition of ungodly men" (2 Pe.3:7).

"And Enoch also, the seventh from Adam, prophesied of these, saying, Behold, the LORD cometh with ten thousands of his saints, To execute judgment upon all, and to convince all that are ungodly among them of all their ungodly deeds which they have ungodly committed, and of all their hard speeches which ungodly sinners have spoken against him" (Jude 14-15).

"But the fearful, and unbelieving, and the abominable, and murderers, and whore-mongers, and sorcerers, and idolaters, and all liars [cursers, false swearers], shall have their part in the lake which burneth with fire and brimstone: which is the second death" (Re.21:8).

4 (5:12-15) **Sabbath—Sunday—Worship—Work—Obedience—Commandment, the Ten**: What is the charge of the fourth commandment? "Observe and keep the Sabbath day holy." Several preliminary facts need to be noted.

First, the word *keep* or *observe* (shamar or samar) means to hedge about; to guard, protect, keep, observe, preserve, obey, watch over, maintain, keep secure, defend. It has the idea of building a guard to protect the Sabbath. The command is imperative, a strong, strong imperative: "You must observe and keep the Sabbath; guard and protect the Sabbath. You must obey the Sabbath day and keep it holy."

Second, the Hebrew word "Sabbath does not mean the seventh day (Saturday) as so many people think. The word *Sabbath* (shabbath) means to rest, to repose, to cease. It means to cease from work, to rest from work.

This is significant, for God is charging us to keep the Sabbath, the day of rest and worship. He is not specifying a particular day of the week when man is to worship and rest. God simply says, work six days and then rest on the seventh day. This fact is important for industrialized and technological societies. Why? Because so many people *have* to work on Saturday or on Sunday, on the day set aside by their religion as the day of worship and rest. In many cases, factories cannot shut down their huge furnaces, boilers, and machines without damaging them mechanically. They have to be operated continually; therefore, thousands upon thousands of people have to work on Saturday and Sunday. The same is true with many service industries and other businesses.

Thought 1. When businesses have to operate seven days a week, what are the employees of these businesses to do about worship and rest? Two very practical things must be done throughout the remaining generations of history:
⇒ The church must provide other services through the week for worship and rest, provide them for people who have to work on Saturday or Sunday.
⇒ People who work on the regular day of worship and rest must still worship God and rest at the alternate services and days scheduled by the church.

"Not forsaking the assembling of ourselves together, as the manner of some is; but exhorting one another: and so much the more, as ye see the day approaching" (He.10:25).
"And they went into Capernaum; and straightway on the sabbath day he [Jesus Christ] entered into the synagogue, and taught" (Mk.1:21).
"And he came to Nazareth, where he had been brought up: and, as his custom was, he went into the synagogue on the sabbath day, and stood up for to read" (Lu.4:16).
"But when they departed from Perga, they came to Antioch in Pisidia, and went into the synagogue on the sabbath day, and sat down" (Ac.13:14).

When the law was given by Moses, the Jews set aside the seventh day, Saturday, as their day of worship and rest. Today, others follow their practice. But the largest body of Christian believers have switched their day of worship and rest from the last day of the week to the first day of the week, from Saturday to Sunday. Why?
⇒ Because Jesus Christ burst loose from the bonds of death on the first day of the week. Believers wish to celebrate His glorious resurrection and the great hope of their salvation on the very day He arose.
⇒ Because the first day of the week is called "the LORD's day" (Re.1:10). Believers wish to worship on the LORD's day.
⇒ Because the early followers of Christ switched their day of worship and rest to the first day of the week. The tradition has continued down through the centuries.

"And upon the first day of the week, when the disciples came together to break bread, Paul preached unto them, ready to depart on the morrow; and continued his speech until midnight" (Ac.20:7).
"Upon the first day of the week let every one of you lay by him in store, as God hath prospered him, that there be no gatherings when I come" (1 Co.16:2).

Third, the Sabbath, the day of rest and worship, is to be kept "holy" (see DEEPER STUDY # 1—De.5:12-15 for more discussion).

OUTLINE	SCRIPTURE	SCRIPTURE	OUTLINE

4. Commandment 4—God's day: Observe & keep the Sabbath day holy^{DS1}
a. The commandment:
  1) Work for six days
  2) Set apart the Sabbath to the LORD for worship
  3) Do no work whatsoever on the Sabbath: No person & no animal
	12 Keep the sabbath day to sanctify it, as the LORD thy God hath commanded thee.
	13 Six days thou shalt labour, and do all thy work:
	14 But the seventh day is the sabbath of the LORD thy God: in it thou shalt not do any work, thou, nor thy son, nor thy daughter, nor thy manservant, nor thy maidservant, nor thine ox, nor thine ass, nor any of thy cattle, nor thy
		stranger that is within thy gates; that thy manservant and thy maidservant may rest as well as thou.
		15 And remember that thou wast a servant in the land of Egypt, and that the LORD thy God brought thee out thence through a mighty hand and by a stretched out arm: therefore the LORD thy God commanded thee to keep the sabbath day.
			b. The reasons
			  1) Because you are to remember the redemption of God: His great deliverance from Egypt (a symbol of the world)
			  2) Because the LORD your God commands you to keep the Sabbath day

a. This commandment includes three clear instructions. God issues three demands, three *you shalls* concerning the Sabbath commandment:
⇒ (You *shall*) observe the Sabbath day by keeping it holy (v.12).
⇒ Six days you *shall* labor and do all your work (v.13).
⇒ The seventh day is a Sabbath to the LORD your God. On it you *shall* not do any work (v.14).

1) You shall work six days but *only* six days a week (v.13). This commandment declares that man is to work, to work diligently. From the very beginning of creation, God commanded man to work.
⇒ God told Adam (man) to dress and keep the Garden of Eden, to develop and maintain it.

"And the LORD God took the man, and put him into the garden of Eden to dress it and to keep it" (Ge.2:15).

⇒ Scripture clearly says that a man must work if he is to eat and meet his needs.

"For even when we were with you, this we commanded you, that if any would not work, neither should he eat. For we hear that there are some which walk among you disorderly, working not at all,

DEUTERONOMY 5:7-15

but are busybodies. Now them that are such we command and exhort by our Lord Jesus Christ, that with quietness they work, and eat their own bread" (2 Th.3:10-12).

⇒ Scripture also says that a person should look after his own affairs and work with his own hands.

"And that ye study to be quiet, and to do your own business, and to work with your own hands, as we commanded you" (1 Th.4:11).

What about people who have enough money, so much that they do not have to work? They have worked hard and earned huge amounts of money or have inherited large estates or won a large sum. Does this commandment apply to them? Yes. No person is ever to sit idle nor live an extravagant lifestyle, wasting and hoarding wealth. Scripture warns us: we are responsible to meet the needs of the world. Every person is to work as long as he lives, helping to conquer the evils of this earth—all the ravaging and destructive forces that bring suffering and destruction to man:

- hunger
- thirst
- disease
- loneliness
- emptiness
- death, both physical and spiritual

"Jesus said unto him, If thou wilt be perfect, go [and] sell that thou hast, and give to the poor, and thou shalt have treasure in heaven: and come [and] follow me. But when the young man heard that saying, he went away sorrowful: for he had great possessions. Then said Jesus unto his disciples, Verily I say unto you, That a rich man shall hardly enter into the kingdom of heaven. And again I say unto you, It is easier for a camel to go through the eye of a needle, than for a rich man to enter into the kingdom of God" (Mt.19:21-24).

"And he spake a parable unto them, saying, The ground of a certain rich man brought forth plentifully: And he thought within himself, saying, What shall I do, because I have no room where to bestow my fruits? And he said, This will I do: I will pull down my barns, and build greater; and there will I bestow all my fruits and my goods. And I will say to my soul, Soul, thou hast much goods laid up for many years; take thine ease, eat, drink, [and] be merry. But God said unto him, [Thou] fool, this night thy soul shall be required of thee: then whose shall those things be, which thou hast provided? So [is] he that layeth up treasure for himself, and is not rich toward God" (Lu.12:16-21).

What about the people who are lazy and slothful, people who do not give an honest day's work or else shun work altogether? Again, Scripture warns the lazy and slothful.

"Yet a little sleep, a little slumber, a little folding of the hands to sleep: So shall thy poverty come as one that travelleth, and thy want as an armed man" (Pr.6:10-11).

"For the drunkard and the glutton shall come to poverty: and drowsiness shall clothe a man with rags" (Pr.23:21).

"He that tilleth his land shall have plenty of bread: but he that followeth after vain persons shall have poverty enough" (Pr.28:19).

Man is to work six days a week. God created man with a nature that must work. There is within man a restlessness, a drive, an energy to be active, to work and achieve and conquer. Man never experiences complete fulfillment and satisfaction unless he works and senses that he achieves something worthwhile. If man does not direct his energy into profitable work, then he directs it to worthless or even destructive activities: to lawlessness, gangs, mobs, war, sex, alcohol, drugs, over-eating—all to the damage of others or himself. It is this—a lack of work and a lack of sensing fulfillment and satisfaction—that causes so much lawlessness and problems for society.

But note this fact: man is to work six days a week, but *only* six days a week.

2) You shall set apart the Sabbath day to the LORD: you are to worship on the Sabbath day (v.12). It is His day...
- a day of special worship
- a day of extended worship and praise
- a day of concentration and focus upon God
- a day of special, very special holiness (See DEEPER STUDY # 1—De.5:12-15 for more discussion.)

3) You shall not do any work on the Sabbath day, none whatsoever (v.14). Note how strongly God expects this commandment to be obeyed: no person is to work seven days a week...
- not you (male or female)
- not your son or daughter
- not your slaves (employees)
- not your animals
- not even a stranger

Thought 1. The fourth commandment was given for our good. Without the Sabbath rest, we would soon break our bodies down. We would be constantly weary, worn out, and burned out. Productivity would soon decline. This has been proven time and again in dictatorial nations and slave markets that have demanded constant, unbroken work with no rest for its labor force. Productivity declined sharply, as well as health, physical strength, and mental alertness and ability.

Resting one day a week is an absolute essential for the human body. Business and labor, individuals and groups—we all must protect our bodies and the productivity of our society and economies. How? By obeying God's fourth commandment: Remember the Sabbath day; keep it holy—do not work on the Sabbath. Allow our bodies and minds to rest one day a week.

DEUTERONOMY 5:7-15

"For in six days the LORD made heaven and earth, the sea, and all that in them is, and rested the seventh day: wherefore the LORD blessed the sabbath day, and hallowed it" (Ex.20:11).

"Six days thou shalt do thy work, and on the seventh day thou shalt rest: that thine ox and thine ass may rest, and the son of thy handmaid, and the stranger, may be refreshed" (Ex.23:12).

"Ye shall keep the sabbath therefore; for it is holy unto you" (Ex.31:14).

b. Why did God give this commandment? God gives two strong reasons why the Sabbath is to be observed and kept holy (v.15).

1) Man is to remember the redemption of God, the mighty hand of His salvation (v.15). God had delivered His people from Egyptian slavery, saved them from the most horrible and terrible fate imaginable. He was therefore worthy of worship and praise.

This was the first purpose of the Sabbath day: to remember and never forget the redemption of God. Man is to take one day a week and focus upon the mighty hand of God's glorious salvation.

"Blessed *be* the LORD God of Israel; for he hath visited and redeemed his people" (Lu.1:68).

"In whom we have redemption through his blood, the forgiveness of sins, according to the riches of his grace" (Ep.1:7).

"Forasmuch as ye know that ye were not redeemed with corruptible things, *as* silver and gold, from your vain conversation *received* by tradition from your fathers" (1 Pe.1:18).

"He sent redemption unto his people: he hath commanded his covenant for ever: holy and reverend *is* his name" (Ps.111:9).

"Let Israel hope in the LORD: for with the LORD *there is* mercy, and with him *is* plenteous redemption" (Ps.130:7).

2) Man is to remember the Sabbath for another very clear reason: because the LORD your God commands you to keep the Sabbath day (v.15). He is "your God." You belong to Him. You are expected, obligated to keep the Sabbath, responsible to worship Him and to rest one day a week.

"For the Son of man is LORD even of the sabbath day" (Mt.12:8).

"Therefore the Son of man is LORD also of the sabbath" (Mk.2:28).

"And thou shalt take no gift: for the gift blindeth the wise, and perverteth the words of the righteous" (Ex.23:8).

"Speak thou also unto the children of Israel, saying, Verily my sabbaths ye shall keep: for it is a sign between me and you throughout your generations; that ye may know that I *am* the LORD that doth sanctify you" (Ex.31:13).

"If thou turn away thy foot from the sabbath, *from* doing thy pleasure on my holy day; and call the sabbath a delight, the holy of the LORD, honourable; and shalt honour him, not doing thine own ways, nor finding thine own pleasure, nor speaking *thine own* words" (Is.58:13-14).

DEEPER STUDY # 1
(5:12-15) **Holy** (qados): means sanctified, separated, set apart, devoted, dedicated, consecrated, hallowed, honored, made sacred. It means to be pure, clean, and free from all pollution and defilement, from all sin and evil. It means to be totally different and distinct from anything else, from all the corruption that is in the world.[12]

- The Sabbath is to be a day set apart, devoted, and dedicated to God, a day for worship and rest.
- The Sabbath is to be a day hallowed, honored, and made sacred in obedience to God and His command.
- The Sabbath is to be a day that *focuses our minds* upon living pure and clean lives, lives free from all pollution and defilement, sin and evil.
- The Sabbath is to be a day that is totally different and distinct from all other days of the week with their busy schedules that pull our thoughts away from God.

"Exalt the LORD our God, and worship at his holy hill; for the LORD our God is holy" (Ps.99:9).

"Wherefore come out from among them, and be ye separate, saith the Lord, and touch not the unclean thing; and I will receive you, And will be a Father unto you, and ye shall be my sons and daughters, saith the Lord Almighty. Having therefore these promises, dearly beloved, let us cleanse ourselves from all filthiness of the flesh and spirit, perfecting holiness in the fear of God" (2 Co.6:17-7:1).

"Follow peace with all men, and holiness, without which no man shall see the Lord" (He.12:14).

"Because it is written, Be ye holy; for I am holy" (1 Pe.1:16).

"Who shall not fear thee, O Lord, and glorify thy name? for thou only art holy: for all nations shall come and worship before thee; for thy judgments are made manifest" (Re.15:4).

---

[12] Harris, Archer, Waltke. *Theological Wordbook of the New Testament*. (Chicago, IL: Moody Bible Institute of Chicago, 1980), pp.786-789; Vine, Unger, White. *Vine's Complete Expository Dictionary of Old and New Testament Words*. (Nashville, TN: Thomas Nelson Publishers, 1985), pp.113-114; Francis Brown. *The New Brown-Driver-Briggs-Gesenius Hebrew-English Lexicon*. (Peabody, MA: Hendrickson Publishers, 1979), pp.872-873.

DEUTERONOMY 5:16-21

OUTLINE	SCRIPTURE	
	C. The Ten Commandments (Part 2): The Laws Governing Man's Duty to Others, 5:16-21	

1. Commandment 5—*man's parents*
 a. The commandment: Honor your father & mother
 b. The reasons
    1) Will live longer
    2) Will help things go better—far better: Live a victorious life
 2. Commandment 6—*man's life*^{DS1,2}
	16 Honour thy father and thy mother, as the LORD thy God hath commanded thee; that thy days may be prolonged, and that it may go well with thee, in the land which the LORD thy God giveth thee.
	 17 Thou shalt not kill.
	 18 Neither shalt thou commit adultery.
	 19 Neither shalt thou steal.
	 20 Neither shalt thou bear false witness against thy neighbour.
	 21 Neither shalt thou desire thy neighbour's wife, neither shalt thou covet thy neighbour's house, his field, or his manservant, or his maidservant, his ox, or his ass, or any *thing* that *is* thy neighbour's.
		3. Commandment 7—*man's family*: Forbids adultery
		 4. Commandment 8—*man's property*
		 5. Commandment 9—*man's word*: Forbids lying or speaking falsely against anyone
		 6. Commandment 10—*man's desires & security*: Forbids coveting anything that belongs to your neighbor—his wife, house, land, servant, animals, or anything else

DIVISION III

THE SECOND GREAT THEME PREACHED BY GOD'S AGED SERVANT (PART 1): REMEMBER THE TEN COMMANDMENTS—THE FUNDAMENTAL LAWS TO GOVERN MAN AND SOCIETY, 4:44–11:32

C. The Ten Commandments (Part 2): The Laws Governing Man's Duty to Others, 5:16-21

(5:16-21) **Introduction—Disrespect of Parents—Murder—Adultery—Stealing—Lying—Covetousness**: evil is sweeping the earth today. Note how these evils attack every area of society and human life:

⇒ Disrespect of parents destroys family life, the men, women, and children of a nation.
⇒ Murder destroys human life as well as the dignity and value of life, destroys the greatest resource that a nation has—its citizens.
⇒ Adultery destroys the most precious qualities of life and relationships—the qualities of love, trust, loyalty, respect, fulfillment, perseverance, care, and self-esteem.
⇒ Stealing destroys property rights and relationships, one of the most basic rights of a neighbor and of the nation and government.
⇒ Lying destroys the very foundation of relationships and society, causes the collapse of any relationship, organization, group, or nation. No relationship can stand upon lies.
⇒ Covetousness destroys all rights upon which everything is based.

Every evil found upon earth can be found in these six basic evils. (See Introductions to each of the commandments—Ex.20:12-17 for more discussion of this fact.) But note a marvelous fact: God counteracts these terrible evils, and He does so in a very simple way, using very simple words. The evils that people do to one another are counteracted in the last six of the Ten Commandments. This is clearly seen in this passage: *The Ten Commandments (Part 2): The Laws Governing Man's Duty to Others*, 5:16-21.

1. Commandment 5 concerns man's parents (v.16).
2. Commandment 6 concerns man's life (v.17).
3. Commandment 7 concerns man's family: forbids adultery (v.18).
4. Commandment 8 concerns man's property (v.19).
5. Commandment 9 concerns man's word: forbids lying or speaking falsely against anyone (v.20).
6. Commandment 10 concerns man's desires and security: forbids coveting anything that belongs to your neighbor—his wife, house, land, servant, animals, or anything else (v.21).

1 (5:16) **Obedience—Children—Parents—Family—Father—Mother—Commandments, the Ten**: commandment five is, "Honor your father and mother." The first four commandments covered our duty to God. Now, once we have done our duty to God, note what our very next duty is: to honor our parents. This is the divine order: God *first*, then our parents.

OUTLINE	SCRIPTURE

1. Commandment 5—*man's parents*
 a. The commandment: Honor your father & mother
 b. The reasons
    1) Will live longer
    2) Will help things go better—far better: Live a victorious life
	16 Honour thy father and thy mother, as the LORD thy God hath commanded thee; that thy days may be prolonged, and that it may go well with thee, in the land which the LORD thy God giveth thee.

DEUTERONOMY 5:16-21

a. Note six points about the charge of this commandment.
1) The Hebrew word *honor* (kabed or kabedl) means to respect, esteem, and highly regard; to set apart and count as distinguished. We are to respect, esteem, and highly regard our parents. We are to set apart our parents and count them as distinct, distinguished. There is even the idea of reverence in the word *honor*: we are to *reverence* our parents. The Greek word for *honor* (timao) pictures exactly what is meant: it means that we are to esteem and value our parents as precious (Amplified Bible); to show them respect, reverence, kindness, and obedience. Matthew Henry says that in practical terms, the commandment means we are to...
- respect our parents, reverence them
- obey our parents
- submit to the rebukes, instructions, and corrections of our parents
- listen to our parents' advice, direction, and concern
- comfort our parents[1]

Thought 1. What does God mean by *honoring our parents*? Scripture tells us:

⇒ To honor means to obey and respect our parents.

"For Moses said, Honour thy father and thy mother; and, Whoso curseth father or mother, let him die the death" (Mk.7:10).
"Children, obey your parents in the LORD: for this is right. Honour thy father and mother; (which is the first commandment with promise;) That it may be well with thee, and thou mayest live long on the earth" (Ep.6:1-3).
"Children, obey your parents in all things: for this is well pleasing unto the LORD" (Col.3:20).
"Honour thy father and thy mother: that thy days may be long upon the land which the LORD thy God giveth thee" (Ex.20:12).
"Honour thy father and thy mother, as the LORD thy God hath commanded thee; that thy days may be prolonged, and that it may go well with thee, in the land which the LORD thy God giveth thee" (De.5:16).
"For God commanded, saying, Honour thy father and mother: and, He that curseth father or mother, let him die the death" (Mt.15:4).

⇒ To honor means to listen to the instructions of our parents; to obey the instructions, never forsaking them.

"My son, hear the instruction of thy father, and forsake not the law of thy mother" (Pr.1:8).
"Hear, ye children, the instruction of a father, and attend to know understanding....Hear, O my son, and receive my sayings; and the years of thy life shall be many. I have taught thee in the way of wisdom; I have led thee in right paths. When thou goest, thy steps shall not be straitened [hampered, NIV]; and when thou runnest, thou shalt not stumble. Take fast hold of instruction; let her not go: keep her; for she is thy life" (Pr.4:1, 10-13).
"My son, keep thy father's commandment, and forsake not the law of thy mother" (Pr.6:20).

⇒ To honor means to listen to our parents and never despise them when they are old.

"Hearken unto thy father that begat thee, and despise not thy mother when she is old" (Pr.23:22).

⇒ To honor means to be wise, never foolish.

"A wise son maketh a glad father: but a foolish son is the heaviness of his mother" (Pr.10:1).
"A wise son maketh a glad father: but a foolish man despiseth his mother" (Pr.15:20).

⇒ To honor means to have a testimony of pure and right behavior.

"Even a child is known by his doings, whether his work [behavior, conduct] be pure, and whether it be right" (Pr.20:11).

⇒ To honor means to respect and reverence our parents when they are elderly.

"Ye shall fear every man his mother, and his father, and keep my sabbaths: I am the LORD your God" (Le.19:3).
"Thou shalt rise up before the hoary [gray] head, and honour the face of the old man, and fear thy God: I am the LORD" (Le.19:32).
"And Elihu the son of Barachel the Buzite answered and said, I am young, and ye are very old; wherefore I was afraid, and durst not show you mine opinion" (Jb.32:6).
"Hearken unto thy father that begat thee, and despise not thy mother when she is old" (Pr.23:22).

---

[1] *Matthew Henry's Commentary*, Vol.1, pp.361-362.

DEUTERONOMY 5:16-21

⇒ To honor means to accept the true faith of our parents, their belief in God's Son, the Lord Jesus Christ.

> "When I call to remembrance the unfeigned faith that is in thee, which dwelt first in thy grandmother Lois, and thy mother Eunice; and I am persuaded that in thee also" (2 Ti.1:5).
>
> "And that from a child thou hast known the holy scriptures, which are able to make thee wise unto salvation through faith which is in Christ Jesus" (2 Ti.3:15).

⇒ To honor means to respect our parents so much that it carries over to others, honoring and respecting all persons.

> "Rebuke not an elder, but intreat him as a father; and the younger men as brethren" (1 Ti.5:1).

2) Note that mothers are to be honored just as much as fathers, and fathers just as much as mothers: "[Children] honor your father and your mother" (v.16; see Ex.20:12). Mothers and fathers are placed on equal footing. God Himself honors and respects mothers as much as fathers and charges all children to honor each equally.

3) Note that every person within the family is mentioned: the child, mother, and father. If our mothers and fathers are living, we are to honor and respect them. But note this fact as well: every person in the world, whether young or old (adult), is the child of some father and mother.

The implication is clear: the families of the earth and the world as a whole are to be filled with honor and respect. Honor and respect are to flood the hearts and lives of our families, flowing out and flooding society and civilization, and spreading throughout the world. This is God's will; this is one of the main reasons God has given this commandment.

Note: the family is the basic unit of society, the very foundation of society. If honor and respect control the behavior of the family, it will help to control the behavior of our communities and society. God wants *honor and respect* to be the prevailing force flowing out from the hearts of people to one another. God knows:

⇒ if we honor and respect one another, then peace and love will prevail upon the earth.
⇒ if we honor and respect one another, then the behavior of men will be controlled.
⇒ if we honor and respect one another, there will be no lawlessness and selfishness. There will be only honor and respect for all people—for all the parents and children of the earth.

Thought 1. William Barclay makes three points that should stir us to keep this commandment, to always honor our parents:

> *With the fifth commandment we come right home, for the fifth commandment is "Honour your father and your mother" (Exodus 20:12). Of all the commandments this should be the easiest to obey.*
>
> *i. It should be easy to obey this commandment because it is natural to do so. This commandment is, as it were, built into the very structure of life. It is not a commandment which we find only in the Bible. There never was a society of any kind in which this commandment was not accepted as binding. In ancient Greece, for instance, Solon the great law-giver laid it down that, if a son did not support his parents in their old age, when they needed support, he should lose his rights as a citizen. The Greeks believed that to honour parents is part of the basic duty of every citizen of the state. Anyone who has good parents and who does not realise the duty of honouring them is an unnatural person. Nature itself demands that we keep this commandment.*
>
> *ii. It is a duty of gratitude to keep this commandment. It was our parents who brought us into this world, and we owe them our lives. Of all living creatures man takes longest to become able to support and look after himself.*
>
> *There is a long time when we cannot get ourselves a home or food or clothes, and when we are entirely dependent on our parents; and there is a considerable part of that time when we are so helpless, that a blow would kill us, and, even if nothing was done to us, and we were just alone, we would certainly die. We ought to find it easy to keep this commandment, if only as a matter of gratitude to those to whom we literally owe the fact that we came into the world, and that we survived through the years when we were quite unable to help ourselves, or to get the things necessary to keep body and soul together.*
>
> *Apart from that purely physical side of life, many of us owe a great deal to the care and the love and even to the sacrifice of our parents to give us a good start in life....We ought to be grateful that in many, many homes the parents do without things and plan and save so that their children should have a chance to do well in life. Of all faults, ingratitude is the ugliest and the most hurting, and not to keep this commandment is to be guilty of ingratitude.*
>
> *iii. To honour our parents is a matter of common sense. They have walked the journey of life before us, and therefore they know the dangers and the pitfalls in the way. If you are going on a journey through what is to you an unknown country, a map and a guide-book will be very useful, but most useful of all will be the advice and the experience of one who has already travelled that way.*
>
> *When parents advise their child to do or not to do something, he should understand that it is not because they wish to show their authority or because they are killjoys or because they are old-fashioned, it is because out of their experience they know that the thing is right or wrong, safe or dangerous.*
>
> *The man who will not listen to the voice of experience will certainly end in trouble—and he will deserve all that is coming to him....*
>
> *It is sensible to listen to what our parents tell us, because they have an experience of life that we do not yet possess.*[2]

---

[2] William Barclay. *The Old Law & The New Law*, pp.24-26.

DEUTERONOMY 5:16-21

4) Note that this commandment emphasizes one of the great lessons of life, that we learn by example. Children are to learn to honor their parents. How? By the parents showing honor to their parents. The commandment charges all children to honor their parents. Even if they are adults and parents themselves, the adult child is to honor and respect his parents. Parents are to create an atmosphere of honor and respect in the home. By so doing, the parent teaches—sets an example—for his child to honor him. This commandment stresses the awesome importance of parents setting the right example before their children.

> **"In all things showing thyself a pattern of good works: in doctrine showing uncorruptness, gravity, sincerity" (Tit.2:7).**
> **"Train up a child in the way he should go: and when he is old, he will not depart from it" (Pr.22:6).**

God makes it clear: parents have the obligation to teach this commandment and all the other commandments to their children.

> **"And thou shalt teach them [the commandments] diligently unto thy children, and shalt talk of them when thou sittest in thine house, and when thou walkest by the way, and when thou liest down, and when thou risest up" (De.6:7).**
> **"And, ye fathers, provoke not your children to wrath: but bring them up in the nurture and admonition of the LORD" (Ep.6:4).**

5) What about parents who neglect their children or who abuse their children? Are children to honor and respect parents who are evil, who live in sin and abuse them? *The Preacher's Outline & Sermon Bible®* (N.T. Vol.9, Galatians—Colossians) has an excellent comment on this point that is quoted at length because of its importance:

> **"Children obey your parents in the LORD: for this is right" (Ep.6:1).**

Children are to obey their parents. The word "obey" (hupakouo) means to submit to; to comply with; to hearken; to heed; to follow the directions or guidance of some instruction. When a parent guides and directs a child, the child is to obey the parent. But what about the problems that are so repulsively evident in society: the problems of parental abuse—the problems of physical abuse, sexual abuse, and mental abuse? Is a child to obey a parent when the parent is so devilishly wrong? No! A thousand times no!

To obey means to obey in the LORD. Note the command again: "Children, obey your parents in the LORD." The phrase "in the LORD" means at least two things.

1) There is a limit to the child's obedience. When a parent is not acting in the LORD, he is not to be obeyed. The LORD has nothing whatsoever to do with the filth of unrighteousness and abuse of precious children. If a child can break away and free himself from such parental corruption, he has every right to be freed from his parent. The LORD came to set men free from the abuse and the filth of sin, not to enslave men to it, and especially not to enslave children to it.

One of the most severe warnings ever issued in all of history was issued by the LORD Jesus to adults who abuse children:

> **"And whosoever shall offend one of these little ones that believe in me, it is better for him that a millstone were hanged about his neck, and he were cast into the sea. And if thy hand offend thee [by abusing a child], cut it off: it is better for thee to enter into life maimed, than having two hands to go into hell, into the fire that never shall be quenched: where their worm dieth not, and the fire is not quenched. And if thy foot offend thee [by abusing a child], cut it off: it is better for thee to enter halt into life, than having two feet to be cast into hell, into the fire that never shall be quenched: where their worm dieth not, and the fire is not quenched. And if thine eye offend thee [by lusting after a child], pluck it out: it is better for thee to enter into the kingdom of God with one eye, than having two eyes to be cast into hell fire: where their worm dieth not, and the fire is not quenched" (Mk.9:42-48).**

The abusing parent had better heed, for one of the things that God will not tolerate—absolutely not tolerate—is the abuse of a child. We must proclaim the Word of God: children are to obey their parents, but they are to obey only if the parents' desire and instructions are in the LORD. If a parent is beating a child black and blue or sexually abusing a child, the child should go to some other adult he feels close to and ask for help. And ministers of the LORD—ministers who are called to proclaim Christ and to do what they can to bring His righteousness to earth—must teach the truth from the pulpits of the world.

2) The phrase "in the LORD" also tells why the child is to obey his parents. "Children, obey your parents in the LORD"—obeying your parents is right; it is of the LORD; it pleases the LORD; therefore, obey them. When they guide and instruct you, follow them (cp. Col.3:20).

Lehman Strauss points out that obedience is the first law of the universe—that the law of obedience regulates everything in the world: the stars, the planets, the seasons. Even man himself tries to govern the world by the law of obedience. He wants obedience in the state, at work, at play, and at home.[3] *The point is simply this: the law of obedience is the very nature of things, at the very core of the universe and of man's life and*

---

[3] Lehman Strauss. *Devotional Studies in Galatians & Ephesians.* (Neptune, NJ: Loizeaux Brothers, 1957), p.212.

behavior upon earth. Therefore, it is to be expected that God would command children to obey their parents. Children are to obey—obey because it pleases the LORD and it is the right thing to do.

Note the emphasis here; it is striking. Children are not told to obey parents because it pleases the parent, but because it pleases the LORD. Pleasing one's parents is, of course, a reason for obeying them. But the first reason for obeying parents is that it pleases the LORD. The child is to know the LORD to such a degree that he is continually thinking about the LORD and about pleasing Him. The child is to walk so closely with the LORD that his mind is constantly upon the LORD—upon what he can do to please the LORD. When the child so knows the LORD, then obeying his parents will become an automatic response.[4]

>   **"For Moses said, Honour thy father and thy mother; and, Whoso curseth father or mother, let him die the death" (Mk.7:10).**
>   **"Children, obey your parents in the LORD: for this is right" (Ep.6:1).**
>   **"Children, obey your parents in all things: for this is well pleasing unto the LORD" (Col.3:20).**
>   **"My son, hear the instruction of thy father, and forsake not the law of thy mother" (Pr.1:8; see Pr.6:20; 23:22).**
>   **"My son keep my words, and lay up my commandments with thee" (Pr.7:1).**
>   **"A wise son maketh a glad father: but a foolish son is the heaviness of his mother" (Pr.10:1).**
>   **"Even a child is known by his doings, whether his work be pure, and whether it be right" (Pr.20:11).**
>   **"Remember now thy Creator in the days of thy youth, while the evil days come not, nor the years draw nigh, when thou shalt say, I have no pleasure in them" (Ec.12:1).**

6) What about abusive children, children who abuse their parents? Again, *The Preacher's Outline & Sermon Bible®* (N.T. Vol.9) has an excellent statement covering this point:

To obey parents means to honor one's father and mother. The word "honor" (timao) means to "esteem and value as precious" (The Amplified New Testament); to show respect, reverence, kindness, courtesy, and obedience.[5] *Scripture is not speaking to any certain age child. It is speaking to all of us who are children with parents still living. We are to honor our fathers and mothers: to esteem and value them as precious—to respect and reverence them. Tragically, this is a rarity today. Too often a child's response to his parent is that of...*

- *talking back*
- *cutting the parent*
- *ignoring the parent*
- *grumbling*
- *speaking disrespectfully*
- *not listening*
- *disregarding instructions*
- *acting like a "know it all"*
- *calling the parent a cute but disrespectful name*

In addition to these, there is the dishonor of delinquency, crime, drugs, alcohol, and the abuse of property; and the list could go on and on. And when it comes to adult children with aged parents, there is the dishonor of neglect, the ignoring of their needs and the shuffling of them to the side and failing to adequately care for them. Too many adult children forget how much their parents have done for them—bringing them into the world and taking care of them for years. Too many children forget the rich experience and knowledge that their parents have gained through the years and that could be put to great use in meeting community and world needs. And even if the parents failed to be and to do all they should have, we as Christian children are instructed to honor them as followers of the Lord Jesus Christ.[6]

>   **"Children, obey your parents in the LORD: for this is right" (Ep.6:1).**
>   **"But if any widow have children or nephews, let them learn first to show piety at home, and to requite [repay, pay back] their parents: for that is good and acceptable before God....But if any provide not for his own, and specially for those of his own house, he hath denied the faith, and is worse than an infidel" (1 Ti.5:4, 8).**
>   **"Whoso curseth his father or his mother, his lamp shall be put out in obscure darkness" (Pr.20:20).**
>   **"The eye that mocketh at his father, and despiseth to obey his mother, the ravens of the valley shall pick it out, and the young eagles shall eat it" (Pr.30:17).**
>   **"Honour thy father and thy mother: that thy days may be long upon the land which the LORD thy God giveth thee" (Ex.20:12).**
>   **"Ye shall fear every man his mother, and his father, and keep my sabbaths: I am the LORD your God" (Le.19:3).**
>   **"Thou shalt rise up before the hoary [gray] head, and honor the face of the old man, and fear thy God: I am the LORD" (Le.19:32).**
>   **"Cursed be he that setteth light by his father or his mother: and all the people shall say, Amen" (De.27:16).**

---

[4] *Galatians, Ephesians, Philippians, Colossians*, Vol.9. "The Preacher's Outline & Sermon Bible®." (Chattanooga, TN: Leadership Ministries Worldwide, 1991), pp.219-220.

[5] Kenneth S. Wuest. *Ephesians and Colossians.* "Word Studies in the Greek New Testament," Vol.1. (Grand Rapids, MI: Eerdmans Publishing Co., 1966), p.136.

[6] *Galatians, Ephesians, Philippians, Colossians*, Vol.9. "The Preacher's Outline & Sermon Bible®," pp.219-220.

DEUTERONOMY 5:16-21

Thought 1. Maxie Dunnam warns us about making a "cult of the child" within society, showing how this attitude teaches children to be disrespectful and disobedient.

> *I'm concerned about the extreme to which we have gone with the cult of the child during the past thirty or forty years in the United States. To be sure, we needed to give more attention to children. The adage "Children are to be seen and not heard" was a caricature of children treated as wards and, in the extreme in many cultures, as chattel. So we needed to get away from that. But as is so often the case, the pendulum swung too far. We reared our children to be self-centered. We ordered our worlds around not only their needs, but their whims. Our thinking about discipline was distorted. We spared the rod and spoiled the child. There was no center of authority around which the child could order his life, no clear guidelines or directions, no well-defined values. And so respect was diminished, especially at the point of children listening and being obedient. This was not so much the child's fault as the parent's default.*[7]

b. Note the two great promises attached to this commandment. Every person should seek ever so diligently to lay hold of these promises.
  1) First, the person who honors his parents will live an extended life upon earth (v.16b). Common sense tells us this. A tension-filled home—a home full of arguments, bickering, abuse, and divisiveness—causes all kinds of physical and emotional problems, shortening the life of family members. Whereas a home filled with love, joy, and peace strengthens the health and emotional stability of a person, thereby adding years to a person's life.

  God knows what He is talking about; He knows exactly what He is promising. If the Israelites would teach their children to honor their parents, then generations of Israelite homes would be filled with love, joy, and peace. Maxie Dunnam has an excellent thought on the importance of the family to Israel that sets a dynamic example for every civilization:

> *I believe one of the primary reasons Judaism has survived across the years is precisely its family structure. The Jews survived the Holocaust and thousands of years of anti-Semitism because the Jewish family had a sense of identity and a sense of order. It doesn't matter where the family is on the Sabbath, when the Sabbath comes, they stop and pray. It didn't matter what Hitler and all the powers of Nazism said, when Passover came it was time to tell the story, even if the family was gathered in a concentration camp and there were no candles to light. There was a sense of order and identity that gave them roots and strength and perspective and discipline. At the heart of that family structure was a reverence for parents, a high regard, a respect, an esteem for the older members of the family. The elderly were honored and cared for.*[8]

  2) Second, things will go well—far better—for the person who honors his parents. Common sense and logic tell us this: if children (youth or adult) honor their parents, disturbance is eliminated. There is far less...
     - conflict
     - tension
     - strife
     - bitterness
     - exhaustion
     - guilt
     - regret
     - hurt
     - pain

  Honor builds love, respect, and esteem. Honor grows people, strengthens them personally and the relationship that binds a family together. As the Israelites prepared to march into the promised land, they needed to know these facts. They needed to build strong families within the promised land. Strong families would help them live a victorious life in the promised land and help keep their nation strong. Therefore, Moses preached this great commandment, drove the truth into their hearts and minds:

> **"Honour thy father and thy mother, as the LORD thy God hath commanded thee; that thy days may be prolonged, and that it may go well with thee, in the land which the LORD thy God giveth thee" (De.5:16).**

Thought 1. In practical terms, Scripture tells us exactly what God means by this commandment.
(1) To honor our parents means to respect and to reverence our parents.
(2) To honor our parents means to obey our parents.

> **"Children, obey your parents in the LORD: for this is right. Honour thy father and mother; (which is the first commandment with promise;) That it may be well with thee, and thou mayest live long on the earth" (Ep.6:1-3).**
> **"Children, obey your parents in all things: for this is well pleasing unto the LORD" (Col.3:20).**

2 (5:17) **Murder—Killing—Violence—Lawlessness—Obedience—Commandments, the Ten**: commandment six is "You shall not murder." What is forbidden by this commandment? How is this commandment broken or violated? Note exactly what the commandment says:

OUTLINE	SCRIPTURE
2. Commandment 6—*man's life*[DS1,2]	17 Thou shalt not kill.

---
[7] Maxie Dunnam. *The Preacher's Commentary on Exodus*, pp.261-262.
[8] *Ibid.*, p.261.

DEUTERONOMY 5:16-21

   a. The purpose for this commandment is to preserve life: to teach people the sanctity of human life, that they are to honor and hold human life in the highest esteem. Man is created in the image and likeness of God; therefore, man's life is of infinite value to God (Ge.1:26-27). Man is...
- God's *master creation*
- God's *royal masterpiece*
- God's *precious possession*
- God's *priceless property*

Why is man to be so highly esteemed? As stated, because man is created in the *image and likeness* of God. God demands that human life be valued above all the wealth in the world (Mt.16:26; Mk.8:36). The sanctity of human life is to be honored above all else.

> "And God said, Let us make man in our image, after our likeness: and let them have dominion over the fish of the sea, and over the fowl of the air, and over the cattle, and over all the earth, and over every creeping thing that creepeth upon the earth. So God created man in his own image, in the image of God created he him; male and female created he them" (Ge.1:26-27).
>
> "And surely your blood of your lives will I require; at the hand of every beast will I require it, and at the hand of man; at the hand of every man's brother will I require the life of man. Whoso sheddeth man's blood, by man shall his blood be shed: for in the image of God made he man. And you, be ye fruitful, and multiply; bring forth abundantly in the earth, and multiply therein" (Ge.9:5-7).
>
> "For what shall it profit a man, if he shall gain the whole world, and lose his own soul?" (Mk.8:36; see Mt.16:26).

   b. The Hebrew word for *kill* or *murder* (rasah) means premeditated, planned, deliberate, intentional, unauthorized murder. This commandment is broken either by a planned murderous attack upon a person(s) or by a rash, reckless attack. This commandment forbids the taking of a life because a person is...
- angry
- bitter
- violent
- uncontrolled
- passionate
- vengeful
- selfish
- stealing
- lusting
- coveting
- rebelling

Murder for such reasons as these is wrong and must always be counted wrong. This is the only way to make our community, society, and civilization safe and secure. The terrifying evils of this earth—lawlessness, violence, and murder—must not be allowed. We must always agree with God's Holy Word: murder for such reasons as anger, robbery, and violence must always be counted wrong and be punished.

But there are also other forms of murder that are just as wrong as lifting one's own hand to kill another person. All over the world, there are people who commit murder...
- by forcing people to work in conditions that will injure or eventually kill them, that lead to their premature death
- by forcing people to live in horrible conditions, so horrible that the environment or lack of basic necessities eventually kills them
- by selling and hooking people on drugs, drugs that eventually enslave and kill the addicts

Man must control and punish the lawless, the violent, and the murderers who roam his streets and in many cases sit in the plush offices of authority and rule. Evil men must be stopped and taught to obey this commandment or else our civilization can never survive. Lawlessness, violence, and murder must be stamped out. We can have safe streets and parks, unlocked doors, and the freedom to move about at night only if we obey this commandment. We will have a satisfying and fruitful life only if we heed this commandment: "You shall not murder [live lawless and violent lives]" (v.13).

But even the above are not the only kinds of murder forbidden by God. The spirit of lawlessness, violence, and murder so sweeps through the societies and history of man that at least two other types of murder need to be discussed. (See DEEPER STUDY # 1, *Abortion*—De.5:17; DEEPER STUDY # 2, *Suicide*—De.5:17 for discussion.)

   c. Note this fact: this commandment is not a blanket commandment against all killing. God's Word clearly says that the taking of life is justified, understandable, and allowed...
- as capital punishment (Ge.9:6)
- in a justified war (De.13:15; 1 S.15:3; 2 S.10:1f)
- in cases of adultery (Le.20:10). This may seem harsh to society today, but this commandment and penalty were given to protect and preserve the family. The very survival of Israel depended upon the family being preserved as the basic unit of society. Loyalty to the family taught the Israelites to be loyal to the nation as a whole.
- in the defense of ourselves, for example, when a thief breaks into our home (Ex.22:2)
- in accidental killing (De.19:5)
- in killing animals for food (Ge.9:3)

   d. What is the ultimate cause, the basic source, of murder? Scripture says that the underlying cause and source of murder is twofold:
   1) Satan, the devil, is the arch-enemy of God and man: he seeks to tempt and arouse people to live greedy and selfish lives, lives of lawlessness, violence, and murder.

> "Ye are of [your] father the devil, and the lusts of your father ye will do. He was a murderer from the beginning, and abode not in the truth, because there is no truth in him. When he speak-eth a lie, he speaketh of his own: for he is a liar, and the father of it" (Jn.8:44).

DEUTERONOMY 5:16-21

2) Lust—the unregulated urges of man's heart—drives some people to rob, assault, and kill. Some people allow the lust of their soul—greed and covetousness—to drive them to lawlessness, violence, and murder.

> "But every man is tempted, when he is drawn away of his own lust, and enticed. Then when lust hath conceived, it bringeth forth sin: and sin, when it is finished, bringeth forth death" (Js.1:14-15).
>
> "From whence come wars and fightings among you? come they not hence, even of your lusts that war in your members? Ye lust, and have not: ye kill, and desire to have, and cannot obtain: ye fight and war, yet ye have not, because ye ask not. Ye ask, and receive not, because ye ask amiss, that ye may consume it upon your lusts" (Js.4:1-3).

e. What will be the eternal judgment of God upon the murderer? Death, spiritual and eternal death.

> "For the wages of sin is death" (Ro.6:23).
>
> "For to be carnally minded is death" (Ro.8:6).
>
> "Now the works of the flesh are manifest, which are these; Adultery, fornication, uncleanness, lasciviousness, Idolatry, witchcraft, hatred, variance, emulations, wrath, strife, seditions, heresies, Envyings, murders, drunkenness, revellings, and such like: of the which I tell you before, as I have also told you in time past, that they which do such things shall not inherit the kingdom of God" (Ga.5:19-21).
>
> "But every man is tempted, when he is drawn away of his own lust, and enticed. Then when lust hath conceived, it bringeth forth sin: and sin, when it is finished, bringeth forth death" (Js.1:14-15).
>
> "But the fearful, and unbelieving, and the abominable, and murderers, and whoremongers, and sorcerers, and idolaters, and all liars, shall have their part in the lake which burneth with fire and brimstone: which is the second death" (Re.21:8).
>
> "The soul that sinneth, it shall die" (Eze.18:4).

f. Can a murderer be saved and forgiven for his sin of murder? Scripture says "yes," a resounding "yes." But the murderer must confess his sin and repent, turning away from the life of sin. He must genuinely give his heart and life to Jesus Christ and live for Jesus Christ.

> "I tell you, Nay: but, except ye repent, ye shall all likewise perish" (Lu.13:3).
>
> "Repent ye therefore, and be converted, that your sins may be blotted out, when the times of refreshing shall come from the presence of the LORD" (Ac.3:19).
>
> "Let the wicked forsake his way, and the unrighteous man his thoughts: and let him return unto the LORD, and he will have mercy upon him; and to our God, for he will abundantly pardon" (Is.55:7).
>
> "But if the wicked will turn from all his sins that he hath committed, and keep all my statutes, and do that which is lawful and right, he shall surely live, he shall not die" (Eze.18:21).
>
> "Then Peter said unto them, Repent, and be baptized every one of you in the name of Jesus Christ for the remission of sins, and ye shall receive the gift of the Holy Ghost" (Ac.2:38).
>
> "For the wages of sin is death; but the gift of God is eternal life through Jesus Christ our LORD" (Ro.6:23).
>
> "For to be carnally minded is death; but to be spiritually minded is life and peace" (Ro.8:6).

g. Jesus Christ taught that this commandment means far more than just prohibiting the killing of people. He enlarged the meaning to include both the anger that is aroused within the heart and the lawless motives that drive a person to kill others.

> "Ye have heard that it was said by them of old time, Thou shalt not kill; and whosoever shall kill shall be in danger of the judgment: But I say unto you, That whosoever is angry with his brother without a cause shall be in danger of the judgment: and whosoever shall say to his brother, Raca, shall be in danger of the council: but whosoever shall say, Thou fool, shall be in danger of hell fire" (Mt.5:21-22).

Note what Christ is saying: He is saying that man has a problem. Man misreads God's law. Man interprets God's law to say what he wishes it to say. Man applies it only to the outward act, in this case to the act of murder. Man fails to look inward—within himself—to the cause (see note—Mt.5:17-18; DEEPER STUDY # 2—Mt.5:17; note—Mk.7:14-23).

Murder is deeper than just an outward act. It is an inward act: an act of anger, bitterness, enmity. Murder is born from within, from an uncontrolled spirit, from an unregulated urge, from an inner anger. Anger itself is the root sin, the sin that first breaks the law of God. Anger is...

- bitterness and enmity
- indignation and wrath
- striking out against a person
- a disappointment or hatred of oneself
- rage and fury
- an uncontrolled spirit
- desiring a person's hurt
- envying and killing a person's happiness
- slandering and destroying a person's image (who is created in God's image)

The growth of anger is dangerous. Unresolved anger will fester. It can become uncontrolled and give birth to murder. There are three steps in the growth of anger given by Christ.

1) The anger that broods, that is selfish. It harbors malice; it will not forget; it lingers; it broods; it wills revenge and sometimes seeks revenge.
2) The anger that holds contempt (raca). It despises; it ridicules; it arrogantly exalts self and calls another person empty and useless. This is an anger that is full of malice. It despises and scorns (raca). It arises from pride—a proud wrath

DEUTERONOMY 5:16-21

(Pr.21:24). Such feelings or anger walk over and trample a person. It says that whatever ill comes upon a person is deserved.

3) The anger that curses. It seeks to destroy a man and his reputation morally, intellectually, and spiritually.

There is a justified anger. In fact, the believer must be an angry person—angry with those who sin and do wrong, who are unjust and selfish in their behavior. However, a justified anger is always disciplined and controlled; it is always limited to those who do wrong either against God or against others. The distinguishing mark between justified and unjustified anger is that a justified anger is never selfish; it is never shown because of what has happened to oneself. It is an anger that is purposeful. The believer knows that he is angry for a legitimate reason, and he seeks to correct the situation in the most peaceful way possible (see notes—Ep.4:26-27; Ro.12:18; Jn.2:14-17. Also see DEEPER STUDY # 1—Jn.2:14.)

"Be ye angry, and sin not: let not the sun go down upon your wrath" (Ep.4:26).

"If it be possible, as much as lieth in you, live peaceably with all men" (Ro.12:18).

"And the Jews' passover was at hand, and Jesus went up to Jerusalem, and found in the temple those that sold oxen and sheep and doves, and the changers of money sitting: and when he had made a scourge of small cords, he drove them all out of the temple, and the sheep, and the oxen; and poured out the changer's money, and overthrew the tables" (Jn.2:13-16).

Thought 1. Anger is cast against many. Too often hurt feelings exist between those who are supposed to be the closest: husband and wife, parent and child, neighbor and friend, employer and employee. The LORD is clear about the matter: we must never allow anger to take hold of us without just cause.

"But now ye also put off all these; anger, wrath, malice, blasphemy, filthy communication out of your mouth" (Col.3:8).

"Wherefore, my beloved brethren, let every man be swift to hear, slow to speak, slow to wrath" (Js.1:19).

"Whosoever hateth his brother is a murderer: and ye know that no murderer hath eternal life abiding in him" (1 Jn.3:15).

"Cease from anger, and forsake wrath: fret not thyself in any wise to do evil" (Ps.37:8).

"He that is soon angry dealeth foolishly; and a man of wicked devices is hated" (Pr.14:17).

"He that is slow to anger is better than the mighty; and he that ruleth his spirit than he that taketh a city" (Pr.16:32).

"The discretion of a man deferreth his anger; and it is his glory to pass over a transgression" (Pr.19:11).

"Be not hasty in thy spirit to be angry: for anger resteth in the bosom of fools" (Ec.7:9).

Thought 2. There are reasons why people get angry and develop feelings against others:
⇒ To seek revenge and to hurt
⇒ To show ego or authority
⇒ To reveal passion or secure some end
⇒ To show hurt, resentment, or bitterness
⇒ To express disagreement or displeasure
⇒ To correct a wrong (a justified anger)
⇒ To give warning

Thought 3. It is a serious matter to hold feelings against another person—a very, very serious matter. There is (1) the *danger of judgment,* (2) the *danger of having to come before earthly courts*, and (3) the *danger of hell fire*. Violence is to be judged—not only before the councils of the world but before the councils of God.

DEEPER STUDY # 1

(5:17) **Abortion—Children—Pregnancy—Unborn, The—Murder—Ministry**: abortion, the killing of unborn babies, is one of the major indictments against the human race down through the centuries. The sanctity of life has been and still is under lethal attack. Tragically, the tide of public opinion usually runs counter to the clear commandment of God, "You shall not kill." Because abortion is legal in so many societies and is so prevalent, it is being discussed at length here.

1. What does the Bible say about the creation of man and the fetus or unborn baby in the womb?

"So God created man in his own image, in the image of God created he him; male and female created he them" (Ge.1:27).

"This is the book of the generations of Adam. In the day that God created man, in the likeness of God made he him" (Ge.5:1).

"Did not he that made me in the womb make him? and did not one fashion us in the womb?" (Jb.31:15).

"Thy hands have made me and fashioned me: give me understanding, that I may learn thy commandments" (Ps.119:73).

"For thou hast possessed my reins: thou hast covered me in my mother's womb. I will praise thee; for I am fearfully and wonderfully made: marvellous are thy works; and that my soul knoweth right well. My substance was not hid from thee, when I was made in secret, and curiously wrought in the lowest parts of the earth. Thine eyes did see my substance, yet being unperfect; and in thy book all my members were written, which in continuance were fashioned, when as yet there was none of them" (Ps.139:13-16).

DEUTERONOMY 5:16-21

"As thou knowest not what is the way of the spirit, nor how the bones do grow in the womb of her that is with child: even so thou knowest not the works of God who maketh all" (Ec.11:5).

"Then the word of the LORD came unto me, saying, Before I formed thee in the belly I knew thee; and before thou camest forth out of the womb I sanctified thee, and I ordained thee a prophet unto the nations" (Je.1:4-5).

"Now the birth of Jesus Christ was on this wise: When as his mother Mary was espoused to Joseph, before they came together, she was found with child of the Holy Ghost. Then Joseph her husband, being a just man, and not willing to make her a public example, was minded to put her away privily. But while he thought on these things, behold, the angel of the LORD appeared unto him in a dream, saying, Joseph, thou son of David, fear not to take unto thee Mary thy wife: for that which is conceived in her is of the Holy Ghost" (Mt.1:18-20).

2. What does the medical profession say about the fetus or unborn child in the mother's womb? The excellent Bible teacher Stuart Briscoe says this:

> *Physicians have given us a wide variety of suggestions about when the fetus becomes human. Seven of them are outlined by Oliver O'Donavan and quoted in Norman Anderson's Issues of Life and Death.*[9]
> 1. *The first group says the fetus becomes fully human at the point of conception. Among those some would say "the point of conception" rather unguardedly, while others would describe it not as a moment, but a process that we cannot accurately measure. But both would agree that, whenever it takes place, the child becomes invested with the divine image.*
> 2. *Others claim that the problem with the first theory is that 50 percent of all impregnated ova disappear in the natural course of events. If that is the case, then 50 percent of unborn, unformed, unimplanted ova have the divine image and simply drift off into eternity without having existed in any sense that is meaningful to us. These people state that the person starts to be formed at implantation; before that it has no meaningful existence at all.*
> 3. *A third group says the fetus becomes human when it takes human shape. They say it will measure at least three centimeters, which will happen between forty-five and forty-nine days after conception.*
> 4. *Still another group claims the fetus becomes human at animation. Old-time theologians used to try to figure out when the body got the soul and when the soul left. They thought of the body having a soul, as opposed to thinking that humans are body, soul, and spirit. When it came to animation, people believed—and in some circumstances still do believe—that a time exists when the fetus becomes ensouled. To give you an idea how things have changed, Aristotle said that took place twenty-five to forty days after conception for the male, but fifty to eighty days after conception for the female.*
> 5. *A fifth way of thinking says the fetus becomes human at viability—the point at which it could survive without its mother. We have a problem with this today because with our rapidly advancing technology the fetus's viability point changes all the time. Supreme Court Justice Sandra Day O'Connor said, "Fetal viability in the first trimester of pregnancy may be possible in the not too distant future." If that happens, it will make the Supreme Court's ruling palpable nonsense.*
> 6. *Another set of people would try to get the problem out of the way simply by declaring the fetus human at birth, not before. If so, how do you take into account the biblical passages we've considered?*
> 7. *Finally, some would claim that the fetus becomes fully human one year after birth. They say that at this stage the human child is comparable to all other animals at the moment of birth, because human children are much more helpless than other animals.*[10]

3. Now, when does the unborn child become a human being? When is the fetus made in the image of God? Having looked at what the Bible says and at what different people in the medical profession say, when does the fetus actually become human? Stuart Briscoe gives an excellent discussion of this question as well.

> *All this speculation leaves us in a great, big fog—because when we look at Scripture, medical science, and our knowledge, we find it very difficult to pinpoint the moment the unborn becomes a human made in the image of God.*
> *Because of this difficulty, people argue about whether the fetus is a person, is fully human, is subhuman, or is potentially human. Those in favor of aborting call it subhuman. They would compare it to an appendix—simply a pile of useless tissue, lacking importance. In the light of Scripture, we cannot accept this position under any circumstances.*
> *Despite the complexity of the issue and the degree of uncertainty that surrounds it, if we allow the fetus to go full term, it will become a human being. Therefore under no circumstances should we feel comfortable in agreeing to any callous or careless interference with that. If I cannot categorically say when something is made in God's image, I'm not even going to get close to tampering with it. It would seem we need to take that minimal position at the very least.*[11]

4. What about the mother whose life is in danger if she bears the child? Or whose unborn child is due to rape or incest? Or who had an abortion without any knowledge of what God says about the mother? Are we as believers to minister to them? Again, Stuart Briscoe's discussion of this point is so excellent that it is well worth quoting at length:

> *If we are in favor of life, we must favor not only the life of the unborn, but also that of the mother. We need to express concern for the mother, her physical well-being, her emotional situation, and her spiritual state.*

---

[9] Stuart Briscoe. *The Ten Commandments*. (Wheaton, IL: Harold Shaw Publishers, 1986), p.96-98.
[10] Norman Anderson. *Issues of Life and Death*. (London, England: Hodder & Stoughton Limited, 1977).
[11] Stuart Briscoe. *The Ten Commandments*, p.98.

DEUTERONOMY 5:16-21

> ⇒ What will that do to her emotions?
> ⇒ How does that affect her spiritually?
> ⇒ How can she look the world in the face again?
>
> If we aggressively go after women who have had abortions, we may well drive them to the point of emotional breakdown or even suicide. Among those who have experienced abortions, there exists a high incidence of depression and an increasingly high level of suicide. It seems to me that if we call ourselves prolife, we must be prolife for the unborn and the born as well. We've got to be for the fetus and for the mother, which complicates the abortion issue quite dramatically.
>
> In some cases that means we must balance out the rights of the unborn against those of the living.
> ⇒ The Roman Catholics have arrived at a simple answer for this: They see the rights of the fetus as the primary ones.
> ⇒ Those in the feminist tradition and with more liberal thinking call that nonsense, saying the rights of the living are far more important than the rights of the potentially living.
> ⇒ Others who grapple with the Word of God ask, "How do we put these together?"
>
> Can we countenance abortion on demand? Emphatically no! Can we ban abortion, period, for all circumstances and conditions? It would seem to me that by doing so we could get ourselves in situations where we cannot adequately deal with the needs for the life of the mother and the life of the unborn. Some people would probably agree that if the mother has a very major medical problem, and carrying the child threatens her life, action needs to be taken. To balance this out, let me quote a British physician: "In forty years of gynecological and obstetric practice, I can only remember a handful of occasions in which the mother's life was in danger because of the birth of the fetus." We need to bear that in mind.
>
> I believe we must uphold the sanctity of life for both the born and the unborn. I believe we must take that position. If we wish to take a stand for the rights of the unborn, potentially made in the image of God, we must be ready at the same time to care for those who have had abortions and feel depression and overwhelming guilt and who might commit suicide. We need to cultivate compassion for both. When we persuade women not to abort the unborn, we should be prepared to help with the steps of the pregnancy that follow. But we also need to aid those who need forgiveness—we must help human lives in many dimensions, not only in the right to be born.[12]

DEEPER STUDY # 2
(5:17) **Suicide—Murder—Ministry**: suicide is viewed differently by different people and societies. For example...
- Can a Christian believer commit suicide? Become so despondent, depressed, and discouraged that he takes his own life?
- Can a person be justified if he is so heroic that he undertakes a suicide mission for his nation or for some great cause? This has happened often down through history. The Japanese kamikaze pilots of the Second World War are a prime example. In fact, many of the surviving men who have fought in war would know of men who gave themselves to undertake suicidal missions.

One thing is sure: a deliberate suicide *to escape* this life with all its trials and problems is a desperate crime, a crime that should never be committed. Suicide happens, happens far too often, but it is never the answer. God has stamped His image upon every human life, and no person should ever destroy himself. There are three strong reasons why a person should never commit suicide.

1. God forbids murder, and suicide is the murdering of oneself.

    "**Thou shalt not kill**" (Ex.20:13).
    "For this, Thou shalt not commit adultery, Thou shalt not kill, Thou shalt not steal, Thou shalt not bear false witness, Thou shalt not covet; and if there be any other commandment, it is briefly comprehended in this saying, namely, Thou shalt love thy neighbor as thyself" (Ro.13:9).
    "But let none of you suffer as a murderer, or as a thief, or as an evildoer, or as a busybody in other men's matters" (1 Pe.4:15).

2. The person destroys the very image of God that is stamped upon his or her life.

    "**So God created man in his own image, in the image of God created he him; male and female created he them**" (Ge.1:27).

3. Jesus Christ, God's very own Son, loves and cares for us. He helps us *conquer* and *overcome* whatever problems confront us, no matter how terrible. He will give us wisdom and show us how to *conquer* the problem.

    "For in that he himself hath suffered being tempted, he is able to succour them that are tempted" (He.2:18).
    "For we have not an high priest which cannot be touched with the feeling of our infirmities; but was in all points tempted like as we are, yet without sin. Let us therefore come boldly unto the throne of grace, that we may obtain mercy, and find grace to help in time of need" (He.4:15-16).

---

[12] *Ibid.*, pp.98-100.

DEUTERONOMY 5:16-21

> "For we have not an high priest which cannot be touched with the feeling of our infirmities; but was in all points tempted like as we are, yet without sin. Let us therefore come boldly unto the throne of grace, that we may obtain mercy, and find grace to help in time of need" (He.4:15-16).
>
> "There hath no temptation taken you but such as is common to man: but God is faithful, who will not suffer you to be tempted above that ye are able; but will with the temptation also make a way to escape, that ye may be able to bear it" (1 Co.10:13).
>
> "If any of you lack wisdom, let him ask of God, that giveth to all men liberally, and upbraideth not; and it shall be given him" (Js.1:5).
>
> Now, having said the above, what should our attitude (and the church's attitude) be toward suicidal people and their families? To the genuine Christian believer, the answer is obvious: we are to minister to them. We are to seek out and help all who hurt and face desperate problems and circumstances. Note what has just been said: we are not to sit around waiting for hurting people to cross our paths. We are to actively seek out, find, and help hurting people. This is the call of every Christian believer and the mission of the church. Christ made this perfectly clear.
>
> > "Even as the Son of man came not to be ministered unto, but to minister, and to give his life a ransom for many" (Mt.20:28; see Lu.4:18).
> >
> > "Let this mind be in you, which was also in Christ Jesus: Who, being in the form of God, thought it not robbery to be equal with God: But made himself of no reputation, and took upon him the form of a servant, and was made in the likeness of men" (Ph.2:5-7; see Lu.4:18).
> >
> > "For the Son of man is come to seek and to save that which was lost" (Lu.19:10; see Jn.20:21).
> >
> > "Peace [be] unto you: as [my] Father hath sent me, even so send I you" (Jn.20:21).

3 (5:18) **Adultery—Immorality—Sex, Illicit—Morality—Marriage—Sin—Commandment, the Ten**: the seventh commandment is, "You shall not commit adultery." How serious a problem is adultery? In just a moment we will see that this commandment refers to all forms of immorality. In light of that, how serious a problem is immorality in our society? Most authorities and polls tell us that...

- adultery is prevalent
- pregnancy among unwed mothers is on a sharp rise
- premarital sex is becoming commonplace, the accepted practice among the young
- sex among unmarried adults—young and old alike—is accepted and even expected by the vast majority of people

Is there a cesspool of immorality in society today? Most honest and thinking observers of history would say that immorality is a very serious problem today. Why? Because it threatens the family, the very foundation of society and civilization. The family is the primary place where trust, loyalty, and love are to be taught and demonstrated. If a person will not be faithful and loyal to his family, how can he be trusted to be loyal to his nation, society, and civilization? It is far easier to be loyal to that which can be physically seen, such as one's family, than for that which is only an ideal such as nation, society, and civilization. Immorality strikes at the very foundation of society, the family. It tears apart the family and causes hurt, suffering, strain, shame, guilt, secrecy, destitution, distrust, disloyalty, and unfaithfulness. Moreover, immorality and adultery teach that certain behavior is acceptable: selfishness, unfaithfulness, distrust, disloyalty, secrecy, irresponsibility, and on and on.

This is the reason God gave us this commandment: to preserve our lives, to preserve the great qualities that bring peace, love, and trust to our lives, qualities that build a healthy mind and heart.

OUTLINE	SCRIPTURE
3. Commandment 7—*man's family*: Forbids adultery	18 Neither shalt thou commit adultery.

a. *Adultery* (naap) or *adulterate* means to debase, to corrupt oneself sexually, to make oneself impure sexually, to have sex outside of marriage. What God is saying is simple, unqualified, and irrevocable: "You shall not commit adultery: you shall not debase yourself, corrupt yourself, nor make yourself impure sexually. You shall not have sex outside of marriage."

1) Scripture teaches that a person becomes sexually impure in at least three ways:
   ⇒ A person has sex with someone other than his or her spouse. This is what is commonly called adultery.
   ⇒ A person has sex before marriage. This is called fornication. Fornication refers to any sexual immorality, either before marriage or after marriage.
   ⇒ A person fantasizes and lusts after a person other than his or her spouse, allows his mind and heart to be set upon another person.

2) Note that the sin of adultery embraces all that leads up to the act of sex, not just the sexual act itself. Adultery is far more than just being sexually unfaithful in marriage. This commandment forbids any immoral thought or act...
   - that makes a person impure for marriage
   - that spots or dirties a person's marriage
   - that causes a person to lose his or her virginity
   - that keeps a person from being able to offer himself or herself as a pure virgin when married

   Illicit sex is a violation against the marriage to be. Illicit sex dirties, corrupts, spots, and makes a person impure either before or after marriage.

3) The thought life of a person is important when dealing with adultery. Adultery is committed in the heart long before the act is committed. Always keep in mind that God's law is spiritual; therefore His law deals with the thoughts of our mind and heart. This commandment forbids committing adultery in the heart. A person is...

DEUTERONOMY 5:16-21

- not to prostitute his thoughts and imaginations
- not to allow impure, lustful thoughts
- not to indulge in illicit fantasies

b. The meaning of adultery was expanded by the Lord Jesus Christ, by God's Son Himself. Christ taught that this commandment means far more than just committing the act of adultery. He enlarged the commandment to include thoughts and lusts, to include the second look when a person is dressed to sexually attract or expose his or her body.

> "Ye have heard that it was said by them of old time, Thou shalt not commit adultery: But I say unto you, That whosoever looketh on a woman to lust after her hath committed adultery with her already in his heart. And if thy right eye offend thee, pluck it out, and cast [it] from thee: for it is profitable for thee that one of thy members should perish, and not [that] thy whole body should be cast into hell. And if thy right hand offend thee, cut it off, and cast [it] from thee: for it is profitable for thee that one of thy members should perish, and not [that] thy whole body should be cast into hell" (Mt.5:27-30).

c. Now, what causes adultery and immorality? There are no doubt many causes, but we can perhaps summarize them all under the following five categories.

1) Immorality is caused by corrupt moral standards or a lack of moral standards.
    ⇒ Some people have never been taught nor are they aware that sex outside of marriage is wrong in the sight of God. Their society has become so corrupted down through the ages that belief in the true and living God has been lost as well as the sanctity of sex and marriage.

2) Immorality is caused by lax or liberal moral standards, or by a selfish, worldly, immoral lifestyle. These people either ignore or deny God's commandment, choosing to live as they wish.

3) Immorality is caused by the need for companionship, attention, or love or by the need for appreciation or fulfillment. Many people reach out to others because of these very basic needs. This is especially true during marriage when a husband or wife fails to meet these needs in his or her spouse.

4) Immorality is caused by anger, hostility, or the seeking of revenge. A host of behaviors can anger a person and arouse him to commit adultery, such things as coldness, indifference, neglect, a biting tongue, harshness, selfishness.

5) Immorality is caused by poor ego strength or by an inflated ego, by a lack of self-esteem or self-worth, by a need to feel important, or by the challenge and conquest of the affair. The most intimate thing a person can give to another is his or her body. Therefore, sex is a challenge or conquest for many people; it is an ego booster, an act that either builds a person's feelings of importance or adds to his or her trophy case of conquests.

Sex is a very normal, natural act, a most precious and cherished act given by God. God has built the desire for sex into the very nature of man. In fact, sex is the most intimate experience God has chosen for man to nourish the great virtues of life and to propagate the human race. But the depraved, sinful heart of man has corrupted sex, so much so that man has developed a sex-crazed society. In very practical terms, immorality is caused...

- by ignoring or denying God and His Word
- by ignoring right vs. wrong
- by lack of teaching and training
- by unsatisfying, inadequate sex with a spouse
- by coldness, the alienation of husband or wife
- by living in a dream or fantasy world due to such things as pornography, films, or suggestive music
- by not guarding relationships, by getting too close and becoming attracted to a person
- by not guarding against loneliness, emptiness, or the disappointment in one's spouse or loved one

d. Now, why does God forbid adultery? Prohibit immorality? What is God's purpose, His reason for giving this commandment? Keep in mind what is stated above: the experience of sex is a gift to man, a gift given by God. God created sex for man, and even went so far as to make sex...

- a part of man's very nature
- the very way man is to propagate the human race

Note what this means: if man failed to have sex, the human race would cease to be. Human life would become extinct within a few generations. God so intertwined sex within man's nature that man must have sex. All this is to say one thing: sex is of critical importance to God. God not only approves of sex: He is the Giver and Creator of the experience of sex. But He put boundaries and limits around sex. Sex was created for marriage, for the home, and only for marriage and the home. This leads us to the purposes for sex, the reasons why God gave this seventh commandment.

1) God gave the seventh commandment to preserve man, to protect and safeguard the value of the individual, the sanctity of man's body and spirit. When a man and woman lie together, they are never more vulnerable, never more exposed. Lying together, their bodies and spirits are more exposed than at any other time. God intended sex to be one of the most intimate, warm, precious, and growing experiences of human life. Sex was created so that two people could grow together, could nourish and nurture each other in...

• love	• loyalty	• care
• joy	• perseverance	• security
• peace	• attractiveness	• self-esteem
• trust	• attention	• a sense of fulfillment

On and on the list could go; but note all the wonderful, positive, and strong qualities that sex is supposed to bring between two people. This is the reason God gave the seventh commandment: "You shall not commit adultery"

DEUTERONOMY 5:16-21

(v.18; see Ex.20:13). These things are so important for a healthy personality that God did something: He ordained that one man and one woman were to give their lives to one another, that they were to focus upon sharing and developing the wonderful qualities in the other. God ordained marriage. Sex outside of marriage never develops these qualities. Illicit sex always causes problems...

- guilt
- jealousy
- a sense of being used
- unwanted pregnancies
- broken marriages
- insecurity
- a false sense of security
- unhappiness
- disease
- a cheapening of sex
- broken trust
- selfishness
- loss of self-esteem
- loss of respect for others
- loss of respect by others
- dissolution of the family
- emotional problems
- disloyalty
- loss of affection and relationships
- a lack of fulfillment

The point: God gave the seventh commandment to preserve the value of human life, the sanctity of man's body and spirit.

2) God gave the seventh commandment to preserve the family and the human race, society itself. The family is the basic unit of any society; therefore, the family has to be protected and preserved for society to survive. This was true for Israel and it is true for us, no matter what our generation. When husbands and wives are living in love and are faithful to each other, the great qualities of life are learned and taught: loyalty, trust, commitment, love, joy, and peace. These are the very qualities that grow and develop fruitful lives, families, and nations. No family, society, or nation can survive without these great qualities.

God demands the *sanctity of marriage*. God demands that husbands and wives be pure and faithful to one another, that they love one another and never commit adultery: "You shall never commit adultery, never commit any act of immorality."

"Thou shalt not commit adultery" (Ex.20:14).

"Flee fornication [all forms of sex outside of marriage]. Every sin that a man doeth is without the body; but he that commiteth fornication sinneth against his own body" (1 Co.6:18).

"Abstain from fornication" (1 Th.4:3).

"Abstain from fleshly lusts, which war against the soul" (1 Pe.2:11).

Thought 1. What is the decision required by this commandment?

Obedience! Very simply, we must never commit adultery, never commit an immoral act. We must live pure, holy lives. But how? How can we guard ourselves and keep from committing sexual sin in a sex-crazed society—a society that uses sex to sell products, provide entertainment, pleasure, recreation, and clothing for day-to-day dress? Scripture says the following:

(1) Never take a second look. And if you can prevent the first look, never look the first time. As the old saying goes, we cannot keep the birds from flying over our heads, but we can prevent them from roosting there.

"But I say unto you, That whosoever looketh on a woman to lust after her hath committed adultery with her already in his heart" (Mt.5:28).

(2) Flee temptation; flee the very appearance of evil. We must always flee at the very first offer, the very first sight, the very first thought, the very first urge (desire).

"Abstain from all appearance of evil" (1 Th.5:22).

(3) Flee immorality—abstain totally.

"Flee fornication [all forms of illicit sex]" (1 Co.6:18).

"For this is the will of God, even your sanctification, that ye should abstain from fornication: That every one of you should know how to possess his vessel in sanctification and honour; Not in the lust of concupiscence, even as the Gentiles which know not God" (1 Th.4:3-5).

(4) Never touch the unclean thing.

"Wherefore come out from among them, and be ye separate, saith the LORD, and touch not the unclean thing; and I will receive you, And will be a Father unto you, and ye shall be my sons and daughters, saith the LORD Almighty" (2 Co.6:17-18).

(5) Never talk about immorality, not even once.

"But fornication, and all uncleanness, or covetousness, let it not be once named among you, as becometh saints; Neither filthiness, nor foolish talking, nor jesting, which are not convenient: but rather giving of thanks" (Ep.5:3-4).

DEUTERONOMY 5:16-21

(6) Never give any part of your body over to sin.

"**Neither yield ye your members [body parts] as instruments of unrighteousness unto sin: but yield yourselves unto God, as those that are alive from the dead, and your members as instruments of righteousness unto God**" (Ro.6:13).

(7) Never let sin control your body.

"**Let not sin therefore reign in your mortal body, that ye should obey it in the lusts thereof**" (Ro.6:12, see vv.11-13).

(8) Do not love the world nor the things of the world.

"**Love not the world, neither the things that are in the world. If any man love the world, the love of the Father is not in him. For all that is in the world, the lust of the flesh, and the lust of the eyes, and the pride of life, is not of the Father, but is of the world**" (1 Jn.2:15-16).

(9) Live a crucified life, a life sacrificed totally to Christ.

"**I am crucified with Christ: nevertheless I live; yet not I, but Christ liveth in me: and the life which I now live in the flesh I live by the faith of the Son of God, who loved me, and gave himself for me**" (Ga.2:20).
"**And he said to [them] all, If any [man] will come after me, let him deny himself, and take up his cross daily, and follow me**" (Lu.9:23).

(10) Sacrifice and commit your body totally to Jesus Christ.

"**I beseech you therefore, brethren, by the mercies of God, that ye present your bodies a living sacrifice, holy, acceptable unto God, which is your reasonable service. And be not conformed to this world: but be ye transformed by the renewing of your mind, that ye may prove what is that good, and acceptable, and perfect, will of God**" (Ro.12:1-2).

(11) Put the sinful acts of the body to death.

"**Likewise reckon ye also yourselves to be dead indeed unto sin, but alive unto God through Jesus Christ our LORD**" (Ro.6:11).
"**For if ye live after the flesh, ye shall die: but if ye through the Spirit do mortify the deeds of the body, ye shall live**" (Ro.8:13).

(12) Discipline yourself—strenuously so—in order to control your body.

"**But I keep under my body, and bring it into subjection: lest that by any means, when I have preached to others, I myself should be a castaway**" (1 Co.9:27).

(13) Be filled with the Spirit of God, bearing His character and His character alone.

"**And be not drunk with wine, wherein is excess; but be filled with the Spirit**" (Ep.5:18).

(14) Guard your spirit.

"**Take heed to your spirit, and let none deal treacherously against the wife of his youth**" (Mal.2:15).

(15) Glorify God in your body.

"**Flee fornication. Every sin that a man doeth is without the body; but he that commiteth fornication sinneth against his own body. What? know ye not that your body is the temple of the Holy Ghost which is in you, which ye have of God, and ye are not your own? For ye are bought with a price: therefore glorify God in your body, and in your spirit, which are God's**" (1 Co.6:18-20).

(16) Captivate and subject every thought to obey Christ.

"**Casting down imaginations, and every high thing that exalteth itself against the knowledge of God, and bringing into captivity every thought to the obedience of Christ**" (2 Co.10:5).

(17) Listen to God's Word: hide His Word in your heart and live by it.

"**Wherewithal shall a young man cleanse his way? by taking heed thereto according to thy word....Thy word have I hid in mine heart, that I might not sin against thee**" (Ps.119:9, 11).

DEUTERONOMY 5:16-21

4 (5:19) **Stealing—Theft—Robbery—Property—Responsibility—Obedience—Commandment, the Ten**: the eighth commandment is, "You shall not steal." Think for a moment: What is *the crime* most often committed within your community? The nation? Around the world? Probably stealing. So many people steal that stealing has become a very commonplace crime of society. If the thief does not assault or kill the victim, he is simply called a *common thief*. Thievery, robbery, and swindling have become epidemic, contributing to the lawlessness within society. And stealing is such a terrible epidemic that it threatens the very foundation of society itself. Just think of...

- government leaders who steal and misuse funds
- employees who steal from their employer
- employers who steal through unfair prices and wages
- dishonest athletes and famous people who steal
- acquaintances and neighbors who steal and are dishonest
- people who steal by living extravagant and indulgent lifestyles, hoarding and banking when so many are in such desperate need throughout the world
- people who steal by taking so much of the earth's wealth and resources

Stealing shows a disrespect for property and for human life. Stealing leads to more and more lawlessness, sometimes even assault and murder. Stealing always creates some havoc, and it can cause devastation. Stealing can bankrupt families, companies, communities, and even nations. Stealing always causes loss, loss for both the victim and the thief. The victim, of course, loses whatever object (physical or otherwise) is stolen; but in addition, the loss can be very painful and sometimes irreplaceable. The thief, though frequently undetected by men, always loses his reputation, integrity, and character before God; and eventually, unless he repents and turns from his sin, he loses his soul. This is the subject of this important commandment:

OUTLINE	SCRIPTURE
4. Commandment 8—*man's property*	19 Neither shalt thou steal.

a. *Stealing* (ganab) means to take and keep something that belongs to another person. William Barclay says:

> [Stealing] *is a "natural" sin. It is human nature to want what we have not got; and the desire may turn to action; and, when it does, a man may steal. We do not need to argue about the rightness of this commandment. Everyone agrees that stealing is wrong.*[13]

God has made man a working being, a being who must work, produce, achieve, accomplish, and possess. The desire to move ahead and progress is planted within man by God. This is the reason we desire things that we do not have. The desire is normal and natural; it is God-given. But the legitimate way to fulfill that desire is to work for what we want and can achieve in life. The illegitimate way to fulfill the desire is to steal. When we act out our desire and take something that does not belong to us—take it either secretly or by force—it is stealing.

b. Note that stealing is a *heart problem*: the cause, the source of stealing, is found in the human heart. Stealing begins with a desire in man. When that desire turns into a passion, a lust, an urge, or covetousness—regardless if the act is carried out—the person is guilty of sin. This is exactly what God says:

> "But every man is tempted, when he is drawn away of his own lust, and enticed. Then when lust hath conceived, it bringeth forth sin: and sin, when it is finished, bringeth forth death" (Js.1:14-15).

Thought 1. Note an excellent example of coveting—of desiring and lusting—in Scripture.

> "When I saw among the spoils a goodly Babylonish garment, and two hundred shekels of silver, and a wedge of gold of fifty shekels weight, then I coveted them, and took them; and, behold, they are hid in the earth in the midst of my tent, and the silver under it" (Jos.7:21).

Thought 2. Arthur W. Pink points out the following:
(1) Stealing was the first sin committed by the human race: Eve took of the forbidden fruit.

> "And when the woman saw that the tree was good for food, and that it was pleasant to the eyes, and a tree to be desired to make one wise, she took of the fruit thereof, and did eat, and gave also unto her husband with her; and he did eat" (Ge.3:6).

(2) Stealing was the first recorded sin committed by Israel after entering Canaan: Achan stole the spoils of war.

> "When I saw among the spoils a goodly Babylonish garment, and two hundred shekels of silver, and a wedge of gold of fifty shekels weight, then I coveted them, and took them; and, behold, they are hid in the earth in the midst of my tent, and the silver under it" (Jos.7:21).

(3) Stealing was the first sin to defile the early church: Ananias and Sapphira kept back some of the money from the sale of their property, money that was to be given to the church.[14]

---

13 William Barclay. *The Old & The New Law*, p.37.
14 Arthur W. Pink. *The Ten Commandments*, p.54.

DEUTERONOMY 5:16-21

"But a certain man named Ananias, with Sapphira his wife, sold a possession, And kept back part of the price, his wife also being privy to it, and brought a certain part, and laid it at the apostles' feet. But Peter said, Ananias, why hath Satan filled thine heart to lie to the Holy Ghost, and to keep back part of the price of the land?" (Ac.5:1-3).

c. God's purpose for commanding people not to steal can be simply stated: it is to protect a person's property and his right to own property, to preserve peace among neighbors and within society. Stealing causes loss—sometimes terrible loss—to the victim. And stealing always leads to hard feelings, broken relationships, and sometimes revenge. This commandment protects a person's right...
- to feed, house, clothe, and provide for himself and his family
- to own property
- to reap and keep the property and rewards of his labor
- to secure enough goods and money to help meet the desperate needs of the poor, the suffering, and the lost of this world

"Let him that stole steal no more: but rather let him labour, working with his hands the thing which is good, that he may have to give to him that needeth" (Ep.4:28).

"For even when we were with you, this we commanded you, that if any would not work, neither should he eat. For we hear that there are some which walk among you disorderly, working not at all, but are busybodies. Now them that are such we command and exhort by our Lord Jesus Christ, that with quietness they work, and eat their own bread" (2 Th.3:10-12).

d. Now, how is this commandment broken, violated? Stealing is so common and so costly to society that the way people go about stealing needs to be studied. Moreover, stealing is not only a sin against society and the people stolen from, stealing is a sin against God. Stealing condemns a person to death, eternal death—unless the person repents and turns to God. For this reason, the various forms of stealing need to be looked at in some detail. A person breaks God's commandment, a person steals...

- by robbing a person, store, company, organization or bank
- by shoplifting
- by loafing on the job
- by not paying bills
- by keeping something borrowed
- by failing to pay debts
- by not paying due taxes
- by stealing the reputation and character of another through lies, gossip, or rumor
- by taking away a person's right to justice (Is.10:1-3)
- by falsely or deceptively advertising
- by keeping an overpayment or excessive refund check, or over-shipment of goods
- by overcharging or price-gouging: charging unfair prices
- by not paying fair and just wages
- by not giving a full day's work on the job
- by taking things from one's employer
- by making unauthorized phone calls
- by padding expense reports
- by unjustly extending business trips at company expense
- by manipulating information or stocks for personal gain
- by abusing sick days
- by arriving at work late or leaving work early without permission
- by stealing and enslaving people for work and profit
- by breaking the rules or cheating to win something, a game or a prize

All acts of stealing are wrong, but there is one form of stealing that is most serious and damning, that of robbing God:
⇒ A person robs God by failing to pay his tithes and offerings to God.

"Even from the days of your fathers ye are gone away from mine ordinances, and have not kept them. Return unto me, and I will return unto you, saith the LORD of hosts. But ye said, Wherein shall we return? Will a man rob God? Yet ye have robbed me. But ye say, Wherein have we robbed thee? In tithes and offerings" (Mal.3:7-8).

⇒ A person robs God by living a hypocritical, inconsistent life. When a person professes to believe and follow God, then fails to follow through, he robs God and other men of a *godly testimony*.

"What? know ye not that your body is the temple of the Holy Ghost which is in you, which ye have of God, and ye are not your own? For ye are bought with a price: therefore glorify God in your body, and in your spirit, which are God's" (1 Co.6:19-20).

⇒ A person robs God by living for self and the world, by choosing not to live for God. God is the great Creator of man; therefore, man owes his life—all he is and has—to God. When a person chooses to live like he wants, he steals his life from God.

"I beseech you therefore, brethren, by the mercies of God, that ye present your bodies a living sacrifice, holy, acceptable unto God, which is your reasonable service. And be not conformed to this world: but be ye transformed by the renewing of your mind, that ye may prove what is that good, and acceptable, and perfect, will of God" (Ro.12:1-2).

"Love not the world, neither the things that are in the world. If any man love the world, the love of the Father is not in him. For all that is in the world, the lust of the flesh, and the lust of the eyes, and the pride of life, is not of the Father, but is of the world" (1 Jn.2:15-16).

DEUTERONOMY 5:16-21

Thought 1. This commandment against stealing is broken when property is taken, no matter how little and insignificant the item may be. F.B. Huey again has an excellent comment on the breaking of this commandment.

> *The spirit of this commandment can be broken in ways other than taking the property of another violently or covertly. The employee who takes paper clips, postage stamps, stationery, etc., from his employer for personal use, the taxpayer who falsifies his tax return, the friend who borrows money or even a cup of sugar without intent of returning it, the shopkeeper who uses dishonest scales or engages in any kind of fraudulent business practice, the student who takes credit for work that was done by someone else, the employee who loafs on the job but accepts full wages, or the nation that takes the land of another by war—all violate this commandment.*[15]

Maxie Dunnam also has an excellent application on this commandment:

> *One of the tragedies of our day is how the justice system treats crimes of stealing. Poor people, with no money to hire legal defense, waste away in prisons for stealing a car or a television, while officers of huge corporate organizations preside in posh board rooms, though it is proven they have manipulated the stock market. Television gives us almost daily reports of defense contract "cost overrides" that steal millions of tax dollars....Ours is a society "on the take," and stealing is one of our most blatant sins....*
>
> *Apart from the obvious ways of seeing this commandment broken, we should think of the more subtle ways we break it.*
> - *by not giving our employers a full day for the pay we receive*
> - *by stealing the good name of another with malicious gossip*
> - *by remaining silent, thus stealing from another the word that might preserve reputation and/or undergird character*
> - *by failing to give to others the support, praise, and credit they're due.*[16]

Thought 2. Scripture is very forceful in dealing with stealing, holding back, and cheating.
(1) We must never steal, not even once.

> **"Thou shalt not steal" (Ex.20:15).**

(2) We must never withhold tithes and offerings from God.

> **"Will a man rob God? Yet ye have robbed me. But ye say, Wherein have we robbed thee? In tithes and offerings. Ye are cursed with a curse: for ye have robbed me, even this whole nation. Bring ye all the tithes into the storehouse, that there may be meat in mine house, and prove me now herewith, saith the LORD of hosts, if I will not open you the windows of heaven, and pour you out a blessing, that there shall not be room enough to receive it" (Mal.3:8-10).**

(3) We must never cheat our brother in anything.

> **"That no man go beyond and defraud his brother in any matter: because that the LORD is the avenger of all such, as we also have forewarned you and testified" (1 Th.4:6).**

(4) We must never steal people (i.e., kidnap, enslave, or put them in bondage): the enslavement of people takes away a person's right to his own life.

> **"And he that stealeth a man, and selleth him, or if he be found in his hand, he shall surely be put to death" (Ex.21:16).**

[5] **(5:20) Lying—Testimony, False—Deception—Perjury—Tongue—Speech, False—Commandment, the Ten—Obedience:** the ninth commandment is, "You shall not lie—never bear false witness against your neighbor." Lying—bearing false testimony against people—is common to all of us. Sometime in the past we have all...

- told a little white lie
- twisted the truth
- told a half-truth
- gossiped, not really knowing the truth
- discredited someone
- slandered someone
- sought to escape blame by skirting around the truth
- tried to place blame elsewhere by failing to come forth with the truth
- cast a suggestive hint or insinuated an untruth about someone
- boasted or exaggerated the truth in order to boost ourselves
- raised an eyebrow, shrugged a shoulder, or made some motion to indicate something was untrue or to keep from disclosing the truth

Scripture emphatically declares: "All men are liars" (Ps.116:11). Lying is so common that it is condoned, accepted, and even expected by many people. But lying is never justified. Silence sometimes is, but not lying, not answering dishonestly. Leaders, both business and political, can say or promise anything, and people either accept or overlook their twisting of the truth. A person's character, his word and integrity, seem to matter little. Making false claims and promises has become a way of life. There is a feeling that a person simply cannot survive or get ahead unless he twists the truth to boost himself. Telling the truth and being honest have fallen by the wayside.

Lying—bearing false witness—threatens the very foundation of society. Nothing can survive when it is filled with lies, not for long: not families, friendships, businesses, clubs, schools, churches, communities, governments. Any organization or group will collapse in the wake of mistrust and broken, severed relationships.

---

[15] F.B. Huey, Jr. *A Study Guide Commentary, Exodus.* (Grand Rapids, MI: Zondervan Publishing House, 1977), p.91.
[16] Maxie Dunnam. *The Preacher's Commentary on Exodus.* pp.265-266.

DEUTERONOMY 5:16-21

This is the great concern of the ninth commandment, the concern for truth, that we build our lives upon truth: build our families, friendships, businesses, clubs, schools, churches, communities, and governments upon truth.

OUTLINE	SCRIPTURE
5. **Commandment 9**—*man's word:* Forbids lying or speaking falsely against anyone	20 Neither shalt thou bear false witness against thy neighbour.

a. This commandment is broken by lying, by telling an untruth of any kind. Man's concept of lying is this: "If I lie, it is justifiable, but if you lie to me, it is unforgivable." But to God, lying is lying. The word *lying* (sheqer) means that which is false, untrue. It is untruthfulness, deception, misrepresentation, exaggeration.

Note how Scripture itself defines a false witness:

⇒ A false witness is a person who breathes out lies.

> "A faithful witness will not lie: but a false witness will utter lies" (Pr.14:5).
> "A false witness shall not be unpunished, and he that speaketh lies shall not escape" (Pr.19:5).

⇒ A false witness is a person who shares a false report.

> "Thou shalt not raise a false report: put not thine hand with the wicked to be an unrighteous witness" (Ex.23:1).

⇒ A false witness is a person who deceives.

> "He that speaketh truth showeth forth righteousness: but a false witness deceit" (Pr.12:17).

As pointed out in note one, when some people look at the ninth commandment, they think of a courtroom scene and think that lying against someone in court is what is being forbidden. But as the Scriptures above show, *bearing false witness* means far more than just lying against someone in court. *Bearing* false witness means any kind of lying. Hosea 4:2 clearly shows this. When Hosea charged the people with breaking several of the commandments, he did not charge them with bearing false witness in court. He charged them with lying in their day-to-day affairs:

> "Hear the word of the LORD, ye children of Israel: for the LORD hath a controversy with the inhabitants of the land, because there is no truth, nor mercy, nor knowledge of God in the land. By swearing, and lying, and killing, and stealing, and committing adultery, they break out, and blood toucheth blood" (Ho.4:1-2).

b. There are several forms or kinds of lies, and they must be diligently guarded against.

1) There is slander: thinking something bad about a person and sharing it; misrepresenting something about someone; tearing down the reputation and life of a person by spreading bad news about him.

> "Whoso privily [secretly] slandereth his neighbour, him will I cut off: him that hath an high look and a proud heart will not I suffer" (Ps.101:5).
> "He that hideth hatred with lying lips, and he that uttereth a slander, is a fool" (Pr.10:18).

2) There is rumor or gossip or tale-bearing: spreading little or big tales, idle or active tales, whether imagined or real; spreading the evil news that one has imagined in his mind or has heard.

> "And withal they learn to be idle, wandering about from house to house; and not only idle, but tattlers also and busybodies, speaking things which they ought not" (1 Ti.5:13).
> "But let none of you suffer as a murderer, or as a thief, or as an evildoer, or as a busybody in other men's matters" (1 Pe.4:15).
> "Thou shalt not go up and down as a talebearer among thy people" (Le.19:16).
> "A talebearer revealeth secrets: but he that is of a faithful spirit concealeth the matter" (Pr.11:13).
> "A froward man soweth strife: and a whisperer separateth chief friends" (Pr.16:28).
> "Where no wood is, there the fire goeth out: so where there is no talebearer, the strife ceaseth" (Pr.26:20).

3) There are suggestive hints or insinuations: arousing a bad impression about someone; stirring the idea that something might possibly be true; planting in the mind the possibility of something improper or indecent.

> "Thou shalt not raise a false report: put not thine hand with the wicked to be an unrighteous witness" (Ex.23:1).
> "Take ye heed every one of his neighbor, and trust ye not in any brother: for every brother will utterly supplant, and every neighbor will walk with slanders" (Je.9:4).

DEUTERONOMY 5:16-21

4) There is deception: thinking or wanting something to be true, accepting it as true and sharing it; tricking oneself and others into thinking something is true; deceiving oneself and others by accepting bad news as true when the truth is really not known; causing oneself and others to believe bad news.

> "He that speaketh truth showeth forth righteousness: but a false witness deceit" (Pr.12:17).
> "Be not a witness against thy neighbor without cause; and deceive not with thy lips" (Pr.24:28).

5) There are false charges and criticism: accusations made against a person to a third party; sharing the faults and failures of a person with someone other than the person himself; talking about the weaknesses and failures of a person with someone else; condemning, blaming, and censoring a person with others.

> "Blessed are ye, when men shall revile you, and persecute you, and shall say all manner of evil against you falsely, for my sake. Rejoice, and be exceeding glad: for great is your reward in heaven: for so persecuted they the prophets which were before you" (Mt.5:11-12).
> "Having a good conscience; that, whereas they speak evil of you, as of evildoers, they may be ashamed that falsely accuse your good conversation in Christ" (1 Pe.3:16).
> "For I have heard the slander of many: fear was on every side: while they took counsel together against me, they devised to take away my life" (Ps.31:13).

6) There is exaggeration and blown-up flattery: stretching the truth about a person; excessively praising someone; falsely representing someone; painting a false picture of a person.

> "Let me not, I pray you, accept any man's person; neither let me give flattering titles unto man" (Jb.32:21).
> "He that goeth about as a talebearer revealeth secrets: therefore meddle not with him that flattereth with his lips" (Pr.20:19).
> "A lying tongue hateth those that are afflicted by it; and a flattering mouth worketh ruin" (Pr.26:28).
> "He that rebuketh a man, afterward shall find more favor than he that flattereth with the tongue" (Pr.28:23).
> "A man that flattereth his neighbor spreadeth a net for his feet" (Pr.29:5).
> "The LORD shall cut off all flattering lips, and the tongue that speaketh proud things" (Ps.12:3).
> "But as we were allowed of God to be put in trust with the gospel, even so we speak; not as pleasing men, but God, which trieth our hearts. For neither at any time used we flattering words, as ye know, nor a cloke of covetousness; God is witness" (1 Th.2:4-5).
> "He that saith unto the wicked, Thou art righteous; him shall the people curse, nations shall abhor him" (Pr.24:24).

7) There are innumerable ways in which we lie, such as...
- perjury
- propaganda
- boasting
- telling half-truths
- breaking vows
- twisting the truth to protect oneself
- shifting blame
- seeking to discredit someone
- sharing a convenient lie
- making up an excuse
- seeking to escape responsibility or punishment
- raising an eyebrow, shrugging the shoulder, or snickering—doing anything that indicates something is untrue or that disavows knowledge of the truth

c. A lie has at least three terrible effects upon people.
  1) Lying misrepresents the truth. It camouflages and hides the truth. The person lied to does not know the truth; therefore, he has to act or live upon a lie. If the lie is serious, it can be very damaging:
  ⇒ A lie about a business deal can cost money and cause terrible loss.
  ⇒ A lie about loving someone can stir emotions that lead to destruction.
  ⇒ A lie about the salvation of the gospel can cost a person the hope of eternal life.

  2) Lying deceives a person. It leads a person astray. A person deceives...
  - to get what he wants
  - to seduce someone
  - to cover up or hide something
  - to cause harm or hurt

  The point to see is that lying is a deception, and deception eventually causes misunderstanding, disappointment, bewilderment, helplessness, emotional upheaval, loss, and sometimes immorality and destruction.

  3) Lying builds a wrong relationship, a relationship built upon sinking sand. Two people cannot possibly be friends or live together if the relationship is based upon lies. Lying destroys...
  - confidence
  - assurance
  - security
  - love
  - trust
  - hope

DEUTERONOMY 5:16-21

    d. Four facts need to be noted about lying or bearing false witness.

      1) False witness is usually shared with loved ones and good friends, with people we feel can be trusted. Therefore, we always feel that our loved ones and friends can be trusted with the *bad news*. However, what is overlooked is that our loved ones and friends have good friends whom they feel can be trusted. And so the bad news is spread further and further afield; more damage and hurt is done to people and to the cause of Christ. God knows this is the way people are. This is the reason God forbids His people from sharing failure, whether true or untrue, except in dealing with the person involved with the issue.

      2) Bearing tales about a person, whether true or untrue, always hurts the person. The person being talked about has a heart just like we do: a heart that is subject to being cut and hurt and suffering pain. Therefore, when tales are shared, we are eventually going to cause pain and hurt, sometimes a great deal of pain, to the person and his loved ones. (Imagine how God feels about this.)

> "All that hate me whisper together against me: against me do they devise my hurt" (Ps.41:7).
>
> "The words of a talebearer are as wounds, and they go down into the innermost parts of the belly" (Pr.18:8).
>
> "A man that beareth false witness against his neighbor is a maul [hammer], and a sword, and a sharp arrow" (Pr.25:18).

      3) The person who bears tales, giving false witness, shall be judged by God, no matter who he is.

> "Being filled with all unrighteousness...deceit...whisperers, backbiters....Who knowing the judgment of God, that they which commit such things are worthy of death, not only do the same, but have pleasure in them that do them" (Ro.1:29-30, 32).
>
> "Whoso privily [secretly] slandereth his neighbour, him will I cut off: him that hath an high look and a proud heart will not I suffer" (Ps.101:5).
>
> "A false witness shall not be unpunished; and he that speaketh lies shall perish" (Pr.19:9).

      4) If a person truly loves, he will not bear false witness about anyone. If there is a problem or some questionable report, he will deal with the person himself, seeking to restore him to the faith. Note: love does not deal with a person in harshness, downgrading him, but in love and tenderness and in *strength*, being guided by the Holy Spirit of God.

> "Brethren, if a man be overtaken in a fault, ye which are spiritual, restore such an one in the spirit of meekness; considering thyself, lest thou also be tempted. Bear ye one another's burdens, and so fulfil the law of Christ" (Ga.6:1-2).
>
> "I have seen his ways, and will heal him: I will lead him also, and restore comforts unto him and to his mourners" (Is.57:18).
>
> "Set a watch, O Lord, before my mouth; keep the door of my lips" (Ps.141:3).

    e. The source of lies and lying is Satan. He was the first ever to lie; therefore, he is called the father of lies. The person who lies follows in the footsteps of Satan and is called by Scripture a "child of the devil."

> "Ye are of [your] father the devil, and the lusts of your father ye will do. He was a murderer from the beginning, and abode not in the truth, because there is no truth in him. When he speaketh a lie, he speaketh of his own: for he is a liar, and the father of it" (Jn.8:44).

    f. The source of truth is God. Note Scripture declares time and again that God is the God of truth.

> "God is not a man, that he should lie; neither the son of man, that he should repent: hath he said, and shall he not do it? or hath he spoken, and shall he not make it good?" (Nu.23:19).
>
> "He is the Rock, his work is perfect: for all his ways are judgment: a God of truth and without iniquity, just and right is he" (De.32:4).
>
> "And now, O Lord GOD, thou art that God, and thy words be true, and thou hast promised this goodness unto thy servant" (2 S.7:28).
>
> "Happy is he that hath the God of Jacob for his help, whose hope is in the LORD his God: Which made heaven, and earth, the sea, and all that therein is: which keepeth truth for ever" (Ps.146:5-6).
>
> "That he who blesseth himself in the earth shall bless himself in the God of truth; and he that sweareth in the earth shall swear by the God of truth; because the former troubles are forgotten, and because they are hid from mine eyes" (Is.65:16).
>
> "God forbid: yea, let God be true, but every man a liar; as it is written, That thou mightest be justified in thy sayings, and mightest overcome when thou art judged" (Ro.3:4).
>
> "In hope of eternal life, which God, that cannot lie, promised before the world began" (Tit.1:2).
>
> "Wherein God, willing more abundantly to show unto the heirs of promise the immutability of his counsel, confirmed it by an oath: That by two immutable things, in which it was impossible for God to lie, we might have a strong consolation, who have fled for refuge to lay hold upon the hope set before us" (He.6:17-18).

    g. The very foundation or basis of society is truth. Families, businesses, organizations, clubs, neighbors, or communities in any society will disintegrate and collapse unless the members are truthful with one another. If we lie and deceive one

DEUTERONOMY 5:16-21

another, the consequences are hurtful, damaging, and often devastating. Wrong decisions are made and wrong actions are taken. Lies and deception—bearing false witness—are often what cause...

- divorce
- job loss
- unemployment
- severed relationships
- pain and hurt
- failure
- bankruptcy
- collapse
- vengeance
- retaliation
- abuse
- accident
- suffering
- imprisonment
- death

h. A critical question needs to be asked when dealing with lying or telling the truth. Should we ever tell the truth bluntly or harshly? In a court of law, the truth must always be spoken straight to the point: directly and straightforward. But when dealing in personal, face-to-face relationships, we should not intentionally cause pain, hurt, embarrassment, or shame. We should never deliberately wound a person with a blunt, harsh statement of the truth. Truth is to be spoken in love and kindness not in harshness and ugliness.

"But speaking the truth in love, may grow up into him in all things, which is the head, even Christ" (Ep.4:15).

"Let all bitterness, and wrath, and anger, and clamour, and evil speaking, be put away from you, with all malice: And be ye kind one to another, tenderhearted, forgiving one another, even as God for Christ's sake hath forgiven you" (Ep.4:31-32).

Thought 1. William Barclay has an excellent statement on this point:

When we speak about telling the truth, one special point arises. Must we always tell the truth baldly and bluntly? For instance, if a person has played a game or sung a song or given some kind of performance, and not done very well, must we say that he was no good, or is there any harm in the polite compliment which will encourage him, even if it is not strictly true? Must we tell the truth, even when it is unpleasant and when it might hurt?

Someone has given us a valuable rule about this. There are three questions we should always ask about anything we say about anyone else, or to anyone else. The first question is: Is it true? And, of course, if it is not true, then it must not be said at all. The second question is: Is it necessary? If it is necessary, it will have to be said, but there are not many times when politeness and courtesy need to be disregarded. The third question is: Is it kind? It is hardly ever a duty to be unkind. There are ways and ways of telling the truth. You can tell it in a way that is deliberately designed to wound and hurt; there are people who take a delight in seeing other people wince when something is said. On the other hand, it was said of Florence Allshorn, a great teacher, that, when she had some criticism to make, she always made it, as it were, with her arm round your shoulder. She spoke the truth; she said what was necessary; but she took care to say it kindly and in a way that would help and not hurt. And that is the best rule of all. [17]

6 (5:21) **Covetousness—Desire—Lust—Craving—Security—Obedience—Commandment, the Ten**: the tenth commandment is, "You shall not covet." What is forbidden by this commandment? How is this commandment broken, violated? Commandment ten concerns man's security. This commandment forbids coveting anything that belongs to our neighbor: his house, wife, servant, workers, animals, or anything else. A man should be able to live in peace and feel secure. He should not have to worry about someone coveting and stealing what he has. God wants man to feel secure and protected. God wants man to know that his wife and family, his property and possessions, his joy and anything else he has is secure and protected against the covetousness and theft of people.

OUTLINE	SCRIPTURE
6. Commandment 10—*man's desires & security*: Forbids coveting anything that belongs to your neighbor—his wife, house, land, servant, animals, or anything else	21 Neither shalt thou desire thy neighbour's wife, neither shalt thou covet thy neighbour's house, his field, or his manservant, or his maidservant, his ox, or his ass, or any *thing* that *is* thy neighbour's.

a. The Hebrew word for *covet* (hamad) means to desire, crave, want, long for, thirst for, yearn for, lust after. *Coveting* is a neutral word; that is, coveting can be good as well as bad, legitimate as well as illegitimate.

1) The Bible clearly says that there is a legitimate covetousness, that God has planted within man certain inalienable desires, desires that we are entitled to, desires that are good. We all have legitimate desires for love, joy, and peace; legitimate desires to be secure, successful, fulfilled, and satisfied.

⇒ The Bible says that every good and perfect gift comes from God Himself. This being so, we should actually *seek after* and *covet* good and perfect gifts.

"Every good gift and every perfect gift is from above, and cometh down from the Father of lights, with whom is no variableness, neither shadow of turning" (Js.1:17).

---

[17] William Barclay. *The Old Law & The New Law*, pp.43-44.

DEUTERONOMY 5:16-21

⇒ The Bible says that the excellent qualities of life and the best gifts of God are to be coveted.

"Blessed [are] they which do hunger and thirst after righteousness: for they shall be filled" (Mt.5:6).

"But covet earnestly the best gifts: and yet show I unto you a more excellent way" (1 Co.12:31).

"The fear of the LORD is clean, enduring for ever: the judgments of the LORD are true and righteous altogether. More to be desired are they than gold, yea, than much fine gold: sweeter also than honey and the honeycomb" (Ps.19:9-10).

⇒ The Bible even says that God gives us the ability to get wealth and that we should work so diligently that we can actually earn enough to meet the needs of others.

"Let him that stole steal no more: but rather let him labour, working with his hands the thing which is good, that he may have to give to him that needeth" (Ep.4:28).

2) The Bible clearly says there is an illegitimate covetousness, that man commits evil when he desires another person's wife or property, or any other possession belonging to the person.

"Thou shalt not covet thy neighbour's house, thou shalt not covet thy neighbour's wife, nor his manservant, nor his maidservant, nor his ox, nor his ass, nor any thing that is thy neighbour's" (Ex.20:17).

"But fornication, and all uncleanness, or covetousness, let it not be once named among you, as becometh saints" (Ep.5:3).

"Mortify [put to death] therefore your members which are upon the earth; fornication, uncleanness, inordinate affection, evil concupiscence, and covetousness, which is idolatry" (Col.3:5).

b. Covetousness is an inward sin, a sin of the heart and mind: it is a *desire*, a *thought* within the heart and mind. This commandment differs from the other commandments in this very fact, differs rather significantly: covetousness is not the outward sin; it is the inward *desire* and *thought* that leads to the outward sin.

Remember, the first nine commandments dealt primarily with outward acts, with such acts as lying, stealing, and killing. But this tenth commandment deals with the human heart, with inward feelings, desires, thoughts, and attitudes. But note: the first nine commandments *also involved* the desires and thoughts of a person. Before a person ever lies, steals, or kills, the desire or thought to take such action arises in his heart and mind. The desire to do something always precedes the actual act. A man commits immorality because he desires a person. A woman steals because she either desires the thing stolen or the excitement of stealing. In dealing with the first nine commandments, we discussed this fact, the fact that the evil forbidden was aroused first of all in the heart and mind of a person, that the evil was basically a heart problem.

This is the very reason God has covered coveting last, listed it as the tenth commandment. Coveting (desire, lust, the covetous thought) is the first thing that happens before a person commits the outward sin. The sin is *aroused* within the heart before it is committed; the evil act is *thought about* before it is done. This commandment underlies all the commandments: coveting—the desire or thought—takes place within the human heart and mind before any of the nine commandments are publicly or secretly committed. Before a person ever commits the sinful act, he desires and thinks about what someone else has, his...

- house
- wife
- servant
- livestock
- horse
- vehicle
- property
- money
- clothing
- appearance
- personality
- looks
- position
- power
- recognition
- job
- promotion
- opportunity
- influence

The list could go on and on. We commit the sin of covetousness when our *hearts and minds* are set on some possession, so set that we...

- crave, long, and lust after it
- are consumed with getting it
- give ourselves over to pursuing it
- give top priority and first attention to it
- focus our hearts, minds, energy, and time to securing it

Covetousness is being so consumed with getting something that we become gripped and enslaved by it. Our hearts become focused upon *a possession, a thing, something other than God*. This is the reason Scripture declares that covetousness is idolatry:

"**For this ye know, that no whoremonger, nor unclean person, nor covetous man, who is an idolater, hath any inheritance in the kingdom of Christ and of God**" (Ep.5:5).

Thought 1. Maxie Dunnam has an excellent application on this commandment:

Most of us are guilty of looking at others, comparing ourselves to them, and seeing ourselves come out on the short end. We torture ourselves in this fashion, drive ourselves to depression by self-pity, thinking we deserve more. When we find ourselves jealous of what life is for someone else, dreaming of how happy we would be if we were in someone else's situation, it's a dead giveaway that we are falling into the subtle, seductive hands of covetousness.

DEUTERONOMY 5:16-21

How often do we convince ourselves that other people always get the breaks and not us? How recently have we thought that we were deprived of opportunity? We look at our peers, friends our own age, and see where they are in life, and we're plagued with the notion that they had far more opportunity than we did.

You probably have not associated that with coveting, but whatever name you give it, it is exactly that, and it is destructive....

We convince ourselves that we have a sort of cosmic right to an equal share of the good things of life. That's a fallacious idea, and it plays folly in our lives. There's no equality to being in the right place at the right time.

There is no cosmic right that is ours to have an equal share of what everybody else has. If you're prone to leaning in that direction, consider how you would feel if you were averaged out with the world's two billion starving people. You see, we always want to be averaged up and not down.[18]

Thought 2. Matthew Henry has a very graphic application:

"O that such a man's house were mine! Such a man's wife mine! Such a man's estate mine!" This is certainly the language of discontent at our own lot, and envy at our neighbour's; and these are the sins principally forbidden here.[19]

Thought 3. The covetous life has been described as follows by an unnamed author:

The passion to possess is an ugly sin no matter how we look at it. But when the object of our passion belongs to some one else, as the Tenth Commandment says thy neighbor, this sin takes on an even uglier hue. When we covet something out there, something that is available and waiting to be claimed, we limit most of the destruction to ourselves. But, when we covet that which belongs to others, we bring those people into the situation, and jeopardize our attitudes toward them and our relationships with them.

Someone may covet a starting position on a sports team or another individual's job. This person, consumed with envy, may scheme and wish for his nemesis to be hurt, or miss a deadline, or lose an account, in order to claim his position. Or, what about coveting someone else's spouse? This person berates their own mate, feeds discontent with insensitive comparisons, and undermines another's marriage with subtle (or, not-so-subtle) advances. Some selfish siblings count the days to their parents' death as they covet the inheritance money.

Coveting what belongs to another person is a serious offense on two counts. First, it indicates our lack of love for our neighbor, our relative, our friend, or whoever owns what we desire. The first and great commandment has to do with love; but, covetousness stands in direct opposition to love. When we place our affections on an inheritance, we remove our love from the person who's bequeathing it to us. When we see our neighbor's wife as the object of our desire, we begin to view our neighbor as the object of our disdain. When we scheme to get someone else's job, we reveal our calloused, insensitive heart. When we wish another person illness, injury, or bad fortune, we make it clear that the ONLY person we care about is "NUMBER ONE", ourselves. When we covet what belongs to someone else, we displace the owner. In our minds, we kick him out of the game, or out of the job, or out of the marriage.[20]

---

18 Maxie Dunnam. *The Preacher's Commentary on Exodus*, pp.267-268.
19 *Matthew Henry's Commentary*, Vol. 1, pp.362-363.
20 As quoted in the Sunday School material: *Ten Overlooked Principles in Building Successful Families*, pp.6-7; derived from Adrian Rogers' *Ten Secrets For A Successful Family*.

DEUTERONOMY 5:22-33

	D. The Purposes of the Law: Why God Gave the Ten Commandments & the Law, 5:22-33	that the LORD our God shall say: and speak thou unto us all that the LORD our God shall speak unto thee; and we will hear *it*, and do *it*.	be their mediator b. The leaders promised to listen & obey God's Word

1. To give man the commandments of the LORD Himself, the commandments that point to a full, victorious life
  a. Were proclaimed by the voice of God Himself: Out from the awesome presence of His glory
  b. Were then written on two stone tablets by God Himself
	22 These words the LORD spake unto all your assembly in the mount out of the midst of the fire, of the cloud, and of the thick darkness, with a great voice: and he added no more. And he wrote them in two tables of stone, and delivered them unto me.	28 And the LORD heard the voice of your words, when ye spake unto me; and the LORD said unto me, I have heard the voice of the words of this people, which they have spoken unto thee: they have well said all that they have spoken.	4. To reveal the very heart of God for man
			  a. He longs to meet man's need for a mediator: Appointed Moses to stand between the people & God

2. To reveal the majestic glory & holiness of God: Showing that a great barrier—a great gulf—exists between man & God
  a. The people saw the glory of God & heard His voice speak: They feared & sent the leaders to Moses for help
  b. The leaders acknowledged God's holiness, the great barrier between God & man: They feared being consumed by God's voice & the fire of His majestic holiness
	23 And it came to pass, when ye heard the voice out of the midst of the darkness, (for the mountain did burn with fire,) that ye came near unto me, *even* all the heads of your tribes, and your elders;
	24 And ye said, Behold, the LORD our God hath showed us his glory and his greatness, and we have heard his voice out of the midst of the fire: we have seen this day that God doth talk with man, and he liveth.
	25 Now therefore why should we die? for this great fire will consume us: if we hear the voice of the LORD our God any more, then we shall die.
		29 O that there were such an heart in them, that they would fear me, and keep all my commandments always, that it might be well with them, and with their children for ever!
		30 Go say to them, Get you into your tents again.
		31 But as for thee, stand thou here by me, and I will speak unto thee all the commandments, and the statutes, and the judgments, which thou shalt teach them, that they may do *them* in the land which I give them to possess it.
			b. He longs for man to fear Him & obey Him: To reverence, worship, & fellowship with Him
			c. He longs for things to go well for man & his family
			d. He longs to give man all the laws he needs to live a full & victorious life
			  1) God had the people sent home
			  2) God kept Moses with Him: To give him the laws the people would need in the promised land

3. To reveal that man must have a mediator to represent him before God
 	
  a. The leaders asked Moses to
	26 For who *is there of* all flesh, that hath heard the voice of the living God speaking out of the midst of the fire, as we *have*, and lived?
	27 Go thou near, and hear all
		32 Ye shall observe to do therefore as the LORD your God hath commanded you: ye shall not turn aside to the right hand or to the left.
		33 Ye shall walk in all the ways which the LORD your God hath commanded you, that ye may live, and *that it may be* well with you, and *that* ye may prolong *your* days in the land which ye shall possess.
			e. He longs for man to obey Him: A reemphasis seen in the exhortation of Moses
			  1) Must not turn aside to the right nor to the left
			  2) Must walk in the path of God's commandments
			  3) The result: Will live, prosper, & prolong your days in the promised land

DIVISION III

THE SECOND GREAT THEME PREACHED BY GOD'S AGED SERVANT (PART 1): REMEMBER THE TEN COMMANDMENTS—THE FUNDAMENTAL LAWS TO GOVERN MAN AND SOCIETY, 4:44–11:32

D. The Purposes of the Law: Why God Gave the Ten Commandments and the Law, 5:22-33

(5:22-33) **Introduction**: Scripture is clear: God gave the Ten Commandments as the basic law to govern all people. But why? Why exactly did God give the Ten Commandments to the world? What were His purposes? What did God have in mind? What were His reasons for instituting the Ten Commandments to be the basic law for all men to obey?

We must understand God's reasons for giving the Ten Commandments in order to gain the greatest benefit from them. A careful study of the present passage tells us why God gave the law. Five very specific purposes can be gleaned from the experience of Israel right after receiving the Ten Commandments. This is the all-important subject of this Scripture: *The Purposes of the Law: Why God Gave the Ten Commandments and the Law*, 5:22-33.

1. To give man the commandments of the LORD Himself, the commandments that point to a full, victorious life (v.22).
2. To reveal the majestic glory and holiness of God: showing that a great barrier—a great gulf—exists between man and God (vv.23-25).
3. To reveal that man must have a mediator to represent him before God (vv.26-27).
4. To reveal the very heart of God for man (vv.28-33).

DEUTERONOMY 5:22-33

1 **(5:22) Commandments, the Ten, Source of—Glory, of God, Revealed—Revelation, of God's Glory—God, Revelation of:** What is the first purpose of the law? To give man the commandments of the LORD Himself, the commandments that point people to a full, victorious life. God loves His people and cares about their welfare, the problems and difficulties, the trials and temptations they face in life. God is deeply concerned about the terrible and appalling evil committed by people:

⇒ dishonoring father and mother
⇒ murdering
⇒ committing adultery and other forms of immorality
⇒ stealing
⇒ lying and speaking falsely against people
⇒ coveting the things of this world, including the wives and husbands of others
⇒ cursing God's name
⇒ committing idolatry and false worship
⇒ believing in false gods

God created man; therefore, He knows how man should live. God knows what it is that gives man a full, victorious life. This is what the Ten Commandments are for: they are the laws that tell man how to live—how to have purpose, meaning, and significance in life—how to have confidence, assurance, satisfaction, and fulfillment in life—how to live a victorious life, conquering all the enemies that stand opposed to life: disease, accident, death, broken relationships, and all the other trials and tribulations that confront us day by day as we walk throughout life. God wants His people conquering all of the difficulties and trials of life. He wants His people living full, victorious lives. This was the reason He gave the Ten Commandments to the people of Israel. He wanted His people to have the laws, the commandments that told them how to live, the commandments that would lead them to full, victorious lives. Note the Scripture and outline:

OUTLINE	SCRIPTURE
1. To give man the commandments of the LORD Himself, the commandments that point to a full, victorious life a. Were proclaimed by the voice of God Himself: Out from the awesome presence of His glory b. Were then written on two stone tablets by God Himself	22 These words the LORD spake unto all your assembly in the mount out of the midst of the fire, of the cloud, and of the thick darkness, with a great voice: and he added no more. And he wrote them in two tables of stone, and delivered them unto me.

a. The voice of God Himself spoke the commandments, proclaiming them out from the spectacular sight of His glory. God wanted no question about the source of the commandments, that they came from Him and Him alone. Therefore, He gave the commandments in the midst of a spectacular revelation of His majestic glory and holiness. By doing this, the commandments would be stamped and engraved upon the minds of the people forever. Remember, the presence of God had descended upon Mt. Sinai, symbolized in a cloud that Scripture describes as *thick, deep darkness*. The cloud was filled with thunder and lightning and the constant blast of a loud trumpet. When it descended upon the mountain, a flaming fire engulfed the mountain with flames shooting up into the deep, dark cloud. There was a violent quaking of the mountain and bellowing smoke that arose as though from a huge, volcanic eruption. (See note 2 below—De.5:23-25 for more discussion.) By giving the law in such a spectacular, dramatic way, it was imprinted forever on the minds of the people. God did all He could to make sure they had the laws they needed to live full, victorious lives.

b. But this was not all God did. He Himself wrote the commandments on two stone tablets and gave the tablets to Moses to give to the people. Obviously, the people of that day could look at the tablets and tell that the wording had not been chiseled by man, but rather by the flaming finger of God's holy hand. This means that the Ten Commandments were given to man in two dramatic ways:

⇒ by the very voice of God Himself, proclaimed out from the awesome presence of His spectacular glory
⇒ by the very finger of God Himself

There could never be any legitimate question, not by a thoughtful, honest person: the Ten Commandments have come from the LORD God Himself. They were given by God to the Israelites and to all other people to show them how to live full, victorious lives.

"For verily I say unto you, Till heaven and earth pass, one jot or one tittle shall in no wise pass from the law, till all be fulfilled" (Mt.5:18).

"Heaven and earth shall pass away: but my words shall not pass away" (Lu.21:33).

"All scripture *is* given by inspiration of God, and *is* profitable for doctrine, for reproof, for correction, for instruction in righteousness" (2 Ti.3:16).

"How shall we escape, if we neglect so great salvation; which at the first began to be spoken by the LORD, and was confirmed unto us by them that heard *him*" (He.2:3).

"For the word of God *is* quick, and powerful, and sharper than any twoedged sword, piercing even to the dividing asunder of soul and spirit, and of the joints and marrow, and *is* a discerner of the thoughts and intents of the heart" (He.4:12).

"But the word of the LORD endureth for ever. And this is the word which by the gospel is preached unto you" (1 Pe.1:25).

DEUTERONOMY 5:22-33

"Ye shall not add unto the word which I command you, neither shall ye diminish *ought* from it, that ye may keep the commandments of the LORD your God which I command you" (De.4:2).

"The statutes of the LORD *are* right, rejoicing the heart: the commandment of the LORD *is* pure, enlightening the eyes" (Ps.19:8).

"For ever, O LORD, thy word is settled in heaven" (Ps.119:89).

"Thy word *is* a lamp unto my feet, and a light unto my path" (Ps.119:105).

"The grass withereth, the flower fadeth: but the word of our God shall stand for ever" (Is.40:8).

2 (5:23-25) **Gulf, Separates Man from God—Separation, from God—Barrier, Between God and Man—Holiness, of God—Majesty, of God—Glory, of God—Law—Commandments, the Ten**: Why did God give the Ten Commandments to man? Second, to reveal the glorious majesty and holiness of God's person, to reveal that a great barrier—a great gulf—exists between man and God. Remember what had happened: God's holy presence had descended to the top of Mt. Sinai in what was probably the most spectacular, terrifying storm and cloud ever witnessed upon earth. Note the glorious description given by Scripture: there was...

- thunder and lightning (Ex.19:16; 20:18)
- a flaming fire that engulfed the cloud and mountain (Ex.19:18)
- a cloud of deep darkness that bellowed smoke arising as though from a huge volcanic eruption (Ex.19:18; 20:18)
- the violent quaking of the mountain that never stopped trembling (Ex.19:18)
- the constant blast of a loud trumpet (Ex.19:16, 19; 20:18)

The people reacted just as any of us would. Note the Scripture and outline:

OUTLINE	SCRIPTURE	SCRIPTURE	OUTLINE
2. To reveal the majestic glory & holiness of God: Showing that a great barrier—a great gulf—exists between man & God a. The people saw the glory of God & heard His voice speak: They feared & sent the leaders to Moses for help b. The leaders acknowledged God's holiness, the great bar-	23 And it came to pass, when ye heard the voice out of the midst of the darkness, (for the mountain did burn with fire,) that ye came near unto me, *even* all the heads of your tribes, and your elders; 24 And ye said, Behold, the LORD our God hath showed us his glory and his greatness,	and we have heard his voice out of the midst of the fire: we have seen this day that God doth talk with man, and he liveth. 25 Now therefore why should we die? for this great fire will consume us: if we hear the voice of the LORD our God any more, then we shall die.	rier between God & man: They feared being consumed by God's voice & the fire of His majestic holiness

a. The people saw the glory of God and heard the voice of God speak (vv.23-24). They were stricken with a terrifying fear and withdrew a great distance from the foot of the mountain. They then sent the leaders of their tribes to Moses for help.

b. When the leaders gathered with Moses, they acknowledged God's majestic glory and holiness, the great barrier—the great gulf—between God and man (vv.24-25). The people had shrunk back from God's holy presence because they feared for their lives. They feared lest the holy presence of God strike out and consume them (v.25; Ex.20:19). Obviously, they were sensing a great gulf between the holy presence of God and their own sinful human nature. They sensed a deep, terrifying distance between the majesty and holiness of God's Person and their own human condition, a condition of weakness, failure, shortcoming, and sinfulness. They knew that the majesty of God being displayed upon the mountain, the majesty they were witnessing, could strike them dead at any moment. Thus they shrunk back and withdrew from God's holy presence.

This was the very point that God wished to convey to the people: He is the very embodiment of *majestic glory and holiness*. There is a great gulf—a chasm, an abyss, a terrifying separation—between Himself and man, between what He Himself is and what man is. Again, God is the very embodiment of *majestic glory and holiness*; therefore, the very law of God—the Ten Commandments, the very *words* which God spoke—were holy and glorious (Ro.7:12, 14, 16). The law of God and the Ten Commandments were the very expression of God's being. Therefore, people were to obey God's law or else face the terrifying glory and holiness of God.

Thought 1. This was the first reason God gave the law: to reveal His majestic glory and holiness, that there is a *great gulf*, a terrifying separation between God and man.

"But your iniquities have separated between you and your God, and your sins have hid his face from you, that he will not hear" (Is.59:2).

"But we are all as an unclean thing, and all our righteousnesses are as filthy rags; and we all do fade as a leaf; and our iniquities, like the wind, have taken us away" (Is.64:6).

"And there is none that calleth upon thy name, that stirreth up himself to take hold of thee: for thou hast hid thy face from us, and hast consumed us, because of our iniquities" (Is.64:7).

"And beside all this, between us [in heaven] and you [in hell] there is a great gulf fixed: so that they which would pass from hence to you cannot; neither can they pass to us, that [would come] from thence" (Lu.16:26).

"For all have sinned, and come short of the glory of God" (Ro.3:23).

"If we say that we have no sin, we deceive ourselves, and the truth is not in us" (1 Jn.1:8).

DEUTERONOMY 5:22-33

"And GOD saw that the wickedness of man was great in the earth, and that every imagination of the thoughts of his heart was only evil continually" (Ge.6:5).

"Who can say, I have made my heart clean, I am pure from my sin?" (Pr.20:9).

3 (5:26-27) **Mediator—Approach, to God—Salvation—Law—Commandments, the Ten**: Why did God give the Ten Commandments to man? Third, to reveal man's need for a *mediator*, for a person who can approach God for man, a person who can represent man before God. Apparently, the people had heard the booming voice of God speaking out from the cloud covering the mountain.

OUTLINE	SCRIPTURE
3. To reveal that man must have a mediator to represent him before God	26 For who *is there of* all flesh, that hath heard the voice of the living God speaking out of the midst of the fire, as we *have*, and lived?
a. The leaders asked Moses to be their mediator b. The leaders promised to listen & obey God's Word	27 Go thou near, and hear all that the LORD our God shall say: and speak thou unto us all that the LORD our God shall speak unto thee; and we will hear *it*, and do *it*.

Scripture suggests that God's booming voice actually spoke and gave the Ten Commandments directly to the people:

"The LORD talked with you face to face in the mount out of the midst of the fire" (De.5:4).

"These words the LORD spake unto all your assembly in the mount out of the midst of the fire, of the cloud, and of the thick darkness, with a great voice: and he added no more. And he wrote them in two tables of stone, and delivered them unto me. And it came to pass, when ye heard the voice out of the midst of the darkness, (for the mountain did burn with fire,) that ye came near unto me, even all the heads of your tribes, and your elders; And ye said, Behold, the LORD our God hath showed us his glory and his greatness, and we have heard his voice out of the midst of the fire: we have seen this day that God doth talk with man, and he liveth. Now therefore why should we die? for this great fire will consume us: if we hear the voice of the LORD our God any more, then we shall die. For who is there of all flesh, that hath heard the voice of the living God speaking out of the midst of the fire, as we have, and lived? Go thou near, and hear all that the LORD our God shall say: and speak thou unto us all that the LORD our God shall speak unto thee; and we will hear it, and do it" (De.5:22-27).

Two terrifying events were happening: the people were witnessing the awesome sight of God's glory and majesty, and they were actually hearing the booming voice of God Himself declare the Ten Commandments. Both struck a deep sense of unworthiness in the people. They became keenly aware of the vast difference—the enormous gulf—between God and man, the vast difference...

- between God's holy nature and man's sinful nature
- between God's awesome power and man's helplessness before that power
- between what God is like and what man is like

The sight of God's majestic glory and the hearing of God's booming voice revealed a startling fact to the people: there was a *great gulf* between man and God, and the people sensed the *gulf* deeply. They were so aware of God's holiness and their sinfulness—so aware of the vast difference between God's awesome person and their humanity—that they did not want God to speak directly to them, not anymore. They obviously feared some pronouncement of judgment upon them (v.27).

The point is this: they sensed the need for a mediator, for a person to approach God for them, a person who could represent them before God. They wanted God's messenger to be their mediator: they wanted Moses to approach God, to receive God's message, and then to bring God's message back to them. Note what the people promised: they would hear and obey the word of God (v.27).

This great sense and need for a mediator led to one of the great promises in Scripture, the promise of God's Perfect Mediator, the Lord Jesus Christ. As God's Perfect Mediator, Jesus Christ was to stand before God for all people of all ages. Note what Moses himself was later to proclaim to the people:

"The LORD thy God will raise up unto thee a Prophet from the midst of thee, of thy brethren, like unto me; unto him ye shall hearken; According to all that thou desiredst of the LORD thy God in Horeb [Mt. Sinai] in the day of the assembly, saying, Let me not hear again the voice of the LORD my God, neither let me see this great fire any more, that I die not. And the LORD said unto me, They have well spoken that which they have spoken. I will raise them up a Prophet from among their brethren, like unto thee, and will put my words in his mouth; and he shall speak unto them all that I shall command him. And it shall come to pass, that whosoever will not hearken unto my words which he shall speak in my name, I will require it of him" (De.18:15-19).

DEUTERONOMY 5:22-33

Thought 1. The law—that is, our failure to keep the law—shows how far short we come, how far away we are from God. The law shows our great need for a mediator, for someone to approach God and to intercede for us. That Someone, that Person, is Jesus Christ. Jesus Christ is our mediator, the person who approaches God for us.

> "For there is one God, and one mediator between God and men, the man Christ Jesus; Who gave himself a ransom for all, to be testified in due time" (1 Ti.2:5-6).

> "Forasmuch then as the children are partakers of flesh and blood, he also himself likewise took part of the same; that through death he might destroy him that had the power of death, that is, the devil; And deliver them who through fear of death were all their lifetime subject to bondage. For verily he took not on him the nature of angels; but he took on him the seed of Abraham. Wherefore in all things it behooved him to be made like unto his brethren, that he might be a merciful and faithful high priest [mediator] in things pertaining to God, to make reconciliation for the sins of the people" (He.2:14-17).

> "Wherefore he is able also to save them to the uttermost that come unto God by him, seeing he ever liveth [as the mediator] to make intercession for them" (He.7:25).

> "But now hath he obtained a more excellent ministry, by how much also he is the mediator of a better covenant, which was established upon better promises" (He.8:6).

> "And for this cause he is the mediator of the new testament, that by means of death, for the redemption of the transgressions that were under the first testament, they which are called might receive the promise of eternal inheritance" (He.9:15).

4 (5:28-33) **Heart, of God—Needs, of Man—Obedience, Results of—Life, Fullness of—Victorious Life:** Why did God give the Ten Commandments to man? Fourth, to reveal the very heart of God for man. This passage opens up the heart of God and shows His consuming passion for people. People are held ever so deeply within the inner recesses of God's being. God loves people, and His love focuses on what is best for His people. Note how the Scripture reveals the very heart of God for man, reveals how the longing of His heart reaches out to help man:

OUTLINE	SCRIPTURE	SCRIPTURE	OUTLINE
4. To reveal the very heart of God for man a. He longs to meet man's need for a mediator: Appointed Moses to stand between the people & God b. He longs for man to fear Him & obey Him: To reverence, worship, & fellowship with Him c. He longs for things to go well for man & his family d. He longs to give man all the laws he needs to live a full & victorious life 1) God had the people sent	28 And the LORD heard the voice of your words, when ye spake unto me; and the LORD said unto me, I have heard the voice of the words of this people, which they have spoken unto thee: they have well said all that they have spoken. 29 O that there were such an heart in them, that they would fear me, and keep all my commandments always, that it might be well with them, and with their children for ever! 30 Go say to them, Get you into your tents again. 31 But as for thee, stand thou here by me, and I will speak	unto thee all the commandments, and the statutes, and the judgments, which thou shalt teach them, that they may do *them* in the land which I give them to possess it. 32 Ye shall observe to do therefore as the LORD your God hath commanded you: ye shall not turn aside to the right hand or to the left. 33 Ye shall walk in all the ways which the LORD your God hath commanded you, that ye may live, and *that it may be* well with you, and *that* ye may prolong *your* days in the land which ye shall possess.	home 2) God kept Moses with Him: To give him the laws the people would need in the promised land e. He longs for man to obey Him: A reemphasis seen in the exhortation of Moses 1) Must not turn aside to the right nor to the left 2) Must walk in the path of God's commandments 3) The result: Will live, prosper, & prolong your days in the promised land

a. God longs to meet man's need for a mediator (v.28). When God heard the people's request for a mediator, note what He did: He immediately granted their request. He appointed Moses to stand between them and God, to intercede for them. In love and compassion, God met the people's need—willingly, immediately met their need. He did exactly what they asked, gave them a mediator to intercede between them and God.

This was exactly what God wanted. He wanted the people to sense the great barrier—the great gulf—between Him and man. He wanted them crying out for someone to stand between them and God so that He could provide a mediator for them. God's purpose was to use the intercession of Moses as a symbol, a type of the coming Savior and Messiah of the world, the Lord Jesus Christ. Just as Moses stood between God and the people of Israel, so Christ stands between God and the human race as the permanent and perfect Mediator. Jesus Christ is the Intercessor, the Advocate who alone stands between God and man. As the eternal and perfect Mediator, He can bring any person to God. In dealing with the Israelites, the longing of God's heart was to provide a mediator for them. In dealing with the human race as a whole, the longing of God's heart is to provide for man the eternal and perfect Mediator, His Son the Lord Jesus Christ.

> "For *there is* one God, and one mediator between God and men, the man Christ Jesus; Who gave himself a ransom for all, to be testified in due time" (1 Ti.2:5-6).

> "But now hath he obtained a more excellent ministry, by how much also he is the mediator of a better covenant, which was established upon better promises" (He.8:6).

> "And for this cause he is the mediator of the new testament, that by means of death, for the redemption of the transgressions *that were* under the first testament, they which are called might receive the promise of eternal inheritance" (He.9:15).

DEUTERONOMY 5:22-33

"For Christ is not entered into the holy places made with hands, *which are* the figures of the true; but into heaven itself, now to appear in the presence of God for us: Nor yet that he should offer himself often, as the high priest entereth into the holy place every year with blood of others; For then must he often have suffered since the foundation of the world: but now once in the end of the world hath he appeared to put away sin by the sacrifice of himself. And as it is appointed unto men once to die, but after this the judgment: So Christ was once offered to bear the sins of many; and unto them that look for him shall he appear the second time without sin unto salvation" (He.9:24-28).

"And to Jesus the mediator of the new covenant, and to the blood of sprinkling, that speaketh better things than *that of* Abel" (He.12:24).

"My little children, these things write I unto you, that ye sin not. And if any man sin, we have an advocate with the Father, Jesus Christ the righteous" (1 Jn.2:1).

b. God longs to have man fear and obey Him (v.29). Note that an outburst of emotion erupts from God's heart in this verse, "O that they had such a heart that would fear and obey me." This is a longing for man to reverence, worship, and fellowship with God. This is a picture of God longing for an intimate relationship with man, for fellowship and communion with man. Instead of cursing Him—rejecting and rebelling against Him—God longs for man to reverence and worship Him. God wants man praying to Him and seeking His face so that there can be a warm, fellowshipping communion between God and man.

"And fear not them which kill the body, but are not able to kill the soul: but rather fear him which is able to destroy both soul and body in hell" (Mt.10:28).

"That which we have seen and heard declare we unto you, that ye also may have fellowship with us: and truly our fellowship *is* with the Father, and with his Son Jesus Christ" (1 Jn.1:3).

"Behold, I stand at the door, and knock: if any man hear my voice, and open the door, I will come in to him, and will sup with him, and he with me" (Re.3:20).

"And now, Israel, what doth the LORD thy God require of thee, but to fear the LORD thy God, to walk in all his ways, and to love him, and to serve the LORD thy God with all thy heart and with all thy soul" (De.10:12).

"And the people said unto Joshua, The LORD our God will we serve, and his voice will we obey" (Jos.24:14).

"The LORD *is* nigh unto them that are of a broken heart; and saveth such as be of a contrite spirit" (Ps.34:18).

"The LORD *is* nigh unto all them that call upon him, to all that call upon him in truth" (Ps.145:18).

"Let us hear the conclusion of the whole matter: Fear God, and keep his commandments: for this *is* the whole *duty* of man" (Ec.12:13).

"*Am* I a God at hand, saith the LORD, and not a God afar off?" (Je.23:23).

c. God longs to have things go well for man and his family (v.29). This is really the result of obedience to God. If a person obeys Gods, things will go well—far, far better—for him. All things work for good to those who love and obey God (Ro.8:28). God floods the person's heart with a full and victorious life, with a deep sense of confidence, assurance, satisfaction, and fulfillment. The person walks through life conquering all of the enemies—the problems, difficulties, trials, and temptations of life—conquering even death itself. God sincerely longs for things to go well for man and his family. And things do go well for the man who fears and obeys God, keeping all His commandments.

"And, behold, I *am* with thee, and will keep thee in all *places* whither thou goest, and will bring thee again into this land; for I will not leave thee, until I have done *that* which I have spoken to thee of" (Ge.28:15).

"And he said, My presence shall go *with thee,* and I will give thee rest" (Ex.33:14).

"Fear thou not; for I *am* with thee: be not dismayed; for I *am* thy God: I will strengthen thee; yea, I will help thee; yea, I will uphold thee with the right hand of my righteousness" (Is.41:10).

"When thou passest through the waters, I *will be* with thee; and through the rivers, they shall not overflow thee: when thou walkest through the fire, thou shalt not be burned; neither shall the flame kindle upon thee" (Is.43:2).

d. God longs to give man all the laws he needs to live a full, victorious life (vv.30-31). As stated earlier, God has created man; therefore, He knows what man needs in order to live a full and victorious life. This was the very reason He gave the Ten Commandments to His people, to show man exactly how to live. Note that God had Moses send the people home from the base of the mountain, but He kept Moses with Himself. He kept Moses in order to give him the laws the people would need in the promised land. This is a reference to the civil and religious laws that the people would need when they reached the promised land. (See note—De.5:22 for more discussion.)

"Search the scriptures; for in them ye think ye have eternal life: and they are they which testify of me" (Jn.5:39).

"Now ye are clean through the word which I have spoken unto you" (Jn.15:3).

"Sanctify them through thy truth: thy word is truth" (Jn.17:17).

"But these are written, that ye might believe that Jesus is the Christ, the Son of God; and that believing ye might have life through his name" (Jn.20:31).

"These were more noble than those in Thessalonica, in that they received the word with all readiness of mind, and searched the scriptures daily, whether those things were so" (Ac.17:11).

DEUTERONOMY 5:22-33

"For whatsoever things were written aforetime were written for our learning, that we through patience and comfort of the scriptures might have hope" (Ro.15:4).

"Now all these things happened unto them for examples: and they are written for our admonition, upon whom the ends of the world are come" (1 Co.10:11).

"All scripture *is* given by inspiration of God, and *is* profitable for doctrine, for reproof, for correction, for instruction in righteousness" (2 Ti.3:16).

"These things have I written unto you that believe on the name of the Son of God; that ye may know that ye have eternal life, and that ye may believe on the name of the Son of God" (1 Jn.5:13).

"Wherewithal shall a young man cleanse his way? by taking heed *thereto* according to thy word" (Ps.119:9).

e. God longs to have man obey Him. This scene is a reemphasis of the exhortation by Moses (vv.32-33). This is a strong exhortation that shows the deep, intense longing of God for the obedience and fellowship of man. Keep in mind that Moses is preaching to the people. He exhorts them to be very careful—to make absolutely sure—that they obey God.
   1) They must not turn aside to the right nor to the left (v.32). They must keep a straight course, following the commandments of God exactly as He dictates. They must not look to the right of the commandments nor to the left of the commandments. They must not add to the commandments nor take away from them. They must do exactly what God says: stay the course and obey the commandments perfectly.
   2) They must walk in all the ways of God's commandments, following the exact path He has laid out. They must not wander off the path of God's commandments—not become distracted, not lose their focus and begin wandering off in another direction. They must not take another path. All other paths are false paths. The only true path to walk in life is the path of God's holy commandments.
   3) The reason is clearly spelled out: the person who obeys God's commandments will live, prosper, and prolong his days in the promised land of God (v.33). He will live a victorious life, experience the fullness of life, and conquer all the enemies that seek to defeat and destroy him.

"Not every one that saith unto me, LORD, LORD, shall enter into the kingdom of heaven; but he that doeth the will of my Father which is in heaven" (Mt.7:21).

"Blessed *are* they that do his commandments, that they may have right to the tree of life, and may enter in through the gates into the city" (Re.22:14).

"This day the LORD thy God hath commanded thee to do these statutes and judgments: thou shalt therefore keep and do them with all thine heart, and with all thy soul" (De.26:16).

"This book of the law shall not depart out of thy mouth; but thou shalt meditate therein day and night, that thou mayest observe to do according to all that is written therein: for then thou shalt make thy way prosperous, and then thou shalt have good success" (Jos.1:8).

"And Samuel said, Hath the LORD *as great* delight in burnt offerings and sacrifices, as in obeying the voice of the LORD? Behold, to obey *is* better than sacrifice, *and* to hearken than the fat of rams" (1 S.15:22).

DEUTERONOMY 6:1-25

CHAPTER 6

E. The Summary of the Commandments—the Greatest Commandment of All: Love the LORD, 6:1-25

1. **The primary charge of God given to families: To teach children to obey His commandments**

    a. The commandments will teach you to fear the LORD: You, your children, & grandchildren—all generations^{DS1}
    b. The commandments will prolong your days—you will enjoy a long life
    c. The commandments will cause all things to go well: Give you a victorious life
    d. The commandments will make you increase (grow in numbers) & assure a full, satisfying life

2. **The greatest commandment**
    a. The LORD our God is One LORD
    b. Love the LORD your God with your whole being—heart, soul, and strength

3. **The duty of the parent**
    a. To place the commandments in your heart
    b. To diligently teach them to your children: Constantly talk about them—all day, every waking hour—at home, while walking, lying down, & getting up
    c. To use them as a witness
        1) Bind them on your hands & forehead
        2) In your home: Write them on your doorposts & on your gates

4. **The blessings promised to the faithful parent: Prosperity**
    a. The gift of the promised land: A symbol of spiritual conquest & rest
    b. The gift of prosperous cities
    c. The gift of houses filled with all kinds of good things

Now these *are* the commandments, the statutes, and the judgments, which the LORD your God commanded to teach you, that ye might do *them* in the land whither ye go to possess it:

2 That thou mightest fear the LORD thy God, to keep all his statutes and his commandments, which I command thee, thou, and thy son, and thy son's son, all the days of thy life; and that thy days may be prolonged.

3 Hear therefore, O Israel, and observe to do *it*; that it may be well with thee, and that ye may increase mightily, as the LORD God of thy fathers hath promised thee, in the land that floweth with milk and honey.

4 Hear, O Israel: The LORD our God *is* one LORD:

5 And thou shalt love the LORD thy God with all thine heart, and with all thy soul, and with all thy might.

6 And these words, which I command thee this day, shall be in thine heart:

7 And thou shalt teach them diligently unto thy children, and shalt talk of them when thou sittest in thine house, and when thou walkest by the way, and when thou liest down, and when thou risest up.

8 And thou shalt bind them for a sign upon thine hand, and they shall be as frontlets between thine eyes.

9 And thou shalt write them upon the posts of thy house, and on thy gates.

10 And it shall be, when the LORD thy God shall have brought thee into the land which he sware unto thy fathers, to Abraham, to Isaac, and to Jacob, to give thee great and goodly cities, which thou buildedst not,

11 And houses full of all good *things*, which thou filledst not, and wells digged, which thou diggedst not, vineyards and olive trees, which thou plantedst not; when thou shalt have eaten and be full;

12 Then beware lest thou forget the LORD, which brought thee forth out of the land of Egypt, from the house of bondage.

13 Thou shalt fear the LORD thy God, and serve him, and shalt swear by his name.

14 Ye shall not go after other gods, of the gods of the people which *are* round about you;

15 (For the LORD thy God *is* a jealous God among you) lest the anger of the LORD thy God be kindled against thee, and destroy thee from off the face of the earth.

16 Ye shall not tempt the LORD your God, as ye tempted *him* in Massah.

17 Ye shall diligently keep the commandments of the LORD your God, and his testimonies, and his statutes, which he hath commanded thee.

18 And thou shalt do *that* which is right and good in the sight of the LORD: that it may be well with thee, and that thou mayest go in and possess the good land which the LORD sware unto thy fathers,

19 To cast out all thine enemies from before thee, as the LORD hath spoken.

20 And when thy son asketh thee in time to come, saying, What *mean* the testimonies, and the statutes, and the judgments, which the LORD our God hath commanded you?

21 Then thou shalt say unto thy son, We were Pharaoh's bondmen in Egypt; and the LORD brought us out of Egypt with a mighty hand:

22 And the LORD showed signs and wonders, great and sore, upon Egypt, upon Pharaoh, and upon all his household, before our eyes:

23 And he brought us out from thence, that he might bring us in, to give us the land which he sware unto our fathers.

24 And the LORD commanded us to do all these statutes, to fear the LORD

   d. The gift of wells & water
   e. The gift of food

5. **The danger of prosperity: Comfort—ease—satisfaction**
    a. The danger of forgetting God & His deliverance from Egypt: A symbol of forgetting God & your salvation

        1) Must fear & serve God
        2) Must take oaths *only* in God's name
    b. The danger of compromise: Following false gods & false worship

        1) Must know the LORD is a jealous God
        2) Must know that one will be judged, condemned to death

    c. The danger of testing God: Being too demanding, going too far, daring, presuming
        1) Must obey God: Keep His commandments—all His stipulations & laws

        2) Must do what is right & good in His eyes
        3) The results
           • Things will go well with you
           • You will inherit the promised land, conquer all the enemies who oppose you

6. **The duty of parents to teach the truth of salvation & of the commandments to children**
    a. The fact: Children will ask about the LORD & His commandments
    b. The parents must teach the wonderful truth of God's deliverance from Egypt: A symbol of salvation, redemption

        1) Delivered by God's power—miraculous signs & wonders—executed against the Egyptians & Pharaoh
        2) Brought to the promised land—inherited the great gift sworn to the forefathers

    c. The parents must teach the truth of God's commandments
        1) Must obey & fear God

DEUTERONOMY 6:1-25

2) The results: 3) Will prosper & be preserved	our God, for our good always, that he might preserve us alive, as *it is* at this day. 25 And it shall be our righ-	teousness, if we observe to do all these commandments before the LORD our God, as he hath commanded us.	4) Will be counted righteous before God

DIVISION III

THE SECOND GREAT THEME PREACHED BY GOD'S AGED SERVANT (PART 1): REMEMBER THE TEN COMMANDMENTS—THE FUNDAMENTAL LAWS TO GOVERN MAN AND SOCIETY, 4:44–11:32

E. The Summary of the Commandments—the Greatest Commandment of All: Love the LORD, 6:1-25

(6:1-25) **Introduction**: What is the greatest force on earth? Some military weapon? The authority of some world leader? The power of some machine? Technology? Economic power? Enormous wealth?

All these possess a dynamic force, enormous power. But they are not the greatest force on earth. The greatest force known to man is *love, true love*. If need be, *true love* drives a person to make the ultimate sacrifice, that of giving his life on behalf of the person or thing loved. Love is defined as affection, admiration, warm attachment, devotion, unselfish concern, and loyalty that seeks the good of another person or cause. It means to hold dear and cherish, to be tender and affectionate toward some person, thing, or cause.

No better description of love has ever been given than the one spelled out by Holy Scripture (1 Co.13:4-8). In the words of Scripture...

- Love suffers long, and is kind.
- Love does not envy.
- Love does not vaunt itself and is not puffed up.
- Love does not behave itself unseemly, does not seek her own, is not easily provoked, and thinks no evil.
- Love does not rejoice in iniquity but rejoices in the truth.
- Love bears all things, believes all things, hopes all things, endures all things.
- Love never fails.

The greatest commandment ever given by God is the commandment dealing with love. This is the great subject of the present passage: *The Summary of the Commandments—the Greatest Commandment of All: Love the LORD, 6:1-25.*
1. The primary charge of God given to families: to teach children to obey His commandments (vv.1-3).
2. The greatest commandment (vv.4-5).
3. The duty of the parent (vv.6-9).
4. The blessings promised to the faithful parent: Prosperity (vv.10-11).
5. The danger of prosperity: comfort—ease—satisfaction (vv.11-19).
6. The duty to teach the truth of salvation and of the commandments to children (vv.20-25).

1 (6:1-3) **Commandments, Duty—Obedience, Results of—Fear, of God—Victorious Life, Source of**: there was the primary charge of God given to families: to teach children to obey His commandments. The commandments were the very foundation of life, telling man exactly how to live. God is the great Creator, the Giver of all life; therefore, He knows exactly how life should be lived. This was the very reason He had given the commandments to man, to show man how to live a full and victorious life. If a person obeys God, he will experience the fullness of life and conquer all the enemies who oppose life, seeking to drag him down into the pit of death. This is clearly seen in the Scripture and outline:

OUTLINE	SCRIPTURE	SCRIPTURE	OUTLINE
1. The primary charge of God given to families: To teach children to obey His commandments a. The commandments will teach you to fear the LORD: You, your children, & grandchildren—all generations[DS1] b. The commandments will	Now these *are* the commandments, the statutes, and the judgments, which the LORD your God commanded to teach you, that ye might do *them* in the land whither ye go to possess it: 2 That thou mightest fear the LORD thy God, to keep all his statutes and his commandments, which I command thee, thou, and	thy son, and thy son's son, all the days of thy life; and that thy days may be prolonged. 3 Hear therefore, O Israel, and observe to do *it*; that it may be well with thee, and that ye may increase mightily, as the LORD God of thy fathers hath promised thee, in the land that floweth with milk and honey.	prolong your days—you will enjoy a long life c. The commandments will cause all things to go well: Give you a victorious life d. The commandments will make you increase (grow in numbers) & assure a full, satisfying life

a. The commandments will teach you to fear the LORD: you, your children, your grandchildren—all generations (v.2). The word *fear* means to honor and reverence God to such a point that a person worships Him. The person who truly fears God surrenders his life to serve God, to obey God just as He commands. But the word means more than just reverence and honor: it means to respect the justice and judgment of God, to fear what God can do to a person if he disobeys the commandments

DEUTERONOMY 6:1-25

of God. Thus the very purpose for teaching the commandments to God's people is just this: to teach the fear of God. Believers are to fear God:

⇒ reverence and worship Him, surrendering their lives to Him, obeying His commandments and living exactly as He says
⇒ respect His holiness and justice, lest their disobedience arouse the judgment of God

b. The commandments will prolong your days, give you the enjoyment of a long life (v.2). God has established the very laws of life to make the truth of this statement a reality. A person who obeys God will experience far less guilt, pressure, and tension. These are things that eat away at life, that cause ulcers and all kinds of other emotional and physical problems. Guilt, pressure, and tension sap the strength out of life and shorten life. One of the wisest things a person can do is to obey God, eliminating the guilt, pressure, and tension that disobedience brings into his life. Not only will obeying God prolong your days, but also it will give you a more enjoyable or abundant life.

c. The commandments will cause all things to go well for you, give you a victorious life (v.3). Just think for a moment: breaking the commandments of God causes all kinds of problems for a person. For example, lying, stealing, adultery, and murder cause all kinds of disturbed relationships and wreck human life. Breaking any of the commandments of God causes all kinds of problems...

- broken relationships
- wrecked lives
- accidents
- unemployment
- disease
- divorce
- bankruptcy
- poverty
- homelessness
- death

The results of disobedience are terrible. The ravages of sin, of disobeying God, are seen within every community in the broken lives and families all around us. But this is the glorious message of this point: obeying God will cause all things to go far better. If people obey the commandments, there will be no lying, stealing, adultery, or murder. There will be far fewer broken lives and families. Things will go well, and people will live a far more victorious life, conquering all the enemies and evil of this world. A life of conquest and victory is solely dependent upon obeying God. This is the reason God gave His commandments, to show man how to live so that he could live a victorious life. Obeying God simply makes things go better. In fact, all things will go well if a person obeys God.

d. The commandments will make you increase and assure a full, satisfying life (v.3). This was a specific promise made to the Israelites, but it is also common sense for any people. As has already been seen, obeying the commandments extends life and improves the quality of that life. Just these facts alone would increase the population of a people, make them far more fruitful. Moreover, God blesses His people, assures them of a full, satisfying life. If a person obeys God, he walks throughout life conquering the temptation to lie, steal, commit adultery, and react in anger and violence when wronged by people. The point is he lives a victorious life over the temptations and trials of life. Therefore, God gives him a sense of confidence, assurance, satisfaction, and fulfillment in life. He grows in love for God and for people, experiencing the fullness of joy, peace, and strength of life.

> "Now therefore, if ye will obey my voice indeed, and keep my covenant, then ye shall be a peculiar treasure unto me above all people: for all the earth *is* mine" (Ex.19:5).
>
> "O that there were such an heart in them, that they would fear me, and keep all my commandments always, that it might be well with them, and with their children for ever" (De.5:29).
>
> "And if thou wilt walk in my ways, to keep my statutes and my commandments, as thy father David did walk, then I will lengthen thy days" (1 K.3:14).
>
> "But whoso looketh into the perfect law of liberty, and continueth *therein,* he being not a forgetful hearer, but a doer of the work, this man shall be blessed in his deed" (Js.1:25).
>
> "Blessed *are* they that do his commandments, that they may have right to the tree of life, and may enter in through the gates into the city" (Re.22:14).
>
> "But seek ye first the kingdom of God, and his righteousness; and all these things shall be added unto you" (Mt.6:33).
>
> "Therefore whosoever heareth these sayings of mine, and doeth them, I will liken him unto a wise man, which built his house upon a rock: And the rain descended, and the floods came, and the winds blew, and beat upon that house: and it fell not: for it was founded upon a rock. And every one that heareth these sayings of mine, and doeth them not, shall be likened unto a foolish man, which built his house upon the sand: And the rain descended, and the floods came, and the winds blew, and beat upon that house; and it fell: and great was the fall of it" (Mt.7:24-27).

DEEPER STUDY # 1

(6:2) **Fear—Reverence—God, Fear of—God, Reverence of**: the word "fear" (yare) means to be afraid; to stand in awe; to revere or reverence; to dread; to be frightened or intimidated; to be stricken with a deep sense of honor, reverence, awe, and worship. The word means recognizing the exalted position of a person and standing in reverence and awe of him, acknowledging the honor due the person. The word also means the psychological reaction of fear; to be afraid of something or of some person.[1]

---

[1] *Vine's Complete Expository Dictionary of Old and New Testament Words.* Edited by W.E. Vine, Merrill F. Unger, William White, Jr. (Nashville, TN: Thomas Nelson Publishers, 1985), p.79.

DEUTERONOMY 6:1-25

2 (6:4-5) **Commandments, the Greatest—Love, for God—Believers, Duty of—God, Nature, Is One**: What is the greatest commandment in the law? Remember that Jesus Christ Himself was asked this question, and He answered without hesitation or equivocation. He answered with all the authority of God Himself, and His answer was an eye-opener: He quoted this passage in Deuteronomy. (See outline and notes—Mt.22:37-38; Mk.12:29-31 for more discussion.) The greatest commandment is this:

OUTLINE	SCRIPTURE
2. The greatest commandment a. The LORD our God is One LORD b. Love the LORD your God with your whole being—heart, soul, and strength	4 Hear, O Israel: The LORD our God *is* one LORD: 5 And thou shalt love the LORD thy God with all thine heart, and with all thy soul, and with all thy might.

a. Know that "the LORD our God is One LORD" (v.4).
  1) He is *the* LORD (Jehovah, Yahweh). God is the great Creator, the Sovereign Majesty of the universe. Therefore, He is the LORD of all. There is not one god of the Jew (religionist) and another god of the Gentile. There are not different gods of the races and nations of the world, not a different god of Africa and a different god of India, and a different god for Arabs, and a different god for Americans and on and on. Imagine the foolishness of such an idea! Yet how common the idea is! There is only one God who created the universe and only one God who is the God of all mankind.
   ⇒ There is only one God who created all things: "One God, the Father of whom are all things and we in Him" (1 Co.8:6).
   ⇒ There is only one God who has made all men alike: "Who made of one blood every nation of men" (Ac.17:26).
   ⇒ There is only one God "in whom we live and move and have our being" (Ac.17:28).

   "And call no man your father [god] upon the earth: for one is your Father, which is in heaven" (Mt.23:9).
   "One God and Father of all, who is above all, and through all, and in you all" (Ep.4:6).
   "Furthermore we have had fathers of our flesh which corrected us, and we gave them reverence: shall we not much rather be in subjection unto the Father of spirits, and live?" (He.12:9).
   "Have we not all one father? hath not one God created us? why do we deal treacherously every man against his brother, by profaning the covenant of our fathers?" (Mal.2:10).

   Note this fact: as the LORD, God is the *only* living and true God, the God of salvation, deliverance, and redemption. This means a most wonderful thing: as the LORD—the only living and true God—all people are saved, redeemed in the same way. God does not play favorites or show partiality. God does not make it more difficult for some to be saved. God is the LORD—the only One—therefore He treats all equally and justly. All people can approach God and be saved in the same way.
   ⇒ There "is [only] one God, who shall justify the circumcision by faith and the uncircumcision through faith" (Ro.3:30).
   ⇒ "There is [only] one God, and one Mediator between God and man, the man Christ Jesus" (1 Ti.2:5).

   "Then Peter opened his mouth, and said, Of a truth I perceive that God is no respecter of persons" (Ac.10:34).
   "And [God] put no difference between us and them, purifying their hearts by faith" (Ac.15:9).
   "For there is no respect of persons with God" (Ro.2:11).
   "For there is no difference between the Jew and the Greek: for the same LORD over all is rich unto all that call upon him" (Ro.10:12-13).

  2) The LORD is *our* God (v.4). This is a personal relationship between a worshipper and the LORD. It is a daily experience. We are related to Him; we are His people, the sheep of His pasture. Therefore, we should love, adore, and worship Him.
  3) The LORD is *one* LORD (v.4). There is no other. Monotheism (one God) is the truth of God, of the true and living God. Polytheism (many gods) is a false belief created in the imaginations of people.

   "There is none other God but one" (1 Co.8:4).
   "One God and Father of all, who is above all, and through all, and in you all" (Ep.4:6).
   "For there is one God, and one mediator between God and men, the man Christ Jesus" (1 Ti.2:5).
   "For there are three that bear record in heaven, the Father, the Word [Jesus Christ], and the Holy Ghost: and these three are one" (1 Jn.5:7).
   "Wherefore thou art great, O LORD God: for there is none like thee, neither is there any God besides thee, according to all that we have heard with our ears" (2 S.7:22).
   "For thou art great, and doest wondrous things: thou art God alone" (Ps.86:10).
   "Ye are my witnesses, saith the LORD, and my servant whom I have chosen: that ye may know and believe me, and understand that I am he: before me there was no God formed, neither shall there be after me. I, even I, am the LORD; and beside me there is no savior" (Is.43:10-11).

DEUTERONOMY 6:1-25

> "Thus saith the LORD the King of Israel, and his Redeemer the LORD of hosts; I am the first, and I am the last; and beside me there is no God" (Is.44:6).
>
> "For thus saith the LORD that created the heavens; God himself that formed the earth and made it; he hath established it, he created it not in vain, he formed it to be inhabited: I am the LORD and there is none else" (Is.45:18).

b. Love the LORD *your* God with your whole being: your heart, soul and strength (v.5). Love God as *your* very own God. This is a personal relationship, not a distant relationship. God is not impersonal, far out in space someplace, distant and removed. God is personal, ever so close, and we are to be personally involved with God on a face-to-face basis. The command is to "*love the LORD thy God.*" Loving God is alive and active, not dead and inactive. Therefore, we are to maintain a personal relationship with God that is alive and active.

Note that Jesus Christ says to love God with all your being. Christ breaks our being down into three parts: the heart, the soul, and strength.

1) The *heart* (lebab) is the inner part, the *inner man* of a person. The heart is the seat of man's affection and will (devotion). The heart attaches and focuses our will and devotion. The heart causes us to give either good things or bad things. The heart causes us to devote ourselves to either good or bad. Therefore, Christ says we are to love God "with all our heart." We are to focus our heart, our affection, and our will (devotion) upon God. We are to love God supremely.

> "For where your treasure [object of affection] is, there will your heart be also" (Mt.6:21).
>
> "...for out of the abundance of the heart the mouth speaketh. A good man out of the good treasure of the heart bringeth forth good things: and an evil man out of the evil treasure bringeth forth evil things" (Mt.12:34-35; see Mt.15:18-19).

2) The *soul* (nephesh) is the seat of man's breath and life or consciousness. The soul is the life of a man, the consciousness, the breath, the essence, the being of a man. The soul is the *animal life* of a man. The soul is the breath and consciousness that distinguishes man and other animals from vegetation. The world of vegetation lives and man and animals live, but there is a difference in their living. Man and animals are *breathing* and *conscious* beings. The essence of their being is breath and consciousness. They are living souls. This is clearly pointed out in the Hebrew language of Ge.1:20: "Let the waters bring forth abundantly *living souls* [nephesh] that hath life. The *living souls* that God created were different from the vegetation He had just created. The *living souls* were creatures (fish) that breathed and possessed consciousness.

Christ said we are to love God *with all our soul,* that is, with all our life, our breath, our consciousness. We are to love God with all the breath and consciousness, all the life and awareness we have.

3) The word *strength* (meod) means the full strength, all the strength of a person. It means to use up one's strength thoroughly, to the point of exhaustion. We are to love God with all our strength—fully, thoroughly, to the point of exhaustion.

Thought 1. The greatest commandment is clear: we must love God with all our hearts, souls, and strength.

> "And Jesus answered him, The first of all the commandments *is,* Hear, O Israel; The LORD our God is one LORD: And thou shalt love the LORD thy God with all thy heart, and with all thy soul, and with all thy mind, and with all thy strength: this is the first commandment" (Mk.12:29-30).
>
> "And the LORD direct your hearts into the love of God, and into the patient waiting for Christ" (2 Th.3:5).
>
> "Keep yourselves in the love of God, looking for the mercy of our Lord Jesus Christ unto eternal life" (Jude 21).
>
> "And now, Israel, what doth the LORD thy God require of thee, but to fear the LORD thy God, to walk in all his ways, and to love him, and to serve the LORD thy God with all thy heart and with all thy soul" (De.10:12).
>
> "Therefore thou shalt love the LORD thy God, and keep his charge, and his statutes, and his judgments, and his commandments, alway" (De.11:1).
>
> "But take diligent heed to do the commandment and the law, which Moses the servant of the LORD charged you, to love the LORD your God, and to walk in all his ways, and to keep his commandments, and to cleave unto him, and to serve him with all your heart and with all your soul" (Jos.22:5).
>
> "O love the LORD, all ye his saints: *for* the LORD preserveth the faithful, and plentifully rewardeth the proud doer" (Ps.31:23).

3 (6:6-9) **Commandments, Duty to Obey—Parent, Duty of—Teaching, Duty—Children, Duty to**: the duty of the parent is stated by Moses in clear, descriptive terms. He laid three important duties upon every believer:

DEUTERONOMY 6:1-25

OUTLINE	SCRIPTURE	SCRIPTURE	OUTLINE

3. The duty of the parent
  a. To place the commandments in your heart
  b. To diligently teach them to your children: Constantly talk about them—all day, every waking hour—at home, while walking, lying down, & getting up
	6 And these words, which I command thee this day, shall be in thine heart:
	7 And thou shalt teach them diligently unto thy children, and shalt talk of them when thou sittest in thine house, and when thou walkest by the way, and when thou liest
		down, and when thou risest up.
		8 And thou shalt bind them for a sign upon thine hand, and they shall be as frontlets between thine eyes.
		9 And thou shalt write them upon the posts of thy house, and on thy gates.
			c. To use them as a witness
			  1) Bind them on your hands & forehead
			  2) In your home: Write them on your doorposts & on your gates

a. The believer is to place the commandments in his heart (v.6). The commandments are to be preeminent in the believer's life. He is to cherish the commandments, cradle them in his heart. Simply stated, the believer is to be totally committed, wholeheartedly committed to the commandments. He is to hold them ever so near and dear to his heart.

> "And these words, which I command thee this day, shall be in thine heart" (De.6:6).
>
> "Therefore shall ye lay up these my words in your heart and in your soul, and bind them for a sign upon your hand, that they may be as frontlets between your eyes" (De.11:18).
>
> "Thy word have I hid in mine heart, that I might not sin against thee" (Ps.119:11).
>
> "But what saith it? The word is nigh thee, *even* in thy mouth, and in thy heart: that is, the word of faith, which we preach; That if thou shalt confess with thy mouth the LORD Jesus, and shalt believe in thine heart that God hath raised him from the dead, thou shalt be saved. For with the heart man believeth unto righteousness; and with the mouth confession is made unto salvation" (Ro.10:8-10).
>
> "Let the word of Christ dwell in you richly in all wisdom; teaching and admonishing one another in psalms and hymns and spiritual songs, singing with grace in your hearts to the LORD" (Col.3:16).
>
> "Neither have I gone back from the commandment of his lips; I have esteemed the words of his mouth more than my necessary *food*" (Jb.23:12).
>
> "And I will delight myself in thy commandments, which I have loved" (Ps.119:47).
>
> "The law of thy mouth *is* better unto me than thousands of gold and silver" (Ps.119:72).
>
> "O how love I thy law! it *is* my meditation all the day" (Ps.119:97).
>
> "Thy word *is* very pure: therefore thy servant loveth it" (Ps.119:140).

b. The believer is to diligently teach the commandments to his children (v.7). The commandments are not automatically taught to children. Educating children is an absolute necessity. And note: education is not just teaching facts and principles, not just passing along information. Teaching is experiencing the truth personally, living out the truth before the children. It is applying the truth of the commandments to one's heart and experiencing the truths within one's own life. The children then see the truth of the commandments lived before their very eyes, and they absorb the truth, pick it up automatically. The truth becomes a part of their lives. This is exactly what Moses was preaching: the believer was constantly to talk about the commandments when he sat at home, when he walked along the road throughout the day, when he laid down, and when he got up. The whole thrust is that he was to live by the commandments, experience them, obey them, and set the dynamic example before his children.

> "Search the scriptures; for in them ye think ye have eternal life: and they are they which testify of me" (Jn.5:39).
>
> "But these are written, that ye might believe that Jesus is the Christ, the Son of God; and that believing ye might have life through his name" (Jn.20:31).
>
> "Now all these things happened unto them for examples: and they are written for our admonition, upon whom the ends of the world are come" (1 Co.10:11).
>
> "And, ye fathers, provoke not your children to wrath: but bring them up in the nurture and admonition of the LORD" (Ep.6:4).
>
> "That they may teach the young women to be sober, to love their husbands, to love their children" (Tit.2:4).
>
> "These things have I written unto you that believe on the name of the Son of God; that ye may know that ye have eternal life, and that ye may believe on the name of the Son of God" (1 Jn.5:13).
>
> "And these words, which I command thee this day, shall be in thine heart: And thou shalt teach them diligently unto thy children, and shalt talk of them when thou sittest in thine house, and when thou walkest by the way, and when thou liest down, and when thou risest up" (De.6:6-7).
>
> "Train up a child in the way he should go: and when he is old, he will not depart from it" (Pr.22:6).

c. The believer is to use the commandments as a strong witness and testimony before the public (vv.8-9). When an Israelite was out in public, he was to bind the commandments on his hands and forehead. Within the home, he was to write them on his doorposts and on his gates. This particular charge has been literally practiced by orthodox Jews down through the centuries. They have copied four sections from the law and put these passages in leather cases and tied them to their arms and on their foreheads during morning prayers (Ex.13:1-10; 13:11-16; De.6:4-9; 11:13-21). Some have also put two passages of Scripture in a metal or glass case and attached it to the right doorpost of every entrance to their homes (De.6:4-5; 11:13-20).[2]

---

[2] John Maxwell. *The Preacher's Commentary on Deuteronomy*, p.128.

DEUTERONOMY 6:1-25

The thrust of Moses' preaching was that the home was to be the center for bearing testimony to the truth of the commandments. Very simply, the believer was to place the commandments in the very core of his heart and diligently teach them to his children both by example and word. Moreover, he was to bear strong testimony to the commandments both outside and inside his home. His home was to be known as a righteous home, a home where the commandments of God were taught and lived.

"For we cannot but speak the things which we have seen and heard" (Ac.4:20).

"Be not thou therefore ashamed of the testimony of our LORD, nor of me his prisoner: but be thou partaker of the afflictions of the gospel according to the power of God" (2 Ti.1:8).

"But sanctify the LORD God in your hearts: and *be* ready always to *give* an answer to every man that asketh you a reason of the hope that is in you with meekness and fear" (1 Pe.3:15).

"Come *and* hear, all ye that fear God, and I will declare what he hath done for my soul" (Ps.66:16).

"They shall speak of the glory of thy kingdom, and talk of thy power" (Ps.145:11).

"Then they that feared the LORD spake often one to another: and the LORD hearkened, and heard *it*, and a book of remembrance was written before him for them that feared the LORD, and that thought upon his name" (Mal.3:16).

4 (6:10-11) **Obedience, Blessings of—Prosperity, Source of**: Moses preached the blessings promised to the faithful parent of prosperity. If the Israelite believers obeyed God, God would pour out His blessings upon them, give them great prosperity. Note the blessings, the gifts God would give if they obeyed Him:

⇒ the gift of the promised land (v.10). He would give them a place they could call their own, a permanent inheritance upon which they could settle and experience the victorious life and rest that had been promised by God. (See outline and note—De.1:8 for more discussion.)
⇒ the gift of prosperous cities (v.10)
⇒ the gift of houses filled with all kinds of good things (v.11)
⇒ the gift of wells and water (v.11)
⇒ the gift of food (v.11)

OUTLINE	SCRIPTURE	SCRIPTURE	OUTLINE
4. The blessings promised to the faithful parent: Prosperity a. The gift of the promised land: A symbol of spiritual conquest & rest b. The gift of prosperous cities	10 And it shall be, when the LORD thy God shall have brought thee into the land which he sware unto thy fathers, to Abraham, to Isaac, and to Jacob, to give thee great and goodly cities, which thou buildedst not,	11 And houses full of all good *things*, which thou filledst not, and wells digged, which thou diggedst not, vineyards and olive trees, which thou plantedst not; when thou shalt have eaten and be full;	c. The gift of houses filled with all kinds of good things d. The gift of wells & water e. The gift of food

Thought 1. The believer who obeys God will be blessed by God, greatly blessed in this life and in the life to come. This is the strong declaration of Scripture.

"But seek ye first the kingdom of God, and his righteousness; and all these things shall be added unto you" (Mt.6:33).

"Not every one that saith unto me, LORD, LORD, shall enter into the kingdom of heaven; but he that doeth the will of my Father which is in heaven" (Mt.7:21).

"If ye keep my commandments, ye shall abide in my love; even as I have kept my Father's commandments, and abide in his love" (Jn.15:10).

"These things have I spoken unto you, that my joy might remain in you, and *that* your joy might be full" (Jn.15:11).

"Ye are my friends, if ye do whatsoever I command you" (Jn.15:14).

"And to know the love of Christ, which passeth knowledge, that ye might be filled with all the fulness of God" (Ep.3:19).

"But whoso looketh into the perfect law of liberty, and continueth *therein,* he being not a forgetful hearer, but a doer of the work, this man shall be blessed in his deed" (Js.1:25).

"Blessed *are* they that do his commandments, that they may have right to the tree of life, and may enter in through the gates into the city" (Re.22:14).

"Now therefore, if ye will obey my voice indeed, and keep my covenant, then ye shall be a peculiar treasure unto me above all people: for all the earth *is* mine" (Ex.19:5).

"And ye shall serve the LORD your God, and he shall bless thy bread, and thy water; and I will take sickness away from the midst of thee" (Ex.23:25).

"O that there were such an heart in them, that they would fear me, and keep all my commandments always, that it might be well with them, and with their children for ever" (De.5:29).

"This book of the law shall not depart out of thy mouth; but thou shalt meditate therein day and night, that thou mayest observe to do according to all that is written therein: for then thou shalt make thy way prosperous, and then thou shalt have good success" (Jos.1:8).

DEUTERONOMY 6:1-25

> "Bring ye all the tithes into the storehouse, that there may be meat in mine house, and prove me now herewith, saith the LORD of hosts, if I will not open you the windows of heaven, and pour you out a blessing, that *there shall* not *be room* enough *to receive it*" (Mal.3:10).

5 (6:11-19) **Prosperity, Danger of—Comfort, Danger of—Satisfaction, Danger of—Ease, Danger of—Plenty, Danger of—Abundance, Danger of—Forget - Forgetting, God, Answer to—Compromise, Answer to—Testing God, Answer to**: Moses preached the danger of prosperity, the danger of being too comfortable, at ease, self-satisfied. The believer must beware, watch, guard against the indulgence of the flesh, the danger of becoming too comfortable or too at ease. Prosperity can ruin the believer. Having plenty can make a believer complacent. Prosperity gives rise to three particular dangers, dangers that the believer must guard against with all vigilance:

OUTLINE	SCRIPTURE	SCRIPTURE	OUTLINE
5. The danger of prosperity: Comfort—ease—satisfaction a. The danger of forgetting God & His deliverance from Egypt: A symbol of forgetting God & one's salvation 1) Must fear & serve God 2) Must take oaths *only* in God's name b. The danger of compromise: Following false gods & false worship 1) Must know the LORD is a jealous God 2) Must know that one will	11 And houses full of all good *things*, which thou filledst not, and wells digged, which thou diggedst not, vineyards and olive trees, which thou plantedst not; when thou shalt have eaten and be full; 12 *Then* beware lest thou forget the LORD, which brought thee forth out of the land of Egypt, from the house of bondage. 13 Thou shalt fear the LORD thy God, and serve him, and shalt swear by his name. 14 Ye shall not go after other gods, of the gods of the people which *are* round about you; 15 (For the LORD thy God *is* a jealous God among you) lest the anger of the LORD thy	God be kindled against thee, and destroy thee from off the face of the earth. 16 Ye shall not tempt the LORD your God, as ye tempted *him* in Massah. 17 Ye shall diligently keep the commandments of the LORD your God, and his testimonies, and his statutes, which he hath commanded thee. 18 And thou shalt do *that* which *is* right and good in the sight of the LORD: that it may be well with thee, and that thou mayest go in and possess the good land which the LORD sware unto thy fathers, 19 To cast out all thine enemies from before thee, as the LORD hath spoken.	be judged, condemned to death c. The danger of testing God: Being too demanding, going too far, daring, presuming 1) Must obey God: Keep His commandments—all His stipulations & laws 2) Must do what is right & good in His eyes 3) The results • Things will go well with you • You will inherit the promised land, conquer all the enemies who oppose you

    a. Prosperity can lead to the danger of forgetting God (vv.12-13). Becoming prosperous, having plenty, and being full can easily dull a person, making him insensitive to God. He can become overly comfortable and satisfied to the point that he forgets God. He forgets that every good and perfect gift comes from God. Therefore, he owes God his life and all that he possesses. Note what Scripture says: prosperity can make the person forget his great salvation, that it was God who delivered him out of Egypt. Keep in mind that Egypt is a symbol of the world. It is God who delivers us from the enslavement of the world.

    The opposite of forgetting God is to fear God and to serve God (v.13). This is the answer to forgetting God. The believer is to fear the LORD his God and serve Him with all his heart, soul, and strength. But this is not all: the believer is to take oaths only in God's name. He is openly to declare himself to be a follower of God, to be a strong witness of God. This would be one way to guard against forgetting God.

    b. Prosperity can lead to the danger of compromise (v.14.). Surrounding neighbors would always be inviting God's people to participate with them in their false worship. Unless God's people stayed close to God and obeyed His commandments, they would end up compromising and accepting the invitations of their neighbors. They would end up participating in false worship and soon begin to follow false gods. Belief in false gods and false worship sweeps the earth—always has and always will—and is a constant temptation to God's people. The warning of Moses to believers is forceful: prosperity can lead to the danger of compromise. You must not follow other gods, the gods of the people who are all around you.

    Note the answer to compromise: the believer must know—keep ever before his mind—that the LORD is a jealous God and His anger will burn against him. If the believer participates in idolatry or false worship, he must know that God will judge him, condemn him to death.

    c. Prosperity could lead to the danger of testing God (vv.16-19). A person could test God by being too demanding or going too far in thinking that God would never judge nor chastise him. A person can go so far in his sinful behavior that he is presuming upon God's goodness, daring God to judge or chastise him. This was what happened in Massah out in the middle of the desert: the people were forced to camp in a place where there was no water to drink. Consequently, they were gripped with a spirit of unbelief and they rebelled against Moses and God. They demanded that Moses prove his leadership and God's guidance by producing water. They were even on the verge of stoning him. They were presuming upon God's goodness, being too demanding and going too far, daring God's judgment to lash out against them (see outline and notes—Ex.17:1-7 for more discussion).

    The answer to the danger of testing God is to obey God, keep His commandments—all His laws (v.17). The believer must do what is right and good in God's eyes, not in his own eyes (v.18). If he obeys God, then things will go well with him and he will inherit the promised land (v.18).

DEUTERONOMY 6:1-25

Thought 1. The believer must guard against prosperity, against becoming overly comfortable, at ease, and self-satisfied. God does bless the believer, but with the blessings come some threatening dangers.

(1) There is the danger of forgetting God.

"Only take heed to thyself, and keep thy soul diligently, lest thou forget the things which thine eyes have seen, and lest they depart from thy heart all the days of thy life: but teach them thy sons, and thy sons' sons" (De.4:9).

"And it shall be, when the LORD thy God shall have brought thee into the land which he sware unto thy fathers, to Abraham, to Isaac, and to Jacob, to give thee great and goodly cities, which thou buildedst not, And houses full of all good *things*, which thou filledst not, and wells digged, which thou diggedst not, vineyards and olive trees, which thou plantedst not; when thou shalt have eaten and be full; *Then* beware lest thou forget the LORD, which brought thee forth out of the land of Egypt, from the house of bondage" (De.6:10-12).

"The wicked shall be turned into hell, *and* all the nations that forget God" (Ps.9:17).

"Now consider this, ye that forget God, lest I tear *you* in pieces, and *there be* none to deliver" (Ps.50:22).

"And forgat his works, and his wonders that he had showed them" (Ps.78:11).

"Because thou hast forgotten the God of thy salvation, and hast not been mindful of the rock of thy strength, therefore shalt thou plant pleasant plants, and shalt set it with strange slips" (Is.17:10).

"And forgettest the LORD thy maker, that hath stretched forth the heavens, and laid the foundations of the earth; and hast feared continually every day because of the fury of the oppressor, as if he were ready to destroy? and where *is* the fury of the oppressor" (Is.51:13).

"A voice was heard upon the high places, weeping *and* supplications of the children of Israel: for they have perverted their way, *and* they have forgotten the LORD their God" (Je.3:21).

(2) There is the danger of compromise, of following false gods and false worship.

"Wherefore come out from among them, and be ye separate, saith the LORD, and touch not the unclean *thing;* and I will receive you, And will be a Father unto you, and ye shall be my sons and daughters, saith the LORD Almighty" (2 Co.6:17-18).

"I beseech you therefore, brethren, by the mercies of God, that ye present your bodies a living sacrifice, holy, acceptable unto God, *which is* your reasonable service. And be not conformed to this world: but be ye transformed by the renewing of your mind, that ye may prove what is that good, and acceptable, and perfect, will of God" (Ro.12:1-2).

"Love not the world, neither the things *that are* in the world. If any man love the world, the love of the Father is not in him. For all that *is* in the world, the lust of the flesh, and the lust of the eyes, and the pride of life, is not of the Father, but is of the world" (1 Jn.2:15-16).

"Little children, keep yourselves from idols. Amen" (1 Jn.5:21).

"Thou shalt not make unto thee any graven image, or any likeness *of any thing* that *is* in heaven above, or that *is* in the earth beneath, or that *is* in the water under the earth" (Ex.20:4).

"Ye shall make you no idols nor graven image, neither rear you up a standing image, neither shall ye set up *any* image of stone in your land, to bow down unto it: for I *am* the LORD your God" (Le.26:1).

"Take heed to yourselves, that your heart be not deceived, and ye turn aside, and serve other gods, and worship them" (De.11:16).

"I *am* the LORD: that *is* my name: and my glory will I not give to another, neither my praise to graven images" (Is.42:8).

(3) There is the danger of testing God. The believer can be too demanding of God and go too far, thinking that God would never judge him. He can presume upon the goodness of God, going so far in sin that he is daring God to judge him.

"Not every one that saith unto me, Lord, Lord, shall enter into the kingdom of heaven; but he that doeth the will of my Father which is in heaven" (Mt.7:21).

"Neither let us tempt Christ, as some of them also tempted, and were destroyed of serpents" (1 Co.10:9).

"Go to now, ye that say, To day or to morrow we will go into such a city, and continue there a year, and buy and sell, and get gain" (Js.4:13).

"But chiefly them that walk after the flesh in the lust of uncleanness, and despise government. Presumptuous *are they*, selfwilled, they are not afraid to speak evil of dignities" (2 Pe.2:10).

"But the soul that doeth *ought* presumptuously, *whether he be* born in the land, or a stranger, the same reproacheth the LORD; and that soul shall be cut off from among his people" (Nu.15:30).

"Ye shall not tempt the LORD your God, as ye tempted *him* in Massah" (De.6:16).

"But the prophet, which shall presume to speak a word in my name, which I have not commanded him to speak, or that shall speak in the name of other gods, even that prophet shall die" (De.18:20).

"This book of the law shall not depart out of thy mouth; but thou shalt meditate therein day and night, that thou mayest observe to do according to all that is written therein: for then thou shalt make thy way prosperous, and then thou shalt have good success" (Jos.1:8).

"Pride *goeth* before destruction, and an haughty spirit before a fall" (Pr.16:18).

"An high look, and a proud heart, *and* the plowing of the wicked, *is* sin" (Pr.21:4).

DEUTERONOMY 6:1-25

"Woe unto him that striveth with his Maker! *Let* the potsherd *strive* with the potsherds of the earth. Shall the clay say to him that fashioneth it, What makest thou? or thy work, He hath no hands" (Is.45:9).
"Woe unto *them that are* wise in their own eyes, and prudent in their own sight" (Is.5:21).

6 (6:20-25) **Salvation, Duty to Teach—Commandments, Duty to—Children, Duty to—Teaching, Duty of—Education, Duty of—Parents, Duty of**: Moses preached the duty to teach the truth of salvation and of the commandments to children. Teaching the truth to children is one of the primary duties of parents. Moses understood children: he knew that children would be asking about God and His commandments when they heard God or the commandments mentioned. This was and is particularly true when a family focuses upon the LORD and His Word or commandments. When children asked an Israelite believer about the wonderful truth of God's deliverance from Egypt, the parents were to explain to the children what had happened. He was to explain how God had delivered His people from Egyptian slavery by miraculous signs and wonders and how God had executed judgment against the Egyptians and Pharaoh (vv.21-22). The parents were also to explain how God had brought them to the promised land, given them the great inheritance sworn to the forefathers, that is, to Abraham, Isaac, and Jacob (v.23).

But explaining salvation was not enough: the parents had to teach the truth of God's commandments to their children (vv.24-25). The parents were to teach the wonderful promise of God—that if they obeyed God, the most wonderful results would happen: they would prosper and be preserved.

⇒ They would be counted righteous before God. The word righteousness, *tsedaqah*, is taken from the root word *tsadaq* or *sadaq* which means to be righteous; to cleanse or clear oneself; to make righteous or to turn to righteousness; to be in the right; to be justified; to be just. The basic meaning of the word righteousness is exactly what the English word says: to be righteous, noble, honest, good. Moses was declaring that the person who obeyed God would be counted righteous before God. He would become acceptable to God.

OUTLINE	SCRIPTURE	SCRIPTURE	OUTLINE
6. The duty of parents to teach the truth of salvation & of the commandments to children	20 And when thy son asketh thee in time to come, saying, What *mean* the testimonies, and the statutes, and the judgments, which the LORD our God hath commanded you?	hold, before our eyes: 23 And he brought us out from thence, that he might bring us in, to give us the land which he sware unto our fathers.	Pharaoh 2) Brought to the promised land—inherited the great gift sworn to the forefathers
a. The fact: Children will ask about the LORD & His commandments			
b. The parents must teach the wonderful truth of God's deliverance from Egypt: A symbol of salvation, redemption	21 Then thou shalt say unto thy son, We were Pharaoh's bondmen in Egypt; and the LORD brought us out of Egypt with a mighty hand:	24 And the LORD commanded us to do all these statutes, to fear the LORD our God, for our good always, that he might preserve us alive, as *it is* at this day.	c. The parents must teach the truth of God's commandments 1) Must obey & fear God 2) The results:
1) Delivered by God's power—miraculous signs & wonders—executed against the Egyptians &	22 And the LORD showed signs and wonders, great and sore, upon Egypt, upon Pharaoh, and upon all his house-	25 And it shall be our righteousness, if we observe to do all these commandments before the LORD our God, as he hath commanded us.	• Will prosper & be preserved • Will be counted righteous before God

Thought 1. There are two strong lessons for us in this point.
(1) Parents must teach their children the truth of salvation and the importance of God's Holy Word or commandments.

"So when they had dined, Jesus saith to Simon Peter, Simon, *son* of Jonas, lovest thou me more than these? He saith unto him, Yea, LORD; thou knowest that I love thee. He saith unto him, Feed my lambs" (Jn.21:15).

"When I call to remembrance the unfeigned faith that is in thee, which dwelt first in thy grandmother Lois, and thy mother Eunice; and I am persuaded that in thee also" (2 Ti.1:5).

"And that from a child thou hast known the holy scriptures, which are able to make thee wise unto salvation through faith which is in Christ Jesus" (2 Ti.3:15).

"Only take heed to thyself, and keep thy soul diligently, lest thou forget the things which thine eyes have seen, and lest they depart from thy heart all the days of thy life: but teach them thy sons, and thy sons' sons" (De.4:9).

"And *that* their children, which have not known *any thing*, may hear, and learn to fear the LORD your God, as long as ye live in the land whither ye go over Jordan to possess it" (De.31:13).

"Train up a child in the way he should go: and when he is old, he will not depart from it" (Pr.22:6).

"Whom shall he teach knowledge? and whom shall he make to understand doctrine? *them that are* weaned from the milk, *and* drawn from the breasts" (Is.28:9).

(2) Since the coming of Jesus Christ, righteousness is by faith through Christ and not by the works of the law. No person can keep the law perfectly; therefore, God accepts a person only when he comes through the righteousness of Christ and through His righteousness alone. A person must approach God through Christ in order to be accepted by God. But once a person has been accepted by God, he must seek to obey God and to fulfill the commandments of God.

DEUTERONOMY 6:1-25

"And by him all that believe are justified from all things, from which ye could not be justified by the law of Moses" (Ac.13:39).

"Therefore being justified by faith, we have peace with God through our Lord Jesus Christ" (Ro.5:1).

"And such were some of you: but ye are washed, but ye are sanctified, but ye are justified in the name of the LORD Jesus, and by the Spirit of our God" (1 Co.6:11).

"For he hath made him *to be* sin for us, who knew no sin; that we might be made the righteousness of God in him" (2 Co.5:21).

"Even as Abraham believed God, and it was accounted to him for righteousness" (Ga.3:6).

"For as many as are of the works of the law are under the curse: for it is written, Cursed *is* every one that continueth not in all things which are written in the book of the law to do them. But that no man is justified by the law in the sight of God, *it is* evident: for, The just shall live by faith. And the law is not of faith: but, The man that doeth them shall live in them. Christ hath redeemed us from the curse of the law, being made a curse for us: for it is written, Cursed *is* every one that hangeth on a tree: That the blessing of Abraham might come on the Gentiles through Jesus Christ; that we might receive the promise of the Spirit through faith" (Ga.3:10-14).

"Wherefore the law was our schoolmaster *to bring us* unto Christ, that we might be justified by faith" (Ga.3:24).

"And he believed in the LORD; and he counted it to him for righteousness" (Ge.15:6).

TYPES, SYMBOLS, AND PICTURES
(Deuteronomy 6:1-25)

Historical Term	Type or Picture (Scriptural Basis for Each)	Life Application for Today's Believer	Biblical Application
Forgetting God and His Deliverance from Egypt De.6:12	*Forgetting God and His deliverance from Egypt is a picture of forgetting God and one's salvation.* "**Then beware lest thou forget the LORD, which brought thee forth out of the land of Egypt, from the house of bondage**" (De.6:12).	⇒ The believer must guard against prosperity, against becoming overly comfortable, at ease, and self-satisfied. God does bless the believer, but with the blessings come some threatening dangers. 1. There is the danger of forgetting God.	*"Only take heed to thyself, and keep thy soul diligently, lest thou forget the things which thine eyes have seen, and lest they depart from thy heart all the days of thy life: but teach them thy sons, and thy sons' sons" (De.4:9).* *"And it shall be, when the LORD thy God shall have brought thee into the land which he sware unto thy fathers, to Abraham, to Isaac, and to Jacob, to give thee great and goodly cities, which thou buildedst not, And houses full of all good things, which thou filledst not, and wells digged, which thou diggedst not, vineyards and olive trees, which thou plantedst not; when thou shalt have eaten and be full; Then beware lest thou forget the LORD, which brought thee forth out of the land of Egypt, from the house of bondage" (De.6:10-12).* *"The wicked shall be turned into hell, and all the nations that forget God" (Ps.9:17).*

DEUTERONOMY 6:1-25

Historical Term	Type or Picture (Scriptural Basis for Each)	Life Application for Today's Believer	Biblical Application
			"Now consider this, ye that forget God, lest I tear you in pieces, and there be none to deliver" (Ps.50:22; See also Ps.78:11; Is. 17:10; Is.51:13; Je.3:21).
		2. There is the danger of compromise, of following false gods and false worship.	"Wherefore come out from among them, and be ye separate, saith the Lord, and touch not the unclean thing; and I will receive you, And will be a Father unto you, and ye shall be my sons and daughters, saith the Lord Almighty" (2 Co.6:17-18). "I beseech you therefore, brethren, by the mercies of God, that ye present your bodies a living sacrifice, holy, acceptable unto God, which is your reasonable service. And be not conformed to this world: but be ye transformed by the renewing of your mind, that ye may prove what is that good, and acceptable, and perfect, will of God" (Ro.12:1-2). "Love not the world, neither the things that are in the world. If any man love the world, the love of the Father is not in him. For all that is in the world, the lust of the flesh, and the lust of the eyes, and the pride of life, is not of the Father, but is of the world" (1 Jn.2:15-16). "Little children, keep yourselves from idols. Amen" (1 Jn.5:21; See also Ex.20:4; Le.26:1; De.11:16; Is.42:8).
		3. There is the danger of testing God. The believer can be too demanding of God and go too far, thinking that God would never judge him. He can presume upon the goodness of God, going so far in sin that he is daring God to judge him.	"Not every one that saith unto me, Lord, Lord, shall enter into the kingdom of heaven; but he that doeth the will of my Father which is in heaven" (Mt.7:21). "Neither let us tempt Christ, as some of them also tempted, and were destroyed of serpents" (1 Co. 10:9). "Go to now, ye that say, To day or to morrow we will go into such a city, and continue there a year, and buy and sell, and get gain" (Js.4:13). "But chiefly them that walk after the flesh in the

DEUTERONOMY 6:1-25

Historical Term	Type or Picture (Scriptural Basis for Each)	Life Application for Today's Believer	Biblical Application
			lust of uncleanness, and despise government. Presumptuous are they, selfwilled, they are not afraid to speak evil of dignities" (2 Pe.2:10; See also Nu.15:30; De.6:16; De.18:20; Jos.1:8; Pr.16:18; Pr. 21:4; Is.45:9; Is.5:21).
Teaching Children the Wonderful Truth of God's Deliverance from Egypt De.6:21	*Parents teaching their children the wonderful truth of God's deliverance from Egypt is a picture of salvation, redemption.* "Then thou shalt say unto thy son, We were Pharaoh's bondmen in Egypt; and the LORD brought us out of Egypt with a mighty hand" (De.6:21).	⇒ Note two important points: 1. Parents must teach their children the truth of salvation and the importance of God's Holy Word or commandments.	*"So when they had dined, Jesus saith to Simon Peter, Simon, son of Jonas, lovest thou me more than these? He saith unto him, Yea, Lord; thou know-est that I love thee. He saith unto him, Feed my lambs" (Jn.21:15).* *"When I call to remembrance the unfeigned faith that is in thee, which dwelt first in thy grandmother Lois, and thy mother Eunice; and I am persuaded that in thee also" (2 Ti.1:5).* *"And that from a child thou hast known the holy scriptures, which are able to make thee wise unto salvation through faith which is in Christ Jesus" (2 Ti. 3:15; See also De.4:9; De.31:13; Pr.22:6; Is.28:9).*
		2. Since the coming of Jesus Christ, righteousness is by faith through Christ and not by the works of the law. No person can keep the law perfectly; therefore, God accepts a person only when he comes through the righteousness of Christ and through His righteousness alone. A person must approach God through Christ in order to be accepted by God. But once a person has been accepted by God, he must seek to obey God and to fulfill the commandments of God.	*"And by him all that believe are justified from all things, from which ye could not be justified by the law of Moses" (Ac.13:39).* *"Therefore being justified by faith, we have peace with God through our Lord Jesus Christ" (Ro.5:1).* *"And such were some of you: but ye are washed, but ye are sanctified, but ye are justified in the name of the Lord Jesus, and by the Spirit of our God" (1 Co.6:11).* *"For he hath made him to be sin for us, who knew no sin; that we might be made the righteousness of God in him" (2 Co.5:21).* *"Even as Abraham believed God, and it was accounted to him for righteousness" (Ga.3:6; see Ga. 3:10-14; Ga.3:24; Ge.15:6).*

DEUTERONOMY 7:1-26

CHAPTER 7

F. The Greatest Hindrance to Obeying the Commandments of God: The Enemies of the Promised Land, 7:1-26

1. **The clear charge of God: Defeat! Conquer! Totally destroy all enemies of the promised land**
   a. The seven major enemies: Were larger & more powerful than Israel (a symbol of believers, God's people)

   b. The careful strategy & charge: A picture that believers must not compromise with sinners & unbelievers[DS1]
   1) Must destroy them totally: Their "cup of iniquity was full" (Ge.15:16)
   2) Must not intermarry with them: Because of their evil influence & unbelief (2 Co.6:14)
      • Will turn one away from God to serve other gods
      • Will result in judgment & death
   3) Must destroy all their false worship: Their altars, sacred stones, Asherah poles, & idols

2. **The reasons why all enemies of the promised land must be completely destroyed: A picture of spiritual separation**
   a. Because God's people are holy—set apart to God: Chosen to be His special treasure
   1) God's people were not chosen because of any merit or value: They were the fewest of all people (Ge.12:1-3; 46:26)
   2) God's people were chosen only because of God's love & oath to Abraham & the forefathers

   b. Because the LORD redeemed, saved His people from the enslavement of Egypt (a symbol of the world)

   c. Because the Lord God is the true God & He is faithful:

1 When the LORD thy God shall bring thee into the land whither thou goest to possess it, and hath cast out many nations before thee, the Hittites, and the Girgashites, and the Amorites, and the Canaanites, and the Perizzites, and the Hivites, and the Jebusites, seven nations greater and mightier than thou;
2 And when the LORD thy God shall deliver them before thee; thou shalt smite them, *and* utterly destroy them; thou shalt make no covenant with them, nor show mercy unto them:
3 Neither shalt thou make marriages with them; thy daughter thou shalt not give unto his son, nor his daughter shalt thou take unto thy son.
4 For they will turn away thy son from following me, that they may serve other gods: so will the anger of the LORD be kindled against you, and destroy thee suddenly.
5 But thus shall ye deal with them; ye shall destroy their altars, and break down their images, and cut down their groves, and burn their graven images with fire.
6 For thou *art* an holy people unto the LORD thy God: the LORD thy God hath chosen thee to be a special people unto himself, above all people that *are* upon the face of the earth.
7 The LORD did not set his love upon you, nor choose you, because ye were more in number than any people; for ye *were* the fewest of all people:
8 But because the LORD loved you, and because he would keep the oath which he had sworn unto your fathers, hath the LORD brought you out with a mighty hand, and redeemed you out of the house of bondmen, from the hand of Pharaoh king of Egypt.
9 Know therefore that the LORD thy God, he *is* God, the faithful God, which keepeth covenant and mercy with them that love him and keep his commandments to a thousand generations;
10 And repayeth them that hate him to their face, to destroy them: he will not be slack to him that hateth him, he will repay him to his face.
11 Thou shalt therefore keep the commandments, and the statutes, and the judgments, which I command thee this day, to do them.
12 Wherefore it shall come to pass, if ye hearken to these judgments, and keep, and do them, that the LORD thy God shall keep unto thee the covenant and the mercy which he sware unto thy fathers:
13 And he will love thee, and bless thee, and multiply thee: he will also bless the fruit of thy womb, and the fruit of thy land, thy corn, and thy wine, and thine oil, the increase of thy kine, and the flocks of thy sheep, in the land which he sware unto thy fathers to give thee.
14 Thou shalt be blessed above all people: there shall not be male or female barren among you, or among your cattle.
15 And the LORD will take away from thee all sickness, and will put none of the evil diseases of Egypt, which thou knowest, upon thee; but will lay them upon all *them* that hate thee.
16 And thou shalt consume all the people which the LORD thy God shall deliver thee; thine eye shall have no pity upon them: neither shalt thou serve their gods; for that *will be* a snare unto thee.
17 If thou shalt say in thine heart, These nations *are* more than I; how can I dispossess them?
18 Thou shalt not be afraid of them: *but* shalt well remember what the LORD thy God did unto Pharaoh, and unto all Egypt;
19 The great temptations which thine eyes saw, and the signs, and the wonders, and the mighty hand, and the stretched out arm, whereby the LORD thy God brought thee out: so shall the LORD

He keeps His covenant of love...
1) To those who love Him
2) To those who obey Him

   d. Because God does not hesitate to execute justice: He destroys all who hate & reject Him

   e. Because obedience is demanded by God: His people must obey all God's commandments, laws, & regulations

3. **The results of obedience: What happens if all the enemies of the promised land are destroyed**
   a. God will keep His covenant of love

   b. God will love & bless His people in a very special way
   1) Increase their number: Make them into a great nation of people—give them many children
   2) Bless their crops & livestock
   3) Give them the promised land
   4) Bless them above all other people (possibly a promise of the Messiah, see Ge.12:2-3)
   5) Give them health; keep them free from disease
   6) Free them from the chastisement & diseases that afflicted Egypt: They will afflict their enemies

   c. The charge reemphasized
   1) Must destroy all enemies, for they will be a snare
   2) Must not turn to their false worship

4. **The solution to doubt & fear: The presence & power of God**
   a. Face the question of fear
   b. Do not be overcome by fear: Remember past victories

   1) The LORD delivered His people from Egypt with miraculous signs & wonders—with amazing power
   2) The LORD will continue to deliver His people from the enemies of the

DEUTERONOMY 7:1-26

Outline	Scripture	Scripture (cont.)	Outline (cont.)

promised land: By His amazing power
c. Know that the LORD will send the hornet (a symbol of some enemy or plague or of God's power) until all enemies are driven out & destroyed
d. Know that the LORD's presence—His great & awesome presence—is among His people: Do not be terrified by the enemy
e. Know that the LORD will drive out the enemy little by little, gradually
  1) To give time for the land to be controlled & cultivated
  2) To keep land from returning to its primitive state
f. Know that the LORD will throw the enemies into total confusion, until they are destroyed
	thy God do unto all the people of whom thou art afraid.
	20 Moreover the LORD thy God will send the hornet among them, until they that are left, and hide themselves from thee, be destroyed.
	21 Thou shalt not be affrighted at them: for the LORD thy God is among you, a mighty God and terrible.
	22 And the LORD thy God will put out those nations before thee by little and little: thou mayest not consume them at once, lest the beasts of the field increase upon thee.
	23 But the LORD thy God shall deliver them unto thee, and shall destroy them with a mighty destruction, until they
		be destroyed.
		24 And he shall deliver their kings into thine hand, and thou shalt destroy their name from under heaven: there shall no man be able to stand before thee, until thou have destroyed them.
		25 The graven images of their gods shall ye burn with fire: thou shalt not desire the silver or gold *that is* on them, nor take *it* unto thee, lest thou be snared therein: for it *is* an abomination to the LORD thy God.
		26 Neither shalt thou bring an abomination into thine house, lest thou be a cursed thing like it: *but* thou shalt utterly detest it, and thou shalt utterly abhor it; for it *is* a cursed thing.
			g. Know that the LORD will give their kings over to His people
			  1) To erase their names
			  2) To defeat them
			
			h. Remove all temptation that ensnares a person or causes him to turn away from God
			  1) Destroy all idols
			  2) Do not covet the silver & gold of idols
			  3) Do not keep the idols: Will ensnare
			  4) Do not take a detestable thing into one's home
			    • Will bring judgment
			    • Must abhor, detest it
			    • God has set it apart for destruction

DIVISION III

THE SECOND GREAT THEME PREACHED BY GOD'S AGED SERVANT (PART 1): REMEMBER THE TEN COMMANDMENTS—THE FUNDAMENTAL LAWS TO GOVERN MAN AND SOCIETY, 4:44–11:32

F. The Most Dangerous Threat Against the Law of God: The Enemies of the Promised Land, 7:1-26

(7:1-26) **Introduction**: enemy after enemy confronts man as he walks throughout life. The enemies are hostile, often attacking and threatening to drain the life out of man. Sometimes the enemies are powerful, far too strong for man to overcome by himself. Without supernatural help, the enemies can easily destroy a person, enemies such as...

- cancer
- heart problems
- other diseases
- accidents
- drugs
- alcohol
- loneliness
- depression
- discouragement
- mental problems
- unemployment
- bankruptcy
- greed
- abuse
- anger
- hostility
- lawlessness
- violence
- war
- death

The list of enemies that attack and threaten to destroy man are almost innumerable. But there is hope, the hope of God's presence and power.

Moses knew this fact, that God would empower His people to conquer the enemies that were to confront them. This is the reason he preached the message of this Scripture to the Israelites. They were camped by the River Jordan in the plain of Moab right across from the great city of Jericho. They were poised to cross over the Jordan and enter into the promised land. But before they could lay claim to their inheritance, they needed to be prepared to face the enemies that were going to oppose them. The enemies were going to be powerful and far more numerous than the Israelites. Fear and doubt were potential problems; therefore, Moses had to challenge the people to obey God. In obeying God, they would assure the presence and power of God. Disobedience would cut them off from God, separating them from Him. But obedience would secure the presence and power of God and assure victory over all the enemies who attacked. This is the subject of this important passage of Scripture: *The Most Dangerous Threat Against the Law of God: the Enemies of the Promised Land*, 7:1-26.

1. The clear charge of God: Defeat! Conquer! Totally destroy all enemies of the promised land (vv.1-5).
2. The reasons why all enemies of the promised land must be completely destroyed: a picture of spiritual separation (vv.6-11).
3. The results of obedience: what happens if all the enemies of the promised land are destroyed (vv.12-16).
4. The solution to doubt and fear: the presence and power of God (vv.17-26).

1 (7:1-5) **Enemies, of a Believer—Believer, Enemies of—Compromise, Duty Not to—Separation, Spiritual—Intermarriage, Forbidden—Idolatry, Duty—Worship, False, Duty—Israel, Enemies of—Canaanites, Nations of**: the charge of God was clear: Defeat! Conquer! Totally destroy all enemies of the promised land. Standing there preaching, Moses warned the people: the conquest of the promised land will not be easy. Some major enemies will oppose them; therefore, a very clear strategy had to be pursued—totally pursued—in order to conquer the enemy. Note the Scripture and outline:

DEUTERONOMY 7:1-26

OUTLINE	SCRIPTURE	SCRIPTURE	OUTLINE
1. The clear charge of God: Defeat! Conquer! Totally destroy all enemies of the promised land a. The seven major enemies: Were larger & more powerful than Israel (a symbol of believers, God's people) b. The careful strategy & charge: A picture that believers must not compromise with sinners & unbelievers^{DS1} 1) Must destroy them totally: Their "cup of iniquity was full" (Ge.15:16)	When the LORD thy God shall bring thee into the land whither thou goest to possess it, and hath cast out many nations before thee, the Hittites, and the Girgashites, and the Amorites, and the Canaanites, and the Perizzites, and the Hivites, and the Jebusites, seven nations greater and mightier than thou; 2 And when the LORD thy God shall deliver them before thee; thou shalt smite them, *and* utterly destroy them; thou shalt make no covenant with them, nor show mercy unto them:	3 Neither shalt thou make marriages with them; thy daughter thou shalt not give unto his son, nor his daughter shalt thou take unto thy son. 4 For they will turn away thy son from following me, that they may serve other gods: so will the anger of the LORD be kindled against you, and destroy thee suddenly. 5 But thus shall ye deal with them; ye shall destroy their altars, and break down their images, and cut down their groves, and burn their graven images with fire.	2) Must not intermarry with them: Because of their evil influence & unbelief (2 Co.6:14) • Will turn one away from God to serve other gods • Will result in judgment & death 3) Must destroy all their false worship: Their altars, sacred stones, Asherah poles, & idols

a. In his sermon, Moses pulled no punches: the enemy was larger and more powerful than Israel. In fact, he listed seven of the major enemies the Israelites were to face (v.1):

⇒ The Hittites had been a very powerful nation that dominated Syria and Asia Minor from 1800 to 900 B.C.[1] A strong remnant of the great empire still dominated a portion of Canaan. Although they were presently just a small, fringe state of the formerly great Hittite empire, they were still a powerful, numerous people.
⇒ The Girgashites were apparently allies of these other nations, but nothing else is known about them. They are mentioned in several other Scriptures in a list with other Canaanite nations (Ge.10:16; 15:21; De.7:1; Jos.3:10; 24:11; 1 Chr.1:14; Ne.9:8).
⇒ The Amorites were the native people of Canaan who were located in the mountains or hill country of Judaea.
⇒ The Canaanites were natives of the land who settled along the coastlands of Canaan. The Canaanites actually lived further north than the Amorites (Jos.11:3; 13:4). Sometimes all of the nations within the land were referred to as Canaanites.
⇒ The Perizzites were also a native population of the land who lived in the southern hill country of Jordan. It was apparently their land that was to be allotted to Judah, Simeon, and Ephraim. Their border reached up into the center of the country (Jud.1:4-5; Jos.17:15).
⇒ The Hivites were the native population occupying the northern region of the land in Gibeon that was south of the Lebanon mountains (Jos.9:7; 11:19). This area apparently also included Lebanon and Hermon.
⇒ The Jebusites were the native people who occupied Jerusalem and the surrounding area (Jos.18:28; Jud.1:21).

As stated, these seven nations were larger and more powerful than the Israelites. The enemy posed a serious threat to the Israelites. A careful, well-thought-out strategy was needed to defeat the enemy. But even more than the strategy, the presence of God—His leadership and guidance—was needed.

b. Moses explained the careful strategy and issued a strong charge to the people (vv.2-5).
1) The Israelites were to destroy the enemy totally: make no treaty with them nor show them any mercy. The enemy was to be totally annihilated. For generations, the Canaanites had been a cruel and savage people. In God's eyes, their "cup of iniquity was full" (Ge.15:16). They had reached the point when they would never repent nor correct their behavior. As a people, they would continue in their sinful ways, continue to spread their evil, brutality, lawlessness, and violence upon the earth. Consequently, God was using the Israelites to execute judgment upon the cruel and savage Canaanites. (See DEEPER STUDY # 1—De.7:2.)
2) The Israelites were not to intermarry with evil unbelievers of the Canaanite nations (vv.3-4). The reason is clearly stated: because of the evil influence and unbelief of the sinful people. Note that the parents themselves were to prevent the intermarriage: they were not to allow their sons or daughters to marry an unbeliever. The unbeliever would become a stumblingblock, lead the believer away from God into false worship. The result would be catastrophic: the anger of God would be aroused and his judgment executed. The disobedient Israelite would be destroyed because of his idolatry and rejection of God.
3) The Israelites must destroy all the false worship of the enemies (v.5). This includes all their altars, sacred stones, Asherah poles, and their idols. The instructions were clear: they were to allow no false gods, no false worship in their midst. They were to destroy the altars of other gods and of false worship. This was an absolute necessity lest the people become contaminated by the false worship and turn away from God.

Thought 1. This is a picture that believers must not compromise with sinners and unbelievers. God's people are to live a life of separation, never becoming associated or tied to unbelievers. The reason is clear: lest they be influenced by the sinful, evil ways of unbelievers. God's people must never be unequally yoked with unbelievers, not in anything. God knows that no believer is strong enough to resist the worldly influence of unbelievers if he is always associated with them. He knows that the worldly ways of unbelievers will eventually wear down the resistance of the believer. The believer will eventually commit spiritual adultery, that is, turn away from God to the gods of this world (the attractions,

---

[1] John Maxwell. *The Preacher's Commentary on Deuteronomy*, p.137.

DEUTERONOMY 7:1-26

possessions, and pleasures of this world). Alliances and permanent associations with unbelievers will lead to intermarriage with unbelievers.

The believer must always remember: it is difficult to remain pure and untainted. It is difficult to always be alert to the lust of the flesh, the lust of the eyes, and the pride of life (1 Jn.2:15-16). It is difficult to continually be growing and maturing in Christ. For this reason, he needs the constant help of other believers, in particular the help of a spouse and other family members who know the LORD. This is the reason the believer absolutely must not carry on a close fellowship with the carnal, fleshly unbelievers of this world.

> "But now I have written unto you not to keep company, if any man that is called a brother be a fornicator, or covetous, or an idolater, or a railer, or a drunkard, or an extortioner; with such an one no not to eat" (1 Co.5:11).
>
> "Be ye not unequally yoked together with unbelievers: for what fellowship hath righteousness with unrighteousness? and what communion hath light with darkness....Wherefore come out from among them, and be ye separate, saith the Lord, and touch not the unclean *thing*; and I will receive you, And will be a Father unto you, and ye shall be my sons and daughters, saith the Lord Almighty" (2 Co.6:14, 17-18).
>
> "And have no fellowship with the unfruitful works of darkness, but rather reprove *them*" (Ep.5:11).
>
> "Love not the world, neither the things *that are* in the world. If any man love the world, the love of the Father is not in him. For all that *is* in the world, the lust of the flesh, and the lust of the eyes, and the pride of life, is not of the Father, but is of the world" (1 Jn.2:15-16).
>
> "Little children, keep yourselves from idols. Amen" (1 Jn.5:21).
>
> "Thou shalt not follow a multitude to *do* evil; neither shalt thou speak in a cause to decline after many to wrest *judgment*" (Ex.23:2).
>
> "Take heed to yourselves, that your heart be not deceived, and ye turn aside, and serve other gods, and worship them" (De.11:16).
>
> "Be not thou envious against evil men, neither desire to be with them" (Pr.24:1).
>
> "Depart ye, depart ye, go ye out from thence, touch no unclean *thing*; go ye out of the midst of her; be ye clean, that bear the vessels of the LORD" (Is.52:11).

DEEPER STUDY # 1

(7:2) Iniquity, Cup of—Nations, Destruction of—Nations, Sin and Evil of—Nations, Judgment of—Canaanites, Destruction of: the words *utterly, totally, completely destroy* (harami) mean to annihilate, exterminate, eliminate, or abolish. The word is related to the Hebrew *herem* which means to *devote to the ban*.[2] Once something had been devoted to God, it was placed under the ban: it could not be removed. If it was a gift, it had to be given to God. If it was the promise to do something, then it had to be done. If it was a vow to devote something to destruction, then it had to be destroyed and terminated. In ancient days, this was known as the *herem principal or law*. Once a person or thing had been *devoted* to the LORD, it could not be removed. It went to the LORD. (See note, pt.4, d—Ge.15:7-21 for more discussion.)

The very idea that God and moral people would be set on the total destruction of a people is offensive to some persons. How could God and moral people possibly endorse such an act? In looking at this, a person needs to keep certain facts in mind:

1. People can become so savage, evil, and corrupt that they are beyond repair or repentance, beyond hope or correction. This is what is known as the *cup of iniquity being full*—filled to the point that it overflows and continues to overflow with...

- savagery
- violence
- brutality
- slavery
- ruthlessness
- lawlessness
- abuse
- cruelty
- atrocities
- barbarism
- corruption
- evil
- immorality

History has shown that such behavior can be true of both individuals and nations. A person's or a nation's "cup of iniquity" can become full—well beyond repair or repentance, well beyond hope or correction. God declares this fact time and again as the Scriptures below show (Ge.15:16).

God wants justice executed against these people. Scripture is clear about this fact: this is the very purpose for the judgment of God.

> "But in the fourth generation they shall come hither again: for the iniquity of the Amorites is not yet full" (Ge.15:16).
>
> "Defile not ye yourselves in any of these things: for in all these the nations are defiled which I cast out before you: And the land is defiled: therefore I do visit the iniquity thereof upon it, and the land itself vomiteth out her inhabitants" (Le.18:24-25).
>
> "And ye shall not walk in the manners of the nation, which I cast out before you: for they committed all these things, and therefore I abhorred them" (Le.20:23).
>
> "Speak not thou in thine heart, after that the LORD thy God hath cast them out from before thee, saying, For my righteousness the LORD hath brought me in to possess this land: but for the wickedness of these nations the LORD doth drive them out from before thee" (De.9:4).
>
> "And he did that which was evil in the sight of the Lord, after the abominations of the heathen, whom the Lord cast out before the children of Israel" (2 K.21:2).

---

2 Frank E. Gaebelein, Editor. *The Expositor's Bible Commentary*, Vol.2., p.874.

> "Moreover he burnt incense in the valley of the son of Hinnom, and burnt his children in the fire, after the abominations of the heathen whom the Lord had cast out before the children of Israel" (2 Chr.28:3).
>
> "But did that which was evil in the sight of the Lord, like unto the abominations of the heathen, whom the LORD had cast out before the children of Israel" (2 Chr.33:2).
>
> "And shed innocent blood, even the blood of their sons and of their daughters, whom they sacrificed unto the idols of Canaan: and the land was polluted with blood" (Ps.106:38).
>
> "The earth also is defiled under the inhabitants thereof; because they have transgressed the laws, changed the ordinance, broken the everlasting covenant" (Is.24:5).
>
> "Lift up thine eyes unto the high places, and see where thou hast not been lien with. In the ways hast thou sat for them, as the Arabian in the wilderness; and thou hast polluted the land with thy whoredoms and with thy wickedness" (Je.3:2).
>
> "And first I will recompense their iniquity and their sin double; because they have defiled my land, they have filled mine inheritance with the carcases of their detestable and abominable things" (Je.16:18).

2. God is a just God as well as a God of love. God loves all people—every individual and all the people of every nation upon earth. His love continually flows out to everyone. But God is also a just God, the Sovereign LORD who executes justice upon the earth. God is not an indulgent grandfather type of person who pampers the evil and savage of this world. If He allowed injustice to go unpunished, He would be a God of evil, a God who showed partiality and favoritism. He would be favoring the evil of the earth by allowing them to go unpunished, and He would be showing injustice to the moral of the earth by allowing them to continue to suffer under the injustices of evil people.

When the "cup of iniquity becomes full"—well beyond repair or repentance, well beyond hope or correction—that person or people are to be judged. Justice is to be executed upon them. God wants justice executed against such persons. This is the reason He has appointed a day in which He will judge the world.

> "When the Son of man shall come in his glory, and all the holy angels with him, then shall he sit upon the throne of his glory: And before him shall be gathered all nations: and he shall separate them one from another, as a shepherd divideth his sheep from the goats: And he shall set the sheep on his right hand, but the goats on the left" (Mt.25:31-33).
>
> "Because he hath appointed a day, in the which he will judge the world in righteousness by that man whom he hath ordained; whereof he hath given assurance unto all men, in that he hath raised him from the dead" (Ac.17:31).
>
> "In the day when God shall judge the secrets of men by Jesus Christ according to my gospel" (Ro.2:16).
>
> "I charge thee therefore before God, and the Lord Jesus Christ, who shall judge the quick and the dead at his appearing and his kingdom" (2 Ti.4:1).
>
> "And as it is appointed unto men once to die, but after this the judgment" (He.9:27).
>
> "The Lord knoweth how to deliver the godly out of temptations, and to reserve the unjust unto the day of judgment to be punished" (2 Pe.2:9).
>
> "Behold, the Lord cometh with ten thousands of his saints, To execute judgment upon all, and to convince all that are ungodly among them of all their ungodly deeds which they have ungodly committed, and of all their hard speeches which ungodly sinners have spoken against him" (Jude 14-15).
>
> "And I saw the dead, small and great, stand before God; and the books were opened: and another book was opened, which is the book of life: and the dead were judged out of those things which were written in the books, according to their works" (Re.20:12).

Thought 1. James Philips makes an excellent statement on the justice and judgment of God that is well worth quoting in full.

> *God was using His people as the rod of His anger against peoples whose cup of iniquity was full to overflowing. They were being judged for their sins and their depravities. This is, of course, stated explicitly more than once in the Old Testament itself (cf. Ge. 15:16 and Lev. 18:24-30). The time of their destruction was ripe. This is why they were thus dealt with, and it was no arbitrary act of injustice that drove them out of their land. They had forfeited the right to live as nations in Canaan by the extremes of their debauchery and depravity, just as Sodom and Gomorrah had done (Ge. 19), and just as the Cainite civilization as a whole had done, bringing upon itself the judgment of the Flood (Ge. 6). Furthermore, it should be remembered that God dealt with His own people in similar fashion when they proved themselves unworthy to life in the land of promise, and He brought them into the captivity of Babylon in 586 B.C. To understand God's burning passion for righteousness in His creatures is to understand the basic reason for these judgments upon men and nations that refused to be righteous, and who rendered themselves incapable of being so by their continued sin.*[3]

---

3 James Philip. *The Preacher's Commentary on Numbers*. (Nashville, TN: Thomas Nelson, 1987, 2003), p.311.

DEUTERONOMY 7:1-26

2 (7:6-11) **Holiness, Position of—Believers, Title of—Treasure, Title of Believers—Possession, Treasured—Covenant, of God—Obedience, Duty:** the reasons why all enemies of the promised land must be completely destroyed are clearly spelled out. Moses wanted to stir up the people to obey God, to make sure they completely destroyed all enemies who would keep them out of the promised land. God's people must march into the promised land and lay claim to the inheritance promised by God. This was their right: to live as conquerors throughout life and to secure their spiritual rest in the promised land of God. Five strong reasons are given for obeying God, for conquering all the enemies who seek to defeat them and keep them out of the promised land.

OUTLINE	SCRIPTURE	SCRIPTURE	OUTLINE

2. The reasons why all enemies of the promised land must be completely destroyed: A picture of spiritual separation
a. Because God's people are holy—set apart to God: Chosen to be His special treasure
  1) God's people were not chosen because of any merit or value: They were the fewest of all people (Ge.12:1-3; 46:26)
  2) God's people were chosen only because of God's love & oath to Abraham & the forefathers
b. Because the LORD redeemed, saved His people from the enslavement of Egypt (a
	6 For thou *art* an holy people unto the LORD thy God: the LORD thy God hath chosen thee to be a special people unto himself, above all people that *are* upon the face of the earth.
	7 The LORD did not set his love upon you, nor choose you, because ye were more in number than any people; for ye *were* the fewest of all people:
	8 But because the LORD loved you, and because he would keep the oath which he had sworn unto your fathers, hath the LORD brought you out with a mighty hand, and redeemed you out of the house of bondmen, from the
		hand of Pharaoh king of Egypt.
		9 Know therefore that the LORD thy God, he *is* God, the faithful God, which keepeth covenant and mercy with them that love him and keep his commandments to a thousand generations;
		10 And repayeth them that hate him to their face, to destroy them: he will not be slack to him that hateth him, he will repay him to his face.
		11 Thou shalt therefore keep the commandments, and the statutes, and the judgments, which I command thee this day, to do them.
			symbol of the world)
			
			c. Because the Lord God is the true God & He is faithful: He keeps His covenant of love...
			  1) to those who love Him
			  2) to those who obey Him
			
			d. Because God does not hesitate to execute justice: He destroys all who hate & reject Him
			
			e. Because obedience is demanded by God: His people must obey all God's commandments, laws, & regulations

a. Standing there preaching with fire in his heart, Moses declared: "You are to obey God. Go forth and conquer all the enemies of the promised land. This you are to do for a very special reason: you are holy, set apart to God. You are chosen to be His special people, His special treasure—the people who are totally committed to God, committed to love and obey Him. You are chosen to be His witnesses to the immoral, lawless, and violent peoples of the earth—witnesses to the only living and true God" (Is.43:10).

Moses declared that God's people are not chosen because of any merit or value within themselves. In fact, the Israelites had been the fewest (smallest in number) of all people when God chose them (see outline and notes—Ge.12:1-3 for more discussion. See Ge.46:26.) Long before—far, far back in antiquity—the whole earth lay in wickedness. Immorality, lawlessness, and violence swept the earth. Few persons, if any, obeyed God. There were no righteous persons upon earth. God had no choice but to start all over, and this He did by choosing one man, Abraham. God made several great promises to Abraham if he would just follow and obey God:

⇒ the promise of the promised land
⇒ the promise of the promised seed, the coming Messiah and Savior of the world
⇒ the promise of a great nation of people (see outline and notes—Ge.12:1-3 for more discussion)

It was from Abraham that God's people had been born. The present generation of Israelites standing before Moses were the descendants of Abraham.

The point is striking: the Israelites were not chosen because of any merit or value within themselves. They were chosen only because of God's love and oath to Abraham and the forefathers (v.8). God had chosen the Israelites to build a new race of people, a people who would belong totally to Him. The Israelites were to be His holy people, that is, a people totally set apart to God. For this reason, the Israelites were to obey God, do exactly what He said: completely conquer and destroy all the enemies who opposed them and tried to keep them out of the promised land.

> "That he would grant unto us, that we being delivered out of the hand of our enemies might serve him without fear, In holiness and righteousness before him, all the days of our life" (Lu.1:74-75).
>
> "Having therefore these promises, dearly beloved, let us cleanse ourselves from all filthiness of the flesh and spirit, perfecting holiness in the fear of God" (2 Co.7:1).
>
> "Follow peace with all *men*, and holiness, without which no man shall see the Lord" (He.12:14).
>
> "But as he which hath called you is holy, so be ye holy in all manner of conversation; Because it is written, Be ye holy; for I am holy" (1 Pe.1:15-16).
>
> "But the day of the Lord will come as a thief in the night; in the which the heavens shall pass away with a great noise, and the elements shall melt with fervent heat, the earth also and the works that are therein shall be burned up. *Seeing* then *that* all these things shall be dissolved, what manner *of persons* ought ye to be in *all* holy conversation and godliness, Looking for and hasting unto the coming of the day of God, wherein the heavens being on fire shall be dissolved, and the elements shall melt with fervent heat? Nevertheless we, according to his promise, look for new heavens and a new earth, wherein dwelleth righteousness. Wherefore, beloved, seeing that ye look for such things, be diligent that ye may be found of him in peace, without spot, and blameless" (2 Pe.3:10-14).

"For I *am* the LORD that bringeth you up out of the land of Egypt, to be your God: ye shall therefore be holy, for I *am* holy" (Le.11:45).

b. You are to obey God, conquer all the enemies of the promised land for another special reason: because the LORD redeemed you and saved you from the enslavement of Egypt (v.8). It was only because of God's salvation that the Israelites stood there before Moses. They would still be slaves in Egypt if God had not saved them. God loved His people; therefore He saved them and redeemed them from a life of enslavement. For this reason, they were to obey God and destroy all the enemies of the promised land, lest they become enslaved again. They owed their lives to God. Having been saved from Egypt and its sinful ways, never again were they to run the risk of becoming entangled with sinful unbelievers. They were now God's people, saved and redeemed by Him.

"But now being made free from sin, and become servants to God, ye have your fruit unto holiness, and the end everlasting life. For the wages of sin *is* death; but the gift of God *is* eternal life through Jesus Christ our Lord" (Ro.6:22-23).

"For by grace are ye saved through faith; and that not of yourselves: *it is* the gift of God: Not of works, lest any man should boast. For we are his workmanship, created in Christ Jesus unto good works, which God hath before ordained that we should walk in them" (Ep.2:8-10).

"The Lord knoweth how to deliver the godly out of temptations, and to reserve the unjust unto the day of judgment to be punished" (2 Pe.2:9).

"The LORD *is* my light and my salvation; whom shall I fear? the LORD *is* the strength of my life; of whom shall I be afraid" (Ps.27:1).

"But the salvation of the righteous *is* of the LORD: *he is* their strength in the time of trouble" (Ps.37:39).

"Behold, God *is* my salvation; I will trust, and not be afraid: for the LORD JEHOVAH *is* my strength and *my* song; he also is become my salvation" (Is.12:2).

c. You are to obey God, conquer all the enemies of the promised land for a third special reason: the LORD *your God is* the true God. There is no other God; all other gods are false. They are lifeless, unable to save or help in times of need, unable to give a full and victorious life as you walk throughout life. There is only one true and living God, the LORD your God. Therefore you owe your obedience to Him.

But this is not all. The LORD your God is faithful: He keeps His covenant of love to all those who love and obey Him (v.9). And He keeps His covenant for one thousand generations. But note that His covenant is conditional: it is kept only for those who love and obey Him. But for those who do love and obey Him, He keeps it eternally, for one thousand generations.

"God *is* faithful, by whom ye were called unto the fellowship of his Son Jesus Christ our Lord" (1 Co.1:9).

"Wherein God, willing more abundantly to show unto the heirs of promise the immutability of his counsel, confirmed *it* by an oath: That by two immutable things, in which *it was* impossible for God to lie, we might have a strong consolation, who have fled for refuge to lay hold upon the hope set before us" (He.6:17-18).

"For this *is* the covenant that I will make with the house of Israel after those days, saith the Lord; I will put my laws into their mind, and write them in their hearts: and I will be to them a God, and they shall be to me a people" (He.8:10).

"Blessed *be* the LORD, that hath given rest unto his people Israel, according to all that he promised: there hath not failed one word of all his good promise, which he promised by the hand of Moses his servant" (1 K.8:56).

"Thy mercy, O LORD, *is* in the heavens; *and* thy faithfulness *reacheth* unto the clouds" (Ps.36:5).

"I will sing of the mercies of the LORD for ever: with my mouth will I make known thy faithfulness to all generations" (Ps.89:1).

d. You are to obey God, conquer all the enemies of the promised land for a fourth special reason: because God does not hesitate to execute justice (v.10). God will destroy all who hate and reject Him. All the Canaanite nations had filled to the brim "their cup of iniquity." Consequently, they were to be destroyed. If any believer—any of the Israelites—turned away from God—demonstrating a hatred and rejection of God—that person would face the judgment of God and be destroyed. God's people were to fear the justice and judgment of God. For this reason, they must obey God and do exactly what He said: conquer all the enemies of the promised land.

"For the wrath of God is revealed from heaven against all ungodliness and unrighteousness of men, who hold the truth in unrighteousness" (Ro.1:18).

"But unto them that are contentious, and do not obey the truth, but obey unrighteousness, indignation and wrath" (Ro.2:8).

"But fornication, and all uncleanness, or covetousness, let it not be once named among you, as becometh saints; Neither filthiness, nor foolish talking, nor jesting, which are not convenient: but rather giving of thanks. For this ye know, that no whoremonger, nor unclean person, nor covetous man, who is an idolater, hath any inheritance in the kingdom of Christ and of God. Let no man deceive you with vain words: for because of these things cometh the wrath of God upon the children of disobedience" (Ep.5:3-6).

"Herein is our love made perfect, that we may have boldness in the day of judgment: because as he is, so are we in this world" (1 Jn.4:17).

DEUTERONOMY 7:1-26

e. You are to obey God, conquer all the enemies of the promised land for a fifth special reason: because obedience is demanded by God (v.11). Simply stated, the believer must obey all God's commandments. The enemies of the promised land must be completely destroyed. Once the enemies are destroyed, God's people will secure the victorious life. They will live a life of conquest and of rest—both physical and spiritual conquest and rest (He.4:1-11).

> "Not every one that saith unto me, Lord, Lord, shall enter into the kingdom of heaven; but he that doeth the will of my Father which is in heaven" (Mt.7:21).
>
> "This day the LORD thy God hath commanded thee to do these statutes and judgments: thou shalt therefore keep and do them with all thine heart, and with all thy soul" (De.26:16).
>
> "This book of the law shall not depart out of thy mouth; but thou shalt meditate therein day and night, that thou mayest observe to do according to all that is written therein: for then thou shalt make thy way prosperous, and then thou shalt have good success" (Jos.1:8).
>
> "And Samuel said, Hath the LORD *as great* delight in burnt offerings and sacrifices, as in obeying the voice of the LORD? Behold, to obey *is* better than sacrifice, *and* to hearken than the fat of rams" (1 S.15:22).

3 (7:12-16) **Obedience, Results of—Blessings, of God—Blessings, Result of Obedience**: the results of obedience are spelled out in practical detail. Point by point Moses spelled out exactly what would happen if God's people obeyed God and destroyed all the enemies of the promised land.

OUTLINE	SCRIPTURE	SCRIPTURE	OUTLINE
3. The results of obedience: What happens if all the enemies of the promised land are destroyed	12 Wherefore it shall come to pass, if ye hearken to these judgments, and keep them, that the LORD thy God shall keep unto thee the covenant and the mercy which he sware unto thy fathers:	above all people: there shall not be male or female barren among you, or among your cattle.	people (possibly a promise of the Messiah, see Ge.12:2-3)
a. God will keep His covenant of love		15 And the LORD will take away from thee all sickness, and will put none of the evil diseases of Egypt, which thou knowest, upon thee; but will lay them upon all *them* that hate thee.	5) Give them health; keep them free from disease
b. God will love & bless His people in a very special way	13 And he will love thee, and bless thee, and multiply thee: he will also bless the fruit of thy womb, and the fruit of thy land, thy corn, and thy wine, and thine oil, the increase of thy kine, and the flocks of thy sheep, in the land which he sware unto thy fathers to give thee.		6) Free them from the chastisement & diseases that afflicted Egypt: They will afflict their enemies
1) Increase their number: Make them into a great nation of people—give them many children			c. The charge reemphasized
2) Bless their crops & livestock		16 And thou shalt consume all the people which the LORD thy God shall deliver thee; thine eye shall have no pity upon them: neither shalt thou serve their gods; for that *will be* a snare unto thee.	1) Must destroy all enemies, for they will be a snare
3) Give them the promised land			2) Must not turn to their false worship
4) Bless them above all other	14 Thou shalt be blessed		

a. God will keep His covenant of love if His people will obey Him (vv.12-14). This was the covenant promised to Abraham, the wonderful blessing God had promised to pour out upon Abraham and his descendants if Abraham would just follow God. Note how the blessings discussed in point two cover the promises given to Abraham (see outline and notes—Ge.12:1-3 for more discussion).

b. God will love and bless you in a very special way (vv.13-15).

1) God will increase your number, make you into a great nation of people (v.13). This was one of the promises given to Abraham, that he would have many descendants. The Israelites standing before Moses as he preached were the descendants of Abraham. But God promised to continue to increase the population of Israel—if the second generation of believers would just continue to obey God and do exactly what He says.

2) God will bless your crops and livestock (v.13). The land will be fruitful, producing enough for food and marketing. And the livestock would produce beyond the normal production rate. If God's people would just obey Him, be faithful to keep His commandments, then God's people would never know hunger nor poverty. They would prosper and prosper greatly.

3) God will give His people the promised land (v.13) if they obey Him (see outline and notes—De.1:8 for more discussion).

4) God will bless you above all other people (v.14). This is definitely a promise of material and spiritual blessings to the obedient believer. Also, it is most likely a promise of the coming Messiah (see Ge.12:2-3). In the promised Messiah and Savior, the descendants of Abraham—all believers—are blessed more than any other people. More than any other blessing, it is Christ who causes them to be blessed more than any other people.

5) God will give His people health and keep them from disease (v.15). Again, this blessing was conditional. God's people had to obey Him in order to experience better than normal health.

6) God will not chastise His people for sin, not with the diseases of Egypt. But the enemies of God's people, the sinful unbelievers of the world, will be afflicted with disease (v.15). The immoral will be afflicted with sexual disease; the glutton and indulgent will be afflicted with bodily diseases; the disobedient and rebellious will suffer the diseases of Egypt, of the world.

DEUTERONOMY 7:1-26

c. Moses reemphasized the charge of God: God's people must destroy all the enemies of the promised land (v.16). This was an absolute necessity, for the enemies would become a snare to the people of God. Therefore God's people must not look upon their enemies with pity. And they must not turn to their false gods and worship.

Thought 1. God blesses the obedient person. If a person will keep God's commandments, God will pour out His blessings upon the person, blessings that are incomprehensible.

"But seek ye first the kingdom of God, and his righteousness; and all these things shall be added unto you" (Mt.6:33).

"If ye keep my commandments, ye shall abide in my love; even as I have kept my Father's commandments, and abide in his love" (Jn.15:10).

"Now unto him that is able to do exceeding abundantly above all that we ask or think, according to the power that worketh in us" (Ep.3:20).

"But my God shall supply all your need according to his riches in glory by Christ Jesus" (Ph.4:19).

"But whoso looketh into the perfect law of liberty, and continueth *therein,* he being not a forgetful hearer, but a doer of the work, this man shall be blessed in his deed" (Js.1:25).

"And whatsoever we ask, we receive of him, because we keep his commandments, and do those things that are pleasing in his sight" (1 Jn.3:22).

"Blessed *are* they that do his commandments, that they may have right to the tree of life, and may enter in through the gates into the city" (Re.22:14).

"O that there were such an heart in them, that they would fear me, and keep all my commandments always, that it might be well with them, and with their children for ever" (De.5:29).

"And it shall come to pass, if thou shalt hearken diligently unto the voice of the LORD thy God, to observe *and* to do all his commandments which I command thee this day, that the LORD thy God will set thee on high above all nations of the earth" (De.28:1).

"This book of the law shall not depart out of thy mouth; but thou shalt meditate therein day and night, that thou mayest observe to do according to all that is written therein: for then thou shalt make thy way prosperous, and then thou shalt have good success" (Jos.1:8).

"I will abundantly bless her provision: I will satisfy her poor with bread" (Ps.132:15).

"Then shall he give the rain of thy seed, that thou shalt sow the ground withal; and bread of the increase of the earth, and it shall be fat and plenteous: in that day shall thy cattle feed in large pastures" (Is.30:23).

4 (7:17-26) **Doubt, Answer to—Fear, Answer to—Victory—Life, Victorious—Idolatry, Duty—Temptation, Duty**: the solution to doubt and fear is clearly spelled out by Moses. The presence and power of God is the answer to doubt and fear. When facing enemies that are more powerful and numerous, there is the danger that a person will shrink back, that a defeatist attitude will grip him and his family. A spirit of fear and doubt in God's presence and promises can grip any person and people. This Moses knew; therefore, he began to deal head-on with the issue. Note what he proclaimed to the people:

OUTLINE	SCRIPTURE	SCRIPTURE	OUTLINE
4. The solution to doubt & fear: The presence & power of God a. Face the question of fear b. Do not be overcome by fear: Remember past victories 1) The LORD delivered His people from Egypt with miraculous signs & wonders—with amazing power 2) The LORD will continue to deliver His people from the enemies of the promised land: By His amazing power c. Know that the LORD will send the hornet (a symbol of some enemy or plague or of God's power) until all enemies are driven out & destroyed	17 If thou shalt say in thine heart, These nations *are* more than I; how can I dispossess them? 18 Thou shalt not be afraid of them: *but* shalt well remember what the LORD thy God did unto Pharaoh, and unto all Egypt; 19 The great temptations which thine eyes saw, and the signs, and the wonders, and the mighty hand, and the stretched out arm, whereby the LORD thy God brought thee out: so shall the LORD thy God do unto all the people of whom thou art afraid. 20 Moreover the LORD thy God will send the hornet among them, until they that are left, and hide themselves from thee, be destroyed.	21 Thou shalt not be affrighted at them: for the LORD thy God *is* among you, a mighty God and terrible. 22 And the LORD thy God will put out those nations before thee by little and little: thou mayest not consume them at once, lest the beasts of the field increase upon thee. 23 But the LORD thy God shall deliver them unto thee, and shall destroy them with a mighty destruction, until they be destroyed. 24 And he shall deliver their kings into thine hand, and thou shalt destroy their name from under heaven: there shall no man be able to stand before thee, until thou have	d. Know that the LORD's presence—His great & awesome presence—is among His people: Do not be terrified by the enemy e. Know that the LORD will drive out the enemy little by little, gradually 1) To give time for the land to be controlled & cultivated 2) To keep land from returning to its primitive state f. Know that the LORD will throw the enemies into total confusion, until they are destroyed g. Know that the LORD will give their kings over to His people 1) To erase their names 2) To defeat them

DEUTERONOMY 7:1-26

OUTLINE	SCRIPTURE	SCRIPTURE	OUTLINE
h. Remove all temptation that ensnares a person—causes them to turn away from God 1) Destroy all idols 2) Do not covet the silver & gold of idols 3) Do not keep the idols:	destroyed them. 25 The graven images of their gods shall ye burn with fire: thou shalt not desire the silver or gold *that is* on them, nor take *it* unto thee, lest thou be a snared therein: for it *is* an abomination to the LORD thy	God. 26 Neither shalt thou bring an abomination into thine house, lest thou be a cursed thing like it: *but* thou shalt utterly detest it, and thou shalt utterly abhor it; for it *is* a cursed thing.	Will ensnare 4) Do not take a detestable thing into one's home • Will bring judgment • Must abhor, detest it • God has set it apart for destruction

a. The question of fear must be faced (v.17). As a wise leader, Moses knew that the major battle fought by men is in the mind, not on the battlefield. Standing there preaching, he confronted the problem of fear head-on. He told the people they were going to be afraid, they were going to ask themselves: "How can we defeat these nations? They are stronger than we are." In confronting the problem of fear, the people were actually taking the first needed step. They were facing the fear. They were standing face to face, toe to toe with their fear. They were confronting their fear and acknowledging that fear is a normal reaction, and by so doing, they were dealing with their fear.

b. Moses declared: Do not be overcome by fear: remember past victories (vv.18-19). Remember that the LORD delivered His people from Egypt with miraculous signs and wonders, with amazing power. Therefore the LORD will deliver you from the enemies of the promised land by doing the very same. The LORD will work in and through you to defeat all the enemies who try to keep you out of the promised land. Conquer doubt and fear by remembering past victories.

c. Know that the LORD will send the hornet among the enemies (v.20). The hornet will sting all the enemies until they are driven out and destroyed. The hornet is a symbol of some plague or of God's power, thus, the meaning is clear: God will see to it that His people are victorious over all the enemies who oppose them. They must not fear nor doubt His presence and power to give victory.

d. Know that the LORD's presence—His great and awesome presence—is among you (v.21). Therefore, do not be terrified by the enemy. God's presence will protect His people; God will give strength to His people, the strength to conquer their enemies. In confronting fear and doubt, keep one thing in mind: God is able (Ep.3:20).

e. Know that the LORD will drive out the enemy little by little, gradually (v.22). This was necessary in order to give time for the land to be controlled and cultivated. A battle to conquer the entire promised land would have taken many months, probably stretching into several years. If this strategy had been followed, there would have been no time for either side to cultivate the land. The land would have returned to its primitive state. Therefore, the strategy established by God is now being explained to the people by Moses. The conquest was not to happen overnight. The people were to fight, then settle down and take care of the land.[4] This strategy would give rest to both the land and the people, and it should encourage the people not to fear but to lay hold of the full inheritance promised by God.

f. Know that the LORD will throw the enemies into total confusion, until they are defeated (v.23). A negative spirit of defeatism will sweep their hearts, and they will be gripped with a terrible fear, knowing that they are to suffer defeat. Destruction will be inevitable, and they will be unable to stop it.

g. Know that God will give their kings and leaders over to you (v.24). You will erase their names from history. No enemy will be able to stand against you. Do not fear nor doubt. Just trust and obey God, and the victory will be yours.

h. Remove all temptations that will ensnare you as you march into the promised land (v.25). Completely destroy the enemy and their possessions—all things that might cause you to turn away from God.
⇒ Destroy all their idols: burn them in the fire.
⇒ Do not covet the silver and gold of the idols.
⇒ Do not keep the idols, for they will ensnare you. You will be running the risk of being tempted to turn to false worship.
⇒ Do not take abominable, detestable things into your home (v.26). Detestable things will bring judgment upon you. You must, therefore, abhor, detest anything that is abominable or contemptible. God has set all idols and detestable things apart for destruction.

Thought 1. The believer faces many enemies throughout life, enemies that strike fear and doubt in his heart. The enemies are often strong and hostile, enemies such as...

- disease
- accident
- drugs
- alcohol
- immorality
- greed
- covetousness
- anger
- discouragement
- depression
- failure
- financial difficulty
- unemployment
- lack of purpose
- loneliness
- emptiness
- death

Some enemies are small and weak, amounting to nothing more than minor problems or difficulties. Such enemies are easy to conquer, even by the arm of the flesh. But there are other enemies that are far more powerful and brutal in their attack. These enemies can never be defeated by man, such enemies as terminal disease, a paralyzing accident, or even death. Such enemies as these can be conquered only by the power of God Himself. This is the lesson we should learn from this passage. The presence and power of God is at our disposal. If we will only obey God, God will give us His presence and power to conquer the enemies of this life. We will be victorious over any enemy that tries to keep us out of the promised land. We will experience a full and victorious life as we march into the promised land of heaven.

---

4 John Maxwell. *The Preacher's Commentary on Deuteronomy*, p.144.

DEUTERONOMY 7:1-26

"Who shall separate us from the love of Christ? *shall* tribulation, or distress, or persecution, or famine, or nakedness, or peril, or sword....Nay, in all these things we are more than conquerors through him that loved us. For I am persuaded, that neither death, nor life, nor angels, nor principalities, nor powers, nor things present, nor things to come, Nor height, nor depth, nor any other creature, shall be able to separate us from the love of God, which is in Christ Jesus our Lord" (Ro.8:35, 37-39).

"But there shall not an hair of your head perish" (Lu.21:18).

"So that we may boldly say, The Lord *is* my helper, and I will not fear what man shall do unto me" (He.13:6).

"The LORD shall fight for you, and ye shall hold your peace" (Ex.14:14).

"I will send my fear before thee, and will destroy all the people to whom thou shalt come, and I will make all thine enemies turn their backs unto thee" (Ex.23:27).

"For the eyes of the LORD run to and fro throughout the whole earth, to show himself strong in the behalf of *them* whose heart *is* perfect toward him" (2 Chr.16:9).

"With him *is* an arm of flesh; but with us *is* the LORD our God to help us, and to fight our battles. And the people rested themselves upon the words of Hezekiah king of Judah" (2 Chr.32:8).

"The LORD *is* my strength and my shield; my heart trusted in him, and I am helped: therefore my heart greatly rejoiceth; and with my song will I praise him" (Ps.28:7).

"For in the time of trouble he shall hide me in his pavilion: in the secret of his tabernacle shall he hide me; he shall set me up upon a rock" (Ps.27:5).

"Thou shalt hide them in the secret of thy presence from the pride of man: thou shalt keep them secretly in a pavilion from the strife of tongues" (Ps.31:20).

"The angel of the LORD encampeth round about them that fear him, and delivereth them" (Ps.34:7).

"He shall cover thee with his feathers, and under his wings shalt thou trust: his truth *shall be thy* shield and buckler" (Ps.91:4).

"Fear thou not; for I *am* with thee: be not dismayed; for I *am* thy God: I will strengthen thee; yea, I will help thee; yea, I will uphold thee with the right hand of my righteousness" (Is.41:10).

Thought 2. All temptation must be removed from our lives and homes. If there is anything that might defile us, we must get rid of it. We must not allow any defiling thing to remain in our presence, not if we can prevent it. Detestable things will ensnare us and arouse the judgment of God against us. We must, therefore, flee temptation.

"Neither yield ye your members *as* instruments of unrighteousness unto sin: but yield yourselves unto God, as those that are alive from the dead, and your members *as* instruments of righteousness unto God" (Ro.6:13).

"For we wrestle not against flesh and blood, but against principalities, against powers, against the rulers of the darkness of this world, against spiritual wickedness in high *places*. Wherefore take unto you the whole armour of God, that ye may be able to withstand in the evil day, and having done all, to stand" (Ep.6:12-13).

"Flee fornication. Every sin that a man doeth is without the body; but he that committeth fornication sinneth against his own body" (1 Co.6:18).

"Wherefore, my dearly beloved, flee from idolatry" (1 Co.10:14).

"Be ye angry, and sin not: let not the sun go down upon your wrath: Neither give place to the devil" (Ep.4:26-27).

"But thou, O man of God, flee these things; and follow after righteousness, godliness, faith, love, patience, meekness. Fight the good fight of faith, lay hold on eternal life, whereunto thou art also called, and hast professed a good profession before many witnesses" (1 Ti.6:11-12).

"Submit yourselves therefore to God. Resist the devil, and he will flee from you" (Js.4:7).

"Be sober, be vigilant; because your adversary the devil, as a roaring lion, walketh about, seeking whom he may devour: Whom resist stedfast in the faith, knowing that the same afflictions are accomplished in your brethren that are in the world" (1 Pe.5:8-9).

"Ye therefore, beloved, seeing ye know *these things* before, beware lest ye also, being led away with the error of the wicked, fall from your own stedfastness" (2 Pe.3:17).

"My son, if sinners entice thee, consent thou not" (Pr.1:10).

"Enter not into the path of the wicked, and go not in the way of evil *men*" (Pr.4:14).

TYPES, SYMBOLS, AND PICTURES
(Deuteronomy 7:1-26)

Historical Term	Type or Picture (Scriptural Basis for Each)	Life Application for Today's Believer	Biblical Application
Complete Destruction of Enemies in the Promised Land De.7:1-5	*Complete destruction of enemies in the promised land is a picture of spiritual separation. This is a picture that believers must not compromise with sinners and unbelievers.*	⇒ God's people are to live a life of separation, never becoming associated or tied to unbelievers. The reason is clear: lest they be influenced by the sinful, evil ways of unbe-	*"But now I have written unto you not to keep company, if any man that is called a brother be a fornicator, or covetous, or an idolater, or a railer, or a drunkard, or an extortioner;*

DEUTERONOMY 7:1-26

Historical Term	Type or Picture (Scriptural Basis for Each)	Life Application for Today's Believer	Biblical Application
	"And when the LORD thy God shall deliver them before thee; thou shalt smite them, *and* utterly destroy them; thou shalt make no covenant with them, nor show mercy unto them" (De.7:2).	lievers. God's people must never be unequally yoked with unbelievers, not in anything. God knows that no believer is strong enough to resist the worldly influence of unbelievers if he is always associated with them. He knows that the worldly ways of unbelievers will eventually wear down the resistance of the believer. The believer will eventually commit spiritual adultery, that is, turn away from God to the gods of this world (the attractions, possessions, and pleasures of this world). Alliances and permanent associations with unbelievers will lead to intermarriage with unbelievers. The believer must always remember: it is difficult to remain pure and untainted. It is difficult to be always alert to the lust of the flesh, the lust of the eyes, and the pride of life (1 Jn.2:15-16). It is difficult to continually be growing and maturing in Christ. For this reason, he needs the constant help of other believers, in particular the help of a spouse and other family members who know the LORD. This is the reason the believer absolutely must not carry on a close fellowship with the carnal, fleshly unbelievers of this world.	with such an one no not to eat" (1 Co.5:11). "Be ye not unequally yoked together with unbelievers: for what fellowship hath righteousness with unrighteousness? and what communion hath light with darkness....Wherefore come out from among them, and be ye separate, saith the Lord, and touch not the unclean thing; and I will receive you, And will be a Father unto you, and ye shall be my sons and daughters, saith the Lord Almighty" (2 Co.6:14, 17-18). "And have no fellowship with the unfruitful works of darkness, but rather reprove them" (Ep.5:11). "Love not the world, neither the things that are in the world. If any man love the world, the love of the Father is not in him. For all that is in the world, the lust of the flesh, and the lust of the eyes, and the pride of life, is not of the Father, but is of the world" (1 Jn.2:15-16). "Little children, keep yourselves from idols. Amen" (1 Jn.5:21). "Thou shalt not follow a multitude to do evil; neither shalt thou speak in a cause to decline after many to wrest judgment" (Ex.23:2). "Take heed to yourselves, that your heart be not deceived, and ye turn aside, and serve other gods, and worship them" (De. 11:16; See also Pr.24:1; Is.42:8; Is.52:11).
Hornet De.7:17-26, esp. v.20	*The hornet is a type or symbol of some enemy or plague or of God's power. The hornet sent by God will sting all the enemies until they are driven out and destroyed.* "Moreover the LORD thy God will send the hornet among them, until they that are left, and hide themselves from thee, be destroyed" (De.7:20).	⇒ God will see to it that His people are victorious over all the enemies who oppose them. They must not fear nor doubt His presence and power to give victory. ⇒ When a severe problem confronts us, a problem that seems to have no solution, what is the natural tendency of our hearts? Often to flee, to get away, to run wherever we can. But this is not God's way. God's way is to stand still, stand firm: watch the salvation of the Lord.	"Who shall separate us from the love of Christ? shall tribulation, or distress, or persecution, or famine, or nakedness, or peril, or sword....Nay, in all these things we are more than conquerors through him that loved us. For I am persuaded, that neither death, nor life, nor angels, nor principalities, nor powers, nor things present, nor things to come, Nor height, nor depth, nor any other creature, shall be able to separate us from the love of God, which is in Christ

DEUTERONOMY 7:1-26

Historical Term	Type or Picture (Scriptural Basis for Each)	Life Application for Today's Believer	Biblical Application
		God wants to deliver us. We must, therefore, stand firm, not give up, cave in, nor flee away. We must be steadfast: stand still, wait upon God's mighty arm to save and deliver us.	Jesus our Lord" (Ro.8:35, 37-39). "So that we may boldly say, The Lord is my helper, and I will not fear what man shall do unto me" (He.13:6). "The LORD shall fight for you, and ye shall hold your peace" (Ex.14:14). "The LORD is my strength and my shield; my heart trusted in him, and I am helped: therefore my heart greatly rejoiceth; and with my song will I praise him" (Ps.28:7).

DEUTERONOMY 8:1-20

CHAPTER 8

G. The Safeguards to Assure Obedience to the Commandments of God: How to Guard Against Forgetting God, 8:1-20

1. **Be careful! Observe! Obey every commandment of God**
   a. Assures life
   b. Assures increase in fruitfulness & population
   c. Assures an inheritance in the promised land
2. **Remember God's guidance through the wilderness wanderings**
   a. God's humbling you & testing you
      1) To prove your character
      2) To prove your obedience or disobedience
   b. God's provision of food
      1) He provided *manna*
      2) His purpose: To teach one great truth
         - Man's life does not depend on bread alone
         - Man's life depends on the Word of God—on every word He speaks
   c. God's provision of clothing & strength
      1) Clothes did not wear out
      2) Feet did not swell
   d. God's discipline: Just as a father loves & corrects, so God loves & corrects
   e. God's expectation: Obedience
      1) Must walk in His ways
      2) Must fear, revere Him
3. **Praise the LORD for the promised land & its wonderful provision**
   a. The great provision of the land
      1) An overflowing supply of water
      2) An abundance of food
      3) A scarcity or lack of nothing
      4) A rich deposit of minerals

   b. The strong charge: Always praise the LORD for the promised land & its wonderful provision
4. **Guard against forgetting God**
   a. The cause of forgetting God
      1) Failing to obey God's commandments
      2) Being prosperous, at ease, satisfied, complacent
         - Plenty to eat
         - Comfortable housing
         - Wealth: large herds & flocks—gold & silver—all has multiplied
      3) Pride, a sense of self-sufficiency
   b. The result of forgetting God
      1) You forget that it was God who saved you
      2) You forget that it was God who led you through the wilderness wanderings (a picture of the world with all its trials)
      3) You forget that it was God who provided for you
         - Provided water
         - Provided food (both physical & spiritual food, v.3)
      4) You forget that it was God who humbled & tested you: Made things go well
      5) You forget humility: Develop a sense of self-sufficiency
   c. The protection against forgetting God
      1) Remember the LORD
         - It is God who gives you the ability to work
         - It is God who fulfills His covenant, the gift of the promised land
      2) Remember the judgment of God
         - Must not forget God nor engage in false worship
         - The result—judgment: Will be destroyed just like the nations & peoples before you

All the commandments which I command thee this day shall ye observe to do, that ye may live, and multiply, and go in and possess the land which the LORD sware unto your fathers.

2 And thou shalt remember all the way which the LORD thy God led thee these forty years in the wilderness, to humble thee, *and* to prove thee, to know what *was* in thine heart, whether thou wouldest keep his commandments, or no.

3 And he humbled thee, and suffered thee to hunger, and fed thee with manna, which thou knewest not, neither did thy fathers know; that he might make thee know that man doth not live by bread only, but by every *word* that proceedeth out of the mouth of the LORD doth man live.

4 Thy raiment waxed not old upon thee, neither did thy foot swell, these forty years.

5 Thou shalt also consider in thine heart, that, as a man chasteneth his son, *so* the LORD thy God chasteneth thee.

6 Therefore thou shalt keep the commandments of the LORD thy God, to walk in his ways, and to fear him.

7 For the LORD thy God bringeth thee into a good land, a land of brooks of water, of fountains and depths that spring out of valleys and hills;

8 A land of wheat, and barley, and vines, and fig trees, and pomegranates; a land of oil olive, and honey;

9 A land wherein thou shalt eat bread without scarceness, thou shalt not lack any *thing* in it; a land whose stones *are* iron, and out of whose hills thou mayest dig brass.

10 When thou hast eaten and art full, then thou shalt bless the LORD thy God for the good land which he hath given thee.

11 Beware that thou forget not the LORD thy God, in not keeping his commandments, and his judgments, and his statutes, which I command thee this day:

12 Lest *when* thou hast eaten and art full, and hast built goodly houses, and dwelt *therein*;

13 And *when* thy herds and thy flocks multiply, and thy silver and thy gold is multiplied, and all that thou hast is multiplied;

14 Then thine heart be lifted up, and thou forget the LORD thy God, which brought thee forth out of the land of Egypt, from the house of bondage;

15 Who led thee through that great and terrible wilderness, *wherein were* fiery serpents, and scorpions, and drought, where *there was* no water; who brought thee forth water out of the rock of flint;

16 Who fed thee in the wilderness with manna, which thy fathers knew not, that he might humble thee, and that he might prove thee, to do thee good at thy latter end;

17 And thou say in thine heart, My power and the might of *mine* hand hath gotten me this wealth.

18 But thou shalt remember the LORD thy God: for *it is* he that giveth thee power to get wealth, that he may establish his covenant which he sware unto thy fathers, as *it is* this day.

19 And it shall be, if thou do at all forget the LORD thy God, and walk after other gods, and serve them, and worship them, I testify against you this day that ye shall surely perish.

20 As the nations which the LORD destroyeth before your face, so shall ye perish; because ye would not be obedient unto the voice of the LORD your God.

DEUTERONOMY 8:1-20

DIVISION III

THE SECOND GREAT THEME PREACHED BY GOD'S AGED SERVANT (PART 1): REMEMBER THE TEN COMMANDMENTS—THE FUNDAMENTAL LAWS TO GOVERN MAN AND SOCIETY, 4:44–11:32

G. The Safeguards to Assure Obedience to the Commandments of God: How to Guard Against Forgetting God, 8:1-20

(8:1-20) **Introduction**: How many people forget God? How many ignore God? Neglect God? Reject God? How many atheists are there, people who say that God does not exist; therefore they seldom if ever think about God? How many agnostics are there, people who say God may or may not exist; therefore they, too, seldom if ever think about God? How many people attempt to push God out of their minds because they want to live in some sin? They want to live like they want, when they want, and not like God says.

How much time throughout the day do you personally think about God? Can it be said that you forget God? Measure yourself. How much time throughout the day do you spend in prayer, thinking about God and talking with Him? How much daily time do you spend reading and studying God's Holy Word, thinking about Him and what He has to say? How much time do you spend in witnessing and sharing Christ with others? Prayer, Bible study, and witnessing are three strong measuring rods to show how much thought you give to God. Do you forget God? Ignore, neglect God?

How can a person guard against forgetting God? This was the great concern of Moses as he stood preaching to the people. Remember, the Israelites were camped in the plain of Moab, close to the Jordan River, right across from the great city of Jericho. They were poised to enter the promised land. But before they entered, Moses was preparing them to lay claim to their inheritance. The success of their campaign depended upon their obedience to God. Moses had to prepare the people, warn them: they must continue to follow God and keep His holy commandments. If they were faithful and obedient, God would give them the promised land. He would guide and protect them, giving them victory over all the enemies who stood opposed to them. One preparation was the message of this sermon, a message that forcefully speaks to our hearts as well. This is the message that Moses now preaches: *The Safeguards to Assure Obedience to the Commandments of God: How to Guard Against Forgetting God,* 8:1-20.

1. Be careful! Observe! Obey every commandment of God (v.1).
2. Remember God's guidance through the wilderness wanderings (vv.2-6).
3. Praise the LORD for the promised land and its wonderful provision (vv.7-10).
4. Guard against forgetting God (vv.11-20).

1 (8:1) **Obedience, Results of—Commandments, Results of Keeping**: How does a person guard against forgetting God? Be careful! Observe! Follow! Obey every commandment of God. If a person obeys the commandments of God, his mind is set upon God. He is not forgetting God; rather, he is thinking about God, seeking to please and fulfill the will of God. If a person is concerned about the commandments of God, his mind and thoughts are upon God. He is meditating, fellowshipping, and communing with God. The energy and drive of his heart is to know God personally and intimately. He gains this knowledge by living in the Word of God and by obeying the commandments of God. How then does a person guard against forgetting God? By obeying every commandment of God, every single commandment.

OUTLINE	SCRIPTURE
1. **Be careful! Observe! Obey every commandment of God** a. Assures life b. Assures increase in fruitfulness & population c. Assures an inheritance in the promised land	All the commandments which I command thee this day shall ye observe to do, that ye may live, and multiply, and go in and possess the land which the LORD sware unto your fathers.

Now note the wonderful gifts promised to the person who obeys God. First, there is the gift of life. The person who places his life into the hands of God is looked after by God. God takes care of the person, guiding and protecting him throughout all of life. Therefore, when it is time for the person to go home to heaven, God takes him. His life is under the care of God until God is ready for him. His life is not cut short by sinful behavior such as drugs, alcohol, gluttony, guilt, and a host of other emotional and health problems caused by sinful behavior. Nothing cuts his life short, for God looks after him, giving him every day he is supposed to live upon the earth.

Second, there is the increase in fruitfulness and in population growth. Common sense tells us that people who obey God's commandments will live longer and healthier lives. And people who live longer and healthier lives will probably bear more children. Keeping God's commandments means less adultery and divorce, less assault and murder, less stealing and bankruptcy, less lying and broken relationships, less gluttony and abuse of the body. All this means longer and healthier lives and the blessing of a larger number of children born out of fruitful lives before God.

Third, there is the gift of an inheritance in the promised land. The person who obeys God will enter and inherit the promised land.

Thought 1. How can we guard against forgetting God? Be careful! Observe! Follow! Obey every commandment of God! Obey ever single commandment!

DEUTERONOMY 8:1-20

"Not every one that saith unto me, Lord, Lord, shall enter into the kingdom of heaven; but he that doeth the will of my Father which is in heaven" (Mt.7:21).

"Blessed *are* they that do his commandments, that they may have right to the tree of life, and may enter in through the gates into the city" (Re.22:14).

"But whoso looketh into the perfect law of liberty, and continueth *therein,* he being not a forgetful hearer, but a doer of the work, this man shall be blessed in his deed" (Js.1:25).

"This day the Lord thy God hath commanded thee to do these statutes and judgments: thou shalt therefore keep and do them with all thine heart, and with all thy soul" (De.26:16).

"This book of the law shall not depart out of thy mouth; but thou shalt meditate therein day and night, that thou mayest observe to do according to all that is written therein: for then thou shalt make thy way prosperous, and then thou shalt have good success" (Jos.1:8).

"O that there were such an heart in them, that they would fear me, and keep all my commandments always, that it might be well with them, and with their children for ever" (De.5:29).

"Now therefore, if ye will obey my voice indeed, and keep my covenant, then ye shall be a peculiar treasure unto me above all people: for all the earth *is* mine" (Ex.19:5).

2 (8:2-6) **Necessities, of Life—Provision, Source—Wilderness Wanderings—Journey, the Wilderness—Israel, Wilderness Wanderings of—Testing, of God—Discipline, of God—Chastisement, of God**: How does a person guard against forgetting God? Remember God's guidance through the wilderness wanderings. The word *remember* (zakar) means to mark out, recognize, be mindful of, recount, record, bring to remembrance, consider, recall, remind, reflect on, review. It also has the idea of keeping or observing. That is, to remember something is to keep, observe, carry it out, do it. Standing there preaching to the people, Moses wanted them to remember God's guidance through the wilderness wanderings. He wanted them to remember and trust God's guidance as they looked forward to entering the promised land.

OUTLINE	SCRIPTURE	SCRIPTURE	OUTLINE

2. Remember God's guidance through the wilderness wanderings
a. God's humbling you & testing you
  1) To prove your character
  2) To prove your obedience or disobedience
 	
b. God's provision of food
  1) He provided *manna*
  2) His purpose: To teach one great truth
    • Man's life does not depend on bread alone
    • Man's life depends on
	2 And thou shalt remember all the way which the Lord thy God led thee these forty years in the wilderness, to humble thee, *and* to prove thee, to know what *was* in thine heart, whether thou wouldest keep his commandments, or no.
	3 And he humbled thee, and suffered thee to hunger, and fed thee with manna, which thou knewest not, neither did thy fathers know; that he might make thee know that man doth not live by bread
		only, but by every *word* that proceedeth out of the mouth of the Lord doth man live.
		4 Thy raiment waxed not old upon thee, neither did thy foot swell, these forty years.
		5 Thou shalt also consider in thine heart, that, as a man chasteneth his son, *so* the Lord thy God chasteneth thee.
		6 Therefore thou shalt keep the commandments of the Lord thy God, to walk in his ways, and to fear him.
			the Word of God—on every word He speaks
			
			c. God's provision of clothing & strength
			  1) Clothes did not wear out
			  2) Feet did not swell
			d. God's discipline: Just as a father loves & corrects, so God loves & corrects
			
			e. God's expectation: Obedience
			  1) Must walk in His ways
			  2) Must fear, revere Him

a. Remember that God humbled and tested you in the wilderness wanderings (v.2). The desert was dry and hot, no doubt sometimes reaching temperatures over 100 degrees. Under such circumstances, perspiration flows freely, soaking a person's clothes and dripping down his face into his eyes. Thirst then becomes a problem. Life and work become uncomfortable and sleep during hot nights almost impossible. There were also poisonous snakes, scorpions, and other dangerous animals that required a constant watch for protection. There were few trees in the desert, little grass, and no vineyards, vegetables, or fish to eat in the desert. Life in the desert was hard and strenuous. The people often experienced...

- hunger
- thirst
- heat exhaustion
- fatigue
- exhausting work
- strain
- pressure
- tension
- distress
- discouragement
- danger
- disgust

Whatever a person would experience by living in the desert, the *second generation* of believers had experienced for forty years. But their parents—the *first generation*—had been condemned because of their sin, condemned to wander about in the desert until they had all died. (See outline and notes—Nu.14:1-45 for more discussion.) They were barred from ever entering the promised land. But not the children: the promised land was to be their inheritance. Now the children, the *second generation* of believers, stand before Moses as he preaches. He reminds them that the oldest among them have wandered about and suffered the hardships of the desert for forty years. But through all the hard, strenuous times God had guided them. He had been humbling and testing them to prove their character, their obedience or disobedience. Would they fail like their parents or would they follow and obey God? Would they complain, murmur, and grumble like their parents or would they praise God? Would they turn away from the promised land and suggest returning to Egypt like their parents or would they go forward and enter the promised land, laying claim to their inheritance? "God is humbling and testing you by these hard, difficult times. What is your decision?"

DEUTERONOMY 8:1-20

b. Remember God's provision of food (v.3). He provided *manna* for you, a bread-like substance that looked like resin or coriander seed. (See outline and note—Ex.16:31-36 for more discussion.) He met your need of hunger. This He did to teach one great truth: man does not live by bread alone, but by every word that comes from the mouth of God. The point is clear: do not forget God like your fathers before you. Do not grumble and complain about having little or no food. But trust God and obey Him. Keep every word He has spoken. And God will give you the provision of food. He will meet your need of hunger.

c. Remember God's provision of clothing and strength (v.4). This is an astonishing statement: the clothes of the Israelites did not wear out and their feet did not swell during the forty years of wilderness wanderings. Obviously, this was a direct miracle of God. For believers down through the generations, the application would be that God would meet the necessities of life for His dear people. Whatever a believer needs, the Word of God declares that God will meet that need.

d. Remember God's discipline in the wilderness wanderings (v.5). Just as a father loves and corrects his child, so God loves and corrects you. When the Israelites went astray, God disciplined and corrected them time and time again. (See DEEPER STUDY #1—Nu.14:22 for a list of the times that the Israelites failed God and God disciplined them.)

e. Remember God's expectation: obedience (v.6). Throughout all the wilderness wanderings, God expected His people to obey Him. He expects no less of you. You must, therefore, walk in His ways, fear and revere Him.

> **Thought 1.** How can we guard against forgetting God? By remembering how God guides us through the wilderness wanderings of this life. God guides us through all the dry, desert experiences of life—through all the trials, tribulations, and temptations of life.
>
> (1) God humbles and tests us through the trials and temptations of life. By helping us to conquer the hard and troublesome experiences, He strengthens us, makes us far stronger and more able to face difficult times in the future. He proves our character, whether we will obey or disobey Him.
>
> > "He is like a man which built an house, and digged deep, and laid the foundation on a rock: and when the flood arose, the stream beat vehemently upon that house, and could not shake it: for it was founded upon a rock" (Lu.6:48).
> >
> > "Every man's work shall be made manifest: for the day shall declare it, because it shall be revealed by fire; and the fire shall try every man's work of what sort it is" (1 Co.3:13).
> >
> > "Blessed *is* the man that endureth temptation: for when he is tried, he shall receive the crown of life, which the LORD hath promised to them that love him" (Js.1:12).
> >
> > "Thou hast proved mine heart; thou hast visited *me* in the night; thou hast tried me, *and* shalt find nothing; I am purposed *that* my mouth shall not transgress" (Ps.17:3).
> >
> > "And I will bring the third part through the fire, and will refine them as silver is refined, and will try them as gold is tried: they shall call on my name, and I will hear them: I will say, It *is* my people: and they shall say, The LORD *is* my God" (Zec.13:9).
> >
> > "And he shall sit *as* a refiner and purifier of silver: and he shall purify the sons of Levi, and purge them as gold and silver, that they may offer unto the LORD an offering in righteousness" (Mal.3:3).
>
> (2) God provides food, clothing, and strength for us. All the necessities of life are promised to the genuine believer who obeys God.
>
> > "But seek ye first the kingdom of God, and his righteousness; and all these things shall be added unto you" (Mt.6:33).
> >
> > "But my God shall supply all your need according to his riches in glory by Christ Jesus" (Ph.4:19).
> >
> > "And ye shall serve the LORD your God, and he shall bless thy bread, and thy water; and I will take sickness away from the midst of thee" (Ex.23:25).
> >
> > "Keep therefore the words of this covenant, and do them, that ye may prosper in all that ye do" (De.29:9).
> >
> > "And the LORD thy God will make thee plenteous in every work of thine hand, in the fruit of thy body, and in the fruit of thy cattle, and in the fruit of thy land, for good: for the LORD will again rejoice over thee for good, as he rejoiced over thy fathers" (De.30:9).
> >
> > "Then shalt thou prosper, if thou takest heed to fulfil the statutes and judgments which the LORD charged Moses with concerning Israel: be strong, and of good courage; dread not, nor be dismayed" (1 Chr.22:13).
> >
> > "But his delight *is* in the law of the LORD; and in his law doth he meditate day and night. And he shall be like a tree planted by the rivers of water, that bringeth forth his fruit in his season; his leaf also shall not wither; and whatsoever he doeth shall prosper" (Ps.1:2-3).
> >
> > "*Oh* how great *is* thy goodness, which thou hast laid up for them that fear thee; *which* thou hast wrought for them that trust in thee before the sons of men" (Ps.31:19).
> >
> > "I will abundantly bless her provision: I will satisfy her poor with bread" (Ps.132:15).
> >
> > "Bring ye all the tithes into the storehouse, that there may be meat in mine house, and prove me now herewith, saith the LORD of hosts, if I will not open you the windows of heaven, and pour you out a blessing, that *there shall* not *be* room enough *to receive it*" (Mal.3:10).
>
> (3) God disciplines us. This too will keep us from forgetting God. Just as a father loves and corrects his child, so God loves and corrects us.
>
> > "Every branch in me that beareth not fruit he taketh away: and every *branch* that beareth fruit, he purgeth it, that it may bring forth more fruit" (Jn.15:2).

DEUTERONOMY 8:1-20

"For this cause many *are* weak and sickly among you, and many sleep. For if we would judge ourselves, we should not be judged. But when we are judged, we are chastened of the LORD, that we should not be condemned with the world" (1 Co.11:30-32).

"And ye have forgotten the exhortation which speaketh unto you as unto children, My son, despise not thou the chastening of the LORD, nor faint when thou art rebuked of him: For whom the LORD loveth he chasteneth, and scourgeth every son whom he receiveth" (He.12:5-6).

"Thou shalt also consider in thine heart, that, as a man chasteneth his son, *so* the LORD thy God chasteneth thee" (De.8:5).

"Blessed *is* the man whom thou chastenest, O LORD, and teachest him out of thy law" (Ps.94:12).

"My son, despise not the chastening of the LORD; neither be weary of his correction: For whom the LORD loveth he correcteth; even as a father the son *in whom* he delighteth" (Pr.3:11-12).

(4) God expects obedience from us. If we profess to know God, we must obey Him. We must revere Him, follow after Him and walk in His ways.

"Therefore we are buried with him by baptism into death: that like as Christ was raised up from the dead by the glory of the Father, even so we also should walk in newness of life" (Ro.6:4).

"I therefore, the prisoner of the LORD, beseech you that ye walk worthy of the vocation wherewith ye are called" (Ep.4:1).

"And walk in love, as Christ also hath loved us, and hath given himself for us an offering and a sacrifice to God for a sweetsmelling savour" (Ep.5:2).

"See then that ye walk circumspectly, not as fools, but as wise" (Ep.5:15).

"*This* I say then, Walk in the Spirit, and ye shall not fulfil the lust of the flesh" (Ga.5:16).

"As ye have therefore received Christ Jesus the LORD, *so* walk ye in him" (Col.2:6).

"But if we walk in the light, as he is in the light, we have fellowship one with another, and the blood of Jesus Christ his Son cleanseth us from all sin" (1 Jn.1:7).

"He that saith he abideth in him ought himself also so to walk, even as he walked" (1 Jn.2:6).

3 (8:7-10) **Thanksgiving, Duty—Praise, Duty—Provision, of God—Necessities, of Life, Provision of**: How does a person guard against forgetting God? By praising the LORD for the promised land and its wonderful provisions. All the hopes of the Israelites were wrapped up in the promised land. Camped by the River Jordan, many an Israelite spent an evening walking along the shores of the Jordan, looking over into the promised land and longing for the day when they would receive their inheritance. Possessing the promised land was the longing and ache of their hearts. Moses knew this. He also knew that as long as the hope stayed alive, the people would remember God. They would obey Him and follow Him. With fire burning in his heart, he preached to the people, challenging them to praise the LORD for the promised land and its wonderful provisions.

OUTLINE	SCRIPTURE	SCRIPTURE	OUTLINE
3. Praise the LORD for the promised land & its wonderful provision a. The great provision of the land 1) An overflowing supply of water 2) An abundance of food 3) A scarcity or lack of	7 For the LORD thy God bringeth thee into a good land, a land of brooks of water, of fountains and depths that spring out of valleys and hills; 8 A land of wheat, and barley, and vines, and fig trees, and pomegranates; a land of oil olive, and honey; 9 A land wherein thou shalt	eat bread without scarceness, thou shalt not lack any *thing* in it; a land whose stones *are* iron, and out of whose hills thou mayest dig brass. 10 When thou hast eaten and art full, then thou shalt bless the LORD thy God for the good land which he hath given thee.	nothing 4) A rich deposit of minerals b. The strong charge: Always praise the LORD for the promised land & its wonderful provision

   a. Moses describes the great provision of the promised land (vv.7-9). Note that he calls it a "good land." It is a land that has everything to meet man's need, a land that will provide a full and fulfilling life for man.

      1) It has an overflowing water supply: brooks or streams, fountains and pools of water, with springs flowing throughout valleys and hills. In contrast to the desert experience, the people will have a full supply of water for themselves, their livestock, and their crops.

      2) It has an abundance of food (v.8). The land is fertile and productive, a land with wheat and barley, fig trees and pomegranates, olives and honey—anything and everything that a person could ever want for food.

      3) It is a land that has no scarcity, no insufficiency, no deficiency—nothing is in short supply. The people will lack nothing in the promised land.

      4) It has a rich deposit of minerals (v.9). Note that iron and copper in particular are mentioned. The note in the NIV says this:

> *The mountains of southern Lebanon and the regions east of the Sea of Galilee and south of the Dead Sea contain iron. Both copper and iron were plentiful in the part of the Arabah south of the Dead Sea. Some of the copper mines date to the time of Solomon and earlier. Zarethan was a center for bronze works in Solomon's*

DEUTERONOMY 8:1-20

time (1 Ki 7:45-46). Some bronze objects from this site precede the Solomonic period, and today there are copper works at Timnah in the Negev.[1]

The Expositor's Bible Commentary says this:

> *The iron (v.9) was probably that in southern Lebanon, in the mountains of Transjordan, and, perhaps, in the Arabah south of the Dead Sea. The basalt of the volcanic region east of the Lake of Galilee was 20 percent iron. The copper mines of Solomon at Ezion Geber are well known. Werner Keller (The Bible as History [New York: Morrow, 1956], pp. 123-25) gives a dramatic description of the discovery in Sinai of ancient Egyptian copper and turquoise mines. See also Baly, pp. 98, 212, 215.*[2]

b. Moses gives a strong charge to the people: always praise the LORD for the promised land and its wonderful provision. Remember the source of your prosperity in the land, God Himself. He is to be praised for the gift of the land and its abundant supplies. Thanksgiving is due Him. Without God, there would be no promised land and no abundant supply of provisions. So praise and give thanks to Him.

Thought 1. How can we guard against forgetting God? By praising the LORD for the promised land of heaven and the wonderful provisions of life. We should always be praising God and giving thanks to Him, for everything we have is from Him. God is the source of all our prosperity: the source of the overflowing water supply of the earth, the abundance of vegetation and food, the rich deposit of minerals. Praise is due God for all His wonderful provisions.

"By him therefore let us offer the sacrifice of praise to God continually, that is, the fruit of *our* lips giving thanks to his name" (He.13:15).

"But ye *are* a chosen generation, a royal priesthood, an holy nation, a peculiar people; that ye should show forth the praises of him who hath called you out of darkness into his marvellous light" (1 Pe.2:9).

"Giving thanks unto the Father, which hath made us meet to be partakers of the inheritance of the saints in light" (Col.1:12).

"And let the peace of God rule in your hearts, to the which also ye are called in one body; and be ye thankful" (Col.3:15).

"In every thing give thanks: for this is the will of God in Christ Jesus concerning you" (1 Th.5:18).

"When thou hast eaten and art full, then thou shalt bless the LORD thy God for the good land which he hath given thee" (De.8:10).

"Sing praises to the LORD, which dwelleth in Zion: declare among the people his doings" (Ps.9:11).

"Praise the LORD with harp: sing unto him with the psaltery *and* an instrument of ten strings" (Ps.33:2).

"And my tongue shall speak of thy righteousness *and* of thy praise all the day long" (Ps.35:28).

"Let the people praise thee, O God; let all the people praise thee" (Ps.67:3).

"Enter into his gates with thanksgiving, *and* into his courts with praise: be thankful unto him, *and* bless his name" (Ps.100:4).

"And let them sacrifice the sacrifices of thanksgiving, and declare his works with rejoicing" (Ps.107:22).

"Let them give glory unto the LORD, and declare his praise in the islands" (Is.42:12).

4 (8:11-20) **Forget - Forgetting, Duty—Pride, Warning Against—Self-sufficiency, Warning Against—Complacency, Warning Against—Being at Ease, Warning Against—Prosperity, Warning Against—Prosperity, Source of**: How can a person guard against forgetting God? He must beware! Be careful! Diligently guard against forgetting God. This is an excellent message on Forgetting God. Note the Scripture and outline:

OUTLINE	SCRIPTURE	SCRIPTURE	OUTLINE
4. Guard against forgetting God a. The cause of forgetting God 1) Failing to obey God's commandments 2) Being prosperous, at ease, satisfied, complacent • Plenty to eat • Comfortable housing • Wealth: large herds &	11 Beware that thou forget not the LORD thy God, in not keeping his commandments, and his judgments, and his statutes, which I command thee this day: 12 Lest *when* thou hast eaten and art full, and hast built goodly houses, and dwelt *therein*; 13 And *when* thy herds and thy flocks multiply, and thy	silver and thy gold is multiplied, and all that thou hast is multiplied; 14 Then thine heart be lifted up, and thou forget the LORD thy God, which brought thee forth out of the land of Egypt, from the house of bondage; 15 Who led thee through that great and terrible wilderness, *wherein were* fiery serpents, and scorpions, and	flocks—gold & silver—all has multiplied 3) Pride, a sense of self-sufficiency b. The result of forgetting God 1) You forget that it was God who saved you 2) You forget that it was God who led you through the wilderness wanderings (a picture of the world with

---

[1] *NIV Study Bible*. (Grand Rapids, MI: Zondervan Bible Publishers, 1985), p.256, note on De.8:9.
[2] Frank E. Gaebelein, Editor. *The Expositor's Bible Commentary*, Vol.2, p.75.

DEUTERONOMY 8:1-20

OUTLINE	SCRIPTURE	SCRIPTURE	OUTLINE
all its trials) 3) You forget that it was God who provided for you • Provided water • Provided food (both physical & spiritual food, v.3) 4) You forget that it was God who humbled & tested you: Made things go well 5) You forget humility: Develop a sense of self-sufficiency c. The protection against forgetting God 1) Remember the LORD	drought, where *there was* no water; who brought thee forth water out of the rock of flint; 16 Who fed thee in the wilderness with manna, which thy fathers knew not, that he might humble thee, and that he might prove thee, to do thee good at thy latter end; 17 And thou say in thine heart, My power and the might of *mine* hand hath gotten me this wealth. 18 But thou shalt remember the LORD thy God: for *it is* he that giveth thee	power to get wealth, that he may establish his covenant which he sware unto thy fathers, as *it is* this day. 19 And it shall be, if thou do at all forget the LORD thy God, and walk after other gods, and serve them, and worship them, I testify against you this day that ye shall surely perish. 20 As the nations which the LORD destroyeth before your face, so shall ye perish; because ye would not be obedient unto the voice of the LORD your God.	• It is God who gives you the ability to work • It is God who fulfills His covenant, the gift of the promised land 2) Remember the judgment of God • Must not forget God nor engage in false worship • The result—judgment: Will be destroyed just like the nations & peoples before you

a. Note the causes of forgetting God (vv.11-14). What is it that makes a person forget God? Some people seldom think about God. Occasionally, the thought of God crosses their minds, but not often. God is not a major subject of their thoughts, neither of their lives. Their world does not include God; their lives are not focused upon God. To them God is way off, out of reach. To some people, God may exist or may not (agnostics). To other people, God does not exist (atheists). Therefore God is not a subject to occupy their minds. God is rejected and denied; thus, there is no need to give thought to God. God is forgotten.

But standing there preaching under the inspiration of God's Holy Spirit, note what Moses proclaimed: Beware! Be careful! Diligently guard against forgetting God. Three things will cause you to forget God.

1) Failing to obey God's holy commandments will cause you to forget God (v.11). You must obey God's commandments, keep your mind upon obeying them. If you neglect and ignore His commandments, you will grow cold and indifferent, soon forgetting God. Your conscience and mind will become dull, insensitive, hard, callous, and dead to God. The thoughts of God will soon pass from your mind. You will forget God.

However, if you obey God's commandments, then God will be active in your heart and life. Your mind and thoughts will focus upon God, seeking to fulfill His commandments. Step by step throughout the day, you will seek to please God by obeying Him. God will be alive in your heart and thoughts. You will not forget God. Keeping God's holy commandments is the way to guard against forgetting God. But failing to obey God's holy commandments will cause a person to forget God.

2) Being prosperous, at ease, satisfied, and complacent can cause a person to forget God (vv.12-13). This was the great concern of Moses for the Israelites. Once they had conquered and settled down in the promised land, there was the danger that their prosperity would cause them to become satisfied and complacent. They would become *at ease* in Zion. Note how Moses warns the people against becoming complacent and satisfied with their prosperity:

⇒ They would have plenty to eat and become full, satisfied (v.12).
⇒ They would have fine housing and be settled down, be perfectly comfortable.
⇒ They would be wealthy in the eyes of the world with large herds and flocks, gold and silver. Everything they had would be multiplied (v.13).

In the midst of all their prosperity, God's people must guard against becoming complacent, self-satisfied, at ease, comfortable. They must not become apathetic, lethargic, indifferent, sluggish, stagnant, cold-hearted, unresponsive to God. They must not forget God.

> "The kingdom of heaven is like unto a certain king, which made a marriage for his son, And sent forth his servants to call them that were bidden to the wedding: and they would not come. Again, he sent forth other servants, saying, Tell them which are bidden, Behold, I have prepared my dinner: my oxen and *my* fatlings *are* killed, and all things *are* ready: come unto the marriage. But they made light of *it,* and went their ways, one to his farm, another to his merchandise....Then said the king to the servants, Bind him hand and foot, and take him away, and cast *him* into outer darkness; there shall be weeping and gnashing of teeth" (Mt.22:2-5, 13).

> "And because iniquity shall abound, the love of many shall wax cold. But he that shall endure unto the end, the same shall be saved" (Mt.24:12-13).

> "Watch ye therefore: for ye know not when the master of the house cometh, at even, or at midnight, or at the cockcrowing, or in the morning: Lest coming suddenly he find you sleeping" (Mk.13:35-36).

> "Therefore let us not sleep, as *do* others; but let us watch and be sober. For they that sleep sleep in the night; and they that be drunken are drunken in the night. But let us, who are of the day, be sober, putting on the breastplate of faith and love; and for an helmet, the hope of salvation. For God hath not appointed us to wrath, but to obtain salvation by our Lord Jesus Christ" (1 Th.5:6-9).

> "That ye be not slothful, but followers of them who through faith and patience inherit the promises" (He.6:12).

> "A brutish man knoweth not; neither doth a fool understand this" (Ps.92:6).

DEUTERONOMY 8:1-20

"Our soul is exceedingly filled with the scorning of those that are at ease, *and* with the contempt of the proud" (Ps.123:4).

"Give not sleep to thine eyes, nor slumber to thine eyelids" (Pr.6:4).

"How long wilt thou sleep, O sluggard? when wilt thou arise out of thy sleep? *Yet* a little sleep, a little slumber, a little folding of the hands to sleep" (Pr.6:9-10).

"For the drunkard and the glutton shall come to poverty: and drowsiness shall clothe *a man* with rags" (Pr.23:21).

"Rise up, ye women that are at ease; hear my voice, ye careless daughters; give ear unto my speech. Many days and years shall ye be troubled, ye careless women: for the vintage shall fail, the gathering shall not come" (Is.32:9-10).

"Therefore hear now this, *thou that art* given to pleasures, that dwellest carelessly, that sayest in thine heart, I *am,* and none else beside me; I shall not sit *as* a widow, neither shall I know the loss of children" (Is.47:8).

"Woe to them *that are* at ease in Zion" (Am. 6:1).

3) Possessing pride and a sense of self-sufficiency can cause a person to forget God (v.14). A person can begin to feel that his prosperity is due to his own knowledge, ability, and skill. He can easily forget that his life, health, and strength—his very existence upon this earth—are due to God. It is God who willed him to be born and who had established the laws of reproduction through which he was born. The believer must guard his heart from becoming proud and self-sufficient, from thinking that it is he himself who has produced the prosperity. He must not forget God: everything he has comes from God. God has willed for him to prosper; therefore, the believer produces the products and possesses the things he owns. God is the primary, ultimate source of everything a man is and has: his ability, skill, health, and possessions. Man does not live upon this earth unless God wills him to live. Consequently, there is no place for pride or self-sufficiency within the heart of man.

b. Note the results of forgetting God (vv.14-17). The results of forgetfulness are tragic, most tragic. They cut the heart of God, grieve His Spirit to the depths of its core.

1) If you forget God, you will forget your salvation (v.14). You did not save yourself nor create the hope for the promised land within your heart. It was God who saved you and gave you the hope of salvation. He delivered you from Egypt, saved you out of the enslavement of this world. This He did to give you the hope of the promised land. But if you forget God, you will forget your salvation. You will forget the very purpose for which God saved you, the very reason why you were living in the promised land.

2) If you forget God, you will forget the guidance and protection of God (v.15). You will forget that it was God who led you through the wilderness wanderings, through all the terrible trials and difficulties of the wilderness. You will forget that He protected you from venomous snakes and scorpions. If you forget God, you will lose the guidance and protection of God. You will be left all alone upon this earth, left only to what you can personally do for yourself and what others are willing to do. In facing the trials of life such as disease, accident, financial difficulty, job or business problems, relationship difficulties, family and school problems—any problem or trial of life—the only help available will be the arm of flesh, only what you or some other person can do to help you. You will have lost the guidance and protection of God—if you forget God.

3) If you forget God, you will forget His provision (v.15). It is God who provides the necessities of life: water to drink and food to eat. But if you forget God, you lose God's day-by-day provision, lose the assurance of having Him look after you. You have no guarantee of the necessities of life. Keep in mind that God had given the Israelites water gushing from a rock and manna to eat day by day out in the desert. They had no excuse for forgetting God.

4) If you forget God, you will forget the humbling experiences (v.16). You forget that God tests you in order to make you stronger and to make things go better for you. (See outline and note, pt.1—De.8:2-6 for more discussion.)

5) If you forget God, you will forget humility (v.17). You develop a sense of self-sufficiency.

Thought 1. Pride and a sense of self-sufficiency will lead a person to forget God; therefore we absolutely must guard against these two terrible sins, sins that cut the heart of God ever so deeply.

"And whosoever shall exalt himself shall be abased; and he that shall humble himself shall be exalted" (Mt.23:12).

"For if a man think himself to be something, when he is nothing, he deceiveth himself" (Ga.6:3).

"And if any man think that he knoweth any thing, he knoweth nothing yet as he ought to know" (1 Co.8:2).

"Love not the world, neither the things *that are* in the world. If any man love the world, the love of the Father is not in him. For all that *is* in the world, the lust of the flesh, and the lust of the eyes, and the pride of life, is not of the Father, but is of the world" (1 Jn.2:15-16).

"Be not wise in thine own eyes: fear the LORD, and depart from evil" (Pr.3:7).

"*When* pride cometh, then cometh shame: but with the lowly *is* wisdom" (Pr.11:2).

"Pride *goeth* before destruction, and an haughty spirit before a fall" (Pr.16:18).

"An high look, and a proud heart, *and* the plowing of the wicked, *is* sin" (Pr.21:4).

"Seest thou a man wise in his own conceit? *there is* more hope of a fool than of him" (Pr.26:12).

"He that is of a proud heart stirreth up strife: but he that putteth his trust in the LORD shall be made fat" (Pr.28:25).

"For thou hast said in thine heart, I will ascend into heaven, I will exalt my throne above the stars of God: I will sit also upon the mount of the congregation, in the sides of the north: I will ascend above the heights of the clouds; I will be like the most High. Yet thou shalt be brought down to hell, to the sides of the pit" (Is.14:13-15).

DEUTERONOMY 8:1-20

"For thou hast trusted in thy wickedness: thou hast said, None seeth me. Thy wisdom and thy knowledge, it hath perverted thee; and thou hast said in thine heart, I *am,* and none else beside me" (Is.47:10).

"Though thou exalt *thyself* as the eagle, and though thou set thy nest among the stars, thence will I bring thee down, saith the LORD" (Ob.4).

c. Note the protection against forgetting God (vv.18-20). With flaming passion, Moses declares the solution, the answer to the problem of forgetting God. Two actions will protect a person from forgetting God.

1) Remember the source of all things: the LORD your God (v.18). It is God who gives you the ability to work and produce. Your ability is due to God, not to you. But even more than this fact, there is another fact that you must grasp: God fulfills His covenant, the gift of the promised land. It is of critical importance to remember this. No person can enter or possess the promised land apart from God. The promised land is a gift of God, not the creation of man. God alone can give the promised land to a person. God and God alone is the source of all things. This fact should keep a person from forgetting God.

"For in him we live, and move, and have our being; as certain also of your own poets have said, For we are also his offspring" (Ac.17:28).

"Neither is [God] worshipped with men's hands, as though he needed any thing, seeing he giveth to all life, and breath, and all things" (Ac.17:25).

"For whether we live, we live unto the LORD; and whether we die, we die unto the LORD: whether we live therefore, or die, we are the LORD's" (Ro.14:8).

"Every good gift and every perfect gift is from above, and cometh down from the Father of lights, with whom is no variableness, neither shadow of turning" (Js.1:17).

"The land shall not be sold for ever: for the land *is* mine; for ye *are* strangers and sojourners with me" (Le.25:23).

"Do ye thus requite the LORD, O foolish people and unwise? *is* not he thy father *that* hath bought thee? hath he not made thee, and established thee" (De.32:6).

"The earth *is* the LORD's, and the fulness thereof; the world, and they that dwell therein" (Ps.24:1).

"Behold, all souls are mine; as the soul of the father, so also the soul of the son is mine: the soul that sinneth, it shall die" (Eze.18:4).

"The silver *is* mine, and the gold *is* mine, saith the LORD of hosts" (Hag.2:8).

2) Remember the judgment of God (vv.19-20). You must not forget God nor engage in false worship lest the judgment of God fall upon you. If you forget God, His judgment will fall upon you, destroying you just like it did the nations and peoples before you (vv.19-20).

"For we must all appear before the judgment seat of Christ; that every one may receive the things *done* in *his* body, according to that he hath done, whether *it be* good or bad" (2 Co.5:10).

"And as it is appointed unto men once to die, but after this the judgment" (He.9:27).

"And if ye call on the Father, who without respect of persons judgeth according to every man's work, pass the time of your sojourning *here* in fear" (1 Pe.1:17).

"The LORD knoweth how to deliver the godly out of temptations, and to reserve the unjust unto the day of judgment to be punished" (2 Pe.2:9).

"I the LORD search the heart, *I* try the reins, even to give every man according to his ways, *and* according to the fruit of his doings" (Je.17:10).

Thought 1. Scripture warns us: we must not forget God. If we forget God, we forsake Him. And if we forsake God, we will suffer the judgment of God.

"Only take heed to thyself, and keep thy soul diligently, lest thou forget the things which thine eyes have seen, and lest they depart from thy heart all the days of thy life: but teach them thy sons, and thy sons' sons" (De.4:9).

"And it shall be, when the LORD thy God shall have brought thee into the land which he sware unto thy fathers, to Abraham, to Isaac, and to Jacob, to give thee great and goodly cities, which thou buildedst not, And houses full of all good *things,* which thou filledst not, and wells digged, which thou diggedst not, vineyards and olive trees, which thou plantedst not; when thou shalt have eaten and be full; *Then* beware lest thou forget the LORD, which brought thee forth out of the land of Egypt, from the house of bondage" (De.6:10-12).

"And he went out to meet Asa, and said unto him, Hear ye me, Asa, and all Judah and Benjamin; The LORD *is* with you, while ye be with him; and if ye seek him, he will be found of you; but if ye forsake him, he will forsake you" (2 Chr.15:2).

"For I was ashamed to require of the king a band of soldiers and horsemen to help us against the enemy in the way: because we had spoken unto the king, saying, The hand of our God *is* upon all them for good that seek him; but his power and his wrath *is* against all them that forsake him" (Ezr. 8:22).

"The wicked shall be turned into hell, *and* all the nations that forget God" (Ps.9:17).

"Now consider this, ye that forget God, lest I tear *you* in pieces, and *there be* none to deliver" (Ps.50:22).

"And forgat his works, and his wonders that he had showed them" (Ps.78:11).

"But my people would not hearken to my voice; and Israel would none of me. So I gave them up unto their own hearts' lust: *and* they walked in their own counsels. Oh that my people had hearkened unto me, *and* Israel had walked in my ways" (Ps.81:11-13).

"Because I have called, and ye refused; I have stretched out my hand, and no man regarded; But ye have set at nought all my counsel, and would none of my reproof: I also will laugh at your calamity; I will mock when your fear cometh; When your fear cometh as desolation, and your destruction cometh as a whirlwind; when distress and anguish cometh upon you. Then shall they call upon me, but I will not answer; they shall seek me early, but they shall not find me: For that they hated knowledge, and did not choose the fear of the LORD: They would none of my counsel: they despised all my reproof. Therefore shall they eat of the fruit of their own way, and be filled with their own devices" (Pr.1:24-31).

"And forgettest the LORD thy maker, that hath stretched forth the heavens, and laid the foundations of the earth" (Is.51:13).

"And I will utter my judgments against them touching all their wickedness, who have forsaken me, and have burned incense unto other gods, and worshipped the works of their own hands" (Je.1:16).

"For my people have committed two evils; they have forsaken me the fountain of living waters, *and* hewed them out cisterns, broken cisterns, that can hold no water" (Je.2:13).

"A voice was heard upon the high places, weeping *and* supplications of the children of Israel: for they have perverted their way, *and* they have forgotten the LORD their God" (Je.3:21).

"And it shall come to pass, when ye shall say, Wherefore doeth the LORD our God all these *things* unto us? then shalt thou answer them, Like as ye have forsaken me, and served strange gods in your land, so shall ye serve strangers in a land *that is* not yours" (Je.5:19).

"Thou hast forsaken me, saith the LORD, thou art gone backward: therefore will I stretch out my hand against thee, and destroy thee; I am weary with repenting" (Je.15:6).

DEUTERONOMY 9:1–10:11

CHAPTER 9

H. The Warnings Against Self-righteousness & Disobedience: Warnings That Must Be Heeded to Inherit the Promised Land, 9:1–10:11

1. **The warning against self-righteousness**
   a. The enemies faced by God's people: Are greater & stronger than believers
      1) Have fortified cities
      2) Are giants: So strong that a saying has been coined about them: "Who can stand up against the Anakites (giants)?"
   b. The promise of victory
      1) By the LORD's action: Will go ahead of His people like a devouring fire—destroy & subdue their enemies
      2) By the people's action: Will drive out & conquer the enemy quickly
   c. The strong warning against self-righteousness: Stated three times for emphasis
      1) It is not because of your righteousness that you receive the promised land
         - It is God who destroys the enemies of the land
         - It is because of their wickedness that He destroys them
      2) It is not because of your righteousness or integrity that you inherit the promised land: The enemies of the land are destroyed by God
         - Because of their evil
         - Because God fulfills His promise to the forefathers (believers)
      3) Understand this: It is not because of your righteousness that God gives you the promised land: On the contrary, you are stiffnecked, stubborn people
2. **The warning against disobedience, against provoking God to anger & judgment**
   a. The strong charge—remember this & never forget it: God was provoked to anger in the wilderness wanderings
      1) The cause: Repeated rebellion

Hear, O Israel: Thou *art* to pass over Jordan this day, to go in to possess nations greater and mightier than thyself, cities great and fenced up to heaven,

2 A people great and tall, the children of the Anakims, whom thou knowest, and *of whom thou hast heard say*, Who can stand before the children of Anak!

3 Understand therefore this day, that the LORD thy God *is* he which goeth over before thee; *as* a consuming fire he shall destroy them, and he shall bring them down before thy face: so shalt thou drive them out, and destroy them quickly, as the LORD hath said unto thee.

4 Speak not thou in thine heart, after that the LORD thy God hath cast them out from before thee, saying, For my righteousness the LORD hath brought me in to possess this land: but for the wickedness of these nations the LORD doth drive them out from before thee.

5 Not for thy righteousness, or for the uprightness of thine heart, dost thou go to possess their land: but for the wickedness of these nations the LORD thy God doth drive them out from before thee, and that he may perform the word which the LORD sware unto thy fathers, Abraham, Isaac, and Jacob.

6 Understand therefore, that the LORD thy God giveth thee not this good land to possess it for thy righteousness; for thou *art* a stiffnecked people.

7 Remember, *and* forget not, how thou provokedst the LORD thy God to wrath in the wilderness: from the day that thou didst depart out of the land of Egypt, until ye came unto this place, ye have been rebellious against the LORD.

8 Also in Horeb ye provoked the LORD to wrath, so that the LORD was angry with you to have destroyed you.

9 When I was gone up into the mount to receive the tables of stone, *even* the tables of the covenant which the LORD made with you, then I abode in the mount forty days and forty nights, I neither did eat bread nor drink water:

10 And the LORD delivered unto me two tables of stone written with the finger of God; and on them *was written* according to all the words, which the LORD spake with you in the mount out of the midst of the fire in the day of the assembly.

11 And it came to pass at the end of forty days and forty nights, *that* the LORD gave me the two tables of stone, *even* the tables of the covenant.

12 And the LORD said unto me, Arise, get thee down quickly from hence; for thy people which thou hast brought forth out of Egypt have corrupted *themselves*; they are quickly turned aside out of the way which I commanded them; they have made them a molten image.

13 Furthermore the LORD spake unto me, saying, I have seen this people, and, behold, it *is* a stiffnecked people:

14 Let me alone, that I may destroy them, and blot out their name from under heaven: and I will make of thee a nation mightier and greater than they.

15 So I turned and came down from the mount, and the mount burned with fire: and the two tables of the covenant *were* in my two hands.

16 And I looked, and, behold, ye had sinned against the LORD your God, *and* had made you a molten calf: ye had turned aside quickly out of the way which the LORD had commanded you.

17 And I took the two tables, and cast them out of my two hands, and brake them before your eyes.

18 And I fell down before the LORD, as at the first, forty days and forty nights: I did

   2) The LORD's anger was aroused enough to destroy His people at Mt. Horeb (Sinai)
   b. The wonderful gift of God at Sinai: The Ten Commandments, the covenant God had made with His people
      1) The LORD kept Moses on Mt. Sinai for 40 days & nights: Fasting, praying & receiving the commandments
      2) The LORD gave Moses the commandments on two stone tablets: Written by the finger of God Himself

      3) The LORD gave the Ten Commandments to Moses at the end of the 40-day fast

   c. The shocking announcement of God
      1) Told Moses to go down to the people: Was disowning them
      2) Charged the people
         - With being corrupt
         - With being quick to disobey
         - With false worship
         - With being stiff-necked

   d. The threat of righteous judgment
      1) To destroy the people
      2) To raise up a new people through Moses' descendants
   e. The righteous anger against terrible sin
      1) Moses turned & went down the mountain: Carried the Ten Commandments with him
      2) Moses saw the terrible sin of the people
         - He saw the idol & false worship
         - He saw how quickly they had turned away from the LORD's commandments
         - He cast the tablets down & broke them

   f. The great intercession for terrible sinners: Moses again prayed & fasted for 40 days

DEUTERONOMY 9:1–10:11

& nights—fell prostrate before the LORD for three reasons
1) Because of their terrible sin & evil

2) Because the LORD was angry enough to destroy them: But He heard the prayer of Moses

3) Because the LORD was angry enough with Aaron to destroy him

g. The destruction of the sinful thing
1) Moses burned the idol
2) Moses ground the idol into powder & threw it into the stream that flowed down the mountain

3. **The warning against continued disobedience & rebellion, against provoking God time & again**
  a. The major examples
  1) Three major examples, v.22
  2) The terrible rebellion at Kadesh Barnea
   - Refused to enter the promised land
   - Rebelled: Did not trust nor obey God
  3) The tragic fact: The people had been rebelling against God from the beginning
  b. Know this: It was intercessory prayer that saved God's people

  1) Moses begged God not to destroy the people
   - They were His people
   - He had saved them

  2) Moses asked God to remember His promises to the forefathers: To overlook the stubbornness & sin of the people

  3) The reasons
   - Because the enemy (Egypt & the world) would falsely charge God: Claim that He did not have the power or honor to fulfill His

neither eat bread, nor drink water, because of all your sins which ye sinned, in doing wickedly in the sight of the LORD, to provoke him to anger.
19 For I was afraid of the anger and hot displeasure, wherewith the LORD was wroth against you to destroy you. But the LORD hearkened unto me at that time also.
20 And the LORD was very angry with Aaron to have destroyed him: and I prayed for Aaron also the same time.
21 And I took your sin, the calf which ye had made, and burnt it with fire, and stamped it, *and* ground *it* very small, *even* until it was as small as dust: and I cast the dust thereof into the brook that descended out of the mount.
22 And at Taberah, and at Massah, and at Kibrothhattaavah, ye provoked the LORD to wrath.
23 Likewise when the LORD sent you from Kadeshbarnea, saying, Go up and possess the land which I have given you; then ye rebelled against the commandment of the LORD your God, and ye believed him not, nor hearkened to his voice.
24 Ye have been rebellious against the LORD from the day that I knew you.
25 Thus I fell down before the LORD forty days and forty nights, as I fell down *at the first*; because the LORD had said he would destroy you.
26 I prayed therefore unto the LORD, and said, O Lord GOD, destroy not thy people and thine inheritance, which thou hast redeemed through thy greatness, which thou hast brought forth out of Egypt with a mighty hand.
27 Remember thy servants, Abraham, Isaac, and Jacob; look not unto the stubbornness of this people, nor to their wickedness, nor to their sin:
28 Lest the land whence thou broughtest us out say, Because the LORD was not able to bring them into the land which he promised them, and because he hated them, he hath brought them out to slay

them in the wilderness.
29 Yet they *are* thy people and thine inheritance, which thou broughtest out by thy mighty power and by thy stretched out arm.

CHAPTER 10

At that time the LORD said unto me, Hew thee two tables of stone like unto the first, and come up unto me into the mount, and make thee an ark of wood.
2 And I will write on the tables the words that were in the first tables which thou brakest, and thou shalt put them in the ark.
3 And I made an ark of shittim wood, and hewed two tables of stone like unto the first, and went up into the mount, having the two tables in mine hand.
4 And he wrote on the tables, according to the first writing, the ten commandments, which the LORD spake unto you in the mount out of the midst of the fire in the day of the assembly: and the LORD gave them unto me.
5 And I turned myself and came down from the mount, and put the tables in the ark which I had made; and there they be, as the LORD commanded me.
6 And the children of Israel took their journey from Beeroth of the children of Jaakan to Mosera: there Aaron died, and there he was buried; and Eleazar his son ministered in the priest's office in his stead.
7 From thence they journeyed unto Gudgodah; and from Gudgodah to Jotbath, a land of rivers of waters.
8 At that time the LORD separated the tribe of Levi, to bear the ark of the covenant of the LORD, to stand before the LORD to minister unto him, and to bless in his name, unto this day.
9 Wherefore Levi hath no part nor inheritance with his brethren; the LORD *is* his inheritance, according as the LORD thy God promised him.
10 And I stayed in the mount, according to the first time, forty days and forty

Word & promises
- Because the Israelites were God's people: His special possession whom He had saved

c. Understand this: It was the wonderful mercy of God that saved you: He heard the prayer & renewed the covenant

1) The LORD instructed Moses to prepare to receive a second copy of the Ten Commandments: To chisel out two tablets & make a wooden chest
2) Moses obeyed
  - Made the ark
  - Chiseled out two stone tablets
  - Climbed Mt. Sinai

3) The LORD rewrote the Ten Commandments: Renewed His covenant with His people (Ex.34:1-35)

4) Moses returned & put the Ten Commandments in the ark he had made

d. Learn this: God led the people step by step as they marched to the promised land
1) Buried Aaron in the wilderness (9:20; see Nu.20:28)

2) Were led to adequate provision by God

e. Remember this: The people were given a permanent corps of ministers to serve them: The Levites
1) To look after the Tabernacle
2) To stand as mediator between God & man
3) To be totally committed to God: This is the reason they were to receive no inherited land—the LORD was to be their share

f. Never forget this: You were saved from judgment by the intercessory ministry of a

mediator 1) The intercessor: Moses prayed for 40 more days (a symbol of Christ) 2) The LORD heard Moses:	nights; and the LORD hearkened unto me at that time also, *and* the LORD would not destroy thee. 11 And the LORD said unto	me, Arise, take *thy* journey before the people, that they may go in and possess the land, which I sware unto their fathers to give unto them.	Charged him to go & lead the people to the promised land

DIVISION III

THE SECOND GREAT THEME PREACHED BY GOD'S AGED SERVANT (PART 1): REMEMBER THE TEN COMMANDMENTS—THE FUNDAMENTAL LAWS TO GOVERN MAN AND SOCIETY, 4:44–11:32

H. The Warnings Against Self-righteousness and Disobedience: Warnings That Must Be Heeded to Inherit the Promised Land, 9:1–10:11

(9:1–10:11) **Introduction**: Is one race of people of more value than another race? Is there a nationality of people who has more merit, more worth than any other nationality? Is there a group of people anyplace who has more qualities within them that makes them more valuable than any other group of people? Within the human heart—the inner recesses of human nature—is there any person anyplace who has more worth, value, goodness, importance, merit, purity, righteousness than any other person?

Not to God. But tragically, some people think so. It is this kind of false reasoning that gives rise to prejudice, discrimination, and atrocities. It is this kind of deceptive philosophy that has given rise to worldwide movements such as the *super-human race* of Nazism, the abuse of the worker by some leaders of capitalism, and the abuse of liberty and freedom by Communism.

When it comes to human nature, no person has any more merit or worth, goodness or righteousness than any other person. We all stand equal before God. God shows no favoritism nor partiality to any person. For a person to think that he is better than someone else, that he has more value and worth than another person, that he is more acceptable and useful to God than others, that God favors him and blesses him more than others—is the height of self-righteousness.

The danger of self-righteousness was of critical concern to Moses. The Israelites were soon to cross the Jordan River and begin their conquest of the promised land. As they conquered their enemies, there was the danger that thoughts of self-sufficiency might begin to arise in their minds. They might begin to think that they had defeated the enemy by *the arm of the flesh*, by their own power—that God had favored them with victory because they were a better people than the enemy, because they were of more value and worth than the enemy. Thoughts of being better and of meriting and deserving God's blessing could begin to penetrate their hearts. A spirit of vanity could consume them. And if vanity consumed them, they would begin to disobey every commandment of God. Contrary to being a righteous people, they were a stiff-necked and stubborn people who continually disobeyed God. A warning was desperately needed, a warning against self-righteousness and disobedience. This is the subject of this important passage of Scripture: *The Warnings Against Self-righteousness and Disobedience: Warnings That Must Be Heeded to Inherit the Promised Land*, 9:1–10:11.

1. The warning against self-righteousness (9:1-6).
2. The warning against disobedience, against provoking God to anger and judgment (9:7-21).
3. The warning against continued disobedience and rebellion, against provoking God time and again (9:22–10:11).

[1] (9:1-6) **Self-righteousness, Warning Against—Israel, Warning to—Israel, Sins of—Faithfulness, of God—Victory, over Enemies—Victory, Source of**: there is the warning against self-righteousness. As the Israelites conquered the promised land, there was the very real danger that they might become self-righteous. Formidable enemies lay ahead. Once they were victorious, the Israelites might begin to think that *the arm of the flesh* had given them the victory, that they had conquered...

- because of their own strength
- because of their own strategy
- because they were more valuable in the eyes of God
- because they merited the favor of God
- because they were a special people in the eyes of God
- because God showed them partiality, favoritism over other people
- because they were a better people, more righteous than other people

Such thoughts are anathema to God, hated and despised by Him. Moses knew this, and somehow he had to drive the point home to the people. Note the Scripture and outline:

OUTLINE	SCRIPTURE	SCRIPTURE	OUTLINE
	CHAPTER 9	greater and mightier than thyself, cities great and fenced up to heaven,	people: Are greater & stronger than believers
1. The warning against self-righteousness a. The enemies faced by God's	Hear, O Israel: Thou *art* to pass over Jordan this day, to go in to possess nations	2 A people great and tall, the children of the Anakims,	1) Have fortified cities 2) Are giants: So strong that a saying has been coined

DEUTERONOMY 9:1–10:11

OUTLINE	SCRIPTURE	SCRIPTURE	OUTLINE

about them: "Who can stand up against the Anakites (giants)?"
b. The promise of victory
  1) By the LORD's action: Will go ahead of His people like a devouring fire—destroy & subdue their enemies
  2) By the people's action: Will drive out & conquer the enemy quickly
c. The strong warning against self-righteousness: Stated three times for emphasis
  1) It is not because of your righteousness that you receive the promised land
    • It is God who destroys
	whom thou knowest, and *of whom* thou hast heard *say*, Who can stand before the children of Anak!
	3 Understand therefore this day, that the LORD thy God *is* he which goeth over before thee; *as* a consuming fire he shall destroy them, and he shall bring them down before thy face: so shalt thou drive them out, and destroy them quickly, as the LORD hath said unto thee.
	4 Speak not thou in thine heart, after that the LORD thy God hath cast them out from before thee, saying, For my righteousness the LORD hath brought me in to possess this land: but
		for the wickedness of these nations the LORD doth drive them out from before thee.
		5 Not for thy righteousness, or for the uprightness of thine heart, dost thou go to possess their land: but for the wickedness of these nations the LORD thy God doth drive them out from before thee, and that he may perform the word which the LORD sware unto thy fathers, Abraham, Isaac, and Jacob.
		6 Understand therefore, that the LORD thy God giveth thee not this good land to possess it for thy righteousness; for thou *art* a stiffnecked people.
			the enemies of the land
			  • It is because of their wickedness that He destroys them
			  2) It is not because of your righteousness or integrity that you inherit the promised land: The enemies of the land are destroyed by God
			    • Because of their evil
			    • Because God fulfills His promise to the forefathers (believers)
			  3) Understand this: It is not because of your righteousness that God gives you the promised land: On the contrary, you are stiffnecked, stubborn people

    a. The enemies to be faced by God's people were far greater and stronger than the Israelites (vv.1-2). They lived in large cities, behind fortified walls that seemed to rise up into the clouds of the sky. But this was not all: the people were as large as giants and very strong. They were so strong that a saying had been coined about them: "Who can stand up against the Anakites (giants)?"

    b. Nevertheless, victory was assured. God's people would be victorious over this formidable enemy (v.3). But note, victory would not come by the arm of the flesh. Not by the strength of the Israelites. True, they had a part to play in the victory, but so did the LORD. Victory would come both by the LORD's action and the people's action. The LORD would go ahead of His people like a devouring fire, destroying and subduing the enemy. But He would use the Israelites as His instruments to achieve victory. The people's action would be to drive out and conquer the enemy quickly. The LORD'S part would be to give the victory—but through the instrument of His people. His people were the instrument through which God Himself would conquer the enemies of the promised land. But note this fact: the people had to march forth trusting God in order to conquer the promised land. They would conquer as they marched forth. By the power of God, the victory was to be achieved as they marched forth.

    c. But note another important point: the strong, strong warning against self-righteousness. The warning is stated three forceful times for emphasis (vv.4-6). Moses drives the point home: he wants to make absolutely sure the people grasp the warning.

      1) Moses emphatically declares, "It is not because of your righteousness that you will receive the promised land. You do not receive the promised land because of some merit or value within yourselves. Not because of your own strength and power. It will be God who destroys the enemies of the promised land, and it is because of their wickedness that He destroys them" (v.4).

        It is critical to note this fact: the enemies of the promised land are destroyed because of their wickedness. They are evil and the "cup of their iniquity" has been filled to the brim. They are now beyond repentance, beyond correction. Their evil must be stopped before any more people are influenced and destroyed. Because of their wickedness, they are to be destroyed, not because of any merit, worth, or value within the Israelites. (See outline and notes—De.20:16-18 for more discussion.)

      2) Again, Moses declares to the people of God: "It is not because of any personal righteousness within you, not because you have pure hearts, that you inherit the promised land (v.5). The enemies of the land are to be conquered and destroyed for two reasons:
⇒ "Because of their wickedness and because they are an evil people; their 'cup of iniquity' is full.
⇒ "Because God is faithful; He fulfills His promise to the forefathers, to Abraham, Isaac, and Jacob. God has promised to give the promised land to their descendants, to all those down through the centuries who believe His Word, His promises."

      3) For a third time, Moses warns the people: "Understand this warning: it is not because of your righteousness that God gives you the promised land. On the contrary, you are a stiff-necked, stubborn people (v.6). You are a sinful people. You have no righteousness within yourselves that merits God's favor. Your hearts are not upright nor pure enough to make God accept you and give you victory over the enemies of the promised land. You are a stiff-necked, stubborn people."

Thought 1. Self-righteousness is a dangerous attitude. It blinds a person and condemns him to be separated forever from God's presence. It prevents a person from ever entering the promised land of heaven. God does not accept or bless a person because of some personal merit, value, or worth. Our righteousness is as filthy rags in the sight of God (Is.64:6). There is no excuse for any person thinking he is better than others, that he has some merit or value or worth that is superior to any other person. God accepts no man's person (Ga.2:6). Scripture is clear: self-righteousness is a terrible evil.

"And when thou prayest, thou shalt not be as the hypocrites *are:* for they love to pray standing in the synagogues and in the corners of the streets, that they may be seen of men. Verily I say unto you, They have their reward" (Mt.6:5).

"The Pharisee stood and prayed thus with himself, God, I thank thee, that I am not as other men *are,* extortioners, unjust, adulterers, or even as this publican" (Lu.18:11).

"Jesus said unto them, If ye were blind, ye should have no sin: but now ye say, We see; therefore your sin remaineth" (Jn.9:41).

"For we dare not make ourselves of the number, or compare ourselves with some that commend themselves: but they measuring themselves by themselves, and comparing themselves among themselves, are not wise" (2 Co.10:12).

"So then because thou art lukewarm, and neither cold nor hot, I will spue thee out of my mouth. Because thou sayest, I am rich, and increased with goods, and have need of nothing; and knowest not that thou art wretched, and miserable, and poor, and blind, and naked" (Re.3:16-17).

"The wicked in *his* pride doth persecute the poor: let them be taken in the devices that they have imagined" (Ps.10:2).

"Thou hast rebuked the proud *that are* cursed, which do err from thy commandments" (Ps.119:21).

"All the ways of a man *are* clean in his own eyes; but the LORD weigheth the spirits" (Pr.16:2).

"Most men will proclaim every one his own goodness: but a faithful man who can find" (Pr.20:6).

"Every way of a man *is* right in his own eyes: but the LORD pondereth the hearts" (Pr.21:2).

"*There is* a generation *that are* pure in their own eyes, and *yet* is not washed from their filthiness" (Pr.30:12).

"But we are all as an unclean *thing,* and all our righteousnesses *are* as filthy rags; and we all do fade as a leaf; and our iniquities, like the wind, have taken us away" (Is.64:6).

"Which say, Stand by thyself, come not near to me; for I am holier than thou. These are a smoke in my nose, a fire that burneth all the day" (Is.65:5).

"If I justify myself, mine own mouth shall condemn me: *if I say, I am* perfect, it shall also prove me perverse" (Jb.9:20).

"Thinkest thou this to be right, *that* thou saidst, My righteousness *is* more than God's" (Jb.35:2).

2 **(9:7-21) Disobedience, Warning Against—Rebellion, Warning Against—Warning, Against Provoking God—Golden Calf—Ten Commandments, Receiving—Idolatry—Worship, False—Israel, Sin of—Stubbornness, Sin of**: there was the warning against disobedience and rebellion, against provoking God to anger and judgment. This point highlights just how stubborn and stiff-necked the Israelites were. Moses warned the people: they must remember how the first generation so miserably failed God. In particular, they must remember the golden calf incident, for it is a compelling example, showing just how stiff-necked and stubborn the people really were.

OUTLINE	SCRIPTURE	SCRIPTURE	OUTLINE
2. The warning against disobedience—against provoking God to anger & judgment a. The strong charge—remember this & never forget it: God was provoked to anger in the wilderness wanderings 1) The cause: Repeated rebellion 2) The LORD's anger was aroused enough to destroy His people at Mt. Horeb (Sinai) b. The wonderful gift of God at Sinai: The Ten Commandments, the covenant God had made with His people 1) The LORD kept Moses on Mt. Sinai for 40 days & nights: Fasting, praying & receiving the commandments 2) The LORD gave Moses the commandments on two stone tablets: Written by the finger of God Himself	7 Remember, *and* forget not, how thou provokedst the LORD thy God to wrath in the wilderness: from the day that thou didst depart out of the land of Egypt, until ye came unto this place, ye have been rebellious against the LORD. 8 Also in Horeb ye provoked the LORD to wrath, so that the LORD was angry with you to have destroyed you. 9 When I was gone up into the mount to receive the tables of stone, *even* the tables of the covenant which the LORD made with you, then I abode in the mount forty days and forty nights, I neither did eat bread nor drink water: 10 And the LORD delivered unto me two tables of stone written with the finger of God; and on them *was written* according to all the words, which the LORD spake	with you in the mount out of the midst of the fire in the day of the assembly. 11 And it came to pass at the end of forty days and forty nights, *that* the LORD gave me the two tables of stone, *even* the tables of the covenant. 12 And the LORD said unto me, Arise, get thee down quickly from hence; for thy people which thou hast brought forth out of Egypt have corrupted *themselves*; they are quickly turned aside out of the way which I commanded them; they have made them a molten image. 13 Furthermore the LORD spake unto me, saying, I have seen this people, and, behold, it *is* a stiffnecked people: 14 Let me alone, that I may destroy them, and blot out their name from under heaven: and I will make of thee a nation mightier and greater	3) The LORD gave the Ten Commandments to Moses at the end of the 40-day fast c. The shocking announcement of God 1) Told Moses to go down to the people: Was disowning them 2) Charged the people • With being corrupt • With being quick to disobey • With false worship • With being stiff-necked d. The threat of righteous judgment 1) To destroy the people 2) To raise up a new people through Moses'

DEUTERONOMY 9:1–10:11

OUTLINE	SCRIPTURE	SCRIPTURE	OUTLINE
descendants e. The righteous anger against terrible sin 1) Moses turned & went down the mountain: Carried the Ten Commandments with him 2) Moses saw the terrible sin of the people • He saw the idol & false worship • He saw how quickly they had turned away from the LORD's commandments • He cast the tablets down & broke them f. The great intercession for terrible sinners: Moses again prayed & fasted for 40 days & nights—fell prostrate before the LORD for three	than they. 15 So I turned and came down from the mount, and the mount burned with fire: and the two tables of the covenant *were* in my two hands. 16 And I looked, and, behold, ye had sinned against the LORD your God, *and* had made you a molten calf: ye had turned aside quickly out of the way which the LORD had commanded you. 17 And I took the two tables, and cast them out of my two hands, and brake them before your eyes. 18 And I fell down before the LORD, as at the first, forty days and forty nights: I did neither eat bread, nor drink water, because of all your	sins which ye sinned, in doing wickedly in the sight of the LORD, to provoke him to anger. 19 For I was afraid of the anger and hot displeasure, wherewith the LORD was wroth against you to destroy you. But the LORD hearkened unto me at that time also. 20 And the LORD was very angry with Aaron to have destroyed him: and I prayed for Aaron also the same time. 21 And I took your sin, the calf which ye had made, and burnt it with fire, and stamped it, *and* ground *it* very small, *even* until it was as small as dust: and I cast the dust thereof into the brook that descended out of the mount.	reasons 1) Because of their terrible sin & evil 2) Because the LORD was angry enough to destroy them: But He heard the prayer of Moses 3) Because the LORD was angry enough with Aaron to destroy him g. The destruction of the sinful thing 1) Moses burned the idol 2) Moses ground the idol into powder & threw it into the stream that flowed down the mountain

a. Moses gave a strong charge: remember the brazen, shameful disobedience and rebellion that took place at Mt. Sinai. Remember that terrible day and never forget it (vv.7-8). God was provoked to anger against the Israelites because of their repeated disobedience and rebellion. In fact, His anger was aroused enough to destroy His people right there at Mt. Sinai (Mt. Horeb).

b. Moses challenged the people to remember the wonderful gift of God at Sinai: the Ten Commandments, the covenant He had made with His people (vv.9-11). The LORD had kept Moses on Mt. Sinai for forty days and nights. During that time, he was fasting, praying, and receiving the Ten Commandments. He ate no bread and drank no water during the forty days (v.9).

The LORD had given Moses the commandments on two stone tablets (v.10). Note that the commandments had been written by the finger of God Himself. They were then given to Moses at the end of the forty-day fast (v.11).

c. Then, all of a sudden, a shocking announcement was made by God (vv.12-13). God told Moses to go down to the people, for He was disowning them. God leveled several charges against the people. He charged them...

- with being corrupt
- with being quick to disobey
- with being false worshippers
- with being stiff-necked

The seriousness of the charges lay in this fact: the people had already accepted the covenant with God, some six weeks earlier, already agreed to the terms of the covenant. But here they were already disobeying God. As God says, being quick to disobey. Remember the covenant, the contract they had made with God:

> **"Now therefore, if ye will obey my voice indeed, and keep my covenant, then ye shall be a peculiar treasure unto me above all people: for all the earth *is* mine: And ye shall be unto me a kingdom of priests, and an holy nation. These *are* the words which thou shalt speak unto the children of Israel" (Ex.19:5-6).**

Imagine the emotions, the utter shock of Moses. For forty days and nights he had been in the presence of God, communing and fellowshipping with God. Then all of a sudden, as though out of nowhere, God made this shocking announcement to Moses: He was disowning the Israelites. Why? Because they were at that very moment corrupting themselves, proving to be a stiff-necked, stubborn people.

d. Moses reminded the second generation of believers standing there before him as he preached, the righteous judgment of God was aroused (v.14). God even announced that he was going to destroy the people. He was going to raise up a new people through Moses' descendants. Keep in mind that God could easily have done this, for the descendants of Moses would have still been the descendants of Abraham. God could still have fulfilled His covenant or promise to Abraham and his descendants.

e. Moses informed the second generations that he was personally filled with a righteous anger against the terrible sin (vv.15-17). Immediately after God's shocking announcement to him, Moses had turned and gone down the mountain carrying the Ten Commandments with him (v.15). What Moses saw shocked him:

⇒ He saw the idol of the golden calf and the false worship of the people.
⇒ He saw how quickly the people had turned away from their covenant with the LORD, turned away from obeying the LORD's commandments.

DEUTERONOMY 9:1–10:11

A righteous, justified anger surged up within his body, and he cast the two stone tablets down and broke them before their very eyes (v.17). The fact that Moses broke the tablets in their presence shows that this was a deliberate act. In fact, this was a custom in the ancient Near East when treaties were broken.[1] It was a visual picture of extreme displeasure over the people's disobedience, of their disobeying the commandments of God. It was a symbol that the covenant with God had been broken.

Note this fact: the people could never make the claim of self-righteousness. They had disobeyed God and broken His commandments on the very day that the commandments were to be delivered to them. However, keep this fact in mind: the commandments had already been given them by the voice of God Himself. From the very midst of the burning fire that symbolized His presence, the voice of God had proclaimed the Ten Commandments to the people (see outline and notes—Ex.20:19; De.5:2-5 for more discussion). The people were without excuse; they were guilty before God. They had disobeyed God. Without question, they were a stiff-necked, stubborn people.

f. After breaking the tablets of the commandments, Moses shared that he got alone with God and began to intercede for the terrible sinners. Note that he once again prayed and fasted for forty days and nights (vv.18-20). He fell prostrate before the LORD for three reasons:

⇒ because of the people's terrible sin and evil that had provoked him to anger
⇒ because the LORD was angry enough to destroy the people (v.19). But note: the LORD heard the prayer of Moses
⇒ because the LORD was angry enough with Aaron to destroy him (v.20). It was only the prayer of Moses that kept God from executing Aaron.

The second generation of believers standing before Moses needed to learn this lesson. It was intercessory prayer that had saved the people and Aaron. It was not because they were righteous and pure in the eyes of God, not because of some personal merit or value or worth. On the contrary, they were guilty of terrible sin and evil. They were a disobedient people, a stiff-necked, stubborn people. It was intercessory prayer and intercessory prayer alone that had saved them. God had mercy upon them only because of the intercessory prayer of Moses.

g. After praying for the people, Moses then destroyed the sinful things of the people: he burned the idol of the golden calf, ground it into powder, and threw it into the stream that flowed down the mountain (v.21).

> **Thought 1.** The golden calf incident must be remembered by all generations of believers. The Israelites broke God's commandments. They disobeyed and rebelled against God. They aroused God's anger, stirred Him to pronounce judgment upon them. This is a strong lesson for us: we must not break the commandments of God. We must not disobey God lest we arouse His anger and judgment against us.
>
> "But after thy hardness and impenitent heart treasurest up unto thyself wrath against the day of wrath and revelation of the righteous judgment of God" (Ro.2:5).
>
> "Let no man deceive you with vain words: for because of these things cometh the wrath of God upon the children of disobedience" (Ep.5:6).
>
> "And to you who are troubled rest with us, when the LORD Jesus shall be revealed from heaven with his mighty angels, In flaming fire taking vengeance on them that know not God, and that obey not the gospel of our Lord Jesus Christ: Who shall be punished with everlasting destruction from the presence of the LORD, and from the glory of his power" (2 Th.1:7-9).
>
> "For if the word spoken by angels was stedfast, and every transgression and disobedience received a just recompence of reward; How shall we escape, if we neglect so great salvation; which at the first began to be spoken by the LORD, and was confirmed unto us by them that heard *him*" (He.2:2-3).
>
> "And a curse, if ye will not obey the commandments of the LORD your God, but turn aside out of the way which I command you this day, to go after other gods, which ye have not known" (De.11:28).
>
> "He, that being often reproved hardeneth *his* neck, shall suddenly be destroyed, and that without remedy" (Pr.29:1).

3 (9:22–10:11) **Disobedience, Warning Against—Warning, Against Rebellion—Warning, Against Provoking God—Intercession, Results of—Mercy, of God—Guidance, of God—Levites, Duty of—Salvation, Source of—Prayer, Intercessory**: there was the warning against continued disobedience and rebellion. Moses warned the people against provoking God time and again. God does forgive His people for disobedience and rebellion, but once forgiven, He expects His people to change their behavior. Once they have repented, turned away from their sin, He expects them to follow Him with their whole hearts, totally and completely. But this was not true with the Israelites. Time and again they disobeyed and rebelled against God. Their repentance and renewed commitments to God did not stick. Throughout this passage, note the mercy of God as well as the continued disobedience of the people.

OUTLINE	SCRIPTURE	SCRIPTURE	OUTLINE
3. The warning against continued disobedience & rebellion—against provoking God time & again a. The major examples 1) Three major examples,	22 And at Taberah, and at Massah, and at Kibrothhattaavah, ye provoked the LORD to wrath. 23 Likewise when the LORD sent you from Kadeshbarnea,	saying, Go up and possess the land which I have given you; then ye rebelled against the commandment of the LORD your God, and ye believed him not, nor hearkened to his	v.22 2) The terrible rebellion at Kadesh Barnea • Refused to enter the promised land • Rebelled: Did not trust

---

[1] J.A. Thompson. *Deuteronomy*. (Leicester, England: Inter-Varsity Press, 1974), p.141.

DEUTERONOMY 9:1–10:11

OUTLINE	SCRIPTURE	SCRIPTURE	OUTLINE
nor obey God 3) The tragic fact: The people had been rebelling against God from the beginning b. Know this: It was intercessory prayer that saved God's people 1) Moses begged God not to destroy the people • They were His people • He had saved them 2) Moses asked God to remember His promises to the forefathers: To overlook the stubbornness & sin of the people 3) The reasons • Because the enemy (Egypt & the world) would falsely charge God: Claim that He did not have the power or honor to fulfill His Word & promises • Because the Israelites were God's people: His special possession whom He had saved c. Understand this: It was the wonderful mercy of God that saved you: He heard the prayer & renewed the covenant 1) The LORD instructed Moses to prepare to receive a second copy of the Ten Commandments: To chisel out two tablets & make a wooden chest 2) Moses obeyed • Made the ark • Chiseled out two stone	voice. 24 Ye have been rebellious against the LORD from the day that I knew you. 25 Thus I fell down before the LORD forty days and forty nights, as I fell down *at the first*; because the LORD had said he would destroy you. 26 I prayed therefore unto the LORD, and said, O Lord GOD, destroy not thy people and thine inheritance, which thou hast redeemed through thy greatness, which thou hast brought forth out of Egypt with a mighty hand. 27 Remember thy servants, Abraham, Isaac, and Jacob; look not unto the stubbornness of this people, nor to their wickedness, nor to their sin: 28 Lest the land whence thou broughtest us out say, Because the LORD was not able to bring them into the land which he promised them, and because he hated them, he hath brought them out to slay them in the wilderness. 29 Yet they *are* thy people and thine inheritance, which thou broughtest out by thy mighty power and by thy stretched out arm. **CHAPTER 10** At that time the LORD said unto me, Hew thee two tables of stone like unto the first, and come up unto me into the mount, and make thee an ark of wood. 2 And I will write on the tables the words that were in the first tables which thou brakest, and thou shalt put them in the ark. 3 And I made an ark *of* shittim wood, and hewed two tables of stone like unto the	first, and went up into the mount, having the two tables in mine hand. 4 And he wrote on the tables, according to the first writing, the ten commandments, which the LORD spake unto you in the mount out of the midst of the fire in the day of the assembly: and the LORD gave them unto me. 5 And I turned myself and came down from the mount, and put the tables in the ark which I had made; and there they be, as the LORD commanded me. 6 And the children of Israel took their journey from Beeroth of the children of Jaakan to Mosera: there Aaron died, and there he was buried; and Eleazar his son ministered in the priest's office in his stead. 7 From thence they journeyed unto Gudgodah; and from Gudgodah to Jotbath, a land of rivers of waters. 8 At that time the LORD separated the tribe of Levi, to bear the ark of the covenant of the LORD, to stand before the LORD to minister unto him, and to bless in his name, unto this day. 9 Wherefore Levi hath no part nor inheritance with his brethren; the LORD *is* his inheritance, according as the LORD thy God promised him. 10 And I stayed in the mount, according to the first time, forty days and forty nights; and the LORD hearkened unto me at that time also, *and* the LORD would not destroy thee. 11 And the LORD said unto me, Arise, take *thy* journey before the people, that they may go in and possess the land, which I sware unto their fathers to give unto them.	tablets • Climbed Mt. Sinai 3) The LORD rewrote the Ten Commandments: Renewed His covenant with His people (see Ex.34:1-35) 4) Moses returned & put the Ten Commandments in the ark he had made d. Learn this: God led the people step by step as they marched to the promised land 1) Buried Aaron in the wilderness (9:20 see Nu.20:28) 2) Were led to adequate provision by God e. Remember this: The people were given a permanent corps of ministers to serve them: The Levites 1) To look after the Tabernacle 2) To stand as mediator between God & man 3) To be totally committed to God: This is the reason they were to receive no inherited land—the LORD was to be their share f. Never forget this: You were saved from judgment by the intercessory ministry of a mediator 1) The intercessor: Moses prayed for 40 more days (a symbol of Christ) 2) The LORD heard Moses: Charged him to go & lead the people to the promised land

a. Moses gave three major examples of disobedience and then covered the terrible rebellion at Kadesh Barnea (vv.22-23).
   ⇒ At Taberah, the people complained and grumbled over their hardships and suffered the judgment of God (see outline and notes—Nu.11:1-3 for more discussion).
   ⇒ At Massah, the people grumbled and distrusted God because they had no water, and they threatened to stone Moses (see outline and notes—Ex.17:1-7 for more discussion).
   ⇒ At Kibroth Hattaavah the people again grumbled against God, distrusting Him because they were tired of the heavenly food provided by God (the manna) and they lusted after the food (delicacies) of Egypt. Again, the judgment of God fell upon the people (see outline and notes—Nu.11:4-35 for more discussion).
   ⇒ At Kadesh Barnea, the sins of disobedience and rebellion reached their summit. God had instructed the people to go up and possess the promised land, but the people refused. They rebelled against God. The result was tragic: this was the final rebellion that God would tolerate from the first generation of believers. They refused to enter the promised land, choosing to remain in the desert. So in the desert they would remain. The judicial judgment of God

fell: they reaped exactly what they had sown. They were condemned to wander about and die in the desert, barred forever from the promised land (see outline and notes—Nu.13:1–14:45; De.1:18-46 for more discussion).

Note the tragic fact: the people did not trust God nor obey Him. They had been rebelling against the LORD ever since Moses had known them (v.24). They were guilty of continued disobedience and rebellion against God, guilty of provoking God time and again. They had obviously confessed their sin after each act of disobedience, but their confession did not include a *lasting repentance*. They were guilty of false confession and false repentance, of not living a changed life. They did not continue to trust and obey God, but were continually slipping back. They were a stiff-necked and stubborn people, filled with unbelief and longing for the things of this world. They wanted to live life as they wanted, when they wanted, not like God demanded. They wanted to do away with the commandments of God. This they had demonstrated time and time again. They were a people who lived lives of continued disobedience and rebellion against the commandments of God. They continued to provoke the anger and judgment of God.

Thought 1. The Israelites were gripped with a spirit of unbelief. They simply did not trust God nor obey Him. Many of the Israelites lived a false profession, not wanting anything to do with the commandments of God. The Scripture warns us against the spirit of unbelief and of a false profession.

"Not every one that saith unto me, LORD, LORD, shall enter into the kingdom of heaven; but he that doeth the will of my Father which is in heaven" (Mt.7:21).

"Give not that which is holy unto the dogs, neither cast ye your pearls before swine, lest they trample them under their feet, and turn again and rend you" (Mk.7:6).

"Harden not your hearts, as in the provocation, in the day of temptation in the wilderness: When your fathers tempted me, proved me, and saw my works forty years. Wherefore I was grieved with that generation, and said, They do alway err in *their* heart; and they have not known my ways. So I sware in my wrath, They shall not enter into my rest. Take heed, brethren, lest there be in any of you an evil heart of unbelief, in departing from the living God. But exhort one another daily, while it is called To day; lest any of you be hardened through the deceitfulness of sin. For we are made partakers of Christ, if we hold the beginning of our confidence stedfast unto the end" (He.3:8-14).

"Let us labour therefore to enter into that rest, lest any man fall after the same example of unbelief" (He.4:11).

"They profess that they know God; but in works they deny *him*, being abominable, and disobedient, and unto every good work reprobate" (Tit.1:16).

"I will therefore put you in remembrance, though ye once knew this, how that the LORD, having saved the people out of the land of Egypt, afterward destroyed them that believed not" (Jude 5).

"And they remembered that God *was* their rock, and the high God their redeemer. Nevertheless they did flatter him with their mouth, and they lied unto him with their tongues" (Ps.78:35-36).

b. Know this: it was intercessory prayer that saved God's people (vv.25-29). At the golden calf incident, God saved the Israelites only because Moses interceded on their behalf. God had already pronounced the judgment, and He was on the verge of executing the sentence. But Moses prostrated himself before the LORD and prayed for the people. For forty days and forty nights, he interceded.
1) Moses begged God not to destroy His people (vv.25-26). He acknowledged God's sovereignty, that He had the power to destroy the people. But he begged God not to destroy them, for they were His people. They were the people He had saved out of Egypt, saved to be His people.
2) Moses asked God to remember His promises to the forefathers, Abraham, Isaac, and Jacob. He begged God to overlook the stubbornness of this people, overlook their wickedness and their sin (v.27).
3) Moses begged God to forgive the sins of the people for two reasons (vv.28-29). If God destroyed the Israelites, the surrounding nations (Egypt and the world) would make false charges against God. They would claim that God was weak, vengeful and evil; that He did not have the power or honor to fulfill His Word and promises to the Israelites. Moses wanted God to preserve His own honor and trust in the eyes of the world, that He keep His name from being slandered, falsely charged with being powerless to fulfill His promises.

But there was another reason why God must give His people another chance: because the Israelites were God's people, His inheritance, His special possession that He had saved with great power. God had saved and delivered His people by His mighty power out of the bondage of Egypt. He had a very special relationship with them, a covenant relationship. Therefore, Moses begged God to turn from His wrath and give His people another chance.

Standing there preaching to the second generation of believers, Moses was doing all he could to teach them the great lesson of intercessory prayer. It was intercessory prayer that moved God to save His people, to give them another chance.

Thought 1. God hears prayer. Prayer is one of the basic laws of the universe established by God. Prayer has been chosen by God to be one of the basic laws that stir Him to act as He governs the universe. Prayer is an act of man that arouses God to move and act in behalf of man. As stated, God answers prayer.

"Ask, and it shall be given you; seek, and ye shall find; knock, and it shall be opened unto you" (Mt.7:7).

"Therefore I say unto you, What things soever ye desire, when ye pray, believe that ye receive *them*, and ye shall have *them*" (Mk.11:24).

"If ye abide in me, and my words abide in you, ye shall ask what ye will, and it shall be done unto you" (Jn.15:7).

DEUTERONOMY 9:1–10:11

"Hitherto have ye asked nothing in my name: ask, and ye shall receive, that your joy may be full" (Jn.16:24).

"Is any among you afflicted? let him pray. Is any merry? let him sing psalms" (Js.5:13).

"Confess *your* faults one to another, and pray one for another, that ye may be healed. The effectual fervent prayer of a righteous man availeth much" (Js.5:16).

"And whatsoever we ask, we receive of him, because we keep his commandments, and do those things that are pleasing in his sight" (1 Jn.3:22).

"He shall call upon me, and I will answer him: I *will be* with him in trouble; I will deliver him, and honour him" (Ps.91:15).

"Then shalt thou call, and the LORD shall answer; thou shalt cry, and he shall say, Here I *am.* If thou take away from the midst of thee the yoke, the putting forth of the finger, and speaking vanity" (Is.58:9).

"And it shall come to pass, that before they call, I will answer; and while they are yet speaking, I will hear" (Is.65:24).

"If my people, which are called by my name, shall humble themselves, and pray, and seek my face, and turn from their wicked ways; then will I hear from heaven, and will forgive their sin, and will heal their land" (2 Chr.7:14).

"And ye shall seek me, and find *me,* when ye shall search for me with all your heart" (Je.29:13).

c. Understand this: it was the wonderful mercy of God that saved God's people. God heard the prayer of Moses and renewed His covenant with His people. God turned away from His wrath and gave them another chance to follow and obey Him (10:1-5).
  1) The LORD immediately instructed Moses to prepare to receive a second copy of the Ten Commandments. He was to chisel out two new tablets and make a wooden chest (vv.1-2).
  2) Moses obeyed God: he made the Ark or chest and chiseled out two stone tablets. Then he climbed Mt. Sinai with the two tablets in his hands (v.3).
  3) Note that the LORD Himself rewrote the Ten Commandments. He renewed His covenant with His people (v.4; see outline and notes—Ex.34:1-35 for more discussion).
  4) God then gave the commandments to Moses, and Moses returned and put the Ten Commandments in the Ark he had made (v.5).

Moses wanted the second generation of believers to grasp and understand this fact: it was the mercy of God that had saved their parents at Mt. Sinai. It was the mercy of God that gave them a second chance, that caused God to turn from His pronounced judgment. God had mercy upon the people, and they were saved. They were given another chance, another opportunity to follow and obey God. God reestablished His covenant, His contract with the people. He would fully restore them and give them every promise He had ever made, but they had to obey Him. They must keep the Ten Commandments.

Thought 1. It is the mercy of God and His wonderful grace that saves us. When we call upon God for forgiveness, He has mercy upon us and forgives us. He gives us a second chance. Another opportunity to follow and obey Him is laid out before us. But once God has mercy upon us, we must obey and follow Him. We must keep the covenant or contract of obedience. We must obey His commandments if we are to inherit the promised land of heaven.

We must always remember this fact: God has mercy upon us, not so that we can live ungodly, disobedient lives upon this earth. We receive God's mercy in order to live holy, righteous, and pure lives before God and the unbelievers of the world.

The point to see is God's mercy. In seeking God's mercy, we must be sincere, genuine. God pours out His mercy upon those who genuinely seek His mercy. A second chance is given to those who genuinely receive His mercy.

"But God, who is rich in mercy, for his great love wherewith he loved us, Even when we were dead in sins, hath quickened us together with Christ, (by grace ye are saved;) And hath raised *us* up together, and made *us* sit together in heavenly *places* in Christ Jesus: That in the ages to come he might show the exceeding riches of his grace in *his* kindness toward us through Christ Jesus" (Ep.2:4-7).

"Not by works of righteousness which we have done, but according to his mercy he saved us, by the washing of regeneration, and renewing of the Holy Ghost" (Tit.3:5).

"But the mercy of the LORD *is* from everlasting to everlasting upon them that fear him, and his righteousness unto children's children" (Ps.103:17).

"For thy mercy *is* great above the heavens: and thy truth *reacheth* unto the clouds" (Ps.108:4).

"*It is of* the LORD'S mercies that we are not consumed, because his compassions fail not. *They are* new every morning: great *is* thy faithfulness" (Lam.3:22-23).

"And rend your heart, and not your garments, and turn unto the LORD your God: for he *is* gracious and merciful, slow to anger, and of great kindness, and repenteth him of the evil" (Joel 2:13).

"Who *is* a God like unto thee, that pardoneth iniquity, and passeth by the transgression of the remnant of his heritage? he retaineth not his anger for ever, because he delighteth *in* mercy" (Mi.7:18).

d. Learn this: God led His people step by step as they marched to the promised land (10:6-7). Once God had forgiven the terrible sin of the people, He renewed His presence among them. He continued to guide and lead them toward the promised land. He led the Israelites to break camp and to march from the wells of the Jaakanites to Moserah. It was there that Aaron died and that his son Eleazar succeeded him as High Priest. From there God continued to lead His people on their march, marching from Gudgodah to Jotbathah where there was an abundance of provision for the people. Apparently the area had a large number of streams, brooks, and perhaps rivers to supply plenty of water for the people. Most likely, so much water also points to the area being cultivated by the residents of the land. This means the Israelites could probably purchase food from the surrounding residents.

DEUTERONOMY 9:1–10:11

The point to see is the renewed presence, guidance, and provision of God. He guided His people as they marched through the wilderness to the promised land.

Thought 1. God leads us step by step as we march to the promised land of heaven. The march through the wilderness of this world is sometimes burdensome and difficult. Trial after trial confronts us, and temptation after temptation threatens to conquer us. But God promises to lead and guide us every step of the way.

"Through the tender mercy of our God; whereby the dayspring from on high hath visited us, To give light to them that sit in darkness and *in* the shadow of death, to guide our feet into the way of peace" (Lu.1:78-79).

"Howbeit when he, the Spirit of truth, is come, he will guide you into all truth: for he shall not speak of himself; but whatsoever he shall hear, *that* shall he speak: and he will show you things to come" (Jn.16:13).

"And, behold, I *am* with thee, and will keep thee in all *places* whither thou goest, and will bring thee again into this land; for I will not leave thee, until I have done *that* which I have spoken to thee of" (Ge.28:15).

"The eternal God *is thy* refuge, and underneath *are* the everlasting arms: and he shall thrust out the enemy from before thee; and shall say, Destroy *them*" (De.33:27).

"He maketh me to lie down in green pastures: he leadeth me beside the still waters" (Ps.23:2).

"The meek will he guide in judgment: and the meek will he teach his way" (Ps.25:9).

"For this God *is* our God for ever and ever: he will be our guide *even* unto death" (Ps.48:14).

"Thou shalt guide me with thy counsel, and afterward receive me *to* glory" (Ps.73:24).

"And thine ears shall hear a word behind thee, saying, This *is* the way, walk ye in it, when ye turn to the right hand, and when ye turn to the left" (Is.30:21).

"And I will bring the blind by a way *that* they knew not; I will lead them in paths *that* they have not known: I will make darkness light before them, and crooked things straight. These things will I do unto them, and not forsake them" (Is.42:16).

"Fear thou not; for I *am* with thee: be not dismayed; for I *am* thy God: I will strengthen thee; yea, I will help thee; yea, I will uphold thee with the right hand of my righteousness" (Is.41:10).

e. Remember this: the people of God were given a permanent corps of ministers to serve them. God appointed the Levites to be the ministers to His people (10:8-9). They were given three very specific tasks:
⇒ to look after the Tabernacle as they marched throughout the wilderness wanderings.
⇒ to stand as mediator between God and man, ministering to the people and pronouncing blessings upon them in the name of God. This they did by leading the people in worship and witness, teaching them the law, and ministering to their need.
⇒ to be totally committed to God and His service. They were not to become entangled in the financial and business affairs of this world. For this reason, they were to receive no inheritance, no share of property in the promised land. The LORD alone was to be their share, their inheritance. Their total focus, energy, and work were to be focused upon God, ministering to Him and to His dear people.

Moses was driving the point home to the hearts of the people: once God's mercy had saved them, He would meet their every need. He had given them an ordained ministry to care for their spiritual welfare, to meet their spiritual needs day by day.

"He saith to him again the second time, Simon, *son* of Jonas, lovest thou me? He saith unto him, Yea, LORD; thou knowest that I love thee. He saith unto him, Feed my sheep" (Jn.21:16).

"Take heed therefore unto yourselves, and to all the flock, over the which the Holy Ghost hath made you overseers, to feed the church of God, which he hath purchased with his own blood" (Ac.20:28).

"Obey them that have the rule over you, and submit yourselves: for they watch for your souls, as they that must give account, that they may do it with joy, and not with grief: for that *is* unprofitable for you" (He.13:17).

"And I will give you pastors according to mine heart, which shall feed you with knowledge and understanding" (Je.3:15).

"And I will set up shepherds over them which shall feed them: and they shall fear no more, nor be dismayed, neither shall they be lacking, saith the LORD" (Je.23:4).

"Son of man, I have made thee a watchman unto the house of Israel: therefore hear the word at my mouth, and give them warning from me" (Eze.3:17).

f. Never forget this: God's people were saved from judgment by the intercessory ministry of a mediator (10:10-11). Because of the importance of intercessory prayer, Moses again drives this point home to the hearts of his listeners. He restates the fact: for forty days and forty nights he stayed on the mountain praying and seeking the LORD. The LORD heard His prayer and did not destroy the Israelites.

Obviously, because of the intercessory ministry of Moses, God chose to forgive the people and give them a second chance. He charged Moses to go and lead the people to the promised land.

Thought 1. There is a great lesson for us in the intercessory ministry of Moses. He stood between God and the people, stood between the judgment and mercy of God. By this act, he is a clear type of the intercession of Jesus Christ. Moses is a picture of Jesus Christ, the Mediator who stands between God and us. Jesus Christ intercedes in our behalf, asking God to accept us because of our faith in His death upon the cross.

"Who *is* he that condemneth? *It is* Christ that died, yea rather, that is risen again, who is even at the right hand of God, who also maketh intercession for us" (Ro.8:34).

"For *there is* one God, and one mediator between God and men, the man Christ Jesus; Who gave himself a ransom for all, to be testified in due time" (1 Ti.2:5-6).

"Wherefore in all things it behooved him to be made like unto *his* brethren, that he might be a merciful and faithful high priest in things *pertaining* to God, to make reconciliation for the sins of the people" (He.2:17).

"Seeing then that we have a great high priest, that is passed into the heavens, Jesus the Son of God, let us hold fast *our* profession. For we have not an high priest which cannot be touched with the feeling of our infirmities; but was in all points tempted like as *we are, yet* without sin" (He.4:14-15).

"Wherefore he is able also to save them to the uttermost that come unto God by him, seeing he ever liveth to make intercession for them" (He.7:25).

"But now hath he obtained a more excellent ministry, by how much also he is the mediator of a better covenant, which was established upon better promises" (He.8:6).

"And for this cause he is the mediator of the new testament, that by means of death, for the redemption of the transgressions *that were* under the first testament, they which are called might receive the promise of eternal inheritance" (He.9:15).

"For Christ is not entered into the holy places made with hands, *which are* the figures of the true; but into heaven itself, now to appear in the presence of God for us: Nor yet that he should offer himself often, as the high priest entereth into the holy place every year with blood of others; For then must he often have suffered since the foundation of the world: but now once in the end of the world hath he appeared to put away sin by the sacrifice of himself. And as it is appointed unto men once to die, but after this the judgment: So Christ was once offered to bear the sins of many; and unto them that look for him shall he appear the second time without sin unto salvation" (He.9:24-28).

"My little children, these things write I unto you, that ye sin not. And if any man sin, we have an advocate with the Father, Jesus Christ the righteous: And he is the propitiation for our sins: and not for ours only, but also for *the sins of* the whole world" (1 Jn.2:1-2).

"Therefore will I divide him *a portion* with the great, and he shall divide the spoil with the strong; because he hath poured out his soul unto death: and he was numbered with the transgressors; and he bare the sin of many, and made intercession for the transgressors" (Is.53:12).

TYPES, SYMBOLS, AND PICTURES
(Deuteronomy 9:1–10:11)

Historical Term	Type or Picture (Scriptural Basis for Each)	Life Application for Today's Believer	Biblical Application
Moses Casting Down the Two Stone Tablets and Breaking them before the People De.9:7-21	This dramatic act was a visual picture of extreme displeasure over the people's disobedience, of their disobeying the commandments of God. It was a symbol that the covenant with God had been broken. A righteous, justified anger surged up within Moses, and he cast the two stone tablets down and broke them before the very eyes of the people (v.17). The fact that Moses broke the tablets in their presence shows that this was a deliberate act. In fact, this was a custom in the ancient Near East when treaties were broken.[2] "And I took the two tables, and cast them out of my two hands, and brake them before your eyes" (De.9:17).	⇒ The golden calf incident must be remembered by all generations of believers. The Israelites broke God's commandments. They disobeyed and rebelled against God. They aroused God's anger, stirred Him to pronounce judgment upon them. This is a strong lesson for us: we must not break the commandments of God. We must not disobey God lest we arouse His anger and judgment against us.	"Let no man deceive you with vain words: for because of these things cometh the wrath of God upon the children of disobedience" (Ep.5:6). "And to you who are troubled rest with us, when the LORD Jesus shall be revealed from heaven with his mighty angels, In flaming fire taking vengeance on them that know not God, and that obey not the gospel of our Lord Jesus Christ: Who shall be punished with everlasting destruction from the presence of the LORD, and from the glory of his power" (2 Th.1:7-9). "For if the word spoken by angels was stedfast, and every transgression and disobedience received a just recompence of reward; How shall we escape, if we

---
[2] J.A. Thompson. *Deuteronomy*, p.141.

DEUTERONOMY 9:1–10:11

Historical Term	Type or Picture (Scriptural Basis for Each)	Life Application for Today's Believer	Biblical Application
			neglect so great salvation; which at the first began to be spoken by the LORD, and was confirmed unto us by them that heard him" (He.2:2-3; See also De. 11:28; Pr.29:1).

DEUTERONOMY 10:12–11:32

1. **Pledge allegiance to the LORD**
   a. The meaning
      1) Fear the LORD
      2) Walk in all His ways
      3) Love Him
      4) Serve Him with all your heart & soul
      5) Keep, obey His commandments
   b. The reasons
      1) God is the glorious Creator & Possessor of the universe
      2) God stooped down to love you & chose you to be His people even though He is the Supreme Owner of the universe

2. **Circumcise or cut sin out of your heart—do not be stiffnecked, stubborn**
   a. Because God is supreme, transcendent over all
   b. Because God is impartial & just: Shows no favoritism whatsoever—never accepts bribes
      1) He defends the poor & helpless & loves the foreigner
      2) He provides for the needy
   c. The expected response: To follow God's example, for they were foreigners in Egypt

3. **Keep close to God: Fear, serve, cling (hold fast) to God—take oaths only in His Name**
   a. Because God is your praise, your God
   b. Because God has done great things for you
      1) Saved you from Egypt
      2) Fulfilled His promise: Multiplied your seed, your descendants from 70 persons to over 3 million (Ge.46:27; see Nu.1:46)

4. **Remember what you have experienced; love & obey God**

I. The Nine Supreme Requirements of Obedience: What is Demanded by God, 10:12–11:32

12 And now, Israel, what doth the LORD thy God require of thee, but to fear the LORD thy God, to walk in all his ways, and to love him, and to serve the LORD thy God with all thy heart and with all thy soul,
13 To keep the commandments of the LORD, and his statutes, which I command thee this day for thy good?
14 Behold, the heaven and the heaven of heavens *is* the LORD's thy God, the earth *also*, with all that therein *is*.
15 Only the LORD had a delight in thy fathers to love them, and he chose their seed after them, *even* you above all people, as *it is* this day.
16 Circumcise therefore the foreskin of your heart, and be no more stiffnecked.
17 For the LORD your God *is* God of gods, and Lord of lords, a great God, a mighty, and a terrible, which regardeth not persons, nor taketh reward:
18 He doth execute the judgment of the fatherless and widow, and loveth the stranger, in giving him food and raiment.
19 Love ye therefore the stranger: for ye were strangers in the land of Egypt.
20 Thou shalt fear the LORD thy God; him shalt thou serve, and to him shalt thou cleave, and swear by his name.
21 He *is* thy praise, and he *is* thy God, that hath done for thee these great and terrible things, which thine eyes have seen.
22 Thy fathers went down into Egypt with threescore and ten persons; and now the LORD thy God hath made thee as the stars of heaven for multitude.

CHAPTER 11

Therefore thou shalt love the LORD thy God, and keep his charge, and his statutes, and his judgments, and his commandments, alway.
2 And know ye this day: for *I speak* not with your children which have not known, and which have not seen the chastisement of the LORD your God, his greatness, his mighty hand, and his stretched out arm,
3 And his miracles, and his acts, which he did in the midst of Egypt unto Pharaoh the king of Egypt, and unto all his land;
4 And what he did unto the army of Egypt, unto their horses, and to their chariots; how he made the water of the Red sea to overflow them as they pursued after you, and how the LORD hath destroyed them unto this day;
5 And what he did unto you in the wilderness, until ye came into this place;
6 And what he did unto Dathan and Abiram, the sons of Eliab, the son of Reuben: how the earth opened her mouth, and swallowed them up, and their households, and their tents, and all the substance that *was* in their possession, in the midst of all Israel:
7 But your eyes have seen all the great acts of the LORD which he did.
8 Therefore shall ye keep all the commandments which I command you this day, that ye may be strong, and go in and possess the land, whither ye go to possess it;
9 And that ye may prolong *your* days in the land, which the LORD sware unto your fathers to give unto them and to their seed, a land that floweth with milk and honey.
10 For the land, whither thou goest in to possess it, *is* not as the land of Egypt, from whence ye came out, where thou sowedst thy seed, and wateredst *it* with thy foot, as a garden of herbs:
11 But the land, whither ye go to possess it, *is* a land of hills and valleys, *and* drinketh water of the rain of heaven:
12 A land which the LORD thy God careth for: the eyes of the LORD thy God *are* always upon it, from the beginning of the year even unto the end of the year.

---

a. Remember: It was not your children who experienced the discipline or chastisement & the greatness & power of God

   1) His power in saving you from Egypt (a symbol of the world): The signs, terrible plagues God did

   2) His power in delivering you from being recaptured & enslaved by the enemy: His power in destroying the pursuing army in the Red Sea

b. Remember: It was not your children who experienced God's guidance through the wilderness wanderings, nor His judgment upon rebellion
   1) The example of the rebellion of Dathan & Abiram
   2) God miraculously caused an earthquake that swallowed them, their families, & all their possessions

c. Remember: It was you who personally experienced the great things God did

5. **Be careful—very careful—to keep all the commandments of God**
   a. Because you will be strong enough to conquer the promised land
   b. Because you will live long in the land: Keep & continue to possess it & to live in it
   c. Because the land will be blessed & cared for by God & made fruitful
      1) Is not a dry desert like Egypt that has to be irrigated

      2) Is a land of beautiful mountains & valleys with plenty of rain providing sufficient water

      3) Is a land watched over by God—day by day

DEUTERONOMY 10:12–11:32

d. Because obedience is the condition for receiving God's blessings upon the promised land: If you faithfully obey God with all your heart & soul

1) God will send rain in its season
2) God will give abundant crops: Plenty of food from the fields & vines & for the livestock
3) God will give satisfaction, fulfillment

6. **Guard against false worship & false gods**
   a. The danger: Will be enticed to turn away from God
   b. The results: The judgment of God
      1) Will suffer loss, scarcity: No water or food—no production
      2) Will perish, die—not survive in the promised land

7. **Be a strong testimony & witness for the LORD**
   a. How to be a testimony
      1) Lock God's commandments in your hearts & minds
      2) Teach the commandments to your children: Talk about them all day long no matter what you are doing
      3) Make your home a strong testimony for the LORD
   b. The result: Will live in the promised land permanently—as long as the heavens are above the earth

8. **Be victorious over all the enemies of the promised land**
   a. The condition: Allegiance
      1) Must obey & love God
      2) Must walk in His ways

13 And it shall come to pass, if ye shall hearken diligently unto my commandments which I command you this day, to love the LORD your God, and to serve him with all your heart and with all your soul,
14 That I will give *you* the rain of your land in his due season, the first rain and the latter rain, that thou mayest gather in thy corn, and thy wine, and thine oil.
15 And I will send grass in thy fields for thy cattle, that thou mayest eat and be full.
16 Take heed to yourselves, that your heart be not deceived, and ye turn aside, and serve other gods, and worship them;
17 And *then* the LORD's wrath be kindled against you, and he shut up the heaven, that there be no rain, and that the land yield not her fruit; and *lest* ye perish quickly from off the good land which the LORD giveth you.
18 Therefore shall ye lay up these my words in your heart and in your soul, and bind them for a sign upon your hand, that they may be as frontlets between your eyes.
19 And ye shall teach them your children, speaking of them when thou sittest in thine house, and when thou walkest by the way, when thou liest down, and when thou risest up.
20 And thou shalt write them upon the door posts of thine house, and upon thy gates:
21 That your days may be multiplied, and the days of your children, in the land which the LORD sware unto your fathers to give them, as the days of heaven upon the earth.
22 For if ye shall diligently keep all these commandments which I command you, to do them, to love the LORD your God, to walk in all his ways,

and to cleave unto him;
23 Then will the LORD drive out all these nations from before you, and ye shall possess greater nations and mightier than yourselves.
24 Every place whereon the soles of your feet shall tread shall be yours: from the wilderness and Lebanon, from the river, the river Euphrates, even unto the uttermost sea shall your coast be.
25 There shall no man be able to stand before you: *for* the LORD your God shall lay the fear of you and the dread of you upon all the land that ye shall tread upon, as he hath said unto you.
26 Behold, I set before you this day a blessing and a curse;
27 A blessing, if ye obey the commandments of the LORD your God, which I command you this day:
28 And a curse, if ye will not obey the commandments of the LORD your God, but turn aside out of the way which I command you this day, to go after other gods, which ye have not known.
29 And it shall come to pass, when the LORD thy God hath brought thee in unto the land whither thou goest to possess it, that thou shalt put the blessing upon mount Gerizim, and the curse upon mount Ebal.
30 *Are* they not on the other side Jordan, by the way where the sun goeth down, in the land of the Canaanites, which dwell in the champaign over against Gilgal, beside the plains of Moreh?
31 For ye shall pass over Jordan to go in to possess the land which the LORD your God giveth you, and ye shall possess it, and dwell therein.
32 And ye shall observe to do all the statutes and judgments which I set before you this day.

3) Must cling to Him
b. The results
   1) Will conquer, drive out all enemies no matter how large or strong—by the power of the LORD
   2) Will conquer a large territory: Every place your foot sets
      • The desert to Lebanon
      • The Euphrates River to the western sea
   3) Will be unstoppable
   4) Will be feared by all

9. **Know the consequence of your choices: A blessing or a curse**
   a. The facts & the choice
      1) To be blessed if one obeys God's commandments
      2) To be cursed if one disobeys God's commandments:
         • By turning away
         • By following false gods or false worship
   b. The charge to hold a ceremony to proclaim the blessings & curses
      1) When: After entering the promised land
      2) Where: On two mountains—to proclaim the blessings from Mt. Gerizim & the cursings from Mount Ebal
   c. The strong encouragement & assurance: You are about to enter the promised land
   d. The final charge: After conquering the promised land, be sure to escape the curses of disobedience—obey all the laws & commandments of God

DIVISION III

THE SECOND GREAT THEME PREACHED BY GOD'S AGED SERVANT (PART 1): REMEMBER THE TEN COMMANDMENTS—THE FUNDAMENTAL LAWS TO GOVERN MAN AND SOCIETY, 4:44–11:32

I. **The Nine Supreme Requirements of Obedience: What is Demanded by God, 10:12–11:32**

DEUTERONOMY 10:12–11:32

(10:12–11:32) Introduction: certain things—requirements—are necessary in order to maintain any relationship. Certain kinds of behavior are required. Requirements are necessary in order to maintain order and build strength of character. For example, what are the requirements established—what kind of behavior is expected—by your parents, school, employer, wife, husband, neighbor, civic club, or government? We become stronger persons when we fulfill those requirements. But before we can fulfill them, we must know what the requirements are.

This was a great concern to Moses as the leader of the Israelites. Certain requirements were demanded by God. Moses was concerned that the Israelites might not understand God's requirements. Yet understanding was absolutely essential, for the requirements would determine their eternal fate. If they fulfilled the requirements of God, they would live victorious lives. But if they failed in the requirements, they would never enter the promised land. They would live defeated lives, becoming engrossed in the world and enslaved by it. They would live immoral, unjust, and corrupt lives and be doomed to face the eternal judgment of God. For this reason, Moses had to make sure—absolutely sure—that the people understood the requirements of God. This is the subject of this great passage of Scripture: *The Nine Supreme Requirements of Obedience: What is Demanded by God*, 10:12-11:32.

1. Pledge allegiance to the LORD (vv.12-15).
2. Circumcise or cut sin out of your heart—do not be stiff-necked, stubborn (vv.16-19).
3. Keep close to God: fear, serve, cling (hold fast) to God—take oaths only in His Name (vv.20-22).
4. Remember what you have experienced; love and obey God (ch.11:1-7).
5. Be careful—very careful—to keep all the commandments of God (vv.8-15).
6. Guard against false worship and false gods (vv.16-17).
7. Be a strong testimony and witness for the LORD (vv.18-21).
8. Be victorious over all the enemies of the promised land (vv.22-25).
9. Know the consequence of your choices: a blessing or a curse (vv.26-32).

1 **(10:12-15) Allegiance, Duty—Commitment, Duty—Dedication, Duty—Believers, Chosen—Chosen, by God—Law, of God—Obedience, Duty—Commandments, Duty to Obey**: What does the LORD God require of you? First, pledge allegiance to the LORD. In building any relationship, allegiance is an absolute necessity. Within marriage, the pledge of allegiance is essential. Friendship requires allegiance; so does belonging to a civic club. A person's employer or his job requires allegiance. A student must give his or her allegiance to the school in order to secure an education. Nations require allegiance. Just as American citizens pledge their allegiance to the flag of the United States of America, so the citizens of other nations pledge their allegiance to their national flag. The point is self-evident: allegiance is an absolute necessity in building any strong relationship. God wants a strong relationship with His people; therefore, He demands the allegiance of His people. Note how Moses stressed this fact as he stood before the people preaching:

OUTLINE	SCRIPTURE	SCRIPTURE	OUTLINE

1. Pledge allegiance to the LORD
  a. The meaning
    1) Fear the LORD
    2) Walk in all His ways
    3) Love Him
    4) Serve Him with all your heart & soul
 	
    5) Keep, obey His commandments
	12 And now, Israel, what doth the LORD thy God require of thee, but to fear the LORD thy God, to walk in all his ways, and to love him, and to serve the LORD thy God with all thy heart and with all thy soul,
	13 To keep the commandments of the LORD, and his statutes, which I command
		thee this day for thy good?
		14 Behold, the heaven and the heaven of heavens *is* the LORD's thy God, the earth *also*, with all that therein *is*.
		15 Only the LORD had a delight in thy fathers to love them, and he chose their seed after them, *even* you above all people, as *it is* this day.
			b. The reasons
			  1) God is the glorious Creator & Possessor of the universe
			  2) God stooped down to love you & chose you to be His people even though He is the Supreme Owner of the universe

  a. Allegiance is an absolute necessity. Moses shouted out, we must pledge allegiance to the LORD. But what does allegiance mean: What is it exactly that the LORD God requires (vv.12-13)?

    1) We must fear the LORD (v.12). To fear means to reverence and honor the LORD, to hold Him in such high esteem that we worship Him. To fear also means to respect the justice and judgment of God, to know that we should shrink back and do whatever is necessary to escape His judgment. The person who pledges his allegiance to the LORD is a person who fears the LORD, truly fears Him.

    2) We must walk in all the ways of God (v.12). There are many ways in life that a person can take. There is the way of worldliness and of the flesh; the way of greed and of possessions; the way of drugs and of alcohol; the way of lawlessness and violence; the way of pride and unbelief; the way of false religion and false worship. There are many, many ways to walk throughout this life. A person can commit his life, his walk to almost anything. But God demands that we walk in all His ways, that we totally dedicate our lives to Him, commit ourselves wholeheartedly to His ways. We owe our utmost devotion to Him, to walk in all His ways.

    3) We must love the LORD (v.12). To love God means that we adore and cherish Him; that He is ever so precious to us and that we want a deep, intense, intimate relationship with Him; that we are devoted and attached to Him and that we hold Him ever so near and dear to our hearts; that we trust Him and are captivated by Him; and that we have an undying fervor to be close to Him. This is what it means to pledge our allegiance to the LORD: we love Him.

    4) We must serve the LORD with all our hearts and souls (v.12). To serve God means to minister and meet the needs of people; to meet their need for the necessities of life such as food, housing, and clothing. To serve God also means to bear strong witness and testimony for Him. A person who pledges His allegiance to the LORD serves the LORD with all his heart and soul.

DEUTERONOMY 10:12–11:32

5) We must keep, obey His commandments (v.13). To pledge allegiance to the LORD means obedience, that we do exactly what He commands, that we keep every single commandment.

b. Now, why does God demand allegiance? Why does the LORD require us to do these things—to fear Him, walk in all His ways, love Him, serve Him, and keep all His commandments? Why must we pledge our allegiance to the LORD? Standing there preaching to the people, Moses answered the question (vv.14-15).

1) The fact that God is the glorious Creator and Possessor of the universe is the reason we owe our allegiance to Him (v.14). It was God who created the universe, both the earth and all the bodies hanging in outer space. It was God who established the laws of reproduction among men and animals. It was God who willed and caused us to be born into the world. All the heavenly bodies above—even the highest heavenly bodies, the earth and everything in it—belong to the LORD. The LORD is the glorious Creator and Possessor of the entire universe. This is the reason God demands that we pledge our allegiance to Him.

2) The fact that God, the Supreme Owner of the universe, stooped down to love us and chose us to be His people is the reason we owe our allegiance to Him (v.15). Just imagine! The great God and glorious Creator of the entire universe has humbled Himself by stooping down to love us. He possesses everything, yet He humbled Himself to reach out and to choose us to be His people, His family, His adopted sons and daughters. He has loved and chosen us. For this reason, He demands our allegiance.

Thought 1. What does the LORD God require of us? That we pledge our allegiance to Him. We must be totally dedicated to the LORD. We must...
- fear the LORD
- walk in all His ways
- love Him
- serve Him wholeheartedly
- keep, obey all His commandments

This is what the LORD God requires of us. He is the great Creator and Sovereign Ruler of the universe. He alone dwells in the majestic glory and splendor of perfection, overlooking the whole universe as Sovereign LORD and Possessor of all things. Yet He stooped down; He humbled Himself to love and choose us—all believers—to be His people. Through Jesus Christ He has made it possible for us to become His sons and daughters, a part of the family of God. For these reasons, we must totally dedicate, wholeheartedly commit our lives to Him. We must pledge our allegiance to the LORD.

> "And he said to *them* all, If any *man* will come after me, let him deny himself, and take up his cross daily, and follow me" (Lu.9:23).
>
> "I beseech you therefore, brethren, by the mercies of God, that ye present your bodies a living sacrifice, holy, acceptable unto God, *which is* your reasonable service. And be not conformed to this world: but be ye transformed by the renewing of your mind, that ye may prove what is that good, and acceptable, and perfect, will of God" (Ro.12:1-2).
>
> "Therefore, my beloved brethren, be ye stedfast, unmovable, always abounding in the work of the LORD, forasmuch as ye know that your labour is not in vain in the LORD" (1 Co.15:58).
>
> "For Moses had said, Consecrate yourselves to day to the LORD, even every man upon his son, and upon his brother; that he may bestow upon you a blessing this day" (Ex.32:29).
>
> "And thou shalt love the LORD thy God with all thine heart, and with all thy soul, and with all thy might" (De.6:5).
>
> "Trust in the LORD with all thine heart; and lean not unto thine own understanding" (Pr.3:5).
>
> "My son, give me thine heart, and let thine eyes observe my ways" (Pr.23:26).
>
> "Blessed *are* they that keep his testimonies, *and that* seek him with the whole heart" (Ps.119:2).
>
> "Therefore also now, saith the LORD, turn ye *even* to me with all your heart, and with fasting, and with weeping, and with mourning" (Joel 2:12).

[2] (10:16-19) **Sin, Duty—Stiff-necked, Duty—Stubborn, Duty—Favoritism, Duty—Partiality, Duty—God, Nature of—Circumcision, Spiritual**: What does the LORD God require of you? Second, circumcise or cut sin out of your heart. Do not be stiff-necked, stubborn. You must be operated upon, undergo a "spiritual circumcision" (Col.2:9-12). Spiritual surgery must be performed on you. The sins of the old nature and of the old life must be removed. This point was of critical importance. Moses knew this. He knew that God's judgment would fall upon the people, that they could never remain in the promised land if sin were in their lives. Unless the sin were circumcised, cut out of their hearts, they would lose the promises of God, lose their inheritance in the promised land. Because of this, Moses drove the point home to the people:

OUTLINE	SCRIPTURE	SCRIPTURE	OUTLINE
2. Circumcise or cut sin out of your heart—do not be stiff-necked, stubborn a. Because God is supreme, transcendent over all	16 Circumcise therefore the foreskin of your heart, and be no more stiffnecked. 17 For the LORD your God *is* God of gods, and Lord of	lords, a great God, a mighty, and a terrible, which regardeth not persons, nor taketh reward: 18 He doth execute the judg-	b. Because God is impartial & just: Shows no favoritism whatsoever—never accepts bribes 1) He defends the poor &

DEUTERONOMY 10:12–11:32

OUTLINE	SCRIPTURE	SCRIPTURE	OUTLINE
helpless & loves the foreigner 2) He provides for the needy	ment of the fatherless and widow, and loveth the stranger, in giving him food and raiment.	19 Love ye therefore the stranger: for ye were strangers in the land of Egypt.	c. The expected response: To follow God's example, for they were foreigners in Egypt

Why must the people circumcise or cut the sin out of their hearts? Why must they not be stiff-necked, stubborn any more? Moses told the people why. Because God is supreme, transcendent over all. The LORD your God is God of gods and LORD of lords. He is the great God, mighty and awesome (v.17). The idea is that God will execute justice and judgment upon the people if they sin and become stiff-necked and stubborn. The disobedient, the person who breaks the commandments of God, will be judged. And note what Moses declared: God is impartial and just. He shows no favoritism whatsoever and never accepts bribes. Among men, the wealthy may be able to buy judges and juries to escape judgment. The wealthy make take advantage of the poor and helpless and foreigners in the courts of this earth. But God never accepts bribes. No person can buy His favor in order to escape judgment. On the contrary, God defends the poor and helpless and loves the foreigner. He provides for the needy. In the matter of justice and judgment, God is impartial and just, perfectly just. This is the point Moses had to get across to the people: they must cut sin out of their hearts. They must not refuse to keep and obey God's commandments. And in dealing with the poor and needy, they must follow God's example: defend them and provide for their needs. This they must do because they were foreigners in Egypt.

Thought 1. The lesson for us is clear and forceful: we too must cut sin out of our hearts. We must not be stiff-necked and stubborn against God, rejecting and refusing to obey Him. The *old man*, the *old life*, must be put out of our lives. We must put away all sin.

> "And that ye put on the new man, which after God is created in righteousness and true holiness. Wherefore putting away lying, speak every man truth with his neighbour: for we are members one of another. Be ye angry, and sin not: let not the sun go down upon your wrath: Neither give place to the devil. Let him that stole steal no more: but rather let him labour, working with *his* hands the thing which is good, that he may have to give to him that needeth. Let no corrupt communication proceed out of your mouth, but that which is good to the use of edifying, that it may minister grace unto the hearers. And grieve not the holy Spirit of God, whereby ye are sealed unto the day of redemption. Let all bitterness, and wrath, and anger, and clamour, and evil speaking, be put away from you, with all malice: And be ye kind one to another, tenderhearted, forgiving one another, even as God for Christ's sake hath forgiven you" (Ep.4:24-32).

> "Mortify [put to death] therefore your members which are upon the earth; fornication, uncleanness, inordinate affection, evil concupiscence, and covetousness, which is idolatry: For which things' sake the wrath of God cometh on the children of disobedience: In the which ye also walked some time, when ye lived in them. But now ye also put off all these; anger, wrath, malice, blasphemy, filthy communication out of your mouth. Lie not one to another, seeing that ye have put off the old man with his deeds; And have put on the new *man,* which is renewed in knowledge after the image of him that created him: Where there is neither Greek nor Jew, circumcision nor uncircumcision, Barbarian, Scythian, bond *nor* free: but Christ *is* all, and in all. Put on therefore, as the elect of God, holy and beloved, bowels of mercies, kindness, humbleness of mind, meekness, longsuffering; Forbearing one another, and forgiving one another, if any man have a quarrel against any: even as Christ forgave you, so also *do* ye" (Col.3:5-13).

Thought 2. What does the ritual of circumcision say to believers today?
(1) Jesus Christ has performed a *spiritual circumcision* upon believers, cutting away the old sinful nature of the believer. But He cuts away more than just a piece of flesh; He performs radical surgery: He cuts away the whole body of sin, all the sin which the believer has committed and for which he stands guilty.

> "In whom also ye are circumcised with the circumcision made without hands, in putting off the body of the sins of the flesh by the circumcision of Christ: buried with him in baptism, wherein also ye are risen with him through the faith of the operation of God, who hath raised him from the dead" (Col.2:11-12).

(2) Circumcision—God's true circumcision—is of the heart, not of the flesh. God never intended circumcision to be only a ritual, a physical sign that one belonged to the people of God. Yes, circumcision was to be a sign, but a sign of spiritual truth, a sign that a person's heart belonged to God, a sign that one was following and living for God fully and completely.

> "For he is not a Jew, which is one outwardly; neither is that circumcision, which is outward in the flesh: but he is a Jew, which is one inwardly; and circumcision is that of the heart, in the spirit, and not in the letter; whose praise is not of men, but of God" (Ro.2:28-29).
> "Circumcise therefore the foreskin of your heart, and be no more stiffnecked" (De.10:16).
> "And the LORD thy God will circumcise thine heart, and the heart of thy seed, to love the LORD thy God with all thine heart, and with all thy soul, that thou mayest live" (De.30:6).

DEUTERONOMY 10:12–11:32

Warren Wiersbe says this about the believer's spiritual circumcision:

> *What does all of this [circumcision] mean to Christian believers today?...We have experienced a "spiritual circumcision" (Col.2:9-12) that makes us part of the "true circumcision" (Ph.3:1-3). When we trusted Christ to save us, the Spirit of God performed "spiritual surgery" that enables us to have victory over the desires of the old nature and the old life. Circumcision removes only a part of the body, but the true "spiritual circumcision" puts off "the body of the sins of the flesh" (Col.2:11) and deals radically with the sin nature.*
>
> *This "spiritual circumcision" is accomplished at conversion when the sinner believes in Christ and is baptized by the Spirit into the body of Christ (1 Co.12:13). This baptism identifies the believer with Christ in His death, burial, resurrection, and ascension, and also in His circumcision (Col.2:11-12; Luke 2:21). It is not "the circumcision of Moses" but "the circumcision of Christ" that is important to the Christian believer.*[1]

(3) Believers are the true circumcision who worship God in the spirit and rejoice in Christ Jesus, in His power to remove sin.

"For we are the circumcision, which worship God in the spirit, and rejoice in Christ Jesus, and have no confidence in the flesh" (Ph.3:3).

3 **(10:20-22) Nearness, to God—Closeness, to God—Hold Fast, Duty—Steadfastness, Duty—Cling, Duty—Fear, Duty—Serve, Duty—Believer, Duty—Oaths, Duty:** What does the LORD God require of you? Third, keep close to God: fear, serve, cling (hold fast) to God. Take oaths only in His name. There is no other living God; therefore, there is no other God by whom to swear oaths in making agreements with other people. The LORD your God is the only living and true God; therefore, oaths are to be taken only in His name. He alone is the One to fear and serve. We are to hold fast to Him and Him alone.

OUTLINE	SCRIPTURE	SCRIPTURE	OUTLINE
3. Keep close to God: Fear, serve, cling (hold fast) to God—take oaths only in His Name	20 Thou shalt fear the LORD thy God; him shalt thou serve, and to him shalt thou cleave, and swear by his name.	things, which thine eyes have seen.	things for you
		22 Thy fathers went down into Egypt with threescore and ten persons; and now the LORD thy God hath made thee as the stars of heaven for multitude.	1) Saved you from Egypt
a. Because God is your praise, your God	21 He *is* thy praise, and he *is* thy God, that hath done for thee these great and terrible		2) Fulfilled His promise: Multiplied your seed, your descendants from 70 persons to over 3 million (Ge.46:27; see Nu.1:46)
b. Because God has done great			

Moses gave two reasons why a person must stay close to God. Standing there preaching, he first of all proclaimed, you must stay close to God because He is the LORD your praise, your God (v.21). He has chosen you and set you apart to be His follower, and you claim that you are a follower of the LORD. As the LORD *your* God, He is your praise, the object of your devotion. You are, therefore, to honor and praise Him, lifting up His name before all the immoral and unrighteous neighbors who surround you.

Second, you are to stay close to God because God has done so much for you (vv.21-22). God has saved you from Egypt, from all the bondages and enslavements of this world. Moreover, God is fulfilling His promises to the forefathers and to you. He has multiplied your seed, your descendants from seventy persons to over three million (Ge.46:27, see Nu.1:46).

> **Thought 1.** What does the LORD require of us? That we stay close to Him, that we fear, serve, and cling to Him. Beyond question, He is the LORD *our* God. He has saved us from the bondages and enslavements of this world: from sin, death, and the condemnation to come. God has saved us, delivered us from so terrible a fate. And He is fulfilling His promises to us: looking after and caring for us day by day, giving us victorious lives. He is empowering us to conquer all the enemies of this life that seek to destroy and keep us out of the promised land. God is doing so much for us that we owe Him our lives. He is our praise, our thanksgiving, our honor, our Savior, our LORD—our God. For this reason we must stay close, ever so near God. We must fear, serve, cling, hold fast to Him. This is what He demands or requires of us: our total allegiance.

> "Therefore, my beloved brethren, be ye stedfast, unmovable, always abounding in the work of the LORD, forasmuch as ye know that your labour is not in vain in the LORD" (1 Co.15:58).
>
> "Stand fast therefore in the liberty wherewith Christ hath made us free, and be not entangled again with the yoke of bondage" (Ga.5:1).
>
> "Let us draw near with a true heart in full assurance of faith, having our hearts sprinkled from an evil conscience, and our bodies washed with pure water" (He.10:22).
>
> "Let us hold fast the profession of *our* faith without wavering; (for he is faithful that promised;)" (He.10:23).
>
> "Draw nigh to God, and he will draw nigh to you. Cleanse *your* hands, *ye* sinners; and purify *your* hearts, *ye* double minded" (Js.4:8).

---

[1] Warren W. Wiersbe. *Be Obedient.* (Wheaton, IL: Victor Books, 1991), pp.69-70.

"Remember therefore how thou hast received and heard, and hold fast, and repent. If therefore thou shalt not watch, I will come on thee as a thief, and thou shalt not know what hour I will come upon thee" (Re.3:3).

"And, behold, I *am* with thee, and will keep thee in all *places* whither thou goest, and will bring thee again into this land; for I will not leave thee, until I have done *that* which I have spoken to thee of" (Ge.28:15).

"And he said, My presence shall go *with thee,* and I will give thee rest" (Ex.33:14).

"I have set the LORD always before me: because *he is* at my right hand, I shall not be moved" (Ps.16:8).

"The LORD *is* nigh unto them that are of a broken heart; and saveth such as be of a contrite spirit" (Ps.34:18).

"But *it is* good for me to draw near to God: I have put my trust in the LORD GOD, that I may declare all thy works" (Ps.73:28).

"The LORD *is* nigh unto all them that call upon him, to all that call upon him in truth" (Ps.145:18).

"*Am* I a God at hand, saith the LORD, and not a God afar off" (Je.23:23).

4 (11:1-7) **Love, Duty—Obedience, Duty—Salvation, Duty—Remember, Duty—Guidance, of God, Duty**: What does the LORD God require of you? Fourth, love and obey God. And remember what you have experienced. Learn from your past and this will help you to love and obey God. Moses exhorted the people to remember the power of God, how God had mightily saved them and guided them in the past. If they would stay focused upon the glorious experiences of the past, this would encourage them to love and obey God.

OUTLINE	SCRIPTURE	SCRIPTURE	OUTLINE
	CHAPTER 11	horses, and to their chariots; how he made the water of the Red sea to overflow them as they pursued after you, and *how* the LORD hath destroyed them unto this day;	tured & enslaved by the enemy: His power in destroying the pursuing army in the Red Sea
4. Remember what you have experienced; love & obey God	Therefore thou shalt love the LORD thy God, and keep his charge, and his statutes, and his judgments, and his commandments, alway.		
a. Remember: It was not your children who experienced the discipline or chastisement & the greatness & power of God	2 And know ye this day: for *I speak* not with your children which have not known, and which have not seen the chastisement of the LORD your God, his greatness, his mighty hand, and his stretched out arm,	5 And what he did unto you in the wilderness, until ye came into this place; 6 And what he did unto Dathan and Abiram, the sons of Eliab, the son of Reuben: how the earth opened her mouth, and swallowed them up, and their households, and their tents, and all the substance that *was* in their possession, in the midst of all Israel:	b. Remember: It was not your children who experienced God's guidance through the wilderness wanderings, nor His judgment upon rebellion 1) The example of the rebellion of Dathan & Abiram 2) God miraculously caused an earthquake that swallowed them, their families, & all their possessions
1) His power in saving you from Egypt (a symbol of the world): The signs, terrible plagues God did	3 And his miracles, and his acts, which he did in the midst of Egypt unto Pharaoh the king of Egypt, and unto all his land;		
2) His power in delivering you from being recap-	4 And what he did unto the army of Egypt, unto their	7 But your eyes have seen all the great acts of the LORD which he did.	c. Remember: It was you who personally experienced the great things God did

a. Note how Moses exhorted the people. He shouted out, it was not your children who experienced the discipline and the greatness and power of God (vv.2-4). It was not your children who experienced the salvation of God from Egypt, who saw the signs and terrible plagues that fell upon Egypt (v.3). It was not your children who witnessed the power of God that kept you from being recaptured and enslaved by the enemy, who witnessed His power in destroying the pursuing army in the Red Sea (v.4).

b. Note how Moses continued to exhort the people: it was not your children who experienced God's guidance through the wilderness wanderings, nor His judgment upon the sinners and rebels who followed Dathan and Abiram (see Map of the Wilderness Wanderings of Israel on page 436). It was not your children who saw God miraculously cause an earthquake that swallowed them, their families, and all their possessions.

c. But remember, it was *you* who personally experienced the great things God did (v.7). It was *you* who were saved by God from Egypt, from its bondage and enslavement. It was *you* who personally saw the terrible judgment of God against the Egyptians. It was *you* who witnessed His power in destroying their pursuing army in the Red Sea. It was *you* who personally experienced God's guidance through the wilderness wanderings. Moreover, *you* witnessed the power of God's judgment against sinners and rebels when He caused an earthquake to swallow the followers of Dathan and Abiram. *You* have personally experienced the discipline or chastisement of God. *You* have personally witnessed God's majesty, His mighty hand, His outstretched arm, His awesome power. Remember what *you* have experienced; love and obey God. This is what the LORD God requires of *you*.

Thought 1. What does the LORD God require of us? That we love and obey Him and that we remember what we have experienced with Him. Remembering the past will stir us to love and obey God. Just think for a moment:

⇒ God has saved us from Egypt, that is, from the world with all its enslavements and bondages: saved us from sin, condemnation, and hell to come. God has marvelously saved us.
⇒ God guides us day by day through the wilderness wanderings of this world, giving us a victorious life. He empowers us to conquer all the enemies—all the trials and temptations of life—that attempt to destroy us and to keep us out of the promised land of heaven.
⇒ God disciplines or chastises us, corrects us when we need it in order to keep us from injuring ourselves or damaging our testimony. God has done so much for us that we owe Him our allegiance. We must, therefore, love and obey Him. And we must remember the past, all the wonderful things He has done for us. Remembering the past will encourage us to love and obey Him.

(1) God demands, requires that we love Him.

"And thou shalt love the LORD thy God with all thine heart, and with all thy soul, and with all thy might" (De.6:5).
"And now, Israel, what doth the LORD thy God require of thee, but to fear the LORD thy God, to walk in all his ways, and to love him, and to serve the LORD thy God with all thy heart and with all thy soul" (De.10:12).
"O love the LORD, all ye his saints: *for* the LORD preserveth the faithful, and plentifully rewardeth the proud doer" (Ps.31:23).
"And the LORD direct your hearts into the love of God, and into the patient waiting for Christ" (2 Th.3:5).
"Keep yourselves in the love of God, looking for the mercy of our Lord Jesus Christ unto eternal life" (Jude 21).

(2) God demands that we keep His commandments, obey Him.

"Not every one that saith unto me, LORD, LORD, shall enter into the kingdom of heaven; but he that doeth the will of my Father which is in heaven" (Mt.7:21).
"Ye are my friends, if ye do whatsoever I command you" (Jn.15:14).
"He that hath my commandments, and keepeth them, he it is that loveth me: and he that loveth me shall be loved of my Father, and I will love him, and will manifest myself to him" (Jn.14:21).
"Then Peter and the *other* apostles answered and said, We ought to obey God rather than men" (Ac.5:29).
"This day the LORD thy God hath commanded thee to do these statutes and judgments: thou shalt therefore keep and do them with all thine heart, and with all thy soul" (De.26:16).
"And Samuel said, Hath the LORD *as great* delight in burnt offerings and sacrifices, as in obeying the voice of the LORD? Behold, to obey *is* better than sacrifice, *and* to hearken than the fat of rams" (1 S.15:22).

[5] (11:8-15) **Obedience, Duty—Commandments, Duty, to Obey**: What does the LORD God require of you? Fifth, be careful—very careful—to keep all the commandments of God. Moses knew that obedience was an absolute essential in order for God's people to live full and victorious lives. Above all else, victory was dependent upon obedience. No believer would ever be allowed to live in the land of God unless he obeyed God. For this reason, Moses exhorted the people to keep all the commandments of God.

OUTLINE	SCRIPTURE	SCRIPTURE	OUTLINE
5. Be careful—very careful—to keep all the commandments of God a. Because you will be strong enough to conquer the promised land b. Because you will live long in the land: Keep & continue to possess it & to live in it c. Because the land will be blessed & cared for by God & made fruitful 1) Is not a dry desert like Egypt that has to be irrigated 2) Is a land of beautiful	8 Therefore shall ye keep all the commandments which I command you this day, that ye may be strong, and go in and possess the land, whither ye go to possess it; 9 And that ye may prolong *your* days in the land, which the LORD sware unto your fathers to give unto them and to their seed, a land that floweth with milk and honey. 10 For the land, whither thou goest in to possess it, *is* not as the land of Egypt, from whence ye came out, where thou sowedst thy seed, and wateredst *it* with thy foot, as a garden of herbs: 11 But the land, whither ye	go to possess it, *is* a land of hills and valleys, *and* drinketh water of the rain of heaven: 12 A land which the LORD thy God careth for: the eyes of the LORD thy God *are* always upon it, from the beginning of the year even unto the end of the year. 13 And it shall come to pass, if ye shall hearken diligently unto my commandments which I command you this day, to love the LORD your God, and to serve him with all your heart and with all your soul, 14 That I will give *you* the rain of your land in his due season, the first rain and the	mountains & valleys with plenty of rain providing sufficient water 3) Is a land watched over by God—day by day d. Because obedience is the condition for receiving God's blessings upon the promised land: If you faithfully obey God with all your heart & soul 1) God will send rain in its season 2) God will give abundant

DEUTERONOMY 10:12–11:32

OUTLINE	SCRIPTURE	SCRIPTURE	OUTLINE
crops: Plenty of food from the fields & vines & for the livestock	latter rain, that thou mayest gather in thy corn, and thy wine, and thine oil.	15 And I will send grass in thy fields for thy cattle, that thou mayest eat and be full.	3) God will give satisfaction, fulfillment

a. Moses declared: obey God. If you obey the commandments of God, you will be strong enough to conquer the promised land (v.8). When you cross the Jordan into the land, God will give you the strength to conquer the enemies who will confront you. You will march forth as conquerors, living victorious lives in the promised land of God. Obedience will make you strong, assure you of God's very special strength.

b. Moses declared: obey God. If you keep the commandments of God, you will live a long time in the promised land (v.9). The idea is that the Israelites would continue to possess the promised land and live in it. But if they were unfaithful, disobedient, then other nations would conquer and deport them as slaves. Disobedience would cause the loss of the promised land.

c. Moses declared: obey God. If you keep the commandments of God, the promised land will be blessed and cared for by God and made fruitful (vv.9-12). God will make sure that the land flows with milk and honey:
 1) The land will not be a dry desert like Egypt that had to be irrigated (v.10).
 2) The land will be a land of beautiful mountains and valleys with plenty of rainfall providing more than sufficient water for the people, livestock, and crops (v.11).
 3) The land will be a land watched over by God day by day (v.12). The eyes of God will continually be upon the land from the beginning of the year to the ending of the year.

d. Moses declared: obey God. You must obey God because obedience is the condition for receiving God's blessings upon the promised land. If you faithfully obey God with all your heart and soul...
- God will send rain in its season (v.14)
- God will give abundant crops, plenty of food from the fields and vines for His people and the livestock (vv.14-15)
- God will give satisfaction, fulfillment to the human heart (v.15)

Thought 1. The lesson is evident and forceful: we must be careful—very careful—to keep all the commandments of God. The blessings of God are dependent upon obedience. If we obey God, we receive the promised land of heaven and will have God's blessings poured out upon us. We walk through life conquering all the enemies that confront us, that is, all the trials and temptations that seek to defeat and destroy us. If we keep the commandments of God, our bodies are healthier and so is society. There is far less lawlessness and violence within a community when its people keep God's commandments. This is the reason God demands obedience. He wants us living victorious lives upon this earth. He wants us marching to the promised land as conquerors, being victorious over all that ever confronts us. But we must remember: obedience is the essential ingredient. Obedience is that which gives us victory. Obedience causes the power of God to work in our lives and in our environment. Obedience arouses God to bless us, to pour His blessings out upon us. This is the reason we must obey God, keep all His commandments.

"Therefore whosoever heareth these sayings of mine, and doeth them, I will liken him unto a wise man, which built his house upon a rock: And the rain descended, and the floods came, and the winds blew, and beat upon that house; and it fell not: for it was founded upon a rock. And every one that heareth these sayings of mine, and doeth them not, shall be likened unto a foolish man, which built his house upon the sand: And the rain descended, and the floods came, and the winds blew, and beat upon that house; and it fell: and great was the fall of it" (Mt.7:24-27).

"Not every one that saith unto me, LORD, LORD, shall enter into the kingdom of heaven; but he that doeth the will of my Father which is in heaven" (Mt.7:21).

"He that hath my commandments, and keepeth them, he it is that loveth me: and he that loveth me shall be loved of my Father, and I will love him, and will manifest myself to him" (Jn.14:21).

"If ye keep my commandments, ye shall abide in my love; even as I have kept my Father's commandments, and abide in his love" (Jn.15:10).

"Jesus answered and said unto him, If a man love me, he will keep my words: and my Father will love him, and we will come unto him, and make our abode with him" (Jn.14:23).

"But whoso looketh into the perfect law of liberty, and continueth *therein*, he being not a forgetful hearer, but a doer of the work, this man shall be blessed in his deed" (Js.1:25).

"Nevertheless we, according to his promise, look for new heavens and a new earth, wherein dwell-eth righteousness. Wherefore, beloved, seeing that ye look for such things, be diligent that ye may be found of him in peace, without spot, and blameless" (2 Pe.3:13-14).

"Blessed *are* they that do his commandments, that they may have right to the tree of life, and may enter in through the gates into the city" (Re.22:14).

"Now therefore, if ye will obey my voice indeed, and keep my covenant, then ye shall be a peculiar treasure unto me above all people: for all the earth *is* mine" (Ex.19:5).

"O that there were such an heart in them, that they would fear me, and keep all my commandments always, that it might be well with them, and with their children for ever" (De.5:29).

"And if thou wilt walk in my ways, to keep my statutes and my commandments, as thy father David did walk, then I will lengthen thy days" (1 K.3:14).

"This book of the law shall not depart out of thy mouth; but thou shalt meditate therein day and night, that thou mayest observe to do according to all that is written therein: for then thou shalt make thy way prosperous, and then thou shalt have good success" (Jos.1:8).

DEUTERONOMY 10:12–11:32

6 **(11:16-17) Idolatry, Duty—False Worship, Duty—Warning, Against False Worship—Warning, Against False Gods:** What does the LORD God require of you? Guard against false worship and false gods. Many of the people surrounding the Israelites were false worshippers who followed false gods, gods of their own imaginations and gods of idols. It was necessary that Moses warn the people against idolatry and false worship. There was the danger that they might be enticed by their neighbors, influenced to join in their false worship (v.16). Being seduced by their neighbors was a real live possibility. For this reason, they must be warned. If they turned to false worship and idolatry, the judgment of God would fall upon them. The LORD's anger would burn against them, and they would suffer loss and scarcity. The LORD would shut the heavens so that it would not rain and the ground would yield no produce. There would be drought and few crops and insufficient water for livestock. The people and the livestock would soon perish or be forced to move out of the land, seeking water. The result would be most tragic: they would perish, lose the promised land (v.17).

OUTLINE	SCRIPTURE	SCRIPTURE	OUTLINE
6. Guard against false worship & false gods a. The danger: Will be enticed to turn away from God b. The results: The judgment of God	16 Take heed to yourselves, that your heart be not deceived, and ye turn aside, and serve other gods, and worship them; 17 And *then* the LORD's wrath be kindled against you,	and he shut up the heaven, that there be no rain, and that the land yield not her fruit; and *lest* ye perish quickly from off the good land which the LORD giveth you.	1) Will suffer loss, scarcity: No water or food—no production 2) Will perish, die—not survive in the promised land

Thought 1. The one demand of God above all other demands is this: we must guard against false worship and false gods. This is exactly what the first two commandments demand.

> **"You shall have no other gods before me" (De.5:7).**
> **"You shall not make for yourself an idol in the form of anything in heaven above or on the earth beneath or in the waters below" (De.5:8).**

If we commit the sins of idolatry and false worship, the judgment of God will fall upon us. We will not inherit the promised land of heaven. Neither will we have the presence of God as we walk day by day throughout life. To worship an idol or a god created by our own imaginations is tragic. To worship an idea of what we think God is instead of who God reveals Himself to be in the Holy Scripture is the depth of folly. Totally unreasonable! To worship some imagination or some idea that we have in our minds or some idol means that we are worshipping nothing. Only the LORD God is reality. He alone is the true and living God who can actually help us in time of need. If we do not worship Him, then we have no help outside of ourselves. We have nothing to help us beyond man himself. And the help of man is limited. Man cannot guarantee the shining of the sun nor the fall of the rain to produce crops. Man cannot even guarantee the air he breathes. And man certainly cannot guarantee life beyond this world. At most, medicine can extend our lives just a few years. As stated, if all we worship is some idol or some idea of God that we imagine in our minds, then we will have nothing to help us in time of need. We must—absolutely must—guard against idolatry and false worship. We must not allow the false worship of our neighbors to influence us. We must not be enticed, seduced to idolatry and false worship.

> **"For the wrath of God is revealed from heaven against all ungodliness and unrighteousness of men, who hold the truth in unrighteousness....Because that, when they knew God, they glorified *him* not as God, neither were thankful; but became vain in their imaginations, and their foolish heart was darkened. Professing themselves to be wise, they became fools, And changed the glory of the uncorruptible God into an image made like to corruptible man, and to birds, and fourfooted beasts, and creeping things. Wherefore God also gave them up to uncleanness through the lusts of their own hearts, to dishonour their own bodies between themselves: Who changed the truth of God into a lie, and worshipped and served the creature more than the Creator, who is blessed for ever. Amen" (Ro.1:18, 21-25).**
> **"Know ye not that the unrighteous shall not inherit the kingdom of God? Be not deceived: neither fornicators, nor idolaters, nor adulterers, nor effeminate, nor abusers of themselves with mankind, Nor thieves, nor covetous, nor drunkards, nor revilers, nor extortioners, shall inherit the kingdom of God" (1 Co.6:9-10).**
> **"Now the works of the flesh are manifest, which are *these;* Adultery, fornication, uncleanness, lasciviousness, Idolatry, witchcraft, hatred, variance, emulations, wrath, strife, seditions, heresies, Envyings, murders, drunkenness, revellings, and such like: of the which I tell you before, as I have also told *you* in time past, that they which do such things shall not inherit the kingdom of God" (Ga.5:19-21).**
> **"Little children, keep yourselves from idols. Amen" (1 Jn.5:21).**
> **"But the fearful, and unbelieving, and the abominable, and murderers, and whoremongers, and sorcerers, and idolaters, and all liars, shall have their part in the lake which burneth with fire and brimstone: which is the second death" (Re.21:8).**
> **"Ye shall make you no idols nor graven image, neither rear you up a standing image, neither shall ye set up *any* image of stone in your land, to bow down unto it: for I *am* the LORD your God" (Le.26:1).**
> **"The graven images of their gods shall ye burn with fire: thou shalt not desire the silver or gold *that is* on them, nor take *it* unto thee, lest thou be snared therein: for it *is* an abomination to the LORD thy God" (De.7:25).**
> **"Take heed to yourselves, that your heart be not deceived, and ye turn aside, and serve other gods, and worship them" (De.11:16).**

DEUTERONOMY 10:12–11:32

"I *am* the LORD: that *is* my name: and my glory will I not give to another, neither my praise to graven images" (Is.42:8).

7 **(11:18-21) Testimony, Duty—Witness, Duty—Phylacteries—Home, Witness of—Family, Witness of—Children, Duty to—Parents, Duty—Education, Duty—Teaching, Duty:** What does the LORD God require of you? Be a strong testimony and witness for the LORD. This was an absolute essential for the Israelites when they entered and settled down in the promised land. Because of this, Moses drove the point home to the hearts of the people. This is the second time he has covered the utter necessity to be a strong witness for the LORD (see outline and note—De.6:6-9 for more discussion).

OUTLINE	SCRIPTURE	SCRIPTURE	OUTLINE

7. Be a strong testimony & witness for the LORD
  a. How to be a testimony
    1) Lock God's commandments in your hearts & minds
    2) Teach the commandments to your children: Talk about them all day long no matter what you are doing
	18 Therefore shall ye lay up these my words in your heart and in your soul, and bind them for a sign upon your hand, that they may be as frontlets between your eyes.
	19 And ye shall teach them your children, speaking of them when thou sittest in thine house, and when thou walkest by the way, when thou liest
		down, and when thou risest up.
		20 And thou shalt write them upon the door posts of thine house, and upon thy gates:
		21 That your days may be multiplied, and the days of your children, in the land which the LORD sware unto your fathers to give them, as the days of heaven upon the earth.
			3) Make your home a strong testimony for the LORD
			
			  b. The result: Will live in the promised land permanently—as long as the heavens are above the earth

  a. Moses told the people how to be a strong witness for the LORD (vv.18-20). Three basic steps were essential:
    1) The believer must lock God's commandments into his heart and mind (v.18). He must study and live in the Word of God, learning the commandments of God, even memorizing them. Then above all else, he must be quick to do the Word of God, quick to keep the commandments of God.

      "But what saith it? The word is nigh thee, *even* in thy mouth, and in thy heart: that is, the word of faith, which we preach; That if thou shalt confess with thy mouth the LORD Jesus, and shalt believe in thine heart that God hath raised him from the dead, thou shalt be saved. For with the heart man believeth unto righteousness; and with the mouth confession is made unto salvation" (Ro.10:8-10).
      "Let the word of Christ dwell in you richly in all wisdom; teaching and admonishing one another in psalms and hymns and spiritual songs, singing with grace in your hearts to the LORD" (Col.3:16).
      "And these words, which I command thee this day, shall be in thine heart" (De.6:6).
      "Therefore shall ye lay up these my words in your heart and in your soul, and bind them for a sign upon your hand, that they may be as frontlets between your eyes" (De.11:18).
      "Neither have I gone back from the commandment of his lips; I have esteemed the words of his mouth more than my necessary *food*" (Jb.23:12).
      "Thy word have I hid in mine heart, that I might not sin against thee" (Ps.119:11).
      "And I will delight myself in thy commandments, which I have loved" (Ps.119:47).
      "The law of thy mouth *is* better unto me than thousands of gold and silver" (Ps.119:72).
      "O how love I thy law! it *is* my meditation all the day" (Ps.119:97).
      "Thy word *is* very pure: therefore thy servant loveth it" (Ps.119:140).

    2) The believer must teach the commandments to his children (v.19). No matter what he does throughout the day, he is to talk about the commandments of God. Educating his children is an absolute essential. The Word of God must be passed down from generation to generation. Therefore, the parents are to make the Word of God, His commandments, a part of their lives. They are to live out the truth before the children so that the children will see the importance of obeying God. For this reason, Moses preaches that the believer must constantly talk about the commandments when he sits at home, when he walks along the road throughout the day, when he lies down, and when he gets up. The believer is to experience the commandments himself, make them a dynamic part of his life. As he obeys them, he will set the living example of obedience before his children.

      "Search the scriptures; for in them ye think ye have eternal life: and they are they which testify of me" (Jn.5:39).
      "But these are written, that ye might believe that Jesus is the Christ, the Son of God; and that believing ye might have life through his name" (Jn.20:31).
      "Now all these things happened unto them for examples: and they are written for our admonition, upon whom the ends of the world are come" (1 Co.10:11).
      "And, ye fathers, provoke not your children to wrath: but bring them up in the nurture and admonition of the LORD" (Ep.6:4).
      "When I call to remembrance the unfeigned faith that is in thee [Timothy], which dwelt first in thy grandmother Lois, and thy mother Eunice; and I am persuaded that in thee also" (2 Ti.1:5).
      "And that from a child thou hast known the holy scriptures, which are able to make thee wise unto salvation through faith which is in Christ Jesus" (2 Ti.3:15).
      "That they may teach the young women to be sober, to love their husbands, to love their children" (Tit.2:4).

DEUTERONOMY 10:12–11:32

"These things have I written unto you that believe on the name of the Son of God; that ye may know that ye have eternal life, and that ye may believe on the name of the Son of God" (1 Jn.5:13).

"And these words, which I command thee this day, shall be in thine heart: And thou shalt teach them diligently unto thy children, and shalt talk of them when thou sittest in thine house, and when thou walkest by the way, and when thou liest down, and when thou risest up" (De.6:6-7).

"Train up a child in the way he should go: and when he is old, he will not depart from it" (Pr.22:6).

3) The believer must make his home a strong testimony for the LORD (v.20). He must write the commandments on the doorframes of his house and on his gates. The thrust of this exhortation is strong: the believer must make his home a living, dynamic witness for the LORD. When the neighbors think or speak of his home, the dominant thought is to be their testimony for the LORD, that they live for the LORD. The neighbors are to know that the believer and his family follow the commandments of God.

"For we cannot but speak the things which we have seen and heard" (Ac.4:20).

"Be not thou therefore ashamed of the testimony of our LORD, nor of me his prisoner: but be thou partaker of the afflictions of the gospel according to the power of God" (2 Ti.1:8).

"But sanctify the LORD God in your hearts: and *be* ready always to *give* an answer to every man that asketh you a reason of the hope that is in you with meekness and fear" (1 Pe.3:15).

"Come *and* hear, all ye that fear God, and I will declare what he hath done for my soul" (Ps.66:16).

"They shall speak of the glory of thy kingdom, and talk of thy power" (Ps.145:11).

"Then they that feared the LORD spake often one to another: and the LORD hearkened, and heard *it*, and a book of remembrance was written before him for them that feared the LORD, and that thought upon his name" (Mal.3:16).

b. Note the result, what happens when the believer has a strong testimony and witness for the LORD: God promises that the believer will live in the promised land permanently, as long as the heavens are above the earth (v.21). What a wonderful promise from God! What assurance! What security!

"But lay up for yourselves treasures in heaven, where neither moth nor rust doth corrupt, and where thieves do not break through nor steal" (Mt.6:20).

"His lord said unto him, Well done, good and faithful servant; thou hast been faithful over a few things, I will make thee ruler over many things: enter thou into the joy of thy lord" (Mt.25:23).

"In my Father's house are many mansions: if *it were* not so, I would have told you. I go to prepare a place for you. And if I go and prepare a place for you, I will come again, and receive you unto myself; that where I am, *there* ye may be also" (Jn.14:2-3).

"For we know that if our earthly house of *this* tabernacle were dissolved, we have a building of God, an house not made with hands, eternal in the heavens" (2 Co.5:1).

"By faith Abraham, when he was called to go out into a place which he should after receive for an inheritance, obeyed; and he went out, not knowing whither he went. By faith he sojourned in the land of promise, as *in* a strange country, dwelling in tabernacles with Isaac and Jacob, the heirs with him of the same promise: For he looked for a city which hath foundations, whose builder and maker *is* God" (He.11:8-10).

"These all died in faith, not having received the promises, but having seen them afar off, and were persuaded of *them,* and embraced *them,* and confessed that they were strangers and pilgrims on the earth. For they that say such things declare plainly that they seek a country. And truly, if they had been mindful of that *country* from whence they came out, they might have had opportunity to have returned. But now they desire a better *country,* that is, an heavenly: wherefore God is not ashamed to be called their God: for he hath prepared for them a city" (He.11:13-16).

"But the day of the LORD will come as a thief in the night; in the which the heavens shall pass away with a great noise, and the elements shall melt with fervent heat, the earth also and the works that are therein shall be burned up. *Seeing* then *that* all these things shall be dissolved, what manner *of persons* ought ye to be in *all* holy conversation and godliness, Looking for and hasting unto the coming of the day of God, wherein the heavens being on fire shall be dissolved, and the elements shall melt with fervent heat? Nevertheless we, according to his promise, look for new heavens and a new earth, wherein dwelleth righteousness" (2 Pe.3:10-13).

"Blessed *are* they that do his commandments, that they may have right to the tree of life, and may enter in through the gates into the city" (Re.22:14).

8 (11:22-25) **Victory, Conditions for—Victory, Promised—Enemies, Conquest of—Israel, Promises to—Promised Land, Territory of**: What does the LORD God require of you? Conquer, be victorious over all the enemies of the promised land. God has promised the inheritance of the land to you, promised to give you victory over all the enemies who oppose you. But you must know this one fact: the promise is conditional. You must pledge your allegiance to the LORD and to Him alone. You must...

- obey and love God
- walk in His ways
- cling to Him

DEUTERONOMY 10:12–11:32

If you obey God, you will conquer and drive out all enemies no matter how large or strong they are. The power of God will enable you to conquer them all. But not only this: you will conquer a large territory. Every place your foot steps, that territory will become yours. Note the boundaries of the territory promised to Israel: the boundaries extended from the desert to Lebanon, and from the Euphrates River to the western sea (Mediterranean Sea) (v.24).

God promised that the Israelites would be unstoppable and feared by all (v.25).

OUTLINE	SCRIPTURE	SCRIPTURE	OUTLINE

8. Be victorious over all the enemies of the promised land
a. The condition: Allegiance
  1) Must obey & love God
  2) Must walk in His ways
  3) Must cling to Him
 	
b. The results
  1) Will conquer, drive out all enemies no matter how large or strong—by the power of the LORD
  2) Will conquer a large terri-
	22 For if ye shall diligently keep all these commandments which I command you, to do them, to love the LORD your God, to walk in all his ways, and to cleave unto him;
	23 Then will the LORD drive out all these nations from before you, and ye shall possess greater nations and mightier than yourselves.
	24 Every place whereon the
		soles of your feet shall tread shall be yours: from the wilderness and Lebanon, from the river, the river Euphrates, even unto the uttermost sea shall your coast be.
		25 There shall no man be able to stand before you: *for* the LORD your God shall lay the fear of you and the dread of you upon all the land that ye shall tread upon, as he hath said unto you.
			tory: Every place your foot sets
			• The desert to Lebanon
			• The Euphrates River to the western sea
			
			3) Will be unstoppable
			4) Will be feared by all

Thought 1. God promises us victory over all the enemies of life. But the promise is conditional. To conquer the enemies of this life, we must pledge our allegiance to God. If we obey and love God and walk in His ways—clinging to Him—He promises to give us the power to conquer throughout life. As we walk throughout life, a barrage of enemies attack us, enemies such as...

- abuse
- ridicule
- hostility
- anger
- wrath
- bitterness
- disturbance

- irritability
- sorrow
- grief
- violence
- persecution
- malice
- a reactionary spirit

- suffering
- accident
- disease
- loneliness
- emptiness
- death

The enemies that attack us throughout life are innumerable. But victory is assured. God promises to give us the power to conquer all the enemies that confront and attack us so that we can walk triumphantly as conquerors throughout life. There is just one condition: obedience to God. By keeping His commandments, a victorious life is possible, because we become more than conquerors through Him who has loved us.

"Nay, in all these things we are more than conquerors through him that loved us. For I am persuaded, that neither death, nor life, nor angels, nor principalities, nor powers, nor things present, nor things to come, Nor height, nor depth, nor any other creature, shall be able to separate us from the love of God, which is in Christ Jesus our LORD" (Ro.8:37-39).

"These things I have spoken unto you, that in me ye might have peace. In the world ye shall have tribulation: but be of good cheer; I have overcome the world" (Jn.16:33).

"And the God of peace shall bruise Satan under your feet shortly. The grace of our Lord Jesus Christ *be* with you. Amen" (Ro.16:20).

"There hath no temptation taken you but such as is common to man: but God *is* faithful, who will not suffer you to be tempted above that ye are able; but will with the temptation also make a way to escape, that ye may be able to bear *it*" (1 Co.10:13).

"Blessed *is* the man that endureth temptation: for when he is tried, he shall receive the crown of life, which the LORD hath promised to them that love him" (Js.1:12).

"My brethren, count it all joy when ye fall into divers temptations; Knowing *this,* that the trying of your faith worketh patience. But let patience have *her* perfect work, that ye may be perfect and entire, wanting nothing. If any of you lack wisdom, let him ask of God, that giveth to all *men* liberally, and upbraideth not; and it shall be given him" (Js.1:2-5).

"Submit yourselves therefore to God. Resist the devil, and he will flee from you" (Js.4:7).

"The LORD knoweth how to deliver the godly out of temptations, and to reserve the unjust unto the day of judgment to be punished" (2 Pe.2:9).

"For whatsoever is born of God overcometh the world: and this is the victory that overcometh the world, *even* our faith. Who is he that overcometh the world, but he that believeth that Jesus is the Son of God" (1 Jn.5:4-5).

"To him that overcometh will I grant to sit with me in my throne, even as I also overcame, and am set down with my Father in his throne" (Re.3:21).

"Through thee will we push down our enemies: through thy name will we tread them under that rise up against us" (Ps.44:5).

DEUTERONOMY 10:12–11:32

9 (11:26-32) **Blessings, Source—Curse, Caused by—Judgment, Caused by—Decision, Result of—Obedience, Result of—Ritual, of Blessings and Cursings—Ceremony, of Blessings and Cursings—Mt. Ebal—Mt. Gerizim—Life, Crossroads of—Decision, Importance of:** What does the LORD God require of you? Know the consequences of your choices, that of being blessed or cursed. The Israelites were at the crossroads of life. They had to make the most important decision of their lives. What they decided would determine their eternal fate in the promised land of God. Moses knew this. Therefore he challenged them: know the consequences of your choices. From this point on you will be blessed or cursed.

OUTLINE	SCRIPTURE	SCRIPTURE	OUTLINE

9. Know the consequence of your choices: A blessing or a curse
 	
a. The facts & the choice
  1) To be blessed if one obeys God's commandments
 	
  2) To be cursed if one disobeys God's commandments:
   • By turning away
   • By following false gods or false worship
 	
b. The charge to hold a ceremony to proclaim the blessings & curses
  1) When: After entering the promised land
	26 Behold, I set before you this day a blessing and a curse;
	27 A blessing, if ye obey the commandments of the LORD your God, which I command you this day:
	28 And a curse, if ye will not obey the commandments of the LORD your God, but turn aside out of the way which I command you this day, to go after other gods, which ye have not known.
	29 And it shall come to pass, when the LORD thy God hath brought thee in unto the land whither thou goest to possess it, that thou shalt put the
		blessing upon mount Gerizim, and the curse upon mount Ebal.
		30 Are they not on the other side Jordan, by the way where the sun goeth down, in the land of the Canaanites, which dwell in the champaign over against Gilgal, beside the plains of Moreh?
		31 For ye shall pass over Jordan to go in to possess the land which the LORD your God giveth you, and ye shall possess it, and dwell therein.
		32 And ye shall observe to do all the statutes and judgments which I set before you this day.
			2) Where: On two mountains—to proclaim the blessings from Mt. Gerizim & the cursings from Mount Ebal
			
			c. The strong encouragement & assurance: You are about to enter the promised land
			d. The final charge: After conquering the promised land, be sure to escape the curses of disobedience—obey all the laws & commandments of God

    a. Note the facts and the choice declared by Moses (vv.26-28). A blessing and a curse are being set before you. You are standing at the crossroads of life, being forced to choose which road to take. There is the road of a blessing, but there is also the road of a curse. You will be blessed if you obey God's commandments. But rest assured, you will be cursed if you disobey God's commandments.
        1) If you allow your friends and neighbors to become a stumblingblock to you, you will be cursed.
        2) If you allow yourself to break the commandments by being enticed or seduced into sin, you will be cursed.
        3) If you turn from the way of the LORD, you will be cursed.
        4) If you follow false gods or false worship, you will be cursed.

No commandment of God is to be broken. No turning away from God will be tolerated. You must face the fact: you are at the crossroads of life. You must make the most important decision of your life: whether you will be blessed or cursed.
    b. Moses charged the Israelites to hold a ceremony to proclaim the blessings and curses (vv.29-30). Note when the ceremony was to be held: after they entered the promised land. This is significant, for it means that Moses would not be present for the ceremony. Thus his charge was to be carried out under the leadership of Joshua, his replacement, after they had entered the promised land. Note that the ceremony was to take place on two mountains, Mt. Gerizim and Mt. Ebal. The blessings were to be proclaimed from the top of Mt. Gerizim and the cursings from Mt. Ebal (vv.29-30). (See outline and notes—De.27:1-26; 28:1-14; 28:15-68 for more discussion.)
    c. Moses gave the people strong encouragement and assurance (v.31). He declared: you are about to enter the promised land. You will cross the Jordan and take possession of the land. The LORD your God is going to give you the inheritance He has promised.
    d. Moses then gave the final charge to the people: after conquering the promised land, be sure to escape the curses of disobedience. The way to escape the curses is to obey all the laws and commandments of God (v.32). Obedience is the requirement of God. God demands this one act on your part: obedience. Pledge your allegiance, your obedience to God.

    Thought 1. The unbeliever and the disobedient stand at the crossroads of life. A major decision has to be made, the most important decision of a person's life. He must face the fact and make the choice. The choice has to be made; it is inevitable. The unbeliever and disobedient must choose between the road of blessing or the road of cursing. He must choose between obeying or disobeying God's holy commandments. If he chooses to obey, he will be blessed. But note this tragic, terrible fact: if he chooses to disobey, he will be cursed.
    (1) A person who obeys God will be blessed.

> "And this is his commandment, That we should believe on the name of his Son Jesus Christ, and love one another, as he gave us commandment" (1 Jn.3:23).
> "Jesus said unto him, If thou canst believe, all things are possible to him that believeth" (Mk.9:23).
> "For God so loved the world, that he gave his only begotten Son, that whosoever believeth in him should not perish, but have everlasting life" (Jn.3:16).
> "And Jesus said unto them, I am the bread of life: he that cometh to me shall never hunger; and he that believeth on me shall never thirst" (Jn.6:35).

Deuteronomy 10:12–11:32

"I am come a light into the world, that whosoever believeth on me should not abide in darkness" (Jn.12:46).

"A new commandment I give unto you, That ye love one another; as I have loved you, that ye also love one another. By this shall all *men* know that ye are my disciples, if ye have love one to another" (Jn.13:34-35).

"For whosoever shall call upon the name of the Lord shall be saved" (Ro.10:13).

"But whoso looketh into the perfect law of liberty, and continueth *therein,* he being not a forgetful hearer, but a doer of the work, this man shall be blessed in his deed" (Js.1:25).

"Blessed *are* they that do his commandments, that they may have right to the tree of life, and may enter in through the gates into the city" (Re.22:14).

"Now therefore, if ye will obey my voice indeed, and keep my covenant, then ye shall be a peculiar treasure unto me above all people: for all the earth *is* mine" (Ex.19:5).

"O that there were such an heart in them, that they would fear me, and keep all my commandments always, that it might be well with them, and with their children for ever!" (De.5:29).

(2) The person who disobeys God will be cursed.

"Let no man deceive you with vain words: for because of these things cometh the wrath of God upon the children of disobedience" (Ep.5:6).

"And to you who are troubled rest with us, when the Lord Jesus shall be revealed from heaven with his mighty angels, In flaming fire taking vengeance on them that know not God, and that obey not the gospel of our Lord Jesus Christ: Who shall be punished with everlasting destruction from the presence of the Lord, and from the glory of his power" (2 Th.1:7-9).

"For if the word spoken by angels was stedfast, and every transgression and disobedience received a just recompence of reward; How shall we escape, if we neglect so great salvation; which at the first began to be spoken by the Lord, and was confirmed unto us by them that heard *him*" (He.2:2-3).

"And a curse, if ye will not obey the commandments of the Lord your God, but turn aside out of the way which I command you this day, to go after other gods, which ye have not known" (De.11:28).

"But if ye will not obey the voice of the Lord, but rebel against the commandment of the Lord, then shall the hand of the Lord be against you, as *it was* against your fathers" (1 S.12:15).

DIVISION IV

THE SECOND GREAT THEME PREACHED BY GOD'S AGED SERVANT (PART 2): REMEMBER THE CIVIL AND RELIGIOUS LAWS OF ISRAEL—HELPFUL PRINCIPLES TO GOVERN MAN AND SOCIETY, 12:1–26:19

(12:1–26:19) **DIVISION OVERVIEW**—Law, of Israel—Law, Civil—Law, Religious—Society, Laws of: this is a continuation of the second theme preached by Moses, a series of messages on the law of God and the utter necessity for people to obey God. Moses had just preached a series of messages on the Ten Commandments. Now, he focused on the civil and religious laws of Israel. These particular laws were given specifically to govern Israel as a nation. However, the principles covered by the laws can often be applied to us today, to our day-to-day behavior and to the legal situations within our communities and societies. In *Exodus*, Vol.2, of *The Preacher's Outline & Sermon Bible®*, several excellent points are given that bear repeating here in *Deuteronomy*. (See Division Overview, Vol.2—Ex.21:1–24:18 for more discussion.)

1. The law was given so God's people could live in security and peace. God gave the law to unify and mold His people into a nation. God already knew what history has shown man: that a nation without laws, or a nation that does not enforce its laws, quickly slips into chaos and anarchy. Thus God gave the law to His people so the nation of Israel would have a firm foundation to govern their relationships with one another and with God.

2. The laws were given by God in order to mold a community of people into law-abiding citizens. The citizen who lives by God's law bears a very special mark: the mark of responsible citizenship to community, society, and nation.

> "By the blessing of the upright the city is exalted: but it is overthrown by the mouth of the wicked" (Pr.11:11).
> "Righteousness exalteth a nation: but sin *is* a reproach to any people" (Pr.14:34).
> "Take away the wicked *from* before the king, and his throne shall be established in righteousness" (Pr.25:5).

3. The laws that God gave to Israel were founded upon His great love and compassion for people. For example, slaves were valued as people who were made in the image of God and slaves were cared for and protected. Moreover, God's love and compassion limited the scope of retaliation against criminals. Life was just too valuable to waste on tempers that overreacted, that caused death and destruction.

The love and compassion of God made it possible for the Israelites to live in peace. They could live in peace because the law was a deterrent to crime and justice was going to be enforced—both for the victim and for the offender.

4. The laws that God gave to Israel were a totally new concept to the world. Remember, the Israelites had just been slaves themselves, subject to the unpredictable, insane dictates of Pharaoh and his cruel taskmasters. At any given moment, the Israelite could have been struck down for no reason at all. Justice in Egypt was dispensed at random and was completely unpredictable. God's people were at the mercy of men who did not know the LORD God of Israel. They did not care about pleasing or displeasing God. The Egyptian masters were not interested in how the Israelites felt nor in what they needed. Egyptian law did not care about personal rights. But God did, and He provided for His people a system of justice that was guaranteed by the very Word of God itself. For the first time in history, a people were given a form of government that would protect the rights of everyone in true justice, peace, security, and understanding—if the people would just follow God and seek to live in the Promised Land of God. God established a *theocracy*, a government that recognized Him as the Sovereign King. And God's government provided a "*Declaration of Independence*" for His people. The establishment of these laws and form of government was only a foreshadowing of things to come. One day in the future, God's Son, the Lord Jesus Christ, the King of kings and LORD of lords, will return to earth and establish His eternal kingdom. The Scriptures declare this fact: Jesus Christ will rule forever and ever in perfect justice.

> "He shall be great, and shall be called the Son of the Highest: and the LORD God shall give unto him the throne of his father David: And he shall reign over the house of Jacob for ever; and of his kingdom there shall be no end" (Lu.1:32-33).
> "But unto the Son *he saith*, Thy throne, O God, *is* for ever and ever: a sceptre of righteousness *is* the sceptre of thy kingdom" (He.1:8).
> "Of the increase of *his* government and peace *there shall be* no end, upon the throne of David, and upon his kingdom, to order it, and to establish it with judgment and with justice from henceforth even for ever. The zeal of the LORD of hosts will perform this" (Is.9:7).
> "I make a decree, That in every dominion of my kingdom men tremble and fear before the God of Daniel: for he is the living God, and stedfast for ever, and his kingdom *that* which shall not be destroyed, and his dominion *shall be even* unto the end" (Da.6:26).

DIVISION IV
12:1–26:19

5. The one thing above all else to look for in studying the civil laws of Israel is this: the *spirit and principle* underlying the laws. Note three facts:
   a. The nation that would work out its laws based upon the spirit and principles of God's laws (given to the Israelites) would be one of the greatest societies in history, a society that would be...
      - just and equitable
      - safe and secure
      - protected and supported (cared for)
      - compassionate and merciful

   b. The spirit and principles lying behind the laws of God could change society if they were written into the laws of a nation. How can this be said? Because the spirit and principles are based upon...
      - true justice and protection
      - true mercy and compassion

   c. A society that would base its laws upon the principles of God's law would be a righteous community. What is a righteous community? The righteous society is a neighborhood, a city, a nation where the *laws of a nation and of God* are applied with *justice toward every person*. The Scripture promises great benefits to the righteous society.

THE BENEFITS TO A RIGHTEOUS SOCIETY

⇒ God will exalt the nation that diligently listens to His voice.

"And it shall come to pass, if thou shalt hearken diligently unto the voice of the LORD thy God, to observe *and* to do all his commandments which I command thee this day, that the LORD thy God will set thee on high above all nations of the earth" (De.28:1).

⇒ God will bless the nation who claims Him. He will claim them for His very own inheritance.

"Blessed *is* the nation whose God *is* the LORD: *and* the people *whom* he hath chosen for his own inheritance" (Ps.33:12).

⇒ God will exalt a righteous nation.

"Righteousness exalteth a nation: but sin *is* a reproach to any people" (Pr.14:34).

⇒ God will bless the city that is filled with righteous people

"When it goeth well with the righteous, the city rejoiceth: and when the wicked perish, *there is* shouting. By the blessing of the upright the city is exalted: but it is overthrown by the mouth of the wicked" (Pr.11:10-11).

⇒ God will protect the city that trusts in Him.

"Except the LORD build the house, they labour in vain that build it: except the LORD keep [protect] the city, the watchman waketh *but* in vain" (Ps.127:1).

⇒ God will make a righteous nation a great nation.

"Keep [the laws] therefore and do *them;* for this *is* your wisdom and your understanding in the sight of the nations, which shall hear all these statutes, and say, Surely this great nation *is* a wise and understanding people. For what nation *is there so* great, who *hath* God *so* nigh unto them, as the LORD our God *is* in all *things that* we call upon him *for?* And what nation *is there so* great, that hath statutes and judgments *so* righteous as all this law, which I set before you this day?" (De.4:6-8).

⇒ God will spare a society from judgment if righteousness is found within its borders.

"And the LORD said, If I find in Sodom fifty righteous within the city, then I will spare all the place for their sakes" (Ge.18:26).
"Peradventure there shall lack five of the fifty righteous: wilt thou destroy all the city for *lack of* five? And he said, If I find there forty and five, I will not destroy *it*....And he said, Oh let not the LORD be angry, and I will speak yet but this once: Peradventure ten shall be found there. And he said, I will not destroy it for ten's sake" (Ge.18:28, 32).

DIVISION IV
12:1–26:19

THE SECOND GREAT THEME PREACHED BY GOD'S AGED SERVANT (PART 2): REMEMBER THE CIVIL AND RELIGIOUS LAWS OF ISRAEL—HELPFUL PRINCIPLES TO GOVERN MAN AND SOCIETY, 12:1–26:19

A. Laws That Regulate the Worship of God: A Picture of True Worship, 12:1-32
B. Laws That Protect a Person from Idolatry: The Dangers of Being Seduced Into False Worship, 13:1-18
C. Laws That Mark the Believer As a Child of God—As Holy, Different, Distinctive, 14:1-29
D. Laws That Demand Generosity and Giving: The Believer Must Not Hoard, Be Hard-hearted Nor Tightfisted, 15:1-23
E. Laws That Govern the Three Pilgrimage Festivals of Worship: Remember the Great Blessings, Salvation, and Guidance of God, 16:1-17
F. Laws That Govern the Administration of Justice and the Appointment of Rulers: Four Major Concerns of Society, 16:18–17:20
G. Laws That Govern the Administration of Religion: Some Concerns of Believers, 18:1-22
H. Laws That Demand Justice for the Defenseless: A Deep Concern for Justice, 19:1-21
I. Laws That Govern the Conduct of War: A Picture of the Believer's Spiritual Warfare against the Enemies of this World, 20:1-20
J. Laws That Govern Some Unique Issues within Families and Society: God's Concern for Human Rights, 21:1-23
K. Laws That Govern Seven Important Social Issues: Being a Good Neighbor and a Strong Testimony for the LORD, 22:1-12
L. Laws That Govern Sexual Behavior: Living a Moral and Pure Life, 22:13-30
M. Laws That Govern Several Social and Religious Issues: God's Concern for Both the Major and Minor Details of Life, 23:1-25
N. Laws That Protect Relationships within Society: How to Prevent Abuse, 24:1-22
O. Laws That Prevent Wrong Behavior and That Demand Justice, 25:1-19
P. Laws That Require Special Confession and Obedience, 26:1-19

DEUTERONOMY 12:1-32

CHAPTER 12

IV. THE SECOND GREAT THEME PREACHED BY GOD'S AGED SERVANT (PART 2): REMEMBER THE CIVIL & RELIGIOUS LAWS OF ISRAEL—HELPFUL PRINCIPLES TO GOVERN MAN & SOCIETY, 12:1–26:19

A. Laws That Regulate the Worship of God: A Picture of True Worship, 12:1-32

1. **True worship obeys the laws & regulations of God**
   a. The charge: Must be careful to obey in the promised land
   b. The obligation: Obey as long as you live

These *are* the statutes and judgments, which ye shall observe to do in the land, which the LORD God of thy fathers giveth thee to possess it, all the days that ye live upon the earth.

2. **True worship must reject all false worship**
   a. The places of Canaanite worship were to be destroyed

2 Ye shall utterly destroy all the places, wherein the nations which ye shall possess served their gods, upon the high mountains, and upon the hills, and under every green tree:

   b. The symbols of false worship were to be destroyed
      1) Their altars & sacred stones
      2) Their Asherah poles & idols

3 And ye shall overthrow their altars, and break their pillars, and burn their groves with fire; and ye shall hew down the graven images of their gods, and destroy the names of them out of that place.

   c. The command: Must not worship the Lord as unbelievers do

4 Ye shall not do so unto the LORD your God.

3. **True worship seeks the place where God's Name is honored**
   a. The worship center chosen by Him, that bears His Name
   b. The charge: Go there
      1) Approach God there through the substitute sacrifice
      2) Bring all tithes, gifts, & offerings there

5 But unto the place which the LORD your God shall choose out of all your tribes to put his name there, *even* unto his habitation shall ye seek, and thither thou shalt come:
6 And thither ye shall bring your burnt offerings, and your sacrifices, and your tithes, and heave offerings of your hand, and your vows, and your freewill offerings, and the firstlings of your herds and of your flocks:

      3) Worship there with one's family

7 And there ye shall eat before the LORD your God, and ye shall rejoice in all that ye put your hand unto, ye and your households, wherein the LORD thy God hath blessed thee.

4. **True worship does not worship as everyone sees fit, but as God dictates**

8 Ye shall not do after all *the things* that we do here this day, every man whatsoever *is* right in his own eyes.
9 For ye are not as yet come to the rest and to the inheritance, which the LORD your God giveth you.
10 But *when* ye go over Jordan, and dwell in the land which the LORD your God giveth you to inherit, and *when* he giveth you rest from all your enemies round about, so that ye dwell in safety;
11 Then there shall be a place which the LORD your God shall choose to cause his name to dwell there; thither shall ye bring all that I command you; your burnt offerings, and your sacrifices, your tithes, and the heave offering of your hand, and all your choice vows which ye vow unto the LORD:
12 And ye shall rejoice before the LORD your God, ye, and your sons, and your daughters, and your menservants, and your maidservants, and the Levite that *is* within your gates; forasmuch as he hath no part nor inheritance with you.
13 Take heed to thyself that thou offer not thy burnt offerings in every place that thou seest:
14 But in the place which the LORD shall choose in one of thy tribes, there thou shalt offer thy burnt offerings, and there thou shalt do all that I command thee.
15 Notwithstanding thou mayest kill and eat flesh in all thy gates, whatsoever thy soul lusteth after, according to the blessing of the LORD thy God which he hath given thee: the unclean and the clean may eat thereof, as of the roebuck, and as of the hart.
16 Only ye shall not eat the blood; ye shall pour it upon the earth as water.
17 Thou mayest not eat within thy gates the tithe of thy corn, or of thy wine, or of thy oil, or the firstlings of thy herds or of thy flock, nor any of thy vows which thou vowest, nor thy freewill offerings, or heave offering of thine hand:
18 But thou must eat them before the LORD thy God in the place which the LORD thy God shall choose, thou, and thy son, and thy daughter,

   a. The past: Worship had been unstructured in the desert, for they had not reached their rest, the promised land
   b. The promise: They will cross the Jordan & settle in the promised land
      1) Will receive their inheritance
      2) Will receive rest from all enemies
   c. The charge: They must then seek God at the worship center where His Name is honored
      1) To bring all offerings there: Burnt offerings, sacrifices, tithes, special gifts, & vow offerings

      2) To worship & rejoice there before the LORD
         • With one's family
         • With one's servants
         • With the Levites, the ministers of God

      3) To be careful: Must approach God through the sacrifice only at the place chosen by God
         • Not to approach God just anyplace (v.13)
         • To worship only at the place honored by the LORD

5. **True worship does not abuse the blood nor misuse the tithe**
   a. The allowance: Could butcher & eat cattle & sheep at home, animals commonly used for sacrifice

   b. The restrictions & regulations
      1) Must not eat the blood: To be poured out on the ground
      2) Must not misuse any tithe or offering once it had been dedicated to God: Not to be eaten at home
         • Not grain, wine, nor oil
         • Not animals

      3) Must worship—take & eat all offerings at the worship center—in the presence of the LORD

DEUTERONOMY 12:1-32

6. True worship supports the ministers of God

7. True worship has a spirit of discernment: Discerns between what is allowed & what is forbidden

   a. The problem
      1) A person desired meat, but he lived too far away from the worship center to offer cattle or sheep in sacrifice (he received part of the sacrifice for food)
      2) The person was allowed to butcher & eat beef & sheep at home: All animals did not have to be used as sacrificial offerings

   b. The strict discernment needed when eating animals: Must not eat the blood
      1) The reason: The blood symbolizes life
      2) The regulation: It was to be poured out upon the ground
      3) The promise: God would bless the obedient person & his children—all things would go well

   c. The strict discernment needed

and thy manservant, and thy maidservant, and the Levite that *is* within thy gates: and thou shalt rejoice before the LORD thy God in all that thou puttest thine hands unto.

19 Take heed to thyself that thou forsake not the Levite as long as thou livest upon the earth.

20 When the LORD thy God shall enlarge thy border, as he hath promised thee, and thou shalt say, I will eat flesh, because thy soul longeth to eat flesh; thou mayest eat flesh, whatsoever thy soul lusteth after.

21 If the place which the LORD thy God hath chosen to put his name there be too far from thee, then thou shalt kill of thy herd and of thy flock, which the LORD hath given thee, as I have commanded thee, and thou shalt eat in thy gates whatsoever thy soul lusteth after.

22 Even as the roebuck and the hart is eaten, so thou shalt eat them: the unclean and the clean shall eat *of* them alike.

23 Only be sure that thou eat not the blood: for the blood *is* the life; and thou mayest not eat the life with the flesh.

24 Thou shalt not eat it; thou shalt pour it upon the earth as water.

25 Thou shalt not eat it; that it may go well with thee, and with thy children after thee, when thou shalt do *that which is* right in the sight of the LORD.

26 Only thy holy things which thou hast, and thy vows, thou shalt take, and go unto the place which the LORD shall choose:

27 And thou shalt offer thy burnt offerings, the flesh and the blood, upon the altar of the LORD thy God: and the blood of thy sacrifices shall be poured out upon the altar of the LORD thy God, and thou shalt eat the flesh.

28 Observe and hear all these words which I command thee, that it may go well with thee, and with thy children after thee for ever, when thou doest *that which is* good and right in the sight of the LORD thy God.

29 When the LORD thy God shall cut off the nations from before thee, whither thou goest to possess them, and thou succeedest them, and dwellest in their land;

30 Take heed to thyself that thou be not snared by following them, after that they be destroyed from before thee; and that thou enquire not after their gods, saying, How did these nations serve their gods? even so will I do likewise.

31 Thou shalt not do so unto the LORD thy God: for every abomination to the LORD, which he hateth, have they done unto their gods; for even their sons and their daughters they have burnt in the fire to their gods.

32 What thing soever I command you, observe to do it: thou shalt not add thereto, nor diminish from it.

with the tithe: Must not personally use the things consecrated to God—but take them to the worship center

   d. The strict discernment needed in approaching God through the sacrifice of the Burnt Offering (Le.1:1-17)
      1) Must offer on the altar
      2) Must pour out the blood of other sacrifices beside the altar

   e. The strict discernment needed in obedience
      1) A person must obey God in all these regulations
      2) The result of obedience: God will bless—all things will go well with a person & his children

8. True worship does not conform to the religious practices of the world

   a. The assurance: God will go ahead of His people & defeat the enemies of the promised land

   b. The warning
      1) A person must not be ensnared, misled by the world's false worship & false gods nor by their religious practices

      2) A person must not worship God by following the world's religious practices
         • Because they do all kinds of abominations, detestable things
         • Because they offer child sacrifices to their gods

      3) A person must obey all of God's commandments: Not add to nor take away from them

DIVISION IV

THE SECOND GREAT THEME PREACHED BY GOD'S AGED SERVANT (PART 2): REMEMBER THE CIVIL AND RELIGIOUS LAWS OF ISRAEL—HELPFUL PRINCIPLES TO GOVERN MAN AND SOCIETY, 12:1–26:19

A. Laws That Regulate the Worship of God: A Picture of True Worship, 12:1-32

(12:1-32) **Introduction**: idolatry and false worship are sweeping the earth today. People are worshipping everything from animals to graven images, from possessions to some idea in their minds of who God is. But even more tragic than this, there are many who are worshipping themselves, that is, man himself. And when man himself is worshipped, this leads to the worship of science, medicine, business, government, and a host of other endeavors created and controlled by man. But the worship of man has one fatal flaw: man dies. After just a few short years upon this earth, man ceases to exist. He leaves this earth. What then?

But there are many prior questions even to this question. What happens to a person when he confronts one of the serious enemies of life:

DEUTERONOMY 12:1-32

⇒ accident?
⇒ disease?
⇒ financial difficulty?
⇒ loss of loved one?
⇒ divorce?

What happens to a person when he faces one of these or a host of other serious problems? The worship of self, of man, ends upon this earth. Humanistic worship is stopped at death. Then what?

True worship was of critical concern to Moses. The Israelites had to understand the difference between false worship and true worship. Their eternal fate depended upon this understanding. If their worship was a true worship, they would inherit the promised land of God. But if their worship was a false worship, they would be excluded from the promised land, never allowed to enter it. Even after entering the promised land, they faced the very real danger of being tempted by the false worship of the world, that of the Canaanites. If they allowed themselves to be seduced into false worship, they would then be expelled from the promised land. It was therefore necessary—absolutely necessary—that they be able to discriminate between true and false worship. This is the all-important subject covered by this Scripture: *Laws That Regulate the Worship of God: A Picture of True Worship*, 12:1-32.

1. True worship obeys the laws and regulations of God (v.1).
2. True worship must reject all false worship (vv.2-4).
3. True worship seeks the place where God's Name is honored (vv.5-7).
4. True worship does not worship as everyone sees fit, but as God dictates (vv.8-14).
5. True worship does not abuse the blood nor misuse the tithe (vv.15-18).
6. True worship supports the ministers of God (v.19).
7. True worship has a spirit of discernment: discerns between what is allowed and what is forbidden (vv.20-28).
8. True worship does not conform to the religious practices of the world (vv.29-32).

1 (12:1) **Worship, Duty—Commandments, Duty—Laws, Duty—Obedience, Duty—Worship, True**: true worship obeys the laws and regulations of God. Moses now begins to cover a long series of laws with the Israelites, a long section of Scripture (12:1–26:19). Verse one is an introduction to the whole section. The person who truly worships God will obey God. *Worship* (shachah or hawah) means to bow and prostrate oneself before God; to highly esteem, pay homage and give reverence to Him. But the word *worship* (abad) also means to serve God. The picture is that of being enslaved to God, of being a bond-slave, bought and paid for by the one worshipped. It has the idea of working and laboring for the one worshipped, of doing exactly what he says in order to please him. The person who worships God holds Him in the highest esteem and shows Him the utmost reverence.

This is the point Moses was preaching to the people. He was getting ready to cover the civil and religious laws that the people must obey in the promised land, and note, they must obey them as long as they live. They are obligated to worship God and obey Him.

OUTLINE	SCRIPTURE
1. True worship obeys the laws & regulations of God	These *are* the statutes and judgments, which ye shall observe to do in the land, which the LORD God of thy fathers giveth thee to possess it, all the days that ye live upon the earth.
a. The charge: Must be careful to obey in the promised land	
b. The obligation: Obey as long as you live	

Thought 1. To worship God means that we bow before Him in reverence and praise of His Holy Name. But it also means that we serve Him, work and labor for Him, doing all that He says in order to please Him. Worship involves obedience. So long as we live upon this earth, we must obey God. We must be careful, very careful, to obey God, to keep all His commandments—His laws and regulations.

"Not every one that saith unto me, LORD, LORD, shall enter into the kingdom of heaven; but he that doeth the will of my Father which is in heaven" (Mt.7:21).

"For this is the love of God, that we keep his commandments: and his commandments are not grievous" (1 Jn.5:3).

"Ye shall diligently keep the commandments of the LORD your God, and his testimonies, and his statutes, which he hath commanded thee" (De.6:17).

"This day the LORD thy God hath commanded thee to do these statutes and judgments: thou shalt therefore keep and do them with all thine heart, and with all thy soul" (De.26:16).

"This book of the law shall not depart out of thy mouth; but thou shalt meditate therein day and night, that thou mayest observe to do according to all that is written therein: for then thou shalt make thy way prosperous, and then thou shalt have good success" (Jos.1:8).

"And Samuel said, Hath the LORD *as great* delight in burnt offerings and sacrifices, as in obeying the voice of the LORD? Behold, to obey *is* better than sacrifice, *and* to hearken than the fat of rams" (1 S.15:22).

DEUTERONOMY 12:1-32

"And keep the charge of the LORD thy God, to walk in his ways, to keep his statutes, and his commandments, and his judgments, and his testimonies, as it is written in the law of Moses, that thou mayest prosper in all that thou doest, and whithersoever thou turnest thyself" (1 K.2:3).

2 (12:2-4) **Worship, False, Duty—Worship, True, Duty—Asherah Poles—Altars, False—Idolatry, Duty**: true worship must reject all false worship. Remember, the Israelites were camped in the plains of Moab by the Jordan River right across from the great city of Jericho. Moses and the people could probably look across the Jordan River and see some of the worship centers that the Canaanites had built on the high mountains and hills. Note the instructions God gave concerning the false worship and idolatry of the Canaanites:

OUTLINE	SCRIPTURE	SCRIPTURE	OUTLINE
2. True worship must reject all false worship	2 Ye shall utterly destroy all the places, wherein the nations which ye shall possess served their gods, upon the high mountains, and upon the hills, and under every green tree:	pillars, and burn their groves with fire; and ye shall hew down the graven images of their gods, and destroy the names of them out of that place.	1) Their altars & sacred stones
a. The places of Canaanite worship were to be destroyed			2) Their Asherah poles & idols
b. The symbols of false worship were to be destroyed	3 And ye shall overthrow their altars, and break their	4 Ye shall not do so unto the LORD your God.	c. The command: Must not worship the Lord as unbelievers do

a. The places of Canaanites worship were to be destroyed (v.2). Their worship was false and it was idolatrous, an affront to God. False worship and idolatry are an insult to God, abusing and slandering His name. For this reason, the worship centers of the Canaanites were to be destroyed. Note this fact: the Canaanites had built their worship centers on high mountains and hills and under every spreading tree to give them prominence. Although false, their worship was very significant in their lives.

b. The symbols of false worship were also to be destroyed (v.3). The Israelites were to destroy all the false altars and sacred stones, all the Asherah poles and idols. They were to allow no false gods, no false worship to remain in their midst. They were to destroy the altars of other gods and of false worship.

c. The command was clear: God's people must not worship the LORD as the unbelievers of the world did (v.4). The Canaanites worshipped false gods, the gods of their own imaginations, and they built worship centers in honor of their false gods which shamed the name of the only living and true God. But this God's people must not do. They must worship only the LORD God Himself, and they must worship Him only at the worship center where His presence was manifested and honored. God's people must not engage in idolatry and false worship. They must not become contaminated with the false worship of the Canaanites, the unbelievers of the world.

Thought 1. The lesson for us is compelling: we must reject all false worship. We must not compromise with the false worship of the world. There is only one living and true God, the LORD God Himself (Jehovah, Yahweh); therefore, we must have nothing to do with the idolatry and false worship of this world. This is the demand of God's Holy Scripture:

"Little children, keep yourselves from idols. Amen" (1 Jn.5:21).

"Thou shalt not make unto thee any graven image, or any likeness *of any thing* that *is* in heaven above, or that *is* in the earth beneath, or that *is* in the water under the earth" (Ex.20:4).

"Ye shall make you no idols nor graven image, neither rear you up a standing image, neither shall ye set up *any* image of stone in your land, to bow down unto it: for I *am* the LORD your God" (Le.26:1).

"The graven images of their gods shall ye burn with fire: thou shalt not desire the silver or gold *that is* on them, nor take *it* unto thee, lest thou be snared therein: for it *is* an abomination to the LORD thy God" (De.7:25).

"Take heed to yourselves, that your heart be not deceived, and ye turn aside, and serve other gods, and worship them" (De.11:16).

"Thou shalt not plant thee a grove of any trees near unto the altar of the LORD thy God, which thou shalt make thee. Neither shalt thou set thee up *any* image; which the LORD thy God hateth" (De.16:21-22).

"There shall no strange god be in thee; neither shalt thou worship any strange god" (Ps.81:9).

"I *am* the LORD: that *is* my name: and my glory will I not give to another, neither my praise to graven images" (Is.42:8).

3 (12:5-7) **Worship, Duty—Church, Duty—Worship Center, Duty—Symbol, of One Worship—Symbol, of One Way to God—Jesus Christ, Symbol of—Worship, Symbol of—Worship, Seeking—Seeking, True Worship**: true worship seeks the place where God's Name is honored. The people of God must worship only at the *place appointed* by God. God and God alone was going to choose where the Tabernacle, the worship center of the Israelites, was to be placed in the promised land. It was at the Tabernacle where God met with His dear people until the temple was built. There was only one Tabernacle, and it would be moved from place to place. It was to the Tabernacle—there and there only—that the people were to go...

- to approach God through the substitute sacrifice (v.6)
- to bring their tithes, gifts, and offerings (v.6)
- to worship with their families (v.7)

DEUTERONOMY 12:1-32

The point to see is that God chose only one place where the people could approach Him through the *substitute sacrifice*. There was to be only one worship center where His holy presence was symbolized: that worship center was to be the Tabernacle, the sanctuary that held the Ark of God's covenant. Just where the Tabernacle was to be erected in the promised land was to be chosen by God and God alone.

What was the purpose for having just one worship center? Why did God handle the worship of the Israelites in this way? One central sanctuary taught the Israelites several significant lessons:
⇒ there is only one living and true God
⇒ there is only one true worship
⇒ there is only one place and one way to approach God
⇒ unity is important—the unity of worship and purpose, of common goals and objectives, of fellowship and celebration (during the times of the annual feasts or festivals)

Moses knew all of this; therefore, he exhorted the people to approach God through the substitute sacrifice only at the appointed place, at the Tabernacle itself. He informed the people that God Himself would choose where the Tabernacle was to be located. When the people reached the promised land, they were to erect the Tabernacle where God instructed and begin to seek Him there and only there, seek Him through the *substitute sacrifice*.

OUTLINE	SCRIPTURE	SCRIPTURE	OUTLINE

3. True worship seeks the place where God's Name is honored
a. The worship center chosen by Him, that bears His Name
b. The charge: Go there
  1) Approach God there through the substitute sacrifice
  2) Bring all tithes, gifts, & offerings there
	5 But unto the place which the LORD your God shall choose out of all your tribes to put his name there, *even* unto his habitation shall ye seek, and thither thou shalt come:
	6 And thither ye shall bring your burnt offerings, and your sacrifices, and your tithes, and heave offerings of
		your hand, and your vows, and your freewill offerings, and the firstlings of your herds and of your flocks:
		7 And there ye shall eat before the LORD your God, and ye shall rejoice in all that ye put your hand unto, ye and your households, wherein the LORD thy God hath blessed thee.
			3) Worship there with one's family

Thought 1. There are several significant lessons in this point for us.
(1) The central worship center or sanctuary of the Tabernacle taught a striking lesson: there is only one true worship, the worship of the only living and true God. The LORD God—He and He alone—is to be worshipped.

    "And Jesus answered him, The first of all the commandments *is*, Hear, O Israel; The LORD our God is one LORD" (Mk.12:29).
    "As concerning therefore the eating of those things that are offered in sacrifice unto idols, we know that an idol *is* nothing in the world, and that *there is* none other God but one" (1 Co.8:4).
    "One God and Father of all, who *is* above all, and through all, and in you all" (Ep.4:6).
    "Unto thee it was showed, that thou mightest know that the LORD he *is* God; *there is* none else beside him" (De.4:35).
    "Hear, O Israel: The LORD our God *is* one LORD" (De.6:4).
    "O LORD, *there is* none like thee, neither *is there any* God beside thee, according to all that we have heard with our ears" (1 Chr.17:20).
    "That *men* may know that thou, whose name alone *is* JEHOVAH, *art* the most high over all the earth" (Ps.83:18).
    "For thou *art* great, and doest wondrous things: thou *art* God alone" (Ps.86:10).
    "Ye *are* my witnesses, saith the LORD, and my servant whom I have chosen: that ye may know and believe me, and understand that I *am* he: before me there was no God formed, neither shall there be after me" (Is.43:10).
    "For thus saith the LORD that created the heavens; God himself that formed the earth and made it; he hath established it, he created it not in vain, he formed it to be inhabited: I *am* the LORD; and *there is* none else" (Is.45:18).

(2) The central worship center taught another striking lesson: there is only one place and one way to approach God. God alone appointed the place and the way to approach Him. Jesus Christ is the Way to God, the Person who leads a person into the presence of God.

    "For God so loved the world, that he gave his only begotten Son, that whosoever believeth in him should not perish, but have everlasting life" (Jn.3:16).
    "Jesus saith unto him, I am the way, the truth, and the life: no man cometh unto the Father, but by me" (Jn.14:6).
    "Neither is there salvation in any other: for there is none other name under heaven given among men, whereby we must be saved" (Ac.4:12).
    "For *there is* one God, and one mediator between God and men, the man Christ Jesus; Who gave himself a ransom for all, to be testified in due time" (1 Ti.2:5-6).

DEUTERONOMY 12:1-32

"Seeing then that we have a great high priest, that is passed into the heavens, Jesus the Son of God, let us hold fast *our* profession. For we have not an high priest which cannot be touched with the feeling of our infirmities; but was in all points tempted like as *we are, yet* without sin" (He.4:14-15).

"Wherefore he is able also to save them to the uttermost that come unto God by him, seeing he ever liveth to make intercession for them" (He.7:25).

(3) We must worship God only in a church where God's Name is honored, truly honored. Tragically, not every church preaches and teaches God's Holy Word. If we have truly approached God through the substitute sacrifice of Christ, then we must offer true worship up to God. We must join other believers in a worship center that proclaims the living Word of the living God.

"For whatsoever things were written aforetime were written for our learning, that we through patience and comfort of the scriptures might have hope" (Ro.15:4).

"Then Philip went down to the city of Samaria, and preached Christ unto them" (Ac.8:5).

"Then Philip opened his mouth, and began at the same scripture, and preached unto him Jesus" (Ac.8:35).

"And straightway he preached Christ in the synagogues, that he is the Son of God" (Ac.9:20).

"The word which *God* sent unto the children of Israel, preaching peace by Jesus Christ: (he is LORD of all" (Ac.10:36).

"These were more noble than those in Thessalonica, in that they received the word with all readiness of mind, and searched the scriptures daily, whether those things were so" (Ac.17:11).

"But we preach Christ crucified, unto the Jews a stumblingblock, and unto the Greeks foolishness" (1 Co.1:23).

"For we preach not ourselves, but Christ Jesus the LORD; and ourselves your servants for Jesus' sake" (2 Co.4:5).

"All scripture *is* given by inspiration of God, and *is* profitable for doctrine, for reproof, for correction, for instruction in righteousness" (2 Ti.3:16).

"But the word of the LORD endureth for ever. And this is the word which by the gospel is preached unto you" (1 Pe.1:25).

4 (12:8-14) **Worship, Duty—Church, Duty**: true worship does not worship as everyone sees fit but as God dictates. There is a right way and a wrong way to worship God. The people of God must worship God exactly as He says, not as they please. True worship is not every person doing what is right in his own eyes. On the contrary, true worship is doing what God dictates. Note the strong warning of Moses against unstructured worship, against every person worshipping God as he sees fit:

OUTLINE	SCRIPTURE	SCRIPTURE	OUTLINE
4. True worship does not worship as everyone sees fit, but as God dictates	8 Ye shall not do after all *the things* that we do here this day, every man whatsoever *is* right in his own eyes.	your tithes, and the heave offering of your hand, and all your choice vows which ye vow unto the LORD:	gifts, & vow offerings
a. The past: Worship had been unstructured in the desert, for they had not reached their rest, the promised land	9 For ye are not as yet come to the rest and to the inheritance, which the LORD your God giveth you.	12 And ye shall rejoice before the LORD your God, ye, and your sons, and your daughters, and your menservants, and your maidservants, and the Levite that *is* within your gates; forasmuch as he hath no part nor inheritance with you.	2) To worship & rejoice there before the LORD • With one's family • With one's servants • With the Levites, the ministers of God
b. The promise: They will cross the Jordan & settle in the promised land 1) Will receive their inheritance 2) Will receive rest from all enemies	10 But *when* ye go over Jordan, and dwell in the land which the LORD your God giveth you to inherit, and *when* he giveth you rest from all your enemies round about, so that ye dwell in safety;		
c. The charge: They must then seek God at the worship center where His Name is honored 1) To bring all offerings there: Burnt offerings, sacrifices, tithes, special	11 Then there shall be a place which the LORD your God shall choose to cause his name to dwell there; thither shall ye bring all that I command you; your burnt offerings, and your sacrifices,	13 Take heed to thyself that thou offer not thy burnt offerings in every place that thou seest: 14 But in the place which the LORD shall choose in one of thy tribes, there thou shalt offer thy burnt offerings, and there thou shalt do all that I command thee.	3) To be careful: Must approach God through the sacrifice only at the place chosen by God • Not to approach God just anyplace (v.13) • To worship only at the place honored by the LORD

a. The worship of the Israelites had been unstructured throughout the wilderness wanderings (vv.8-9). Ever since their deliverance from Egyptian slavery, the people had no permanent resting place; they lived an unsettled, itinerant lifestyle. Therefore, their worship had to be adapted to their situation. Their worship was supposed to be centered around the Tabernacle even during the wilderness wanderings, but apparently some leniency was allowed.

DEUTERONOMY 12:1-32

b. Whatever the case, the Israelites were soon to cross the Jordan and settle in the promised land (v.10). They were going to receive their inheritance. They were going to conquer all their enemies and experience the physical and spiritual rest promised by God.

c. Moses issued a forceful charge: when the people settled in the promised land, they were no longer to worship God as they saw fit. In worshipping God, a person could no longer do whatever was right in his own eyes, whatever he pleased. He had to seek God only at the worship center where His Name was honored (vv.11-14). The sanctuary of the Tabernacle was to be the only place where a person could approach God through the *substitute sacrifice*. Note the strong exhortation of Moses:

⇒ You must bring all your offerings to the central worship center: Burnt Offerings, sacrifices, tithes, special gifts and vow offerings (v.11).
⇒ You must worship and rejoice before the LORD only at the central worship center: worship with one's family, one's servants, and with the Levites, the ministers of God (v.12).
⇒ You must be careful—very careful—to approach God through the sacrifice only at the place chosen by God (vv.13-14). You are not to approach God just any place. You are to approach God and worship only at the place honored by Him, the place where His presence is manifested.

Thought 1. The lesson is important, very important: true worship does not worship as everyone sees fit but as God dictates. Scripture is clear: we are not to worship God as we please, in an unstructured manner. Worship is not every man doing whatever is right in his own eyes.

(1) True worship is approaching God through the substitute sacrifice of Jesus Christ and Him alone.

"I said therefore unto you, that ye shall die in your sins: for if ye believe not that I am *he,* ye shall die in your sins" (Jn.8:24).

"Jesus saith unto him, I am the way, the truth, and the life: no man cometh unto the Father, but by me" (Jn.14:6).

"Neither is there salvation in any other: for there is none other name under heaven given among men, whereby we must be saved" (Ac.4:12).

"For other foundation can no man lay than that is laid, which is Jesus Christ" (1 Co.3:11).

"For *there is* one God, and one mediator between God and men, the man Christ Jesus; Who gave himself a ransom for all, to be testified in due time" (1 Ti.2:5-6).

(2) True worship is worshipping God in spirit and in truth.

"God *is* a Spirit: and they that worship him must worship *him* in spirit and in truth" (Jn.4:24).

(3) True worship is teaching and preaching the truth, the Word of God itself.

"Sanctify them through thy truth: thy word is truth" (Jn.17:17).

"And straightway he preached Christ in the synagogues, that he is the Son of God" (Ac.9:20).

"For we preach not ourselves, but Christ Jesus the LORD; and ourselves your servants for Jesus' sake" (2 Co.4:5).

"All scripture *is* given by inspiration of God, and *is* profitable for doctrine, for reproof, for correction, for instruction in righteousness" (2 Ti.3:16).

(4) True worship is living a holy life, fearing and reverencing God.

"O worship the LORD in the beauty of holiness: fear before him, all the earth" (Ps.96:9).

(5) True worship is humbling oneself before God.

"O come, let us worship and bow down: let us kneel before the LORD our maker" (Ps.95:6).

(6) True worship is giving God the glory due His Name.

"Give unto the LORD the glory *due* unto his name: bring an offering, and come before him: worship the LORD in the beauty of holiness" (1 Chr.16:29).

"Saying with a loud voice, Fear God, and give glory to him; for the hour of his judgment is come: and worship him that made heaven, and earth, and the sea, and the fountains of waters" (Re.14:7).

(7) True worship is giving the tithes and offerings to the LORD.

"And now, behold, I have brought the firstfruits of the land, which thou, O LORD, hast given me. And thou shalt set it before the LORD thy God, and worship before the LORD thy God" (De.26:10).

(8) True worship is serving the LORD and Him only.

"Then saith Jesus unto him, Get thee hence, Satan: for it is written, Thou shalt worship the LORD thy God, and him only shalt thou serve" (Mt.4:10).

"Then saith he unto me, See *thou do it* not: for I am thy fellowservant, and of thy brethren the prophets, and of them which keep the sayings of this book: worship God" (Re.22:9).

DEUTERONOMY 12:1-32

(9) True worship is acknowledging the holiness of God and keeping silent before Him; it is standing in awe of Him.

> "And he said, Draw not nigh hither: put off thy shoes from off thy feet, for the place whereon thou standest is holy ground" (Ex.3:5).
> "Stand in awe, and sin not: commune with your own heart upon your bed, and be still. Selah" (Ps.4:4).
> "Let all the earth fear the LORD: let all the inhabitants of the world stand in awe of him" (Ps.33:8).
> "But the LORD *is* in his holy temple: let all the earth keep silence before him" (Hab.2:20).

5 **(12:15-18) Worship, Duty—Blood, Duty—Tithe, Duty—Blood, Respect for—Blood, Symbol of Christ's Death**: true worship does not abuse the blood nor misuse the tithe. Throughout Scripture, great respect is shown for the blood of any animal or person. There are two reasons for this:
⇒ The life of a creature is in its blood, and God expects the dignity of life to be respected. Therefore, the blood is to be honored.
⇒ The blood was a symbol of the substitute sacrifice, of the atoning sacrifice that was made through the death of the animal. Of course, this was a symbol of the atoning sacrifice of Jesus Christ upon the cross.

OUTLINE	SCRIPTURE	SCRIPTURE	OUTLINE
5. True worship does not abuse the blood nor misuse the tithe a. The allowance: Could butcher & eat cattle & sheep at home, animals commonly used for sacrifice b. The restrictions & regulations 1) Must not eat the blood: To be poured out on the ground 2) Must not misuse any tithe or offering once it had been dedicated to God: Not to be eaten at home	15 Notwithstanding thou mayest kill and eat flesh in all thy gates, whatsoever thy soul lusteth after, according to the blessing of the LORD thy God which he hath given thee: the unclean and the clean may eat thereof, as of the roebuck, and as of the hart. 16 Only ye shall not eat the blood; ye shall pour it upon the earth as water. 17 Thou mayest not eat within thy gates the tithe of thy corn, or of thy wine, or of thy oil, or the firstlings of thy	herds or of thy flock, nor any of thy vows which thou vowest, nor thy freewill offerings, or heave offering of thine hand: 18 But thou must eat them before the LORD thy God in the place which the LORD thy God shall choose, thou, and thy son, and thy daughter, and thy manservant, and thy maidservant, and the Levite that *is* within thy gates: and thou shalt rejoice before the LORD thy God in all that thou puttest thine hands unto.	• Not grain, wine, nor oil • Not animals 3) Must worship—take & eat all offerings at the worship center—in the presence of the LORD

a. Note the allowance made for the Israelites. When they reached the promised land, they could butcher and eat cattle and sheep at home (v.15). The point to note is that these were animals commonly used for sacrifice.

b. Note the restrictions and regulations (vv.16-18). First, they must not eat the blood of any animal but, rather, pour it out upon the ground (v.16). The blood was never to be eaten nor drank.

Second, they must not misuse the tithe or offering once it had been dedicated to God. Remember that the tithes and offerings of that day were not money but, instead, the offering of the firstfruits—the first of the harvest or the first of the animals born (v.17). They must never eat any of the animals that had been dedicated to God nor any of the grain, wine, or oil committed to God.

Third, any crop or animal dedicated to God was to be taken and eaten at the worship center in the presence of the LORD (v.18).

> **Thought 1.** True worship never abuses the blood of Jesus Christ. The person who truly worships God respects and honors the blood of Christ. He acknowledges and knows several facts:
> (1) Jesus Christ shed His blood for the forgiveness of sins.
>
>> "For this is my blood of the new testament, which is shed for many for the remission of sins" (Mt.26:28).
>> "Unto him that loved us, and washed us from our sins in his own blood" (Re.1:5).
>
> (2) Jesus Christ shed His own blood to purchase the church.
>
>> "Take heed therefore unto yourselves, and to all the flock, over the which the Holy Ghost hath made you overseers, to feed the church of God, which he hath purchased with his own blood" (Ac.20:28).
>
> (3) Jesus Christ shed His blood that we might be justified.
>
>> "Much more then, being now justified by his blood, we shall be saved from wrath through him" (Ro.5:9).

(4) Jesus Christ shed His blood to purge our consciences from dead works to serve God.

> "How much more shall the blood of Christ, who through the eternal Spirit offered himself without spot to God, purge your conscience from dead works to serve the living God" (He.9:14).

(5) Jesus Christ shed His blood to redeem us.

> "Forasmuch as ye know that ye were not redeemed with corruptible things, *as* silver and gold, from your vain conversation *received* by tradition from your fathers; But with the precious blood of Christ, as of a lamb without blemish and without spot" (1 Pe.1:18-19).

(6) Jesus Christ shed His blood to continually cleanse us from sin as we walk through life day by day.

> "But if we walk in the light, as he is in the light, we have fellowship one with another, and the blood of Jesus Christ his Son cleanseth us from all sin" (1 Jn.1:7).

(7) The believer knows that there is no forgiveness apart from the shed blood of Christ.

> "And almost all things are by the law purged with blood; and without shedding of blood is no remission" (He.9:22).

Thought 2. The believer must not misuse the tithe, the offerings that belong to God. He must obey God by tithing and giving offerings to the LORD.

> "And he looked up, and saw the rich men casting their gifts into the treasury. And he saw also a certain poor widow casting in thither two mites. And he said, Of a truth I say unto you, that this poor widow hath cast in more than they all: For all these have of their abundance cast in unto the offerings of God: but she of her penury hath cast in all the living that she had" (Lu.21:1-4).
>
> "Neither was there any among them that lacked: for as many as were possessors of lands or houses sold them, and brought the prices of the things that were sold, And laid *them* down at the apostles' feet: and distribution was made unto every man according as he had need" (Ac.4:34-35).
>
> "I have showed you all things, how that so labouring ye ought to support the weak, and to remember the words of the LORD Jesus, how he said, It is more blessed to give than to receive" (Ac.20:35).
>
> "Who goeth a warfare any time at his own charges? who planteth a vineyard, and eateth not of the fruit thereof? or who feedeth a flock, and eateth not of the milk of the flock" (1 Co.9:7).
>
> "Upon the first *day* of the week let every one of you lay by him in store, as *God* hath prospered him, that there be no gatherings when I come" (1 Co.16:2).
>
> "But this *I say,* He which soweth sparingly shall reap also sparingly; and he which soweth bountifully shall reap also bountifully" (2 Co.9:6).
>
> "And all the tithe of the land, *whether* of the seed of the land, *or* of the fruit of the tree, *is* the LORD'S: *it is* holy unto the LORD" (Le.27:30).
>
> "Honour the LORD with thy substance, and with the firstfruits of all thine increase" (Pr.3:9).
>
> "Will a man rob God? Yet ye have robbed me. But ye say, Wherein have we robbed thee? In tithes and offerings. Ye *are* cursed with a curse: for ye have robbed me, *even* this whole nation. Bring ye all the tithes into the storehouse, that there may be meat in mine house, and prove me now herewith, saith the LORD of hosts, if I will not open you the windows of heaven, and pour you out a blessing, that *there shall* not *be room* enough *to receive it.*" (Mal.3:8-10).

6 (12:19) **Worship, Duty—Stewardship, Duty—Ministers, Support of—Tithing, Duty**: true worship supports the ministers of God. This is a strong exhortation from Moses to the Israelites. They must take heed, be very careful not to neglect the Levites, the ministers of their day. They must not fail to support the Levites by forgetting to financially honor them for their work and ministry. They were worthy of payment, and they were to be paid.

OUTLINE	SCRIPTURE
6. True worship supports the ministers of God	19 Take heed to thyself that thou forsake not the Levite as long as thou livest upon the earth.

Thought 1. Ministers of God are to be financially supported. And note: it is the people of God who are to support them. The minister has been appointed and ordained by God to serve the people of God. His work is often burdensome and difficult, involving long, long hours that demand...
- visiting the sick
- visiting unbelievers
- visiting church members
- visiting the shut-ins
- counseling

- managing committees
- planning and managing the overall vision and goals of the church
- supervising the overall administration of the church
- conducting the marriages of the church
- conducting the funerals of the church
- spending hours and hours in preparation for preaching and teaching

On and on the duties of the minister could be listed. But the point is well seen: he is due support. The people of God must support and give a livelihood to the minister of God.

"For the workman is worthy of his meat" (Mt.10:10).

"Let him that is taught in the word communicate [give] unto him that teacheth in all good things" (Ga.6:6).

"Notwithstanding ye have well done, that ye did communicate with my affliction" (Ph.4:14).

"Even so hath the LORD ordained that they which preach the gospel should live of the gospel" (1 Co.9:14).

"Let the elders that rule well be counted worthy of double honour, especially they who labour in the word and doctrine. For the scripture saith, Thou shalt not muzzle the ox that treadeth out the corn. And, The labourer *is* worthy of his reward" (1 Ti.5:17-18).

7 (12:20-28) **Worship, Duty—Discernment, Duty—Blood, Duty—Blood, Respect for—Tithe, Duty—Sacrifice, Animal, Duty—Obedience, Results of:** true worship has a spirit of discernment. It discerns between what is allowed and what is forbidden. Permission to butcher and eat cattle and sheep that were not used for sacrifice is now expanded by Moses. He strongly exhorted the people to learn how to discern between what was allowed and what was forbidden. Note his exhortation:

OUTLINE	SCRIPTURE	SCRIPTURE	OUTLINE
7. True worship has a spirit of discernment: Discerns between what is allowed & what is forbidden	20 When the LORD thy God shall enlarge thy border, as he hath promised thee, and thou shalt say, I will eat flesh, because thy soul longeth to eat flesh; thou mayest eat flesh, whatsoever thy soul lusteth after.	shalt pour it upon the earth as water. 25 Thou shalt not eat it; that it may go well with thee, and with thy children after thee, when thou shalt do *that which is* right in the sight of the LORD.	be poured out upon the ground 3) The promise: God would bless the obedient person & his children—all things would go well
a. The problem 1) A person desired meat, but he lived too far away from the worship center to offer cattle or sheep in sacrifice (he received part of the sacrifice for food) 2) The person was allowed to butcher & eat beef & sheep at home: All animals did not have to be used as sacrificial offerings	21 If the place which the LORD thy God hath chosen to put his name there be too far from thee, then thou shalt kill of thy herd and of thy flock, which the LORD hath given thee, as I have commanded thee, and thou shalt eat in thy gates whatsoever thy soul lusteth after. 22 Even as the roebuck and the hart is eaten, so thou shalt eat them: the unclean and the clean shall eat *of* them alike.	26 Only thy holy things which thou hast, and thy vows, thou shalt take, and go unto the place which the LORD shall choose: 27 And thou shalt offer thy burnt offerings, the flesh and the blood, upon the altar of the LORD thy God: and the blood of thy sacrifices shall be poured out upon the altar of the LORD thy God, and thou shalt eat the flesh.	c. The strict discernment needed with the tithe: Must not personally use the things consecrated to God—but take them to the worship center d. The strict discernment needed in approaching God through the sacrifice of the Burnt Offering (Le.1:1-17) 1) Must offer on the altar 2) Must pour out the blood of other sacrifices beside the altar
b. The strict discernment needed when eating animals: Must not eat the blood 1) The reason: The blood symbolizes life 2) The regulation: It was to	23 Only be sure that thou eat not the blood: for the blood *is* the life; and thou mayest not eat the life with the flesh. 24 Thou shalt not eat it; thou	28 Observe and hear all these words which I command thee, that it may go well with thee, and with thy children after thee for ever, when thou doest *that which is* good and right in the sight of the LORD thy God.	e. The strict discernment needed in obedience 1) A person must obey God in all these regulations 2) The result of obedience: God will bless—all things will go well with a person & his children

a. Moses anticipates a problem that might arise once the Israelites have settled down in the promised land. A person might desire meat but live too far away from the worship center to offer cattle or sheep in sacrifice (vv.20-21). Keep in mind that the person who offered a sacrifice was given part of the sacrifice for food. When the Israelites were out in the desert wilderness, they were apparently not allowed to eat any of their livestock except when they sought the LORD through sacrifice at the Tabernacle. Obviously, this was for the purpose of building up their wills for the future (Le.17:3-4). However, once they had settled down in the promised land, they naturally would begin to desire meat and want to slaughter some of their cattle and sheep for food. This they would be allowed to do: they could butcher and eat beef and sheep at home. All cattle and sheep did not have to be used as sacrificial offerings. And not only this, but *every Israelite* could eat some of the livestock, both the clean and unclean person. Remember, the person who was ceremonially unclean was not allowed to eat any of the holy offering, not any of the meat dedicated to God.

b. Note the strict discernment needed when eating animals: a person must not eat or drink the blood (vv.23-25). The reason is clearly stated: the blood symbolizes life. The dignity of life is to be respected and honored; therefore, the blood was to be poured out upon the ground just like water. Note the great promise attached to this law: if a person honored the blood, God would make all things go well for him and his children (v.25). Things would simply go better for him and his household if he honored the blood.

c. Strict discernment was also needed with the tithe (v.26). A person must never personally use anything that had been consecrated to God. He must take the tithes and offerings to the worship center.

d. Strict discernment was especially needed in approaching God through the sacrifice of the Burnt Offering (v.27). Remember, the Burnt Offering was the primary offering to secure *atonement* for the people of God. The Burnt Offering symbolized the atonement of the Lord Jesus Christ. The Burnt Offering was to be offered only on the altar of the LORD—all the meat and all the blood. However, the blood of other sacrifices was to be poured out beside the altar and some of the sacrificed meat could be eaten.

e. Note the strict discernment needed in obedience (v.28). Moses declares that a person must obey God in all these regulations. If a person obeyed, then God would richly bless him. All things would go well for him and his children down through the generations.

Thought 1. Discernment is an absolute essential in true worship. We must be able to discern between what is allowed and what is forbidden. When a person accepts Jesus Christ as his Savior, God demands a life of separation and of holiness. A person must separate from the worldliness of his neighbors and never again touch unclean things, things such as...

- drugs
- alcohol
- illicit sex
- lying
- stealing
- cheating
- profanity
- abuse
- hostility
- unjustified anger
- covetousness
- murder

List any sin or evil, and the believer is to have absolutely nothing to do with it after he has accepted Jesus Christ. Once saved by Christ, the believer becomes a new creation in Christ. Old things pass away, and all things become new. Instead of living a life of sin and disobedience, the believer lives a life of holiness and righteousness. He lives a life of purity, and he bears strong testimony to Christ. He discerns between what is right and wrong; discerns between the good and the bad; even discerns between the acceptable and the excellent. This is the great lesson of this point: developing a keen, strong spirit of discernment, being able to discern between good and evil, between right and wrong.

"Therefore whosoever heareth these sayings of mine, and doeth them, I will liken him unto a wise man, which built his house upon a rock" (Mt.7:24).

"And ye shall know the truth, and the truth shall make you free" (Jn.8:32).

"But the natural man receiveth not the things of the Spirit of God: for they are foolishness unto him: neither can he know *them*, because they are spiritually discerned" (1 Co.2:14).

"But strong meat belongeth to them that are of full age, *even* those who by reason of use have their senses exercised to discern both good and evil" (He.5:14).

"If any of you lack wisdom, let him ask of God, that giveth to all *men* liberally, and upbraideth not; and it shall be given him" (Js.1:5).

"Give therefore thy servant an understanding heart to judge thy people, that I may discern between good and bad: for who is able to judge [discern] this thy so great a people" (1 K.3:9).

"And shall make him of quick understanding in the fear of the LORD: and he shall not judge after the sight of his eyes, neither reprove after the hearing of his ears" (Is.11:3).

"And unto man he said, Behold, the fear of the LORD, that *is* wisdom; and to depart from evil *is* understanding" (Jb.28:28).

"Wisdom *is* the principal thing; *therefore* get wisdom: and with all thy getting get understanding" (Pr.4:7).

"For *God* giveth to a man that *is* good in his sight wisdom, and knowledge, and joy" (Ec.2:26).

"Who *is* wise, and he shall understand these *things?* prudent, and he shall know them? for the ways of the LORD *are* right, and the just shall walk in them: but the transgressors shall fall therein" (Ho.14:9).

8 (12:29-32) **Worship, Duty—Conform, Duty—Worldliness, Duty—Worship, False, Duty—Religion, False, Duty—Seduction, Duty—Stumblingblock, Duty—Enticement, Duty—Canaanite, Worship of:** true worship does not conform to the religious practices of the world. The seduction of false worship is a constant problem for the believer of any generation. This Moses knew; therefore, he gave a strong warning to the Israelites.

DEUTERONOMY 12:1-32

OUTLINE	SCRIPTURE	SCRIPTURE	OUTLINE

8. True worship does not conform to the religious practices of the world
  a. The assurance: God will go ahead of His people & defeat the enemies of the promised land
    1) A person must not be ensnared, misled by the world's false worship & false gods nor by their religious practices
	29 When the LORD thy God shall cut off the nations from before thee, whither thou goest to possess them, and thou succeedest them, and dwellest in their land;
	30 Take heed to thyself that thou be not snared by following them, after that they be destroyed from before thee; and that thou enquire not after their gods, saying, How did these nations serve their gods? even so will I do like-
		wise.
		31 Thou shalt not do so unto the LORD thy God: for every abomination to the LORD, which he hateth, have they done unto their gods; for even their sons and their daughters they have burnt in the fire to their gods.
		32 What thing soever I command you, observe to do it: thou shalt not add thereto, nor diminish from it.
			2) A person must not worship God by following the world's religious practices
			  • Because they do all kinds of abominations, detestable things
			  • Because they offer child sacrifices to their gods
			3) A person must obey all of God's commandments: Not add to nor take away from them

a. God was going to give His people a great victory over the enemies of the promised land (v.29). Once they had achieved victory, they were going to face an enticing temptation, a strong, strong seduction: the seduction of false worship and false gods. They were going to be tempted to participate in the false worship of the Canaanites by adopting their religious practices, at least some forms of their worship.

b. But the warning from Moses is forceful: they must not worship the LORD God by following the false religious practices of the Canaanites (vv.30-31). The Canaanite religion was full of all kinds of abominations, detestable things, things such as...

- prostitution provided by women serving as temple priestesses
- child sacrifice
- idol gods scattered all over the land
- priests who encouraged false worship
- worship centers enticing people to false worship, worship centers on the high mountains and hills and under every major tree

The Canaanites had many gods, but the highest god was El. The god that was most worshipped day by day was Baal. The word *Baal* simply means lord. Other false gods and idols were Hadad (the storm god), Dagon, and the goddesses Asherah, Astarte, and Anath. Archaeological discoveries show pictures of gross gods and goddesses with mixed bodies of animals and men as well as characters including serpents, cultic doves, bulls, goats, lions, and others.

As Scripture declares, the false worship and religious practices of the Canaanites were abominable, detestable to God. In particular, note that Moses stresses the practice of child sacrifice (v.31). This heinous crime was a capital offense in the eyes of God (Le.18:21; 20:2-5). Child sacrifice was murder, and the offender was to be executed. In fact, God warned the Israelites: if they ever began to practice child sacrifice, they would be expelled from the land (see 2 K.17:17-18).

The warning was clear and forceful: God's people must obey all of God's commandments. The believer must not add to the commandments nor take away from them. There must never be any idolatry or false worship among God's people.

Thought 1. True worship does not conform to the religious practices of the world. The warning is clear:
⇒ No church must ever conform to the religious practices of the world.
⇒ No church must ever adopt or allow a false religious practice or ritual.
⇒ No believer must ever allow himself to be seduced or enticed by some practice of false worship.

Idolatry and false worship permeate society. Most people have created a god within their minds that allows them to live as they want, that justifies their morality and behavior. And tragically, carnal, fleshly behavior is the lifestyle that most people wish to live. When they have need or a desire, they want the right...

- to tell little white lies
- to give way to the flesh
- to satisfy some craving
- to live as they want
- to secure what they want
- to do what they desire
- to react as they feel
- to accept and reject people as they wish
- to curse or use profanity
- to ignore, neglect, deny God as they will
- to use the tithe themselves
- to attend worship as they wish
- to put off accepting Christ until they are ready

The point is this: people create a false god within their minds, a false god that allows them to live as they want. There is no difference between the false god of the Canaanites and the false god created within the minds of so many people. False gods lead to disobedience, and disobedience is an abomination, detestable to God. Believers must not conform to the practices of false worship. On the contrary, believers must obey God; they must do everything God says. They must never add to what God commands nor take away from what He commands. Believers must conform exactly to the commandments of God, not conform to the religious practices of the world. Both the New and Old Testaments state the principle perfectly:

"And with many other words did he testify and exhort, saying, Save yourselves from this untoward generation" (Ac.2:40).

"I beseech you therefore, brethren, by the mercies of God, that ye present your bodies a living sacrifice, holy, acceptable unto God, *which is* your reasonable service. And be not conformed to this world: but be ye transformed by the renewing of your mind, that ye may prove what is that good, and acceptable, and perfect, will of God" (Ro.12:1-2).

"And they that use this world, as not abusing *it:* for the fashion of this world passeth away" (1 Co.7:31).

"But he that is joined unto the LORD is one spirit. Flee fornication. Every sin that a man doeth is without the body; but he that committeth fornication sinneth against his own body" (1 Co.6:17-18).

"Therefore if any man *be* in Christ, *he is* a new creature: old things are passed away; behold, all things are become new" (2 Co.5:17).

"And have no fellowship with the unfruitful works of darkness, but rather reprove *them*" (Ep.5:11).

"And they rejected his statutes, and his covenant that he made with their fathers, and his testimonies which he testified against them; and they followed vanity, and became vain, and went after the heathen that *were* round about them, *concerning* whom the LORD had charged them, that they should not do like them" (2 K.17:15).

"And the children of Israel, which were come again out of captivity, and all such as had separated themselves unto them from the filthiness of the heathen of the land, to seek the LORD God of Israel, did eat" (Ezr. 6:21).

"Depart from me, ye evildoers: for I will keep the commandments of my God" (Ps.119:115).

DEUTERONOMY 13:1-18

CHAPTER 13

B. Laws That Protect a Person from Idolatry: The Dangers of Being Seduced into False Worship, 13:1-18

1. **The danger of a false prophet, or an interpreter of dreams, seducing you into false worship**
   a. The proof that he is a prophet: Miraculous works
   b. The seduction: Declares that following other gods is acceptable, that becoming involved in false worship is acceptable
   c. The warning: Must not listen to the words of this prophet
   d. The purpose of the seduction: The LORD allows the temptation to test (prove, strengthen) your love for Him
   e. The charge
      1) Must follow the LORD God & fear Him
      2) Must obey His commands
      3) Must serve and cling to Him
   f. The judicial judgment or penalty: Death
      1) Because he encouraged rebellion against the LORD
      2) Because God delivered & redeemed you
      3) Because the false prophet tried to turn you from the way of the LORD
   g. The judgment stressed again: Remove the evil from your midst

2. **The danger of a loved one or close friend seducing you into false worship**
   a. The seduction: Is a secret, quiet suggestion that worshipping other gods is acceptable
   b. The warning:
      1) Are false gods
         - Were not worshipped by the forefathers
         - Are gods of the people
         - Are gods of the world
      2) Must not yield to the seduction
      3) Must not pity him, but turn him over to the authorities

1 If there arise among you a prophet, or a dreamer of dreams, and giveth thee a sign or a wonder,
2 And the sign or the wonder come to pass, whereof he spake unto thee, saying, Let us go after other gods, which thou hast not known, and let us serve them;
3 Thou shalt not hearken unto the words of that prophet, or that dreamer of dreams: for the LORD your God proveth you, to know whether ye love the LORD your God with all your heart and with all your soul.
4 Ye shall walk after the LORD your God, and fear him, and keep his commandments, and obey his voice, and ye shall serve him, and cleave unto him.
5 And that prophet, or that dreamer of dreams, shall be put to death; because he hath spoken to turn *you* away from the LORD your God, which brought you out of the land of Egypt, and redeemed you out of the house of bondage, to thrust thee out of the way which the LORD thy God commanded thee to walk in. So shalt thou put the evil away from the midst of thee.
6 If thy brother, the son of thy mother, or thy son, or thy daughter, or the wife of thy bosom, or thy friend, which *is* as thine own soul, entice thee secretly, saying, Let us go and serve other gods, which thou hast not known, thou, nor thy fathers;
7 *Namely*, of the gods of the people which *are* round about you, nigh unto thee, or far off from thee, from the *one* end of the earth even unto the *other* end of the earth;
8 Thou shalt not consent unto him, nor hearken unto him; neither shall thine eye pity him, neither shalt thou spare, neither shalt thou conceal him:
9 But thou shalt surely kill him; thine hand shall be first upon him to put him to death, and afterwards the hand of all the people.
10 And thou shalt stone him with stones, that he die; because he hath sought to thrust thee away from the LORD thy God, which brought thee out of the land of Egypt, from the house of bondage.
11 And all Israel shall hear, and fear, and shall do no more any such wickedness as this is among you.
12 If thou shalt hear *say* in one of thy cities, which the LORD thy God hath given thee to dwell there, saying,
13 *Certain* men, the children of Belial, are gone out from among you, and have withdrawn the inhabitants of their city, saying, Let us go and serve other gods, which ye have not known;
14 Then shalt thou enquire, and make search, and ask diligently; and, behold, *if it be* truth, *and* the thing certain, *that* such abomination is wrought among you;
15 Thou shalt surely smite the inhabitants of that city with the edge of the sword, destroying it utterly, and all that *is* therein, and the cattle thereof, with the edge of the sword.
16 And thou shalt gather all the spoil of it into the midst of the street thereof, and shalt burn with fire the city, and all the spoil thereof every whit, for the LORD thy God: and it shall be an heap for ever; it shall not be built again.
17 And there shall cleave nought of the cursed thing to thine hand: that the LORD may turn from the fierceness of his anger, and show thee mercy, and have compassion upon thee, and multiply thee, as he hath sworn unto thy fathers;
18 When thou shalt hearken to the voice of the LORD thy God, to keep all his commandments which I command thee this day, to do *that which is* right in the eyes of the LORD thy God.

   c. The judicial judgment or penalty: Death
      1) The personal responsibility: Must take the lead in executing justice
      2) The execution: Stoning
      3) The reasons
         - Because he tried to turn you away
         - Because the LORD saved you
         - Because justice & execution will be a deterrent to evil

3. **The danger of an entire city or community seducing you into false worship**
   a. The seduction: Wicked men arose & seduced the entire community or city to worship other gods
   b. The judicial process to be followed: To carefully investigate the case
   c. The judicial judgment or penalty: To be corporate punishment because of corporate responsibility
      1) To execute all the people & livestock
      2) To burn the entire city with all its plunder: To be a burnt offering to God—a sacrifice for atonement, for reconciliation
      3) To leave the city as a ruin forever, never to be rebuilt: To stand as a warning, a deterrent
   d. The charge: To execute the judgment & keep no plunder
      1) Result one: God will turn from His anger & have mercy
      2) Result two: God will make you a great nation of people
      3) The reason: Because you obey & keep all His commandments

DEUTERONOMY 13:1-18

DIVISION IV

THE SECOND GREAT THEME PREACHED BY GOD'S AGED SERVANT (PART 2): REMEMBER THE CIVIL AND RELIGIOUS LAWS OF ISRAEL—HELPFUL PRINCIPLES TO GOVERN MAN AND SOCIETY, 12:1–26:19

B. Laws That Protect a Person from Idolatry: The Dangers of Being Seduced into False Worship, 13:1-18

(13:1-18) **Introduction**: deceiving, seducing, enticing people to do wrong is a terrible evil. Seduction and enticement mislead people to break the commandments of God and, in many cases, doom them to a life of suffering. One of the most severe judgments of God is reserved for the person who deceives and seduces another person. This is especially true when the seduction leads to false worship. The enticement to disobey God's holy commandments—to turn away from God—to commit sin will be severely judged by God. *Laws That Protect a Person from Idolatry: The Dangers of Being Seduced into False Worship*, 13:1-18.

1. The danger of a false prophet or an interpreter of dreams seducing you into false worship (vv.1-5).
2. The danger of a loved one or close friend seducing you into false worship (vv.6-11).
3. The danger of an entire city or community seducing you into false worship (vv.12-18).

1 (13:1-5) **Warning, against False Prophets—Warning, against False Teachers—Seduction, Warning against—Enticement, Warning against—Worship, False, Warning against—Test, of God**: there is the danger of a false prophet, or an interpreter of dreams, seducing you into false worship. Prophets or interpreters of dreams have always impressed or intrigued people, aroused their curiosity. Sometimes a person who proclaims to tell the future has been able to secure a large following, deceiving and misleading people. This was a very real danger with the Israelites just as it is with any generation of people. False prophets and the leaders of the occult are everywhere, and their deceptions pose a real threat to the masses who are seduced. For this reason, Moses warned the Israelites: you must guard against the false prophet and the interpreter of dreams, guard against their seducing you into false worship.

OUTLINE	SCRIPTURE	SCRIPTURE	OUTLINE
1. The danger of a false prophet, or an interpreter of dreams, seducing you into false worship a. The proof that he is a prophet: Miraculous works b. The seduction: Declares that following other gods is acceptable, that becoming involved in false worship is acceptable c. The warning: Must not listen to the words of this prophet d. The purpose of the seduction: The LORD allows the temptation to test (prove, strengthen) your love for Him e. The charge	If there arise among you a prophet, or a dreamer of dreams, and giveth thee a sign or a wonder, 2 And the sign or the wonder come to pass, whereof he spake unto thee, saying, Let us go after other gods, which thou hast not known, and let us serve them; 3 Thou shalt not hearken unto the words of that prophet, or that dreamer of dreams: for the LORD your God proveth you, to know whether ye love the LORD your God with all your heart and with all your soul. 4 Ye shall walk after the	LORD your God, and fear him, and keep his commandments, and obey his voice, and ye shall serve him, and cleave unto him. 5 And that prophet, or that dreamer of dreams, shall be put to death; because he hath spoken to turn *you* away from the LORD your God, which brought you out of the land of Egypt, and redeemed you out of the house of bondage, to thrust thee out of the way which the LORD thy God commanded thee to walk in. So shalt thou put the evil away from the midst of thee.	1) Must follow the LORD God & fear Him 2) Must obey His commands 3) Must serve and cling to Him f. The judicial judgment or penalty: Death 1) Because he encouraged rebellion against the LORD 2) Because God delivered & redeemed you 3) Because the false prophet tried to turn you from the way of the LORD g. The judgment stressed again: Remove the evil from your midst

a. Moses warned that the person will prove that he is a prophet: he will actually perform miraculous works (v.1).

b. After performing the miraculous works, the prophet will suggest that you follow other gods and participate in their worship (v.2). Down through the centuries, the suggestion has often been that all people worship the same God; they just call Him by different names.

The false prophet suggests that no matter what name is used to address God, He is still the same God. We all worship the same God; we just call Him by different names.

c. Moses issued a strong warning: you must not listen to the words of this prophet (v.3). His words betray him: no true prophet could ever speak such words. This is a direct violation of the first commandment:

> "Thou shalt have none other gods before me" (De.5:7).

This is also a direct violation of the greatest of all commandments, that you love the LORD wholeheartedly—with all your heart, soul, and strength:

> "And thou shalt love the LORD thy God with all thine heart, and with all thy soul, and with all thy might" (De.6:5).

DEUTERONOMY 13:1-18

The standard of truth is not miraculous works, not spectacular signs or wonders, not the prediction of future events. The standard of truth is God's Holy Word, not the words of a prophet or psychic or fortune-teller or palm-reader or astrologer or any other person who delves into the world of the occult and the prediction of future events.

The test of a prophet is this one thing: does he lead people to follow the LORD by obeying His Holy Word. No true prophet would ever encourage people to violate God's Holy Word or commandments. Neither would a true prophet ever suggest that people turn to other gods. There is no other God than the LORD God Himself (Jehovah, Yahweh). And there is no other true worship than the worship dictated by the Holy Word of God. He and He alone stands as the only living and true God, as the great Creator and Sovereign Owner of the universe. Therefore, He and He alone knows how He is to be worshipped. This is the very reason God revealed the truth of Himself and of true worship to man. Therefore, man is to worship Him and Him alone exactly as He has revealed. Any other worship of another god is a false worship. No matter what the prophet or the leader of the occult might claim: the true worship is the worship of God as revealed in His Holy Word and commandments.

d. Note the purpose of this particular seduction, why the LORD allowed the temptation of the false prophet to entice you (v.3). The purpose was to test you, to find out if you truly love God with all your heart and soul. The temptation to participate in false worship is allowed by God for this one reason: to strengthen you, to make you stronger in your faith. By standing upon God's Word against the temptation, you defeat the seduction. You overcome the enticement, and by overcoming it, you become stronger. You stand forth as a strong testimony for God, bearing witness to the unbelievers who surround you. This is the reason God allows the seduction of false worship and idolatry, to strengthen you and to make you a stronger testimony and witness for Him. By testing you, God gives you the opportunity to prove your love for Him, that you love Him with all your heart and with all your soul.

e. Note the charge given by Moses (v.4). You must do three things to conquer the seduction of false prophets and the occult leaders who predict the future. If you do these three things, you will overcome and triumph over the seduction to false worship and idolatry.

1) You must follow the LORD God and fear Him. The LORD is the only true and living God, the Creator and Sovereign Majesty of the universe. There is no other; therefore, you must follow Him and Him alone. Moreover, you must fear Him, revere and stand in awe of Him, acknowledging His justice and judgment, and doing all you can to escape His judgment.
2) You must obey the LORD God and keep all His commandments. You must seek to please Him and Him alone, not some false prophet or occult leader who predicts future events. The false prophet and predictor of future events are not to be obeyed, not to be followed or feared. The LORD God Himself is the One who is to be obeyed, followed, and feared.
3) You must serve and cling to the LORD God, hold fast to Him. It is He who gives you life, and the strength and ability to work and carry on activity upon this earth. Therefore, it is He who deserves the energy and service of your life, the focus of your strength, not some false prophet or predictor of future events. You owe the LORD God your life and service.

f. Now note the judicial judgment or penalty pronounced upon the false prophets or occult leaders who seduce God's people. The penalty was to be death (v.5). Capital punishment was the verdict because of the seriousness of the crime. The false prophet or occult leader was to be executed...
- because he encouraged rebellion against the LORD
- because it was God who had delivered and redeemed His people out of Egypt, not the false prophet
- because the false prophet tried to turn the people away from the LORD, leading them to disobey His Holy Word and commandments.

g. Note that Moses stressed the judgment once again: remove, put away the evil from you (v.5). Purge the evil from among you. Reject the seduction to idolatry and false worship. Remove it! Get rid of it!

Thought 1. One of the greatest dangers faced by believers is that of false prophets and occult leaders who predict the future. They seduce us into false worship, the worship of other gods. False prophets will suggest that we all worship the same God; we just call Him by different names. They use the name of God as though it possesses magic: that is, if a person professes the name of God and attends worship services, he is automatically accepted by God. But this is not the teaching of Holy Scripture. Scripture declares that God has revealed Himself and revealed the way to become acceptable to Him. God has revealed that He is the Sovereign Creator of the universe, the Creator of all that is in heaven and earth, including man. As the Creator of man, He alone knows how man can become acceptable to Him.

God knew that man could never penetrate the spiritual world and dimension of being, never be able to reach into the spiritual world and find God or see God face to face. If man was ever to meet God, God had to reveal Himself to man, enter into the physical, material dimension of being. God had to come to earth in order for man to meet God. This God did in the person of His Son, the Lord Jesus Christ. It is God who has revealed to man how to become acceptable to Him, revealed what life has to be in order to live a full and victorious life upon this earth. If any prophet preaches any other gospel other than the gospel of the Lord Jesus Christ, he is a false prophet. Moreover, if he teaches anything that contradicts the Holy Word of God and His commandments, he is a false prophet (Ga.1:6-9).

Another danger that combats the believer is the world of the occult: the person who dreams and predicts future events—psychic, palm-reader, fortune-teller, astrologer, stargazer, sorcerer, diviner, and any other person who contradicts the Holy Word and commandments of God. The tragic error of the occult leaders is this: they teach people...
- to trust them and their predictions
- to put their faith in them and their ability to predict the future
- to entrust their lives into their hands and their predictions

The error is clearly seen and tragic: the occult leaders turn people away from God, seducing people to trust them instead of God. Even more dangerous is the insidious suggestion that a person may follow God and also trust the occult leaders' predictions. But Holy Scripture is clear: anything—anything whatsoever—that turns a person away from God and His Holy Word is false.

(1) God warns us, there is the danger of a false prophet seducing us into false worship.

> "I marvel that ye are so soon removed from him that called you into the grace of Christ unto another gospel: Which is not another; but there be some that trouble you, and would pervert the gospel of Christ. But though we, or an angel from heaven, preach any other gospel unto you than that which we have preached unto you, let him be accursed. As we said before, so say I now again, If any *man* preach any other gospel unto you than that ye have received, let him be accursed" (Ga.1:6-9).

(2) There is the danger of the occult leaders seducing us to turn away from God and to place our trust in them and their predictions.

> "And it came to pass, as we went to prayer, a certain damsel possessed with a spirit of divination met us, which brought her masters much gain by soothsaying: The same followed Paul and us, and cried, saying, These men are the servants of the most high God, which show unto us the way of salvation. And this did she many days. But Paul, being grieved, turned and said to the spirit, I command thee in the name of Jesus Christ to come out of her. And he came out the same hour. And when her masters saw that the hope of their gains was gone, they caught Paul and Silas, and drew *them* into the marketplace unto the rulers" (Ac.16:16-19).

> "Now the works of the flesh are manifest, which are *these;* Adultery, fornication, uncleanness, lasciviousness, Idolatry, witchcraft, hatred, variance, emulations, wrath, strife, seditions, heresies, Envyings, murders, drunkenness, revellings, and such like: of the which I tell you before, as I have also told *you* in time past, that they which do such things shall not inherit the kingdom of God" (Ga.5:19-21).

> "But the fearful, and unbelieving, and the abominable, and murderers, and whoremongers, and sorcerers, and idolaters, and all liars, shall have their part in the lake which burneth with fire and brimstone: which is the second death" (Re.21:8).

> "When thou art come into the land which the LORD thy God giveth thee, thou shalt not learn to do after the abominations of those nations. There shall not be found among you *any one* that maketh his son or his daughter to pass through the fire, or that useth divination, *or* an observer of times, or an enchanter, or a witch, Or a charmer, or a consulter with familiar spirits, or a wizard, or a necromancer. For all that do these things *are* an abomination unto the LORD: and because of these abominations the LORD thy God doth drive them out from before thee. Thou shalt be perfect with the LORD thy God" (De.18:9-13).

> "And they caused their sons and their daughters to pass through the fire, and used divination and enchantments, and sold themselves to do evil in the sight of the LORD, to provoke him to anger" (2 K.17:17).

> "And he made his son pass through the fire, and observed times, and used enchantments, and dealt with familiar spirits and wizards: he wrought much wickedness in the sight of the LORD, to provoke *him* to anger" (2 K.21:6).

> "But these two *things* shall come to thee in a moment in one day, the loss of children, and widowhood: they shall come upon thee in their perfection for the multitude of thy sorceries, *and* for the great abundance of thine enchantments" (Is.47:9).

> "And I will cut off witchcrafts out of thine hand; and thou shalt have no *more* soothsayers" (Mi.5:12).

> "For the idols have spoken vanity, and the diviners have seen a lie, and have told false dreams; they comfort in vain: therefore they went their way as a flock, they were troubled, because *there was* no shepherd" (Zec.10:2).

2 (13:6-11) **Seduction, Warning Against—Enticement, Warning Against—Warning, Against False worship—Family, Dangers Confronting—Stumblingblock, Warning Against—Friendship, Dangers Confronting—Warning, Against Family Being a Stumblingblock**: there is the danger of a loved one or close friend seducing you into false worship. The intimacy of family and the bond of friends can be used to seduce a believer into false worship. In fact, the strongest influence to false worship is often suggested by a loved one. Family members and close friends influence one another; therefore, if a person turned to false worship, he would most likely lead other family members and friends to join him in various functions of worship. There would be the invitation to join in social functions, study classes, recreational activities, and worship services. This was a very real danger among the Israelites. A little participation would eventually lead to apostasy, the turning away from God. Above all other dangers, Moses knew that this was the most threatening danger of all: the danger of a loved one or close friend seducing a person into false worship.

DEUTERONOMY 13:1-18

OUTLINE	SCRIPTURE	SCRIPTURE	OUTLINE
2. The danger of a loved one or close friend seducing you into false worship a. The seduction: Is a secret, quiet suggestion that worshipping other gods is acceptable b. The warning: 1) Are false gods • Were not worshipped by the forefathers • Are gods of the people • Are gods of the world 2) Must not yield to the seduction 3) Must not pity him, but turn	6 If thy brother, the son of thy mother, or thy son, or thy daughter, or the wife of thy bosom, or thy friend, which *is* as thine own soul, entice thee secretly, saying, Let us go and serve other gods, which thou hast not known, thou, nor thy fathers; 7 *Namely*, of the gods of the people which *are* round about you, nigh unto thee, or far off from thee, from the *one* end of the earth even unto the *other* end of the earth; 8 Thou shalt not consent unto him, nor hearken unto him; neither shall thine eye	pity him, neither shalt thou spare, neither shalt thou conceal him: 9 But thou shalt surely kill him; thine hand shall be first upon him to put him to death, and afterwards the hand of all the people. 10 And thou shalt stone him with stones, that he die; because he hath sought to thrust thee away from the LORD thy God, which brought thee out of the land of Egypt, from the house of bondage. 11 And all Israel shall hear, and fear, and shall do no more any such wickedness as this is among you.	him over to the authorities c. The judicial judgment or penalty: Death 1) The personal responsibility: Must take the lead in executing justice 2) The execution: Stoning 3) The reasons • Because he tried to turn you away • Because the LORD saved you • Because justice & execution will be a deterrent to evil

    a. The seduction of a family member or close friend into false worship is a secret enticement (v.6). It is a simple, off-the-cuff suggestion such as...
- worshipping other gods is acceptable
- engaging in other worship is acceptable
- a person does not have to approach God through the substitute sacrifice: there are other ways to approach Him.

  b. Note the strong, forceful warning given by Moses to the Israelites.
    1) All other gods are false gods. They were not worshipped by the forefathers, Abraham, Isaac, and Jacob (v.6). They are the gods of the people who surround you, the gods of your neighbors, and the gods of the other peoples of the world.
    2) You must not yield to the seduction of your family member or friend. You must not even listen to him (v.8).
    3) You must not pity him nor spare him. But you must turn him over to the authorities to keep his seduction from spreading and causing others to turn away from God (v.8).
        Of course, this was most difficult to do. It would be far easier for a person to rationalize the behavior of his loved one or at least to overlook and minimize the dangerous threat of the seduction to false worship. But not to God: the greatest danger that faces a human being is to turn away from Him. Turning away from God dooms a person to eternal separation from God, to eternal judgment and condemnation.

  c. Moses declared the judicial judgment or penalty: the verdict was death (vv.9-10). Note that the seduced person was to take the lead in executing justice. By law, he was to cast the first stone. As painful as this was, it was his responsibility. His relative or friend had done a terrible evil against him. The loved one had tried to turn him away from the LORD. Moreover, the LORD had saved him; therefore, he was to show his allegiance, his loyalty to the LORD. This was demonstrated by taking the lead in purging the evil from among God's people. The execution of justice would be a deterrent to evil; all Israel would hear about the execution and fear. The seduction to false worship would be stopped.

    Thought 1. The influence of family members and friends is strong, very strong. If we are close, we greatly influence each other. For this reason, we must watch for the suggestions of our loved ones, the suggestions that are contrary to the Word of God. If a family member or friend offers a quiet suggestion that seduces us to break one of God's commandments, we must reject the seduction. We must never allow ourselves to be enticed to turn away from God, to disobey His Holy Word and commandments.
    ⇒ Any suggestion that any other worship is acceptable is false.
    ⇒ Any suggestion that we can approach God through some way other than the atoning sacrifice of Christ is false.
    ⇒ Any suggestion that we all worship the same God—no matter what we call Him—is false.
    ⇒ Any suggestion that we put our trust in any other person other than the LORD Himself is false.

    Even if the suggestion comes from a family member or friend, the suggestion is a seduction into false worship and idolatry. It is a suggestion that leads to the trust of something else other than God Himself. And to trust something else is false, a lie. It will doom us, cause the judgment of God to fall upon our heads. A family member or loved one who has been deceived into false worship can seduce us. Their influence is tremendous, ever so strong. Therefore, we must be vigilant, on guard against the seduction of loved ones, against even the slightest suggestion that we not obey God's Holy Word and commandments. We must reject all seductions to false worship even if the suggestion comes quietly from our family members and close friends.

    "Let us not therefore judge one another any more: but judge this rather, that no man put a stumblingblock or an occasion to fall in *his* brother's way" (Ro.14:13).
    "But if thy brother be grieved with *thy* meat, now walkest thou not charitably. Destroy not him with thy meat, for whom Christ died" (Ro.14:15).
    "A little leaven leaveneth the whole lump" (Ga.5:9).

DEUTERONOMY 13:1-18

"But now I have written unto you not to keep company, if any man that is called a brother be a fornicator, or covetous, or an idolater, or a railer, or a drunkard, or an extortioner; with such an one no not to eat" (1 Co.5:11).

"For if any man see thee which hast knowledge sit at meat in the idol's temple, shall not the conscience of him which is weak be emboldened to eat those things which are offered to idols" (1 Co.8:10).

"Be ye not unequally yoked together with unbelievers: for what fellowship hath righteousness with unrighteousness? and what communion hath light with darkness" (2 Co.6:14).

"But whoso keepeth his word, in him verily is the love of God perfected: hereby know we that we are in him" (1 Jn.2:5).

"Thou shalt not follow a multitude to *do* evil; neither shalt thou speak in a cause to decline after many to wrest *judgment*" (Ex.23:2).

"Blessed *is* the man that walketh not in the counsel of the ungodly, nor standeth in the way of sinners, nor sitteth in the seat of the scornful" (Ps.1:1).

"Enter not into the path of the wicked, and go not in the way of evil *men* [friends]" (Pr.4:14).

3 (13:12-18) **Seduction, Warning Against—Warning, Against Enticement—Warning, Against False worship—Community, Warning to—City, Warning to—Nation, Warning to—Israel, Warning to**: there is the danger of an entire city or community seducing you into false worship. What happened if an entire city or town committed apostasy against God? Nothing is any more horrible than for an entire community or body of people to be engrossed in false worship. To be engrossed in false worship means to be separated from God. It means that a person has to live without God's presence, provision, and protection from the ills and evil of this world. For an entire community or town to be completely cut off from God means the outbreak of all forms...

- of lawlessness and violence
- of immorality and sexual perversion
- of brutality and savagery
- of lust and passion
- of greed and covetousness
- of bondage and slavery

This has been demonstrated and is still being demonstrated in many of the communities, cities, and towns of the world. Where the LORD and His Holy Word are honored, that place is able to control the sins and evil of people. But the evil, greed, and domination of men run rampant where the people do not obey the Holy Word and commandments of God. This was a very real danger that threatened the Israelites. The whole world of their day lay in wickedness. Their neighbors were immoral, lawless, and violent. It was going to be difficult, very difficult for Israel to preserve its holiness, to escape the seduction of the surrounding world, its pleasures and bright lights. If the Israelites adopted the seductive, immoral, and worldly lifestyle of their neighbors, if they allowed entire cities or communities to turn away from God, their fate would be sealed. They would be expelled from the promised land. Moses knew this; therefore, he laid out the measures that were to be taken against large-scale apostasy.

OUTLINE	SCRIPTURE	SCRIPTURE	OUTLINE
3. The danger of an entire city or community seducing you into false worship	12 If thou shalt hear *say* in one of thy cities, which the LORD thy God hath given thee to dwell there, saying,	16 And thou shalt gather all the spoil of it into the midst of the street thereof, and shalt burn with fire the city, and all the spoil thereof every whit, for the LORD thy God: and it shall be an heap for ever; it shall not be built again.	2) To burn the entire city with all its plunder: To be a burnt offering to God—a sacrifice for atonement, for reconciliation
a. The seduction: Wicked men arose & seduced the entire community or city to worship other gods	13 *Certain* men, the children of Belial, are gone out from among you, and have withdrawn the inhabitants of their city, saying, Let us go and serve other gods, which ye have not known;		3) To leave the city as a ruin forever, never to be rebuilt: To stand as a warning, a deterrent
b. The judicial process to be followed: To carefully investigate the case	14 Then shalt thou enquire, and make search, and ask diligently; and, behold, *if it be* truth, *and* the thing certain, *that* such abomination is wrought among you;	17 And there shall cleave nought of the cursed thing to thine hand: that the LORD may turn from the fierceness of his anger, and show thee mercy, and have compassion upon thee, and multiply thee, as he hath sworn unto thy fathers;	d. The charge: To execute the judgment & keep no plunder 1) Result one: God will turn from His anger & have mercy 2) Result two: God will make you a great nation of people
c. The judicial judgment or penalty: To be corporate punishment because of corporate responsibility 1) To execute all the people & livestock	15 Thou shalt surely smite the inhabitants of that city with the edge of the sword, destroying it utterly, and all that *is* therein, and the cattle thereof, with the edge of the sword.	18 When thou shalt hearken to the voice of the LORD thy God, to keep all his commandments which I command thee this day, to do *that which is* right in the eyes of the LORD thy God.	3) The reason: Because you obey & keep all His commandments

DEUTERONOMY 13:1-18

a. The scene painted is that of a few wicked men arising and beginning to seduce their friends into false worship (v.13). As time passes, the wickedness grows rapidly: more and more people join into the seduction of false worship. Eventually the entire community or city turns away from God and His holy commandments. The only true and living God is no longer worshipped and His holy commandments are no longer obeyed. The people are following false gods and involved in false worship.

b. Moses laid down the judicial process to be followed. Before any action could be taken against the community or city, a careful investigation of the case was necessary (v.14). The *supreme court* or *central tribunal* of the nation was to oversee the investigation (De.17:8-13).

c. If the charge against the community or city was confirmed, the judicial judgment or penalty was severe (vv.15-16). The verdict was to be corporate punishment because of corporate responsibility. All the people and livestock were to be executed, and the entire city burned with all of its plunder.

Note that this judgment was to be offered to God as a Burnt Offering, that is, as a sacrifice for reconciliation with God (v.16). No greater offense could be committed against God. A whole city or community of people had turned away, rejecting and rebelling against Him. They were not only refusing to obey His commandments, they were rejecting Him personally by turning to false worship and to other gods. They had rejected and rebelled against the only living and true God, the Giver of life Himself. This was the most terrible, horrible evil that could be committed against the LORD God (Jehovah, Yahweh). Consequently, if a community or city committed such a dishonoring evil against God, they could expect nothing less than *utter destruction*. Note that the city was to be left in ruins forever, never to be rebuilt (v.16). It was to stand as a warning to all other communities and cities: they must not turn away from God and His holy commandments, must not turn to false worship and idolatry.

d. Note the strong charge given by Moses to the Israelites: they were to execute the judgment and keep no plunder (vv.17-18). If all the people within the city or community were guilty of this horrible, terrible sin, they were to be treated just like those in a Canaanite city. They were no different from the Canaanites who were engrossed in idolatry. It was because of false worship that the Canaanites were to be exterminated; therefore, the same judgment was to be executed against the apostate Israelites who had turned to false worship.

The point is this: God shows no partiality or favoritism to people. All stand equally before Him, the obedient to be blessed and the disobedient to be judged. If the Israelites obeyed this law, two results would take place. First, God would turn from His anger and have mercy upon the rest of the nation. Second, God would make the Israelites into a great nation of people. He would do these two great things for His people because they obeyed and kept all His commandments. They did what is right in His eyes (v.18).

Thought 1. There are several lessons for us in this point.
(1) Righteousness exalts a nation, but sin brings disgrace to it.

> "Righteousness exalteth a nation: but sin *is* a reproach to any people" (Pr.14:34).

(2) The nations and the rulers of the world are to face a special judgment for the way they have governed.

> "When the Son of man shall come in his glory, and all the holy angels with him, then shall he sit upon the throne of his glory: And before him shall be gathered all nations: and he shall separate them one from another, as a shepherd divideth *his* sheep from the goats: And he shall set the sheep on his right hand, but the goats on the left. Then shall the King say unto them on his right hand, Come, ye blessed of my Father, inherit the kingdom prepared for you from the foundation of the world: For I was an hungred, and ye gave me meat: I was thirsty, and ye gave me drink: I was a stranger, and ye took me in: Naked, and ye clothed me: I was sick, and ye visited me: I was in prison, and ye came unto me. Then shall the righteous answer him, saying, LORD, when saw we thee an hungred, and fed *thee*? or thirsty, and gave *thee* drink? When saw we thee a stranger, and took *thee* in? or naked, and clothed *thee*? Or when saw we thee sick, or in prison, and came unto thee? And the King shall answer and say unto them, Verily I say unto you, Inasmuch as ye have done *it* unto one of the least of these my brethren, ye have done *it* unto me. Then shall he say also unto them on the left hand, Depart from me, ye cursed, into everlasting fire, prepared for the devil and his angels: For I was an hungred, and ye gave me no meat: I was thirsty, and ye gave me no drink: I was a stranger, and ye took me not in: naked, and ye clothed me not: sick, and in prison, and ye visited me not. Then shall they also answer him, saying, LORD, when saw we thee an hungred, or athirst, or a stranger, or naked, or sick, or in prison, and did not minister unto thee? Then shall he answer them, saying, Verily I say unto you, Inasmuch as ye did *it* not to one of the least of these, ye did *it* not to me. And these shall go away into everlasting punishment: but the righteous into life eternal" (Mt.25:31-46).

(3) God warns us against apostasy, against turning away from the living God.

> "Knowing this, that the law is not made for a righteous man, but for the lawless and disobedient, for the ungodly and for sinners, for unholy and profane, for murderers of fathers and murderers of mothers, for manslayers" (1 Ti.1:9).
>
> "Now the Spirit speaketh expressly, that in the latter times some shall depart from the faith, giving heed to seducing spirits, and doctrines of devils" (1 Ti.4:1).
>
> "And they shall turn away *their* ears from the truth, and shall be turned unto fables" (2 Ti.4:4).
>
> "Take heed, brethren, lest there be in any of you an evil heart of unbelief, in departing from the living God" (He.3:12).

DEUTERONOMY 13:1-18

"Ye therefore, beloved, seeing ye know *these things* before, beware lest ye also, being led away with the error of the wicked, fall from your own stedfastness" (2 Pe.3:17).

(4) There is one warning that a man must heed: the warning against misleading people, against deliberately misleading people. Deceiving, seducing, and enticing others into sin has provoked one of the most severe warnings from God. Listen to the warnings:

"And whosoever shall offend one of *these* little ones that believe in me, it is better for him that a millstone were hanged about his neck, and he were cast into the sea. And if thy hand offend thee, cut it off: it is better for thee to enter into life maimed, than having two hands to go into hell, into the fire that never shall be quenched: Where their worm dieth not, and the fire is not quenched. And if thy foot offend thee, cut it off: it is better for thee to enter halt into life, than having two feet to be cast into hell, into the fire that never shall be quenched: Where their worm dieth not, and the fire is not quenched. And if thine eye offend thee, pluck it out: it is better for thee to enter into the kingdom of God with one eye, than having two eyes to be cast into hell fire: Where their worm dieth not, and the fire is not quenched" (Mk.9:42-48).

DEUTERONOMY 14:1-29

CHAPTER 14

C. Laws That Mark the Believer As a Child of God—As Holy, Different, Distinctive, 14:1-29

1. **Law 1: Must not bear the marks of false religion**
   a. The fact: Are a child of God
   b. The mark: Concerns the way one mourns for the dead
   c. The reason for being different
      1) Are holy
      2) Are chosen to be God's treasured possession

2. **Law 2: Must not eat detestable things, only clean things**
   a. The land animals
      1) May eat these animals
         - Ox, sheep, goat
         - Deer, gazelle, roe deer
         - Wild goat, mountain goat, antelope
         - Mountain sheep
         - Any animal that has a split hoof & that chews the cud
      2) May not eat these animals
         - The camel, rabbit, coney or rock badger: Do not have a split hoof
         - The pig
   b. The water creatures
      1) May eat any with fins & scales
      2) May not eat any without fins & scales
   c. The birds
      1) May eat any clean bird
      2) May not eat these birds
         - Eagle, vulture, buzzard
         - Red kite, black kite, falcon
         - Raven
         - Ostrich, screech owl, sea gull, hawk
         - Little owl, great owl, white owl
         - Pelican, osprey, cormorant
         - Stork, heron, hoopoe, bat
   d. The insects
      1) May not eat flying insects that swarm
      2) May eat any winged insect that is clean
   e. The animals found dead
      1) The law: May not eat
      2) The allowance: May give it or sell it to a foreigner
      3) The reason: Are holy—distinctive, different
   f. The young goat: Must not cook in its mother's milk

3. **Law 3: Must tithe**
   a. Tithing is to be a regular practice
   b. Tithing is to be offered at the worship center
   c. Tithing is to be a spiritual testimony: Tithing strengthens & teaches reverence & fear for the LORD
   d. Tithing is to be a flexible law: Circumstances of a person's situation are to be considered
      1) The circumstance: A person lived too far away to carry his tithe
      2) The person could exchange the tithe—crops & animals—for silver
      3) The person could then use the silver to buy whatever he wished as a tithe at the worship center
   e. Tithing is to be a joyful experience
   f. Tithing is to be a benevolent witness
      1) The law: To store all

Ye *are* the children of the LORD your God: ye shall not cut yourselves, nor make any baldness between your eyes for the dead.

2 For thou *art* an holy people unto the LORD thy God, and the LORD hath chosen thee to be a peculiar people unto himself, above all the nations that *are* upon the earth.

3 Thou shalt not eat any abominable thing.

4 These *are* the beasts which ye shall eat: the ox, the sheep, and the goat,

5 The hart, and the roebuck, and the fallow deer, and the wild goat, and the pygarg, and the wild ox, and the chamois.

6 And every beast that parteth the hoof, and cleaveth the cleft into two claws, *and* cheweth the cud among the beasts, that ye shall eat.

7 Nevertheless these ye shall not eat of them that chew the cud, or of them that divide the cloven hoof; *as* the camel, and the hare, and the coney: for they chew the cud, but divide not the hoof; therefore they *are* unclean unto you.

8 And the swine, because it divideth the hoof, yet cheweth not the cud, it *is* unclean unto you: ye shall not eat of their flesh, nor touch their dead carcase.

9 These ye shall eat of all that *are* in the waters: all that have fins and scales shall ye eat:

10 And whatsoever hath not fins and scales ye may not eat; it *is* unclean unto you.

11 *Of* all clean birds ye shall eat.

12 But these *are* they of which ye shall not eat: the eagle, and the ossifrage, and the ospray,

13 And the glede, and the kite, and the vulture after his kind,

14 And every raven after his kind,

15 And the owl, and the night hawk, and the cuckow, and the hawk after his kind,

16 The little owl, and the great owl, and the swan,

17 And the pelican, and the gier eagle, and the cormorant,

18 And the stork, and the heron after her kind, and the lapwing, and the bat.

19 And every creeping thing that flieth *is* unclean unto you: they shall not be eaten.

20 *But of* all clean fowls ye may eat.

21 Ye shall not eat *of* any thing that dieth of itself: thou shalt give it unto the stranger that *is* in thy gates, that he may eat it; or thou mayest sell it unto an alien: for thou *art* an holy people unto the LORD thy God. Thou shalt not seethe a kid in his mother's milk.

22 Thou shalt truly tithe all the increase of thy seed, that the field bringeth forth year by year.

23 And thou shalt eat before the LORD thy God, in the place which he shall choose to place his name there, the tithe of thy corn, of thy wine, and of thine oil, and the firstlings of thy herds and of thy flocks; that thou mayest learn to fear the LORD thy God always.

24 And if the way be too long for thee, so that thou art not able to carry it; *or* if the place be too far from thee, which the LORD thy God shall choose to set his name there, when the LORD thy God hath blessed thee:

25 Then shalt thou turn *it* into money, and bind up the money in thine hand, and shalt go unto the place which the LORD thy God shall choose:

26 And thou shalt bestow that money for whatsoever thy soul lusteth after, for oxen, or for sheep, or for wine, or for strong drink, or for whatsoever thy soul desireth: and thou shalt eat there before the LORD thy God, and thou shalt rejoice, thou, and thine household,

27 And the Levite that *is* within thy gates; thou shalt not forsake him; for he hath no part nor inheritance with thee.

28 At the end of three years

tithing produce in each town every third year	thou shalt bring forth all the tithe of thine increase the same year, and shalt lay *it* up within thy gates:	stranger, and the fatherless, and the widow, which *are* within thy gates, shall come, and shall eat and be satisfied;	
2) The purpose: To provide for the ministers & needy of every town	29 And the Levite, (because he hath no part nor inheritance with thee,) and the	that the LORD thy God may bless thee in all the work of thine hand which thou doest.	g. Tithing is to be a fruitful exercise: The tither will be blessed by God—all his work & labor

DIVISION IV

THE SECOND GREAT THEME PREACHED BY GOD'S AGED SERVANT (PART 2): REMEMBER THE CIVIL AND RELIGIOUS LAWS OF ISRAEL—HELPFUL PRINCIPLES TO GOVERN MAN AND SOCIETY, 12:1–26:19

C. Laws That Mark the Believer As a Child of God—As Holy, Different, Distinctive, 14:1-29

(14:1-29) **Introduction**: evil is sweeping the earth today—arrogance, selfishness, covetousness, greed, immorality, sexual perversion, abuse, brutality, lawlessness, and violence. Lives are being wrecked and people slaughtered because of the rampage of evil upon this earth.

This was the situation that confronted the Israelite believers. They were soon to enter the promised land and lay claim to their inheritance. Once they entered, they would face temptation after temptation to indulge in the immoral and lawless behavior of their neighbors. Therefore, Moses had to prepare them for the onslaught of temptation that would attack them. He had to prepare them to stand strong as the people of God. They were to live holy lives, lives that were set apart totally to God. They were the people of God; therefore they were to be *marked* by the character of God. As God was holy, so they were to be holy; as God was pure and righteous, so they were to be pure and righteous. They were not to be conformed to the immoral and lawless ways of this world, but they were to demonstrate a transformed life, a life of righteousness. They were to bear a strong testimony to the immoral and lawless neighbors who surrounded them, a testimony of holy living. This is the subject of this important passage: *Laws That Mark the Believer As a Child of God—As Holy, Different, Distinctive,* 14:1-29.

1. Law 1: must not bear the marks of false religion (vv.1-2).
2. Law 2: must not eat detestable things, only clean things (vv.3-21).
3. Law 3: must tithe (vv.22-29).

1 (14:1-2) **Testimony, Duty—Witness, Duty—Religion, False, Marks of—Rituals, Pagan, Example of—Unbelievers, Practices of—Believers, Identified As**: the believer must not bear the marks of false religion. Once a person becomes a follower of the LORD, he must put off the works of darkness. He must have nothing to do with false worship and false religion. He must not participate in the rituals, ceremonies, practices, ordinances, sacraments, services, or social activities of false religion. No practice of false religion is ever to be participated in by a believer. The believer is not to be identified with nor bear the marks of false religion. The Israelites had been saved from Egypt, delivered from the slavery of the world to become followers of the LORD God Himself. Therefore the Israelites were to bear the marks of God, not the marks of false religion. Note the Scripture and outline:

OUTLINE	SCRIPTURE

1. **Law 1: Must not bear the marks of false religion**
a. The fact: Are a child of God
b. The mark: Concerns the way one mourns for the dead
c. The reason for being different
   1) Are holy
   2) Are chosen to be God's treasured possession
	Ye *are* the children of the LORD your God: ye shall not cut yourselves, nor make any baldness between your eyes for the dead.
	2 For thou *art* an holy people unto the LORD thy God, and the LORD hath chosen thee to be a peculiar people unto himself, above all the nations that *are* upon the earth.

a. Moses declared the wonderful truth to the Israelites: you are the *children* of the LORD your God (v.1). God had saved the Israelites out of Egyptian slavery to become His *children*, the family of God. As the *children* of God, the Israelites were to honor God and bear strong testimony to His name. They were to take on the nature of God, live as a new creation transformed by God. The old behavior of the world was to pass away and all behavior was to become new. They were to bear the marks of God's character not the marks of the world and its false religions.

b. Note the particular mark of false religion used by Moses to illustrate the point. It concerns the way a person mourned for the dead (v.1). When a person died, loved ones mourned by disfiguring their bodies in pagan-like rituals. It was a common practice for a person to cut his hair on the sides or to make himself completely bald or to clip off the edges of his beard during the mourning ritual. It was also a common practice for a person to cut himself and draw blood.

DEUTERONOMY 14:1-29

"For thus saith the LORD, Enter not into the house of mourning, neither go to lament nor bemoan them: for I have taken away my peace from this people, saith the LORD, *even* lovingkindness and mercies. Both the great and the small shall die in this land: they shall not be buried, neither shall *men* lament for them, nor cut themselves, nor make themselves bald for them: Neither shall *men* tear *themselves* for them in mourning, to comfort them for the dead; neither shall *men* give them the cup of consolation to drink for their father or for their mother" (Je.16:5-7).

"That there came certain from Shechem, from Shiloh, and from Samaria, *even* fourscore men, having their beards shaven, and their clothes rent, and having cut themselves, with offerings and incense in their hand, to bring *them* to the house of the LORD" (Je.41:5).

Down through the centuries, mutilation of the body has been a common practice, a ritual among some false religions. But this is not to be so, not among God's people. They must not bear the marks of false religion. There is to be no participation in false worship, no practice adopted from false religion. The believer is not to be conformed to the false religions and practices of this world. He is to live a transformed life, a life that turns away from the practices of false religion and that turns to God. The true believer becomes a follower of God, obeying God and keeping His commandments. He takes on the nature and character of God, bearing strong testimony to the immoral, lawless, and false worshippers who surround him.

c. Note the two reasons why God's people must not bear the marks of false religion.
  1) First, because they are holy (v.2). This simply means they are set apart to God, dedicated and consecrated to Him. They are to live different lives—pure and righteous lives that honor and bear strong testimony to God's holy name. To be holy means that a person lives a *different kind* of life. He lives a distinctive life, distinctive in that it is pure and righteous, distinctive in that it shuns the immoral and wicked things of this world. The genuine believer has nothing to do with the false religions and worship of this world. God had chosen the Israelites to be His holy people; therefore, this was the kind of life they were to live before Him, a life that was totally set apart to Him.
  2) Second, God's people were chosen to be a people for Himself, a very *special treasure*, a *treasured possession* of His (v.2; see De.4:20; 7:6). Note this fact: God did not choose the Israelites because they were special. On the contrary, they were a stiff-necked, stubborn people (De.9:6; 9:13; 10:16; 31:27). God chose the Israelites to be His special people, His special witnesses and missionary force to the lost of the world. When God saved the Israelites out of Egypt, there was nothing special about them. They were slaves, poor and destitute, considered to be the scum of the earth by the other nations of the world. Nevertheless, God saved them, saved them to become His special treasure, the people who would become the true witnesses of God upon this earth. He chose them by His grace, not because of any merit or value within them. It was His sovereign choice and will alone that chose them to be His special people. Because of this—because God had chosen them, because they were His special people, His treasured possession—they must not bear the marks of false religion. They must live holy and pure lives, obeying God and keeping His commandments. They were to be a strong testimony and strong witness for Him to the immoral and lawless of this earth. They were to bear the marks of God Himself not the marks of false religion and worship.

Thought 1. We must not participate in any practice of false religion or worship, not participate in any...
- ritual
- study
- service
- worship
- social or recreational activity

As believers, we are to be holy, separated and set apart unto God. We are to live lives that are distinct and different, that differ entirely from the immoral and lawless of this world. We are to live lives that are holy and righteous, pure and just, that bear strong testimony and witness to the immoral, the wicked, and the false worshippers of this world.
(1) We must live holy lives, lives that are totally set apart to God, lives that are righteous and pure.

"That he would grant unto us, that we being delivered out of the hand of our enemies might serve him without fear, In holiness and righteousness before him, all the days of our life" (Lu.1:74-75).

"What? know ye not that your body is the temple of the Holy Ghost *which is* in you, which ye have of God, and ye are not your own? For ye are bought with a price: therefore glorify God in your body, and in your spirit, which are God's" (1 Co.6:19-20).

"But as he which hath called you is holy, so be ye holy in all manner of conversation; Because it is written, Be ye holy; for I am holy" (1 Pe.1:15-16).

"For I *am* the LORD that bringeth you up out of the land of Egypt, to be your God: ye shall therefore be holy, for I *am* holy" (Le.11:45).

(2) We are chosen to be the people of God, His special treasure, His treasured possession.

"But ye *are* a chosen generation, a royal priesthood, an holy nation, a peculiar people; that ye should show forth the praises of him who hath called you out of darkness into his marvellous light" (1 Pe.2:9).

"Now therefore, if ye will obey my voice indeed, and keep my covenant, then ye shall be a peculiar treasure unto me above all people: for all the earth *is* mine: And ye shall be unto me a kingdom of priests, and an holy nation. These *are* the words which thou shalt speak unto the children of Israel" (Ex.19:5-6).

DEUTERONOMY 14:1-29

"For thou *art* an holy people unto the LORD thy God: the LORD thy God hath chosen thee to be a special people unto himself, above all people that *are* upon the face of the earth" (De.7:6).

(3) We must not ever participate in any practice of false worship.

"Little children, keep yourselves from idols. Amen" (1 Jn.5:21).

"Ye shall not round the corners of your heads, neither shalt thou mar the corners of thy beard. Ye shall not make any cuttings in your flesh for the dead, nor print any marks upon you: I *am* the LORD" (Le.19:27-28).

"Take heed to yourselves, that your heart be not deceived, and ye turn aside, and serve other gods, and worship them" (De.11:16).

"Ye *are* the children of the LORD your God: ye shall not cut yourselves, nor make any baldness between your eyes for the dead. for thou *art* an holy people unto the LORD thy God, and the LORD hath chosen thee to be a peculiar people unto himself, above all the nations that *are* upon the earth" (De.14:1-2).

[2] **(14:3-21) Cleanliness, Spiritual—Spiritual Cleanliness, Duty—Holiness, Duty—Cleanliness, Duty—Undefiled, Duty—Defilement, Duty—Animals, Land—Animals, Clean—Animals, Unclean—Food, Clean and Unclean—Animals, Edible and Inedible**: the believer must not eat detestable things, only clean things. God cares about man's body; this is the reason He gave this law to the Israelites. God created the human body for man; therefore, God insists that man must take care of his body. This is clearly seen in the food laws discussed in this passage. Obviously, God gave the laws for health reasons, to protect His people from disease, bad diet, and parasites. Medicine had not yet advanced enough for the people to fully understand the reasons for the food laws. Nevertheless, God knew, so He protected His people by giving them laws to govern what they ate. Animals that were more likely to carry parasites or disease were forbidden: they were designated as unclean food. Animals that were less likely to carry parasites or disease were edible: they were called clean animals.

But note this fact: God had more than health in mind when He gave the cleansing laws. God had a spiritual purpose in mind. The laws of cleanliness and defilement were symbolic of spiritual truth, of being spiritually clean and undefiled. The laws of cleanliness set God's people apart as a clean, holy people. God's people were to be distinct and different from the surrounding people and nations. The surrounding nations and people were living unholy lives, lives of immorality and lawlessness. But God's people were to be distinct and different in this very fact: they were to live holy lives. They were to bear a strong testimony that they followed God and obeyed His commandments. They ate only clean food: they took care of their bodies. They kept them clean and healthy—all in *obedience* to God's law governing cleanliness. Simply stated, holiness demands that God's people conform to the laws of God, including the laws of cleanliness. The laws of cleanliness were a visible sign that the people of God were not "conformed to this world" (Ro.12:2). They lived a different kind of life from the people who surrounded them, lives that obeyed God and His commandments. The food laws were a testimony, a strong witness that the people of God had a very special relationship to the LORD. (See outline and notes—Le.11:1-47 for more discussion.) The commentator John Maxwell says this:

> *The food laws provided an opportunity to exercise faith and obedience. Very clearly, God has assured them that this is His will concerning their dietary habits, and whether the regulations seemed reasonable or not, they were to obey. Such a test is quite similar to the one given to Adam and Eve concerning the forbidden fruit. Apart from God's command to the contrary, both they and Israel could have chosen to eat or not eat without any violation of conscience. From a human stand point, God's rules made no sense. Therefore, according to this explanation, this was a higher test of obedience. To obey this command meant no sacrifice or hunger since many good meats were allowed. Here then was a true test of whether Israel would simply obey God's word. It was not the observance of the food laws per se that distinguished Israel as holy, but an attitude of total and willing allegiance to God in love and obedience. This obedience transcended human reasons; it relied not upon outward conditions.*[1]

OUTLINE	SCRIPTURE	SCRIPTURE	OUTLINE

2. Law 2: Must not eat detestable things, only clean things
a. The land animals
  1) May eat these animals
    • Ox, sheep, goat
    • Deer, gazelle, roe deer
    • Wild goat, mountain goat, antelope
    • Mountain sheep
 	
    • Any animal that has a split hoof & that chews the cud
	3 Thou shalt not eat any abominable thing.
	4 These *are* the beasts which ye shall eat: the ox, the sheep, and the goat,
	5 The hart, and the roebuck, and the fallow deer, and the wild goat, and the pygarg, and the wild ox, and the chamois.
	6 And every beast that parteth the hoof, and cleaveth the cleft into two claws, *and*
		cheweth the cud among the beasts, that ye shall eat.
		7 Nevertheless these ye shall not eat of them that chew the cud, or of them that divide the cloven hoof; *as* the camel, and the hare, and the coney: for they chew the cud, but divide not the hoof; *therefore* they *are* unclean unto you.
		8 And the swine, because it divideth the hoof, yet cheweth not the cud, it *is* un-
			2) May not eat these animals
			• The camel, rabbit, coney or rock badger: Do not have a split hoof
			
			• The pig

---

[1] John Maxwell. *The Preacher's Commentary on Deuteronomy*, p.200.

DEUTERONOMY 14:1-29

OUTLINE	SCRIPTURE	SCRIPTURE	OUTLINE
b. The water creatures 1) May eat any with fins & scales 2) May not eat any without fins & scales c. The birds 1) May eat any clean bird 2) May not eat these birds • Eagle, vulture, buzzard • Red kite, black kite, falcon • Raven • Ostrich, screech owl,	clean unto you: ye shall not eat of their flesh, nor touch their dead carcase. 9 These ye shall eat of all that *are* in the waters: all that have fins and scales shall ye eat: 10 And whatsoever hath not fins and scales ye may not eat; it *is* unclean unto you. 11 *Of* all clean birds ye shall eat. 12 But these *are they* of which ye shall not eat: the eagle, and the ossifrage, and the ospray, 13 And the glede, and the kite, and the vulture after his kind, 14 And every raven after his kind, 15 And the owl, and the night hawk, and the cuckow,	and the hawk after his kind, 16 The little owl, and the great owl, and the swan, 17 And the pelican, and the gier eagle, and the cormorant, 18 And the stork, and the heron after her kind, and the lapwing, and the bat. 19 And every creeping thing that flieth *is* unclean unto you: they shall not be eaten. 20 *But of* all clean fowls ye may eat. 21 Ye shall not eat *of* any thing that dieth of itself: thou shalt give it unto the stranger that *is* in thy gates, that he may eat it; or thou mayest sell it unto an alien: for thou *art* an holy people unto the LORD thy God. Thou shalt not seethe a kid in his mother's milk.	sea gull, hawk • Little owl, great owl, white owl • Pelican, osprey, cormorant • Stork, heron, hoopoe, bat d. The insects 1) May not eat flying insects that swarm 2) May eat any winged insect that is clean e. The animals found dead 1) The law: May not eat 2) The allowance: May give it or sell it to a foreigner 3) The reason: Are holy—distinctive, different f. The young goat: Must not cook in its mother's milk

a. The land animals that the Israelites could eat had two characteristics or traits (vv.4-6): they were to be animals that had a split hoof and chewed the cud. Note that both traits were an absolute necessity. The animals included...
- ox, sheep, goat
- deer, gazelle, roe deer
- wild goat, mountain goat, antelope
- mountain sheep

The land animals that could not be eaten were animals that had only one of the two traits (vv.7-8). For example, some animals only chew the cud and others only have a split hoof. These were not to be eaten at all. Several examples are given...
- the camel
- the rabbit
- the coney or rock badger
- the pig

b. The water creatures could include animals that lived in the seas, lakes, rivers, pools, and streams (vv.9-10). The Israelites could eat any water creature that had both fins and scales. However, they were not allowed to eat any water creature that had only fins or only scales (v.10). A water creature with only one of these traits was counted unclean, that is, ceremonially or spiritually unclean. The believer was never to eat its meat.

c. The Israelites could eat any bird that was clean (v.11). Note that no example of clean birds is given, and no trait or characteristic as to what makes a bird clean or unclean is given. The unclean birds alone are listed. Keep in mind that this is a symbol of being spiritually, ceremonially unclean. The birds that were to be counted unclean are...
- eagle, vulture, buzzard
- red kite, black kite, falcon
- raven
- ostrich, screech owl, sea gull, hawk
- little owl, great owl, white owl
- pelican, osprey, cormorant
- stork, heron, hoopoe, bat

d. The Israelites were forbidden to eat any insect that flew or swarmed (v.19). The flying or swarming insects were counted unclean to the believer. Note that Scripture is emphatically clear: the Israelites must not eat them. However, they could eat any winged insect that was clean (v.20). Although no list is given here in *Deuteronomy,* the book of *Leviticus* does list all varieties of locusts, katydids, crickets, and grasshoppers (see outline and note—Le.11:20-23 for more discussion).

e. The Israelites could not eat any animal that was found dead (v.21). However, they could give the meat to a foreigner. The reason is clearly stated: God's people are a holy people, a people totally set apart to God. They are a people who are to live distinctive, different lives, that is, lives that are pure and righteous, bearing strong witness to the immoral and lawless neighbors who surround them. (See outline and note—Lev.11:24-40 for more discussion.)

f. The Israelites were not to cook a young goat in its mothers milk (v.21). The picture is that of a kid, a baby lamb or goat, that was being taken away from its mother, the very mother who had given it life. The kid was being cooked in its mother's milk. The point is probably this: life is precious to God; therefore, the dignity of life is to be respected and protected by man. The very sight of taking a young goat or sheep from its mother and then cooking it in its mother's milk is a distasteful, detestable thought. God did allow the killing of goats and sheep, but only for food. The killing had a deliberate purpose, a necessary purpose, that of providing food for man. But in the killing, man was still to demonstrate the dignity of life.

DEUTERONOMY 14:1-29

He was to show by this simple act that he was distinctive, different from the peoples of the world. He did not believe in the taking of life except for the necessary purpose of food.

Thought 1. The true believers of Israel were to be strict in keeping these laws governing food. This means that every time a believer saw a clean or unclean animal, the thought of God was to enter his mind. He was to think about the commandment to live a holy and clean life before God. What a lesson for us today, for all believers. When we see the unclean and clean things of this earth, we should immediately think of God. We should focus upon God's call to us, that we live holy and clean lives.

"And that ye put on the new man, which after God is created in righteousness and true holiness" (Ep.4:24).

"Therefore if any man *be* in Christ, *he is* a new creature: old things are passed away; behold, all things are become new" (2 Co.5:17).

"Wherefore come out from among them, and be ye separate, saith the LORD, and touch not the unclean *thing*; and I will receive you, And will be a Father unto you, and ye shall be my sons and daughters, saith the LORD Almighty" (2 Co.6:17-18).

"Having therefore these promises, dearly beloved, let us cleanse ourselves from all filthiness of the flesh and spirit, perfecting holiness in the fear of God" (2 Co.7:1).

"Draw nigh to God, and he will draw nigh to you. Cleanse *your* hands, *ye* sinners; and purify *your* hearts, *ye* double minded" (Js.4:8).

"For I *am* the LORD that bringeth you up out of the land of Egypt, to be your God: ye shall therefore be holy, for I *am* holy" (Le.11:45).

3 (14:22-29) **Tithing, Duty—Offerings, Duty—Benevolence, Duty**: the believer must tithe. Seldom does a subject grab the attention of a congregation as much as money. In this Scripture, Moses gives a strong sermon on stewardship. Standing there preaching to the people, he covers seven truths about tithing, truths that are applicable to any generation of believers.[2]

OUTLINE	SCRIPTURE	SCRIPTURE	OUTLINE
3. Law 3: Must tithe a. Tithing is to be a regular practice b. Tithing is to be offered at the worship center c. Tithing is to be a spiritual testimony: Tithing strengthens & teaches reverence & fear for the LORD d. Tithing is to be a flexible law: Circumstances of a person's situation are to be considered 1) The circumstance: A person lived too far away to carry his tithe 2) The person could exchange the tithe—crops & animals—for silver 3) The person could then use	22 Thou shalt truly tithe all the increase of thy seed, that the field bringeth forth year by year. 23 And thou shalt eat before the LORD thy God, in the place which he shall choose to place his name there, the tithe of thy corn, of thy wine, and of thine oil, and the firstlings of thy herds and of thy flocks; that thou mayest learn to fear the LORD thy God always. 24 And if the way be too long for thee, so that thou art not able to carry it; *or* if the place be too far from thee, which the LORD thy God shall choose to set his name there, when the LORD thy God hath blessed thee: 25 Then shalt thou turn *it* into money, and bind up the money in thine hand, and shalt go unto the place which the LORD thy God shall choose: 26 And thou shalt bestow	that money for whatsoever thy soul lusteth after, for oxen, or for sheep, or for wine, or for strong drink, or for whatsoever thy soul desireth: and thou shalt eat there before the LORD thy God, and thou shalt rejoice, thou, and thine household, 27 And the Levite that *is* within thy gates; thou shalt not forsake him; for he hath no part nor inheritance with thee. 28 At the end of three years thou shalt bring forth all the tithe of thine increase the same year, and shalt lay *it* up within thy gates: 29 And the Levite, (because he hath no part nor inheritance with thee,) and the stranger, and the fatherless, and the widow, which *are* within thy gates, shall come, and shall eat and be satisfied; that the LORD thy God may bless thee in all the work of thine hand which thou doest.	the silver to buy whatever he wished as a tithe at the worship center e. Tithing is to be a joyful experience f. Tithing is to be a benevolent witness 1) The law: To store all tithing produce in each town every third year 2) The purpose: To provide for the ministers & needy of every town g. Tithing is to be a fruitful exercise: The tither will be blessed by God—all his work & labor

a. Tithing is to be a *regular practice*. The Israelites were to set aside one tenth of their produce *each year* as a tithe to the LORD. Through Moses, God told His people exactly how much they could keep and how much they were to give, and note, the tithe was to be given *year by year* (v.22).

b. Tithing is to be *offered at the worship center* in the presence of the LORD (v.23). The Israelites were to take a tithe of their grain, new wine, oil, and the firstborn of their herds and flocks to the worship center and offer them to the LORD. Note

---

[2] The idea for this particular outline on tithing was gleaned from John Maxwell's *The Preacher's Commentary on Deuteronomy*, pp.203-205.

exactly where the tithe was to be offered: at the *worship center* chosen by God, that is, the worship center that He honored and where He chose to place His name. The central worship center chosen by God was the Tabernacle and later the temple. Wherever these were to be located in the future, God's people were to take their tithes there.

c. Tithing is to be a *spiritual testimony* (v.23). Tithing strengthens a person's reverence and fear for the LORD; it also teaches others to reverence and fear the LORD. When an Israelite tithed, he was declaring that he trusted God and depended upon God. He knew that he was dependent upon God for health to work and earn a living. Moreover, he knew that he was dependent upon God for a job, for the strength of the economy, for rain, and for a fruitful crop and food. He was totally dependent upon God for the necessities of life. This was the very reason he was tithing: to demonstrate his love, dependence, and trust in God. Thus his tithing served to strengthen his own faith as well as to teach others to reverence and fear the LORD.

d. Tithing is to be a *flexible law*. Circumstances of a person's situation are to be considered (v.24). The circumstances covered by Moses involved a person who lived too far away to carry his tithe to the worship center. In such a situation, a person could exchange the tithe—his crops and animals—for silver (v.25). He could then use the silver to buy whatever offering he needed to tithe at the worship center (v.26). Note this fact: it was this flexibility that led the priests of later generations to place money-changers in the temple courts (see Jn.2:14-16).

The point to see is the concern of God for the extreme circumstances of His people. Living in an imperfect world, God's people sometimes get themselves in financial binds. In such circumstances, the law of tithing has to be flexible until the person can get out from under the financial difficulty. However, a person must never use circumstances as an excuse for not giving offerings to the LORD. If a believer is ever so irresponsible that he gets himself into a financial bind, he must immediately attack the problem. He must correct the situation, for God does not want any believer under the pressure of financial difficulties. The believer is to straighten out any financial predicament so that he may tithe and have enough to give to the needy.

e. Tithing is to be a *joyful experience* (v.26). When the Israelites took their offerings to the central worship center, they were to eat and rejoice around a fellowship meal cooked from part of the tithe. This was to be a joyful time shared with other believers at the worship center.

f. Tithing is to be a *benevolent witness* for the LORD (vv.27-29). Note the law: every third year, the Israelite believers were to take the tithe of their produce and store it in each town (v.28). The purpose for this storage was to provide for the Levite ministers and the needy of every town: the foreigners, the fatherless, and the widows of the community (v.29). Note that the support of the Levite ministers is emphasized: the people were never to neglect the Levite ministers. Supporting them was an absolute necessity, for they were to receive no allotment or inheritance in the promised land. They were to focus totally upon the LORD not upon financial and business matters. Their call was to minister to the people and teach them the ways of God. Therefore, the people must support them.

g. Tithing is to be a *beneficial exercise*. If the Israelite believer was faithful in tithing, God promised to bless him, to bless all the work of his hands. Whatever he did with his hands—his job or employment—would be blessed by God (v.29).

> "Give, and it shall be given unto you; good measure, pressed down, and shaken together, and running over, shall men give into your bosom. For with the same measure that ye mete withal it shall be measured to you again" (Lu.6:38).
>
> "And he looked up, and saw the rich men casting their gifts into the treasury. And he saw also a certain poor widow casting in thither two mites. And he said, Of a truth I say unto you, that this poor widow hath cast in more than they all: For all these have of their abundance cast in unto the offerings of God: but she of her penury hath cast in all the living that she had" (Lu.21:1-4).
>
> "Neither was there any among them that lacked: for as many as were possessors of lands or houses sold them, and brought the prices of the things that were sold, And laid *them* down at the apostles' feet: and distribution was made unto every man according as he had need" (Ac.4:34-35).
>
> "I have showed you all things, how that so labouring ye ought to support the weak, and to remember the words of the LORD Jesus, how he said, It is more blessed to give than to receive" (Ac.20:35).
>
> "Upon the first *day* of the week let every one of you lay by him in store, as *God* hath prospered him, that there be no gatherings when I come" (1 Co.16:2).
>
> "But this *I say*, He which soweth sparingly shall reap also sparingly; and he which soweth bountifully shall reap also bountifully" (2 Co.9:6).
>
> "Every man according as he purposeth in his heart, *so let him give;* not grudgingly, or of necessity: for God loveth a cheerful giver" (2 Co.9:7).
>
> "Every man *shall give* as he is able, according to the blessing of the LORD thy God which he hath given thee" (De.16:17).
>
> "And all the tithe of the land, *whether* of the seed of the land, *or* of the fruit of the tree, *is* the LORD'S: *it is* holy unto the LORD" (Le.27:30).
>
> "And as soon as the commandment came abroad, the children of Israel brought in abundance the firstfruits of corn, wine, and oil, and honey, and of all the increase of the field; and the tithe of all *things* brought they in abundantly" (2 Chr.31:5).
>
> "Honour the LORD with thy substance, and with the firstfruits of all thine increase" (Pr.3:9).
>
> "The liberal soul shall be made fat: and he that watereth shall be watered also himself" (Pr.11:25).
>
> "He that hath a bountiful eye shall be blessed; for he giveth of his bread to the poor" (Pr.22:9).
>
> "Bring ye all the tithes into the storehouse, that there may be meat in mine house, and prove me now herewith, saith the LORD of hosts, if I will not open you the windows of heaven, and pour you out a blessing, that *there shall* not *be room* enough *to receive it*" (Mal.3:10).

DEUTERONOMY 14:1-29

TYPES, SYMBOLS, AND PICTURES
(Deuteronomy 14:1-29)

Historical Term	Type or Picture (Scriptural Basis for Each)	Life Application for Today's Believer	Biblical Application
Cleansing Laws De.14:3-21	*The laws of cleanliness and defilement were symbolic of spiritual truth, of being spiritually clean and undefiled. The laws of cleanliness set God's people apart as a clean, holy people.* *"Thou shalt not eat any abominable thing" (De.14:3).*	⇒ The true believers of Israel were to be strict in keeping these laws governing food. This means that every time a believer saw a clean or unclean animal, the thought of God was to enter his mind. He was to think about the commandment to live a holy and clean life before God. What a lesson for us today, for all believers. When we see the unclean and clean things of this earth, we should immediately think of God. We should focus upon God's call to us, that we live holy and clean lives.	*"And that ye put on the new man, which after God is created in righteousness and true holiness" (Ep. 4:24).* *"Therefore if any man be in Christ, he is a new creature: old things are passed away; behold, all things are become new" (2 Co.5:17).* *"Wherefore come out from among them, and be ye separate, saith the Lord, and touch not the unclean thing; and I will receive you, And will be a Father unto you, and ye shall be my sons and daughters, saith the Lord Almighty" (2 Co.6:17-18).* *"Having therefore these promises, dearly beloved, let us cleanse ourselves from all filthiness of the flesh and spirit, perfecting holiness in the fear of God" (2 Co.7:1).* *"Draw nigh to God, and he will draw nigh to you. Cleanse your hands, ye sinners; and purify your hearts, ye double minded" (Js.4:8; See also Le. 11:45).*

DEUTERONOMY 15:1-23

CHAPTER 15

D. Laws That Demand Generosity & Giving: The Believer Must Not Hoard, Be Hard-hearted Nor Tightfisted, 15:1-23

1. **The law of debt release: Must not be hard-hearted nor tightfisted against debtors**
   a. The law: To cancel all loans made to fellow Israelites or brothers—every seven years
      1) May require payment from a foreigner
      2) Must cancel any debt owed by a brother
   b. The motivation for keeping the law
      1) The elimination of poverty: No poor
      2) The blessing is conditional: Must obey the LORD in order to be blessed
      3) The promise of financial prosperity & freedom—both individually & nationally

2. **The law of generosity, of giving to the poor: Must not be hard-hearted nor tightfisted against the poor**
   a. The law: To be generous, openhanded, & freely lend whatever a brother needs
   b. The warning
      1) Must not show ill will by giving nothing to a needy brother: Some might refuse if the year of debt release was near
      2) The reason: He will cry out to God against your hardness; you will be guilty of sin
   c. The motivation for giving generously—without a grudging heart: The blessing of God
      1) In one's work or labor
      2) In everything one does
   d. The tragic fact—the failure to be generous is foreseen: There will always be poor people
   e. The command reemphasized: Be generous, openhanded to the poor & needy

3. **The law of releasing slaves: Must not be hard-hearted nor tightfisted against workers**[DS1]
   a. The law: Must set a slave free in the seventh year—after six years of service
      1) Must not send him away empty-handed
      2) Must give him ample supplies (finances) to begin life on his own
   b. The motivation
      1) The blessing of God
      2) The redemption of God: His deliverance from Egypt & its slavery (a symbol of the world)
   c. The compassion demanded: A slave wished to stay
      1) His reason: Because he loved the owner's family & was doing well
      2) The contract of a lifetime commitment to a property owner
   d. The attitude encouraged: Freeing a slave was not a hardship
      1) Because the slave's labor was worth twice as much as a paid worker
      2) Because God will bless all you do

4. **The law of giving all firstborn animals to the LORD: Must not be hard-hearted nor tightfisted against God**
   a. Must set apart all firstborn males—for sacrifice
   b. Must not work them or shear them
   c. Must take the firstborn to the worship center, sacrifice & eat the meat only there
   d. Must offer only perfect

At the end of *every* seven years thou shalt make a release.
2 And this *is* the manner of the release: Every creditor that lendeth *ought* unto his neighbour shall release *it*; he shall not exact *it* of his neighbour, or of his brother; because it is called the LORD'S release.
3 Of a foreigner thou mayest exact *it again*: but *that* which is thine with thy brother thine hand shall release;
4 Save when there shall be no poor among you; for the LORD shall greatly bless thee in the land which the LORD thy God giveth thee *for* an inheritance to possess it:
5 Only if thou carefully hearken unto the voice of the LORD thy God, to observe to do all these commandments which I command thee this day.
6 For the LORD thy God blesseth thee, as he promised thee: and thou shalt lend unto many nations, but thou shalt not borrow; and thou shalt reign over many nations, but they shall not reign over thee.
7 If there be among you a poor man of one of thy brethren within any of thy gates in thy land which the LORD thy God giveth thee, thou shalt not harden thine heart, nor shut thine hand from thy poor brother:
8 But thou shalt open thine hand wide unto him, and shalt surely lend him sufficient for his need, *in that* which he wanteth.
9 Beware that there be not a thought in thy wicked heart, saying, The seventh year, the year of release, is at hand; and thine eye be evil against thy poor brother, and thou givest him nought; and he cry unto the LORD against thee, and it be sin unto thee.
10 Thou shalt surely give him, and thine heart shall not be grieved when thou givest unto him: because that for this thing the LORD thy God shall bless thee in all thy works, and in all that thou puttest thine hand unto.
11 For the poor shall never cease out of the land: therefore I command thee, saying, Thou shalt open thine hand wide unto thy brother, to thy poor, and to thy needy, in thy land.
12 *And* if thy brother, an Hebrew man, or an Hebrew woman, be sold unto thee, and serve thee six years; then in the seventh year thou shalt let him go free from thee.
13 And when thou sendest him out free from thee, thou shalt not let him go away empty:
14 Thou shalt furnish him liberally out of thy flock, and out of thy floor, and out of thy winepress: *of that* wherewith the LORD thy God hath blessed thee thou shalt give unto him.
15 And thou shalt remember that thou wast a bondman in the land of Egypt, and the LORD thy God redeemed thee: therefore I command thee this thing to day.
16 And it shall be, if he say unto thee, I will not go away from thee; because he loveth thee and thine house, because he is well with thee;
17 Then thou shalt take an aul, and thrust *it* through his ear unto the door, and he shall be thy servant for ever. And also unto thy maidservant thou shalt do likewise.
18 It shall not seem hard unto thee, when thou sendest him away free from thee; for he hath been worth a double hired servant *to thee*, in serving thee six years: and the LORD thy God shall bless thee in all that thou doest.
19 All the firstling males that come of thy herd and of thy flock thou shalt sanctify unto the LORD thy God: thou shalt do no work with the firstling of thy bullock, nor shear the firstling of thy sheep.
20 Thou shalt eat *it* before the LORD thy God year by year in the place which the LORD shall choose, thou and thy household.
21 And if there be *any*

sacrifices, none with a blemish or defect (a symbol of Christ's perfect sacrifice) e. Must treat all defective animals as wild game: Eat them	blemish therein, *as if it be* lame, or blind, *or have* any ill blemish, thou shalt not sacrifice it unto the LORD thy God. 22 Thou shalt eat it within thy gates: the unclean and the	clean *person shall eat it* alike, as the roebuck, and as the hart. 23 Only thou shalt not eat the blood thereof; thou shalt pour it upon the ground as water.	at home f. Must not eat the blood: To be poured out on the ground

DIVISION IV

THE SECOND GREAT THEME PREACHED BY GOD'S AGED SERVANT (PART 2): REMEMBER THE CIVIL AND RELIGIOUS LAWS OF ISRAEL—HELPFUL PRINCIPLES TO GOVERN MAN AND SOCIETY, 12:1–26:19

D. Laws That Demand Generosity and Giving: The Believer Must Not Hoard, Be Hard-hearted Nor Tightfisted, 15:1-23

(15:1-23) **Introduction**: poverty is a reality. Some people are poor, genuinely poor. As children, they never received the education or training that enabled them to earn a decent living. No one was around to encourage them to secure adequate education or job training skills. All kinds of things can cause poverty:
- lack of education
- health problems
- age
- accident
- loss of job
- some natural disaster
- economic recession or depression
- divorce or desertion

The causes of poverty are innumerable. As Scripture declares, "There will always be poor people" among you (De.15:11). What is to be our attitude toward the poor? Toward helping them? Toward meeting their needs: feeding, clothing, housing them? Are we going to be hard-hearted and tightfisted? Or compassionate, generous, and giving? Poverty—the poor among us—was of great concern to God. For this reason, God led Moses to preach the message of this compassionate section of Scripture: *Laws that Demand Generosity and Giving: the Believer Must Not Hoard, Be Hard-hearted Nor Tightfisted*, 15:1-23.
1. The law of debt release: must not be hard-hearted nor tightfisted against debtors (vv.1-6).
2. The law of generosity, of giving to the poor: must not be hard-hearted nor tightfisted against the poor (vv.7-11).
3. The law of releasing slaves: must not be hard-hearted nor tightfisted against workers (vv.12-18).
4. The law of giving all firstborn to the LORD: must not be hard-hearted nor tightfisted against God (vv.19-23).

1 (15:1-6) **Debt, Release of—Loans, Release of—Cancellation, of Debts—Release, of Debts—Law, Civil—Israel, Laws of—Law, of Debt Release—Sabbatical Year—Year, Sabbatical—Hard-hearted, Remedy Against—Tightfisted, Remedy Against**: there was the law of debt release. The believer must not be hard-hearted nor tightfisted against debtors. Remember, one of the very first institutions established by God was the Sabbath day, which stated that man was to rest and worship one day out of every seven. Sometime later, God established an additional Sabbath institution for His people, the Sabbath year or what is commonly known as the *Sabbatical year*. The law of debt release was to take place during the Sabbatical year. The purpose of the Sabbath year was fourfold:
⇒ to give the land a year of rest, one year out of every seven when the land was to lie fallow, untilled and undisturbed (see outline and notes—Ex.23:10-19; Le.25:2-7 for more discussion)
⇒ to show special compassion for the poor every seven years, special compassion by allowing them and the animals of the field to eat freely from whatever grew naturally
⇒ to set aside one year out of every seven for special worship and study of God's Word (De.31:10-13)
⇒ to provide a year of debt release—one year out of every seven—one year of freedom from the pressure of all debt for all of God's people

This latter purpose, the release from all debt, is the concern of the present passage. Debt causes all kinds of pressure for people and can cause some of the most agonizing tension known to man. If a person does not have the money to pay his debts, he is often left destitute, unable to provide food and housing for himself and his family. The pressure of debt can cause all kinds of health problems such as ulcers, high blood pressure, and strokes. Moreover, the pressure of debt and financial difficulties gnaw away at human relationships, consuming them. It can rip families and friendships apart. For this reason, release from the pressure of debt is a vital concern to God. Through His servant Moses, God attacks the problem head-on in this passage. Moses preaches to God's people: there is to be a law governing debt release during the Sabbatical year. You must not be hard-hearted nor tightfisted against debtors.

DEUTERONOMY 15:1-23

OUTLINE	SCRIPTURE	SCRIPTURE	OUTLINE
1. **The law of debt release: Must not be hard-hearted nor tightfisted against debtors** a. The law: To cancel all loans made to fellow Israelites or brothers—every seven years 1) May require payment from a foreigner 2) Must cancel any debt owed by a brother b. The motivation for keeping the law	At the end of *every* seven years thou shalt make a release. 2 And this *is* the manner of the release: Every creditor that lendeth *ought* unto his neighbour shall release *it*; he shall not exact *it* of his neighbour, or of his brother; because it is called the LORD'S release. 3 Of a foreigner thou mayest exact *it again*: but *that* which is thine with thy brother thine hand shall release; 4 Save when there shall be no poor among you; for the	LORD shall greatly bless thee in the land which the LORD thy God giveth thee *for* an inheritance to possess it: 5 Only if thou carefully hearken unto the voice of the LORD thy God, to observe to do all these commandments which I command thee this day. 6 For the LORD thy God blesseth thee, as he promised thee: and thou shalt lend unto many nations, but thou shalt not borrow; and thou shalt reign over many nations, but they shall not reign over thee.	1) The elimination of poverty: No poor 2) The blessing is conditional: Must obey the LORD in order to be blessed 3) The promise of financial prosperity & freedom—both individually & nationally

a. The law was simply stated: all loans made to fellow Israelites or brothers were canceled every seven years, that is, during the observance of the Sabbatical year. However, the Israelites could require payment of a foreigner. He only had to cancel any debt owed by an Israelite brother (v.3). Now, does this mean that the debts were permanently, forever terminated? Or, does it mean that the debts were just suspended during the course of the seventh year and were to be repaid after that, during the following six years? This issue is debated among commentators; however, the latter alternative seems to be the intent of the law because of the Year of Jubilee. All debts were released during the Year of Jubilee (every 50th year. See outline and notes—Le.25:1-55 for more discussion.)

b. There was strong motivation for keeping the law of debt release (vv.4-6). Poverty would be eliminated. There would be no poor among them. Every person would have enough to eat, enough clothing, housing, and whatever else he needed. The land, the nation, and its people would be greatly blessed. Pressure caused by debt and financial difficulties would be erased. The strain, the tension that causes so many health problems and broken relationships would be greatly eased. This is the purpose for this law, and it is the motivation, the very reason the Israelites were to keep this law.

But note, Moses declared that this blessing is conditional: the people must obey the LORD in order to receive the blessing. They must obey all the commandments of God. If they will obey the law of debt release and all the other commandments of God, poverty will be eliminated from their land. There will be no poor among them.

Note also the promise of financial prosperity and freedom, both individually and nationally. If the Israelites obey, the LORD God will bless them just as He has promised. In fact, they will find themselves lending to many nations but having to borrow from none. And even more significant, they will rule many nations and be ruled by none. They will be a great people and a great nation, all because they obey God. Imagine! A nation with no poverty, a people with no poor among them.

Thought 1. The law of debt release had one specific purpose: to eliminate poverty among the Israelites. There should be no poor among God's people. Every person must have at least the necessities of life, that is, food to eat, clothes to wear, and a roof over his head. God's Holy Word is clear: we are to take care of the poor, not take advantage of them. We are not to deliberately set low wages for the poor nor steal their wages. Neither are we to allow the execution of injustice against them just because they do not have the authority or money to defend themselves. The needs of the poor are to be met.

"Jesus said unto him, If thou wilt be perfect, go *and* sell that thou hast, and give to the poor, and thou shalt have treasure in heaven: and come *and* follow me" (Mt.19:21).

"Only *they would* that we should remember the poor; the same which I also was forward to do" (Ga.2:10).

"Pure religion and undefiled before God and the Father is this, To visit the fatherless and widows in their affliction, *and* to keep himself unspotted from the world" (Js.1:27).

"But the seventh *year* thou shalt let it rest and lie still; that the poor of thy people may eat: and what they leave the beasts of the field shall eat. In like manner thou shalt deal with thy vineyard, *and* with thy oliveyard" (Ex.23:11).

"If there be among you a poor man of one of thy brethren within any of thy gates in thy land which the LORD thy God giveth thee, thou shalt not harden thine heart, nor shut thine hand from thy poor brother" (De.15:7).

"Thou shalt not pervert the judgment of the stranger, *nor* of the fatherless; nor take a widow's raiment to pledge" (De.24:17).

"Defend the poor and fatherless: do justice to the afflicted and needy" (Ps.82:3).

"Blessed *is* he that considereth the poor: the LORD will deliver him in time of trouble" (Ps.41:1).

"He that hath pity upon the poor lendeth unto the LORD; and that which he hath given will he pay him again" (Pr.19:17).

"Whoso stoppeth his ears at the cry of the poor, he also shall cry himself, but shall not be heard" (Pr.21:13).

"The king that faithfully judgeth the poor, his throne shall be established for ever" (Pr.29:14).

DEUTERONOMY 15:1-23

"He judged the cause of the poor and needy; then *it was* well *with him: was* not this to know me? saith the LORD" (Je.22:16).

2 **(15:7-11) Generosity, Duty—Poor, Duty—Hard-hearted, Remedy—Tightfisted, Duty—Loans, Duty—Stewardship, Duty—Giving, Duty**: there was the law of generosity, of giving to the poor. The believer must not be hard-hearted nor tightfisted against the poor. This law is a *heart issue*: it deals with the human heart and speaks to the human heart. The issue is not about outright gifts to the poor but about making loans to the poor, lending the poor person whatever he needs. Standing there preaching to the Israelites, Moses declares: you must not be hard-hearted nor tightfisted toward your poor brother.

OUTLINE	SCRIPTURE	SCRIPTURE	OUTLINE
2. The law of generosity, of giving to the poor: Must not be hard-hearted nor tightfisted against the poor	7 If there be among you a poor man of one of thy brethren within any of thy gates in thy land which the LORD thy God giveth thee, thou shalt not harden thine heart, nor shut thine hand from thy poor brother:	givest him nought; and he cry unto the LORD against thee, and it be sin unto thee. 10 Thou shalt surely give him, and thine heart shall not be grieved when thou givest unto him: because that for this thing the LORD thy God shall bless thee in all thy works, and in all that thou puttest thine hand unto.	2) The reason: He will cry out to God against your hardness; you will be guilty of sin c. The motivation for giving generously—without a grudging heart: The blessing of God 1) In one's work or labor 2) In everything one does
a. The law: To be generous, openhanded, & freely lend whatever a brother needs	8 But thou shalt open thine hand wide unto him, and shalt surely lend him sufficient for his need, *in that* which he wanteth.		
b. The warning 1) Must not show ill will by giving nothing to a needy brother: Some might refuse if the year of debt release was near	9 Beware that there be not a thought in thy wicked heart, saying, The seventh year, the year of release, is at hand; and thine eye be evil against thy poor brother, and thou	11 For the poor shall never cease out of the land: therefore I command thee, saying, Thou shalt open thine hand wide unto thy brother, to thy poor, and to thy needy, in thy land.	d. The tragic fact—the failure to be generous is foreseen: There will always be poor people e. The command reemphasized: Be generous, openhanded to the poor & needy

    a. The law is clearly stated: you are to be generous, openhanded, and freely lend whatever a brother needs (v.8). As stated, the law deals with making loans not with free gifts. This does not mean that free gifts are never to be given to the poor. Of course, there are times when free gifts are needed just as there are times when loans are needed. Some poor could never pay back loans due to being physically handicapped, helpless, unemployed, too young or old, or a host of other reasons. At such times, free gifts must be made to the poor; they must be fed, clothed, and housed. This is the direct responsibility of society so long as the poor are among us. But when the poor are able to pay back loans, then loans are to be made to them and not free gifts. They are to be responsible citizens within the community. This is the law God is declaring through His servant Moses.

    b. But note the warning that Moses gives to the Israelites: the believer must not show ill will by giving nothing to a needy brother (v.9). Some Israelites might refuse to help the needy if the year of debt release was near. A loan to the poor during the sixth year would mean that the creditor would have to bear the loan for an extra year: he would not be able to collect the loan during the seventh year. Because of the year of debt release, a tendency not to make loans to the poor could easily arise within the hearts of the Israelites. This law was given to combat the tendency to be hard-hearted and tightfisted.

    c. Moses declares the strong motivation for giving generously, for giving without a grudging heart. If God's people will give generously to the poor, He promises to bless them in their work and labor. Everything they put their hands to will be blessed: their work, employment, and all their other activities. God will prosper them and do so significantly (v.10).

    d. But note the tragic fact: Moses is very aware of the seed of selfishness and covetousness that is within the heart of man. Consequently, he foresees the failure of God's people to be generous, foresees their failure to obey this commandment (v.11). He declares: there will always be poor people among you.

    e. However, the command stands, and Moses reemphasizes it. He cries out: "I command you: be generous—be openhanded to your brothers and to the poor and needy in your land" (v.11).

Thought 1. The lesson for us is clear. We must be generous to the poor, give to meet their needs. We must not be hard-hearted nor tightfisted against the poor. Our hands must never be closed; rather, they must be open to help the needy of the world. However, we must never indulge the poor nor give license to them if they are able to work and earn a living, yet they do not. We must never indulge nor give license to irresponsibility. Indulging laziness and slothfulness only causes the growth of irresponsible behavior, the corruption and deterioration of society. The poor must be responsible human beings, responsible for doing what they can to strengthen society. They owe a debt to society, and they must pay that debt, making every contribution they can. They are a part of society, and they are responsible for strengthening society—just as much as any other person. Therefore, they must work if they are able.

    Nevertheless, there will always be poor among us who have little and are unable to provide for themselves. Scripture is clear: it is our duty to meet their needs. We must help them. We must be generous and openhanded to them. If they are able to pay back loans, we must freely lend to them. But if they are unable to pay back loans, we must freely give to them. We must not be hard-hearted nor tightfisted against the poor.

"Jesus said unto him, If thou wilt be perfect, go *and* sell that thou hast, and give to the poor, and thou shalt have treasure in heaven: and come *and* follow me" (Mt.19:21).

"But rather give alms of such things as ye have; and, behold, all things are clean unto you" (Lu.11:41).

"Neither was there any among them that lacked: for as many as were possessors of lands or houses sold them, and brought the prices of the things that were sold, And laid *them* down at the apostles' feet: and distribution was made unto every man according as he had need" (Ac.4:34-35).

"Then the disciples, every man according to his ability, determined to send relief unto the brethren which dwelt in Judaea" (Ac.11:29).

"I have showed you all things, how that so labouring ye ought to support the weak, and to remember the words of the LORD Jesus, how he said, It is more blessed to give than to receive" (Ac.20:35).

"Distributing to the necessity of saints; given to hospitality" (Ro.12:13).

"How that in a great trial of affliction the abundance of their joy and their deep poverty abounded unto the riches of their liberality" (2 Co.8:2).

"As we have therefore opportunity, let us do good unto all *men,* especially unto them who are of the household of faith" (Ga.6:10).

"For even in Thessalonica ye sent once and again unto my necessity" (Ph.4:16).

"If there be among you a poor man of one of thy brethren within any of thy gates in thy land which the LORD thy God giveth thee, thou shalt not harden thine heart, nor shut thine hand from thy poor brother" (De.15:7).

"Whoso stoppeth his ears at the cry of the poor, he also shall cry himself, but shall not be heard" (Pr.21:13).

"He that giveth unto the poor shall not lack: but he that hideth his eyes shall have many a curse" (Pr.28:27).

3 (15:12-18) **Slavery, Law Governing—Workers, Duty Toward—Laws, of Israel—Bondage, Laws Governing—Hard-hearted, Duty—Tightfisted, Duty—Compassion, Duty**: there was the law of releasing slaves. The believer must not be hard-hearted nor tightfisted against workers. This law does not deal with slavery in general but, rather, with a particular type of slavery. Sometimes a person sinks to the depths of poverty because he simply has nothing. He as no money with which to buy food or clothing or to keep a roof over his head. Neither does he have the money to pay his debts. When an Israelite faced such dire circumstances, he could sell himself and his labor to his creditor or to anyone else who would take him in and give him employment. He could serve the creditor, and his service would substitute for the repayment of the money he owed to the creditor (see DEEPER STUDY # 1—De.15:12-18 for more discussion on the subject of slavery. Also see notes—Ex.21:2-6; 21:7-11.)

OUTLINE	SCRIPTURE	SCRIPTURE	OUTLINE

3. **The law of releasing slaves: Must not be hard-hearted nor tightfisted against workers**[DS1]
a. The law: Must set a slave free in the seventh year—after six years of service
  1) Must not send him away empty-handed
 	
  2) Must give him ample supplies (finances) to begin life on his own
b. The motivation
  1) The blessing of God
 	
  2) The redemption of God: His deliverance from Egypt & its slavery (a symbol of the world)
	12 And if thy brother, an Hebrew man, or an Hebrew woman, be sold unto thee, and serve thee six years; then in the seventh year thou shalt let him go free from thee.
	13 And when thou sendest him out free from thee, thou shalt not let him go away empty:
	14 Thou shalt furnish him liberally out of thy flock, and out of thy floor, and out of thy winepress: *of that* wherewith the LORD thy God hath blessed thee thou shalt give unto him.
	15 And thou shalt remember that thou wast a bondman in the land of Egypt, and the LORD thy God redeemed
		thee: therefore I command thee this thing to day.
		16 And it shall be, if he say unto thee, I will not go away from thee; because he loveth thee and thine house, because he is well with thee;
		17 Then thou shalt take an aul, and thrust *it* through his ear unto the door, and he shall be thy servant for ever. And also unto thy maidservant thou shalt do likewise.
		18 It shall not seem hard unto thee, when thou sendest him away free from thee; for he hath been worth a double hired servant *to thee*, in serving thee six years: and the LORD thy God shall bless thee in all that thou doest.
			c. The compassion demanded: A slave wished to stay
			  1) His reason: Because he loved the owner's family & was doing well
			  2) The contract of a lifetime commitment to a property owner
			
			d. The attitude encouraged: Freeing a slave was not a hardship
			  1) Because the slave's labor was worth twice as much as a paid worker
			  2) Because God will bless all you do

a. Moses declared the law to the Israelites: they must set a slave free in the seventh year (v.12). This is not a reference to the Sabbatical year but to the seventh year after six years of service. Immediately after laboring for six years, the person's debt was considered paid. He was to be freed on the seventh year. Note the compassion of the law: a person was not to send a slave away empty-handed (vv.13-14). The person was to give the slave ample supplies or finances to begin life on his own.

b. There was strong motivation for God's people to obey this law (vv.14-15). God had blessed them richly, making them prosperous and financially independent. Just as God had blessed them, so they were to bless—be generous—to the poor slave who was stepping out into the world to begin life on his own. But there was a second reason, a far more important reason why a person was to obey this law: God had redeemed Israel, had delivered them from Egypt and its slavery. Consequently, just as God had freed their forefathers, they were to free the slaves after they had worked to pay off their debts (v.15). This law was to be obeyed: every person who was forced to sell himself and his labor to pay off a debt was to be freed.

c. But note the compassion and the understanding heart that were demanded: if a slave wished to stay because he loved the owner's family and was doing well with the owner, he was to be kept. His wish to stay was to be granted. In such a circumstance, the contract of a lifetime commitment to a property owner was to be sealed. The contract was the piercing of his ear and the pledge to serve his master for life (v.17).

d. Moses encouraged a compassionate attitude: freeing a slave was not to be considered a hardship (v.18). The person had labored for six years without any direct income. He had labored as a slave not as a common worker or employee. As a slave, he was available twenty-four hours a day not just a set number of hours as a common laborer would work. Moreover, the debt he owed had been recovered through labor. If he had not served during the six years, the debt would have been lost. The difference between the debt lost and the debt recovered by labor plus the difference between the available hours of a slave and a common worker—all equal twice as much service as a hired hand. Think about this fact: this is the attitude you are to have toward freeing the slave. But not only this, if you obey this law and free the slave after six years of service, God will bless in all that you do.

DEEPER STUDY # 1

(15:12-18) **Slavery—Bondage**: slavery has been a part of society since the earliest days of human history. Every generation has witnessed the enslavement of millions of people. Men of power, the rulers and the wealthy of the world, have always sought more and more of everything:

- ⇒ more power
- ⇒ more recognition
- ⇒ more honor
- ⇒ more land
- ⇒ more wealth
- ⇒ more property
- ⇒ more possessions
- ⇒ more pleasure
- ⇒ more fame

One of the easiest ways to gain more of these things is through slave labor. Slave labor is cheap labor. Slave labor means more for the slave owner, whether the owner is the ruler of a nation, the Board of a corporation, a wealthy individual, or a crime syndicate.

In the ancient world, the entire economy of the world was based upon slavery. Slavery was the very way of life, the fiber and fabric of society itself. When nations conquered people in war, the people were enslaved by the conquering nation. The economy of that day was not a monetary economy (based upon money), but a *goods or materials* economy. That is, people swapped labor for housing, food, clothes. The poor people (the have-nots) of the earth had no way to survive apart from becoming the slave laborers of the rulers and the wealthy of society. They received housing, food, and clothing by becoming the slaves of the powerful of the earth, by selling their labor (themselves) to the rulers and wealthy. As stated, this was just the way of life in the ancient world, the way the peoples of the earth lived and formed the society of their day. The very economy of the world—the trading of goods, merchandise, possessions—was based upon slavery. As in any society, there were both good and evil slave owners. However, as history has proven, the vast majority of slave owners exposed the evil of the human heart. The rulers and wealthy of the world took advantage of slave labor...

- housing the slaves in run-down, dilapidated shanties
- paying few if any wages
- giving little attention to medical treatment
- forcing the people to struggle for food and clothing
- demanding exhaustive labor
- giving little attention to working conditions and the environment
- mistreating through abuse, violence, and rape

The one fact to remember above all others in dealing with slavery is this: most people in the ancient world had to hire themselves out as slaves in order to survive. They just had no other way to secure housing, food, and clothing—the very basic necessities of life. This is the background that must be looked at when studying this particular law governing Hebrew slaves. When this background is understood, the purpose of God in giving this particular law is clearly seen. God set out to correct the terrible evil of human slavery throughout the world. This is seen throughout the entire Old Testament and the New Testament as well. (See note—Ep.6:5-9 for more discussion.) However, in correcting the evil of slavery, keep one clear fact in mind: God could not demand the elimination of slavery all at once. This act would have caused terrible pain and suffering for the majority of people in the world.

⇒ Slaves would have immediately lost the housing, food, clothing, and what little income, if any, they were receiving from their owners.

⇒ The rulers and wealthy of the earth would have reacted by law or violence against any slave who demanded that he be freed because he was following the commandment of the LORD God.

Very simply, if God had given a clear-cut commandment that all slavery was to be eliminated, the ancient world would have been thrown into a terrifying revolution and holocaust. Multiplied millions of people—any mass of slaves who attempted to follow the command of God—would have been slaughtered by the armies of the rulers and wealthy of the earth. This is the reason God moved progressively—ever so slowly, but progressively—in demanding that slavery be eliminated from the face of the earth. The commentator John Maxwell makes this observation:

> In studying the bond-servant law...one could ask why it was that Moses, a divinely commissioned leader, tolerated a form of slavery. The answer is to be found in [the] Scriptures....We can see that he was slowly educating his people away from this form of servitude. Notice the following regulations:
> 1. The Hebrew servant was held for six years only; in the seventh year he or she was freed.

"And if thy brother, an Hebrew man, or an Hebrew woman, be sold unto thee, and serve thee six years; then in the seventh year thou shalt let him go free from thee" (De.15:12).

DEUTERONOMY 15:1-23

2. *Rigorous demands and harshness were forbidden.*

"Thou shalt not rule over him with rigour; but shalt fear thy God" (Le.25:43).

3. *If a master inflicted serious bodily injury on a servant, that servant was to have his freedom.*

"And if a man smite the eye of his servant, or the eye of his maid, that it perish; he shall let him go free for his eye's sake. And if he smite out his manservant's tooth, or his maidservant's tooth; he shall let him go free for his tooth's sake" (Ex.21:26-27).

4. *A servant could acquire assets and might even save enough money to buy his or her own freedom.*

"And if a sojourner or stranger wax rich by thee, and thy brother that dwelleth by him wax poor, and sell himself unto the stranger or sojourner by thee, or to the stock of the stranger's family: After that he is sold he may be redeemed again; one of his brethren may redeem him: Either his uncle, or his uncle's son, may redeem him, or any that is nigh of kin unto him of his family may redeem him; or if he be able, he may redeem himself" (Le.25:47-49).

5. *Two special privileges were given to the servants: They were to be free from work on the Sabbath, and they were to participate in the great national feast times.*

"Six days thou shalt do thy work, and on the seventh day thou shalt rest: that thine ox and thine ass may rest, and the son of thy handmaid, and the stranger, may be refreshed" (Ex.23:12).
"And thou shalt rejoice before the Lord thy God, thou, and thy son, and thy daughter, and thy manservant, and thy maidservant, and the Levite that is within thy gates, and the stranger, and the fatherless, and the widow, that are among you, in the place which the Lord thy God hath chosen to place his name there....And thou shalt rejoice in thy feast, thou, and thy son, and thy daughter, and thy manservant, and thy maidservant, and the Levite, the stranger, and the fatherless, and the widow, that are within thy gates" (De.16:11, 14).

6. *Upon the seventh year, a servant was to be freed and supplied "liberally" with food and other provisions.*

"And when thou sendest him out free from thee, thou shalt not let him go away empty: Thou shalt furnish him liberally out of thy flock, and out of thy floor, and out of thy winepress: of that wherewith the Lord thy God hath blessed thee thou shalt give unto him" (De.15:13-14).

7. *As the nation matured, its laws toward slavery became more progressive. During Moses' lifetime, provisions which were at first intended only for male servants were extended to female servants.*

"And if a man sell his daughter to be a maidservant, she shall not go out as the menservants do" (Ex.21:7).
"Then thou shalt take an aul, and thrust it through his ear unto the door, and he shall be thy servant for ever. And also unto thy maidservant thou shalt do likewise" (De.15:17).

8. *The idea of freedom (through seventh-year release) was continually kept before the master and his servant.*
9. *When a slave escaped from his master, the moment he touched Hebrew soil, he was free.*[1]

"Thou shalt not deliver unto his master the servant which is escaped from his master unto thee: He shall dwell with thee, even among you, in that place which he shall choose in one of thy gates, where it liketh him best: thou shalt not oppress him" (De.23:15-16).

4 **(15:19-23) Giving, Duty—Firstborn, Law Governing—Law, Governing the Firstborn—Hard-hearted, Duty—Tightfisted, Duty—Animal Sacrifice, Common Requirements—Jesus Christ, Symbol of—Offerings, Requirement**: there was the law of giving all the firstborn animals to the LORD. The believer must not be hard-hearted nor tightfisted against God. The only living and true God is the LORD God Himself (Jehovah, Yahweh). He is the Creator of the universe, the Sovereign Majesty who owns everything. Therefore, He lays claims upon man, claims that must be paid:

⇒ He claims the first day of the week as a day of worship.
⇒ He claims the firstfruits of the harvest as an offering to support His ministers and to carry out His purposes upon this earth.
⇒ He claims the commitment of man's heart, that man love Him wholeheartedly.
⇒ He claims the firstborn males from the herds and the flocks to serve as atoning sacrifices offered up to Him.

As the Majestic Creator and Owner of the universe, God has the perfect right to claim the firstborn male of the Israelite's herds and flocks. But this was not all; God was also the Savior of His people. He had saved the Israelites out of Egyptian bondage. As both Creator and Savior, He had the right to demand the very best from His people. Because of His glorious

---
[1] John Maxwell. *The Preacher's Commentary on Deuteronomy*, pp.211-212. (Scripture references given by Maxwell are written out by us for the reader's benefit.)

DEUTERONOMY 15:1-23

salvation, they owed Him the firstborn male (see outline and notes—Ex.13:1-16; 22:29-30; Nu.18:15-18 for more discussion).

OUTLINE	SCRIPTURE	SCRIPTURE	OUTLINE
4. The law of giving all firstborn animals to the LORD: Must not be hard-hearted nor tightfisted against God a. Must set apart all firstborn males—for sacrifice b. Must not work them or shear them c. Must take the firstborn to the worship center, sacrifice & eat the meat only there	19 All the firstling males that come of thy herd and of thy flock thou shalt sanctify unto the LORD thy God: thou shalt do no work with the firstling of thy bullock, nor shear the firstling of thy sheep. 20 Thou shalt eat *it* before the LORD thy God year by year in the place which the LORD shall choose, thou and thy household.	21 And if there be *any* blemish therein, *as if it be* lame, or blind, *or have* any ill blemish, thou shalt not sacrifice it unto the LORD thy God. 22 Thou shalt eat it within thy gates: the unclean and the clean *person shall eat it* alike, as the roebuck, and as the hart. 23 Only thou shalt not eat the blood thereof; thou shalt pour it upon the ground as water.	d. Must offer only perfect sacrifices, none with a blemish or defect (a symbol of Christ's perfect sacrifice) e. Must treat all defective animals as wild game: Eat them at home f. Must not eat the blood: To be poured out on the ground

a. A person was to set apart all firstborn male animals for sacrifice to the LORD (v.19). No animal other than the firstborn was to be used as a sacrifice.

b. A person was not to work the firstborn animal nor shear it (v.19). From birth, the firstborn was counted holy, sanctified, that is, set apart totally to God and His service. Thus the animal was not to be used for any other purpose, nor was its wool to be sheared for profit. The firstborn belonged to God and to God alone.

c. A person was to take the firstborn to the central worship center, that is, the Tabernacle and in future years the temple (v.20). The firstborn was to be sacrificed there and only there, and the fellowship meal was to be shared there and only there.

d. A person was to offer perfect sacrifices. He was not to offer any animal with a blemish or defect (v.21). This was a clear symbol of the perfect sacrifice of the Lord Jesus Christ upon the cross.

e. Moses declares that any defective firstborn animal was to be treated as wild game. The defective animal could be eaten at home (v.22).

f. But note: the person was not to eat the blood. The blood was to be poured out upon the ground (v.23). The life of the animal was in the blood; therefore, the blood was to be respected. The dignity of life was to be highly esteemed. It was not to be consumed as part of the meal.

Thought 1. The application to us is twofold:

(1) We are to give the first of everything to God, the very best that we have.

"Upon the first *day* of the week let every one of you lay by him in store, as *God* hath prospered him, that there be no gatherings when I come" (1 Co.16:2).

"Every man according as he purposeth in his heart, *so let him give;* not grudgingly, or of necessity: for God loveth a cheerful giver" (2 Co.9:7).

"For if there be first a willing mind, *it is* accepted according to that a man hath, *and* not according to that he hath not" (2 Co.8:12).

"And this stone, which I have set *for* a pillar, shall be God's house: and of all that thou shalt give me I will surely give the tenth unto thee" (Ge.28:22).

"Speak unto the children of Israel, that they bring me an offering: of every man that giveth it willingly with his heart ye shall take my offering" (Ex.25:2).

"And all the tithe of the land, *whether* of the seed of the land, *or* of the fruit of the tree, *is* the LORD's: *it is* holy unto the LORD" (Le.27:30).

"That thou shalt take of the first of all the fruit of the earth, which thou shalt bring of thy land that the LORD thy God giveth thee, and shalt put *it* in a basket, and shalt go unto the place which the LORD thy God shall choose to place his name there. And thou shalt go unto the priest that shall be in those days, and say unto him, I profess this day unto the LORD thy God, that I am come unto the country which the LORD sware unto our fathers for to give us. And the priest shall take the basket out of thine hand, and set it down before the altar of the LORD thy God" (De.26:2-4).

"Then the people rejoiced, for that they offered willingly, because with perfect heart they offered willingly to the LORD: and David the king also rejoiced with great joy" (1 Chr.29:9).

"Honour the LORD with thy substance, and with the firstfruits of all thine increase: So shall thy barns be filled with plenty, and thy presses shall burst out with new wine" (Pr.3:9-10).

"Bring ye all the tithes into the storehouse, that there may be meat in mine house, and prove me now herewith, saith the LORD of hosts, if I will not open you the windows of heaven, and pour you out a blessing, that *there shall* not *be room* enough *to receive it*" (Mal.3:10).

(2) The animal was a substitute sacrifice offered to God, offered to make atonement for the people. As the substitute sacrifice, the firstborn was a symbol of the perfect sacrifice of the Lord Jesus Christ.

"Who gave himself for our sins, that he might deliver us from this present evil world, according to the will of God and our Father" (Ga.1:4).

DEUTERONOMY 15:1-23

"And walk in love, as Christ also hath loved us, and hath given himself for us an offering and a sacrifice to God for a sweetsmelling savour" (Ep.5:2).

"Who gave himself for us, that he might redeem us from all iniquity, and purify unto himself a peculiar people, zealous of good works" (Tit.2:14).

"Forasmuch as ye know that ye were not redeemed with corruptible things, *as* silver and gold, from your vain conversation *received* by tradition from your fathers; But with the precious blood of Christ, as of a lamb without blemish and without spot" (1 Pe.1:18-19).

"Who his own self bare our sins in his own body on the tree, that we, being dead to sins, should live unto righteousness: by whose stripes ye were healed" (1 Pe.2:24).

"For Christ also hath once suffered for sins, the just for the unjust, that he might bring us to God, being put to death in the flesh, but quickened by the Spirit" (1 Pe.3:18).

"And ye know that he was manifested to take away our sins; and in him is no sin" (1 Jn.3:5).

"But he *was* wounded for our transgressions, *he was* bruised for our iniquities: the chastisement of our peace *was* upon him; and with his stripes we are healed" (Is.53:5).

(3) God has saved us through the substitute sacrifice of Christ. Because of the glorious salvation He has provided for us, we must give our lives totally to Him. We must present our bodies as a living sacrifice to God.

"And he said to *them* all, If any *man* will come after me, let him deny himself, and take up his cross daily, and follow me" (Lu.9:23).

"Knowing this, that our old man is crucified with *him*, that the body of sin might be destroyed, that henceforth we should not serve sin" (Ro.6:6).

"Likewise reckon ye also yourselves to be dead indeed unto sin, but alive unto God through Jesus Christ our LORD" (Ro.6:11).

"I beseech you therefore, brethren, by the mercies of God, that ye present your bodies a living sacrifice, holy, acceptable unto God, *which is* your reasonable service. And be not conformed to this world: but be ye transformed by the renewing of your mind, that ye may prove what is that good, and acceptable, and perfect, will of God" (Ro.12:1-2).

"For ye are dead, and your life is hid with Christ in God" (Col.3:3).

"I am crucified with Christ: nevertheless I live; yet not I, but Christ liveth in me: and the life which I now live in the flesh I live by the faith of the Son of God, who loved me, and gave himself for me" (Ga.2:20).

"But what things were gain to me, those I counted loss for Christ. Yea doubtless, and I count all things *but* loss for the excellency of the knowledge of Christ Jesus my LORD: for whom I have suffered the loss of all things, and do count them *but* dung, that I may win Christ" (Ph.3:7-8).

"For we which live are alway delivered unto death for Jesus' sake, that the life also of Jesus might be made manifest in our mortal flesh" (2 Co.4:11).

TYPES, SYMBOLS, AND PICTURES
(Deuteronomy 15:1-23)

Historical Term	Type or Picture (Scriptural Basis for Each)	Life Application for Today's Believer	Biblical Application
The Substitute Sacrifice: The Animal Was a Substitute Sacrifice Offered to God, Offered to Make Atonement for the People De.15:19-23	*As the substitute sacrifice, the firstborn animal was a symbol of the perfect sacrifice of the* LORD *Jesus Christ.* "All the firstling males that come of thy herd and of thy flock thou shalt sanctify unto the LORD thy God: thou shalt do no work with the firstling of thy bullock, nor shear the firstling of thy sheep" (De.15:19).	⇒ God has saved us through the substitute sacrifice of Christ. Because of the glorious salvation He has provided for us, we must give our lives totally to Him. We must present our bodies as a living sacrifice to God.	*"Who gave himself for our sins, that he might deliver us from this present evil world, according to the will of God and our Father" (Ga.1:4).* *"And walk in love, as Christ also hath loved us, and hath given himself for us an offering and a sacrifice to God for a sweetsmelling savour" (Ep.5:2).* *"Who gave himself for us, that he might redeem us from all iniquity, and purify unto himself a peculiar people, zealous of good works" (Tit.2:14).* *"I beseech you therefore, brethren, by the mercies of God, that ye present your bodies a living sacrifice, holy, acceptable unto God, which is your reasonable service. And be not conformed*

DEUTERONOMY 15:1-23

Historical Term	Type or Picture (Scriptural Basis for Each)	Life Application for Today's Believer	Biblical Application
			to this world: but be ye transformed by the renewing of your mind, that ye may prove what is that good, and acceptable, and perfect, will of God" (Ro.12:1-2).

DEUTERONOMY 16:1-17

CHAPTER 16

E. Laws That Govern the Three Pilgrimage Festivals of Worship: Remember the Great Blessings, Salvation, & Guidance of God, 16:1-17

1. **The Passover—remember the great deliverance of God from Egypt through the sacrifice of the lamb: A symbol of Christ, the Lamb of God**
   a. The date: Month of Abib
   b. The regulations
      1) To approach God at the place chosen by God, the sanctuary: To approach through the sacrifice: A symbol of Christ
      2) To eat unleavened bread—the bread of affliction—for seven days: A symbol of urgency to get out of Egypt & begin the march to the promised land (they had no time to leaven the bread)

      3) To let no yeast be found in their possession for seven days: A symbol of corruption
      4) To let no sacrificial meat remain until morning: A symbol of the entire sacrifice being consumed
      5) To celebrate the Passover in no place other than the place where God's Name is honored
         • Sacrifice the Passover at God's place in the evening on the anniversary of your deliverance

         • Roast & eat the Passover at God's place

      6) To gather on the seventh day for worship

2. **The Festival of Weeks—**

Observe the month of Abib, and keep the passover unto the LORD thy God: for in the month of Abib the LORD thy God brought thee forth out of Egypt by night.
2 Thou shalt therefore sacrifice the passover unto the LORD thy God, of the flock and the herd, in the place which the LORD shall choose to place his name there.
3 Thou shalt eat no leavened bread with it; seven days shalt thou eat unleavened bread therewith, *even* the bread of affliction; for thou camest forth out of the land of Egypt in haste: that thou mayest remember the day when thou camest forth out of the land of Egypt all the days of thy life.
4 And there shall be no leavened bread seen with thee in all thy coast seven days; neither shall there *any thing* of the flesh, which thou sacrificedst the first day at even, remain all night until the morning.
5 Thou mayest not sacrifice the passover within any of thy gates, which the LORD thy God giveth thee:
6 But at the place which the LORD thy God shall choose to place his name in, there thou shalt sacrifice the passover at even, at the going down of the sun, at the season that thou camest forth out of Egypt.
7 And thou shalt roast and eat *it* in the place which the LORD thy God shall choose: and thou shalt turn in the morning, and go unto thy tents.
8 Six days thou shalt eat unleavened bread: and on the seventh day *shall be* a solemn assembly to the LORD thy God: thou shalt do no work *therein*.
9 Seven weeks shalt thou number unto thee: begin to number the seven weeks from *such time as* thou beginnest *to put* the sickle to the corn.
10 And thou shalt keep the feast of weeks unto the LORD thy God with a tribute of a freewill offering of thine hand, which thou shalt give *unto the LORD thy God,* according as the LORD thy God hath blessed thee:
11 And thou shalt rejoice before the LORD thy God, thou, and thy son, and thy daughter, and thy manservant, and thy maidservant, and the Levite that *is* within thy gates, and the stranger, and the fatherless, and the widow, that *are* among you, in the place which the LORD thy God hath chosen to place his name there.
12 And thou shalt remember that thou wast a bondman in Egypt: and thou shalt observe and do these statutes.
13 Thou shalt observe the feast of tabernacles seven days, after that thou hast gathered in thy corn and thy wine:
14 And thou shalt rejoice in thy feast, thou, and thy son, and thy daughter, and thy manservant, and thy maidservant, and the Levite, the stranger, and the fatherless, and the widow, that *are* within thy gates.
15 Seven days shalt thou keep a solemn feast unto the LORD thy God in the place which the LORD shall choose: because the LORD thy God shall bless thee in all thine increase, and in all the works of thine hands, therefore thou shalt surely rejoice.
16 Three times in a year shall all thy males appear before the LORD thy God in the place which he shall choose; in the feast of unleavened bread, and in the feast of weeks, and in the feast of tabernacles: and they shall not appear before the LORD empty:
17 Every man *shall give* as he is able, according to the blessing of the LORD thy God which he hath given thee.

remember the great day of harvest, the first fruits: A symbol of Pentecost

a. To celebrate 50 days after the Passover
b. To give a freewill offering: The amount was based upon God's blessings

c. To rejoice before the LORD—at the place where God's Name was honored
d. To join others in celebrating God's goodness in the provision of food for another year

e. To remember one's enslavement in Egypt & to obey God

3. **The Festival of Tabernacles—remember the wilderness wanderings: A symbol of the march through this world to the promised land (heaven)**
   a. To celebrate for 7 days at the end of the harvest, v.13
   b. To be a joyful occasion for the entire community

   c. To conduct the celebration at the worship center chosen by God—for 7 full days
      1) To express thanksgiving to God
      2) To express great joy

4. **The strong command to celebrate the three pilgrimage festivals**
   a. All men must appear before the LORD at all three festivals: Each had to appear at the worship center chosen by Him
   b. No man was to appear empty-handed: Each had to bring a contribution based upon the blessings of God

DEUTERONOMY 16:1-17

DIVISION IV

THE SECOND GREAT THEME PREACHED BY GOD'S AGED SERVANT (PART 2): REMEMBER THE CIVIL AND RELIGIOUS LAWS OF ISRAEL—HELPFUL PRINCIPLES TO GOVERN MAN AND SOCIETY, 12:1–26:19

E. Laws That Govern the Three Pilgrimage Feasts or Festivals of Worship: Remember the Great Blessings, Salvation, and Guidance of God, 16:1-17

(16:1-17) **Introduction**: imagine this situation—the government requiring all citizens to make an annual pilgrimage to the capitol in order to pay their taxes and offer appreciation for their freedom. If you were required by law to make such an annual pilgrimage, to offer appreciation for your freedom, to pay your taxes, what would be your attitude? How would you feel about such a law?

There was a *pilgrimage law* in Israel. Just as the Muslims are required to make an annual pilgrimage to Mecca, so the Israelites were required to make an annual pilgrimage to their central worship center. In fact, the Israelites were to make *three annual pilgrimages*. No matter how far away the Israelite believer lived—on the west coast of the sea or in the east on the other side of the Jordan or the farthest border of the north or south—he was to make three yearly pilgrimages a year to the central worship center.

Why such a demand, a requirement that would be so hard and strenuous for some people to keep? This is the subject of this passage of Scripture: *Laws That Govern the Three Pilgrimage Feasts or Festivals of Worship: Remember the Great Blessings, Salvation, and Guidance of God, 16:1-17.*

1. The Passover—remember the great deliverance of God from Egypt through the sacrifice of the lamb: a symbol of Christ, the Lamb of God (vv.1-8).
2. The Festival of Weeks—remember the great day of harvest, the first fruits: a symbol of Pentecost (vv.9-12).
3. The Festival of Tabernacles—remember the wilderness wanderings: a symbol of the march through this world to the promised land (heaven) (vv.13-15).
4. The strong command to celebrate the three pilgrimage festivals (vv.16-17).

1 (16:1-8) **Passover—Feast, of Passover—Feast, of Unleavened Bread—Passover, Festival of—Symbol, of Christ—Passover, Symbol of**: God's people must remember the Passover. Moses preached: remember the great deliverance of God from Egypt, His wonderful deliverance through the sacrifice of the lamb. Keep in mind that the Passover lamb is a symbol of Christ, the Lamb of God (Jn.1:29). Until that time, the greatest event in Israel's history had been its wonderful deliverance from Egyptian slavery. Just the mention of the Passover was bound to remind the Israelites how God had told His people that the Egyptians had gone too far, well beyond repentance. They had become so evil, brutal, and savage that He was going to execute severe judgment upon them, sending the angel of death throughout the land to execute the firstborn son of every Egyptian family. Then and only then would Pharaoh release God's people from their four hundred years of enslavement. But God's people could escape the judgment. How? By believing God and trusting the blood of the sacrificial substitute, the blood of the Passover lamb. (See outline and notes—Ex.12:1–13:16, Division IV; 12:1-13 for more discussion.) Those who believed God took the blood and smeared it on the doorposts of their homes, and those who did not believe God refused to cover their homes with the blood of the substitute sacrifice. Those who believed and obeyed God were passed over by the angel of death: they were saved. But those who did not believe and obey God were visited by the angel of death who took the firstborn son of all unbelieving families. On that very night, God's terrifying judgment fell. But the Egyptians were humbled, humbled by God's mighty judgment, and they let God's people go. They freed the Israelites. At long last, after four hundred years of enslavement, God's people were liberated, set free. As a result, the Passover celebrates the most wonderful event in Israel's history. God's people must never forget the wonderful deliverance by God from Egyptian slavery. They must remember God's wonderful deliverance and His glorious salvation. They must observe and celebrate the Passover. This is the first point of Moses' message:

OUTLINE	SCRIPTURE	SCRIPTURE	OUTLINE

1. The Passover—remember the great deliverance of God from Egypt through the sacrifice of the lamb: A symbol of Christ, the Lamb of God
a. The date: Month of Abib
b. The regulations
  1) To approach God at the place chosen by God, the sanctuary: To approach through the sacrifice: A symbol of Christ
  2) To eat unleavened bread—the bread of affliction—for seven days: A symbol of
	Observe the month of Abib, and keep the passover unto the LORD thy God: for in the month of Abib the LORD thy God brought thee forth out of Egypt by night.
	2 Thou shalt therefore sacrifice the passover unto the LORD thy God, of the flock and the herd, in the place which the LORD shall choose to place his name there.
	3 Thou shalt eat no leavened bread with it; seven days shalt thou eat unleav-
		ened bread therewith, *even* the bread of affliction; for thou camest forth out of the land of Egypt in haste: that thou mayest remember the day when thou camest forth out of the land of Egypt all the days of thy life.
		4 And there shall be no leavened bread seen with thee in all thy coast seven days; neither shall there *any thing* of the flesh, which thou sacrificedst the first day at even, remain all night until the
			urgency to get out of Egypt & begin the march to the promised land (they had no time to leaven the bread)
			
			3) To let no yeast be found in their possession for seven days: A symbol of corruption
			4) To let no sacrificial meat remain until morning: A symbol of the entire

DEUTERONOMY 16:1-17

OUTLINE	SCRIPTURE	SCRIPTURE	OUTLINE
sacrifice being consumed 5) To celebrate the Passover in no place other than the place where God's Name is honored • Sacrifice the Passover at God's place in the evening on the anniversary of your deliverance	morning. 5 Thou mayest not sacrifice the passover within any of thy gates, which the LORD thy God giveth thee: 6 But at the place which the LORD thy God shall choose to place his name in, there thou shalt sacrifice the passover at even, at the going down of the sun, at the season that thou camest forth out of	Egypt. 7 And thou shalt roast and eat *it* in the place which the LORD thy God shall choose: and thou shalt turn in the morning, and go unto thy tents. 8 Six days thou shalt eat unleavened bread: and on the seventh day *shall be* a solemn assembly to the LORD thy God: thou shalt do no work *therein*.	• Roast & eat the Passover at God's place 6) To gather on the seventh day for worship

a. The Passover was to be celebrated in the very first month of the year, the month of Abib (v.1). As stated, the Passover was the most significant event in Israel's history. In fact, it was so significant that God used the Passover to change the very calendar of Israel (Ex.12:1-2). This was done so the Passover would be the first feast of the new year, the very feast that celebrated the beginning of the new year for His people. As such, the Passover would never be forgotten. It would always be remembered, celebrated by His dear people.

b. In his sermon, Moses briefly covered the regulations that were to govern the Passover (vv.2-8).
   1) The believer was to approach God at the place chosen by God, that is, the sanctuary. He was to approach God through the substitute sacrifice (v.2). Again, remember that the substitute sacrifice is a symbol of Christ, the Passover Lamb who was sacrificed for us. There was only one place where the sacrifice offering could be made, the place chosen by God Himself. God and God alone determined where and how He was to be approached. There was only one place appointed by Him and only one way appointed by Him. This was a picture that pointed to Jesus Christ, the only place and the only way that a person could ever become acceptable to God.
   2) The believer was to eat unleavened bread at the feast of the Passover for seven days (v.3). Note that the unleavened bread is called "the bread of affliction." The unleavened bread is a symbol of the urgency of the Israelites to get out of Egypt and begin their march to the promised land. They quite frankly did not have time to put yeast in the bread. This is a symbol of the urgency for a person to flee the slavery of the world and begin his march to the promised land of heaven.
   3) The believer was to make sure there was no yeast in his possession for seven days (v.4). Keep in mind that yeast is a symbol of corruption.
   4) The believer was to let no sacrificial meat remain until morning (v.4). The entire sacrifice was to be consumed. This is a symbol of Jesus Christ paying the ultimate and complete sacrifice for the sins of man.
   5) The believer was never to celebrate the Passover in any place other than the place where God's name was honored (vv.5-7). As the great Creator and Savior of man, God alone has the right to determine where and how He is to be approached. Therefore, He was never to be approached anyplace other than the place chosen by Him. Note that the sacrifice was to be made in the evening on the anniversary of the Israelite's deliverance from Egypt (v.6). The Passover sacrifice was then to be roasted and eaten only at the place chosen by God, the sanctuary (v.7).
   6) The believer was to gather together with other believers for a day of worship seven days after the Passover celebration itself (v.8).

Thought 1. The Passover is a symbol of Jesus Christ our Passover who was sacrificed for us. Jesus Christ is the perfect fulfillment of the Passover Lamb that was slain in behalf of God's people. Through the blood of Jesus Christ, a person escapes the judgment of God. God accepts the blood of the substitute sacrifice as full payment for the sins committed by a person. Note that the Passover is His sign or prophetic picture of the coming Savior, of His salvation and redemption.

> "The next day John seeth Jesus coming unto him, and saith, Behold the Lamb of God, which taketh away the sin of the world" (Jn.1:29).

> "Purge out therefore the old leaven, that ye may be a new lump, as ye are unleavened. For even Christ our passover is sacrificed for us" (1 Co.5:7).

> "Who gave himself for our sins, that he might deliver us from this present evil world, according to the will of God and our Father" (Ga.1:4).

> "And walk in love, as Christ also hath loved us, and hath given himself for us an offering and a sacrifice to God for a sweetsmelling savour" (Ep.5:2).

> "Who gave himself for us, that he might redeem us from all iniquity, and purify unto himself a peculiar people, zealous of good works" (Tit.2:14).

> "Forasmuch as ye know that ye were not redeemed with corruptible things, *as* silver and gold, from your vain conversation *received* by tradition from your fathers; But with the precious blood of Christ, as of a lamb without blemish and without spot" (1 Pe.1:18-19).

> "But he *was* wounded for our transgressions, *he was* bruised for our iniquities: the chastisement of our peace *was* upon him; and with his stripes we are healed. All we like sheep have gone astray; we have turned every one to his own way; and the LORD hath laid on him the iniquity of us all. He was oppressed, and he was afflicted, yet he opened not his mouth: he is brought as a lamb to the slaughter, and as a sheep before her shearers is dumb, so he openeth not his mouth" (Is.53:5-7).

DEUTERONOMY 16:1-17

Thought 2. The Feast or Festival of Unleavened Bread paints a clear picture for the believer. It symbolizes the need and urgency for the believer to be freed from the world and its enslavement to sin and death. There is a need—an urgent, desperate need—to be delivered from all the oppressions and pollutions of this world, from all the sin and evil, immorality and lawlessness, corruption and death of this world. There is a need and urgency to be set free and liberated to live for God. There is a desperate need and urgency to begin the march to the promised land of heaven. Note the prophetic picture:

⇒ The Passover pictures salvation, deliverance, and redemption.
⇒ The Festival of Unleavened Bread pictures the immediate need and urgency to begin the march to the promised land.

"Seek ye the LORD while he may be found, call ye upon him while he is near" (Is.55:6).

"...Behold, now *is* the accepted time; behold, now *is* the day of salvation" (2 Co.6:2).

"But this I say, brethren, the time *is* short" (1 Co.7:29).

"See then that ye walk circumspectly, not as fools, but as wise, Redeeming the time, because the days are evil" (Ep.5:15-16).

"For our conversation [citizenship] is in heaven; from whence also we look for the Saviour, the Lord Jesus Christ" (Ph.3:20).

"Henceforth there is laid up for me a crown of righteousness, which the Lord, the righteous judge, shall give me at that day: and not to me only, but unto all them also that love his appearing" (2 Ti.4:8).

"Blessed *be* the God and Father of our Lord Jesus Christ, which according to his abundant mercy hath begotten us again unto a lively hope by the resurrection of Jesus Christ from the dead, To an inheritance incorruptible, and undefiled, and that fadeth not away, reserved in heaven for you" (1 Pe.1:3-4).

"But the day of the Lord will come as a thief in the night; in the which the heavens shall pass away with a great noise, and the elements shall melt with fervent heat, the earth also and the works that are therein shall be burned up. *Seeing* then *that* all these things shall be dissolved, what manner *of persons* ought ye to be in *all* holy conversation and godliness, Looking for and hasting unto the coming of the day of God, wherein the heavens being on fire shall be dissolved, and the elements shall melt with fervent heat?" (2 Pe.3:10-12).

2 (16:9-12) **Weeks, Festival of—Harvest, Festival of—Feast, of Harvest or Pentecost—Pentecost, Feast of—Dedication—Witnessing—Soul-winning, Harvest of—Salvation, Harvest of:** the believer must celebrate the Festival of Weeks, remember the great day of harvest. The purpose of this festival was to give thanksgiving to God for the harvest and to dedicate one's life anew to God. The Festival of Weeks is sometimes called the Festival of Harvest (Ex.23:16) or "the firstfruits of the harvest" (Ex.34:22) or the "day of firstfruits" (Nu.28:26). Later, it became known as the "Festival of Pentecost" based upon the translation of the Septuagint. The word "pentecost" means fifty days. This festival is a strong symbol of Pentecost, of the great harvest of souls that took place when the Holy Spirit came upon the disciples in the upper room (Ac.2:1f). It was a joyful occasion celebrating the end of the harvest season and the dedication of one's life anew to God. Note the Scripture and outline:

OUTLINE	SCRIPTURE	SCRIPTURE	OUTLINE
2. The Festival of Weeks—remember the great day of harvest, the first fruits: A symbol of Pentecost	9 Seven weeks shalt thou number unto thee: begin to number the seven weeks from *such time as* thou beginnest *to put* the sickle to the corn.	fore the LORD thy God, thou, and thy son, and thy daughter, and thy manservant, and thy maidservant, and the Levite that *is* within thy gates, and the stranger, and the fatherless, and the widow, that *are* among you, in the place which the LORD thy God hath chosen to place his name there.	LORD—at the place where God's name was honored
			d. To join others in celebrating God's goodness in the provision of food for another year
a. To celebrate 50 days after the Passover	10 And thou shalt keep the feast of weeks unto the LORD thy God with a tribute of a freewill offering of thine hand, which thou shalt give unto the LORD thy God, according as the LORD thy God hath blessed thee:		
b. To give a freewill offering: The amount was based upon God's blessings			
		12 And thou shalt remember that thou wast a bondman in Egypt: and thou shalt observe and do these statutes.	e. To remember one's enslavement in Egypt & to obey God
c. To rejoice before the	11 And thou shalt rejoice be-		

a. The believer was to celebrate the Festival of Weeks fifty days after the Passover (v.10). Note that it was exactly fifty days after the resurrection of Christ that the great day of Pentecost in the New Testament took place, exactly fifty days when the great harvest of souls took place as the Holy Spirit came upon the disciples in the upper room.

b. The believer was to give a freewill offering based upon God's blessings (v.10). The offering was to be in proportion to the blessings of God. It was to be given as an expression of thanksgiving and of one's dependence upon God for prosperity in the future.

c. The believer was to rejoice before the LORD at the place where God's name was honored (v.11). There was only one true place to approach God, only one place where a person could give true thanks to God and offer his life in a spirit of true dedication. That place was the place chosen by God Himself, the sanctuary where His presence dwelt. Again, note the symbolism that points to the Lord Jesus Christ. Jesus Christ alone is the place where a person can offer true thanksgiving and true dedication to God. The offering of thanksgiving and the dedication of one's life at any other place avails nothing. It is not accepted by God. The only thanksgiving and dedication accepted by God is that which is offered through Jesus Christ.

d. The believer was to join others in celebrating God's goodness (v.11). The whole community of Israel was to gather together once a year to celebrate the Festival of Weeks. Making the annual pilgrimage to the worship center—either the Tabernacle at that time or the temple in the future—would remind the people of God's wonderful blessings to them. Note this fact as well: coming together as a community stressed the unity of the nation.

e. The believer was to remember his enslavement in Egypt and obey God (v.12). The Israelite was obligated to God because of God's wonderful salvation from the enslavement of Egypt. By remembering His wonderful salvation, the believer would be stirred to offer more thanks to God and even more commitment to God.

> **Thought 1.** The Festival of Weeks is also known as the Festival of Pentecost. The Festival of Pentecost is a clear prophetic picture of salvation. Fifty days after the resurrection of Christ, the dramatic day of Pentecost took place. The disciples were filled with the Holy Spirit, filled with so much power that they went forth immediately witnessing to everyone walking along the streets or standing in the doorways of their homes. This scene was so dramatic that several thousand people gathered and Peter preached to them. The result: three thousand people were saved and became followers of the Lord Jesus Christ—all because the Spirit of God came upon a handful of believers and they became powerful witnesses for God.
>
> > "And Jesus returned in the power of the Spirit into Galilee: and there went out a fame of him through all the region round about" (Lu.4:14).
> > "But ye shall receive power, after that the Holy Ghost is come upon you: and ye shall be witnesses unto me both in Jerusalem, and in all Judaea, and in Samaria, and unto the uttermost part of the earth" (Ac.1:8).
> > "And with great power gave the apostles witness of the resurrection of the Lord Jesus: and great grace was upon them all" (Ac.4:33).
> > "I beseech you therefore, brethren, by the mercies of God, that ye present your bodies a living sacrifice, holy, acceptable unto God, *which is* your reasonable service. And be not conformed to this world: but be ye transformed by the renewing of your mind, that ye may prove [bear witness to] what is that good, and acceptable, and perfect, will of God" (Ro.12:1-2).
> > "But truly I am full of power by the spirit of the LORD, and of judgment, and of might, to declare unto Jacob his transgression, and to Israel his sin" (Mi.3:8).
> > "Then he answered and spake unto me, saying, This *is* the word of the LORD unto Zerubbabel, saying, Not by might, nor by power, but by my spirit, saith the LORD of hosts" (Zec.4:6).

3 (16:13-15) **Festival, of Tabernacles—Wilderness Wanderings—Journeys, the Wilderness—Heaven, Journey to**: the believer was to celebrate the Festival of Tabernacles, the trials of the wilderness wanderings (see Map of the Wilderness Wanderings of Israel on page 436). This festival was a symbol of the believer's march through this world to the promised land of heaven. To the Israelites, the Festival of Tabernacles reminded them of the wilderness wanderings when the people of God had to live in tents on their way to the promised land. It also celebrated a gathering of the harvest at the end of the year; therefore, it was to be a period of thanksgiving to God for the harvest (Ex.23:16). It took God forty years to teach the people of Israel to follow Him and obey His commandments through trial after trial. It was during this forty years that the people were forced to live in tents. They had to be able to pitch camp and to break camp on the spur of the moment when the need to escape some trial arose. Moreover, the desert or wilderness was not to be their permanent home; consequently, they were not allowed to build any kind of permanent housing. Living in tents was a hard, strenuous life. Because they were forced to wander about so long in the wilderness, their journey is referred to as the *wilderness wanderings* or *wilderness journeys*. As stated, the Festival of Tabernacles was to celebrate the wilderness wanderings when they lived in tents on their way to the promised land. They were to be forever thankful to God and to keep their minds focused upon the promised land. Note the Scripture and outline:

OUTLINE	SCRIPTURE	SCRIPTURE	OUTLINE
3. The Festival of Tabernacles—remember the wilderness wanderings: A symbol of the march through this world to the promised land (heaven) a. To celebrate for 7 days at the end of the harvest, v.13 b. To be a joyful occasion for the entire community	13 Thou shalt observe the feast of tabernacles seven days, after that thou hast gathered in thy corn and thy wine: 14 And thou shalt rejoice in thy feast, thou, and thy son, and thy daughter, and thy manservant, and thy maidservant, and the Levite, the stranger, and the fatherless,	and the widow, that *are* within thy gates. 15 Seven days shalt thou keep a solemn feast unto the LORD thy God in the place which the LORD shall choose: because the LORD thy God shall bless thee in all thine increase, and in all the works of thine hands, therefore thou shalt surely rejoice.	c. To conduct the celebration at the worship center chosen by God—for 7 full days 1) To express thanksgiving to God 2) To express great joy

a. The believer was to celebrate the Festival of Tabernacles for seven days at the end of the harvest season (v.13). There was to be a full week of festivities and worship. For seven days, the people actually lived in booths or shelters they had built from tree leaves.

b. The believer was to join other believers in the joyful occasion. It was to be celebrated by the entire community (v.14). All the Israelites were to make the annual pilgrimage to the Tabernacle and later to the temple to celebrate the festival.

c. The believer was to conduct the celebration at the worship center chosen by God. It was there and there alone where thanksgiving and joy were to be offered up to God (v.15). The festival was to be a celebration of great joy and rejoicing

DEUTERONOMY 16:1-17

before the LORD. But again note: there was only one place where the thanksgiving and joy were acceptable. That place was the worship center, the sanctuary chosen by God Himself.

Thought 1. As the believer marches to the promised land, he is to focus upon God, ever learning to trust God more and more, proclaiming the message of joy for the atonement or reconciliation with God. God has saved him; consequently, the believer is to joy in his salvation, joy in the atonement and reconciliation with God. Moreover, the Festival of Trumpets pictures the rapture, the great salvation of God's people when Christ returns. Christ will sound the trumpet; the dead in Christ will be raised, and then all who are alive and remain will be caught up together with Him in the clouds to meet the LORD in the air—to be with Him forever (1 Th.4:16-17). Simply stated, the believer is to grow in his trust and joy; he is to be ever maturing, learning to focus more and more upon the LORD.

"Hitherto have ye asked nothing in my name: ask, and ye shall receive, that your joy may be full" (Jn.16:24).

"Now he that ministereth seed to the sower both minister bread for *your* food, and multiply your seed sown, and increase the fruits of your righteousness" (2 Co.9:10).

"But speaking the truth in love, may grow up into him in all things, which is the head, *even* Christ" (Ep.4:15).

"Rejoice in the Lord always: *and* again I say, Rejoice" (Ph.4:4).

"For the Lord himself shall descend from heaven with a shout, with the voice of the archangel, and with the trump of God: and the dead in Christ shall rise first: Then we which are alive *and* remain shall be caught up together with them in the clouds, to meet the Lord in the air: and so shall we ever be with the Lord" (1 Th.4:16-17).

"As newborn babes, desire the sincere milk of the word, that ye may grow thereby: If so be ye have tasted that the Lord *is* gracious" (1 Pe.2:2-3).

"But grow in grace, and *in* the knowledge of our Lord and Saviour Jesus Christ. To him *be* glory both now and for ever. Amen" (2 Pe.3:18).

"The LORD *is* my light and my salvation; whom shall I fear? the LORD *is* the strength of my life; of whom shall I be afraid?" (Ps.27:1).

"*Oh* how great *is* thy goodness, which thou hast laid up for them that fear thee; *which* thou hast wrought for them that trust in thee before the sons of men!" (Ps.31:19).

"Trust in the LORD, and do good; *so* shalt thou dwell in the land, and verily thou shalt be fed" (Ps.37:3).

"Trust in the LORD with all thine heart; and lean not unto thine own understanding" (Pr.3:5).

"Behold, God *is* my salvation; I will trust, and not be afraid: for the LORD JEHOVAH *is* my strength and *my* song; he also is become my salvation" (Is.12:2).

"And it shall be said in that day, Lo, this *is* our God; we have waited for him, and he will save us: this *is* the LORD; we have waited for him, we will be glad and rejoice in his salvation" (Is.25:9).

"Thou wilt keep *him* in perfect peace, *whose* mind *is* stayed *on thee:* because he trusteth in thee" (Is.26:3).

Thought 2. As the believer marches to heaven, he faces trial after trial, difficulty after difficulty, problem after problem, temptation after temptation. There is no end to the diseases, accidents, broken relationships, lawlessness, immoralities, and death that sweep the earth. Consequently, there is no end to the trials and temptations that confront the true believer who seeks to follow God day by day. But no matter how terrible the trial or temptation, there is the glorious truth of God's wonderful promise: the promise of His presence and guidance. God will *be with us* and will *guide* us as we march to the promised land of heaven. God will enable us to conquer all the trials and temptations of life. No matter how strong and ferocious, no matter how terrified, how frightful—God will guide us right through the trial or temptation. God will be with us, guiding us step by step and giving us a victorious march until that glorious day of redemption in heaven. He will guide us through the wilderness of this world.

"Through the tender mercy of our God; whereby the dayspring from on high hath visited us, To give light to them that sit in darkness and *in* the shadow of death, to guide our feet into the way of peace" (Lu.1:78-79).

"Howbeit when he, the Spirit of truth, is come, he will guide you into all truth: for he shall not speak of himself; but whatsoever he shall hear, *that* shall he speak: and he will show you things to come" (Jn.16:13).

"Lo, I am with you alway, *even* unto the end of the world. Amen" (Mt.28:20).

"And, behold, I *am* with thee, and will keep thee in all *places* whither thou goest, and will bring thee again into this land; for I will not leave thee, until I have done *that* which I have spoken to thee of" (Ge.28:15).

"And he said, My presence shall go *with thee,* and I will give thee rest" (Ex.33:14).

"When thou goest out to battle against thine enemies, and seest horses, and chariots, *and* a people more than thou, be not afraid of them: for the LORD thy God *is* with thee, which brought thee up out of the land of Egypt" (De.20:1).

"For this God *is* our God for ever and ever: he will be our guide *even* unto death" (Ps.48:14).

"Thou shalt guide me with thy counsel, and afterward receive me *to* glory" (Ps.73:24).

"And thine ears shall hear a word behind thee, saying, This *is* the way, walk ye in it, when ye turn to the right hand, and when ye turn to the left" (Is.30:21).

DEUTERONOMY 16:1-17

"And I will bring the blind by a way *that* they knew not; I will lead them in paths *that* they have not known: I will make darkness light before them, and crooked things straight. These things will I do unto them, and not forsake them" (Is.42:16).

"When thou passest through the waters, I *will be* with thee; and through the rivers, they shall not overflow thee: when thou walkest through the fire, thou shalt not be burned; neither shall the flame kindle upon thee" (Is.43:2).

4 **(16:16-17) Remembrance, Duty—Festivals, Duty—Pilgrimage, Festivals of—Obedience, Duty**: the believer must celebrate the three pilgrimage festivals every year. Note the persons responsible for making sure the families celebrated the feast every year: the men of the nation. The fathers of the nation were to make sure that their families were faithful in remembering these special occasions of worship before the LORD. Not a man was exempted. No matter where a family lived nor how far away they were from the worship center, the man had to take his family to celebrate the three pilgrimage festivals. Note, no man was to appear empty-handed. He had to bring a contribution based upon the blessings of God throughout the year (v.17). Why would God make such a demand upon the men and families of Israel? God's purpose for these three national celebrations was threefold:

⇒ to bring the people together in a spirit of unity and oneness, thereby building a strong, unified nation
⇒ to keep before the people the great salvation and blessings of God, His great deliverance and guidance day by day
⇒ to arouse the people to give thanks, to praise God and to give their tithes and offerings to Him in a spirit of recommitment to Him

OUTLINE	SCRIPTURE	SCRIPTURE	OUTLINE
4. The strong command to celebrate the three pilgrimage festivals a. All men must appear before the LORD at all three festivals: Each had to appear at the worship center chosen by	16 Three times in a year shall all thy males appear before the LORD thy God in the place which he shall choose; in the feast of unleavened bread, and in the feast of weeks, and in the feast of	tabernacles: and they shall not appear before the LORD empty: 17 Every man *shall give* as he is able, according to the blessing of the LORD thy God which he hath given thee.	Him b. No man was to appear empty-handed: Each had to bring a contribution based upon the blessings of God

Thought 1. We must worship the LORD and be faithful in our worship. It is God who has saved us and who guides us day by day, looking after and taking care of us. God gives us His presence and guidance, and He abundantly provides for us day by day. It is He who has saved us and not we ourselves. Therefore, we owe Him the worship of our hearts and lives.

"Then saith Jesus unto him, Get thee hence, Satan: for it is written, Thou shalt worship the Lord thy God, and him only shalt thou serve" (Mt.4:10).

"And he came to Nazareth, where he had been brought up: and, as his custom was, he went into the synagogue on the sabbath day, and stood up for to read" (Lu.4:16).

"And they worshipped him, and returned to Jerusalem with great joy: And were continually in the temple, praising and blessing God. Amen" (Lu.24:52-53).

"God *is* a Spirit: and they that worship him must worship *him* in spirit and in truth" (Jn.4:24).

"Not forsaking the assembling of ourselves together, as the manner of some *is;* but exhorting *one another:* and so much the more, as ye see the day approaching" (He.10:25).

"Fear God, and give glory to him; for the hour of his judgment is come: and worship him that made heaven, and earth, and the sea, and the fountains of waters" (Re.14:7).

"But unto the place which the LORD your God shall choose out of all your tribes to put his name there, *even* unto his habitation shall ye seek, and thither thou shalt come" (De.12:5).

"And now, behold, I have brought the firstfruits of the land, which thou, O LORD, hast given me. And thou shalt set it before the LORD thy God, and worship before the LORD thy God" (De.26:10).

"Give unto the LORD the glory *due* unto his name: bring an offering, and come before him: worship the LORD in the beauty of holiness" (1 Chr.16:29).

"LORD, I have loved the habitation of thy house, and the place where thine honour dwelleth" (Ps.26:8).

"One *thing* have I desired of the LORD, that will I seek after; that I may dwell in the house of the LORD all the days of my life, to behold the beauty of the LORD, and to enquire in his temple" (Ps.27:4).

"Blessed *are* they that dwell in thy house: they will be still praising thee. Selah" (Ps.84:4).

"For a day in thy courts *is* better than a thousand. I had rather be a doorkeeper in the house of my God, than to dwell in the tents of wickedness" (Ps.84:10).

"O come, let us worship and bow down: let us kneel before the LORD our maker" (Ps.95:6).

"O worship the LORD in the beauty of holiness: fear before him, all the earth" (Ps.96:9).

"I was glad when they said unto me, Let us go into the house of the LORD" (Ps.122:1).

DEUTERONOMY 16:1-17

TYPES, SYMBOLS, AND PICTURES
(Deuteronomy 16:1-17)

Historical Term	Type or Picture (Scriptural Basis for Each)	Life Application for Today's Believer	Biblical Application
The Passover De.16:1-17 (See also Le. 23:5; Nu.28:16-25)	The Passover is a symbol of Christ, our Passover who was sacrificed for us. ⇒ The Passover is a type or symbol of Christ the Lamb of God who takes away the sins of the world. ⇒ The Passover pictures salvation, deliverance, and redemption. **"Thou shalt therefore sacrifice the passover unto the LORD thy God, of the flock and the herd, in the place which the LORD shall choose to place his name there" (De.16:2).**	⇒ Jesus Christ is the perfect fulfillment of the Passover Lamb that was slain in behalf of God's people. Through the blood of Jesus Christ, a person escapes the judgment of God. God accepts the substitute sacrifice of His Son as full payment for the sins committed by a person. Note that the Passover is a picture, a prophetic picture, of salvation and redemption.	"The next day John seeth Jesus coming unto him, and saith, Behold the Lamb of God, which taketh away the sin of the world" (Jn.1:29). "...For even Christ our passover is sacrificed for us" (1 Co.5:7). "He was oppressed, and he was afflicted, yet he opened not his mouth: he is brought as a lamb to the slaughter, and as a sheep before her shearers is dumb, so he openeth not his mouth" (Is.53:7). "Forasmuch as ye know that ye were not redeemed with corruptible things, as silver and gold, from your vain conversation received by tradition from your fathers; But with the precious blood of Christ, as of a lamb without blemish and without spot" (1 Pe.1:18-19).
The Festival of Tabernacles or Booths or Shelters De.16:13-15	The Festival of Tabernacles is a symbol of the believer's short, temporary life and march through this world to the promised land of heaven. This festival celebrated the wilderness wanderings when the people of God had to live in tents on their way to the promised land. It also celebrated a gathering of the harvest at the end of the year; therefore it was to be a period of thanksgiving to God for the harvest (Ex.23:16). **"Thou shalt observe the feast of tabernacles seven days, after that thou hast gathered in thy corn and thy wine" (De.16:13).**	⇒ We are to be forever thanking God and keeping our minds on the promised land of heaven. ⇒ As the believer marches to heaven his dwelling is only temporary. No matter what kind of house he lives in, it is temporary. It is made out of decaying, corruptible materials. It will waste away and some day, perhaps decades or even a few centuries, it will cease to be. Earthly homes are only temporary structures. Moreover, the believer is living in a temporary body, a body that the Bible describes as a temporary tent or tabernacle. The body is corruptible and will decay and cease to exist. The believer's journey or pilgrimage through this world is only temporary. He is marching to his permanent and eternal home in heaven, living forever in the presence of God.	"Wherefore seeing we also are compassed about with so great a cloud of witnesses, let us lay aside every weight, and the sin which doth so easily beset us, and let us run with patience the race that is set before us, Looking unto Jesus the author and finisher of our faith; who for the joy that was set before him endured the cross, despising the shame, and is set down at the right hand of the throne of God" (He.12:1-2). "For we know that if our earthly house of this tabernacle were dissolved, we have a building of God, an house not made with hands, eternal in the heavens" (2 Co.5:1). "But lay up for yourselves treasures in heaven, where neither moth nor rust doth corrupt, and where thieves do not break through nor steal" (Mt. 6:20). "Notwithstanding in this rejoice not, that the spirits are subject unto you; but rather rejoice, because your names are written in heaven" (Lu.10:20).

DEUTERONOMY 16:1-17

Historical Term	Type or Picture (Scriptural Basis for Each)	Life Application for Today's Believer	Biblical Application
			"For we know that if our earthly house of this tabernacle were dissolved, we have a building of God, an house not made with hands, eternal in the heavens" (2 Co.5:1).
The Festival of Unleavened Bread De.16:1-8, Thgt.2	*The Feast or Festival of Unleavened Bread symbolizes the need and urgency for the believer to be free from the world and it's enslavement to sin and death, the urgency for a person to begin the march to the promised land.* *This festival recalled the need and urgency of God's people to leave Egypt. After God's hand of judgment fell, events moved rapidly. The Egyptians were desperate for Pharaoh to release the Israelites and get rid of them. In fact, the Israelites were forced to leave so quickly that they had no time to adequately prepare. They did not even have time to let their dough rise; they had no time to put yeast or leaven in their bread. They were forced to take unleavened bread. There was the need, the urgency to get out of Egypt immediately.* **"Six days thou shalt eat unleavened bread: and on the seventh day** *shall be* **a solemn assembly to the LORD thy God: thou shalt do no work** *therein*" **(De.16:8).**	⇒ There is a need—an urgent, desperate need—to be delivered from all the oppressions and pollutions of this world, from all the sin and evil, immorality and lawlessness, corruption and death of this world. There is a need and urgency to be set free and liberated to live for God. There is a desperate need and urgency to begin the march to the promised land of heaven.	"Seek ye the LORD while he may be found, call ye upon him while he is near" (Is.55:6). "...Behold, now is the accepted time; behold, now is the day of salvation" (2 Co.6:2). "See then that ye walk circumspectly, not as fools, but as wise, Redeeming the time, because the days are evil" (Ep.5:15-16). "For our conversation [citizenship] is in heaven; from whence also we look for the Saviour, the Lord Jesus Christ" (Ph.3:20). "Henceforth there is laid up for me a crown of righteousness, which the Lord, the righteous judge, shall give me at that day: and not to me only, but unto all them also that love his appearing" (2 Ti.4:8). "Blessed be the God and Father of our Lord Jesus Christ, which according to his abundant mercy hath begotten us again unto a lively hope by the resurrection of Jesus Christ from the dead, To an inheritance incorruptible, and undefiled, and that fadeth not away, reserved in heaven for you" (1 Pe.1:3-4). "But the day of the Lord will come as a thief in the night; in the which the heavens shall pass away with a great noise, and the elements shall melt with fervent heat, the earth also and the works that are therein shall be burned up. Seeing then that all these things shall be dissolved, what manner of persons ought ye to be in all holy conversation and godliness, Looking for and hasting unto the coming of the day of God, wherein the heavens being on fire shall be dissolved, and the elements shall melt with fervent heat?" (2 Pe.3:10-12).

DEUTERONOMY 16:1-17

Historical Term	Type or Picture (Scriptural Basis for Each)	Life Application for Today's Believer	Biblical Application
The Festival of Harvest or Pentecost De.16:9-12 (See also Le.23:15-22)	*The Festival of Harvest or Pentecost is a symbol of Pentecost, of the great harvest of souls and of people giving their lives to God.* *"And thou shalt keep the feast of weeks [Harvest] unto the LORD thy God with a tribute of a freewill offering of thine hand, which thou shalt give unto the LORD thy God, according as the LORD thy God hath blessed thee"* (De.16:10).	⇒ As the believer marches to the promised land, he is to be filled with God's Spirit and bear strong testimony, seeking a great harvest of souls. ⇒ The Festival of Pentecost is a clear prophetic picture of salvation. Fifty days after the resurrection of Christ, the dramatic day of Pentecost took place. The disciples were filled with the Holy Spirit, filled with so much power that they went forth immediately witnessing to everyone walking along the streets or standing in the doorways of their homes. This scene was so dramatic that several thousand people gathered and Peter preached to them. The result: three thousand people were saved and became followers of the Lord Jesus Christ. As stated, the Festival of Harvest or Pentecost was a strong prophetic picture of salvation. It symbolized the great harvest of souls, of people giving their lives to God on the great Day of Pentecost when the Holy Spirit was to come upon men.	*"But ye shall receive power, after that the Holy Ghost is come upon you: and ye shall be witnesses unto me both in Jerusalem, and in all Judaea, and in Samaria, and unto the uttermost part of the earth"* (Ac.1:8). *"And when the day of Pentecost was fully come, they were all with one accord in one place. And suddenly there came a sound from heaven as of a rushing mighty wind, and it filled all the house where they were sitting. And there appeared unto them cloven tongues like as of fire, and it sat upon each of them. And they were all filled with the Holy Ghost, and began to speak with other tongues, as the Spirit gave them utterance"* (Ac.2:1-4). *"Now when they heard this, they were pricked in their heart, and said unto Peter and to the rest of the apostles, Men and brethren, what shall we do? Then Peter said unto them, Repent, and be baptized every one of you in the name of Jesus Christ for the remission of sins, and ye shall receive the gift of the Holy Ghost"* (Ac.2:37-38). *"Then they that gladly received his word were baptized: and the same day there were added unto them about three thousand souls"* (Ac.2:41). *"But sanctify the Lord God in your hearts: and be ready always to give an answer to every man that asketh you a reason of the hope that is in you with meekness and fear"* (1 Pe.3:15).

DEUTERONOMY 16:18–17:20

F. Laws That Govern the Administration of Justice & the Appointment of Rulers: Four Major Concerns of Society, 16:18–17:20

1. Concern 1: The administration of justice
    a. The law: To appoint judges & officers for every town
    b. The duties of judges
        1) Must be fair & just
        2) Must never twist justice nor show partiality
        3) Must never accept a bribe: Bribes blind the wise & twist the words of the righteous
        4) Must follow justice & justice alone: Will be blessed by God with life & the promised land
        5) Must guard the people from idolatry & false worship
            • The law: Must not allow anything to be set up beside God's altar
            • The reason: God hates it
        6) Must guard the people from greed
            • The law: Not to keep the best & give God the least (defective)
            • The reason: God hates it

2. Concern 2: The execution of justice against the major crime
    a. The fact: A person who commits false worship does evil, violates God's covenant
    b. The terrible evil: The person worships other gods (sun, moon, or stars, zodiac, astrology, the occult)
    c. The execution of justice & judgment
        1) The charge: Must be thoroughly investigated
        2) The judgment: If guilty, must be executed

18 Judges and officers shalt thou make thee in all thy gates, which the LORD thy God giveth thee, throughout thy tribes: and they shall judge the people with just judgment.
19 Thou shalt not wrest judgment; thou shalt not respect persons, neither take a gift: for a gift doth blind the eyes of the wise, and pervert the words of the righteous.
20 That which is altogether just shalt thou follow, that thou mayest live, and inherit the land which the LORD thy God giveth thee.
21 Thou shalt not plant thee a grove of any trees near unto the altar of the LORD thy God, which thou shalt make thee.
22 Neither shalt thou set thee up *any* image; which the LORD thy God hateth.

CHAPTER 17

Thou shalt not sacrifice unto the LORD thy God *any* bullock, or sheep, wherein is blemish, *or* any evilfavouredness: for that *is* an abomination unto the LORD thy God.
2 If there be found among you, within any of thy gates which the LORD thy God giveth thee, man or woman, that hath wrought wickedness in the sight of the LORD thy God, in transgressing his covenant,
3 And hath gone and served other gods, and worshipped them, either the sun, or moon, or any of the host of heaven, which I have not commanded;
4 And it be told thee, and thou hast heard *of it*, and enquired diligently, and, behold, *it be* true, *and* the thing certain, *that* such abomination is wrought in Israel:
5 Then shalt thou bring forth that man or that woman, which have committed that wicked thing, unto thy gates, *even* that man or that woman, and shalt stone them with stones, till they die.
6 At the mouth of two witnesses, or three witnesses, shall he that is worthy of death be put to death; *but* at the mouth of one witness he shall not be put to death.
7 The hands of the witnesses shall be first upon him to put him to death, and afterward the hands of all the people. So thou shalt put the evil away from among you.
8 If there arise a matter too hard for thee in judgment, between blood and blood, between plea and plea, and between stroke and stroke, *being* matters of controversy within thy gates: then shalt thou arise, and get thee up into the place which the LORD thy God shall choose;
9 And thou shalt come unto the priests the Levites, and unto the judge that shall be in those days, and enquire; and they shall show thee the sentence of judgment:
10 And thou shalt do according to the sentence, which they of that place which the LORD shall choose shall show thee; and thou shalt observe to do according to all that they inform thee:
11 According to the sentence of the law which they shall teach thee, and according to the judgment which they shall tell thee, thou shalt do: thou shalt not decline from the sentence which they shall show thee, *to* the right hand, nor *to* the left.
12 And the man that will do presumptuously, and will not hearken unto the priest that standeth to minister there before the LORD thy God, or unto the judge, even that man shall die: and thou shalt put away the evil from Israel.
13 And all the people shall hear, and fear, and do no more presumptuously.
14 When thou art come unto the land which the LORD thy God giveth thee, and shalt possess it, and shalt dwell therein, and shalt say, I will set a king over me, like as all the nations that *are* about me;
15 Thou shalt in any wise set *him* king over thee, whom the LORD thy God shall choose:

    3) The safeguards to assure justice
       • The testimony of two or more witnesses was required
       • The witnesses & the community were themselves to be the executioners
    4) The insistence of God: The evil must be purged from among you

3. Concern 3: Difficult legal cases
    a. The law
        1) To take all cases too difficult for a local judge to the central court of law: Held at the sanctuary & presided over by some priests & a civil judge
        2) To present one's case & receive a verdict from the High Court
    b. The verdict or decision of the High Court
        1) Must carry out the verdict—everything the court says
        2) Must execute their sentence & interpretation of the law
        3) Must execute any arrogant person who shows contempt for the judge or priest
            • Must purge such evil from the nation
            • Such discipline will serve as a deterrent

4. Concern 4: The appointment of kings or rulers
    a. The prediction of Israel's future desire for a king
    b. The establishment of the law: The king must be appointed by God Himself

1) To be an Israelite brother 2) Never to be a foreigner c. The duties or responsibilities of the king 1) Must never depend upon horses for military strength nor go to Egypt (the world) for help: Never go back to Egypt—the way of the world—seeking an alliance 2) Must not seek pleasure nor depend upon alliances through many wives 3) Must not lust for nor depend upon wealth 4) Must personally copy the law of God: Study & learn	*one* from among thy brethren shalt thou set king over thee: thou mayest not set a stranger over thee, which *is* not thy brother. 16 But he shall not multiply horses to himself, nor cause the people to return to Egypt, to the end that he should multiply horses: forasmuch as the LORD hath said unto you, Ye shall henceforth return no more that way. 17 Neither shall he multiply wives to himself, that his heart turn not away: neither shall he greatly multiply to himself silver and gold. 18 And it shall be, when he sitteth upon the throne of	his kingdom, that he shall write him a copy of this law in a book out of *that which is* before the priests the Levites: 19 And it shall be with him, and he shall read therein all the days of his life: that he may learn to fear the LORD his God, to keep all the words of this law and these statutes, to do them: 20 That his heart be not lifted up above his brethren, and that he turn not aside from the commandment, *to* the right hand, or *to* the left: to the end that he may prolong *his* days in his kingdom, he, and his children, in the midst of Israel.	the law or Word of God d. The results of learning & ruling by the Word of God 1) Result 1: He will learn to fear God 2) Result 2: He will learn to be a good leader—learn to follow & rule by the law 3) Result 3: He will guard against pride, arrogance, & abuse of the people 4) Result 4: He & his descendants will have a long rule

DIVISION IV

THE SECOND GREAT THEME PREACHED BY GOD'S AGED SERVANT (PART 2): REMEMBER THE CIVIL AND RELIGIOUS LAWS OF ISRAEL—HELPFUL PRINCIPLES TO GOVERN MAN AND SOCIETY, 12:1–26:19

F. **Laws That Govern the Administration of Justice and the Appointment of Rulers: Four Major Concerns of Society, 16:18–17:20**

(16:18–17:20) **Introduction**: the first major concern of society is the administration of justice. Justice is the foundation of society, the tie that binds society together. Without justice, society could not exist; there would be utter chaos. Human relationships would break down; lawlessness and violence would prevail. People would be running around lying, stealing, and cheating; breaking into stores and homes to get whatever they needed or wanted; assaulting and even killing people when they needed. There would be no laws to prevent lawless behavior. Every conceivable sin and evil would be running rampant upon the earth without the controls of justice. Justice is the very foundation of society, of human relationships. Of all the laws covered in this sermon by Moses, these laws that established justice throughout the land are some of the most important. Justice is the great concern of this important passage of Scripture: *Laws That Govern the Administration of Justice and the Appointment of Rulers: Four Major Concerns of Society,* 16:18–17:20.
  1. Concern 1: the administration of justice (16:18–17:1).
  2. Concern 2: the execution of justice against the major crime (17:2-7).
  3. Concern 3: difficult legal cases (17:8-13).
  4. Concern 4: the appointment of kings or rulers (17:14-20).

1 (16:18–17:1) **Justice, Duty—Judges, Duty—Officers of the Law, Duty—Justice, Administration of**: the first major concern of society is the administration of justice. This subject was an absolute necessity for Moses to cover in his sermon. The Israelites had to be a just people, a people ruled by law and justice, or else God would expel them from the promised land. They would lose their inheritance in the promised land. All their hopes and dreams would be dashed against the rocks of disobedience, all because they allowed sin and evil, lawlessness and violence to sweep across the land. God would never tolerate the rule of evil and wickedness. Therefore, it was absolutely necessary for the Israelites to establish the organization, the administration of justice once they were settled in the promised land. (See outline and notes, pt.4—De.1:9-17 for more discussion.)

OUTLINE	SCRIPTURE	SCRIPTURE	OUTLINE
1. Concern 1: The administration of justice a. The law: To appoint judges & officers for every town b. The duties of judges 1) Must be fair & just 2) Must never twist justice nor show partiality	18 Judges and officers shalt thou make thee in all thy gates, which the LORD thy God giveth thee, throughout thy tribes: and they shall judge the people with just judgment. 19 Thou shalt not wrest judgment; thou shalt not	respect persons, neither take a gift: for a gift doth blind the eyes of the wise, and pervert the words of the righteous. 20 That which is altogether just shalt thou follow, that thou mayest live, and inherit the land which the LORD thy	3) Must never accept a bribe: Bribes blind the wise & twist the words of the righteous 4) Must follow justice & justice alone: Will be blessed by God with life & the promised land

DEUTERONOMY 16:18–17:20

OUTLINE	SCRIPTURE	SCRIPTURE	OUTLINE
5) Must guard the people from idolatry & false worship • The law: Must not allow anything to be set up beside God's altar • The reason: God hates it	God giveth thee. 21 Thou shalt not plant thee a grove of any trees near unto the altar of the LORD thy God, which thou shalt make thee. 22 Neither shalt thou set thee up *any* image; which the LORD thy God hateth.	**CHAPTER 17** Thou shalt not sacrifice unto the LORD thy God *any* bullock, or sheep, wherein is blemish, *or* any evilfavouredness: for that *is* an abomination unto the LORD thy God.	6) Must guard the people from greed • The law: Not to keep the best & give God the least (defective) • The reason: God hates it

a. Moses declared the basic law of justice to the Israelites: they were to appoint judges and officers for every town (v.18). This meant that each town within the district of each tribe would have its own legal authorities and court system to handle legal cases. The judges would sit in court, hear the cases, and determine who was right and who was wrong; then they would pass judgment. Note that "officers" of the court were also appointed. These were obviously subordinate officers of the court appointed to carry out the orders of the judges.

b. Moses explained the duties of the judges (ch.16:18-17:1). The oversight of justice, the very management of justice within the land, lay in the hands of judges. It was, therefore, absolutely necessary to spell out their duties. Both the judge and the people needed to understand the function of the judge, exactly what he was to do. They needed to understand the power of his position.

1) The judge must be fair and just (v.18). His duty was to view each case with an open mind in order to be fair and just to both parties.
2) The judge must never twist justice nor show partiality (v.19). The word *partiality* or *respect* (panah or paneh) means to face, appear, look, regard, respect, behold. Literally the idea is "you must not recognize faces." The judge was to treat both parties as though he did not recognize them, and he was not to acknowledge either party. He was not to show partiality to a person because of his friendship, position, wealth, influence, threats, or any other reason. There was to be no favoritism whatsoever shown. Justice was not to be twisted to favor the rich over the poor, the powerful over the weak, the friend over the enemy, the neighbor over the citizen, the resident over the foreigner. The judge was never to twist justice, never to show partiality.
3) The judge must never accept a bribe (v.19). Accepting bribes is one of the worst evils that a judge can commit. Bribes blind the wise judgment of the jury. Bribes cause a judge to twist the words of the innocent and righteous. Bribes lead to injustice, wrong verdicts, loss of property, the imprisonment of the innocent, and sometimes even the death penalty for the innocent. Bribes cause all kinds of evil, unjust treatment, and suffering for innocent people. God despises the taking of bribes so much that He declares this truth: He Himself never takes a bribe. Moreover, the judge or person who takes a bribe that causes the execution of an innocent person will be cursed.

> "For the LORD your God *is* God of gods, and LORD of lords, a great God, a mighty, and a terrible, which regardeth not persons, nor taketh reward" (De.10:17).
>
> "Cursed *be* he that taketh reward to slay an innocent person. And all the people shall say, Amen" (De.27:25).

4) The judge must follow justice and justice alone (v.20). He must pursue justice and nothing else, never perverting it. Above all else, he must be a person of character and integrity, with the highest ethical standards and values. Note the two promises given to the judge of high character and integrity: he will be blessed by God with life and inherit the promised land of God.
5) The judge must guard the people from idolatry and false worship (v.21). The oversight of Israel's religion was obviously placed in the hands of the judges. They lived as neighbors to the people in the cities and towns. Therefore, they would be the first leaders to observe the seepage of any idolatry and false worship into the nation. They were to guard and protect the people from this terrible evil lest they be doomed by the judgment of God. They were not to allow any Asherah pole or sacred stone—no idol whatsoever—to be placed beside the altar of the LORD, not in the sanctuary of the Tabernacle nor in a future temple. The people of God were not to engage in false worship of any kind, and they were certainly not to desecrate the worship center of the LORD God Himself. False worship and desecration of His worship center is an act that is hated, despised by God. The idea is that it would bring the judgment of God down upon the heads of the offenders. The judges must, therefore, guard the people from idolatry and false worship.
6) The judge must guard the people from greed and from false approaches toward God (ch.17:1). The judge was to keep the people from offering defective sacrifices to the LORD. There was the temptation to keep the best animals for oneself and offer the defective animals to God. Note that this too was an abomination, a detestable act to God. He would never accept a defective offering or sacrifice. Giving God less than the best is failing to acknowledge Him as the Supreme Creator and Owner, Sustainer and Provider of the universe. It is He and He alone who sustains and provides, in particular for His own people; therefore, God's people are to give Him the best offering.

Thought 1. There are several lessons in this point for us:
(1) Judges must never pervert justice nor show partiality to any person because of their friendship, position, wealth, threats, or any other reason.

"He that is faithful in that which is least is faithful also in much: and he that is unjust in the least is unjust also in much" (Lu.16:10).

"I charge *thee* before God, and the Lord Jesus Christ, and the elect angels, that thou observe these things without preferring one before another, doing nothing by partiality" (1 Ti.5:21).

"Are ye not then partial in yourselves, and are become judges of evil thoughts" (Js.2:4).

"Ye shall do no unrighteousness in judgment: thou shalt not respect the person of the poor, nor honour the person of the mighty: *but* in righteousness shalt thou judge thy neighbour" (Le.19:15).

"Thou shalt not pervert the judgment of the stranger, *nor* of the fatherless; nor take a widow's raiment to pledge" (De.24:17).

"He will surely reprove you, if ye do secretly accept persons" (Jb.13:10).

"How long will ye judge unjustly, and accept the persons of the wicked? Selah" (Ps.82:2).

"An unjust man *is* an abomination to the just: and *he that is* upright in the way *is* abomination to the wicked" (Pr.29:27).

"Therefore have I also made you contemptible and base before all the people, according as ye have not kept my ways, but have been partial in the law" (Mal.2:9).

(2) Judges must never accept bribes.

"And thou shalt take no gift: for the gift blindeth the wise, and perverteth the words of the righteous" (Ex.23:8).

"Woe unto them that call evil good, and good evil; that put darkness for light, and light for darkness; that put bitter for sweet, and sweet for bitter! Woe unto *them that are* wise in their own eyes, and prudent in their own sight! Woe unto *them that are* mighty to drink wine, and men of strength to mingle strong drink: Which justify the wicked for reward, and take away the righteousness of the righteous from him" (Is.5:20-23).

"A wicked *man* taketh a gift out of the bosom to pervert the ways of judgment" (Pr.17:23).

"Gather not my soul with sinners, nor my life with bloody men: In whose hands *is* mischief, and their right hand is full of bribes. But as for me, I will walk in mine integrity: redeem me, and be merciful unto me. My foot standeth in an even place: in the congregations will I bless the LORD" (Ps.26:9-12).

"For I know your manifold transgressions and your mighty sins: they afflict the just, they take a bribe, and they turn aside the poor in the gate *from their right*" (Am. 5:12).

(3) Judges must follow the example of the LORD Himself in the administration of justice.

"For the Father loveth the Son, and showeth him all things that himself doeth: and he will show him greater works than these, that ye may marvel" (Jn.5:20).

"But we are sure that the judgment of God is according to truth against them which commit such things" (Ro.2:2).

"Render therefore to all their dues: tribute to whom tribute *is due;* custom to whom custom; fear to whom fear; honour to whom honour" (Ro.13:7).

"That which is altogether just shalt thou follow, that thou mayest live, and inherit the land which the LORD thy God giveth thee" (De.16:20).

"The LORD executeth righteousness and judgment for all that are oppressed" (Ps.103:6).

"To do justice and judgment *is* more acceptable to the LORD than sacrifice" (Pr.21:3).

"The just LORD *is* in the midst thereof; he will not do iniquity: every morning doth he bring his judgment to light, he faileth not; but the unjust knoweth no shame" (Zep.3:5).

"Thus saith the LORD, Keep ye judgment, and do justice: for my salvation *is* near to come, and my righteousness to be revealed" (Is.56:1).

2 (17:2-7) **Justice, Duty—Judges, Execution of—Idolatry, Penalty of—Justice, Safeguards to Assure—Worship, False, Warning Against—Warning, Against Idolatry**: the second major concern of justice is the execution of justice against the major crime of society, that of idolatry and false worship. Note this fact: the local judges were to handle every conceivable case they could on a day-by-day basis (16:18-17:1). But the difficult cases were referred to the Supreme Court or Central Tribunal (17:8-13). This took care of all legal cases that arose within the nation. However, there was one crime that deserved special attention. That crime is the subject of this point. The execution of justice against this crime was a major concern to both God and Moses. The Israelites were a theocracy, that is, a government that acknowledged God as the Supreme Ruler, a society that was based upon the commandments of God Himself. God had already given His people both the *civil* and *religious laws* that were to govern them as a nation. But among all the laws given by God, there was one supreme commandment:

"Thou shalt have no other gods before me" (Ex.20:3).

When this commandment was broken, the execution of justice was to be carried out. A person had violated, dishonored the LORD God Himself (Jehovah, Yahweh), the only living and true God. (See outline and notes—De.4:15-31; 13:1-18 for more discussion.)

DEUTERONOMY 16:18–17:20

OUTLINE	SCRIPTURE	SCRIPTURE	OUTLINE
2. Concern 2: The execution of justice against the major crime a. The fact: A person who commits false worship does evil, violates God's covenant b. The terrible evil: The person worships other gods (sun, moon, or stars, zodiac, astrology, the occult) c. The execution of justice & judgment 1) The charge: Must be thoroughly investigated	2 If there be found among you, within any of thy gates which the LORD thy God giveth thee, man or woman, that hath wrought wickedness in the sight of the LORD thy God, in transgressing his covenant, 3 And hath gone and served other gods, and worshipped them, either the sun, or moon, or any of the host of heaven, which I have not commanded; 4 And it be told thee, and thou hast heard *of it*, and enquired diligently, and, behold, *it be* true, *and* the thing certain, *that* such abomination is wrought in Israel:	5 Then shalt thou bring forth that man or that woman, which have committed that wicked thing, unto thy gates, *even* that man or that woman, and shalt stone them with stones, till they die. 6 At the mouth of two witnesses, or three witnesses, shall he that is worthy of death be put to death; *but* at the mouth of one witness he shall not be put to death. 7 The hands of the witnesses shall be first upon him to put him to death, and afterward the hands of all the people. So thou shalt put the evil away from among you.	2) The judgment: If guilty, must be executed 3) The safeguards to assure justice • The testimony of two or more witnesses was required • The witnesses & the community were themselves to be the executioners 4) The insistence of God: The evil must be purged from among you

a. Moses declared this fact: a person who commits false worship does evil, violates God's covenant (v.2). The Israelites had entered a covenant with God, just as every believer down through the generations enters a covenant with God. If a person will believe and obey God, God will save him and give him an inheritance in the promised land of God (Ex.19:4-6). The Israelites had promised to follow God, to obey Him and keep His commandments. God had saved them from Egypt, from the slavery of this world; therefore, the Israelites professed to be followers of God. By professing God, they committed themselves to obey God, to keep His commandments.

b. Moses declared the terrible evil of false worship and idolatry (v.3). The person who turns to false worship actually turns away from God to worship other gods. He looks for help or guidance from such things as the sun, moon, or stars of the sky. He seeks to know the future, his destiny and fate through such things as the zodiac, astrology, and the occult. A terrible evil—depending upon such things—trusting such things instead of trusting God! This is a terrible breach of the first commandment. The person owed God total allegiance, yet he cut the heart of God causing ever so much pain.

c. Moses declared the execution of justice and judgment against the false worshipper and idolater (vv.4-7). The commentator Peter C. Craigie points out that the idolater and false worshipper deserves the penalty of capital punishment because his evil threatened the very existence of the Israelite nation. The crime, though religious in form, had the most severe political consequences. It destroyed the unity of the people and the assurance of God's presence and blessings. False worship and idolatry would destroy the nation. These terrible evils could be compared to the crime of espionage or treason in the time of war, acts that would weaken the security of the nation.[1]

    1) A charge of false worship or idolatry against a person was to be thoroughly investigated (v.4). This was absolutely necessary since the crime was a capital crime: the person was to be executed. The accused could not be convicted solely on the accusation of a single witness. The accused was innocent until proven guilty.

    2) However, if he was found guilty, he was to be executed (v.5). The person was to be taken out to the city gate and stoned to death.

    3) Note the safeguards to assure justice, to make absolutely sure that an innocent person was not executed (vv.6-7).
        ⇒ The testimony of two or more witnesses was required (v.6).
        ⇒ The witnesses and the community were themselves to be the executioners (v.7). Note how this was a safeguard against false accusations. A person would think twice before falsely accusing someone since he himself had to cast the first stone.

    4) Note the insistence of God: the evil of idolatry and false worship must be purged from among you (v.7).

Thought 1. Since false worship and idolatry are forbidden by God, they are to suffer the most severe consequences imaginable.
(1) False worship and idolatry are forbidden by God.

> "Little children, keep yourselves from idols. Amen" (1 Jn.5:21).
> "Thou shalt not make unto thee any graven image, or any likeness *of any thing* that *is* in heaven above, or that *is* in the earth beneath, or that *is* in the water under the earth" (Ex.20:4).
> "Ye shall make you no idols nor graven image, neither rear you up a standing image, neither shall ye set up *any* image of stone in your land, to bow down unto it: for I *am* the LORD your God" (Le.26:1).
> "Take heed to yourselves, that your heart be not deceived, and ye turn aside, and serve other gods, and worship them" (De.11:16).
> "I *am* the LORD: that *is* my name: and my glory will I not give to another, neither my praise to graven images" (Is.42:8).

---
[1] Peter C. Craigie. *The Book of Deuteronomy*, p.250.

(2) The judgment of God against idolatry will be severe.

"For the wrath of God is revealed from heaven against all ungodliness and unrighteousness of men, who hold the truth in unrighteousness; Because that which may be known of God is manifest in them; for God hath showed *it* unto them. For the invisible things of him from the creation of the world are clearly seen, being understood by the things that are made, *even* his eternal power and Godhead; so that they are without excuse: Because that, when they knew God, they glorified *him* not as God, neither were thankful; but became vain in their imaginations, and their foolish heart was darkened. Professing themselves to be wise, they became fools, And changed the glory of the uncorruptible God into an image made like to corruptible man, and to birds, and fourfooted beasts, and creeping things" (Ro.1:18-23).

"Know ye not that the unrighteous shall not inherit the kingdom of God? Be not deceived: neither fornicators, nor idolaters, nor adulterers, nor effeminate, nor abusers of themselves with mankind, Nor thieves, nor covetous, nor drunkards, nor revilers, nor extortioners, shall inherit the kingdom of God" (1 Co.6:9-10).

"Now the works of the flesh are manifest, which are *these;* Adultery, fornication, uncleanness, lasciviousness, Idolatry, witchcraft, hatred, variance, emulations, wrath, strife, seditions, heresies, Envyings, murders, drunkenness, revellings, and such like: of the which I tell you before, as I have also told *you* in time past, that they which do such things shall not inherit the kingdom of God" (Ga.5:19-21).

"But the fearful, and unbelieving, and the abominable, and murderers, and whoremongers, and sorcerers, and idolaters, and all liars, shall have their part in the lake which burneth with fire and brimstone: which is the second death" (Re.21:8).

Thought 2. There is a lesson in this point for the church: the church must keep itself pure. It must deal with and correct any person who sins, especially one who becomes involved in some false worship or form of idolatry. (See outline and notes—Mt.18:15-20 for the steps to take in correcting offending brothers.)

"Moreover if thy brother shall trespass against thee, go and tell him his fault between thee and him alone: if he shall hear thee, thou hast gained thy brother. But if he will not hear *thee, then* take with thee one or two more, that in the mouth of two or three witnesses every word may be established. And if he shall neglect to hear them, tell *it* unto the church: but if he neglect to hear the church, let him be unto thee as an heathen man and a publican" (Mt.18:15-17).

"Brethren, if a man be overtaken in a fault, ye which are spiritual, restore such an one in the spirit of meekness; considering thyself, lest thou also be tempted" (Ga.6:1).

"A man that is an heretick after the first and second admonition reject" (Tit.3:10).

"To deliver such an one unto Satan for the destruction of the flesh, that the spirit may be saved in the day of the LORD Jesus" (1 Co.5:5).

"I told you before, and foretell you, as if I were present, the second time; and being absent now I write to them which heretofore have sinned, and to all other, that, if I come again, I will not spare" (2 Co.13:2).

3 (17:8-13) **Justice, Duty—Legal Cases, Duty—Court, the High or Supreme—Tribunal, the Central**: the third major concern of society is difficult legal cases. Throughout the wilderness wanderings, the difficult legal cases had been brought to Moses; but after the people had entered the promised land, a central court of law, a central tribunal or Supreme Court was to be established. Note the Scripture and outline:

OUTLINE	SCRIPTURE	SCRIPTURE	OUTLINE
3. Concern 3: Difficult legal cases a. The law 1) To take all cases too difficult for a local judge to the central court of law: Held at the sanctuary & presided over by some priests & a civil judge	8 If there arise a matter too hard for thee in judgment, between blood and blood, between plea and plea, and between stroke and stroke, *being* matters of controversy within thy gates: then shalt thou arise, and get thee up into the place which the LORD thy God shall choose;	they inform thee: 11 According to the sentence of the law which they shall teach thee, and according to the judgment which they shall tell thee, thou shalt do: thou shalt not decline from the sentence which they shall show thee, *to* the right hand, nor *to* the left.	2) Must execute their sentence & interpretation of the law
2) To present one's case & receive a verdict from the High Court	9 And thou shalt come unto the priests the Levites, and unto the judge that shall be in those days, and enquire; and they shall show thee the sentence of judgment:	12 And the man that will do presumptuously, and will not hearken unto the priest that standeth to minister there before the LORD thy God, or unto the judge, even that man shall die: and thou shalt put away the evil from Israel.	3) Must execute any arrogant person who shows contempt for the judge or priest • Must purge such evil from the nation
b. The verdict or decision of the High Court 1) Must carry out the verdict—everything the court says	10 And thou shalt do according to the sentence, which they of that place which the LORD shall choose shall show thee; and thou shalt observe to do according to all that	13 And all the people shall hear, and fear, and do no more presumptuously.	• Such discipline will serve as a deterrent

DEUTERONOMY 16:18–17:20

a. Moses declared that all cases too difficult for a local judge were to be brought to the central court of law (vv.8-9). Where was the Supreme Court to be located? At the sanctuary or the Tabernacle and later at the temple after it had been built. The sanctuary was to serve as the spiritual, social, and political center of the nation (see De.16:18-20; Mt.18:16). Note the categories of cases that could be brought to this High Court: cases of bloodshed, lawsuits, and assaults. These three categories cover the full span of criminal and civil law.[2]

The High Court was to be presided over by a civil judge and several priests. Obviously, they rendered joint judgments on religious, civil, and criminal law.

b. Moses declared that the verdict or decision of the High Court had to be carried out (vv.10-13). The local judges and officials no longer had a say in the matter: by law, they were to execute the verdict passed down by the High Court. They were to execute the sentence or interpretation of the law as explained by the High Court (v.11). And note: they were to execute any arrogant judge or person who showed contempt for the officials of the High Court. By law, the High Court had the power to settle all legal conflicts and problems throughout the nation. The unity of the nation lay in their hands. Therefore, their verdict must be executed. No anarchy or revolt against their authority must be allowed, no attempt to manipulate the law to achieve selfish purposes or advantages. Consequently, if a person rebelled or caused an uprising of anarchy, he was to be executed. This evil was to be purged from the nation. Note this fact: the execution would serve as a deterrent to rebellion and anarchy. By this action, the people would learn to respect the High Court and to highly esteem the judges.

> **Thought 1**. Civic duties are the duties of us all. We are all responsible to uphold the civic laws of our communities and nations. Citizens and rulers, judges and court officials are all held accountable by God to obey the laws. No person is above the law, not even judges. This is the thrust of this point: once the Supreme Court, the High Court of a nation, has rendered a verdict, it is to be obeyed. Even the judges of the land are to obey the rulings of the High Court. There is to be no rebellion or anarchy against the law, unless it is an evil law that is in direct violation of God's Holy Word. The point to note is this: every person is obligated to obey the law, even the judges themselves.
>
> "Notwithstanding, lest we should offend them, go thou to the sea, and cast an hook, and take up the fish that first cometh up; and when thou hast opened his mouth, thou shalt find a piece of money: that take, and give unto them for me and thee" (Mt.17:27).
>
> "Show me the tribute money. And they brought unto him a penny. And he saith unto them, Whose *is* this image and superscription? They say unto him, Caesar's. Then saith he unto them, Render therefore unto Caesar the things which are Caesar's; and unto God the things that are God's" (Mt.22:19-21).
>
> "Let every soul be subject unto the higher powers. For there is no power but of God: the powers that be are ordained of God" (Ro.13:1).
>
> "Put them in mind to be subject to principalities and powers, to obey magistrates, to be ready to every good work" (Tit.3:1).
>
> "Submit yourselves to every ordinance of man for the LORD's sake: whether it be to the king, as supreme; Or unto governors, as unto them that are sent by him for the punishment of evildoers, and for the praise of them that do well" (1 Pe.2:13-14).
>
> "And whosoever will not do the law of thy God, and the law of the king, let judgment be executed speedily upon him, whether *it be* unto death, or to banishment, or to confiscation of goods, or to imprisonment" (Ezr.7:26).
>
> "*I counsel thee* to keep the king's commandment, and *that* in regard of the oath of God" (Ec.8:2).

4 (17:14-20) **King, Duty of—Rulers, Duty of—Israel, Kings of—King, Appointment of**: the fourth major concern of society is the appointment of kings or rulers. These are the only laws dealing with kings in the Pentateuch (first five books of the Bible). Note the Scripture and outline:

OUTLINE	SCRIPTURE	SCRIPTURE	OUTLINE
4. Concern 4: The appointment of kings or rulers a. The prediction of Israel's future desire for a king	14 When thou art come unto the land which the LORD thy God giveth thee, and shalt possess it, and shalt dwell therein, and shalt say, I will set a king over me, like as all the nations that *are* about me;	horses to himself, nor cause the people to return to Egypt, to the end that he should multiply horses: forasmuch as the LORD hath said unto you, Ye shall henceforth return no more that way.	of the king 1) Must never depend upon horses for military strength nor go to Egypt (the world) for help: Never go back to Egypt—the way of the world—seeking an alliance
b. The establishment of the law: The king must be appointed by God Himself 1) To be an Israelite brother 2) Never to be a foreigner	15 Thou shalt in any wise set *him* king over thee, whom the LORD thy God shall choose: *one* from among thy brethren shalt thou set king over thee: thou mayest not set a stranger over thee, which *is* not thy brother.	17 Neither shall he multiply wives to himself, that his heart turn not away: neither shall he greatly multiply to himself silver and gold. 18 And it shall be, when he sitteth upon the throne of his kingdom, that he shall write him a copy of this law in a	2) Must not seek pleasure nor depend upon alliances through many wives 3) Must not lust for nor depend upon wealth 4) Must personally copy the law of God: Study & learn the law or Word of God
c. The duties or responsibilities	16 But he shall not multiply		

---

[2] Frank E Gaebelein, Editor. *The Expositor's Bible Commentary*, Vol.2, p.114.

DEUTERONOMY 16:18–17:20

OUTLINE	SCRIPTURE	SCRIPTURE	OUTLINE
d. The results of learning & ruling by the Word of God 1) Result 1: He will learn to fear God 2) Result 2: He will learn to be a good leader—learn to follow & rule by the	book out of *that which is* before the priests the Levites: 19 And it shall be with him, and he shall read therein all the days of his life: that he may learn to fear the LORD his God, to keep all the words of this law and these statutes, to do them:	20 That his heart be not lifted up above his brethren, and that he turn not aside from the commandment, *to* the right hand, or *to* the left: to the end that he may prolong *his* days in his kingdom, he, and his children, in the midst of Israel.	law 3) Result 3: He will guard against pride, arrogance, & abuse of the people 4) Result 4: He & his descendants will have a long rule

    a. Standing there preaching to the Israelites, Moses predicted that someday lying out in the future Israel would desire a king (v.14). The people would approach their leaders, requesting a king to rule over them like all the nations that surrounded them. They would desire the royal pomp and power, the authority and rule of a king.

    b. Moses declared the establishment of the law: the king must be appointed by God Himself (v.15). Note a significant fact: God does not tie His people to one form of government. He does not oppose the establishment of a monarchy in Israel. God has only one concern: that His Word and commandments be obeyed. If God's people would take His holy commandments and obey them, they would be permitted to establish a monarchy, have a king rule over them.[3] But note, the people had to seek God's direction in choosing a king. The person whom God chose was the person to be placed upon the throne. Another restriction also had to be closely observed: the king must always be an Israelite brother, never a foreigner. They were not to choose a foreigner to strengthen some alliance or to gain a greater security.

    c. Moses declared the duties or responsibilities of the king (vv.16-18). Simply stated, the king was to guard against doing anything that would divert him from serving God and the people.

    1) The king must never depend upon horses—the cavalry—for military strength nor go to Egypt for help. He must never go back to Egypt, the way of the world, to seek an alliance with the world. His dependence was not to be in military strength but in God. Victory over the enemies of the world was to be found in God not in the *arm of the flesh*. Therefore, the king must depend upon God not military power.

    2) The king must not seek pleasure nor depend upon alliances through the marriage of many wives (v.17). Pleasure and wives would divert his affections from God and the citizens of his country. There was the danger he would become enslaved to sex and the worldly ways of foreign wives. Down through history, alliances and security have often been sought through the intermarriage of royalty among the nations of the world. Once a king had been appointed to rule Israel, the temptation to take many wives would confront the king. This would especially be true if a nation's security were threatened and war could be averted by marrying a daughter or relative of the threatening king. But God forbids this. The king of Israel must neither seek pleasure nor depend upon alliances through many wives.

    3) The king must not lust for nor depend upon wealth (v.17). Economic prosperity always gives a great sense of independence, and a sense of independence can easily cause a person to forget God. The king must depend upon God not upon economic prosperity.

    4) Note this most interesting requirement: the king must personally copy the law of God (v.18). He was to take the law and copy it for himself. The idea is that he was to study and learn the law, the Word of God, in order to govern his people just as God dictated. Obviously, he was personally to copy the law right after his inauguration upon the throne. This requirement is interesting, for there would be other copies of the law available to him. Moreover, he would have assistants available to copy the law if he wished a personal copy. But despite this, God insisted that the king have his own personal copy of the law and that he write it out himself, law by law and commandment by commandment.

    d. Moses proclaimed the results of learning the law and ruling by the law of God (vv.19-20). Note that the king was to keep the law with him at all times, and to read it all every day of his life. By doing this, some wonderful results would occur.

    1) By learning the law and ruling by the law, the king would learn to fear God (v.19). He would reverence and worship God, stand in awe of Him. He would be very aware of the justice and judgment of God and demonstrate a respect and need to escape the judgment of God.

    2) If the king learned the law and ruled by the law, he would be a good leader. He would follow the law himself and rule the citizens of his nation by the law. He would not attempt to rule through selfish desires or the whims of the moment, seeking personal gain, wealth, and power. He would rule in order to serve the people. His purpose would be to build a stronger society that would meet the needs of his people more and more.

    3) If the king learned the law and ruled by the law, he would guard against pride, arrogance, and abuse of the people (v.20). He would not consider himself better than the citizens, considering them to exist for his benefit. On the contrary, he would consider himself to be the servant of the people. He would count himself as existing for the people and not the people for him.

    4) If the king learned the law and ruled by the law, he and his descendants would have a long rule over the kingdom of Israel (v.20). God would establish his rule and the rule of his heirs for generations to come. Just remember: the promise is conditional. The king must learn the law and rule by the law.

---

[3] *Matthew Henry's Commentary*, Vol.1, p.796.

DEUTERONOMY 16:18–17:20

Thought 1. Rulers are to heed the Word of God. Scripture is clear, very clear, about the duties of rulers.

"The God of Israel said, the Rock of Israel spake to me, He that ruleth over men *must be* just, ruling in the fear of God" (2 S.23:3).

"Then I consulted with myself, and I rebuked the nobles, and the rulers, and said unto them, Ye exact usury, every one of his brother. And I set a great assembly against them" (Ne.5:7).

"Be wise now therefore, O ye kings: be instructed, ye judges of the earth. Serve the LORD with fear, and rejoice with trembling" (Ps.2:10-11).

"Righteousness exalteth a nation: but sin *is* a reproach to any people" (Pr.14:34).

"*It is* an abomination to kings to commit wickedness: for the throne is established by righteousness" (Pr.16:12).

"Mercy and truth preserve the king: and his throne is upholden by mercy" (Pr.20:28).

"The king by judgment establisheth the land: but he that receiveth gifts overthroweth it" (Pr.29:4).

"The king that faithfully judgeth the poor, his throne shall be established for ever" (Pr.29:14).

"The LORD will enter into judgment with the ancients of his people, and the princes thereof: for ye have eaten up the vineyard; the spoil of the poor *is* in your houses" (Is.3:14).

"Woe unto them [kings, rulers] that decree unrighteous decrees, and that write grievousness *which* they have prescribed" (Is.10:1).

"Thus saith the LORD GOD; Let it suffice you, O princes of Israel: remove violence and spoil, and execute judgment and justice, take away your exactions from my people, saith the LORD GOD" (Eze.45:9).

DEUTERONOMY 18:1-22

CHAPTER 18

G. Laws That Govern the Administration of Religion: Some Concerns of Believers, 18:1-22

1. **Concern 1: The dedication & support of priests or ministers of God**
   a. The law: To receive no inheritance of land with the other tribes, but to be supported by the offerings
   b. The reason: The LORD is their inheritance; they are to focus totally on the LORD & His ministry
   c. The provision for the priest (minister)
      1) Certain parts of the sacrifice
      2) Firstfruit offerings of grain, wine, oil, & the first wool sheared from sheep
   d. The reason the priest (minister) is to be supported
      1) Because God has chosen him
      2) Because he stands & ministers in God's name
   e. The special cases of priests (ministers) who move or who have wealth: Are to be supported
      1) He may move from a local town to the central worship center & minister there: Was still to be equally supported
      2) He may have a private source of income or be wealthy: Was still to be equally supported

2. **Concern 2: The detestable practices & ways of the occult world**
   a. The law: Must not follow the detestable practices of the occult world
      1) Child sacrifice
      2) Divination
      3) Sorcery
      4) Interpreting omens
      5) Witchcraft
      6) Casting spells
      7) Mediums
      8) Spiritists or psychics
      9) Consulting the dead
   b. The warning
      1) These things make a person detestable
      2) These things arouse God's judgment
   c. The strong charge
      1) You must be blameless
      2) You must fear the judgment of God that will fall upon those who practice the occult

3. **Concern 3: A permanent prophet to replace Moses (a prediction of Christ)**
   a. The declaration by Moses: God will raise up a special Prophet: You must listen to Him
   b. The work of the special Prophet
      1) To be the mediator between God & the people
      2) To fulfill the will of God
      3) To be the spokesman for God, declaring the Word of God
   c. The warning: A person must heed the words of the Prophet (Christ) or face the judgment of God

4. **Concern 4: False prophets**
   a. The law: Must execute all false prophets
      1) Any who proclaim a message other than God's
      2) Any who speak in the name of another god
   b. The way to tell if a message is not of God: The message or prophecy does not come true
   c. The charge:
      1) The false prophet speaks his own man-made message
      2) The false prophet is not to be feared

The priests the Levites, *and* all the tribe of Levi, shall have no part nor inheritance with Israel: they shall eat the offerings of the LORD made by fire, and his inheritance.

2 Therefore shall they have no inheritance among their brethren: the LORD *is* their inheritance, as he hath said unto them.

3 And this shall be the priest's due from the people, from them that offer a sacrifice, whether *it be* ox or sheep; and they shall give unto the priest the shoulder, and the two cheeks, and the maw.

4 The firstfruit *also* of thy corn, of thy wine, and of thine oil, and the first of the fleece of thy sheep, shalt thou give him.

5 For the LORD thy God hath chosen him out of all thy tribes, to stand to minister in the name of the LORD, him and his sons for ever.

6 And if a Levite come from any of thy gates out of all Israel, where he sojourned, and come with all the desire of his mind unto the place which the LORD shall choose;

7 Then he shall minister in the name of the LORD his God, as all his brethren the Levites *do*, which stand there before the LORD.

8 They shall have like portions to eat, beside that which cometh of the sale of his patrimony.

9 When thou art come into the land which the LORD thy God giveth thee, thou shalt not learn to do after the abominations of those nations.

10 There shall not be found among you *any one* that maketh his son or his daughter to pass through the fire, *or that* useth divination, *or* an observer of times, or an enchanter, or a witch,

11 Or a charmer, or a consulter with familiar spirits, or a wizard, or a necromancer.

12 For all that do these things *are* an abomination unto the LORD: and because of these abominations the LORD thy God doth drive them out from before thee.

13 Thou shalt be perfect with the LORD thy God.

14 For these nations, which thou shalt possess, hearkened unto observers of times, and unto diviners: but as for thee, the LORD thy God hath not suffered thee so *to do*.

15 The LORD thy God will raise up unto thee a Prophet from the midst of thee, of thy brethren, like unto me; unto him ye shall hearken;

16 According to all that thou desiredst of the LORD thy God in Horeb in the day of the assembly, saying, Let me not hear again the voice of the LORD my God, neither let me see this great fire any more, that I die not.

17 And the LORD said unto me, They have well *spoken that* which they have spoken.

18 I will raise them up a Prophet from among their brethren, like unto thee, and will put my words in his mouth; and he shall speak unto them all that I shall command him.

19 And it shall come to pass, *that* whosoever will not hearken unto my words which he shall speak in my name, I will require *it* of him.

20 But the prophet, which shall presume to speak a word in my name, which I have not commanded him to speak, or that shall speak in the name of other gods, even that prophet shall die.

21 And if thou say in thine heart, How shall we know the word which the LORD hath not spoken?

22 When a prophet speaketh in the name of the LORD, if the thing follow not, nor come to pass, that *is* the thing which the LORD hath not spoken, *but* the prophet hath spoken it presumptuously: thou shalt not be afraid of him.

DEUTERONOMY 18:1-22

DIVISION IV

THE SECOND GREAT THEME PREACHED BY GOD'S AGED SERVANT (PART 2): REMEMBER THE CIVIL AND RELIGIOUS LAWS OF ISRAEL—HELPFUL PRINCIPLES TO GOVERN MAN AND SOCIETY, 12:1–26:19

G. Laws That Govern the Administration of Religion: Some Concerns of Believers, 18:1-22

(18:1-22) **Introduction**: religion is and always has been one of the dominant forces in the world. Within every major city of the world, some worship center sits within just a few blocks of its citizens. Moreover, every major city has a host of charismatic personalities claiming the supernatural ability to see into the future and to help people control the events and destiny of their lives. This is the world of the occult. The occult is followed by masses within most nations of the world. With so many religions and different voices of the occult claiming to know the true path of life, how can a person discern who or what is right? Who really knows the truth? Which religion, which voice can really lead us to God and give us a full, victorious life upon this earth? Which voice can honestly point to and prepare us for eternity? Which message can lead us to heaven, to live eternally with God?

These are the concerns of the LORD as well as of man. God wants man to know the truth. For this reason, God gave the present Scripture to help His people discern between true and false religions and true and false voices in the world. This passage is: *Laws that Govern the Administration of Religion: some Concerns of Believers,* 18:1-22.

1. Concern 1: The dedication and support of priests or ministers of God (vv.1-8).
2. Concern 2: The detestable practices and ways of the occult world (vv.9-14).
3. Concern 3: A permanent prophet to replace Moses (a prediction of Christ) (vv.15-19).
4. Concern 4: False prophets (vv.20-22).

1 (18:1-8) **Ministers, Support of—Dedication, of Priests—Ministers, Dedication of—Stewardship, Duty—Priests, Support of—Believers, Duty—Ministers, Dedication of—Ministry, Focus of—Ministers, Focus of—Inheritance, of Priests**: the first concern is the dedication and support of the priests, the ministers of God. There is a destructive danger always confronting the minister of God. This destructive danger was faced by the priests of Israel, and it has been faced by ministers down through the ages. What is this destructive danger? That of becoming entangled with the affairs of this life, of focusing upon the things of this world instead of upon God and the ministry. If a minister has to focus upon business and financial affairs, it affects his focus upon the ministry. If a minister becomes wrapped up in a secular job day by day, if he has to be concerned about earning a living for himself and his family—it affects his focus, the time he can spend in serving the LORD and the people of God. Becoming entangled with the affairs of this world can be destructive to the minister and his service to God. For this reason, God led Moses to institute this important law for His people.

OUTLINE	SCRIPTURE	SCRIPTURE	OUTLINE
1. Concern 1: The dedication & support of priests or ministers of God a. The law: To receive no inheritance of land with the other tribes, but to be supported by the offerings b. The reason: The LORD is their inheritance; they are to focus totally on the LORD & His ministry c. The provision for the priest (minister) 1) Certain parts of the sacrifice 2) Firstfruit offerings of grain, wine, oil, & the first wool sheared from sheep	The priests the Levites, and all the tribe of Levi, shall have no part nor inheritance with Israel: they shall eat the offerings of the LORD made by fire, and his inheritance. 2 Therefore shall they have no inheritance among their brethren: the LORD *is* their inheritance, as he hath said unto them. 3 And this shall be the priest's due from the people, from them that offer a sacrifice, whether *it be* ox or sheep; and they shall give unto the priest the shoulder, and the two cheeks, and the maw. 4 The firstfruit *also* of thy corn, of thy wine, and of thine oil, and the first of the fleece of thy sheep, shalt thou	give him. 5 For the LORD thy God hath chosen him out of all thy tribes, to stand to minister in the name of the LORD, him and his sons for ever. 6 And if a Levite come from any of thy gates out of all Israel, where he sojourned, and come with all the desire of his mind unto the place which the LORD shall choose; 7 Then he shall minister in the name of the LORD his God, as all his brethren the Levites *do*, which stand there before the LORD. 8 They shall have like portions to eat, beside that which cometh of the sale of his patrimony.	d. The reason the priest (minister) is to be supported 1) Because God has chosen him 2) Because he stands & ministers in God's name e. The special cases of priests (ministers) who move or who have wealth: Are to be supported 1) He may move from a local town to the central worship center & minister there: Was still to be equally supported 2) He may have a private source of income or be wealthy: Was still to be equally supported

a. The law governing the tribe of Levi (the priests or ministers of God) was restrictive, very restrictive: they were to receive no inheritance within the promised land. All the land was to be divided among the other eleven tribes. The Levites were to be supported by the offerings the people gave to the LORD (v.1).

b. The reason for this law should touch the heart and challenge every believer. The priest (minister) was to receive no allotment of land because *the LORD was to be His inheritance* (v.2). The priest was to focus totally upon the LORD and his ministry to the people of God. Very simply, if he had land to manage, he would have to look after the land: the planning, tending, harvesting, and marketing of the crops. He would be concerned about the rain, disease, fruitfulness, and marketing price of the crops. The focus of his thoughts would be upon business and financial affairs. He would be wrapped up in money matters, in the management of day-to-day details of profit and loss margins, and in earning a living. The time and energy of the priest would be given to the management of the property and not to God. For this reason, God established this law. The priest was not to receive an inheritance in the promised land. His inheritance was to be the LORD Himself: he was to be totally focused upon the LORD and his ministry. All his time and energy belonged to the LORD and to the people of God. He was to spend his time before the face of the LORD, serving the people by teaching them the Word of God and ministering to their needs. The priests were to be supported by the offerings of God's people.

c. The priest (minister) was to receive an adequate living (vv.3-4). What exactly did he receive? When a bull or sheep was used in sacrifice, the priest received the shoulder, the cheeks, and the stomach. In addition to the animal sacrifices, they received all the firstfruit offerings of grain, wine, oil, and the first wool sheared from the sheep (v.4).

d. Note that Moses gave two clear reasons why the people must support the priests (ministers) of God:
⇒ because God has chosen them to be His ministers
⇒ because the priests stand and minister in God's Name (v.5).

The priest (minister) was the representative of God upon the earth, chosen by God to be His appointed minister to the people of God. Moreover, the priest (minister) stood before the people of God and ministered in the name of God. The people were to allow the priest to carry on his ministry for God, to focus his time and energy upon God and the ministry to the people. For this reason, the people were to willingly and gladly support the priest (minister).

e. Note that the special case of priests (ministers) who moved or who had wealth is covered. They, too, were to be supported (vv.6-8). A priest was given the right to move from a local town to the central worship center (the Tabernacle) and minister there. If he chose to do this, he was to be equally supported along with his fellow Levites. Even if he had a private source of income or was wealthy, he was to be equally supported. He was to receive his share of the offerings just as the other priests (v.8).

Thought 1. There are two strong lessons in this point for us, one for the minister of God and the other for the people of God.

(1) The minister of God has been called to serve the people of God. He must be faithful and committed to his call, serving ever so diligently.

"I beseech you therefore, brethren, by the mercies of God, that ye present your bodies a living sacrifice, holy, acceptable unto God, *which is* your reasonable service. And be not conformed to this world: but be ye transformed by the renewing of your mind, that ye may prove what is that good, and acceptable, and perfect, will of God" (Ro.12:1-2).

"Let a man so account of us, as of the ministers of Christ, and stewards of the mysteries of God. But have renounced the hidden things of dishonesty, not walking in craftiness, nor handling the word of God deceitfully; but by manifestation of the truth commending ourselves to every man's conscience in the sight of God" (2 Co.4:1-2).

"But in all *things* approving ourselves as the ministers of God, in much patience, in afflictions, in necessities, in distresses" (2 Co.6:4).

"But as we were allowed of God to be put in trust with the gospel, even so we speak; not as pleasing men, but God, which trieth our hearts" (1 Th.2:4).

"Now we exhort you, brethren, warn them that are unruly, comfort the feebleminded, support the weak, be patient toward all *men*" (1 Th.5:14).

"A bishop [minister] then must be blameless, the husband of one wife, vigilant, sober, of good behaviour, given to hospitality, apt to teach" (1 Ti.3:2).

"Let no man despise thy youth [Timothy]; but be thou an example of the believers, in word, in conversation, in charity, in spirit, in faith, in purity" (1 Ti.4:12).

"Preach the word; be instant in season, out of season; reprove, rebuke, exhort with all longsuffering and doctrine" (2 Ti.4:2).

"For a bishop [minister] must be blameless, as the steward of God; not selfwilled, not soon angry, not given to wine, no striker, not given to filthy lucre" (Tit.1:7).

"In all things showing thyself a pattern of good works: in doctrine *showing* uncorruptness, gravity, sincerity" (Tit.2:7).

(2) The people of God must support the minister of God. Scripture is clear: just as a layperson deserves to be paid for his labor, so the minister of God is to be compensated for his labor. The minister is to receive his livelihood from the offerings given to God by the people.

"Even so hath the LORD ordained that they which preach the gospel should live of the gospel" (1 Co.9:14).

"Let him that is taught in the word communicate [give] unto him that teacheth in all good things" (Ga.6:6).

"Notwithstanding ye have well done, that ye did communicate with my [Paul] affliction" (Ph.4:14).

"Let the elders that rule well be counted worthy of double honour, especially they who labour in the word and doctrine. For the scripture saith, Thou shalt not muzzle the ox that treadeth out the corn. And, The labourer *is* worthy of his reward" (1 Ti.5:17-18).

DEUTERONOMY 18:1-22

2 (18:9-14) **Occult, Warning Against—Child Sacrifice, Warning Against—Divination, Warning Against—Sorcery, Warning Against—Witchcraft, Warning Against—Mediums, Warning Against—Psychics, Warning Against—Consulting the Dead, Warning Against—Warning, Against the Occult**: the second concern is the world of occult—the detestable practices and ways of the occult world. People want a full and satisfying life. Because of this, people seek to know their destiny, future events that might affect their lives. If they can know future events, they feel they might be able to manipulate or change the future so as to have a better life. The world of the occult claims to have insight into the future and into the destiny of people. Because of their claims, people by the millions turn to the world of the occult, seeking to control their lives and their future. As the Israelites entered the promised land, there was the danger that they would adopt the occult practices of the Canaanites. To prevent this, God established this law against the world of the occult:

OUTLINE	SCRIPTURE	SCRIPTURE	OUTLINE

2. Concern 2: The detestable practices & ways of the occult world
a. The law: Must not follow the detestable practices of the occult world
  1) Child sacrifice
  2) Divination
  3) Sorcery
  4) Interpreting omens
  5) Witchcraft
  6) Casting spells
 	
  7) Mediums
  8) Spiritists or psychics
	9 When thou art come into the land which the LORD thy God giveth thee, thou shalt not learn to do after the abominations of those nations.
	10 There shall not be found among you *any one* that maketh his son or his daughter to pass through the fire, *or* that useth divination, *or* an observer of times, or an enchanter, or a witch,
	11 Or a charmer, or a consulter with familiar spirits, or
		a wizard, or a necromancer.
		12 For all that do these things *are* an abomination unto the LORD: and because of these abominations the LORD thy God doth drive them out from before thee.
		13 Thou shalt be perfect with the LORD thy God.
		14 For these nations, which thou shalt possess, hearkened unto observers of times, and unto diviners: but as for thee, the LORD thy God hath not suffered thee so *to do*.
			9) Consulting the dead
			b. The warning
			  1) These things make a person detestable
			  2) These things arouse God's judgment
			
			c. The strong charge
			  1) You must be blameless
			  2) You must fear the judgment of God that will fall upon those who practice the occult

  a. Moses declared the law: you must not follow the detestable practices of the occult world (vv.9-11).
    1) There was the occult practice of child sacrifice (v.10). A child was sacrificed in order to secure the favor of some false god or to seek the revelation of some future event.[1]
    2) There was the occult practice of divination or fortune-telling (v.10). This was an attempt to foresee or foretell future events or to discover some hidden knowledge.
    3) There was the occult practice of sorcery which was the attempt to learn or control future events by the power of evil spirits (v.10).
    4) There was the occult practice of interpreting omens (v.10). This was the attempt to tell future events based upon signs such as fire, rain, or the movement of birds.[2]
    5) There was the occult practice of witchcraft (v.10). This was an attempt to influence people or events through sorcery or magic. This they do by using some supernatural method or by consulting the devil or some familiar spirit.
    6) There was the occult practice of casting spells upon people (v.11). A person who casts spells is literally "one who ties others in knots." The idea is that of binding other people by magical utterings.[3]
    7) There was the occult practice of a medium (v.11). This is a person who seeks to communicate with the dead or the world of spirits and actually ends up communicating with evil spirits.
    8) There was the occult practice of a spiritist or psychic (v.11). This was a person who claimed to be sensitive to supernatural forces and influences; a person who claimed to know the forces and events that would affect a person's future.
    9) There was the occult practice of consulting the dead (v.11). In some cases, this person claimed to be able to predict future events by communicating with the dead.
  b. Moses strongly warned the people: these things make a person detestable in the sight of God. The person who practices these things will arouse the judgment of God, and God's judgment will fall upon him. This was the very reason God's judgment was falling upon the Canaanites. The Canaanites were being destroyed and expelled from their land because they had become consumed with the terrible evil of the occult world.

God's people must never allow this to happen to them. They must reject the practices of the occult world. They must never participate nor engage in any practice of the occult.

> **Thought 1.** Psychics, fortune-tellers, palm-readers, sorcerers, diviners, self-proclaimed prophets of new-age movements or of the zodiac—the whole world of the occult—have all been sought by people down through the centuries of human history. People want to know their destiny, what the future holds. They want the blessings of the gods that be, or else they want some enemy cursed. They want only good things to happen to them, not bad things. They want good experiences, not bad experiences. They want plenty, not the bare necessities. They want more, not less. They want acceptance, not rejection. They want to be highly esteemed, not put down. They want position and power, not servitude and enslavement.
>
> For these reasons, and for so many more, people seek the leaders of the occult. They seek the help of any person who claims to have the power of astrology, the power to read the stars, the zodiac, or any other medium. If a

---

[1] Peter C. Craigie. *The Book of Deuteronomy*, p.260.
[2] John Maxwell. *The Preacher's Commentary on Deuteronomy*, p.229.
[3] *Ibid.*, p.230.

person claims to have the answer to the future or to people's problems, they flock to him. But Scripture is clear: the world of the occult is a world of sin and evil. Man is to have nothing—absolutely nothing—to do with the world of the occult.

"And it came to pass, as we went to prayer, a certain damsel possessed with a spirit of divination met us, which brought her masters much gain by soothsaying: The same followed Paul and us, and cried, saying, These men are the servants of the most high God, which show unto us the way of salvation. And this did she many days. But Paul, being grieved, turned and said to the spirit, I command thee in the name of Jesus Christ to come out of her. And he came out the same hour. And when her masters saw that the hope of their gains was gone, they caught Paul and Silas, and drew them into the marketplace unto the rulers" (Ac.16:16-19).

"Now the works of the flesh are manifest, which are these; Adultery, fornication, uncleanness, lasciviousness, Idolatry, witchcraft, hatred, variance, emulations, wrath, strife, seditions, heresies, Envyings, murders, drunkenness, revellings, and such like: of the which I tell you before, as I have also told you in time past, that they which do such things shall not inherit the kingdom of God" (Ga.5:19-21).

"But the fearful, and unbelieving, and the abominable, and murderers, and whoremongers, and sorcerers, and idolaters, and all liars, shall have their part in the lake which burneth with fire and brimstone: which is the second death" (Re.21:8).

"When thou art come into the land which the LORD thy God giveth thee, thou shalt not learn to do after the abominations of those nations. There shall not be found among you any one that maketh his son or his daughter to pass through the fire, or that useth divination, or an observer of times, or an enchanter, or a witch, Or a charmer, or a consulter with familiar spirits, or a wizard, or a necromancer. For all that do these things are an abomination unto the LORD: and because of these abominations the LORD thy God doth drive them out from before thee. Thou shalt be perfect with the LORD thy God" (De.18:9-13).

"And they caused their sons and their daughters to pass through the fire, and used divination and enchantments, and sold themselves to do evil in the sight of the LORD, to provoke him to anger" (2 K.17:17).

"And he [king Manasseh] made his son pass through the fire, and observed times, and used enchantments, and dealt with familiar spirits and wizards: he wrought much wickedness in the sight of the LORD, to provoke him to anger" (2 K.21:6).

"But these two things shall come to thee in a moment in one day, the loss of children, and widowhood: they shall come upon thee in their perfection for the multitude of thy sorceries, and for the great abundance of thine enchantments" (Is.47:9).

"And I will cut off witchcrafts out of thine hand; and thou shalt have no more soothsayers" (Mi.5:12).

"For the idols have spoken vanity, and the diviners have seen a lie, and have told false dreams; they comfort in vain: therefore they went their way as a flock, they were troubled, because there was no shepherd" (Zec.10:2).

"And now we call the proud happy; yea, they that work wickedness are set up; yea, they that tempt God are even delivered" (Mal.3:15).

3 (18:15-19) **Prophet, Call—Prophet, Duty—Prophecy, of Christ—Minister, Duty—Jesus Christ, Prophet**: the third concern is that of a permanent prophet to replace Moses. Moses was old, very old, and he was soon to pass off the scene. What were the Israelites to do once he was gone? Who was going to stand as a prophet before them to proclaim the will of God? Who was going to keep them on the straight and narrow path of holiness? Who was going to protect them from the world of the occult and from the other evils of this world? Who was going to warn them and call them back when they began to go astray? Who was going to stand before them as the spokesman for God, declaring the Word of God? Standing there preaching to the Israelites, Moses answers these questions, and in so doing, he makes an astounding prophecy of the Lord Jesus Christ:

OUTLINE	SCRIPTURE	SCRIPTURE	OUTLINE

3. Concern 3: A permanent prophet to replace Moses (a prediction of Christ)
a. The declaration by Moses: God will raise up a special Prophet: You must listen to Him
b. The work of the special Prophet
  1) To be the mediator between God & the people
 	
  2) To fulfill the will of God
	15 The LORD thy God will raise up unto thee a Prophet from the midst of thee, of thy brethren, like unto me; unto him ye shall hearken;
	16 According to all that thou desiredst of the LORD thy God in Horeb in the day of the assembly, saying, Let me not hear again the voice of the LORD my God, neither let me see this great fire any more, that I die not.
	17 And the LORD said unto
		me, They have well *spoken that* which they have spoken.
		18 I will raise them up a Prophet from among their brethren, like unto thee, and will put my words in his mouth; and he shall speak unto them all that I shall command him.
		19 And it shall come to pass, *that* whosoever will not hearken unto my words which he shall speak in my name, I will require *it* of him.
			3) To be the spokesman for God, declaring the Word of God
			
			c. The warning: A person must heed the words of the Prophet (Christ) or face the judgment of God

DEUTERONOMY 18:1-22

    a. Moses assured the people that God would raise up a special prophet from among their own brothers. Once he appeared, the people must listen to him (v.15).
    b. The work of the special Prophet was to be threefold:
        1) The prophet was to be the mediator between the people and God (v.16). Moses reminded the people that this was exactly what they had requested at Mt. Sinai. When they heard the voice of God speaking from the midst of the fire proclaiming the Ten Commandments, they were stricken with terror. They shrunk back from the mountain, fearing the holiness of God, and begged Moses to stand as mediator between them and God. They begged Moses to approach God on their behalf, receiving the Word of God and then proclaiming His Word to them. Thus Moses was not only God's mediator to the people, he was also God's prophet to the people.
        2) Moses reminded the people that God agreed with their request. It was His will for Moses to be their mediator and prophet (v.17).
        3) Moses then declared that God made a wonderful promise to the people: He would raise up a prophet just like Moses from among the Israelites (v.18). That prophet would be the spokesman for God, declaring the Word of God.
    c. But note: after making the wonderful promise, God had Moses issue a strong warning to the people (v.19). A person must heed the words of the prophet or else face the judgment of God.

Now note: this passage obviously has a double reference. God was promising a permanent line of prophets who would be His spokesmen to declare the Word of God to His people. But He was also promising a very special Prophet who would be the preeminent spokesman for God. This Prophet would be the Divine Communicator in revealing God and His will to the people. Note nine facts:
    1) The great *Pulpit Commentary* says this: "The use of the singular here is remarkable, for nowhere else is the singular, *nabhi*, employed to designate more than one individual."[4]
    2) This passage continues God's wonderful promise of the "promised seed" that was first given to Adam and Eve, and through them to all believers down through the centuries.

> **"And I will put enmity between thee and the woman, and between thy seed and her seed; it shall bruise thy head, and thou shalt bruise his heel" (Ge.3:15;** see outline and notes—Ge.3:15 for more discussion).
>
> **"And I will bless them that bless thee, and curse him that curseth thee: and in thee shall all families of the earth be blessed [through the "promised seed" of Christ]" (Ge.12:3;** see outline and notes—Ge.12:1-3 for more discussion).
>
> **"And in thy seed shall all the nations of the earth be blessed; because thou hast obeyed my voice" (Ge.22:18).**
>
> **"And the scripture, foreseeing that God would justify the heathen through faith, preached before the gospel unto Abraham,** *saying,* **In thee shall all nations be blessed" (Ga.3:8).**
>
> **"Now to Abraham and his seed were the promises made. He saith not, And to seeds, as of many; but as of one, And to thy seed, which is Christ" (Ga.3:16).**

    3) In the days of Christ, the religious leaders were still looking for the fulfillment of this prophecy, and John the Baptist said that he was not the promised Prophet.

> **"And they asked him, What then? Art thou Elias? And he saith, I am not. Art thou that prophet? And he answered, No.... And they asked him, and said unto him, Why baptizest thou then, if thou be not that Christ, nor Elias, neither that prophet" (Jn.1:21, 25).**

    4) Philip, one of the twelve apostles, declared that Jesus Christ was the promised Prophet.

> **"Philip findeth Nathanael, and saith unto him, We have found him, of whom Moses in the law, and the prophets, did write, Jesus of Nazareth, the son of Joseph" (Jn.1:45).**

    5) The people thought that Jesus was the Prophet promised by God.

> **"Then those men, when they had seen the miracle that Jesus did, said, This is of a truth that prophet that should come into the world" (Jn.6:14).**
>
> **"Many of the people therefore, when they heard this saying, said, Of a truth this is the Prophet" (Jn.7:40).**

    6) Jesus Christ Himself was obviously claiming that He was the Prophet Moses predicted.

> **"For had ye believed Moses, ye would have believed me: for he wrote of me" (Jn.5:46).**

    7) Jesus Christ claimed to fulfill the requirements of the promised Prophet.

> **"For I have not spoken of myself; but the Father which sent me, he gave me a commandment, what I should say, and what I should speak. And I know that his commandment is life everlasting: whatsoever I speak therefore, even as the Father said unto me, so I speak" (Jn.12:49-50).**

---

[4] *The Pulpit Commentary*, Vol.3. Edited by H.D.M. Spence & Joseph S. Exell. (Grand Rapids, MI: Eerdmans Publishing Company, 1950), p.304.

DEUTERONOMY 18:1-22

8) Peter declared that Jesus Christ was the Prophet predicted by Moses.

> "For Moses truly said unto the fathers, A prophet shall the LORD your God raise up unto you of your brethren, like unto me; him shall ye hear in all things whatsoever he shall say unto you. And it shall come to pass, *that* every soul, which will not hear that prophet, shall be destroyed from among the people. Yea, and all the prophets from Samuel and those that follow after, as many as have spoken, have likewise foretold of these days" (Ac.3:22-24).

9) Stephen, at his execution trial, boldly proclaimed that Jesus Christ was the promised Prophet.

> "This [Jesus Christ] is that Moses, which said unto the children of Israel, A prophet shall the LORD your God raise up unto you of your brethren, like unto me; him shall ye hear" (Ac.7:37).

4 (18:20-22) **Prophets, False—Tests, Purpose of—Message, Test of—Message, False**: the fourth concern is that of false prophets. How does a person tell whether a prophet is true or false? Whether or not what he preaches or predicts is of God? This was of great concern to God; therefore, He led Moses to establish a very clear law to help the people discern between true and false prophets.

OUTLINE	SCRIPTURE	SCRIPTURE	OUTLINE

4. Concern 4: False prophets
 a. The law: Must execute all false prophets
   1) Any who proclaim a message other than God's
   2) Any who speak in the name of another god
 b. The way to tell if a message is not of God: The message or prophecy does not come
	20 But the prophet, which shall presume to speak a word in my name, which I have not commanded him to speak, or that shall speak in the name of other gods, even that prophet shall die.
	 21 And if thou say in thine heart, How shall we know the word which the LORD hath
		not spoken?
		 22 When a prophet speaketh in the name of the LORD, if the thing follow not, nor come to pass, that *is* the thing which the LORD hath not spoken, *but* the prophet hath spoken it presumptuously: thou shalt not be afraid of him.
			true
			 c. The charge:
			   1) The false prophet speaks his own man-made message
			   2) The false prophet is not to be feared

    a. The law was a strong warning to all false prophets (v.20). Two acts will clearly identify a false prophet:
⇒ proclaiming a message other than God's Word or commandments
⇒ speaking in the name of another god

Note the seriousness of this crime in God's eyes. The false prophet was to be executed.

    b. But how could a person tell if a message was really of God? By the outcome of the message or prophecy (v.21): Did it come true? J. Vernon McGee gives an excellent statement and illustration on this passage that enables the reader to see just how the test of prophets was applied:

> *Let us take time to look at this for a moment. Isaiah is a prophet of God, a true prophet of God. How do we know? He prophesied that a virgin would conceive and bring forth a son. He clearly marked out the coming of the LORD Jesus, His birth, His life, His death [Is.7:14; 53:1ff]. Suppose someone had asked Isaiah when all this would take place. He would have answered that he was not quite sure but that it could be hundreds of years. (Actually, it was seven hundred years.) Well, that crowd would laugh and say they would never be around to know whether he was telling the truth or not. The test of the prophets was that they had to give a prediction about a local situation that would come to pass right away, and they had to be completely accurate. They couldn't miss on any point of their predictions. Any inaccuracy at all would immediately disqualify them as a true prophet of God.*
>
> *Now let us look at Isaiah again. He prophesied the virgin birth, and we today can look back 1900 years to the fulfillment of that and know that he was accurate. But how could the people in his day know that? They could know because Isaiah went to the king, Hezekiah, with a prophecy concerning a local current event. There was a great Assyrian army of trigger-happy soldiers surrounding the city, but Isaiah said that not one arrow would enter the city. Those Assyrians had conquered other nations and they were there to conquer Jerusalem and to carry Israel into captivity. Isaiah told them what God had said about it:*

> "Therefore thus saith the LORD concerning the king of Assyria, He shall not come into this city, nor shoot an arrow there, nor come before it with shields, nor cast a bank against it. By the way that he came, by the same shall he return, and shall not come into this city, saith the LORD" (Isa. 37:33-34).

> *All of...the Assyrian army had bows and arrows. You'd think that just one of them might let an arrow fly over the wall just to see if he could hit someone. Now if one arrow was shot into the city, Isaiah would lose his job as a true prophet of God. He would be out of business. That was one of the tests which Isaiah passed. There were others where Isaiah spoke to a local situation, and it came to pass just as he had said. The true prophet had to be correct 100 percent of the time.*[5]

---

[5] J. Vernon McGee. *Thru the Bible*, Vol.1, pp.579-580.

c. The charge against the false prophet is a strong indictment and warning (v.22): what he says is his own man-made message. His message is not the message of God, not the Word of God. The false prophet is not to be feared. What he predicts—whether encouraging or threatening predictions—will not come true.

Thought 1. False prophets and teachers are everywhere, both inside and outside the church. There are many charismatic, attractive personalities with fluent, soothing messages that appeal to human nature, to the desires of our flesh. But there is only one true message from God Himself, the message of His Holy Word. God loves us, cares so much for us that He would never leave us in the dark, grasping about seeking the truth of life and death. This is the reason He sent Christ into the world and gave us the Word of God, to reveal the truth to us. Any other message is false. Any person who preaches or teaches another message is a false prophet or teacher. Note how strongly Scripture proclaims this:

"Whosoever therefore shall break one of these least commandments, and shall teach men so, he shall be called the least in the kingdom of heaven: but whosoever shall do and teach *them*, the same shall be called great in the kingdom of heaven" (Mt.5:19).

"Beware of false prophets, which come to you in sheep's clothing, but inwardly they are ravening wolves. Ye shall know them by their fruits. Do men gather grapes of thorns, or figs of thistles? Even so every good tree bringeth forth good fruit; but a corrupt tree bringeth forth evil fruit. A good tree cannot bring forth evil fruit, neither *can* a corrupt tree bring forth good fruit. Every tree that bringeth not forth good fruit is hewn down, and cast into the fire. Wherefore by their fruits ye shall know them" (Mt.7:15-20).

"And many false prophets shall rise, and shall deceive many" (Mt.24:11).

"For false Christs and false prophets shall rise, and shall show signs and wonders, to seduce, if *it were* possible, even the elect" (Mk.13:22).

"I marvel that ye are so soon removed from him that called you into the grace of Christ unto another gospel: Which is not another; but there be some that trouble you, and would pervert the gospel of Christ. But though we, or an angel from heaven, preach any other gospel unto you than that which we have preached unto you, let him be accursed. As we said before, so say I now again, If any *man* preach any other gospel unto you than that ye have received, let him be accursed" (Ga.1:6-9).

"For our exhortation *was* not of deceit, nor of uncleanness, nor in guile: But as we were allowed of God to be put in trust with the gospel, even so we speak; not as pleasing men, but God, which trieth our hearts. For neither at any time used we flattering words, as ye know, nor a cloke of covetousness; God *is* witness: Nor of men sought we glory, neither of you, nor *yet* of others, when we might have been burdensome, as the apostles of Christ. But we were gentle among you, even as a nurse cherisheth her children: So being affectionately desirous of you, we were willing to have imparted unto you, not the gospel of God only, but also our own souls, because ye were dear unto us" (1 Th.2:3-8).

"Desiring to be teachers of the law; understanding neither what they say, nor whereof they affirm" (1 Ti.1:7).

"Speaking lies in hypocrisy; having their conscience seared with a hot iron" (1 Ti.4:2).

"If any man teach otherwise, and consent not to wholesome words, *even* the words of our Lord Jesus Christ, and to the doctrine which is according to godliness; He is proud, knowing nothing, but doting about questions and strifes of words, whereof cometh envy, strife, railings, evil surmisings, Perverse disputings of men of corrupt minds, and destitute of the truth, supposing that gain is godliness: from such withdraw thyself" (1 Ti.6:3-5).

"For the time will come when they will not endure sound doctrine; but after their own lusts shall they heap to themselves teachers, having itching ears; And they shall turn away *their* ears from the truth, and shall be turned unto fables" (2 Ti.4:3-4).

"Holding fast the faithful word as he hath been taught, that he may be able by sound doctrine both to exhort and to convince the gainsayers. For there are many unruly and vain talkers and deceivers, specially they of the circumcision: Whose mouths must be stopped, who subvert whole houses, teaching things which they ought not, for filthy lucre's sake" (Tit.1:9-11).

"But there were false prophets also among the people, even as there shall be false teachers among you, who privily shall bring in damnable heresies, even denying the Lord that bought them, and bring upon themselves swift destruction" (2 Pe.2:1).

"And that prophet, or that dreamer of dreams, shall be put to death; because he hath spoken to turn *you* away from the Lord your God, which brought you out of the land of Egypt, and redeemed you out of the house of bondage, to thrust thee out of the way which the Lord thy God commanded thee to walk in. So shalt thou put the evil away from the midst of thee" (De.13:5).

"Then the Lord said unto me, The prophets prophesy lies in my name: I sent them not, neither have I commanded them, neither spake unto them: they prophesy unto you a false vision and divination, and a thing of nought, and the deceit of their heart" (Je.14:14).

"Thus saith the Lord of hosts, Hearken not unto the words of the prophets that prophesy unto you: they make you vain: they speak a vision of their own heart, *and* not out of the mouth of the Lord" (Je.23:16).

CHAPTER 19

H. Laws That Demand Justice for the Defenseless: A Deep Concern for Justice, 19:1-21

1. **Justice for the unintentional killer, for manslaughter: The cities of refuge (a picture of Christ, our refuge from death & from the storms & threats of life)**
   a. The law: To build three cities of refuge
      1) To be centrally located
      2) To build roads to the cities

   b. The purpose: To be a place of safety for a person guilty of accidental manslaughter

   c. The clear illustration: A man & his neighbor are in the forest cutting trees
      1) The man swings the ax & the head flies off & kills his neighbor
      2) The man may flee to a city of refuge for safety from the "avenger of blood" (usually the victim's nearest male relative)

   d. The purpose reemphasized: God gave this commandment to provide a place of safety
   e. The provision for three more cities—if the territory was enlarged by God
      1) The enlarged territory was promised to the forefathers, but it was conditional:
         • Had to obey God
         • Had to love God
         • Had to walk in His ways
      2) The reason for the additional cities
         • To prevent the death of

When the LORD thy God hath cut off the nations, whose land the LORD thy God giveth thee, and thou succeedest them, and dwellest in their cities, and in their houses;
2 Thou shalt separate three cities for thee in the midst of thy land, which the LORD thy God giveth thee to possess it.
3 Thou shalt prepare thee a way, and divide the coasts of thy land, which the LORD thy God giveth thee to inherit, into three parts, that every slayer may flee thither.
4 And this is the case of the slayer, which shall flee thither, that he may live: Whoso killeth his neighbour ignorantly, whom he hated not in time past;
5 As when a man goeth into the wood with his neighbour to hew wood, and his hand fetcheth a stroke with the axe to cut down the tree, and the head slippeth from the helve, and lighteth upon his neighbour, that he die; he shall flee unto one of those cities, and live:
6 Lest the avenger of the blood pursue the slayer, while his heart is hot, and overtake him, because the way is long, and slay him; whereas he was not worthy of death, inasmuch as he hated him not in time past.
7 Wherefore I command thee, saying, Thou shalt separate three cities for thee.
8 And if the LORD thy God enlarge thy coast, as he hath sworn unto thy fathers, and give thee all the land which he promised to give unto thy fathers;
9 If thou shalt keep all these commandments to do them, which I command thee this day, to love the LORD thy God, and to walk ever in his ways; then shalt thou add three cities more for thee, beside these three:
10 That innocent blood be not shed in thy land, which the LORD thy God giveth thee *for* an inheritance, and *so* blood be upon thee.
11 But if any man hate his neighbour, and lie in wait for him, and rise up against him, and smite him mortally that he die, and fleeth into one of these cities:
12 Then the elders of his city shall send and fetch him thence, and deliver him into the hand of the avenger of blood, that he may die.
13 Thine eye shall not pity him, but thou shalt put away *the guilt of* innocent blood from Israel, that it may go well with thee.
14 Thou shalt not remove thy neighbour's landmark, which they of old time have set in thine inheritance, which thou shalt inherit in the land that the LORD thy God giveth thee to possess it.
15 One witness shall not rise up against a man for any iniquity, or for any sin, in any sin that he sinneth: at the mouth of two witnesses, or at the mouth of three witnesses, shall the matter be established.
16 If a false witness rise up against any man to testify against him *that which is* wrong;
17 Then both the men, between whom the controversy *is,* shall stand before the LORD, before the priests and the judges, which shall be in those days;
18 And the judges shall make diligent inquisition: and, behold, *if* the witness *be* a false witness, *and* hath testified falsely against his brother;
19 Then shall ye do unto him, as he had thought to have done unto his brother: so shalt thou put the evil away from among you.
20 And those which remain shall hear, and fear, and shall henceforth commit no more any such evil among you.
21 And thine eye shall not pity; *but* life *shall go* for life, eye for eye, tooth for tooth, hand for hand, foot for foot.

   innocent people
   • To avoid personal responsibility for the death of the innocent
   f. The law to prevent the abuse of the refuge cities
      1) The law: A murderer was not to be allowed to remain in the refuge city
         • The officials were to have him arrested & returned to his own city
         • The officials were to see that he was executed
      2) The murderer was to be shown no pity: The guilt of shedding innocent blood had to be purged from the people to receive God's blessing

2. **Justice for the land owner**
   a. The law: Must not steal land by moving a boundary stone
   b. The warning:
      1) Is the command of God
      2) Will be cursed (27:17)

3. **Justice for the accused**
   a. The law governing any crime or offense: Two or more witnesses are necessary for the conviction

   b. The law governing perjury: A false witness must bear the penalty that the accused would have borne
      1) The two men must stand in God's presence before the legal court of priests & judges

      2) The judges must make a thorough investigation: To see if he is a liar, giving false testimony

      3) The penalty: Equal justice
      4) The reasons for equal justice being executed
         • To purge away evil
         • To serve as a deterrent

      5) The false witness must be shown no pity: Equal justice must be executed

DEUTERONOMY 19:1-21

DIVISION IV

THE SECOND GREAT THEME PREACHED BY GOD'S AGED SERVANT (PART 2): REMEMBER THE CIVIL AND RELIGIOUS LAWS OF ISRAEL—HELPFUL PRINCIPLES TO GOVERN MAN AND SOCIETY, 12:1–26:19

H. Laws That Demand Justice for the Defenseless: A Deep Concern for Justice, 19:1-21

(19:1-21) **Introduction**: accidentally killing a person, stealing land from neighbors, falsely accusing someone of a crime—all three of these acts place a person in terrible jeopardy. A person who commits any of these crimes has to face the bar of justice. Think of the crimes again: manslaughter, theft of property, and perjury. Terrible crimes to commit against a person. Yet they are crimes that are committed every day throughout our communities and nations. These three crimes are of special concern to God. God cares about the person who accidentally kills a neighbor. If a person is driving down the road and accidentally kills a person, the person may be charged with manslaughter. God cares for the driver of a car who is charged with manslaughter. If a land owner has had land stolen from him, God cares for the land owner. If a person has been falsely accused and dragged into court, God cares for the person who has been falsely accused. This is the important subject of this passage: *Laws That Demand Justice for the Defenseless: A Deep Concern for Justice,* 19:1-21.

1. Justice for the unintentional killer, for manslaughter: the cities of refuge (a picture of Christ, our refuge from death and from the storms and threats of life) (vv.1-13).
2. Justice for the land owner (v.14).
3. Justice for the accused (vv.15-21).

1 (19:1-13) **Justice, for Manslaughter—Manslaughter, Justice of—Refuge, Cities of—Cities of Refuge—Christ, Our Refuge—Symbol, of Christ—Life, Storms of—Storms, of Life, Deliverance from**: there was justice for the unintentional killer, for the person who committed manslaughter. Accidents do occur; people are killed without malice or forethought. Unintentional killing does take place within every community. This was the purpose for the cities of refuge: to provide a place of safety for the person who accidentally killed someone. The cities of refuge were to be an asylum, a place of safety for persons guilty of accidental murder. They were to provide a place for the murderer to flee from any avenger who might seek revenge. The cities of refuge were a place of safety until a trial could be set by a community court. Keep in mind that the cities of refuge are a picture of Christ, our refuge from death and from the storms and threats of life. Note the Scripture and outline:

OUTLINE	SCRIPTURE	SCRIPTURE	OUTLINE
1. Justice for the unintentional killer, for manslaughter: The cities of refuge (a picture of Christ, our refuge from death & from the storms & threats of life)	When the LORD thy God hath cut off the nations, whose land the LORD thy God giveth thee, and thou succeedest them, and dwellest in their cities, and in their houses;	6 Lest the avenger of the blood pursue the slayer, while his heart is hot, and overtake him, because the way is long, and slay him; whereas he *was* not worthy of death, inasmuch as he hated him not in time past.	tim's nearest male relative)
a. The law: To build three cities of refuge	2 Thou shalt separate three cities for thee in the midst of thy land, which the LORD thy God giveth thee to possess it.	7 Wherefore I command thee, saying, Thou shalt separate three cities for thee.	d. The purpose reemphasized: God gave this commandment to provide a place of safety
1) To be centrally located			
2) To build roads to the cities	3 Thou shalt prepare thee a way, and divide the coasts of thy land, which the LORD thy God giveth thee to inherit, into three parts, that every slayer may flee thither.	8 And if the LORD thy God enlarge thy coast, as he hath sworn unto thy fathers, and give thee all the land which he promised to give unto thy fathers;	e. The provision for three more cities—if the territory was enlarged by God
			1) The enlarged territory was promised to the forefathers, but it was conditional:
b. The purpose: To be a place of safety for a person guilty of accidental manslaughter	4 And this *is* the case of the slayer, which shall flee thither, that he may live: Whoso killeth his neighbour ignorantly, whom he hated not in time past;	9 If thou shalt keep all these commandments to do them, which I command thee this day, to love the LORD thy God, and to walk ever in his ways; then shalt thou add three cities more for thee, beside these three:	• Had to obey God • Had to love God • Had to walk in His ways
c. The clear illustration: A man & his neighbor are in the forest cutting trees	5 As when a man goeth into the wood with his neighbour to hew wood, and his hand fetcheth a stroke with the axe to cut down the tree, and the head slippeth from the helve, and lighteth upon his neighbour, that he die; he shall flee unto one of those cities, and live:		2) The reason for the additional cities
1) The man swings the ax & the head flies off & kills his neighbor		10 That innocent blood be not shed in thy land, which the LORD thy God giveth thee *for* an inheritance, and *so* blood be upon thee.	• To prevent the death of innocent people • To avoid personal responsibility for the death of the innocent
2) The man may flee to a city of refuge for safety from the "avenger of blood" (usually the vic-		11 But if any man hate his neighbour, and lie in wait for	f. The law to prevent the abuse of the refuge cities

Deuteronomy 19:1-21

OUTLINE	SCRIPTURE	SCRIPTURE	OUTLINE
1) The law: A murderer was not to be allowed to remain in the refuge city • The officials were to have him arrested & returned to his own city • The officials were to	him, and rise up against him, and smite him mortally that he die, and fleeth into one of these cities: 12 Then the elders of his city shall send and fetch him thence, and deliver him into	the hand of the avenger of blood, that he may die. 13 Thine eye shall not pity him, but thou shalt put away *the guilt of* innocent blood from Israel, that it may go well with thee.	see that he was executed 2) The murderer was to be shown no pity: The guilt of shedding innocent blood had to be purged from the people to receive God's blessing

    a. Moses instructed the people to build three cities of refuge as soon as they settled in the promised land (vv.2-3). Remember, the Israelites were camped close by the Jordan River in the plain of Moab, right across from the great city of Jericho. They were poised to cross the Jordan to enter the promised land. They had already conquered and distributed the land of East Jordan to the tribes of Reuben, Gad, and the half-tribe of Manasseh. After distributing the land, Moses had established three cities of refuge to serve these three tribes. Now, standing there preaching to the other tribes, he instructed them to establish three more cities as soon as they conquered West Jordan and settled in their towns and houses. The importance of the cities is seen in the emphasis placed upon them: they were to be centrally located so that a man-slayer could quickly reach them. Moreover, the people were to build special roads to the cities so that they would be accessible, easily reached (v.3).

    b. Moses declared the purpose for the cities of refuge: they were to be places of safety for the person guilty of accidental manslaughter (vv.3-4). Anyone who killed a person could flee to a city of refuge. But note: the cities were only for those who had unintentionally killed a neighbor, killed a person without malice or forethought.

    c. A clear illustration was given: a man and his neighbor were in the forest cutting trees. As one man swung the ax, the head flew off and killed his neighbor (vv.5-6). The man could flee to a city of refuge for safety from the *avenger of blood*. In ancient days it was the responsibility of the nearest relative to protect the family rights of any victim who had been killed. The nearest relative was known as the *revenger of blood* or the *redeemer* or *kinsman*. The nearest relative or *kinsman* was responsible by law to save his relative from any trouble he faced. He was essentially the *protector* of the family. For example, the *kinsman* or *redeemer* was responsible...

- for buying or redeeming a relative from slavery (Le.25:48-49)
- for buying back or redeeming the property of a relative (Le.25:25)
- for marrying a dead relative's widow and bearing children in order to carry on the name of the deceased (Ru.3:12-13; 4:5-10)
- for avenging the death of a relative (Nu.35:19; De.19:6)[1]

    The *kinsman* or the *avenger of blood* became the avenger for the person who had been killed. By law, it was the responsibility of the avenger to execute justice upon the person who had committed the killing. But revenge would run wild and sweep the nation without a place of safety for the manslayer. Accidental killings do happen: the heads of axes do fly off and kill neighbors; cut trees do fall and accidentally kill bystanders. All kinds of accidental killings occur. Consequently, to take revenge against the person who accidentally killed a neighbor is to commit a gross injustice. This was the purpose for establishing the cities of refuge.

    d. Moses reemphasized the purpose: God gave this commandment to provide a place of safety for the accidental manslayer (v.7). The cities of refuge were to be built to provide places of safety until a trial could be set by the community courts.

    e. Note that another provision was made for three more cities of refuge if the territory was enlarged by God (vv.8-10). This point again stresses the importance of justice and shows God's concern for justice among His people. God looked ahead to the day when the promised land would be enlarged and His people would need three more cities of refuge, need the cities in order to assure justice for innocent people.

    1) Note that the enlarged territory was promised to the forefathers, but it was conditional. The people had to obey and love God, walking in His ways (vv.8-9).

    2) The reason for the additional cities is clearly stated:
  ⇒ to prevent the death of innocent people
  ⇒ to avoid personal responsibility for the death of the innocent

    There is national responsibility for this law. God was speaking to the nation as a whole: every person must make sure that innocent blood was not shed in the land. If innocent blood was shed, every person became guilty. For this reason, every person had to make sure that the cities of refuge were built and made available as asylums or places of safety for persons guilty of accidental murder.

    f. Moses declared the law to prevent the abuse of the refuge cities (vv.11-13). A deliberate murderer could not remain in the city of refuge. If a person hated his neighbor and ambushed him, assaulting and killing him, he was guilty of premeditated murder. He was not to be allowed to remain in the city of refuge. The officials were to have him arrested and returned to his own city, where he was handed over to the avenger for execution (v.12). The murderer was to be shown no pity (v.13).

    Note that the guilt of shedding innocent blood had to be purged from the people in order to receive God's blessing. If the people executed justice throughout the land, things would go well for them—far, far better. The execution of justice, not injustice, makes things go far better for any nation. Just as Scripture declares: the execution of justice will cause things to "go well with you" (v.13).

    Thought 1. In a fallen world, accidents happen. Sometimes the accidents cause the death of loved ones. When we lose a loved one, our thoughts should never be upon revenge but upon seeking help from God. God is our refuge and

---

[1] John Maxwell. *The Preacher's Commentary on Deuteronomy*, p.236

strength. He loves and cares for us, and He will take care of us even in the most painful and grieving experiences of life. As stated, God Himself is our refuge and strength. He will sustain us through the loss of our loved ones.

"And we know that all things work together for good to them that love God, to them who are the called according to *his* purpose" (Ro.8:28).

"Casting all your care upon him; for he careth for you" (1 Pe.5:7).

"The eternal God *is thy* refuge, and underneath *are* the everlasting arms" (De.33:27).

"For in the time of trouble he shall hide me in his pavilion: in the secret of his tabernacle shall he hide me; he shall set me up upon a rock" (Ps.27:5).

"But I *am* poor and needy; *yet* the LORD thinketh upon me: thou *art* my help and my deliverer; make no tarrying, O my God" (Ps.40:17).

"God *is* our refuge and strength, a very present help in trouble" (Ps.46:1).

"Be merciful unto me, O God, be merciful unto me: for my soul trusteth in thee: yea, in the shadow of thy wings will I make my refuge, until *these* calamities be overpast" (Ps.57:1).

"Be thou my strong habitation, whereunto I may continually resort: thou hast given commandment to save me; for thou *art* my rock and my fortress" (Ps.71:3).

"In the fear of the LORD *is* strong confidence: and his children shall have a place of refuge" (Pr.14:26).

"The name of the LORD *is* a strong tower: the righteous runneth into it, and is safe" (Pr.18:10).

"For thou hast been a strength to the poor, a strength to the needy in his distress, a refuge from the storm, a shadow from the heat, when the blast of the terrible ones *is* as a storm *against* the wall" (Is.25:4).

"Fear thou not; for I *am* with thee: be not dismayed; for I *am* thy God: I will strengthen thee; yea, I will help thee; yea, I will uphold thee with the right hand of my righteousness" (Is.41:10).

"And *even* to *your* old age I *am* he; and *even* to hoar hairs will I carry *you:* I have made, and I will bear; even I will carry, and will deliver *you*" (Is.46:4).

Thought 2. The LORD is our Refuge from the threats and storms of life. Scripture declares four wonderful truths about the protection the LORD gives us.

(1) The LORD is our Refuge.

"The eternal God *is thy* refuge, and underneath *are* the everlasting arms: and he shall thrust out the enemy from before thee; and shall say, Destroy *them*" (De.33:27).

"God *is* our refuge and strength, a very present help in trouble" (Ps.46:1).

"Be thou my strong habitation, whereunto I may continually resort: thou hast given commandment to save me; for thou *art* my rock and my fortress" (Ps.71:3).

"The name of the LORD *is* a strong tower: the righteous runneth into it, and is safe" (Pr.18:10).

"For thou hast been a strength to the poor, a strength to the needy in his distress, a refuge from the storm, a shadow from the heat, when the blast of the terrible ones *is* as a storm *against* the wall" (Is.25:4).

"Turn you to the strong hold, ye prisoners of hope" (Zec.9:12).

(2) The LORD is our Hiding Place.

"Keep me as the apple of the eye, hide me under the shadow of thy wings" (Ps.17:8).

"For in the time of trouble he shall hide me in his pavilion: in the secret of his tabernacle shall he hide me; he shall set me up upon a rock" (Ps.27:5).

"Thou shalt hide them in the secret of thy presence from the pride of man: thou shalt keep them secretly in a pavilion from the strife of tongues" (Ps.31:20).

"Thou *art* my hiding place; thou shalt preserve me from trouble; thou shalt compass me about with songs of deliverance. Selah" (Ps.32:7).

"Hide me from the secret counsel of the wicked; from the insurrection of the workers of iniquity" (Ps.64:2).

"Thou *art* my hiding place and my shield: I hope in thy word" (Ps.119:114).

"Deliver me, O LORD, from mine enemies: I flee unto thee to hide me" (Ps.143:9).

"And a man shall be as an hiding place from the wind, and a covert from the tempest; as rivers of water in a dry place, as the shadow of a great rock in a weary land" (Is.32:2).

(3) The LORD is our Shield in protecting us.

"After these things the word of the LORD came unto Abram in a vision, saying, Fear not, Abram: I *am* thy shield, *and* thy exceeding great reward" (Ge.15:1).

"Our soul waiteth for the LORD: he *is* our help and our shield" (Ps.33:20).

"For the LORD God *is* a sun and shield: the LORD will give grace and glory: no good *thing* will he withhold from them that walk uprightly" (Ps.84:11).

"O Israel, trust thou in the LORD: he *is* their help and their shield" (Ps.115:9).

DEUTERONOMY 19:1-21

(4) The LORD is our Atoning Sacrifice who delivers us from the avenger of death.

> "For God so loved the world, that he gave his only begotten Son, that whosoever believeth in him should not perish, but have everlasting life" (Jn.3:16).
> "And whosoever liveth and believeth in me shall never die. Believest thou this" (Jn.11:26).
> "The last enemy that shall be destroyed is death" (1 Co.15:26).
> "For this corruptible must put on incorruption, and this mortal must put on immortality. So when this corruptible shall have put on incorruption, and this mortal shall have put on immortality, then shall be brought to pass the saying that is written, Death is swallowed up in victory" (1 Co.15:53-54).
> "For we know that if our earthly house of this tabernacle were dissolved, we have a building of God, an house not made with hands, eternal in the heavens" (2 Co.5:1).
> "For the LORD himself shall descend from heaven with a shout, with the voice of the archangel, and with the trump of God: and the dead in Christ shall rise first: then we which are alive and remain shall be caught up together with them in the clouds, to meet the LORD in the air: and so shall we ever be with the LORD" (1 Th.4:16-17).
> "But is now made manifest by the appearing of our Saviour Jesus Christ, who hath abolished death, and hath brought life and immortality to light through the gospel" (2 Ti.1:10).
> "But we see Jesus, who was made a little lower than the angels for the suffering of death, crowned with glory and honour; that he by the grace of God should taste death for every man" (He.2:9).
> "Forasmuch then as the children are partakers of flesh and blood, he also himself likewise took part of the same; that through death he might destroy him that had the power of death, that is, the devil; And deliver them who through fear of death were all their lifetime subject to bondage" (He.2:14-15).
> "And God shall wipe away all tears from their eyes; and there shall be no more death, neither sorrow, nor crying, neither shall there be any more pain: for the former things are passed away" (Re.21:4).
> "He will swallow up death in victory; and the LORD God will wipe away tears from off all faces; and the rebuke of his people shall he take away from off all the earth: for the LORD hath spoken it" (Is.25:8).

2 (19:14) **Stealing, Duty—Justice, Duty—Land Owner, Wrongs Against—Thieves, Duty**: there was the law governing justice for the land owner. God's law protects the rights and properties of people, and His law puts a hedge around them. Down through the centuries, the boundaries of property lines have probably been one of the most controversial issues among men, causing conflict after conflict. No doubt, this was especially true before the development of accurate surveys and property maps. It was far easier for a person to move a boundary stone than it is today.

When the Israelites entered the promised land, they would be distributing the land among the tribes. Property lines were to be determined and boundary stones set to clearly mark the property. The law was clear: a person must not steal any land by moving a boundary stone. If any person moved a landmark, he was a thief according to the law of God. Note the warning given: this law is the command of God (v.14). The person who breaks this law will be cursed (see De.27:17).

OUTLINE	SCRIPTURE

2. Justice for the land owner
  a. The law: Must not steal land by moving a boundary stone
  b. The warning:
    1) Is the command of God
    2) Will be cursed (27:17)
	14 Thou shalt not remove thy neighbour's landmark, which they of old time have set in thine inheritance, which thou shalt inherit in the land that the LORD thy God giveth thee to possess it.

Thought 1. Scripture is clear about stealing property. Landmarks or property lines are not to be moved. Note what Scripture says about the stealing of property.
(1) The stealing of property is forbidden.

> "Let him that stole steal no more: but rather let him labour, working with *his* hands the thing which is good, that he may have to give to him that needeth" (Ep.4:28).
> "Not purloining [stealing], but showing all good fidelity; that they may adorn the doctrine of God our Saviour in all things" (Tit.2:10).
> "But let none of you suffer as a murderer, or *as* a thief, or *as* an evildoer, or as a busybody in other men's matters" (1 Pe.4:15).
> "Thou shalt not steal" (Ex.20:15).
> "*Some* remove the landmarks; they violently take away flocks, and feed *thereof*" (Jb.24:2).
> "Remove not the ancient landmark, which thy fathers have set" (Pr.22:28).
> "Remove not the old landmark; and enter not into the fields of the fatherless" (Pr.23:10).

(2) The person who steals property will be judged, cursed by God.

> "But the fearful, and unbelieving, and the abominable, and murderers, and whoremongers, and sorcerers, and idolaters, and all liars, shall have their part in the lake which burneth with fire and brimstone: which is the second death" (Re.21:8).

DEUTERONOMY 19:1-21

"Know ye not that the unrighteous shall not inherit the kingdom of God? Be not deceived: neither fornicators, nor idolaters, nor adulterers, nor effeminate, nor abusers of themselves with mankind, Nor thieves, nor covetous, nor drunkards, nor revilers, nor extortioners, shall inherit the kingdom of God" (1 Co.6:9-10).

"Cursed *be* he that removeth his neighbour's landmark. And all the people shall say, Amen" (De.27:17).

"The princes of Judah were like them that remove the bound: *therefore* I will pour out my wrath upon them like water" (Ho.5:10).

3 (19:15-21) **Perjury—Justice, for the Accused—Accused, Justice for—Court, Witnesses in—Witnesses, in Court**: there was justice for the accused. Rules to govern evidence are essential in any court case. The truth must be established, and the number of witnesses must be sufficient to prove that the case against the accused is either just or unjust. Note the Scripture and outline:

OUTLINE	SCRIPTURE	SCRIPTURE	OUTLINE

3. Justice for the accused
a. The law governing any crime or offense: Two or more witnesses are necessary for the conviction
 	
b. The law governing perjury: A false witness must bear the penalty that the accused would have borne
  1) The two men must stand in God's presence before the legal court of priests & judges
 	
  2) The judges must make a
	15 One witness shall not rise up against a man for any iniquity, or for any sin, in any sin that he sinneth: at the mouth of two witnesses, or at the mouth of three witnesses, shall the matter be established.
	16 If a false witness rise up against any man to testify against him *that which is* wrong;
	17 Then both the men, between whom the controversy *is*, shall stand before the LORD, before the priests and the judges, which shall be in those days;
	18 And the judges shall
		make diligent inquisition: and, behold, *if* the witness *be* a false witness, *and* hath testified falsely against his brother;
		19 Then shall ye do unto him, as he had thought to have done unto his brother: so shalt thou put the evil away from among you.
		20 And those which remain shall hear, and fear, and shall henceforth commit no more any such evil among you.
		21 And thine eye shall not pity; *but* life *shall go* for life, eye for eye, tooth for tooth, hand for hand, foot for foot.
			thorough investigation: To see if he is a liar, giving false testimony
			
			3) The penalty: Equal justice
			4) The reasons for equal justice being executed
			  • To purge away evil
			  • To serve as a deterrent
			
			5) The false witness must be shown no pity: Equal justice must be executed

a. Moses declared one of the basic laws governing any crime or offense: two or more witnesses are necessary for conviction (v.15). A single witness was never to be admitted to give evidence in a criminal case. This law is so important that Moses stressed it for a second time in this same series of sermons (see De.17:6). No person's life or honor should lie at the mercy of one witness. The one witness who might be making a false accusation because of some complaint or hostility against the accused. The charge was to be established by the testimony of two or more witnesses.

"But if he will not hear *thee, then* take with thee one or two more, that in the mouth of two or three witnesses every word may be established" (Mt.18:16).

"This *is* the third *time* I am coming to you. In the mouth of two or three witnesses shall every word be established" (2 Co.13:1).

"Whoso killeth any person, the murderer shall be put to death by the mouth of witnesses: but one witness shall not testify against any person *to cause him* to die" (Nu.35:30).

"At the mouth of two witnesses, or three witnesses, shall he that is worthy of death be put to death; *but* at the mouth of one witness he shall not be put to death" (De.17:6).

b. Truth has to be established in a legal case. Perjury must never be allowed to rule the courts of the land. For this reason, Moses declared the law governing perjury: a false witness must bear the penalty that the accused person would have borne (vv.16-21). Whatever penalty would have been inflicted upon the accused, the false witness was to bear that punishment. Note the procedure to be followed if a malicious witness took the stand to accuse a man of a crime.

  1) The two persons involved in the dispute must stand in God's presence before the legal court of priests and judges (v.17).
  2) The judges were then to make a thorough investigation of the case (v.18). They were to determine if the accuser was lying, making a false charge against the accused.
  3) If the accuser was found guilty of lying and giving false testimony, equal justice was to be executed against him. That is, the false witness was to bear the penalty that the accused would have borne. The same punishment was to be inflicted upon him that would have fallen upon the accused.
  4) Note the reasons for equal justice being executed (vv.19-20). Equal justice would purge away the evil from the people, and serve as a *deterrent*. People who heard about the execution of equal justice against false witnesses would

DEUTERONOMY 19:1-21

fear. Equal justice would make them think twice, think long and hard before they would personally bear false witness. Equal justice would protect the public, punish the offenders, and deter crime.[2]

5) Moses declared that the false witnesses must be shown no pity: equal justice must be executed for every citizen within the nation (v.21). Note that equal justice meant "life for life, eye for eye, tooth for tooth, hand for hand, foot for foot."

Throughout the legal system of the Bible and some of the Near Eastern nations, there is this fundamental principle of law: the punishment must match the crime. This is known as the principle of *lex talionis*. It is sometimes called the principle of retaliation or retribution. In the Bible, however, it should be noted that the principle was seldom carried out literally. The basic principle in the Holy Scripture is that of restitution, except in the case of deliberate murder. Premeditated murder and serious sins against the family in God's holy name did merit the death penalty. But in most, if not all, other cases of crime, restitution that equaled the crime had to be paid. (See outline and notes—Ex.21:1-23:19; Le.24:10-23 for more discussion.)

Thought 1. Above all else, we must tell the truth. We must never lie. One of the worst evils among men is that of perjury, bearing false witness against a person. Lying or bearing false witness injures the innocent person by damaging his reputation, stealing his property, or taking his life. A false witness will be shown no mercy, not by God. This is the strong declaration of Scripture.

"For the wrath of God is revealed from heaven against all ungodliness and unrighteousness of men, who hold the truth in unrighteousness....Being filled with all unrighteousness, fornication, wickedness, covetousness, maliciousness; full of envy, murder, debate, deceit, malignity; whisperers, Backbiters, haters of God, despiteful, proud, boasters, inventors of evil things, disobedient to parents, Without understanding, covenantbreakers, without natural affection, implacable, unmerciful: Who knowing the judgment of God, that they which commit such things are worthy of death, not only do the same, but have pleasure in them that do them" (Ro.1:18, 29-32).

"Know ye not that the unrighteous shall not inherit the kingdom of God? Be not deceived: neither fornicators, nor idolaters, nor adulterers, nor effeminate, nor abusers of themselves with mankind, Nor thieves, nor covetous, nor drunkards, nor revilers, nor extortioners, shall inherit the kingdom of God" (1 Co.6:9-10).

"But the fearful, and unbelieving, and the abominable, and murderers, and whoremongers, and sorcerers, and idolaters, and all liars, shall have their part in the lake which burneth with fire and brimstone: which is the second death" (Re.21:8).

"Thou shalt not bear false witness against thy neighbour" (Ex.20:16).

"Thou shalt not raise a false report: put not thine hand with the wicked to be an unrighteous witness" (Ex.23:1).

"A false witness shall not be unpunished, and he that speaketh lies shall perish" (Pr.19:9).

TYPES, SYMBOLS, AND PICTURES
(Deuteronomy 19:1-21)

Historical Term	Type or Picture (Scriptural Basis for Each)	Life Application for Today's Believer	Biblical Application
Cities of Refuge De.19:1-13	*The cities of refuge are a picture of Christ, our refuge from the threats and storms of life.* *Accidents do occur; people are killed without malice or forethought. Unintentional killing does take place within every community. This was the purpose for the cities of refuge: to provide a place of safety for the person who accidentally killed someone. The cities of refuge were to be an asylum, a place of safety for persons guilty of accidental murder. They were to provide a place for the murderer to flee from any avenger who might seek revenge. He was to remain in the city until a trial could be set by a community court.*	⇒ The LORD is our Refuge from the threats and storms of life. Scripture declares four wonderful truths about the protection the LORD gives us. 1. The LORD is our Refuge. 2. The LORD is our Hiding Place.	"The eternal God is thy refuge, and underneath are the everlasting arms: and he shall thrust out the enemy from before thee; and shall say, Destroy them" (De. 33:27). "The God of my rock; in him will I trust: he is my shield, and the horn of my salvation, my high tower, and my refuge, my saviour; thou savest me from violence" (2 S.22:3; See Ps.9:9; Ps.46:1; Ps.91:9). "Thou art my hiding place; thou shalt preserve

---

[2] Frank E. Gaebelein, Editor. *The Expositor's Bible Commentary*, p.126.

DEUTERONOMY 19:1-21

Historical Term	Type or Picture (Scriptural Basis for Each)	Life Application for Today's Believer	Biblical Application
	"And this *is* the case of the slayer, which shall flee thither, that he may live: Whoso killeth his neighbour ignorantly, whom he hated not in time past" (De.19:4).		me from trouble; thou shalt compass me about with songs of deliverance" (Ps.32:7). "Thou art my hiding place and my shield: I hope in thy word" (Ps.119:114).
		3. The LORD is our Shield of protection.	"After these things the word of the LORD came unto Abram in a vision, saying, Fear not, Abram: I am thy shield, and thy exceeding great reward" (Ge.15:1; See De. 33:29; 2 S. 22:3; 2 S.22:36). "But thou, O LORD, art a shield for me; my glory, and the lifter up of mine head" (Ps.3:3; See Ps.5:12; Ps.18:35; Ps.28:7; Ps. 144:2; Pr.30:5).
		4. The LORD is our Atoning Sacrifice who delivers us from the avenger of death.	"For God so loved the world, that he gave his only begotten Son, that whosoever believeth in him should not perish, but have everlasting life" (Jn.3:16). "For if, when we were enemies, we were reconciled to God by the death of his Son, much more, being reconciled, we shall be saved by his life. And not only so, but we also joy in God through our Lord Jesus Christ, by whom we have now received the atonement" (Ro.5:10-11; See Jn.11:26).

DEUTERONOMY 20:1-20

CHAPTER 20

I. Laws That Govern the Conduct of War: A Picture of the Believer's Spiritual Warfare Against the Enemies of This World, 20:1-20

1. **The assurance of victory**
   a. The charge: Do not fear the enemy
   b. The encouragements
      1) The assurance of God's presence & power: Proven by His deliverance from Egypt (a symbol of salvation)
      2) The message of the appointed priest (a picture of Christ): Before the battle, he was to charge the army

   - Do not be fainthearted
   - Do not be afraid
   - Do not be terrified
   - Do not panic
   - God is with you & will give you victory

2. **The exemptions from military service: The need for total commitment by all in mobilizing for war**
   a. An exemption due to home life: Necessary to maintain life in the land
   b. An exemption due to employment: Necessary to maintain food production
   c. An exemption due to marriage: Necessary to maintain life & families in the nation
   d. An exemption due to cowardice: Necessary to maintain the courage & loyalty of the army
   e. After the exemptions, the officers were appointed: Necessary to wait in order to show who was available to fight

3. **The strategy for conquest**
   a. The conquest of distant enemies
      1) Must first seek peace
      2) Must have control over the enemy if they accept the peace offer: Put the enemy to work for you
      3) Must lay siege to the city if the enemy rejects peace & makes war
         - Execute all the men
         - Save all the women, children, livestock, & other plunder as spoils of war
      4) Must know that this strategy applies only to enemies far away—outside the promised land
   b. The conquest of immediate enemies, enemies within the promised land^{DS1}
      1) The rule of war: Must be completely destroyed
      2) The reasons
         - Because this is the command of God
         - Because of their evil influence
         - Because their cup of iniquity was full—beyond repentance (see Ge.15:16; Nu.21:2-3)
   c. The strategy of conservation, of preserving the land for the public good
      1) The law: Must not destroy the fruit trees (lay waste the land)
      2) The purpose: To preserve the trees (& land) for food
      3) The allowance: Could use non-fruit trees as needed until the enemy was conquered

When thou goest out to battle against thine enemies, and seest horses, and chariots, *and* a people more than thou, be not afraid of them: for the LORD thy God *is* with thee, which brought thee up out of the land of Egypt.
2 And it shall be, when ye are come nigh unto the battle, that the priest shall approach and speak unto the people,
3 And shall say unto them, Hear, O Israel, ye approach this day unto battle against your enemies: let not your hearts faint, fear not, and do not tremble, neither be ye terrified because of them;
4 For the LORD your God *is* he that goeth with you, to fight for you against your enemies, to save you.
5 And the officers shall speak unto the people, saying, What man *is there* that hath built a new house, and hath not dedicated it? let him go and return to his house, lest he die in the battle, and another man dedicate it.
6 And what man *is he* that hath planted a vineyard, and hath not *yet* eaten of it? let him *also* go and return unto his house, lest he die in the battle, and another man eat of it.
7 And what man *is there* that hath betrothed a wife, and hath not taken her? let him go and return unto his house, lest he die in the battle, and another man take her.
8 And the officers shall speak further unto the people, and they shall say, What man *is there that is* fearful and fainthearted? let him go and return unto his house, lest his brethren's heart faint as well as his heart.
9 And it shall be, when the officers have made an end of speaking unto the people, that they shall make captains of the armies to lead the people.
10 When thou comest nigh unto a city to fight against it, then proclaim peace unto it.
11 And it shall be, if it make thee answer of peace, and open unto thee, then it shall be, *that* all the people *that is* found therein shall be tributaries unto thee, and they shall serve thee.
12 And if it will make no peace with thee, but will make war against thee, then thou shalt besiege it:
13 And when the LORD thy God hath delivered it into thine hands, thou shalt smite every male thereof with the edge of the sword:
14 But the women, and the little ones, and the cattle, and all that is in the city, *even* all the spoil thereof, shalt thou take unto thyself; and thou shalt eat the spoil of thine enemies, which the LORD thy God hath given thee.
15 Thus shalt thou do unto all the cities *which are* very far off from thee, which *are* not of the cities of these nations.
16 But of the cities of these people, which the LORD thy God doth give thee *for* an inheritance, thou shalt save alive nothing that breatheth:
17 But thou shalt utterly destroy them; *namely*, the Hittites, and the Amorites, the Canaanites, and the Perizzites, the Hivites, and the Jebusites; as the LORD thy God hath commanded thee:
18 That they teach you not to do after all their abominations, which they have done unto their gods; so should ye sin against the LORD your God.
19 When thou shalt besiege a city a long time, in making war against it to take it, thou shalt not destroy the trees thereof by forcing an axe against them: for thou mayest eat of them, and thou shalt not cut them down (for the tree of the field *is* man's *life*) to employ *them* in the siege:
20 Only the trees which thou knowest that they *be* not trees for meat, thou shalt destroy and cut them down; and thou shalt build bulwarks against the city that maketh war with thee, until it be subdued.

DEUTERONOMY 20:1-20

DIVISION IV

THE SECOND GREAT THEME PREACHED BY GOD'S AGED SERVANT (PART 2): REMEMBER THE CIVIL AND RELIGIOUS LAWS OF ISRAEL—HELPFUL PRINCIPLES TO GOVERN MAN AND SOCIETY, 12:1–26:19

I. Laws That Govern the Conduct of War: A Picture of the Believer's Spiritual Warfare Against the Enemies of This World, 20:1-20

(20:1-20) **Introduction**: war is hell, the cutting loose of hell upon earth. War unlocks the chains of hell and sets free the demonic spirits of killing, slaughter, maiming, rape, brutality, savagery, pain, suffering, starvation, destruction of property, economic collapse, and a host of other demonic spirits that destroy the earth and human life. But despite these terrible, horrible evils, there are times when war is necessary. There are times when we must protect ourselves from those who attack and seek either to dominate us or to slaughter our children, wives, and husbands. Because we are living in a sinful world where the heart of man is desperately wicked, there are times when we must declare war and fight for our very survival. There are wars in which the LORD God (Jehovah, Yahweh)—the true and living God—is on one side. Because of this fact, before ever declaring a war, a nation should seek the LORD God to make absolutely sure that the war is God's will. If it is not God's will, the war should never be declared.

The present passage concerns the conduct of war waged by the Israelites. God gave very specific laws to govern the wars the Israelites fought. This is the subject of the present passage: *Laws That Govern the Conduct of War: A Picture of the Believer's Spiritual Warfare Against the Enemies of This World*, 20:1-20.
1. The assurance of victory (vv.1-4).
2. The exemptions from military service: the need for total commitment by all in mobilizing for war (vv.5-9).
3. The strategy for conquest (vv.10-20).

1 (20:1-4) **Victory, Assurance of—Assurance, of Victory—Enemies, Victory over—Fear, Duty—Faint-hearted, Duty**: there was the assurance of victory given by God, victory over all enemies. Remember, the Israelites were camped close by the Jordan River in the plain of Moab, right across from the great city of Jericho. They were soon to march across the river and face the enemies of the promised land. The terror of war was staring them in the face. Battle was soon to be waged. As with any people facing battle, apprehension and fear arose and become a threat to the mental and emotional preparedness of the army. Moses knew the importance of preparing the army mentally and emotionally; therefore, he encouraged the people to conquer their fears. Note what he said to them:

OUTLINE	SCRIPTURE	SCRIPTURE	OUTLINE

1. The assurance of victory
a. The charge: Do not fear the enemy
b. The encouragements
  1) The assurance of God's presence & power: Proven by His deliverance from Egypt (a symbol of salvation)
  2) The message of the appointed priest (a picture of Christ): Before the battle, he was to charge the
	When thou goest out to battle against thine enemies, and seest horses, and chariots, *and* a people more than thou, be not afraid of them: for the LORD thy God *is* with thee, which brought thee up out of the land of Egypt.
	2 And it shall be, when ye are come nigh unto the battle, that the priest shall approach and speak unto the
		people,
		3 And shall say unto them, Hear, O Israel, ye approach this day unto battle against your enemies: let not your hearts faint, fear not, and do not tremble, neither be ye terrified because of them;
		4 For the LORD your God *is* he that goeth with you, to fight for you against your enemies, to save you.
			army
			
			• Do not be fainthearted
			• Do not be afraid
			• Do not be terrified
			• Do not panic
			• God is with you & will give you victory

a. Moses charged the people: do not fear the enemy (v.1). He warned them that the enemy will have greater numbers and superior military equipment, horses, and chariots. But the superior numbers and equipment were not to strike fear in their hearts. Victory was to be theirs. However, it was not to be achieved through superior numbers or equipment, but rather through God Himself.

b. Note the two strong encouragements that Moses gave the people (vv.1-4).
  1) Moses assured the people that God's presence and power would be with them. God would deliver them just as He had delivered them from Egyptian slavery. And they were always to remember: Egypt was a far more powerful nation than they. Yet, God delivered them. The implication was clear: if God had delivered them from such a powerful nation as Egypt, He could give them victory over any enemy.
  2) The message of the appointed priests was also to be a strong encouragement to the people (vv.2-4). Before going into battle, the priest was to address the army, giving four charges to them.
     ⇒ Do not be faint-hearted; do not lose heart.
     ⇒ Do not be afraid.
     ⇒ Do not be terrified.
     ⇒ Do not tremble, panic.

Moses assured the people: God would be with them and would give them victory over all their enemies (v.4). In the thick of battle, they were to remember this one fact: victory was theirs through the presence and power of God.

DEUTERONOMY 20:1-20

Thought 1. The language of warfare is a picture of the believer's spiritual warfare against the enemies of this world. The war fought by the Christian believer is not an *earthly war* but a spiritual warfare. As the believer marches to the promised land of heaven, enemy after enemy attacks him, subtle temptations and trials such as...

- disease
- accident
- immorality
- greed
- covetousness
- anger
- discouragement
- depression
- failure
- financial difficulty
- loneliness
- emptiness
- loss of job
- lack of purpose
- death

Some enemies are small and weak, amounting to nothing more than minor temptations or trials. Such enemies are easy to conquer, sometimes even by the *arm of the flesh*. But there are other enemies that are far more powerful and brutal in their attacks. These enemies could never be defeated by man, such enemies as a terminal disease, a paralyzing accident, the face of death, or the powerful seduction and lust of some sin that so easily entangles us (He.12:1). Such enemies as these can be conquered only by the presence and power of God Himself.

> "There hath no temptation taken you but such as is common to man: but God *is* faithful, who will not suffer you to be tempted above that ye are able; but will with the temptation also make a way to escape, that ye may be able to bear *it*" (1 Co.10:13).
>
> "Now unto him that is able to do exceeding abundantly above all that we ask or think, according to the power that worketh in us" (Ep.3:20).
>
> "So that we may boldly say, The LORD *is* my helper, and I will not fear what man shall do unto me" (He.13:6).
>
> "The LORD shall fight for you, and ye shall hold your peace" (Ex.14:14).
>
> "When thou goest out to battle against thine enemies, and seest horses, and chariots, *and* a people more than thou, be not afraid of them: for the LORD thy God *is* with thee, which brought thee up out of the land of Egypt" (De.20:1).
>
> "The LORD *is* my strength and my shield; my heart trusted in him, and I am helped: therefore my heart greatly rejoiceth; and with my song will I praise him" (Ps.28:7).
>
> "But I *am* poor and needy; *yet* the LORD thinketh upon me: thou *art* my help and my deliverer; make no tarrying, O my God" (Ps.40:17).
>
> "Fear thou not; for I *am* with thee: be not dismayed; for I *am* thy God: I will strengthen thee; yea, I will help thee; yea, I will uphold thee with the right hand of my righteousness" (Is.41:10).
>
> "When thou passest through the waters, I *will be* with thee; and through the rivers, they shall not overflow thee: when thou walkest through the fire, thou shalt not be burned; neither shall the flame kindle upon thee" (Is.43:2).

Thought 2. John Maxwell has an excellent statement dealing with the treatment of holy war. The statement is well worth quoting in its entirety:

Holy war is marked by a number of distinctives which set it apart from other types of wars:
(1) A holy war was not undertaken without consulting Yahweh (1 Sam. 28:5-6; 30:7-8; 2 Sam. 5:19, 22-23).
(2 The men of Israel were consecrated to the LORD before (and during) battle (1 Sam. 21:5; 2 Sam. 11:11; Isa. 13:3).
(3 Men that would offend God were removed from camp (Deut. 23:9-11).
(4) Yahweh was present in the camp (Deut. 23:14), and He gave His leader special powers, although it was God Himself who was the Captain of the hosts of Israel and could alone deliver His people (Judg. 4:14-15; 7:2ff; 1 Sam. 13:5, 15; 14:6-23).
(5) At the climax of the battle God sent terror and panic into the midst of the enemy, thus bringing about their overthrow (Deut. 2:25; Josh. 2:9; 5:1; 1 Sam. 5:11; 7:10).
(6) The spoils of war were under the ban of sacred consecration and were the exclusive right of God. [1]

2 **(20:5-9) Military, Exemptions from—Exemptions, from Military Service—War, Commitment to:** there were the exemptions from military service. The exemptions were allowed because of the need for total commitment by every soldier. Distractions could not be allowed. Anything that might distract a soldier had to be eliminated. Commitment was an absolute necessity when marching into battle. Without commitment, the battle was lost even before it began. For this reason, the basic qualification for a soldier was personal commitment to the army and its purpose. It was not necessary to have the *largest* possible army but the *best* possible army. The best possible army was the army totally committed to God, and absolutely confident that God would give them the victory over the enemy.[2] Note the exemptions in the Scripture and outline:

---

[1] John Maxwell. *The Preacher's Commentary on Deuteronomy*, p.239. Points are set apart for clarity.
[2] Peter C. Craigie. *The Book of Deuteronomy*, p.273.

DEUTERONOMY 20:1-20

OUTLINE	SCRIPTURE	SCRIPTURE	OUTLINE
2. The exemptions from military service: The need for total commitment by all in mobilizing for war a. An exemption due to home life: Necessary to maintain life in the land b. An exemption due to employment: Necessary to maintain food production c. An exemption due to marriage: Necessary to maintain	5 And the officers shall speak unto the people, saying, What man *is there* that hath built a new house, and hath not dedicated it? let him go and return to his house, lest he die in the battle, and another man dedicate it. 6 And what man *is he* that hath planted a vineyard, and hath not *yet* eaten of it? let him *also* go and return unto his house, lest he die in the battle, and another man eat of it. 7 And what man *is there* that hath betrothed a wife,	and hath not taken her? let him go and return unto his house, lest he die in the battle, and another man take her. 8 And the officers shall speak further unto the people, and they shall say, What man *is there that is* fearful and fainthearted? let him go and return unto his house, lest his brethren's heart faint as well as his heart. 9 And it shall be, when the officers have made an end of speaking unto the people, that they shall make captains of the armies to lead the people.	life & families in the nation d. An exemption due to cowardice: Necessary to maintain the courage & loyalty of the army e. After the exemptions, the officers were appointed: Necessary to wait in order to show who was available to fight

a. There was an exemption due to home life (v.5). If a person had just built a house but had not started to live in it, he was allowed to return home. This exemption was necessary to maintain life in the promised land. Remember, as the Israelites conquered the land, they were to immediately settle down and begin to farm the land. Building homes, growing food, and marrying and having children—all these were necessary to carry on life in the promised land. Without these very basic functions of life, war would be pointless.[3] There would be no need to conquer the promised land, no need to seek a full and victorious life in the land promised by God.

b. There was an exemption due to employment (v.6). If a person had just begun to farm his land, he was allowed to go home.

c. There was an exemption due to marriage (v.7). Again, this was necessary to maintain life and families within the nation of Israel.

d. There was an exemption due to cowardice (v.8). This was an absolute essential to maintain the courage and loyalty of the army. A coward was a threat to the courage of the other soldiers. In the rage of battle, especially in a hard fought battle, fear and cowardice can spread like wildfire. Fear and cowardice in the rage of a battle can destroy morale and lead to a fatal retreat. It was, therefore, absolutely necessary to exempt the faint-hearted, the coward. Note this fact: fear and cowardice were spiritual problems. God promised the victory; victory was assured. Going into battle, a person was bound to feel some apprehension, but there was no need to allow the fear to conquer one's heart and cause panic and terror. God promised His presence and power to help every soldier fight against the enemies of the promised land. Therefore, fear and cowardice were inexcusable. Nevertheless, after all the encouragement, if a person was still faint-hearted, gripped with the spirit of a coward, he was exempt from service.

e. Note that the commanders were appointed only after the exemptions had taken place (v.9). It was necessary to wait in order to show who was available for military service. Only the loyal and courageous were left: from among them the officers and commanders were to be appointed.

Thought 1. Commitment, courage, and loyalty are absolute essentials in any warfare. This is true of earthly warfare and of spiritual warfare. No matter who the enemy is—man, temptation, or trial—we must be committed to God, loyal to Him, and courageous in order to be victorious. We can conquer the enemies of this life only by the presence and the power of God. Victorious courage—the kind of courage that gives a full and victorious life—can come only from God. Therefore, we must be committed and loyal to God. If we will give Him our hearts and lives, God will infuse us with enormous courage, enough courage to conquer all the enemies of this life.

"Therefore, my beloved brethren, be ye stedfast, unmovable, always abounding in the work of the LORD, forasmuch as ye know that your labour is not in vain in the LORD" (1 Co.15:58).

"Now unto him that is able to do exceeding abundantly above all that we ask or think, according to the power that worketh in us" (Ep.3:20).

"And in nothing terrified by your adversaries: which is to them an evident token of perdition, but to you of salvation, and that of God" (Ph.1:28).

"For God hath not given us the spirit of fear; but of power, and of love, and of a sound mind" (2 Ti.1:7).

"Be strong and of a good courage, fear not, nor be afraid of them: for the LORD thy God, he *it is* that doth go with thee; he will not fail thee, nor forsake thee" (De.31:6).

"Be strong and of a good courage: for unto this people shalt thou divide for an inheritance the land, which I sware unto their fathers to give them" (Jos.1:6).

"And Joshua said unto them, Fear not, nor be dismayed, be strong and of good courage: for thus shall the LORD do to all your enemies against whom ye fight" (Jos.10:25).

"Be ye therefore very courageous to keep and to do all that is written in the book of the law of Moses, that ye turn not aside therefrom *to* the right hand or *to* the left; That ye come not among these nations, these that remain among you; neither make mention of the names of their gods, nor cause to swear

---
[3] John Maxwell. *The Preacher's Commentary on Deuteronomy*, p.244.

by them, neither serve them, nor bow yourselves unto them: But cleave unto the LORD your God, as ye have done unto this day" (Jos.23:6-8).

"Be of good courage, and let us play the men for our people, and for the cities of our God: and the LORD do that which seemeth him good" (2 S.10:12).

"Be of good courage, and let us behave ourselves valiantly for our people, and for the cities of our God: and let the LORD do *that which is* good in his sight" (1 Chr.19:13).

"Then shalt thou prosper, if thou takest heed to fulfil the statutes and judgments which the LORD charged Moses with concerning Israel: be strong, and of good courage; dread not, nor be dismayed" (1 Chr.22:13).

"And David said to Solomon his son, Be strong and of good courage, and do *it:* fear not, nor be dismayed: for the LORD God, *even* my God, *will be* with thee; he will not fail thee, nor forsake thee, until thou hast finished all the work for the service of the house of the LORD" (1 Chr.28:20).

"Trust in the LORD with all thine heart; and lean not unto thine own understanding" (Pr.3:5).

"My son, give me thine heart, and let thine eyes observe my ways" (Pr.23:26).

3 (20:10-20) **War, Strategy—Strategy, for War—Israel, Strategy of Warfare—Conservation, of Land—War, Rules of—Iniquity, Cup of—Land, Conservation of**: there was the strategy for warfare. As Israel launched its campaign to conquer the promised land, God laid down a very specific strategy for the army to follow. A different strategy was to be followed when facing *distant enemies* from that of facing the Canaanite enemies within the promised land. In addition, a deliberate strategy of conservation was to be made in preserving the land for the public good. Note these three different strategies as covered by the Scripture and outline:

OUTLINE	SCRIPTURE	SCRIPTURE	OUTLINE
3. The strategy for conquest a. The conquest of distant enemies 1) Must first seek peace 2) Must have control over the enemy if they accept the peace offer: Put the enemy to work for you 3) Must lay siege to the city if the enemy rejects peace & makes war • Execute all the men • Save all the women, children, livestock, & other plunder as spoils of war 4) Must know that this strategy applies only to enemies far away—outside the promised land b. The conquest of immediate enemies, enemies within the	10 When thou comest nigh unto a city to fight against it, then proclaim peace unto it. 11 And it shall be, if it make thee answer of peace, and open unto thee, then it shall be, *that* all the people *that is* found therein shall be tributaries unto thee, and they shall serve thee. 12 And if it will make no peace with thee, but will make war against thee, then thou shalt besiege it: 13 And when the LORD thy God hath delivered it into thine hands, thou shalt smite every male thereof with the edge of the sword: 14 But the women, and the little ones, and the cattle, and all that is in the city, *even* all the spoil thereof, shalt thou take unto thyself; and thou shalt eat the spoil of thine enemies, which the LORD thy God hath given thee. 15 Thus shalt thou do unto all the cities *which are* very far off from thee, which *are* not of the cities of these nations. 16 But of the cities of these people, which the LORD thy	God doth give thee *for* an inheritance, thou shalt save alive nothing that breatheth: 17 But thou shalt utterly destroy them; *namely,* the Hittites, and the Amorites, the Canaanites, and the Perizzites, the Hivites, and the Jebusites; as the LORD thy God hath commanded thee: 18 That they teach you not to do after all their abominations, which they have done unto their gods; so should ye sin against the LORD your God. 19 When thou shalt besiege a city a long time, in making war against it to take it, thou shalt not destroy the trees thereof by forcing an axe against them: for thou mayest eat of them, and thou shalt not cut them down (for the tree of the field *is* man's *life*) to employ *them* in the siege: 20 Only the trees which thou knowest that they *be* not trees for meat, thou shalt destroy and cut them down; and thou shalt build bulwarks against the city that maketh war with thee, until it be subdued.	promised land^{DS1} 1) The rule of war: Must be completely destroyed 2) The reasons • Because this is the command of God • Because of their evil influence • Because their cup of iniquity was full—beyond repentance (see Ge.15:16; Nu.21:2-3) c. The strategy of conservation, of preserving the land for the public good 1) The law: Must not destroy the fruit trees (lay waste the land) 2) The purpose: To preserve the trees (& land) for food 3) The allowance: Could use non-fruit trees as needed until the enemy was conquered

a. There was the strategy for conquering distant enemies (vv.10-15).
  1) The Israelites must first seek peace with the distant enemy (v.10). They were not to launch a secret, sneak attack. They were first to seek terms of peace.
  2) The Israelites must have control over the enemy if they accepted the peace offering (v.11). They had to guard against deception and intrigue, for the enemy could accept the offer of peace in order to lull the Israelites into a false security and disarmament. The enemy could then stage an uprising, a revolt against Israel, and end up conquering them. For this reason, the citizens of a distant enemy were to become servants of Israel.
  3) The Israelites were to lay siege to the city if the distant city rejected peace and made war (vv.12-14). Once the city had been conquered, all the men were to be executed. They were not to be taken back to Israel as slaves lest they

DEUTERONOMY 20:1-20

cause uprisings and revolts. However, all the women, children, livestock, and other plunder were to be saved as spoils of war (v.14).

4) The Israelites must understand that this strategy applied only to enemies that were far away, outside the promised land (v.15).

b. There was the strategy for conquering immediate enemies, that is, enemies within the promised land, the Canaanites (vv.16-18).

1) In dealing with the Canaanites, the rule of war was clear: every enemy must be completely destroyed (vv.16-17). No living or breathing creature was to be left alive, neither man nor animal. Most likely, animals were destroyed because some of them had been set apart to be sacrificed to idol gods. It would have been impossible to know which of these animals had been dedicated to idols; therefore, all animals were destroyed. Whatever the case, no breathing creature was to be left alive.

2) Three specific reasons are given for the execution of the Canaanites (vv.17-18).
   ⇒ The Canaanites must be destroyed because this is the direct command of God. Because of their terrible evil and brutality, their shameful rejection and rebellion against God down through the centuries, it was now God's will for the Canaanites to be destroyed.
   ⇒ The Canaanites were to be destroyed because of their evil influence upon other people and the great threat they posed to the Israelites (v.18). If they were allowed to survive as hostages of war, they would teach the Israelites to follow all the detestable things they did. The Israelites would become an immoral, lawless, and violent society just like that of the Canaanites. Simply stated, the Canaanites would become stumblingblocks to the people of God.
   ⇒ The Canaanites were to be destroyed because their *cup of iniquity* was full. They were beyond repentance, beyond correction. Their evil must be stopped before any more people could be influenced and destroyed. (See DEEPER STUDY # 1—De.20:16-18. See note, pt.3—De.9:1-6 for more discussion.)

c. There was the strategy of conservation, of preserving the land for the public good (vv.19-20). When the Israelites were laying siege to a city, the siege could last for months. An army often decimates the land of its enemy. But this was not to be true with the Israelites. They were to conserve and preserve the land for the public good. The law was clear: they must not destroy the fruit trees, that is, lay waste to the land. They could eat the fruit of the trees, but they were not to cut them down. They were to preserve the trees and land for food for future generations. However, note: non-fruit trees could be cut as they were needed for firewood, battering rams, or other purposes. But even then, the non-fruit trees could be used only until the enemy was conquered (v.20).

Thought 1. Note three strong lessons for us in this point.
(1) God is good, and He expects us to be good in our treatment of people. Israel was first to seek peace with distant enemies. God expects us to seek peace with our neighbors, whether distant or next door. We are to seek peace with all persons and do good to them.

> "Blessed *are* the peacemakers: for they shall be called the children of God" (Mt.5:9).
> "Salt *is* good: but if the salt have lost his saltness, wherewith will ye season it? Have salt in yourselves, and have peace one with another" (Mk.9:50).
> "But love ye your enemies, and do good, and lend, hoping for nothing again; and your reward shall be great, and ye shall be the children of the Highest: for he is kind unto the unthankful and *to* the evil" (Lu.6:35).
> "If it be possible, as much as lieth in you, live peaceably with all men" (Ro.12:18).
> "Let us therefore follow after the things which make for peace, and things wherewith one may edify another" (Ro.14:19).
> "Follow peace with all *men*, and holiness, without which no man shall see the LORD" (He.12:14).
> "*Let your* conversation [behavior] *be* without covetousness; *and be* content with such things as ye have: for he hath said, I will never leave thee, nor forsake thee" (He.13:6).
> "Therefore to him that knoweth to do good, and doeth *it* not, to him it is sin" (Js.4:17).
> "Depart from evil, and do good; seek peace, and pursue it" (Ps.34:14).
> "Trust in the LORD, and do good; *so* shalt thou dwell in the land, and verily thou shalt be fed" (Ps.37:3).
> "Deceit *is* in the heart of them that imagine evil: but to the counsellors of peace *is* joy" (Pr.12:20).

(2) God will judge every evil and brutal person upon the earth. A person will die; after that he faces the judgment of God. The Canaanites were an evil and brutal people, a people who had reached the point of no repentance, no return. They would never turn from their immoral, lawless, and savage ways, never turn back to God. Therefore, the judgment of God fell upon them. So it will be with every evil and brutal person upon the earth: the judgment of God will fall upon him. He will face the eternal judgment of God and be separated from God forever.

> "Marvel not at this: for the hour is coming, in the which all that are in the graves shall hear his voice, And shall come forth; they that have done good, unto the resurrection of life; and they that have done evil, unto the resurrection of damnation" (Jn.5:28-29).
> "Now the works of the flesh are manifest, which are *these*; Adultery, fornication, uncleanness, lasciviousness, Idolatry, witchcraft, hatred, variance, emulations, wrath, strife, seditions, heresies, Envyings, murders, drunkenness, revellings, and such like: of the which I tell you before, as I have also told *you* in time past, that they which do such things shall not inherit the kingdom of God" (Ga.5:19-21).

DEUTERONOMY 20:1-20

"For this ye know, that no whoremonger, nor unclean person, nor covetous man, who is an idolater, hath any inheritance in the kingdom of Christ and of God" (Ep.5:5).

"Know ye not that the unrighteous shall not inherit the kingdom of God? Be not deceived: neither fornicators, nor idolaters, nor adulterers, nor effeminate, nor abusers of themselves with mankind, Nor thieves, nor covetous, nor drunkards, nor revilers, nor extortioners, shall inherit the kingdom of God" (1 Co.6:9-10).

"And as it is appointed unto men once to die, but after this the judgment" (He.9:27).

"The LORD knoweth how to deliver the godly out of temptations, and to reserve the unjust unto the day of judgment to be punished" (2 Pe.2:9).

"And Enoch also, the seventh from Adam, prophesied of these, saying, Behold, the LORD cometh with ten thousands of his saints, To execute judgment upon all, and to convince all that are ungodly among them of all their ungodly deeds which they have ungodly committed, and of all their hard *speeches* which ungodly sinners have spoken against him" (Jude 14-15).

"But the fearful, and unbelieving, and the abominable, and murderers, and whoremongers, and sorcerers, and idolaters, and all liars, shall have their part in the lake which burneth with fire and brimstone: which is the second death" (Re.21:8).

(3) God demands conservation, the preservation of the land of the earth—all for the public good. This is seen throughout Scripture.
  (a) When God created man, He assigned man the task of looking after the Garden of Eden, the paradise in which God placed man. God had given Adam the Garden—the most perfect, beautiful, and bountiful paradise imaginable—and God expected Adam to work and keep up the garden. He was to *dress* (abhadh) the garden. The word means to work, till, cultivate, dress, and serve the garden. Man was also to *keep* (shamar) the garden. This word means to watch over; to guard; to keep; to look after; to take care of. The point is this: man was made responsible—personally responsible—for the Garden of Eden. The garden was a paradise just as the earth is. God has assigned man the task of *dressing* and *keeping* the earth.

  "And the LORD God took the man, and put him into the garden of Eden to dress it and to keep it" (Ge.2:15).

  "And God blessed them, and God said unto them, Be fruitful, and multiply, and replenish the earth, and subdue it: and have dominion over the fish of the sea, and over the fowl of the air, and over every living thing that moveth upon the earth" (Ge.1:28).

  "I went by the field of the slothful, and by the vineyard of the man void of understanding; And, lo, it was all grown over with thorns, *and* nettles had covered the face thereof, and the stone wall thereof was broken down" (Pr.24:30-31).

  "By much slothfulness the building decayeth; and through idleness of the hands the house droppeth through" (Ec.10:18).

  (b) Scripture declares that the creation is suffering and held in bondage because of the sin and corruption of man. Creation is pictured as living and longing for the glorious day of redemption, for the new heavens and earth in which there will be no corruption. The implication is clear: we must prevent corruption, take care of the earth; stop the pollution and corruption of the air, the lakes, the rivers, the oceans, and the land.

  "For the earnest expectation of the creature waiteth for the manifestation of the sons of God. For the creature was made subject to vanity, not willingly, but by reason of him who hath subjected *the same* in hope, Because the creature itself also shall be delivered from the bondage of corruption into the glorious liberty of the children of God. For we know that the whole creation groaneth and travaileth in pain together until now" (Ro.8:19-22).

  "Hurt not the earth, neither the sea, nor the trees, till we have sealed the servants of our God in their foreheads" (Re.7:3).

  (c) God loves the earth and the sun, moon, and stars. God loves the universe so much that He is going to make a new heavens and earth in which the redeemed believers of the earth and all the spiritual beings of heaven will live.

  "But the day of the LORD will come as a thief in the night; in the which the heavens shall pass away with a great noise, and the elements shall melt with fervent heat, the earth also and the works that are therein shall be burned up. *Seeing* then *that* all these things shall be dissolved, what manner *of persons* ought ye to be in *all* holy conversation and godliness, Looking for and hasting unto the coming of the day of God, wherein the heavens being on fire shall be dissolved, and the elements shall melt with fervent heat? Nevertheless we, according to his promise, look for new heavens and a new earth, wherein dwelleth righteousness" (2 Pe.3:10-13).

  "And I saw a new heaven and a new earth: for the first heaven and the first earth were passed away; and there was no more sea" (Re.21:1).

  "Of old hast thou laid the foundation of the earth: and the heavens *are* the work of thy hands. They shall perish, but thou shalt endure: yea, all of them shall wax old like a garment; as a vesture shalt thou change them, and they shall be changed: But thou *art* the same, and thy years shall have no end" (Ps.102:25-27).

"For, behold, I create new heavens and a new earth: and the former shall not be remembered, nor come into mind" (Is.65:17).

"For as the new heavens and the new earth, which I will make, shall remain before me, saith the LORD, so shall your seed and your name remain" (Is.66:22).

"And all the host of heaven shall be dissolved, and the heavens shall be rolled together as a scroll: and all their host shall fall down, as the leaf falleth off from the vine, and as a falling *fig* from the fig tree" (Is.34:4).

"Lift up your eyes to the heavens, and look upon the earth beneath: for the heavens shall vanish away like smoke, and the earth shall wax old like a garment, and they that dwell therein shall die in like manner: but my salvation shall be for ever, and my righteousness shall not be abolished" (Is.51:6).

DEEPER STUDY # 1
(20:16-18) Iniquity, Cup of—Nations, Destruction of—Nations, Evil of—Nations, Judgment of—Canaanites, Destruction of: the words *utterly, totally, completely destroy* (harami or charam) mean to annihilate, exterminate, eliminate, or abolish. The word is related to the Hebrew *herem* which means "to devote to the ban."[4] Once something had been promised or devoted to God, it was placed under the ban: it could not be removed. If it was a gift, it had to be given to God. If it was the promise to do something, then it had to be done. If it was a vow to devote something to destruction, then it had to be destroyed or exterminated. In ancient days, this was known as the *harem principal or law*. Once a person or thing had been *devoted* to the LORD, it could not be removed. It went to the LORD.

The very idea that God and moral people would be set on the total destruction of a people is offensive to some persons. How could God and moral people possibly endorse such an act? In looking at this, a person needs to keep certain factors in mind:

1. People can become so savage, evil, and corrupt that they are beyond repair or repentance, beyond hope or correction. This is what is known as the *cup of iniquity being full*—filled to the point that it overflows and continues to overflow with...

- savagery
- violence
- brutality
- slavery
- rape
- ruthlessness
- lawlessness
- abuse
- cruelty
- atrocities
- barbarism
- corruption
- evil
- immorality
- injustice

History has shown that such behavior can be true of both individuals and nations. A person's or a nation's *cup of iniquity* can become full—well beyond repair or repentance, well beyond hope or correction. God declares this fact time and again as the Scriptures below show (Ge.15:16).

God wants justice executed against these people. Scripture is clear about this fact: this is the very purpose for the judgment of God.

"But in the fourth generation they shall come hither again: for the iniquity of the Amorites is not yet full" (Ge.15:16).

"Defile not ye yourselves in any of these things: for in all these the nations are defiled which I cast out before you: And the land is defiled: therefore I do visit the iniquity thereof upon it, and the land itself vomiteth out her inhabitants" (Le.18:24-25).

"And ye shall not walk in the manners of the nation, which I cast out before you: for they committed all these things, and therefore I abhorred them" (Le.20:23).

"Speak not thou in thine heart, after that the LORD thy God hath cast them out from before thee, saying, For my righteousness the LORD hath brought me in to possess this land: but for the wickedness of these nations the LORD doth drive them out from before thee. Not for thy righteousness, or for the uprightness of thine heart, dost thou go to possess their land: but for the wickedness of these nations the LORD thy God doth drive them out from before thee, and that he may perform the word which the LORD sware unto thy fathers, Abraham, Isaac, and Jacob" (De.9:4-5).

"And he did that which was evil in the sight of the LORD, after the abominations of the heathen, whom the LORD cast out before the children of Israel" (2 K.21:2).

"Moreover he burnt incense in the valley of the son of Hinnom, and burnt his children in the fire, after the abominations of the heathen whom the LORD had cast out before the children of Israel" (2 Chr.28:3).

"But did that which was evil in the sight of the LORD, like unto the abominations of the heathen, whom the LORD had cast out before the children of Israel" (2 Chr.33:2).

"And shed innocent blood, even the blood of their sons and of their daughters, whom they sacrificed unto the idols of Canaan: and the land was polluted with blood" (Ps.106:38).

"The earth also is defiled under the inhabitants thereof; because they have transgressed the laws, changed the ordinance, broken the everlasting covenant" (Is.24:5).

"...thou hast polluted the land with thy whoredoms and with thy wickedness" (Je.3:2).

"And first I will recompense their iniquity and their sin double; because they have defiled my land, they have filled mine inheritance with the carcases of their detestable and abominable things" (Je.16:18).

---

[4] Frank E. Gaebelein, Editor. *The Expository Bible Commentary*, p.874.

DEUTERONOMY 20:1-20

2. God is a just God as well as a God of love. God loves all people—every individual and every nation upon earth. His love continually flows out to everyone. But God is also a just God, the Sovereign LORD who executes justice upon the earth. God is not an *indulgent grandfather* who pampers the evil and savage of this world. To allow injustice to go unpunished, He would be a God of evil, a God who showed partiality and favoritism. He would be favoring the evil of the earth by allowing them to go unpunished, showing injustice to the moral of the earth by allowing them to continue to suffer under the injustices of evil people.

When the *cup of iniquity* becomes full—well beyond repair or repentance, well beyond hope or correction—that person or people are to be judged. Justice is to be executed upon them. God wants justice executed against such persons. This is the reason He has appointed a day in which He will judge the world.

> "For the Son of man shall come in the glory of his Father with his angels; and then he shall reward every man according to his works" (Mt.16:27).
>
> "When the Son of man shall come in his glory, and all the holy angels with him, then shall he sit upon the throne of his glory: And before him shall be gathered all nations: and he shall separate them one from another, as a shepherd divideth his sheep from the goats: And he shall set the sheep on his right hand, but the goats on the left" (Mt.25:31-33).
>
> "Because he hath appointed a day, in the which he will judge the world in righteousness by that man whom he hath ordained; whereof he hath given assurance unto all men, in that he hath raised him from the dead" (Ac.17:31).
>
> "In the day when God shall judge the secrets of men by Jesus Christ according to my gospel" (Ro.2:16).
>
> "I charge thee therefore before God, and the Lord Jesus Christ, who shall judge the quick and the dead at his appearing and his kingdom" (2 Ti.4:1).
>
> "And as it is appointed unto men once to die, but after this the judgment" (He.9:27).
>
> "The LORD knoweth how to deliver the godly out of temptations, and to reserve the unjust unto the day of judgment to be punished" (2 Pe.2:9).
>
> "The LORD is not slack concerning his promise, as some men count slackness; but is longsuffering to us-ward, not willing that any should perish, but that all should come to repentance" (2 Pe.3:9).
>
> "And Enoch also, the seventh from Adam, prophesied of these, saying, Behold, the LORD cometh with ten thousands of his saints, To execute judgment upon all, and to convince all that are ungodly among them of all their ungodly deeds which they have ungodly committed, and of all their hard speeches which ungodly sinners have spoken against him" (Jude 14-15).
>
> "And I saw the dead, small and great, stand before God; and the books were opened: and another book was opened, which is the book of life: and the dead were judged out of those things which were written in the books, according to their works" (Re.20:12).

3. Israel was used by God as His instrument of justice and judgment against the nations of Canaan. The Israelites did not receive the promised land of Canaan because of some merit or value within themselves nor because of their own strength or power. In justice and judgment, God Himself destroyed the Canaanites, and it was because of their wickedness that He destroyed them.

Again, it is critical to note this fact: Israel as a people did not receive the promised land because of their merit or value nor because of some righteousness they possessed. The Canaanites were destroyed because they were evil and their *cup of iniquity* had been filled to the brim. They reached the point of no repentance; they were beyond correction. Moses himself declared to the Israelites:

a. It is not because of any personal righteousness within you, not because you have pure hearts, that you inherit the promised land (De.9:5). The enemies of the land are to be conquered and destroyed for two reasons:
 ⇒ Because of their wickedness and because they are an evil people; their *cup of iniquity* is full.
 ⇒ Because God is faithful; He fulfills His promise to the forefathers, to Abraham, Isaac, and Jacob. God has promised to give the promised land to their descendants, to all those down through the centuries who believe His Word, His promises.

b. Understand this warning: it is not because of your righteousness that God gives you the promised land. On the contrary, you are a stiff-necked, stubborn people (De.9:6). You are a sinful people. You have no righteousness within yourselves that merits God's favor. Your hearts are not upright nor pure enough to make God accept you and give you victory over the enemies of the promised land. You are a stiff-necked, stubborn people.

> "Not for thy righteousness, or for the uprightness of thine heart, dost thou go to possess their land: but for the wickedness of these nations the LORD thy God doth drive them out from before thee, and that he may perform the word which the LORD sware unto thy fathers, Abraham, Isaac, and Jacob. Understand therefore, that the LORD thy God giveth thee not this good land to possess it for thy righteousness; for thou *art* a stiffnecked people" (De.9:5-6).

4. God shows no partiality, no favoritism—not to any person nor to any nation. God warned the Israelites that they too would face the justice and judgment of God if they disobeyed Him, if they failed to keep His commandments.

The Canaanites were destroyed because they lived immoral and unrighteous lives. If the Israelites adopted the immoral and unrighteous lifestyle of the Canaanites, they too would be destroyed.

> "Defile not ye yourselves in any of these things: for in all these the nations are defiled which I cast out before you: And the land is defiled: therefore I do visit the iniquity thereof upon it, and the land

itself vomiteth out her inhabitants. Ye shall therefore keep my statutes and my judgments, and shall not commit *any* of these abominations; *neither* any of your own nation, nor any stranger that sojourn-eth among you: (For all these abominations have the men of the land done, which *were* before you, and the land is defiled;) That the land spue not you out also, when ye defile it, as it spued out the nations that *were* before you. For whosoever shall commit any of these abominations, even the souls that commit *them* shall be cut off from among their people. Therefore shall ye keep mine ordinance, that *ye* commit not *any one* of these abominable customs, which were committed before you, and that ye defile not yourselves therein: I *am* the LORD your God" (Le.18:24-30).

"Ye shall therefore keep all my statutes, and all my judgments, and do them: that the land, whither I bring you to dwell therein, spue you not out. And ye shall not walk in the manners of the nation, which I cast out before you: for they committed all these things, and therefore I abhorred them. But I have said unto you, Ye shall inherit their land, and I will give it unto you to possess it, a land that floweth with milk and honey: I *am* the LORD your God, which have separated you from *other* people" (Le.20:22-24).

"When the LORD thy God shall bring thee into the land whither thou goest to possess it, and hath cast out many nations before thee, the Hittites, and the Girgashites, and the Amorites, and the Canaanites, and the Perizzites, and the Hivites, and the Jebusites, seven nations greater and mightier than thou; And when the LORD thy God shall deliver them before thee; thou shalt smite them, *and* utterly destroy them; thou shalt make no covenant with them, nor show mercy unto them: Neither shalt thou make marriages with them; thy daughter thou shalt not give unto his son, nor his daughter shalt thou take unto thy son. For they will turn away thy son from following me, that they may serve other gods: so will the anger of the LORD be kindled against you, and destroy thee suddenly" (De.7:1-4).

"Speak not thou in thine heart, after that the LORD thy God hath cast them out from before thee, saying, For my righteousness the LORD hath brought me in to possess this land: but for the wickedness of these nations the LORD doth drive them out from before thee. Not for thy righteousness, or for the uprightness of thine heart, dost thou go to possess their land: but for the wickedness of these nations the LORD thy God doth drive them out from before thee, and that he may perform the word which the LORD sware unto thy fathers, Abraham, Isaac, and Jacob. Understand therefore, that the LORD thy God giveth thee not this good land to possess it for thy righteousness; for thou *art* a stiffnecked people" (De.9:4-6).

Thought 1. James Philips makes an excellent statement on the justice and judgment of God that is well worth quoting in full.

> *God was using His people as the rod of His anger against peoples whose cup of iniquity was full to overflowing. They were being judged for their sins and their depravities. This is, of course, stated explicitly more than once in the Old Testament itself (cf. Gen. 15:16 and Lev. 18:24-30). The time of their destruction was ripe. This is why they were thus dealt with, and it was no arbitrary act of injustice that drove them out of their land. They had forfeited the right to live as nations in Canaan by the extremes of their debauchery and depravity, just as Sodom and Gomorrah had done (Gen. 19), and just as the Cainite civilization as a whole had done, bringing upon itself the judgment of the Flood (Gen. 6). Furthermore, it should be remembered that God dealt with His own people in similar fashion when they proved themselves unworthy to life in the land of promise, and He brought them into the captivity of Babylon in 586 B.C. To understand God's burning passion for righteousness in His creatures is to understand the basic reason for these judgments upon men and nations that refused to be righteous, and who rendered themselves incapable of being so by their continued sin.*[5]

Thought 2. *The Nelson Study Bible* says this:

> *Of Israel's attacks on the northern part of Canaanite cities, the Bible states, "but they struck every man with the edge of the sword until they had destroyed them, and they left none breathing. As the LORD had commanded Moses his servant, so Moses commanded Joshua, and so Joshua did" (Josh. 11:14, 15). God clearly commanded Israel to annihilate the Canaanites, and that is exactly what Joshua did.*
>
> *Headlines such as this have caused many people to question God's basic justice. How can a holy, just, and loving God command such extreme violence? Indeed, many have thought of this issue as the Old Testament's biggest challenge to modern readers. Some have gone so far as to allege that there is no connection between the "God of the Old Testament" and "God of the New Testament revealed in Jesus."*
>
> *However, this stereotype breaks down under examination. The Bible gives reasons for the Canaanites' destruction—and these reasons are in concert with the whole tenor of the Bible in both Testaments.*
>
> *The primary reason for the Canaanites' destruction was that they were guilty of gross sin. Abraham got a preview of this when God promised him the land. God said fulfillment of the promise would be delayed in part because "the iniquity of the Amorites is not yet complete" (Ge. 15:16; the Amorites were the Canaanites). For many years, the Canaanites' sins would not justify annihilation. But that time would arrive, and it did arrive by the time of Joshua.*
>
> *What were the sins of the Canaanites? The gruesome list in Lev. 18 gives some of the details, including incest, adultery, child sacrifice, homosexuality, and bestiality. Of course, every person has sinned in some fashion (Ps. 14:3). On this level, the Canaanites only received what all peoples deserved; others were spared only by God's*

---

[5] James Philip. *The Preacher's Commentary on Numbers*, p.311.

DEUTERONOMY 20:1-20

grace. But Canaan was not a community of upstanding citizens. It was a thoroughly debased society, hostile to all God's ways (Deut. 9:4, 5).

To a lesser degree, God was merely protecting His people. God promised Abraham that He would curse anyone who cursed Israel (Gen. 12:3). The Canaanites sought to destroy Israel on at least two occasions (Josh. 9:1, 2; 11:1-5), and God would not allow that.

The stereotype also breaks down because it overlooks the highly localized nature of the judgment on Canaan. The Israelites did not have a license to kill. They had no right to do the same to whatever peoples they encountered, at any time or in any place. This destruction targeted the sinful Canaanites of that time only. As harsh as it may seem to us, the Canaanites brought God's judgment on themselves by their own sin.

The New Testament states that one day Jesus Christ will judge the wicked nations of the earth (Matt. 25:31-46). God once judged all the wicked with an overwhelming flood (Gen. 6-9), and the same God will one day again judge everyone who has ever lived (2 Pet. 3:10-13). The judgment against the Canaanites is merely one instance of His judgment on the wicked even as He extends forgiveness to others.[6]

Thought 3. Warren Wiersbe gives an excellent statement on God's command to exterminate the Canaanite nations.

But wasn't it cruel and unjust for God to command Israel to exterminate the nations in Canaan? Not in the least! To begin with, He had been patient with these nations for centuries and had mercifully withheld His judgment (Gen. 15:16; 2 Peter 3:9). Their society, and especially their religion, was unspeakably wicked (Rom. 1:18ff) and should have been wiped out years before Israel appeared on the scene.

Something else is true: These nations had been warned by the judgments God had inflicted on others, especially on Egypt and the nations east of the Jordan (Josh. 2:8-13). Rahab and her family had sufficient information to be able to repent and believe, and God saved them (Josh. 2; 6:22-25). Therefore, we have every right to conclude that God would have saved anybody who had turned to Him. These nations were sinning against a flood of light in rejecting God's truth and going their own way.

God didn't want the filth of the Canaanite society and religion to contaminate His people Israel. Israel was God's special people, chosen to fulfill divine purposes in this world. Israel would give the world the knowledge of the true God, the Holy Scriptures, and the Savior. In order to accomplish God's purposes, the nation had to be separated from all other nations; for if Israel was polluted, how could the Holy Son of God come into the world? "God is perpetually at war with sin," wrote G. Campbell Morgan. "That is the whole explanation of the extermination of the Canaanites.[7]

The main deity in Canaan was Baal, god of rainfall and fertility, and Ashtoreth was his spouse. If you wanted to have fruitful orchards and vineyards, flourishing crops, and increasing flocks and herds, you worshiped Baal by visiting a temple prostitute. This combination of idolatry, immorality, and agricultural success was difficult for men to resist, which explains why God told Israel to wipe out the Canaanite religion completely (Num. 33:51-56; Deut. 7:1-5).[8]

TYPES, SYMBOLS, AND PICTURES
(Deuteronomy 20:1-20)

Historical Term	Type or Picture (Scriptural Basis for Each)	Life Application for Today's Believer	Biblical Application
Conducting a Just War De.20:1-20	The law governing the conduct of war is a picture of the believer's spiritual warfare against the enemies of this world. There are times when we must protect ourselves from those who attack and seek either to dominate us or to slaughter our children, wives, and husbands. Because we are living in a sinful world where the heart of man is desperately wicked, there are times when we must declare war and fight for our very survival. There are wars in which the LORD God (Jehovah, Yahweh)—the true and living God—is on one side. Because of this	⇒ Commitment, courage, and loyalty are absolute essentials in any warfare. This is true of earthly warfare and of spiritual warfare. No matter who the enemy is—man, temptation, or trial—we must be committed to God, loyal to Him, and courageous in order to be victorious. We can conquer the enemies of this life only by the presence and the power of God. Victorious courage—the kind of courage that gives a full and victorious life—can come only from God. Therefore, we must be committed and loyal to	*"Therefore, my beloved brethren, be ye stedfast, unmovable, always abounding in the work of the LORD, forasmuch as ye know that your labour is not in vain in the LORD"* (1 Co.15:58). *"Now unto him that is able to do exceeding abundantly above all that we ask or think, according to the power that worketh in us"* (Ep.3:20). *"And in nothing terrified by your adversaries: which is to them an evident token of perdition, but to you of salvation, and that of God"* (Ph.1:28). *"For God hath not given us the spirit of fear; but of*

---

6 *The Nelson Study Bible, New King James Version*, p.375.
7 G. Campbell Morgan. *Living Messages of the Books of the Bible*, Vol.1 (Old Tappan, NJ: Fleming H. Revell, 1912), p.104.
8 Warren Wiersbe, *Judges*, pp.15-16.

DEUTERONOMY 20:1-20

Historical Term	Type or Picture (Scriptural Basis for Each)	Life Application for Today's Believer	Biblical Application
	fact, before ever declaring a war, a nation should seek the LORD God to make absolutely sure that the war is God's will. If it is not God's will, the war should never be declared. "When thou goest out to battle against thine enemies, and seest horses, and chariots, and a people more than thou, be not afraid of them: for the LORD thy God is with thee, which brought thee up out of the land of Egypt" (De.20:1).	God. If we will give Him our hearts and lives, God will infuse us with enormous courage, enough courage to conquer all the enemies of this life.	*power, and of love, and of a sound mind" (2 Ti.1:7).* *"Be strong and of a good courage, fear not, nor be afraid of them: for the LORD thy God, he it is that doth go with thee; he will not fail thee, nor forsake thee" (De.31:6).* *"Be strong and of a good courage: for unto this people shalt thou divide for an inheritance the land, which I sware unto their fathers to give them" (Jos.1:6).*
The Message of the Appointed Priest De.20:1-20	*The message of the appointed priest is a picture of Christ, our great High Priest. Before going into battle, the priest was to address the army, giving four charges to them.* ⇒ *Do not be faint-hearted; do not lose heart.* ⇒ *Do not be afraid.* ⇒ *Do not be terrified.* ⇒ *Do not tremble, panic.* "And it shall be, when ye are come nigh unto the battle, that the priest shall approach and speak unto the people" (De.20:2).	⇒ Jesus Christ, the great High Priest, issues four *strong* charges to us as we struggle against the enemies of life: • We must not be faint-hearted; must not lose heart. • We must not be afraid. • We must not be terrified. • We must not tremble, panic.	*"Finally, my brethren, be strong in the LORD, and in the power of his might. Put on the whole armour of God, that ye may be able to stand against the wiles of the devil. For we wrestle not against flesh and blood, but against principalities, against powers, against the rulers of the darkness of this world, against spiritual wickedness in high places. Wherefore take unto you the whole armour of God, that ye may be able to withstand in the evil day, and having done all, to stand" (Ep.6:10-13; see He.13:6; Ps.28:7).* *"Fear thou not; for I am with thee: be not dismayed; for I am thy God: I will strengthen thee; yea, I will help thee; yea, I will uphold thee with the right hand of my righteousness" (Is.41:10; see Is.43:2).*

DEUTERONOMY 21:1-23

CHAPTER 21

J. Laws That Govern Some Unique Issues within Families & Society: God's Concern for Human Rights, 21:1-23

1. **The law that governed unsolved murders: A lesson on the sanctity of life**

   a. The leaders & judges of a district court were to determine the nearest town to the murder

   b. The leaders of the nearest town were to accept responsibility for the murder & undergo a cleansing ritual

   1) The leaders were to offer a young unworked cow by breaking its neck: A symbol that murder deserved punishment—was a terrible evil
   2) The priests—the ministers of God—were to step forth & participate in the ritual
   3) The leaders were to wash their hands over the young cow: A symbol of cleansing, being washed from guilt
   4) The leaders were to declare their innocence
   5) The leaders were to pray that God would accept the offering as atonement (reconciliation) for the people—not hold them guilty of the murder

   c. The assurance of answered prayer: Atonement & forgiveness are secured

2. **The law that protected female war prisoners: A lesson on sexual purity & the respect for women (even in helpless, dire circumstances)**

   a. The law: A soldier who desired a female war prisoner could have her—but only through marriage

   b. The requirements of the law
   1) She had to shave her head, trim her nails, put on new clothes, & mourn for her parents for one month: A symbol that she was putting off her old life & beginning a new life
   2) He could then take her as his wife
   3) He had to free her if he ever divorced her: She could go wherever she wished

3. **The law that protected the inheritance rights of the firstborn son: A lesson on justice & showing partiality**

   a. The terrible wrong of polygamy: Loves or favors one wife more
   b. The law: The father must not give the rights of the firstborn to a son of the loved wife unless he is the firstborn

   1) He must give the double share to the firstborn of the unloved wife
   2) The reason: Because the firstborn is the first picture of the father's strength, of his procreative power to bring life into the world

4. **The law that dealt with the stubborn & rebellious son: A striking lesson for children**

   a. The parents were to take the son before the court & present their case
   1) That he is stubborn & rebellious: A threat & dangerous
   2) That he is a glutton & a worthless drunkard

   b. The judgment: Execution
   c. The reasons
   1) To purge the evil of a rebellious spirit
   2) To serve as a deterrent

If *one* be found slain in the land which the LORD thy God giveth thee to possess it, lying in the field, *and* it be not known who hath slain him: 2 Then thy elders and thy judges shall come forth, and they shall measure unto the cities which *are* round about him that is slain: 3 And it shall be, *that* the city which *is* next unto the slain man, even the elders of that city shall take an heifer, which hath not been wrought with, *and* which hath not drawn in the yoke; 4 And the elders of that city shall bring down the heifer unto a rough valley, which is neither eared nor sown, and shall strike off the heifer's neck there in the valley: 5 And the priests the sons of Levi shall come near; for them the LORD thy God hath chosen to minister unto him, and to bless in the name of the LORD; and by their word shall every controversy and every stroke be *tried*: 6 And all the elders of that city, *that are* next unto the slain *man*, shall wash their hands over the heifer that is beheaded in the valley: 7 And they shall answer and say, Our hands have not shed this blood, neither have our eyes seen *it*. 8 Be merciful, O LORD, unto thy people Israel, whom thou hast redeemed, and lay not innocent blood unto thy people of Israel's charge. And the blood shall be forgiven them. 9 So shalt thou put away the *guilt of* innocent blood from among you, when thou shalt do *that which is* right in the sight of the LORD. 10 When thou goest forth to war against thine enemies, and the LORD thy God hath delivered them into thine hands, and thou hast taken them captive, 11 And seest among the captives a beautiful woman, and hast a desire unto her, that thou wouldest have her to thy wife; 12 Then thou shalt bring her home to thine house; and she shall shave her head, and pare her nails; 13 And she shall put the raiment of her captivity from off her, and shall remain in thine house, and bewail her father and her mother a full month: and after that thou shalt go in unto her, and be her husband, and she shall be thy wife. 14 And it shall be, if thou have no delight in her, then thou shalt let her go whither she will; but thou shalt not sell her at all for money, thou shalt not make merchandise of her, because thou hast humbled her. 15 If a man have two wives, one beloved, and another hated, and they have born him children, *both* the beloved and the hated; and *if* the firstborn son be hers that was hated: 16 Then it shall be, when he maketh his sons to inherit *that* which he hath, *that* he may not make the son of the beloved firstborn before the son of the hated, which *is indeed* the firstborn: 17 But he shall acknowledge the son of the hated *for* the firstborn, by giving him a double portion of all that he hath: for he *is* the beginning of his strength; the right of the firstborn *is* his. 18 If a man have a stubborn and rebellious son, which will not obey the voice of his father, or the voice of his mother, and *that*, when they have chastened him, will not hearken unto them: 19 Then shall his father and his mother lay hold on him, and bring him out unto the elders of his city, and unto the gate of his place; 20 And they shall say unto the elders of his city, This our son *is* stubborn and rebellious, he will not obey our voice; *he is* a glutton, and a drunkard. 21 And all the men of his city shall stone him with stones, that he die: so shalt thou put evil away from among you; and all Israel shall hear,

DEUTERONOMY 21:1-23

5. The law that dealt with a man hung on a tree: A picture of Christ (Ga.5:13) a. The body was to be buried, not left on the tree overnight	and fear. 22 And if a man have committed a sin worthy of death, and he be to be put to death, and thou hang him on a tree: 23 His body shall not remain all night upon the tree, but	thou shalt in any wise bury him that day; (for he that is hanged *is* accursed of God;) that thy land be not defiled, which the LORD thy God giveth thee *for* an inheritance.	b. The reason 1) Because the body hung on a tree pictured the curse of God—His judgment 2) Because the body would defile the land—through undue attention to the judgment

DIVISION IV

THE SECOND GREAT THEME PREACHED BY GOD'S AGED SERVANT (PART 2): REMEMBER THE CIVIL AND RELIGIOUS LAWS OF ISRAEL—HELPFUL PRINCIPLES TO GOVERN MAN AND SOCIETY, 12:1–26:19

J. Laws That Govern Some Unique Issues within Families and Society: God's Concern for Human Rights, 21:1-23

(21:1-23) **Introduction—Human Rights, Laws Governing**: human rights are abused all over the world. People are mistreated everywhere. In some cases, the rights of individuals are abused; in other cases, it is the rights of a group that are abused. Sometimes the abuse is brutal:

⇒ A person is assaulted, injured, or killed.
⇒ A person is seduced, forced, or raped.
⇒ A person is overlooked, ignored, or neglected.
⇒ A person is not looked after, taken care of, nor provided for.
⇒ A person is not fed, clothed, or housed.
⇒ A person's property is stolen.
⇒ A person's reputation is destroyed by rumors or lies.

The abuse of human rights includes every evil that a person commits against others: lying, stealing, cheating, assaulting, gossiping. Any evil done against another person abuses his rights as a human being. Human rights are a vital concern to God. How we treat one another matters to God. This is the important subject of this passage of Scripture: *Laws That Govern Some Unique Issues within Families and Society: God's Concern for Human Rights*, 21:1-23.

1. The law that governed unsolved murders: a lesson on the sanctity of life (vv.1-9).
2. The law that protected female war prisoners: a lesson on sexual purity and the respect for women (even in helpless, dire circumstances) (vv.10-14).
3. The law that protected the inheritance rights of the firstborn son: a lesson on justice and showing partiality (vv.15-17).
4. The law dealing with the stubborn and rebellious son: a striking lesson for children (vv.18-21).
5. The law dealing with a man hung on a tree: a picture of Christ (Ga.5:13) (vv.22-23).

1 (21:1-9) **Murder, Unsolved—Homicide, Unsolved—Guilt, Corporate—Community, Duty—Ritual, Cleansing—Cleansing, Necessity of—Life, Sanctity of—Law, of Israel—Israel, Law of**: there was the law that governed unsolved murders. This law stresses the sanctity of life. Life is precious to God. God created man and breathed the breathe of life into his nostrils. Life is from God; He is the source of life. Therefore, life is precious, the most precious commodity upon earth. Life is sacred, the most precious gift man can possess. For this reason, the sanctity of life must be respected, held in the highest esteem and be protected at all costs. No price tag can be placed on the value of life. Life is the most valuable possession upon earth, the most precious treasure a person can possess. This is the reason murder concerns God so much, the reason murder is covered in one of the Ten Commandments. There is a sanctity to life: life is sacred to God, and it is to be sacred to man. Man is not to commit murder. When murder is committed, it is a gross offense against God: it is a terrible evil committed against His creation of life. The present point deals with unsolved homicide. When a body is found murdered out in a field and there are no eyewitnesses, what is to be done? Note the Scripture and outline:

OUTLINE	SCRIPTURE	SCRIPTURE	OUTLINE
1. The law that governed unsolved murders: A lesson on the sanctity of life a. The leaders & judges of a district court were to determine the nearest town to the murder b. The leaders of the nearest town were to accept respon-	If *one* be found slain in the land which the LORD thy God giveth thee to possess it, lying in the field, *and* it be not known who hath slain him: 2 Then thy elders and thy judges shall come forth, and they shall measure unto the cities which *are* round about him that is slain: 3 And it shall be, *that* the city which *is* next unto the	slain man, even the elders of that city shall take an heifer, which hath not been wrought with, *and* which hath not drawn in the yoke; 4 And the elders of that city shall bring down the heifer unto a rough valley, which is neither eared nor sown, and shall strike off the heifer's neck there in the valley: 5 And the priests the sons	sibility for the murder & undergo a cleansing ritual 1) The leaders were to offer a young unworked cow by breaking its neck: A symbol that murder deserved punishment—was a terrible evil 2) The priests—the ministers

DEUTERONOMY 21:1-23

OUTLINE	SCRIPTURE	SCRIPTURE	OUTLINE
of God—were to step forth & participate in the ritual 3) The leaders were to wash their hands over the young cow: A symbol of cleansing, being washed from guilt 4) The leaders were to declare their innocence	of Levi shall come near; for them the LORD thy God hath chosen to minister unto him, and to bless in the name of the LORD; and by their word shall every controversy and every stroke be *tried*: 6 And all the elders of that city, *that are* next unto the slain *man*, shall wash their hands over the heifer that is beheaded in the valley: 7 And they shall answer and say, Our hands have not	shed this blood, neither have our eyes seen *it*. 8 Be merciful, O LORD, unto thy people Israel, whom thou hast redeemed, and lay not innocent blood unto thy people of Israel's charge. And the blood shall be forgiven them. 9 So shalt thou put away the *guilt of* innocent blood from among you, when thou shalt do *that which is* right in the sight of the LORD.	5) The leaders were to pray that God would accept the offering as atonement (reconciliation) for the people—not hold them guilty of the murder c. The assurance of answered prayer: Atonement & forgiveness are secured

a. The leaders and judges of a district court were to determine the nearest town to the murder (v.2). The implication is that they were to conduct a thorough investigation into the crime, but they were still unable to uncover the murderer.

b. At this point, the leaders of the nearest town were to accept responsibility for the murder and undergo a cleansing ritual (vv.3-8). The cleansing ritual was necessary because of the sanctity of life that has just been discussed, but there was a second reason, a reason that every generation must heed: the unity of the human race. In God's eyes the human race is one—one body of people, one community, one family. No person lives as an island to himself. We are all neighbors, a part of one large family, the family of the human race, the family of God's holy creation. Consequently, we are responsible for one another—for the care, development, and growth of one another. When a person does wrong, we are all to varying degrees responsible. There is community guilt, corporate guilt.

But this is not all: the universe, including all the heavens and earth, is God's creation. He created the earth to be man's home; therefore, the earth belongs to God, but God has placed it under the care of man. Man is the *caretaker* of the earth. Thus, when the earth is polluted by sin and corruption, it has to be cleansed from the defilement of man. This is the reason the earth and the universe are to be recreated, made into a new heavens and earth (2 Pe.3:10-13).

There is community responsibility, a responsibility of neighbors for one another. Consequently, there was community guilt for the murder that had taken place. Since it was unsolved, the leaders of the nearest town had to accept responsibility for the murder and undergo the cleansing ritual. This had to be done in order to make atonement, reconciliation with God. God's holy creation had been violated; evil had been committed against God's creation. A life had been taken. Therefore, atonement or reconciliation had to be made with God. Note the cleansing that was necessary in order to secure reconciliation.

1) The leaders were to offer a young unworked cow by breaking its neck (v.4). They were to secure the cow and lead her down into a valley that had never been farmed or worked by man, a valley where there was a flowing stream. It was there that they were to break the cow's neck. This was a strong object lesson to the people, stressing just how terrible murder was. Murder was a terrible crime that deserved punishment. Since the murderer could not be found, the cow's life was given to show that murder deserved the most severe punishment. It was a terrible, horrible evil.
2) The priests, the ministers of God, were to step forth and participate in the ritual (v.5). This was a religious ritual; therefore, as God's representatives, they were to be the presiding officials at the ceremony.
3) The leaders were then to wash their hands over the young cow (v.6). This was a symbol of cleansing, of being washed from the guilt of the murder.
4) The leaders were then to declare their innocence (v.7). Note what it was that they testified: that they were not personally guilty of the crime, nor were they eyewitnesses of the crime.
5) The leaders were then to pray that God would accept the offering as atonement or reconciliation for the people, that He would not hold them guilty of the murder (v.8).

c. Note the assurance of answered prayer: atonement and forgiveness were secured by following this ritual (vv.8-9). By this ritual, the community acknowledged their responsibility for one another. They were responsible for the care, development, and growth of one another. And they also shared in the community or corporate guilt of one another. They did bear some of the guilt for the unsolved murder. Consequently, they had sought atonement or reconciliation with God. For this reason they were purged, cleansed from the guilt of the innocent blood of the murdered victim.

Thought 1. We are neighbors of one another. We are neighbors with every citizen of our community, city, state, and nation. But we are also neighbors of every human being upon the earth. We are all members of the same community, the same human race, the same earth and universe. But this is not the only fact to note: we are also neighbors with the same kind of heart and body. As a man or woman, we are all the creation of God, brought into this world by the law of reproduction put into operation by God Himself. By the ordination of God, we are neighbors of one another. Therefore, as neighbors, God expects a certain behavior from us. Just as there is a community or corporate guilt, there is a community or corporate responsibility for one another. This is the strong declaration of Holy Scripture.

> **"And the second *is* like unto it, Thou shalt love thy neighbour as thyself"** (Mt.22:39).
> **"And the second *is* like, *namely* this, Thou shalt love thy neighbour as thyself. There is none other commandment greater than these"** (Mk.12:31).
> **"And hath made of one blood all nations of men for to dwell on all the face of the earth, and hath determined the times before appointed, and the bounds of their habitation"** (Ac.17:26).
> **"*Let* love be without dissimulation [hypocrisy]. Abhor that which is evil; cleave to that which is good"** (Ro.12:9).
> **"Love worketh no ill to his neighbour: therefore love *is* the fulfilling of the law"** (Ro.13:10).

DEUTERONOMY 21:1-23

"Let us not therefore judge one another any more: but judge this rather, that no man put a stumblingblock or an occasion to fall in *his* brother's way" (Ro.14:13).

"We then that are strong ought to bear the infirmities of the weak, and not to please ourselves. Let every one of us please *his* neighbour for *his* good to edification" (Ro.15:1-2).

"Wherefore, if meat make my brother to offend, I will eat no flesh while the world standeth, lest I make my brother to offend" (1 Co.8:13).

"For all the law is fulfilled in one word, *even* in this; Thou shalt love thy neighbour as thyself" (Ga.5:14).

"And be ye kind one to another, tenderhearted, forgiving one another, even as God for Christ's sake hath forgiven you" (Ep.4:32).

"Put on therefore, as the elect of God, holy and beloved, bowels of mercies, kindness, humbleness of mind, meekness, longsuffering" (Col.3:12).

"If ye fulfil the royal law according to the scripture, Thou shalt love thy neighbour as thyself, ye do well" (Js.2:8).

"And the LORD make you to increase and abound in love one toward another, and toward all *men*, even as we *do* toward you" (1 Th.3:12).

"And this is his commandment, That we should believe on the name of his Son Jesus Christ, and love one another, as he gave us commandment" (1 Jn.3:23).

"The rich and poor meet together: the LORD is the maker of them all" (Pr.22:2).

"Have we not all one father? hath not one God created us? why do we deal treacherously every man against his brother, by profaning the covenant of our fathers" (Mal.2:10).

2 (21:10-14) **Prisoners, of War—Sex, Duty—Purity, Duty—Women, Respect for—Respect, for Women—War, Prisoners of—Marriage, Importance of:** there was the law that protected female war prisoners. This law stressed marriage and sexual purity and respect for women. Women were to be respected and protected even if they were caught in helpless, dire circumstances. Note the Scripture and outline:

OUTLINE	SCRIPTURE	SCRIPTURE	OUTLINE
2. The law that protected female war prisoners: A lesson on sexual purity & the respect for women (even in helpless, dire circumstances) a. The law: A soldier who desired a female war prisoner could have her—but only through marriage b. The requirements of the law 1) She had to shave her head, trim her nails, put on new clothes, & mourn for her parents for one	10 When thou goest forth to war against thine enemies, and the LORD thy God hath delivered them into thine hands, and thou hast taken them captive, 11 And seest among the captives a beautiful woman, and hast a desire unto her, that thou wouldest have her to thy wife; 12 Then thou shalt bring her home to thine house; and she shall shave her head, and pare her nails; 13 And she shall put the rai-	ment of her captivity from off her, and shall remain in thine house, and bewail her father and her mother a full month: and after that thou shalt go in unto her, and be her husband, and she shall be thy wife. 14 And it shall be, if thou have no delight in her, then thou shalt let her go whither she will; but thou shalt not sell her at all for money, thou shalt not make merchandise of her, because thou hast humbled her.	month: A symbol that she was putting off her old life & beginning a new life 2) He could then take her as his wife 3) He had to free her if he ever divorced her: She could go wherever she wished

a. A soldier who desired a female war prisoner could have her, but only through marriage (v.11). Assault, rape, and the mistreatment of women in general are common occurrences during war. But such behavior was not allowed among Israelite soldiers. If a soldier saw a beautiful women and was attracted to her, he was allowed to have her but only through marriage. And even then, he had to undergo a waiting period just to make sure that his attraction was genuine love and not infatuation. Note how this law protected the human rights of women, their dignity and the strength of marriage or home as the basis of society.

b. Moses declared the requirements of the law (vv.12-14). The soldier had to bring the woman into his home, but not touch her before the marriage, a period of one month. During this month, the woman had to shave her head, trim her nails, put on new clothes, and mourn for her parents (vv.12-14). All this symbolized that she was putting off her old life and starting a new life, a new life with God and her husband.

The soldier could then take the women as his wife (v.13). Note this fact: if he ever decided to divorce her, he had to free her to go wherever she wished. She was no longer a prisoner and could not be treated as such. The soldier was not allowed to sell her as a slave nor to mistreat her in any way whatsoever (v.14). By being a freed woman, she was able to retain her honor and dignity wherever she lived.

Thought 1. Marriage is honorable and is to be protected at all costs. This is an absolute essential, for the family is the very foundation of society. Without the family, society cannot long exist. God Himself instituted marriage when He placed Adam and Eve together and charged them to bear children. Marriage is of God, ordained by God. Therefore, marriage is to be respected, held in the highest esteem. We are to honor marriage and protect marriage. This is the strong declaration of Scripture.

"What therefore God hath joined together, let not man put asunder" (Mk.10:9).

"Wives, submit yourselves unto your own husbands, as unto the LORD" (Ep.5:22).

"Husbands, love your wives, even as Christ also loved the church, and gave himself for it" (Ep.5:25).

"So ought men to love their wives as their own bodies. He that loveth his wife loveth himself" (Ep.5:28).

"Husbands, love *your* wives, and be not bitter against them" (Col.3:19).

"And unto the married I command, *yet* not I, but the LORD, Let not the wife depart from *her* husband" (1 Co.7:10).

"Marriage *is* honourable in all, and the bed undefiled: but whoremongers and adulterers God will judge" (He.13:4).

"I will therefore that the younger women marry, bear children, guide the house, give none occasion to the adversary to speak reproachfully" (1 Ti.5:14).

"Likewise, ye wives, *be* in subjection to your own husbands; that, if any obey not the word, they also may without the word be won by the conversation of the wives" (1 Pe.3:1).

"Likewise, ye husbands, dwell with *them* according to knowledge, giving honour unto the wife, as unto the weaker vessel, and as being heirs together of the grace of life; that your prayers be not hindered" (1 Pe.3:7).

"Therefore shall a man leave his father and his mother, and shall cleave unto his wife: and they shall be one flesh" (Ge.2:24).

"*Whoso* findeth a wife findeth a good *thing,* and obtaineth favour of the LORD" (Pr.18:22).

3 (21:15-17) **Inheritance, Rights of—Firstborn, Inheritance of—Polygamy—Monogamy—Partiality, Evil of—Favoritism, Evil of**: there was the law that protected the inheritance rights of the firstborn son. This is a clear lesson on justice and on showing partiality and favoritism. Note that polygamy is accepted, condoned in this passage. Why was it condoned? Probably for three reasons:

⇒ probably for the same reason that divorce was allowed by God: because of the hardness of man's heart (Mt.19:8; Mk.10:5).

⇒ perhaps because polygamy had been practiced from the very earliest of times, almost from the day of creation (Ge.4:19). It was, apparently, the common practice in the ancient world.

⇒ perhaps because there was a shortage of men due to the savagery and loss of life during ancient wars.

Whatever the reason, polygamy was condoned even among the Israelites. Therefore, the law that protected the inheritance rights of the firstborn son had to deal with the problem of polygamy. Note the Scripture and outline:

OUTLINE	SCRIPTURE	SCRIPTURE	OUTLINE
3. **The law that protected the inheritance rights of the firstborn son: A lesson on justice & showing partiality** a. The terrible wrong of polygamy: Loves or favors one wife more b. The law: The father must not give the rights of the firstborn to a son of the loved wife unless he is the	15 If a man have two wives, one beloved, and another hated, and they have born him children, *both* the beloved and the hated; and *if* the firstborn son be hers that was hated: 16 Then it shall be, when he maketh his sons to inherit *that* which he hath, *that* he may not make the son of the	beloved firstborn before the son of the hated, *which is indeed* the firstborn: 17 But he shall acknowledge the son of the hated *for* the firstborn, by giving him a double portion of all that he hath: for he *is* the beginning of his strength; the right of the firstborn *is* his.	firstborn 1) He must give the double share to the firstborn of the unloved wife 2) The reason: Because the firstborn is the first picture of the father's strength, of his procreative power to bring life into the world

a. There was the terrible wrong that arose from polygamy (v.15). A man would soon love and prefer one wife over the other, thereby favoring her. The inevitable result was hurt feelings, jealousy, strife, partiality, favoritism.

b. The law governing the inheritance was clear: the father must not give the rights of the firstborn to a son of the loved wife unless he was the firstborn son. If the husband loved one wife over the other, there would be the tendency to favor and show partiality to her children. He might desire to give the greater inheritance to the oldest son of his favorite wife. This was absolutely forbidden. By law he was to give the double share to the firstborn of the unloved wife (v.17). Note the reason why: the firstborn son was the first picture of the father's strength, of his procreative power, his power to bring life into the world.

This law protected the rights of the firstborn son and assured that justice would be done. Partiality and favoritism were not to enter the picture when dealing with the inheritance rights of the firstborn son.

Thought 1. There are two lessons that can be gleaned from this point:

(1) We must not show partiality or favoritism to our children nor to anyone else.

"*Let* love be without dissimulation [hypocrisy]. Abhor that which is evil; cleave to that which is good" (Ro.12:9).

"I charge *thee* before God, and the Lord Jesus Christ, and the elect angels, that thou observe these things without preferring one before another, doing nothing by partiality" (1 Ti.5:21).

"Are ye not then partial in yourselves, and are become judges of evil thoughts" (Js.2:4).

"Ye shall do no unrighteousness in judgment: thou shalt not respect the person of the poor, nor honour the person of the mighty: *but* in righteousness shalt thou judge thy neighbour" (Le.19:15).

"He will surely reprove you, if ye do secretly accept persons" (Jb.13:10).

"These *things* also *belong* to the wise. *It is* not good to have respect of persons in judgment" (Pr.24:23).

(2) We must be just, do what is right, uphold justice in all our dealings. We must be fair and just in dealing with our children and with everyone else.

"Render therefore to all their dues: tribute to whom tribute *is due;* custom to whom custom; fear to whom fear; honour to whom honour" (Ro.13:7).

"That which is altogether just shalt thou follow, that thou mayest live, and inherit the land which the LORD thy God giveth thee" (De.16:20).

"And, ye fathers, provoke not your children to wrath: but bring them up in the nurture and admonition of the LORD" (Ep.6:4).

"Look not every man on his own things, but every man also on the things of others" (Ph.2:4).

"Defend the poor and fatherless: do justice to the afflicted and needy" (Ps.82:3).

"To do justice and judgment *is* more acceptable to the LORD than sacrifice" (Pr.21:3).

"Thus saith the LORD, Keep ye judgment, and do justice: for my salvation *is* near to come, and my righteousness to be revealed" (Is.56:1).

4 (21:18-21) **Children, Behavior of—Rebellion, of Children—Parents, Duty of—Law, Governing Children—Israel, Law of—Children, Discipline of**: there was the law dealing with the stubborn and rebellious son. This is a striking lesson for children, a lesson that is based upon the fifth commandment to honor one's parents (De.5:16). To modern society, this is a harsh law. But note the illustration given: it deals with a stubborn and rebellious son. The idea is that of constant stubbornness, persistent rebellion, a rebellion so ugly and evil that it gnaws away at the security of the family and threatens to destroy them. The son has no respect whatsoever for the parents, cursing and raging against them, being defiant and threatening the parents. Keep in mind God's will and honor for parents. Parents are His major representatives upon the earth, responsible for bringing children into the world and for nourishing, teaching, and instructing them. By their example, the child can come to know a full and victorious life and preserve the human race down through succeeding generations. Standing as God's primary representatives upon the earth, the parent is to be honored by all children. A child must honor his father and mother. To dishonor is to stand under the curse of God Himself (De.27:16).

OUTLINE	SCRIPTURE	SCRIPTURE	OUTLINE
4. **The law that dealt with the stubborn & rebellious son: A striking lesson for children**	18 If a man have a stubborn and rebellious son, which will not obey the voice of his father, or the voice of his mother, and *that,* when they have chastened him, will not hearken unto them:	20 And they shall say unto the elders of his city, This our son *is* stubborn and rebellious, he will not obey our voice; *he is* a glutton, and a drunkard.	2) That he is a glutton & a worthless drunkard
a. The parents were to take the son before the court & present their case 1) That he is stubborn & rebellious: A threat & dangerous	19 Then shall his father and his mother lay hold on him, and bring him out unto the elders of his city, and unto the gate of his place;	21 And all the men of his city shall stone him with stones, that he die: so shalt thou put evil away from among you; and all Israel shall hear, and fear.	b. The judgment: Execution c. The reasons 1) To purge the evil of a rebellious spirit 2) To serve as a deterrent

a. If parents ever reached the point when they could not control their son—the point where he was threatening the very stability and security of the family—the parents were to take the son before the local court (vv.19-20). They were to present their case to the court: that the child was stubborn and rebellious, that he was totally undisciplined and could not be controlled, at least not by them. Note the charges against the son: despite being so young, the child had already deteriorated into a gluttonous, licentious (uncontrolled passions), and immoral person, into a worthless drunkard.

b. The judgment upon the son was to be execution (v.21). And note: all the men of the city were to participate in carrying out the execution. This suggests that the son's rebellion was affecting, doing significant damage to, the entire community. He had become totally useless, of no value to the community. Therefore, every person within the community was to give witness to this by participating in the execution.

c. Moses declared the reasons why the son was to be executed (v.21). The evil of *constant stubbornness* and of *a rebellious spirit* had to be purged from the community. As long as it persisted, the dishonor and rebellion of the son against his parents would become a *stumblingblock* to other children. If the rebellious son was allowed to dishonor his parents, other children would soon follow his lead and begin to dishonor theirs. For this reason, the terrible evil of dishonoring and rebelling against parents had to be purged, removed from the community. Moreover, the son was executed as an example to all other children: a stubborn spirit, rebellion against parents was not to be tolerated, not by the community nor by God. This judgment upon the stubborn, rebellious son who so dishonored, cursed, and threatened his parents stands as a picture of the judgment of God that is going to fall upon all children who are defiant toward their parents.

Thought 1. A child must honor and obey his parents. This is the clear commandment of God.

"Children, obey your parents in the LORD: for this is right. Honour thy father and mother; (which is the first commandment with promise" (Ep.6:1-2).

"Children, obey *your* parents in all things: for this is well pleasing unto the LORD" (Col.3:20).

"Let no man despise thy youth; but be thou an example of the believers, in word, in conversation, in charity, in spirit, in faith, in purity" (1 Ti.4:12).

"But if any widow have children or nephews, let them learn first to show piety at home, and to requite their parents: for that is good and acceptable before God" (1 Ti.5:4).

"Honour thy father and thy mother: that thy days may be long upon the land which the LORD thy God giveth thee" (Ex.20:12).

"Ye shall fear every man his mother, and his father, and keep my sabbaths: I *am* the LORD your God" (Le.19:3).

"Cursed *be* he that setteth light by his father or his mother. And all the people shall say, Amen" (De.27:16).

"My son, hear the instruction of thy father, and forsake not the law of thy mother" (Pr.1:8).

"My son, keep thy father's commandment, and forsake not the law of thy mother" (Pr.6:20).

"Be not among winebibbers; among riotous eaters of flesh: For the drunkard and the glutton shall come to poverty: and drowsiness shall clothe *a man* with rags. Hearken unto thy father that begat thee, and despise not thy mother when she is old" (Pr.23:20-22).

"The eye *that* mocketh at *his* father, and despiseth to obey *his* mother, the ravens of the valley shall pick it out, and the young eagles shall eat it" (Pr.30:17).

5 (21:22-23) **Execution, Method Used—Criminal, Execution of—Capital Crime, Penalty of—Curse, of God—Tree, Execution upon—Execution, upon a Tree—Jesus Christ, Symbol of Death—Symbol, of Christ's Death**: there was the law dealing with a man hung on a tree. This was a picture of the crucifixion of Christ (Ga.3:13). Note that the criminal was not executed by hanging but by some other method. He was only hung upon the tree after his execution, hung as a lesson or a deterrent to the public. Seeing the criminal hang upon a tree was a gruesome sight, a strong warning against breaking the law. Note the Scripture and outline:

OUTLINE	SCRIPTURE	SCRIPTURE	OUTLINE
5. The law that dealt with a man hung on a tree: A picture of Christ (Ga.5:13) a. The body was to be buried, not left on the tree overnight b. The reason	22 And if a man have committed a sin worthy of death, and he be to be put to death, and thou hang him on a tree: 23 His body shall not remain all night upon the tree, but	thou shalt in any wise bury him that day; (for he that is hanged *is* accursed of God;) that thy land be not defiled, which the LORD thy God giveth thee *for* an inheritance.	1) Because the body hung on a tree pictured the curse of God—His judgment 2) Because the body would defile the land—through undue attention to the judgment

The body was to be buried on the very day that the person had been executed. It was not to be left hanging on the tree overnight (v.23). Why? Because the body hung on a tree pictured the curse of God. It pictured the judgment of God that was going to fall upon all who broke God's holy commandments, all who lived evil and wicked lives upon this earth. If the body was left hanging upon the tree, it would decompose and decay. This defilement would become the focus of attention, not the judgment.

Thought 1. The criminal hanging upon the tree publicly demonstrated the judgment of God against sin. So it was with Christ hanging upon the cross: Christ took upon Himself the curse of the law, the penalty that was due us. He died upon the cross bearing our sin, condemnation, and punishment. He bore the wrath of God against sin that was due us, bore the judgment in our behalf.

"Who gave himself for our sins, that he might deliver us from this present evil world, according to the will of God and our Father" (Ga.1:4).

"Christ hath redeemed us from the curse of the law, being made a curse for us: for it is written, Cursed *is* every one that hangeth on a tree" (Ga.3:13).

"But we see Jesus, who was made a little lower than the angels for the suffering of death, crowned with glory and honour; that he by the grace of God should taste death for every man" (He.2:9).

"For Christ also hath once suffered for sins, the just for the unjust, that he might bring us to God, being put to death in the flesh, but quickened by the Spirit" (1 Pe.3:18).

"Who his own self bare our sins in his own body on the tree, that we, being dead to sins, should live unto righteousness: by whose stripes ye were healed" (1 Pe.2:24).

"But he *was* wounded for our transgressions, *he was* bruised for our iniquities: the chastisement of our peace *was* upon him; and with his stripes we are healed" (Is.53:5).

DEUTERONOMY 21:1-23

TYPES, SYMBOLS, AND PICTURES
(Deuteronomy 21:1-23)

Historical Term	Type or Picture (Scriptural Basis for Each)	Life Application for Today's Believer	Biblical Application
The Offering of a Young Unworked Cow Whose Neck Was Broken De.21:4	Offering a young unworked cow whose neck was broken was a symbol that murder deserved punishment, severe punishment, for it was a terrible evil. The leaders were to secure the cow and lead her down into a valley that had never been formed or worked by man, a valley where there was a flowing stream. It was there that they were to break the cow's neck. This was a strong object lesson to the people, stressing just how terrible murder was. Murder was a terrible crime that deserved punishment. Since the murderer could not be found, the cow's life was given to show that murder deserved the most severe punishment. It was a terrible, horrible evil. "And the elders of that city shall bring down the heifer unto a rough valley, which is neither eared nor sown, and shall strike off the heifer's neck there in the valley" (De.21:4).	⇒ Life is precious to God. God created man and breathed the breathe of life into his nostrils. Life is from God; He is the source of life. Therefore, life is the most precious commodity upon earth, is the most precious gift man can possess. For this reason, the sanctity of life is to be respected, held in the highest esteem and to be protected at all costs. No price tag can be placed on the value of life. Life is the most valuable possession upon earth, the most precious treasure a person can possess. This is the reason murder concerns God so much, the reason murder is covered in one of the Ten Commandments. There is a sanctity to life: life is sacred to God, and it is to be sacred to man. Man is not to commit murder. When murder is committed, it is a gross offense against God: it is a terrible evil committed against His creation of life.	"And the LORD God formed man of the dust of the ground, and breathed into his nostrils the breath of life; and man became a living soul" (Ge.2:7). "Neither is worshipped with men's hands, as though he needed any thing, seeing he giveth to all life, and breath, and all things" (Ac.17:25). "For thou hast possessed my reins: thou hast covered me in my mother's womb. I will praise thee; for I am fearfully and wonderfully made: marvellous are thy works; and that my soul knoweth right well. My substance was not hid from thee, when I was made in secret, and curiously wrought in the lowest parts of the earth" (Ps.139:13-15). "For God so loved the world, that he gave his only begotten Son, that whosoever believeth in him should not perish, but have everlasting life" (Jn.3:16). "Fear ye not therefore, ye are of more value than many sparrows" (Mt.10:31).
The Leaders Who Washed Their Hands over the Young Cow De.21:6	Leaders washing their hands over the young cow symbolized cleansing, being washed from guilt. "And all the elders of that city, *that are* next unto the slain *man*, shall wash their hands over the heifer that is beheaded in the valley" (De.21:6).	⇒ Our hearts just flow in full assurance and confidence knowing that all things are well with God. There is no more condemnation or guilt. We know that we are forgiven and cleansed through Jesus Christ. We know that we are acceptable to God and our hearts revel in the confidence and assurance of Him.	"He that believeth on him is not condemned: but he that believeth not is condemned already, because he hath not believed in the name of the only begotten Son of God" (Jn.3:18). "Verily, verily, I say unto you, He that heareth my word, and believeth on him that sent me, hath everlasting life, and shall not come into condemnation; but is passed from death unto life" (Jn.5:24). "There is therefore now no condemnation to them which are in Christ Jesus, who walk not after the flesh, but after the Spirit" (Ro.8:1; See also Ro.8:34; 1 Jn1:9; 1 Jn.3:24).
The Female War Prisoner Who Was to Be Wed Had to Shave Her Head, Trim Her Nails, Put on New Clothes, and Mourn for Her Parents for One Month De.21:13	The actions of the engaged female war prisoner were a symbol that she was putting off her old life and beginning a new life with God and her husband.	⇒ Marriage is the beginning of a new life, a new life being wedded by the joining together of a man and woman. Marriage is honorable and is to be protected at all costs. This is	"What therefore God hath joined together, let not man put asunder" (Mk.10:9). "Wives, submit yourselves unto your own husbands, as unto the LORD" (Ep.5:22).

DEUTERONOMY 21:1-23

Historical Term	Type or Picture (Scriptural Basis for Each)	Life Application for Today's Believer	Biblical Application
	"And she shall put the raiment of her captivity from off her, and shall remain in thine house, and bewail her father and her mother a full month: and after that thou shalt go in unto her, and be her husband, and she shall be thy wife" (De.21:13).	an absolute essential, for the family is the very foundation of society. Without the family, society cannot long exist. God Himself instituted marriage when He placed Adam and Eve together and charged them to bear children. Marriage is of God, ordained by God. Therefore, marriage is to be respected, held in the highest esteem. We are to honor marriage and protect marriage. This is the strong declaration of Scripture.	*"Husbands, love your wives, even as Christ also loved the church, and gave himself for it"* (Ep.5:25). *"So ought men to love their wives as their own bodies. He that loveth his wife loveth himself"* (Ep.5:28). *"Husbands, love your wives, and be not bitter against them"* (Col.3:19). *"Marriage is honourable in all, and the bed undefiled: but whoremongers and adulterers God will judge"* (He.13:4; see 1 Co.7:10; 1 Ti.5:14; 1 Pe.3:1; 1 Pe.3:7; Ge.2:24; Pr.18:22).
The Law Dealing with a Man Hung on a Tree De.21:22-23	*The law dealing with a man hung on a tree was a picture of the crucifixion of Christ (Ga.3:13). Note that the criminal was not executed by hanging but by some other method. He was only hung upon the tree after his execution, hung as a lesson or a deterrent to the public. Seeing the criminal hang upon a tree was a gruesome sight, a strong warning against breaking the law.* "And if a man have committed a sin worthy of death, and he be to be put to death, and thou hang him on a tree: His body shall not remain all night upon the tree, but thou shalt in any wise bury him that day; (for he that is hanged *is* accursed of God;) that thy land be not defiled, which the LORD thy God giveth thee *for* an inheritance" (De.21:22-23).	⇒ The criminal hanging upon the tree publicly demonstrated the judgment of God against sin. So it was with Christ hanging upon the cross: Christ took upon Himself the curse of the law, the penalty that was due us. He died upon the cross bearing our sin, condemnation, and punishment. He bore the wrath of God against sin that was due us, bore the judgment in our behalf.	*"Christ hath redeemed us from the curse of the law, being made a curse for us: for it is written, Cursed is every one that hangeth on a tree"* (Ga.3:13; see Ga.1:4). *"But we see Jesus, who was made a little lower than the angels for the suffering of death, crowned with glory and honour; that he by the grace of God should taste death for every man"* (He.2:9). *"For Christ also hath once suffered for sins, the just for the unjust, that he might bring us to God, being put to death in the flesh, but quickened by the Spirit"* (1 Pe.3:18). *"Who his own self bare our sins in his own body on the tree, that we, being dead to sins, should live unto righteousness: by whose stripes ye were healed"* (1 Pe.2:24; Is. 53:5).

DEUTERONOMY 22:1-12

CHAPTER 22

K. Laws That Govern Seven Important Social Issues: Being a Good Neighbor & a Strong Testimony for the LORD, 22:1-12

1. **Issue 1: The restoration of lost property**
   a. Must return a lost animal to its owner
   b. Must keep the animal if the owner lives far away or is unknown
      1) To keep it until he comes for it
      2) To give it back; to readily return it
   c. Must apply the law to all lost property: Not to ignore it or pretend you do not see it

2. **Issue 2: Assisting a neighbor**
   a. Must help a neighbor in a crisis
   b. Must not look the other way

3. **Issue 3: Transvestism**
   a. Must not wear the clothes of the other sex: Is unnatural, deviant, offensive behavior
   b. Is an abomination, detested by God

4. **Issue 4: The conservation of animal life & of food**
   a. Must not take a mother bird for food when it is sitting on the young
      1) May take the young
      2) Must let the mother go
   b. The reason: To provide a permanent source of food, well-being, & long life
   c. The result: Things will go well & life will be extended

5. **Issue 5: Building codes & public safety**
   a. Must build a railing around one's roof porch
   b. The reason: To prevent accidents & personal liability

6. **Issue 6: Unnatural, inappropriate, impure mixing (a symbol of spiritual separation, of living a pure, distinctive life)**
   a. Must not mix seed: Defiles the crops
   b. Must not mix animals in plowing
   c. Must not mix clothes of two different materials

7. **Issue 7: Distinctive clothing (a symbol to stir holiness & obedience, see Nu.15:37-41)**

Thou shalt not see thy brother's ox or his sheep go astray, and hide thyself from them: thou shalt in any case bring them again unto thy brother.

2 And if thy brother *be* not nigh unto thee, or if thou know him not, then thou shalt bring it unto thine own house, and it shall be with thee until thy brother seek after it, and thou shalt restore it to him again.

3 In like manner shalt thou do with his ass; and so shalt thou do with his raiment; and with all lost thing of thy brother's, which he hath lost, and thou hast found, shalt thou do likewise: thou mayest not hide thyself.

4 Thou shalt not see thy brother's ass or his ox fall down by the way, and hide thyself from them: thou shalt surely help him to lift *them* up again.

5 The woman shall not wear that which pertaineth unto a man, neither shall a man put on a woman's garment: for all that do so *are* abomination unto the LORD thy God.

6 If a bird's nest chance to be before thee in the way in any tree, or on the ground, *whether they be* young ones, or eggs, and the dam sitting upon the young, or upon the eggs, thou shalt not take the dam with the young:

7 *But* thou shalt in any wise let the dam go, and take the young to thee; that it may be well with thee, and *that* thou mayest prolong *thy* days.

8 When thou buildest a new house, then thou shalt make a battlement for thy roof, that thou bring not blood upon thine house, if any man fall from thence.

9 Thou shalt not sow thy vineyard with divers seeds: lest the fruit of thy seed which thou hast sown, and the fruit of thy vineyard, be defiled.

10 Thou shalt not plow with an ox and an ass together.

11 Thou shalt not wear a garment of divers sorts, *as* of woollen and linen together.

12 Thou shalt make thee fringes upon the four quarters of thy vesture, wherewith thou coverest *thyself*.

DIVISION IV

THE SECOND GREAT THEME PREACHED BY GOD'S AGED SERVANT (PART 2): REMEMBER THE CIVIL AND RELIGIOUS LAWS OF ISRAEL—HELPFUL PRINCIPLES TO GOVERN MAN AND SOCIETY, 12:1–26:19

K. Laws That Govern Seven Important Social Issues: Being a Good Neighbor and a Strong Testimony for the LORD, 22:1-12

(22:1-12) **Introduction**: What kind of neighbor are you? A good or bad neighbor? A concerned or indifferent neighbor? An involved or distant neighbor? Are you a neighbor who looks away when a person needs help or a neighbor who reaches out and helps in times of need? Are you concerned or unconcerned about the welfare of your neighbors? Are you just indifferent—the welfare of your neighbors simply does not matter? Being a good neighbor is the subject of this important passage of Scripture: *Laws That Govern Seven Important Social Issues: Being a Good Neighbor and a Strong Testimony for the LORD,* 22:1-12.

1. Issue 1: the restoration of lost property (vv.1-3).
2. Issue 2: assisting a neighbor (v.4).
3. Issue 3: transvestism (v.5).
4. Issue 4: the conservation of animal life and of food (vv.6-7).
5. Issue 5: building codes and public safety (v.8).
6. Issue 6: unnatural, inappropriate, impure mixing (a symbol of spiritual separation, of living a pure, distinctive life) (vv.9-11).
7. Issue 7: distinctive clothing (a symbol to stir holiness and obedience, see Nu.15:37-41) (v.12).

DEUTERONOMY 22:1-12

1 (22:1-3) **Neighbor, a Good—Love, of Neighbor—Relationship, with Neighbor—Law, Governing Relationships with Neighbor—Law, Governing Lost Property**: the first issue concerns the restoration of lost property. People are always misplacing or losing things. If an item is ever found by a neighbor, it is to be returned to the rightful owner. Note the legal case covered by Moses, the case that was to serve as a precedent for lost property:

OUTLINE	SCRIPTURE	SCRIPTURE	OUTLINE
1. Issue 1: The restoration of lost property a. Must return a lost animal to its owner b. Must keep the animal if the owner lives far away or is unknown 1) To keep it until he comes for it	Thou shalt not see thy brother's ox or his sheep go astray, and hide thyself from them: thou shalt in any case bring them again unto thy brother. 2 And if thy brother *be* not nigh unto thee, or if thou know him not, then thou shalt bring it unto thine own house, and it shall be with thee until	thy brother seek after it, and thou shalt restore it to him again. 3 In like manner shalt thou do with his ass; and so shalt thou do with his raiment; and with all lost thing of thy brother's, which he hath lost, and thou hast found, shalt thou do likewise: thou mayest not hide thyself.	2) To give it back; to readily return it c. Must apply the law to all lost property: Not to ignore it or pretend you do not see it

Moses stated the law in very simple terms. If a lost animal was found, it was not to be ignored. It was to be taken back to the owner. If the owner was unknown or lived far away, the animal was to be kept until the owner came for it. When the owner came for his animal, the animal was to be readily returned.

Note that the law applied to all lost property, not only to animals. No matter what the lost property was, the finder was not to keep the property. He was not to lie, pretending that he did not have the property nor that he had not seen it. The law was clear: he was to return the property; he was to be a good neighbor. He was obligated to help his neighbor in recovering his property. This law was not to be ignored.

> **Thought 1**. Every adult upon earth, at one time or another, has misplaced or lost some property. All kinds of things are misplaced or lost, things such as...
> - purses
> - billfolds
> - money
> - credit cards
> - dogs
> - cats
> - clothes
> - jewelry
> - pencils or pens
> - important papers
> - eyeglasses
> - keys
>
> When a lost item is found, the law of God is clear: it is to be returned. The found property is not to be stolen. It is to be returned to the rightful owner.
>
>> "Thou shalt not steal" (Ex.20:15).
>> "Ye shall not steal, neither deal falsely, neither lie one to another" (Le.19:11).
>> "The getting of treasures by a lying tongue *is* a vanity tossed to and fro of them that seek death" (Pr.21:6).
>> "And they will deceive every one his neighbour, and will not speak the truth: they have taught their tongue to speak lies, *and* weary themselves to commit iniquity" (Je.9:5).
>> "Let him that stole steal no more: but rather let him labour, working with *his* hands the thing which is good, that he may have to give to him that needeth" (Ep.4:28).
>> "But let none of you suffer as a murderer, or *as* a thief, or *as* an evildoer, or as a busybody in other men's matters" (1 Pe.4:15).
>> "Not purloining [stealing], but showing all good fidelity; that they may adorn the doctrine of God our Saviour in all things" (Tit.2:10).

2 (22:4) **Neighbor, a Good—Love, of Neighbor—Relationship, with Neighbor—Law, Governing Relationship with Neighbor—Law, Assisting a Neighbor**: the second issue concerns assisting a neighbor who faces a crisis. Note the example given by Moses to illustrate the law:

OUTLINE	SCRIPTURE
2. Issue 2: Assisting a neighbor a. Must help a neighbor in a crisis b. Must not look the other way	4 Thou shalt not see thy brother's ass or his ox fall down by the way, and hide thyself from them: thou shalt surely help him to lift *them* up again.

Simply stated, if a person saw a neighbor who needed help, he was to go help the neighbor. If a neighbor's animal had fallen under the weight of a heavy load, the animal was to be helped to its feet. A person was not to look the other way, ignoring his neighbor's need for help. He was not to pretend that he did not see the need for help. A person is to go help his neighbor in his hour of need. He was to be a good neighbor, give assistance and supply what help he could. (See outline and note—Ex.23:4-5 for more discussion.)

DEUTERONOMY 22:1-12

Thought 1. Throughout life, we face all kinds of crises. We face crises such as...
- the loss of a loved one
- some injury due to an accident
- some financial crisis
- the loss of property due to fire
- damage to our homes due to some natural disaster
- becoming bedridden due to sickness or disease or aging

A host of crises could be listed, for tragedies are a common occurrence upon this earth that witnesses so much evil and depravity. But in the midst of crises and tragedies, God cares. This is the reason God established this law, and it is the reason He has established the eternal law of loving our neighbors as ourselves (Mt.22:39). When a neighbor faces a crisis, we are not to look the other way, not ignore his need. We are to help our neighbor in his hour of crisis.

> "And the second *is* like, *namely* this, Thou shalt love thy neighbour as thyself. There is none other commandment greater than these" (Mk.12:31).
> "Love worketh no ill to his neighbour: therefore love *is* the fulfilling of the law" (Ro.13:10).
> "We then that are strong ought to bear the infirmities of the weak, and not to please ourselves. Let every one of us please *his* neighbour for *his* good to edification" (Ro.15:1-2).
> "For all the law is fulfilled in one word, *even* in this; Thou shalt love thy neighbour as thyself" (Ga.5:14).
> "If ye fulfil the royal law according to the scripture, Thou shalt love thy neighbour as thyself, ye do well" (Js.2:8).

3 (22:5) **Transvestism—Homosexuality—Life, Created Order of—Deviancy, Behavior of—Behavior, Unnatural—Clothing, Cross-dressing—Deviancy, Cross-dressing—Deviancy, Transvestism—Law, Governing Transvestism—Law, Governing Clothing**: the third issue concerns transvestism, that of wearing the clothes and often adopting the behavior of the opposite sex. This is strictly forbidden by God and His holy law:

OUTLINE	SCRIPTURE

3. Issue 3: Transvestism
  a. Must not wear the clothes of the other sex: Is unnatural, deviant, offensive behavior
  b. Is an abomination, detested by God
	5 The woman shall not wear that which pertaineth unto a man, neither shall a man put on a woman's garment: for all that do so *are* abomination unto the LORD thy God.

God has created man and woman to be male and female. This is the order of God's holy creation; this is the created order of life (Ge.1:27). Therefore, the distinctiveness between male and female is to be maintained. There is a clear, distinct difference between man and woman, and this clear, distinct difference is to be respected and honored. The clothing worn by people during the days of Moses was similar, very similar. Both men and women wore robes that differed primarily only in their decoration or ornamentation. Even when there was little difference in dress, God demanded that the distinctiveness between man and woman be respected and maintained. The created order of life was not to be violated. Wearing the clothes and adopting the behavior of the opposite sex is unnatural. It is deviant, offensive, distasteful behavior. But even more serious, transvestism is an abomination to God. It is detested by God. The idea is that the judgment of God will fall upon the person who seeks fleshly pleasure through transvestism.

Transvestism sometimes leads to homosexuality; moreover, the deviant behavior is often associated with homosexuality. The law of God is clear: the order of God's holy creation, that of male and female, is not to be dishonored nor camouflaged. Women are to be women and men are to be men. The distinction is to be protected, respected, and honored.

> "So God created man in his *own* image, in the image of God created he him; male and female created he them" (Ge.1:27).
> "For this cause God gave them up unto vile affections: for even their women did change the natural use into that which is against nature: And likewise also the men, leaving the natural use of the woman, burned in their lust one toward another; men with men working that which is unseemly, and receiving in themselves that recompence of their error which was meet" (Ro.1:26-27).
> "Wherefore lay apart all filthiness and superfluity of naughtiness, and receive with meekness the engrafted word, which is able to save your souls" (Js.1:21).
> "Thou shalt not lie with mankind, as with womankind: it *is* abomination" (Le.18:22).
> "If a man also lie with mankind, as he lieth with a woman, both of them have committed an abomination: they shall surely be put to death; their blood *shall be* upon them" (Le.20:13).
> "For all that do such things, *and* all that do unrighteously, *are* an abomination unto the LORD thy God" (De.25:16).
> "Every one of them is gone back: they are altogether become filthy; *there is* none that doeth good, no, not one" (Ps.53:3).
> "He that turneth away his ear from hearing the law, even his prayer *shall be* abomination" (Pr.28:9).

DEUTERONOMY 22:1-12

[4] **(22:6-7) Conservation, of Animals—Conservation, of Food—Law, Governing Conservation—Food, Conservation of**: the fourth issue concerns the conservation of animal life and of food. The Israelites were soon to cross the Jordan River and engage the enemies of the promised land. One of the devastating effects of war is the killing of animals and the destruction of the land and its food supply. For this reason, the Israelites needed to practice the conservation of animal life and of their food. Note how this law helped to meet the need of the Israelites for food:

OUTLINE	SCRIPTURE	SCRIPTURE	OUTLINE

4. Issue 4: The conservation of animal life & of food
  a. Must not take a mother bird for food when it is sitting on the young
    1) May take the young
    2) Must let the mother go
	6 If a bird's nest chance to be before thee in the way in any tree, or on the ground, *whether they be* young ones, or eggs, and the dam sitting upon the young, or upon the eggs, thou shalt not take the	dam with the young:
		7 *But* thou shalt in any wise let the dam go, and take the young to thee; that it may be well with thee, and *that* thou mayest prolong *thy* days.
			b. The reason: To provide a permanent source of food, well-being, & long life
			c. The result: Things will go well & life will be extended

Keep in mind that these laws are examples of daily life that were to serve as legal precedents covering all the situations that would arise in the future. Conservation was of concern to God; therefore, He gave this law to serve as a precedent in the conservation of animal life and of food supplies. The law is clearly stated: if a person found a mother bird who was sitting on her young or eggs, the person could take the young but he had to let the mother go. Of course, the natural thing would be to take both the mother and the young, as well as the eggs. Such action would have a devastating effect. In the words of Peter C. Craigie:

> *The effect of such action, however, would be bad; in commercial language, it would be exchanging a long-term profit for an immediate gain. To take and kill the mother would be to terminate a potential future supply of food. To take the mother and leave the others would not be possible, for they would not be able to survive without the mother. Thus by taking the young birds (or eggs), but letting the mother go, food was acquired without the source of food for the future being cut off. The legislation thus has something in common with modern conservation laws. The large-scale killing of any species can lead to a serious diminution in its numbers and to eventual extinction.*[1]

The law of God was intended to conserve His creation, in particular animal life and the food supply of man. Note that the result of conservation is stated in a simple but straightforward statement: "Let the mother go, so that it may go well for you, and you may have a long life." Conservation of animal life and of the earth (air, water, trees, nature) will make things go better—far, far better—and give us a richer and longer life upon earth. This is the promise of God.

Thought 1. God has created animals for man (Ge.2:18-20). Man should, therefore, be pleased with the animal creation of God and act responsibly toward them. He must practice the laws of conservation, the conservation of the earth and of animal life. We must always remember that God cares not only for man but also for animals. He even cares for the little sparrow that falls to the ground.

> "Behold the fowls of the air: for they sow not, neither do they reap, nor gather into barns; yet your heavenly Father feedeth them. Are ye not much better than they" (Mt.6:26).
> "Are not five sparrows sold for two farthings, and not one of them is forgotten before God? But even the very hairs of your head are all numbered. Fear not therefore: ye are of more value than many sparrows" (Lu.12:6-7).
> "And God saw every thing that he had made [including the earth and animals], and, behold, *it was* very good. And the evening and the morning were the sixth day" (Ge.1:31).
> "And out of the ground the LORD God formed every beast of the field, and every fowl of the air; and brought *them* unto Adam to see what he would call them: and whatsoever Adam called every living creature, that *was* the name thereof" (Ge.2:19).

[5] **(22:8) Building, Codes of—Public Safety, Duty—Laws, Governing Building Codes and Public Safety—Construction, Building Codes**: the fifth issue concerns building codes and public safety. The Israelites would soon be entering the promised land and building permanent homes. In constructing their homes, they were to be concerned with protecting the safety of visiting neighbors. Public safety is a vital issue to God, even in the construction of the believer's home:

OUTLINE	SCRIPTURE

5. Issue 5: Building codes & public safety
  a. Must build a railing around one's roof porch
  b. The reason: To prevent accidents & personal liability
	8 When thou buildest a new house, then thou shalt make a battlement for thy roof, that thou bring not blood upon thine house, if any man fall from thence.

---

[1] Peter C. Craigie. *The Book of Deuteronomy*, p.289.

DEUTERONOMY 22:1-12

Many people would be constructing a porch on their roof that would be used for evening relaxation, conversation, entertaining, cooking, and as a play area for small children. Simply stated, they would be using their roof porches for the very same purposes that all generations have used porches. Since the roof sat so high off the ground, it was necessary to build a railing to prevent accidents and personal liability.

Thought 1. Building codes and public safety are of concern to God. We must be responsible citizens, protecting the lives of our families as well as of our neighbors. The houses and buildings we construct can either be of good quality or bad quality. Buildings can either be a place of safety or a death trap during storms and natural disasters. But God is clear: if we are to obey Him, then we must protect our families and our neighbors. We must be responsible and diligent in establishing strong building codes and in providing for public safety. We must not deal with a slack hand nor be sluggish.

"Not slothful in business; fervent in spirit; serving the LORD" (Ro.12:11).

"And whatsoever ye do in word or deed, *do* all in the name of the LORD Jesus, giving thanks to God and the Father by him" (Col.3:17).

"And whatsoever ye do, do *it* heartily, as to the LORD, and not unto men" (Col.3:23).

"Bear ye one another's burdens, and so fulfil the law of Christ....As we have therefore opportunity, let us do good unto all *men*, especially unto them who are of the household of faith" (Ga.6:2, 10).

"Therefore to him that knoweth to do good, and doeth *it* not, to him it is sin" (Js.4:17).

"Wherefore, beloved, seeing that ye look for such things, be diligent that ye may be found of him in peace, without spot, and blameless" (2 Pe.3:14).

"Seest thou a man diligent in his business? he shall stand before kings; he shall not stand before mean *men*" (Pr.22:29).

"Whatsoever thy hand findeth to do, do *it* with thy might; for *there is* no work, nor device, nor knowledge, nor wisdom, in the grave, whither thou goest" (Ec.9:10).

"Trust in the LORD, and do good; *so* shalt thou dwell in the land, and verily thou shalt be fed" (Ps.37:3).

6 (22:9-11) **Spiritual Separation—Separation, Spiritual—Lifestyle, Distinctive—Seed, Mixing of:** the sixth issue concerned the unnatural, impure mixing of life. This is a symbol of spiritual separation, of the believer living a pure, distinctive life from the immoral and lawless behavior of the world. The Israelites were to live lives that were distinct, totally separated to God. This law drove the truth of spiritual separation into their minds and hearts through everything they did. God wanted His people separated, set apart to Him, not to the world and its sinful ways. Therefore, God commanded...

- that there be no mixing of seed when planting a field
- that there be no mixing of animals in plowing
- that there be no mixing of clothes made from two different materials

OUTLINE	SCRIPTURE	SCRIPTURE	OUTLINE
6. Issue 6: Unnatural, inappropriate, impure mixing (a symbol of spiritual separation, of living a pure, distinctive life) a. Must not mix seed: Defiles the crops	9 Thou shalt not sow thy vineyard with divers seeds: lest the fruit of thy seed which thou hast sown, and the fruit of thy vineyard, be defiled.	10 Thou shalt not plow with an ox and an ass together. 11 Thou shalt not wear a garment of divers sorts, *as* of woollen and linen together.	b. Must not mix animals in plowing c. Must not mix clothes of two different materials

This law was to give a daily reminder to God's people, a reminder that they were to live a life of spiritual separation. Everything was to maintain its difference and distinctiveness. There was to be no mixture of truth and error, no mixture of morality and immorality, no mixture of obedience and disobedience. God's people were to live lives that were distinctively different from that of their immoral and lawless neighbors. They were not to have any mixed behavior, not adopt any of the sinful and evil practices of their wicked neighbors. They were to live lives of spiritual separation, lives that were distinctively different from the rest of the world. (See outline and note, pt.8—Le.19:9-22 for more discussion.)

"And take heed to yourselves, lest at any time your hearts be overcharged with surfeiting, and drunkenness, and cares of this life, and so that day come upon you unawares" (Lu.21:34).

"I beseech you therefore, brethren, by the mercies of God, that ye present your bodies a living sacrifice, holy, acceptable unto God, *which is* your reasonable service. And be not conformed to this world: but be ye transformed by the renewing of your mind, that ye may prove what is that good, and acceptable, and perfect, will of God" (Ro.12:1-2).

"No man that warreth entangleth himself with the affairs of *this* life; that he may please him who hath chosen him to be a soldier" (2 Ti.2:4).

"And have no fellowship with the unfruitful works of darkness, but rather reprove *them*" (Ep.5:11).

"Wherefore come out from among them, and be ye separate, saith the LORD, and touch not the unclean *thing*; and I will receive you, And will be a Father unto you, and ye shall be my sons and daughters, saith the LORD Almighty" (2 Co.6:17-18).

"Now we command you, brethren, in the name of our Lord Jesus Christ, that ye withdraw yourselves from every brother that walketh disorderly, and not after the tradition which he received of us" (2 Th.3:6).

"Love not the world, neither the things *that are* in the world. If any man love the world, the love of the Father is not in him. For all that *is* in the world, the lust of the flesh, and the lust of the eyes, and the pride of life, is not of the Father, but is of the world" (1 Jn.2:15-16).

"Depart from me, ye evildoers: for I will keep the commandments of my God" (Ps.119:115).

7 (22:12) **Clothing, Distinctive—Holiness, of Life—Holy, Duty—Mind, Duty to Protect—Thoughts, Duty to Protect—Concentration, Duty—Separation, Spiritual—Mind, Duty to Concentrate**: the seventh issue concerned distinctive clothing. This commandment to wear tassels on the four corners of a person's cloak or outer garment shows that God cares about the dress of His people. Note the simple statement of the law:

OUTLINE	SCRIPTURE
7. Issue 7: Distinctive clothing (a symbol to stir holiness & obedience, see Nu.15:37-41)	12 Thou shalt make thee fringes upon the four quarters of thy vesture, wherewith thou coverest *thyself*.

Other Scripture tells us that the purpose for the tassels was to remind the believer to obey God's commandments and to live a life of holiness, a life of separation from the world (see outline and notes—Nu.15:37-41 for more discussion). As the believer walked throughout the day, the tassels would be flapping about, occasionally attracting his attention. At that point he was to focus, for just a moment, upon the fact that he was to obey God's commandments and live a life of holiness before God. He was not to seek after the lust of his flesh and eyes. He was to focus his mind upon God, concentrate upon the commandments of God. The tassels were to remind him to obey all the commandments of God.

Thought 1. There are two significant lessons for us in this point:
(1) We do not wear tassels on our clothing today; nevertheless, our clothing should be distinctive, distinctive in the sense of demonstrating modesty, morality, and purity. Our clothing should be a testimony for Christ, not a degrading of His name. Our clothing should never arouse immoral, lustful thoughts in the minds of another person. Our clothing should never cause another person to sin. Our concern should be the clothing of righteousness not the clothing of enticement and of immorality. We should be clothed with the new man of Christ not with the old man of sin and shame.

"Neither yield ye your members *as* instruments of unrighteousness unto sin: but yield yourselves unto God, as those that are alive from the dead, and your members *as* instruments of righteousness unto God" (Ro.6:13).

"And have put on the new *man*, which is renewed in knowledge after the image of him that created him" (Col.3:10).

"And that ye put on the new man, which after God is created in righteousness and true holiness" (Ep.4:24).

"Therefore if any man *be* in Christ, *he is* a new creature: old things are passed away; behold, all things are become new" (2 Co.5:17).

"In like manner also, that women adorn themselves in modest apparel, with shamefacedness and sobriety; not with broided hair, or gold, or pearls, or costly array; But (which becometh women professing godliness) with good works" (1 Ti.2:9-10).

"Whose adorning let it not be that outward *adorning* of plaiting the hair, and of wearing of gold, or of putting on of apparel; But *let it be* the hidden man of the heart, in that which is not corruptible, *even the ornament* of a meek and quiet spirit, which is in the sight of God of great price. For after this manner in the old time the holy women also, who trusted in God, adorned themselves, being in subjection unto their own husbands" (1 Pe.3:3-5).

"I counsel thee to buy of me gold tried in the fire, that thou mayest be rich; and white raiment, that thou mayest be clothed, and *that* the shame of thy nakedness do not appear; and anoint thine eyes with eyesalve, that thou mayest see" (Re.3:18).

"And to her was granted that she should be arrayed in fine linen, clean and white: for the fine linen is the righteousness of saints" (Re.19:8).

"I put on righteousness, and it clothed me: my judgment *was* as a robe and a diadem" (Jb.29:14).

(2) We must control our minds throughout the day and occasionally take just a moment to think upon God, acknowledging and giving thanks to Him. The basic thrust of our lives must be to focus upon His commandments and bear a strong testimony for Him.

"For to be carnally minded *is* death; but to be spiritually minded *is* life and peace" (Ro.8:6).

"Casting down imaginations, and every high thing that exalteth itself against the knowledge of God, and bringing into captivity every thought to the obedience of Christ" (2 Co.10:5).

"Let this mind be in you, which was also in Christ Jesus" (Ph.2:5).

"For this *is* the covenant that I will make with the house of Israel after those days, saith the LORD; I will put my laws into their mind, and write them in their hearts: and I will be to them a God, and they shall be to me a people" (He.8:10; see He.10:16).

"Meditate upon these things; give thyself wholly to them; that thy profiting may appear to all" (1 Ti.4:15).

DEUTERONOMY 22:1-12

"This book of the law shall not depart out of thy mouth; but thou shalt meditate therein day and night, that thou mayest observe to do according to all that is written therein: for then thou shalt make thy way prosperous, and then thou shalt have good success" (Jos.1:8).

"But his delight *is* in the law of the LORD; and in his law doth he meditate day and night" (Ps.1:2).

"Stand in awe, and sin not: commune with your own heart upon your bed, and be still. Selah" (Ps.4:4).

"Let the words of my mouth, and the meditation of my heart, be acceptable in thy sight, O LORD, my strength, and my redeemer" (Ps.19:14).

"Wherewithal shall a young man cleanse his way? by taking heed *thereto* according to thy word" (Ps.119:9).

"Thy word have I hid in mine heart, that I might not sin against thee" (Ps.119:11).

TYPES, SYMBOLS, AND PICTURES
(Deuteronomy 22:1-12)

Historical Term	Type or Picture (Scriptural Basis for Each)	Life Application for Today's Believer	Biblical Application
Unnatural, Inappropriate, Impure Mixing De.22:9-11	Unnatural, inappropriate, impure mixing was a symbol of spiritual separation, of living a pure, distinctive life from the immoral and lawless behavior of the world. The Israelites were to live lives that were distinct, totally separated to God. This law drove the truth of spiritual separation into their minds and hearts through everything they did. God wanted His people separated, set apart to Him, not to the world and its sinful ways. Note the three warnings: 1. A person must not mix seed, for it defiles the crops. 2. A person must not mix animals in plowing. 3. A person must not mix the clothes of two different materials. "**Thou shalt not sow thy vineyard with divers seeds: lest the fruit of thy seed which thou hast sown, and the fruit of thy vineyard, be defiled. Thou shalt not plow with an ox and an ass together. Thou shalt not wear a garment of divers sorts, as of woollen and linen together**" (De.22:9-11).	⇒ This law was to give a daily reminder to God's people, a reminder that they were to live a life of spiritual separation. Everything was to maintain its difference and distinctiveness. There was to be no mixture of truth and error, no mixture of morality and immorality, no mixture of obedience and disobedience. God's people were to live lives that were distinctively different from that of their immoral and lawless neighbors. They were not to have any mixed behavior, not adopt any of the sinful and evil practices of their wicked neighbors. They were to live lives of spiritual separation, lives that were distinctively different from the rest of the world. (See outline and note, pt.8—Le.19:9-22 for more discussion.)	*"I beseech you therefore, brethren, by the mercies of God, that ye present your bodies a living sacrifice, holy, acceptable unto God, which is your reasonable service. And be not conformed to this world: but be ye transformed by the renewing of your mind, that ye may prove what is that good, and acceptable, and perfect, will of God"* (Ro.12:1-2). *"No man that warreth entangleth himself with the affairs of this life; that he may please him who hath chosen him to be a soldier"* (2 Ti.2:4). *"And have no fellowship with the unfruitful works of darkness, but rather reprove them"* (Ep.5:11; see 2 Co.6:17-18; 2 Th. 3:6; 1 Jn.2:15-16; Ps.119:115).
Distinctive Clothing De.22:12	Distinctive clothing is a symbol to stir holiness and obedience, (see Nu.15:37-41). This commandment to wear tassels on the four corners of a person's cloak or outer garment shows that God cares about the dress of His people. "**Thou shalt make thee fringes upon the four quarters of thy vesture, wherewith thou coverest *thyself***	⇒ There are two significant lessons for us in this point: 1. We do not wear tassels on our clothing today; nevertheless, our clothing should be distinctive, distinctive in the sense of demonstrating modesty, morality, and purity. Our clothing should be a testimony for Christ, not a degrading of	*"Neither yield ye your members as instruments of unrighteousness unto sin: but yield yourselves unto God, as those that are alive from the dead, and your members as instruments of righteousness unto God"* (Ro.6:13). *"And have put on the new man, which is renewed in knowledge after the image of him that created him"* (Col.3:10).

DEUTERONOMY 22:1-12

Historical Term	Type or Picture (Scriptural Basis for Each)	Life Application for Today's Believer	Biblical Application
	(De.22:12).	His name. Our clothing should never arouse immoral, lustful thoughts in the minds of another person. Our clothing should never cause another person to sin. Our concern should be the clothing of righteousness not the clothing of enticement and of immorality. We should be clothed with the new man of Christ not with the old man of sin and shame.	*"And that ye put on the new man, which after God is created in righteousness and true holiness"* (Ep. 4:24). *"Therefore if any man be in Christ, he is a new creature: old things are passed away; behold, all things are become new"* (2 Co.5:17; see 1 Ti.2:9-10; 1 Pe.3:3-5; Re.3:18; Re. 19:8; Jb.29:14).
		2. We must control our minds throughout the day and occasionally take a moment to think upon God, acknowledging and giving thanks to Him. The basic thrust of our lives must be to focus upon His commandments and bear a strong testimony for Him.	*"For to be carnally minded is death; but to be spiritually minded is life and peace"* (Ro.8:6). *"Casting down imaginations, and every high thing that exalteth itself against the knowledge of God, and bringing into captivity every thought to the obedience of Christ"* (2 Co.10:5). *"Let this mind be in you, which was also in Christ Jesus"* (Ph.2:5). *"Meditate upon these things; give thyself wholly to them; that thy profiting may appear to all"* (1 Ti. 4:15; see Jos.1:8; Ps.1:2; Ps.4:4; Ps.19:14; Ps.119:9; Ps.119:11).

DEUTERONOMY 22:13-30

	L. Laws That Govern Sexual Behavior: Living a Moral & Pure Life, 22:13-30		
1. The issue of premarital immorality a. Case 1: A newly married man seeks to get rid of his wife by falsely accusing her of not being a virgin 1) The wife's parents were to present proof to the court • To declare that he gave his daughter to the husband in good faith • To charge the husband with slander • To present proof of his daughter's virginity (perhaps a sheet or garment stained with the blood of her broken hymen) 2) The judges were to execute justice • Punish (flog) the man • Fine him 100 pieces of silver: Given to the father • Charge him with slander • Refuse to grant the divorce b. Case 2: The charge of premarital immorality is true 1) The woman was to be executed: She had disgraced her parents by being immoral while under their care 2) The evil was to be purged from God's people	13 If any man take a wife, and go in unto her, and hate her, 14 And give occasions of speech against her, and bring up an evil name upon her, and say, I took this woman, and when I came to her, I found her not a maid: 15 Then shall the father of the damsel, and her mother, take and bring forth *the tokens of* the damsel's virginity unto the elders of the city in the gate: 16 And the damsel's father shall say unto the elders, I gave my daughter unto this man to wife, and he hateth her; 17 And, lo, he hath given occasions of speech *against her*, saying, I found not thy daughter a maid; and yet these *are the tokens of* my daughter's virginity. And they shall spread the cloth before the elders of the city. 18 And the elders of that city shall take that man and chastise him; 19 And they shall amerce him in an hundred *shekels* of silver, and give *them* unto the father of the damsel, because he hath brought up an evil name upon a virgin of Israel: and she shall be his wife; he may not put her away all his days. 20 But if this thing be true, *and the tokens of* virginity be not found for the damsel: 21 Then they shall bring out the damsel to the door of her father's house, and the men of her city shall stone her with stones that she die: because she hath wrought folly in Israel, to play the whore in	her father's house: so shalt thou put evil away from among you. 22 If a man be found lying with a woman married to an husband, then they shall both of them die, *both* the man that lay with the woman, and the woman: so shalt thou put away evil from Israel. 23 If a damsel *that is* a virgin be betrothed unto an husband, and a man find her in the city, and lie with her; 24 Then ye shall bring them both out unto the gate of that city, and ye shall stone them with stones that they die; the damsel, because she cried not, *being* in the city; and the man, because he hath humbled his neighbour's wife: so thou shalt put away evil from among you. 25 But if a man find a betrothed damsel in the field, and the man force her, and lie with her: then the man only that lay with her shall die: 26 But unto the damsel thou shalt do nothing; *there is* in the damsel no sin *worthy* of death: for as when a man riseth against his neighbour, and slayeth him, even so *is* this matter: 27 For he found her in the field, *and* the betrothed damsel cried, and *there was* none to save her. 28 If a man find a damsel *that is* a virgin, which is not betrothed, and lay hold on her, and lie with her, and they be found; 29 Then the man that lay with her shall give unto the damsel's father fifty *shekels* of silver, and she shall be his wife; because he hath humbled her, he may not put her away all his days. 30 A man shall not take his father's wife, nor discover his father's skirt.	**2. The issue of adultery** a. The case: A man sleeps with a married woman b. The judgment: Execution c. The reason: To purge the evil from God's people **3. The issue of the seduction of an engaged woman (or man)** a. The case: A man has sex with an engaged woman b. The judgment: Execution of both 1) The woman because she did not scream for help 2) The man because he violated another man's wife c. The reason: To purge the evil from God's people **4. The issue of rape** a. Case 1: A man rapes an engaged woman out in the country 1) He is to be executed 2) She is innocent • Was an unwilling victim (just like a murder victim) • Screamed, but there was no one to rescue her b. Case 2: A man rapes a young girl 1) He must pay 50 pieces of silver 2) He must marry her & never divorce **5. The issue of incest** a. Must not marry a stepmother b. The reason: Violated his father

DIVISION IV

THE SECOND GREAT THEME PREACHED BY GOD'S AGED SERVANT (PART 2): REMEMBER THE CIVIL AND RELIGIOUS LAWS OF ISRAEL—HELPFUL PRINCIPLES TO GOVERN MAN AND SOCIETY, 12:1–26:19

L.   Laws That Govern Sexual Behavior: Living a Moral and Pure Life, 22:13-30

(22:13-30) Introduction: living a moral and pure life is of critical importance. Why? For one strong reason: immorality tears down the very nature of man, man who is the summit of God's creation. Immorality causes great pain and suffering: it destroys wives, husbands, and children, and eventually society itself. Immorality destroys the family, the very foundation of

DEUTERONOMY 22:13-30

society, the institution God ordained to give purpose and meaning, form and structure to society. Immorality does irreparable harm to all parties involved. Immorality breaks up families and destroys homes and when it destroys homes, it causes a part of society to crumble. Moreover, immorality corrupts the mind and conscience of the offender, enslaving him to unbridled lust. And when a mind becomes enslaved by unbridled lust, it is far more subject to committing all forms of lawlessness and corrupt behavior. The sins of immorality and the utter necessity for living a moral and pure life are the subjects of this important passage of Scripture: *Laws That Govern Sexual Behavior: Living a Moral and Pure Life,* 22:13-30.

1. The issue of premarital immorality (vv.13-21).
2. The issue of adultery (v.22).
3. The issue of the seduction of an engaged woman (or man) (vv.23-24).
4. The issue of rape (vv.25-29).
5. The issue of incest (v.30).

1 **(22:13-21) Immorality, Premarital—Immorality, Judgment of—Sex, Premarital—Premarital Sex—Morality, Duty—Purity, Duty—Marriage, Sanctity of—Sexual Purity, Sanctity of—Virgin, Duty**: the first issue concerns premarital immorality. Young men and women are to keep themselves sexually pure, and parents are to teach their children the importance of being sexually pure. The importance of premarital purity cannot be overstressed, not in the eyes of God. This is clearly seen in the two cases covered by Moses:

OUTLINE	SCRIPTURE	SCRIPTURE	OUTLINE
1. The issue of premarital immorality a. Case 1: A newly married man seeks to get rid of his wife by falsely accusing her of not being a virgin 1) The wife's parents were to present proof to the court • To declare that he gave his daughter to the husband in good faith • To charge the husband with slander • To present proof of his daughter's virginity (perhaps a sheet or garment stained with the blood of her broken	13 If any man take a wife, and go in unto her, and hate her, 14 And give occasions of speech against her, and bring up an evil name upon her, and say, I took this woman, and when I came to her, I found her not a maid: 15 Then shall the father of the damsel, and her mother, take and bring forth *the tokens of* the damsel's virginity unto the elders of the city in the gate: 16 And the damsel's father shall say unto the elders, I gave my daughter unto this man to wife, and he hateth her; 17 And, lo, he hath given occasions of speech *against her,* saying, I found not thy daughter a maid; and yet these *are the tokens of* my daughter's virginity. And they shall spread the cloth before	the elders of the city. 18 And the elders of that city shall take that man and chastise him; 19 And they shall amerce him in an hundred *shekels* of silver, and give *them* unto the father of the damsel, because he hath brought up an evil name upon a virgin of Israel: and she shall be his wife; he may not put her away all his days. 20 But if this thing be true, *and the tokens of* virginity be not found for the damsel: 21 Then they shall bring out the damsel to the door of her father's house, and the men of her city shall stone her with stones that she die: because she hath wrought folly in Israel, to play the whore in her father's house: so shalt thou put evil away from among you.	hymen) 2) The judges were to execute justice • Punish (flog) the man • Fine him 100 pieces of silver: Given to the father • Charge him with slander • Refuse to grant the divorce b. Case 2: The charge of premarital immorality is true 1) The woman was to be executed: She had disgraced her parents by being immoral while under their care 2) The evil was to be purged from God's people

a. The first case concerns a newly married man who becomes displeased with his wife and wishes to divorce her. Just what displeased him is not stated, but he launches a false accusation against her. He charges her with not being a virgin. Being a virgin when married was important to an Israelite, just as it is to most people. Most people would prefer by far that their new wife or husband be a virgin, be sexually pure. Few people want a person who has been handled by others, who has shared the intimacy, love, and preciousness of his or her body with others. Body to body engagement—the intimacy of sex—is for marriage and marriage alone. Therefore, being a virgin was of extreme importance to the Israelites, just as it is to most of us. Thus the charge of this newly married man against his wife was extremely serious.

1) It was the responsibility of the wife's parents to prove to the court that their daughter was a virgin (vv.15-17). They were responsible because they had given their daughter to the man in marriage. By this act they declared that their daughter was fit for marriage, that she was a virgin. Note the defense that the parents were to give to the court:
   ⇒ The father was to declare that he gave his daughter to the husband in good faith (v.16).
   ⇒ The father was to charge the husband with slander (v.17).
   ⇒ The father was to present proof of his daughter's virginity (v.17). This was apparently a sheet or garment stained with the blood of her broken hymen that would have taken place on the night of their first sexual experience. The blood would have been proof that the woman was a virgin.[1]
2) After the wife's virginity had been established, the judges were to execute justice upon the lying husband (vv.18-19). Four actions were to be taken:
   ⇒ They were to punish the man (v.18). Most likely, this refers to the man being publicly flogged.
   ⇒ They were to fine the man 100 pieces of silver, giving the silver to the father (v.19).

---
[1] Peter C. Craigie. *The Book of Deuteronomy*, pp.292-293.

⇒ They were to charge the man with slander (v.19).
⇒ They were to refuse the man's request for divorce (v.19). Note that he was not allowed to divorce the wife as long as he lived.

b. The second case concerns the charge of premarital sex that is proven to be true (vv.20-21). Very simply stated, if the woman was found guilty, she was to be executed. She had disgraced her parents by being immoral while under their care (v.21). Therefore, she was to be stoned to death by the community. The evil was to be purged from God's people (v.21). The severity of the punishment shows how serious God considers premarital immorality. The immoral person is to face the judgment of God. John Maxwell makes the statement that needs to be heeded by us all:

The entire community became involved in a private sin. Today, although the stigma and the punishment of premarital sex have been greatly reduced, others are still affected by one person's immorality. There is no such thing as a "casual affair." One need only read the statistics concerning abortions, sexually transmitted diseases, and government assistance for unwed mothers to realize that private sexual sins quickly become public matters of concern.[2]

Thought 1. This is a strong warning to young men and women to flee fornication, that is, premarital sex. Premarital sex robs a person of the most precious gift he or she has to give to the future husband or wife—the intimacy and preciousness of one's body. Premarital sex means that a person's body has become engaged with another body, that a person's body has been handled and shared with another person, that the intimacy of the sharing that belonged to the future spouse has been lost forever. The *initial* engagement, intimacies, and sharing of one's body with a future spouse can never be experienced—all because a person has already shared the intimacies of his or her body with a passing or at least 'temporary' acquaintance—sometimes even with a perfect stranger—with whom there is no permanent commitment. Premarital sex is wrong in the eyes of God. This is the strong declaration of Scripture.

"But fornication, and all uncleanness, or covetousness, let it not be once named among you, as becometh saints" (Ep.5:3).
"Mortify therefore your members which are upon the earth; fornication, uncleanness, inordinate affection, evil concupiscence, and covetousness, which is idolatry" (Col.3:5).
"Know ye not that the unrighteous shall not inherit the kingdom of God? Be not deceived: neither fornicators, nor idolaters, nor adulterers, nor effeminate, nor abusers of themselves with mankind, Nor thieves, nor covetous, nor drunkards, nor revilers, nor extortioners, shall inherit the kingdom of God" (1 Co.6:9-10).
"Nevertheless, *to avoid* fornication, let every man have his own wife, and let every woman have her own husband" (1 Co.7:2).
"For this is the will of God, *even* your sanctification, that ye should abstain from fornication" (1 Th.4:3).

2 (22:22) **Adultery, Judgment of—Adultery, Duty—Judgment, of Adultery—Laws, Governing Adultery—Adultery, Laws Governing**: the second issue concerned adultery.

OUTLINE	SCRIPTURE
2. The issue of adultery a. The case: A man sleeps with a married woman b. The judgment: Execution c. The reason: To purge the evil from God's people	22 If a man be found lying with a woman married to an husband, then they shall both of them die, *both* the man that lay with the woman, and the woman: so shalt thou put away evil from Israel.

Adultery is the breaking of the seventh commandment, "You shall not commit adultery" (De.5:18). If any man, single or married, was found sleeping with another man's wife, both the man and the woman were to be put to death. This was the most serious of crimes in the eyes of God, for the man was violating the most precious possession of the husband. Moreover, the wife was willingly and deliberately giving herself to another man, thereby cutting the hearts of her husband and children to the deepest core possible. For this reason, the adulterous couple was to be executed. This evil was to be purged from the midst of God's people.

Thought 1. Such a terrible act as adultery causes great pain and suffering: adultery destroys wives, husbands, children, and eventually society itself. Adultery breaks up families and destroys homes. Adulterers will bear the judicial judgment of God: what they sow they will reap. Adulterers sow lust and immorality; therefore, they burn in their lust and immorality as long as they live upon the earth. But then once they die, they face the eternal judgment and condemnation of God.

"For the wrath of God is revealed from heaven against all ungodliness and unrighteousness of men, who hold the truth in unrighteousness....Wherefore God also gave them up to uncleanness through the lusts of their own hearts, to dishonour their own bodies between themselves: Who changed the truth of

---
[2] John Maxwell. *The Preacher's Commentary on Deuteronomy*, pp.262-263.

God into a lie, and worshipped and served the creature more than the Creator, who is blessed for ever. Amen. For this cause God gave them up unto vile affections: for even their women did change the natural use into that which is against nature: And likewise also the men, leaving the natural use of the woman, burned in their lust one toward another; men with men working that which is unseemly, and receiving in themselves that recompence of their error which was meet. And even as they did not like to retain God in *their* knowledge, God gave them over to a reprobate mind, to do those things which are not convenient; Being filled with all unrighteousness, fornication, wickedness, covetousness, maliciousness; full of envy, murder, debate, deceit, malignity; whisperers, Backbiters, haters of God, despiteful, proud, boasters, inventors of evil things, disobedient to parents, Without understanding, covenantbreakers, without natural affection, implacable, unmerciful: Who knowing the judgment of God, that they which commit such things are worthy of death, not only do the same, but have pleasure in them that do them" (Ro.1:18, 24-32).

"Know ye not that the unrighteous shall not inherit the kingdom of God? Be not deceived: neither fornicators, nor idolaters, nor adulterers, nor effeminate, nor abusers of themselves with mankind, Nor thieves, nor covetous, nor drunkards, nor revilers, nor extortioners, shall inherit the kingdom of God" (1 Co.6:9-10).

"Now the works of the flesh are manifest, which are these; Adultery, fornication, uncleanness, lasciviousness, Idolatry, witchcraft, hatred, variance, emulations, wrath, strife, seditions, heresies, Envyings, murders, drunkenness, revellings, and such like: of the which I tell you before, as I have also told *you* in time past, that they which do such things shall not inherit the kingdom of God" (Ga.5:19-21).

"But the fearful, and unbelieving, and the abominable, and murderers, and whoremongers, and sorcerers, and idolaters, and all liars, shall have their part in the lake which burneth with fire and brimstone: which is the second death" (Re.21:8).

3 (22:23-24) **Seduction, of an Engaged Man or Woman—Engagement, Marital, Abuse of—Law, Governing the Seduction of an Engaged Woman or Man—Immorality, Seduction to**: the third concern was the seduction of an engaged woman or man.

OUTLINE	SCRIPTURE	SCRIPTURE	OUTLINE
3. The issue of the seduction of an engaged woman (or man) a. The case: A man has sex with an engaged woman b. The judgment: Execution of both 1) The woman because she	23 If a damsel *that is* a virgin be betrothed unto an husband, and a man find her in the city, and lie with her; 24 Then ye shall bring them both out unto the gate of that city, and ye shall stone them	with stones that they die; the damsel, because she cried not, *being* in the city; and the man, because he hath humbled his neighbour's wife: so thou shalt put away evil from among you.	did not scream for help 2) The man because he violated another man's wife c. The reason: To purge the evil from God's people

An engaged person in Israelite society was treated as though he were married, for the dowry had been paid and the marriage was being finalized.[3] If a man had sex with an engaged woman within the boundaries of a city or town, they were both to be executed. The case could not be considered rape, for the woman could have screamed out for help. Being within the city limits, her screams would have been heard and help would have come. Consequently, both the woman and the man were to be executed, the man because he had violated the engaged woman and the woman because she had willingly consented to his advances. The evil of immorality was to be purged from God's people.

Thought 1. Engaged men and women are to keep themselves pure for the marriage. They have promised their love and their bodies to another person; therefore, they are to keep their promises. They are not to be unfaithful by sharing the intimacies of their bodies and love with a passing acquaintance. They are to keep themselves pure for their lifetime companion, their husband or wife. The engagement period is to be a time of drawing closer, learning more and more about one another, and growing together in development of the future relationship that is to be consummated in marriage. All this is to be done so that the spiritual union that can be given by God alone will be experienced by the engaged couple. The engaged woman and man are not to allow themselves to be seduced by another person, not to commit immorality with a passing acquaintance. Such evil is to be purged.

"But I say unto you, That whosoever looketh on a woman to lust after her hath committed adultery with her already in his heart" (Mt.5:28).

"I speak after the manner of men because of the infirmity of your flesh: for as ye have yielded your members servants to uncleanness and to iniquity unto iniquity; even so now yield your members servants to righteousness unto holiness" (Ro.6:19).

"Wherefore come out from among them, and be ye separate, saith the LORD, and touch not the unclean *thing;* and I will receive you, And will be a Father unto you, and ye shall be my sons and daughters, saith the LORD Almighty" (2 Co.6:17-18).

"But fornication, and all uncleanness, or covetousness, let it not be once named among you, as becometh saints" (Ep.5:3).

---

3 John Maxwell. *The Preacher's Commentary on Deuteronomy*, p.263.

DEUTERONOMY 22:13-30

"For this is the will of God, *even* your sanctification, that ye should abstain from fornication: That every one of you should know how to possess his vessel in sanctification and honour; Not in the lust of concupiscence, even as the Gentiles which know not God" (1 Th.4:3-5).

"For God hath not called us unto uncleanness, but unto holiness" (1 Th.4:7).

"Abstain from all appearance of evil" (1 Th.5:22).

"Flee also youthful lusts: but follow righteousness, faith, charity, peace, with them that call on the LORD out of a pure heart" (2 Ti.2:22).

"Marriage *is* honourable in all, and the bed undefiled: but whoremongers and adulterers God will judge" (He.13:4).

"Abstain from fleshly lusts, which war against the soul" (1 Pe.2:11).

"Lust not after her beauty in thine heart; neither let her take thee with her eyelids" (Pr.6:25).

[4] (22:25-29) **Rape, Judgment of—Law, Governing Rape—Rape, Law Governing**: the fourth issue concerned rape. Note that two examples are given to serve as cases of precedence in governing the terrible acts of rape.

OUTLINE	SCRIPTURE	SCRIPTURE	OUTLINE
4. The issue of rape a. Case 1: A man rapes an engaged woman out in the country 1) He is to be executed 2) She is innocent • Was an unwilling victim (just like a murder victim) • Screamed, but there was no one to rescue her	25 But if a man find a betrothed damsel in the field, and the man force her, and lie with her: then the man only that lay with her shall die: 26 But unto the damsel thou shalt do nothing; *there is* in the damsel no sin *worthy* of death: for as when a man riseth against his neighbour, and slayeth him, even so *is* this matter: 27 For he found her in the field, *and* the betrothed dam-	sel cried, and *there was* none to save her. 28 If a man find a damsel *that is* a virgin, which is not betrothed, and lay hold on her, and lie with her, and they be found; 29 Then the man that lay with her shall give unto the damsel's father fifty *shekels* of silver, and she shall be his wife; because he hath humbled her, he may not put her away all his days.	 b. Case 2: A man rapes a young girl 1) He must pay 50 pieces of silver 2) He must marry her & never divorce

a. The first case concerns a man who rapes an engaged woman out in the country (vv.25-27). The man alone was to be executed, for the woman was innocent. She was an unwilling victim; in fact, her case is comparable to the case of a murder victim. Her body was taken from her just like the body of a murder victim, both unwillingly. She screamed for help, but there was no one out in the country who could hear and rescue her (v.27). The point to note is the seriousness of this crime in the eyes of God: rape is just as serious a crime as murder. The woman was an unwilling victim of the attacker just as a person who is murdered is an unwilling victim of an attacker.

b. The second case concerns a man who rapes a young girl who is neither engaged nor married (vv.28-29). In this particular situation, the man must pay 50 pieces of silver to the girl's father and marry her, never divorcing her (v.29). Note how this protects the girls honor and assures her of permanent support for herself and for any child who might be born from the rape. This law was, no doubt, a deterrent to rape.

Thought 1. What would happen in today's society if a man or woman who raped another person would be executed soon thereafter? What would happen if the guilty rapist had to pay a large amount of money for victimizing a virgin? If he had to marry the person he raped? If he had to take care of the child that resulted from the union for the rest of his life? If such laws existed and were executed today, would men and women behave differently, knowing that a large sum of money and marriage were directly tied to their mistreatment of one another? Note how a man and woman are to keep themselves pure in today's society.

"Flee fornication. Every sin that a man doeth is without the body; but he that committeth fornication sinneth against his own body" (1 Co.6:18).

"But fornication, and all uncleanness, or covetousness, let it not be once named among you, as becometh saints" (Ep.5:3).

"*Let* nothing *be done* through strife or vainglory; but in lowliness of mind let each esteem other better than themselves. Look not every man on his own things, but every man also on the things of others" (Ph.2:3-4).

"Mortify therefore your members which are upon the earth; fornication, uncleanness, inordinate affection, evil concupiscence, and covetousness, which is idolatry" (Col.3:5).

"For God hath not called us unto uncleanness, but unto holiness" (1 Th.4:7).

"Wherewithal shall a young man cleanse his way? by taking heed *thereto* according to thy word" (Ps.119:9).

"Thy word have I hid in mine heart, that I might not sin against thee" (Ps.119:11).

Thought 2. Note a significant fact: neither the marriage nor the payment of money removed the guilt and coming judgment of God from the rapist. Guilt and forgiveness of sin come only through confession of sin and repentance, only by turning to God and beginning to follow Him.

DEUTERONOMY 22:13-30

"I tell you, nay: but, except you repent, ye shall all likewise perish" (Lu.13:3).

"And the publican, standing afar off, would not lift up so much as *his* eyes unto heaven, but smote upon his breast, saying, God be merciful to me a sinner" (Lu.18:13).

"Repent ye therefore, and be converted, that your sins may be blotted out, when the times of refreshing shall come from the presence of the LORD;" (Ac.3:19).

"Repent therefore of this thy wickedness, and pray God, if perhaps the thought of thine heart may be forgiven thee" (Ac.8:22).

"If my people, which are called by my name, shall humble themselves, and pray, and seek my face, and turn from their wicked ways; then will I hear from heaven, and will forgive their sin, and will heal their land" (2 Chr.7:14).

"Then Job answered the LORD, and said....Wherefore I abhor *myself*, and repent in dust and ashes" (Jb. 42:1, 6).

5 (22:30) **Incest, Law Governing—Law, Governing Incest—Stepmother, Duty to—Stepfather, Duty to**: the fifth issue concerned the sin of incest. Simply stated, a man must not marry his stepmother. The implication or legal precedent would also prohibit a woman from marrying her stepfather. Note why: such an act would defile the bed of a person's father.

OUTLINE	SCRIPTURE

5. The issue of incest
  a. Must not marry a stepmother
  b. The reason: Violated his father
	30 A man shall not take his father's wife, nor discover his father's skirt.

Thought 1. God warns both His people and the people of the world: He is going to execute justice and judgment upon the immoral of the world. The judgment of God will fall upon those who commit sins of immorality, sins such as...
- incest
- rape
- the seduction of an engaged woman or man
- adultery
- premarital sex

"For the wrath of God is revealed from heaven against all ungodliness and unrighteousness of men, who hold the truth in unrighteousness....For this cause God gave them up unto vile affections: for even their women did change the natural use into that which is against nature: And likewise also the men, leaving the natural use of the woman, burned in their lust one toward another; men with men working that which is unseemly, and receiving in themselves that recompence of their error which was meet. And even as they did not like to retain God in *their* knowledge, God gave them over to a reprobate mind, to do those things which are not convenient; Being filled with all unrighteousness, fornication, wickedness, covetousness, maliciousness; full of envy, murder, debate, deceit, malignity; whisperers, Backbiters, haters of God, despiteful, proud, boasters, inventors of evil things, disobedient to parents, Without understanding, covenantbreakers, without natural affection, implacable, unmerciful: Who knowing the judgment of God, that they which commit such things are worthy of death, not only do the same, but have pleasure in them that do them" (Ro.1:18, 26-32).

"Know ye not that the unrighteous shall not inherit the kingdom of God? Be not deceived: neither fornicators, nor idolaters, nor adulterers, nor effeminate, nor abusers of themselves with mankind, Nor thieves, nor covetous, nor drunkards, nor revilers, nor extortioners, shall inherit the kingdom of God" (1 Co.6:9-10).

"Now the works of the flesh are manifest, which are *these;* Adultery, fornication, uncleanness, lasciviousness, Idolatry, witchcraft, hatred, variance, emulations, wrath, strife, seditions, heresies, Envyings, murders, drunkenness, revellings, and such like: of the which I tell you before, as I have also told *you* in time past, that they which do such things shall not inherit the kingdom of God" (Ga.5:19-21).

"But the fearful, and unbelieving, and the abominable, and murderers, and whoremongers, and sorcerers, and idolaters, and all liars, shall have their part in the lake which burneth with fire and brimstone: which is the second death" (Re.21:8).

Thought 2. God demands that the believer separate himself, have nothing to do with the sexual immorality of his neighbors and the world. The believer is to live a holy, moral, righteous, and pure life, a life that is different from those in the world, a life that is separated and set apart to God.

"And take heed to yourselves, lest at any time your hearts be overcharged with surfeiting, and drunkenness, and cares of this life, and so that day come upon you unawares" (Lu.21:34).

"I beseech you therefore, brethren, by the mercies of God, that ye present your bodies a living sacrifice, holy, acceptable unto God, *which is* your reasonable service. And be not conformed to this world: but be ye transformed by the renewing of your mind, that ye may prove what is that good, and acceptable, and perfect, will of God" (Ro.12:1-2).

"Wherefore come out from among them, and be ye separate, saith the LORD, and touch not the unclean *thing;* and I will receive you, And will be a Father unto you, and ye shall be my sons and daughters, saith the LORD Almighty" (2 Co.6:17-18).

"And have no fellowship with the unfruitful works of darkness, but rather reprove *them*. For it is a shame even to speak of those things which are done of them in secret" (Ep.5:11-12).

"Love not the world, neither the things *that are* in the world. If any man love the world, the love of the Father is not in him. For all that *is* in the world, the lust of the flesh, and the lust of the eyes, and the pride of life, is not of the Father, but is of the world" (1 Jn.2:15-16).

"Depart ye, depart ye, go ye out from thence, touch no unclean *thing;* go ye out of the midst of her; be ye clean, that bear the vessels of the LORD" (Is.52:11).

DEUTERONOMY 23:1-25

CHAPTER 23

M. Laws That Govern Several Social & Religious Issues: God's Concern for Both the Major & Minor Details of Life, 23:1-25

1. **Issue 1: Who is to be excluded from the assembly (a lesson on the need for pure worship)**
   a. The castrated man

   b. The illegitimate child or child born of a forbidden marriage & his descendants—through ten generations

   c. The Ammonite or the Moabite & his descendants—through ten generations

   1) Because they did not help God's people during the wilderness wanderings
   2) Because they hired the false prophet Balaam to curse God's people

   3) Because God loves His people: Demonstrated by turning the curse into a blessing

   4) Because God has issued a permanent decree: No treaty is ever to be made with them
   d. The Edomite & the Egyptian & their descendants—through two generations
   1) Must not abhor them

   2) Must allow their generation to assemble & worship

2. **Issue 2: Purity in the military camp (a picture of being spiritually clean)**
   a. Must flee everything impure
   b. The two examples given
   1) A man is unclean due to a nighttime discharge

   • To go outside the camp

   • To wash himself

He that is wounded in the stones, or hath his privy member cut off, shall not enter into the congregation of the LORD.
2 A bastard shall not enter into the congregation of the LORD; even to his tenth generation shall he not enter into the congregation of the LORD.
3 An Ammonite or Moabite shall not enter into the congregation of the LORD; even to their tenth generation shall they not enter into the congregation of the LORD for ever:
4 Because they met you not with bread and with water in the way, when ye came forth out of Egypt; and because they hired against thee Balaam the son of Beor of Pethor of Mesopotamia, to curse thee.
5 Nevertheless the LORD thy God would not hearken unto Balaam; but the LORD thy God turned the curse into a blessing unto thee, because the LORD thy God loved thee.
6 Thou shalt not seek their peace nor their prosperity all thy days for ever.
7 Thou shalt not abhor an Edomite; for he *is* thy brother: thou shalt not abhor an Egyptian; because thou wast a stranger in his land.
8 The children that are begotten of them shall enter into the congregation of the LORD in their third generation.
9 When the host goeth forth against thine enemies, then keep thee from every wicked thing.
10 If there be among you any man, that is not clean by reason of uncleanness that chanceth him by night, then shall he go abroad out of the camp, he shall not come within the camp:
11 But it shall be, when evening cometh on, he shall wash *himself* with water: and when the sun is down, he shall come into the camp *again*.
12 Thou shalt have a place also without the camp, whither thou shalt go forth abroad:
13 And thou shalt have a paddle upon thy weapon; and it shall be, when thou wilt ease thyself abroad, thou shalt dig therewith, and shalt turn back and cover that which cometh from thee:
14 For the LORD thy God walketh in the midst of thy camp, to deliver thee, and to give up thine enemies before thee; therefore shall thy camp be holy: that he see no unclean thing in thee, and turn away from thee.
15 Thou shalt not deliver unto his master the servant which is escaped from his master unto thee:
16 He shall dwell with thee, *even* among you, in that place which he shall choose in one of thy gates, where it liketh him best: thou shalt not oppress him.
17 There shall be no whore of the daughters of Israel, nor a sodomite of the sons of Israel.
18 Thou shalt not bring the hire of a whore, or the price of a dog, into the house of the LORD thy God for any vow: for even both these *are* abomination unto the LORD thy God.
19 Thou shalt not lend upon usury to thy brother; usury of money, usury of victuals, usury of any thing that is lent upon usury:
20 Unto a stranger thou mayest lend upon usury; but unto thy brother thou shalt not lend upon usury: that the LORD thy God may bless thee in all that thou settest thine hand to in the land whither thou goest to possess it.
21 When thou shalt vow a vow unto the LORD thy God, thou shalt not slack to pay it: for the LORD thy God will surely require it of thee; and it would be sin in thee.
22 But if thou shalt forbear to vow, it shall be no sin in thee.
23 That which is gone out of thy lips thou shalt keep and

• To return at sunset

2) A place for a latrine was to be marked off: Were to cover the waste with each relief

c. The reasons why God gave this law on purity
1) To protect God's people
2) To teach the truth that God is holy & cannot look upon any unclean thing

3. **Issue 3: Escaped slaves (a lesson on mercy—life, liberty, & justice)**
   a. Must be given sanctuary & allowed to live wherever he wished
   b. Must not be oppressed

4. **Issue 4: Prostitution**
   a. Must not become a prostitute

   b. Must not bring money secured by prostitution (nor by any other evil means) into the house of God nor use the money to pay vows or pledges
   c. The reason: God detests this
5. **Issue 5: Charging interest**
   a. Must lend freely, not charge interest to a brother in need: Not on anything

   b. May charge interest to foreigners
   c. The reason: God will bless your labor

6. **Issue 6: Vows**
   a. Must not be slow to pay your vows or pledges to God
   1) Because God demands payment
   2) Because refusal is sin
   b. Must know that it is better not to make a vow than to make it & not fulfill it
   c. Must do exactly what you vow or pledge: Because all

DEUTERONOMY 23:1-25

vows are freely made, never demanded by God	perform; *even* a freewill offering, according as thou hast vowed unto the LORD thy God, which thou hast promised with thy mouth. 24 When thou comest into thy neighbour's vineyard, then thou mayest eat grapes thy fill at thine own pleasure;	but thou shalt not put *any* in thy vessel. 25 When thou comest into the standing corn of thy neighbour, then thou mayest pluck the ears with thine hand; but thou shalt not move a sickle unto thy neighbour's standing corn.	grapes but not fill a basket
7. Issue 7: Property rights a. Example 1: If you pass through a neighbor's vineyard, you may eat some			b. Example 2: If you pass through a field, you may fill your hand with grain but not harvest & steal the grain

DIVISION IV

THE SECOND GREAT THEME PREACHED BY GOD'S AGED SERVANT (PART 2): REMEMBER THE CIVIL AND RELIGIOUS LAWS OF ISRAEL—HELPFUL PRINCIPLES TO GOVERN MAN AND SOCIETY, 12:1–26:19

M. Laws That Govern Several Social and Religious Issues of Life: God's Concern for Both the Major and Minor Details of Life, 23:1-25

(23:1-25) **Introduction**: the major and minor details of life, in fact, all the details of life, are of vital concern to God. Take just a moment. Think of the interesting subjects covered by this Scripture:
⇒ property rights
⇒ vows
⇒ making loans and charging interest
⇒ prostitution
⇒ escaped slaves—life, liberty, and justice
⇒ purity in military camps or keeping the barracks clean

Such social and religious issues of life make an interesting discussion among any group of people. This passage shows that God is concerned, deeply concerned, about the day-to-day details of human life. This is the discussion of the present passage: *Laws That Govern Several Social and Religious Issues of Life: God's Concern for Both the Major and Minor Details of Life, 23:1-25.*
1. Issue 1: who is to be excluded from the assembly (a lesson on the need for pure worship) (vv.1-8).
2. Issue 2: purity in the military camp (a picture of being spiritually clean) (vv.9-14).
3. Issue 3: escaped slaves (a lesson on mercy—life, liberty, and justice) (vv.15-16).
4. Issue 4: prostitution (vv.17-18).
5. Issue 5: charging interest (vv.19-20).
6. Issue 6: vows (vv.21-23).
7. Issue 7: property rights (vv.24-25).

1 (23:1-8) **Worship, Duty—Discipline, Spiritual—Church Discipline**: the first issue concerns just who is to be excluded from the assembly of God's people, from their worship. This point is a strong lesson on the need for pure worship. The word *assembly* (qahal) refers to the people of God, particularly when they gather together for worship.[1] Not all people are allowed to worship God. Why? Because they are unclean. The worship of God is to be kept clean, for God is pure and holy. Therefore, various categories of unclean people were not allowed to approach and worship God at their whim, as they wished and willed. Note the people who were to be excluded from the assembly of worship:

OUTLINE	SCRIPTURE	SCRIPTURE	OUTLINE
1. Issue 1: Who is to be excluded from the assembly (a lesson on the need for pure worship) a. The castrated man b. The illegitimate child or child born of a forbidden marriage & his descendants—through ten generations c. The Ammonite or the Moabite & his descendants—through ten generations	He that is wounded in the stones, or hath his privy member cut off, shall not enter into the congregation of the LORD. 2 A bastard shall not enter into the congregation of the LORD; even to his tenth generation shall he not enter into the congregation of the LORD. 3 An Ammonite or Moabite shall not enter into the congregation of the LORD; even to their tenth generation shall	they not enter into the congregation of the LORD for ever: 4 Because they met you not with bread and with water in the way, when ye came forth out of Egypt; and because they hired against thee Balaam the son of Beor of Pethor of Mesopotamia, to curse thee. 5 Nevertheless the LORD thy God would not hearken unto Balaam; but the LORD	 1) Because they did not help God's people during the wilderness wanderings 2) Because they hired the false prophet Balaam to curse God's people 3) Because God loves His people: Demonstrated by turning the curse into a

---
[1] Peter C. Craigie, *The Book of Deuteronomy*, p.296.

DEUTERONOMY 23:1-25

OUTLINE	SCRIPTURE	SCRIPTURE	OUTLINE
blessing	thy God turned the curse into a blessing unto thee, because the LORD thy God loved thee.	Edomite; for he *is* thy brother: thou shalt not abhor an Egyptian; because thou wast a stranger in his land.	& their descendants—through two generations 1) Must not abhor them
4) Because God has issued a permanent decree: No treaty is ever to be made with them d. The Edomite & the Egyptian	6 Thou shalt not seek their peace nor their prosperity all thy days for ever. 7 Thou shalt not abhor an	8 The children that are begotten of them shall enter into the congregation of the LORD in their third generation.	2) Must allow their generation to assemble & worship

    a. The castrated man was to be excluded (v.1). Obviously, this refers to the person who had himself castrated for pagan religious purposes. This castrated man had been involved in false worship, the worship of a false god or idol. Consequently, he was forbidden to enter the congregation of God's people, prohibited from worshipping the only true and living LORD (Jehovah, Yahweh). What about the person whose reproductive organs had been damaged or mutilated by accident or illness? Knowing the mercy of God, this person was most likely allowed to participate in the worship of the LORD.

    b. The illegitimate child or child born of a forbidden marriage and his descendants were forbidden to worship with God's people. Note that this included ten generations of the person (v.2). The Hebrew word for *illegitimate birth* or *bastard* or *forbidden marriage* (mamzer) is used only twice in the Old Testament and its specific meaning is unknown. Most likely, it refers to children who were born as a result of some incestuous relationship or to some cult prostitute.[2] It could also refer to a child who had been born to a mixed marriage between an Israelite and a foreign unbeliever. Two facts should be noted:

⇒ This law was a strong deterrent against adulterous, immoral behavior.
⇒ This law stressed the importance of pure worship in the eyes of God.

    c. The Ammonites or Moabites and their descendants were not allowed to worship with God's people, even down through ten generations (vv.3-6). Four reasons are given for their exclusion:

⇒ because they did not help God's people during the wilderness wanderings (v.4; see outline and notes—De.2:24-3:11 for more discussion).
⇒ because they hired the false prophet Balaam to curse God's people (v.4; see outline and notes—Nu.22:1-24:25 for more discussion).
⇒ because God loved the Israelites. His love was demonstrated by turning the curse of Balaam into a blessing (v.5).
⇒ because God had issued a permanent decree, that no treaty was ever to be made with these two nations (v.6).

    The Ammonites and Moabites were an evil, cruel, savage people. It would take generations of righteous influence before their hearts could be softened enough to undergo a permanent change for righteousness. Therefore, they were not allowed to worship with God's people down through ten generations.

    d. The Edomites and Egyptians and their descendants were not allowed to worship with God's people, down through two generations (vv.7-8). Note the instructions given to the Israelites: they were not to abhor the Egyptians, because they had lived as aliens in their country (v.7). Remember that the Egyptians had exalted Joseph to be second only to Pharaoh, and they had allowed Jacob and his descendants to live in Egypt as free citizens for some time. For this reason, if an Egyptian became a true convert to the LORD God, he was to be allowed to worship with God's people after two generations.

    Thought 1. The lessons for us are clear:
(1) We must know that God will not share His glory with another.

> "I *am* the LORD: that *is* my name: and my glory will I not give to another, neither my praise to graven images" (Is.42:8).

(2) We must guard ourselves against the deception of false worship, against turning aside and serving false gods.

> "Take heed to yourselves, that your heart be not deceived, and ye turn aside, and serve other gods, and worship them" (De.11:16).

(3) We must worship and bow before the only living and true God.

> "O come, let us worship and bow down: let us kneel before the LORD our maker" (Ps.95:6).
> "Ye *are* my witnesses, saith the LORD, and my servant whom I have chosen: that ye may know and believe me, and understand that I *am* he: before me there was no God formed, neither shall there be after me. I, *even* I, *am* the LORD; and beside me *there is* no saviour" (Is.43:10-11).

(4) We must worship God in spirit and in truth.

> "God *is* a Spirit: and they that worship him must worship *him* in spirit and in truth" (Jn.4:24).
> "Saying with a loud voice, Fear God, and give glory to him; for the hour of his judgment is come: and worship him that made heaven, and earth, and the sea, and the fountains of waters" (Re.14:7).
> "O worship the LORD in the beauty of holiness: fear before him, all the earth" (Psalm 96:9).

---

[2] Peter C. Craigie. *The Book of Deuteronomy*, p.297.

DEUTERONOMY 23:1-25

(5) We must fear God and give glory to Him and Him alone.

"Saying with a loud voice, Fear God, and give glory to him; for the hour of his judgment is come: and worship him that made heaven, and earth, and the sea, and the fountains of waters" (Re.14:7).
"O worship the LORD in the beauty of holiness: fear before him, all the earth" (Ps.96:9).

(6) We must worship the LORD our God and Him only.

"Then saith Jesus unto him, Get thee hence, Satan: for it is written, Thou shalt worship the LORD thy God, and him only shalt thou serve" (Mt.4:10).
"LORD, I have loved the habitation of thy house, and the place where thine honour dwelleth" (Ps.26:8).
"One *thing* have I desired of the LORD, that will I seek after; that I may dwell in the house of the LORD all the days of my life, to behold the beauty of the LORD, and to enquire in his temple" (Ps.27:4).

(7) We must know that the unrighteous are not accepted by God, that they are excluded from the presence of God and will be excluded forever.

"For I say unto you, That except your righteousness shall exceed *the righteousness* of the scribes and Pharisees, ye shall in no case enter into the kingdom of heaven" (Mt.5:20).
"Not every one that saith unto me, LORD, LORD, shall enter into the kingdom of heaven; but he that doeth the will of my Father which is in heaven. Many will say to me in that day, LORD, LORD, have we not prophesied in thy name? and in thy name have cast out devils? and in thy name done many wonderful works? And then will I profess unto them, I never knew you: depart from me, ye that work iniquity" (Mt.7:21-23).
"Verily I say unto you, Whosoever shall not receive the kingdom of God as a little child, he shall not enter therein" (Mk.10:15).
"Know ye not that the unrighteous shall not inherit the kingdom of God? Be not deceived: neither fornicators, nor idolaters, nor adulterers, nor effeminate, nor abusers of themselves with mankind" (1 Co.6:9).
"Now this I say, brethren, that flesh and blood cannot inherit the kingdom of God; neither doth corruption inherit incorruption" (1 Co.15:50).
"And there shall in no wise enter into it any thing that defileth, neither *whatsoever* worketh abomination, or *maketh* a lie: but they which are written in the Lamb's book of life" (Re.21:27).

2 (23:9-14) **Cleanliness, Duty—Military, Camp of—Spiritual Cleanliness, Duty—Cleanliness, Spiritual:** the second issue concerns purity in the military camp. Very simply, when the Israelites were engaged in a military campaign, they were to maintain a clean camp. Personal hygiene and sanitation are of concern to God. The practicality of this passage is clearly seen:

OUTLINE	SCRIPTURE	SCRIPTURE	OUTLINE

2. Issue 2: Purity in the military camp (a picture of being spiritually clean)
 a. Must flee everything impure
 b. The two examples given
   1) A man is unclean due to a nighttime discharge
 	
     • To go outside the camp
 	
     • To wash himself
     • To return at sunset
 	
   2) A place for a latrine was
	9 When the host goeth forth against thine enemies, then keep thee from every wicked thing.
	 10 If there be among you any man, that is not clean by reason of uncleanness that chanceth him by night, then shall he go abroad out of the camp, he shall not come within the camp:
	 11 But it shall be, when evening cometh on, he shall wash *himself* with water: and when the sun is down, he shall come into the camp *again*.
	 12 Thou shalt have a place
		also without the camp, whither thou shalt go forth abroad:
		 13 And thou shalt have a paddle upon thy weapon; and it shall be, when thou wilt ease thyself abroad, thou shalt dig therewith, and shalt turn back and cover that which cometh from thee:
		 14 For the LORD thy God walketh in the midst of thy camp, to deliver thee, and to give up thine enemies before thee; therefore shall thy camp be holy: that he see no unclean thing in thee, and turn away from thee.
			to be marked off: Were to cover the waste with each relief
			
			 c. The reasons why God gave this law on purity
			   1) To protect God's people
			   2) To teach the truth that God is holy & cannot look upon any unclean thing

a. The Israelite soldier was to keep away or flee from everything impure (v.9). He was to protect himself from anything that was unclean, from all pollution. He was not to pollute the streams, air, water, or ground. He was to protect the environment.
b. Note the two examples given to illustrate exactly what God meant by this law (vv.10-13).
  1) A man was considered unclean due to a nighttime discharge (vv.10-11). This refers either to the accidental wetting of a bed at night or to what is commonly known as a "wet dream," that is, a nighttime emission of semen (see Le.15:16-17). If some emission occurred during the night, the soldier was to go outside the camp and wash himself.

He was not allowed to return until sunset (v.11). Note how this law prevented uncleanness and the possible spread of disease. Having to stay up all night outside the camp served as a deterrent to pollution and uncleanness.

    2) A latrine was to be marked off (vv.12-13). Note that a soldier was to dig a hole and bury his excrement.
- c. Three reasons are given for this law (v.14).
  1) God gave this law to protect His people. God is interested in cleanliness. In fact, Scripture teaches that cleanliness is closely related to godliness. God wants His people clean in body, and He wants the environment of His people to be clean. Pollution and contamination cause disease, plagues, and death. Therefore, personal hygiene is of critical concern to God. He wants His people protected by eliminating pollution and keeping the earth and its water and air clean and pure.
  2) God gave this law to His people because God is holy and He cannot look upon any unclean, indecent thing. Therefore, God's people must be holy. They must keep their camp and environment clean and pure, free from pollution and contamination. God moves about the camp and throughout the environment of His people; therefore, the camp and environment must be kept clean for His presence. God will not tolerate uncleanness, pollution, or contamination. He withdraws His presence from filth and defilement.
  3) Note that the living quarters and the environment of God's people are to be kept clean, for God's eyes are always looking upon His people. If there is any defilement, any uncleanness whatsoever, God sees it. And God will not look upon evil, upon any defilement or uncleanness.

Thought 1. This is a picture of personal hygiene, but it is also a picture of spiritual cleansing. The body of the believer is the temple of the Holy Spirit: that is, the Spirit of God lives within the human body of the believer. Consequently, the believer is to keep both his body and his spirit clean. But not only this: when God created the earth, He put the earth under the dominion and control of man. Man is responsible for looking after the earth, guarding it against pollution and contamination. Man is to keep the earth clean, maintaining pure air, water, forests, and soil. This is the clear declaration of Scripture:

> "What? know ye not that your body is the temple of the Holy Ghost *which is* in you, which ye have of God, and ye are not your own? For ye are bought with a price: therefore glorify God in your body, and in your spirit, which are God's" (1 Co.6:19-20).
>
> "Having therefore these promises, dearly beloved, let us cleanse ourselves from all filthiness of the flesh and spirit, perfecting holiness in the fear of God" (2 Co.7:1).
>
> "In the beginning God created the heaven and the earth" (Ge.1:1).
>
> "And God blessed them, and God said unto them, Be fruitful, and multiply, and replenish the earth, and subdue it: and have dominion over the fish of the sea, and over the fowl of the air, and over every living thing that moveth upon the earth. And God said, Behold, I have given you every herb bearing seed, which *is* upon the face of all the earth, and every tree, in the which *is* the fruit of a tree yielding seed; to you it shall be for meat. And to every beast of the earth, and to every fowl of the air, and to every thing that creepeth upon the earth, wherein *there is* life, *I have given* every green herb for meat: and it was so. And God saw every thing that he had made, and, behold, *it was* very good. And the evening and the morning were the sixth day" (Ge.1:28-31).
>
> "Thou madest him to have dominion over the works of thy hands; thou hast put all *things* under his feet" (Ps.8:6).
>
> "The earth *is* the LORD's, and the fulness thereof; the world, and they that dwell therein" (Ps.24:1).
>
> "Wash you, make you clean; put away the evil of your doings from before mine eyes; cease to do evil" (Is.1:16).

3 (23:15-16) **Slavery, Duty—Liberty, Duty—Justice, Duty—Slaves, Escape—Laws, Governing Escaped Slaves**: the third issued concerns escaped slaves who sought refuge with God's people. The land of Israel was made a sanctuary for slaves who were wronged by their masters. The Israelites were to become a shelter, a refuge from the storm of slavery abuse. Giving sanctuary to slaves was contrary to all known laws in the ancient world. Escaped slaves and other fugitives were to be returned to their masters. But not among God's people. Slaves were to be given sanctuary among God's people and even allowed to live wherever they wished within the nation of Israel. Under no circumstances were they to be oppressed (v.16).

OUTLINE	SCRIPTURE	SCRIPTURE	OUTLINE
3. Issue 3: Escaped slaves (a lesson on mercy—life, liberty, & justice)	15 Thou shalt not deliver unto his master the servant which is escaped from his master unto thee:	*even* among you, in that place which he shall choose in one of thy gates, where it liketh him best: thou shalt not oppress him.	allowed to live wherever he wished b. Must not be oppressed
a. Must be given sanctuary &	16 He shall dwell with thee,		

Thought 1. This is a strong lesson on the mercy of God, on His concern for life, liberty, and justice. No human being is to be enslaved. God's people are to have mercy and give sanctuary to any person who has escaped slavery. But the meaning of this law can be extended much further. The believer is to reach out and provide sanctuary and help to any person in need. Mercy is to fill the heart of the believer. We are to show compassion to any person who is in need.

> "Jesus said unto him, If thou wilt be perfect, go *and* sell that thou hast, and give to the poor, and thou shalt have treasure in heaven: and come *and* follow me" (Mt.19:21).
>
> "And the second *is* like unto it, Thou shalt love thy neighbour as thyself" (Mt.22:39).

"If I then, *your* LORD and Master, have washed your feet; ye also ought to wash one another's feet" (Jn.13:14).

"A new commandment I give unto you, That ye love one another; as I have loved you, that ye also love one another. By this shall all *men* know that ye are my disciples, if ye have love one to another" (Jn.13:34-35).

"This is my commandment, That ye love one another, as I have loved you" (Jn.15:12).

"*Let* love be without dissimulation. Abhor that which is evil; cleave to that which is good" (Ro.12:9).

"Only *they would* that we should remember the poor; the same which I also was forward to do" (Ga.2:10).

"Bear ye one another's burdens, and so fulfil the law of Christ" (Ga.6:2).

"As we have therefore opportunity, let us do good unto all *men*, especially unto them who are of the household of faith" (Ga.6:10).

"With good will doing service, as to the LORD, and not to men" (Ep.6:7).

"If a brother or sister be naked, and destitute of daily food, And one of you say unto them, Depart in peace, be ye warmed and filled; notwithstanding ye give them not those things which are needful to the body; what *doth it* profit? Even so faith, if it hath not works, is dead, being alone. Yea, a man may say, Thou hast faith, and I have works: show me thy faith without thy works, and I will show thee my faith by my works" (Js.2:15-18).

"But whoso hath this world's good, and seeth his brother have need, and shutteth up his bowels *of compassion* from him, how dwelleth the love of God in him" (1 Jn.3:17).

"Defend the poor and fatherless: do justice to the afflicted and needy" (Ps.82:3).

"Whoso stoppeth his ears at the cry of the poor, he also shall cry himself, but shall not be heard" (Pr.21:13).

4 (23:17-18) **Prostitution, Duty—Law, Governing Prostitution—Prostitution, Law Governing—Stewardship, Duty—Offerings, What Is Acceptable and Not Acceptable**: the fourth issue concerns prostitution and the money earned from prostitution. In the ancient world, religious or temple prostitution became a common practice. Prostitution became a corruption of worship, a fertility ritual that celebrated the harvesting of the crops. The worshipper offered his thanksgiving by participating in the fertility ritual of prostitution. God's people were forbidden to participate in such corruption, prohibited from participating in the wicked practice of prostitution. Note also that no man or woman was to become a religious or temple prostitute; neither were they allowed to bring the money from prostitution into the house of the LORD. They were not to use the money gained from prostitution to pay vows or pledges. The reason is clearly stated: God detests prostitution. And He detests the money that comes from prostitution. Such money is looked upon by God as *corrupt money* or *dirty money*.

OUTLINE	SCRIPTURE	SCRIPTURE	OUTLINE
4. Issue 4: Prostitution a. Must not become a prostitute b. Must not bring money secured by prostitution (nor by	17 There shall be no whore of the daughters of Israel, nor a sodomite of the sons of Israel. 18 Thou shalt not bring the hire of a whore, or the price	of a dog, into the house of the LORD thy God for any vow: for even both these *are* abomination unto the LORD thy God.	any other evil means) into the house of God nor use the money to pay vows or pledges c. The reason: God detests this

Thought 1. Lax morals are sweeping the world today. Prostitution is a common practice within every nation. A people must remember that society can become so immoral that God is forced to give up on them, turning them over to their unbridled lusts. If people refuse to repent of their immorality, God has to give them up to the burning of their passion and lusts. And once God has given them up to do their own thing, they are doomed to bear the judgment of God. They are to bear the eternal judgment and condemnation of God. This is the clear declaration of Scripture:

"For the wrath of God is revealed from heaven against all ungodliness and unrighteousness of men, who hold the truth in unrighteousness....Wherefore God also gave them up to uncleanness through the lusts of their own hearts, to dishonour their own bodies between themselves: Who changed the truth of God into a lie, and worshipped and served the creature more than the Creator, who is blessed for ever. Amen. For this cause God gave them up unto vile affections: for even their women did change the natural use into that which is against nature: And likewise also the men, leaving the natural use of the woman, burned in their lust one toward another; men with men working that which is unseemly, and receiving in themselves that recompence of their error which was meet. And even as they did not like to retain God in *their* knowledge, God gave them over to a reprobate mind, to do those things which are not convenient; Being filled with all unrighteousness, fornication, wickedness, covetousness, maliciousness; full of envy, murder, debate, deceit, malignity; whisperers, Backbiters, haters of God, despiteful, proud, boasters, inventors of evil things, disobedient to parents, Without understanding, covenantbreakers, without natural affection, implacable, unmerciful: Who knowing the judgment of God, that they which commit such things are worthy of death, not only do the same, but have pleasure in them that do them" (Ro.1:18, 24-32).

"Know ye not that the unrighteous shall not inherit the kingdom of God? Be not deceived: neither fornicators, nor idolaters, nor adulterers, nor effeminate, nor abusers of themselves with mankind, Nor thieves, nor covetous, nor drunkards, nor revilers, nor extortioners, shall inherit the kingdom of God" (1 Co.6:9-10).

DEUTERONOMY 23:1-25

"Now the works of the flesh are manifest, which are *these;* Adultery, fornication, uncleanness, lasciviousness, Idolatry, witchcraft, hatred, variance, emulations, wrath, strife, seditions, heresies, Envyings, murders, drunkenness, revellings, and such like: of the which I tell you before, as I have also told *you* in time past, that they which do such things shall not inherit the kingdom of God" (Ga.5:19-21).

"But the fearful, and unbelieving, and the abominable, and murderers, and whoremongers, and sorcerers, and idolaters, and all liars, shall have their part in the lake which burneth with fire and brimstone: which is the second death" (Re.21:8).

5 (23:19-20) **Law, Civil—Loans, Duty—Poverty, Duty—Society, Duty—Needy, the—Poor, the—Interest, Charging, Duty**: the fifth issue concerns making loans and charging interest to a needy brother. Very simply, interest was not to be charged to the needy. Note that this passage is not dealing with what the modern world calls commercial loans. It is dealing with...

- a neighbor becoming poverty-stricken and needing help
- some person within the community being poor due to a handicap or being unskilled and unable to find employment; therefore, he has to borrow in order to eat

In such situations, the believer was to lend freely. He was not to charge interest to a brother in need, not to charge interest on anything. However, he could charge interest to foreigners. No doubt, the loan made to a foreigner would be for business purposes and interest would be expected.

A very special promise was made to the person who obeyed this law. If a person obeyed, God would bless his labor, bless everything he did.

OUTLINE	SCRIPTURE	SCRIPTURE	OUTLINE
5. Issue 5: Charging interest a. Must lend freely, not charge interest to a brother in need: Not on anything b. May charge interest to foreigners	19 Thou shalt not lend upon usury to thy brother; usury of money, usury of victuals, usury of any thing that is lent upon usury: 20 Unto a stranger thou mayest lend upon usury; but	unto thy brother thou shalt not lend upon usury: that the LORD thy God may bless thee in all that thou settest thine hand to in the land whither thou goest to possess it.	c. The reason: God will bless your labor

Thought 1. Believers are to show compassion for the needy of this earth, doing all they can to meet their needs. We are never to take advantage of the poor and needy, not by charging them interest on money loaned or given to them.

"And if thy brother be waxen poor, and fallen in decay with thee; then thou shalt relieve him: *yea, though he be* a stranger, or a sojourner; that he may live with thee. Take thou no usury of him, or increase: but fear thy God; that thy brother may live with thee. Thou shalt not give him thy money upon usury, nor lend him thy victuals for increase" (Le.25:35-37).

"If there be among you a poor man of one of thy brethren within any of thy gates in thy land which the LORD thy God giveth thee, thou shalt not harden thine heart, nor shut thine hand from thy poor brother" (De.15:7).

"Thou shalt not lend upon usury [interest] to thy brother; usury of money, usury of victuals, usury of any thing that is lent upon usury: Unto a stranger thou mayest lend upon usury; but unto thy brother thou shalt not lend upon usury: that the LORD thy God may bless thee in all that thou settest thine hand to in the land whither thou goest to possess it" (De.23:19-20).

"And I was very angry when I heard their cry and these words. Then I consulted with myself, and I rebuked the nobles, and the rulers, and said unto them, Ye exact usury, every one of his brother. And I set a great assembly against them. And I said unto them, We after our ability have redeemed our brethren the Jews, which were sold unto the heathen; and will ye even sell your brethren? or shall they be sold unto us? Then held they their peace, and found nothing *to answer.* Also I said, It *is* not good that ye do: ought ye not to walk in the fear of our God because of the reproach of the heathen our enemies? I likewise, *and* my brethren, and my servants, might exact of them money and corn: I pray you, let us leave off this usury. Restore, I pray you, to them, even this day, their lands, their vineyards, their oliveyards, and their houses, also the hundredth *part* of the money, and of the corn, the wine, and the oil, that ye exact of them. Then said they, We will restore *them,* and will require nothing of them; so will we do as thou sayest. Then I called the priests, and took an oath of them, that they should do according to this promise" (Ne.5:6-12).

"*He that* putteth not out his money to usury, nor taketh reward against the innocent. He that doeth these *things* shall never be moved" (Ps.15:5).

"He that by usury and unjust gain increaseth his substance, he shall gather it for him that will pity the poor" (Pr.28:8).

"He *that* hath not given forth upon usury, neither hath taken any increase, *that* hath withdrawn his hand from iniquity, hath executed true judgment between man and man" (Eze.18:8; see vv.13, 17).

"Hath given forth upon usury, and hath taken increase: shall he then live? he shall not live: he hath done all these abominations; he shall surely die; his blood shall be upon him" (Eze.18:13).

"In thee have they taken gifts to shed blood; thou hast taken usury and increase, and thou hast greedily gained of thy neighbours by extortion, and hast forgotten me, saith the LORD GOD" (Eze.22:12).

DEUTERONOMY 23:1-25

6 (23:21-23) **Vows, Duty—Pledges, Duty—Law, Governing Vows—Pledges, Laws Governing**: the sixth issue concerns the making and keeping of vows. Once a person had made a vow or pledge to the LORD, he was to keep it as soon as possible. Note the Scripture and outline:

OUTLINE	SCRIPTURE	SCRIPTURE	OUTLINE

6. Issue 6: Vows
a. Must not be slow to pay your vows or pledges to God
  1) Because God demands payment
  2) Because refusal is sin
b. Must know that it is better not to make a vow than to
	21 When thou shalt vow a vow unto the LORD thy God, thou shalt not slack to pay it: for the LORD thy God will surely require it of thee; and it would be sin in thee.
	22 But if thou shalt forbear to vow, it shall be no sin in
		thee.
		23 That which is gone out of thy lips thou shalt keep and perform; *even* a freewill offering, according as thou hast vowed unto the LORD thy God, which thou hast promised with thy mouth.
			make it & not fulfill it
			c. Must do exactly what you vow or pledge: Because all vows are freely made, never demanded by God

Vows are to be taken seriously, for God accepts a vow or pledge when it is made. He expects the vow to be kept. He expects the pledge to be paid. Three clear expectations are given in this passage:

⇒ A person must not be slow to pay his vow or pledge to God (v.21). The reason is clear: because God demands payment, and refusing to pay one's vow is sin.
⇒ A person must know that it is better not to make a vow than to make it and not fulfill it (v.22).
⇒ A person must do exactly what he vows or pledges, for all vows are freely made. They are never demanded by God (v.23). All vows are voluntary, made of a person's own free will, not requested by God. No person is ever forced to make a vow or pledge to God. Consequently, when a pledge or vow is made, a person must keep his vow and pay his pledge. His word—integrity and character—is at stake.

"For if there be first a willing mind, *it is* accepted according to that a man hath, *and* not according to that he hath not" **(2 Co.8:12).**

"But this *I say*, He which soweth sparingly shall reap also sparingly; and he which soweth bountifully shall reap also bountifully" **(2 Co.9:6).**

"Every man according as he purposeth in his heart, *so let him give;* not grudgingly, or of necessity: for God loveth a cheerful giver" **(2 Co.9:7).**

"When thou shalt vow a vow unto the LORD thy God, thou shalt not slack to pay it: for the LORD thy God will surely require it of thee; and it would be sin in thee. But if thou shalt forbear to vow, it shall be no sin in thee. That which is gone out of thy lips thou shalt keep and perform; *even* a freewill offering, according as thou hast vowed unto the LORD thy God, which thou hast promised with thy mouth" **(De.23:21-23).**

"What shall I render unto the LORD *for* all his benefits toward me" **(Ps.116:12).**

"*It is* a snare to the man *who* devoureth *that which is* holy, and after vows to make enquiry" **(Pr.20:25).**

"When thou vowest a vow unto God, defer not to pay it; for *he hath* no pleasure in fools: pay that which thou hast vowed. Better *is it* that thou shouldest not vow, than that thou shouldest vow and not pay. Suffer not thy mouth to cause thy flesh to sin; neither say thou before the angel, that it *was* an error: wherefore should God be angry at thy voice, and destroy the work of thine hands" **(Ec.5:4-6).**

7 (23:24-25) **Property Rights, Protection of—Rights, of Property—Laws, Governing Property Rights—Mercy, Duty of—Compassion, Duty of**: the seventh issued concerns property rights. The example given illustrates how carefully a person's property was to be protected. If a traveler from some distance away was passing through a neighbor's (Israelite's) vineyard, he could refresh himself by eating some grapes, but he could not fill his basket (v.24). If he passed through a field, he could fill his hand with grain, but he could not harvest or steal the grain (v.25). Note two significant facts in this law:

⇒ A person's property was protected.
⇒ A property owner was to show compassion to a long-distance traveler by letting him refresh himself in his fields.

OUTLINE	SCRIPTURE	SCRIPTURE	OUTLINE
7. Issue 7: Property rights a. Example 1: If you pass through a neighbor's vineyard, you may eat some grapes but not fill a basket	24 When thou comest into thy neighbour's vineyard, then thou mayest eat grapes thy fill at thine own pleasure; but thou shalt not put *any* in thy vessel. 25 When thou comest into	the standing corn of thy neighbour, then thou mayest pluck the ears with thine hand; but thou shalt not move a sickle unto thy neighbour's standing corn.	b. Example 2: If you pass through a field, you may fill your hand with grain but not harvest & steal the grain

Thought 1. Two clear lessons are seen in this point:
(1) We must respect the property rights of others. We must never damage nor destroy the property of others. Neither are we to steal the property of others.

"Not purloining [stealing], but showing all good fidelity; that they may adorn the doctrine of God our Saviour in all things" **(Tit.2:10).**

"But let none of you suffer as a murderer, or *as* a thief, or *as* an evildoer, or *as* a busybody in other men's matters" **(1 Pe.4:15).**

"Let him that stole steal no more: but rather let him labour, working with *his* hands the thing which is good, that he may have to give to him that needeth" (Ep.4:28).

"Thou shalt not steal" (Ex.20:15).

"Trust not in oppression, and become not vain in robbery: if riches increase, set not your heart *upon them*" (Ps.62:10).

(2) We must be compassionate to those in need, doing all we can to meet their needs. Whatever property or money we have, it has been given by God. We must, therefore, willingly share our blessings with others, in particular with those who are in need.

"Neither was there any among them that lacked: for as many as were possessors of lands or houses sold them, and brought the prices of the things that were sold, And laid *them* down at the apostles' feet: and distribution was made unto every man according as he had need" (Ac.4:34-35).

"Then the disciples, every man according to his ability, determined to send relief unto the brethren which dwelt in Judaea" (Ac.11:29).

"I have showed you all things, how that so labouring ye ought to support the weak, and to remember the words of the LORD Jesus, how he said, It is more blessed to give than to receive" (Ac.20:35).

"Distributing to the necessity of saints; given to hospitality" (Ro.12:13).

"Therefore if thine enemy hunger, feed him; if he thirst, give him drink: for in so doing thou shalt heap coals of fire on his head" (Ro.12:20).

"How that in a great trial of affliction the abundance of their joy and their deep poverty abounded unto the riches of their liberality" (2 Co.8:2).

"For ye know the grace of our Lord Jesus Christ, that, though he was rich, yet for your sakes he became poor, that ye through his poverty might be rich" (2 Co.8:9).

"And let us not be weary in well doing: for in due season we shall reap, if we faint not. As we have therefore opportunity, let us do good unto all *men,* especially unto them who are of the household of faith" (Ga.6:9-10).

"For even in Thessalonica ye sent once and again unto my necessity" (Ph.4:16).

"But to do good and to communicate [give] forget not: for with such sacrifices God is well pleased" (He.13:16).

TYPES, SYMBOLS, AND PICTURES
(Deuteronomy 23:1-25)

Historical Term	Type or Picture (Scriptural Basis for Each)	Life Application for Today's Believer	Biblical Application
Purity in the Military Camp De.23:9-14	*Purity in the military camp is a picture of personal hygiene, but it is also a picture of spiritual cleansing.* "For the LORD thy God walketh in the midst of thy camp, to deliver thee, and to give up thine enemies before thee; therefore shall thy camp be holy: that he see no unclean thing in thee, and turn away from thee" (De.23:14).	⇒ The body of the believer is the temple of the Holy Spirit: that is, the Spirit of God lives within the human body of the believer. Consequently, the believer is to keep both his body and his spirit clean. But not only this: when God created the earth, He put the earth under the dominion and control of man. Man is responsible for looking after the earth, guarding it against pollution and contamination. Man is to keep the earth clean, maintaining pure air, water, forests, and soil. This is the clear declaration of Scripture.	*"What? know ye not that your body is the temple of the Holy Ghost which is in you, which ye have of God, and ye are not your own? For ye are bought with a price: therefore glorify God in your body, and in your spirit, which are God's"* (1 Co.6:19-20). *"Having therefore these promises, dearly beloved, let us cleanse ourselves from all filthiness of the flesh and spirit, perfecting holiness in the fear of God"* (2 Co. 7:1). *"In the beginning God created the heaven and the earth"* (Ge.1:1). *"And God blessed them, and God said unto them, Be fruitful, and multiply, and replenish the earth, and subdue it: and have dominion over the fish of the sea, and over the fowl of the air, and over every living thing that moveth upon the earth. And God said, Behold, I have given you every herb bearing seed, which is upon*

DEUTERONOMY 23:1-25

Historical Term	Type or Picture (Scriptural Basis for Each)	Life Application for Today's Believer	Biblical Application
			the face of all the earth, and every tree, in the which is the fruit of a tree yielding seed; to you it shall be for meat. And to every beast of the earth, and to every fowl of the air, and to every thing that creepeth upon the earth, wherein there is life, I have given every green herb for meat: and it was so. And God saw every thing that he had made, and, behold, it was very good. And the evening and the morning were the sixth day" (Ge.1:28-31). *"Thou madest him to have dominion over the works of thy hands; thou hast put all things under his feet"* (Ps.8:6). *"The earth is the LORD's, and the fulness thereof; the world, and they that dwell therein"* (Ps.24:1). *"Wash you, make you clean; put away the evil of your doings from before mine eyes; cease to do evil"* (Is.1:16).

DEUTERONOMY 24:1-22

CHAPTER 24

N. Laws That Protect Relationships within Society: How to Prevent Abuse, 24:1-22

1. **The protection of marriage, the issue of divorce & remarriage**
   a. The example or situation
      1) A man marries a woman
         - She later becomes unclean, indecent, a shame
         - He divorces her
      2) The woman later remarries & one of two things happens: The second husband either divorces her or dies
   b. The law: The first husband must not remarry her—they are forbidden to remarry
   c. The reasons
      1) Is detestable to God
      2) Brings sin upon the land: Condones—shows approval of divorce

2. **The protection of a newly married couple**
   a. The law: To be exempted from the military & any other social responsibility
   b. The reason: To nourish the marriage

3. **The protection of livelihood**
   a. Must not take a man's tools as security for debt
   b. The reason: Takes away a man's livelihood

4. **The protection from kidnapping**
   a. The law: To be executed if the kidnapper enslaved the victim
   b. The reason: To purge away the evil

5. **The protection from people with infectious diseases (leprosy)**
   a. Must obey all the laws governing infectious disease (see Le.chs.13-14)
   b. The warning: Must obey or suffer the judgment of God—just as Miriam did

6. **The protection from loan collectors**
   a. The law

When a man hath taken a wife, and married her, and it come to pass that she find no favour in his eyes, because he hath found some uncleanness in her: then let him write her a bill of divorcement, and give *it* in her hand, and send her out of his house.

2 And when she is departed out of his house, she may go and be another man's *wife*.

3 And *if* the latter husband hate her, and write her a bill of divorcement, and giveth *it* in her hand, and sendeth her out of his house; or if the latter husband die, which took her *to be* his wife;

4 Her former husband, which sent her away, may not take her again to be his wife, after that she is defiled; for that *is* abomination before the LORD: and thou shalt not cause the land to sin, which the LORD thy God giveth thee *for* an inheritance.

5 When a man hath taken a new wife, he shall not go out to war, neither shall he be charged with any business: *but* he shall be free at home one year, and shall cheer up his wife which he hath taken.

6 No man shall take the nether or the upper millstone to pledge: for he taketh *a man's* life to pledge.

7 If a man be found stealing any of his brethren of the children of Israel, and maketh merchandise of him, or selleth him; then that thief shall die; and thou shalt put evil away from among you.

8 Take heed in the plague of leprosy, that thou observe diligently, and do according to all that the priests the Levites shall teach you: as I commanded them, *so* ye shall observe to do.

9 Remember what the LORD thy God did unto Miriam by the way, after that ye were come forth out of Egypt.

10 When thou dost lend thy brother any thing, thou shalt not go into his house to fetch his pledge.

11 Thou shalt stand abroad, and the man to whom thou dost lend shall bring out the pledge abroad unto thee.

12 And if the man *be* poor, thou shalt not sleep with his pledge:

13 In any case thou shalt deliver him the pledge again when the sun goeth down, that he may sleep in his own raiment, and bless thee: and it shall be righteousness unto thee before the LORD thy God.

14 Thou shalt not oppress an hired servant *that is* poor and needy, *whether he be* of thy brethren, or of thy strangers that *are* in thy land within thy gates:

15 At his day thou shalt give *him* his hire, neither shall the sun go down upon it; for he *is* poor, and setteth his heart upon it: lest he cry against thee unto the LORD, and it be sin unto thee.

16 The fathers shall not be put to death for the children, neither shall the children be put to death for the fathers: every man shall be put to death for his own sin.

17 Thou shalt not pervert the judgment of the stranger, *nor* of the fatherless; nor take a widow's raiment to pledge:

18 But thou shalt remember that thou wast a bondman in Egypt, and the LORD thy God redeemed thee thence: therefore I command thee to do this thing.

19 When thou cuttest down thine harvest in thy field, and hast forgot a sheaf in the field, thou shalt not go again to fetch it: it shall be for the stranger, for the fatherless, and for the widow: that the LORD thy God may bless thee in all the work of thine hands.

20 When thou beatest thine olive tree, thou shalt not go over the boughs again: it shall be for the stranger, for the fatherless, and for the widow.

21 When thou gatherest the grapes of thy vineyard, thou shalt not glean it afterward: it shall be for the stranger, for the fatherless, and for the widow.

22 And thou shalt remember that thou wast a bondman in the land of Egypt: therefore I command thee to do this thing.

   1) Must respect a borrower's privacy & his home: Not to enter his home to claim the security or pledge, but let him bring it
   2) Must not devastate a needy or poor borrower: Not to keep his cloak as security if he needs it for warmth (to survive)

   b. The reason: Will stir gratitude & the approval of God

7. **The protection of the poor worker**
   a. The law
      1) Must not take advantage of the poor or needy worker
      2) Must pay him full wages & pay on time
   b. The warning: God will hear the cry of the poor & charge you with sin—condemn & judge you

8. **The protection of justice**
   a. The law: A father or child must not be punished for the other
   b. The reason: Each is individually, personally responsible

9. **The protection of the defenseless: Foreigner, orphan, & widow**
   a. The law: Must grant true justice & show compassion
   b. The reason: God delivered, redeemed you from Egypt (a symbol of salvation)

10. **The protection of the food supply for the poor & underprivileged**
    a. The law
       1) Must leave some grain for the poor: Assures the blessing of God upon your work
       2) Must leave some olives for the poor
       3) Must leave some grapes for the poor

    b. The reason: God is the One who has blessed you—saved you from slavery & poverty

DIVISION IV

THE SECOND GREAT THEME PREACHED BY GOD'S AGED SERVANT (PART 2): REMEMBER THE CIVIL AND RELIGIOUS LAWS OF ISRAEL—HELPFUL PRINCIPLES TO GOVERN MAN AND SOCIETY, 12:1–26:19

N. Laws That Protect Relationships within Society: How to Prevent Abuse, 24:1-22

(24:1-22) Introduction: one thing is an absolute essential within any society: good and healthy relationships. No nation can survive without healthy relationships among its citizens. Broken relationships lead to ill will, anger, strife, lawlessness, violence, and killing among neighbors. Sometimes it even leads to insurrection against government. Broken relationships result in the ruin and collapse of any society. The greatest threat to any nation's survival is not from without but from within. A nation of people—in fact, any body of people—can remain strong only if the relationships between people are strong and healthy.

Moses, the aged servant of God, knew the importance of healthy relationships among God's people. Remember, the Israelites were camped in the plains of Moab close to the Jordan River, camped right across from the great city of Jericho. The Israelites are poised to cross the Jordan River into the promised land. But before they enter the land promised by God, one thing is essential: the people must understand the importance of building strong relationships among themselves. They must protect relationships within society, protect the relationships between the various categories of people. They must learn the laws of God that protect these relationships. God revealed these laws for two purposes: to show the Israelites how their society was to be governed, and to show all future societies the very spirit and principles that were to underlie their laws. God gave His law to all people to illustrate the principles that were to govern their relationships to one another. God Himself has a very significant role to play in every society. This is the subject of this most important passage of Scripture: *Laws That Protect Relationships within Society: How to Prevent Abuse,* 24:1-22.

1. The protection of marriage, the issue of divorce and remarriage (vv.1-4).
2. The protection of a newly married couple (v.5).
3. The protection of livelihood (v.6).
4. The protection from kidnapping (v.7).
5. The protection from people with infectious diseases (leprosy) (vv.8-9).
6. The protection from loan collectors (vv.10-13).
7. The protection of the poor worker (vv.14-15).
8. The protection of justice (v.16).
9. The protection of the defenseless: Foreigner, orphan, and widow (vv.17-18).
10. The protection of the food supply for the poor and underprivileged (vv.19-22).

1 **(24:1-4) Marriage, Protection—Remarriage, Law Governing—Law, Governing Marriage, Divorce, and Remarriage—Divorce, Law Governing:** the first law concerned the protection of marriage, in particular the issue of divorce and remarriage. Simply stated, the law governs a man who divorces his wife, who then marries another man who later dies or divorces her. The first husband is not allowed to remarry the woman. Note the Scripture and outline:

OUTLINE	SCRIPTURE	SCRIPTURE	OUTLINE
1. The protection of marriage, the issue of divorce & remarriage a. The example or situation 1) A man marries a woman • She later becomes unclean, indecent, a shame • He divorces her 2) The woman later remarries & one of two things happens: The second husband either divorces her or dies	When a man hath taken a wife, and married her, and it come to pass that she find no favour in his eyes, because he hath found some uncleanness in her: then let him write her a bill of divorcement, and give *it* in her hand, and send her out of his house. 2 And when she is departed out of his house, she may go and be another man's *wife.* 3 And *if* the latter husband hate her, and write her a bill	of divorcement, and giveth *it* in her hand, and sendeth her out of his house; or if the latter husband die, which took her *to be* his wife; 4 Her former husband, which sent her away, may not take her again to be his wife, after that she is defiled; for that *is* abomination before the LORD: and thou shalt not cause the land to sin, which the LORD thy God giveth thee *for* an inheritance.	 b. The law: The first husband must not remarry her—they are forbidden to remarry c. The reasons 1) Is detestable to God 2) Brings sin upon the land: Condones—shows approval of divorce

a. The example given by Moses clearly illustrates the law. A man marries a woman who later becomes unclean and indecent, becoming a shame and an embarrassment to her husband. Consequently, he divorces her. After the divorce, the woman later remarries and one of two things happens: the second husband either dies or divorces her (vv.2-3).

b. The law is clearly stated: the first husband must not remarry her. They are forbidden to remarry because she has become defiled through intercourse with a second man. The reasons for this law were twofold: such a remarriage was detestable to God and would bring sin upon the land. It would condone "cheap marriage," show approval of divorce. It would abuse the covenant of marriage and make divorce too easy. Simply stated, marriage and divorce would become so easy that it would become a *legal* form of committing adultery.[1]

Note this fact: God is not condoning divorce in this passage. He is giving a law to control the problem of divorce and remarriage that already existed within society. From almost the very beginning of human history, the covenant of marriage had been abused through gross acts of immorality and divorce, long before the great book of Deuteronomy was written. Note this fact as well: divorce stems from sin, but divorce itself is not sin. Sometimes divorce is justified due to adultery and life-threatening abuse. God hates divorce, but He loves the divorced person. In fact, God loves all people, regardless of their terrible sins.[2]

"But I say unto you, That whosoever shall put away his wife, saving for the cause of fornication, causeth her to commit adultery: and whosoever shall marry her that is divorced committeth adultery" (Mt.5:32).

"They say unto him, Why did Moses then command to give a writing of divorcement, and to put her away? He saith unto them, Moses because of the hardness of your hearts suffered you to put away your wives: but from the beginning it was not so. And I say unto you, Whosoever shall put away his wife, except *it be* for fornication, and shall marry another, committeth adultery: and whoso marrieth her which is put away doth commit adultery" (Mt.19:7-9).

"What therefore God hath joined together, let not man put asunder" (Mk.10:9).

"Whosoever putteth away his wife, and marrieth another, committeth adultery: and whosoever marrieth her that is put away from *her* husband committeth adultery" (Lu.16:18).

"And unto the married I command, *yet* not I, but the LORD, Let not the wife depart from *her* husband: But and if she depart, let her remain unmarried, or be reconciled to *her* husband: and let not the husband put away *his* wife" (1 Co.7:10-11).

"I will therefore that the younger women marry, bear children, guide the house, give none occasion to the adversary to speak reproachfully" (1 Ti.5:14).

"For every house is builded by some *man;* but he that built all things *is* God" (He.13:4).

2 (24:5) **Marriage, Protection of—Military, Exemption from—Law, Governing a Newly Married Couple—Law, Governing Exemptions from Military Duty**: the second law concerned the protection of a newly married couple from military duty. The newly married couple had one whole year to adjust to married life and to become established as a family. Note also that no other civic duty could be assigned him. The newlyweds were completely free to nurture and nourish their love and union throughout the year. They were to be totally focused upon one another, seeking the happiness that only marriage can bring to a young couple.

OUTLINE	SCRIPTURE

2. The protection of a newly married couple
  a. The law: To be exempted from the military & any other social responsibility
  b. The reason: To nourish the marriage
	5 When a man hath taken a new wife, he shall not go out to war, neither shall he be charged with any business: *but* he shall be free at home one year, and shall cheer up his wife which he hath taken.

Thought 1. What a dynamic lesson for our society! How different marriage would be if we allowed all newlyweds one full year to adjust to marriage! How fewer divorces there would be! This is a strong point stressing the importance of marriage in the eyes of God.

"Wives, submit yourselves unto your own husbands, as unto the LORD" (Ep.5:22).

"Husbands, love your wives, even as Christ also loved the church, and gave himself for it" (Ep.5:25).

"So ought men to love their wives as their own bodies. He that loveth his wife loveth himself" (Ep.5:28).

"Likewise, ye husbands, dwell with *them* according to knowledge, giving honour unto the wife, as unto the weaker vessel, and as being heirs together of the grace of life; that your prayers be not hindered" (1 Pe.3:7).

"And Adam said, This *is* now bone of my bones, and flesh of my flesh: she shall be called Woman, because she was taken out of Man. Therefore shall a man leave his father and his mother, and shall cleave unto his wife: and they shall be one flesh" (Ge.2:23-24).

"Let thy fountain be blessed: and rejoice with the wife of thy youth" (Pr.5:18).

"She looketh well to the ways of her household, and eateth not the bread of idleness" (Pr.31:27).

"Live joyfully with the wife whom thou lovest all the days of the life of thy vanity, which he hath given thee under the sun, all the days of thy vanity: for that *is* thy portion in *this* life, and in thy labour which thou takest under the sun" (Ec.9:9).

---

[1] Peter C. Craigie. *The Book of Deuteronomy*, p.305.
[2] John Maxwell. *The Preacher's Commentary on Deuteronomy*, p.273.

DEUTERONOMY 24:1-22

3 (24:6) **Livelihood, Protection of—Debtor, Protection of—Security, for Debts—Law, Governing the Protection of a Man's Livelihood—Law, Protecting Security for a Debt—Collateral, Law Governing**: the third law concerned the protection of a man's livelihood. When a loan was made to a person in need, some collateral or security was given to the lender. This was necessary to show the good intentions of repaying the loan. This law puts a limit on the collateral or security that could be demanded. The lender must not take a man's tools as security or collateral. The reason is clear: if a man's tools were taken away, he would have no way to earn a livelihood. The example given involves the millstones that were used to grind grain in order to make flour for bread. The millstone was one of the basic tools needed to provide a family's daily bread or living.

OUTLINE	SCRIPTURE

3. The protection of livelihood
  a. Must not take a man's tools as security for debt
  b. The reason: Takes away a man's livelihood
	6 No man shall take the nether or the upper millstone to pledge: for he taketh *a man's* life to pledge.

Thought 1. The believer must never put another person in a state of destitution, a state whereby he cannot earn a livelihood for himself and his family. No matter what his debt to us, we must make sure that the man has the tools necessary to earn a living. We must treat our neighbors just as Scripture declares:

(1) We must do to others what we would have them do to us.

"Therefore all things whatsoever ye would that men should do to you, do ye even so to them: for this is the law and the prophets" (Mt.7:12).

"And as ye would that men should do to you, do ye also to them likewise" (Lu.6:31).

(2) We must love our neighbors as ourselves.

"Thou shalt love thy neighbour as thyself" (Mt.19:19).

"For all the law is fulfilled in one word, *even* in this; Thou shalt love thy neighbour as thyself" (Ga.5:14).

"If ye fulfil the royal law according to the scripture, Thou shalt love thy neighbour as thyself, ye do well" (Js.2:8).

4 (24:7) **Kidnapping, Punishment of—Law, Governing Kidnapping—Kidnapping, Law Governing**: the fourth law concerned the protection from kidnapping. Kidnapping was a common crime in the ancient world, primarily for the purpose of selling the person into slavery or else enslaving the person on one's own property in order to receive cheap labor. The penalty for kidnapping was execution. The evil of kidnapping was to be purged from God's people.

OUTLINE	SCRIPTURE

4. The protection from kidnapping
  a. The law: To be executed if the kidnapper enslaved the victim
  b. The reason: To purge away the evil
	7 If a man be found stealing any of his brethren of the children of Israel, and maketh merchandise of him, or selleth him; then that thief shall die; and thou shalt put evil away from among you.

Thought 1. God keeps an accurate account of abuse and will be swift to judge the kidnapper. Swift and severe judgment is demanded, for the kidnapper...
- abuses the victim
- dehumanizes the victim
- puts the victim at personal risk
- robs the victim of his ability to make choices
- breaks the hearts of loved ones
- often kills or causes the early death of the victim

"If a man be found stealing any of his brethren of the children of Israel, and maketh merchandise of him, or selleth him; then that thief shall die; and thou shalt put evil away from among you" (De.24:7).

"The LORD executeth righteousness and judgment for all that are oppressed" (Ps.103:6).

"And he that stealeth a man, and selleth him, or if he be found in his hand, he shall surely be put to death" (Ex.21:16).

"Know ye not that the unrighteous shall not inherit the kingdom of God? Be not deceived: neither fornicators, nor idolaters, nor adulterers, nor effeminate, nor abusers of themselves with mankind, Nor thieves, nor covetous, nor drunkards, nor revilers, nor extortioners, shall inherit the kingdom of God" (1 Co.6:9-10).

DEUTERONOMY 24:1-22

5 (24:8-9) **Leprosy, Protection from—Infectious Skin Diseases, Protection from—Law, Governing Leprosy—Law, Governing Infectious Skin Diseases**: the fifth law concerned the protection from people with leprosy or infectious skin diseases.

OUTLINE	SCRIPTURE
5. The protection from people with infectious diseases (leprosy)	8 Take heed in the plague of leprosy, that thou observe diligently, and do according to all that the priests the Levites shall teach you: as I commanded them, *so* ye shall observe to do.
a. Must obey all the laws governing infectious disease (see Le.chapters 13-14)	
b. The warning: Must obey or suffer the judgment of God—just as Miriam did	9 Remember what the LORD thy God did unto Miriam by the way, after that ye were come forth out of Egypt.

Note that Moses did not actually cover the laws governing leprosy or skin diseases. Instead, he encouraged the people to do exactly as the priest instructed them (v.8). The laws governing infectious skin diseases were detailed, very detailed; therefore, the priests were to guide the people in protecting themselves from citizens who had leprosy or infectious skin diseases. Standing there preaching, Moses simply instructed the people to obey all the laws as dictated by the priests or Levites. Note the warning: they must obey or else suffer the judgment of God just as Miriam had borne His judgment (v.9). Remember, Miriam had opposed Moses, seeking some of his authority and power in ruling over the people. As a result, God had afflicted Miriam with leprosy (see outline and notes—Nu.12:1-16 for more discussion).

Thought 1. Leprosy or infectious skin disease is a symbol of sin throughout the Bible. The infectious diseases among men paint a picture of just how terrible sin is. Sin is ever present with man, spreading, contaminating, arousing concern and fear among people. Infectious skin disease or leprosy strikes others with hopelessness and death. Sin is exceedingly vile and contagious.

"And he said unto him, Arise, go thy way: thy faith hath made thee whole" (Lu.17:19).

"*There is* no soundness in my flesh because of thine anger; neither *is there any* rest in my bones because of my sin....My wounds stink *and* are corrupt because of my foolishness....For my loins are filled with a loathsome *disease:* and *there is* no soundness in my flesh....For I will declare mine iniquity; I will be sorry for my sin" (Ps.38:3, 5, 7, 18).

"Purge me with hyssop, and I shall be clean: wash me, and I shall be whiter than snow" (Ps.51:7).

"Wash you, make you clean; put away the evil of your doings from before mine eyes; cease to do evil" (Is.1:16).

6 (24:10-13) **Loan Collectors, Protection from—Respect, of Privacy—Privacy, Respect of—Property Rights, Respect of—Law, Governing Loan Collectors—Respect, for the Poor**: the sixth law concerned the protection from loan collectors. When a person made a loan to a neighbor, he was to respect the neighbor and his home. Under no circumstance—no matter how poverty-stricken or destitute—was the lender to enter the home of the borrower, not even to secure collateral or to collect a payment or pledge. Simply stated, he was to respect the privacy and home of the loan recipient. Moreover, if the man was poor or needy, the lender could not keep his cloak as security overnight. Why? Because a poor person needed his garment for warmth by day and by night. Therefore, if the poor person had given his cloak as a pledge or collateral, it was not to be kept overnight. It was to be returned to the person. The reason for this generosity is clearly stated: the lender's act would stir gratitude and be counted as a righteous act in the sight of God.

OUTLINE	SCRIPTURE	SCRIPTURE	OUTLINE
6. The protection from loan collectors	10 When thou dost lend thy brother any thing, thou shalt not go into his house to fetch his pledge.	thou shalt not sleep with his pledge:	needy or poor borrower: Not to keep his cloak as security if he needs it for warmth (to survive)
a. The law		13 In any case thou shalt deliver him the pledge again when the sun goeth down, that he may sleep in his own raiment, and bless thee: and it shall be righteousness unto thee before the LORD thy God.	
1) Must respect a borrower's privacy & his home: Not to enter his home to claim the security or pledge, but let him bring it	11 Thou shalt stand abroad, and the man to whom thou dost lend shall bring out the pledge abroad unto thee.		b. The reason: Will stir gratitude & the approval of God
2) Must not devastate a	12 And if the man *be* poor,		

Thought 1. Believers are to show compassion and care for the needy of this earth. We are to do all we can to meet their needs. We must never devastate a needy brother by demanding so much collateral that he cannot survive. To devastate a person is wrong, a terrible evil.

"Jesus said unto him, If thou wilt be perfect, go *and* sell that thou hast, and give to the poor, and thou shalt have treasure in heaven: and come *and* follow me" (Mt.19:21).

"But so shall it not be among you: but whosoever will be great among you, shall be your minister: And whosoever of you will be the chiefest, shall be servant of all" (Mk.10:43-44).

"Which now of these three, thinkest thou, was neighbour unto him that fell among the thieves? And he said, He that showed mercy on him. Then said Jesus unto him, Go, and do thou likewise" (Lu.10:36-37).

"Only *they would* that we should remember the poor; the same which I also was forward to do" (Ga.2:10).

"Bear ye one another's burdens, and so fulfil the law of Christ" (Ga.6:2).

"As we have therefore opportunity, let us do good unto all *men,* especially unto them who are of the household of faith" (Ga.6:10).

"That they do good, that they be rich in good works, ready to distribute, willing to communicate" (1 Ti.6:18).

"In all things showing thyself a pattern of good works: in doctrine *showing* uncorruptness, gravity, sincerity" (Tit.2:7).

"But to do good and to communicate [give] forget not: for with such sacrifices God is well pleased" (He.13:16).

"Therefore to him that knoweth to do good, and doeth *it* not, to him it is sin" (Js.4:17).

"If there be among you a poor man of one of thy brethren within any of thy gates in thy land which the LORD thy God giveth thee, thou shalt not harden thine heart, nor shut thine hand from thy poor brother" (De.15:7).

"Blessed *is* he that considereth the poor: the LORD will deliver him in time of trouble" (Ps.41:1).

"He that hath pity upon the poor lendeth unto the LORD; and that which he hath given will he pay him again" (Pr.19:17).

[7] **(24:14-15) Worker, Duty toward—Employee, Duty toward—Wages, Duty—Law, Governing the Protection of the Poor—Law, Governing the Protection of the Worker—Employee, Law Governing Wages**: the seventh law concerned the protection of the poor worker.

OUTLINE	SCRIPTURE	SCRIPTURE	OUTLINE

7. The protection of the poor worker
a. The law
  1) Must not take advantage of the poor or needy worker
 	
  2) Must pay him full wages
	14 Thou shalt not oppress an hired servant *that is* poor and needy, *whether he be* of thy brethren, or of thy strangers that *are* in thy land within thy gates:
	15 At his day thou shalt
		give *him* his hire, neither shall the sun go down upon it; for he *is* poor, and setteth his heart upon it: lest he cry against thee unto the LORD, and it be sin unto thee.	& pay on time
			
			b. The warning: God will hear the cry of the poor & charge you with sin—condemn & judge you

This law is clearly stated: you must not take advantage of the poor and needy worker, no matter who he is, even if he is an alien or foreigner. You must pay him full wages and pay him on time. Within Israelite society, the wages were to be paid each day before sunset. This was necessary so that a person could purchase enough food to feed his family for that day. The poor would not have enough money to buy food ahead of time. They survived day by day.

Note the warning: the person who disobeys this law will become guilty of sin and face the judgment of God. The poor man who is cheated out of his wages will cry out to God against his oppressor, and God will hear his cry. The poor man has no one else to whom he can appeal. His only resource is God. Consequently, if he is cheated out of his wages, he is forced to cry out for help from the only person who will hear him, God Himself. Scripture is clear: God will vindicate the cry of the poor who are oppressed. The oppressor is guilty of sin and will face the eternal judgment of God.

"**Masters, give unto *your* servants that which is just and equal; knowing that ye also have a Master in heaven**" (Col.4:1).

"**Go to now, *ye* rich men, weep and howl for your miseries that shall come upon *you.* Your riches are corrupted, and your garments are motheaten. Your gold and silver is cankered; and the rust of them shall be a witness against you, and shall eat your flesh as it were fire. Ye have heaped treasure together for the last days. Behold, the hire of the labourers who have reaped down your fields, which is of you kept back by fraud, crieth: and the cries of them which have reaped are entered into the ears of the LORD of sabaoth. Ye have lived in pleasure on the earth, and been wanton; ye have nourished your hearts, as in a day of slaughter. Ye have condemned *and* killed the just; *and* he doth not resist you**" (Js.5:1-6).

"**Behold, the hire of the labourers who have reaped down your fields, which is of you kept back by fraud, crieth: and the cries of them which have reaped are entered into the ears of the LORD of sabaoth**" (Js.5:4).

"Thou shalt not defraud thy neighbour, neither rob *him:* the wages of him that is hired shall not abide with thee all night until the morning" (Le.19:13).

"Woe unto him that buildeth his house by unrighteousness, and his chambers by wrong; *that* useth his neighbour's service without wages, and giveth him not for his work" (Je.22:13).

"And I will come near to you to judgment; and I will be a swift witness against the sorcerers, and against the adulterers, and against false swearers, and against those that oppress the hireling in *his* wages, the widow, and the fatherless, and that turn aside the stranger *from his right,* and fear not me, saith the LORD of hosts" (Mal.3:5).

DEUTERONOMY 24:1-22

8 (24:16) **Justice, Duty—Responsibility, Personal—Law, Governing the Protection of Justice—Justice, Law Governing Personal Responsibility**: the eighth law concerned the protection of justice, true justice—a justice that declares personal responsibility for crimes committed.

OUTLINE	SCRIPTURE
8. The protection of justice a. The law: A father or child must not be punished for the other b. The reason: Each is individually, personally responsible	16 The fathers shall not be put to death for the children, neither shall the children be put to death for the fathers: every man shall be put to death for his own sin.

Each person is individually, personally responsible for his own crime; therefore, he must personally bear the punishment for the crime. Moses gives the example of a father or a child who steps forth to bear the punishment for the other. There is a tendency among parents to protect their children or among older children to protect their parents when facing the responsibility for a particular crime. The father or child willingly accepts responsibility for the crime in order to protect the other. But God is clear: each individual is responsible for his own behavior, and each individual is to bear the punishment for his behavior. If a parent is guilty, the parent is to bear the punishment of the crime. If the child is guilty, then the child is to bear the punishment of the crime. Every person is responsible for his own behavior. Justice is to be upheld and protected, true justice. The guilty are to be held responsible for their crimes, and they are to bear the punishment for their crimes. Again, a person is to be held individually, personally responsible for his own behavior.

"So then every one of us shall give account of himself to God" (Ro.14:12).

"That which is altogether just shalt thou follow, that thou mayest live, and inherit the land which the LORD thy God giveth thee" (De.16:20).

"And be it indeed *that* I have erred, mine error remaineth with myself" (Jb. 19:4).

"If thou be wise, thou shalt be wise for thyself: but *if* thou scornest, thou alone shalt bear *it*" (Pr.9:12).

"To do justice and judgment *is* more acceptable to the LORD than sacrifice" (Pr.21:3).

"Thus saith the LORD, Keep ye judgment, and do justice: for my salvation *is* near to come, and my righteousness to be revealed" (Is.56:1).

"But every one shall die for his own iniquity: every man that eateth the sour grape, his teeth shall be set on edge" (Je.31:30).

"The soul that sinneth, it shall die. The son shall not bear the iniquity of the father, neither shall the father bear the iniquity of the son: the righteousness of the righteous shall be upon him, and the wickedness of the wicked shall be upon him" (Eze.18:20).

9 (24:17-18) **Defenseless, the, Protection of—Foreigner, Law Governing—Orphan, Law Governing—Widow, Law Governing—Law, Governing the Defenseless—Law, Governing the Needy**: the ninth law concerned the protection of the defenseless—the foreigner, orphan, and widow. The law is clear: a person must grant true justice and show compassion to the underprivileged and defenseless of society. The foreigner has absolutely no way to protect himself; neither does an orphan or poor widow. They are somewhat helpless within society, completely dependent upon the laws and compassion of a community. When dealing with the underprivileged and defenseless, the law of God is clear: they must be granted true justice and shown compassion. The Israelites knew exactly what it meant to be helpless and defenseless, for they had been slaves in Egypt. But they also knew what it was to experience mercy, for God had mercy upon them and delivered them from Egyptian slavery. For this reason, the Israelites were to show compassion upon the less fortunate, the underprivileged, and the defenseless of society.

OUTLINE	SCRIPTURE	SCRIPTURE	OUTLINE
9. The protection of the defenseless: Foreigner, orphan, & widow a. The law: Must grant true justice & show compassion b. The reason: God delivered,	17 Thou shalt not pervert the judgment of the stranger, *nor* of the fatherless; nor take a widow's raiment to pledge: 18 But thou shalt remember	that thou wast a bondman in Egypt, and the LORD thy God redeemed thee thence: therefore I command thee to do this thing.	redeemed you from Egypt (a symbol of salvation)

Thought 1. God has shown compassion to us and redeemed us from the enslavement of sin and death. The lesson for us is clear: we must show compassion and grant true justice to the underprivileged, the defenseless, and the needy of this world. In compassion and mercy, we must reach out to the foreigners, orphans, and widows of our communities. We must do all we can to help them and to meet their needs.

"Give, and it shall be given unto you; good measure, pressed down, and shaken together, and running over, shall men give into your bosom. For with the same measure that ye mete withal it shall be measured to you again" (Lu.6:38).

"Sell that ye have, and give alms; provide yourselves bags which wax not old, a treasure in the heavens that faileth not, where no thief approacheth, neither moth corrupteth" (Lu.12:33).

"And I was afraid, and went and hid thy talent in the earth: lo, *there* thou hast *that is* thine" (Mt.25:35).

DEUTERONOMY 24:1-22

"I have showed you all things, how that so labouring ye ought to support the weak, and to remember the words of the LORD Jesus, how he said, It is more blessed to give than to receive" (Ac.20:35).

"Distributing to the necessity of saints; given to hospitality" (Ro.12:13).

"But this *I say*, He which soweth sparingly shall reap also sparingly; and he which soweth bountifully shall reap also bountifully" (2 Co.9:6).

"As we have therefore opportunity, let us do good unto all *men*, especially unto them who are of the household of faith" (Ga.6:10).

"Pure religion and undefiled before God and the Father is this, To visit the fatherless and widows in their affliction, *and* to keep himself unspotted from the world" (Js.1:27).

"Thou shalt neither vex a stranger, nor oppress him: for ye were strangers in the land of Egypt" (Ex.22:21).

"Ye shall not afflict any widow, or fatherless child" (Ex.22:22).

"*But* the stranger that dwelleth with you shall be unto you as one born among you, and thou shalt love him as thyself; for ye were strangers in the land of Egypt: I *am* the LORD your God" (Le.19:34).

"And if thy brother be waxen poor, and fallen in decay with thee; then thou shalt relieve him: *yea, though he be* a stranger, or a sojourner; that he may live with thee" (Le.25:35).

"Thou shalt not pervert the judgment of the stranger, *nor* of the fatherless; nor take a widow's raiment to pledge: But thou shalt remember that thou wast a bondman in Egypt, and the LORD thy God redeemed thee thence: therefore I command thee to do this thing" (De.24:17-18).

"When thou hast made an end of tithing all the tithes of thine increase the third year, *which is* the year of tithing, and hast given *it* unto the Levite, the stranger, the fatherless, and the widow, that they may eat within thy gates, and be filled" (De.26:12).

"Cursed *be* he that perverteth the judgment of the stranger, fatherless, and widow. And all the people shall say, Amen" (De.27:19).

"Gather the people together, men, and women, and children, and thy stranger that *is* within thy gates, that they may hear, and that they may learn, and fear the LORD your God, and observe to do all the words of this law" (De.31:12).

"*Is* not this the fast that I have chosen? to loose the bands of wickedness, to undo the heavy burdens, and to let the oppressed go free, and that ye break every yoke? *Is it* not to deal thy bread to the hungry, and that thou bring the poor that are cast out to thy house? when thou seest the naked, that thou cover him; and that thou hide not thyself from thine own flesh" (Is.58:6-7).

"The liberal soul shall be made fat: and he that watereth shall be watered also himself" (Pr.11:25).

"He that hath a bountiful eye shall be blessed; for he giveth of his bread to the poor" (Pr.22:9).

"Learn to do well; seek judgment, relieve the oppressed, judge the fatherless, plead for the widow" (Is.1:17).

"And *if* thou draw out thy soul to the hungry, and satisfy the afflicted soul; then shall thy light rise in obscurity, and thy darkness *be* as the noonday" (Is.58:10).

10 (24:19-22) **Poor, Duty Toward—Underprivileged, Duty Toward—Law, Governing the Poor and Underprivileged—Needy, Law Governing**: the tenth law concerned the protection of the food supply for the poor and underprivileged. When Israel crossed the Jordan River and entered the promised land, there would be some persons who would eventually become poor. Poverty is caused by a host of reasons: bad judgment, poor business skills, bad health, accident, natural disaster, laziness, or sin. Consequently, some Israelites would not be sharing directly in the land promised by God, not sharing in the fruit of the land, not having a part in the joy and rejoicing over the harvest of the land. This law was established so the poor and underprivileged would have a part in the land promised by God. This law allowed them to participate in the fruit of the land.

OUTLINE	SCRIPTURE	SCRIPTURE	OUTLINE

10. The protection of the food supply for the poor & underprivileged
a. The law
  1) Must leave some grain for the poor: Assures the blessing of God upon your work
 	
  2) Must leave some olives for the poor
	19 When thou cuttest down thine harvest in thy field, and hast forgot a sheaf in the field, thou shalt not go again to fetch it: it shall be for the stranger, for the fatherless, and for the widow: that the LORD thy God may bless thee in all the work of thine hands.
	20 When thou beatest thine olive tree, thou shalt not go over the boughs again: it shall
		be for the stranger, for the fatherless, and for the widow.
		21 When thou gatherest the grapes of thy vineyard, thou shalt not glean *it* afterward: it shall be for the stranger, for the fatherless, and for the widow.
		22 And thou shalt remember that thou wast a bondman in the land of Egypt: therefore I command thee to do this thing.
			3) Must leave some grapes for the poor
			
			b. The reason: God is the One who has blessed you—saved you from slavery & poverty

a. The law stipulated that a landowner must leave some grain for the poor (vv.19-21). When harvesting the field, the landowner was not to pick the field clean. He was not to go back over the field a second time. Whatever had been missed was to be left. Note the promise of God: the landowner who obeyed this law would be richly blessed by God, blessed in all his work.

The landowner was also to leave some olives and grapes for the poor (vv.20-21). He was to harvest the olive trees and the grape vines only once, leaving whatever had been missed. This law meant several significant things:

⇒ The poor had to work, harvest their own food, to eat.
⇒ The work gave the poor a sense of purpose, fulfillment, and satisfaction.
⇒ The poor were protected from the humiliation and shame of having to beg and depend upon welfare.

b. The reason why the landowner must obey this law is significant: God is the one who has blessed the landowner. God had compassion upon the landowner of Israel, saved him from slavery and poverty in Egypt (v.22). The implication is clear: the landowner was to show compassion to the poor and underprivileged. He was to protect the food supply in the fields, make sure there was enough for the poor and underprivileged to harvest, enough to provide a livelihood for themselves and their families.

Thought 1. Work or employment must be provided for the poor and underprivileged. Any person who is able to work must be given the opportunity to earn a livelihood for himself and his family. If a person is not able to work—such as a foreigner, orphan, widow or widower—that person must be looked after and fed. We must protect the food supply for the poor and underprivileged, provide for whatever needs they have. This is the strong declaration of Scripture:

"Jesus said unto him, If thou wilt be perfect, go *and* sell that thou hast, and give to the poor, and thou shalt have treasure in heaven: and come *and* follow me" (Mt.19:21).

"I have showed you all things, how that so labouring ye ought to support the weak, and to remember the words of the LORD Jesus, how he said, It is more blessed to give than to receive" (Ac.20:35).

"Only *they would* that we should remember the poor; the same which I also was forward to do" (Ga.2:10).

"If there be among you a poor man of one of thy brethren within any of thy gates in thy land which the LORD thy God giveth thee, thou shalt not harden thine heart, nor shut thine hand from thy poor brother" (De.15:7).

"Every man *shall give* as he is able, according to the blessing of the LORD thy God which he hath given thee" (De.16:17).

"Blessed *is* he that considereth the poor: the LORD will deliver him in time of trouble" (Ps.41:1).

"Defend the poor and fatherless: do justice to the afflicted and needy" (Ps.82:3).

"He that hath pity upon the poor lendeth unto the LORD; and that which he hath given will he pay him again" (Pr.19:17).

"Whoso stoppeth his ears at the cry of the poor, he also shall cry himself, but shall not be heard" (Pr.21:13).

TYPES, SYMBOLS, AND PICTURES
(Deuteronomy 24:1-22)

Historical Term	Type or Picture (Scriptural Basis for Each)	Life Application for Today's Believer	Biblical Application
Leprosy De.24:8-9 (See also Le.13:1-59; Nu.5:1-4; 12:13-16)	Leprosy symbolizes the disease of sin, how contagious it is, and the need to prevent the spread of sin. Leprosy or infectious skin disease is a symbol of sin throughout the Bible. The infectious diseases among men paint a picture of just how terrible sin is. Sin is ever present with man, spreading, contaminating, arousing concern and fear among people. Infectious skin disease or leprosy strikes its victims with hopelessness and death. Sin is exceedingly vile and contagious. "Take heed in the plague of leprosy, that thou observe diligently, and do according to all that the priests the Levites shall teach you: as I commanded them, so ye shall observe to do. Remember what the LORD thy God did unto Miriam by the way, after	⇒ God gave Israel the law governing leprosy or infectious skin disease because He loves His people. God loves us and cares for us; therefore He wants us healthy. He wants us experiencing the fullness of life, worshipping and serving Him. He wants us bearing strong testimony to a world lost and reeling under the weight of desperate need. He wants all of His people throughout all generations healthy.	"And he said unto him, Arise, go thy way: thy faith hath made thee whole" (Lu.17:19). "There is no soundness in my flesh because of thine anger; neither is there any rest in my bones because of my sin....My wounds stink and are corrupt because of my foolishness....For my loins are filled with a loathsome disease: and there is no soundness in my flesh....For I will declare mine iniquity; I will be sorry for my sin" (Ps.38:3, 5, 7, 18). "Purge me with hyssop, and I shall be clean: wash me, and I shall be whiter than snow" (Ps.51:7). "Wash you, make you clean; put away the evil of your doings from before mine eyes; cease to do evil" (Is.1:16; See also Lu.4:18; 3 Jn.1:2; Ex.15:26; De.7:15; Je.30:17). "When Jesus heard it, he saith unto them, They that

DEUTERONOMY 24:1-22

Historical Term	Type or Picture (Scriptural Basis for Each)	Life Application for Today's Believer	Biblical Application
	that ye were come forth out of Egypt" (De.24:8-9).		are whole have no need of the physician, but they that are sick: I came not to call the righteous, but sinners to repentance" (Mk.2:17). "Come, and let us return unto the LORD: for he hath torn, and he will heal us; he hath smitten, and he will bind us up" (Ho.6:1).

DEUTERONOMY 25:1-19

CHAPTER 25

O. Laws That Prevent Wrong Behavior & That Demand Justice, 25:1-19

1. **The wrong of abusive punishment in legal disputes**
   a. The fact: Must take legal disputes before the judge to decide who is wrong & who is right
   b. The law: Limits of corporeal, physical punishment
      1) If flogging was the verdict, two rules were to be observed
         - To be flogged lying down before the judge
         - To limit the flogging to match the crime—not more than 40 lashes
      2) The reason: Inhumane, humiliating punishment

2. **The wrong of muzzling an ox while working: Deserves to eat**

3. **The wrong of refusing to help the wife of a dead brother**
   a. The law: Concerned brothers living on the same property & one of them died without a son
      1) The surviving brother was to marry the widow
      2) The first son was to be counted as the son of the dead brother: To inherit his property & carry on his name
   b. The law if a man refused to marry his brother's widow
      1) The widow was to take the case to court

      2) The judges were to summon & reason with him
      3) The punishment if he continued to refuse: The widow was to symbolically pronounce a curse upon him

If there be a controversy between men, and they come unto judgment, that *the judges* may judge them; then they shall justify the righteous, and condemn the wicked.
2 And it shall be, if the wicked man *be* worthy to be beaten, that the judge shall cause him to lie down, and to be beaten before his face, according to his fault, by a certain number.
3 Forty stripes he may give him, *and* not exceed: lest, *if* he should exceed, and beat him above these with many stripes, then thy brother should seem vile unto thee.
4 Thou shalt not muzzle the ox when he treadeth out *the corn*.
5 If brethren dwell together, and one of them die, and have no child, the wife of the dead shall not marry without unto a stranger: her husband's brother shall go in unto her, and take her to him to wife, and perform the duty of an husband's brother unto her.
6 And it shall be, *that* the firstborn which she beareth shall succeed in the name of his brother *which is* dead, that his name be not put out of Israel.
7 And if the man like not to take his brother's wife, then let his brother's wife go up to the gate unto the elders, and say, My husband's brother refuseth to raise up unto his brother a name in Israel, he will not perform the duty of my husband's brother.
8 Then the elders of his city shall call him, and speak unto him: and *if* he stand *to it*, and say, I like not to take her;
9 Then shall his brother's wife come unto him in the presence of the elders, and loose his shoe from off his foot, and spit in his face, and shall answer and say, So shall it be done unto that man that will not build up his brother's house.
10 And his name shall be called in Israel, The house of him that hath his shoe loosed.
11 When men strive together one with another, and the wife of the one draweth near for to deliver her husband out of the hand of him that smiteth him, and putteth forth her hand, and taketh him by the secrets:
12 Then thou shalt cut off her hand, thine eye shall not pity *her*.
13 Thou shalt not have in thy bag divers weights, a great and a small.
14 Thou shalt not have in thine house divers measures, a great and a small.
15 *But* thou shalt have a perfect and just weight, a perfect and just measure shalt thou have: that thy days may be lengthened in the land which the LORD thy God giveth thee.
16 For all that do such things, *and* all that do unrighteously, *are* an abomination unto the LORD thy God.
17 Remember what Amalek did unto thee by the way, when ye were come forth out of Egypt;
18 How he met thee by the way, and smote the hindmost of thee, *even* all *that were* feeble behind thee, when thou *wast* faint and weary; and he feared not God.
19 Therefore it shall be, when the LORD thy God hath given thee rest from all thine enemies round about, in the land which the LORD thy God giveth thee *for* an inheritance to possess it, *that* thou shalt blot out the remembrance of Amalek from under heaven; thou shalt not forget *it*.

- Remove one of his sandals (symbolized a failure of duty)
- Spit in his face (showed humiliation)

- Given a humiliating title: Known as an irresponsible family

4. **The wrong of excessive force**
   a. The law: Excessive force is not to be used in fights—not even by a woman who seeks to aid her husband

   b. The penalty: A just, equal punishment for the crime (*Lex Talionis*)

5. **The wrong of dishonesty in business dealings**
   a. The law
      1) Must not overcharge when selling (use large weights)
      2) Must not underpay when buying (use smaller weights)
      3) Must be honest in all business dealings
   b. The reasons
      1) Because honesty assures the blessings of God, a longer life
      2) Because God detests any person who cheats & is dishonest

6. **The wrong of a cruel, savage, & inhumane people**
   a. The case of the Amalekites: Stand as an example of cruelty
      1) They brutally attacked the sick, disabled, & elderly who lagged behind the marching divisions of Israel
      2) They did not fear God
   b. The insistence of God: Such cruelty must be judged
      1) To be blotted out
      2) Not to forget this judgment

DIVISION IV

THE SECOND GREAT THEME PREACHED BY GOD'S AGED SERVANT (PART 2): REMEMBER THE CIVIL AND RELIGIOUS LAWS OF ISRAEL—HELPFUL PRINCIPLES TO GOVERN MAN AND SOCIETY, 12:1–26:19

O. **Laws That Prevent Wrong Behavior and That Demand Justice, 25:1-19**

DEUTERONOMY 25:1-19

(25:1-19) **Introduction**: How much wrong or bad behavior is there around us? How much bad behavior occurs in our homes? In our schools? At work? At play? In our times of leisure and recreation? In our churches? In our community? In our society as a whole? In our nation? How much inappropriate or dishonest behavior takes place every day within the world, behavior leading to...

- turmoil
- disease
- coldness
- violence
- cruelty
- pollution
- abuse
- indifference
- excessive force
- savagery
- injury
- injustice
- lawlessness
- dishonesty
- inhumane treatment

Right behavior leads to a life of achievement, success, and fruitfulness. Right behavior gives a person a sense of purpose, satisfaction, and fulfillment in life. But wrong behavior causes all kinds of problems for a person and for his family and friends. Moreover, wrong behavior contributes to the increase of evil behavior throughout society. This is the important subject of this passage of Scripture: *Laws That Prevent Wrong Behavior and That Demand Justice,* 25:1-19.

1. The wrong of abusive punishment in legal disputes (vv.1-3).
2. The wrong of muzzling an ox while working: the animal deserves to eat (v.4).
3. The wrong of refusing to help the wife of a dead brother (vv.5-10).
4. The wrong of excessive force (vv.11-12).
5. The wrong of dishonesty in business dealings (vv.13-16).
6. The wrong of a cruel, savage, and inhumane people (vv.17-19).

1 (25:1-3) **Legal Disputes, Punishment—Legal Punishment, Limits of—Punishment, Limits of Legal—Law, Governing Abuse of Punishment—Crime, Punishment of, Limited**: the first law prevents the wrong of abusive punishment in legal disputes. This law stipulates that legal disputes must be carried before the judge to decide who is right and who is wrong (v.1).

OUTLINE	SCRIPTURE	SCRIPTURE	OUTLINE
1. **The wrong of abusive punishment in legal disputes** a. The fact: Must take legal disputes before the judge to decide who is wrong & who is right b. The law: Limits of corporeal, physical punishment 1) If flogging was the verdict,	If there be a controversy between men, and they come unto judgment, that *the judges* may judge them; then they shall justify the righteous, and condemn the wicked. 2 And it shall be, if the wicked man *be* worthy to be beaten, that the judge shall	cause him to lie down, and to be beaten before his face, according to his fault, by a certain number. 3 Forty stripes he may give him, *and* not exceed: lest, *if* he should exceed, and beat him above these with many stripes, then thy brother should seem vile unto thee.	two rules were to be observed • To be flogged lying down before the judge • To limit the flogging to match the crime—not more than 40 lashes 2) The reason: Inhumane, humiliating punishment

The law that appointed judges to settle legal disputes had already been established. The present law is given to limit corporeal, physical punishment upon the guilty party (vv.2-3). If the guilty party deserved to be flogged, two rules were to be observed:

⇒ The guilty person was to be flogged while lying down before the judge.
⇒ The judge was to limit the flogging to match the crime, never allowing more than forty lashes (v.3). The Jews usually limited the flogging to thirty-nine lashes or less just to make sure that this law was obeyed (see 2 Co.11:24).

The point of this law was to *prevent abusive punishment* in legal cases. Physical, corporeal punishment or flogging could be executed only after a fair trial, and then it had to be carried out before the judge himself. This made sure that the criminal received fair justice, exactly what he deserved—nothing more, nothing less. This law prevented inhumane, humiliating punishment and abusive mistreatment.

Thought 1. Justice—fair and equal justice—is an absolute essential for a strong and healthy society. No partiality or favoritism should ever be shown in the execution of justice. A person found guilty is to receive justice: he is to be treated fairly and equally along with all other citizens. His punishment is to equal the crime, nothing more, nothing less.

"I charge *thee* before God, and the Lord Jesus Christ, and the elect angels, that thou observe these things without preferring one before another, doing nothing by partiality" (1 Ti.5:21).
"Ye shall do no unrighteousness in judgment: thou shalt not respect the person of the poor, nor honour the person of the mighty: *but* in righteousness shalt thou judge thy neighbour" (Le.19:15).
"That which is altogether just shalt thou follow, that thou mayest live, and inherit the land which the LORD thy God giveth thee" (De.16:20).
"He will surely reprove you, if ye do secretly accept persons" (Jb.13:10).
"How long will ye judge unjustly, and accept the persons of the wicked?" (Ps.82:2).
"To do justice and judgment *is* more acceptable to the LORD than sacrifice" (Pr.21:3).

DEUTERONOMY 25:1-19

2 (25:4) **Work, Wages of—Wages, Payment of—Law, Governing the Muzzling of an Ox While Working—Law, Governing the Payment of Wages**: the second law prevents the wrong of muzzling an ox while working. An ox was often used to trample across a threshing floor in order to separate the ears of grain from the stalk. Sometimes the oxen pulled a large millstone that crushed the grain for the making of flour. Whatever the case, the law stipulated that the oxen could not be muzzled while he was treading out the grain. The oxen was working; therefore, he deserved to eat.

OUTLINE	SCRIPTURE
2. The wrong of muzzling an ox while working: Deserves to eat	4 Thou shalt not muzzle the ox when he treadeth out *the* corn.

Thought 1. The lesson for us is clear: the person who works deserves to be paid. If a person is harvesting, he deserves to share in the harvest. All laborers who truly work are to be paid, both those who labor within the church and those who labor within the business world.

"Let the elders that rule well be counted worthy of double honour, especially they who labour in the word and doctrine. For the scripture saith, Thou shalt not muzzle the ox that treadeth out the corn. And, The labourer *is* worthy of his reward" (1 Ti.5:17-18).

"Say not ye, There are yet four months, and *then* cometh harvest? behold, I say unto you, Lift up your eyes, and look on the fields; for they are white already to harvest. And he that reapeth receiveth wages, and gathereth fruit unto life eternal: that both he that soweth and he that reapeth may rejoice together" (Jn.4:35-36).

"Let him that stole steal no more: but rather let him labour, working with *his* hands the thing which is good, that he may have to give to him that needeth" (Ep.4:28).

"Masters, give unto *your* servants that which is just and equal; knowing that ye also have a Master in heaven" (Col.4:1).

"Now them that are such we command and exhort by our Lord Jesus Christ, that with quietness they work, and eat their own bread" (2 Th.3:12).

"Thou shalt not defraud thy neighbour, neither rob *him*: the wages of him that is hired shall not abide with thee all night until the morning" (Le.19:13).

"Whoso keepeth the fig tree shall eat the fruit thereof: so he that waiteth on his master shall be honoured" (Pr.27:18).

3 (25:5-10) **Marriage—Levirate Marriage, Duty of—Ministering, to the Grieving—Death, of Family Member—Law, Governing the Wife of a Dead Brother**: the third law prevents the wrong of refusing to help the wife of a dead brother. This law stipulated that a man was to marry his deceased brother's widow if she was childless. The purpose was to protect the property: she was to bear a son who would carry on the name of the dead brother and inherit his property. The Scripture and outline clearly spell out the law:

OUTLINE	SCRIPTURE	SCRIPTURE	OUTLINE
3. The wrong of refusing to help the wife of a dead brother a. The law: Concerned brothers living on the same property & one of them died without a son 1) The surviving brother was to marry the widow 2) The first son was to be counted as the son of the dead brother: To inherit his property & carry on his name b. The law if a man refused to marry his brother's widow 1) The widow was to take the case to court	5 If brethren dwell together, and one of them die, and have no child, the wife of the dead shall not marry without unto a stranger: her husband's brother shall go in unto her, and take her to him to wife, and perform the duty of an husband's brother unto her. 6 And it shall be, *that* the firstborn which she beareth shall succeed in the name of his brother *which is* dead, that his name be not put out of Israel. 7 And if the man like not to take his brother's wife, then let his brother's wife go up to the gate unto the elders, and say, My husband's brother	refuseth to raise up unto his brother a name in Israel, he will not perform the duty of my husband's brother. 8 Then the elders of his city shall call him, and speak unto him: and *if* he stand *to it*, and say, I like not to take her; 9 Then shall his brother's wife come unto him in the presence of the elders, and loose his shoe from off his foot, and spit in his face, and shall answer and say, So shall it be done unto that man that will not build up his brother's house. 10 And his name shall be called in Israel, The house of him that hath his shoe loosed.	2) The judges were to summon & reason with him 3) The punishment if he continued to refuse: The widow was to symbolically pronounce a curse upon him • Remove one of his sandals (symbolized a failure of duty) • Spit in his face (showed humiliation) • Given a humiliating title: Known as an irresponsible family

a. Note that the law concerned brothers who lived on the same property and one of them died without a son (vv.5-6). The surviving brother was to marry the widow. As soon as the first son was born, the child was to be counted as the son of the dead brother. That is, he was to inherit the dead brother's property and carry on his name. This prevented the name from being blotted out from Israel, and it kept the property and estate in the family's name.

b. Note that the man had a legal right to refuse to marry his brother's widow (vv.7-10). However, if he refused, certain legal steps were to be taken:

DEUTERONOMY 25:1-19

1) The widow was to take the case to the court (v.7).
2) The judges were to summon the brother and reason with him (v.8).
3) If the brother continued to refuse, the widow was to symbolically pronounce a curse upon him:
   ⇒ She was to remove one of the brother's sandals which symbolized that he had forsaken his responsibility, the responsibility to maintain the name of his brother (v.9).
   ⇒ She was to spit in his face, symbolizing that he deserved to be publicly humiliated and shamed (v.9).
   ⇒ The brother and his family were then given a humiliating title: "the family of the unsandaled" (NIV) or "the house of him who had his sandal removed" (NKJV).

Why would a man refuse to marry his brother's widow and undergo this disgraceful punishment? Because of the inheritance. The closest male relative was to inherit the property of a childless brother. Therefore, if the inheritance or estate was large, the temptation for some would be strong not to marry the woman to give her a son. So long as no son was born, he himself would inherit the property. Understanding this helps to explain why the punishment involved *public humiliation*. If a brother's motive was the estate of his deceased brother, he deserved punishment that involved public shame.

Thought 1. There is a strong lesson for us in this point: we must give very special help and close attention both to our earthly families and to our brothers and sisters in Christ. Help is especially needed when a loved one dies and our brothers and sisters are left all alone, without children. In their hour of need, we must be there for them—helping and doing all we can to meet their needs.

"And whosoever shall give to drink unto one of these little ones a cup of cold *water* only in the name of a disciple, verily I say unto you, he shall in no wise lose his reward" (Mt.10:42).

"But so shall it not be among you: but whosoever will be great among you, shall be your minister: And whosoever of you will be the chiefest, shall be servant of all" (Mk.10:43-44).

"If I then, *your* Lord and Master, have washed your feet; ye also ought to wash one another's feet" (Jn.13:14).

"I have showed you all things, how that so labouring ye ought to support the weak, and to remember the words of the Lord Jesus, how he said, It is more blessed to give than to receive" (Ac.20:35).

"We then that are strong ought to bear the infirmities of the weak, and not to please ourselves" (Ro.15:1).

"Bear ye one another's burdens, and so fulfil the law of Christ" (Ga.6:2).

"As we have therefore opportunity, let us do good unto all *men,* especially unto them who are of the household of faith" (Ga.6:10).

"And I intreat thee also, true yokefellow, help those women which laboured with me in the gospel, with Clement also, and *with* other my fellowlabourers, whose names *are* in the book of life" (Ph.4:3).

"Pure religion and undefiled before God and the Father is this, To visit the fatherless and widows in their affliction, *and* to keep himself unspotted from the world" (Js.1:27).

"The Lord GOD hath given me the tongue of the learned, that I should know how to speak a word in season to *him that is* weary: he wakeneth morning by morning, he wakeneth mine ear to hear as the learned" (Is.50:4).

4 (25:11-12) **Justice, Equal—Legal Punishment, Duty—Law, Governing the Wrong of Excessive Force—Protection, Duty**: the fourth law prevents the wrong of excessive force. This is the only place in the Old Testament where mutilation is stipulated as punishment for a crime.[1] Note the Scripture and outline:

OUTLINE	SCRIPTURE
4. The wrong of excessive force a. The law: Excessive force is not to be used in fights—not even by a woman who seeks to aid her husband	11 When men strive together one with another, and the wife of the one draweth near for to deliver her husband out of the hand of him that smiteth him, and putteth forth her hand, and taketh him by the secrets:
b. The penalty: A just, equal punishment for the crime (*Lex Talionis*)	12 Then thou shalt cut off her hand, thine eye shall not pity *her*.

This law is to prevent excessive force from being used in fights. Excessive force was never to be used, not even by a wife who came to the aid of her husband. If she struck her husband's opponent in the private parts of his body, damaging his testicles, she was to be legally tried and punished. Her hand was to be cut off, and she was to be shown no pity. This penalty is what is known as a just, equal punishment for the crime, the law of *Lex Talionis*. Note this fact: the *Lex Talionis* law of the ancient world demanded that an equal punishment be executed for a crime; that is, if a person damaged a certain part of another person's body, then he was to suffer the same punishment. That same part of his body was to be equally injured. This

---
[1] John Maxwell. *The Preachers's Commentary on Deuteronomy*, p.279.

was the law of *Lex Talionis*: an eye for an eye; a tooth for a tooth; a life for a life. However, in this particular situation, considering the different sexes of the two parties, the law of equal punishment could not be carried out. Peter C. Craigie points out that this particular law may be an example of how *Lex Talionis* was able to be interpreted when it could not be literally applied.[2]

> **Thought 1.** We should never use excessive force in any situation. In a sinful and evil world where many persons seek to lie, steal, cheat, assault, and kill, a person must protect himself. But in protecting himself, he must not use excessive force. This is particularly true of the Christian believer. We must never use excessive force in protecting ourselves: on the contrary, whenever possible, we must show compassion and mercy, turning the other cheek—all for the purpose of being a strong testimony and of reaching the person for Christ.
>
>> "And unto him that smiteth thee on the *one* cheek offer also the other; and him that taketh away thy cloke forbid not *to take thy* coat also" (Lu.6:29).
>>
>> "Recompense to no man evil for evil. Provide things honest in the sight of all men" (Ro.12:17).
>>
>> "[Love] beareth all things, believeth all things, hopeth all things, endureth all things" (1 Co.13:7).
>>
>> "And, ye masters, do the same things unto them, forbearing threatening: knowing that your Master also is in heaven; neither is there respect of persons with him" (Ep.6:9).
>>
>> "*Let* nothing *be done* through strife or vainglory; but in lowliness of mind let each esteem other better than themselves" (Ph.2:3).
>>
>> "Forbearing one another, and forgiving one another, if any man have a quarrel against any: even as Christ forgave you, so also *do* ye" (Col.3:13).
>>
>> "And the servant of the Lord must not strive; but be gentle unto all *men,* apt to teach, patient" (2 Ti.2:24).
>>
>> "Not rendering evil for evil, or railing for railing: but contrariwise blessing; knowing that ye are thereunto called, that ye should inherit a blessing" (1 Pe.3:9).
>>
>> "Thou shalt not avenge, nor bear any grudge against the children of thy people, but thou shalt love thy neighbour as thyself: I *am* the LORD" (Le.19:18).
>>
>> "Strive not with a man without cause, if he have done thee no harm" (Pr.3:30).
>>
>> "Say not thou, I will recompense evil; *but* wait on the LORD, and he shall save thee" (Pr.20:22).
>>
>> "Go not forth hastily to strive, lest *thou know not* what to do in the end thereof, when thy neighbour hath put thee to shame" (Pr.25:8).
>>
>> "Seek ye the LORD, all ye meek of the earth, which have wrought his judgment; seek righteousness, seek meekness: it may be ye shall be hid in the day of the LORD'S anger" (Zep.2:3).

5 **(25:13-16) Dishonesty, Wrong of—Business Dealings, Duty—Honesty, Duty—Weights, Duty—Measures, Duty—Law, Governing Dishonesty in Business Dealings**: the fifth law prevents the wrong of dishonesty in business dealings. A customer is always at the mercy of a merchant. It is very easy for a business to exploit and take advantage of its customers. But such is prohibited by God:

OUTLINE	SCRIPTURE	SCRIPTURE	OUTLINE

5. The wrong of dishonesty in business dealings
a. The law
  1) Must not overcharge when selling (use large weights)
  2) Must not underpay when buying (use smaller weights)
  3) Must be honest in all business dealings
	13 Thou shalt not have in thy bag divers weights, a great and a small.
	14 Thou shalt not have in thine house divers measures, a great and a small.
	15 *But* thou shalt have a perfect and just weight, a perfect and just measure shalt thou
		have: that thy days may be lengthened in the land which the LORD thy God giveth thee.
		16 For all that do such things, *and* all that do unrighteously, *are* an abomination unto the LORD thy God.
			b. The reasons
			  1) Because honesty assures the blessings of God, a longer life
			  2) Because God detests any person who cheats & is dishonest

The law is clearly stated: a business—whether merchant or vendor—must not overcharge when selling merchandise nor underpay when buying merchandise. Moses gives the example of two weights used in measuring merchandise in the ancient world. It was easy for a merchant to use a larger weight in order to overcharge and to use a lighter weight in order to underpay when purchasing merchandise. But the stipulation of the law is clear: the merchant must always be honest in all his business dealings, both in selling and in purchasing (vv.14-15). Note that two strong reasons are given for honesty in business dealings:

1) Honest business dealings will assure the blessings of God. A society that is honest in its business dealings will survive for a long, long time. Fair and equal justice will be built into the fabric of the nation and peace will reign within the nation.
2) Dishonest business dealings are detested by God. God actually declares that He detests any person who cheats and is dishonest in business dealings (v.16). This is a strong warning to the dishonest person: the judgment of God will fall upon him unless he repents and begins to deal with people fairly and honestly.

> "And he said unto them, Exact no more than that which is appointed you" (Lu.3:13).
>
> "Recompense to no man evil for evil. Provide things honest in the sight of all men" (Ro.12:17).

---

[2] Peter C. Craigie. *The Book of Deuteronomy,* p. 316.

DEUTERONOMY 25:1-19

"Owe no man any thing, but to love one another: for he that loveth another hath fulfilled the law" (Ro.13:8).

"Ye shall do no unrighteousness in judgment, in meteyard, in weight, or in measure. Just balances, just weights, a just ephah, and a just hin, shall ye have: I *am* the LORD your God, which brought you out of the land of Egypt" (Le.19:35-36).

"Thou shalt not have in thy bag divers weights, a great and a small" (De.25:13).

"*But* thou shalt have a perfect and just weight, a perfect and just measure shalt thou have: that thy days may be lengthened in the land which the LORD thy God giveth thee" (De.25:15).

"A false balance *is* abomination to the LORD: but a just weight *is* his delight" (Pr.11:1).

"Better *is* a little with righteousness than great revenues without right" (Pr.16:8).

"*It is* naught, *it is* naught, saith the buyer: but when he is gone his way, then he boasteth" (Pr.20:14).

"The getting of treasures by a lying tongue *is* a vanity tossed to and fro of them that seek death" (Pr.21:6).

"*He is* a merchant, the balances of deceit *are* in his hand: he loveth to oppress" (Ho.12:7).

"Behold, therefore I have smitten mine hand at thy dishonest gain which thou hast made, and at thy blood which hath been in the midst of thee" (Eze.22:13).

6 (25:17-19) **Judgment, Surety of—Judicial Judgment, Surety of—Cruelty, Judgment of—Savagery, Judgment of—War, Inhumane, Judgment of—Inhumane, Judgment of—Law, Governing the Wrong of a Cruel People**: the Amalekites stand as an example of a cruel, savage people. Consequently, they were to bear the severe judgment of God. (See outline and notes—Ex.17:8-16 for more discussion.)

OUTLINE	SCRIPTURE	SCRIPTURE	OUTLINE
6. **The wrong of a cruel, savage, & inhumane people** a. The case of the Amalekites: Stand as an example of cruelty 1) They brutally attacked the sick, disabled, & elderly who lagged behind the marching divisions of Israel 2) They did not fear God	17 Remember what Amalek did unto thee by the way, when ye were come forth out of Egypt; 18 How he met thee by the way, and smote the hindmost of thee, *even* all *that were* feeble behind thee, when thou *wast* faint and weary; and he feared not God.	19 Therefore it shall be, when the LORD thy God hath given thee rest from all thine enemies round about, in the land which the LORD thy God giveth thee *for* an inheritance to possess it, *that* thou shalt blot out the remembrance of Amalek from under heaven; thou shalt not forget *it*.	b. The insistence of God: Such cruelty must be judged 1) To be blotted out 2) Not to forget this judgment

Right after the Israelites had fled from their Egyptian slavery, the Amalekites had secretly attacked the sick, disabled, and elderly who lagged behind the marching divisions of Israel. Note what Scripture says: they had no fear of God. Their hearts were hard, insensitive, savage, and cruel. Attacking and killing the helpless and disadvantaged did not bother them at all. Consequently, God stipulates that such cruelty and savagery must be judged. Justice must be executed against such a savage and cruel people. Once Israel had settled in the promised land, they were then to march against the Amalekites and blot them out, executing every single person. And note: the Israelites were never to forget that this judgment was to be executed. (See outline and notes—Nu.21:1-3; DEEPER STUDY #1—De.20:16-18 for more discussion.)

Thought 1. The Amalekites were the descendants of Esau, the brother of Jacob. This means that they came from the same godly roots, the same godly forefathers as the Israelites. But they squandered and forsook their godly roots. They turned away from God and turned to the ways of the world, the ways of immorality, lawlessness, and violence. As a result, they became a cruel and savage people, a people with hard hearts who abused and brutalized the weak and helpless. They had become a people who did not fear God, a people who did not believe in God nor His judgment. But the judgment of God was a living reality, and God pronounced His judgment. The Amalekites were to be wiped off the face of the earth. Note this fact: the Amalekites ceased to exist as a nation under the reign of King Hezekiah (1 Chr.4:43).

The judgment of God is sure. His judgment falls upon any who turn away from Him to the ways of the world. This is the strong declaration of Scripture: we will all face the judgment of God.

"But I say unto you, It shall be more tolerable for Tyre and Sidon at the day of judgment, than for you" (Mt.11:22).

"When the Son of man shall come in his glory, and all the holy angels with him, then shall he sit upon the throne of his glory: And before him shall be gathered all nations: and he shall separate them one from another, as a shepherd divideth *his* sheep from the goats: And he shall set the sheep on his right hand, but the goats on the left" (Mt.25:31-33).

"Marvel not at this: for the hour is coming, in the which all that are in the graves shall hear his voice, And shall come forth; they that have done good, unto the resurrection of life; and they that have done evil, unto the resurrection of damnation" (Jn.5:28-29).

"For the wrath of God is revealed from heaven against all ungodliness and unrighteousness of men, who hold the truth in unrighteousness" (Ro.1:18).

"But fornication, and all uncleanness, or covetousness, let it not be once named among you, as becometh saints; Neither filthiness, nor foolish talking, nor jesting, which are not convenient: but rather giving of thanks. For this ye know, that no whoremonger, nor unclean person, nor covetous man, who is an idolater, hath any inheritance in the kingdom of Christ and of God. Let no man deceive you with vain words: for because of these things cometh the wrath of God upon the children of disobedience" (Ep.5:3-6).

"And to you who are troubled rest with us, when the Lord Jesus shall be revealed from heaven with his mighty angels, In flaming fire taking vengeance on them that know not God, and that obey not the gospel of our Lord Jesus Christ" (2 Th.1:7-8).

"And as it is appointed unto men once to die, but after this the judgment" (He.9:27).

"The Lord knoweth how to deliver the godly out of temptations, and to reserve the unjust unto the day of judgment to be punished" (2 Pe.2:9).

"But the heavens and the earth, which are now, by the same word are kept in store, reserved unto fire against the day of judgment and perdition of ungodly men" (2 Pe.3:7).

"And Enoch also, the seventh from Adam, prophesied of these, saying, Behold, the Lord cometh with ten thousands of his saints, To execute judgment upon all, and to convince all that are ungodly among them of all their ungodly deeds which they have ungodly committed, and of all their hard *speeches* which ungodly sinners have spoken against him" (Jude 14-15).

"And I saw the dead, small and great, stand before God; and the books were opened: and another book was opened, which is *the book* of life: and the dead were judged out of those things which were written in the books, according to their works" (Re.20:12).

DEUTERONOMY 26:1-19

CHAPTER 26

P. Laws That Require Special Confession & Obedience, 26:1-19

1. **The confession to be made during the offering of the firstfruit: Thanking God for His salvation & blessings**
   a. The law: Must celebrate after entering the promised land
      1) To set aside the very first of one's harvest for God
      2) To take the offering to the worship center, the place where God's name is honored

   b. The confession
      1) To declare that one has entered the promised land: A symbol of trusting God & resting in God

      2) To have the priest take & present the offering of firstfruits to the LORD

      3) To declare the great salvation of God
         - That Israel had been born of one man, Jacob
         - That Israel had grown into a great nation, mighty & numerous
         - That Israel had been enslaved by the Egyptians
         - That Israel had cried out to God for deliverance

         - That God had heard their cry & delivered them

         - That God had led & given them the promised land, the most fruitful land imaginable

      4) To declare one's thanksgiving to God & to bow down & present the firstfruit offering to God

And it shall be, when thou art come in unto the land which the LORD thy God giveth thee *for* an inheritance, and possessest it, and dwellest therein;
2 That thou shalt take of the first of all the fruit of the earth, which thou shalt bring of thy land that the LORD thy God giveth thee, and shalt put *it* in a basket, and shalt go unto the place which the LORD thy God shall choose to place his name there.
3 And thou shalt go unto the priest that shall be in those days, and say unto him, I profess this day unto the LORD thy God, that I am come unto the country which the LORD sware unto our fathers for to give us.
4 And the priest shall take the basket out of thine hand, and set it down before the altar of the LORD thy God.
5 And thou shalt speak and say before the LORD thy God, A Syrian ready to perish *was* my father, and he went down into Egypt, and sojourned there with a few, and became there a nation, great, mighty, and populous:
6 And the Egyptians evil entreated us, and afflicted us, and laid upon us hard bondage:
7 And when we cried unto the LORD God of our fathers, the LORD heard our voice, and looked on our affliction, and our labour, and our oppression:
8 And the LORD brought us forth out of Egypt with a mighty hand, and with an outstretched arm, and with great terribleness, and with signs, and with wonders:
9 And he hath brought us into this place, and hath given us this land, *even* a land that floweth with milk and honey.
10 And now, behold, I have brought the firstfruits of the land, which thou, O LORD, hast given me. And thou shalt set it before the LORD thy God, and worship before the LORD thy God:
11 And thou shalt rejoice in every good *thing* which the LORD thy God hath given unto thee, and unto thine house, thou, and the Levite, and the stranger that *is* among you.
12 When thou hast made an end of tithing all the tithes of thine increase the third year, *which is* the year of tithing, and hast given *it* unto the Levite, the stranger, the fatherless, and the widow, that they may eat within thy gates, and be filled;
13 Then thou shalt say before the LORD thy God, I have brought away the hallowed things out of *mine* house, and also have given them unto the Levite, and unto the stranger, to the fatherless, and to the widow, according to all thy commandments which thou hast commanded me: I have not transgressed thy commandments, neither have I forgotten *them*:
14 I have not eaten thereof in my mourning, neither have I taken away *ought* thereof for *any* unclean *use*, nor given *ought* thereof for the dead: but I have hearkened to the voice of the LORD my God, *and* have done according to all that thou hast commanded me.
15 Look down from thy holy habitation, from heaven, and bless thy people Israel, and the land which thou hast given us, as thou swarest unto our fathers, a land that floweth with milk and honey.
16 This day the LORD thy God hath commanded thee to do these statutes and judgments: thou shalt therefore keep and do them with all thine heart, and with all thy soul.
17 Thou hast avouched the LORD this day to be thy God, and to walk in his ways, and to keep his statutes, and his commandments, and his judgments, and to hearken unto his voice:
18 And the LORD hath avouched thee this day to be his peculiar people, as he hath promised thee, and that *thou* shouldest keep all his commandments;
19 And to make thee high

   c. The purpose: To have a worship service where everyone could rejoice together & give thanks to God—thanks for their new life in the promised land of God

2. **The confession to be made when offering the three-year tithe: Being faithful in giving**
   a. The law
      1) To set aside a special tithe every third year
      2) To give the tithe to the Levites (local ministers) foreigners, orphans, & widows
   b. The confession before the LORD
      1) To declare that one is faithful in giving the tithe, in supporting the ministers & needy

      2) To declare that one has not misused any of the tithe
         - Not while he was in mourning & not working
         - Not while he was ceremonially unclean & not working
         - Not for the dead (funeral expenses)
      3) To seek the LORD in prayer: Asking the LORD to bless His people & the fruitfulness of the land

3. **The strong charge to obey God**
   a. The charge: To obey all these laws—without reservation—with all your heart & soul
   b. The reasons
      1) Your confession, declaration of faith
         - That the LORD is *your* God
         - That you will obey Him
      2) God's confession & demand
         - You are His people, His special treasure
         - You are to obey Him

      3) God's promise & guarantee

• To make His people great: Exalt them in praise, name, & honor	above all nations which he hath made, in praise, and in name, and in honour;	and that thou mayest be an holy people unto the LORD thy God, as he hath spoken.	• To make His people holy—totally set apart to God

DIVISION IV

THE SECOND GREAT THEME PREACHED BY GOD'S AGED SERVANT (PART 2): REMEMBER THE CIVIL AND RELIGIOUS LAWS OF ISRAEL—HELPFUL PRINCIPLES TO GOVERN MAN AND SOCIETY, 12:1–26:19

P. Laws That Require Special Confession and Obedience, 26:1-19

(26:1-19) **Introduction**: what a person confesses is important—of critical importance. A sincere confession determines how a person lives upon this earth and how a person walks and behaves day by day. For example, if a person truly believes in the pleasures and material possessions of this world, then he attaches himself to pleasures and possessions. He confesses his belief in worldliness by his behavior and by the words he speaks. If a person believes in humanism, that man is the ultimate authority and power in the universe, then he attaches himself to the humanistic philosophy. By his behavior and words he confesses humanism. If a person believes that science and technology are the keys to success and achievement, then he attaches himself to technology and science. By his behavior and words, he confesses that his hope lies in technology and science.

Again, what a person confesses is of critical importance, for it determines how a person lives. But even more than this, what a person confesses determines his eternal destiny. Just think about the fact: a person's fate—whether or not he lives eternally in the promised land of heaven—is determined by what he confesses. Because of this, a wise and honest person will study his confession. He will make sure that what he confesses is reality, that it is the truth.

What a person confesses matters to God. For this reason, God established two special services of confession for the Israelites. Two times a year they were to approach God with hearts filled with gratitude, making a strong confession of faith in Him. This is the subject of the present passage, a strong lesson on the importance of a true confession: *Laws That Require Special Confession and Obedience*, 26:1-19.

1. The confession to be made during the offering of the firstfruit: thanking God for His salvation and blessings (vv.1-11).
2. The confession to be made when offering the three-year tithe: being faithful in giving (vv.12-15).
3. The strong charge to obey God (vv.16-19).

1 (26:1-11) **Confession, of Salvation—Firstfruit, Offering of—Ceremony, of Firstfruit Offering—Thanksgiving, to God—Ritual, of the Firstfruit Offering**: there was the confession to be made during the offering of the firstfruit. This confession declared the great salvation of God and the wonderful blessings of God. God's people were always to show gratitude for God's salvation and blessings, but there were two specific times during the year when a very special confession was to be made. One of these times was the service where the firstfruit offering was presented to God. Note the ceremony of the service:

OUTLINE	SCRIPTURE	SCRIPTURE	OUTLINE

1. The confession to be made during the offering of the firstfruit: Thanking God for His salvation & blessings
a. The law: Must celebrate after entering the promised land
  1) To set aside the very first of one's harvest for God
  2) To take the offering to the worship center, the place where God's name is honored
 	
b. The confession
  1) To declare that one has entered the promised land: A symbol of trusting God & resting in God
 	
  2) To have the priest take &
	And it shall be, when thou *art* come in unto the land which the LORD thy God giveth thee *for* an inheritance, and possessest it, and dwellest therein;
	2 That thou shalt take of the first of all the fruit of the earth, which thou shalt bring of thy land that the LORD thy God giveth thee, and shalt put *it* in a basket, and shalt go unto the place which the LORD thy God shall choose to place his name there.
	3 And thou shalt go unto the priest that shall be in those days, and say unto him, I profess this day unto the LORD thy God, that I am come unto the country which the LORD sware unto our fathers for to give us.
	4 And the priest shall take
		the basket out of thine hand, and set it down before the altar of the LORD thy God.
		5 And thou shalt speak and say before the LORD thy God, A Syrian ready to perish *was* my father, and he went down into Egypt, and sojourned there with a few, and became there a nation, great, mighty, and populous:
		6 And the Egyptians evil entreated us, and afflicted us, and laid upon us hard bondage:
		7 And when we cried unto the LORD God of our fathers, the LORD heard our voice, and looked on our affliction, and our labour, and our oppression:
		8 And the LORD brought us forth out of Egypt with a mighty hand, and with an
			present the offering of firstfruits to the LORD
			
			3) To declare the great salvation of God
			• That Israel had been born of one man, Jacob
			• That Israel had grown into a great nation, mighty & numerous
			
			• That Israel had been enslaved by the Egyptians
			
			• That Israel had cried out to God for deliverance
			
			• That God had heard their cry & delivered them

DEUTERONOMY 26:1-19

OUTLINE	SCRIPTURE	SCRIPTURE	OUTLINE
• That God had led & given them the promised land, the most fruitful land imaginable 4) To declare one's thanksgiving to God & to bow down & present the	outstretched arm, and with great terribleness, and with signs, and with wonders: 9 And he hath brought us into this place, and hath given us this land, *even* a land that floweth with milk and honey. 10 And now, behold, I have brought the firstfruits of the land, which thou, O LORD,	hast given me. And thou shalt set it before the LORD thy God, and worship before the LORD thy God: 11 And thou shalt rejoice in every good *thing* which the LORD thy God hath given unto thee, and unto thine house, thou, and the Levite, and the stranger that is among you.	firstfruit offering to God c. The purpose: To have a worship service where everyone could rejoice together & give thanks to God—thanks for their new life in the promised land of God

a. The Festival of Firstfruits was to be celebrated after the Israelites had entered and taken possession of the promised land (vv.1-2). The very first celebration was to take place right after the first harvest. A person was to take some of the very first produce from the harvest, put it in a basket, and take it as an offering to the worship center. Note that the worship center is said to be the place that God has chosen to place His Name, the place where His Name is honored. This was the sanctuary where the Ark of the covenant was placed, the Ark that symbolized God's very own presence.

b. The confession was a strong declaration.
1) The person declared that he had now entered the promised land, the very land that the Lord Himself had sworn to give His people (v.3). The person was confessing that he trusted God and rested in God. His trust and rest were demonstrated by the very fact that he was standing there in the promised land: he was there because he had trusted and was resting in the presence and power of God.
2) The person was to have the priest take the basket and present the offerings of firstfruit to the Lord (v.4).
3) The worshipper was then to declare the great salvation of God before the priest and all others standing around (vv.5-9). Note the strong confession declared by the worshipper:
⇒ He confessed that Israel had been born of just one man, Jacob (v.5). The implication is that God alone could cause a nation to be born of one person.
⇒ He confessed that Israel had become a great nation, a mighty and numerous people (v.5).
⇒ He confessed that Israel had been enslaved by the Egyptians and been mistreated, afflicted and forced into hard, exhausting labor (v.6).
⇒ He confessed that the Israelites had cried out for God to deliver them in the midst of their misery, toil, and oppression (v.7).
⇒ He confessed that God had heard the cry of His people and delivered them with great power and miraculous signs and wonders (v.8).
⇒ He confessed that God had led His people and given them the promised land, the most fruitful land imaginable—a land that actually flowed with milk and honey (v.9).

4) The worshipper was then to declare his thanksgiving to God. This he did by bowing down and presenting the firstfruit offering to God (v.10).

c. Note why the firstfruit offering was established as a law: to have a worship service where everyone could rejoice together and give thanks to God for his new life in the promised land. Every citizen, Levite, and foreigner among the Israelites was to celebrate the Festival of Firstfruits. The people of God were...
- to celebrate the new life given by God
- to celebrate the rest, both physical and spiritual rest, that God had given them in the promised land
- to celebrate the gift of the promised land itself

The celebration of the firstfruit was to be a strong confession of God's great salvation and wonderful blessings that He poured out upon His people.

Thought 1. We are to offer thanksgiving to God for His wonderful salvation and for His continued blessings. Everything we have is due to God. We have been delivered from the sin, enslavement, and death of this world—saved to live eternally with God in the promised land of heaven. But not only this: the strength and skill to work and all the good things we possess—they have all come from the hand of God. God has poured out His blessings upon us.

There is only one confession that can flow from our lips, the confession of thanksgiving to God for His glorious salvation and wonderful blessings. This is the great lesson of the firstfruit offering.

"Giving thanks always for all things unto God and the Father in the name of our Lord Jesus Christ" (Ep.5:20).

"Giving thanks unto the Father, which hath made us meet to be partakers of the inheritance of the saints in light" (Col.1:12).

"And let the peace of God rule in your hearts, to the which also ye are called in one body; and be ye thankful" (Col.3:15).

"And whatsoever ye do in word or deed, do all in the name of the Lord Jesus, giving thanks to God and the Father by him" (Col.3:17).

"In every thing give thanks: for this is the will of God in Christ Jesus concerning you" (1 Th.5:18).

"For every creature of God is good, and nothing to be refused, if it be received with thanksgiving" (1 Ti.4:4).

"By him therefore let us offer the sacrifice of praise to God continually, that is, the fruit of our lips giving thanks to his name" (He.13:15).

"But ye are a chosen generation, a royal priesthood, an holy nation, a peculiar people; that ye should show forth the praises of him who hath called you out of darkness into his marvellous light" (1 Pe.2:9).

"When thou hast eaten and art full, then thou shalt bless the Lord thy God for the good land which he hath given thee" (De.8:10).

"Give thanks unto the Lord, call upon his name, make known his deeds among the people" (1 Chr.16:8).

"Sing praises to the Lord, which dwelleth in Zion: declare among the people his doings" (Ps.9:11).

"Offer unto God thanksgiving; and pay thy vows unto the most High" (Ps.50:14).

"It is a good thing to give thanks unto the Lord, and to sing praises unto thy name, O most High" (Ps.92:1).

"Enter into his gates with thanksgiving, and into his courts with praise: be thankful unto him, and bless his name" (Ps.100:4).

"And let them sacrifice the sacrifices of thanksgiving, and declare his works with rejoicing" (Ps.107:22).

2 (26:12-15) **Tithing, Duty—Benevolence, Duty—Offerings, Duty—Confession, Duty—Giving, Faithfulness in**: there was the confession to be made when offering the three-year tithe. A person was to make a strong declaration of faithfulness, that he was faithful in giving a true tithe. Note the Scripture and outline.

OUTLINE	SCRIPTURE	SCRIPTURE	OUTLINE

2. The confession to be made when offering the three-year tithe: Being faithful in giving
a. The law
  1) To set aside a special tithe every third year
  2) To give the tithe to the Levites (local ministers) foreigners, orphans, & widows
b. The confession before the LORD
  1) To declare that one is faithful in giving the tithe, in supporting the ministers & needy
	12 When thou hast made an end of tithing all the tithes of thine increase the third year, *which is* the year of tithing, and hast given *it* unto the Levite, the stranger, the fatherless, and the widow, that they may eat within thy gates, and be filled;
	13 Then thou shalt say before the LORD thy God, I have brought away the hallowed things out of *mine* house, and also have given them unto the Levite, and unto the stranger, to the fatherless, and to the widow, according to all thy commandments which thou hast commanded me: I have
		not transgressed thy commandments, neither have I forgotten *them*:
		14 I have not eaten thereof in my mourning, neither have I taken away *ought* thereof for *any* unclean *use*, nor given *ought* thereof for the dead: *but* I have hearkened to the voice of the LORD my God, *and* have done according to all that thou hast commanded me.
		15 Look down from thy holy habitation, from heaven, and bless thy people Israel, and the land which thou hast given us, as thou swarest unto our fathers, a land that floweth with milk and honey.
			2) To declare that one has not misused any of the tithe
			  • Not while he was in mourning & not working
			  • Not while he was ceremonially unclean & not working
			  • Not for the dead (funeral expenses)
			3) To seek the LORD in prayer: Asking the LORD to bless His people & the fruitfulness of the land

a. The law governing the three-year tithe had already been given to the people (see outline and note pt.6—De.14:22-29 for more discussion). Simply stated, every third year a special tithe was to be given to support the Levites or local ministers, the foreigners, the orphans, and the widows (v.12).

b. As a person was presenting his offering to the Lord through the priest, he was to make a strong confession of faithfulness.

1) He was to confess that he had been faithful in the tithe, in supporting the ministers and needy throughout the land (v.13). He was to declare that he had kept the commandment of God to tithe and that he had not turned aside from any of God's commandments.
2) The worshipper was also to declare that he had not misused any of the tithe (v.14). Note the detail of the confession. He was to declare:
⇒ that he had not used any of the tithe for himself.
⇒ that he had not used any of the tithe while he was in mourning. During periods of mourning, there were days that he was not allowed to work; consequently, the need for some of the tithe could have arisen.
⇒ that he had not used any of the tithe while he was unclean; that is, spiritually, ceremonially unclean. Again, he would not have been working during this period, and a need for the tithe could have arisen.
⇒ that he had not used any of the tithe for the dead, perhaps referring to funeral expenses.

3) After making his confession, the worshipper was to seek the LORD in prayer (v.15). He was to ask the LORD to look down from heaven and to bless all His people and the fruitfulness of the land.

Thought 1. The believer must tithe. We must all support the ministers of God, the foreigners, orphans, widows, and the needy of this world. We must meet the needs of people and carry the glorious message of the gospel to the world. All this takes money, a tithe of our income. Without money—without a tithe—the needs of people will not be met and the gospel will not be taken to the ends of the world. Our money is needed. It was needed during the days of God's aged servant Moses, and it is needed today. This is the reason God requires us to be generous, benevolent—to possess a giving heart.

> "Give, and it shall be given unto you; good measure, pressed down, and shaken together, and running over, shall men give into your bosom. For with the same measure that ye mete withal it shall be measured to you again" (Lu.6:38).

> "And he looked up, and saw the rich men casting their gifts into the treasury. And he saw also a certain poor widow casting in thither two mites. And he said, Of a truth I say unto you, that this poor widow hath cast in more than they all: For all these have of their abundance cast in unto the offerings of God: but she of her penury hath cast in all the living that she had" (Lu.21:1-4).

> "Neither was there any among them that lacked: for as many as were possessors of lands or houses sold them, and brought the prices of the things that were sold, And laid *them* down at the apostles' feet: and distribution was made unto every man according as he had need" (Ac.4:34-35).

> "I have showed you all things, how that so labouring ye ought to support the weak, and to remember the words of the Lord Jesus, how he said, It is more blessed to give than to receive" (Ac.20:35).

> "Upon the first *day* of the week let every one of you lay by him in store, as *God* hath prospered him, that there be no gatherings when I come" (1 Co.16:2).

> "But this *I say,* He which soweth sparingly shall reap also sparingly; and he which soweth bountifully shall reap also bountifully" (2 Co.9:6).

> "And all the tithe of the land, *whether* of the seed of the land, *or* of the fruit of the tree, *is* the LORD'S: *it is* holy unto the LORD" (Le.27:30).

> "Honour the LORD with thy substance, and with the firstfruits of all thine increase" (Pr.3:9).

> "Bring ye all the tithes into the storehouse, that there may be meat in mine house, and prove me now herewith, saith the LORD of hosts, if I will not open you the windows of heaven, and pour you out a blessing, that *there shall* not *be room* enough *to receive it*" (Mal.3:10).

3 **(26:16-19) Obedience, Duty—Confession, Duty—Believer, Treasured Possession—Believer, Special Treasure—Promises, of Greatness and Holiness—Laws, Duty:** there was the strong charge to obey God. Remember that Moses had been preaching a series of messages on the commandments and laws of God, a series of sermons that have covered the major portion of the great book of Deuteronomy (De.4:44-26:19). Did Moses preach the series of sermons just to the leadership who in turn conveyed his messages to the three million plus Israelites? Or, did he personally preach to all of the Israelites himself, tribe by tribe, splitting them up into manageable groups? The answer is not known. Whatever the case, Moses now comes to the conclusion of his series of messages on the commandments and laws. The reader can just picture Moses standing before a mass of people and preaching from the depths of his heart. He is soon to go home to be with the Lord; thus every word he speaks is of critical importance. This he knows, and his heart reaches out to the people, wanting them to hang upon every word being preached. This is especially true with the present charge he is about to give. Above all other exhortations, this one charge must be heeded: the people must—absolutely must—obey God.

OUTLINE	SCRIPTURE	SCRIPTURE	OUTLINE

3. The strong charge to obey God
a. The charge: To obey all these laws—without reservation—with all your heart & soul
b. The reasons
  1) Your confession, declaration of faith
    • That the LORD is *your* God
    • That you will obey Him
	16 This day the LORD thy God hath commanded thee to do these statutes and judgments: thou shalt therefore keep and do them with all thine heart, and with all thy soul.
	17 Thou hast avouched the LORD this day to be thy God, and to walk in his ways, and to keep his statutes, and his commandments, and his judgments, and to hearken unto his voice:
		18 And the LORD hath avouched thee this day to be his peculiar people, as he hath promised thee, and that *thou* shouldest keep all his commandments;
		19 And to make thee high above all nations which he hath made, in praise, and in name, and in honour; and that thou mayest be an holy people unto the LORD thy God, as he hath spoken.
			2) God's confession & demand
			  • You are His people, His special treasure
			  • You are to obey Him
			3) God's promise & guarantee
			  • To make His people great: Exalt them in praise, name, & honor
			  • To make His people holy—totally set apart to God

a. The charge was forceful: the people must obey all the commandments and laws of God. Moses cried out: without reservation, you must obey the laws of God with all your heart and with all your soul (v.16).

b. Note the reasons why obedience is necessary.
1) You must obey because of your confession, your declaration of faith (v.17). You have declared that the Lord is *your God,* that you will obey Him. You have declared that you will keep all His commandments and laws.
2) Because of your declaration and confession, God has established His covenant with you. God has declared this day that you are His people, His treasured possession, His very special treasure. Moreover, He has declared that you are to do just as you have promised: obey Him (v.18).
3) If you are true to your word—if you keep God's commandments—then the most wonderful promise and guarantee is given you (v.19). God will exalt you above all the peoples of the earth and make you a great nation. You will be exalted in praise, name, and honor. Moreover, you will become God's holy people: a people totally set apart to God.

DEUTERONOMY 26:1-19

Thought 1: There are two strong lessons in this point for us:
(1) We must obey God without reservation, we must obey Him with all our heart and soul.

> "Not every one that saith unto me, Lord, Lord, shall enter into the kingdom of heaven; but he that doeth the will of my Father which is in heaven" (Mt.7:21).

> "He that hath my commandments, and keepeth them, he it is that loveth me: and he that loveth me shall be loved of my Father, and I will love him, and will manifest myself to him" (Jn.14:21).

> "Jesus answered and said unto him, If a man love me, he will keep my words: and my Father will love him, and we will come unto him, and make our abode with him" (Jn.14:23).

> "If ye keep my commandments, ye shall abide in my love; even as I have kept my Father's commandments, and abide in his love" (Jn.15:10).

> "Ye are my friends, if ye do whatsoever I command you" (Jn.15:14).

> "Then Peter and the *other* apostles answered and said, We ought to obey God rather than men" (Ac.5:29).

> "For this is the love of God, that we keep his commandments: and his commandments are not grievous" (1 Jn.5:3).

> "Blessed *are* they that do his commandments, that they may have right to the tree of life, and may enter in through the gates into the city" (Re.22:14).

> "Ye shall diligently keep the commandments of the LORD your God, and his testimonies, and his statutes, which he hath commanded thee" (De.6:17).

> "This day the LORD thy God hath commanded thee to do these statutes and judgments: thou shalt therefore keep and do them with all thine heart, and with all thy soul" (De.26:16).

> "This book of the law shall not depart out of thy mouth; but thou shalt meditate therein day and night, that thou mayest observe to do according to all that is written therein: for then thou shalt make thy way prosperous, and then thou shalt have good success" (Jos.1:8).

(2) If we obey God—follow Him with our whole heart and soul—God promises to exalt us. We become His very special treasure, His treasured possession.

> "But ye *are* a chosen generation, a royal priesthood, an holy nation, a peculiar people; that ye should show forth the praises of him who hath called you out of darkness into his marvellous light: Which in time past *were* not a people, but *are* now the people of God: which had not obtained mercy, but now have obtained mercy" (1 Pe.2:9-10).

> "For I reckon that the sufferings of this present time *are* not worthy *to be compared* with the glory which shall be revealed in us" (Ro.8:18).

> "For our light affliction, which is but for a moment, worketh for us a far more exceeding *and* eternal weight of glory" (2 Co.4:17).

> "Therefore I endure all things for the elect's sakes, that they may also obtain the salvation which is in Christ Jesus with eternal glory" (2 Ti.2:10).

> "To him that overcometh will I grant to sit with me in my throne, even as I also overcame, and am set down with my Father in his throne" (Re.3:21).

> "Now therefore, if ye will obey my voice indeed, and keep my covenant, then ye shall be a peculiar treasure unto me above all people: for all the earth *is* mine" (Ex.19:5).

> "But know that the LORD hath set apart him that is godly for himself: the LORD will hear when I call unto him" (Ps.4:3).

> "Because he hath set his love upon me, therefore will I deliver him: I will set him on high, because he hath known my name" (Ps.91:14).

> "Then shalt thou delight thyself in the LORD; and I will cause thee to ride upon the high places of the earth, and feed thee with the heritage of Jacob thy father: for the mouth of the LORD hath spoken *it*" (Is.58:14).

> "And they that be wise shall shine as the brightness of the firmament; and they that turn many to righteousness as the stars for ever and ever" (Da.12:3).

DIVISION V

THE THIRD GREAT THEME PREACHED BY GOD'S AGED SERVANT: THE CHARGE TO RENEW THE COVENANT WITH GOD, 27:1–30:20

(27:1–30:20) **DIVISION OVERVIEW**: the aged servant of God now came to the heart of preparing the people. Moses now preached a series of messages that challenged the people to recommit their lives to God, urging them to renew their covenant with Him. In the past they had promised to follow and obey God. Now, right before they crossed the Jordan and entered the promised land, it was time for them to renew their promise to God. They must keep their covenant with God, their promise to obey and follow Him wholeheartedly.

THE THIRD GREAT THEME PREACHED BY GOD'S AGED SERVANT: THE CHARGE TO RENEW THE COVENANT WITH GOD, 27:1–30:20

A. The Charge to Renew the Covenant: The Command to Obey God, and Those to Be Cursed for Disobeying God, 27:1-26

B. The Results of Obeying the Covenant: The Blessings of God, 28:1-14

C. The Results of Disobeying God: The Curses for Disobedience, 28:15-68

D. The Terms of the Covenant: Obey God or Face His Judgment, 29:1-29

E. The Strong Appeal and Hope of the Covenant: Restoration—Repentance and Forgiveness, 30:1-20

DEUTERONOMY 27:1-26

CHAPTER 27

V. THE THIRD GREAT THEME PREACHED BY GOD'S AGED SERVANT: THE CHARGE TO RENEW THE COVENANT WITH GOD, 27:1–30:20

A. The Charge to Renew the Covenant: The Command to Obey God, & Those to Be Cursed for Disobeying God, 27:1-26

1. **The strong charge: Keep the covenant, God's commandments, & write them down as a memorial**
   a. The charge to write the covenant, the commandments, on a stone memorial
      1) To do this after entering the promised land
      2) To write all the words of the law on the memorial: Do this because the LORD has fulfilled His promise, given you the promised land
      3) To set up the stone memorial on Mt. Ebal

   b. The charge to dedicate the covenant memorial by building an altar of stones & offering sacrifices to God
      1) To offer Burnt Offerings: A symbol of seeking atonement, reconciliation through Christ's sacrifice
      2) To sacrifice Fellowship Offerings: A symbol of seeking more of the peace & fellowship of God
      3) To clearly write the covenant, the commandments, on the stone memorial: Make them readable

2. **The strong challenge: Be silent & listen to the covenant**
   a. Know God's part in the covenant: God makes you His people—you have become the people of God
   b. Know your part, your duty
      1) Keep the covenant
      2) Obey the LORD your God
      3) Follow His commandments

3. **The results of obeying & disobeying the covenant: Blessings & curses**
   a. The striking ceremony that was to picture the covenant renewal
      1) Six tribes were to stand on Mt. Gerizim^{DS1} to pronounce the blessings for obeying
      2) Six tribes were to stand on Mt. Ebal^{DS2} to proclaim the curses for disobeying
      3) The Levites—standing between the two—were to recite the blessings & curses
      4) The people were to respond, "Amen"

   b. Those cursed for disobedience
      1) Those who commit idolatry & false worship
         - Is detestable to God
         - The people's response: "Amen!" They understand & agree to the terms
      2) Those who dishonor parents
      3) Those who steal
      4) Those who lead the blind astray—taking advantage of the disabled
      5) Those who mistreat of the foreigner, orphan, & widows—symbolizing all the poor, weak, & disadvantaged
      6) Those who commit incest—sexual relations with one's mother (or father)
      7) Those who commit bestiality
      8) Those who commit incest—sexual relations with one's sister (or brother)
      9) Those who commit incest—sexual relations with one's mother-in-law (or father-in-law)

And Moses with the elders of Israel commanded the people, saying, Keep all the commandments which I command you this day.

2 And it shall be on the day when ye shall pass over Jordan unto the land which the LORD thy God giveth thee, that thou shalt set thee up great stones, and plaister them with plaister:

3 And thou shalt write upon them all the words of this law, when thou art passed over, that thou mayest go in unto the land which the LORD thy God giveth thee, a land that floweth with milk and honey; as the LORD God of thy fathers hath promised thee.

4 Therefore it shall be when ye be gone over Jordan, that ye shall set up these stones, which I command you this day, in mount Ebal, and thou shalt plaister them with plaister.

5 And there shalt thou build an altar unto the LORD thy God, an altar of stones: thou shalt not lift up any iron tool upon them.

6 Thou shalt build the altar of the LORD thy God of whole stones: and thou shalt offer burnt offerings thereon unto the LORD thy God:

7 And thou shalt offer peace offerings, and shalt eat there, and rejoice before the LORD thy God.

8 And thou shalt write upon the stones all the words of this law very plainly.

9 And Moses and the priests the Levites spake unto all Israel, saying, Take heed, and hearken, O Israel; this day thou art become the people of the LORD thy God.

10 Thou shalt therefore obey the voice of the LORD thy God, and do his commandments and his statutes, which I command thee this day.

11 And Moses charged the people the same day, saying,

12 These shall stand upon mount Gerizim to bless the people, when ye are come over Jordan; Simeon, and Levi, and Judah, and Issachar, and Joseph, and Benjamin:

13 And these shall stand upon mount Ebal to curse; Reuben, Gad, and Asher, and Zebulun, Dan, and Naphtali.

14 And the Levites shall speak, and say unto all the men of Israel with a loud voice,

15 Cursed *be* the man that maketh *any* graven or molten image, an abomination unto the LORD, the work of the hands of the craftsman, and putteth *it* in *a* secret *place*. And all the people shall answer and say, Amen.

16 Cursed *be* he that setteth light by his father or his mother. And all the people shall say, Amen.

17 Cursed *be* he that removeth his neighbour's landmark. And all the people shall say, Amen.

18 Cursed *be* he that maketh the blind to wander out of the way. And all the people shall say, Amen.

19 Cursed *be* he that perverteth the judgment of the stranger, fatherless, and widow. And all the people shall say, Amen.

20 Cursed *be* he that lieth with his father's wife; because he uncovereth his father's skirt. And all the people shall say, Amen.

21 Cursed *be* he that lieth with any manner of beast. And all the people shall say, Amen.

22 Cursed *be* he that lieth with his sister, the daughter of his father, or the daughter of his mother. And all the people shall say, Amen.

23 Cursed *be* he that lieth with his mother in law. And all the people shall say, Amen.

OUTLINE	SCRIPTURE	SCRIPTURE	OUTLINE
10) Those who commit murder—secret murder that is never discovered or put on trial 11) Those who commit murder for hire—who get paid	24 Cursed *be* he that smiteth his neighbour secretly. And all the people shall say, Amen. 25 Cursed *be* he that taketh reward to slay an innocent	person. And all the people shall say, Amen. 26 Cursed *be* he that confirmeth not *all* the words of this law to do them. And all the people shall say, Amen.	to take an innocent person's life 12) Those who are disobedient—who do not obey all the laws given by God

DIVISION V

THE THIRD GREAT THEME PREACHED BY GOD'S AGED SERVANT: THE CHARGE TO RENEW THE COVENANT WITH GOD, 27:1–30:20

A. The Charge to Renew the Covenant: The Command to Obey God, and Those to Be Cursed for Disobeying God, 27:1-26

(27:1-26) **Introduction—Judgment—Curses, of Judgment**: the curses of God and His judgment are a living reality. God is going to judge the world. Every human being who has ever lived will face the judgment of God. If a person has not approached God through the LORD Jesus Christ, that person will face God's judgment. No matter what he professes, he will stand and give an account for rejecting God's Son, give an account because profession is not what matters to God. What matters to God is not what a person professes or says but what he does. A person may say that he knows God, but if he does not have the righteous life to back up his words, his unrighteous life will cause him to face the judgment of God. What God is after is genuine faith, belief, and obedience. God wants people who will genuinely love and worship Him in all sincerity and truth. God wants obedience. Genuine belief and faith that lead to obedience are the only things that will keep a person from facing the judgment of God's curse.

Moses knew this in dealing with the Israelites. For this reason, he had just finished preaching a series of messages on the commandments and laws of God. He had to make sure that the people understood the commandments of God. Once they understood, they could live in a way that would please God. Now, having just completed the messages on the commandments, it was time for a decision. The people needed to make a rededication of their lives to God. They needed to recommit their lives to obey the covenant, the commandments of God. And so Moses now begins a brief series of messages challenging the people to make a strong decision for God. He challenges them to renew their covenant with God, to rededicate their lives. This is the subject of this great passage of Scripture: *The Charge to Renew the Covenant: The Command to Obey God, and Those to Be Cursed for Disobeying God*, 27:1-26.

1. The strong charge: keep the covenant, God's commandments, and write them down as a memorial (vv.1-8).
2. The strong challenge: be silent and listen to the covenant (vv.9-10).
3. The results of obeying and disobeying the covenant: blessings and curses (vv.11-26).

1 (27:1-8) **Commandments, Duty—Obedience, Duty—Covenant, Duty—Worship Service, Dedication of Covenant Memorial—Memorial Service, Dedication of Covenant Renewal—Altar, Built for Dedication Service—Covenant, Renewal of**: a strong charge was given to keep the covenant, God's commandments, and write them down as a memorial. Note that both Moses and the elders or national leaders gave this charge. Why would the leaders of the nation now join Moses as he preached to the people? Keep in mind that Moses was soon to die, go home to be with the LORD; therefore, Moses would not be present at the renewal of the covenant. The covenant was to be renewed after the Israelites crossed the Jordan into the promised land (v.3). The national leaders were to be responsible for leading the people in the covenant renewal. By having the national leaders join him in giving these charges, two things would happen: the people would look to them for leadership, and the leaders would sense a greater responsibility for the welfare of the people. The leaders would be more conscientious, committed to godly leadership. Two very specific charges were given to prepare the people for the renewal of the covenant.

OUTLINE	SCRIPTURE	SCRIPTURE	OUTLINE
1. The strong charge: Keep the covenant, God's commandments, & write them down as a memorial a. The charge to write the covenant, the commandments, on a stone memorial 1) To do this after entering the promised land 2) To write all the words of the law on the memorial: Do this because the LORD has fulfilled His promise,	And Moses with the elders of Israel commanded the people, saying, Keep all the commandments which I command you this day. 2 And it shall be on the day when ye shall pass over Jordan unto the land which the LORD thy God giveth thee, that thou shalt set thee up great stones, and plaister them with plaister: 3 And thou shalt write upon them all the words of this law, when thou art passed over, that thou mayest go in	unto the land which the LORD thy God giveth thee, a land that floweth with milk and honey; as the LORD God of thy fathers hath promised thee. 4 Therefore it shall be when ye be gone over Jordan, *that* ye shall set up these stones, which I command you this day, in mount Ebal, and thou shalt plaister them with plaister. 5 And there shalt thou build an altar unto the LORD thy God, an altar of stones: thou	given you the promised land 3) To set up the stone memorial on Mt. Ebal b. The charge to dedicate the covenant memorial by building an altar of stones &

DEUTERONOMY 27:1-26

OUTLINE	SCRIPTURE	SCRIPTURE	OUTLINE
offering sacrifices to God 1) To offer Burnt Offerings: A symbol of seeking atonement, reconciliation through Christ's sacrifice	shalt not lift up *any* iron tool upon them. 6 Thou shalt build the altar of the LORD thy God of whole stones: and thou shalt offer burnt offerings thereon unto the LORD thy God:	7 And thou shalt offer peace offerings, and shalt eat there, and rejoice before the LORD thy God. 8 And thou shalt write upon the stones all the words of this law very plainly.	2) To sacrifice Fellowship Offerings: A symbol of seeking more of the peace & fellowship of God 3) To clearly write the covenant, the commandments, on the stone memorial: Make them readable

a. The first charge was to write the covenant, the commandments, on a stone memorial (vv.2-4). Some large stones were to be taken and whitewashed, coated with white plaster, and then the covenant or commandments were to be engraved upon the white stones. Note that all the words of the law were to be written on the memorial stones. What is meant by all the words of the law? Does this mean the entire book of *Deuteronomy* was to be written? Or all the laws that were given at Mt. Sinai? Or just the Ten Commandments? Just what is meant by *all the law* is not clearly stated anyplace. However, the covenant was based upon the laws that were given at Mt. Sinai, which included both the Ten Commandments and the civil and religious laws (see outline and notes—Ex.20:1-24:18 for more discussion).

Note that the memorial stones were to be prepared after the people had crossed the Jordan and entered the promised land. They were to be set up as a stone memorial on Mt. Ebal (v.4). This location is significant, for at the base of Mt. Ebal sat the city of Shechem. Shechem was one of the very first places where God appeared to Abraham and gave him the great promise of the promised land (Ge.12:6-7). For this reason, God's people had always attached great significance to the area. It was no doubt being deliberately chosen by God for this very reason: it was an ideal place for the covenant to be renewed between Him and the people.

b. A second charge was given to the people: they were to dedicate the covenant memorial, dedicate it by building an altar of stones and offering sacrifices up to God (vv.5-8). Note that no iron tool was to be used to shape the stones of the altar (v.5). Only undressed field stones were to be used. No stone was to be touched by any tool of man. Touching the stones with any tool or giving any shape to the stone was considered by God to be a defilement (see outline and notes, pt.2—Ex.20:23-26 for more discussion). The point is that worship was to be totally free of man, free from man's thought or the effort of man to shape the alter of worship like he thought it should be. Worship is shaped and determined by God, not man. Therefore, the altar was not to be shaped by man. It was to be natural, free of any ostentation and flashiness dreamed up by man.

Note that the people were to approach God through the sacrifice of the Burnt Offerings and the Fellowship Offerings (vv.6-7). The sacrifice of the Burnt Offerings symbolized their seeking atonement, reconciliation through the substitute sacrifice. And the sacrifice of the Fellowship Offerings symbolized the people's seeking more of the peace and fellowship of God. (See outlines and notes—Le.1:1-17; 3:1-17 for more discussion.)

Note the reemphasis upon the memorial stone for the covenant renewal. The people were to make sure that the covenant, the commandments, were clearly written on the stones. The very reason the memorial stone was being erected was to emphasize the importance of the covenant, the commandments. Therefore, the commandments had to be readable (v.8).

Thought 1. When we accept Jesus Christ as our LORD and Savior, we are making a covenant with God that we will follow Him and obey Him—keep His commandments. The commandments of God must be a memorial written upon our hearts, a memorial that we can read anytime throughout the day. As a memorial written upon our hearts, the commandments can be a guide to us as we walk throughout the day and keep us obedient and faithful to the LORD. The commandments need to be so engraved within us that we will become a dynamic testimony and witness for Christ. The charge of God is clear: His commandments are to be engraved upon our hearts. We are, therefore, to heed His commandments, to keep them as we walk throughout the day.

"If thou wilt enter into life, keep the commandments" (Mt.19:17).

"He that hath my commandments, and keepeth them, he it is that loveth me: and he that loveth me shall be loved of my Father, and I will love him, and will manifest myself to him" (Jn.14:21).

"Jesus answered and said unto him, If a man love me, he will keep my words: and my Father will love him, and we will come unto him, and make our abode with him" (Jn.14:23).

"If ye keep my commandments, ye shall abide in my love; even as I have kept my Father's commandments, and abide in his love" (Jn.15:10).

"Ye are my friends, if ye do whatsoever I command you" (Jn.15:14).

"For I delight in the law of God after the inward man" (Ro.7:22).

"For by one offering he [Christ] hath perfected for ever them that are sanctified [set apart to God]. *Whereof* the Holy Ghost also is a witness to us: for after that he had said before, This *is* the covenant that I will make with them after those days, saith the Lord, I will put my laws into their hearts, and in their minds will I write them; And their sins and iniquities will I remember no more. Now where remission of these *is, there is* no more offering for sin. Having therefore, brethren, boldness to enter into the holiest by the blood of Jesus, By a new and living way, which he hath consecrated for us, through the veil, that is to say, his flesh; And *having* an high priest over the house of God; Let us draw near with a true heart in full assurance of faith, having our hearts sprinkled from an evil conscience, and our bodies washed with pure water. Let us hold fast the profession of *our* faith without wavering; (for he is faithful that promised" (He.10:14-23).

"For this is the love of God, that we keep his commandments: and his commandments are not grievous" (1 Jn.5:3).

DEUTERONOMY 27:1-26

"Here is the patience of the saints: here *are* they that keep the commandments of God, and the faith of Jesus" (Re.14:12).

"The law of his God *is* in his heart; none of his steps shall slide" (Ps.37:31).

"I delight to do thy will, O my God: yea, thy law *is* within my heart" (Ps.40:8).

"Ye shall diligently keep the commandments of the LORD your God, and his testimonies, and his statutes, which he hath commanded thee" (De.6:17).

"This book of the law shall not depart out of thy mouth; but thou shalt meditate therein day and night, that thou mayest observe to do according to all that is written therein: for then thou shalt make thy way prosperous, and then thou shalt have good success" (Jos.1:8).

"But this *shall be* the covenant that I will make with the house of Israel; After those days, saith the LORD, I will put my law in their inward parts, and write it in their hearts; and will be their God, and they shall be my people" (Je.31:33).

"And I will make an everlasting covenant with them, that I will not turn away from them, to do them good; but I will put my fear in their hearts, that they shall not depart from me" (Je.32:40).

2 (27:9-10) **Covenant, Duty—Obedience, Duty—Commandments, Duty—Covenant, Renewal of**: Moses and the priests gave a strong challenge to the people: be silent and listen to the covenant. There are two parts to the covenant, God's part and the people's part:

OUTLINE	SCRIPTURE

2. **The strong challenge: Be silent & listen to the covenant**
a. Know God's part in the covenant: God makes you His people—you have become the people of God
b. Know your part, your duty
  1) Keep the covenant
  2) Obey the LORD your God
  3) Follow His commandments
	9 And Moses and the priests the Levites spake unto all Israel, saying, Take heed, and hearken, O Israel; this day thou art become the people of the LORD thy God.
	10 Thou shalt therefore obey the voice of the LORD thy God, and do his commandments and his statutes, which I command thee this day.

a. There was God's part in the covenant. The people were to know God's part, that God had made them His people and set them apart to be His very special followers and witnesses to the world. The Lord had challenged the Israelites to believe and follow Him, and the Israelites had become the people of God because they had made the commitment to follow God. Because of their commitment, God had accepted them as His people, His treasured possession. Because of their faith, they had become the people of the LORD God (v.9).

b. There was the people's part in the covenant (v.10). They had one strict responsibility, one strong duty to fulfill: they must keep the covenant, obey the LORD God, follow His commandments.

Once the Israelites had crossed the Jordan into the promised land, they were to renew this covenant with God. As they renewed the covenant, they were to acknowledge God's part: that by faith they had become the people of God. Because of their faith God had accepted them and made them His *treasured possession*, His very special people and witnesses upon this earth. But knowing God's part was not enough: they, too, had a part in the covenant. Their responsibility was to keep the covenant, obey the LORD their God, following all of His commandments. Note that it is the love of God that was to stir obedience. The fact that God accepted their faith and made them His people was to stir the people to obey God and keep His commandments. Knowing the wonderful grace of God was to arouse a deep sense of responsibility in the people. This was to be the renewal of the covenant with God once the Israelites had crossed the Jordan into the promised land.

Thought 1. The wonderful grace of God in saving us through faith—the fact that He has accepted us and made us His people and witnesses upon this earth—should arouse us to keep the covenant, to obey the LORD and follow His commandments. The love of God should stir a deep sense of responsibility within us. God's part in the great covenant of grace is to accept us by faith in His Son, the LORD Jesus Christ, making us His people. Our part in the cov-enant is to obey God. It is the love of God—His wonderful grace—that stirs us to obey Him. We must, therefore, keep the picture of His grace in our minds and obey Him. If we keep the grace of God before our minds, we will obey Him. His love, His grace will stir us to obedience.

"We love him, because he first loved us" (1 Jn.4:19).

"Not every one that saith unto me, Lord, Lord, shall enter into the kingdom of heaven; but he that doeth the will of my Father which is in heaven" (Mt.7:21).

"For the love of Christ constraineth us; because we thus judge, that if one died for all, then were all dead: And that he died for all, that they which live should not henceforth live unto themselves, but unto him which died for them, and rose again" (2 Co.5:14-15).

"Keep yourselves in the love of God, looking for the mercy of our Lord Jesus Christ unto eternal life" (Jude 21).

"Blessed are they that do his commandments, that they may have right to the tree of life, and may enter in through the gates into the city" (Re.22:14).

DEUTERONOMY 27:1-26

"And now, Israel, what doth the Lord thy God require of thee, but to fear the Lord thy God, to walk in all his ways, and to love him, and to serve the Lord thy God with all thy heart and with all thy soul" (De.10:12).

"This day the Lord thy God hath commanded thee to do these statutes and judgments: thou shalt therefore keep and do them with all thine heart, and with all thy soul" (De.26:16).

"And Samuel said, Hath the Lord as great delight in burnt offerings and sacrifices, as in obeying the voice of the Lord? Behold, to obey is better than sacrifice, and to hearken than the fat of rams" (1 S.15:22).

3 (27:11-26) **Obedience, Results of—Disobedience, Results of—Covenant, Renewal of—Blessings, Source of—Curses, Source of—Curses, Caused by**: the results of obeying and disobeying the covenant were spelled out by Moses. If they obeyed God, they would be blessed; but if they disobeyed God, they would be cursed. Note that Moses instructed the people to conduct a worship service during which they would renew the covenant with God. The worship service was actually to be a ceremony of recommitment to the covenant, and the ceremony was to be a recitation shouted out by the people. During the renewal ceremony, the people were actually to shout out the blessings for obedience and the curses for disobedience. Note how the ceremony is described in the Scripture and outline:

OUTLINE	SCRIPTURE	SCRIPTURE	OUTLINE
3. The results of obeying & disobeying the covenant: Blessings & curses	11 And Moses charged the people the same day, saying,	way. And all the people shall say, Amen.	of the disabled
a. The striking ceremony that was to picture the covenant renewal	12 These shall stand upon mount Gerizim to bless the people, when ye are come over Jordan; Simeon, and Levi, and Judah, and Issachar, and Joseph, and Benjamin:	19 Cursed *be* he that perverteth the judgment of the stranger, fatherless, and widow. And all the people shall say, Amen.	5) Those who mistreat of the foreigner, orphan, & widows—symbolizing all the poor, weak, & disadvantaged
1) Six tribes were to stand on Mt. Gerizim^{DS1} to pronounce the blessings for obeying		20 Cursed *be* he that lieth with his father's wife; because he uncovereth his father's skirt. And all the people shall say, Amen.	6) Those who commit incest—sexual relations with one's mother (or father)
2) Six tribes were to stand on Mt. Ebal^{DS2} to proclaim the curses for disobeying	13 And these shall stand upon mount Ebal to curse; Reuben, Gad, and Asher, and Zebulun, Dan, and Naphtali.	21 Cursed *be* he that lieth with any manner of beast. And all the people shall say, Amen.	7) Those who commit bestiality
3) The Levites—standing between the two—were to recite the blessings & curses	14 And the Levites shall speak, and say unto all the men of Israel with a loud voice,	22 Cursed *be* he that lieth with his sister, the daughter of his father, or the daughter of his mother. And all the people shall say, Amen.	8) Those who commit incest—sexual relations with one's sister (or brother)
4) The people were to respond, "Amen"			
b. The curses for disobedience	15 Cursed *be* the man that maketh *any* graven or molten image, an abomination unto the LORD, the work of the hands of the craftsman, and putteth *it* in *a* secret *place*. And all the people shall answer and say, Amen.	23 Cursed *be* he that lieth with his mother in law. And all the people shall say, Amen.	9) Those who commit incest—sexual relations with one's mother-in-law (or father-in-law)
1) Those who commit idolatry & false worship		24 Cursed *be* he that smiteth his neighbour secretly. And all the people shall say, Amen.	10) Those who commit murder—secret murder that is never discovered or put on trial
• Is detestable to God			
• The people's response: "Amen!" They understand & agree to the terms			
2) Those who dishonor parents	16 Cursed *be* he that setteth light by his father or his mother. And all the people shall say, Amen.	25 Cursed *be* he that taketh reward to slay an innocent person. And all the people shall say, Amen.	11) Those who commit murder for hire—who get paid to take an innocent person's life
3) Those who steal	17 Cursed *be* he that removeth his neighbour's landmark. And all the people shall say, Amen.	26 Cursed *be* he that confirmeth not *all* the words of this law to do them. And all the people shall say, Amen.	12) Those who are disobedient—who do not obey all the laws given by God
4) Those who lead the blind astray—taking advantage	18 Cursed *be* he that maketh the blind to wander out of the		

a. The ceremony that was to picture the covenant renewal was striking (vv.12-14). The scene was to be very dramatic. It was to be conducted in an extraordinary manner—a moving, emotional event that would stir the people to make a renewed commitment to the covenant or commandments of God. Note how the ceremony was to be conducted:

⇒ Six tribes were to gather on Mt. Gerizim to pronounce the blessings upon the people if they were obedient (v.12).
⇒ Six tribes were to gather on Mt. Ebal to pronounce the curses if they disobeyed God (v.13).
⇒ The Levites were to stand between the two mountains and actually shout out the blessings and curses (v.14). It should be noted that the Levites who stood in the valley between the two mountains were the priests who took care of the Ark of the Covenant. They stood there beside the ark and shouted out the blessings and curses. This is significant, for it means that the people were in fact looking down upon the ark that contained the law of the covenant or the Ten Commandments while they were shouting their understanding of the blessings and curses. The Ark of the Covenant was a dramatic visual reminder of their responsibility to obey the commandments of God.

DEUTERONOMY 27:1-26

⇒ Right after the Levites shouted out a blessing or a curse, the people were to respond by shouting out, "Amen" (see vv.15-26).

b. Scripture now covers the categories of people who will be cursed due to their disobedience (vv.15-26). Peter C. Craigie points out that the theme running throughout these curses seems to be *secrecy*.[1] They seem to cover certain crimes that are not easily discovered and, therefore, could not be brought to trial before a human court. However, the crimes are always known to God. Nothing can be hidden from Him, nothing ever done that is kept secret from Him. God sees and knows all; therefore, every crime, every sinful act will be brought before God. There are no secrets to God: those who commit sinful acts behind closed doors and in secret will face the eternal judgment of God.

1) The first curse concerned idolatry and false worship (v.15). This was detestable to God, and it broke both the first and second commandments (see outlines and notes—Ex.20:3; 20:4-6 for more discussion). Once the priests shouted out that idolatry and false worship were to be cursed, judged by God, the people were to respond by shouting out, "Amen!" By shouting out "amen," they were declaring that they understood and agreed to the terms of this curse. Never would they be disobedient by engaging in idolatry or false worship.
2) The second curse concerned dishonoring parents (v.16). This was a violation of the fifth commandment (see outline and notes—Ex.20:12; De.5:16 for more discussion). The person who dishonored his parents was to face the judgment of God and be cursed. Once this curse had been shouted out by the priest standing by the ark, the people were to shout out, "Amen!" They fully understood their duty and agreed to the terms of the curse with God.
3) The third curse concerned stealing (v.17). If a person stole, he broke the eighth commandment (see outlines and notes—Ex.20:15; De.5:19 for more discussion). Note the example given, an example that stands as an illustration for all forms of stealing: a man moves his neighbor's boundary stone. He steals a portion of his neighbor's property. The priests were to shout out that the person who stole was to be cursed by God. Then all the people were to cry out, "Amen!" They fully understood and agreed. They were not to steal the property of other people.
4) The fourth curse concerned leading the blind astray, that is, taking advantage of the disabled (v.18). The priests were to shout out that the person who took advantage of the disabled was to face the judgment of God and be cursed. Understanding and agreeing to the terms, the people were to respond by shouting, "Amen!"
5) The fifth curse concerned the mistreatment of foreigners, orphans, and widows. The mentioning of these three classifications of people symbolizes all the poor, weak, and disadvantaged of society (v.19). The people were to fully understand their responsibility to help the poor and suffering of society. The priests were to shout out that any person who failed to help the weak of society would be cursed by God. Upon hearing the curse, the people were to respond by saying, "Amen!"
6) The sixth curse concerned incest, that of having sexual relations with one's mother and, by implication, one's father (v.20). This is a terrible sin in the eyes of God, a sin that dishonors the father's bed. The priests were to shout out God's curse upon any person who had sexual relations with his parents, and the people were to respond that they fully understood God's curse, respond by shouting out, "Amen!"
7) The seventh curse concerned bestiality, having sexual relations with any animal (v.21). This is the most repulsive, disgusting, and foul sin that can be imagined. It is so disgusting that even the thought of such an evil act is offensive. Nevertheless, the curse was to be shouted out by the priests and the people were to respond by crying out, "Amen!" They fully understood and agreed to the terms of this curse.
8) The eighth curse also concerned incest, in particular having sexual relations with one's sister and, by implication, one's brother (v.22). Upon hearing this curse pronounced, the people were to respond, "Amen!"
9) The ninth curse also concerned incest, having sexual relations with one's mother-in-law or, by implication, one's father-in-law (v.23). All of these sexual sins that have been mentioned involve the breaking of the seventh commandment that forbids adultery or immorality (see outlines and notes—Ex.20:14; De.5:18 for more discussion). The people were to clearly understand that God condemns and curses the person who commits adultery or immorality. Once the priests had shouted out this curse, the people were to cry out, "Amen!" They fully understood and agreed that adultery or immorality would be cursed and judged by God.
10) The tenth curse concerned murder, the secret murder that is never discovered or taken to trial by man (v.24). Murder is a violation of the sixth commandment, "You shall not kill" (see outline and notes—Ex.20:13; De.5:17 for more discussion). The murderer may never be discovered by man, but God knows. He even saw the murder when it was committed, the agonizing pain of the victim and the grief and suffering of loved ones. The priests were to shout out that the murderer would be cursed by God and bear His eternal judgment, and the people were to respond by saying, "Amen!"
11) The eleventh curse also concerned murder, but in this case murder that is hired out and never discovered (v.25). The point that was to be driven into the hearts of the people is a fact that must be known by all men of all generations: all murderers, even the person who hires out a murder, will be cursed and judged eternally by God (v.25). But this is not all: the person who accepts the bribe to kill an innocent person will also be judged and cursed by God. The priests were to shout out this curse, and then the people were to respond by saying, "Amen!"
12) The twelfth curse is an all-inclusive curse, a curse against all disobedience (v.26). The priests were to shout out that any person who did not obey all the laws given by God would suffer the curse and judgment of God. Standing there upon the mountains, all the people were to respond by shouting out, "Amen!" They fully understood and agreed to obey and carry out all the laws of God.

Thought 1. There are two strong lessons for us in this passage:
(1) No person can keep the law in every detail, not perfectly. Consequently, every human person is under the curse of God. This is exactly what the New Testament declares:

---

[1] Peter C. Craigie. *The Book of Deuteronomy*, p.331.

"For as many as are of the works of the law are under the curse: for it is written, Cursed *is* every one that continueth not in all things which are written in the book of the law to do them" (Ga.3:10).

Frankly, the law covers too much for a person to follow every commandment. The law includes and embraces all of human nature, every possible thought as well as act. We all stand guilty before God for breaking the law. This was the very reason Christ came. He came to deliver us from the curse of the law. This He did by becoming a curse for us, that is, by bearing the penalty and curse that was due us—all in our behalf. When we place our faith in Him, God sees Christ bearing the curse for us. And He sees us standing there in the righteousness of Christ, free from the curse. Therefore, we become acceptable to Him—all because we trust Christ, trust the fact that He bore the curse of the law for us.

"Therefore by the deeds of the law there shall no flesh be justified in his sight: for by the law *is* the knowledge of sin. But now the righteousness of God without the law is manifested, being witnessed by the law and the prophets; Even the righteousness of God *which is* by faith of Jesus Christ unto all and upon all them that believe: for there is no difference" (Ro.3:20-22).

"*There is* therefore now no condemnation to them which are in Christ Jesus, who walk not after the flesh, but after the Spirit. For the law of the Spirit of life in Christ Jesus hath made me free from the law of sin and death. For what the law could not do, in that it was weak through the flesh, God sending his own Son in the likeness of sinful flesh, and for sin, condemned sin in the flesh: That the righteousness of the law might be fulfilled in us, who walk not after the flesh, but after the Spirit" (Ro.8:1-4).

"For he hath made him *to be* sin for us, who knew no sin; that we might be made the righteousness of God in him" (2 Co.5:21).

"For as many as are of the works of the law are under the curse: for it is written, Cursed *is* every one that continueth not in all things which are written in the book of the law to do them. But that no man is justified by the law in the sight of God, *it is* evident: for, The just shall live by faith. And the law is not of faith: but, The man that doeth them shall live in them. Christ hath redeemed us from the curse of the law, being made a curse for us: for it is written, Cursed *is* every one that hangeth on a tree" (Ga.3:10-13).

"Christ hath redeemed us from the curse of the law, being made a curse for us: for it is written, Cursed *is* every one that hangeth on a tree" (Ga.3:13).

"But before faith came, we were kept under the law, shut up unto the faith which should afterwards be revealed. Wherefore the law was our schoolmaster *to bring us* unto Christ, that we might be justified by faith" (Ga.3:23-24).

"For we have not an high priest which cannot be touched with the feeling of our infirmities; but was in all points tempted like as *we are, yet* without sin" (He.4:15).

"For this *is* the covenant that I will make with the house of Israel after those days, saith the Lord; I will put my laws into their mind, and write them in their hearts: and I will be to them a God, and they shall be to me a people" (He.8:10).

"*Whereof* the Holy Ghost also is a witness to us: for after that he had said before, This *is* the covenant that I will make with them after those days, saith the Lord, I will put my laws into their hearts, and in their minds will I write them; And their sins and iniquities will I remember no more. Now where remission of these *is, there is* no more offering for sin. Having therefore, brethren, boldness to enter into the holiest by the blood of Jesus, By a new and living way, which he hath consecrated for us, through the veil, that is to say, his flesh" (He.10:15-20).

(2) We must obey God, keep His commandments. Being saved does not free us from our responsibility to obey God. In fact, our salvation lays more of an obligation upon us. We are to obey God even more because of our salvation. The death of Jesus Christ does not erase the law of God nor our responsibility to obey God. What happened was this: the law was fulfilled in Christ. He came to fulfill the law, not to destroy it. This means that the law is wrapped up in Christ. He fulfilled the law, embraced it, laid hold of it, made it a part of His very being. Christ embraces the law and so much more. He is the full embodiment of righteousness, of all that God Himself is. Therefore, when we follow Christ, we follow all that Christ is, all of His righteousness which includes both the commandments and the very nature of God itself. The point is clear: we must obey all the righteousness of God which includes the commandments of God.

"Think not that I am come to destroy the law, or the prophets: I am not come to destroy, but to fulfil" (Mt.5:17).

"Not every one that saith unto me, Lord, Lord, shall enter into the kingdom of heaven; but he that doeth the will of my Father which is in heaven" (Mt.7:21).

"He that hath my commandments, and keepeth them, he it is that loveth me: and he that loveth me shall be loved of my Father, and I will love him, and will manifest myself to him" (Jn.14:21).

"Jesus answered and said unto him, If a man love me, he will keep my words: and my Father will love him, and we will come unto him, and make our abode with him" (Jn.14:23).

"If ye keep my commandments, ye shall abide in my love; even as I have kept my Father's commandments, and abide in his love" (Jn.15:10).

"Ye are my friends, if ye do whatsoever I command you" (Jn.15:14).

"Let no man deceive you with vain words: for because of these things cometh the wrath of God upon the children of disobedience" (Ep.5:6).

"And to you who are troubled rest with us, when the Lord Jesus shall be revealed from heaven with his mighty angels, In flaming fire taking vengeance on them that know not God, and that obey not the

DEUTERONOMY 27:1-26

gospel of our Lord Jesus Christ: Who shall be punished with everlasting destruction from the presence of the Lord, and from the glory of his power" (2 Th.1:7-9).

"But whoso looketh into the perfect law of liberty, and continueth *therein,* he being not a forgetful hearer, but a doer of the work, this man shall be blessed in his deed" (Js.1:25).

"Blessed *are* they that do his commandments, that they may have right to the tree of life, and may enter in through the gates into the city" (Re.22:14).

"O that there were such an heart in them, that they would fear me, and keep all my commandments always, that it might be well with them, and with their children for ever" (De.5:29).

DEEPER STUDY # 1

(27:12) **Gerizim, Mount**: a mountain that sits across from Mount Ebal and along with Mount Ebal forms the valley of Shechem. Mount Gerizim is 2,849 feet above the Mediterranean, 700 feet above the valley, and today is called Jebel el-Tor.[2] Mount Gerizim is commonly known as the "Mountain of Blessings." It is well-known for several historical events:

⇒ It was the place where the *blessings for obedience* to God were pronounced by six of the tribes (De.11:29; 27:12).
⇒ It was the place where Jotham shared his parable and prophetic curse upon Abimelech and the people of Shechem (Jud.9:7-15).
⇒ It became the place of false worship after the Northern Kingdom of Israel fell to the Assyrians (2 K.17:33).

DEEPER STUDY # 2

(27:13) **Ebal, Mount**: a mountain that sits across from Mount Gerizim and along with Mount Gerizim forms the valley of Shechem. Mount Ebal is 2,950 feet above sea level and today is called Jebel Eslamiyeh.[3] Mount Ebal is commonly known as the "Mountain of Curses." It is well-known for several historical events:

⇒ It was the place where the *curses for disobedience* to God were pronounced by six of the tribes (De.11:29; 27:13).
⇒ It was the place where the law of Moses was recorded and read by Joshua along with the blessings and the cursings (Jos.8:30-35).[4]

TYPES, SYMBOLS, AND PICTURES
(Deuteronomy 27:1-26)

Historical Term	Type or Picture (Scriptural Basis for Each)	Life Application for Today's Believer	Biblical Application
The Sacrifice of the Burnt Offerings De.27:1-8 (See also Le. 1:1-17; 6:8-13; 8:18-21; 16:24; Nu.6:3-12; 15:1-16; 28:11-15)	The sacrifice of the Burnt Offerings symbolized Israel's seeking atonement or reconciliation through the substitute sacrifice. The Burnt Offering is a type of Christ, a symbol or picture of Christ dying as the substitute sacrifice for us. By dying for us: ⇒ Christ bore the full judgment of God against sin—paid the ransom price to deliver us from sin and death ⇒ Christ secured the atonement for us, reconciling us to God

"Thou shalt build the altar of the LORD thy God of whole stones: and thou shalt offer burnt offerings thereon unto the LORD thy God" (De.27:6). | ⇒ Jesus Christ died for us as our substitute sacrifice. He died to secure the atonement or reconciliation with God for us. A person can now approach God and be reconciled with God; a person can now become acceptable to God. How? By approaching God through the sacrifice of Christ. | "But God commendeth his love toward us, in that, while we were yet sinners, Christ died for us. Much more then, being now justified by his blood, we shall be saved from wrath through him. For if, when we were enemies, we were reconciled to God by the death of his Son, much more, being reconciled, we shall be saved by his life. And not only so, but we also joy in God through our Lord Jesus Christ, by whom we have now received the atonement." (Ro.5:8-11). "And he shall put his hand upon the head of the burnt offering; and it shall be accepted for him to make atonement for him" (Le.1:4). "Wherefore in all things it behooved him to be made like unto his brethren, that he might be a merciful and faithful high priest in things pertaining to God, to make reconciliation for the sins of the people" (He.2:17). |

---

2 *New Unger's Bible Dictionary.* Chicago, IL: Moody Press, 1988.
3 *Holman Bible Dictionary.* Nashville, TN: Holman Bible Publishers, 1991.
4 *New Unger's Bible Dictionary.*

Deuteronomy 27:1-26

Historical Term	Type or Picture (Scriptural Basis for Each)	Life Application for Today's Believer	Biblical Application
The Sacrifice of the Fellowship Offerings De.27:1-8 (See also Le.3:1-17; Nu.6:13-20; 15:1-16)	*The Fellowship Or Peace Offering is a type of Christ, a symbol or picture of Christ, the One who died on the cross bearing the judgment of God for man. The sacrifice of Christ made peace between a holy God and an alienated, fallen, depraved people. The sacrifice of Christ and Christ alone brings peace and fellowship between man and God.* **"And thou shalt offer peace offerings, and shalt eat there, and rejoice before the Lord thy God"** (De.27:7).	⇒ How do we grow in the fellowship and peace of God? Very simply, by seeking more of the fellowship and peace of God. We must stand upon the completed work of Christ's sacrifice on the cross. Because of Christ... • we can enjoy the fellowship of the Lord • we can experience the peace of God (See outlines and notes—Le.1:1-17; 3:1-17 for more discussion.)	*"That which we have seen and heard declare we unto you, that ye also may have fellowship with us: and truly our fellowship is with the Father, and with his Son Jesus Christ"* (1 Jn.1:3). *"But if we walk in the light, as he is in the light, we have fellowship one with another, and the blood of Jesus Christ his Son cleanseth us from all sin"* (1 Jn.1:7).

DEUTERONOMY 28:1-14

Outline	Scripture	Outline
	CHAPTER 28 **B. The Results of Obeying the Covenant: The Blessings of God, 28:1-14**	

1. The blessings of God are conditional
  a. Must obey the LORD
  b. The result of obedience
    1) Will be exalted
 	
    2) Will experience all the blessings of God
 	
    3) Will be continually blessed—no matter where you are
2. The blessing of fruitfulness
  a. The fruitfulness of population growth
  b. The fruitfulness of livestock
  c. The fruitfulness of crops
  d. The fruitfulness of daily food
3. The blessing of all daily activities
 	
4. The blessing of victory over all enemies (see Ep.6:10-18)
 	
5. The blessing of labor, work, employment
  a. The promise: God will bless all you put your hand to
	And it shall come to pass, if thou shalt hearken diligently unto the voice of the LORD thy God, to observe *and* to do all his commandments which I command thee this day, that the LORD thy God will set thee on high above all nations of the earth:
	2 And all these blessings shall come on thee, and overtake thee, if thou shalt hearken unto the voice of the LORD thy God.
	3 Blessed *shalt* thou *be* in the city, and blessed *shalt* thou *be* in the field.
	4 Blessed *shall be* the fruit of thy body, and the fruit of thy ground, and the fruit of thy cattle, the increase of thy kine, and the flocks of thy sheep.
	5 Blessed *shall be* thy basket and thy store.
	6 Blessed *shalt* thou *be* when thou comest in, and blessed *shalt* thou *be* when thou goest out.
	7 The LORD shall cause thine enemies that rise up against thee to be smitten before thy face: they shall come out against thee one way, and flee before thee seven ways.
	8 The LORD shall command the blessing upon thee in thy storehouses, and in all that thou settest thine hand unto; and he shall bless thee in the land which the LORD thy God giveth thee.
	9 The LORD shall establish thee an holy people unto himself, as he hath sworn unto thee, if thou shalt keep the commandments of the LORD thy God, and walk in his ways.
	10 And all people of the earth shall see that thou art called by the name of the LORD; and they shall be afraid of thee.
	11 And the LORD shall make thee plenteous in goods, in the fruit of thy body, and in the fruit of thy cattle, and in the fruit of thy ground, in the land which the LORD sware unto thy fathers to give thee.
	12 The LORD shall open unto thee his good treasure, the heaven to give the rain unto thy land in his season, and to bless all the work of thine hand: and thou shalt lend unto many nations, and thou shalt not borrow.
	13 And the LORD shall make thee the head, and not the tail; and thou shalt be above only, and thou shalt not be beneath; if that thou hearken unto the commandments of the LORD thy God, which I command thee this day, to observe and to do *them*:
	14 And thou shalt not go aside from any of the words which I command thee this day, *to* the right hand, or *to* the left, to go after other gods to serve them.
		b. The result: Will experience purpose, achievement, accomplishment, fulfillment
		6. The blessing of spiritual growth
		  a. The promise: God will establish you as His holy people
		  b. The condition: Must obey God
		
		  c. The result: A strong testimony & witness for the LORD—the exaltation of the LORD's name
		7. The blessing of prosperity, an excess of good things
		  a. The good things such as children, livestock, crops
		
		  b. The LORD will open the storehouse, the treasury, of His provision: Rain & a blessing upon all the work of your hands
		  c. The blessing of a prosperous, wealthy economy
		8. The blessing of exaltation
		  a. The promise: Will become the head or leader, not the tail
		  b. The condition: Must obey God
		  c. The promise reemphasized: Will always be on top, not on bottom
		9. The strong charge: A person must not turn away from any of the commandments to follow false gods or false worship

DIVISION V

THE THIRD GREAT THEME PREACHED BY GOD'S AGED SERVANT: THE CHARGE TO RENEW THE COVENANT WITH GOD, 27:1–30:20

B. The Results of Obeying the Covenant: The Blessings of God, 28:1-14

(28:1-14) **Introduction**: the blessings of God are not automatically poured out upon people. God is not a robot, not a mechanical being that acts impulsively, on the spur of the moment without thought or purpose. The blessings of God are not the result of a reflex emotion that arouses God to bless this and that person. The blessings of God are not poured out indiscriminately, at random, in a chaotic manner. God demands something of a person before He blesses that person. God's blessings are conditional. A person has to do something in order to receive God's blessings. The blessings of God are the subject of the present passage.

Remember, the children of Israel were camped in the plains of Moab close by the river Jordan, right across from the great city of Jericho. They were poised to cross the river and enter the promised land. But before they entered, Moses felt the need to preach a series of messages to the people. He needed to make sure that the people understood exactly how they were to live in the promised land of God. His messages were later compiled into the book of Deuteronomy. In essence, Deuteronomy is the preaching of Moses during the days when the Israelites were camped beside the Jordan River, preparing to enter the promised land. At this point, the messages are nearing completion. Moses has almost accomplished his purpose. The people are prepared, as much so as Moses is capable of preparing them. Only one more thing remains: the people need to renew their covenant with God. They need to make a rededication, a recommitment to God, before actually entering the promised

DEUTERONOMY 28:1-14

land. The present passage deals with the blessings and cursings of the covenant. The people were to be blessed if they obeyed God, but cursed if they disobeyed Him. First, the blessings of God are to be preached; then next, the curses of God will be preached. This is the subject of this great passage of Scripture: *The Results of Obeying the Covenant: The Blessings of God,* 28:1-14.

1. The blessings of God are conditional (vv.1-3).
2. The blessing of fruitfulness (vv.4-5).
3. The blessing of all daily activities (v.6).
4. The blessing of victory over all enemies (v.7).
5. The blessing of labor, work, employment (v.8).
6. The blessing of spiritual growth (vv.9-10).
7. The blessing of prosperity, an excess of good things (vv.11-12).
8. The blessing of exaltation (v.13).
9. The strong charge: must not turn away from any of the commandments to follow false gods or false worship (v.14).

1 (28:1-3) **Blessings, of God, Conditional—Obedience, Results of—Exhortation, of Believer—Honor, of Believer**: the blessings of God are conditional. Being a human being does not automatically qualify a person for God's blessings. God does not mechanically or impulsively pour out His blessings upon people. He is not a robot who is ordered or programmed to help people when they cry out to Him. Certain conditions have to be met before a person can receive the blessings of God. Note what the Scripture says:

OUTLINE	SCRIPTURE
1. The blessings of God are conditional a. Must obey the LORD b. The result of obedience 1) Will be exalted	And it shall come to pass, if thou shalt hearken diligently unto the voice of the LORD thy God, to observe *and* to do all his commandments which I command thee this day, that the LORD thy God will set thee on high above all nations of the earth:
2) Will experience all the blessings of God	2 And all these blessings shall come on thee, and overtake thee, if thou shalt hearken unto the voice of the LORD thy God.
3) Will be continually blessed—no matter where you are	3 Blessed *shalt* thou *be* in the city, and blessed *shalt* thou *be* in the field.

  a. A person must obey the LORD: fully, diligently obey the LORD, carefully observe and follow all His commandments. Obedience is the one condition that has to be met to receive the blessings of God.
  b. Note the results of obedience declared by Moses:
    ⇒ If the people obeyed God, God would exalt them above all the nations on earth (v.1). They would be a great nation, a great people to whom all other nations and peoples would look.
    ⇒ If the people obeyed God, they would experience all the blessings of God (v.2). No blessing would be withheld from them. They would walk in all the fullness and victory of life.
    ⇒ If the people obeyed God, they would be continually blessed, no matter where they were (v.3). If they lived in the city they would be blessed, and if they lived in the country they would be blessed. The blessings of God would flow from heaven no matter where they lived.

Thought 1. The blessings of God are conditional. Promise after promise is given to the believer, but the believer has to believe God to receive the promises. He has to stay focused upon God and His promises, keep his mind upon them. Only if he stays focused upon God will he obey God and receive the promises. Obedience is an absolute essential to receive the blessings of God.

Think about this: if a person is not obeying God, he is not staying focused upon the blessings or promises given by God. Consequently, it is only a *natural outcome* that he will not receive the blessings of God. But if the person is obeying God, he is focused upon the promises of God's blessings. Walking throughout the day, he is honoring God by staying focused upon Him and His blessings. Therefore, God is bound to bless him, for it is the honor, worship, and obedience of man that God wants. This is the very purpose for which God created man.

Again, the man who is obeying God stays focused upon God. Consequently, God blesses him, pours out blessing after blessing upon him. All because the man walks obediently before Him. The declaration of Scripture is forceful:

> "Not every one that saith unto me, Lord, Lord, shall enter into the kingdom of heaven; but he that doeth the will of my Father which is in heaven" (Mt.7:21).
> "Therefore whosoever heareth these sayings of mine, and doeth them, I will liken him unto a wise man, which built his house upon a rock: And the rain descended, and the floods came, and the winds blew, and beat upon that house; and it fell not: for it was founded upon a rock. And every one that

DEUTERONOMY 28:1-14

heareth these sayings of mine, and doeth them not, shall be likened unto a foolish man, which built his house upon the sand: And the rain descended, and the floods came, and the winds blew, and beat upon that house; and it fell: and great was the fall of it" (Mt.7:24-27).

"He that hath my commandments, and keepeth them, he it is that loveth me: and he that loveth me shall be loved of my Father, and I will love him, and will manifest myself to him" (Jn.14:21).

"Jesus answered and said unto him, If a man love me, he will keep my words: and my Father will love him, and we will come unto him, and make our abode with him" (Jn.14:23).

"If ye keep my commandments, ye shall abide in my love; even as I have kept my Father's commandments, and abide in his love" (Jn.15:10).

"Ye are my friends, if ye do whatsoever I command you" (Jn.15:14).

"But whoso looketh into the perfect law of liberty, and continueth *therein,* he being not a forgetful hearer, but a doer of the work, this man shall be blessed in his deed" (Js.1:25).

"Blessed *are* they that do his commandments, that they may have right to the tree of life, and may enter in through the gates into the city" (Re.22:14).

"Now therefore, if ye will obey my voice indeed, and keep my covenant, then ye shall be a peculiar treasure unto me above all people: for all the earth *is* mine" (Ex.19:5).

"O that there were such an heart in them, that they would fear me, and keep all my commandments always, that it might be well with them, and with their children for ever" (De.5:29).

"This book of the law shall not depart out of thy mouth; but thou shalt meditate therein day and night, that thou mayest observe to do according to all that is written therein: for then thou shalt make thy way prosperous, and then thou shalt have good success" (Jos.1:8).

2 (28:4-5) **Necessities of Life, Source—Food, Provision of—Fruitfulness, Source of—Blessing, of Fruitfulness—Necessities, Blessing of**: the blessing of fruitfulness is promised to the obedient person. Keep in mind that Moses was addressing the Israelites as a whole, but the nation was made up of individuals. Therefore, the blessings are applicable to the individual as well as to the nation. The nation is blessed by the citizens being blessed. If the people obeyed God...
- their population would grow, overflow with fruitfulness
- their livestock would grow and increase
- their crops would grow and increase
- their daily food would always be provided

OUTLINE	SCRIPTURE

2. The blessing of fruitfulness
  a. The fruitfulness of population growth
  b. The fruitfulness of livestock
  c. The fruitfulness of crops
  d. The fruitfulness of daily food
	4 Blessed *shall be* the fruit of thy body, and the fruit of thy ground, and the fruit of thy cattle, the increase of thy kine, and the flocks of thy sheep.
	5 Blessed *shall be* thy basket and thy store.

The point is striking: the people of God would always have an abundance of everything. Everything they owned would be fruitful and increase in value. They would grow as a people and as a nation. Moreover, their livestock would increase more and more, and their crops would produce an abundant harvest. They would develop a strong economy, be financially secure. And note the blessing of daily food: the very basic necessities of human life—food and water—would always be provided for them. Just keep in mind, there was one condition to receive this blessing of fruitfulness: obedience.

Thought 1. The blessing of fruitfulness, of plenty, is ours. But there is a condition: obedience. If we obey God, truly keep His commandments and follow Him, then God promises always to provide the necessities of life for us. We will always have the blessing of plenty.

"But seek ye first the kingdom of God, and his righteousness; and all these things shall be added unto you" (Mt.6:33).

"But my God shall supply all your need according to his riches in glory by Christ Jesus" (Ph.4:19).

"If ye walk in my statutes, and keep my commandments, and do them; Then I will give you rain in due season, and the land shall yield her increase, and the trees of the field shall yield their fruit. And your threshing shall reach unto the vintage, and the vintage shall reach unto the sowing time: and ye shall eat your bread to the full, and dwell in your land safely" (Le.26:3-5).

"And thou shalt return and obey the voice of the LORD, and do all his commandments which I command thee this day. And the LORD thy God will make thee plenteous in every work of thine hand, in the fruit of thy body, and in the fruit of thy cattle, and in the fruit of thy land, for good: for the LORD will again rejoice over thee for good, as he rejoiced over thy fathers" (De.30:8-9).

"I will abundantly bless her provision: I will satisfy her poor with bread" (Ps.132:15).

3 (28:6) **Blessings, Promised—Walk, of the Believer—Believer's Walk, Blessings of—Life, of Believer, Blessings of**: the blessing of all daily activities is promised to the obedient person. No matter where a person is—coming into or going out of the home—God will bless him. The only condition is obedience. If the person is walking with God, following God with all his heart, then God blesses him. Where the believer is, at home or away, does not matter. What matters is obedience. If the believer is walking after God, obeying Him, then God blesses his daily activities—all of them.

OUTLINE	SCRIPTURE
3. The blessing of all daily activities	6 Blessed *shalt* thou *be* when thou comest in, and blessed *shalt* thou *be* when thou goest out.

Thought 1. There is a strong lesson in this point for believers. If we walk day after day, obeying God wholeheartedly, then God will bless us richly in Himself. He will bless all our daily activities. He promises to grant us His presence and guidance as we walk throughout the day.

"Lo, I am with you alway, *even* unto the end of the world. Amen" (Mt.28:20).

"Through the tender mercy of our God; whereby the dayspring from on high hath visited us, To give light to them that sit in darkness and *in* the shadow of death, to guide our feet into the way of peace" (Lu.1:78-79).

"Howbeit when he, the Spirit of truth, is come, he will guide you into all truth: for he shall not speak of himself; but whatsoever he shall hear, *that* shall he speak: and he will show you things to come" (Jn.16:13).

"And, behold, I *am* with thee, and will keep thee in all *places* whither thou goest, and will bring thee again into this land; for I will not leave thee, until I have done *that* which I have spoken to thee of" (Ge.28:15).

"And he said, My presence shall go *with thee,* and I will give thee rest" (Ex.33:14).

"When thou passest through the waters, I *will be* with thee; and through the rivers, they shall not overflow thee: when thou walkest through the fire, thou shalt not be burned; neither shall the flame kindle upon thee" (Is.43:2).

"He maketh me to lie down in green pastures: he leadeth me beside the still waters" (Ps.23:2).

"For this God *is* our God for ever and ever: he will be our guide *even* unto death" (Ps.48:14).

"Thou shalt guide me with thy counsel, and afterward receive me *to* glory" (Ps.73:24).

"And thine ears shall hear a word behind thee, saying, This *is* the way, walk ye in it, when ye turn to the right hand, and when ye turn to the left" (Is.30:21).

4 (28:7) **Victory, Promised—Victory, Blessing of—Victory, Condition of—Blessing, of Victory**: the blessing of victory over all enemies is promised to the obedient person. Protection or security is a most wonderful promise given by God to the believer.

OUTLINE	SCRIPTURE
4. The blessing of victory over all enemies (see Ep.6:10-18)	7 The LORD shall cause thine enemies that rise up against thee to be smitten before thy face: they shall come out against thee one way, and flee before thee seven ways.

Note exactly what is said to the Israelites about this wonderful promise: if an enemy rises up against you, that enemy will be defeated before your very presence. No matter who the enemy is nor how strong and numerous, the enemy will be defeated. Note the graphic description: the enemy will come at you from one direction, but he will flee from you in seven directions, flee as a defeated, scattered foe.

Thought 1. The enemies who confronted the Israelites were a symbol of the spiritual enemies that confront the believer. As the believer marches to the promised land of heaven, enemy after enemy confronts him, enemies such as...

- backbiters
- despisers
- accident
- immorality
- temptation
- stealing
- mockers
- persecutors
- loss of loved ones
- loss of job
- stormy or continuous trials
- haters
- disease
- financial difficulties
- doubt and unbelief
- lying

The enemies that attempt to overthrow and conquer the believer are innumerable. But the promise of God is strong: if the believer will obey God, keep His holy commandments, God will give him victory over the enemies that oppose him. Victory is assured, assured if the believer will just obey God.

"Who shall separate us from the love of Christ? *shall* tribulation, or distress, or persecution, or famine, or nakedness, or peril, or sword....Nay, in all these things we are more than conquerors through him that loved us. For I am persuaded, that neither death, nor life, nor angels, nor principalities, nor powers, nor things present, nor things to come, Nor height, nor depth, nor any other creature, shall be able to separate us from the love of God, which is in Christ Jesus our Lord" (Ro.8:35, 37-39).

"There hath no temptation taken you but such as is common to man: but God *is* faithful, who will not suffer you to be tempted above that ye are able; but will with the temptation also make a way to escape, that ye may be able to bear *it*" (1 Co.10:13).

"Now unto him that is able to do exceeding abundantly above all that we ask or think, according to the power that worketh in us" (Ep.3:20).

"For we wrestle not against flesh and blood, but against principalities, against powers, against the rulers of the darkness of this world, against spiritual wickedness in high *places.* Wherefore take unto you the whole armour of God, that ye may be able to withstand in the evil day, and having done all, to stand" (Ep.6:12-13).

"Wherefore in all things it behooved him to be made like unto *his* brethren, that he might be a merciful and faithful high priest in things *pertaining* to God, to make reconciliation for the sins of the people. For in that he himself hath suffered being tempted, he is able to succour them that are tempted" (He.2:17-18).

"Submit yourselves therefore to God. Resist the devil, and he will flee from you" (Js.4:7).

"For whatsoever is born of God overcometh the world: and this is the victory that overcometh the world, *even* our faith" (1 Jn.5:4).

"To him that overcometh will I grant to sit with me in my throne, even as I also overcame, and am set down with my Father in his throne" (Re.3:21).

"Through thee will we push down our enemies: through thy name will we tread them under that rise up against us" (Ps.44:5).

5 (28:8) **Labor, Blessings of—Work, Blessings of—Employment, Blessings of—Blessings, of Employment—Blessings, of Work**: the blessing of labor, work, and employment is promised to the obedient person. Note that God will bless not only what a believer has in his barns, but He will bless everything the believer puts his hand to. This means that God will bless all his labor and work, all his employment. And the result will be the experience of purpose, achievement, accomplishment, and fulfillment in the promised land.

OUTLINE	SCRIPTURE

5. The blessing of labor, work, employment
  a. The promise: God will bless all you put your hand to
  b. The result: Will experience purpose, achievement, accomplishment, fulfillment
	8 The LORD shall command the blessing upon thee in thy storehouses, and in all that thou settest thine hand unto; and he shall bless thee in the land which the LORD thy God giveth thee.

Note this fact: meaningful work stirs a sense of purpose within a person. Work produces a sense of achievement and success, a sense of fulfillment and satisfaction. This means a most wonderful thing: if God blesses our work and labor, then we will have the deepest sense of purpose, significance, and meaning in life. We will achieve and be successful. This is the wonderful promise of God that was first given to the Israelites but is applicable to every believer of all generations. If God's people will simply obey Him, He will bless all that they put their hands to.

"If ye keep my commandments, ye shall abide in my love; even as I have kept my Father's commandments, and abide in his love. These things have I spoken unto you, that my joy might remain in you, and *that* your joy might be full" (Jn.15:10-11).

"With good will doing service, as to the Lord, and not to men" (Ep.6:7).

"And whatsoever ye do in word or deed, *do* all in the name of the Lord Jesus, giving thanks to God and the Father by him" (Col.3:17).

"Servants [employees, workers], obey in all things *your* masters [employers] according to the flesh; not with eyeservice, as menpleasers; but in singleness of heart, fearing God: And whatsoever ye do, do *it* heartily, as to the Lord, and not unto men; Knowing that of the Lord ye shall receive the reward of the inheritance: for ye serve the Lord Christ" (Col.3:22-24).

"Wherefore we receiving a kingdom which cannot be moved, let us have grace, whereby we may serve God acceptably with reverence and godly fear" (He.12:28).

"And ye shall serve the LORD your God, and he shall bless thy bread, and thy water; and I will take sickness away from the midst of thee" (Ex.23:25).

"And now, Israel, what doth the LORD thy God require of thee, but to fear the LORD thy God, to walk in all his ways, and to love him, and to serve the LORD thy God with all thy heart and with all thy soul" (De.10:12).

"Serve the LORD with fear, and rejoice with trembling" (Ps.2:11).

"Thou wilt show me the path of life: in thy presence *is* fulness of joy; at thy right hand *there are* pleasures for evermore" (Ps.16:11).

"They that sow in tears shall reap in joy" (Ps.126:5).

DEUTERONOMY 28:1-14

6 **(28:9-10) Spiritual Growth, Conditional—Growth, Spiritual, Conditional—Blessing, of Spiritual Growth—Obedience, Result of:** the blessing of spiritual growth is promised to the obedient person. The promise is phenomenal: God would establish the Israelites as His holy people, as the people who followed the only living and true God, the LORD Himself (Jehovah, Yahweh). But note: this blessing of spiritual growth was conditional. Spiritual growth—being set apart as God's holy people—was to be a reality only if the people obeyed God. They had to keep His commandments and walk in His ways in order to grow spiritually. If they would just obey God, then they would bear a strong testimony and witness for the LORD before all the peoples of the earth. Obedience would exalt the name of the LORD. If a believer obeyed God, his neighbors would see that he lived a holy life, a life that was totally set apart to God. He would bear a testimony of holiness to his immoral and lawless neighbors, bear a strong witness of holiness for God.

OUTLINE	SCRIPTURE	SCRIPTURE	OUTLINE
6. The blessing of spiritual growth a. The promise: God will establish you as His holy people b. The condition: Must obey God	9 The LORD shall establish thee an holy people unto himself, as he hath sworn unto thee, if thou shalt keep the commandments of the LORD thy God, and walk in his ways.	10 And all people of the earth shall see that thou art called by the name of the LORD; and they shall be afraid of thee.	c. The result: A strong testimony & witness for the LORD—the exaltation of the LORD's name

Thought 1. God is holy; therefore, we must be holy. Holiness simply means *being set apart to God*. If a person is set apart to God, he is following and obeying God. He is keeping the commandments of God, doing all that God says. Since God is holy, we must be holy. We must be set apart to obey God in all that He says. This is the witness, the strong testimony that we are to have for God: the witness and testimony of holiness. It is holiness that will cause us to grow spiritually. Spiritual growth is a direct result of holy living. Holiness bears the fruit of spiritual growth.

> "That he would grant unto us, that we being delivered out of the hand of our enemies might serve him without fear, In holiness and righteousness before him, all the days of our life" (Lu.1:74-75).
> "Having therefore these promises, dearly beloved, let us cleanse ourselves from all filthiness of the flesh and spirit, perfecting holiness in the fear of God" (2 Co.7:1).
> "Follow peace with all *men*, and holiness, without which no man shall see the Lord" (He.12:14).
> "But as he which hath called you is holy, so be ye holy in all manner of conversation; Because it is written, Be ye holy; for I am holy" (1 Pe.1:15-16).
> "*Seeing* then *that* all these things shall be dissolved, what manner *of persons* ought ye to be in *all* holy conversation and godliness, Looking for and hasting unto the coming of the day of God, wherein the heavens being on fire shall be dissolved, and the elements shall melt with fervent heat? Nevertheless we, according to his promise, look for new heavens and a new earth, wherein dwelleth righteousness. Wherefore, beloved, seeing that ye look for such things, be diligent that ye may be found of him in peace, without spot, and blameless" (2 Pe.3:11-14).
> "For I *am* the LORD that bringeth you up out of the land of Egypt, to be your God: ye shall therefore be holy, for I *am* holy" (Le.11:45).

7 **(28:11-12) Prosperity, Blessing of—Rain, Blessing of—Provision, Blessing of—Necessities, Abundance of, Promised—Blessings, Abundance of, Promised:** the blessing of prosperity, an excess of good things, is promised to the obedient person.

OUTLINE	SCRIPTURE	SCRIPTURE	OUTLINE
7. The blessing of prosperity, an excess of good things a. The good things such as children, livestock, crops	11 And the LORD shall make thee plenteous in goods, in the fruit of thy body, and in the fruit of thy cattle, and in the fruit of thy ground, in the land which the LORD sware unto thy fathers to give thee.	12 The LORD shall open unto thee his good treasure, the heaven to give the rain unto thy land in his season, and to bless all the work of thine hand: and thou shalt lend unto many nations, and thou shalt not borrow.	b. The LORD will open the storehouse, the treasury, of His provision: Rain & a blessing upon all the work of your hands c. The blessing of a prosperous, wealthy economy

The thrust of this point is entirely different from that mentioned earlier (see v.4). In the ancient world, prosperity depended primarily upon one thing: rain. Rain is the focus of this promise. Without rain, nothing could survive: not children, livestock, or crops. But with an abundance of rain, in particular at the right time, there would be an abundance of crops and plenty to eat for the children and the livestock. This is the promise of the blessing: the LORD promised to open the heavens and pour out abundant rain, the storehouse of His bounty, that would nourish the crops, livestock, and His children. In fact, He would pour out so much rain and the people would prosper so much that they would have a wealthy economy throughout the whole nation. The economy of the Israelites would be healthy, strong, and prosperous. They would have so much as a nation that two things would happen economically: they would lend to many nations and have to borrow from none.

Thought 1. The needs of the believer will be met. This is the sure promise of God. There is only one condition: we must obey God. If we obey God, then He meets all our needs. We never suffer a need, not a true need, that is not met. God promises to meet our needs and to meet them abundantly.

DEUTERONOMY 28:1-14

"But seek ye first the kingdom of God, and his righteousness; and all these things shall be added unto you" (Mt.6:33).

"The thief cometh not, but for to steal, and to kill, and to destroy: I am come that they might have life, and that they might have *it* more abundantly" (Jn.10:10).

"But my God shall supply all your need according to his riches in glory by Christ Jesus" (Ph.4:19).

"Blessed *are* they that do his commandments, that they may have right to the tree of life, and may enter in through the gates into the city" (Re.22:14).

"And ye shall serve the LORD your God, and he shall bless thy bread, and thy water; and I will take sickness away from the midst of thee" (Ex.23:25).

"Keep therefore the words of this covenant, and do them, that ye may prosper in all that ye do" (De.29:9).

"Then shalt thou prosper, if thou takest heed to fulfil the statutes and judgments which the LORD charged Moses with concerning Israel: be strong, and of good courage; dread not, nor be dismayed" (1 Chr.22:13).

"Blessed *is* the man that walketh not in the counsel of the ungodly, nor standeth in the way of sinners, nor sitteth in the seat of the scornful. But his delight *is* in the law of the LORD; and in his law doth he meditate day and night. And he shall be like a tree planted by the rivers of water, that bring-eth forth his fruit in his season; his leaf also shall not wither; and whatsoever he doeth shall prosper" (Ps.1:1-3).

"Thou visitest the earth, and waterest it: thou greatly enrichest it with the river of God, *which* is full of water: thou preparest them corn, when thou hast so provided for it" (Ps.65:9).

"Blessed *be* the Lord, *who* daily loadeth us *with benefits, even* the God of our salvation. Selah" (Ps.68:19).

"Then shall he give the rain of thy seed, that thou shalt sow the ground withal; and bread of the increase of the earth, and it shall be fat and plenteous: in that day shall thy cattle feed in large pastures" (Is.30:23).

8 (28:13) **Leadership, Blessings of—Obedience, Result of—Blessing, of Leadership—Leadership, Provision of—Provision, of Leadership**: the blessing of being exalted is promised to the obedient person. This is a confidence-building promise: the people of God would become the head or leader, not the tail. They would always be on top, have the upper hand, and never be on bottom. God's people would be exalted, become a prince among the nations of the world. But note: the promise of the blessing is qualified once again. There is a stinging condition: the blessing of being exalted is not to be given automatically. Obedience is the condition. The people of God must obey God to become a prince among the nations and peoples of the earth. Obedience to God is an absolute essential to be exalted by God.

OUTLINE	SCRIPTURE

8. The blessing of exaltation
  a. The promise: Will become the head or leader, not the tail
  b. The condition: Must obey God
  c. The promise reemphasized: Will always be on top, not on bottom
	13 And the LORD shall make thee the head, and not the tail; and thou shalt be above only, and thou shalt not be beneath; if that thou hearken unto the commandments of the LORD thy God, which I command thee this day, to observe and to do *them*:

Thought 1. One of the great promises of God to the believer is just this: the believer will be exalted by God. If a person has truly trusted Christ—honestly following and obeying God—then he will be greatly rewarded by God. God will exalt the genuine believer beyond the highest of the high. The exaltation of the believer is assured. This is the promise of God.

"His lord said unto him, Well done, good and faithful servant; thou hast been faithful over a few things, I will make thee ruler over many things: enter thou into the joy of thy lord" (Mt.25:23).

"And he said unto him, Well, thou good servant: because thou hast been faithful in a very little, have thou authority over ten cities" (Lu.19:17).

"In my Father's house are many mansions: if *it were* not so, I would have told you. I go to prepare a place for you. And if I go and prepare a place for you, I will come again, and receive you unto myself; that where I am, *there* ye may be also" (Jn.14:2-3).

"But glory, honour, and peace, to every man that worketh good, to the Jew first, and also to the Gentile" (Ro.2:10).

"Do ye not know that the saints shall judge the world? and if the world shall be judged by you, are ye unworthy to judge the smallest matters" (1 Co.6:2).

"And every man that striveth for the mastery is temperate in all things. Now they *do it* to obtain a corruptible crown; but we an incorruptible" (1 Co.9:25).

"Henceforth there is laid up for me a crown of righteousness, which the Lord, the righteous judge, shall give me at that day: and not to me only, but unto all them also that love his appearing" (2 Ti.4:8).

"If we suffer, we shall also reign with *him:* if we deny *him,* he also will deny us" (2 Ti.2:12).

"Esteeming the reproach of Christ greater riches than the treasures in Egypt: for he [Moses] had respect unto the recompence of the reward" (He.11:26).

"Blessed *is* the man that endureth temptation: for when he is tried, he shall receive the crown of life, which the Lord hath promised to them that love him" (Js.1:12).

"And when the chief Shepherd shall appear, ye shall receive a crown of glory that fadeth not away" (1 Pe.5:4).

"Behold, I come quickly: hold that fast which thou hast, that no man take thy crown" (Re.3:11).

"To him that overcometh will I grant to sit with me in my throne, even as I also overcame, and am set down with my Father in his throne" (Re.3:21).

"The four and twenty elders fall down before him that sat on the throne, and worship him that liveth for ever and ever, and cast their crowns before the throne, saying" (Re.4:10).

"And hast made us unto our God kings and priests: and we shall reign on the earth" (Re.5:10).

"And they heard a great voice from heaven saying unto them, Come up hither. And they ascended up to heaven in a cloud; and their enemies beheld them" (Re.11:12).

"Because he hath set his love upon me, therefore will I deliver him: I will set him on high, because he hath known my name" (Ps.91:14).

"And they that be wise shall shine as the brightness of the firmament; and they that turn many to righteousness as the stars for ever and ever" (Da.12:3).

9 (28:14) **Obedience, Duty—Commandments, Duty—Idolatry, Forbidden—Worship, False, Forbidden**: the wonderful blessings of God conclude with a strong charge. Moses declared that God's people must not turn away from any of the commandments. They must not turn to the right nor to the left. They must obey God, in particular by refusing to follow false gods and false worship. Above all other evils, following false gods and false worship were the most horrible evils that a person could commit. The believer must never deviate from the path of God's commandments. He must follow the LORD God and Him alone, never straying toward false gods and false worship.

OUTLINE	SCRIPTURE
9. The strong charge: A person must not turn away from any of the commandments to follow false gods or false worship	14 And thou shalt not go aside from any of the words which I command thee this day, *to* the right hand, or *to* the left, to go after other gods to serve them.

"For the wrath of God is revealed from heaven against all ungodliness and unrighteousness of men, who hold the truth in unrighteousness; Because that which may be known of God is manifest in them; for God hath showed *it* unto them. For the invisible things of him from the creation of the world are clearly seen, being understood by the things that are made, *even* his eternal power and Godhead; so that they are without excuse: Because that, when they knew God, they glorified *him* not as God, neither were thankful; but became vain in their imaginations, and their foolish heart was darkened. Professing themselves to be wise, they became fools, And changed the glory of the uncorruptible God into an image made like to corruptible man, and to birds, and fourfooted beasts, and creeping things" (Ro.1:18-23).

"Know ye not that the unrighteous shall not inherit the kingdom of God? Be not deceived: neither fornicators, nor idolaters, nor adulterers, nor effeminate, nor abusers of themselves with mankind, Nor thieves, nor covetous, nor drunkards, nor revilers, nor extortioners, shall inherit the kingdom of God" (1 Co.6:9-10).

"Now the works of the flesh are manifest, which are *these;* Adultery, fornication, uncleanness, lasciviousness, Idolatry, witchcraft, hatred, variance, emulations, wrath, strife, seditions, heresies, Envyings, murders, drunkenness, revellings, and such like: of the which I tell you before, as I have also told *you* in time past, that they which do such things shall not inherit the kingdom of God" (Ga.5:19-21).

"Little children, keep yourselves from idols. Amen" (1 Jn.5:21).

"Thou shalt not make unto thee any graven image, or any likeness *of any thing* that *is* in heaven above, or that *is* in the earth beneath, or that *is* in the water under the earth" (Ex.20:4).

"Ye shall make you no idols nor graven image, neither rear you up a standing image, neither shall ye set up *any* image of stone in your land, to bow down unto it: for I *am* the LORD your God" (Le.26:1).

"Take heed to yourselves, that your heart be not deceived, and ye turn aside, and serve other gods, and worship them" (De.11:16).

"There shall no strange god be in thee; neither shalt thou worship any strange god" (Ps.81:9).

"I *am* the LORD: that *is* my name: and my glory will I not give to another, neither my praise to graven images" (Is.42:8).

DEUTERONOMY 28:15-68

1. **The first set of curses: Cursed due to disobedience, refusing to listen to God**

    a. The curse of being continually cursed—wherever you are
    b. The curse of inadequate daily food
    c. The curse on production: Being infertile & fruitless

    d. The curse on all daily activities

    e. The curse of confusion (panic) & frustration in every activity
        1) The result: Utter destruction & ruin
        2) The reason: Forsook God

    f. The curse of deadly diseases, plagues

        1) Wasting disease or consumption
        2) Fever & inflammation
    g. The curse on crops, all plant life & vegetation
        1) Heat & drought
        2) Blight & mildew
        3) No rain & hard, iron-like soil

        4) Sand & powder coming down in rain-like dust storms

    h. The curse of being defeated by one's enemies
        1) Will be an object of horror to all the kingdoms of the earth

        2) Will die a terrible death: One's corpse will be eaten

C. The Results of Disobeying God: The Curses for Disobedience, 28:15-68

15 But it shall come to pass, if thou wilt not hearken unto the voice of the LORD thy God, to observe to do all his commandments and his statutes which I command thee this day; that all these curses shall come upon thee, and overtake thee:
16 Cursed *shalt* thou *be* in the city, and cursed *shalt* thou *be* in the field.
17 Cursed *shall be* thy basket and thy store.
18 Cursed *shall be* the fruit of thy body, and the fruit of thy land, the increase of thy kine, and the flocks of thy sheep.
19 Cursed *shalt* thou *be* when thou comest in, and cursed *shalt* thou *be* when thou goest out.
20 The LORD shall send upon thee cursing, vexation, and rebuke, in all that thou settest thine hand unto for to do, until thou be destroyed, and until thou perish quickly; because of the wickedness of thy doings, whereby thou hast forsaken me.
21 The LORD shall make the pestilence cleave unto thee, until he have consumed thee from off the land, whither thou goest to possess it.
22 The LORD shall smite thee with a consumption, and with a fever, and with an inflammation, and with an extreme burning, and with the sword, and with blasting, and with mildew; and they shall pursue thee until thou perish.
23 And thy heaven that *is* over thy head shall be brass, and the earth that is under thee *shall be* iron.
24 The LORD shall make the rain of thy land powder and dust: from heaven shall it come down upon thee, until thou be destroyed.
25 The LORD shall cause thee to be smitten before thine enemies: thou shalt go out one way against them, and flee seven ways before them: and shalt be removed into all the kingdoms of the earth.
26 And thy carcase shall be meat unto all fowls of the air, and unto the beasts of the earth, and no man shall fray *them* away.
27 The LORD will smite thee with the botch of Egypt, and with the emerods, and with the scab, and with the itch, whereof thou canst not be healed.
28 The LORD shall smite thee with madness, and blindness, and astonishment of heart:
29 And thou shalt grope at noonday, as the blind gropeth in darkness, and thou shalt not prosper in thy ways: and thou shalt be only oppressed and spoiled evermore, and no man shall save *thee*.
30 Thou shalt betroth a wife, and another man shall lie with her: thou shalt build an house, and thou shalt not dwell therein: thou shalt plant a vineyard, and shalt not gather the grapes thereof.
31 Thine ox *shall be* slain before thine eyes, and thou shalt not eat thereof: thine ass *shall be* violently taken away from before thy face, and shall not be restored to thee: thy sheep *shall be* given unto thine enemies, and thou shalt have none to rescue *them*.
32 Thy sons and thy daughters *shall be* given unto another people, and thine eyes shall look, and fail *with longing* for them all the day long: and *there shall be* no might in thine hand.
33 The fruit of thy land, and all thy labours, shall a nation which thou knowest not eat up; and thou shalt be only oppressed and crushed alway:
34 So that thou shalt be mad for the sight of thine eyes which thou shalt see.
35 The LORD shall smite thee in the knees, and in the legs, with a sore botch that cannot be healed, from the sole of thy foot unto the top of thy head.
36 The LORD shall bring thee, and thy king which thou shalt set over thee, unto a nation which neither thou nor thy fathers have known; and there shalt thou serve other gods, wood and stone.
37 And thou shalt become an astonishment, a proverb, and a byword, among all nations whither the LORD shall lead

by the birds & beasts of the earth

i. The curse of incurable physical afflictions
   1) Boils & tumors
   2) Festering sores & the itch

   3) Madness, blindness, confusion, or panic

j. The curse of failure: One will be like a blind man groping about in the dark
   1) Will be unsuccessful
   2) Will be oppressed & robbed continually

k. The curse of becoming plunder for a conquering nation
   1) One's fiancée or wife will be raped
   2) One's house will be destroyed
   3) One's vineyard will not be harvested: The fruit will be taken
   4) One's livestock will be forcibly taken

   5) One's sons & daughters will be enslaved

   6) One's land will be ravaged of all crops
   7) One will reap cruel oppression

   8) One will be driven mad or insane by what one sees

   9) One will suffer unbearable afflictions—such as boils

l. The curse of exile, deportation to a foreign nation
   1) Will be led to worship other gods

   2) Will become an object of horror, scorn, & ridicule

Deuteronomy 28:15-68

m. The curse of a devastated economy
  1) Will work hard but harvest little because of locusts
  2) Will harvest little fruit because of worms

  3) Will harvest few olives because of disease

  4) Will lose the labor & continued growth of the young because they are taken captive
  5) Will lose all trees & crops because of locusts
  6) Will suffer steady decline; sink lower & lower, far below the foreigners living among you
  7) Will suffer great debt
  8) Will become the dregs of society: Lose your exalted position

n. The curses—all of them—will come upon you, pursue & overtake you until you are destroyed
  1) The reason: Disobedience—you refused to obey the LORD

  2) The purpose of the curses: To be a sign, a warning

2. **The second set of curses: Cursed due to lack of service, failing to serve God**

  a. The curse of serving one's enemies
    1) Will leave you hungry, thirsty, naked, & in poverty
    2) Will enslave & destroy you

    3) Will quickly & forcefully conquer you

    4) Will be a fierce, heartless nation

    5) Will devour the food supply—the livestock & crops—until you starve & are destroyed

    6) Will lay siege & destroy all your cities

  b. The curse of suffering untold horror because of one's enemy: The ghastly, repulsive horror of eating the flesh of dead sons & daughters

    1) Even the most tenderhearted man will have no compassion for his family: Starvation will make him so degenerate & depraved that he will eat the flesh of his own children & not share with his family

    2) Even the most tender & delicate woman will become callous & cruel: She will secretly eat the afterbirth & the newborn child from her womb

3. **The third set of curses: Cursed due to lack of fear & reverence for God—failing to fear His glorious & awesome name, THE LORD YOUR GOD**

  a. The curse of fearful plagues, harsh & prolonged disasters, & severe & lingering sicknesses

thee. 38 Thou shalt carry much seed out into the field, and shalt gather *but* little in; for the locust shall consume it. 39 Thou shalt plant vineyards, and dress *them*, but shalt neither drink *of* the wine, nor gather *the grapes*; for the worms shall eat them. 40 Thou shalt have olive trees throughout all thy coasts, but thou shalt not anoint *thyself* with the oil; for thine olive shall cast *his fruit*. 41 Thou shalt beget sons and daughters, but thou shalt not enjoy them; for they shall go into captivity. 42 All thy trees and fruit of thy land shall the locust consume. 43 The stranger that *is* within thee shall get up above thee very high; and thou shalt come down very low. 44 He shall lend to thee, and thou shalt not lend to him: he shall be the head, and thou shalt be the tail. 45 Moreover all these curses shall come upon thee, and shall pursue thee, and overtake thee, till thou be destroyed; because thou hearkenedst not unto the voice of the LORD thy God, to keep his commandments and his statutes which he commanded thee: 46 And they shall be upon thee for a sign and for a wonder, and upon thy seed for ever. 47 Because thou servedst not the LORD thy God with joyfulness, and with gladness of heart, for the abundance of all *things*; 48 Therefore shalt thou serve thine enemies which the LORD shall send against thee, in hunger, and in thirst, and in nakedness, and in want of all *things*: and he shall put a yoke of iron upon thy neck, until he have destroyed thee. 49 The LORD shall bring a nation against thee from far, from the end of the earth, *as swift* as the eagle flieth; a nation whose tongue thou shalt not understand; 50 A nation of fierce countenance, which shall not regard the person of the old, nor show favour to the young: 51 And he shall eat the fruit of thy cattle, and the fruit of thy land, until thou be destroyed: which *also* shall not leave thee *either* corn, wine, or oil, *or* the increase of thy kine, or flocks of thy sheep, until he have destroyed thee. 52 And he shall besiege thee in all thy gates, until thy high and fenced walls come down, wherein thou trustedst, throughout all thy land: and he shall besiege thee in all thy gates throughout all thy land, which the LORD thy God hath given thee. 53 And thou shalt eat the fruit of thine own body, the flesh of thy sons and of thy daughters, which the LORD thy God hath given thee, in the siege, and in the straitness, wherewith thine enemies shall distress thee: 54 *So that* the man *that is* tender among you, and very delicate, his eye shall be evil toward his brother, and toward the wife of his bosom, and toward the remnant of his children which he shall leave: 55 So that he will not give to any of them of the flesh of his children whom he shall eat: because he hath nothing left him in the siege, and in the straitness, wherewith thine enemies shall distress thee in all thy gates. 56 The tender and delicate woman among you, which would not adventure to set the sole of her foot upon the ground for delicateness and tenderness, her eye shall be evil toward the husband of her bosom, and toward her son, and toward her daughter, 57 And toward her young one that cometh out from between her feet, and toward her children which she shall bear: for she shall eat them for want of all *things* secretly in the siege and straitness, wherewith thine enemy shall distress thee in thy gates. 58 If thou wilt not observe to do all the words of this law that are written in this book, that thou mayest fear this glorious and fearful name, THE LORD THY GOD; 59 Then the LORD will make thy plagues wonderful, and the plagues of thy seed, *even* great plagues, and of long

1) Will suffer all the dreaded diseases of Egypt, & the diseases will cling to them	continuance, and sore sicknesses, and of long continuance. 60 Moreover he will bring upon thee all the diseases of Egypt, which thou wast afraid of; and they shall cleave unto thee.	thou shalt serve other gods, which neither thou nor thy fathers have known, *even* wood and stone. 65 And among these nations shalt thou find no ease, neither shall the sole of thy foot have rest: but the LORD shall	2) Will find no security or resting place
2) Will suffer every kind of disease & disaster, even those not recorded in the Book of the Law	61 Also every sickness, and every plague, which *is* not written in the book of this law, them will the LORD bring upon thee, until thou be destroyed.	give thee there a trembling heart, and failing of eyes, and sorrow of mind: 66 And thy life shall hang in doubt before thee; and thou shalt fear day and night, and	3) Will have a mind gripped by anxiety, eyes that are weary & longing, & a heart that is filled with sorrow & despair 4) Will live in constant doubt, fear, & hopelessness
b. The curse of being almost annihilated, exterminated—reduced to a very small population	62 And ye shall be left few in number, whereas ye were as the stars of heaven for multitude; because thou wouldest not obey the voice of the LORD thy God.	shalt have none assurance of thy life: 67 In the morning thou shalt say, Would God it were even! and at even thou shalt say, Would God it were	
1) The LORD had increased your number 2) The LORD will decrease your population	63 And it shall come to pass, *that* as the LORD rejoiced over you to do you good, and to multiply you; so the LORD will rejoice over you to destroy you, and to bring you to	morning! for the fear of thine heart wherewith thou shalt fear, and for the sight of thine eyes which thou shalt see.	5) Will be gripped by terror: In the morning one will wish it were evening & in the evening wish it were morning
c. The curse of being uprooted & scattered among all nations	nought; and ye shall be plucked from off the land whither thou goest to possess it.	68 And the LORD shall bring thee into Egypt again with ships, by the way whereof I spake unto thee, Thou shalt see it no more again: and	6) Will even be scattered in Egypt & offer oneself for sale as a slave: But no one will buy you
1) Will worship false gods: Commit idolatry & false worship	64 And the LORD shall scatter thee among all people, from the one end of the earth even unto the other; and there	there ye shall be sold unto your enemies for bondmen and bondwomen, and no man shall buy *you*.	

DIVISION V

THE THIRD GREAT THEME PREACHED BY GOD'S AGED SERVANT: THE CHARGE TO RENEW THE COVENANT WITH GOD, 27:1–30:20

C. The Results of Disobeying God: The Curses for Disobedience, 28:15-68

(28:15-68) **Introduction**: one of the major ways God has chosen to deal with us is speaking with us, giving us His Words. God wants to fellowship with us; therefore, He communicates with us in the same way we communicate with one another: by word of mouth. God has spoken to us by giving us a permanent form of communication: the written Word. God has given us His Word because He wants us to know how to live a full and victorious life, how to fellowship and commune with Him and worship Him.

As the Sovereign Creator and Supreme Ruler of the universe, God has every right to expect us to follow His Word, to keep His commandments and decrees, to live exactly as He says. To disobey God is the height of contempt, the summit of wickedness. Disobedience against the LORD God is...

- shameful and despicable
- disrespectful and disgraceful
- disgusting and detestable
- abhorrent and abominable
- cruel and hateful
- mean and vile
- rejection and rebellion

Disobedience is an abomination, detestable to God. Disobedience shows the utmost contempt and disrespect for God. For this reason, disobedience will be judged and cursed by God.

Remember, Moses is challenging the people to make a decision for God. It is time for the people to renew their covenant with God, to rededicate their lives to Him. If they obey the covenant, His commandments, they will be richly blessed and receive all the promises of God. The blessings of God will be poured out upon them (see outline and notes—De.28:1-14). However, if the people disobey the covenant, His commandments, they will be cursed. The curses of God will fall upon them.

The importance of these curses cannot be overestimated, for this is the final warning that Moses will ever give to the Israelites. He is soon to die, go home to be with the LORD. Therefore, he seizes this opportunity to give one final warning to the

DEUTERONOMY 28:15-68

people: the whole future of the Israelite nation depends upon their faithful obedience to God. They must keep the commandments of God to receive the blessings of God and to inherit the promised land. This lengthy warning—these curses that are heaped one upon another—should arouse the Israelites to make a decision for God. Focusing upon the curses of judgment should stir the people to renew their covenant with God, to rededicate their lives and recommit themselves to keep the covenant, obeying the commandments of God. This is the subject of this great passage of Scripture:

The Results of Disobeying God: The Curses for Disobedience, 28:15-68.
1. The first set of curses: cursed due to disobedience, refusing to listen to God (vv.15-46).
2. The second set of curses: cursed due to lack of service, failing to serve God (vv.47-57).
3. The third set of curses: cursed due to lack of fear and reverence for God—failing to fear His glorious and awesome name, "the Lord your God" (vv.58-68).

1 (28:15-46) **Disobedience, Results of—Curses, for Disobedience—Listen, Refusing to—Rejection, Results of—Judgment, Results of**: the first set of curses was due to disobedience, refusing to listen to God. Moses declared a tragic fact: if a person refuses to listen and disobeys the Sovereign Creator of the universe, this person will suffer the curses of God. To disobey the LORD God, the only living and true God, is the highest contempt imaginable, a despicable, detestable act of rebellion. Judgment is bound to fall upon the disobedient. A person who treats God with such contempt is bound to suffer the curses of God. Note exactly what Scripture says: the curses will *come upon* you and *overtake* you (v.15). Later Moses declared to the disobedient, "all these curses will *come upon* you. They will *pursue, overtake,* and *destroy* you—all because you did not obey the LORD your God." Note the Scripture and outline:

OUTLINE	SCRIPTURE	SCRIPTURE	OUTLINE
1. The first set of curses: Cursed due to disobedience, refusing to listen to God	15 But it shall come to pass, if thou wilt not hearken unto the voice of the LORD thy God, to observe to do all his commandments and his statutes which I command thee this day; that all these curses shall come upon thee, and overtake thee:	thee until thou perish. 23 And thy heaven that *is* over thy head shall be brass, and the earth that is under thee *shall be* iron. 24 The LORD shall make the rain of thy land powder and dust: from heaven shall it come down upon thee, until thou be destroyed.	3) No rain & hard, iron-like soil 4) Sand & powder coming down in rain-like dust storms
a. The curse of being continually cursed—wherever you are	16 Cursed *shalt* thou *be* in the city, and cursed *shalt* thou *be* in the field.	25 The LORD shall cause thee to be smitten before thine enemies: thou shalt go out one way against them, and flee seven ways before them: and shalt be removed into all the kingdoms of the earth.	h. The curse of being defeated by one's enemies 1) Will be an object of horror to all the kingdoms of the earth
b. The curse of inadequate daily food	17 Cursed *shall be* thy basket and thy store.		
c. The curse on production: Being infertile & fruitless	18 Cursed *shall be* the fruit of thy body, and the fruit of thy land, the increase of thy kine, and the flocks of thy sheep.	26 And thy carcase shall be meat unto all fowls of the air, and unto the beasts of the earth, and no man shall fray *them* away.	2) Will die a terrible death: One's corpse will be eaten by the birds & beasts of the earth
d. The curse on all daily activities	19 Cursed *shalt* thou *be* when thou comest in, and cursed *shalt* thou *be* when thou goest out.	27 The LORD will smite thee with the botch of Egypt, and with the emerods, and with the scab, and with the itch, whereof thou canst not be healed.	i. The curse of incurable physical afflictions 1) Boils & tumors 2) Festering sores & the itch
e. The curse of confusion (panic) & frustration in every activity	20 The LORD shall send upon thee cursing, vexation, and rebuke, in all that thou settest thine hand unto for to do, until thou be destroyed, and until thou perish quickly; because of the wickedness of thy doings, whereby thou hast forsaken me.	28 The LORD shall smite thee with madness, and blindness, and astonishment of heart:	3) Madness, blindness, confusion, or panic
1) The result: Utter destruction & ruin			
2) The reason: Forsook God			
f. The curse of deadly diseases, plagues	21 The LORD shall make the pestilence cleave unto thee, until he have consumed thee from off the land, whither thou goest to possess it.	29 And thou shalt grope at noonday, as the blind gropeth in darkness, and thou shalt not prosper in thy ways: and thou shalt be only oppressed and spoiled evermore, and no man shall save *thee*.	j. The curse of failure: One will be like a blind man groping about in the dark 1) Will be unsuccessful 2) Will be oppressed & robbed continually
1) Wasting disease or consumption	22 The LORD shall smite thee with a consumption, and with a fever, and with an inflammation, and with an extreme burning, and with the sword, and with blasting, and with mildew; and they shall pursue		
2) Fever & inflammation		30 Thou shalt betroth a wife, and another man shall lie with her: thou shalt build an house, and thou shalt not dwell therein: thou	k. The curse of becoming plunder for a conquering nation 1) One's fiancée or wife will be raped 2) One's house will be
g. The curse on crops, all plant life & vegetation			
1) Heat & drought			
2) Blight & mildew			

DEUTERONOMY 28:15-68

OUTLINE	SCRIPTURE	SCRIPTURE	OUTLINE
destroyed 3) One's vineyard will not be harvested: The fruit will be taken 4) One's livestock will be forcibly taken 5) One's sons & daughters will be enslaved 6) One's land will be ravaged of all crops 7) One will reap cruel oppression 8) One will be driven mad or insane by what one sees 9) One will suffer unbearable afflictions—such as boils l. The curse of exile, deportation to a foreign nation 1) Will be led to worship other gods 2) Will become an object of horror, scorn, & ridicule	shalt plant a vineyard, and shalt not gather the grapes thereof. 31 Thine ox *shall be* slain before thine eyes, and thou shalt not eat thereof: thine ass *shall be* violently taken away from before thy face, and shall not be restored to thee; thy sheep *shall be* given unto thine enemies, and thou shalt have none to rescue *them*. 32 Thy sons and thy daughters *shall be* given unto another people, and thine eyes shall look, and fail *with longing* for them all the day long: and *there shall be* no might in thine hand. 33 The fruit of thy land, and all thy labours, shall a nation which thou knowest not eat up; and thou shalt be only oppressed and crushed alway: 34 So that thou shalt be mad for the sight of thine eyes which thou shalt see. 35 The LORD shall smite thee in the knees, and in the legs, with a sore botch that cannot be healed, from the sole of thy foot unto the top of thy head. 36 The LORD shall bring thee, and thy king which thou shalt set over thee, unto a nation which neither thou nor thy fathers have known; and there shalt thou serve other gods, wood and stone. 37 And thou shalt become an astonishment, a proverb, and a byword, among all nations whither the LORD shall lead	thee. 38 Thou shalt carry much seed out into the field, and shalt gather *but* little in; for the locust shall consume it. 39 Thou shalt plant vineyards, and dress *them*, but shalt neither drink *of* the wine, nor gather *the grapes*; for the worms shall eat them. 40 Thou shalt have olive trees throughout all thy coasts, but thou shalt not anoint *thyself* with the oil; for thine olive shall cast *his fruit*. 41 Thou shalt beget sons and daughters, but thou shalt not enjoy them; for they shall go into captivity. 42 All thy trees and fruit of thy land shall the locust consume. 43 The stranger that *is* within thee shall get up above thee very high; and thou shalt come down very low. 44 He shall lend to thee, and thou shalt not lend to him: he shall be the head, and thou shalt be the tail. 45 Moreover all these curses shall come upon thee, and shall pursue thee, and overtake thee, till thou be destroyed; because thou hearkenedst not unto the voice of the LORD thy God, to keep his commandments and his statutes which he commanded thee: 46 And they shall be upon thee for a sign and for a wonder, and upon thy seed for ever.	m. The curse of a devastated economy 1) Will work hard but harvest little because of locusts 2) Will harvest little fruit because of worms 3) Will harvest few olives because of disease 4) Will lose the labor & continued growth of the young because they are taken captive 5) Will lose all trees & crops because of locusts 6) Will suffer steady decline; sink lower & lower, far below the foreigners living among you 7) Will suffer great debt 8) Will become the dregs of society: Lose your exalted position n. The curses—all of them—will come upon you, pursue & overtake you until you are destroyed 1) The reason: Disobedience—you refused to obey the LORD 2) The purpose of the curses: To be a sign, a warning

a. There will be the curse of being continually cursed (v.16). Disobedience will cause you to be cursed wherever you are, in the city or in the country.

b. There will be the curse of inadequate daily food (v.17). The promise of God to provide the necessities of life will no longer be true. You will be left without the care of God, without His looking after you. You will no longer have the presence, guidance, and help of God. Disobedience separates you from God, from His care and provision.

c. There will be the curse on production or fruitfulness (v.18). Disobedience will cause you, your livestock, and your crops to be fruitless. The blessing of a fruitful and rich production will no longer be true. A curse will rest upon your production.

d. There will be the curse on all daily activities (v.19). As you come into your home you will be cursed, and as you go out of your home you will be cursed. Whether at home or out in the community or business world you will be cursed. A curse will rest upon your life: neither your home, community, or employment will be able to shelter you from the curse. Note that these verses just covered are parallel to the first four blessings preached by Moses earlier (28:1-6).

e. There will be the curse of confusion or panic and frustration in every activity you undertake (v.20). Disobedience will cause you to be confused and frustrated until you are utterly destroyed and ruined. All this will come upon you because of the evil of your disobedience. You forsook the LORD God.

f. There will be the curse of deadly diseases or plagues that will sweep across entire populations (v.21). Disobedience will cause you to suffer some wasting disease or consumption, and diseases of high fever and inflammation.

g. There will be the curse on crops, on all plant life and vegetation (v.22). Disobedience will cause a scorching heat and drought, blight and mildew to strike your land and destroy your crops (v.22). The idea is that there will be little harvest and starvation will strike the land. But this is not all: there will be no rain, for the sky over your head will be like bronze, and the soil beneath you will be as hard as iron (v.23). In fact, God will change the rain into sand and powder that will come down in rain-like dust storms (v.24).

DEUTERONOMY 28:15-68

h. There will be the curse of being defeated by your enemies (vv.25-26). Note that this curse is the opposite of the blessing given earlier (28:7, 10). Instead of victory, God's people would be defeated before their enemies. The army would attack in one direction, but the soldiers would panic and be routed and scattered in seven different directions. The number seven simply indicates a complete, full flight and defeat. Disobedience separated the people from God; therefore, they could not expect God to be present and to give victory to their army. The very opposite was true: disobedience would lead to utter defeat and destruction. They would, in fact, be so devastated that they would become an object of horror to all the kingdoms of the earth (v.25). They would die terrible deaths: their corpses would be eaten by the birds and beasts of the earth (v.26).

i. There will be the curse of incurable physical afflictions (vv.27-28). Disobedience will cause the most horrible, miserable afflictions:

⇒ boils and tumors
⇒ festering sores and the itch, from which one cannot be cured (v.27)
⇒ madness, blindness, and confusion or panic (v.28)

Keep in mind that physical afflictions or illnesses made a person unclean in the eyes of the Israelites, spiritually and ceremonially unclean. Therefore, the diseased person was not able to participate in the worship services of the LORD. In fact, the diseased person had to be quarantined—removed and put out of the camp—until he was cured. Various commentators try to identify the various afflictions mentioned here, suggesting various stages of several sexual diseases such as syphilis, herpes, or AIDS (acquired immunodeficiency syndrome), and various kinds of leprosy or other cancerous growths. However, an exact identification is impossible. The point to note is that these various afflictions are debilitating, making a person totally incapacitated, unable to function normally.

j. There will be the curse of failure (v.29). The disobedient person will be like a blind man groping about in the dark, unable to find his way. He will be unable to see and not know where to go nor what to do. He will be unsuccessful in everything he does. Day by day he will be just like a blind man who is oppressed and robbed, with no one to rescue him.

k. There will be the curse of becoming plunder for a conquering nation (vv.30-35). What follows now is a series of curses that fall upon a people who have been defeated in battle. They suffer a miserable existence. If Israel disobeyed God, her future would be very bleak. The possibility of future blessings still existed for Israel, but the possibility of the horrors of the curses seemed even more sure. For this reason, Moses preached with fire in his heart, heaping calamity upon calamity, warning the people against disobedience to God.[1] If the Israelites ever began to continually disobey God, they would become plunder for a conquering nation. Moses graphically described the horrible curses that fall upon a people who are defeated by a wicked nation:

⇒ A person's fiancée or wife would be raped (v.30).
⇒ A person's house would be destroyed (v.30).
⇒ A person's vineyard would not be harvested. The fruit would be taken (v.30).
⇒ A person's livestock would be forcibly taken for food by the invading army (v.31).
⇒ A person's sons and daughters would be enslaved (v.32). Day by day the parents would helplessly watch for their return but be powerless to secure their return.
⇒ A person's land would be ravaged of all crops (v.33). The foreign invaders would eat what a person's own hands and labor have produced.
⇒ Cruel oppression would be reaped, and a person would know nothing but oppression all his days (v.33).
⇒ A person would be driven mad or insane by what he sees (v.34). The devastated land, the death or affliction of so many with incurable diseases, the bankruptcy and collapse of families and businesses, the loss of possessions, the enslavement of children and adults would literally drive many mad or insane.
⇒ A person would suffer unbearable afflictions such as boils that could not be cured, boils that would spread from the soles of his feet to the top of his head (v.35).

l. There will be the curse of exile, deportation to a foreign nation (vv.36-37). Disobedience would lead to defeat by a foreign nation and to exile or deportation. Note that the disobedient will be led into false worship, to worshipping false gods. Moreover, the disobedient will become an object of horror, scorn, and ridicule (v.37). They will be the target of jokes and cutting remarks, the laughingstock of society.

Note this fact: the situation just described here actually happened to the Israelites. They suffered the Babylonian captivity (see the books of *Ezra, Nehemiah, Haggai, Zechariah, Malachi*, and Is.13:1–14:23; 2 Chr.36:2-7; Je.45:1; Da.1:1-3; 2 K.25:2-21).

m. There will be the curse of a devastated economy (vv.38-44). Disobedience will cause a steady decline of the economy, a steady decline in production and fruitfulness. The disobedient will sink lower and lower into debt, suffering a steady decline until recovery is impossible. Standing there preaching to the people, Moses graphically described the picture of economic collapse:

⇒ There will be little harvest because of locusts (v.38).
⇒ There will be little fruit to harvest because of worms (v.39).
⇒ There will be few olives to harvest because of disease (v.40).
⇒ There will be little labor and continued economic growth because the young—the sons and daughters—will be taken captive (v.41).
⇒ There will be few crops and trees surviving because of locusts (v.42).
⇒ There will be a steady decline of the economy, and the disobedient will sink lower and lower, even below the foreigners living among them (v.43).
⇒ There will be the need to borrow over and over again, leading to terrible debt that causes a continued deterioration and decline of the economy (v.44).

---

[1] Frank E. Gaebelein, Editor. *The Expositor's Bible Commentary*, p.172.

DEUTERONOMY 28:15-68

⇒ There will be the loss of their exalted position: they will no longer be the head, but instead the dregs, of society (v.44).

n. There will be all of these curses coming upon you—pursuing and overtaking you until you are destroyed (v.45). Disobedience will lead to disaster, inevitable destruction. All because you refused to obey the LORD. Note the purpose for the curses: Moses declared that they were a sign, a warning to God's people and their descendants. God's people must obey Him or else they will suffer these curses.

Thought 1. There is a strong warning in these verses for us and for all believers of all generations. The warning is against disobedience, against refusing to listen to God. Disobedience is a high crime committed against God. It is the height of contempt, the summit of wickedness. Disobedience is despicable and shameful, showing the utmost spite and disrespect for God. Holy Scripture warns us:

"And these [the disobedient] shall go away into everlasting punishment: but the righteous into life eternal" (Mt.25:46).

"Let no man deceive you with vain words: for because of these [wicked things] things cometh the wrath of God upon the children of disobedience" (Ep.5:6).

"And to you who are troubled rest with us, when the Lord Jesus shall be revealed from heaven with his mighty angels, In flaming fire taking vengeance on them that know not God, and that obey not the gospel of our Lord Jesus Christ: Who shall be punished with everlasting destruction from the presence of the Lord, and from the glory of his power" (2 Th.1:7-9).

"For if the word spoken by angels was stedfast, and every transgression and disobedience received a just recompence of reward; How shall we escape, if we neglect so great salvation; which at the first began to be spoken by the Lord, and was confirmed unto us by them that heard *him*" (He.2:2-3).

"But if ye will not obey the voice of the LORD, but rebel against the commandment of the LORD, then shall the hand of the LORD be against you, as *it was* against your fathers" (1 S.12:15).

2 (28:47-57) **Judgment, Described—Curses, Described—Service, Failure in—Ministry, Failure in—Judgment, Caused by:** the second set of curses was due to lack of service, the failure to serve God. Note verse 47: Moses began to warn the people against failing to serve God. If they failed to serve Him, a series of horrible curses would fall upon them. The Sovereign Creator of the universe expects to be served. Therefore, it is the height of folly to refuse to serve the LORD God Almighty. Rejecting Him and His call to service will cause curse after curse to come upon a person, a barrage of horrible calamities.

Note this fact: the Hebrew uses the future perfect tense, which simply means that the events are being predicted. However, Moses is speaking as though the people had already come under the curses: they are future events, but it as though the events had already been put into effect.[2] The future perfect tense is also used in verse 45.

OUTLINE	SCRIPTURE	SCRIPTURE	OUTLINE
2. The second set of curses: Cursed due to lack of service, failing to serve God	47 Because thou servedst not the LORD thy God with joyfulness, and with gladness of heart, for the abundance of all *things*;	of thy cattle, and the fruit of thy land, until thou be destroyed: which *also* shall not leave thee *either* corn, wine, or oil, *or* the increase of thy	ply—the livestock & crops—until you starve & are destroyed
a. The curse of serving one's enemies	48 Therefore shalt thou serve thine enemies which the LORD shall send against thee,	kine, or flocks of thy sheep, until he have destroyed thee.	
1) Will leave you hungry, thirsty, naked, & in poverty	in hunger, and in thirst, and in nakedness, and in want of	52 And he shall besiege thee in all thy gates, until thy high and fenced walls come down,	6) Will lay siege & destroy all your cities
2) Will enslave & destroy you	all *things*: and he shall put a yoke of iron upon thy neck, until he have destroyed thee.	wherein thou trustedst, throughout all thy land: and he shall besiege thee in all thy	
3) Will quickly & forcefully conquer you	49 The LORD shall bring a nation against thee from far, from the end of the earth, *as* swift as the eagle flieth; a nation whose tongue thou shalt not understand;	gates throughout all thy land, which the LORD thy God hath given thee. 53 And thou shalt eat the fruit of thine own body, the flesh of thy sons and of thy	b. The curse of suffering untold horror because of one's enemy: The ghastly, repulsive horror of eating the flesh of dead sons & daughters
4) Will be a fierce, heartless nation	50 A nation of fierce countenance, which shall not regard the person of the old, nor show favour to the young:	daughters, which the LORD thy God hath given thee, in the siege, and in the straitness, wherewith thine ene-	
5) Will devour the food sup-	51 And he shall eat the fruit	mies shall distress thee:	

---

[2] Peter C. Craigie. *The Book of Deuteronomy*, p.348.

DEUTERONOMY 28:15-68

OUTLINE	SCRIPTURE	SCRIPTURE	OUTLINE
1) Even the most tenderhearted man will have no compassion for his family: Starvation will make him so degenerate & depraved that he will eat the flesh of his own children & not share with his family	54 *So that* the man *that is* tender among you, and very delicate, his eye shall be evil toward his brother, and toward the wife of his bosom, and toward the remnant of his children which he shall leave: 55 So that he will not give to any of them of the flesh of his children whom he shall eat: because he hath nothing left him in the siege, and in the straitness, wherewith thine enemies shall distress thee in all thy gates. 56 The tender and delicate	woman among you, which would not adventure to set the sole of her foot upon the ground for delicateness and tenderness, her eye shall be evil toward the husband of her bosom, and toward her son, and toward her daughter, 57 And toward her young one that cometh out from between her feet, and toward her children which she shall bear: for she shall eat them for want of all *things* secretly in the siege and straitness, wherewith thine enemy shall distress thee in thy gates.	delicate woman will become callous & cruel: She will secretly eat the afterbirth & the newborn child from her womb
2) Even the most tender &			

a. There was the curse of serving one's enemies (vv.48-52). Moses declared that failing to serve God would result in serving various enemies. And the enemies would bring curse after curse upon the head of a person or nation who failed to serve God. The curses brought about by the enemy are the worst curses imaginable:
⇒ The enemy would leave them hungry, thirsty, naked, and in poverty (v.48).
⇒ The enemy would enslave and destroy them (v.48). His oppression would be so severe that it would be as though an iron yoke has been put on their necks until they were destroyed.
⇒ The enemy would quickly and forcefully conquer them (v.49). Note that a particular nation is being spoken about, a nation that would swoop down upon the Israelites just like an eagle, a nation whose language the Israelites would not understand. Both the Assyrians and the Babylonians were referred to in Scripture as eagles (Ho.8:1; Je.48:40). The soaring of an eagle pictures the speed and strength of military power.
⇒ The enemy would be a fierce, heartless nation (v.50). They would enslave and slaughter both the old and the young as well as the middle-aged adults.
⇒ The enemy would devour the food supply, the livestock and crops, until they starved and were destroyed. They would leave absolutely nothing, plundering and ransacking and destroying everything (v.51).
⇒ The enemy would lay siege and destroy all their cities (v.52). Note the reference to the Israelites trusting in their fortified cities. But their fortifications could not secure them; their cities could not make them safe nor give them victory. Only God could provide security. But they had refused to serve Him; therefore, they were to serve a foreign nation of people.

b. There was the curse of suffering untold horror because of one's enemy. The Israelites would suffer the ghastly, repulsive horror of eating the flesh of dead sons and daughters (vv.53-57). The siege of the fiercest looking nation would reach its climax in cannibalism. Starving to death, the Israelites would actually eat their own children.
1) Even the most tenderhearted man would have no compassion for his family (vv.54-55). Starvation would make him so degenerate and depraved that he would eat the flesh of his own children, not sharing any with his family.
2) Even the most tender and delicate woman would become callous and cruel (vv.56-57). She would secretly eat the afterbirth and the newborn child from her womb.

Note why Moses predicted that the people would turn to cannibalism: because of the suffering the enemy would inflict on them (vv.53, 55, 57). Three times the suffering is mentioned. The frightful horror of starvation would stare people in the face, and they would become utterly depraved, degenerate. Shockingly, they would begin to eat the flesh of the dead. Then, when there were no more dead, they would begin to turn upon the weak and helpless children, slaughtering them and eating their flesh—the most horrible, repulsive, sickening thought that can be imagined. Nevertheless, it happened (see 2 K.6:24-31; La.2:20; 4:10).

Thought 1. Refusing to serve and failing to serve God are serious offenses. One thing God will not tolerate: the neglect of our duty. We must not neglect our responsibility, our service for Him. If we fail to serve God—if we neglect our duty—we will face the terrifying judgment of God.

"And every one that heareth these sayings of mine, and doeth them not, shall be likened unto a foolish man, which built his house upon the sand: And the rain descended, and the floods came, and the winds blew, and beat upon that house; and it fell: and great was the fall of it" (Mt.7:26-27).
"Thou oughtest therefore to have put my money to the exchangers, and *then* at my coming I should have received mine own with usury. Take therefore the talent from him, and give *it* unto him which hath ten talents....And cast ye the unprofitable servant into outer darkness: there shall be weeping and gnashing of teeth" (Mt.25:27-28, 30).
"When the Son of man shall come in his glory, and all the holy angels with him, then shall he sit upon the throne of his glory: And before him shall be gathered all nations: and he shall separate them one from another, as a shepherd divideth *his* sheep from the goats....Then shall he say also unto them on the left hand, Depart from me, ye cursed, into everlasting fire, prepared for the devil and his angels: For I was an hungred, and ye gave me no meat: I was thirsty, and ye gave me no drink: I was a stranger, and

DEUTERONOMY 28:15-68

ye took me not in: naked, and ye clothed me not: sick, and in prison, and ye visited me not. Then shall they also answer him, saying, Lord, when saw we thee an hungred, or athirst, or a stranger, or naked, or sick, or in prison, and did not minister unto thee? Then shall he answer them, saying, Verily I say unto you, Inasmuch as ye did *it* not to one of the least of these, ye did *it* not to me. And these shall go away into everlasting punishment: but the righteous into life eternal" (Mt.25:31-32, 41-46).

"And that servant, which knew his lord's will, and prepared not *himself,* neither did according to his will, shall be beaten with many *stripes*" (Lu.12:47).

"There was a certain rich man, which was clothed in purple and fine linen, and fared sumptuously every day: And there was a certain beggar named Lazarus, which was laid at his gate, full of sores, And desiring to be fed with the crumbs which fell from the rich man's table: moreover the dogs came and licked his sores. And it came to pass, that the beggar died, and was carried by the angels into Abraham's bosom: the rich man also died, and was buried; And in hell he lift up his eyes, being in torments, and seeth Abraham afar off, and Lazarus in his bosom. And he cried and said, Father Abraham, have mercy on me, and send Lazarus, that he may dip the tip of his finger in water, and cool my tongue; for I am tormented in this flame. But Abraham said, Son, remember that thou in thy lifetime receivedst thy good things, and likewise Lazarus evil things: but now he is comforted, and thou art tormented" (Lu.16:19-25).

"How shall we escape, if we neglect so great salvation; which at the first began to be spoken by the Lord, and was confirmed unto us by them that heard *him*" (He.2:3).

"What *doth it* profit, my brethren, though a man say he hath faith, and have not works? can faith save him" (Js.2:14).

"Therefore to him that knoweth to do good, and doeth *it* not, to him it is sin" (Js.4:17).

"Whoso stoppeth his ears at the cry of the poor, he also shall cry himself, but shall not be heard" (Pr.21:13).

3 (28:58-68) **Fear, of God—Reverence, of God—Judgment, Caused by—Curses, of Judgment**: the third set of curses was due to lack of fear and reverence for God. The curses would fall upon a person because he failed to fear the glorious and awesome name, "the LORD your God." The LORD (Jehovah, Yahweh) is the only living and true God. He is living and true; He actually exists. He is the Sovereign Creator of the universe, the Majestic Prince who has created every human being upon earth. Therefore, He is to be *your* God. You are to stand in awe of Him, honor and worship Him. You are to reverence Him, hold Him in the highest esteem. And you are to fear Him, acknowledging your own sinfulness and the light of His holy justice. Failing to fear and reverence God is the height of pride and arrogance, insolence and disdain. The haughty, high-handed person who scorns the fear and reverence of God will face the judgment of God. He will be cursed. Note that Moses now focused upon the failure of people to revere the glorious and awesome name of "the LORD your God" (v.58).

OUTLINE	SCRIPTURE	SCRIPTURE	OUTLINE
3. The third set of curses: Cursed due to lack of fear & reverence for God—failing to fear His glorious & awesome name, THE LORD YOUR GOD	58 If thou wilt not observe to do all the words of this law that are written in this book, that thou mayest fear this glorious and fearful name, THE LORD THY GOD;	63 And it shall come to pass, *that* as the LORD rejoiced over you to do you good, and to multiply you; so the LORD will rejoice over you to destroy you, and to bring you to nought; and ye shall be plucked from off the land whither thou goest to possess it.	1) The LORD had increased your number 2) The LORD will decrease your population
a. The curse of fearful plagues, harsh & prolonged disasters, & severe & lingering sicknesses	59 Then the LORD will make thy plagues wonderful, and the plagues of thy seed, *even* great plagues, and of long continuance, and sore sicknesses, and of long continuance.		c. The curse of being uprooted & scattered among all nations
1) Will suffer all the dreaded diseases of Egypt, & the diseases will cling to them	60 Moreover he will bring upon thee all the diseases of Egypt, which thou wast afraid of; and they shall cleave unto thee.	64 And the LORD shall scatter thee among all people, from the one end of the earth even unto the other; and there thou shalt serve other gods, which neither thou nor thy fathers have known, *even* wood and stone.	1) Will worship false gods: Commit idolatry & false worship
2) Will suffer every kind of disease & disaster, even those not recorded in the Book of the Law	61 Also every sickness, and every plague, which *is* not written in the book of this law, them will the LORD bring upon thee, until thou be destroyed.	65 And among these nations shalt thou find no ease, neither shall the sole of thy foot have rest: but the LORD shall give thee there a trembling heart, and failing of eyes, and sorrow of mind:	2) Will find no security or resting place 3) Will have a mind gripped by anxiety, eyes that are weary & longing, & a heart that is filled with sorrow & despair
b. The curse of being almost annihilated, exterminated—reduced to a very small population	62 And ye shall be left few in number, whereas ye were as the stars of heaven for multitude; because thou wouldest not obey the voice of the LORD thy God.	66 And thy life shall hang in doubt before thee; and thou shalt fear day and night, and shalt have none assurance of	4) Will live in constant doubt, fear, & hopelessness

DEUTERONOMY 28:15-68

OUTLINE	SCRIPTURE	SCRIPTURE	OUTLINE
5) Will be gripped by terror: In the morning one will wish it were evening & in the evening wish it were morning	thy life: 67 In the morning thou shalt say, Would God it were even! and at even thou shalt say, Would God it were morning! for the fear of thine heart wherewith thou shalt fear, and for the sight of thine eyes which thou shalt see.	68 And the LORD shall bring thee into Egypt again with ships, by the way whereof I spake unto thee, Thou shalt see it no more again: and there ye shall be sold unto your enemies for bondmen and bondwomen, and no man shall buy *you*.	6) Will even be scattered in Egypt & offer oneself for sale as a slave: But no one will buy you

a. They would face the curse of fearful plagues, harsh and prolonged disasters, and severe and lingering sicknesses (vv.59-61). What Moses now proclaimed to the Israelites is most frightening: if they failed to fear God's holy and awesome name...

- they would suffer all the dreaded diseases of Egypt, and the diseases would cling to them (v.60)
- they would suffer every kind of disease and disaster, even those not recorded in the book of the law (v.61)

b. They would suffer the curse of being almost annihilated, exterminated—reduced to a very small population (vv.62-63). If they refused to obey the LORD, refused to fear and reverence His holy name, they would suffer the most horrible curses imaginable. Just as the LORD had increased their number, so He would decrease their population.

c. They would suffer the curse of being uprooted and scattered all over the world, among all nations (vv.63-68). Note how literally this has been fulfilled in the persecution of the Jews down through the centuries—all because of their continued disobedience, their refusing to acknowledge, fear, and reverence the LORD. Moses declared that the result would be catastrophic:

⇒ They would worship false gods, engage in idolatry and false worship (v.64).
⇒ They would find no security or resting place no matter where they set the soles of their feet (v.65).
⇒ They would have minds gripped by anxiety; their eyes would be weary and lonely, and their hearts would be filled with sorrow and despair (v.65).
⇒ They would live in constant doubt, fear, and hopelessness (v.66). They would never be sure of their lives.
⇒ They would be gripped by terror (v.67). In the morning they would wish it were evening, and in the evening they would wish it were morning.
⇒ They would even be scattered in Egypt and offer themselves for sale as slaves, but no one would buy them (v.68).

Thought 1. This is the conclusion of the curses, the conclusion of the warning preached by Moses. This graphic picture of the curses for disobedience should be enough to stir any person to rededicate his life. The curses for disobedience stand as a severe warning to all people of all generations. Moses warned the Israelites and, through them, he warns us all. There are consequences for disobedience, curses that will fall upon the head of all disobedient people. The warning of God is clear: we must fear God and reverence Him.

> "And fear not them which kill the body, but are not able to kill the soul: but rather fear him which is able to destroy both soul and body in hell" (Mt.10:28).
>
> "And if ye call on the Father, who without respect of persons judgeth according to every man's work, pass the time of your sojourning *here* in fear" (1 Pe.1:17).
>
> "Honour all *men*. Love the brotherhood. Fear God. Honour the king" (1 Pe.2:17).
>
> "And now, Israel, what doth the LORD thy God require of thee, but to fear the LORD thy God, to walk in all his ways, and to love him, and to serve the LORD thy God with all thy heart and with all thy soul" (De.10:12).
>
> "Now therefore fear the LORD, and serve him in sincerity and in truth: and put away the gods which your fathers served on the other side of the flood, and in Egypt; and serve ye the LORD" (Jos.24:14).
>
> "Stand in awe, and sin not: commune with your own heart upon your bed, and be still. Selah" (Ps.4:4).
>
> "Let all the earth fear the LORD: let all the inhabitants of the world stand in awe of him" (Ps.33:8).
>
> "God is greatly to be feared in the assembly of the saints, and to be had in reverence of all *them that are* about him" (Ps.89:7).
>
> "Let us hear the conclusion of the whole matter: Fear God, and keep his commandments: for this *is* the whole *duty* of man" (Ec.12:13).
>
> "Sanctify the LORD of hosts himself; and *let* him *be* your fear, and *let* him *be* your dread" (Is.8:13).
>
> "For thus saith the high and lofty One that inhabiteth eternity, whose name *is* Holy; I dwell in the high and holy *place,* with him also *that is* of a contrite and humble spirit, to revive the spirit of the humble, and to revive the heart of the contrite ones" (Is.57:15).
>
> "But the LORD *is* in his holy temple: let all the earth keep silence before him" (Hab.2:20).

Thought 2. One supreme fact must always be remembered: Jesus Christ bore the curse of the law for us (Ga.3:13). The curse of the law is the penalty that we must bear for having broken the law, the penalty of corruption and of death. Every time we commit a sin, we add more sin to the evil that already exists. We heap sin upon sin. The corruption of sin is one of the penalties for breaking the law. But this is not all; death is also one of the penalties for disobedience. We die because we have disobeyed God. The first man and woman upon earth, Adam and Eve, disobeyed God;

DEUTERONOMY 28:15-68

consequently, God pronounced the judgment of death upon them. Death simply means separation; it does not mean annihilation, ceasing to exist. There are three types of death mentioned in the Bible:

⇒ *Spiritual death*, which we experience while living on the earth. *Spiritual death* simply means that we are separated, alienated from God.
⇒ *Physical death*, which simply means the separation of the spirit from the body. This is what people usually refer to as death.
⇒ *Eternal death*, which is also referred to as the *second death*. This means that we will be eternally separated from God unless we have trusted Jesus Christ as our Savior.

The point is this: death is the curse of the law, the penalty for having broken the law. But Jesus Christ has borne the curse for us, taking the penalty of the law upon Himself. He took the curse of the law that was due us and suffered the curse for us. He died upon the cross, bearing the penalty for disobedience. This means a most wonderful thing: if we will simply trust Jesus Christ, we will be saved from the curse of the law. God will accept us in the righteousness of Jesus Christ, His one and only Son. What Jesus Christ has done for us by bearing the curse of the law is beyond imagination! Incomprehensible!

> "For as many as are of the works of the law are under the curse: for it is written, Cursed *is* every one that continueth not in all things which are written in the book of the law to do them. But that no man is justified by the law in the sight of God, *it is* evident: for, The just shall live by faith. And the law is not of faith: but, The man that doeth them shall live in them. Christ hath redeemed us from the curse of the law, being made a curse for us: for it is written, Cursed *is* every one that hangeth on a tree" (Ga.3:10-13).
>
> "But we see Jesus, who was made a little lower than the angels for the suffering of death, crowned with glory and honour; that he by the grace of God should taste death for every man" (He.2:9).
>
> "So Christ was once offered to bear the sins of many; and unto them that look for him shall he appear the second time without sin unto salvation" (He.9:28).
>
> "Who his own self bare our sins in his own body on the tree, that we, being dead to sins, should live unto righteousness: by whose stripes ye were healed" (1 Pe.2:24).
>
> "For Christ also hath once suffered for sins, the just for the unjust, that he might bring us to God, being put to death in the flesh, but quickened by the Spirit" (1 Pe.3:18).
>
> "And ye know that he was manifested to take away our sins; and in him is no sin" (1 Jn.3:5).
>
> "But he *was* wounded for our transgressions, *he was* bruised for our iniquities: the chastisement of our peace *was* upon him; and with his stripes we are healed" (Is.53:5).

DEUTERONOMY 29:1-29

CHAPTER 29

D. The Terms of the Covenant: Obey God or Face His Judgment, 29:1-29

1. **The parties of the covenant**
   a. The parties: The LORD, the Israelites, & Moses
   b. The covenant: To include additional terms added to the covenant made at Mt. Sinai

2. **The basis of the covenant: Why the covenant was needed**
   a. The salvation & works of God: The people had been saved by the power of God from the slavery of Egypt (a symbol of being saved from the world)

   b. The hard hearts of the people: Kept the LORD from giving them a deeper understanding of His salvation
   c. The need for God's guidance & provision: He had led His people day by day through the wilderness wanderings
      1) Provided clothes & sandals
      2) Provided food & water
      3) The reason: To demonstrate that He was the LORD their God

   d. The need for victory over all enemies: God had given a great victory over two strong kings, Kings Sihon & Og

   e. The hope of the promised land: The conquered land of the two kings had been given as an inheritance to several of the tribes
   f. The necessity of obedience: Must carefully obey the terms of the covenant in order to prosper

3. **The purpose of the covenant**
   a. The covenant embraced every person who stood in the presence of the LORD
      1) The leaders, elders, officers, men, children, wives, & foreigners

      2) The point: The very reason the people stood before the LORD was to enter into

These *are* the words of the covenant, which the LORD commanded Moses to make with the children of Israel in the land of Moab, beside the covenant which he made with them in Horeb.
2 And Moses called unto all Israel, and said unto them, Ye have seen all that the LORD did before your eyes in the land of Egypt unto Pharaoh, and unto all his servants, and unto all his land;
3 The great temptations which thine eyes have seen, the signs, and those great miracles:
4 Yet the LORD hath not given you an heart to perceive, and eyes to see, and ears to hear, unto this day.
5 And I have led you forty years in the wilderness: your clothes are not waxen old upon you, and thy shoe is not waxen old upon thy foot.
6 Ye have not eaten bread, neither have ye drunk wine or strong drink: that ye might know that I *am* the LORD your God.
7 And when ye came unto this place, Sihon the king of Heshbon, and Og the king of Bashan, came out against us unto battle, and we smote them:
8 And we took their land, and gave it for an inheritance unto the Reubenites, and to the Gadites, and to the half tribe of Manasseh.
9 Keep therefore the words of this covenant, and do them, that ye may prosper in all that ye do.
10 Ye stand this day all of you before the LORD your God; your captains of your tribes, your elders, and your officers, *with* all the men of Israel,
11 Your little ones, your wives, and thy stranger that *is* in thy camp, from the hewer of thy wood unto the drawer of thy water:
12 That thou shouldest enter into covenant with the LORD thy God, and into his oath, which the LORD thy God maketh with thee this day:
13 That he may establish thee to day for a people unto himself, and *that* he may be unto thee a God, as he hath said unto thee, and as he hath sworn unto thy fathers, to Abraham, to Isaac, and to Jacob.
14 Neither with you only do I make this covenant and this oath;
15 But with *him* that standeth here with us this day before the LORD our God, and also with *him* that *is* not here with us this day:
16 (For ye know how we have dwelt in the land of Egypt; and how we came through the nations which ye passed by;
17 And ye have seen their abominations, and their idols, wood and stone, silver and gold, which *were* among them:)
18 Lest there should be among you man, or woman, or family, or tribe, whose heart turneth away this day from the LORD our God, to go *and* serve the gods of these nations; lest there should be among you a root that beareth gall and wormwood;
19 And it come to pass, when he heareth the words of this curse, that he bless himself in his heart, saying, I shall have peace, though I walk in the imagination of mine heart, to add drunkenness to thirst:
20 The LORD will not spare him, but then the anger of the LORD and his jealousy shall smoke against that man, and all the curses that are written in this book shall lie upon him, and the LORD shall blot out his name from under heaven.
21 And the LORD shall separate him unto evil out of all the tribes of Israel, according to all the curses of the covenant that are written in this book of the law:
22 So that the generation to come of your children that shall rise up after you, and the stranger that shall come from a far land, shall say,

a covenant with Him, to seal the covenant with an oath that very day
   b. The covenant had one purpose only: To establish that they were God's people & that He was their God—just as He promised

   c. The covenant included future generations as well

      1) Was made with the Israelites standing there

      2) Was also made with all future generations
4. **The warning against breaking the covenant & against hypocrisy**
   a. Must remember the false gods & false worship of the world: You have seen them in Egypt (the world) & in the wilderness wanderings

   b. Must make sure—absolutely sure—that you do not turn away from the LORD
      1) By worshipping the false gods of the world
      2) By planting a seed that bears such poisonous & bitter fruit

   c. Must make absolutely sure that you are not a hypocrite, feeling that you are safe & immune from God's judgment
      1) You are not safe
      2) You will bring disaster on yourself, on everyone else, & even upon the land
5. **The judgment for breaking the covenant, for turning away to false gods & false worship**[DS1]
   a. The LORD will severely judge the violator
      1) Will never forgive him & will blot out his name

      2) Will separate him for special judgment: Pour out upon him all the curses written in the Book of the Law (the Word of God)

   b. The nation will become a spectacle to succeeding generations & nations

      1) The land will suffer

DEUTERONOMY 29:1-29

calamities & diseases	when they see the plagues of that land, and the sicknesses which the LORD hath laid upon it;	them forth out of the land of Egypt:	He saved them from Egypt (the world)
2) The land will be a burning waste with no vegetation growing	23 And that the whole land thereof is brimstone, and salt, and burning, that it is not sown, nor beareth, nor any grass groweth therein, like the overthrow of Sodom, and Gomorrah, Admah, and Zeboim, which the LORD overthrew in his anger, and in his wrath:	26 For they went and served other gods, and worshipped them, gods whom they knew not, and whom he had not given unto them:	• Because the people turned away from the LORD to false gods & false worship
3) The land will suffer the same destruction that fell upon Sodom & Gomorrah, upon Admah & Zeboim		27 And the anger of the LORD was kindled against this land, to bring upon it all the curses that are written in this book:	3) The result of apostasy • The LORD's anger burned: Devastated the land itself
c. The judgment will be so fierce that people will ask, "Why?" 1) The question	24 Even all nations shall say, Wherefore hath the LORD done thus unto this land? what meaneth the heat of this great anger?	28 And the LORD rooted them out of their land in anger, and in wrath, and in great indignation, and cast them into another land, as it is this day.	• The LORD's wrath: Allowed a nation to conquer, uproot, & exile the people
2) The answer • Because the people broke the covenant, the promise they made with the LORD when	25 Then men shall say, Because they have forsaken the covenant of the LORD God of their fathers, which he made with them when he brought	29 The secret things belong unto the LORD our God: but those things which are revealed belong unto us and to our children for ever, that we may do all the words of this law.	d. The prediction of these things is said to be secret 1) The secret things belong to God 2) The things revealed belong to us: That we may know God's will & obey

DIVISION V

THE THIRD GREAT THEME PREACHED BY GOD'S AGED SERVANT: THE CHARGE TO RENEW THE COVENANT WITH GOD, 27:1–30:20

D. The Terms of the Covenant: Obey God or Face the Judgment of God, 29:1-29

(29:1-29) **Introduction**: this is the hour of decision, the hour for salvation and the rededication of our lives to God. Our commitment and covenant with God need to be renewed. People within the church have come short of what they should be, and sin and evil are sweeping throughout our communities. Lawlessness and violence are engulfing our states and nations. People everywhere are living unholy and ungodly lives, committing all forms of sin and wickedness:

- ⇒ abuse of children and spouses
- ⇒ prostitution and homosexuality
- ⇒ premarital sex and adultery
- ⇒ atheism and agnosticism
- ⇒ pride and arrogance
- ⇒ bitterness and hatred
- ⇒ incest
- ⇒ forced labor and enslavement
- ⇒ secularism and humanism
- ⇒ intoxication and drunkenness
- ⇒ anger and hostility
- ⇒ greed and covetousness

There is no end to the list of our shortcomings and failures before the face of God's holiness. If there has ever been a day when repentance was needed, it is today. This is the day for rededication, the day when we must renew our commitment and covenant with God.

This was exactly what Moses was facing: a stubborn, stiff-necked, hard-hearted people. Israel stood before him as he was preaching and doing all he could to prepare them to march victoriously into the promised land. They had failed so often in the past throughout the wilderness wanderings. But here they stood: in the plains of Moab, close by the Jordan River, almost ready to cross the Jordan and enter the promised land. They were soon to lay claim to the inheritance given them by God. What could Moses do to prepare them, to make sure that the hand of God remained upon them, blessed them, and kept them in the promised land? There was only one thing Moses could do: challenge the people to rededicate their lives to God, to renew their commitment and covenant with God. This Moses did. This is the subject of this great passage of Scripture: *The Terms of the Covenant: Obey God or Face the Judgment of God,* 29:1-29.

1. The parties of the covenant (v.1).
2. The basis of the covenant: why the covenant was needed (vv.2-9).
3. The purpose of the covenant (vv.10-15).
4. The warning against breaking the covenant and against hypocrisy (vv.16-19).
5. The judgment for breaking the covenant, for turning away to false gods and false worship (vv.20-29).

1 (29:1) **Covenant, Mosaic, Parties**: the first term of the covenant spelled out the parties who were to agree to the contract.
  a. There were three parties involved in renewing the covenant:
    ⇒ God Himself
    ⇒ the people (Israelites)
    ⇒ Moses, the mediator who stood between God and the people

DEUTERONOMY 29:1-29

The LORD appointed Moses to share the terms of the covenant with the Israelites. As the mediator of the covenant of the law, Moses is a clear type of Christ, the Mediator of the new covenant of grace.

b. Note this fact: the covenant being renewed in the plains of Moab was now to be enlarged. Additional terms were to be added to the covenant made at Mt. Sinai. A new revelation, more information about the covenant, was now to be revealed by God. What was the new information, the added terms? The *restoration of Israel*. This is what is called by some commentators the *Palestinian Covenant*. Note these facts:

⇒ The utter failure of Israel and their dispersion or scattering the people among the nations of the world had just been predicted (28:63-68).

⇒ Now the additional information about the restoration of Israel was to be revealed. The restoration involved some future repentance and their return to the promised land (De.30:1-10. See outlines and notes—Ro.11:1-36 for more discussion.)

It should be noted that some commentators refer to chapters 29–30 as the Palestinian covenant; whereas other commentators prefer to look upon these chapters as a renewal and reaffirmation of the covenant given at Mt. Sinai. Whatever the case, the new information about the restoration of Israel is definitely a new revelation, a new promise to be added to the covenant given to God's people. (For a full discussion of what some commentators call the Palestinian covenant, see all of De.29:1-29; 30:1-20.)

OUTLINE	SCRIPTURE

1. The parties of the covenant
   a. The parties: The LORD, the Israelites, & Moses
   b. The covenant: To include additional terms added to the covenant made at Mt. Sinai
	These *are* the words of the covenant, which the LORD commanded Moses to make with the children of Israel in the land of Moab, beside the covenant which he made with them in Horeb.

Thought 1. Moses was the mediator who stood between God and man. He preached the covenant of the law to man, the fact that man must obey the commandments of God to receive the great promises of God. As the mediator between God and man, Moses is a type of Jesus Christ, the Mediator who represents us before God. Jesus Christ is the Mediator of the covenant of grace. He brought the gospel of grace to man, proclaimed the fact that we are saved by the grace of God through faith.

"Who *is* he that condemneth? *It is* Christ that died, yea rather, that is risen again, who is even at the right hand of God, who also maketh intercession for us" (Ro.8:34).

"For by grace are ye saved through faith; and that not of yourselves: *it is* the gift of God: Not of works, lest any man should boast" (Ep.2:8-9).

"For this *is* good and acceptable in the sight of God our Saviour; Who will have all men to be saved, and to come unto the knowledge of the truth. For *there is* one God, and one mediator between God and men, the man Christ Jesus" (1 Ti.2:3-5).

"Wherefore in all things it behooved him to be made like unto *his* brethren, that he might be a merciful and faithful high priest in things *pertaining* to God, to make reconciliation for the sins of the people" (He.2:17).

"Seeing then that we have a great high priest, that is passed into the heavens, Jesus the Son of God, let us hold fast *our* profession. For we have not an high priest which cannot be touched with the feeling of our infirmities; but was in all points tempted like as *we are, yet* without sin" (He.4:14-15).

"Wherefore he is able also to save them to the uttermost that come unto God by him, seeing he ever liveth to make intercession for them" (He.7:25).

"But now hath he obtained a more excellent ministry, by how much also he is the mediator of a better covenant, which was established upon better promises" (He.8:6).

"Neither by the blood of goats and calves, but by his own blood he entered in once into the holy place, having obtained eternal redemption *for us*. For if the blood of bulls and of goats, and the ashes of an heifer sprinkling the unclean, sanctifieth to the purifying of the flesh: How much more shall the blood of Christ, who through the eternal Spirit offered himself without spot to God, purge your conscience from dead works to serve the living God? And for this cause he is the mediator of the new testament, that by means of death, for the redemption of the transgressions *that were* under the first testament, they which are called might receive the promise of eternal inheritance" (He.9:12-15).

"For Christ is not entered into the holy places made with hands, *which are* the figures of the true; but into heaven itself, now to appear in the presence of God for us" (He.9:24).

"My little children, these things write I unto you, that ye sin not. And if any man sin, we have an advocate with the Father, Jesus Christ the righteous: And he is the propitiation for our sins: and not for ours only, but also for *the sins of* the whole world" (1 Jn.2:1-2).

2 (29:2-9) **Covenant, Basis—Works of God, Among Israel**: the covenant spelled out the basis or the reasons for the covenant. Moses declared that there were five basic reasons why the covenant between God and man was needed, five reasons why the people must renew their commitment, their covenant with God.

DEUTERONOMY 29:1-29

OUTLINE	SCRIPTURE	SCRIPTURE	OUTLINE

2. The basis of the covenant: Why the covenant was needed
a. The salvation & works of God: The people had been saved by the power of God from the slavery of Egypt (a symbol of being saved from the world)
 	
b. The hard hearts of the people: Kept the LORD from giving them a deeper understanding of His salvation
c. The need for God's guidance & provision: He had led His people day by day through the wilderness wanderings
  1) Provided clothes & sandals
	2 And Moses called unto all Israel, and said unto them, Ye have seen all that the LORD did before your eyes in the land of Egypt unto Pharaoh, and unto all his servants, and unto all his land;
	3 The great temptations which thine eyes have seen, the signs, and those great miracles:
	4 Yet the LORD hath not given you an heart to perceive, and eyes to see, and ears to hear, unto this day.
	5 And I have led you forty years in the wilderness: your clothes are not waxen old upon you, and thy shoe is not waxen old upon thy foot.
		6 Ye have not eaten bread, neither have ye drunk wine or strong drink: that ye might know that I am the LORD your God.
		7 And when ye came unto this place, Sihon the king of Heshbon, and Og the king of Bashan, came out against us unto battle, and we smote them:
		8 And we took their land, and gave it for an inheritance unto the Reubenites, and to the Gadites, and to the half tribe of Manasseh.
		9 Keep therefore the words of this covenant, and do them, that ye may prosper in all that ye do.
			2) Provided food & water
			  3) The reason: To demonstrate that He was the LORD their God
			
			d. The need for victory over all enemies: God had given a great victory over two strong kings, kings Sihon & Og
			
			e. The hope of the promised land: The conquered land of the two kings had been given as an inheritance to several of the tribes
			f. The necessity of obedience: Must carefully obey the terms of the covenant in order to prosper

    a. The covenant was needed because of the *salvation and works of God* (vv.2-3). The people had actually seen and experienced the saving power of God from the slavery of Egypt. Remember, Israel's deliverance from Egypt is a symbol of the believer being saved from the enslavements of the world. God had done so much for the Israelite believers. Moses reviewed the wonderful salvation of God, knowing that the goodness of God would help stir the people to rededicate their lives, to renew their covenant with God.

    Note this fact: not every person standing in front of Moses had actually been in Egypt, but many had. At the time of the Exodus, many were 18 years of age or younger, which means that they were now around 40 to 58 years old. These were the ones who had actually seen and witnessed the saving power of God from Egyptian slavery. Everyone else had been born in the desert, but they knew one evident fact: if God had not saved their parents from Egypt, they would have been born in slavery. Thus the preaching of Moses was correct: every Israelite had been delivered from Egyptian slavery by the hand of God. It was the wonderful salvation of God that had saved them. This was the first basis of the covenant, the first reason why the people should renew their commitment, their covenant with God. Their salvation should stir them to rededicate their lives to God, to renew their covenant to obey God.

    b. The covenant was needed because of the *hard hearts* of the people (v.4). They wanted to do their own thing and live as they wanted, not as God said. Consequently, they disobeyed and rebelled against God. They closed their minds, eyes, and ears against God. They did not seek to understand the salvation and works of God. They refused to look and see the hand of God at work in nature and in the lives of people. They refused to listen to the commandments and Word of God. Because of the hardness of their hearts, the LORD was not able to open their minds, eyes, and ears so that they could understand His commandments and Word—all because the people had become hard, stiff-necked, and stubborn against God. This was a second reason why the people needed to renew their commitment, their covenant with God. They needed to repent of their stubborn, hard hearts and heed the Word of God.

    c. The covenant was needed because the people needed the *guidance and provision of God* (vv.5-6). God had led His people day by day through the wilderness wanderings, taking care of their every need. This included all the necessities of life: clothes, food, and water. Note that God miraculously kept their clothes and sandals from wearing out. The clothing lasted as long as it was needed. The reason why God used miracles to provide for His people is clearly stated: to demonstrate that He and He alone is "the LORD your God." Moses declared that this fact—the miraculous guidance and provision of God—should stir the people to renew their covenant with God. God would be with His people—guide and provide for them—only if they obeyed the covenant, kept His commandments. Rededication and recommitment to God—renewing one's life to the covenant—was therefore an absolute essential.

    d. The covenant was needed because the people needed to be *victorious over all their enemies* (v.7). The LORD had given a great victory over two strong kings who had opposed the Israelites, King Sihon and King Og (see outline and note—De.2:24-3:11 for more discussion). Victory over enemies—living a victorious life, a life that conquers—is the reason why God's people need to make a covenant with God. The only way God's people can secure victory over their enemies is to keep their covenant with God. For this reason, Moses declares that the people of God must renew their covenant with God. They must honor their part of the contract agreement: they must obey God, keep His commandments.

    e. The covenant was needed because of the *hope of the promised land* (v.8). Note that the conquered land of the two kings had been given as an inheritance to several of the tribes. None of the other tribes had received their inheritance. The promised land still lay out in the future for them. But they were soon to cross the Jordan River and enter the promised land, laying claim to their inheritance. Standing there preaching to the people, Moses knew that the hope of the promised land was alive in the hearts of the people. Therefore, he reminded the people that only a few of the tribes had received their inheritance; the other tribes still had to conquer theirs. It was, therefore, absolutely necessary to renew their covenant with God.

    f. The covenant was needed because of the *necessity for obedience* (v.9). The people must obey God, follow all the terms of the covenant. Obedience is absolutely necessary in order to prosper throughout life. Therefore, the people must rededicate their lives to God. They must renew their commitment to obey God, renew their covenant with God.

DEUTERONOMY 29:1-29

3 (29:10-15) **Covenant, Purpose of—Rededication, Purpose of—Commitment, Purpose of—Covenant, Renewal of—Israel, Renewal of the Covenant—Israel, Rededication of**: the purpose of the covenant was spelled out. Standing before the Israelites preaching to them, the heart of Moses was tender toward the people. Yet, his heart was burning with zeal, longing for the people to rededicate their lives to the LORD, to renew their covenant and commitment with God. Note the Scripture and outline:

OUTLINE	SCRIPTURE	SCRIPTURE	OUTLINE
3. The purpose of the covenant a. The covenant embraced every person who stood in the presence of the LORD 1) The leaders, elders, officers, men, children, wives, & foreigners 2) The point: The very reason the people stood before the LORD was to enter into a covenant with Him, to seal the covenant with an	10 Ye stand this day all of you before the LORD your God; your captains of your tribes, your elders, and your officers, *with* all the men of Israel, 11 Your little ones, your wives, and thy stranger that *is* in thy camp, from the hewer of thy wood unto the drawer of thy water: 12 That thou shouldest enter into covenant with the LORD thy God, and into his oath, which the LORD thy God maketh with thee this	day: 13 That he may establish thee to day for a people unto himself, and *that* he may be unto thee a God, as he hath said unto thee, and as he hath sworn unto thy fathers, to Abraham, to Isaac, and to Jacob. 14 Neither with you only do I make this covenant and this oath; 15 But with *him* that standeth here with us this day before the LORD our God, and also with *him* that *is* not here with us this day:	oath that very day b. The covenant had one purpose only: To establish that they were God's people & that He was their God—just as He promised c. The covenant included future generations as well 1) Was made with the Israelites standing there 2) Was also made with all future generations

    a. The covenant embraced every person who stood in the presence of the LORD (vv.10-12). All of the Israelites stood before God as Moses proclaimed the terms of the covenant to them. Standing there were the leaders, elders, officers, men, children, wives, and foreigners (vv.10-11).

    Note that this is a formal ceremony. It is a very special worship service where all the people are renewing their covenant with God. Just picture the scene: all the leaders, elders, officers, and armed forces of the government are standing there with all the citizens of the nation—the men, women, children, and foreigners—all three million plus stretched out across the valley floor tribe by tribe. They stand there together to renew their commitment, their covenant with God. What a sight! What a dynamic example and lesson for the peoples of the world! There the people stood to renew their cov-enant with God, to renew it with an oath. And note the urgency stressed by Moses: it was necessary to renew their commitment and covenant "this day" (v.12). The word *today* is stressed five times in these six verses (vv.10, 12, 13, 15 [two times]).

    b. Moses declared that the covenant had one purpose and one purpose only: to establish that the believers—those who truly followed God—were God's people and that He was their God (v.13). This is the core, the essence, the summary statement of the covenant. The people were to confirm that they were God's people, that God had chosen and raised them up to be a people for Himself. In the covenant, God was taking an oath that He was choosing the Israelites to be His people and His witnesses upon the earth. They were to be His missionary force to the world, declaring that there is only one living and true God. In response, the people were to declare that the LORD was their God. They were to promise that they would follow and obey the LORD and bear strong testimony to the truth of His Holy Word.

    Note how both God and the people were undertaking obligations to one another. The people were responsible to obey God, and God was responsible to accept the true believer, the obedient person. God was to make him His treasured possession and witness upon the earth. This is clearly stated in this verse (v.13), but it is spelled out in more detail at Mt. Sinai where God first shared the covenant:

> "Now therefore, if ye will obey my voice indeed, and keep my covenant, then ye shall be a peculiar treasure unto me above all people: for all the earth *is* mine: And ye shall be unto me a kingdom of priests, and an holy nation. These *are* the words which thou shalt speak unto the children of Israel" (Ex.19:5-6).

Note the wonderful assurance given by God: He promises to fulfill His part of the covenant. God will not fail in His obligations to the people. He will do exactly as He promises. Just as He swore to the forefathers Abraham, Isaac, and Jacob, so He swears to the Israelites standing there this day. He will not fail. He will fulfill His promise, His part of the covenant.

    c. But this was not all: the covenant included future generations as well (vv.14-15). The covenant with its oath was being made with the Israelites there in the formal ceremony of rededication and renewal. But the covenant was also being confirmed with all future generations of believers, even those who had not yet been born.

    Thought 1. There are three meaningful lessons for us in this point.
    (1) God will keep His promises to us. Every promise He has made will be fulfilled. God is faithful; God will not fail us.

> "For verily I say unto you, Till heaven and earth pass, one jot or one tittle shall in no wise pass from the law, till all be fulfilled" (Mt.5:18).
> "Heaven and earth shall pass away: but my words shall not pass away" (Lu.21:33).
> "God *is* faithful, by whom ye were called unto the fellowship of his Son Jesus Christ our LORD" (1 Co.1:9).
> "Wherein God, willing more abundantly to show unto the heirs of promise the immutability of his counsel, confirmed *it* by an oath: That by two immutable things, in which *it was* impossible for God to lie,

we might have a strong consolation, who have fled for refuge to lay hold upon the hope set before us" (He.6:17-18).

"Wherefore let them that suffer according to the will of God commit the keeping of their souls *to him* in well doing, as unto a faithful Creator" (1 Pe.4:19).

"Know therefore that the LORD thy God, he *is* God, the faithful God, which keepeth covenant and mercy with them that love him and keep his commandments to a thousand generations" (De.7:9).

"And now, O LORD GOD, thou *art* that God, and thy words be true, and thou hast promised this goodness unto thy servant" (2 S.7:28).

"Blessed *be* the LORD, that hath given rest unto his people Israel, according to all that he promised: there hath not failed one word of all his good promise, which he promised by the hand of Moses his servant" (1 K.8:56).

"Thy mercy, O LORD, *is* in the heavens; *and* thy faithfulness *reacheth* unto the clouds" (Ps.36:5).

"I will sing of the mercies of the LORD for ever: with my mouth will I make known thy faithfulness to all generations" (Ps.89:1).

(2) We must be faithful to keep our promises to God. When we first accepted Christ as our Savior, we made a covenant with God, a covenant to follow and obey Him. We must do just what we promised: obey—follow and walk after Him.

"Not every one that saith unto me, LORD, LORD, shall enter into the kingdom of heaven; but he that doeth the will of my Father which is in heaven" (Mt.7:21).

"He that hath my commandments, and keepeth them, he it is that loveth me: and he that loveth me shall be loved of my Father, and I will love him, and will manifest myself to him" (Jn.14:21).

"Jesus answered and said unto him, If a man love me, he will keep my words: and my Father will love him, and we will come unto him, and make our abode with him" (Jn.14:23).

"*This* I say then, Walk in the Spirit, and ye shall not fulfil the lust of the flesh" (Ga.5:16).

"I therefore, the prisoner of the LORD, beseech you that ye walk worthy of the vocation wherewith ye are called" (Ep.4:1).

"See then that ye walk circumspectly, not as fools, but as wise" (Ep.5:15).

"As ye have therefore received Christ Jesus the LORD, *so* walk ye in him" (Col.2:6).

"But if we walk in the light, as he is in the light, we have fellowship one with another, and the blood of Jesus Christ his Son cleanseth us from all sin" (1 Jn.1:7).

"He that saith he abideth in him ought himself also so to walk, even as he walked" (1 Jn.2:6).

"Blessed *are* they that do his commandments, that they may have right to the tree of life, and may enter in through the gates into the city" (Re.22:14).

(3) The genuine believer—the person who truly believes and follows after Christ—is accepted by God and becomes one of God's people. Scripture describes the most wonderful relationship:
(a) The genuine believer is adopted by God, adopted as one of His very own children, as a son or daughter of God.

"But as many as received him, to them gave he power to become the sons of God, *even* to them that believe on his name: Which were born, not of blood, nor of the will of the flesh, nor of the will of man, but of God" (Jn.1:12-13).

"For ye have not received the spirit of bondage again to fear; but ye have received the Spirit of adoption, whereby we cry, Abba, Father. The Spirit itself beareth witness with our spirit, that we are the children of God: And if children, then heirs; heirs of God, and joint-heirs with Christ; if so be that we suffer with *him,* that we may be also glorified together" (Ro.8:15-17).

"Wherefore come out from among them, and be ye separate, saith the LORD, and touch not the unclean *thing;* and I will receive you, And will be a Father unto you, and ye shall be my sons and daughters, saith the LORD Almighty" (2 Co.6:17-18).

"But when the fulness of the time was come, God sent forth his Son, made of a woman, made under the law, To redeem them that were under the law, that we might receive the adoption of sons. And because ye are sons, God hath sent forth the Spirit of his Son into your hearts, crying, Abba, Father" (Ga.4:4-6).

(b) The genuine believer—the person who truly believes and follows after Christ—becomes a very special person to God: His treasured possession.

"According as he hath chosen us in him before the foundation of the world, that we should be holy and without blame before him in love" (Ep.1:4).

"Ye also, as lively stones, are built up a spiritual house, an holy priesthood, to offer up spiritual sacrifices, acceptable to God by Jesus Christ" (1 Pe.2:5).

"But ye are a chosen generation, a royal priesthood, an holy nation, a peculiar people; that ye should show forth the praises of him who hath called you out of darkness into his marvellous light" (1 Pe.2:9).

"Which in time past were not a people, but are now the people of God: which had not obtained mercy, but now have obtained mercy" (1 Pe.2:10).

"And hath made us kings and priests unto God and his Father; to him be glory and dominion for ever and ever. Amen" (Re.1:6).

DEUTERONOMY 29:1-29

"Blessed and holy is he that hath part in the first resurrection: on such the second death hath no power, but they shall be priests of God and of Christ, and shall reign with him a thousand years" (Re.20:6).

"Now therefore, if ye will obey my voice indeed, and keep my covenant, then ye shall be a peculiar treasure unto me above all people: for all the earth is mine" (Ex.19:5).

"And ye shall be unto me a kingdom of priests, and an holy nation. These *are* the words which thou shalt speak unto the children of Israel" (Ex.19:6).

"For thou *art* an holy people unto the LORD thy God: the LORD thy God hath chosen thee to be a special people unto himself, above all people that *are* upon the face of the earth" (De.7:6).

"For thou *art* an holy people unto the LORD thy God, and the LORD hath chosen thee to be a peculiar people unto himself, above all the nations that *are* upon the earth" (De.14:2).

"But know that the LORD hath set apart him that is godly for himself: the LORD will hear when I call unto him" (Ps.4:3).

"But ye shall be named the Priests of the LORD: *men* shall call you the Ministers of our God: ye shall eat the riches of the Gentiles, and in their glory shall ye boast yourselves" (Is.61:6).

Thought 2. Note that the covenant included future generations as well as those who were standing before Moses. Over three million Israelites were standing there being challenged to renew their commitment and covenant with God. The decision they made would affect the future of the nation, affect the destiny of all future generations. John Maxwell gives an excellent illustration of this:

> *This covenant is for future generations as well for those who are now being challenged to make this commitment to God. The decision today will affect Israel's destiny for generations to come. At crucial times throughout history, nations have made decisions that have either enhanced or destroyed their futures.*
>
> *An example of this occurred during World War II. Following the fall of France in 1940, the German Third Reich claimed victory in Europe. Hitler appealed to Great Britain: 'I am the victor; I can see no reason why this war need go on.' LORD Halifax officially responded that no peace which gave Germany control of non-German territory would be acceptable to Britain.*
>
> *However, the decision leading to this reply had been made a few weeks earlier, as the fall of France was anticipated. Addressing the nation, Churchill noted, "The battle of France is over; I expect that the battle of Britain is about to begin. Upon this battle depends the survival of Christian civilization....Let us therefore brace ourselves to our duties and so bear ourselves that if the British Empire and its commonwealth last for a thousand years, men will say 'This was the finest hour.'"*[1]

4 (29:16-19) **Hypocrisy, Warning Against—Disobedience, Warning Against—Warning, Against Breaking the Covenant—Covenant, Warning Against Breaking—Warning, Against Hypocrisy**: the terms of the covenant included a strong warning against breaking the covenant and against hypocrisy. The warning is personal, very personal, and very descriptive:

OUTLINE	SCRIPTURE	SCRIPTURE	OUTLINE
4. The warning against breaking the covenant & against hypocrisy a. Must remember the false gods & false worship of the world: You have seen them in Egypt (the world) & in the wilderness wanderings b. Must make sure—absolutely sure—that you do not turn away from the LORD 1) By worshipping the false	16 (For ye know how we have dwelt in the land of Egypt; and how we came through the nations which ye passed by; 17 And ye have seen their abominations, and their idols, wood and stone, silver and gold, which *were* among them:) 18 Lest there should be among you man, or woman, or family, or tribe, whose heart turneth away this day	from the LORD our God, to go and serve the gods of these nations; lest there should be among you a root that beareth gall and wormwood; 19 And it come to pass, when he heareth the words of this curse, that he bless himself in his heart, saying, I shall have peace, though I walk in the imagination of mine heart, to add drunkenness to thirst:	gods of the world 2) By planting a seed that bears such poisonous & bitter fruit c. Must make absolutely sure that you are not a hypocrite, feeling that you are safe & immune from God's judgment 1) You are not safe 2) You will bring disaster on yourself, on everyone else, & even upon the land

a. Zeal, fervor, urgency, and a burning passion were ablaze in the heart of Moses as he warned the people. He cried out: "You must remember the false gods and false worship of the world." The people had lived among the idols and false worship of the Egyptians when they were enslaved by Egypt. Moreover, they had seen the detestable worship of idolatry and false worship among the nations throughout their wilderness wanderings (vv.16-17).

b. Moses shouted out: "You must make sure—absolutely sure—that you do not turn away from the LORD. You must not worship the false gods of the world, must not engage in the false worship of your neighbors" (v.18).

Note how personal the warning is: no man or woman, family or tribe, must ever turn away from the LORD and engage in false worship.

Note the fruit of idolatry and false worship: it is a root that bears bitter and poisonous fruit (wormwood). The picture is that of a flowing, permeating evil that will contaminate and grow. No person is "an island to himself." He influences other people. Therefore, if he turns away from God and engages in false worship, he will influence and lead others to rebel and

---

[1] John Maxwell. *The Preacher's Commentary on Deuteronomy*, p.313

forsake God. One individual can poison the whole community, even become a stumblingblock to a nation. The poison of his sin and evil can ruin the whole tree.

c. A person must make sure—absolutely sure—that he is not a hypocrite, feeling that he is safe and immune from God's judgment (v.19). Again, note how personal Moses makes this point: an individual must make sure that he does not think, "I will be safe and experience peace of heart and security, even though I do my own thing and live as I want." This person will bring disaster upon himself and everyone else and even upon the land.

Thought 1. There are two clear warnings in this passage applicable to us:
(1) The warning against idolatry and false worship.

> "Forasmuch then as we are the offspring of God, we ought not to think that the Godhead is like unto gold, or silver, or stone, graven by art and man's device" (Ac.17:29).
>
> "For the wrath of God is revealed from heaven against all ungodliness and unrighteousness of men, who hold the truth in unrighteousness; Because that which may be known of God is manifest in them; for God hath showed *it* unto them. For the invisible things of him from the creation of the world are clearly seen, being understood by the things that are made, *even* his eternal power and Godhead; so that they are without excuse: Because that, when they knew God, they glorified *him* not as God, neither were thankful; but became vain in their imaginations, and their foolish heart was darkened. Professing themselves to be wise, they became fools, And changed the glory of the uncorruptible God into an image made like to corruptible man, and to birds, and fourfooted beasts, and creeping things" (Ro.1:18-23).
>
> "Little children, keep yourselves from idols. Amen" (1 Jn.5:21).
>
> "Take heed to yourselves, that your heart be not deceived, and ye turn aside, and serve other gods, and worship them" (De.11:16).
>
> "There shall no strange god be in thee; neither shalt thou worship any strange god" (Ps.81:9).
>
> "I *am* the LORD: that *is* my name: and my glory will I not give to another, neither my praise to graven images" (Is.42:8).
>
> "Assemble yourselves and come; draw near together, ye *that are* escaped of the nations: they have no knowledge that set up the wood of their graven image, and pray unto a god *that* cannot save" (Is.45:20).

(2) The warning against feeling that we are safe and immune from God's judgment. Few people actually think they will ever have to bear God's judgment. Most people think they are good enough to be acceptable to God, that God would never reject them. They feel they do not do enough bad or evil to be kept out of heaven, out of God's presence. They feel safe and secure, immune from God's judgment. They feel that they can, for the most part, do their own thing and live life as they wish, even if they do break the commandments of God. But the warning of God is clear: we must make sure—absolutely sure—that we do not live hypocritical lives. We must not profess to follow God and then not follow Him. If we say that we follow God, then we must follow Him. We must obey Him, keep His commandments. The warning is clear: we must not break our commitment and covenant with God; we must not live lives of hypocrisy.

> "Even so every good tree bringeth forth good fruit; but a corrupt tree bringeth forth evil fruit. A good tree cannot bring forth evil fruit, neither *can* a corrupt tree bring forth good fruit. Every tree that bringeth not forth good fruit is hewn down, and cast into the fire. Wherefore by their fruits ye shall know them" (Mt.7:17-20).
>
> "Even so ye also outwardly appear righteous unto men, but within ye are full of hypocrisy and iniquity" (Mt.23:28).
>
> "In the mean time, when there were gathered together an innumerable multitude of people, insomuch that they trode one upon another, he began to say unto his disciples first of all, Beware ye of the leaven of the Pharisees, which is hypocrisy" (Lu.12:1).
>
> "Wherefore let him that thinketh he standeth take heed lest he fall" (1 Co.10:12).
>
> "They profess that they know God; but in works they deny *him*, being abominable, and disobedient, and unto every good work reprobate" (Tit.1:16).
>
> "He that trusteth in his own heart is a fool: but whoso walketh wisely, he shall be delivered" (Pr.28:26).

DEUTERONOMY 29:1-29

5 (29:20-29) **Judgment, Caused by—Covenant, Judgment for Breaking—Idolatry, Results of—Worship, False, Results of—Disobedience, Results of:** the judgment for breaking the covenant is spelled out in descriptive terms. The person who turns away to false gods and false worship will suffer the awesome weight of terrifying judgment. Note the graphic description in the Scripture:

OUTLINE	SCRIPTURE	SCRIPTURE	OUTLINE
5. **The judgment for breaking the covenant, for turning away to false gods & false worship**^{DS1}	20 The LORD will not spare him, but then the anger of the LORD and his jealousy shall smoke against that man, and all the curses that are written in this book shall lie upon him, and the LORD shall blot out his name from under heaven.	Wherefore hath the LORD done thus unto this land? what *meaneth* the heat of this great anger?	fierce that people will ask, "Why?"
a. The LORD will severely judge the violator			1) The question
1) Will never forgive him & will blot out his name			2) The answer
		25 Then men shall say, Because they have forsaken the covenant of the LORD God of their fathers, which he made with them when he brought them forth out of the land of Egypt:	• Because the people broke the covenant, the promise they made with the LORD when He saved them from Egypt (the world)
2) Will separate him for special judgment: Pour out upon him all the curses written in the Book of the Law (the Word of God)	21 And the LORD shall separate him unto evil out of all the tribes of Israel, according to all the curses of the covenant that are written in this book of the law:	26 For they went and served other gods, and worshipped them, gods whom they knew not, and *whom* he had not given unto them:	• Because the people turned away from the LORD to false gods & false worship
b. The nation will become a spectacle to succeeding generations & nations	22 So that the generation to come of your children that shall rise up after you, and the stranger that shall come from a far land, shall say, when they see the plagues of that land, and the sicknesses which the LORD hath laid upon it;	27 And the anger of the LORD was kindled against this land, to bring upon it all the curses that are written in this book:	3) The result of apostasy
1) The land will suffer calamities & diseases			• The LORD's anger burned: Devastated the land itself
2) The land will be a burning waste with no vegetation growing			
3) The land will suffer the same destruction that fell upon Sodom & Gomorrah, upon Admah & Zeboim	23 *And that* the whole land thereof *is* brimstone, and salt, *and* burning, *that* it is not sown, nor beareth, nor any grass groweth therein, like the overthrow of Sodom, and Gomorrah, Admah, and Zeboim, which the LORD overthrew in his anger, and in his wrath:	28 And the LORD rooted them out of their land in anger, and in wrath, and in great indignation, and cast them into another land, as *it is* this day.	• The LORD's wrath: Allowed a nation to conquer, uproot, & exile the people
		29 The secret *things belong* unto the LORD our God: but those *things which are* revealed *belong* unto us and to our children for ever, that *we* may do all the words of this law.	d. The prediction of these things is said to be secret
			1) The secret things belong to God
c. The judgment will be so	24 Even all nations shall say,		2) The things revealed belong to us: That we may know God's will & obey

a. The LORD will severely judge the violator, the idolater and false worshipper (vv.20-21). If a person lives a hypocritical life, feeling that he is safe and secure, immune from God's judgment—that person will bear the awesome weight of God's terrifying judgment. Note what Moses declared:

1) The LORD will never forgive him and will blot his name out from under heaven (v.20). The LORD's wrath and jealousy will burn against that person.
2) The LORD will separate him for very special judgment (v.21). The LORD will pour out upon him all the curses written in the Book of the Law, the Word of God.

    Why so severe a judgment against the hypocrite, the idolater and false worshipper? The answer is given above: because the person turned away from the LORD, turned away to false worship, to worship the gods of this world. By so turning away, he misled others to turn away from God and to engage in false worship. He became a hypocrite, claiming to follow God, while all the time he was following a false, lifeless, and senseless god. Following the false god, he felt safe and secure, immune from the holy judgment of the only living and true God. But the judgment of God is sure: this person will suffer all the curses of God's judgment.

b. Moses declares that the nation of Israel will become a spectacle (vv.22-23). Note that this is a prediction of what will happen to Israel in the future. The people will be chastised as a nation because they allowed idolatry to infiltrate and permeate the nation, because they allowed so many to be swept away by the hypocrites, swept away into false worship. The judgment upon the nation will be severe:

⇒ The land will suffer calamity after calamity and disease after disease (v.22).
⇒ The land will become a burning waste, unproductive, with no vegetation growing (v.23).
⇒ The land will suffer the same destruction that fell upon Sodom and Gomorrah, Admah and Zeboim (v.23).

c. The judgment will be so fierce and catastrophic that people will question why (vv.24-28). Very simply, the answer will be because the people broke the covenant of the LORD God. The people broke the promise they made to God when He saved them from Egypt (v.25). Remember, this is a symbol of the believer being saved from the enslavement of the world. The Israelites broke their promise, turning away from the LORD to false gods and false worship. Tragically, they abandoned their commitment and covenant with the LORD.

The result of their apostasy would be catastrophic and tragic: the LORD's anger would burn against them and devastate the land itself. In furious anger and wrath, the LORD would allow a nation to conquer and uproot them. They would be transported into a foreign nation. The people of Israel would be conquered and taken as slaves into the foreign nation (v.28).

d. The prediction of these things is said to be secret (v.29). The secret things belong to the LORD and are known only by Him. The hypocritical spirit and apostasy of the Israelites would happen just as God reveals in Holy Scripture. The judgment upon Israel would also happen just as God predicted and history has now shown. But when the events were revealed for the first time here in Scripture—back in the days of Deuteronomy—they were secret things. The fact that they would actually happen, especially to those standing there before Moses, was incomprehensible. But today, history has shown that they did happen.

Now note this fact: Moses declares that the things revealed in God's Holy Word belong to us. But God has revealed them to us for a very specific purpose: that we may follow His Holy Word, keep His commandments.

Thought 1. The judgment of God will fall upon any person who lives a hypocritical life. No matter what a person professes, if he does not live for Christ, following and obeying Him, he will suffer the judgment of God. But not only the hypocrite: the idolater and false worshipper will also bear the judgment of God. The judgment of God is sure: the wrath of God will be executed against all ungodliness and unrighteousness of men, in particular against those who hold the truth in unrighteousness.

"For the wrath of God is revealed from heaven against all ungodliness and unrighteousness of men, who hold the truth in unrighteousness" (Ro.1:18).

"When the Son of man shall come in his glory, and all the holy angels with him, then shall he sit upon the throne of his glory: And before him shall be gathered all nations: and he shall separate them one from another, as a shepherd divideth *his* sheep from the goats: And he shall set the sheep on his right hand, but the goats on the left" (Mt.25:31-33).

"He that believeth on the Son hath everlasting life: and he that believeth not the Son shall not see life; but the wrath of God abideth on him" (Jn.3:36).

"But unto them that are contentious, and do not obey the truth, but obey unrighteousness, indignation and wrath" (Ro.2:8).

"But fornication, and all uncleanness, or covetousness, let it not be once named among you, as becometh saints; Neither filthiness, nor foolish talking, nor jesting, which are not convenient: but rather giving of thanks. For this ye know, that no whoremonger, nor unclean person, nor covetous man, who is an idolater, hath any inheritance in the kingdom of Christ and of God. Let no man deceive you with vain words: for because of these things cometh the wrath of God upon the children of disobedience" (Ep.5:3-6).

"The LORD knoweth how to deliver the godly out of temptations, and to reserve the unjust unto the day of judgment to be punished" (2 Pe.2:9).

"But the heavens and the earth, which are now, by the same word are kept in store, reserved unto fire against the day of judgment and perdition of ungodly men" (2 Pe.3:7).

"And Enoch also, the seventh from Adam, prophesied of these, saying, Behold, the LORD cometh with ten thousands of his saints, To execute judgment upon all, and to convince all that are ungodly among them of all their ungodly deeds which they have ungodly committed, and of all their hard *speeches* which ungodly sinners have spoken against him" (Jude 14-15).

DEEPER STUDY # 1
(29:20-29) Captivity of Israel—Restoration, of Israel—Judgment, of Israel: when studying prophecies such as these, a person must keep in mind the captivity of the ten tribes in 722 B.C. and the captivity of Judah in 586 B.C. Both captivities took place in stages. The ten tribes of the northern kingdom suffered a series of invasions by the Assyrians over a number of years and were eventually taken captive by the great Assyrian king, Sargon the Second (2 K.17:6-7; see 2 K.15:29; 1 Chr.5:26; 2 K.17:3-5; Ezr.2:10). The southern kingdom was conquered and taken into captivity by Nebuchadnezzar, the great Babylonian king:

⇒ In 605 B.C., he deported or exiled some members of the nobility, including Daniel the prophet (2 Chr.36:2-7; Je.45:1; Da.1:1-3).
⇒ In 597 B.C., he deported king Jehoiachin and thousands of the leaders and nobility, including the prophet Ezekiel (2 K.24:14-16).
⇒ In 586 B.C., he destroyed Jerusalem and exiled all the population except the very poorest of the land (2 K.25:2-21).
⇒ In 581 B.C., he deported thousands more.

The Israelites were allowed to return to the promised land after the Persians conquered the Babylonians in 537 B.C.. Just one year later, King Cyrus of Persia issued a decree allowing the enslaved captives to return to the promised land (Ezr.1:1-4). Scripture says that 43,000 returned with Zerubbabel (Ezr.2:64). In 458 B.C., Ezra led 1800 more enslaved captives back to their homeland.[2]

---

[2] *The New Compact Bible Dictionary.* Edited by T. Alton Bryant. (Grand Rapids, MI: Zondervan Publishing House, 1967).

DEUTERONOMY 30:1-20

1. The conditions of the covenant
  a. Must sense the need for repentance: Call to mind, meditate upon the blessings & judgments of God
  b. Must repent, return to the LORD
  c. Must obey the LORD—obey with all your heart & soul (see v.10)

2. The promises of the covenant: Restoration—forgiveness & acceptance
  a. The LORD will have compassion & restore His people
    1) Restore them from all nations—even from the most distant lands
    2) Restore them to the promised land
  b. The LORD will make them more prosperous & numerous than ever before

  c. The LORD will circumcise, cut away the sins of their heart: Forgive them
    1) That they may love God
    2) That they may live
  d. The LORD will transfer all the curses upon the enemies of His people

  e. The LORD will stir His people to obey all His commandments

  f. The LORD will pour out His blessings upon His people: Bless their lives, work, & property
    1) Will make them prosperous & successful
    2) Will take joy & rejoice in His people

E. The Strong Appeal & Hope of the Covenant: Restoration—Repentance & Forgiveness, 30:1-20

And it shall come to pass, when all these things are come upon thee, the blessing and the curse, which I have set before thee, and thou shalt call *them* to mind among all the nations, whither the LORD thy God hath driven thee,
2 And shalt return unto the LORD thy God, and shalt obey his voice according to all that I command thee this day, thou and thy children, with all thine heart, and with all thy soul;
3 That then the LORD thy God will turn thy captivity, and have compassion upon thee, and will return and gather thee from all the nations, whither the LORD thy God hath scattered thee.
4 If *any* of thine be driven out unto the outmost *parts* of heaven, from thence will the LORD thy God gather thee, and from thence will he fetch thee:
5 And the LORD thy God will bring thee into the land which thy fathers possessed, and thou shalt possess it; and he will do thee good, and multiply thee above thy fathers.
6 And the LORD thy God will circumcise thine heart, and the heart of thy seed, to love the LORD thy God with all thine heart, and with all thy soul, that thou mayest live.
7 And the LORD thy God will put all these curses upon thine enemies, and on them that hate thee, which persecuted thee.
8 And thou shalt return and obey the voice of the LORD, and do all his commandments which I command thee this day.
9 And the LORD thy God will make thee plenteous in every work of thine hand, in the fruit of thy body, and in the fruit of thy cattle, and in the fruit of thy land, for good: for the LORD will again rejoice over thee for good, as he rejoiced over thy fathers:

10 If thou shalt hearken unto the voice of the LORD thy God, to keep his commandments and his statutes which are written in this book of the law, *and* if thou turn unto the LORD thy God with all thine heart, and with all thy soul.
11 For this commandment which I command thee this day, it *is* not hidden from thee, neither *is* it far off.
12 It *is* not in heaven, that thou shouldest say, Who shall go up for us to heaven, and bring it unto us, that we may hear it, and do it?
13 Neither *is* it beyond the sea, that thou shouldest say, Who shall go over the sea for us, and bring it unto us, that we may hear it, and do it?
14 But the word *is* very nigh unto thee, in thy mouth, and in thy heart, that thou mayest do it.
15 See, I have set before thee this day life and good, and death and evil;
16 In that I command thee this day to love the LORD thy God, to walk in his ways, and to keep his commandments and his statutes and his judgments, that thou mayest live and multiply: and the LORD thy God shall bless thee in the land whither thou goest to possess it.
17 But if thine heart turn away, so that thou wilt not hear, but shalt be drawn away, and worship other gods, and serve them;
18 I denounce unto you this day, that ye shall surely perish, *and that* ye shall not prolong *your* days upon the land, whither thou passest over Jordan to go to possess it.
19 I call heaven and earth to record this day against you, *that* I have set before you life and death, blessing and cursing: therefore choose life, that both thou and thy seed may live:
20 That thou mayest love the LORD thy God, *and* that thou mayest obey his voice, and that thou mayest cleave unto him: for he *is* thy life, and the length of thy days: that thou mayest dwell in the land which the LORD sware unto thy fathers, to Abraham, to Isaac, and to Jacob, to give them.

  g. The promises of the new covenant are conditional; the restoration & blessings are conditional
    1) You must obey the LORD & His commandments
    2) You must repent, turn to the LORD wholeheartedly

3. The appeal of the covenant: The call to love & obey the LORD
  a. The call to obey is not unreasonable nor impossible
    1) The commandment is not in some inaccessible place
      • Not up in heaven—still unrevealed & hidden in God's heart
      • Not beyond the sea in a foreign land

    2) The Word is near, has been revealed to you: So you can obey it

  b. The call is to make a decision
    1) Between life & death
    2) Between good & evil
  c. The call is spelled out
    1) To love the LORD
    2) To walk in His ways
    3) To obey His commandments & laws
  d. The results of heeding the call are positive
    1) Will live & multiply
    2) Will be blessed

4. The final warning against breaking the covenant
  a. The transgressions named: Turning away, idolatry, & false worship
  b. The judgment
    1) Will perish, be destroyed
    2) Will not live long in the promised land

5. The final appeal to accept the covenant
  a. The choice to be made: Life or death, blessings or curses
  b. The appeal: Choose life—so you & your children will live

    1) Choose to love God
    2) Choose to obey Him
    3) Choose to cling to Him
  c. The reason
    1) The LORD is your life
    2) The LORD will give you a long life in the promised land

DEUTERONOMY 30:1-20

DIVISION V

THE THIRD GREAT THEME PREACHED BY GOD'S AGED SERVANT: THE CHARGE TO RENEW THE COVENANT WITH GOD, 27:1–30:20

E. The Strong Appeal and Hope of the Covenant: Restoration—Repentance and Forgiveness, 30:1-20

(30:1-20) **Introduction**: decisions sometimes confront us that are very difficult to make. We simply do not know what to do. Difficult decisions often involve health or personal difficulty; marital, family, or employment problems; or some business, national, or world issue. There are events that happen in life that are simply impossible to predict. At other times an event occurs because we have made a wrong decision; we just could not see into the future.

This is not the case with God: the future is known by God, even the details of future events. Because He knows all things—God was able to predict the *terrible apostasy* of the Israelites referred to in the recent message preached by Moses (see outline and notes—De.28:1-68 for more discussion). Now, one of the most interesting and captivating prophecies in all of Scripture is to be made. Speaking through Moses, God predicts the restoration of Israel, a day when the Jews will return to the promised land, modern-day Palestine. Has this prophecy been fulfilled? Was the return of the Jews to Palestine in 1948 a fulfillment of this prophecy? Some Bible commentators say, "Yes!" But if the return of the Jews to Palestine is a fulfillment of this prophecy, then the conditions that are covered by this passage have not yet been met. The Jewish people as a whole community or nation have not yet renewed their commitment to God; they have not yet rededicated their lives to the new covenant established by God. This is the discussion of this important passage of Scripture: *The Strong Appeal and Hope of the Covenant: Restoration—Repentance and Forgiveness,* 30:1-20.

1. The conditions of the covenant (vv.1-2).
2. The promises of the covenant: restoration—forgiveness and acceptance (vv.3-10).
3. The appeal of the covenant: the call to love and obey the LORD (vv.11-16).
4. The final warning against breaking the covenant (vv.17-18).
5. The final appeal to accept the covenant (vv.19-20).

1 (30:1-2) **Covenant, Conditions of—Repentance, Conditions of—Restoration, of Israel—Israel, Restoration of—Conditions, of Repentance—Returning, to the LORD, Conditions of—Restoration, Conditions of**: the conditions of the covenant are spelled out. Keep in mind what Moses had just preached: the terrible apostasy of the Israelites. A day was coming when the Israelites would turn away from God and turn to idolatry and false worship. As a result, the judgment of God would fall upon their heads. A foreign nation was to conquer the Israelites and enslave them. The Israelites were to become exiles in a foreign nation that they knew nothing about (28:36).

But now, Moses predicted that a glorious day of restoration would come. After suffering the terrible judgment and curses of God, the people would fulfill the conditions of the covenant. Note the Scripture and outline:

OUTLINE	SCRIPTURE	SCRIPTURE	OUTLINE
1. The conditions of the covenant a. Must sense the need for repentance: Call to mind, meditate upon the blessings & judgments of God	And it shall come to pass, when all these things are come upon thee, the blessing and the curse, which I have set before thee, and thou shalt call *them* to mind among all the nations, whither the LORD thy God hath driven	thee, 2 And shalt return unto the LORD thy God, and shalt obey his voice according to all that I command thee this day, thou and thy children, with all thine heart, and with all thy soul;	b. Must repent, return to the LORD c. Must obey the LORD—obey with all your heart & soul (see v.10)

a. The people must sense the need for repentance (v.1). They must come to their senses and recall the blessings and curses of God. Note the great hope laid out by Moses: eventually the people would recall the blessings of God as well as the curses for disobedience. By meditating upon the blessings and judgments of God, they would begin to sense their need for repentance. A deep sense of need would grip their hearts but, tragically, only after they had been enslaved by the world and suffered a broken heart.

b. The people must repent, return to the LORD (v.2). They must turn away from their hypocrisy and from engaging in idolatry and false worship. They must turn away from their lives of sin and shame and return to God.

c. The people must obey the LORD, obey Him with their whole hearts and souls (v.2). Obedience is an absolute essential for restoration and forgiveness.

If the people were going to rededicate their lives to God, if they were going to renew their commitment and covenant with God, the people must repent and obey the LORD.

> **Thought 1.** A *renewal* or *rededication* of life involves two things: repentance and obedience to the LORD. No matter how terrible a sin we have committed, God will forgive us and restore us. But we must sense the need for repentance and actually repent. True repentance is an absolute essential. So is obedience. To be forgiven and restored before God, we must repent and obey God.

DEUTERONOMY 30:1-20

(1) Repentance is necessary.

"And saying, Repent ye: for the kingdom of heaven is at hand" (Mt.3:2).

"I tell you, Nay: but, except ye repent, ye shall all likewise perish" (Lu.13:3).

"Repent ye therefore, and be converted, that your sins may be blotted out, when the times of refreshing shall come from the presence of the LORD" (Ac.3:19).

"Repent therefore of this thy wickedness, and pray God, if perhaps the thought of thine heart may be forgiven thee" (Ac.8:22).

"If my people, which are called by my name, shall humble themselves, and pray, and seek my face, and turn from their wicked ways; then will I hear from heaven, and will forgive their sin, and will heal their land" (2 Chr.7:14).

"Let the wicked forsake his way, and the unrighteous man his thoughts: and let him return unto the LORD, and he will have mercy upon him; and to our God, for he will abundantly pardon" (Is.55:7).

"Cast away from you all your transgressions, whereby ye have transgressed; and make you a new heart and a new spirit: for why will ye die, O house of Israel" (Eze.18:31).

"Therefore also now, saith the LORD, turn ye *even* to me with all your heart, and with fasting, and with weeping, and with mourning" (Joel 2:12).

"But if the wicked will turn from all his sins that he hath committed, and keep all my statutes, and do that which is lawful and right, he shall surely live, he shall not die" (Eze.18:21).

(2) Obedience—obeying God will all of one's heart and soul—is necessary to be restored to God.

"Not every one that saith unto me, LORD, LORD, shall enter into the kingdom of heaven; but he that doeth the will of my Father which is in heaven" (Mt.7:21).

"If ye keep my commandments, ye shall abide in my love; even as I have kept my Father's commandments, and abide in his love" (Jn.15:10).

"Ye are my friends, if ye do whatsoever I command you" (Jn.15:14).

"Blessed *are* they that do his commandments, that they may have right to the tree of life, and may enter in through the gates into the city" (Re.22:14).

"This day the LORD thy God hath commanded thee to do these statutes and judgments: thou shalt therefore keep and do them with all thine heart, and with all thy soul" (De.26:16).

2 (30:3-10) **Covenant, Promise of—Restoration, Promise of—Forgiveness, Promise of—Israel, Restoration of—Restoration, of Israel—Covenant, Given to Israel—Promise, Given to Israel**: the promise of the covenant is clearly stated, the wonderful promise of restoration—forgiveness and acceptance by the LORD. This is the great promise of *restoration* given to Israel, and through Israel, given to every person who ever repents and turns to the LORD to follow Him wholeheartedly. Note the wonderful promise given by God:

OUTLINE	SCRIPTURE	SCRIPTURE	OUTLINE
2. **The promises of the covenant: Restoration—forgiveness & acceptance** a. The LORD will have compassion & restore His people 1) Restore them from all nations—even from the most distant lands	3 That then the LORD thy God will turn thy captivity, and have compassion upon thee, and will return and gather thee from all the nations, whither the LORD thy God hath scattered thee. 4 If *any* of thine be driven out unto the outmost *parts* of heaven, from thence will the LORD thy God gather thee, and from thence will he fetch thee:	7 And the LORD thy God will put all these curses upon thine enemies, and on them that hate thee, which persecuted thee. 8 And thou shalt return and obey the voice of the LORD, and do all his commandments which I command thee this day.	d. The LORD will transfer all the curses upon the enemies of His people e. The LORD will stir His people to obey all His commandments

2) Restore them to the promised land
b. The LORD will make them more prosperous & numerous than ever before
	5 And the LORD thy God will bring thee into the land which thy fathers possessed, and thou shalt possess it; and he will do thee good, and multiply thee above thy fathers.	9 And the LORD thy God will make thee plenteous in every work of thine hand, in the fruit of thy body, and in the fruit of thy cattle, and in the fruit of thy land, for good: for the LORD will again rejoice over thee for good, as he rejoiced over thy fathers:	f. The LORD will pour out His blessings upon His people: Bless their lives, work, & property
			  1) Will make them prosperous & successful
			  2) Will joy & rejoice in His people

c. The LORD will circumcise, cut away the sins of their heart: Forgive them
  1) That they may love God
  2) That they may live
	6 And the LORD thy God will circumcise thine heart, and the heart of thy seed, to love the LORD thy God with all thine heart, and with all thy soul, that thou mayest live.	10 If thou shalt hearken unto the voice of the LORD thy God, to keep his commandments and his statutes which are written in this book of the law, *and* if thou turn unto the LORD thy God with all thine heart, and with all thy soul.	g. The promises of the new covenant are conditional; the restoration & blessings are conditional
			  1) You must obey the LORD & His commandments
			  2) You must repent, turn to the LORD wholeheartedly

DEUTERONOMY 30:1-20

    a. The LORD will have compassion and restore His people (vv.3-5). He will restore the Israelites from all nations, even the most distant lands (v.4). He will restore them to the promised land (v.5). Once they have repented of their sins, they will again lay claim to their inheritance and walk victoriously in the promised land of God.
    b. The LORD will make His people more prosperous and numerous than ever before (v.5).
    c. The LORD will circumcise or cut away the sins of their hearts and forgive them (v.6). He will chisel away at their hard, stubborn hearts. He will enable them to love Him completely and to live forever before Him.
    d. The LORD will actually transfer all the curses of His judgment upon the enemies of His people (v.7). The very people who had ridiculed, mocked, enslaved, and persecuted His people will suffer the terrible curses of God's judgment.
    e. The LORD will stir His people to obey all His commandments (v.8). At long last—sometime in the future—the people of God will become obedient. They will keep the commandments of God, obey His Holy Word.
    f. The LORD will pour out His blessings upon His people. He will bless their lives, work, and property (v.9). The LORD will make His people prosperous and successful, causing Him to joy and rejoice in them.
    g. But note: the warning is again issued. The promises of the new covenant are conditional; the restoration and blessings are conditional (v.10). Standing before the people and preaching his heart out, Moses declared: to be forgiven and restored before God...

- you must obey the LORD and His commandments
- you must repent, turn to the LORD with your whole heart and soul

Thought 1. This Scripture covers one of the great promises of God, the promise of forgiveness. But note: the promise is conditional. If we confess and repent of our sins, God will forgive us. He will restore us before His face.

> "Him hath God exalted with his right hand *to be* a Prince and a Saviour, for to give repentance to Israel, and forgiveness of sins" (Ac.5:31).
>
> "Be it known unto you therefore, men *and* brethren, that through this man is preached unto you the forgiveness of sins" (Ac.13:38).
>
> "In whom we have redemption through his blood, the forgiveness of sins, according to the riches of his grace" (Ep.1:7).
>
> "If we confess our sins, he is faithful and just to forgive us *our* sins, and to cleanse us from all unrighteousness" (1 Jn.1:9).
>
> "Restore unto me the joy of thy salvation; and uphold me *with thy* free spirit" (Ps.51:12).
>
> "I, *even* I, *am* he that blotteth out thy transgressions for mine own sake, and will not remember thy sins" (Is.43:25).
>
> "I have blotted out, as a thick cloud, thy transgressions, and, as a cloud, thy sins: return unto me; for I have redeemed thee" (Is.44:22).
>
> "Let the wicked forsake his way, and the unrighteous man his thoughts: and let him return unto the LORD, and he will have mercy upon him; and to our God, for he will abundantly pardon" (Is.55:7).
>
> "Return, ye backsliding children, *and* I will heal your backslidings. Behold, we come unto thee; for thou *art* the LORD our God" (Je.3:22).
>
> "I will heal their backsliding, I will love them freely: for mine anger is turned away from him" (Ho.14:4).
>
> "He will turn again, he will have compassion upon us; he will subdue our iniquities; and thou wilt cast all their sins into the depths of the sea" (Mi.7:19).

Thought 2. The restoration of Israel is one of the great prophecies of the Bible. Scripture after Scripture predicted that the Jews, the Israelites, would someday return to the land promised them by God, the land that is known today as Palestine.

> "And so all Israel shall be saved: as it is written, There shall come out of Sion the Deliverer, and shall turn away ungodliness from Jacob: For this *is* my covenant unto them, when I shall take away their sins" (Ro.11:26-27).
>
> "That then the LORD thy God will turn thy captivity, and have compassion upon thee, and will return and gather thee from all the nations, whither the LORD thy God hath scattered thee. If *any* of thine be driven out unto the outmost *parts* of heaven, from thence will the LORD thy God gather thee, and from thence will he fetch thee: And the LORD thy God will bring thee into the land which thy fathers possessed, and thou shalt possess it; and he will do thee good, and multiply thee above thy fathers" (De.30:3-5).
>
> "And I will restore thy judges as at the first, and thy counsellors as at the beginning: afterward thou shalt be called, The city of righteousness, the faithful city" (Is.1:26).
>
> "And it shall come to pass in that day, *that* the LORD shall set his hand again the second time to recover the remnant of his people, which shall be left, from Assyria, and from Egypt, and from Pathros, and from Cush, and from Elam, and from Shinar, and from Hamath, and from the islands of the sea. And he shall set up an ensign for the nations, and shall assemble the outcasts of Israel, and gather together the dispersed of Judah from the four corners of the earth" (Is.11:11-12).
>
> "And it shall come to pass in that day, *that* the great trumpet shall be blown, and they shall come which were ready to perish in the land of Assyria, and the outcasts in the land of Egypt, and shall worship the LORD in the holy mount at Jerusalem" (Is.27:13).
>
> "Thus saith the LORD GOD, Behold, I will lift up mine hand to the Gentiles, and set up my standard to the people: and they shall bring thy sons in *their* arms, and thy daughters shall be carried upon *their* shoulders" (Is.49:22).

"And the sons of strangers shall build up thy walls, and their kings shall minister unto thee: for in my wrath I smote thee, but in my favour have I had mercy on thee" (Is.60:10).

"And I will gather the remnant of my flock out of all countries whither I have driven them, and will bring them again to their folds; and they shall be fruitful and increase. And I will set up shepherds over them which shall feed them: and they shall fear no more, nor be dismayed, neither shall they be lacking, saith the LORD. Behold, the days come, saith the LORD, that I will raise unto David a righteous Branch, and a King shall reign and prosper, and shall execute judgment and justice in the earth. In his days Judah shall be saved, and Israel shall dwell safely: and this *is* his name whereby he shall be called, THE LORD OUR RIGHTEOUSNESS. Therefore, behold, the days come, saith the LORD, that they shall no more say, The LORD liveth, which brought up the children of Israel out of the land of Egypt; But, The LORD liveth, which brought up and which led the seed of the house of Israel out of the north country, and from all countries whither I had driven them; and they shall dwell in their own land" (Je.23:3-8).

"Behold, the days come, saith the LORD, that I will make a new covenant with the house of Israel, and with the house of Judah: Not according to the covenant that I made with their fathers in the day *that* I took them by the hand to bring them out of the land of Egypt; which my covenant they brake, although I was an husband unto them, saith the LORD: But this *shall be* the covenant that I will make with the house of Israel; After those days, saith the LORD, I will put my law in their inward parts, and write it in their hearts; and will be their God, and they shall be my people" (Je.31:31-33).

"For in mine holy mountain, in the mountain of the height of Israel, saith the LORD GOD, there shall all the house of Israel, all of them in the land, serve me: there will I accept them, and there will I require your offerings, and the firstfruits of your oblations, with all your holy things" (Eze.20:40).

"And say unto them, Thus saith the LORD GOD; Behold, I will take the children of Israel from among the heathen, whither they be gone, and will gather them on every side, and bring them into their own land: And I will make them one nation in the land upon the mountains of Israel; and one king shall be king to them all: and they shall be no more two nations, neither shall they be divided into two kingdoms any more at all: Neither shall they defile themselves any more with their idols, nor with their detestable things, nor with any of their transgressions: but I will save them out of all their dwellingplaces, wherein they have sinned, and will cleanse them: so shall they be my people, and I will be their God. And David my servant *shall be* king over them; and they all shall have one shepherd: they shall also walk in my judgments, and observe my statutes, and do them. And they shall dwell in the land that I have given unto Jacob my servant, wherein your fathers have dwelt; and they shall dwell therein, *even* they, and their children, and their children's children for ever: and my servant David *shall be* their prince for ever. Moreover I will make a covenant of peace with them; it shall be an everlasting covenant with them: and I will place them, and multiply them, and will set my sanctuary in the midst of them for evermore. My tabernacle also shall be with them: yea, I will be their God, and they shall be my people. And the heathen shall know that I the LORD do sanctify Israel, when my sanctuary shall be in the midst of them for evermore" (Eze.37:21-28).

"Therefore, behold, I will allure her, and bring her into the wilderness, and speak comfortably unto her. And I will give her her vineyards from thence, and the valley of Achor for a door of hope: and she shall sing there, as in the days of her youth, and as in the day when she came up out of the land of Egypt. And it shall be at that day, saith the LORD, *that* thou shalt call me Ishi; and shalt call me no more Baali" (Ho.2:14-16).

"Cry yet, saying, Thus saith the LORD of hosts; My cities through prosperity shall yet be spread abroad; and the LORD shall yet comfort Zion, and shall yet choose Jerusalem" (Zec.1:17).

"And *men* shall dwell in it, and there shall be no more utter destruction; but Jerusalem shall be safely inhabited" (Zec.14:11).

"Then shall the offering of Judah and Jerusalem be pleasant unto the LORD, as in the days of old, and as in former years" (Mal.3:4).

---

3 (30:11-16) **Covenant, Appeal of—Appeal, to Obey the Covenant—Call, of the Covenant—Call, to Love and Obey God—Obedience, Call to—Love, Duty**: the appeal of the covenant is a strong call, a call to love and obey the LORD. Moses now turned away from prediction and prophecy and focused upon the audience before him. As he faced them, he knew that they desperately needed to rededicate their lives to the LORD. They had a dire need to renew their covenant, their commitment to the LORD. With a strong sense of urgency burning within his heart, he challenged the people to love and obey the LORD:

OUTLINE	SCRIPTURE	SCRIPTURE	OUTLINE
3. The appeal of the covenant: The call to love & obey the LORD a. The call to obey is not unreasonable nor impossible 1) The commandment is not	11 For this commandment which I command thee this day, it *is* not hidden from thee, neither *is* it far off. 12 It *is* not in heaven, that	thou shouldest say, Who shall go up for us to heaven, and bring it unto us, that we may hear it, and do it? 13 Neither *is* it beyond the	in some inaccessible place • Not up in heaven—still unrevealed & hidden in God's heart • Not beyond the sea in a

DEUTERONOMY 30:1-20

OUTLINE	SCRIPTURE	SCRIPTURE	OUTLINE

foreign land	sea, that thou shouldest say, Who shall go over the sea for us, and bring it unto us, that we may hear it, and do it?	death and evil; 16 In that I command thee this day to love the LORD thy God, to walk in his ways, and to keep his commandments and his statutes and his judgments, that thou mayest live and multiply: and the LORD thy God shall bless thee in the land whither thou goest to possess it.	2) Between good & evil
			c. The call is spelled out
			  1) To love the LORD
			  2) To walk in His ways
			  3) To obey His commandments & laws
			d. The results of heeding the call are positive
			  1) Will live & multiply
			  2) Will be blessed

2) The Word is near, has been revealed to you: So you can obey it	14 But the word *is* very nigh unto thee, in thy mouth, and in thy heart, that thou mayest do it.		
b. The call is to make a decision 1) Between life & death	15 See, I have set before thee this day life and good, and		

    a. The call to obey God is not unreasonable nor impossible (vv.11-14). The commandments of God are not in some distant, inaccessible place (vv.12-13). They are not up in heaven, still unrevealed and hidden in the heart of God. The commandments are not beyond the sea in a foreign land (v.13). No! The Word of God is near us. It has been revealed by God so that we can obey it (v.14).
    God has demonstrated His love to us in a most wonderful way. He has not left us in the dark, groping, grasping, and stumbling about, seeking the answers to life on our own. No! God has revealed His Holy Word to us, telling us how to live life, how to find God, and how to have the assurance of living forever. The Word of God is near, very near, right at our fingertips.
    b. All of a sudden, with passion burning in his soul, Moses called upon the people to make a decision (v.15)...
- between life and death
- between good and evil

    c. Moses spelled out exactly what he meant by the call of the covenant (v.16). The call was...
- to love the LORD
- to walk in His ways
- to obey His commandments

    d. The decision to love and obey the LORD will result in the most wonderful life. A person will live a full and fruitful life and be wonderfully blessed in the promised land (v.16).

    Thought 1. The call to us is direct and forceful: we must love and obey the LORD. We who live today are without defense, totally without excuse. For God has not only given us the *Written Word* but also the *Living Word*. The Written Word is the Holy Bible, the Scriptures that have been written down for us to obey. The Living Word is the Lord Jesus Christ, the greatest witness to the truth that could ever be conceived by the mind of man. Yes, God did a marvelous thing in giving us the *Written Word* of God. But God did a far more marvelous thing by giving us the *Living Word* of God. Jesus Christ actually lived out the Written Word of God. He obeyed every commandment in the Holy Scripture, and by obeying, showed us how to obey God. By living upon this earth, Jesus Christ showed us how to live life. But not only this: being the Perfect Man—obeying all of the commandments of God and being sinless—He became the *Ideal Man*. As the Ideal Man, He was able to bear all our sins and pay the penalty of our condemnation. He was able to take the judgment that was due us—take it and bear it for us.
    As the *Living Word of God*, Jesus Christ is a far greater gift from God than even the *Written Word of God*. Because of living in this day and time, we are of all people without excuse. If a people were ever confronted with a decision that desperately needed to be made, it is we who live today. We must make the decision to love and obey the LORD.

    "If ye love me, keep my commandments. And I will pray the Father, and he shall give you another Comforter, that he may abide with you for ever" (Jn.14:15-16).
    "Jesus answered and said unto him, If a man love me, he will keep my words: and my Father will love him, and we will come unto him, and make our abode with him" (Jn.14:23).
    "For the Father himself loveth you, because ye have loved me, and have believed that I came out from God" (Jn.16:27).
    "Grace *be* with all them that love our Lord Jesus Christ in sincerity. Amen" (Ep.6:24).
    "And the LORD direct your hearts into the love of God, and into the patient waiting for Christ" (2 Th.3:5).
    "Whom having not seen, ye love; in whom, though now ye see *him* not, yet believing, ye rejoice with joy unspeakable and full of glory" (1 Pe.1:8).
    "Keep yourselves in the love of God, looking for the mercy of our Lord Jesus Christ unto eternal life" (Jude 21).
    "And thou shalt love the LORD thy God with all thine heart, and with all thy soul, and with all thy might" (De.6:5).
    "And now, Israel, what doth the LORD thy God require of thee, but to fear the LORD thy God, to walk in all his ways, and to love him, and to serve the LORD thy God with all thy heart and with all thy soul" (De.10:12).
    "O love the LORD, all ye his saints: *for* the LORD preserveth the faithful, and plentifully rewardeth the proud doer" (Ps.31:23).

DEUTERONOMY 30:1-20

4 **(30:17-18) Warning, Against Breaking the Covenant—Covenant, Warning Against Breaking—Judgment, Results**: the final warning against breaking the covenant was issued. Stressing the judgment of God would again show the people the desperate need to rededicate their lives to God, to renew their covenant and commitment to Him.

Sensing deep compassion and love for the people, Moses warned them against turning away from God and becoming disobedient. They must—absolutely must—guard against idolatry and false worship (v.17). Moses shouted that they would surely perish and be destroyed if they turned away from God. They would not live long in the promised land, not live full and victorious lives (v.18).

OUTLINE	SCRIPTURE	SCRIPTURE	OUTLINE
4. The final warning against breaking the covenant a. The transgressions named: Turning away, idolatry, & false worship b. The judgment	17 But if thine heart turn away, so that thou wilt not hear, but shalt be drawn away, and worship other gods, and serve them; 18 I denounce unto you this	day, that ye shall surely perish, *and that* ye shall not prolong *your* days upon the land, whither thou passest over Jordan to go to possess it.	1) Will perish, be destroyed 2) Will not live long in the promised land

Thought 1. The warning to us is as clear as it can be stated: if we do not trust the LORD—follow and obey Him—we will perish, be utterly destroyed. We will not live long in the promised land of God.

"For God so loved the world, that he gave his only begotten Son, that whosoever believeth in him should not perish, but have everlasting life. For God sent not his Son into the world to condemn the world; but that the world through him might be saved. He that believeth on him is not condemned: but he that believeth not is condemned already, because he hath not believed in the name of the only begotten Son of God" (Jn.3:16-18).

"He that believeth on the Son hath everlasting life: and he that believeth not the Son shall not see life; but the wrath of God abideth on him" (Jn.3:36).

"I said therefore unto you, that ye shall die in your sins: for if ye believe not that I am *he,* ye shall die in your sins" (Jn.8:24).

"And when he is come, he will reprove the world of sin, and of righteousness, and of judgment: Of sin, because they believe not on me" (Jn.16:8-9).

"Harden not your hearts, as in the provocation, in the day of temptation in the wilderness: When your fathers tempted me, proved me, and saw my works forty years. Wherefore I was grieved with that generation, and said, They do alway err in *their* heart; and they have not known my ways. So I sware in my wrath, They shall not enter into my rest.) Take heed, brethren, lest there be in any of you an evil heart of unbelief, in departing from the living God" (He.3:8-12).

"Let us therefore fear, lest, a promise being left *us* of entering into his rest, any of you should seem to come short of it. For unto us was the gospel preached, as well as unto them: but the word preached did not profit them, not being mixed with faith in them that heard *it*....Let us labour therefore to enter into that rest, lest any man fall after the same example of unbelief" (He.4:1-2, 11).

5 **(30:19-20) Covenant, Appeal to Obey—Appeal, to Obey God—Choice, Essential—Decision, Essential—Decision, Call to—Call, to Decision**: the final appeal to accept the covenant was urged upon the people. Urgency and immediate attention were called for. Every compelling fact Moses could impress upon the people he had preached. Only one thing remained: the decision. The people had a choice to make: life or death, blessings or curses (v.19). Having a heart broken with compassion and a gripping sense of urgency, he appealed to the people: "Choose life! Choose life so that you and your children will live" (vv.19-20).

⇒ Choose to love God.
⇒ Choose to obey His voice, His Word.
⇒ Choose to cling, to hold fast to Him.

OUTLINE	SCRIPTURE	SCRIPTURE	OUTLINE
5. The final appeal to accept the covenant a. The choice to be made: Life or death, blessings or curses b. The appeal: Choose life—so you & your children will live 1) Choose to love God 2) Choose to obey Him	19 I call heaven and earth to record this day against you, *that* I have set before you life and death, blessing and cursing: therefore choose life, that both thou and thy seed may live: 20 That thou mayest love the LORD thy God, *and* that thou	mayest obey his voice, and that thou mayest cleave unto him: for he *is* thy life, and the length of thy days: that thou mayest dwell in the land which the LORD sware unto thy fathers, to Abraham, to Isaac, and to Jacob, to give them.	3) Choose to cling to Him c. The reason 1) The LORD is your life 2) The LORD will give you a long life in the promised land

Note that Moses gave two strong reasons why the people must choose life, why they must rededicate their lives to God, renew their commitment and covenant with God. First, because "the LORD is your life" (v.20). The LORD "gives life, preserves life, restores life, and prolongs life by His power."[1] The fullness of life that overflows with blessing after blessing, and the victorious life that conquers all the trials, temptations, and enemies of this world all come from "the LORD [who] is your life."

But this is not the only reason to make a decision of rededication; there is a second strong reason. If you will renew your covenant and commitment, the LORD will give you a long life in the promised land. You will walk victoriously throughout all of life, conquering all the trials, temptations, and enemies that confront you. You will march victoriously through and over all, march right into the promised land of God.

> **Thought 1**. The choice is ours. A decision has to be made. We choose either life or death, either blessings or curses. The appeal of God's Holy Word is this: Choose life! Choose life so that you and your children will live full and victorious lives over all the trials, temptations, and enemies of this world.

> "Then Jesus beholding him loved him, and said unto him, One thing thou lackest: go thy way, sell whatsoever thou hast, and give to the poor, and thou shalt have treasure in heaven: and come, take up the cross, and follow me" (Mk.10:21).

> "For the Father loveth the Son, and sheweth him all things that himself doeth: and he will show him greater works than these, that ye may marvel" (Jn.5:20).

> "Then said Jesus unto the twelve, Will ye also go away" (Jn.6:67).

> "(For he saith, I have heard thee in a time accepted, and in the day of salvation have I succoured thee: behold, now *is* the accepted time; behold, now *is* the day of salvation)" (2 Co.6:2).

> "See, I have set before thee this day life and good, and death and evil" (De.30:15).

> "I call heaven and earth to record this day against you, *that* I have set before you life and death, blessing and cursing: therefore choose life, that both thou and thy seed may live: That thou mayest love the LORD thy God, *and* that thou mayest obey his voice, and that thou mayest cleave unto him: for he *is* thy life, and the length of thy days: that thou mayest dwell in the land which the LORD sware unto thy fathers, to Abraham, to Isaac, and to Jacob, to give them. (De.30:19-20).

> "And if it seem evil unto you to serve the LORD, choose you this day whom ye will serve; whether the gods which your fathers served that *were* on the other side of the flood, or the gods of the Amorites, in whose land ye dwell: but as for me and my house, we will serve the LORD" (Jos.24:15).

> "And Elijah came unto all the people, and said, How long halt ye between two opinions? if the LORD *be* God, follow him: but if Baal, *then* follow him. And the people answered him not a word" (1 K.18:21).

---

[1] *Matthew Henry's Commentary*, Vol.1, p.855.

DIVISION VI

THE FINAL ACTS AND DEATH OF MOSES, GOD'S AGED SERVANT: REMEMBER THE ENCOURAGEMENT AND THE WARNING OF GOD, 31:1–34:12

(31:1–34:12) **DIVISION OVERVIEW**: the final days of Moses upon earth now become the focus of Deuteronomy. Moses had to take care of some very practical matters, matters such as passing the mantle of leadership over to Joshua, making sure the law of God was permanently stored for future generations, and writing a song of strong warning and witness for the people. Then one final act had to be performed: the dear aged servant had to pronounce his prophetic blessing upon the twelve tribes of Israel. Once these things were done, the people would be prepared for his death and ready to follow the strong leadership of Joshua. They would be spiritually prepared, ready to cross the Jordan and enter the promised land. They would be ready to lay claim to the wonderful inheritance promised by God long, long ago.

The task of this great servant of God was now done. He could now die. The LORD could now take Moses to his reward in the promised land of heaven, that "heavenly country" for which his soul had so long sought (He.11:13-16).

THE FINAL ACTS AND DEATH OF MOSES, GOD'S AGED SERVANT: REMEMBER THE ENCOURAGEMENT AND THE WARNING OF GOD, 31:1–34:12

A. The Final Preparations for Entering the Promised Land: Five Strong Charges of Encouragement and Warning, 31:1-29

B. The Song of Moses: A Strong Warning and Witness to God's People and to Those Who Reject Him, 31:30–32:52

C. The Prophetic Blessing of Moses: The Last Words Spoken by the Man of God—a Message of Great Assurance and Encouragement, 33:1-29

D. The Death of Moses: The Joyful Yet Sorrowful Passing of God's Dear Servant, 34:1-12

DEUTERONOMY 31:1-29

CHAPTER 31

VI. THE FINAL ACTS & DEATH OF MOSES, GOD'S AGED SERVANT: REMEMBER THE ENCOURAGEMENT & THE WARNING OF GOD, 31:1–34:12

A. The Final Preparations for Entering the Promised Land: Five Strong Charges of Encouragement & Warning, 31:1-29

1. **The charge & strong encouragement given to the people**
   a. The death of Moses was rapidly approaching: Was 120 years old & forbidden to enter the promised land
   b. The encouragement: God's constant presence & guidance was assured
      1) God would lead—go ahead of His people
         - To destroy the enemy
         - To secure the land
      2) God would raise up a new leader, Joshua

      3) God would give complete & total victory over all the enemies of His people: The kind of victory He gave over Sihon & Og

   c. The charge: Be strong & courageous! Do not fear nor be terrified!
      1) Because God will be with you
      2) Because God will never leave nor forsake you
2. **The charge & encouragement given to Joshua: The commissioning service to appoint him as the new leader**
   a. The charge: Be strong & courageous
      1) He was the appointed leader of God's people
      2) He was the one appointed to divide the land among them
   b. The encouragement
      1) The LORD's presence & guidance
      2) The expectation: That he would not fear nor be discouraged
3. **The charge given to the leaders & priests, the ministers of God: To read & teach the law**
   a. The law was written down by Moses & entrusted to the care of the priests & leaders
   b. The charge
      1) To read the entire law in a very special service: Read every seven years—during the sabbatical year—at the Festival of Tabernacles
      2) To read at the central worship center

      3) To assemble & teach all the people
         - Teach them to fear the LORD & to carefully obey all the law

         - Teach the children in particular
         - Teach the law as long as they lived

4. **The charge of God to Moses & Joshua—given by God Himself**
   a. The LORD reminded His dear servant that his death was near
      1) God summoned Moses & Joshua to the Tabernacle
      2) God was personally to commission Joshua
      3) God appeared in the cloud above the Tabernacle

   b. The LORD gave a prophetic warning to Moses & Joshua
      1) The people would forsake God & break the covenant: Turn to false gods & false worship

      2) The LORD would become angry & forsake the people: Hide His face
         - They would be destroyed
         - They would suffer disasters & difficulties

And Moses went and spake these words unto all Israel.
2 And he said unto them, I *am* an hundred and twenty years old this day; I can no more go out and come in: also the LORD hath said unto me, Thou shalt not go over this Jordan.
3 The LORD thy God, he will go over before thee, *and* he will destroy these nations from before thee, and thou shalt possess them: *and* Joshua, he shall go over before thee, as the LORD hath said.
4 And the LORD shall do unto them as he did to Sihon and to Og, kings of the Amorites, and unto the land of them, whom he destroyed.
5 And the LORD shall give them up before your face, that ye may do unto them according unto all the commandments which I have commanded you.
6 Be strong and of a good courage, fear not, nor be afraid of them: for the LORD thy God, he *it is* that doth go with thee; he will not fail thee, nor forsake thee.
7 And Moses called unto Joshua, and said unto him in the sight of all Israel, Be strong and of a good courage: for thou must go with this people unto the land which the LORD hath sworn unto their fathers to give them; and thou shalt cause them to inherit it.
8 And the LORD, he *it is* that doth go before thee; he will be with thee, he will not fail thee, neither forsake thee: fear not, neither be dismayed.
9 And Moses wrote this law, and delivered it unto the priests the sons of Levi, which bare the ark of the covenant of the LORD, and unto all the elders of Israel.
10 And Moses commanded them, saying, At the end of *every* seven years, in the solemnity of the year of release, in the feast of tabernacles,
11 When all Israel is come to appear before the LORD thy God in the place which he shall choose, thou shalt read this law before all Israel in their hearing.
12 Gather the people together, men, and women, and children, and thy stranger that *is* within thy gates, that they may hear, and that they may learn, and fear the LORD your God, and observe to do all the words of this law:
13 And *that* their children, which have not known *any thing*, may hear, and learn to fear the LORD your God, as long as ye live in the land whither ye go over Jordan to possess it.
14 And the LORD said unto Moses, Behold, thy days approach that thou must die: call Joshua, and present yourselves in the tabernacle of the congregation, that I may give him a charge. And Moses and Joshua went, and presented themselves in the tabernacle of the congregation.
15 And the LORD appeared in the tabernacle in a pillar of a cloud: and the pillar of the cloud stood over the door of the tabernacle.
16 And the LORD said unto Moses, Behold, thou shalt sleep with thy fathers; and this people will rise up, and go a whoring after the gods of the strangers of the land, whither they go *to be* among them, and will forsake me, and break my covenant which I have made with them.
17 Then my anger shall be kindled against them in that day, and I will forsake them, and I will hide my face from them, and they shall be devoured, and many evils and troubles shall befall them; so that they will say in that day, Are not these evils come upon us, because our God *is* not among us?

DEUTERONOMY 31:1-29

• The LORD would be forced to hide His face because of all their evil
 	
c. The LORD gave a final charge to Moses: To write a *Song of Warning & Witness*—a song to stand as a permanent warning to the people
  1) The people needed the song because they would be given the promised land, but they would commit apostasy
 	
    • Would turn to false gods & worship
    • Would break the covenant
  2) The people needed the song to warn them & testify against them
  3) The people needed the song because God knew their hearts, knew exactly what they would do
 	
  4) Moses obeyed God: Gave the *Song of Warning & Witness* to the people
d. The LORD Himself commissioned & charged Joshua
  1) The charge: Be strong & courageous
	18 And I will surely hide my face in that day for all the evils which they shall have wrought, in that they are turned unto other gods.
	19 Now therefore write ye this song for you, and teach it the children of Israel: put it in their mouths, that this song may be a witness for me against the children of Israel.
	20 For when I shall have brought them into the land which I sware unto their fathers, that floweth with milk and honey; and they shall have eaten and filled themselves, and waxen fat; then will they turn unto other gods, and serve them, and provoke me, and break my covenant.
	21 And it shall come to pass, when many evils and troubles are befallen them, that this song shall testify against them as a witness; for it shall not be forgotten out of the mouths of their seed: for I know their imagination which they go about, even now, before I have brought them into the land which I sware.
	22 Moses therefore wrote this song the same day, and taught it the children of Israel.
	23 And he gave Joshua the son of Nun a charge, and said, Be strong and of a good courage: for thou shalt bring
		the children of Israel into the land which I sware unto them: and I will be with thee.
		24 And it came to pass, when Moses had made an end of writing the words of this law in a book, until they were finished,
		25 That Moses commanded the Levites, which bare the ark of the covenant of the LORD, saying,
		26 Take this book of the law, and put it in the side of the ark of the covenant of the LORD your God, that it may be there for a witness against thee.
		27 For I know thy rebellion, and thy stiff neck: behold, while I am yet alive with you this day, ye have been rebellious against the LORD; and how much more after my death?
		28 Gather unto me all the elders of your tribes, and your officers, that I may speak these words in their ears, and call heaven and earth to record against them.
		29 For I know that after my death ye will utterly corrupt *yourselves*, and turn aside from the way which I have commanded you; and evil will befall you in the latter days; because ye will do evil in the sight of the LORD, to provoke him to anger through the work of your hands.
			2) The assurance: God's presence & guidance
			
			5. **The final charge given to the Levites (ministers)**
			a. The writing of the law was completed
			
			b. The charge: To take responsibility for keeping the *Book of the Law*—to place it beside the Ark of the Covenant
			c. The *Book of the Law* was to be kept as a permanent witness against the people: Because they had proven they had rebellious & stubborn hearts
			
			d. The summons was given to assemble all the leaders together for the *Song of Warning & Witness*
			  1) The purpose: To warn & to testify against them
			  2) The reasons
			    • Because they would become corrupt after Moses' death: Turn away from the path of the commandments
			    • Because they would suffer disaster & judgment due to their evil behavior

DIVISION VI

THE FINAL ACTS AND DEATH OF MOSES, GOD'S AGED SERVANT: REMEMBER THE ENCOURAGEMENT AND THE WARNING OF GOD, 31:1–34:12

A. The Final Preparations for Entering the Promised Land: Five Strong Charges of Encouragement and Warning, 31:1-29

(31:1-29) **Introduction**: there are occasions when a person needs to be stirred to arise and carry out his duties. At times, the person needs strong encouragement. At other times, the same person needs a strong warning. He needs to be warned of the consequences of his behavior in order to stir him into action.

The Israelites needed both the charge of encouragement and a strong warning. Moses, the dear servant of God, was aged—now 120 years old. He was soon to pass from the scene. These are the last days of his life upon earth. He will have only a few more meetings to share with the people; therefore, he has to prepare them for his departure.

The Israelites must be encouraged in their faith, encouraged to hang on to the hope of the promised land, to the wonderful inheritance to be given them by God. Moreover, there are some practical matters that the people must handle before Moses leaves them. The mantle of leadership is to be passed on to Joshua, so a commissioning service must be held. Also, the *Book of the Law* needs to be entrusted into the hands of the nation's leadership. A special worship service also needs to be established for the reading and learning of the law. So much to be done in so little time.

How could the dear aged servant of God do all this with just a few days remaining upon earth? How could he both encourage and warn the people—do all he could to strengthen their faith—and handle all the practical matters in so brief a time? How was the dear aged servant of God going to close out his ministry in the most effective way possible? What was he going to say to the people? What were to be his last words?

DEUTERONOMY 31:1-29

Keep in mind that Moses, this dear aged servant of God, was one of the greatest men of human history, not only in the minds of men, but also in the estimation of God. Moses was one of the two men who appeared with God's own Son, the Lord Jesus Christ, on the mount of transfiguration. With this passage begins some of the final words of Moses to the people of God: a message for people of all generations. Note that he gives five strong charges of encouragement and a strong warning to the people of God: *The Final Preparations for Entering the Promised Land: Five Strong Charges of Encouragement and Warning, 31:1-29.*

1. The charge and strong encouragement given to the people (vv.1-6).
2. The charge and encouragement given to Joshua: the commissioning service to appoint him as the new leader (vv.7-8).
3. The charge given to the leaders and priests, the ministers of God: to read and teach the law (vv.9-13).
4. The charge of God to Moses and Joshua—given by God Himself (vv.14-23).
5. The final charge by God's servant to the Levites (ministers) (vv.24-29).

1 (31:1-6) **Charge, to Be Strong and Courageous—Strong, Duty—Courageous, Duty—Fear, Duty—Encouragement, Source of—Presence, of God, Assurance of—Assurance, of God's Guidance**: a strong charge and encouragement was given to the people by the aged servant of God. Moses had summoned all the people together, and now he was about to address them, knowing that his days upon earth were rapidly drawing to a close. This is a touching scene, for it is the picture of an aged leader spending his last days upon earth with the dear people he loved so much. For 40 years he had led the Israelites, living with them day in and day out and struggling with them through all the trials and temptations of life. He had personally experienced the mighty hand of God using him to deliver the people out of Egyptian slavery. He had walked hand in hand with the people for forty years, suffering through the wilderness wanderings. He had experienced both victory and defeat with the people, and he knew that they were basically a stubborn and stiff-necked people toward God. Nevertheless, this aged servant loved his dear people, the Israelites. What would he say to them in one of his final hours with them? What was upon his heart? His heart was obviously tender toward them; yet knowing they were hard and stiff-necked, what could he say in these final days that would arouse them to follow God wholeheartedly? Note the Scripture and outline:

OUTLINE	SCRIPTURE	SCRIPTURE	OUTLINE

1. **The charge & strong encouragement given to the people**
a. The death of Moses was rapidly approaching: Was 120 years old & forbidden to enter the promised land
b. The encouragement: God's constant presence & guidance was assured
  1) God would lead—go ahead of His people
   • To destroy the enemy
   • To secure the land
  2) God would raise up a new leader, Joshua
 	
  3) God would give complete
	And Moses went and spake these words unto all Israel.
	2 And he said unto them, I am an hundred and twenty years old this day; I can no more go out and come in: also the LORD hath said unto me, Thou shalt not go over this Jordan.
	3 The LORD thy God, he will go over before thee, and he will destroy these nations from before thee, and thou shalt possess them: and Joshua, he shall go over before thee, as the LORD hath said.
	4 And the LORD shall do
		unto them as he did to Sihon and to Og, kings of the Amorites, and unto the land of them, whom he destroyed.
		5 And the LORD shall give them up before your face, that ye may do unto them according unto all the commandments which I have commanded you.
		6 Be strong and of a good courage, fear not, nor be afraid of them: for the LORD thy God, he *it is* that doth go with thee; he will not fail thee, nor forsake thee.
			& total victory over all the enemies of His people: The kind of victory He gave over Sihon & Og
			
			c. The charge: Be strong & courageous! Do not fear nor be terrified!
			  1) Because God will be with you
			  2) Because God will never leave nor forsake you

a. Moses declared that his death was rapidly approaching (v.2). He was soon to go home to be with the LORD. This he knew, for he was 120 years old. But there was another fact that the people needed to know: he was forbidden by God to enter the promised land. Why? Because years before he had disobeyed God and shown arrogance before the people at the waters of Meribah. The Israelites had apparently been forced to camp at Meribah, a place where there was little or no water. As a result, they began to grumble and complain, even to the point of threatening the life of Moses. But in mercy, God stepped forth and instructed Moses to gather the people before a particular rock. There Moses was to speak to the rock before the very eyes of the people, and water would come gushing out of the rock. However, in anger and hostility toward the people, Moses began to speak to the people and not to the rock, accusing the people of being rebels. Displaying a shameful arrogance, he failed to give God the full credit and honor for producing the water: he claimed that it was both he and God who had provided the miracle for the people. This was a disobedience and arrogance that God could not accept, for the evil was committed in a public meeting right before the people. As a result, God had to chastise His dear servant. He was barred from ever entering the promised land. (See outline and note—Nu.20:7-13 for more discussion.)

Moses was heartbroken. No doubt, every time he thought about or had to mention his chastisement, it cut him to the core. But now, it was time to get the point across to his dear people, for they were soon to cross the Jordan. When they entered the promised land, he would not be with them. This fact must be settled in their minds and hearts.

b. Moses knew that the people must be encouraged. God Himself would be with them. They could rest assured of His presence and guidance (vv.3-5). In fact, the LORD would actually cross over ahead of them and do three wonderful things for them:

  1) God would lead the Israelites and destroy the enemies of the promised land. The people could rest assured that they would secure the land promised by God (v.3).
  2) God would raise up a new leader, Joshua, to take the place of Moses (v.3). God would not leave the people stranded, without leadership. He would give them a very capable leader, a man who had already proven himself:

DEUTERONOMY 31:1-29

⇒ as a military leader (Ex.17:9-16)
⇒ as a spy (Nu.13:1-16)
⇒ as a leader of strong faith, decision, obedience, and courage, standing up for the truth—even against all odds (Nu.14:6-9)
⇒ through training and service in leadership, being personally trained by Moses (Nu.11:28; Jos.1:1)

Joshua had been prepared for leadership as much as a person could be. The people could rest assured in his guidance, for they had witnessed the proof of his leadership for years.

3) God would give total and complete victory over all the enemies of His people (v.4). Moses declares that the LORD will give the very same kind of victory He had given over the Amorites, over King Sihon and Og (v.4).

The people had every right to stand encouraged. They had the wonderful promise of God's presence and guidance, the promise of a new leader, and the glorious promise of complete victory over all enemies who stood before them. This was the strong encouragement the aged servant of God, facing the final days of his ministry, gave to his dear people.

c. Now, he gave them a very straightforward charge: be strong and courageous (v.6)! As you march into the promised land, do not fear nor be terrified by the enemies who oppose you. The LORD your God will be with you. He will never leave you nor forsake you.

Note that the people's strength and courage would not come from the power of their armed forces nor from their own abilities and strategies to conquer the enemy. On the contrary, their strength and courage would come from God Himself. This is a strong charge for the people to be focused upon God, not upon the enemy; to be focused upon trusting God for victory instead of the arm of the flesh. They were to believe and have confidence in God, in His presence and power.

Thought 1. As we march to the promised land of heaven, the one thing we want is a full and victorious life. We want to experience all the abundance of life, walking triumphantly through all the trials and temptations that confront us. Simply stated, we want fullness of life and victory over all the enemies that attempt to defeat us, enemies such as...

- accidents
- abuse
- lawlessness
- drug addiction
- unemployment
- disease
- mistreatment
- violence
- death
- financial difficulty
- broken relationships
- anger
- immorality
- war

The enemies that confront and attempt to defeat us are innumerable. But victory over all enemies can be attained. The power to conquer each one is at our disposal. We can be victorious throughout life and experience the fullness of life. This is the promise of God. The same charge and encouragement given to the Israelites is applicable to us. Note what Scripture says:

(1) We must be strong and courageous. We must not fear nor be terrified by the enemies who confront us throughout life.

"Watch ye, stand fast in the faith, quit you like men, be strong" (1 Co.16:13).

"Finally, my brethren, be strong in the LORD, and in the power of his might. Put on the whole armour of God, that ye may be able to stand against the wiles of the devil. For we wrestle not against flesh and blood, but against principalities, against powers, against the rulers of the darkness of this world, against spiritual wickedness in high *places*. Wherefore take unto you the whole armour of God, that ye may be able to withstand in the evil day, and having done all, to stand." (Ep.6:10-13).

"And in nothing terrified by your adversaries: which is to them an evident token of perdition, but to you of salvation, and that of God" (Ph.1:28).

"Thou therefore, my son, be strong in the grace that is in Christ Jesus" (2 Ti.2:1).

"Be sober, be vigilant; because your adversary the devil, as a roaring lion, walketh about, seeking whom he may devour: Whom resist stedfast in the faith, knowing that the same afflictions are accomplished in your brethren that are in the world. But the God of all grace, who hath called us unto his eternal glory by Christ Jesus, after that ye have suffered a while, make you perfect, stablish, strengthen, settle *you*" (1 Pe.5:8-10).

"I go the way of all the earth: be thou strong therefore, and show thyself a man" (1 K.2:2).

"Be ye strong therefore, and let not your hands be weak: for your work shall be rewarded" (2 Chr.15:7).

"Be strong and of a good courage: for unto this people shalt thou divide for an inheritance the land, which I sware unto their fathers to give them" (Jos.1:6).

"And Joshua said unto them, Fear not, nor be dismayed, be strong and of good courage: for thus shall the LORD do to all your enemies against whom ye fight" (Jos.10:25).

"Be ye therefore very courageous to keep and to do all that is written in the book of the law of Moses, that ye turn not aside therefrom *to* the right hand or *to* the left" (Jos.23:6).

(2) We can be strong and courageous because of God's presence and guidance. As we face the enemies of this world, God will be with us and never forsake us.

"Lo, I am with you alway, *even* unto the end of the world. Amen" (Mt.28:20).

"Howbeit when he, the Spirit of truth, is come, he will guide you into all truth: for he shall not speak of himself; but whatsoever he shall hear, *that* shall he speak: and he will show you things to come" (Jn.16:13).

DEUTERONOMY 31:1-29

"And, behold, I *am* with thee, and will keep thee in all *places* whither thou goest, and will bring thee again into this land; for I will not leave thee, until I have done *that* which I have spoken to thee of" (Ge.28:15).

"And he said, My presence shall go *with thee,* and I will give thee rest" (Ex.33:14).

"When thou goest out to battle against thine enemies, and seest horses, and chariots, *and* a people more than thou, be not afraid of them: for the LORD thy God *is* with thee, which brought thee up out of the land of Egypt" (De.20:1).

"He maketh me to lie down in green pastures: he leadeth me beside the still waters" (Ps.23:2).

"The meek will he guide in judgment: and the meek will he teach his way" (Ps.25:9).

"For this God *is* our God for ever and ever: he will be our guide *even* unto death" (Ps.48:14).

"Thou shalt guide me with thy counsel, and afterward receive me *to* glory" (Ps.73:24).

"And thine ears shall hear a word behind thee, saying, This *is* the way, walk ye in it, when ye turn to the right hand, and when ye turn to the left" (Is.30:21).

"When thou passest through the waters, I *will be* with thee; and through the rivers, they shall not overflow thee: when thou walkest through the fire, thou shalt not be burned; neither shall the flame kindle upon thee" (Is.43:2).

2 (31:7-8) **Charge, Duty—Joshua, Charge to—Joshua, Commissioning of—Courage, Duty—Encouragement, Source of**: there was the strong charge and encouragement given to Joshua. This was the commissioning service to appoint Joshua as the new leader of the Israelites. A public commissioning service was needed so the people would know that the mantle of leadership was now being passed to Joshua. By witnessing the commissioning service and seeing the confidence of Moses in Joshua, the people would be encouraged. They would begin to look to Joshua for leadership.

OUTLINE	SCRIPTURE	SCRIPTURE	OUTLINE
2. The charge & encouragement given to Joshua: The commissioning service to appoint him as the new leader a. The charge: Be strong & courageous 　1) He was the appointed leader of God's people	7 And Moses called unto Joshua, and said unto him in the sight of all Israel, Be strong and of a good courage: for thou must go with this people unto the land which the LORD hath sworn unto their fathers to give them; and	thou shalt cause them to inherit it. 8 And the LORD, he *it is* that doth go before thee; he will be with thee, he will not fail thee, neither forsake thee: fear not, neither be dismayed.	2) He was the one appointed to divide the land among them b. The encouragement 　1) The LORD's presence & guidance 　2) The expectation: That he would not fear nor be discouraged

a. The commissioning charge was strong and clear: be strong and courageous (v.7). Both strength and courage were needed, for Joshua would bear two heavy responsibilities:
⇒ the responsibility of leading the Israelites into the promised land
⇒ the responsibility of dividing the land among the tribes

But Joshua was given not only responsibility, he was given a most wonderful privilege. He was the person chosen to lead God's people in the fulfillment of the ancient promise made to the forefathers, Abraham, Isaac, and Jacob. What was the wonderful privilege, the ancient promise? The inheritance of the promised land. The ancient promise was now to be fulfilled in the lives of God's dear people. They were soon to cross over the Jordan and enter the promised land, receiving their long awaited inheritance. And Joshua was the appointed leader to guide them into the land.

b. The commissioning service also included a strong encouragement (v.8). Standing before the people with his hands resting upon the head of Joshua, Moses gave the most wonderful encouragement to Joshua. He was being divinely appointed, and he could rest assured that he would be divinely led. In commissioning Joshua, Moses declared that the LORD's presence and guidance would always rest upon Joshua. The LORD would go before him and be with him, never leaving nor forsaking him. He must, therefore, not be afraid nor ever be discouraged. This was the strong expectation of God.

Thought 1. The genuine believer has the most wonderful promise from God: that of His presence and guidance. God promises never to leave nor forsake us. Because of this wonderful promise, God expects one thing from us: that we not fear nor be discouraged. If God be with us, who can be against us (Ro.8:31)? God's presence assures fullness of life and a victorious life. The presence and guidance of God should eliminate all fear from our hearts and lives. God is with us and He guides us. Consequently, the charge is to us as well as to Joshua: we must not fear nor be discouraged.

"But the very hairs of your head are all numbered. Fear ye not therefore, ye are of more value than many sparrows" (Mt.10:30-31).

"What shall we then say to these things? If God *be* for us, who *can be* against us? He that spared not his own Son, but delivered him up for us all, how shall he not with him also freely give us all things....Who shall separate us from the love of Christ? *shall* tribulation, or distress, or persecution, or famine, or nakedness, or peril, or sword....Nay, in all these things we are more than conquerors through him that loved us. For I am persuaded, that neither death, nor life, nor angels, nor principalities, nor powers, nor things present, nor things to come, Nor height, nor depth, nor any other creature, shall be able to separate us from the love of God, which is in Christ Jesus our LORD" (Ro.8:31-32, 35, 37-39).

"And in nothing terrified by your adversaries: which is to them an evident token of perdition, but to you of salvation, and that of God" (Ph.1:28).

"For God hath not given us the spirit of fear; but of power, and of love, and of a sound mind" (2 Ti.1:7).

"Ye are of God, little children, and have overcome them: because greater is he that is in you, than he that is in the world" (1 Jn.4:4).

"Be strong and of a good courage, fear not, nor be afraid of them: for the LORD thy God, he *it is* that doth go with thee; he will not fail thee, nor forsake thee" (De.31:6).

"Be strong and of a good courage: for unto this people shalt thou divide for an inheritance the land, which I sware unto their fathers to give them" (Jos.1:6).

"And Joshua said unto them, Fear not, nor be dismayed, be strong and of good courage: for thus shall the LORD do to all your enemies against whom ye fight" (Jos.10:25).

"Be ye therefore very courageous to keep and to do all that is written in the book of the law of Moses, that ye turn not aside therefrom *to* the right hand or *to* the left; That ye come not among these nations, these that remain among you; neither make mention of the names of their gods, nor cause to swear *by them,* neither serve them, nor bow yourselves unto them: But cleave unto the LORD your God, as ye have done unto this day" (Jos.23:6-8).

"Be of good courage, and let us play the men for our people, and for the cities of our God: and the LORD do that which seemeth him good" (2 S.10:12).

"Be of good courage, and let us behave ourselves valiantly for our people, and for the cities of our God: and let the LORD do *that which is* good in his sight" (1 Chr.19:13).

"Then shalt thou prosper, if thou takest heed to fulfil the statutes and judgments which the LORD charged Moses with concerning Israel: be strong, and of good courage; dread not, nor be dismayed" (1 Chr.22:13).

"And David said to Solomon his son, Be strong and of good courage, and do *it:* fear not, nor be dismayed: for the LORD God, *even* my God, *will be* with thee; he will not fail thee, nor forsake thee, until thou hast finished all the work for the service of the house of the LORD" (1 Chr.28:20).

"Fear thou not; for I *am* with thee: be not dismayed; for I *am* thy God: I will strengthen thee; yea, I will help thee; yea, I will uphold thee with the right hand of my righteousness" (Is.41:10).

"Fear not: for I have redeemed thee, I have called *thee* by thy name; thou *art* mine. When thou passest through the waters, I *will be* with thee; and through the rivers, they shall not overflow thee: when thou walkest through the fire, thou shalt not be burned; neither shall the flame kindle upon thee" (Is.43:1-2).

3 (31:9-13) **Charge, to Ministers—Charge, to Priests—Ministers, Charge to—Moses, Writings of—Ministers, Duty of—Priests, Duty of—Word of God, Duty to—Scriptures, Duty to—Bible, Duty to**: there was the charge given to the leaders and the priests, the ministers of God. They were to read and teach the law to the people. God's Word was to hold the most prominent place in their lives. They were to obey the Word of God, live it out in their lives. To do this, they had to learn the commandments of God.

OUTLINE	SCRIPTURE	SCRIPTURE	OUTLINE

3. The charge given to the leaders & priests, the ministers of God: To read & teach the law
a. The law was written down by Moses & entrusted to the care of the priests & leaders
b. The charge
  1) To read the entire law in a very special service: Read every seven years—during the sabbatical year—at the Festival of Tabernacles
  2) To read at the central worship center
	9 And Moses wrote this law, and delivered it unto the priests the sons of Levi, which bare the ark of the covenant of the LORD, and unto all the elders of Israel.
	10 And Moses commanded them, saying, At the end of *every* seven years, in the solemnity of the year of release, in the feast of tabernacles,
	11 When all Israel is come to appear before the LORD thy God in the place which he shall choose, thou shalt read
		this law before all Israel in their hearing.
		12 Gather the people together, men, and women, and children, and thy stranger that *is* within thy gates, that they may hear, and that they may learn, and fear the LORD your God, and observe to do all the words of this law:
		13 And *that* their children, which have not known *any thing*, may hear, and learn to fear the LORD your God, as long as ye live in the land whither ye go over Jordan to possess it.
			3) To assemble & teach all the people
			  • Teach them to fear the LORD & to carefully obey all the law
			  • Teach the children in particular
			  • Teach the law as long as they lived

a. The law was written down by Moses and given to the priests (v.9). Is this a reference to the entire Pentateuch (the first five books of the Bible)? Or a reference to the whole book of *Deuteronomy* (at least chapters 1-30)? Or is this a reference to the laws that were given in *Exodus, Leviticus,* and *Deuteronomy* dealing with the behavior of people? Scripture does not say. The point to see is that the law was entrusted to the priests who carried the Ark of the Covenant and to the leaders of Israel.

b. The charge focused upon the law, the Word of God. The importance of the law in the life of the Israelites could never be over-stressed. Conquering and remaining in the promised land depended upon one thing: their obedience to the law. If they kept the commandments of God, the presence and guidance of God would be available to them. But if they disobeyed the law, the presence and guidance of God would be removed. They would be left on their own.

Simply stated, the eternal fate of Israel in the promised land depended upon their response to the law of God. For this reason, the law was placed under the care of both *the political and the religious leaders* of the nation. Making sure that the

people learned the Word of God was as much the responsibility of the government leaders as of the priests (ministers). Three charges were given to these leaders:
1) They were to make sure that the entire law was read in a very special service (vv.10-13). The law was to be read every seven years during the sabbatical year at the Festival of Tabernacles (v.10).
2) The law was to be read at the central worship center (v.11).
3) All the people were to assemble together and be taught the law. This included the men, women, children, and foreigners. Through this ceremony of publicly reading God's law, the people would learn to fear the LORD and to obey His commandments. Note that special attention and instruction in the Word of God was to be given to the children (v.13). The law was to be taught as long as they lived in the promised land.

It must be kept in mind that most people did not possess a copy of the law. No doubt, copies were written and made available to as many people as possible. However, most people would not have day-to-day access to the Word of God. In light of this, the public reading of the law was very important for learning the commandments. Thus, the purpose of this special service was educational as well as a time of rededication to the covenant of God. By hearing the Word of God read, a person would learn more of the commandments and be stirred to renew his commitment and covenant with God.

Note this fact as well: by teaching the covenant to children at such an early age, they would soon grasp the importance of the Word of God in the lives of individuals as well as within the community. Being gathered up and leaving their homes to go to the central worship center would be an exciting time for children. They would know that the event was significant, very important. Being in the presence of the whole congregation of God's people would build a deep sense of community within them, of the importance of the body of God's people acting and standing together. The children would soon realize that it was the covenant, the Word of God, that held the people together, held them together as a community of believers. They would soon learn to obey God, to keep His covenant and commandments for the sake of the community as well as for themselves personally.

Thought 1. The importance of the Word of God cannot be over-stressed. God gave His Word in order to show us how to live.

Experiencing the fullness of life and living a victorious life that conquers and triumphs over all—this is the longing of every human heart. Life, real life, is found in the Word of God. It is the Word of God that tells us how to secure a full and victorious life. If a person will do what the Word of God says, he will be flooded with all the blessings of life and conquer all the trials and temptations that confront him. This is the importance of learning the Word of God.

"For verily I say unto you, Till heaven and earth pass, one jot or one tittle shall in no wise pass from the law, till all be fulfilled" (Mt.5:18).

"Heaven and earth shall pass away, but my words shall not pass away" (Mt.24:35).

"Now ye are clean through the word which I have spoken unto you" (Jn.15:3).

"Sanctify them through thy truth: thy word is truth" (Jn.17:17).

"But these are written, that ye might believe that Jesus is the Christ, the Son of God; and that believing ye might have life through his name" (Jn.20:31).

"For I am not ashamed of the gospel of Christ: for it is the power of God unto salvation to every one that believeth; to the Jew first, and also to the Greek" (Ro.1:16).

"For whatsoever things were written aforetime were written for our learning, that we through patience and comfort of the scriptures might have hope" (Ro.15:4).

"Let the word of Christ dwell in you richly in all wisdom; teaching and admonishing one another in psalms and hymns and spiritual songs, singing with grace in your hearts to the LORD" (Col.3:16).

"Study to show thyself approved unto God, a workman that needeth not to be ashamed, rightly dividing the word of truth" (2 Ti.2:15).

"All scripture *is* given by inspiration of God, and *is* profitable for doctrine, for reproof, for correction, for instruction in righteousness" (2 Ti.3:16).

"For the word of God *is* quick, and powerful, and sharper than any twoedged sword, piercing even to the dividing asunder of soul and spirit, and of the joints and marrow, and *is* a discerner of the thoughts and intents of the heart" (He.4:12).

"As newborn babes, desire the sincere milk of the word, that ye may grow thereby" (1 Pe.2:2).

"These things have I written unto you that believe on the name of the Son of God; that ye may know that ye have eternal life, and that ye may believe on the name of the Son of God" (1 Jn.5:13).

"Wherewithal shall a young man cleanse his way? by taking heed *thereto* according to thy word" (Ps.119:9).

"How sweet are thy words unto my taste! *yea, sweeter* than honey to my mouth" (Ps.119:103).

"The grass withereth, the flower fadeth: but the word of our God shall stand for ever" (Is.40:8).

DEUTERONOMY 31:1-29

4 (31:14-23) **Song, of Moses—Song of Warning and Witness, of Moses—Charge, of God, to Moses—Moses, Charge to, by God—Moses, Writings of—Writings, of Moses**: there was the charge of God Himself to Moses and Joshua. Up to this point, Moses had been issuing the charges. He had issued a charge to the people, then to Joshua who was to replace him as leader of the Israelites, and finally to the leaders and priests of the nation. Now, God Himself steps forth and issues a clear charge to Moses and Joshua. This is a private, intimate meeting between God and His two dear servants. Note the Scripture and outline:

OUTLINE	SCRIPTURE	SCRIPTURE	OUTLINE

4. The charge of God to Moses & Joshua—given by God Himself
a. The LORD reminded His dear servant that his death was near
  1) God summoned Moses & Joshua to the Tabernacle
  2) God was personally to commission Joshua
  3) God appeared in the cloud above the Tabernacle
 	
b. The LORD gave a prophetic warning to Moses & Joshua
  1) The people would forsake God & break the covenant: Turn to false gods & false worship
 	
2) The LORD would become angry & forsake the people: Hide His face
  • They would be destroyed
  • They would suffer disasters & difficulties
 	
  • The LORD would be forced to hide His face because of all their evil
	14 And the LORD said unto Moses, Behold, thy days approach that thou must die: call Joshua, and present yourselves in the tabernacle of the congregation, that I may give him a charge. And Moses and Joshua went, and presented themselves in the tabernacle of the congregation.
	15 And the LORD appeared in the tabernacle in a pillar of a cloud: and the pillar of the cloud stood over the door of the tabernacle.
	16 And the LORD said unto Moses, Behold, thou shalt sleep with thy fathers; and this people will rise up, and go a whoring after the gods of the strangers of the land, whither they go *to be* among them, and will forsake me, and break my covenant which I have made with them.
	17 Then my anger shall be kindled against them in that day, and I will forsake them, and I will hide my face from them, and they shall be devoured, and many evils and troubles shall befall them; so that they will say in that day, Are not these evils come upon us, because our God *is* not among us?
	18 And I will surely hide my face in that day for all the evils which they shall have wrought, in that they are
		turned unto other gods.
		19 Now therefore write ye this song for you, and teach it the children of Israel: put it in their mouths, that this song may be a witness for me against the children of Israel.
		20 For when I shall have brought them into the land which I sware unto their fathers, that floweth with milk and honey; and they shall have eaten and filled themselves, and waxen fat; then will they turn unto other gods, and serve them, and provoke me, and break my covenant.
		21 And it shall come to pass, when many evils and troubles are befallen them, that this song shall testify against them as a witness; for it shall not be forgotten out of the mouths of their seed: for I know their imagination which they go about, even now, before I have brought them into the land which I sware.
		22 Moses therefore wrote this song the same day, and taught it the children of Israel.
		23 And he gave Joshua the son of Nun a charge, and said, Be strong and of a good courage: for thou shalt bring the children of Israel into the land which I sware unto them: and I will be with thee.
			c. The LORD gave a final charge to Moses: To write a *Song of Warning & Witness*—a song to stand as a permanent warning to the people
			  1) The people needed the song because they would be given the promised land, but they would commit apostasy
			    • Would turn to false gods & worship
			    • Would break the covenant
			
			  2) The people needed the song to warn them & testify against them
			  3) The people needed the song because God knew their hearts, knew exactly what they would do
			
			  4) Moses obeyed God: Gave the *Song of Warning & Witness* to the people
			
			d. The LORD Himself commissioned & charged Joshua
			  1) The charge: Be strong & courageous
			  2) The assurance: God's presence & guidance

    a. The LORD spoke to Moses and reminded His dear servant that his death was near (v.14). Most likely, the LORD took some time to discuss the matter with Moses, making this a most precious and hallowed experience. At some point, God broke off the discussion of Moses' death and told him to summon Joshua to the Tabernacle: God wanted to personally commission Joshua in a private meeting with just the three of them. When Moses and Joshua presented themselves at the Tabernacle, the LORD appeared in the pillar of cloud above the Tabernacle (v.15).

    b. Note what happened: the LORD did not immediately begin the commission of Joshua. Instead, the LORD gave a prophetic warning to Moses and Joshua (vv.16-18). The words must have broken the heart of Moses while arousing some apprehension in Joshua. Sadness must have filled the room as the LORD began to speak and prophesy the future behavior of the Israelites. Keep in mind that this is a prophecy of what would happen to them, a prophecy that we today are able to look back upon and understand. History has shown that the prophecy was fulfilled precisely as the LORD predicted..

      1) The LORD revealed that the people of Israel would forsake God and break the covenant with Him. And note, the breaking of the covenant would happen soon (v.16). The people would soon turn to false gods and false worship. The neighbors surrounding the Israelites would influence them and lead them into apostasy. The people would soon begin to follow the immoral and lawless ways of their neighbors. They would soon forsake the LORD.

      2) The LORD revealed that He would become angry and forsake the people (v.17). He would hide His face from them, and they would be destroyed. They would suffer problems and disasters beyond imagination. The LORD would be forced to hide His face because of all their evil (v.18). Having forsaken God, they would in turn be forsaken by God.

DEUTERONOMY 31:1-29

Note that neither Moses nor Joshua spoke. They were stone silent. During the entire interview, they were speechless. To hear these words after so many years of faithful service, God's aged servant must have been gripped with emotions beyond description. Sad and brokenhearted, Moses could say nothing. Neither could Joshua, the man upon whom the mantle of leadership had fallen. Being all alone with the LORD in the Tabernacle and hearing such a revelation from the LORD Himself no doubt prostrated the two men, weeping and sobbing before the LORD.

But in His eternal compassion and mercy, God wanted to do everything He could to warn the people. Therefore, He began to address Moses personally.

c. The LORD gave a final charge to Moses (vv.19-22). God wanted Moses to write a *song of warning and witness* to the Israelites. This song would stand as a permanent warning to the people. Note that the song was to be taught to the Israelites: they were to sing it, apparently many times, in order to commit it to memory. Just why the people needed the song is clearly spelled out by God.

1) The people needed the song because even though they would be given the promised land, they would commit apostasy (v.20). They would turn to false gods and false worship. They would break the covenant with God, rejecting Him and His commandments.
2) The people needed the song to warn them and to testify against them. The song could stand as a warning to all future generations, a warning not to forsake the LORD.
3) The song was needed because God knew the hearts of the people, knew exactly what they would do (v.21). God understands the nature of man—his imaginations and inclinations of behavior, exactly what he is like.
4) Note that Moses obeyed God (v.22). He wrote down the *Song of Warning and Witness* and later taught it to the people. The song is discussed in detail in the next chapter (De.31:30-32:52).

d. After giving the above charge to Moses, the LORD Himself commissioned and charged Joshua (v.23). The charge was clear and forceful: be strong and courageous. These words were desperately needed in light of the sad revelation that the Israelites would miserably fail. Nevertheless, even if most of the people failed and turned away from God, Joshua was not to fail. He was personally responsible for his own life and call. Above all others, as the leader of God's people, he was to be strong and courageous. He was to set a dynamic example of strength and courage. Note the wonderful assurance given by God, the assurance of His presence and guidance. The presence of God would empower him to conquer and triumph over all the trials and temptations that lay ahead. By God's presence and power, he would be able to lead the people into the promised land.

Thought 1. God knows everything about us. He knows our coming in and going out, where we are and where we are going. He even knows where we have been. Nothing can be hidden from God. Secret places and secret acts are known to God. God even knows the future, every minute detail that will happen, including what we will do. God's knowledge is complete and perfect. He is omniscient—all-knowing and without limits.

"Be not ye therefore like unto them: for your Father knoweth what things ye have need of, before ye ask him" (Mt.6:8).

"Nathanael saith unto him, Whence knowest thou me? Jesus answered and said unto him, Before that Philip called thee, when thou wast under the fig tree, I saw thee" (Jn.1:48).

"And again, The LORD knoweth the thoughts of the wise, that they are vain" (1 Co.3:20).

"Nevertheless the foundation of God standeth sure, having this seal, The LORD knoweth them that are his. And, Let every one that nameth the name of Christ depart from iniquity" (2 Ti.2:19).

"Talk no more so exceeding proudly; let *not* arrogancy come out of your mouth: for the LORD is a God of knowledge, and by him actions are weighed" (1 S.2:3).

"For his eyes *are* upon the ways of man, and he seeth all his goings" (Jb. 34:21).

"For the LORD knoweth the way of the righteous: but the way of the ungodly shall perish" (Ps.1:6).

"I have kept thy precepts and thy testimonies: for all my ways *are* before thee" (Ps.119:168).

"Thou compassest my path and my lying down, and art acquainted *with* all my ways" (Ps.139:3).

"When my spirit was overwhelmed within me, then thou knewest my path. In the way wherein I walked have they privily [secretly] laid a snare for me" (Ps.142:3).

"For the ways of man *are* before the eyes of the LORD, and he pondereth all his goings" (Pr.5:21).

"I the LORD search the heart, *I* try the reins, even to give every man according to his ways, *and* according to the fruit of his doings" (Je.17:10).

"For mine eyes *are* upon all their ways: they are not hid from my face, neither is their iniquity hid from mine eyes" (Je.16:17).

"Can any hide himself in secret places that I shall not see him? saith the LORD. Do not I fill heaven and earth? saith the LORD" (Je.23:24).

"Great in counsel, and mighty in work: for thine eyes *are* open upon all the ways of the sons of men: to give every one according to his ways, and according to the fruit of his doings" (Je.32:19).

"He revealeth the deep and secret things: he knoweth what *is* in the darkness, and the light dwelleth with him" (Da.2:22).

Thought 2. God warns us against apostasy, against turning away from Him.

"Holding faith, and a good conscience; which some having put away concerning faith have made shipwreck" (1 Ti.1:19).

"Now the Spirit speaketh expressly, that in the latter times some shall depart from the faith, giving heed to seducing spirits, and doctrines of devils" (1 Ti.4:1).

"And they shall turn away *their* ears from the truth, and shall be turned unto fables" (2 Ti.4:4).

"Take heed, brethren, lest there be in any of you an evil heart of unbelief, in departing from the living God" (He.3:12).

"For *it is* impossible for those who were once enlightened, and have tasted of the heavenly gift, and were made partakers of the Holy Ghost, And have tasted the good word of God, and the powers of the world to come, If they shall fall away, to renew them again unto repentance; seeing they crucify to themselves the Son of God afresh, and put *him* to an open shame" (He.6:4-6).

"For if after they have escaped the pollutions of the world through the knowledge of the LORD and Saviour Jesus Christ, they are again entangled therein, and overcome, the latter end is worse with them than the beginning. For it had been better for them not to have known the way of righteousness, than, after they have known *it*, to turn from the holy commandment delivered unto them" (2 Pe.2:20-21).

"Ye therefore, beloved, seeing ye know *these things* before, beware lest ye also, being led away with the error of the wicked, fall from your own stedfastness" (2 Pe.3:17).

"They went out from us, but they were not of us; for if they had been of us, they would *no doubt* have continued with us: but *they went out*, that they might be made manifest that they were not all of us" (1 Jn.2:19).

"Nevertheless they were disobedient, and rebelled against thee, and cast thy law behind their backs, and slew thy prophets which testified against them to turn them to thee, and they wrought great provocations" (Ne.9:26).

"Thou hast forsaken me, saith the LORD, thou art gone backward: therefore will I stretch out my hand against thee, and destroy thee; I am weary with repenting" (Je.15:6).

Thought 3. John Maxwell gives an excellent statement dealing with the LORD's commission of Joshua. The statement is well worth quoting in its entirety:

> *Perhaps the most sobering fact of leadership is that it is a lonely position. A leader has no one with whom he shares the responsibility of final decisions. It is human to stand with the crowd; it is divine to stand alone. It is manlike to follow the people, to drift with the tide; it is Godlike to follow a principle and stem the time. Noah built and voyaged alone; his neighbors laughed at his strangeness and perished. Abraham wandered and worshiped alone; Sodomites smiled at the simple shepherd, followed the fashion, and fed the flames. Daniel dined and prayed alone. Elijah sacrificed and witnessed alone. Jeremiah prophesied and wept alone. Jesus loved and died alone. 'No man stood with me, but all forsook me' wrote the battle-scarred apostle in describing his appearance before the emperor. Joshua, too, must stand alone. Yet in that vacant spot he will find God: "I will be with you" (v.23).* [1]

5 (31:24-29) **Ministers, Duty—Charge, of Moses—Book of the Law, Preserved—Moses, Charges of—Writings, the Book of the Law—Writings, of Moses—Moses, Writings of—Word of God, Importance of:** there was the final charge by God's aged servant to the Levites, the ministers of God. These few verses cover the actual delivery of *The Book of the Law* to the Levites.

OUTLINE	SCRIPTURE	SCRIPTURE	OUTLINE
5. The final charge given to the Levites (ministers) a. The writing of the law was completed b. The charge: To take responsibility for keeping the *Book of the Law*—to place it beside the Ark of the Covenant c. The *Book of the Law* was to be kept as a permanent witness against the people: Because they had rebellious & stubborn hearts—this they had proven	24 And it came to pass, when Moses had made an end of writing the words of this law in a book, until they were finished, 25 That Moses commanded the Levites, which bare the ark of the covenant of the LORD, saying, 26 Take this book of the law, and put it in the side of the ark of the covenant of the LORD your God, that it may be there for a witness against thee. 27 For I know thy rebellion, and thy stiff neck: behold, while I am yet alive with you this day, ye have been rebel-	lious against the LORD; and how much more after my death? 28 Gather unto me all the elders of your tribes, and your officers, that I may speak these words in their ears, and call heaven and earth to record against them. 29 For I know that after my death ye will utterly corrupt *yourselves*, and turn aside from the way which I have commanded you; and evil will befall you in the latter days; because ye will do evil in the sight of the LORD, to provoke him to anger through the work of your hands.	d. The summons was given to assemble all the leaders together for the *Song of Warning & Witness* 1) The purpose: To warn & to testify against them 2) The reasons • Because they would become corrupt after Moses' death: Turn away from the path of the commandments • Because they would suffer disaster & judgment due to their evil behavior

a. The writing of the law was completed by Moses (v.24). God had called him to write *The Book of the Law*, and he was faithful to that call. He wrote exactly as God instructed him.

b. After completing the writing, he issued a strong charge to the Levites, who were responsible for the Ark of the Covenant: they were to be the trustees of the *Book of the Law*. They were to place this book beside the Ark of the Covenant (vv.25-26). Remember, only the two tables of the law, the Ten Commandments, were placed inside the Ark. This particular book was also to be preserved, but it was to be placed beside the Ark, not in it.

---

[1] John Maxwell. *The Preacher's Commentary on Deuteronomy*, p.329.

DEUTERONOMY 31:1-29

c. Moses instructed the Levites to keep the *Book of the Law* as a permanent witness against the people (vv.26-27). This was an important duty, very important. To stress the fact—so they would fully understand the importance of preserving the book—Moses briefly shared the revelation that God had given to Joshua and him.

Moses told the priest that he knew how rebellious and stiff-necked the people were. If they had been that rebellious against the LORD while he, Moses, was alive and with them, how much more would they rebel after he died. Moses knew the spirit of the people: he was an eyewitness of their rebellion. He knew that their hearts were hard, that a spirit of unbelief and grumbling gripped their hearts. He knew that they would rebel in the future.

d. Moses instructed the priests to assemble all the leaders together for the *Song of Warning and Witness*. It was necessary to teach the song to them first so they could help him teach it to the people. He told the priests that the song was an absolute essential in order to warn the people and to serve as a testimony against them. The song was essential...

- because the people would become corrupt after his death. They would turn away from the path of the commandments.
- because the judgment of God would fall upon the people, and they would suffer disaster and judgment due to their evil behavior (v.29).

Thought 1. The way of sin is hard. This is one reason God has given us the Word of God, to warn us against sin. Sin leads to misery and results in death. This was the warning that Moses had to convey to the priests and leaders and, through them, to the people. It is also the warning that must be conveyed to us. This is the strong declaration of Holy Scripture, the very Word of God Himself.

"Tribulation and anguish, upon every soul of man that doeth evil, of the Jew first, and also of the Gentile" (Ro.2:9).

"Destruction and misery *are* in their ways" (Ro.3:16).

"For all have sinned, and come short of the glory of God" (Ro.3:23).

"The wicked man travaileth with pain all *his* days, and the number of years is hidden to the oppressor" (Jb.15:20).

"Fools because of their transgression, and because of their iniquities, are afflicted" (Ps.107:17).

"Good understanding giveth favour: but the way of transgressors *is* hard" (Pr.13:15).

"For all his days *are* sorrows, and his travail grief; yea, his heart taketh not rest in the night. This is also vanity" (Ec.2:23).

"*There is* no peace, saith the LORD, unto the wicked" (Is.48:22).

"But the wicked *are* like the troubled sea, when it cannot rest, whose waters cast up mire and dirt" (Is.57:20).

"The way of peace they know not; and *there is* no judgment in their goings: they have made them crooked paths: whosoever goeth therein shall not know peace" (Is.59:8).

"Destruction cometh; and they shall seek peace, and *there shall be* none" (Eze.7:25).

B. The Song of Moses: A Strong Warning & Witness to God's People & to Those Who Reject Him, 31:30–32:52

1. **The introduction of the song: Moses recited the song, declared the message to all the people**

   30 And Moses spake in the ears of all the congregation of Israel the words of this song, until they were ended.

   CHAPTER 32

   a. The appeal for heaven & earth to hear the words of the song & its message
   b. The appeal for the message to bear fruit, stir people to grow in the LORD—just like the rain or dew falling on grass & tender plants

   Give ear, O ye heavens, and I will speak; and hear, O earth, the words of my mouth.
   2 My doctrine shall drop as the rain, my speech shall distil as the dew, as the small rain upon the tender herb, and as the showers upon the grass:

2. **The name of God is to be proclaimed & the greatness of God praised**
   a. Because God is the Rock
      1) His works are perfect
      2) His ways are just
   b. Because God is faithful: Does no wrong—is just & upright

   3 Because I will publish the name of the LORD: ascribe ye greatness unto our God.
   4 *He is* the Rock, his work *is* perfect: for all his ways *are* judgment: a God of truth and without iniquity, just and right *is* he.

3. **The charge & indictment against Israel (unbelievers): Corruption**
   a. Were blemished (evil)—no longer God's children
   b. Were deceitful & crooked
   c. Were unthankful—foolish & unwise
   d. Were neglectful of God, ignoring & rejecting Him as the Father who created them

   5 They have corrupted themselves, their spot *is* not *the spot* of his children: *they are* a perverse and crooked generation.
   6 Do ye thus requite the LORD, O foolish people and unwise? *is* not he thy father *that* hath bought thee? hath he not made thee, and established thee?

4. **The challenge to remember the goodness of God**

   7 Remember the days of old, consider the years of many generations: ask thy father, and he will show thee; thy elders, and they will tell thee.

   a. God—the Most High—divided & set the boundaries for the people of the earth: All based upon the inheritance needed for His people

   8 When the most High divided to the nations their inheritance, when he separated the sons of Adam, he set the bounds of the people according to the number of the children of Israel.

   b. God chose Israel to be His people, His witnesses upon the earth
   c. God saved His people from a desert land & from the wilderness of this world
      1) God protected & instructed His people: Shielded, taught, & kept them—just like an eagle teaches & protects its young while they are learning to fly

   9 For the LORD's portion *is* his people; Jacob *is* the lot of his inheritance.
   10 He found him in a desert land, and in the waste howling wilderness; he led him about, he instructed him, he kept him as the apple of his eye.
   11 As an eagle stirreth up her nest, fluttereth over her young, spreadeth abroad her wings, taketh them, beareth them on her wings:
   12 *So* the LORD alone did lead him, and *there was* no strange god with him.
   13 He made him ride on the high places of the earth, that he might eat the increase of the fields; and he made him to suck honey out of the rock, and oil out of the flinty rock;
   14 Butter of kine, and milk of sheep, with fat of lambs, and rams of the breed of Bashan, and goats, with the fat of kidneys of wheat; and thou didst drink the pure blood of the grape.

      2) God guided His people—He & He alone, not some false god
   d. God gave victory & provided for His people
      1) Made them ride over the heights of the earth: A picture of victors & conquerors over the enemies of this world
      2) Fed & nourished them: Met their needs & gave them an abundance of food

5. **The tragic response to God's goodness: The people forgot & rejected God**
   a. The people prospered & became affluent, but they kicked against God: Forsook & rejected Him

   15 But Jeshurun waxed fat, and kicked: thou art waxen fat, thou art grown thick, thou art covered *with fatness*; then he forsook God *which* made him, and lightly esteemed the Rock of his salvation.

   b. The people committed idolatry & detestable acts: Made God jealous & angered Him

   16 They provoked him to jealousy with strange *gods*, with abominations provoked they him to anger.

   c. The people sacrificed to demons, not to God: Sacrificed to false gods

   17 They sacrificed unto devils, not to God; to gods whom they knew not, to new *gods that* came newly up, whom your fathers feared not.

   d. The people neglected the Rock who fathered them & forgot the God who gave birth to them

   18 Of the Rock *that* begat thee thou art unmindful, and hast forgotten God that formed thee.

6. **The terrible result of apostasy, of turning away from God: Rejection & judgment**
   a. God saw & became angered
   b. God hid His face from His people (in pain & sorrow): Because they were perverse & unfaithful children

   19 And when the LORD saw *it*, he abhorred *them*, because of the provoking of his sons, and of his daughters.
   20 And he said, I will hide my face from them, I will see what their end *shall be*: for they *are* a very froward generation, children in whom *is* no faith.

   c. God became jealous & angered by their idolatry & false worship
   d. God would turn away from the Israelites & choose other people to be His witnesses (see Ro.11:11-12)

   21 They have moved me to jealousy with *that which is* not God; they have provoked me to anger with their vanities: and I will move them to jealousy with *those which are* not a people; I will provoke them to anger with a foolish nation.

   e. God aroused His wrath to know no limits
      1) To burn to the very realm of hell itself
      2) To consume the earth
      3) To destroy the foundations of the mountains
      4) To heap disasters on His people

   22 For a fire is kindled in mine anger, and shall burn unto the lowest hell, and shall consume the earth with her increase, and set on fire the foundations of the mountains.
   23 I will heap mischiefs upon them; I will spend mine arrows upon them.

- Hunger & famine
- Pestilence, disease, plague, & death
- Wild beasts & poisonous snakes
- War & terror & death

f. God would completely destroy His sinful, disobedient people—but for one thing: The enemy might misunderstand
  1) Might feel they triumphed
  2) Would fail to see God's sovereign hand

7. The major reason God's judgment falls: The people's lack of sense, discernment
  a. A lack of wisdom & understanding in discerning their fate
  b. A failure to discern the presence & power of God
    1) That it was God & God alone who had given victory over their enemies
    2) That the rock (false god) of the enemy is not like our Rock, the LORD God Himself

8. The surety of judgment against the enemies of God's people
  a. Their character comes from Sodom & Gomorrah
    1) Is poisonous & bitter, evil & repulsive
    2) Is deadly
  b. Their judgment is being stored up by God
    1) He will avenge & repay
    2) He will bring the day of disaster & doom upon them

9. The compassion of God for His people
  a. God will show compassion when several things happen
    1) One's strength—self-sufficiency—is gone
    2) One acknowledges his sin, his trust in false gods or rocks
      - False help

24 *They shall be* burnt with hunger, and devoured with burning heat, and with bitter destruction: I will also send the teeth of beasts upon them, with the poison of serpents of the dust.
25 The sword without, and terror within, shall destroy both the young man and the virgin, the suckling *also* with the man of gray hairs.
26 I said, I would scatter them into corners, I would make the remembrance of them to cease from among men:
27 Were it not that I feared the wrath of the enemy, lest their adversaries should behave themselves strangely, *and* lest they should say, Our hand *is* high, and the LORD hath not done all this.
28 For they *are* a nation void of counsel, neither *is there any* understanding in them.
29 O that they were wise, *that* they understood this, *that* they would consider their latter end!
30 How should one chase a thousand, and two put ten thousand to flight, except their Rock had sold them, and the LORD had shut them up?
31 For their rock *is* not as our Rock, even our enemies themselves *being* judges.
32 For their vine *is* of the vine of Sodom, and of the fields of Gomorrah: their grapes *are* grapes of gall, their clusters *are* bitter:
33 Their wine *is* the poison of dragons, and the cruel venom of asps.
34 *Is* not this laid up in store with me, *and* sealed up among my treasures?
35 To me *belongeth* vengeance, and recompence; their foot shall slide in *due* time: for the day of their calamity *is* at hand, and the things that shall come upon them make haste.
36 For the LORD shall judge his people, and repent himself for his servants, when he seeth that *their* power is gone, and *there is* none shut up, or left.
37 And he shall say, Where *are* their gods, *their* rock in whom they trusted,
38 Which did eat the fat of their sacrifices, *and* drank the wine of their drink offerings? let them rise up and help you, *and* be your protection.
39 See now that I, *even* I, *am* he, and *there is* no god with me: I kill, and I make alive; I wound, and I heal: neither *is there any* that can deliver out of my hand.
40 For I lift up my hand to heaven, and say, I live for ever.
41 If I whet my glittering sword, and mine hand take hold on judgment; I will render vengeance to mine enemies, and will reward them that hate me.
42 I will make mine arrows drunk with blood, and my sword shall devour flesh; *and that* with the blood of the slain and of the captives, from the beginning of revenges upon the enemy.
43 Rejoice, O ye nations, *with* his people: for he will avenge the blood of his servants, and will render vengeance to his adversaries, and will be merciful unto his land, *and* to his people.
44 And Moses came and spake all the words of this song in the ears of the people, he, and Hoshea the son of Nun.
45 And Moses made an end of speaking all these words to all Israel:
46 And he said unto them, Set your hearts unto all the words which I testify among you this day, which ye shall command your children to observe to do, all the words of this law.
47 For it *is* not a vain thing for you; because it *is* your life: and through this thing ye shall prolong *your* days in the land, whither ye go over Jordan to possess it.
48 And the LORD spake unto Moses that selfsame day, saying,
49 Get thee up into this mountain Abarim, *unto* mount Nebo, which *is* in the land of Moab, that *is* over against Jericho; and behold the land of Canaan, which I give unto the children of Israel for a possession:
50 And die in the mount whither thou goest up, and be gathered unto thy people; as

- False protection, shelter, refuge

3) One sees the only living & true God: That He alone holds the power of life & death, sickness & health, victory & deliverance

b. God will show compassion for His people by executing justice upon their enemies
  1) He will take the position of a warrior & execute judgment upon His enemies—those who reject & hate Him
  2) He will demonstrate His superior strength & execute full & complete judgment
  3) He will spare no one, not slave nor leader
  4) He will cause the nations to rejoice with His people
    - Because He will avenge them
    - Because He will make atonement for them & their land

10. The message of the song & of the law must be heeded
  a. Moses was faithful to God's instructions: He finished sharing the warning & witness of the song (31:19)
  b. Moses issued a strong charge: You must set your heart upon the law of God, all His Words, all His commandments
    1) So you may teach your children to obey
    2) So you may know they are not idle words but your life
    3) So you may live long in the promised land

11. The immediate example of God's compassion & judgment
  a. God's compassion: Instructed His dear servant Moses to climb to the peak of Mt. Nebo & look out across the promised land
  b. God's judgment or chastisement: Moses was to die on the mountain—be gathered

to his people—just as Aaron had 1) Because they had disobeyed God 2) Because they did not honor God as holy in the sight of the people (see	Aaron thy brother died in mount Hor, and was gathered unto his people: 51 Because ye trespassed against me among the children of Israel at the waters of Meribah-Kadesh, in the wilderness of Zin; because	ye sanctified me not in the midst of the children of Israel. 52 Yet thou shalt see the land before *thee*; but thou shalt not go thither unto the land which I give the children of Israel.	Nu.20:7-13) c. God's compassion & judgment are clearly demonstrated: God's dear servant was allowed to view the promised land, but he was barred from experiencing the victory & rest of the land

DIVISION VI

THE FINAL ACTS AND DEATH OF MOSES, GOD'S AGED SERVANT: REMEMBER THE ENCOURAGEMENT AND THE WARNING OF GOD, 31:1–34:12

B. **The Song of Moses: A Strong Warning and Witness to God's People and to Those Who Reject Him, 31:30–32:52**

(31:30-32:52) **Introduction**: a strong warning and witness to God's people and to those who reject Him—this is the message of this Scripture. Almost the entire chapter—43 verses to be exact—is what is known as "the song of Moses." This was a song written by Moses that was to be learned and sung by the people. It was not just a song for the people of Moses' day but one that was to be passed down from generation to generation, passed down to be sung so that its message would stand as a permanent warning. The message is striking:

⇒ It covers the commitment of the people to the covenant and commandments of God and their failure to keep the covenant and commandments.
⇒ It also covers a prediction about their future—their future failure and their restoration and return to Palestine or the promised land.

The last restoration of Israel occurred in 1948, when the Jew returned to Palestine. There were other restorations prior to 1948, and there may be more restorations yet to occur in coming centuries if the LORD tarries. But the message of the song is the same: it is a strong warning to any people who turn away from God, disobeying His commandments and following false idols and false worship. They will all suffer the hand of God's judgment. But if they return to their senses and repent, God will forgive their sins and restore them back into His favor. This is the great subject of this most important passage of Scripture: *The Song of Moses: A Strong Warning and Witness to God's People and to Those Who Reject Him*, 31:30–32:52.

1. The introduction of the song: Moses recited the song, declared the message to all the people (31:30–32:2).
2. The name of God is to be proclaimed and the greatness of God praised (32:3-4).
3. The charge and indictment against Israel (unbelievers): Corruption (32:5-6).
4. The challenge to remember the goodness of God (32:7-14).
5. The tragic response to God's goodness: the people forgot and rejected God (32:15-18).
6. The terrible result of apostasy, of turning away from God: rejection and judgment (32:19-27).
7. The major reason God's judgment falls: the people's lack of sense, discernment (32:28-31).
8. The surety of judgment against the enemies of God's people (32:32-35).
9. The compassion of God for His people (32:36-43).
10. The message of the song and of the law must be heeded (32:44-47).
11. The immediate example of God's compassion and judgment (32:48-52).

1 (31:30–32:2) **Growth, Spiritual—Message, Purpose of—Song, of Moses—Heaven and Earth, Appeal to—Witnesses, Heaven and Earth**: the introduction of the song was given by Moses himself. It was he who personally recited the song and shared the message with the people. Remember that he had already taught the song to all the elders or leaders or officials of the tribes so that they could help teach the song to the people (De.31:28). Note the Scripture and outline:

OUTLINE	SCRIPTURE	SCRIPTURE	OUTLINE
1. **The introduction of the song: Moses recited the song, declared the message to all the people** a. The appeal for heaven &	30 And Moses spake in the ears of all the congregation of Israel the words of this song, until they were ended. **CHAPTER 32** Give ear, O ye heavens, and I	will speak; and hear, O earth, the words of my mouth. 2 My doctrine shall drop as the rain, my speech shall distil as the dew, as the small rain upon the tender herb, and as the showers upon the grass:	earth to hear the words of the song & its message b. The appeal for the message to bear fruit, stir people to grow in the LORD—just like the rain or dew falling on grass & tender plants

The first line of the song was an appeal for heaven and earth to hear the words and the message of the song (v.1). Keep in mind that the song was being taught to the people so that they could sing it down through the coming generations. They were to call upon heaven and earth to act as witnesses to their testimony, to what they were saying. Heaven and earth would see and be silent witnesses both to the commitment and the failures of God's people. When God's people renewed their commitment and covenant with God, heaven and earth would witness their rededication. But when God's people disobeyed God by breaking His covenant and commandments, heaven and earth would stand in silent condemnation of their lack of discernment. The people were to appeal for the message of the song to bear fruit, to stir all the people to grow in the LORD (v.2). The people were appealing for the words of the song to penetrate their lives, making them grow—just like the rain or dew falls and penetrates the grass and tender plants, making them grow.

Thought 1. Spiritual growth is to be the objective of the believer. We must grow in the LORD. We must seek to be like Christ, to be conformed to His image more and more. We are either moving forward in the LORD or moving backward, either living righteously or living wickedly. We are either maturing in the LORD or else our growth has been stymied. Heaven and earth see and bear witness as to our growth.

But this is not all. Our friends and neighbors see what kind of lives we are living, whether we are growing in the LORD or not growing, whether we are living righteously or wickedly. All of heaven—God, angels, and our loved ones—all see and bear witness to our spiritual growth. The call of Scripture is for us to grow in the LORD, for us to be conformed more and more to His image.

"I beseech you therefore, brethren, by the mercies of God, that ye present your bodies a living sacrifice, holy, acceptable unto God, *which is* your reasonable service. And be not conformed to this world: but be ye transformed by the renewing of your mind, that ye may prove what is that good, and acceptable, and perfect, will of God" (Ro.12:1-2).

"But we all, with open face beholding as in a glass the glory of the LORD, are changed into the same image from glory to glory, *even* as by the Spirit of the LORD" (2 Co.3:18).

"That we *henceforth* be no more children, tossed to and fro, and carried about with every wind of doctrine, by the sleight of men, *and* cunning craftiness, whereby they lie in wait to deceive; But speaking the truth in love, may grow up into him in all things, which is the head, *even* Christ" (Ep.4:14-15).

"And the LORD make you to increase and abound in love one toward another, and toward all *men*, even as we *do* toward you" (1 Th.3:12).

"Therefore leaving the principles of the doctrine of Christ, let us go on unto perfection; not laying again the foundation of repentance from dead works, and of faith toward God" (He.6:1).

"As newborn babes, desire the sincere milk of the word, that ye may grow thereby: If so be ye have tasted that the LORD *is* gracious" (1 Pe.2:2-3).

"But grow in grace, and *in* the knowledge of our LORD and Saviour Jesus Christ. To him *be* glory both now and for ever. Amen" (2 Pe.3:18).

2 (32:3-4) **God, Name of—God, Greatness of—Praise, of God—Warning, of God—Rock, Title of God**: the name of God is to be proclaimed and the greatness of God praised. Note that the singer of the song praises God and then calls upon others to proclaim the name and greatness of God. Two clear reasons are given for praising God:

OUTLINE	SCRIPTURE
2. The name of God is to be proclaimed & the greatness of God praised	3 Because I will publish the name of the LORD: ascribe ye greatness unto our God.
a. Because God is the Rock	4 *He is* the Rock, his work *is* perfect: for all his ways *are* judgment: a God of truth and without iniquity, just and right *is* he.
1) His works are perfect	
2) His ways are just	
b. Because God is faithful: Does no wrong—is just & upright	

a. God is to be praised because He is the Rock (v.4). This is a title that is often ascribed to God throughout Scripture, in particular the Psalms. It is a title of God that has been set to the music of the church in such songs as *Rock of Ages* and *The Solid Rock*. The picture of a large rock is that of being solid, stable, permanent, immovable, unchangeable. A solid rock is a picture of a sure foundation. As the Rock, God's works are perfect and His ways just.

b. God is to be praised because He is faithful (v.4). His faithfulness is as solid as a rock: He does no wrong; He is just and upright in all His dealings.

Thought 1. The name of God is to be proclaimed and the greatness of God praised. All because He is the *Rock of ages* and *the solid Rock* upon which we can stand and live a full and victorious life.

"Therefore whosoever heareth these sayings of mine, and doeth them, I will liken him unto a wise man, which built his house upon a rock: And the rain descended, and the floods came, and the winds blew, and beat upon that house; and it fell not: for it was founded upon a rock. And every one that heareth these sayings of mine, and doeth them not, shall be likened unto a foolish man, which built his house upon the sand: And the rain descended, and the floods came, and the winds blew, and beat upon that house; and it fell: and great was the fall of it" (Mt.7:24-27).

"For other foundation can no man lay than that is laid, which is Jesus Christ" (1 Co.3:11).

"Laying up in store for themselves a good foundation against the time to come, that they may lay hold on eternal life" (1 Ti.6:19).

"Nevertheless the foundation of God standeth sure, having this seal, The LORD knoweth them that are his. And, Let every one that nameth the name of Christ depart from iniquity" (2 Ti.2:19).

"*He is* the Rock, his work *is* perfect: for all his ways *are* judgment: a God of truth and without iniquity, just and right *is* he" (De.32:4).

"For their rock *is* not as our Rock, even our enemies themselves *being* judges" (De.32:31).

"*There is* none holy as the LORD: for *there is* none beside thee: neither *is there* any rock like our God" (1 S.2:2).

"The LORD liveth; and blessed *be* my rock; and exalted be the God of the rock of my salvation" (2 S.22:47).

"For who *is* God save the LORD? or who *is* a rock save our God" (Ps.18:31).

"Unto thee will I cry, O LORD my rock; be not silent to me: lest, *if* thou be silent to me, I become like them that go down into the pit" (Ps.28:1).

"He only *is* my rock and my salvation; *he is* my defence; I shall not be greatly moved" (Ps.62:2).

"But the LORD is my defence; and my God *is* the rock of my refuge" (Ps.94:22).

"Therefore thus saith the LORD GOD, Behold, I lay in Zion for a foundation a stone, a tried stone, a precious corner *stone*, a sure foundation: he that believeth shall not make haste" (Is.28:16).

Thought 2. God is faithful. He fulfills every promise He has ever made, never breaking a single promise. He does no wrong; He is upright and just.

"God *is* faithful, by whom ye were called unto the fellowship of his Son Jesus Christ our LORD" (1 Co.1:9).

"But the LORD is faithful, who shall stablish you, and keep *you* from evil" (2 Th.3:3).

"If we believe not, *yet* he abideth faithful: he cannot deny himself" (2 Ti.2:13).

"Wherein God, willing more abundantly to show unto the heirs of promise the immutability of his counsel, confirmed *it* by an oath: That by two immutable things, in which *it was* impossible for God to lie, we might have a strong consolation, who have fled for refuge to lay hold upon the hope set before us" (He.6:17-18).

"Let us hold fast the profession of *our* faith without wavering; (for he is faithful that promised" (He.10:23).

"Know therefore that the LORD thy God, he *is* God, the faithful God, which keepeth covenant and mercy with them that love him and keep his commandments to a thousand generations" (De.7:9).

"Blessed *be* the LORD, that hath given rest unto his people Israel, according to all that he promised: there hath not failed one word of all his good promise, which he promised by the hand of Moses his servant" (1 K.8:56).

"Thy mercy, O LORD, *is* in the heavens; *and* thy faithfulness *reacheth* unto the clouds" (Ps.36:5).

"I will sing of the mercies of the LORD for ever: with my mouth will I make known thy faithfulness to all generations" (Ps.89:1).

3 (32:5-6) **Charge, Against Israel—Israel, Indictment Against—Corruption, of Israel—Israel, Sin of:** there was the charge and indictment against Israel, that of corruption. This is a high charge against the Israelites, a charge that their character was the exact opposite of God *the solid Rock.* Note how corrupt the Israelites had become:

OUTLINE	SCRIPTURE
3. The charge & indictment against Israel (unbelievers): Corruption a. Were blemished (evil)—no longer God's children b. Were deceitful & crooked c. Were unthankful—foolish & unwise d. Were neglectful of God, ignoring & rejecting Him as the Father who created them	5 They have corrupted themselves, their spot *is* not *the spot* of his children: they *are* a perverse and crooked generation. 6 Do ye thus requite the LORD, O foolish people and unwise? *is* not he thy father *that* hath bought thee? hath he not made thee, and established thee?

a. The Israelites had become spotted, blemished, corrupted (v.5). They had become so corrupted that they were no longer the children of God.

b. The Israelites had become perverse or deceitful, a crooked or twisted generation of people (v.5).

c. The Israelites were an unthankful people (v.6). They were dealing with the LORD as an evil people, living corrupt lives. They were acting in a foolish and unwise manner.

d. The Israelites were neglectful of God, ignoring and rejecting Him as the Father who created them (v.6). Note that the word *bought* or *creator* or *created* (qanah) is not the more familiar Hebrew word used for *created* (bara), which is used in Genesis 1:1. This is the same word qanah that is used in Exodus 15:16 in the song that celebrated the Israelites' salvation from Egypt. Thus the reference to the Father being the One who created or bought the Israelites can refer to God as the Creator or to God as the One who saved the Israelites to be His people.

Thought 1. The Israelites became a sinful and corrupt people. But Scripture declares that we are all sinners, short of the glory of God. Sin is universal: the charge and indictment of corruption stands against every human being. We are all guilty of being spotted, blemished, and corrupted by evil. At some time, we have all been deceitful and crooked and unthankful toward God, acting in a foolish or unwise fashion. We have all neglected God, ignoring and rejecting Him as the Father who created us.

"Because that, when they knew God, they glorified *him* not as God, neither were thankful; but became vain in their imaginations, and their foolish heart was darkened" (Ro.1:21).

"For all have sinned, and come short of the glory of God" (Ro.3:23).

"If we say that we have no sin, we deceive ourselves, and the truth is not in us" (1 Jn.1:8).

"And GOD saw that the wickedness of man *was* great in the earth, and *that* every imagination of the thoughts of his heart *was* only evil continually" (Ge.6:5).

"Every one of them is gone back: they are altogether become filthy; *there is* none that doeth good, no, not one" (Ps.53:3).

"Who can say, I have made my heart clean, I am pure from my sin" (Pr.20:9).

"All we like sheep have gone astray; we have turned every one to his own way; and the LORD hath laid on him the iniquity of us all" (Is.53:6).

"But we are all as an unclean *thing*, and all our righteousnesses *are* as filthy rags; and we all do fade as a leaf; and our iniquities, like the wind, have taken us away" (Is.64:6).

4 (32:7-14) **Goodness, of God—God, Goodness of—Challenge, Duty**: there was the challenge to remember the goodness of God. This is a challenge to reflect on the past, to learn from the lessons of history. Note that a person is encouraged to ask his father and the elders to explain the lessons of past history to them.

OUTLINE	SCRIPTURE	SCRIPTURE	OUTLINE
4. The challenge to remember the goodness of God	7 Remember the days of old, consider the years of many generations: ask thy father, and he will show thee; thy elders, and they will tell thee.	11 As an eagle stirreth up her nest, fluttereth over her young, spreadeth abroad her wings, taketh them, beareth them on her wings:	like an eagle teaches & protects its young while they are learning to fly
a. God—the Most High—divided & set the boundaries for the people of the earth: All based upon the inheritance needed for His people	8 When the most High divided to the nations their inheritance, when he separated the sons of Adam, he set the bounds of the people according to the number of the children of Israel.	12 *So* the LORD alone did lead him, and *there was* no strange god with him. 13 He made him ride on the high places of the earth, that he might eat the increase of the fields; and he made him to suck honey out of the rock, and oil out of the flinty rock;	2) God guided His people—He & He alone, not some false god d. God gave victory & provided for His people 1) Made them ride over the heights of the earth: A picture of victors & conquerors over the enemies of this world
b. God chose Israel to be His people, His witnesses upon the earth	9 For the LORD'S portion *is* his people; Jacob *is* the lot of his inheritance.		
c. God saved His people from a desert land & from the wilderness of this world 1) God protected & instructed His people: Shielded, taught, & kept them—just	10 He found him in a desert land, and in the waste howling wilderness; he led him about, he instructed him, he kept him as the apple of his eye.	14 Butter of kine, and milk of sheep, with fat of lambs, and rams of the breed of Bashan, and goats, with the fat of kidneys of wheat; and thou didst drink the pure blood of the grape.	2) Fed & nourished them: Met their needs & gave them an abundance of food

a. A person is to remember that God, the Most High, divided and set the boundaries for the people of the earth (v.8). Note that God based the boundaries of races upon the inheritance needed for His people, the Israelites. It should be noted that the exact phrase *the children [or sons] of Israel* in the Hebrew is uncertain. It could be translated as *the sons of God*, referring to angelic beings or the divine counsel of the LORD consisting of *holy ones*.[1]

b. A person was to remember that God chose Israel to be His people, His inheritance, His witnesses upon the earth (v.9).

c. A person was to remember that God saved His people from a desert land and from the wilderness of this world (vv.10-12). The desert land is a picture of God saving His people from the slavery of Egypt. The barren wasteland and howling wilderness is a picture of the *wilderness wanderings*. A person was to remember...

- that God protected and instructed His people in saving them from Egypt and through the wilderness wanderings: He shielded, taught, and kept them—just like an eagle teaches and protects its young while they are learning to fly (vv.10-11).
- that God guided His people, He and He alone, not some false god (v.12).

---

[1] Peter C. Craigie. *The Book of Deuteronomy*, p.379.

d. A person was to remember that God gave victory and provided for His people (vv.13-14). Note that the focus now switches to the future, to the people's being in the promised land. In just a few days, when the people cross the Jordan River and enter the promised land, God will give them victory over the enemies who confront them, and He will provide for them.
    1) God will make His people ride over the heights of the earth (v.13). This is a picture of God's people being victors and conquerors over the enemies of this world, over all the enemies who try to keep them out of the promised land.
    2) God will feed and nourish His people (v.14). Note the statement is actually made from the position of the future, as though God had already provided for His people. Keep in mind that the song was to be sung down through the coming generations; therefore, many of the people would have already experienced the fruitfulness of the promised land and the wonderful provision of God. God met their needs and gave them an abundance of food. As stated, this is a prediction, but it is a prediction that will look back upon the past and see God's wonderful provision.

Thought 1. The goodness of God is to be remembered and praised. God is good to His people down through all generations. God is good to us today. Note what God has done for us:
⇒ God has saved us to be His people, His very special possession, His treasured possession—His witnesses upon the earth.
⇒ God is leading us through the wilderness of this world to the promised land of heaven. He is protecting and instructing us, shielding, teaching, and keeping us—just like an eagle teaches and protects its young while they are learning to fly.
⇒ God and God alone is guiding us, not some false god.
⇒ God is giving us a full and victorious life, providing all good things for us. And He is giving us victory over all the enemies of this world.

The goodness of God is beyond imagination and beyond description.

> "Or despisest thou the riches of his goodness and forbearance and longsuffering; not knowing that the goodness of God leadeth thee to repentance" (Ro.2:4).
> "So that we may boldly say, The LORD *is* my helper, and I will not fear what man shall do unto me" (He.13:6).
> "Show thy marvellous lovingkindness, O thou that savest by thy right hand them which put their trust *in thee* from those that rise up *against them*" (Ps.17:7).
> "Good and upright *is* the LORD: therefore will he teach sinners in the way" (Ps.25:8).
> "For thy lovingkindness *is* before mine eyes: and I have walked in thy truth" (Ps.26:3).
> "The LORD *is* my strength and my shield; my heart trusted in him, and I am helped: therefore my heart greatly rejoiceth; and with my song will I praise him" (Ps.28:7).
> "He loveth righteousness and judgment: the earth is full of the goodness of the LORD" (Ps.33:5).
> "O taste and see that the LORD *is* good: blessed *is* the man *that* trusteth in him" (Ps.34:8).
> "But I *am* poor and needy; *yet* the LORD thinketh upon me: thou *art* my help and my deliverer; make no tarrying, O my God" (Ps.40:17).
> "Because thy lovingkindness *is* better than life, my lips shall praise thee" (Ps.63:3).
> "Fear thou not; for I *am* with thee: be not dismayed; for I *am* thy God: I will strengthen thee; yea, I will help thee; yea, I will uphold thee with the right hand of my righteousness" (Is.41:10).
> "Behold, the LORD GOD will help me; who *is* he *that* shall condemn me? lo, they all shall wax old as a garment; the moth shall eat them up" (Is.50:9).
> "I will mention the lovingkindnesses of the LORD, *and* the praises of the LORD, according to all that the LORD hath bestowed on us, and the great goodness toward the house of Israel, which he hath bestowed on them according to his mercies, and according to the multitude of his lovingkindnesses" (Is.63:7).
> "The LORD hath appeared of old unto me, *saying*, Yea, I have loved thee with an everlasting love: therefore with lovingkindness have I drawn thee" (Je.31:3).
> "Thou showest lovingkindness unto thousands, and recompensest the iniquity of the fathers into the bosom of their children after them: the Great, the Mighty God, the LORD of hosts, *is* his name" (Je.32:18).
> "And I will betroth thee unto me for ever; yea, I will betroth thee unto me in righteousness, and in judgment, and in lovingkindness, and in mercies" (Ho.2:19).
> "The LORD *is* good, a strong hold in the day of trouble; and he knoweth them that trust in him" (Na.1:7).

5 (32:15-18) **Rejection, of God—Apostasy—Forgetting, of God—Response, Rejection of God**: there was the tragic response to God's goodness. The people would forget and reject God. Keep in mind that this is a prediction of the future, a prophecy of the apostasy of the Israelites once they had settled in the promised land. This song of Moses is a warning to the people, a warning that they must heed the Word of God and stay faithful to Him. They must guard their lives and not forget Him. Note the word *Jeshurun*: it was a favored name that means *uprighteousness*.

DEUTERONOMY 31:30–32:52

OUTLINE	SCRIPTURE	SCRIPTURE	OUTLINE
5. The tragic response to God's goodness: The people forgot & rejected God a. The people prospered & became affluent, but they kicked against God: Forsook & rejected Him b. The people committed idolatry & detestable acts: Made God jealous & angered Him	15 But Jeshurun waxed fat, and kicked: thou art waxen fat, thou art grown thick, thou art covered *with fatness*; then he forsook God *which* made him, and lightly esteemed the Rock of his salvation. 16 They provoked him to jealousy with strange *gods*, with abominations provoked	they him to anger. 17 They sacrificed unto devils, not to God; to gods whom they knew not, to new *gods that* came newly up, whom your fathers feared not. 18 Of the Rock *that* begat thee thou art unmindful, and hast forgotten God that formed thee.	c. The people sacrificed to demons, not to God: Sacrificed to false gods d. The people neglected the Rock who fathered them & forgot the God who gave birth to them

a. It is predicted that the people will prosper and become affluent, but they will kick against God (v.15). They will forsake and reject Him. Note exactly who it is they forsake: the Creator, the God who created them and the Rock of their salvation. What a terrible indictment! What kind of life can a person expect—what kind of future and destiny can a person expect—if he rejects the Creator of the universe and the Rock of salvation?

b. The people would commit idolatry and detestable acts (v.16). They would turn to the false gods and false worship of their neighbors. The result would be catastrophic and tragic: they would arrows the jealousy of God and provoke Him to anger.

c. The people would sacrifice to demons, not to God (v.17). They would actually serve false gods.

d. The people would neglect the Rock who fathered them and forget the God who gave birth to them (v.18). God had given birth to His people, become a father to them, treating them as His sons and daughters; but despite His fatherly relationship to them, they would neglect and desert Him. They would commit apostasy, what amounted to high treason, against God, the Rock of their salvation.

Thought 1. This is a strong warning to us: we must not forget and reject God. We must not kick against Him nor forsake Him. We must not commit apostasy against God.

"Holding faith, and a good conscience; which some having put away concerning faith have made shipwreck" (1 Ti.1:19).

"Now the Spirit speaketh expressly, that in the latter times some shall depart from the faith, giving heed to seducing spirits, and doctrines of devils" (1 Ti.4:1).

"For the time will come when they will not endure sound doctrine; but after their own lusts shall they heap to themselves teachers, having itching ears; And they shall turn away *their* ears from the truth, and shall be turned unto fables" (2 Ti.4:3-4).

"For Demas hath forsaken me, having loved this present world, and is departed unto Thessalonica; Crescens to Galatia, Titus unto Dalmatia" (2 Ti.4:10).

"Harden not your hearts, as in the provocation, in the day of temptation in the wilderness: When your fathers tempted me, proved me, and saw my works forty years. Wherefore I was grieved with that generation, and said, They do alway err in *their* heart; and they have not known my ways. So I sware in my wrath, They shall not enter into my rest.) Take heed, brethren, lest there be in any of you an evil heart of unbelief, in departing from the living God" (He.3:8-12).

"For *it is* impossible for those who were once enlightened, and have tasted of the heavenly gift, and were made partakers of the Holy Ghost, And have tasted the good word of God, and the powers of the world to come, If they shall fall away, to renew them again unto repentance; seeing they crucify to themselves the Son of God afresh, and put *him* to an open shame" (He.6:4-6).

"Having eyes full of adultery, and that cannot cease from sin; beguiling unstable souls: an heart they have exercised with covetous practices; cursed children: Which have forsaken the right way, and are gone astray, following the way of Balaam *the son* of Bosor, who loved the wages of unrighteousness; But was rebuked for his iniquity: the dumb ass speaking with man's voice forbad the madness of the prophet. These are wells without water, clouds that are carried with a tempest; to whom the mist of darkness is reserved for ever" (2 Pe.2:14-17).

"Ye therefore, beloved, seeing ye know *these things* before, beware lest ye also, being led away with the error of the wicked, fall from your own stedfastness" (2 Pe.3:17).

"Little children, it is the last time: and as ye have heard that antichrist shall come, even now are there many antichrists; whereby we know that it is the last time. They went out from us, but they were not of us; for if they had been of us, they would *no doubt* have continued with us: but *they went out*, that they might be made manifest that they were not all of us" (1 Jn.2:18-19).

"Nevertheless they were disobedient, and rebelled against thee, and cast thy law behind their backs, and slew thy prophets which testified against them to turn them to thee, and they wrought great provocations" (Ne.9:26).

6 (32:19-27) **Judgment, Described—Israel, Judgment upon—Apostasy, Result of—Rejection, of God, Result of:** there was the terrible result of apostasy, of turning away from God. The Israelites were to be rejected and suffer the judgment of God. Again, this is a prophecy, a prediction of the terrible apostasy of the Israelites that was to take place sometime in the future. The Scripture speaks as though the events were taking place or had already.

DEUTERONOMY 31:30–32:52

OUTLINE	SCRIPTURE	SCRIPTURE	OUTLINE
6. The terrible result of apostasy, of turning away from God: Rejection & judgment a. God saw & became angered b. God hid His face from His people (in pain & sorrow): Because they were perverse & unfaithful children c. God became jealous & angered by their idolatry & false worship d. God would turn away from the Israelites & choose other people to be His witnesses (see Ro.11:11-12) e. God aroused His wrath to know no limits 1) To burn to the very realm of hell itself 2) To consume the earth 3) To destroy the foundations of the mountains	19 And when the LORD saw it, he abhorred them, because of the provoking of his sons, and of his daughters. 20 And he said, I will hide my face from them, I will see what their end shall be: for they are a very froward generation, children in whom is no faith. 21 They have moved me to jealousy with that which is not God; they have provoked me to anger with their vanities: and I will move them to jealousy with those which are not a people; I will provoke them to anger with a foolish nation. 22 For a fire is kindled in mine anger, and shall burn unto the lowest hell, and shall consume the earth with her increase, and set on fire the foundations of the mountains.	23 I will heap mischiefs upon them; I will spend mine arrows upon them. 24 They shall be burnt with hunger, and devoured with burning heat, and with bitter destruction: I will also send the teeth of beasts upon them, with the poison of serpents of the dust. 25 The sword without, and terror within, shall destroy both the young man and the virgin, the suckling also with the man of gray hairs. 26 I said, I would scatter them into corners, I would make the remembrance of them to cease from among men: 27 Were it not that I feared the wrath of the enemy, lest their adversaries should behave themselves strangely, and lest they should say, Our hand is high, and the LORD hath not done all this.	4) To heap disasters on His people • Hunger & famine • Pestilence, disease, plague, & death • Wild beasts & poisonous snakes • War & terror & death f. God would completely destroy His sinful, disobedient people—but for one thing: The enemy might misunderstand 1) Might feel they triumphed 2) Would fail to see God's sovereign hand

a. God saw the repulsive sin and apostasy of His people, and His anger was aroused (v.19). Note exactly what aroused His anger: these were His sons and daughters, the very people whom He had created and adopted as His family upon the earth. They were to be His special people and treasured possession who were to be His witnesses to the immoral and wicked people of the world. But here they were committing apostasy, committing terrible evil against Him. They were breaking the covenant they had made, the promise that they would obey Him. Instead of obeying, they rejected Him. Consequently, God had no choice; He had to chastise them by rejecting them.

b. God hid His face from His people (v.20). This is a picture of pain and sorrow, revealing not only the anger of God, but also the love of God for His people. As a loving Father, it was difficult to look upon the sin and shame of His children who were so unfaithful.

c. God became jealous and angry at their idolatry and false worship (v.21). Note that idolatry and false worship are totally worthless, useless, empty, and foolish.

d. God will turn away from the Israelites and choose other people to be His witnesses (v.21; see Ro.11:11-12).

e. God aroused His wrath to know no limits (vv.22-25). This is a graphic description of the judgment of God that was to fall upon the Israelites, a warning that stands to all generations of people down through the centuries.
  1) The judgment of God will burn to the very realm of death and hell itself (v.22).
  2) The judgment of God will consume the earth with all its harvest (v.22).
  3) The judgment of God will destroy the very foundations of the mountains themselves. Although the mountains seem to be immovable, seem to be that part of the earth that cannot be shaken—they will be shaken. Even their very foundations will be set on fire. The picture is that of earthquake after earthquake, of one volcanic eruption after another.
  4) The judgment of God will heap disasters upon His people, disasters such as...
    • hunger and famine (vv.23-24)
    • pestilence, disease, plagues, and death
    • wild beasts and poisonous snakes
    • war, terror, and death (v.25)

f. God would completely destroy His sinful, disobedient people—but for one thing: the enemy might misunderstand (vv.26-27). They might begin to feel that their own military power had triumphed over the Israelites, failing to see that it was God's sovereign hand of judgment that had destroyed them. One of the purposes for the song was to stand as a witness and testimony, a warning of God's judgment upon sin and evil and upon those who reject Him. Consequently, God could do nothing that would keep the lesson of the song from making its intended impact. The people of the world were to stand warned: judgment would fall upon the heads of any people who rejected Him. Moreover, the honor of God was at stake. God is love, but He is also just. It was the execution of His justice that destroyed the Israelites, exiling them from the promised land. Everyone was to know and learn this lesson; therefore, God could not completely destroy His sinful, disobedient people. He had to save and preserve a remnant to later bring them back into the land. The mighty hand of God at work in both judgment and forgiveness or restoration had to be seen and witnessed by the world. Note how this was fulfilled before the very eyes of the world in the generations from the date of this prophecy up until the present. The Israelites did witness the utter destruction of their land under the Assyrians, the Babylonians, and the Romans. But the world has also witnessed the restoration of the Israelites in their return to Palestine in 1948. (See Introduction to this outline, De.31:30–32:52, for more discussion.)

DEUTERONOMY 31:30–32:52

Thought 1. The judgment of God falls upon all who reject Him. This is the clear declaration of Holy Scripture.

"And before him shall be gathered all nations: and he shall separate them one from another, as a shepherd divideth *his* sheep from the goats: And he shall set the sheep on his right hand, but the goats on the left....Then shall he say also unto them on the left hand, Depart from me, ye cursed, into everlasting fire, prepared for the devil and his angels" (Mt.25:32-33, 41).

"He that believeth on him is not condemned: but he that believeth not is condemned already, because he hath not believed in the name of the only begotten Son of God" (Jn.3:18).

"Because he hath appointed a day, in the which he will judge the world in righteousness by *that* man whom he hath ordained; *whereof* he hath given assurance unto all *men,* in that he hath raised him from the dead" (Ac.17:31).

"In the day when God shall judge the secrets of men by Jesus Christ according to my gospel" (Ro.2:16).

"So then every one of us shall give account of himself to God" (Ro.14:12).

"For we must all appear before the judgment seat of Christ; that every one may receive the things *done* in *his* body, according to that he hath done, whether *it be* good or bad" (2 Co.5:10).

"And to you who are troubled rest with us, when the LORD Jesus shall be revealed from heaven with his mighty angels, In flaming fire taking vengeance on them that know not God, and that obey not the gospel of our Lord Jesus Christ: Who shall be punished with everlasting destruction from the presence of the LORD, and from the glory of his power" (2 Th.1:7-9).

"And I saw the dead, small and great, stand before God; and the books were opened: and another book was opened, which is *the book* of life: and the dead were judged out of those things which were written in the books, according to their works" (Re.20:12).

"And I will execute vengeance in anger and fury upon the heathen, such as they have not heard" (Mi.5:15).

"And I will execute great vengeance upon them with furious rebukes; and they shall know that I *am* the LORD, when I shall lay my vengeance upon them" (Eze.25:17).

7 (32:28-31) **Judgment, Caused by—Discernment, Lack of, Results**: there was the major reason why God's judgment fell upon His people. His people simply lacked sense, discernment. Note the Scripture and outline:

OUTLINE	SCRIPTURE	SCRIPTURE	OUTLINE
7. The major reason God's judgment falls: The people's lack of sense, discernment a. A lack of wisdom & understanding in discerning their fate b. A failure to discern the pres-	28 For they *are* a nation void of counsel, neither *is there any* understanding in them. 29 O that they were wise, *that* they understood this, *that* they would consider their latter end! 30 How should one chase a	thousand, and two put ten thousand to flight, except their Rock had sold them, and the LORD had shut them up? 31 For their rock *is* not as our Rock, even our enemies themselves *being* judges.	ence & power of God 1) That it was God & God alone who had given victory over their enemies 2) That the rock (false god) of the enemy is not like our Rock, the LORD God Himself

    a. God's judgment fell because the people lacked wisdom and understanding in discerning their fate (vv.28-29). They just could not grasp that their sin and evil would result in the judgment of God. They were not wise enough to understand that God does not play around with sin and evil, that He means exactly what He says and that people must obey Him. They did not have sense enough nor enough wisdom and understanding to foresee the day of God's impending judgment.

    b. The people failed to discern the presence and power of God (vv.30-31). Keep in mind that this was a prediction of what would happen when the Israelites entered the promised land. Enemy after enemy was going to confront them, but God was going to empower them to defeat all the enemies. One Israelite was going to chase a thousand soldiers and two Israelites were going to put ten thousand soldiers to flight. How could the survival of the Israelites be attributed to anything other than their Rock, the LORD Himself? It was God and God alone who had given the Israelites victory over their enemies. The rock of the enemy was nothing like the Rock of the Israelites, nothing like the LORD God Himself (v.31).

Thought 1. What an indictment against all who reject God! An indictment that charges the unbeliever with a lack of sense, a lack of discernment. Not having enough wisdom or understanding to foresee the judgment of God upon sin—this is the height of ignorance. A person is gripped by a spirit of dullness to God and His holy commandments. This is the clear teaching of Holy Scripture:

"Therefore speak I to them in parables: because they seeing see not; and hearing they hear not, neither do they understand" (Mt.13:13).

"*Ye* hypocrites, ye can discern the face of the sky and of the earth; but how is it that ye do not discern this time [the day of Christ]" (Lu.12:56).

"Why do ye not understand my speech? *even* because ye cannot hear my word" (Jn.8:43).

"There is none that understandeth, there is none that seeketh after God" (Ro.3:11).

"For the heart of this people is waxed gross, and their ears are dull of hearing, and their eyes have they closed; lest they should see with *their* eyes, and hear with *their* ears, and understand with *their* heart, and should be converted, and I should heal them" (Ac.28:27).

DEUTERONOMY 31:30–32:52

"This I say therefore, and testify in the LORD, that ye henceforth walk not as other Gentiles walk, in the vanity of their mind, Having the understanding darkened, being alienated from the life of God through the ignorance that is in them, because of the blindness of their heart: Who being past feeling have given themselves over unto lasciviousness, to work all uncleanness with greediness" (Ep.4:17-19).

"Now the Spirit speaketh expressly, that in the latter times some shall depart from the faith, giving heed to seducing spirits, and doctrines of devils; Speaking lies in hypocrisy; having their conscience seared with a hot iron" (1 Ti.4:1-2).

"Ever learning, and never able to come to the knowledge of the truth" (2 Ti.3:7).

"They know not, neither will they understand; they walk on in darkness: all the foundations of the earth are out of course" (Ps.82:5).

"O LORD, how great are thy works! *and* thy thoughts are very deep. A brutish man knoweth not; neither doth a fool understand this. When the wicked spring as the grass, and when all the workers of iniquity do flourish; *it is* that they shall be destroyed for ever: But thou, LORD, *art most* high for evermore. For, lo, thine enemies, O LORD, for, lo, thine enemies shall perish; all the workers of iniquity shall be scattered" (Ps.92:5-9).

"But they know not the thoughts of the LORD, neither understand they his counsel: for he shall gather them as the sheaves into the floor" (Mi.4:12).

8 (32:32-35) **Judgment, Surety of—Enemies, Judgment of**: there was the surety of judgment against the enemies of God's people. All enemies who ridicule and persecute the people of God will suffer the vengeance of God. A day of calamity and disaster will come, the plagues of God's wrath will fall upon their heads.

OUTLINE	SCRIPTURE	SCRIPTURE	OUTLINE

8. The surety of judgment against the enemies of God's people
a. Their character comes from Sodom & Gomorrah
  1) Is poisonous & bitter, evil & repulsive
  2) Is deadly
b. Their judgment is being
	32 For their vine *is* of the vine of Sodom, and of the fields of Gomorrah: their grapes *are* grapes of gall, their clusters *are* bitter:
	33 Their wine *is* the poison of dragons, and the cruel venom of asps.
	34 *Is* not this laid up in store
		with me, *and* sealed up among my treasures?
		35 To me *belongeth* vengeance, and recompence; their foot shall slide in *due* time: for the day of their calamity *is* at hand, and the things that shall come upon them make haste.
			stored up by God
			
			1) He will avenge & repay
			2) He will bring the day of disaster & doom upon them

a. The enemies of God bear the very character of Sodom and Gomorrah (vv.32-33). This is a graphic description of a person or people who ridicule and persecute others. They are said to have the heart and character of Sodom and Gomorrah. That is, the fruit of their lives is filled with poison and bitterness, evil and wickedness that is repulsive and will be spit out. Note that the venom of their hearts and character is deadly, just as deadly as the poison of asps or cobras.

b. The judgment that is to fall upon the enemies of God's people is actually being stored up by God (vv.34-35). Vengeance belongs to God, and He will avenge all the ridicule and persecution against His people. He will bring the day of disaster and doom upon all enemies. And the day of their calamities—the day of their disaster and doom—is rapidly drawing near and rushing upon them.

Thought 1. The judgment of God is sure. It will fall, and it will fall upon all ungodliness and unrighteousness of people. Any person who rejects God—turning away from Him to the world with its immoral, unrighteous ways—will suffer the judgment of God falling upon his head. But note this fact: the person who ridicules and persecutes the believer will particularly suffer the vengeance of God. This is the clear teaching of Holy Scripture:

"And to you who are troubled [persecuted] rest with us, when the LORD Jesus shall be revealed from heaven with his mighty angels, In flaming fire taking vengeance on them that know not God, and that obey not the gospel of our Lord Jesus Christ: Who shall be punished with everlasting destruction from the presence of the LORD, and from the glory of his power" (2 Th.1:7-9).

"But I say unto you, It shall be more tolerable for Tyre and Sidon at the day of judgment, than for you. And thou, Capernaum, which art exalted unto heaven, shalt be brought down to hell: for if the mighty works, which have been done in thee, had been done in Sodom, it would have remained until this day. But I say unto you, That it shall be more tolerable for the land of Sodom in the day of judgment, than for thee" (Mt.11:22-24).

"And whosoever shall not receive you, nor hear you, when ye depart thence, shake off the dust under your feet for a testimony against them. Verily I say unto you, It shall be more tolerable for Sodom and Gomorrha in the day of judgment, than for that city" (Mk.6:11).

"For the wrath of God is revealed from heaven against all ungodliness and unrighteousness of men, who hold the truth in unrighteousness" (Ro.1:18).

"The LORD knoweth how to deliver the godly out of temptations, and to reserve the unjust unto the day of judgment to be punished" (2 Pe.2:9).

"And Enoch also, the seventh from Adam, prophesied of these, saying, Behold, the LORD cometh with ten thousands of his saints, To execute judgment upon all, and to convince all that are ungodly among them of all their ungodly deeds which they have ungodly committed, and of all their hard *speeches* which ungodly sinners have spoken against him" (Jude 14-15).

DEUTERONOMY 31:30–32:52

9 (32:36-43) **Compassion, of God—God, Compassion of**: this is a prediction of the restoration of Israel and the execution of judgment upon their enemies. Note the Scripture and outline:

OUTLINE	SCRIPTURE	SCRIPTURE	OUTLINE

9. **The compassion of God for His people**
a. God will show compassion when several things happen
  1) One's strength—self-sufficiency—is gone
  2) One acknowledges his sin, his trust in false gods or rocks
    • False help
    • False protection, shelter, refuge
 	
  3) One sees the only living & true God: That He alone holds the power of life & death, sickness & health, victory & deliverance
b. God will show compassion
	36 For the LORD shall judge his people, and repent himself for his servants, when he seeth that *their* power is gone, and *there is* none shut up, or left.
	37 And he shall say, Where *are* their gods, *their* rock in whom they trusted,
	38 Which did eat the fat of their sacrifices, *and* drank the wine of their drink offerings? let them rise up and help you, *and* be your protection.
	39 See now that I, *even* I, am he, and *there is* no god with me: I kill, and I make alive; I wound, and I heal: neither *is there any* that can deliver out of my hand.
	40 For I lift up my hand to
		heaven, and say, I live for ever.
		41 If I whet my glittering sword, and mine hand take hold on judgment; I will render vengeance to mine enemies, and will reward them that hate me.
		42 I will make mine arrows drunk with blood, and my sword shall devour flesh; *and that* with the blood of the slain and of the captives, from the beginning of revenges upon the enemy.
		43 Rejoice, O ye nations, *with* his people: for he will avenge the blood of his servants, and will render vengeance to his adversaries, and will be merciful unto his land, *and* to his people.
			for His people by executing justice upon their enemies
			  1) He will take the position of a warrior & execute judgment upon His enemies—those who reject & hate Him
			
			  2) He will demonstrate His superior strength & execute full & complete judgment
			  3) He will spare no one, not slave nor leader
			
			  4) He will cause the nations to rejoice with His people
			    • Because He will avenge them
			    • Because He will make atonement for them & their land

a. God will show compassion upon the Israelites when several things happen (vv.36-39).
  1) The people of God will be restored when their strength, their self-sufficiency, is gone (v.36). Remember, the Israelites had forsaken God when they were full, when they had plenty of everything. Being so blessed, they began to feel as though they had achieved success by the *arm of the flesh*. Prosperity flooded the land and the people became comfortable and self-sufficient. They began to feel that they were wise and knowledgeable enough to control the economy and prosperity that flooded the nation. Self-sufficiency and pride caused the people to forget God, that all blessings actually flow from Him. It was this self-sufficiency and pride that had caused the judgment of God to fall upon the people. The people would have to suffer the loss of all they had before they would ever realize their need for God's strength. All sense of self-sufficiency and pride would first have to be wiped out.
  2) The people would then acknowledge their sin, that they had trusted in false gods and taken refuge in false rocks. Once the people had been exiled, deported into foreign nations, then they would realize the weakness of the false gods and false worship they had been following. They would realize that they had been trusting in false protection, false shelter and refuge (vv.36-38).
  3) Once these calamities had come upon the people—once they had lost all sense of self-sufficiency and pride—they would then turn to the living and true God. They would see that the LORD (Jehovah, Yahweh) is truly the only living God. There is no god beside Him. It is He alone who holds the power of life and death, sickness and health, victory and deliverance. Again, keep in mind that this is a prediction of the future restoration of the Israelites.
b. God will show compassion for His people by executing justice upon their enemies (vv.40-43). Note that God raises His hand to heaven, indicating that He is declaring an eternal oath. The oath is an *oath of vengeance*: the LORD is saying that His judgment will definitely fall upon the enemies of God's people. Nothing will stop His judgment nor cause Him to change His mind from executing this judgment upon all enemies. Note how the judgment is described:
  1) The LORD will take the position of a warrior and execute judgment upon all adversaries, all those who reject and hate Him (v.41). Note how God identifies His people with Himself: to hate His people is to hate Him.
  2) The LORD will demonstrate His superior strength, executing full and complete judgment (v.42).
  3) The LORD will spare no one, not slave nor leader (v.42).
  4) The LORD will cause the nations to rejoice with His people (v.43). The nations of the world will rejoice because God avenged the Israelites and because He made atonement for them and their land. The Israelites would have a new beginning in the promised land.

Thought 1. There is a strong lesson in this passage for us. We can hit rock bottom by losing...
- our strength and self-sufficiency
- our job or business
- our home or property
- our finances or security
- our physical or emotional health
- our attractiveness or appeal
- our spouse or child

No matter what the loss is, if we call out to God, He will have compassion upon us. He wants to forgive us and restore us back into His favor. He wants to pour out His blessings upon us. The LORD is compassionate, full of tenderness and mercy.

DEUTERONOMY 31:30–32:52

"Seeing then that we have a great high priest, that is passed into the heavens, Jesus the Son of God, let us hold fast *our* profession. For we have not an high priest which cannot be touched with the feeling of our infirmities; but was in all points tempted like as *we are, yet* without sin. Let us therefore come boldly unto the throne of grace, that we may obtain mercy, and find grace to help in time of need" (He.4:14-16).

"The LORD is not slack concerning his promise, as some men count slackness; but is longsuffering to us-ward, not willing that any should perish, but that all should come to repentance. But the day of the LORD will come as a thief in the night; in the which the heavens shall pass away with a great noise, and the elements shall melt with fervent heat, the earth also and the works that are therein shall be burned up" (2 Pe.3:9-10).

"But he, *being* full of compassion, forgave *their* iniquity, and destroyed *them* not: yea, many a time turned he his anger away, and did not stir up all his wrath" (Ps.78:38).

"But thou, O LORD, *art* a God full of compassion, and gracious, longsuffering, and plenteous in mercy and truth" (Ps.86:15).

"Like as a father pitieth *his* children, *so* the LORD pitieth them that fear him" (Ps.103:13).

"In all their affliction he was afflicted, and the angel of his presence saved them: in his love and in his pity he redeemed them; and he bare them, and carried them all the days of old" (Is.63:9).

"And it shall come to pass, after that I have plucked them out I will return, and have compassion on them, and will bring them again, every man to his heritage, and every man to his land" (Je.12:15).

"But though he cause grief, yet will he have compassion according to the multitude of his mercies" (La.3:32).

"I drew them with cords of a man, with bands of love: and I was to them as they that take off the yoke on their jaws, and I laid meat unto them" (Ho.11:4).

"He will turn again, he will have compassion upon us; he will subdue our iniquities; and thou wilt cast all their sins into the depths of the sea" (Mi.7:19).

10 (32:44-47) **Warning, Message of—Message, Warning of—Song, of Moses, Warning of:** the message of the song and of the law must be heeded by God's people. The song has now ended. Note what happened:

OUTLINE	SCRIPTURE	SCRIPTURE	OUTLINE
10. The message of the song & of the law must be heeded a. Moses was faithful to God's instructions: He finished sharing the warning & witness of the song (31:19) b. Moses issued a strong charge: Must set your hearts upon the law of God,	44 And Moses came and spake all the words of this song in the ears of the people, he, and Hoshea the son of Nun. 45 And Moses made an end of speaking all these words to all Israel: 46 And he said unto them, Set your hearts unto all the words which I testify among	you this day, which ye shall command your children to observe to do, all the words of this law. 47 For it *is* not a vain thing for you; because it *is* your life: and through this thing ye shall prolong *your* days in the land, whither ye go over Jordan to possess it.	all His Words—all His commandments 1) So you may teach your children to obey 2) So you may know they are not idle words but your life 3) So you may live long in the promised land

a. Moses was faithful to God's instructions to share the song with the people (vv.44-45). With Joshua standing by his side, he had recited the song and started the process of teaching the song to all the people. Just as God had commanded, Moses finished sharing the warning and witness of the song (31:19).

b. Next Moses issued a strong charge to the people: they must set their hearts upon the law of God (v.46a). They must wholeheartedly commit themselves to the covenant, to the holy commandments of God. Note this fact: "the words" can refer either to the words of the song or to all the law and commandments of God (v.46b). The people were to be wholeheartedly committed to the law and commandments for three reasons:

⇒ so they could teach their children to obey the law.
⇒ so they might know that the law and commandments were not idle words, but their very life (v.47). The very purpose for the law and commandments was to impart life to the people, a life that experienced the fullness of being, that conquered all the trials and temptations of life.
⇒ so they could live long lives in the promised land. Only as they obeyed God would God continue to bless them and allow them to remain in the promised land (v.47).

Thought 1. The commandment of God is clear: we must be wholeheartedly committed to the LORD. When we were first saved, we made a commitment, a covenant to give our lives to the LORD and to follow Him. We made this significant promise to the LORD: if He would save us, we would follow Him with our whole heart. If we were genuinely sincere, God kept His promise. He saved us. Therefore, the strong expectation of God is that we will keep our promise. We will wholeheartedly follow Him.

"I beseech you therefore, brethren, by the mercies of God, that ye present your bodies a living sacrifice, holy, acceptable unto God, *which is* your reasonable service. And be not conformed to this world: but be ye transformed by the renewing of your mind, that ye may prove what is that good, and acceptable, and perfect, will of God" (Ro.12:1-2).

"And thou shalt love the LORD thy God with all thine heart, and with all thy soul, and with all thy might" (De.6:5).

DEUTERONOMY 31:30–32:52

"Blessed *are* they that keep his testimonies, *and that* seek him with the whole heart" (Ps.119:2).
"Trust in the LORD with all thine heart; and lean not unto thine own understanding" (Pr.3:5).
"My son, give me thine heart, and let thine eyes observe my ways" (Pr.23:26).
"And ye shall seek me, and find *me,* when ye shall search for me with all your heart" (Je.29:13).
"Therefore also now, saith the LORD, turn ye *even* to me with all your heart, and with fasting, and with weeping, and with mourning" (Joel 2:12).

11 (32:48-52) **Compassion, of God—Chastisement, of God—Moses, Death of**: these verses provide an immediate example of God's compassion and judgment. The ministry of Moses was now over. Only one more thing needed to be done. Moses needed to pronounce the prophetic blessings upon the twelve tribes. After that, this dear aged servant of God would go home to be with the LORD. It was now time for God to personally prepare Moses for this eventful moment.

What happened next was a private, personal time between God and His dear aged servant. On the very same day that Moses recited the song to the people of God, the LORD led Moses to seclude himself for a most precious and hallowed time with Him. The Scripture gives us the very words that God shared with him:

OUTLINE	SCRIPTURE	SCRIPTURE	OUTLINE
11. The immediate example of God's compassion & judgment a. God's compassion: Instructed His dear servant Moses to climb to the peak of Mt. Nebo & look out across the promised land b. God's judgment or chastisement: Moses was to die on the mountain—be gathered to his people—just as	48 And the LORD spake unto Moses that selfsame day, saying, 49 Get thee up into this mountain Abarim, *unto* mount Nebo, which *is* in the land of Moab, that *is* over against Jericho; and behold the land of Canaan, which I give unto the children of Israel for a possession: 50 And die in the mount whither thou goest up, and be gathered unto thy people; as Aaron thy brother died in	mount Hor, and was gathered unto his people: 51 Because ye trespassed against me among the children of Israel at the waters of Meribah-Kadesh, in the wilderness of Zin; because ye sanctified me not in the midst of the children of Israel. 52 Yet thou shalt see the land before *thee*; but thou shalt not go thither unto the land which I give the children of Israel.	Aaron had 1) Because they had disobeyed God 2) Because they did not honor God as holy in the sight of the people (see Nu. 20:7-13) c. God's compassion & judgment are clearly demonstrated: God's dear servant was allowed to view the promised land, but he was barred from experiencing the victory & rest of the land

a. God's compassion flowed out to Moses (v.49). The LORD instructed him to climb to the peak of Mt. Nebo and look out across the promised land. This was a compassionate and touching act on the part of God, for Moses did not deserve to see the promised land. As we will be reminded in just a moment, Moses had committed a terrible sin against God that barred him from the promised land. But as always, the compassion and mercy of God reached out to one of His dear believers who had repented and returned to the fold. *The Expositor's Bible Commentary* gives an excellent description of Mt. Nebo and the sight that Moses could see from that vantage point:

> Mount Nebo is in the Abarim Mountains, a range running in a general north and south direction about ten miles east of the most northern part of the Dead Sea, rising to about 4,000 feet above the Dead Sea, which would be about 2,700 feet above the Mediterranean (sea level). Nebo is 2,631 feet above sea level. From Nebo Moses could see Canaan in the north beyond Lake Galilee, on the west the mountains of Judea, and toward the south as far as the area south of the Dead Sea (Zoar).[2]

b. God's judgment that had been pronounced earlier upon His faithful servant was now to be executed (vv.50-51). The chastisement was to be carried out exactly as God had said. Moses was to be an example to all generations as well as to Israel, an example that a lack of discernment would cause the judgment and chastisement of God to fall upon a person.

With compassion and mercy flooding His heart, God obviously spoke ever so softly and gently to this man of God. With warmth and tenderness, the LORD told Moses that he was to die on the mountain and be gathered to his people just as Aaron had. What a glorious promise to give to this dear man of God, the promise that he would join the other saints who had gone before him and who were living in the presence of God. A spirit of rejoicing must have surged through the heart of Moses, hearing these words that he was soon to join the LORD and all the other believers who had gone on before. But there was also bound to be a sadness, a regret surging through the mind of Moses, for Moses was being barred from entering the promised land. Note that God spelled out the reasons why:

⇒ because Moses and Aaron had broken faith with God, disobeying and rebelling against God.
⇒ because Moses and Aaron had not honored God as holy in the sight of the people at the waters of Meribah. Instead of speaking only to the rock—charging water to gush out from the rock—Moses had spoken to the people, charging them with being rebels. And with anger against the people raging up within him, he had taken his rod and struck the rock twice. Moses had shown that God could not trust him to follow His instructions—not entirely, not always. Moreover, Moses had claimed some of the credit for himself. He declared that it was both the LORD and he who were performing the miracle of causing water to gush out of the rock. He had not honored God as holy, as being totally set apart from any act or ability of man.

Moses had left God no choice: the chastisement of God had to fall upon him. And now, after so many years, the chastisement and judgment were being executed. The dear aged servant of God was not to be allowed to enter the

---
[2] Frank E. Gaebelein, Editor. *The Expositor's Bible Commentary*, p.217

promised land—not ever. He would never experience the victory and rest of the land for which he had so long sought. For forty years, he had served the LORD ever so faithfully, except on this one very serious occasion. He had given his heart and soul to God and His people, labored ever so diligently to the point of exhaustion day after day in order to lead the people to the promised land. If a person had ever committed his life totally and wholly to the LORD, it was this dear aged servant. All for the purpose of leading the people of God to the victory and rest of the promised land. And now, as the people were poised to enter the promised land in just a few days, he could no longer march with them. He would personally never experience the victory and rest of the promised land, that for which he had sought so long.

c. In this single event, God's compassion and judgment were clearly demonstrated (v.52). God's beloved servant was allowed to view the promised land, but he was barred from experiencing the victory and rest of the land (v.52; see outline and notes—Nu.20:7-13 for more discussion).

Thought 1. The death of God's dear people—their going home to be with the LORD—is a most wonderful and precious experience. It is far, far different from the horrible, terrifying experience that unbelievers will undergo the moment they pass from this life into the next. For the genuine believer, death is not to be dreaded nor feared. Death is not to be recoiled from nor withdrawn from. At the moment of passing from this life into the next, quicker than the eye can blink, God transfers His dear believer into His very presence. The believer enters heaven, the other world, the eternal and spiritual dimension of being.

"And these shall go away into everlasting punishment: but the righteous into life eternal" (Mt.25:46).

"And it came to pass, that the beggar died, and was carried by the angels into Abraham's bosom: the rich man also died, and was buried" (Lu.16:22).

"He that believeth on the Son hath everlasting life: and he that believeth not the Son shall not see life; but the wrath of God abideth on him" (Jn.3:36).

"And I give unto them eternal life; and they shall never perish, neither shall any *man* pluck them out of my hand" (Jn.10:28).

"To them who by patient continuance in well doing seek for glory and honour and immortality, eternal life" (Ro.2:7).

"For whether we live, we live unto the LORD; and whether we die, we die unto the LORD: whether we live therefore, or die, we are the LORD's" (Ro.14:8).

"For to me to live *is* Christ, and to die *is* gain....For I am in a strait betwixt two, having a desire to depart, and to be with Christ; which is far better: Nevertheless to abide in the flesh *is* more needful for you" (Ph.1:21, 23-24).

"Through faith we understand that the worlds were framed by the word of God, so that things which are seen were not made of things which do appear" (He.11:3).

"And this is the promise that he hath promised us, *even* eternal life" (1 Jn.2:25).

"Keep yourselves in the love of God, looking for the mercy of our Lord Jesus Christ unto eternal life" (Jude 21).

"And I heard a voice from heaven saying unto me, Write, Blessed *are* the dead which die in the LORD from henceforth: Yea, saith the Spirit, that they may rest from their labours; and their works do follow them" (Re.14:13).

"Yea, though I walk through the valley of the shadow of death, I will fear no evil: for thou *art* with me; thy rod and thy staff they comfort me" (Ps.23:4).

"Precious in the sight of the LORD *is* the death of his saints" (Ps.116:15).

"The wicked is driven away in his wickedness: but the righteous hath hope in his death" (Pr.14:32).

TYPES, SYMBOLS, AND PICTURES
(Deuteronomy 31:30–32:52)

Historical Term	Type or Picture (Scriptural Basis for Each)	Life Application for Today's Believer	Biblical Application
The Wilderness Wanderings (Journey) De.32:7-14 (See also Ex.13:17-18:27; Nu.14:33; De.8:2-3, 5-6)	The Wilderness Wanderings is a symbol of the pilgrimage of the believer... • as he turns away from Egypt (the world) and leaves behind his old life. • as he turns to begin his new life by marching to the promised land. • as he marches through the wilderness [trials] of this world and conquers all that the wilderness throws against him.	⇒ Once a person has been saved—turned to God from the world (Egypt), turned away from his old life—he begins his *new life* in Christ. He immediately begins to march to the promised land of heaven. His new life is the *pilgrimage* of the Christian believer: a march through the *wilderness* of this world, through all that the wilderness throws up against him...	"Now all these things happened unto them for examples: and they are written for our admonition, upon whom the ends of the world are come" (1 Co. 10:11). "And, behold, I am with thee, and will keep thee in all places whither thou goest, and will bring thee again into this land; for I will not leave thee, until I have done that which I have spoken to thee of" (Ge.28:15).

DEUTERONOMY 31:30–32:52

Historical Term	Type or Picture (Scriptural Basis for Each)	Life Application for Today's Believer	Biblical Application
	"He found him in a desert land, and in the waste howling wilderness; he led him about, he instructed him, he kept him as the apple of his eye" (De. 32:10).	<ul><li>trials</li><li>temptations</li><li>problems</li><li>difficulties</li><li>obstacles</li><li>accidents</li><li>sufferings</li><li>death</li></ul>	*"When thou passest through the waters, I will be with thee; and through the rivers, they shall not overflow thee: when thou walkest through the fire, thou shalt not be burned; neither shall the flame kindle upon thee"* (Is.43:2). *"There hath no temptation taken you but such as is common to man: but God is faithful, who will not suffer you to be tempted above that ye are able; but will with the temptation also make a way to escape, that ye may be able to bear it"* (1 Co.10:13). (See Mt.4:1-11; Lu.4:1-13; 2 S.22:2; Je.1:8; He.2:14-15.)

DEUTERONOMY 33:1-29

CHAPTER 33

C. The Prophetic Blessing of Moses: The Last Words Spoken by the Man of God—a Message of Great Assurance & Encouragement, 33:1-29

1. **The great blessings of God: Pronounced by Moses, the man of God**

   a. God's glorious, majestic presence
   1) Appeared on Mt. Sinai & continued with His people everywhere
   2) Came with innumerable heavenly beings

   b. God's love & care: He holds His people in His hands

   c. God's gift of worship

   d. God's instruction—His law

   e. God's kingship—His rule & reign over His people (Jeshurun is another name for Israel. It means the upright, righteous one)

2. **The blessing of Reuben: To live & not die or become extinct**

3. **The blessing of Judah**
   a. To be heard by God
   b. To be settled as a people in the promised land
   c. To be victorious in defending himself—with the help of God

4. **The blessing of Levi**
   a. To be responsible for the Thummim & Urim, for seeking the will of God
   1) Because they had been faithful (Ex.17:7; Nu. 20:1-13)
   2) Because they obeyed God & guarded His covenant when threatened: Executed impartial justice (even against loved ones) at the golden calf tragedy (Ex.32:25-29)
   b. To be the teachers of God's law
   c. To be the representatives of the people, the priests who offer sacrifice to God
   d. To be greatly blessed
   1) In their substance
   2) In their work (ministry)
   3) In their victory over enemies

And this *is* the blessing, wherewith Moses the man of God blessed the children of Israel before his death.
2 And he said, The LORD came from Sinai, and rose up from Seir unto them; he shined forth from mount Paran, and he came with ten thousands of saints: from his right hand *went* a fiery law for them.
3 Yea, he loved the people; all his saints *are* in thy hand: and they sat down at thy feet; every one shall receive of thy words.
4 Moses commanded us a law, *even* the inheritance of the congregation of Jacob.
5 And he was king in Jeshurun, when the heads of the people *and* the tribes of Israel were gathered together.
6 Let Reuben live, and not die; and let *not* his men be few.
7 And this *is the blessing* of Judah: and he said, Hear, LORD, the voice of Judah, and bring him unto his people: let his hands be sufficient for him; and be thou an help *to him* from his enemies.
8 And of Levi he said, *Let* thy Thummim and thy Urim *be* with thy holy one, whom thou didst prove at Massah, *and with* whom thou didst strive at the waters of Meribah;
9 Who said unto his father and to his mother, I have not seen him; neither did he acknowledge his brethren, nor knew his own children: for they have observed thy word, and kept thy covenant.
10 They shall teach Jacob thy judgments, and Israel thy law: they shall put incense before thee, and whole burnt sacrifice upon thine altar.
11 Bless, LORD, his substance, and accept the work of his hands: smite through the loins of them that rise against him, and of them that hate him, that they rise not again.
12 *And* of Benjamin he said, The beloved of the LORD shall dwell in safety by him; *and the* LORD shall cover him all the day long, and he shall dwell between his shoulders.
13 And of Joseph he said, Blessed of the LORD *be* his land, for the precious things of heaven, for the dew, and for the deep that coucheth beneath,
14 And for the precious fruits *brought forth* by the sun, and for the precious things put forth by the moon,
15 And for the chief things of the ancient mountains, and for the precious things of the lasting hills,
16 And for the precious things of the earth and fulness thereof, and *for* the good will of him that dwelt in the bush: let *the blessing* come upon the head of Joseph, and upon the top of the head of him *that was* separated from his brethren.
17 His glory *is like* the firstling of his bullock, and his horns *are like* the horns of unicorns: with them he shall push the people together to the ends of the earth: and they *are* the ten thousands of Ephraim, and they *are* the thousands of Manasseh.
18 And of Zebulun he said, Rejoice, Zebulun, in thy going out; and, Issachar, in thy tents.
19 They shall call the people unto the mountain; there they shall offer sacrifices of righteousness: for they shall suck of the abundance of the seas, and *of* treasures hid in the sand.
20 And of Gad he said, Blessed *be* he that enlargeth Gad: he dwelleth as a lion, and teareth the arm with the crown of the head.
21 And he provided the first part for himself, because there, *in* a portion of the lawgiver, *was he* seated; and he came with the heads of the people, he executed the justice of the LORD, and his judgments with Israel.
22 And of Dan he said, Dan *is* a lion's whelp: he shall leap from Bashan.
23 And of Naphtali he said,

5. **The blessing of Benjamin**
   a. Was the beloved of God
   b. To rest secure (be faithful) in the LORD
   c. To be carried, supported by God

6. **The blessing of Joseph (Ephraim & Manasseh)**
   a. To have material prosperity
   1) The precious water from dew, rivers, & streams
   2) The best crops that the sun & seasons could produce
   3) The precious materials from the mountains & hills (wood & minerals)
   4) The precious things of the earth
   5) The favor of the LORD
   6) The assurance of prosperity

   b. To possess great power—be blessed with military strength
   1) Will be strong as a bull & as the horns of an ox
   2) Will slaughter & defeat the enemy
   3) Will be a large army

7. **The blessing of Zebulun & Issachar**
   a. To rejoice in all their activities
   b. To call people to seek God through worship & sacrifice
   c. To grow rich from sea & land trade

8. **The blessing of Gad**
   a. To stand as praise to God
   b. To have the military strength of a lion & be victorious
   c. To choose & possess the best land
   d. To fight alongside the other tribes until victory was secured over the enemies of the promised land (see Nu.32:1-42)

9. **The blessing of Dan: To be courageous & ferocious in military conflicts**

10. **The blessing of Naphtali**

DEUTERONOMY 33:1-29

a. To be favored & filled with God's blessing
b. To inherit the fertile land down to the Lake of Galilee
11. **The blessing of Asher**
   a. To be most blessed, happy, & favored by others
   b. To be prosperous
 	
   c. To have military protection—fortification & strength
 	
12. **The greatness of God & His wonderful blessings**
   a. The greatness of God
      1) He is incomparable: Dwells in sovereign power & majesty
	O Naphtali, satisfied with favour, and full with the blessing of the LORD: possess thou the west and the south.
	24 And of Asher he said, *Let* Asher *be* blessed with children; let him be acceptable to his brethren, and let him dip his foot in oil.
	25 Thy shoes *shall be* iron and brass; and as thy days, *so shall* thy strength *be*.
	26 *There is* none like unto the God of Jeshurun, *who* rideth upon the heaven in thy help, and in his excellency on the sky.
	27 The eternal God *is* thy refuge, and underneath *are*
		the everlasting arms: and he shall thrust out the enemy from before thee; and shall say, Destroy *them*.
		28 Israel then shall dwell in safety alone: the fountain of Jacob *shall be* upon a land of corn and wine; also his heavens shall drop down dew.
		29 Happy *art* thou, O Israel: who *is* like unto thee, O people saved by the LORD, the shield of thy help, and who *is* the sword of thy excellency! and thine enemies shall be found liars unto thee; and thou shalt tread upon their high places.
			2) He is the eternal God
			b. The wonderful blessings of God
			   1) Refuge & support
			   2) Victory, conquest, triumph
			   3) Security, safety
			   4) Provision, supply, prosperity
			
			5) Salvation
			6) Protection: Shielded, defended, feared
			7) Spiritual victory & purity

DIVISION VI

THE FINAL ACTS AND DEATH OF MOSES, GOD'S AGED SERVANT: REMEMBER THE ENCOURAGEMENT AND THE WARNING OF GOD, 31:1–34:12

C. The Prophetic Blessing of Moses: The Last Words Spoken by the Man of God—a Message of Great Assurance and Encouragement, 33:1-29

(33:1-29) **Introduction**: conflicts rage all over the world. Down through history, on any given day, there have always been several nations waging war against one another. But war is not the only conflict that is continually being waged on the world scene. There are political conflicts, religious strife, power struggles, racial hostility, organizational clashes, family divisions, neighborhood disputes, and marital separation and divorce.

The conflicts that are constantly being waged throughout society are innumerable. There are literally millions of people engaged in conflict at any given moment throughout the world. And where conflict is, there is always division, pain, suffering, maiming, and death. Conflict results in broken hearts and broken spirits, discouragement and grief, distress and failure.

The great leader of Israel, Moses, the aged servant of God, knew the terrible results of conflict. In just a few days, the Israelites were going to be marching across the Jordan River, marching into the promised land. They would be entering into conflict with the enemies who stood opposed to God and opposed to their inheritance of the promised land. The raging conflict could discourage God's people and lead to their defeat. Moses would not be present to rally the forces. Within hours, he was to die and go home to be with the LORD. What could he say that would give long-lasting encouragement to the people, the perfect assurance that they would be victorious? What should his message be? This was to be the final message he would ever preach to God's people, the last opportunity he would ever have to encourage and assure them.

Moses was one of the greatest men in history, not only in the eyes of man, but in the eyes of God. It is this that makes his final words so important, not only to the Israelites of his day but to the people of God down through all generations. His final message was not a typical one. It was a message that would be preached only once in a person's lifetime, in the final hours of a person's life. Moses proclaimed a *prophetic blessing* upon each of the twelve tribes. This is what is commonly known as the *prophetic blessing of Moses*. It should be compared with the prophetic blessings of the patriarchs Isaac and Jacob (Ge.27:7; 49:1-28). Note that the prophetic blessing of Moses was written in poetic form. It was both a prayer of Moses and a prophecy of what would happen to the tribes, the people of God, in the future. This is the subject of the final message, the last words Moses ever spoke to the Israelites: *The Prophetic Blessing of Moses: The Last Words Spoken by the Man of God—a Message of Great Assurance and Encouragement, 33:1-29*.

1. The great blessings of God: pronounced by Moses the man of God (vv.1-5).
2. The blessing of Reuben: to live and not die or become extinct (v.6).
3. The blessing of Judah (v.7).
4. The blessing of Levi (vv.8-11).
5. The blessing of Benjamin (v.12).
6. The blessing of Joseph (Ephraim and Manasseh) (vv.13-17).
7. The blessing of Zebulun and Issachar (vv.18-19).
8. The blessing of Gad (vv.20-21).
9. The blessing of Dan: to be courageous and ferocious in military attacks (v.22).
10. The blessing of Naphtali (v.23).
11. The blessing of Asher (vv.24-25).
12. The greatness of God and His wonderful blessings (vv.26-29).

DEUTERONOMY 33:1-29

1 (33:1-5) **Blessings, of God—God, Blessings of—Israel, Blessings of—Blessings, of Israel**: the great blessings of God were pronounced by Moses, the man of God. Never before had a man been called *the man of God*. This is the first time the term is used of a man. Later in the Old Testament, others will be called men of God, especially the prophets. However, it is significant that Moses is the first person to be called *the man of God* (see Jud.13:6, 8; 1 S.9:6; 1 K.13:1-3; 2 K.4:7, 16). The titles given to Moses throughout Scripture are:

⇒ the servant of God (Nu.12:6-8; Heb.3:5)
⇒ the friend of God (Ex.33:11)
⇒ the prophet of God (De.18:15; 34:10)
⇒ the man of God (De.33:1; Jos.14:6)

Moses, the man of God, will soon die and go home to be with the LORD. But before he dies, he is to carry out one final duty: he must give a personal blessing to each of the tribes of Israel just as the great patriarchs Isaac and Jacob had done (Ge.27:7; 49:1-28). Moses had served God for over forty years now, years that were blessed beyond imagination and had witnessed the wonderful miracles of God. Nevertheless, because of the hard hearts and disobedience of the people, the years had been long and difficult. But now, the end of Moses' life and ministry with the people was drawing to a rapid close. It was time for him to conclude his ministry with them, time for him to complete his one final act, that of pronouncing the prophetic blessings upon each of the tribes. Throughout the years, Moses had faithfully looked after the people whom God had committed to his charge. The LORD had just informed him that he was to leave his people for the final time, climb Mt. Nebo where he would view the land, and then die, being carried into the presence of the LORD. It was now time to carry out his last function upon the earth: the pronouncement of the prophetic blessings upon the dear people of God, tribe by tribe.

Moses began by covering the *great blessings* of God that had been poured out upon the Israelites. Note the Scripture and outline:

OUTLINE	SCRIPTURE	SCRIPTURE	OUTLINE
1. The great blessings of God: Pronounced by Moses, the man of God	And this is the blessing, wherewith Moses the man of God blessed the children of Israel before his death.	all his saints are in thy hand: and they sat down at thy feet; every one shall receive of thy words.	His people in His hands c. God's gift of worship
a. God's glorious, majestic presence 1) Appeared on Mt. Sinai & continued with His people everywhere 2) Came with innumerable heavenly beings	2 And he said, The LORD came from Sinai, and rose up from Seir unto them; he shined forth from mount Paran, and he came with ten thousands of saints: from his right hand went a fiery law for them.	4 Moses commanded us a law, even the inheritance of the congregation of Jacob. 5 And he was king in Jeshurun, when the heads of the people and the tribes of Israel were gathered together.	d. God's instruction—His law e. God's kingship—His rule & reign over His people (Jeshurun is another name for Israel. It means the upright, righteous one)
b. God's love & care: He holds	3 Yea, he loved the people;		

a. There was the blessing of God's glorious, majestic presence (vv.1-2). God had given His dear people a visible and illustrious revelation of His majestic glory on Mt. Sinai. This passage describes His presence as shining forth like the sun that flooded the desert. God's majestic presence was so bright that it shot rays of light from Mt. Sinai on the south all the way over to Seir on the northeast and to Paran on the north.[1] The picture is that of the LORD's presence shining forth with the brightness of the noonday sun, covering the whole floor of the desert with the grandeur of His glory. Note also that the LORD came with innumerable heavenly beings.

b. There was the blessing of God's love and care (v.3). God had loved His dear people and held them in His hands. He had given the Israelites all the provision they needed, meeting the necessities of their lives. And He had given them security and protection, making sure they were safe from all harm and enemies.

c. There was the blessing of God's gift of worship. His people were given the privilege of bowing down at His feet and worshipping Him, giving thanks and praise to Him for His great salvation, for His love and care.

d. There was the blessing of God's instruction, the gift of the law that He had given His people (vv.3-4). It was the law of God that told His people how to live, how to secure the fullness of life, and how to live a victorious life over all the enemies, trials, and temptations of life.

e. There was the blessing of God's kingship, His rule and reign over His people (v.5). God Himself was to be the Ruler, the King over the state of Israel. The leaders of the nation were to seek the counsel of God in all decisions. The law was to serve as the constitution of the nation, and the Giver of the law, God Himself, was to be the Ruler of the state of Israel. Note that Jeshurun is another name for Israel. It means the upright, the righteous one. Peter C. Craigie has an excellent statement on the rule of God as the King of Israel that is well worth quoting in full:

> *The law received at Sinai was to be the constitution of the new state of Israel, which was to come into existence in the near future; the lawgiver would be the head of the new state. Hence the people acclaim their leader, namely, God (the lawgiver): Let there be a King in Jeshurun. The kingship of God in early Israel rests on three basic premises: (i) the liberation of his people in the Exodus (see Exod. 15:18); (ii) the giving of the law at Sinai; (iii) the victory (still lying in the future) by which God would grant to his people the promised land. The affirmation of God's kingship at the beginning of the blessings, in the context of a gathering of the tribes with their chiefs, points up that although Moses would utter the blessings, their fulfilment would lie in the hands of God, provided that the people continued to acknowledge and serve him as their King. And Moses, about to die, could leave his people with the knowledge that*

---

[1] Frank E. Gaebelein, Editor. *The Expositor's Bible Commentary*, p.219.

DEUTERONOMY 33:1-29

they recognized God as their King, so that his death did not mean that the Israelites were bereft of a leader; his departure might even make them depend more heavily on God.[2]

Thought 1. The blessings of God upon Israel were beyond imagination. God poured His blessings out upon them day by day and year by year. And one of the most wonderful things about God is just this fact: He blesses His people, the believers of the world. No matter who the believer is nor where the believer is, God blesses him. God loves us and cares for us, looking after all of our affairs. His presence, His provision, His protection and security—all these wonderful blessings belong to God's people. Every necessity of life is met by God.

"But seek ye first the kingdom of God, and his righteousness; and all these things shall be added unto you" (Mt.6:33).

"Come unto me, all *ye* that labour and are heavy laden, and I will give you rest. Take my yoke upon you, and learn of me; for I am meek and lowly in heart: and ye shall find rest unto your souls" (Mt.11:28-29).

"If ye then, being evil, know how to give good gifts unto your children: how much more shall *your* heavenly Father give the Holy Spirit to them that ask him" (Lu.11:13).

"For God so loved the world, that he gave his only begotten Son, that whosoever believeth in him should not perish, but have everlasting life" (Jn.3:16).

"And I give unto them eternal life; and they shall never perish, neither shall any *man* pluck them out of my hand" (Jn.10:28).

"There hath no temptation taken you but such as is common to man: but God *is* faithful, who will not suffer you to be tempted above that ye are able; but will with the temptation also make a way to escape, that ye may be able to bear *it*" (1 Co.10:13).

"And the LORD shall deliver me from every evil work, and will preserve *me* unto his heavenly kingdom: to whom *be* glory for ever and ever. Amen" (2 Ti.4:18).

"Casting all your care upon him; for he careth for you" (1 Pe.5:7).

"And, behold, I *am* with thee, and will keep thee in all *places* whither thou goest, and will bring thee again into this land; for I will not leave thee, until I have done *that* which I have spoken to thee of" (Ge.28:15).

"And ye shall serve the LORD your God, and he shall bless thy bread, and thy water; and I will take sickness away from the midst of thee" (Ex.23:25).

"The eternal God *is thy* refuge, and underneath *are* the everlasting arms: and he shall thrust out the enemy from before thee; and shall say, Destroy *them*" (De.33:27).

"Salvation *belongeth* unto the LORD: thy blessing *is* upon thy people" (Ps.3:8).

"He shall receive the blessing from the LORD, and righteousness from the God of his salvation" (Ps.24:5).

"Thou visitest the earth, and waterest it: thou greatly enrichest it with the river of God, *which* is full of water: thou preparest them corn, when thou hast so provided for it" (Ps.65:9).

"Blessed *be* the LORD, *who* daily loadeth us *with benefits, even* the God of our salvation. Selah" (Ps.68:19).

"The LORD hath been mindful of us: he will bless *us;* he will bless the house of Israel; he will bless the house of Aaron" (Ps.115:12).

"The blessing of the LORD, it maketh rich, and he addeth no sorrow with it" (Pr.10:22).

"For thou hast been a strength to the poor, a strength to the needy in his distress, a refuge from the storm, a shadow from the heat, when the blast of the terrible ones *is* as a storm *against* the wall" (Is.25:4).

"Fear thou not; for I *am* with thee: be not dismayed; for I *am* thy God: I will strengthen thee; yea, I will help thee; yea, I will uphold thee with the right hand of my righteousness" (Is.41:10).

"And *even* to *your* old age I *am* he; and *even* to hoar [gray] hairs will I carry *you:* I have made, and I will bear; even I will carry, and will deliver *you*" (Is.46:4).

2 (33:6) **Blessing, of Reuben—Reuben, Blessing of—Israel, Prophecy of—Prophecy, of Reuben**: there was the prophetic blessing of Reuben. Reuben was to live and not die as a tribe or state of Israel. The tribe was not to become extinct. Note that this was a prayer of Moses as well as a prophecy that the tribe would be preserved. Centuries before, Jacob's blessing had predicted that Reuben would be as unstable as water, and the prediction had proven to be true (Ge.49:4).

⇒ Some of the tribe showed a lack of restraint and leadership when they joined in the rebellion of Korah against Moses (Nu.16).
⇒ The tribe showed weakness and instability by refusing to fight when they were called to battle (Jud.5:15f).
⇒ The tribe showed a lack of restraint by being the first to request a place to settle in the promised land. They did not cross the Jordan river with the other tribes but prematurely settled on the east side of the river. The east was far less valuable than the west side (Nu.32).
⇒ The tribe showed a lack of godly discipline by helping to erect a false place of worship (Jos.22:10-34).
⇒ The tribe was never important in the history of Israel and never produced a leader of any stature whatsoever for the nation.

---

[2] Peter C. Craigie. *The Book of Deuteronomy*, pp.393-394.

DEUTERONOMY 33:1-29

The prayer and prophetic blessing of Moses was also fulfilled. The tribe of Reuben did survive, but because of its unstable nature, the tribe became smaller and smaller down through the generations. However, they are mentioned in the book of Ezekiel the prophet (Eze.48:7).

OUTLINE	SCRIPTURE
2. The blessing of Reuben: To live & not die or become extinct	6 Let Reuben live, and not die; and let *not* his men be few.

Thought 1. The fact that the tribe of Reuben survived is a picture that God answers prayer. Moses had prayed for God to let the tribe live despite its instability. God heard Moses' prayer and kept the tribe alive. The lesson for us is clear: God hears and answers prayer. If a person truly follows and serves God faithfully, just as Moses did, God hears and answers his prayer. God will answer the prayers of His dear people, of those who love and obey Him.

> "Ask, and it shall be given you; seek, and ye shall find; knock, and it shall be opened unto you" (Mt.7:7).
>
> "And I say unto you, Ask, and it shall be given you; seek, and ye shall find; knock, and it shall be opened unto you" (Lu.11:9).
>
> "If ye abide in me, and my words abide in you, ye shall ask what ye will, and it shall be done unto you" (Jn.15:7).
>
> "Hitherto have ye asked nothing in my name: ask, and ye shall receive, that your joy may be full" (Jn.16:24).
>
> "Is any among you afflicted? let him pray. Is any merry? let him sing psalms" (Js.5:13).
>
> "He shall call upon me, and I will answer him: I *will be* with him in trouble; I will deliver him, and honour him" (Ps.91:15).
>
> "Then shalt thou call, and the LORD shall answer; thou shalt cry, and he shall say, Here I *am*. If thou take away from the midst of thee the yoke, the putting forth of the finger, and speaking vanity" (Is.58:9).
>
> "And it shall come to pass, that before they call, I will answer; and while they are yet speaking, I will hear" (Is.65:24).

3 (33:7) **Prophecy, of Judah—Israel, Prophecy Concerning—Judah, Prophecy Concerning**: there was the blessing of Judah, the leading tribe of Israel. Keep in mind that the Israelites were camped in the plains of Moab close by the river Jordan, straight across from the great city of Jericho. They were poised to cross the Jordan River and enter the promised land to lay claim to their inheritance. Enemy after enemy was to be faced; year after year of conflict lay ahead. Because of this, the military struggle facing the Israelites was flooding the mind of Moses as he pronounced these prophetic blessings. This was the thrust of the blessing given to Judah. Judah marched at the head of the Israelite army; they were the vanguard of all military action. Keeping these facts in mind, note the prayer of the aged servant for this great tribe:

⇒ Moses prayed that God would hear the prayers of the families and the soldiers as they marched to war. Being the vanguard of the army, the soldiers would naturally be seeking God's help.

⇒ Moses prayed that God would settle the tribe of Judah in the promised land, that is, that the soldiers of Judah would return from battle back to their homes.

⇒ Moses prayed that the tribe of Judah would be victorious in defending itself—with the help of God.

OUTLINE	SCRIPTURE
3. The blessing of Judah a. To be heard by God b. To be settled as a people in the promised land c. To be victorious in defending himself—with the help of God	7 And this *is the blessing* of Judah: and he said, Hear, LORD, the voice of Judah, and bring him unto his people: let his hands be sufficient for him; and be thou an help *to him* from his enemies.

Thought 1. God promises to give victory to the believer. As we march to the promised land of heaven, enemy after enemy, conflict after conflict, trial after trial, temptation after temptation—all the enemies that can be conceived—will confront us. But God gives us the glorious promise of victory. The genuine believer will conquer all the enemies that attempt to defeat him throughout life. The believer will be triumphant, more than a conqueror. This is the great promise of God.

> "And the LORD said, Simon, Simon, behold, Satan hath desired *to have* you, that he may sift *you* as wheat: But I have prayed for thee, that thy faith fail not: and when thou art converted, strengthen thy brethren" (Lu.22:31-32).
>
> "Who shall separate us from the love of Christ? *shall* tribulation, or distress, or persecution, or famine, or nakedness, or peril, or sword....Nay, in all these things we are more than conquerors through him that loved us. For I am persuaded, that neither death, nor life, nor angels, nor principalities, nor powers, nor things present, nor things to come, Nor height, nor depth, nor any other

creature, shall be able to separate us from the love of God, which is in Christ Jesus our LORD" (Ro.8:35, 37-39).

"And the God of peace shall bruise Satan under your feet shortly. The grace of our Lord Jesus Christ *be* with you. Amen" (Ro.16:20).

"There hath no temptation taken you but such as is common to man: but God *is* faithful, who will not suffer you to be tempted above that ye are able; but will with the temptation also make a way to escape, that ye may be able to bear *it*" (1 Co.10:13).

"Submit yourselves therefore to God. Resist the devil, and he will flee from you" (Js.4:7).

"For whatsoever is born of God overcometh the world: and this is the victory that overcometh the world, *even* our faith. Who is he that overcometh the world, but he that believeth that Jesus is the Son of God" (1 Jn.5:4-5).

"To him that overcometh will I grant to sit with me in my throne, even as I also overcame, and am set down with my Father in his throne" (Re.3:21).

"Through thee will we push down our enemies: through thy name will we tread them under that rise up against us" (Ps.44:5).

4 (33:8-11) **Blessing, of Levi—Levi, Tribe of, Prophetic Blessing of—Prophecy, Concerning the Tribe of Levi—Priests, Duties of—Ministers, Duties of—Ministers, Blessings of**: there was the blessing of Levi, the priests and ministers of God to the people. This was the tribe of Moses himself and of his brother, Aaron. Moses spelled out the three major duties of the priests or ministers and then pronounced the prayer of blessing upon them.

OUTLINE	SCRIPTURE	SCRIPTURE	OUTLINE
4. The blessing of Levi a. To be responsible for the Thummim & Urim, for seeking the will of God 1) Because they had been faithful (Ex.17:7; Nu. 20:1-13) 2) Because they obeyed God & guarded His covenant when threatened: Executed impartial justice (even against loved ones) at the golden calf tragedy	8 And of Levi he said, *Let* thy Thummim and thy Urim *be* with thy holy one, whom thou didst prove at Massah, *and with* whom thou didst strive at the waters of Meribah; 9 Who said unto his father and to his mother, I have not seen him; neither did he acknowledge his brethren, nor knew his own children: for they have observed thy	word, and kept thy covenant. 10 They shall teach Jacob thy judgments, and Israel thy law: they shall put incense before thee, and whole burnt sacrifice upon thine altar. 11 Bless, LORD, his substance, and accept the work of his hands: smite through the loins of them that rise against him, and of them that hate him, that they rise not again.	(Ex.32:25-29) b. To be the teachers of God's law c. To be the representatives of the people, the priests who offer sacrifice to God d. To be greatly blessed 1) In their substance 2) In their work (ministry) 3) In their victory over enemies

a. The tribe of Levi or the priests and ministers of God were responsible for revealing the will of God to the people (vv.8-9). This was done through the Thummim and Urim, two precious stones placed in the breastpiece of the High Priest right next to his heart. These two stones symbolized the High Priest seeking God's will for the people. Some commentators feel they were used as dice or lots, that they were cast upon the ground with the decision being made based upon which stone turned up a certain way. However, this seems unlikely; it is, frankly, contrary to the way God works throughout Scripture. God reveals His will through prayer, His Word, and the Holy Spirit. It is unlikely that He ever bases His will upon the turn of stones like dice. More likely, they symbolized the special revelation opened up to the High Priest through the seeking of God's will through prayer. Just imagine the scene as the High Priest entered into the Holy Place. The Urim and Thummim reminded him and the dear people that God would speak and give him direction, revealing the will of God to him. The High Priest was in the sanctuary seeking God on behalf of the people; therefore, God would hear and answer him. God would make His will and direction known to the High Priest. (See note, pt.3,b—Ex.28:15-30.)

There were two reasons God chose the tribe of Levi for this awesome responsibility of serving His dear people, serving them as their priests and ministers. First, Moses and Aaron, the two leading members of the tribe, had been faithful at Massah and the waters of Meribah where the people had revolted against God due to lack of water (Ex.17:7; Nu.20:1-13). Second, during the golden-calf incident, many within the tribe of Levi stood faithful. They demonstrated very special devotion to the LORD by executing justice upon the disobedient rebels, including even some of their own loved ones (Ex.32:25-29).

b. The tribe of Levi served as the teachers of God's law (v.10).

c. The tribe of Levi was responsible for leading the people in their worship of God, including the offering of sacrifice to God (v.10).

d. The Levites were to be greatly blessed by God (v.11). This was the prayer of blessing pronounced by Moses. He cried out for God to bless the Levites...
- in all their substance or skills
- in all their work or ministry
- in giving them victory over all their enemies

Thought 1. The minister of God will be greatly blessed if he is faithful to the LORD. God longs to pour out His blessings upon His dear servants. And He will. But faithfulness is a condition, a prerequisite to His blessings.

"His lord said unto him, Well done, good and faithful servant; thou hast been faithful over a few things, I will make thee ruler over many things: enter thou into the joy of thy lord" (Mt.25:23).

"Let a man so account of us, as of the ministers of Christ, and stewards of the mysteries of God. Moreover it is required in stewards, that a man be found faithful" (1 Co.4:1-2).

"Therefore, my beloved brethren, be ye stedfast, unmovable, always abounding in the work of the LORD, forasmuch as ye know that your labour is not in vain in the LORD" (1 Co.15:58).

"For I am now ready to be offered, and the time of my departure is at hand. I have fought a good fight, I have finished *my* course, I have kept the faith: Henceforth there is laid up for me a crown of righteousness, which the LORD, the righteous judge, shall give me at that day: and not to me only, but unto all them also that love his appearing" (2 Ti.4:6-8).

"But whoso looketh into the perfect law of liberty, and continueth *therein,* he being not a forgetful hearer, but a doer of the work, this man shall be blessed in his deed" (Js.1:25).

"Behold, I come quickly: hold that fast which thou hast, that no man take thy crown" (Re.3:11).

"And they that be wise shall shine as the brightness of the firmament; and they that turn many to righteousness as the stars for ever and ever" (Da.12:3).

[5] **(33:12) Blessing, of Benjamin—Prophecy, Concerning Benjamin**: there was the blessing of the tribe of Benjamin. There is a tenderness in this prophetic blessing. The people of this tribe are said to be the beloved of the LORD, a people who were especially loved by God. Perhaps this is a reference back to the special love that Jacob held for his youngest son (Ge.44:20). Whatever the case, Moses prayed that the tribe of Benjamin would rest secure and be safe in the LORD. Note that their security would rest in the presence of God Himself. The picture is that of the LORD carrying the tribe between His shoulders, that of a father carrying his son upon his shoulders, protecting and taking care of him.

OUTLINE	SCRIPTURE
5. The blessing of Benjamin a. Was the beloved of God b. To rest secure (be faithful) in the LORD c. To be carried, supported by God	12 And of Benjamin he said, The beloved of the LORD shall dwell in safety by him; *and the LORD* shall cover him all the day long, and he shall dwell between his shoulders.

Thought 1. The LORD keeps His dear people, keeps them safe and secure. As we walk throughout life day by day, God looks after us and cares for us, protecting and shielding us. Even through the trials and temptations of life—no matter how terrible and ferocious—God carries us on His shoulders, walking us through the pain and suffering. God will so carry us and secure us until we reach the promised land of heaven.

"For the which cause I also suffer these things: nevertheless I am not ashamed: for I know whom I have believed, and am persuaded that he is able to keep that which I have committed unto him against that day" (2 Ti.1:12).

"*Let your* conversation [behavior, conduct] *be* without covetousness; *and be* content with such things as ye have: for he hath said, I will never leave thee, nor forsake thee. So that we may boldly say, The LORD *is* my helper, and I will not fear what man shall do unto me" (He.13:5-6).

"And, behold, I *am* with thee, and will keep thee in all *places* whither thou goest, and will bring thee again into this land; for I will not leave thee, until I have done *that* which I have spoken to thee of" (Ge.28:15).

"The LORD shall fight for you, and ye shall hold your peace" (Ex.14:14).

"And thou shalt be secure, because there is hope; yea, thou shalt dig *about thee, and* thou shalt take thy rest in safety" (Jb.11:18).

"The angel of the LORD encampeth round about them that fear him, and delivereth them" (Ps.34:7).

"He shall cover thee with his feathers, and under his wings shalt thou trust: his truth *shall be thy* shield and buckler" (Ps.91:4).

"Thou shalt not be afraid for the terror by night; *nor* for the arrow *that* flieth by day" (Ps.91:5).

"He shall not be afraid of evil tidings: his heart is fixed, trusting in the LORD" (Ps.112:7).

"Behold, he that keepeth Israel shall neither slumber nor sleep" (Ps.121:4).

"As the mountains *are* round about Jerusalem, so the LORD *is* round about his people from henceforth even for ever" (Ps.125:2).

"When thou liest down, thou shalt not be afraid: yea, thou shalt lie down, and thy sleep shall be sweet" (Pr.3:24).

DEUTERONOMY 33:1-29

6 (33:13-17) **Blessing, of Joseph—Joseph, Blessing of—Prophecy, Concerning Israel—Ephraim, Tribe of, Prophecy Concerning—Manasseh, Tribe of, Prophecy Concerning**: there was the blessing of the tribes of Joseph, Ephraim and Manasseh. Remember, Ephraim and Manasseh were the two sons of Joseph. Note that this prophetic blessing deals with two critical areas of life: material prosperity and military strength.

OUTLINE	SCRIPTURE	SCRIPTURE	OUTLINE

6. The blessing of Joseph (Ephraim & Manasseh)
a. To have material prosperity
  1) The precious water from dew, rivers, & streams
 	
  2) The best crops that the sun & seasons could produce
 	
  3) The precious materials from the mountains & hills (wood & minerals)
 	
  4) The precious things of the earth
	13 And of Joseph he said, Blessed of the LORD *be* his land, for the precious things of heaven, for the dew, and for the deep that coucheth beneath,
	14 And for the precious fruits *brought forth* by the sun, and for the precious things put forth by the moon,
	15 And for the chief things of the ancient mountains, and for the precious things of the lasting hills,
	16 And for the precious things of the earth and fulness
		thereof, and *for* the good will of him that dwelt in the bush: let *the blessing* come upon the head of Joseph, and upon the top of the head of him *that was* separated from his brethren.
		17 His glory *is like* the firstling of his bullock, and his horns *are like* the horns of unicorns: with them he shall push the people together to the ends of the earth: and they *are* the ten thousands of Ephraim, and they *are* the thousands of Manasseh.
			5) The favor of the LORD
			6) The assurance of prosperity
			
			b. To possess great power—be blessed with military strength
			  1) Will be strong as a bull & as the horns of an ox
			  2) Will slaughter & defeat the enemy
			  3) Will be a large army

    a. Moses prayed that these two tribes would have material prosperity (vv.13-16). And note a most interesting point: the request was for the ultimate, the highest degree of prosperity. Depending upon which translation is being used in the study of this particular passage of Scripture, such words as these are used: precious, best, choice, chief, richest, finest. For example, the King James Version uses the word *precious* five times and the word *chief* one time. Moses prayed that God would bless these tribes...
- with the choice, precious water from dew, rivers, and streams (v.13)
- with the precious, finest, and best fruits that the sun and seasons could produce (v.14)
- with the best, most precious materials from the mountains and hills such as wood and minerals (v.15)
- with the best, most precious things the earth could yield (v.16)
- with the favor of the LORD (v.16). Note the reference to the presence of the LORD in the burning bush. This was a prayer for these two tribes to be blessed with the very special presence of God.
- with the assurance of prosperity (v.16). Moses was asking God to give these two tribes an assurance of prosperity because of what Joseph had meant to the Israelites. He had been a prince among his brothers; therefore, Moses was requesting that the tribes of Manasseh and Ephraim be princes among the other tribes.

    b. Moses prayed that these two tribes would be blessed with military might (v.17). The request is descriptive: that they would be as strong as a bull and as the horns of an ox that gores its enemies, totally destroying them. Note the prediction of Moses: such would be the ten thousands of Ephraim and the thousands of Manasseh. It should be noted that Ephraim here takes precedence over Manasseh. This was to be true throughout history.

Thought 1. The blessings that God pours out upon His true follower are unlimited. Just a few are listed here.
(1) There is the blessing of the necessities of life.

> "But seek ye first the kingdom of God, and his righteousness; and all these things shall be added unto you" (Mt.6:33).
> "Blessed be the LORD, who daily loadeth us with benefits, even the God of our salvation" (Ps.68:19).

(2) There is the blessing of joy.

> "These things have I spoken unto you, that my joy might remain in you, and [that] your joy might be full" (Jn.15:11).

(3) There is the blessing of health.

> "And ye shall serve the LORD your God, and he shall bless thy bread, and thy water; and I will take sickness away from the midst of thee" (Ex.23:25).
> "But he was wounded for our transgressions, he was bruised for our iniquities: the chastisement of our peace was upon him; and with his stripes we are healed" (Is.53:5).

(4) There is the blessing of all provision.

> "The LORD is my shepherd; I shall not want. He maketh me to lie down in green pastures: he leadeth me beside the still waters. He restoreth my soul: he leadeth me in the paths of righteousness for his name's sake. Yea, though I walk through the valley of the shadow of death, I will fear no evil: for thou

art with me; thy rod and thy staff they comfort me. Thou preparest a table before me in the presence of mine enemies: thou anointest my head with oil; my cup runneth over" (Ps.23:1-5).

(5) There is the blessing of spiritual fullness.

"Bring ye all the tithes into the storehouse, that there may be meat in mine house, and prove me now herewith, saith the LORD of hosts, if I will not open you the windows of heaven, and pour you out a blessing, that there shall not be room enough to receive it" (Mal.3:10).
"And to know the love of Christ, which passeth knowledge, that ye might be filled with all the fulness of God" (Ep.3:19).
"And be not drunk with wine, wherein is excess; but be filled with the Spirit" (Ep.5:18).
"For this cause we also, since the day we heard it, do not cease to pray for you, and to desire that ye might be filled with the knowledge of his will in all wisdom and spiritual understanding" (Col.1:9).

7 (33:18-19) **Zebulun, Tribe of, Prophecy Concerning—Issachar, Tribe of, Prophecy Concerning**: there was the blessing of the tribe of Zebulun and the tribe of Issachar. These were the two sons of Leah, and the youngest, Zebulun, was blessed first. The younger son had also been blessed first by Jacob (see notes—Ge.49:13; 49:14-15 for more discussion). Note that they were called upon to rejoice in all their activities (v.18). The meaning seems to be this: the two tribes would greatly prosper, so much so that from time to time they would hold sacrificial festivals of thanksgiving to God. An invitation would be extended for the other tribes to join them in their festival of thanksgiving and sacrificial worship. Note their source of wealth: they would grow rich from sea and land trade. It seems that they were to serve the other tribes by providing trade and goods to them.

OUTLINE	SCRIPTURE
7. **The blessing of Zebulun & Issachar**	18 And of Zebulun he said, Rejoice, Zebulun, in thy going out; and, Issachar, in thy tents.
a. To rejoice in all their activities	
b. To call people to seek God through worship & sacrifice	19 They shall call the people unto the mountain; there they shall offer sacrifices of righteousness: for they shall suck *of* the abundance of the seas, and *of* treasures hid in the sand.
c. To grow rich from sea & land trade	

Thought 1. God blessed the tribe of Zebulun with the unique opportunity to serve the other tribes by providing goods for them. The lesson for us is clear: God is the source of our blessings. It is He who has set the laws of nature in place, the laws that give us rain, sunshine, seed, growth, and harvest. It is God who has given us life, health, and the ability to work, to produce, and to know purpose and fulfillment. All that we have is due to God. We must, therefore, serve Him, using our blessings wisely. We must do what Zebulun was to do: use what we have to serve and help those who are around us. We must become a center of service, a center for helping all those who surround us.

"As we have therefore opportunity, let us do good unto all men, especially unto them who are of the household of faith" (Ga.6:10).
"But so shall it not be among you: but whosoever will be great among you, shall be your minister: and whosoever of you will be the chiefest, shall be servant of all" (Mk.10:43-44).
"That they do good, that they be rich in good works, ready to distribute, willing to communicate" (1 Ti.6:18).
"But to do good and to communicate [give] forget not: for with such sacrifices God is well pleased" (He.13:16).
"Trust in the LORD, and do good; so shalt thou dwell in the land, and verily thou shalt be fed" (Ps.37:3).

8 (33:20-21) **Gad, Tribe of, Prophetic Blessing—Prophecy, Concerning the Tribe of Gad**: there was the blessing of the tribe of Gad. Moses began by praising the LORD who had given this tribe the conquered territory east of the Jordan River (see outline and notes—Nu.32:1-42 for more discussion). Gad stood forth as a strong reason for God to be praised. The LORD had enlarged the territory of Gad. This tribe was to be surrounded by the nomadic tribes of the Midianites, Ammonites, and Arabians—roving marauders from the desert. Therefore, Moses prayed that they would have the military strength of a lion and be victorious over their enemies.

Note: this tribe had chosen the best land for itself; therefore, Moses had demanded that they fight right alongside the other tribes until victory was secure over the enemies of the promised land (see Nu.32:1-42). History was to show that the tribe fulfilled the charge that Moses had laid upon it. The soldiers of this tribe remained with the Israelite army until all of the tribes had secured their inheritance in the promised land. Gad was faithful in carrying out the will of the LORD by helping the other tribes.

DEUTERONOMY 33:1-29

OUTLINE	SCRIPTURE

8. The blessing of Gad
  a. To stand as praise to God
  b. To have the military strength of a lion & be victorious
  c. To choose & possess the best land
  d. To fight alongside the other tribes until victory was secured over the enemies of the promised land (see Nu.32:1-42)
	20 And of Gad he said, Blessed *be* he that enlargeth Gad: he dwelleth as a lion, and teareth the arm with the crown of the head.
	21 And he provided the first part for himself, because there, *in* a portion of the lawgiver, *was he* seated; and he came with the heads of the people, he executed the justice of the LORD, and his judgments with Israel.

Thought 1. Helping other people, serving and meeting the needs of others—this is the lesson that can be gleaned from this blessing upon Gad. We must stretch our hands out to others: lifting them up, pulling them along, meeting their needs.

Whatever is needed, we must help people. Needs are all around us, sometimes desperate needs. Every community has people who are hurting and suffering from oppressive and wrenching pain—pain that wrings and wracks the body, mind, and emotions. In many cases, the need is not only mental and physical, but financial. Some persons have suffered bankruptcy or devastating loss, having lost homes and the money to feed, clothe, and house themselves. People need the LORD, and they need help, our help—our ministry, our service, our hands reaching out to help them in whatever way possible.

"And whosoever shall give to drink unto one of these little ones a cup of cold *water* only in the name of a disciple, verily I say unto you, he shall in no wise lose his reward" (Mt.10:42).

"Jesus said unto him, If thou wilt be perfect, go *and* sell that thou hast, and give to the poor, and thou shalt have treasure in heaven: and come *and* follow me" (Mt.19:21).

"But so shall it not be among you: but whosoever will be great among you, shall be your minister: And whosoever of you will be the chiefest, shall be servant of all" (Mk.10:43-44).

"But a certain Samaritan, as he journeyed, came where he was: and when he saw him, he had compassion *on him,* And went to *him,* and bound up his wounds, pouring in oil and wine, and set him on his own beast, and brought him to an inn, and took care of him. And on the morrow when he departed, he took out two pence, and gave *them* to the host, and said unto him, Take care of him; and whatsoever thou spendest more, when I come again, I will repay thee" (Lu.10:33-35).

"If I then, *your* LORD and Master, have washed your feet; ye also ought to wash one another's feet" (Jn.13:14).

"He saith to him again the second time, Simon, *son* of Jonas, lovest thou me? He saith unto him, Yea, LORD; thou knowest that I love thee. He saith unto him, Feed my sheep" (Jn.21:16).

"Bear ye one another's burdens, and so fulfil the law of Christ" (Ga.6:2).

"As we have therefore opportunity, let us do good unto all *men,* especially unto them who are of the household of faith" (Ga.6:10).

"But to do good and to communicate [give] forget not: for with such sacrifices God is well pleased" (He.13:16).

"Pure religion and undefiled before God and the Father is this, To visit the fatherless and widows in their affliction, *and* to keep himself unspotted from the world" (Js.1:27).

"If there be among you a poor man of one of thy brethren within any of thy gates in thy land which the LORD thy God giveth thee, thou shalt not harden thine heart, nor shut thine hand from thy poor brother" (De.15:7).

"I was eyes to the blind, and feet *was* I to the lame" (Jb.29:15).

"Trust in the LORD, and do good; *so* shalt thou dwell in the land, and verily thou shalt be fed" (Ps.37:3).

"Blessed *is* he that considereth the poor: the LORD will deliver him in time of trouble" (Ps.41:1).

"They that sow in tears shall reap in joy. He that goeth forth and weepeth, bearing precious seed, shall doubtless come again with rejoicing, bringing his sheaves *with him*" (Ps.126:5-6).

"He that hath pity upon the poor lendeth unto the LORD; and that which he hath given will he pay him again" (Pr.19:17).

"She stretcheth out her hand to the poor; yea, she reacheth forth her hands to the needy" (Pr.31:20).

"The LORD GOD hath given me the tongue of the learned, that I should know how to speak a word in season to *him that is* weary: he wakeneth morning by morning, he wakeneth mine ear to hear as the learned" (Is.50:4).

9 (33:22) **Dan, Tribe of, Prophetic Blessing of—Tribes, of Israel**: there was the blessing pronounced upon the tribe of Dan. This tribe was to be courageous and ferocious in military conflicts. The character of this tribe was to be that of a lion's cub that springs out from an ambush to consume its prey.

DEUTERONOMY 33:1-29

OUTLINE	SCRIPTURE
9. The blessing of Dan: To be courageous & ferocious in military conflicts	22 And of Dan he said, Dan *is* a lion's whelp: he shall leap from Bashan.

Thought 1. Courage is needed in defeating the enemies that confront us. As we march to the promised land of heaven, enemy after enemy will attack us, seeking to keep us out of the promised land. Trial after trial and temptation after temptation will attempt to overthrow us. In some cases, the affliction or difficulty will be severe. In such moments, courage is needed—a ferocious courage. No matter the strength of the enemy—no matter the severity of these testings—we must not fear, withdraw, or collapse under the onslaught. We must be courageous and stand fast. This is the strong encouragement of Scripture:

"Watch ye, stand fast in the faith, quit you like men, be strong" (1 Co.16:13).

"Finally, my brethren, be strong in the LORD, and in the power of his might" (Ep.6:10).

"And in nothing terrified by your adversaries: which is to them an evident token of perdition, but to you of salvation, and that of God. For unto you it is given in the behalf of Christ, not only to believe on him, but also to suffer for his sake" (Ph.1:28-29).

"Thou therefore, my son, be strong in the grace that is in Christ Jesus" (2 Ti.2:1).

"Be strong and of a good courage, fear not, nor be afraid of them: for the LORD thy God, he *it is* that doth go with thee; he will not fail thee, nor forsake thee" (De.31:6).

"Be strong and of a good courage: for unto this people shalt thou divide for an inheritance the land, which I sware unto their fathers to give them" (Jos.1:6).

"And Joshua said unto them, Fear not, nor be dismayed, be strong and of good courage: for thus shall the LORD do to all your enemies against whom ye fight" (Jos.10:25).

"Be ye therefore very courageous to keep and to do all that is written in the book of the law of Moses, that ye turn not aside therefrom *to* the right hand or *to* the left; That ye come not among these nations, these that remain among you; neither make mention of the names of their gods, nor cause to swear *by them,* neither serve them, nor bow yourselves unto them: But cleave unto the LORD your God, as ye have done unto this day" (Jos.23:6-8).

"Be of good courage, and let us play the men for our people, and for the cities of our God: and the LORD do that which seemeth him good" (2 S.10:12).

"Be of good courage, and let us behave ourselves valiantly for our people, and for the cities of our God: and let the LORD do *that which is* good in his sight" (1 Chr.19:13).

"Then shalt thou prosper, if thou takest heed to fulfil the statutes and judgments which the LORD charged Moses with concerning Israel: be strong, and of good courage; dread not, nor be dismayed" (1 Chr.22:13).

"And David said to Solomon his son, Be strong and of good courage, and do *it:* fear not, nor be dismayed: for the LORD God, *even* my God, *will be* with thee; he will not fail thee, nor forsake thee, until thou hast finished all the work for the service of the house of the LORD" (1 Chr.28:20).

"Be ye strong therefore, and let not your hands be weak: for your work shall be rewarded" (2 Chr.15:7).

"The LORD *is* my light and my salvation; whom shall I fear? the LORD *is* the strength of my life; of whom shall I be afraid? When the wicked, *even* mine enemies and my foes, came upon me to eat up my flesh, they stumbled and fell. Though an host should encamp against me, my heart shall not fear: though war should rise against me, in this *will* I *be* confident" (Ps.27:1-3).

"I will say of the LORD, *He is* my refuge and my fortress: my God; in him will I trust. Surely he shall deliver thee from the snare of the fowler, *and* from the noisome pestilence. He shall cover thee with his feathers, and under his wings shalt thou trust: his truth *shall be thy* shield and buckler. Thou shalt not be afraid for the terror by night; *nor* for the arrow *that* flieth by day; *Nor* for the pestilence *that* walketh in darkness; *nor* for the destruction *that* wasteth at noonday" (Ps.91:2-6).

10 (33:23) **Naphtali, Tribe of, Prophetic Blessing of**: there was the blessing of the tribe of Naphtali. This tribe was to be favored by God and filled with the LORD's blessings. Part of the blessing was to be the inheritance of a very fertile land. The tribe's territory would reach from north of Galilee to the area west and south of Galilee.

OUTLINE	SCRIPTURE
10. The blessing of Naphtali 　a. To be favored & filled with God's blessing 　b. To inherit the fertile land down to the Lake of Galilee	23 And of Naphtali he said, O Naphtali, satisfied with favour, and full with the blessing of the LORD: possess thou the west and the south.

Thought 1. The favor of God is the lesson gleaned from the blessing of this tribe. God favors His people, pouring favor after favor out upon us. He promises to favor us with all the necessities of life.

"For all the promises of God in him *are* yea, and in him Amen, unto the glory of God by us" (2 Co.1:20).

"Whereby are given unto us exceeding great and precious promises: that by these ye might be partakers of the divine nature, having escaped the corruption that is in the world through lust" (2 Pe.1:4).

"And this is the promise that he hath promised us, *even* eternal life" (1 Jn.2:25).

"Blessed *be* the LORD, that hath given rest unto his people Israel, according to all that he promised: there hath not failed one word of all his good promise, which he promised by the hand of Moses his servant" (1 K.8:56).

"Blessed *is* the people that know the joyful sound: they shall walk, O LORD, in the light of thy countenance. In thy name shall they rejoice all the day: and in thy righteousness shall they be exalted. For thou *art* the glory of their strength: and in thy favour our horn shall be exalted" (Ps.89:15-17).

"And therefore will the LORD wait, that he may be gracious unto you, and therefore will he be exalted, that he may have mercy upon you: for the LORD *is* a God of judgment: blessed *are* all they that wait for him" (Is.30:18).

"When thou passest through the waters, I *will be* with thee; and through the rivers, they shall not overflow thee: when thou walkest through the fire, thou shalt not be burned; neither shall the flame kindle upon thee" (Is.43:2).

"Yea, I will rejoice over them to do them good, and I will plant them in this land [the promised land] assuredly with my whole heart and with my whole soul" (Je.32:41).

11 (33:24-25) **Asher, Tribe of, Prophetic Blessing**: there was the blessing of the tribe of Asher. The very name of Asher means *blessed, happy*. This tribe was to be most blessed, happy, and highly favored by the other tribes. Note why: because of their prosperity. The tribe of Asher sat along the seacoast north of Carmel and reached all the way to Tyre and Sidon (Jos.19:24-31). The territory included some of the most fertile land anywhere. It was crisscrossed with trade routes to the sea. The tribe became industrious, energetic, making good use of what it had, so much so that it was called upon to provide a yearly quota for the palace (De.33:24; see 1 K.4:7). Moreover, note that they were to have military protection as well, strong fortifications to protect themselves against attacking enemies (v.25).

The people of Asher became wealthy and lived in luxury. However, during the days of the judges, they were consumed by their luxury and their wealth. They refused to help the other tribes in fighting against the enemies of Israel. They were too caught up in the worldly pleasures, bright lights, and comforts of this world to worry about the needs of their brothers under attack on some far-away border (Jud.5:17-18).

OUTLINE	SCRIPTURE
11. The blessing of Asher	24 And of Asher he said, Let Asher *be* blessed with children; let him be acceptable to his brethren, and let him dip his foot in oil.
a. To be most blessed, happy, & favored by others	
b. To be prosperous	
c. To have military protection—fortification & strength	25 Thy shoes *shall be* iron and brass; and as thy days, *so shall* thy strength *be*.

Thought 1. Scripture warns against worldliness, against becoming too attached to the luxury, pleasures, bright lights, and greed of this earth. True believers are to live separated lives, lives that are different—drastically different—from the worldly of this earth.

"Wherefore come out from among them, and be ye separate, saith the LORD, and touch not the unclean thing; and I will receive you, and will be a Father unto you, and ye shall be my sons and daughters, saith the LORD Almighty" (2 Co.6:17-18).

"And have no fellowship with the unfruitful works of darkness, but rather reprove them" (Ep.5:11).

"If ye were of the world, the world would love his own: but because ye are not of the world, but I have chosen you out of the world, therefore the world hateth you" (Jn.15:19).

"And with many other words did he testify and exhort, saying, Save yourselves from this untoward generation" (Ac.2:40).

"But now I have written unto you not to keep company, if any man that is called a brother be a fornicator, or covetous, or an idolater, or a railer, or a drunkard, or an extortioner; with such an one no not to eat" (1 Co.5:11).

"Be ye not unequally yoked together with unbelievers: for what fellowship hath righteousness with unrighteousness? and what communion hath light with darkness?" (2 Co.6:14).

"Love not the world, neither the things *that are* in the world. If any man love the world, the love of the Father is not in him. For all that *is* in the world, the lust of the flesh, and the lust of the eyes, and the pride of life, is not of the Father, but is of the world" (1 Jn.2:15-16).

DEUTERONOMY 33:1-29

12 **(33:26-29) Blessings, of God—God, Greatness of—God, Nature, Incomparable—God, Nature, Eternal—Moses, Last Words of:** these are the last words ever spoken to the Israelites by the aged servant of God. With these words, Moses closed his ministry upon earth.

OUTLINE	SCRIPTURE	SCRIPTURE	OUTLINE

12. The greatness of God & His wonderful blessings
  a. The greatness of God
    1) He is incomparable: Dwells in sovereign power & majesty
    2) He is the eternal God
  b. The wonderful blessings of God
    1) Refuge & support
    2) Victory, conquest, triumph
    3) Security, safety
    4) Provision, supply,
	26 *There is* none like unto the God of Jeshurun, *who* rideth upon the heaven in thy help, and in his excellency on the sky.
	27 The eternal God *is* thy refuge, and underneath *are* the everlasting arms: and he shall thrust out the enemy from before thee; and shall say, Destroy *them*.
	28 Israel then shall dwell in safety alone: the fountain
		of Jacob *shall be* upon a land of corn and wine; also his heavens shall drop down dew.
		29 Happy *art* thou, O Israel: who *is* like unto thee, O people saved by the LORD, the shield of thy help, and who *is* the sword of thy excellency! and thine enemies shall be found liars unto thee; and thou shalt tread upon their high places.
			prosperity
			
			5) Salvation
			6) Protection: Shielded, defended, feared
			7) Spiritual victory & purity

    The *incomparable greatness* of God and the *wonderful blessings* of God make up the final message that overflows from the lips of this dear aged man of God.

  a. Moses declared the *incomparable greatness* of God (vv.26-27). God is incomparable: there is no one like the God of Israel (Jeshurun).

    1) God dwells in sovereign power, riding across the heavens in majestic glory and splendor (v.26). Note that Moses made a breathtaking statement: the power of God is available to help His people. God is not off in the distance, high in the heavens, out of reach. The people of God are not left helpless and hopeless, not left to handle their problems by themselves. On the contrary, the power of God is available to help in meeting the needs of His dear people.

    2) God is the eternal God (v.27). He had no beginning and will have no end. He is everlasting. Again, the aged servant of God made a startling statement: the fact that God is eternal is not an abstract truth. Being eternal, God has arms that are everlasting. This means a most wonderful thing: the *everlasting arms* of God are able to hold and support His precious people.

  b. Moses proclaimed the wonderful blessings of God (vv.27-29). He had just finished pronouncing the prophetic blessings of God upon each of the twelve tribes of Israel. Now he preached the blessings that God pours out upon all His people, upon all who have truly dedicated their lives to God. These are the blessings that God will pour out upon all who have renewed their covenant and commitment with God.

    1) The first blessing of God is that of refuge and support (v.27). The eternal God is the refuge for His people. He places His everlasting arms underneath them, holding them up and supporting them through all the trials and temptations of life.

    2) The second blessing of God is that of victory, conquest, and triumph over all enemies who oppose His people. Note that God is so active in the defense of His people that He Himself actually drives the enemy out before them and cries out, "Destroy the enemy!" The Israelites were about to enter the promised land and face strong and formidable enemies. As they faced the evil and brutal armies, they could rest assured that the LORD would empower them to defeat the enemy.

    3) The third blessing of God is that of security, of safety (v.28). Herein lies another marvelous promise: the Israelites would live in safety, and note: they would be able to live standing alone, without having to enter alliances with surrounding nations. The *sovereign power* and *everlasting arms* of God would secure His people, make them perfectly safe from all enemies.

    4) The fourth blessing of God is that of provision, supply, and prosperity (v.28). The water supply of the nation would produce a fruitful land that would yield an abundance of grain and new wine. The result would be a prosperous economy.

    5) The fifth blessing of God is that of salvation (v.29). A burst of joy sprang from the heart of the dear servant of God, shouting out how blessed the Israelites were, blessed because they had been saved by the LORD. Note that their salvation made them a very special people to the LORD. They were distinct, different from all other people of the world—all because of their salvation.

    6) The sixth blessing of God is that of protection (v.29). The LORD is their shield and defender. When the people of God need help, God shields them; and when they need to be defended, God takes up the sword of His majesty to protect them.

    7) The seventh promise of God is that of spiritual victory and purity (v.29). Note a very important fact: it is the worship centers of high places that will be trampled under the feet of the Israelites. The *high places* refers to the Canaanite worship centers built on the hills and mountains throughout the land of Canaan. The LORD had instructed the Israelites to destroy these places once the land had been conquered. There was to be spiritual purity among God's people, the worship of Him and Him alone. There was to be no idolatry and no false worship. One of the wonderful blessings of God was to be spiritual victory and purity over all the enemies who opposed God's people.

    The ministry of Moses to God's dear people was now closed, closed on a victorious note. God's people would be victorious over all enemies. They would be more than conquerors through Him who loved them and called them according to His eternal purpose (see Ro.8:28).

DEUTERONOMY 33:1-29

Thought 1. The last words of Moses speak to the hearts of all.
(1) Moses declared the greatness of God.
    (a) God is incomparable: He dwells in sovereign power and majesty.

"For thine is the kingdom, and the power, and the glory, for ever. Amen" (Mt.6:13).

"But Jesus beheld *them,* and said unto them, With men this is impossible; but with God all things are possible" (Mt.19:26).

"For with God nothing shall be impossible" (Lu.1:37).

"God that made the world and all things therein, seeing that he is LORD of heaven and earth, dwelleth not in temples made with hands" (Ac.17:24).

"Thou wilt say then unto me, Why doth he yet find fault? For who hath resisted his will? Nay but, O man, who art thou that repliest against God? Shall the thing formed say to him that formed *it,* Why hast thou made me thus? Hath not the potter power over the clay, of the same lump to make one vessel unto honour, and another unto dishonour" (Ro.9:19-21).

"Now unto him that is able to do exceeding abundantly above all that we ask or think, according to the power that worketh in us" (Ep.3:20).

"Who shall change our vile body, that it may be fashioned like unto his glorious body, according to the working whereby he is able even to subdue all things unto himself" (Ph.3:21).

"Know therefore this day, and consider *it* in thine heart, that the LORD he *is* God in heaven above, and upon the earth beneath: *there is* none else" (De.4:39).

"Both riches and honour *come* of thee, and thou reignest over all; and in thine hand *is* power and might; and in thine hand *it is* to make great, and to give strength unto all" (1 Chr.29:12).

"The LORD sitteth upon the flood; yea, the LORD sitteth King for ever" (Ps.29:10).

"For the LORD most high *is* terrible; *he is* a great King over all the earth" (Ps.47:2).

"That *men* may know that thou, whose name alone *is* JEHOVAH, *art* the most high over all the earth" (Ps.83:18).

"The LORD reigneth, he is clothed with majesty; the LORD is clothed with strength, *wherewith* he hath girded himself: the world also is stablished, that it cannot be moved" (Ps.93:1).

"For I know that the LORD *is* great, and *that* our LORD *is* above all gods. Whatsoever the LORD pleased, *that* did he in heaven, and in earth, in the seas, and all deep places" (Ps.135:5-6).

"Yea, before the day *was* I *am* he; and *there is* none that can deliver out of my hand: I will work, and who shall let [hinder] it" (Is.43:13).

"Daniel answered and said, Blessed be the name of God for ever and ever: for wisdom and might are his: And he changeth the times and the seasons: he removeth kings, and setteth up kings: he giveth wisdom unto the wise, and knowledge to them that know understanding: He revealeth the deep and secret things: he knoweth what *is* in the darkness, and the light dwelleth with him" (Da.2:20-22).

"And all the inhabitants of the earth *are* reputed as nothing: and he doeth according to his will in the army of heaven, and *among* the inhabitants of the earth: and none can stay his hand, or say unto him, What doest thou" (Da.4:35).

    (b) God is the eternal God.

"But, beloved, be not ignorant of this one thing, that one day *is* with the LORD as a thousand years, and a thousand years as one day" (2 Pe.3:8).

"I am Alpha and Omega, the beginning and the ending, saith the LORD, which is, and which was, and which is to come, the Almighty" (Re.1:8).

"For I lift up my hand to heaven, and say, I live for ever" (De.32:40).

"The eternal God *is thy* refuge, and underneath *are* the everlasting arms: and he shall thrust out the enemy from before thee; and shall say, Destroy *them*" (De.33:27).

"Thy name, O LORD, *endureth* for ever; *and* thy memorial, O LORD, throughout all generations" (Ps.135:13).

"Thy kingdom *is* an everlasting kingdom, and thy dominion *endureth* throughout all generations" (Ps.145:13).

    (c) There is no one like God.

"And the scribe said unto him, Well, Master, thou hast said the truth: for there is one God; and there is none other but he" (Mk.12:32).

"And he said, To morrow. And he said, *Be it* according to thy word: that thou mayest know that *there is* none like unto the LORD our God" (Ex.8:10).

"Who *is* like unto thee, O LORD, among the gods? who *is* like thee, glorious in holiness, fearful *in* praises, doing wonders" (Ex.15:11).

"Wherefore thou art great, O LORD God: for *there is* none like thee, neither *is there any* God beside thee, according to all that we have heard with our ears" (2 S.7:22).

"And he said, LORD God of Israel, *there is* no God like thee, in heaven above, or on earth beneath, who keepest covenant and mercy with thy servants that walk before thee with all their heart" (1 K.8:23).

DEUTERONOMY 33:1-29

"O LORD, *there is* none like thee, neither *is there any* God beside thee, according to all that we have heard with our ears" (1 Chr.17:20).

"For who in the heaven can be compared unto the LORD? *who* among the sons of the mighty can be likened unto the LORD" (Ps.89:6).

"To whom then will ye liken God? or what likeness will ye compare unto him? The workman melteth a graven image, and the goldsmith spreadeth it over with gold, and casteth silver chains. He that *is* so impoverished that he hath no oblation chooseth a tree *that* will not rot; he seeketh unto him a cunning workman to prepare a graven image, *that* shall not be moved. Have ye not known? have ye not heard? hath it not been told you from the beginning? have ye not understood from the foundations of the earth? *It is* he that sitteth upon the circle of the earth, and the inhabitants thereof *are* as grasshoppers; that stretcheth out the heavens as a curtain, and spreadeth them out as a tent to dwell in: That bringeth the princes to nothing; he maketh the judges of the earth as vanity" (Is.40:18-23).

(2) Moses proclaimed the wonderful blessings that God pours out upon His people.

  (a) God is our refuge and support. Underneath are His everlasting arms that hold us up and support us.

"The eternal God *is thy* refuge, and underneath *are* the everlasting arms: and he shall thrust out the enemy from before thee; and shall say, Destroy *them*" (De.33:27).

"For in the time of trouble he shall hide me in his pavilion: in the secret of his tabernacle shall he hide me; he shall set me up upon a rock" (Ps.27:5).

"Thou shalt hide them in the secret of thy presence from the pride of man: thou shalt keep them secretly in a pavilion from the strife of tongues" (Ps.31:20).

"God *is* our refuge and strength, a very present help in trouble" (Ps.46:1).

"Be thou my strong habitation, whereunto I may continually resort: thou hast given commandment to save me; for thou *art* my rock and my fortress" (Ps.71:3).

"In the fear of the LORD *is* strong confidence: and his children shall have a place of refuge" (Pr.14:26).

"The name of the LORD *is* a strong tower: the righteous runneth into it, and is safe" (Pr.18:10).

"For thou hast been a strength to the poor, a strength to the needy in his distress, a refuge from the storm, a shadow from the heat, when the blast of the terrible ones *is* as a storm *against* the wall" (Is.25:4).

  (b) God gives us victory over all the enemies of this life. As we march to the promised land of heaven, God empowers us to conquer all the trials and temptations of life.

"Who shall separate us from the love of Christ? *shall* tribulation, or distress, or persecution, or famine, or nakedness, or peril, or sword....Nay, in all these things we are more than conquerors through him that loved us. For I am persuaded, that neither death, nor life, nor angels, nor principalities, nor powers, nor things present, nor things to come, Nor height, nor depth, nor any other creature, shall be able to separate us from the love of God, which is in Christ Jesus our LORD" (Ro.8:35, 37-39).

"There hath no temptation taken you but such as is common to man: but God *is* faithful, who will not suffer you to be tempted above that ye are able; but will with the temptation also make a way to escape, that ye may be able to bear *it*" (1 Co.10:13).

"Wherefore in all things it behooved him to be made like unto *his* brethren, that he might be a merciful and faithful high priest in things *pertaining* to God, to make reconciliation for the sins of the people. For in that he himself hath suffered being tempted, he is able to succour them that are tempted" (He.2:17-18).

"For whatsoever is born of God overcometh the world: and this is the victory that overcometh the world, *even* our faith. Who is he that overcometh the world, but he that believeth that Jesus is the Son of God" (1 Jn.5:4-5).

"Through thee will we push down our enemies: through thy name will we tread them under that rise up against us" (Ps.44:5).

  (c) God gives us security, safety. No matter what may confront us, God secures us and delivers us from overwhelming fear.

"For God hath not given us the spirit of fear; but of power, and of love, and of a sound mind" (2 Ti.1:7).

"*Let your* conversation [conduct, behavior] *be* without covetousness; *and be* content with such things as ye have: for he hath said, I will never leave thee, nor forsake thee. So that we may boldly say, The LORD *is* my helper, and I will not fear what man shall do unto me" (He.13:5-6).

"And who *is* he that will harm you, if ye be followers of that which is good" (1 Pe.3:13).

"And thou shalt be secure, because there is hope; yea, thou shalt dig *about thee, and* thou shalt take thy rest in safety" (Jb. 11:18).

"Thou shalt not be afraid for the terror by night; *nor* for the arrow *that* flieth by day" (Ps.91:5).

"I will say of the LORD, *He is* my refuge and my fortress: my God; in him will I trust. Surely he shall deliver thee from the snare of the fowler, *and* from the noisome pestilence. He shall cover thee with his feathers, and under his wings shalt thou trust: his truth *shall be thy* shield and buckler. Thou

DEUTERONOMY 33:1-29

shalt not be afraid for the terror by night; *nor* for the arrow *that* flieth by day; *Nor* for the pestilence *that* walketh in darkness; *nor* for the destruction *that* wasteth at noonday" (Ps.91:2-6).

"He shall not be afraid of evil tidings: his heart is fixed, trusting in the LORD" (Ps.112:7).

"The LORD *is* on my side; I will not fear: what can man do unto me" (Ps.118:6).

"When thou liest down, thou shalt not be afraid: yea, thou shalt lie down, and thy sleep shall be sweet" (Pr.3:24).

"Behold, God *is* my salvation; I will trust, and not be afraid: for the LORD JEHOVAH *is* my strength and *my* song; he also is become my salvation" (Is.12:2).

(d) God is our provision, supply, and prosperity. He meets every necessity and need of life.

"But seek ye first the kingdom of God, and his righteousness; and all these things shall be added unto you" (Mt.6:33).

"But my God shall supply all your need according to his riches in glory by Christ Jesus" (Ph.4:19).

"And ye shall serve the LORD your God, and he shall bless thy bread, and thy water; and I will take sickness away from the midst of thee" (Ex.23:25).

"Thou preparest a table before me in the presence of mine enemies: thou anointest my head with oil; my cup runneth over" (Ps.23:5).

"Blessed *be* the LORD, *who* daily loadeth us *with benefits, even* the God of our salvation" (Ps.68:19).

"I will abundantly bless her provision: I will satisfy her poor with bread" (Ps.132:15).

"Bring ye all the tithes into the storehouse, that there may be meat in mine house, and prove me now herewith, saith the LORD of hosts, if I will not open you the windows of heaven, and pour you out a blessing, that *there shall* not *be room* enough *to receive it*" (Mal.3:10).

(e) God gives us the wonderful gift of salvation (v.29). This is the basis, the very foundation of the blessings of God.

"For God so loved the world, that he gave his only begotten Son, that whosoever believeth in him should not perish, but have everlasting life" (Jn.3:16).

"And it shall come to pass, *that* whosoever shall call on the name of the LORD shall be saved" (Ac.2:21).

"That if thou shalt confess with thy mouth the LORD Jesus, and shalt believe in thine heart that God hath raised him from the dead, thou shalt be saved. For with the heart man believeth unto righteousness; and with the mouth confession is made unto salvation" (Ro.10:9-10).

"For whosoever shall call upon the name of the LORD shall be saved" (Ro.10:13).

"For by grace are ye saved through faith; and that not of yourselves: *it is* the gift of God: Not of works, lest any man should boast" (Ep.2:8-9).

"For the grace of God that bringeth salvation hath appeared to all men, Teaching us that, denying ungodliness and worldly lusts, we should live soberly, righteously, and godly, in this present world" (Tit.2:11-12).

"The LORD *is* my light and my salvation; whom shall I fear? the LORD *is* the strength of my life; of whom shall I be afraid" (Ps.27:1).

"But the salvation of the righteous *is* of the LORD: *he is* their strength in the time of trouble" (Ps.37:39).

"Behold, God *is* my salvation; I will trust, and not be afraid: for the LORD JEHOVAH *is* my strength and *my* song; he also is become my salvation" (Is.12:2).

"And it shall be said in that day, Lo, this *is* our God; we have waited for him, and he will save us: this *is* the LORD; we have waited for him, we will be glad and rejoice in his salvation" (Is.25:9).

"The LORD thy God in the midst of thee *is* mighty; he will save, he will rejoice over thee with joy; he will rest in his love, he will joy over thee with singing" (Zep.3:17).

(f) God blesses us with protection. He Himself is our shield and defender.

"After these things the word of the LORD came unto Abram in a vision, saying, Fear not, Abram: I *am* thy shield, *and* thy exceeding great reward" (Ge.15:1).

"But let all those that put their trust in thee rejoice: let them ever shout for joy, because thou defendest them: let them also that love thy name be joyful in thee" (Ps.5:11).

"Bow down thine ear to me; deliver me speedily: be thou my strong rock, for an house of defence to save me" (Ps.31:2).

"Our soul waiteth for the LORD: he *is* our help and our shield" (Ps.33:20).

"For the LORD God *is* a sun and shield: the LORD will give grace and glory: no good *thing* will he withhold from them that walk uprightly" (Ps.84:11).

"O Israel, trust thou in the LORD: he *is* their help and their shield" (Ps.115:9).

"Every word of God *is* pure: he *is* a shield unto them that put their trust in him" (Pr.30:5).

"As birds flying, so will the LORD of hosts defend Jerusalem; defending also he will deliver *it*; *and* passing over he will preserve *it*" (Is.31:5).

DEUTERONOMY 33:1-29

(g) God gives us spiritual victory and purity. He forgives our sins and empowers us to live a victorious life as we march to the promised land of heaven.

"These things I have spoken unto you, that in me ye might have peace. In the world ye shall have tribulation: but be of good cheer; I have overcome the world" (Jn.16:33).

"For though we walk in the flesh, we do not war after the flesh: (For the weapons of our warfare *are* not carnal, but mighty through God to the pulling down of strong holds;) Casting down imaginations, and every high thing that exalteth itself against the knowledge of God, and bringing into captivity every thought to the obedience of Christ" (2 Co.10:3-5).

"Now unto him that is able to do exceeding abundantly above all that we ask or think, according to the power that worketh in us" (Ep.3:20).

"Finally, my brethren, be strong in the LORD, and in the power of his might. Put on the whole armour of God, that ye may be able to stand against the wiles of the devil. For we wrestle not against flesh and blood, but against principalities, against powers, against the rulers of the darkness of this world, against spiritual wickedness in high *places*. Wherefore take unto you the whole armour of God, that ye may be able to withstand in the evil day, and having done all, to stand" (Ep.6:10-13).

"But thou, O man of God, flee these things; and follow after righteousness, godliness, faith, love, patience, meekness. Fight the good fight of faith, lay hold on eternal life, whereunto thou art also called, and hast professed a good profession before many witnesses" (1 Ti.6:11-12).

"Thou therefore endure hardness, as a good soldier of Jesus Christ. No man that warreth entangleth himself with the affairs of *this* life; that he may please him who hath chosen him to be a soldier" (2 Ti.2:3-4).

"Be sober, be vigilant; because your adversary the devil, as a roaring lion, walketh about, seeking whom he may devour: Whom resist stedfast in the faith, knowing that the same afflictions are accomplished in your brethren that are in the world. But the God of all grace, who hath called us unto his eternal glory by Christ Jesus, after that ye have suffered a while, make you perfect, stablish, strengthen, settle *you*" (1 Pe.5:8-10).

"He that hath an ear, let him hear what the Spirit saith unto the churches; To him that overcometh will I give to eat of the tree of life, which is in the midst of the paradise of God" (Re.2:7).

"He that hath an ear, let him hear what the Spirit saith unto the churches; To him that overcometh will I give to eat of the hidden manna, and will give him a white stone, and in the stone a new name written, which no man knoweth saving he that receiveth *it*" (Re.2:17).

"And he that overcometh, and keepeth my works unto the end, to him will I give power over the nations" (Re.2:26).

"He that overcometh, the same shall be clothed in white raiment; and I will not blot out his name out of the book of life, but I will confess his name before my Father, and before his angels" (Re.3:5).

"Him that overcometh will I make a pillar in the temple of my God, and he shall go no more out: and I will write upon him the name of my God, and the name of the city of my God, *which is* new Jerusalem, which cometh down out of heaven from my God: and *I will write upon him* my new name" (Re.3:12).

"To him that overcometh will I grant to sit with me in my throne, even as I also overcame, and am set down with my Father in his throne" (Re.3:21).

"He that overcometh shall inherit all things; and I will be his God, and he shall be my son" (Re.21:7).

DEUTERONOMY 34:1-12

CHAPTER 34

D. The Death of Moses: The Joyful Yet Sorrowful Passing of God's Dear Servant, 34:1-12

1. **The tender compassion & justice of God toward His dear servant**
   a. The exciting but sad climb up Mt. Pisgah^{DS1}: Moses viewed the promised land but died without ever entering it
   b. The tender compassion of God
      1) Showed Moses all the land

      2) Assured Moses that this was the promised land sworn to the forefathers of faith
   c. The sure justice of God: Moses was not allowed to enter the promised land because of his terrible sin (Nu.20:7-13)

   d. The presence of God during the death of His dear servant
      1) Died as God said (appointed)
      2) Died & was buried in the

And Moses went up from the plains of Moab unto the mountain of Nebo, to the top of Pisgah, that *is* over against Jericho. And the LORD showed him all the land of Gilead, unto Dan,
2 And all Naphtali, and the land of Ephraim, and Manasseh, and all the land of Judah, unto the utmost sea,
3 And the south, and the plain of the valley of Jericho, the city of palm trees, unto Zoar.
4 And the LORD said unto him, This *is* the land which I sware unto Abraham, unto Isaac, and unto Jacob, saying, I will give it unto thy seed: I have caused thee to see *it* with thine eyes, but thou shalt not go over thither.
5 So Moses the servant of the LORD died there in the land of Moab, according to the word of the LORD.
6 And he buried him in a valley in the land of Moab, over against Bethpeor: but no man knoweth of his sepulchre unto this day.
7 And Moses *was* an hundred and twenty years old when he died: his eye was not dim, nor his natural force abated.
8 And the children of Israel wept for Moses in the plains of Moab thirty days: so the days of weeping *and* mourning for Moses were ended.
9 And Joshua the son of Nun was full of the spirit of wisdom; for Moses had laid his hands upon him: and the children of Israel hearkened unto him, and did as the LORD commanded Moses.
10 And there arose not a prophet since in Israel like unto Moses, whom the LORD knew face to face,
11 In all the signs and the wonders, which the LORD sent him to do in the land of Egypt to Pharaoh, and to all his servants, and to all his land,
12 And in all that mighty hand, and in all the great terror which Moses showed in the sight of all Israel.

   presence of God
   - Was buried by God
   - Grave site is unknown

   3) Died when he was 120 years old
   - Was still healthy & strong

   - Was grieved over for 30 days

2. **The smooth transition of leadership from God's dear servant to Joshua^{DS2}**
   a. Joshua was qualified
      1) Filled with wisdom
      2) Commissioned by Moses
   b. Joshua was willingly followed

3. **The legacy of God's dear servant: The greatest of prophets**
   a. A legacy of strong, intimate fellowship with God: So close, God knew him face-to-face
   b. A legacy of saving God's people from Egyptian slavery (a symbol of salvation)—using miraculous signs & wonders
   c. A legacy of leading God's people through the wilderness journeys to the promised land (a symbol of heaven, of spiritual victory & rest)—all thru the mighty power of God

DIVISION VI

THE FINAL ACTS AND DEATH OF MOSES, GOD'S AGED SERVANT: REMEMBER THE ENCOURAGEMENT AND THE WARNING OF GOD, 31:1–34:12

D. The Death of Moses: The Joyful Yet Sorrowful Passing of God's Dear Servant, 34:1-12

(34:1-12) **Introduction**: the ministry of Moses had come to an end. He knew that he was now to die. He had just preached his last message to the people of God, the people he loved so much. For forty long and difficult years he had ministered to the Israelites, his very own people. By the presence and power of God, he had led them out of Egyptian slavery and through the wilderness wanderings. He had marched with them step by step, rejoicing over their successes and weeping and suffering with them through their defeats. He had often been the victim of their complaints, grumbling, and murmuring, and even of their threats against his life. The people were a stiff-necked, stubborn people who continually disobeyed and rebelled against God. Nevertheless, Moses loved the dear people of God. He had poured out his life as an offering in service to the people of God; he had totally sacrificed himself in ministry to them. But now he had just proclaimed his last message to them. He had walked out, away from the congregation. No doubt, he briefly stopped to give a final word of exhortation to Joshua, his appointed replacement, and Eleazar, and to the rest of the national cabinet consisting of the twelve tribal leaders and their judges. But most likely with tears in his eyes, he said farewell and turned to begin the long climb up Mt. Pisgah where he was to meet the LORD face to face and go home to be with the Him forever. This Scripture is: *The Death of Moses: The Joyful Yet Sorrowful Passing of God's Dear Servant,* 34:1-12.
1. The tender compassion and justice of God toward His dear servant (vv.1-8).
2. The smooth transition of leadership from God's dear servant to Joshua (v.9).
3. The legacy of God's dear servant: The greatest of prophets (vv.10-12).

1 (34:1-8) **Compassion, of God—Justice, of God—Moses, Hope Fulfilled—Moses, Death of—Promised Land, Seen by Moses**: there was the tender compassion and justice of God toward His dear servant. No better description of the scene could be given than that of Scripture:

425

DEUTERONOMY 34:1-12

OUTLINE	SCRIPTURE	SCRIPTURE	OUTLINE
1. **The tender compassion & justice of God toward His dear servant**	And Moses went up from the plains of Moab unto the mountain of Nebo, to the top of Pisgah, that *is* over against Jericho. And the LORD showed him all the land of Gilead, unto Dan,	thee to see *it* with thine eyes, but thou shalt not go over thither.	enter the promised land because of his terrible sin (Nu.20:7-13)
a. The exciting but sad climb up Mt. Pisgah^{DS1}: Moses viewed the promised land but died without ever entering it		5 So Moses the servant of the LORD died there in the land of Moab, according to the word of the LORD.	d. The presence of God during the death of His dear servant
b. The tender compassion of God			1) Died as God said (appointed)
1) Showed Moses all the land	2 And all Naphtali, and the land of Ephraim, and Manasseh, and all the land of Judah, unto the utmost sea,	6 And he buried him in a valley in the land of Moab, over against Bethpeor: but no man knoweth of his sepulchre unto this day.	2) Died & was buried in the presence of God • Was buried by God • Grave site is unknown
	3 And the south, and the plain of the valley of Jericho, the city of palm trees, unto Zoar.	7 And Moses *was* an hundred and twenty years old when he died: his eye was not dim, nor his natural force abated.	3) Died when he was 120 years old • Was still healthy & strong
2) Assured Moses that this was the promised land sworn to the forefathers of faith	4 And the LORD said unto him, This *is* the land which I sware unto Abraham, unto Isaac, and unto Jacob, saying, I will give it unto thy seed: I have caused	8 And the children of Israel wept for Moses in the plains of Moab thirty days: so the days of weeping *and* mourning for Moses were ended.	• Was grieved over for 30 days
c. The sure justice of God: Moses was not allowed to			

a. The climb up Mt. Pisgah was obviously an exciting time, but a sad time as well. Moses was to view the promised land from the top of the mountain, but he was also to die on the mountain without ever entering the land (v.1). He was climbing the mountain to be all alone with God: his ministry was to end just as it had begun—in the very presence of God Himself.[1] When Moses was only a shepherd in the desert, God first confronted him in the burning bush. But now God was going to confront him on Mt. Nebo as the great leader who had faithfully obeyed and served Him for forty long years. God was now ready to take His dear servant to the eternal promised land of heaven. He was now to be face to face with the LORD God forever.

b. In tender compassion, God granted Moses the right to gaze out over the promised land for which he had so long sought (vv.1-3). As he viewed the land, all sorts of joyful emotions must have surged through his mind, for there lying before him was the wonderful promised land of God. From the top of Mt. Nebo, Moses had a panoramic view of the promised land, the inheritance that God had promised to give to His people. *The Expositor's Bible Commentary* describes exactly what Moses could see:

> *The description indicates the area one would see from Nebo when looking first northward (from Gilead to Dan), turning his gaze northwest (all of Naphtali; the territory of Ephraim and Manasseh), and west (all the land of Judah as far as the western sea), and then looking southward (the Negev and the whole region from the Valley of Jericho, the City of Palms, as far as Zoar).*[2]

Note the assurance God gave Moses: this was the promised land sworn to the forefathers of faith. This was the very land God had promised to Abraham, Isaac, and Jacob and to their descendants who would follow in the steps of their faith (see Ro.4:1-25; Ga.3:6-9).

c. Even in the midst of this touching scene that so graphically pictures the death of God's dear servant, the sure justice of God must be remembered (v.4). The justice of God has to be executed. Even the dear servant of God had to face the judgment of God. Moses was not allowed to cross the Jordan River and enter the promised land, all because of his haughty, prideful, reactionary spirit and terrible disobedience at the waters of Meribah (see outline and notes—Nu.20:7-13).

d. God was present during the death of His dear servant (vv.5-8). Moses died just as God had said or appointed (v.5). Jewish rabbis give a descriptive interpretation of this verse, saying that "He died with a kiss from the LORD."[3] Note that Moses died in the very presence of God Himself, and that no man had a part in his burial. Scripture says that God Himself buried Moses and that his grave sight was unknown from the very beginning. There was obviously a very special reason for this private burial. Being prone to idolatry, the Israelites would have made a shrine and worshipped the dead body of Moses, the great founder and father of their nation. From the very beginning, God prevented His people from worshipping Moses.[4]

Moses died when he was 120 years old (vv.7-8). Scripture clearly says that he died while he was still healthy and strong (v.7). Nevertheless, his work for God upon earth was done, so God took him on home to be with Him, took him home to the eternal promised land of heaven. The Israelites grieved over his passing for thirty days, just as they had done for Aaron.

> **Thought 1.** The death of a believer is precious in the sight of God. Suffering, sin, and evil break the heart of God; therefore, when it is time for a dear believer to go home to heaven—this is a most precious moment to God. He is able to take one of His people out of the suffering and shame of this world. God would go ahead and end world history now in order to stop the suffering, the shame, the sin and evil but for one thing: He wants more and more people to be saved

---
1 John Maxwell. *The Preacher's Commentary on Deuteronomy*, p.347.
2 Frank E. Gaebelein, Editor. *The Expositor's Bible Commentary*, p.233.
3 *Matthew Henry's Commentary, Vol.1*, p.886.
4 *Ibid.*, p.886.

so they can live with Him in the bliss of heaven and in His presence forever. When God took Moses home, it was a most precious experience. And when God takes any of us who truly believe and trust Him, it will likewise be a most precious moment.

"Precious in the sight of the LORD *is* the death of his saints" (Ps.116:15).

"Yea, though I walk through the valley of the shadow of death, I will fear no evil: for thou *art* with me; thy rod and thy staff they comfort me" (Ps.23:4).

"The wicked is driven away in his wickedness: but the righteous hath hope in his death" (Pr.14:32).

"For none of us liveth to himself, and no man dieth to himself. For whether we live, we live unto the LORD; and whether we die, we die unto the LORD: whether we live therefore, or die, we are the LORD's. For to this end Christ both died, and rose, and revived, that he might be LORD both of the dead and living" (Ro.14:7-9).

"We are confident, *I say,* and willing rather to be absent from the body, and to be present with the LORD" (2 Co.5:8).

"For to me to live *is* Christ, and to die *is* gain. But if I live in the flesh, this *is* the fruit of my labour: yet what I shall choose I wot not. For I am in a strait betwixt two, having a desire to depart, and to be with Christ; which is far better" (Ph.1:21-23).

"These all died in faith, not having received the promises, but having seen them afar off, and were persuaded of *them,* and embraced *them,* and confessed that they were strangers and pilgrims on the earth. For they that say such things declare plainly that they seek a country....But now they desire a better *country,* that is, an heavenly: wherefore God is not ashamed to be called their God: for he hath prepared for them a city" (He.11:13-14, 16).

"And I heard a voice from heaven saying unto me, Write, Blessed *are* the dead which die in the LORD from henceforth: Yea, saith the Spirit, that they may rest from their labours; and their works do follow them" (Re.14:13).

"And God shall wipe away all tears from their eyes; and there shall be no more death, neither sorrow, nor crying, neither shall there be any more pain: for the former things are passed away" (Re.21:4).

DEEPER STUDY # 1
(34:1) **Pisgah, Mount**: a mountain that is located on the east side of the Jordan River and is part of the same mountain range that is associated with Mt. Nebo. Mount Pisgah...
- was the place where God showed Moses the spectacular view of the promised land (De.34:1)
- was the place where the prophet Balaam was taken by Balak to curse Israel (Nu.23:14)
- was included in Sihon's domain, king of the Ammorites (Jos.12:2-3)
- became the border of the promised land for the tribe of Reuben (Jos.13:20)

---

2 (34:9) **Leadership, of Joshua—Joshua, Qualification of—Joshua, Leadership of**: there was a smooth transition of leadership from God's dear servant Moses to Joshua. Joshua was eminently qualified to lead the Israelites into the promised land. He had been appointed by God and filled with the spirit of wisdom by God. Moreover, Moses had publicly commissioned Joshua before all the people. They knew beyond question that the mantle of leadership had been passed to him. Therefore the Israelites willingly followed Joshua now that Moses was dead. His leadership and ministry will be studied in the next great book of Holy Scripture, the book of Joshua.

OUTLINE	SCRIPTURE

2. The smooth transition of leadership from God's dear servant to Joshua^{DS2}
a. Joshua was qualified
  1) Filled with wisdom
  2) Commissioned by Moses
b. Joshua was willingly followed
	9 And Joshua the son of Nun was full of the spirit of wisdom; for Moses had laid his hands upon him: and the children of Israel hearkened unto him, and did as the LORD commanded Moses.

Thought 1. The Israelites followed Joshua because he had been appointed by God to be the ruler of their nation, and he was eminently qualified. Scripture says this about the wisdom and integrity of rulers, both of which are essential.

"Now therefore let Pharaoh look out a man discreet and wise, and set him over the land of Egypt" (Ge.41:33).

"Moreover thou shalt provide out of all the people able men, such as fear God, men of truth, hating covetousness; and place *such* over them, *to be* rulers of thousands, *and* rulers of hundreds, rulers of fifties, and rulers of tens" (Ex.18:21).

"Take you wise men, and understanding, and known among your tribes, and I will make them rulers over you" (De.1:13).

"Judges and officers shalt thou make thee in all thy gates, which the LORD thy God giveth thee, throughout thy tribes: and they shall judge the people with just judgment" (De.16:18).

DEUTERONOMY 34:1-12

"That which is altogether just shalt thou follow, that thou mayest live, and inherit the land which the LORD thy God giveth thee" (De.16:20).

"The God of Israel said, the Rock of Israel spake to me, He that ruleth over men *must be* just, ruling in the fear of God" (2 S.23:3).

"Be wise now therefore, O ye kings: be instructed, ye judges of the earth. Serve the LORD with fear, and rejoice with trembling" (Ps.2:10-11).

"Mercy and truth preserve the king: and his throne is upholden by mercy" (Pr.20:28).

"To do justice and judgment *is* more acceptable to the LORD than sacrifice" (Pr.21:3).

"These *things* also *belong* to the wise. *It is* not good to have respect of persons in judgment" (Pr.24:23).

"*It is* the glory of God to conceal a thing: but the honour of kings *is* to search out a matter" (Pr.25:2).

"The king by judgment establisheth the land: but he that receiveth gifts overthroweth it" (Pr.29:4).

"The king that faithfully judgeth the poor, his throne shall be established for ever" (Pr.29:14).

"*It is* not for kings, O Lemuel, *it is* not for kings to drink wine; nor for princes strong drink" (Pr.31:4).

"Thus saith the LORD, Keep ye judgment, and do justice: for my salvation *is* near to come, and my righteousness to be revealed" (Is.56:1).

DEEPER STUDY # 2

(34:9) Moses—Joshua—Leadership, Transition of: training future leaders is of critical importance. The success or failure of the younger generation is in the hands of today's leaders. As a leader, Moses took his responsibility seriously and prepared his young aide Joshua to succeed him. He carefully mixed his many years of formal training with his many years of life experiences and prepared Joshua to lead God's people into the promised land.[5]

COMPARISONS AND CONTRASTS OF MOSES WITH JOSHUA

	MOSES	JOSHUA
Meaning Of Name	⇒ "Drawn out of the water" (Ex.2:10)	⇒ "God Saves" (Nu.13:1-25; 27:18-23)
Character Of	⇒ He was not reactionary nor combative but humble (Nu.12:1-3, esp. v.3) ⇒ He had the spirit of a humble minister, of a true servant of God (Nu.11:4-35, esp. vv.26-30)	⇒ He was a man after God's own heart (Nu.27:18-23)
Type - Symbol Of	⇒ Christ, the perfect Mediator who stands between God and man (Nu.36:13, Thgt.1)	⇒ Christ, the person who saves us and leads us into the promised land forever (Nu.13:1-25, Thgt.3)
Tribe Of / Family	⇒ Tribe of Levi, Son of Amram and Jochebed (Ex.6:20)	⇒ Tribe of Ephraim, Son of Nun (Nu.13:1-25, esp.v.8)
Most Significant Contribution	⇒ Used by God to deliver Israel from the bondage of Egyptian slavery ⇒ Used by God to present God's law to His people ⇒ Used by God to build the Tabernacle, the place of worship, teaching how God was to be approached by man ⇒ Used by God to constitute Israel as a nation governed by law	⇒ Used by God to lead Israel into the promised land ⇒ Used by God to conquer the promised land and to divide the inheritance of the land among the tribes
Similarities	⇒ Moses took his sandals off in God's presence (Ex.3:1-6)	⇒ Joshua took his sandals off in the presence of the Captain of the LORD's Host (Jos.5:13-15)

---

[5] NOTE: we would like to acknowledge the help of *The Nelson Study Bible (NKJV)* in preparing the similarities portion of this chart. Thomas Nelson Publishers: Nashville, TN, 1997, p.353.

DEUTERONOMY 34:1-12

	MOSES	JOSHUA
	⇒ Moses at first was hesitant to lead God's people	⇒ Joshua at first needed encouragement to lead God's people
	⇒ Moses assumed the leadership of Israel when he was around 80 years old (Ac.7:23, 30)	⇒ Joshua assumed the leadership of Israel when he was around the age of 80 years old
	⇒ Moses led God's people through the waters of the Red Sea	⇒ Joshua led God's people through the waters of the Jordan River
	⇒ Moses interceded, prayed before God on behalf of Israel (Ex.32:30-34)	⇒ Joshua interceded, prayed before God on behalf of Israel (Jos.7:6-9)
	⇒ Moses presented God's law to Israel and charged the people to obey God's law (De.30:15-20)	⇒ Joshua charged Israel to obey God's law (Jos.23:6-8)
	⇒ Moses issued a stirring farewell message (The book of Deuteronomy)	⇒ Joshua issued a stirring farewell message (Jos.23)
	⇒ Moses was called "the servant of the LORD" (Jos.1:1)	⇒ Joshua was called "the servant of the LORD" (Jos.24:29)
Differences	⇒ Moses was raised in Pharaoh's household, in the lap of luxury (Ex.2:3-4; 2:5-8; 2:9-10; 2:11; 2:11-12; 2:13-15; He.11:26-27)	⇒ Joshua was raised in slavery, in poverty
Length of Life	⇒ 120 years	⇒ 110 years

3 (34:10-12) **Legacy, of Moses—Moses, Legacy of—Prophet, Listed, Moses—Moses, a Prophet**: the legacy of God's dear servant is a challenging testimony. The legacy of Moses arouses the reader to rededicate his life to God, to renew his covenant to follow God as never before. No prophet had ever risen in Israel like Moses; he was the greatest of prophets, especially in the eyes of God. Three reasons are given for his greatness:

OUTLINE	SCRIPTURE	SCRIPTURE	OUTLINE
3. The legacy of God's dear servant: The greatest of prophets a. A legacy of strong, intimate fellowship with God: So close, God knew him face-to-face b. A legacy of saving God's people from Egyptian slavery (a symbol of salvation)—using	10 And there arose not a prophet since in Israel like unto Moses, whom the LORD knew face to face, 11 In all the signs and the wonders, which the LORD sent him to do in the land of	Egypt to Pharaoh, and to all his servants, and to all his land, 12 And in all that mighty hand, and in all the great terror which Moses showed in the sight of all Israel.	miraculous signs & wonders c. A legacy of leading God's people through the wilderness journeys to the promised land (a symbol of heaven, of spiritual victory & rest)—all thru the mighty power of God

 a. The legacy of Moses was that of a strong, intimate fellowship with God. He fellowshipped and drew so close to God that Scripture makes this startling statement: God knew Moses face to face (v.10). How and what did Moses do to fellowship with the LORD? Obviously, he did just what the Word of God says to do: he prayed, confessed his sins continually, and studied the Word of God that was available to him, the first five books that God had given him to write. The reader can just picture Moses studying and pouring over God's Word, praying and seeking the LORD's face—for continued forgiveness, for the LORD's presence, for God's guidance and power in his life and ministry. Moses knew that the primary reason God created man was for the purpose of fellowship. Consequently, Moses drew near to the LORD—ever so close—and fellowshipped with Him. He fellowshipped so much in prayer and the study of God's Holy Word that the LORD knew him face to face.
 b. The legacy of Moses was that of saving God's people from the slavery of Egypt (v.11). This he did through the power of God.
 c. The legacy of Moses was that of leading God's people through the wilderness journey to the promised land of God (v.12). All the miracles performed by the hand of Moses and the necessary inner strength to lead God's people through the temptations and trials of the wilderness—all this was given by the mighty power of God.
 Moses was the great *liberator, prophet, lawgiver,* and *father* of Israel. It was he who had liberated the Israelites from Egypt through the laws given at Mt. Sinai. Under his leadership, the greatest events in Israel's history took place: the setting free of over three million Israelites from slavery and the forming of the nation into the state of Israel. All this was done under the hand of God who was to be acknowledged as the king of Israel.

> "The LORD shall reign for ever and ever" (Ex.15:18).
> "And he was king in Jeshurun, when the heads of the people and the tribes of Israel were gathered together" (De.33:5).

Thought 1. Moses longed to know the LORD personally and intimately. The driving force of his heart and life was to fellowship with God. Above all else, Moses longed for a sense or awareness of God's presence, for an unbroken consciousness of His presence. He wanted what Paul was later to express, that every thought and imagination would be captured and made obedient to the LORD (2 Co.10:3-5). Moses knew that God had chosen His people for one purpose and one purpose only: that they might know Him, believe Him, and understand Him (Is.43:10). This Moses wanted to the ultimate degree: to know, believe, and understand his LORD. Moses wanted to live in a continued, unbroken consciousness of God's holy presence; therefore, he prayed and lived in God's Holy Word as often as he could make time. In addition to these times, he prayed all throughout the day as he went about his daily activities. He learned to capture his thoughts and imaginations, subjecting them to obey God's holy commandments. This dear aged servant of God had learned what it meant to walk throughout the day in an unbroken consciousness of God's holy presence. As Holy Scripture teaches us, devotion to the LORD is the prerequisite, the condition for serving the LORD. Moses was wholeheartedly devoted to the LORD—so much so that the LORD knew him face to face.

(1) Moses' fellowship with God.

"And the people stood afar off, and Moses drew near unto the thick darkness where God was" (Ex.20:21).

"And Moses alone shall come near the LORD: but they shall not come nigh; neither shall the people go up with him" (Ex.24:2).

"And there I will meet with thee, and I will commune with thee from above the mercy seat, from between the two cherubims which are upon the ark of the testimony, of all things which I will give thee in commandment unto the children of Israel" (Ex.25:22).

"And it came to pass, as Moses entered into the tabernacle, the cloudy pillar descended, and stood at the door of the tabernacle, and the LORD talked with Moses" (Ex.33:9).

"With him will I speak mouth to mouth, even apparently, and not in dark speeches; and the similitude of the LORD shall he behold: wherefore then were ye not afraid to speak against my servant Moses" (Nu.12:8).

"And there arose not a prophet since in Israel like unto Moses, whom the LORD knew face to face" (De.34:10).

(2) The believer's fellowship with God.

"He that hath my commandments, and keepeth them, he it is that loveth me: and he that loveth me shall be loved of my Father, and I will love him, and will manifest myself to him" (Jn.14:21).

"For they that are after the flesh do mind the things of the flesh; but they that are after the Spirit the things of the Spirit" (Ro.8:5).

"What? know ye not that your body is the temple of the Holy Ghost which is in you, which ye have of God, and ye are not your own? For ye are bought with a price: therefore glorify God in your body, and in your spirit, which are God's" (1 Co.6:19-20).

"Casting down imaginations, and every high thing that exalteth itself against the knowledge of God, and bringing into captivity every thought to the obedience of Christ" (2 Co.10:5).

"I am crucified with Christ: nevertheless I live; yet not I, but Christ liveth in me: and the life which I now live in the flesh I live by the faith of the Son of God, who loved me, and gave himself for me" (Ga.2:20).

"That I may know him, and the power of his resurrection, and the fellowship of his sufferings, being made conformable unto his death; If by any means I might attain unto the resurrection of the dead" (Ph.3:10-11).

"Let us draw near with a true heart in full assurance of faith, having our hearts sprinkled from an evil conscience, and our bodies washed with pure water" (He.10:22).

"Draw nigh to God, and he will draw nigh to you." (Js.4:8).

"Behold, I stand at the door, and knock: if any man hear my voice, and open the door, I will come in to him, and will sup with him, and he with me" (Re.3:20).

"But if from thence thou shalt seek the LORD thy God, thou shalt find him, if thou seek him with all thy heart and with all thy soul" (De.4:29).

"I have set the LORD always before me: because he is at my right hand, I shall not be moved" (Ps.16:8).

"The LORD is nigh unto them that are of a broken heart; and saveth such as be of a contrite spirit" (Ps.34:18).

"But it is good for me to draw near to God: I have put my trust in the LORD GOD, that I may declare all thy works" (Ps.73:28).

"The LORD is nigh unto all them that call upon him, to all that call upon him in truth" (Ps.145:18).

"Seek ye the LORD while he may be found, call ye upon him while he is near" (Is.55:6).

Thought 2. The excellent expositor J.A. Thompson says this about Moses:

He was the greatest of Israel's prophets (18:15-22; Nu.12:6-8). He possessed an intimacy of fellowship with God unknown to others, for Yahweh knew (him) face to face. He was unequaled in the performance of the signs...and wonders...which Yahweh sent him to perform in Egypt. He was unequaled, too, in the display of great and awesome power among the people of Israel. In short, he was God's chosen charismatic leader in Israel, God's spokesman,

DEUTERONOMY 34:1-12

God's agent. In him were concentrated all the great offices of Israel—prophet, ruler, judge and priest. If some who held these offices were great, Moses was the greatest of them all.[6]

Thought 3. The excellent expositor Peter C. Craigie says this:

For the Christian reader, Deuteronomy ends with a pointer toward the future. The earthly kingdom of God, in the founding of which Moses played so important a part, came to an end as an independent state early in the sixth century BC. The prophets who followed Moses at a later date began to point forward to a New Covenant (see 18:15-22 and commentary). It was in the formation of the New Covenant that at last a prophet like Moses appeared again, but he was more than a prophet. Whereas Moses was a servant in the household of God, the coming prophet was a son, Jesus Christ (He.3:1-6).[7]

Thought 4. The great expositor Matthew Henry says this:

By Moses God gave the law, and moulded and formed the Jewish church; by the other prophets he only sent particular reproofs, directions, and predictions. The last of the prophets concludes with a charge to remember the law of Moses, Mal. iv. 4. Christ himself often appealed to the writings of Moses....[but] our LORD Jesus went beyond him. His doctrine was more excellent, his miracles were more illustrious, and his communion with his Father was more intimate, for he had lain in his bosom from eternity, and by him God does now in these last days speak to us. Moses was faithful as a servant, but Christ as a Son. The history of Moses leaves him buried in the plains of Moab, and concludes with the period of his government; but the history of our Saviour leaves him sitting at the right hand of the Majesty on high, and we are assured that of the increase of his government and peace there shall be no end. The apostle, in his epistle to the Hebrews, largely proves the pre-eminence of Christ above Moses, as a good reason why we that are Christians should be obedient, faithful, and constant, to that holy religion which we make profession of. God, by his grace, make us all so![8]

Thought 5. Donald F. Ackland makes an excellent statement about Moses that needs to be noted:

Moses' faithfulness was that of a servant. The term implies recognized inferiority to the one served and submission to his will. But servant is a glorious word when applied to those who dedicate themselves to God's purpose. There is no anticlimax between the eulogy of Moses with which Deuteronomy ends (34:10-12) and the opening words of the book of Joshua: 'Now after the death of Moses the servant of the LORD...' This man's greatness was in his service.

Yet a son is greater than a servant, and the Son of God greater than all others who do the Father's will. Did not Moses, in fact, serve the Son? Through him was given the law, and that law is 'our schoolmaster to bring us unto Christ, that we might be justified by faith' (Ga.3:24). The faithful servant prepared the way for the glorious Saviour.

And so it was, in John's Patmos vision, that the redeemed of heaven sang not only 'the song of Moses the servant of God' but also 'the song of the Lamb.' The first song needed the second. For great as was Moses' theme of deliverance, greater still is the deliverance wrought in Christ. The song of Moses told of Egypt's bondage ended, of victory against human foes, of God's righteous judgments in the earth, of a Promised Land possessed, and of a prospect depending on obedience. But the song of the Lamb—that new song with which the courts of heaven ring—tells of salvation from sin, of powers of darkness conquered, of righteousness gained by a perfect Victim's death and imputed by the grace of a loving God, and of life everlasting in a kingdom of eternal glory.[9]

Thought 6. *The Thompson Chain Reference Bible* gives an excellent parallel between Moses and Christ that is well worth studying:[10]

(1) Both Moses and Christ were preserved in childhood.

> "And there went a man of the house of Levi, and took to wife a daughter of Levi. And the woman conceived, and bare a son: and when she saw him that he was a goodly child, she hid him three months. And when she could not longer hide him, she took for him an ark of bulrushes, and daubed it with slime and with pitch, and put the child therein; and she laid it in the flags by the river's brink. And his sister stood afar off, to wit what would be done to him. And the daughter of Pharaoh came down to wash herself at the river; and her maidens walked along by the river's side; and when she saw the ark among the flags, she sent her maid to fetch it. And when she had opened it, she saw the child: and, behold, the babe wept. And she had compassion on him, and said, This is one of the Hebrews' children. Then said his sister to Pharaoh's daughter, Shall I go and call to thee a nurse of the Hebrew women, that she may nurse the child for thee? And Pharaoh's daughter said to her, Go. And the maid went and called the child's mother. And Pharaoh's daughter said unto her, Take this child away, and nurse it for me, and I will give thee thy wages. And the woman took the child, and nursed it. And the child grew, and she brought him unto Pharaoh's daughter, and he became her son. And she called his name Moses: and she said, Because I drew him out of the water" (Ex.2:2-10).

---

6 J.A. Thompson. *Deuteronomy*, p.320.
7 Peter C. Craigie. *The Book of Deuteronomy*, pp.406-407.
8 *Matthew Henry's Commentary*, Vol.1, p.888.
9 Donald F. Ackland. *Studies in Deuteronomy*. (Nashville, TN: Convention Press, 1964), pp.139-140.
10 *The New Thompson Chain Reference Bible*. (Indianapolis, IN: B.B. Kirkbride Bible Co., Inc., 1964), #2421.

Deuteronomy 34:1-12

"When he arose, he took the young child and his mother by night, and departed into Egypt...And was there until the death of Herod: that it might be fulfilled which was spoken of the LORD by the prophet, saying, Out of Egypt have I called my son" (Mt.2:14-15).

(2) Both Moses and Christ contended with masters of evil.

"Then Pharaoh also called the wise men and the sorcerers: now the magicians of Egypt, they also did in like manner with their enchantments" (Ex.7:11).
"Then was Jesus led up of the Spirit into the wilderness to be tempted of the devil" (Mt.4:1).

(3) Both Moses and Christ fasted forty days.

"And he was there with the LORD forty days and forty nights; he did neither eat bread, nor drink water. And he wrote upon the tables the words of the covenant, the ten commandments" (Ex.34:28).
"And when he had fasted forty days and forty nights, he was afterward an hungred" (Mt.4:2).

(4) Both Moses and Christ controlled the sea.

"And Moses stretched out his hand over the sea; and the LORD caused the sea to go back by a strong east wind all that night, and made the sea dry land, and the waters were divided" (Ex.14:21).
"And he saith unto them, Why are ye fearful, O ye of little faith? Then he arose, and rebuked the winds and the sea; and there was a great calm" (Mt.8:26).

(5) Both Moses and Christ fed a multitude.

"And when the children of Israel saw it, they said one to another, It is manna: for they wist not what it was. And Moses said unto them, This is the bread which the Lord hath given you to eat" (Ex.16:15).
"And they did all eat, and were filled: and they took up of the fragments that remained twelve baskets full" (Mt.14:20).
"And they that had eaten were about five thousand men, beside women and children" (Mt.14:21).

(6) Both Moses and Christ had radiant faces.

"And the children of Israel saw the face of Moses, that the skin of Moses' face shone: and Moses put the vail upon his face again, until he went in to speak with him" (Ex.34:35).
"And was transfigured before them: and his face did shine as the sun, and his raiment was white as the light" (Mt.17:2).

(7) Both Moses and Christ endured grumbling,

"And the people murmured against Moses, saying, What shall we drink" (Ex.15:24).
"And when they saw some of his disciples eat bread with defiled, that is to say, with unwashen, hands, they found fault" (Mk7:2).

(8) Both Moses and Christ were discredited in the home.

"And Miriam and Aaron spake against Moses because of the Ethiopian woman whom he had married: for he had married an Ethiopian woman" (Nu.12:1).
"For neither did his brethren believe in him" (Jn.7:5).

(9) Both Moses and Christ made intercessory prayers.

"Yet now, if thou wilt forgive their sin--; and if not, blot me, I pray thee, out of thy book which thou hast written" (Ex.32:32).
"I pray for them: I pray not for the world, but for them which thou hast given me; for they are thine" (Jn.17:9).

(10) Both Moses and Christ spoke as oracles.

"I will raise them up a Prophet [Jesus Christ] from among their brethren, like unto thee, and will put my words in his mouth; and he shall speak unto them all that I shall command him" (De.18:18).

DEUTERONOMY 34:1-12

(11) Both Moses and Christ had seventy helpers.

"And the LORD said unto Moses, Gather unto me seventy men of the elders of Israel, whom thou knowest to be the elders of the people, and officers over them; and bring them unto the tabernacle of the congregation, that they may stand there with thee" (Nu.11:16).

"And I will come down and talk with thee there: and I will take of the spirit which is upon thee, and will put it upon them; and they shall bear the burden of the people with thee, that thou bear it not thyself alone" (Nu.11:17).

"After these things the Lord appointed other seventy also, and sent them two and two before his face into every city and place, whither he himself would come" (Lu.10:1).

(12) Both Moses and Christ established memorials.

"And this day shall be unto you for a memorial; and ye shall keep it a feast to the Lord throughout your generations; ye shall keep it a feast by an ordinance for ever" (Ex.12:14).

"And he took bread, and gave thanks, and brake it, and gave unto them, saying, This is my body which is given for you: this do in remembrance of me" (Lu.22:19).

(13) Both Moses and Christ reappeared after death.

"And, behold, there appeared unto them Moses and Elias talking with him" (Mt.17:3).

"To whom also he showed himself alive after his passion by many infallible proofs, being seen of them forty days, and speaking of the things pertaining to the kingdom of God" (Ac.1:3).

RESOURCES
DEUTERONOMY

	PAGE
PRACTICAL BIBLE HELPS AND RESOURCES	435
MAP 1: Map of the Wilderness Wanderings of Israel	436
CHART 1: An Overview of the Life of Moses	437
CHART 2: The Blessings for Obedience to God and the Curses for Disobedience	450
TYPES IN DEUTERONOMY	
➢ Alphabetical Outline	464
➢ Chronological Outline	466
OUTLINE AND SUBJECT INDEX: DEUTERONOMY	468

THE DESERT OR WILDERNESS WANDERINGS OF ISRAEL

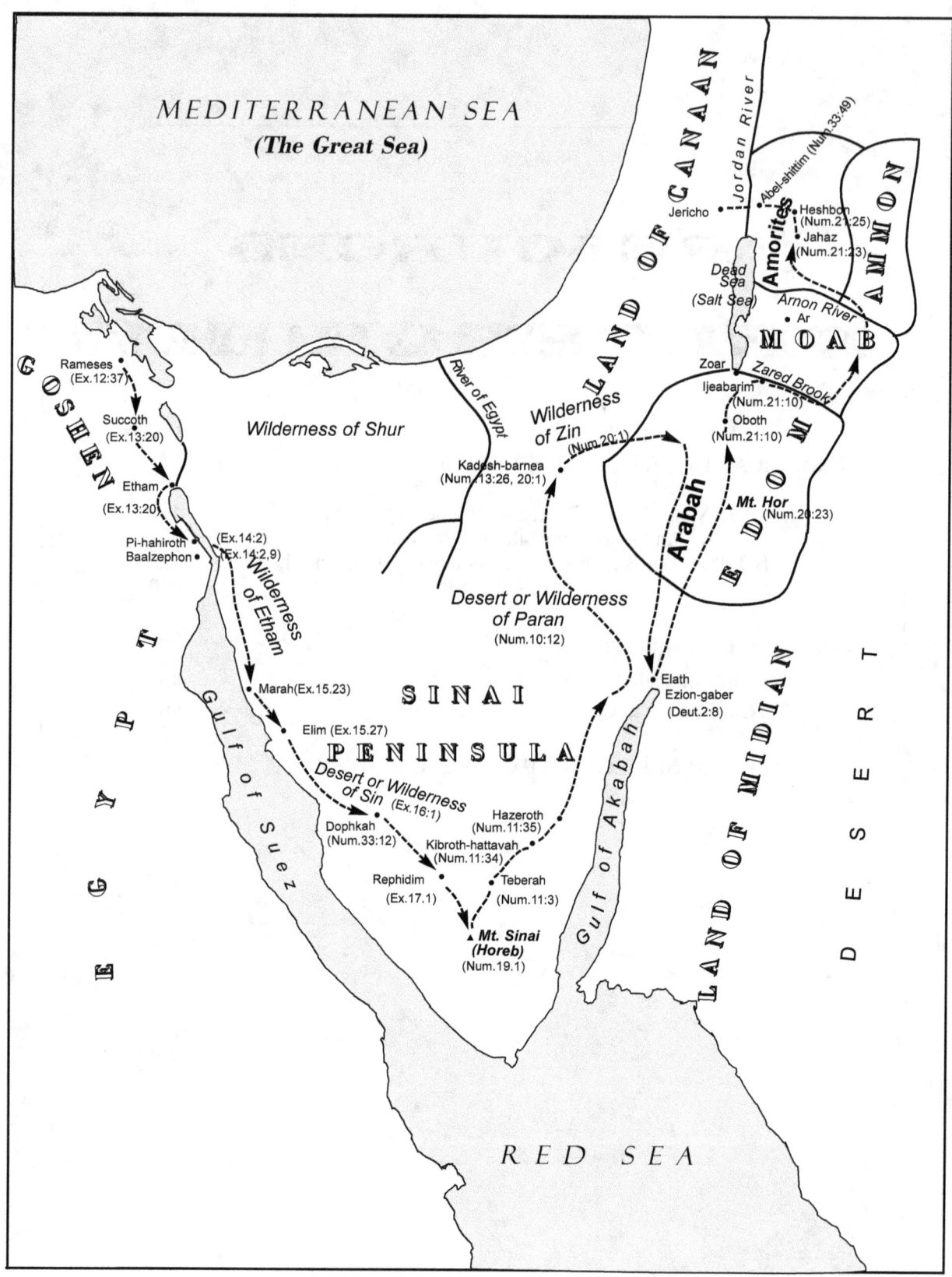

An Overview of
The Life of Moses

CONTENTS

1. Moses' Family
2. Moses' First, Formative Years
3. Moses' Young Adult Years
4. Moses' Life in Midian
5. Moses' Call to Service: At the Burning Bush—His Excuses and His Surrender to Serve God
6. Moses' Return to Egypt: To Deliver Israel
7. The Exodus: Where the Journey Begins—the Crossing of the Red Sea and the Wilderness Wanderings
8. Moses' Time at Mount Sinai
9. The Journey from Mount Sinai to Kadesh-Barnea
10. The Horrible Choices Made at Kadesh-Barnea
11. Forty Lost Years of Wandering in the Desert Wilderness
12. Moses' Appearance at the Transfiguration of Christ
13. The Faith of Moses
14. The Body of Moses

AN OVERVIEW OF
THE LIFE OF MOSES

Moses is one of the most important men in history. Every believer should seek to grasp the great contributions of Moses, a man who walked with the LORD God like few men have ever done.

SUBJECT	FACTS	SUPPORTING SCRIPTURE
1. Moses' Family	• His tribe was Levi.	"And there went a man of the house of Levi, and took *to wife* a daughter of Levi" (Ex.2:1).
	• His father was Amram	"And Amram took him Jochebed his father's sister to wife; and she bare him Aaron and Moses: and the years of the life of Amram *were* an hundred and thirty and seven years" (Ex.6:20).
	• His brother was Aaron.	"And the anger of the LORD was kindled against Moses, and he said, *Is* not Aaron the Levite thy brother? I know that he can speak well. And also, behold, he cometh forth to meet thee: and when he seeth thee, he will be glad in his heart" (Ex.4:14).
	• His sister was Miriam.	"And Miriam the prophetess, the sister of Aaron, took a timbrel in her hand; and all the women went out after her with timbrels and with dances" (Ex.15:20).
	• His wife was Zipporah.	"And Moses was content to dwell with the man: and he gave Moses Zipporah his daughter" (Ex.2:21).
	• His first son was Gershom.	"And she bare *him* a son, and he called his name Gershom: for he said, I have been a stranger in a strange land" (Ex.2:22; see Ex.18:3).
	• His youngest son was Eliezer.	"And the name of the other *was* Eliezer; for the God of my father, *said he, was* mine help, and delivered me from the sword of Pharaoh" (Ex.18:4).
	• His father-in-law was Reuel or Jethro.	"When Jethro, the priest of Midian, Moses' father in law, heard of all that God had done for Moses, and for Israel his people, *and* that the LORD had brought Israel out of Egypt" (Ex.18:1; see Ex.2:21).
2. Moses' First, Formative Years	• He was born in Egypt.	"And the woman conceived, and bare a son: and when she saw him that he *was a* goodly *child*, she hid him three months" (Ex.2:2).
	• He was hidden in the Ark.	"And when she could not longer hide him, she took for him an ark of bulrushes, and daubed it with slime and with pitch, and put the child therein; and she laid *it* in the flags by the river's brink" (Ex.2:3).
	• He was adopted by Pharaoh's daughter and was given a special name meaning, *Drawn out of the water*.	"And the child grew, and she brought him unto Pharaoh's daughter, and he became her son. And she called his name Moses: and she said, Because I drew him out of the water" (Ex.2:10).

AN OVERVIEW OF
THE LIFE OF MOSES

SUBJECT	FACTS	SUPPORTING SCRIPTURE
3. Moses' Young-Adult Years	• He was highly educated.	"And Moses was learned in all the wisdom of the Egyptians, and was mighty in words and in deeds" (Ac.7:22).
	• He was a Hebrew, not an Egyptian.	"By faith Moses, when he was come to years, refused to be called the son of Pharaoh's daughter; Choosing rather to suffer affliction with the people of God, than to enjoy the pleasures of sin for a season" (He.11:24-25).
	• He was a murderer.	"And it came to pass in those days, when Moses was grown, that he went out unto his brethren, and looked on their burdens: and he spied an Egyptian smiting an Hebrew, one of his brethren. And he looked this way and that way, and when he saw that *there was* no man, he slew the Egyptian, and hid him in the sand" (Ex.2:11-12).
	• He fled Egypt for refuge in Midian.	"Now when Pharaoh heard this thing, he sought to slay Moses. But Moses fled from the face of Pharaoh, and dwelt in the land of Midian: and he sat down by a well" (Ex.2:15).
4. Moses' Life in Midian	• He married Zipporah.	"And Moses was content to dwell with the man: and he gave Moses Zipporah his daughter" (Ex.2:21).
	• He lived on the back side of the desert—in Midian—for 40 years, 40 long, inconspicuous years.	"Then fled Moses at this saying, and was a stranger in the land of Midian, where he begat two sons. And when forty years were expired, there appeared to him in the wilderness of mount Sinai an angel of the Lord in a flame of fire in a bush" (Ac.7:29-30).
	• He sensed the need to leave Midian and visit his own people, the Israelites, in Egypt at the age of 40.	"And when he was full forty years old, it came into his heart to visit his brethren the children of Israel" (Ac.7:23).
5. Moses' Call To Service: At the Burning Bush—His Excuses and His Surrender To Serve God	God called Moses to lead the Israelites out of Egyptian slavery. Moses rejected God's call to leadership by offering several excuses.	
	• He had serious questions about his qualifications for such a task.	"And Moses said unto God, Who *am* I, that I should go unto Pharaoh, and that I should bring forth the children of Israel out of Egypt?" (Ex.3:11).
	• He felt the people would not believe him.	"And Moses answered and said, But, behold, they will not believe me, nor hearken unto my voice: for they will say, The LORD hath not appeared unto thee" (Ex.4:1).
	• He felt he was not a good speaker.	"And Moses said unto the LORD, O my Lord, I *am* not eloquent, neither heretofore, nor since thou hast spoken unto thy servant: but I *am* slow of speech, and of a slow tongue" (Ex.4:10).

AN OVERVIEW OF
THE LIFE OF MOSES

SUBJECT	FACTS	SUPPORTING SCRIPTURE
5. Moses' Call To Service: At the Burning Bush—His Excuses and His Surrender To Serve God (continued)	• He felt he needed to escape from his responsibility by suggesting that God send Aaron.	"And he said, O my Lord, send, I pray thee, by the hand *of him whom* thou wilt send" (Ex.4:13).
	• He finally surrendered to God's call.	"And the LORD said unto Moses in Midian, Go, return into Egypt: for all the men are dead which sought thy life. And Moses took his wife and his sons, and set them upon an ass, and he returned to the land of Egypt: and Moses took the rod of God in his hand" (Ex.4:19-20).
6. Moses' Return to Egypt: To Deliver Israel	• Moses' first confrontation with Pharaoh: "Let my people go!..." Pharaoh said, "No!"	"And afterward Moses and Aaron went in, and told Pharaoh, Thus saith the LORD God of Israel, Let my people go, that they may hold a feast unto me in the wilderness. And Pharaoh said, Who *is* the LORD, that I should obey his voice to let Israel go? I know not the LORD, neither will I let Israel go" (Ex.5:1-2).
	As God hardened Pharaoh's heart, the Ten Plagues were sent in judgment. • The water of the Nile was changed to blood.	"And Moses and Aaron did so, as the LORD commanded; and he lifted up the rod, and smote the waters that *were* in the river, in the sight of Pharaoh, and in the sight of his servants; and all the waters that *were* in the river were turned to blood" (Ex.7:20).
	• A plague of frogs covered the land.	"And Aaron stretched out his hand over the waters of Egypt; and the frogs came up, and covered the land of Egypt" (Ex.8:6).
	• Lice or gnats infested the land.	"And they did so; for Aaron stretched out his hand with his rod, and smote the dust of the earth, and it became lice in man, and in beast; all the dust of the land became lice throughout all the land of Egypt" (Ex.8:17).
	• Flies swarmed over the land.	"And the LORD did so; and there came a grievous swarm *of flies* into the house of Pharaoh, and *into* his servants' houses, and into all the land of Egypt: the land was corrupted by reason of the swarm *of flies*" (Ex.8:24).
	• A severe disease struck and killed all livestock in the field.	"And the LORD did that thing on the morrow, and all the cattle of Egypt died: but of the cattle of the children of Israel died not one" (Ex.9:6).
	• Festering boils afflicted man and animal.	"And they took ashes of the furnace, and stood before Pharaoh; and Moses sprinkled it up toward heaven; and it became a boil breaking forth *with* blains upon man, and upon beast" (Ex.9:10).

AN OVERVIEW OF
THE LIFE OF MOSES

SUBJECT	FACTS	SUPPORTING SCRIPTURE
6. Moses' Return to Egypt: To Deliver Israel (continued)	• A severe hail and thunderstorm broke loose.	"And Moses stretched forth his rod toward heaven: and the LORD sent thunder and hail, and the fire ran along upon the ground; and the LORD rained hail upon the land of Egypt. So there was hail, and fire mingled with the hail, very grievous, such as there was none like it in all the land of Egypt since it became a nation" (Ex.9:23-24).
	• Locusts swarmed over the land.	"And the locusts went up over all the land of Egypt, and rested in all the coasts of Egypt: very grievous were they; before them there were no such locusts as they, neither after them shall be such" (Ex.10:14).
	• Darkness covered the land.	"And Moses stretched forth his hand toward heaven; and there was a thick darkness in all the land of Egypt three days: They saw not one another, neither rose any from his place for three days: but all the children of Israel had light in their dwellings" (Ex.10:22-23).
	• The severe judgment fell upon the firstborn.	"And it came to pass, that at midnight the LORD smote all the firstborn in the land of Egypt, from the firstborn of Pharaoh that sat on his throne unto the firstborn of the captive that was in the dungeon; and all the firstborn of cattle. And Pharaoh rose up in the night, he, and all his servants, and all the Egyptians; and there was a great cry in Egypt; for there was not a house where there was not one dead" (Ex.12:29-30).
7. The Exodus: Where the Journey Begins—The Crossing of the Red Sea and the Wilderness Wanderings	• There was God's guidance by day and night.	"And the LORD went before them by day in a pillar of a cloud, to lead them the way; and by night in a pillar of fire, to give them light; to go by day and night" (Ex.13:21).
	• There was the crossing of the Red Sea—God's great deliverance.	"But the children of Israel walked upon dry land in the midst of the sea; and the waters were a wall unto them on their right hand, and on their left. Thus the LORD saved Israel that day out of the hand of the Egyptians; and Israel saw the Egyptians dead upon the sea shore" (Ex.14:29-30).
	• There was Moses' great song of praise.	"Then sang Moses and the children of Israel this song unto the LORD, and spake, saying, I will sing unto the LORD, for he hath triumphed gloriously: the horse and his rider hath he thrown into the sea. The LORD is my strength and song, and he is become my salvation: he is my God, and I will prepare him an habitation; my father's God, and I will exalt him" (Ex.15:1-2).

AN OVERVIEW OF
THE LIFE OF MOSES

SUBJECT	FACTS	SUPPORTING SCRIPTURE
7. The Exodus: Where the Journey Begins—The Crossing of the Red Sea and the Wilderness Wanderings (continued)	• There was the bitter water of Marah.	"And when they came to Marah, they could not drink of the waters of Marah, for they *were* bitter: therefore the name of it was called Marah. And the people murmured against Moses, saying, What shall we drink? And he cried unto the LORD; and the LORD showed him a tree, *which* when he had cast into the waters, the waters were made sweet: there he made for them a statute and an ordinance, and there he proved them" (Ex.15:23-25).
	• There was hunger in the wilderness.	"And the children of Israel did eat manna forty years, until they came to a land inhabited; they did eat manna, until they came unto the borders of the land of Canaan" (Ex.16:35).
	• There was the water from the rock: Moses struck the rock for water at Rephidim (later called Massah or Meribah).	"Behold, I will stand before thee there upon the rock in Horeb; and thou shalt smite the rock, and there shall come water out of it, that the people may drink. And Moses did so in the sight of the elders of Israel" (Ex.17:6).
	• There was victory through prevailing prayer.	"And it came to pass, when Moses held up his hand, that Israel prevailed: and when he let down his hand, Amalek prevailed. But Moses' hands *were* heavy; and they took a stone, and put *it* under him, and he sat thereon; and Aaron and Hur stayed up his hands, the one on the one side, and the other on the other side; and his hands were steady until the going down of the sun" (Ex.17:11-12).
	• There was a need for improved administration: Moses heeded Jethro's advice concerning organization and overwork.	"And Moses chose able men out of all Israel, and made them heads over the people, rulers of thousands, rulers of hundreds, rulers of fifties, and rulers of tens. And they judged the people at all seasons: the hard causes they brought unto Moses, but every small matter they judged themselves" (Ex.18:25-26).
8. Moses' Time at Mount Sinai	• First, the LORD called Moses to go up Mount Sinai.	"And the LORD came down upon mount Sinai, on the top of the mount: and the LORD called Moses *up* to the top of the mount; and Moses went up" (Ex.19:20).
	• Second, Moses received the Ten Commandments from the LORD.	"And he gave unto Moses, when he had made an end of communing with him upon mount Sinai, two tables of testimony, tables of stone, written with the finger of God" (Ex.31:18; see Ex.20:2-17).
	• Third, the conquest of the promised land was guaranteed by God.	"And I will set thy bounds from the Red sea even unto the sea of the Philistines, and from the desert unto the river: for I will deliver the inhabitants of the land into your hand; and thou shalt drive them out before thee" (Ex.23:31).

AN OVERVIEW OF
THE LIFE OF MOSES

SUBJECT	FACTS	SUPPORTING SCRIPTURE
8. Moses' Time at Mount Sinai (continued)	• Fourth, Moses sprinkled blood upon the people, confirming that the blood covenant between the LORD and His people had been sealed.	"And he took the book of the covenant, and read in the audience of the people: and they said, All that the LORD hath said will we do, and be obedient. And Moses took the blood, and sprinkled *it* on the people, and said, Behold the blood of the covenant, which the LORD hath made with you concerning all these words" (Ex.24:7-8).
	• Fifth, on the mountain, Moses was covered by the glory of the LORD for 40 days and 40 nights.	"And Moses went up into the mount, and a cloud covered the mount. And the glory of the LORD abode upon mount Sinai, and the cloud covered it six days: and the seventh day he called unto Moses out of the midst of the cloud. And the sight of the glory of the LORD *was* like devouring fire on the top of the mount in the eyes of the children of Israel. And Moses went into the midst of the cloud, and gat him up into the mount: and Moses was in the mount forty days and forty nights" (Ex.24:15-18).
	• Sixth, Moses received the blueprints for the construction of the Tabernacle.	"And let them make me a sanctuary; that I may dwell among them. According to all that I show thee, *after* the pattern of the tabernacle, and the pattern of all the instruments thereof, even so shall ye make *it*" (Ex.25:8-9).
	• Seventh, the people built a golden calf while Moses was away on the mountain.	"And when the people saw that Moses delayed to come down out of the mount, the people gathered themselves together unto Aaron, and said unto him, Up, make us gods, which shall go before us; for *as for* this Moses, the man that brought us up out of the land of Egypt, we wot not what is become of him" (Ex.32:1).
	• Eighth, Moses interceded for Israel while he was on the mountain.	"Wherefore should the Egyptians speak, and say, For mischief did he bring them out, to slay them in the mountains, and to consume them from the face of the earth? Turn from thy fierce wrath, and repent of this evil against thy people....And the LORD repented of the evil which he thought to do unto his people" (Ex.32:12, 14).
	• Ninth, Moses shattered the tablets after seeing the golden calf.	"And it came to pass, as soon as he came nigh unto the camp, that he saw the calf, and the dancing: and Moses' anger waxed hot, and he cast the tables out of his hands, and brake them beneath the mount" (Ex.32:19).
	• Tenth, Moses interceded for Israel at the foot of the mountain and offered his life as a sacrifice.	"Yet now, if thou wilt forgive their sin—; and if not, blot me, I pray thee, out of thy book which thou hast written" (Ex.32:32).

AN OVERVIEW OF
THE LIFE OF MOSES

SUBJECT	FACTS	SUPPORTING SCRIPTURE
8. Moses' Time at Mount Sinai (continued)	• Eleventh, God spoke face to face with Moses at the tent of meeting with the LORD.	"And all the people saw the cloudy pillar stand *at* the tabernacle door: and all the people rose up and worshipped, every man *in* his tent door. And the LORD spake unto Moses face to face, as a man speaketh unto his friend. And he turned again into the camp: but his servant Joshua, the son of Nun, a young man, departed not out of the tabernacle" (Ex.33:10-11).
	• Twelfth, Moses interceded for Israel again and asked for God's divine presence.	"And he said, My presence shall go *with thee*, and I will give thee rest. And he said unto him, If thy presence go not *with me*, carry us not up hence" (Ex.33:14-15).
	• Thirteenth, Moses saw God's glory from the cleft of the rock.	"And it shall come to pass, while my glory passeth by, that I will put thee in a clift of the rock, and will cover thee with my hand while I pass by: And I will take away mine hand, and thou shalt see my back parts: but my face shall not be seen" (Ex.33:22-23).
	• Fourteenth, God replaced the shattered tablets.	"And the LORD said unto Moses, Hew thee two tables of stone like unto the first: and I will write upon *these* tables the words that were in the first tables, which thou brakest" (Ex.34:1).
	• Fifteenth, Moses shared the commandments with the people.	"And afterward all the children of Israel came nigh: and he gave them in commandment all that the LORD had spoken with him in mount Sinai" (Ex.34:32).
	• Sixteenth, Moses' face shone after spending time with the LORD.	"But when Moses went in before the LORD to speak with him, he took the vail off, until he came out. And he came out, and spake unto the children of Israel *that* which he was commanded. And the children of Israel saw the face of Moses, that the skin of Moses' face shone: and Moses put the vail upon his face again, until he went in to speak with him" (Ex.34:34-35).
	• Seventeenth, the Tabernacle was constructed according to God's precise instructions.	"And he reared up the court round about the tabernacle and the altar, and set up the hanging of the court gate. So Moses finished the work. Then a cloud covered the tent of the congregation, and the glory of the LORD filled the tabernacle. And Moses was not able to enter into the tent of the congregation, because the cloud abode thereon, and the glory of the LORD filled the tabernacle" (Ex.40:33-35).
9. The Journey from Mount Sinai to Kadesh-Barnea	• Israel moved away from Sinai: During the second year, on the twentieth day in the second month.	"And it came to pass on the twentieth *day* of the second month, in the second year, that the cloud was taken up from off the tabernacle of the testimony. And the children of Israel took their journeys out of the wilderness of

AN OVERVIEW OF
THE LIFE OF MOSES

SUBJECT	FACTS	SUPPORTING SCRIPTURE
9. The Journey from Mount Sinai to Kadesh-Barnea (continued)		Sinai; and the cloud rested in the wilderness of Paran. And they first took their journey according to the commandment of the LORD by the hand of Moses" (Nu.10:11-13).
	• The people complained and God destroyed some of the people with fire because of their complaining.	"And *when* the people complained, it displeased the LORD: and the LORD heard *it;* and his anger was kindled; and the fire of the LORD burnt among them, and consumed *them that were* in the uttermost parts of the camp" (Nu.11:1).
	• Sometime later, the people again complained about food, and Moses cried out to God for help in dealing with the people.	"And the mixed multitude that *was* among them fell a lusting: and the children of Israel also wept again, and said, Who shall give us flesh to eat?" (Nu.11:4). "I am not able to bear all this people alone, because *it is* too heavy for me" (Nu.11:14).
	• God judged the complaining and they became violently sick because of their greedy, gluttonous appetite.	"And while the flesh (the quail) *was* yet between their teeth, ere it was chewed, the wrath of the LORD was kindled against the people, and the LORD smote the people with a very great plague. And he called the name of that place Kibroth-hattaavah: because there they buried the people that lusted" (Nu.11:33-34).
	• At some point, Miriam and Aaron murmured against Moses.	"And Miriam and Aaron spake against Moses because of the Ethiopian woman whom he had married: for he had married an Ethiopian woman" (Nu.12:1).
	• A strong trait of humility or meekness was demonstrated by Moses when he was judged by his sister and brother.	"(Now the man Moses *was* very meek, above all the men which *were* upon the face of the earth)" (Nu.12:3).
	• It was at this point in time that Moses sent out spies to view the promised land.	"And the LORD spake unto Moses, saying, Send thou men, that they may search the land of Canaan, which I give unto the children of Israel: of every tribe of their fathers shall ye send a man, every one a ruler among them" (Nu.13:1-2).
10. The Horrible Choices Made at Kadesh-Barnea	• The majority of the spies gave a report of unbelief, not believing God could give them victory over the enemies of the promised land.	"But the men that went up with him said, We be not able to go up against the people; for they are stronger than we. And they brought up an evil report of the land which they had searched unto the children of Israel, saying, The land, through which we have gone to search it, is a land that eateth up the inhabitants thereof; and all the people that we saw in it *are* men of a great stature. And there we saw the giants, the sons of Anak, *which come* of the giants: and we were in our own sight as grasshoppers, and so we were in their sight" (Nu.13:31-33).

AN OVERVIEW OF
THE LIFE OF MOSES

SUBJECT	FACTS	SUPPORTING SCRIPTURE
10. The Horrible Choices Made at Kadesh-Barnea (continued)	• The people rebelled against Moses and Aaron.	"And all the children of Israel murmured against Moses and against Aaron: and the whole congregation said unto them, Would God that we had died in the land of Egypt! or would God we had died in this wilderness! And wherefore hath the LORD brought us unto this land, to fall by the sword, that our wives and our children should be a prey? were it not better for us to return into Egypt? And they said one to another, Let us make a captain, and let us return into Egypt" (Nu.14:2-4).
	• The great intercessor, Moses, interceded for Israel at Kadesh.	"Pardon, I beseech thee, the iniquity of this people according unto the greatness of thy mercy, and as thou hast forgiven this people, from Egypt even until now" (Nu.14:19).
	• The final judgment of God would fall upon the first generation of Israelite believers.	"I the LORD have said, I will surely do it unto all this evil congregation, that are gathered together against me: in this wilderness they shall be consumed, and there they shall die" (Nu.14:35; see Nu.4:26-34).
	• The Israelites made an incomplete confession and attempted to enter the promised land without God's presence.	"And they rose up early in the morning, and gat them up into the top of the mountain, saying, Lo, we *be here*, and will go up unto the place which the LORD hath promised: for we have sinned. And Moses said, Wherefore now do ye transgress the commandment of the LORD? but it shall not prosper. Go not up, for the LORD *is* not among you; that ye be not smitten before your enemies....But they presumed to go up unto the hill top: nevertheless the ark of the covenant of the LORD, and Moses, departed not out of the camp. (Nu.14:40-42, 44).
	• The Israelites were soundly defeated.	"Then the Amalekites came down, and the Canaanites which dwelt in that hill, and smote them, and discomfited them, *even* unto Hormah" (Nu.14:45).
11. Forty Lost Years of Wandering in the Desert Wilderness	• The judgment of the wilderness wandering was pronounced on everyone except Caleb and Joshua and the next generation of children. Note: even the children suffered in the wilderness.	"But *as for* you, your carcases, they shall fall in this wilderness. And your children shall wander in the wilderness forty years, and bear your whoredoms, until your carcases be wasted in the wilderness" (Nu.14:32-33).
	• At some point, a Sabbath-breaker was punished.	"And while the children of Israel were in the wilderness, they found a man that gathered sticks upon the sabbath day....And all the congregation brought him without the camp, and stoned him with stones, and he died; as the LORD commanded Moses" (Nu.15:32, 36).
	• A serious rebellion threatened the life of Moses and Aaron, led by the three leaders: Korah, Dathan,	"And they gathered themselves together against Moses and against Aaron, and said unto them, *Ye take*

AN OVERVIEW OF
THE LIFE OF MOSES

SUBJECT	FACTS	SUPPORTING SCRIPTURE
11. Forty Lost Years of Wandering in the Desert Wilderness (continued)	and Abiram.	too much upon you, seeing all the congregation *are* holy, every one of them, and the LORD *is* among them: wherefore then lift ye up yourselves above the congregation of the LORD?" (Nu.16:3).
	• Israel continued to grumble against Moses and Aaron.	"But on the morrow all the congregation of the children of Israel murmured against Moses and against Aaron, saying, Ye have killed the people of the LORD" (Nu.16:41).
	• Moses, once again, was forced to place his life on the line for the sake of Israel.	"And Moses and Aaron came before the tabernacle of the congregation. And the LORD spake unto Moses, saying, Get you up from among this congregation, that I may consume them as in a moment. And they fell upon their faces" (Nu.16:43-45).
	• Miriam, Moses' sister, died in Kadesh.	"Then came the children of Israel, *even* the whole congregation, into the desert of Zin in the first month: and the people abode in Kadesh; and Miriam died there, and was buried there" (Nu.20:1).
	• The people continued to complain of thirst.	"And there was no water for the congregation: and they gathered themselves together against Moses and against Aaron. And the people chode with Moses, and spake, saying, Would God that we had died when our brethren died before the LORD! And why have ye brought up the congregation of the LORD into this wilderness, that we and our cattle should die there?" (Nu.20:2-4).
	• At this point, Moses finally reached the end of his patience with the people and committed his great and awful sin: God told him to *speak* to the rock, not *strike* the rock: In anger at the people and rebellion against God, he lashed out against the people and struck the rock.	"Take the rod, and gather thou the assembly together, thou, and Aaron thy brother, and speak ye unto the rock before their eyes; and it shall give forth his water, and thou shalt bring forth to them water out of the rock: so thou shalt give the congregation and their beasts drink" (Nu.20:8). "And Moses lifted up his hand, and with his rod he smote the rock twice: and the water came out abundantly, and the congregation drank, and their beasts *also*. And the LORD spake unto Moses and Aaron, Because ye believed me not, to sanctify me in the eyes of the children of Israel, therefore ye shall not bring this congregation into the land which I have given them" (Nu.20:11-12).
	• Aaron, Moses' brother, died.	"Aaron shall be gathered unto his people: for he shall not enter into the land which I have given unto the children of Israel, because ye rebelled against my word at the water of Meribah" (Nu.20:24).

AN OVERVIEW OF
THE LIFE OF MOSES

SUBJECT	FACTS	SUPPORTING SCRIPTURE
11. *Forty Lost Years of Wandering in the Desert Wilderness (continued)*	• Sometime later, Israel was attacked by the Canaanites, but they were able to counter-attack the Canaanites and win a smashing victory.	"And *when* king Arad the Canaanite, which dwelt in the south, heard tell that Israel came by the way of the spies; then he fought against Israel, and took *some* of them prisoners. And Israel vowed a vow unto the LORD, and said, If thou wilt indeed deliver this people into my hand, then I will utterly destroy their cities. And the LORD hearkened to the voice of Israel, and delivered up the Canaanites; and they utterly destroyed them and their cities: and he called the name of the place Hormah" (Nu.21:1-3).
	• The people continued to complain and grumble, speaking out against God and Moses.	"And the people spake against God, and against Moses, Wherefore have ye brought us up out of Egypt to die in the wilderness? for *there is* no bread, neither *is there any* water; and our soul loatheth this light bread" (Nu.21:5).
	• God was forced to continue chastening the people.	"And the LORD sent fiery serpents among the people, and they bit the people; and much people of Israel died" (Nu.21:6).
	• The people repented and the LORD continued to provide a way of deliverance: Moses made a bronze serpent.	"And the LORD said unto Moses, Make thee a fiery serpent, and set it upon a pole: and it shall come to pass, that every one that is bitten, when he looketh upon it, shall live. And Moses made a serpent of brass, and put it upon a pole, and it came to pass, that if a serpent had bitten any man, when he beheld the serpent of brass, he lived" (Nu.21:8-9).
	• As ordered, Moses defeated Sihon, king of the Amorites.	"And Israel smote him with the edge of the sword, and possessed his land from Arnon unto Jabbok, even unto the children of Ammon: for the border of the children of Ammon *was* strong" (Nu.21:24).
	• As ordered, Moses defeated Og, the king of Bashan.	"So they smote him, and his sons, and all his people, until there was none left him alive: and they possessed his land" (Nu.21:35).
	• At some point, God instructed Moses to take a census.	"Take the sum of all the congregation of the children of Israel, from twenty years old and upward, throughout their fathers' house, all that are able to go to war in Israel" (Nu.26:2).
	• God gave Moses the privilege of seeing the promised land from a distance.	"And the LORD said unto Moses, Get thee up into this mount Abarim, and see the land which I have given unto the children of Israel. And when thou hast seen it, thou also shalt be gathered unto thy people, as Aaron thy brother was gathered. For ye rebelled against my commandment in the desert of Zin, in the strife of the congregation, to sanctify me at the water before their eyes: that *is* the water of Meribah in Kadesh in the wilderness of Zin" (Nu.27:12-14).

AN OVERVIEW OF
THE LIFE OF MOSES

SUBJECT	FACTS	SUPPORTING SCRIPTURE
11. Forty Lost Years of Wandering in the Desert Wilderness (continued)	• The LORD set apart Joshua to succeed Moses.	"And Moses did as the LORD commanded him: and he took Joshua, and set him before Eleazar the priest, and before all the congregation: And he laid his hands upon him, and gave him a charge, as the LORD commanded by the hand of Moses" (Nu.27:22-23).
	• Israel fought and defeated the Midianites.	"And they warred against the Midianites, as the LORD commanded Moses; and they slew all the males" (Nu.31:7).
	• Moses died on Mount Nebo in the land of Moab, after giving Israel his blessing.	"So Moses the servant of the LORD died there in the land of Moab, according to the word of the LORD. And he buried him in a valley in the land of Moab, over against Beth-peor: but no man knoweth of his sepulchre unto this day" (De.34:5-6).
	• Scripture itself declares the great legacy of Moses' life.	"And there arose not a prophet since in Israel like unto Moses, whom the LORD knew face to face, In all the signs and the wonders, which the LORD sent him to do in the land of Egypt to Pharaoh, and to all his servants, and to all his land, And in all that mighty hand, and in all the great terror which Moses showed in the sight of all Israel" (De.34:10-12).
12. Moses' Appearance at the Transfiguration of Christ	• Moses reappeared with Elijah at the transfiguration of Christ.	"And, behold, there appeared unto them Moses and Elias talking with him" (Mt.17:3).
13. The Faith of Moses	• Moses gave up the riches of Egypt and the pleasures of sin in order to inherit the wonderful promises and rewards of God.	"Esteeming the reproach of Christ greater riches than the treasures in Egypt: for he had respect unto the recompence of the reward" (He.11:26).
14. The Body of Moses	• The body of Moses was argued over by Michael the Archangel and Satan.	"Yet Michael the archangel, when contending with the devil he disputed about the body of Moses, durst not bring against him a railing accusation, but said, The Lord rebuke thee" (Jude 9).

Note: We deeply appreciate the help *The Thompson Chain-Reference Bible* gave us in organizing some of our thoughts for this study on the life of Moses. (*The Thompson Chain-Reference Bible, 5th Improved Edition*. Indianapolis, IN: B. B. Kirkbride Bible Co., Inc., 1988, p.1665.)

THE BLESSINGS FOR OBEDIENCE TO GOD
AND THE CURSES FOR DISOBEDIENCE
Deuteronomy 28:1-68

NOTE: this information is being put into chart form...
- to summarize the lesson from chapter 28 in a simple-to-read chart for easy reference
- to raise the awareness of believers to the importance of the *blessings for obedience* and the *curses for disobedience*
- to learn from the life and history of Israel, from their example: they are a people who failed to obey God and suffered the judgment of God, the *curses for disobedience* (Ro.15:4; 1 Co.10:11)

THE BLESSINGS FOR OBEDIENCE
Deuteronomy 28:1-14

THE BLESSING AND THE BIBLICAL BASIS	THE RESULTS OF OBEDIENCE AND THE PRACTICAL APPLICATION	THE SUPPORTING SCRIPTURE
The Blessing of Fruitfulness "Blessed *shall be* the fruit of thy body, and the fruit of thy ground, and the fruit of thy cattle, the increase of thy kine, and the flocks of thy sheep. Blessed *shall be* thy basket and thy store" (De.28:4-5).	The blessings are applicable to the individual as well as to the nation. The nation is blessed by the citizens being blessed. If the people obeyed God... • their population would grow, overflow with fruitfulness • their livestock would grow and increase • their crops would grow and increase • their daily food would always be provided The blessing of fruitfulness, of plenty, is ours. But there is a condition: obedience. If we obey God, truly keep His commandments and follow Him, then God promises always to provide the necessities of life for us. We will always have the blessing of plenty.	"But seek ye first the kingdom of God, and his righteousness; and all these things shall be added unto you" (Mt.6:33). "But my God shall supply all your need according to his riches in glory by Christ Jesus" (Ph.4:19). "If ye walk in my statutes, and keep my commandments, and do them; Then I will give you rain in due season, and the land shall yield her increase, and the trees of the field shall yield their fruit. And your threshing shall reach unto the vintage, and the vintage shall reach unto the sowing time: and ye shall eat your bread to the full, and dwell in your land safely" (Le.26:3-5; see De.30:8-9; Ps.132:15).
The Blessing of All Daily Activities "Blessed *shalt* thou *be* when thou comest in, and blessed *shalt* thou *be* when thou goest out" (De.28:6).	No matter where a person is—coming into or going out of the home—God will bless him. The only condition is obedience. If the person is walking with God, following God with all his heart, then God blesses him. Where the believer is, at home or away, does not matter. What matters is obedience. If the believer is walking after God, obeying Him, then God blesses his daily activities—all of them. There is a strong lesson in this point for believers. If we walk day after day, obeying God wholeheartedly, then God will bless us richly in Himself. He will bless all our daily activities. He promises to grant us His presence and guidance as we walk throughout the day.	"Lo, I am with you alway, even unto the end of the world. Amen" (Mt.28:20). "Through the tender mercy of our God; whereby the dayspring from on high hath visited us, To give light to them that sit in darkness and in the shadow of death, to guide our feet into the way of peace" (Lu.1:78-79). "Howbeit when he, the Spirit of truth, is come, he will guide you into all truth: for he shall not speak of himself; but whatsoever he shall hear, that shall he speak: and he will show you things to come" (Jn.16:13). "And, behold, I am with thee, and will keep thee in all places whither thou goest, and will bring thee again into this land; for I will not leave thee, until I have done that which I have spoken to thee of" (Ge.28:15; see Ex.33:14; Is.43:2; Ps.23:2; Ps.48:14; Ps.73:24; Is.30:21).
The Blessing of Victory over All Enemies "The LORD shall cause thine enemies that rise up against thee to be smitten before thy face: they shall come out against thee one way, and flee before thee seven ways" (De.28:7).	The blessing of victory over all enemies is promised to the obedient person. Protection or security is a most wonderful promise given by God to the believer. Note exactly what is said to the Israelites about this wonderful promise: if an enemy rises up against you, that enemy will be defeated before your very presence. No matter who the en-	"Who shall separate us from the love of Christ? shall tribulation, or distress, or persecution, or famine, or nakedness, or peril, or sword....Nay, in all these things we are more than conquerors through him that loved us. For I am persuaded, that neither death, nor life, nor angels, nor principalities, nor powers, nor things present, nor things to come, Nor height,

THE BLESSINGS
Deuteronomy 28:1-14

THE BLESSING AND THE BIBLICAL BASIS	THE RESULTS OF OBEDIENCE AND THE PRACTICAL APPLICATION	THE SUPPORTING SCRIPTURE
	emy is nor how strong and numerous, the enemy will be defeated. Note the graphic description: the enemy will come at you from one direction, but he will flee from you in seven directions, flee as a defeated, scattered foe. The enemies that attempt to overthrow and conquer the believer are innumerable. But the promise of God is strong: if the believer will obey God, keep His holy commandments, God will give him victory over the enemies that oppose him. Victory is assured, assured if the believer will just obey God.	*nor depth, nor any other creature, shall be able to separate us from the love of God, which is in Christ Jesus our LORD" (Ro.8:35, 37-39).* *"There hath no temptation taken you but such as is common to man: but God is faithful, who will not suffer you to be tempted above that ye are able; but will with the temptation also make a way to escape, that ye may be able to bear it" (1 Co.10:13).* *"Now unto him that is able to do exceeding abundantly above all that we ask or think, according to the power that worketh in us" (Ep.3:20).* *"For we wrestle not against flesh and blood, but against principalities, against powers, against the rulers of the darkness of this world, against spiritual wickedness in high places. Wherefore take unto you the whole armour of God, that ye may be able to withstand in the evil day, and having done all, to stand" (Ep.6:12-13; See also He.2:17-18; Js.4:7; 1 Jn. 5:4; Re.3:21; Ps.44:5).*
The Blessing of Labor, Work, Employment **"The LORD shall command the blessing upon thee in thy storehouses, and in all that thou settest thine hand unto; and he shall bless thee in the land which the LORD thy God giveth thee" (De.28:8).**	The blessing of labor, work, and employment is promised to the obedient person. Note that God will bless not only what a believer has in his barns, but He will bless everything the believer puts his hand to. This means that God will bless all his labor and work, all his employment. And the result will be the experience of purpose, achievement, accomplishment, and fulfillment in the promised land. Note this fact: meaningful work stirs a sense of purpose within a person. Work produces a sense of achievement and success, a sense of fulfillment and satisfaction. This means a most wonderful thing: if God blesses our work and labor, then we will have the deepest sense of purpose, significance, and meaning in life. We will achieve and be successful. We will be flooded with a sense of purpose, fulfillment, and satisfaction. This is the wonderful promise of God that was first given to the Israelites, but is applicable to every believer of all generations. If God's people will simply obey Him, He will bless all that they put their hands to. They will have a sense of purpose, meaning, and significance in life. They will experience achievement and success. They will be flooded with the deepest sense of fulfillment and satisfaction imaginable.	*"If ye keep my commandments, ye shall abide in my love; even as I have kept my Father's commandments, and abide in his love. These things have I spoken unto you, that my joy might remain in you, and that your joy might be full" (Jn.15:10-11).* *"With good will doing service, as to the LORD, and not to men" (Ep.6:7).* *"And whatsoever ye do in word or deed, do all in the name of the LORD Jesus, giving thanks to God and the Father by him" (Col.3:17).* *"Servants [employees, workers], obey in all things your masters [employers] according to the flesh; not with eyeservice, as menpleasers; but in singleness of heart, fearing God: And whatsoever ye do, do it heartily, as to the LORD, and not unto men; Knowing that of the LORD ye shall receive the reward of the inheritance: for ye serve the LORD Christ" (Col.3:22-24; see He.12:28; Ex.23:25; De.10:12; Ps.2:11; Ps. 16:11; Ps. 126:5).*
The Blessing of Spiritual Growth **"The LORD shall establish thee an holy people unto himself, as he hath**	The blessing of spiritual growth is promised to the obedient person. The promise is phenomenal: God would establish the Israelites as His holy	*"That he would grant unto us, that we being delivered out of the hand of our enemies might serve him without fear, In holiness and righteousness*

THE BLESSINGS
Deuteronomy 28:1-14

THE BLESSING AND THE BIBLICAL BASIS	THE RESULTS OF OBEDIENCE AND THE PRACTICAL APPLICATION	THE SUPPORTING SCRIPTURE
sworn unto thee, if thou shalt keep the commandments of the LORD thy God, and walk in his ways. And all people of the earth shall see that thou art called by the name of the LORD; and they shall be afraid of thee" (De.28:9-10).	people, as the people who followed the only living and true God, the LORD Himself (Jehovah, Yahweh). But note: this blessing of spiritual growth was conditional. Spiritual growth—being set apart as God's holy people—was to be a reality only if the people obeyed God. They had to keep His commandments and walk in His ways in order to grow spiritually. If they would just obey God, then they would bear a strong testimony and witness for the LORD before all the peoples of the earth. Obedience would exalt the name of the LORD. If a believer obeyed God, his neighbors would see that he lived a holy life, a life that was totally set apart to God. He would bear a testimony of holiness to his immoral and lawless neighbors, bear a strong witness of holiness for God. God is holy; therefore, we must be holy. Holiness simply means *being set apart to God*. If a person is set apart to God, he is following and obeying God. He is keeping the commandments of God, doing all that God says. Since God is holy, we must be holy. We must be set apart to obey God in all that He says. This is the witness, the strong testimony that we are to have for God: the witness and testimony of holiness. It is holiness that will cause us to grow spiritually. Spiritual growth is a direct result of holy living. Holiness bears the fruit of spiritual growth.	*before him, all the days of our life"* (Lu.1:74-75). *"Having therefore these promises, dearly beloved, let us cleanse ourselves from all filthiness of the flesh and spirit, perfecting holiness in the fear of God"* (2 Co.7:1). *"Follow peace with all men, and holiness, without which no man shall see the LORD"* (He.12:14). *"But as he which hath called you is holy, so be ye holy in all manner of conversation; Because it is written, Be ye holy; for I am holy"* (1 Pe.1:15-16). *"For I am the LORD that bringeth you up out of the land of Egypt, to be your God: ye shall therefore be holy, for I am holy"* (Le.11:45; See also 2 Pe.3:11-14).
The Blessing of Prosperity, an Excess of Good Things "And the LORD shall make thee plenteous in goods, in the fruit of thy body, and in the fruit of thy cattle, and in the fruit of thy ground, in the land which the LORD sware unto thy fathers to give thee. The LORD shall open unto thee his good treasure, the heaven to give the rain unto thy land in his season, and to bless all the work of thine hand: and thou shalt lend unto many nations, and thou shalt not borrow" (De.28:11-12).	The blessing of prosperity, an excess of good things, is promised to the obedient person. The thrust of this point is entirely different from that mentioned earlier (see v.4). In the ancient world, prosperity depended primarily upon one thing: rain. Rain is the focus of this promise. Without rain, nothing could survive: not children, livestock, or crops. But with an abundance of rain, in particular at the right time, there would be an abundance of crops and plenty to eat for the children and the livestock. This is the promise of the blessing: the LORD promised to open the heavens and pour out abundant rain, the storehouse of His bounty, that would nourish the crops, livestock, and His children. In fact, He would pour out so much rain and the people would prosper so much that they would have a wealthy economy throughout the whole nation. The economy of the Israelites would be healthy, strong, and prosperous. They would have so much as a nation that two things would happen economically:	*"But seek ye first the kingdom of God, and his righteousness; and all these things shall be added unto you"* (Mt.6:33). *"The thief cometh not, but for to steal, and to kill, and to destroy: I am come that they might have life, and that they might have it more abundantly"* (Jn.10:10). *"But my God shall supply all your need according to his riches in glory by Christ Jesus"* (Ph.4:19). *"Blessed are they that do his commandments, that they may have right to the tree of life, and may enter in through the gates into the city"* (Re.22:14). *"Keep therefore the words of this covenant, and do them, that ye may prosper in all that ye do"* (De.29:9). *"And ye shall serve the LORD your God, and he shall bless thy bread, and thy water; and I will take sickness away from the midst of thee"* (Ex.23:25). *"Then shalt thou prosper, if thou takest heed to fulfil the statutes and judgments which the LORD charged*

THE BLESSINGS
Deuteronomy 28:1-14

THE BLESSING AND THE BIBLICAL BASIS	THE RESULTS OF OBEDIENCE AND THE PRACTICAL APPLICATION	THE SUPPORTING SCRIPTURE
	they would lend to many nations and have to borrow from none. The needs of the believer will be met. This is the sure promise of God. There is only one condition: we must obey God. If we obey God, then He meets all our needs. We never suffer a need, not a true need, that is not met. God promises to meet our needs and to meet them abundantly.	*Moses with concerning Israel: be strong, and of good courage; dread not, nor be dismayed" (1 Chr.22:13; See also Ps.1:1-3; Ps.65:9; Ps.68:19; Is.30:23).*
The Blessing of Exaltation "And the LORD shall make thee the head, and not the tail; and thou shalt be above only, and thou shalt not be beneath; if that thou hearken unto the commandments of the LORD thy God, which I command thee this day, to observe and to do them" (De.28:13).	The blessing of being exalted is promised to the obedient person. This is a confidence-building promise: the people of God would become the head or leader, not the tail. They would always be on top, have the upper hand, and never be on bottom. God's people would be exalted, become a prince among the nations of the world. But note: the promise of the blessing is qualified once again. There is a stinging condition: the blessing of being exalted is not to be given automatically. Obedience is the condition. The people of God must obey God to become princes among the nations and peoples of the earth. Obedience to God is an absolute essential to be exalted by God. One of the great promises of God to the believer is just this: the believer will be exalted by God. If a person has truly trusted Christ—honestly following and obeying God—then he will be greatly rewarded by God. God will exalt the genuine believer beyond the highest of the high. The exaltation of the believer is assured. This is the promise of God.	*"His lord said unto him, Well done, good and faithful servant; thou hast been faithful over a few things, I will make thee ruler over many things: enter thou into the joy of thy lord" (Mt.25:23).* *"And he said unto him, Well, thou good servant: because thou hast been faithful in a very little, have thou authority over ten cities" (Lu.19:17).* *"In my Father's house are many mansions: if it were not so, I would have told you. I go to prepare a place for you. And if I go and prepare a place for you, I will come again, and receive you unto myself; that where I am, there ye may be also" (Jn.14:2-3).* *"But glory, honour, and peace, to every man that worketh good, to the Jew first, and also to the Gentile" (Ro.2:10; See also 1 Co.6:2; 1 Co. 9:25; 2 Ti.4:8; 2 Ti.2:12; He. 11:26; Js.1:12; 1 Pe.5:4; Re.3:21; Re.3:11; Re.4:10; Re.5:10; Re. 11:12; Ps.91:14; Da.12:3).*

THE CURSES FOR DISOBEDIENCE
Deuteronomy 28:15-68

INTRODUCTION

A. THE FIRST SET OF CURSES (DE.28:15-46): The first set of curses was due to disobedience, refusing to listen to God. Moses declared a tragic fact: if a person refuses to listen and disobeys the Sovereign Creator of the universe, this person will suffer the curses of God. To disobey the LORD God, the only living and true God, is the highest contempt imaginable, a despicable, detestable act of rebellion. Judgment is bound to fall upon the disobedient. A person who treats God with such contempt is bound to suffer the curses of God. Note exactly what Scripture says: the curses will come upon you and overtake you (v.15). Later Moses declared to the disobedient, "all these curses will come upon you. They will pursue, overtake, and destroy you—all because you did not obey the LORD your God."

There is a strong warning in these verses for us and for all believers of all generations. The warning is against disobedience, against refusing to listen to God. Disobedience is a high crime committed against God. It is the height of contempt, the summit of wickedness. Disobedience is despicable and shameful, showing the utmost spite and disrespect for God.

> "And these [the disobedient] shall go away into everlasting punishment: but the righteous into life eternal" (Mt.25:46).
>
> "Let no man deceive you with vain words: for because of these [wicked] things cometh the wrath of God upon the children of disobedience" (Ep.5:6).
>
> "And to you who are troubled rest with us, when the LORD Jesus shall be revealed from heaven with his mighty angels, In flaming fire taking vengeance on them that know not God, and that obey not the gospel of our Lord Jesus Christ: Who shall be punished with everlasting destruction from the presence of the LORD, and from the glory of his power" (2 Th.1:7-9; see He.2:2-3; 1 S.12:15).

THE CURSES AND THE BIBLICAL BASIS	THE RESULTS OF OBEDIENCE AND THE PRACTICAL APPLICATION	THE SUPPORTING SCRIPTURE
The Curse of Being Continually Cursed "Cursed *shalt* thou *be* in the city, and cursed *shalt* thou *be* in the field" (De.28:16).	Disobedience will cause you to be cursed wherever you are, in the city or in the country. There is a strong warning to all believers: there is no escape from a life that is constantly cursed. The cursed life is marked by unbelief, of rejecting God's Word and walking in a perverted path.	"And a curse, if ye will not obey the commandments of the LORD your God, but turn aside out of the way which I command you this day, to go after other gods, which ye have not known" (De.11:28). "For such as be blessed of him shall inherit the earth; and they that be cursed of him shall be cut off" (Ps.37:22). "The curse of the LORD is in the house of the wicked: but he blesseth the habitation of the just" (Pr.3:33). "And say thou unto them, Thus saith the LORD God of Israel; Cursed be the man that obeyeth not the words of this covenant" (Je.11:3).
The Curse of Inadequate Daily Food "Cursed *shall be* thy basket and thy store" (De.28:17).	The promise of God to provide the necessities of life will no longer be true. You will be left without the care of God, without His looking after you. You will no longer have the presence, guidance, and help of God. Disobedience separates you from God, from His care and provision. Disobedience will rob us from receiving the blessings for God's provision. We must never allow sin to quench God's endless supply of provision.	"But seek ye first the kingdom of God, and his righteousness; and all these things shall be added unto you" (Mt.6:33). "The thief cometh not, but for to steal, and to kill, and to destroy: I am come that they might have life, and that they might have it more abundantly" (Jn.10:10). "And God is able to make all grace abound toward you; that ye, always having all sufficiency in all things, may abound to every good work" (2 Co.9:8). "Now unto him that is able to do exceeding abundantly above all that we ask or think, according to the power that worketh in us" (Ep.3:20). "But my God shall supply all your need according to his riches in glory by Christ Jesus" (Ph.4:19).

THE CURSES
Deuteronomy 28:15-68

THE CURSES AND THE BIBLICAL BASIS	THE RESULTS OF OBEDIENCE AND THE PRACTICAL APPLICATION	THE SUPPORTING SCRIPTURE
The Curse on Production or Fruitfulness "Cursed *shall be* the fruit of thy body, and the fruit of thy land, the increase of thy kine, and the flocks of thy sheep" (De.28:18).	Disobedience will cause you, your livestock, and your crops to be fruitless. The blessing of a fruitful and rich production will no longer be true. A curse will rest upon your production. Disobedience leads to the tragic result of a fruitless life. Time, energy, and resources will bear no fruit—not for eternity, not in God's eyes.	"Then I looked on all the works that my hands had wrought, and on the labour that I had laboured to do: and, behold, all was vanity and vexation of spirit, and there was no profit under the sun" (Ec.2:11). "All the labour of man is for his mouth, and yet the appetite is not filled" (Ec.6:7). "Labour not for the meat which perisheth, but for that meat which endureth unto everlasting life, which the Son of man shall give unto you: for him hath God the Father sealed" (Jn.6:27).
The Curse on All Daily Activities "Cursed *shalt* thou *be* when thou comest in, and cursed *shalt* thou *be* when thou goest out" (De.28:19).	As you come into your home you will be cursed, and as you go out of your home you will be cursed. Whether at home or out in the community or business world you will be cursed. A curse will rest upon your life: neither your home, community, or employment will be able to shelter you from the curse. Note that the verses just covered are parallel to the first four blessings preached by Moses earlier (28:1-6). When God's judgment is pronounced upon a person, there is no hiding place, no escape, no rescue from the justice and holiness of God.	"But we are sure that the judgment of God is according to truth against them which commit such things" (Ro.2:2). "Cursed be he that doeth the work of the LORD deceitfully, and cursed be he that keepeth back his sword from blood" (Je.48:10). "If ye will not hear, and if ye will not lay it to heart, to give glory unto my name, saith the LORD of hosts, I will even send a curse upon you, and I will curse your blessings: yea, I have cursed them already, because ye do not lay it to heart" (Mal.2:2). "Ye are cursed with a curse: for ye have robbed me, even this whole nation" (Mal.3:9).
The Curse of Confusion or Panic and Frustration in Every Activity You Undertake "The LORD shall send upon thee cursing, vexation, and rebuke, in all that thou settest thine hand unto for to do, until thou be destroyed, and until thou perish quickly; because of the wickedness of thy doings, whereby thou hast forsaken me" (De.28:20).	Disobedience will cause you to be confused and frustrated until you are utterly destroyed and ruined. All this will come upon you because of the evil of your disobedience. You forsook the LORD God. The disobedient person will be constantly filled with fear, confusion, and panic. This curse will bring to judgment and ruin even the most prideful, arrogant person.	"My confusion is continually before me, and the shame of my face hath covered me" (Ps.44:15). "Therefore shall the strength of Pharaoh be your shame, and the trust in the shadow of Egypt your confusion" (Is.30:3). "We lie down in our shame, and our confusion covereth us: for we have sinned against the LORD our God, we and our fathers, from our youth even unto this day, and have not obeyed the voice of the LORD our God" (Je.3:25). "For where envying and strife is, there is confusion and every evil work" (Js.3:16). "Because he hath appointed a day, in the which he will judge the world in righteousness by that man whom he hath ordained; whereof he hath given assurance unto all men, in that he hath raised him from the dead" (Ac.17:31).
The Curse of Deadly Diseases or Plagues That Will Sweep Across Entire Populations "The LORD shall make the pestilence cleave unto thee, until he have consumed thee from off the land,	Disobedience will cause you to suffer some wasting disease or consumption, and diseases of high fever and inflammation. Scripture is clear: disobedience to God can have an impact upon our physical health. God is not to be	"Also every sickness, and every plague, which is not written in the book of this law, them will the LORD bring upon thee, until thou be destroyed" (De.28:61). "Fools because of their transgression, and because of their iniquities,

THE CURSES
Deuteronomy 28:15-68

THE CURSES AND THE BIBLICAL BASIS	THE RESULTS OF OBEDIENCE AND THE PRACTICAL APPLICATION	THE SUPPORTING SCRIPTURE
whither thou goest to possess it. The LORD shall smite thee with a consumption, and with a fever, and with an inflammation, and with an extreme burning, and with the sword..." (De.28:21-22a).	mocked; His judgment will come to the fool, to the one who disobeys Him.	are afflicted" (Ps.107:17). "Therefore also will I make thee sick in smiting thee, in making thee desolate because of thy sins" (Mi.6:13).
The Curse on Crops, on All Plant Life and Vegetation "The LORD shall smite thee...with blasting, and with mildew; and they shall pursue thee until thou perish. And thy heaven that *is* over thy head shall be brass, and the earth that is under thee *shall be* iron. The LORD shall make the rain of thy land powder and dust: from heaven shall it come down upon thee, until thou be destroyed" (De.28:22b-24).	There will be the curse on crops, on all plant life and vegetation (v.22). The idea is that there will be little harvest, and starvation will strike the land. But this is not all: there will be no rain, for the sky over your head will be like bronze, and the soil beneath you will be as hard as iron (v.23). Disobedience will cause a scorching heat and drought, blight and mildew to strike your land and destroy your crops (v.22). There will be no rain, for the sky over your head will be like bronze, and the soil beneath you will be as hard as iron (v.23). The soil will be nothing more than dust and powder blowing about in rain-like dust storms (v.24). The severe judgment of God often strikes through the weather. In judging sin, God often closes the heavens from rain and sends drought to soak the life out of man's existence.	"And then the LORD'S wrath be kindled against you, and he shut up the heaven, that there be no rain, and that the land yield not her fruit; and lest ye perish quickly from off the good land which the LORD giveth you" (De.11:17). "When heaven is shut up, and there is no rain, because they have sinned against thee; if they pray toward this place, and confess thy name, and turn from their sin, when thou afflictest them" (1 K.8:35). "And I will lay it waste: it shall not be pruned, nor digged; but there shall come up briers and thorns: I will also command the clouds that they rain no rain upon it" (Is.5:6). "Neither said they, Where is the LORD that brought us up out of the land of Egypt, that led us through the wilderness, through a land of deserts and of pits, through a land of drought, and of the shadow of death, through a land that no man passed through, and where no man dwelt?" (Je.2:6). "I did know thee in the wilderness, in the land of great drought" (Ho.13:5).
The Curse of Being Defeated by Your Enemies "The LORD shall cause thee to be smitten before thine enemies: thou shalt go out one way against them, and flee seven ways before them: and shalt be removed into all the kingdoms of the earth. And thy carcase shall be meat unto all fowls of the air, and unto the beasts of the earth, and no man shall fray *them* away" (De.28:25-26).	There will be the curse of being defeated by your enemies (vv.25-26). Note that this curse is the opposite of the blessing given earlier (28:7, 10). Instead of victory, God's people would be defeated before their enemies. The army would attack in one direction, but the soldiers would panic and be routed and scattered in seven different directions. The number seven simply indicates a complete, full flight and defeat. Disobedience separated the people from God; therefore, they could not expect God to be present and to give victory to their army. The very opposite was true: disobedience would lead to utter defeat and destruction. They would, in fact, be so devastated that they would become an object of horror to all the kingdoms of the earth (v.25). They would die terrible deaths: their corpses would be eaten by the birds and beasts of the earth (v.26).	"(For the weapons of our warfare are not carnal, but mighty through God to the pulling down of strong holds;)" (2 Co.10:4). "For we wrestle not against flesh and blood, but against principalities, against powers, against the rulers of the darkness of this world, against spiritual wickedness in high places" (Ep.6:12). "No man that warreth entangleth himself with the affairs of this life; that he may please him who hath chosen him to be a soldier" (2 Ti.2:4). "Be sober, be vigilant; because your adversary the devil, as a roaring lion, walketh about, seeking whom he may devour" (1 Pe.5:8).
The Curse of Incurable Physical Afflictions "The LORD will smite thee with the botch of Egypt, and with the emerods, and with the scab, and	Disobedience will cause the most horrible, miserable afflictions: ⇒ boils and tumors ⇒ festering sores and the itch, from which a person cannot be cured (v.27)	"And they took ashes of the furnace, and stood before Pharaoh; and Moses sprinkled it up toward heaven; and it became a boil breaking forth with blains upon man, and upon beast" (Ex.9:10).

THE CURSES
Deuteronomy 28:15-68

THE CURSES AND THE BIBLICAL BASIS	THE RESULTS OF OBEDIENCE AND THE PRACTICAL APPLICATION	THE SUPPORTING SCRIPTURE

with the itch, whereof thou canst not be healed. The LORD shall smite thee with madness, and blindness, and astonishment of heart" (De.28:27-28).	⇒ madness, blindness, and confusion or panic (v.28)
	
	The point to note is that these various afflictions are debilitating, making a person totally incapacitated, unable to function normally.
	  God often gets the attention of people who are disobedient by permitting plagues to perform His judgment. Just think of the abuses caused by…
	• alcohol abuse
	• drug addictions
	• sexually transmitted diseases
	
	The warning of Scripture is clear: disobedience causes God's judgment.
		"And Aaron took as Moses commanded, and ran into the midst of the congregation; and, behold, the plague was begun among the people: and he put on incense, and made an atonement for the people" (Nu.16:47).
		  "But the hand of the LORD was heavy upon them of Ashdod, and he destroyed them, and smote them with emerods, even Ashdod and the coasts thereof" (1 S.5:6).
		  "And immediately the angel of the LORD smote him, because he gave not God the glory: and he was eaten of worms, and gave up the ghost" (Ac.12:23).

The Curse of Failure
 	
"And thou shalt grope at noonday, as the blind gropeth in darkness, and thou shalt not prosper in thy ways: and thou shalt be only oppressed and spoiled evermore, and no man shall save *thee*" (De.28:29).
	The disobedient person will be like a blind man groping about in the dark, unable to find his way. He will be unable to see and not know where to go nor what to do. He will be unsuccessful in everything he does. Day by day he will be just like a blind man who is oppressed and robbed, with no one to rescue him.	"Therefore night shall be unto you, that ye shall not have a vision; and it shall be dark unto you, that ye shall not divine; and the sun shall go down over the prophets, and the day shall be dark over them" (Mi.3:6).
		  "But if thine eye be evil, thy whole body shall be full of darkness. If therefore the light that is in thee be darkness, how great is that darkness!" (Mt.6:23).
		  "And the light shineth in darkness; and the darkness comprehended it not" (Jn.1:5).
		  "And this is the condemnation, that light is come into the world, and men loved darkness rather than light, because their deeds were evil" (Jn.3:19).
		  "If we say that we have fellowship with him, and walk in darkness, we lie, and do not the truth" (1 Jn.1:6).

The Curse of Becoming Plunder for a Conquering Nation
 	
"Thou shalt betroth a wife, and another man shall lie with her: thou shalt build an house, and thou shalt not dwell therein: thou shalt plant a vineyard, and shalt not gather the grapes thereof. Thine ox *shall be* slain before thine eyes, and thou shalt not eat thereof: thine ass *shall be* violently taken away from before thy face, and shall not be restored to thee: thy sheep *shall be* given unto thine enemies, and thou shalt have none to rescue *them*. Thy sons and thy daughters *shall be* given unto another people, and thine eyes shall look, and fail *with* longing for them all the day long: and *there shall be* no might in thine hand. The fruit of thy land, and all thy labours, shall a nation which thou knowest not eat up; and thou shalt be only oppressed and crushed alway: So that thou shalt be mad for the sight of thine
	Moses graphically described the horrible curses that fall upon a people who are defeated by a wicked nation:
	⇒ A person's fiancée or wife would be raped (v.30).
	⇒ A person's house would be destroyed (v.30).
	⇒ A person's vineyard would not be harvested. The fruit would be taken (v.30).
	⇒ A person's livestock would be forcibly taken for food by the invading army (v.31).
	⇒ One's sons and daughters would be enslaved (v.32). Day by day the parents would helplessly watch for their return, but be powerless to secure their return.
	⇒ One's land would be ravaged of all crops (v.33). The foreign invaders would eat what one's own hands and labor have produced.
	⇒ Cruel oppression would be reaped, and one would know nothing but cruel oppression all his days (v.33).
		"The wicked man travaileth with pain all his days, and the number of years is hidden to the oppressor" (Jb.15:20).
		  "Fools because of their transgression, and because of their iniquities, are afflicted" (Ps.107:17).
		  "Good understanding giveth favour: but the way of transgressors is hard" (Pr.13:15).
		  "Tribulation and anguish, upon every soul of man that doeth evil, of the Jew first, and also of the Gentile" (Ro.2:9).
		  "Destruction and misery are in their ways" (Ro.3:16).
		  "For to be carnally minded is death; but to be spiritually minded is life and peace" (Ro.8:6).
		  "But the fearful, and unbelieving, and the abominable, and murderers, and whoremongers, and sorcerers, and idolaters, and all liars, shall have their part in the lake which burneth with fire and brimstone: which is the second death" (Re.21:8).

THE CURSES
Deuteronomy 28:15-68

THE CURSES AND THE BIBLICAL BASIS	THE RESULTS OF OBEDIENCE AND THE PRACTICAL APPLICATION	THE SUPPORTING SCRIPTURE
eyes which thou shalt see. The LORD shall smite thee in the knees, and in the legs, with a sore botch that cannot be healed, from the sole of thy foot unto the top of thy head" (De.28:30-35).	⇒ One would be driven mad or insane by what he sees (v.34). The devastation of so much land, the death of so many, the affliction of so many with incurable diseases, the bankruptcy and collapse of so many families and businesses, the loss of all possessions by so many, the enslavement of so many children and adults, and the death of so many people—seeing all this would literally drive many mad or insane. ⇒ One would suffer unbearable afflictions such as boils that could not be cured, boils that would spread from the soles of a person's feet to the top of his head (v.35).	
The Curse of Exile, Deportation to a Foreign Nation "The LORD shall bring thee, and thy king which thou shalt set over thee, unto a nation which neither thou nor thy fathers have known; and there shalt thou serve other gods, wood and stone. And thou shalt become an astonishment, a proverb, and a byword, among all nations whither the LORD shall lead thee" (De.28:36-37).	Disobedience would lead to defeat by a foreign nation and to exile or deportation. Note that the disobedient will be led into false worship, to worshipping false gods. Moreover, the disobedient will become an object of horror, scorn, and ridicule (v.37). They will be the target of jokes and cutting remarks, the laughingstock of society. Note this fact: the situation just described here actually happened to the Israelites. They suffered the Babylonian captivity (see the books of *Ezra, Nehemiah, Haggai, Zechariah, Malachi,* and Is.13:1-14:23; 2 Chr.36:2-7; Je.45:1; Da.1:1-3; 2 K.25:2-21).	*"Holding faith, and a good conscience; which some having put away concerning faith have made shipwreck" (1 Ti.1:19).* *"Now the Spirit speaketh expressly, that in the latter times some shall depart from the faith, giving heed to seducing spirits, and doctrines of devils" (1 Ti.4:1).* *"And they shall turn away their ears from the truth, and shall be turned unto fables" (2 Ti.4:4).* *"Take heed, brethren, lest there be in any of you an evil heart of unbelief, in departing from the living God" (He.3:12).* *"Ye therefore, beloved, seeing ye know these things before, beware lest ye also, being led away with the error of the wicked, fall from your own stedfastness" (2 Pe.3:17).*
The Curse of a Devastated Economy "Thou shalt carry much seed out into the field, and shalt gather *but* little in; for the locust shall consume it. Thou shalt plant vineyards, and dress *them*, but shalt neither drink *of* the wine, nor gather *the grapes;* for the worms shall eat them. Thou shalt have olive trees throughout all thy coasts, but thou shalt not anoint *thyself* with the oil; for thine olive shall cast *his fruit.* Thou shalt beget sons and daughters, but thou shalt not enjoy them; for they shall go into captivity. All thy trees and fruit of thy land shall the locust consume. The stranger that *is* within thee shall get up above thee very high; and thou shalt come down very low. He shall lend to thee, and thou shalt not lend to him: he shall be the head, and thou shalt be the tail" (De.28:38-44).	Disobedience will cause a steady decline of the economy, a steady decline in production and fruitfulness. The disobedient will sink lower and lower into debt, suffering a steady decline until recovery is impossible. Standing there preaching to the people, Moses graphically described the picture of economic collapse: ⇒ There will be little harvest because of locusts (v.38). ⇒ There will be little fruit to harvest because of worms (v.39). ⇒ There will be few olives to harvest because of disease (v.40). ⇒ There will be little labor and continued economic growth because the young—the sons and daughters—will be taken captive (v.41). ⇒ There will be few crops and trees surviving because of locusts (v.42). ⇒ There will be a steady decline	*"The increase of his house shall depart, and his goods shall flow away in the day of his wrath" (Jb.20:28).* *"For he seeth that wise men die, likewise the fool and the brutish person perish, and leave their wealth to others" (Ps.49:10).* *"Wilt thou set thine eyes upon that which is not? for riches certainly make themselves wings; they fly away as an eagle toward heaven" (Pr.23:5).* *"For riches are not for ever: and doth the crown endure to every generation?" (Pr.27:24).* *"As the partridge sitteth on eggs, and hatcheth them not; so he that getteth riches, and not by right, shall leave them in the midst of his days, and at his end shall be a fool" (Je.17:11).* *"Your gold and silver is cankered; and the rust of them shall be a witness against you, and shall eat your*

THE CURSES
Deuteronomy 28:15-68

THE CURSES AND THE BIBLICAL BASIS	THE RESULTS OF OBEDIENCE AND THE PRACTICAL APPLICATION	THE SUPPORTING SCRIPTURE
	of the economy, and the disobedient will sink lower and lower, even below the foreigners living among them (v.43). ⇒ There will be the need to borrow over and over again, leading to terrible debt that causes a continued deterioration and decline of the economy (v.44). ⇒ There will be the loss of their exalted position: they will no longer be the head but the dregs of society instead (v.44). People tend to go about their daily lives without much disturbance until the economy is shaken. Throughout history, God has brought judgment upon the disobedient by striking the economy. Individuals as well as nations have suffered great financial loss and/or economic collapse.	*flesh as it were fire. Ye have heaped treasure together for the last days"* (Js.5:3). *"Therefore shalt thou serve thine enemies which the LORD shall send against thee, in hunger, and in thirst, and in nakedness, and in want of all things: and he shall put a yoke of iron upon thy neck, until he have destroyed thee"* (De.28:48).

THE CURSES
Deuteronomy 28:15-68

INTRODUCTION

B. THE SECOND SET OF CURSES (DE.28:47-57): The second set of curses was due to lack of service, the failure to serve God. Note verse 47: Moses began to warn the people against failing to serve God. If they failed to serve Him, a series of horrible curses would fall upon them. The Sovereign Creator of the universe expects to be served. Therefore, it is the height of folly to refuse to serve the LORD God Almighty. Rejecting Him and His call to service will cause curse after curse to come upon a person, a barrage of horrible calamities.

One thing God will not tolerate: the neglect of our duty. We must not neglect our responsibility, our service for Him. If we fail to serve God—if we neglect our duty—we will face the terrifying judgment of God.

"And every one that heareth these sayings of mine, and doeth them not, shall be likened unto a foolish man, which built his house upon the sand: And the rain descended, and the floods came, and the winds blew, and beat upon that house; and it fell: and great was the fall of it" (Mt.7:26-27).

"Thou oughtest therefore to have put my money to the exchangers, and then at my coming I should have received mine own with usury [interest, growth]. Take therefore the talent from him, and give it unto him which hath ten talents....And cast ye the unprofitable servant into outer darkness: there shall be weeping and gnashing of teeth" (Mt.25:27-28, 30; see Mt.25:31-32, 41-46; Lu.12:47; Lu.16:19-25; He.2:3; Js.2:14; Js.4:17; Pr.21:13).

THE CURSES AND THE BIBLICAL BASIS	THE RESULTS OF OBEDIENCE AND THE PRACTICAL APPLICATION	THE SUPPORTING SCRIPTURE
The Curse of Serving One's Enemies "Therefore shalt thou serve thine enemies which the LORD shall send against thee, in hunger, and in thirst, and in nakedness, and in want of all *things*: and he shall put a yoke of iron upon thy neck, until he have destroyed thee. The LORD shall bring a nation against thee from far, from the end of the earth, *as swift* as the eagle flieth; a nation whose tongue thou shalt not understand; A nation of fierce countenance, which shall not regard the person of the old, nor show favour to the young: And he shall eat the fruit of thy cattle, and the fruit of thy land, until thou be destroyed: which *also* shall not leave thee *either* corn, wine, or oil, *or* the increase of thy kine, or flocks of thy sheep, until he have destroyed thee. And he shall besiege thee in all thy gates, until thy high and fenced walls come down, wherein thou trustedst, throughout all thy land: and he shall besiege thee in all thy gates throughout all thy land, which the LORD thy God hath given thee" (De.28:48-52).	The curses brought about by the enemy are the worst curses imaginable: ⇒ The enemy would leave them hungry, thirsty, naked, and in poverty (v.48). ⇒ The enemy would enslave and destroy them (v.48). His oppression would be so severe that it would be as though an iron yoke has been put on their necks until they were destroyed. ⇒ The enemy would quickly and forcefully conquer them (v.49). Note that a particular nation is being spoken about, a nation that would swoop down upon the Israelites just like an eagle, a nation whose language the Israelites would not understand. Both the Assyrians and the Babylonians were referred to in Scripture as eagles (Ho.8:1; Je.48:40). The soaring of an eagle pictures the speed and strength of military power. ⇒ The enemy would be a fierce, heartless nation (v.50). They would enslave and slaughter both the old and the young as well as the middle-aged adults. ⇒ The enemy would devour the food supply, the livestock and crops, until they starved and were destroyed. They would leave absolutely nothing, plundering and ransacking and destroying everything. ⇒ The enemy would lay siege and destroy all their cities (v.52). Note the reference to the Israelites trusting in their fortified cities. But their fortifications could not secure them; their cities could not make them safe nor	"His own iniquities shall take the wicked himself, and he shall be holden with the cords of his sins" (Pr.5:22). "Jesus answered them, Verily, verily, I say unto you, Whosoever committeth sin is the servant of sin" (Jn.8:34). "Know ye not, that to whom ye yield yourselves servants to obey, his servants ye are to whom ye obey; whether of sin unto death, or of obedience unto righteousness?" (Ro.6:16). "But I see another law in my members, warring against the law of my mind, and bringing me into captivity to the law of sin which is in my members" (Ro.7:23). "And that they may recover themselves out of the snare of the devil, who are taken captive by him at his will" (2 Ti.2:26). "While they promise them liberty, they themselves are the servants of corruption: for of whom a man is overcome, of the same is he brought in bondage" (2 Pe.2:19). "But your iniquities have separated between you and your God, and your sins have hid his face from you, that he will not hear" (Is.59:2). "For the wages of sin is death; but the gift of God is eternal life through Jesus Christ our LORD" (Ro.6:23).

THE CURSES
Deuteronomy 28:15-68

THE CURSES AND THE BIBLICAL BASIS	THE RESULTS OF OBEDIENCE AND THE PRACTICAL APPLICATION	THE SUPPORTING SCRIPTURE
	give them victory. Only God could provide security. But they had refused to serve Him; therefore, they were to serve a foreign nation of people. Sin is an evil foe. It shows no mercy to any sinner. Sin… • entangles • accuses • attacks • destroys • kills …all those who are enslaved to it. We must make every effort to flee from the snare of sin and become a slave to Christ.	
The Curse of Suffering Untold Horror Because of One's Enemy. "And thou shalt eat the fruit of thine own body, the flesh of thy sons and of thy daughters, which the LORD thy God hath given thee, in the siege, and in the straitness, wherewith thine enemies shall distress thee: *So that* the man *that is* tender among you, and very delicate, his eye shall be evil toward his brother, and toward the wife of his bosom, and toward the remnant of his children which he shall leave: So that he will not give to any of them of the flesh of his children whom he shall eat: because he hath nothing left him in the siege, and in the straitness, wherewith thine enemies shall distress thee in all thy gates. The tender and delicate woman among you, which would not adventure to set the sole of her foot upon the ground for delicateness and tenderness, her eye shall be evil toward the husband of her bosom, and toward her son, and toward her daughter, And toward her young one that cometh out from between her feet, and toward her children which she shall bear: for she shall eat them for want of all *things* secretly in the siege and straitness, wherewith thine enemy shall distress thee in thy gates" (De.28:53-57).	The Israelites would suffer the ghastly, repulsive horror of eating the flesh of dead sons and daughters (vv.53-57). The siege of the fiercest looking nation would reach its climax in cannibalism. Starving to death, the Israelites would actually eat their own children. ⇒ Even the most tender-hearted man would have no compassion for his family (vv.54-55). Starvation would make him so degenerate and depraved that he would eat the flesh of his own children, not sharing any with his family. ⇒ Even the most tender and delicate woman would become callous and cruel (vv.56-57). She would secretly eat the afterbirth and the newborn child from her womb. Note why Moses predicted that the people would turn to cannibalism: because of the suffering the enemy would inflict on them (vv.53, 55, 57). Three times the suffering is mentioned. The frightful horror of starvation would stare people in the face, and they would become utterly depraved, degenerate. Shockingly, they would begin to eat the flesh of the dead. Then, when there were no more dead, they would begin to turn upon the weak and helpless children, slaughtering them and eating their flesh—the most horrible, repulsive, sickening thought that can be imagined. Nevertheless, it happened (see 2 K.6:24-31; La.2:20; 4:10).	"And turn ye not aside: for *then* should ye go after vain things, which cannot profit nor deliver; for they are vain" (1 S.12:21). "Treasures of wickedness profit nothing: but righteousness delivereth from death" (Pr.10:2). "For there shall be no reward to the evil man; the candle of the wicked shall be put out" (Pr.24:20). "They have sown wheat, but shall reap thorns: they have put themselves to pain, but shall not profit: and they shall be ashamed of your revenues because of the fierce anger of the LORD" (Je.12:13). "For what is a man advantaged, if he gain the whole world, and lose himself, or be cast away?" (Lu.9:25). "For the wages of sin is death; but the gift of God is eternal life through Jesus Christ our LORD" (Ro.6:23).

THE CURSES
Deuteronomy 28:15-68

INTRODUCTION

C.   THE THIRD SET OF CURSES (DE.28:58-68): The third set of curses was due to fear and lack of reverence for God. The curses would fall upon a person because he failed to fear the glorious and awesome name, "the LORD your God." This graphic picture of the curses for disobedience should be enough to stir any person to rededicate his life. The curses for disobedience stand as a severe warning to all people of all generations. Moses warned the Israelites and, through them, he warns us all. There are consequences for disobedience, curses that will fall upon the heads of all disobedient people. The warning of God is clear: we must fear God and reverence Him.

"And fear not them which kill the body, but are not able to kill the soul: but rather fear him which is able to destroy both soul and body in hell" (Mt.10:28).

"And if ye call on the Father, who without respect of persons judgeth according to every man's work, pass the time of your sojourning here in fear" (1 Pe.1:17).

"Honour all men. Love the brotherhood. Fear God. Honour the king" (1 Pe.2:17).

"And now, Israel, what doth the LORD thy God require of thee, but to fear the LORD thy God, to walk in all his ways, and to love him, and to serve the LORD thy God with all thy heart and with all thy soul" (De.10:12).

"Now therefore fear the LORD, and serve him in sincerity and in truth: and put away the gods which your fathers served on the other side of the flood, and in Egypt; and serve ye the LORD" (Jos.24:14; Ps.4:4; Ps.33:8; Ps.89:7; Ec.12:13; Is.8:13; Is.57:15; Hab.2:20).

THE CURSES AND THE BIBLICAL BASIS	THE RESULTS OF OBEDIENCE AND THE PRACTICAL APPLICATION	THE SUPPORTING SCRIPTURE
The Curse of Fearful Plagues, Harsh and Prolonged Disasters, and Severe and Lingering Sicknesses "Then the LORD will make thy plagues wonderful, and the plagues of thy seed, *even* great plagues, and of long continuance, and sore sicknesses, and of long continuance. Moreover he will bring upon thee all the diseases of Egypt, which thou wast afraid of; and they shall cleave unto thee. Also every sickness, and every plague, which *is* not written in the book of this law, them will the LORD bring upon thee, until thou be destroyed" (De.28:59-61).	What Moses now proclaimed to the Israelites is most frightening: if they failed to fear God's holy and awesome name... • they would suffer all the dreaded diseases of Egypt, and the diseases would cling to them (v.60) • they would suffer every kind of disease and disaster, even those not recorded in the book of the law (v.61) The records of history are clear: disobedience will lead to awful plagues and all kinds of sicknesses.	"I also will do this unto you; I will even appoint over you terror, consumption, and the burning ague, that shall consume the eyes, and cause sorrow of heart: and ye shall sow your seed in vain, for your enemies shall eat it" (Le.26:16). "Fools because of their transgression, and because of their iniquities, are afflicted. Their soul abhorreth all manner of meat; and they draw near unto the gates of death" (Ps.107:17-18). "Therefore also will I make thee sick in smiting thee, in making thee desolate because of thy sins" (Mi.6:13).
The Curse of Being Almost Annihilated, Exterminated—Reduced to a Very Small Population "And ye shall be left few in number, whereas ye were as the stars of heaven for multitude; because thou wouldest not obey the voice of the LORD thy God. And it shall come to pass, *that* as the LORD rejoiced over you to do you good, and to multiply you; so the LORD will rejoice over you to destroy you, and to bring you to nought; and ye shall be plucked from off the land whither thou goest to possess it" (De.28:62-63).	If they refused to obey the LORD, refused to fear and reverence His holy name; they would suffer the most horrible curses imaginable. Just as the LORD had increased their number, so He would decrease their population. There is no protection for those who rebel against God, for those who refuse to fear and reverence His holy name. God's judgment will be sure and swift.	"Thou shalt not take the name of the LORD thy God in vain; for the LORD will not hold him guiltless that taketh his name in vain" (Ex.20:7). "He that keepeth his mouth keepeth his life: but he that openeth wide his lips shall have destruction" (Pr.13:3). "O generation of vipers, how can ye, being evil, speak good things? for out of the abundance of the heart the mouth speaketh. A good man out of the good treasure of the heart bringeth forth good things: and an evil man out of the evil treasure bringeth forth evil things. But I say unto you, That every idle word that men shall speak, they shall give account thereof in the day of judgment" (Mt.12:34-36).
The Curse of Being Uprooted and Scattered All over the World, Among All Nations	Moses declared that the result would be catastrophic: ⇒ They would worship false gods, engage in idolatry and false worship (v.64).	"But I keep under my body, and bring it into subjection: lest that by any means, when I have preached to others, I myself should be a castaway" (1 Co.9:27).

THE CURSES
Deuteronomy 28:15-68

THE CURSES AND THE BIBLICAL BASIS	THE RESULTS OF OBEDIENCE AND THE PRACTICAL APPLICATION	THE SUPPORTING SCRIPTURE
"And it shall come to pass, *that* as the LORD rejoiced over you to do you good, and to multiply you; so the LORD will rejoice over you to destroy you, and to bring you to nought; and ye shall be plucked from off the land whither thou goest to possess it. And the LORD shall scatter thee among all people, from the one end of the earth even unto the other; and there thou shalt serve other gods, which neither thou nor thy fathers have known, *even* wood and stone. And among these nations shalt thou find no ease, neither shall the sole of thy foot have rest: but the LORD shall give thee there a trembling heart, and failing of eyes, and sorrow of mind: And thy life shall hang in doubt before thee; and thou shalt fear day and night, and shalt have none assurance of thy life: In the morning thou shalt say, Would God it were even! and at even thou shalt say, Would God it were morning! for the fear of thine heart wherewith thou shalt fear, and for the sight of thine eyes which thou shalt see. And the LORD shall bring thee into Egypt again with ships, by the way whereof I spake unto thee, Thou shalt see it no more again: and there ye shall be sold unto your enemies for bondmen and bondwomen, and no man shall buy *you*" (De.28:63-68).	⇒ They would find no security or resting place no matter where they set the soles of their feet (v.65). ⇒ They would have minds gripped by anxiety; their eyes would be weary and lonely, and their hearts would be filled with sorrow and despair (v.65). ⇒ They would live in constant doubt, fear, and hopelessness (v.66). They would never be sure of their lives. ⇒ They would be gripped by terror (v.67). In the morning they would wish it were evening, and in the evening they would wish it were morning. ⇒ They would even be scattered in Egypt and offer themselves for sale as slaves, but no one would buy them (v.68). Sin separates us from a holy God. A life that is marked by unrepentant sin will be cast away from communion with the LORD. This is the clear teaching of Scripture.	*"But the children of the kingdom shall be cast out into outer darkness: there shall be weeping and gnashing of teeth"* (Mt.8:12). *"Then said the king to the servants, Bind him hand and foot, and take him away, and cast him into outer darkness; there shall be weeping and gnashing of teeth"* (Mt.22:13). *"And cast ye the unprofitable servant into outer darkness: there shall be weeping and gnashing of teeth"* (Mt.25:30). *"If a man abide not in me, he is cast forth as a branch, and is withered; and men gather them, and cast them into the fire, and they are burned"* (Jn.15:6).

TYPES, SYMBOLS, AND PICTURES
THE BOOK OF DEUTERONOMY

ALPHABETICAL OUTLINE

What is a biblical type or symbol? Simply put, a *biblical type* is a *foreshadowing* of what was to come at a later time in history. Through a person, place, or thing, a biblical type points toward a New Testament fulfillment.

In addition to biblical types, there are what we may call *biblical pictures*. A biblical picture is a lesson that we can see in the Scriptures *without distorting the truth*. The study of biblical types and pictures is a valuable tool in that it helps us apply the truth of the Scriptures in our lives. Scripture itself tells us this:

"Now all these things happened unto them for examples: and they are written for our admonition, upon whom the ends of the world are come" (1 Co.10:11).

"For whatsoever things were written aforetime were written for our learning, that we through patience and comfort of the scriptures might have hope" (Ro.15:4).

PERSON/PLACE/THING	SCRIPTURE, OUTLINE AND DISCUSSION
ABRAHAM	De.1:6-8
ALL ISRAEL	De.1:1
BURNT OFFERINGS, THE SACRIFICE OF THE	De.27:1-8; See also Le.1:1-17; 6:8-13; 8:18-21; 16:24; Nu.6:3-12; 15:1-16; 28:11-15
CITIES OF REFUGE	De.19:1-13
CLEANSING LAWS	De.14:3-21
CLOTHING, DISTINCTIVE	De.22:12
DISTRIBUTION OF THE CONQUERED LAND OF EAST JORDAN, THE	De.3:12-20
EGYPT	De.1:3; See also Nu.3:5-13; 9:1-14; Le.11:44-47; Le.19:33-34
ENEMIES IN THE PROMISED LAND, COMPLETE DESTRUCTION OF	De.7:1-5
EXODUS, THE	De.1:3; See also De.20:1-20
FELLOWSHIP OFFERINGS, THE SACRIFICE OF THE	De.27:1-8; See also Le.3:1-17; Nu.6:13-20; 15:1-16
FEMALE WAR PRISONER WHO WAS TO BE WED HAD TO SHAVE HER HEAD, TRIM HER NAILS, PUT ON NEW CLOTHES, AND MOURN FOR HER PARENTS FOR ONE MONTH, THE	De.21:13
FESTIVAL OF HARVEST OR PENTECOST, THE	De.16:9-12; See also Le.23:15-22
FESTIVAL OF TABERNACLES OR BOOTHS OR SHELTERS, THE	De.16:13-15
FESTIVAL OF UNLEAVENED BREAD, THE	De.16:1-8, Thgt.2
FORGETTING GOD AND HIS DELIVERANCE FROM EGYPT	De.6:12
HORNET	De.7:17-26, esp. v.20
LAW DEALING WITH A MAN HUNG ON A TREE, THE	De.21:22-23
LEADERS WHO WASHED THEIR HANDS OVER THE YOUNG COW, THE	De.21:6
LEPROSY	De.24:8-9; See also Le.13:1-59; Nu.5:1-4; 12:13-16
MARCH TO THE PROMISED LAND, THE	De.1:6-8
MESSAGE OF THE APPOINTED PRIEST, THE	De.20:1-20

TYPES, SYMBOLS, AND PICTURES
Alphabetical Outline

PERSON/PLACE/THING	SCRIPTURE, OUTLINE AND DISCUSSION
MESSENGER—MOSES, THE SERVANT OF GOD, THE	De.1:1
MOSES AS THE MEDIATOR OF THE COVENANT	De.5:2-5; See also De.29:1
MOSES CASTING DOWN THE TWO STONE TABLETS AND BREAKING THEM BEFORE THE PEOPLE	De.9:7-21
OFFERING OF A YOUNG UNWORKED COW WHOSE NECK WAS BROKEN, THE	De.21:4
PASSOVER, THE	De.16:1-17; See also Le. 23:5; Nu.28:16-25
PROMISED LAND, THE	De.1:1-5; See also De.4:1-5; De.26:3
PURITY IN THE MILITARY CAMP	De.23:9-14
SCATTERED AMONG THE PEOPLES OF THE WORLD	De.4:27
SUBSTITUTE SACRIFICE, THE: THE ANIMAL WAS A SUBSTITUTE SACRIFICE OFFERED TO GOD, OFFERED TO MAKE ATONEMENT FOR THE PEOPLE	De.15:19-23
TEACHING CHILDREN THE WONDERFUL TRUTH OF GOD'S DELIVERANCE FROM EGYPT	De.6:21
UNNATURAL, INAPPROPRIATE, IMPURE MIXING	De.22:9-11
VICTORIOUS MARCH OVER THE CANAANITE ENEMIES, THE	De.2:24-3:11; See also De.28:7
WAR, CONDUCTING A JUST	De.20:1-20
WILDERNESS WANDERINGS (JOURNEY), THE	De.32:7-14; See also Ex.13:17-18:27; Nu.14:33; De.8:2-3, 5-6

TYPES, SYMBOLS, AND PICTURES
THE BOOK OF DEUTERONOMY

CHRONOLOGICAL OUTLINE

What is a biblical type or symbol? Simply put, a *biblical type* is a *foreshadowing* of what was to come at a later time in history. Through a person, place, or thing, a biblical type points toward a New Testament fulfillment.

In addition to biblical types, there are what we may call *biblical pictures*. A biblical picture is a lesson that we can see in the Scriptures *without distorting the truth*. The study of biblical types and pictures is a valuable tool in that it helps us apply the truth of the Scriptures in our lives. Scripture itself tells us this:

"Now all these things happened unto them for examples: and they are written for our admonition, upon whom the ends of the world are come" (1 Co.10:11).

"For whatsoever things were written aforetime were written for our learning, that we through patience and comfort of the scriptures might have hope" (Ro.15:4).

PERSON/PLACE/THING	SCRIPTURE, OUTLINE AND DISCUSSION
THE MESSENGER—MOSES, THE SERVANT OF GOD	1:1
ALL ISRAEL	1:1
THE PROMISED LAND	1:1-5; See also 4:1-5; 26:3
THE EXODUS	1:3; See also 20:1-20
EGYPT	1:3; See also Nu.3:5-13; 9:1-14; Le.11:44-47; Le.19:33-34
ABRAHAM	1:6-8
THE MARCH TO THE PROMISED LAND	1:6-8
THE VICTORIOUS MARCH OVER THE CANAANITE ENEMIES	2:24-3:11; See also 28:7
THE DISTRIBUTION OF THE CONQUERED LAND OF EAST JORDAN	3:12-20
SCATTERED AMONG THE PEOPLES OF THE WORLD	4:27
MOSES AS THE MEDIATOR OF THE COVENANT	5:2-5; See also 29:1
FORGETTING GOD AND HIS DELIVERANCE FROM EGYPT	6:12
TEACHING CHILDREN THE WONDERFUL TRUTH OF GOD'S DELIVERANCE FROM EGYPT	6:21
COMPLETE DESTRUCTION OF ENEMIES IN THE PROMISED LAND	7:1-5
HORNET	7:17-26, esp. v.20
MOSES CASTING DOWN THE TWO STONE TABLETS AND BREAKING THEM BEFORE THE PEOPLE	9:7-21
CLEANSING LAWS	14:3-21
THE SUBSTITUTE SACRIFICE: THE ANIMAL WAS A SUBSTITUTE SACRIFICE OFFERED TO GOD, OFFERED TO MAKE ATONEMENT FOR THE PEOPLE	15:19-23
PASSOVER, THE	16:1-17; See also Le.23:5; Nu.28:16-25
THE FESTIVAL OF TABERNACLES OR BOOTHS OR SHELTERS	16:13-15
THE FESTIVAL OF UNLEAVENED BREAD	16:1-8, Thgt.2

TYPES, SYMBOLS, AND PICTURES
Chronological Outline

PERSON/PLACE/THING	SCRIPTURE, OUTLINE AND DISCUSSION
THE FESTIVAL OF HARVEST OR PENTECOST	16:9-12; See also Le.23:15-22
CITIES OF REFUGE	19:1-13
CONDUCTING A JUST WAR	20:1-20
THE MESSAGE OF THE APPOINTED PRIEST	20:1-20
THE OFFERING OF A YOUNG UNWORKED COW WHOSE NECK WAS BROKEN	21:4
THE LEADERS WHO WASHED THEIR HANDS OVER THE YOUNG COW	21:6
THE FEMALE WAR PRISONER WHO WAS TO BE WED HAD TO SHAVE HER HEAD, TRIM HER NAILS, PUT ON NEW CLOTHES, AND MOURN FOR HER PARENTS FOR ONE MONTH	21:13
THE LAW DEALING WITH A MAN HUNG ON A TREE	21:22-23
UNNATURAL, INAPPROPRIATE, IMPURE MIXING	22:9-11
DISTINCTIVE CLOTHING	22:12
PURITY IN THE MILITARY CAMP	23:9-14
LEPROSY	24:8-9; See also Le. 13:1-59; Nu.5:1-4; 12:13-16
THE SACRIFICE OF THE BURNT OFFERINGS	27:1-8; See also Le. 1:1-17; 6:8-13; 8:18-21; 16:24; Nu.6:3-12; 15:1-16; 28:11-15
THE SACRIFICE OF THE FELLOWSHIP OFFERINGS	27:1-8; See also Le. 3:1-17; Nu.6:13-20; 15:1-16
THE WILDERNESS WANDERINGS JOURNEY	32:7-14; See also Ex.13:17-18:27; Nu.14:33; 8:2-3, 5-6

DEUTERONOMY
OUTLINE & SUBJECT INDEX

REMEMBER: When you look up a subject and turn to the Scripture reference, you have not just the Scripture but also an outline and a discussion (commentary) of the Scripture and subject.

This is one of the GREAT FEATURES of *The Preacher's Outline & Sermon Bible®*. Once you have all the volumes, you will have not only what all other Bible indexes give you, that is, a list of all the subjects and their Scripture references, but in addition you will have...

- an outline of every Scripture and subject in the Bible
- a discussion (commentary) on every Scripture and subject
- every subject supported by other Scripture, already written out or cross referenced

DISCOVER THE UNIQUE VALUE for yourself. Quickly glance below to the first subject of the Index. It is:

AARON
Death of. In Moserah. 9:22–10:11, esp. v.10:6
Discussion. It was only the prayer of Moses that kept God from executing Aaron. 9:7-21, esp. v.20
Judgment of. Was prevented because of Moses' intercession. 9:7-21, esp. v.20
Sin of. God was angry enough to destroy him. 9:7-21, esp. v.20
Was gathered to his people. 32:50

Turn to the first reference. Glance at the Scripture and the outline, then read the commentary. You will immediately see the TREMENDOUS BENEFIT of the INDEX of *The Preacher's Outline & Sermon Bible®*.

OUTLINE AND SUBJECT INDEX

A

AARON
Death of. In Moserah. 9:22-10:11, esp. v.10:6
Discussion. It was only the prayer of Moses that kept God from executing Aaron. 9:7-21, esp. v.20
Judgment of. Was prevented because of Moses' intercession. 9:7-21, esp. v.20
Sin of. God was angry enough to destroy him. 9:7-21, esp. v.20
Was gathered to his people. 32:50

ABORTION
Meaning of. 5:17, D.S. #1
Ministry to. Women with an unwanted pregnancy. 5:17, D.S. #1
Question.
  What does the Bible say about the creation of man & the fetus or unborn baby in the womb? 5:17, D.S. #1
  What does the medical profession say about the fetus or unborn child in the mother's womb? 5:17, D.S. #1
  When does the unborn child become a human being? 5:17, D.S. #1

ABRAHAM
Assurance of. God's presence. Symbolizes the believer's experience. 1:8, D.S.#1
Type - Symbol of. All believers. 1:6-8, Types Chart

ABRAHAMIC COVENANT
Abraham's perspective.
  The assurance of a personal inheritance. 1:8, D.S.#1
  The assurance of conquest & rest, of spiritual victory & spiritual rest. 1:8, D.S.#1
  The assurance of God's own presence, His love, care, provision, & protection. 1:8, D.S.#1
Discussed. The call & promises. 5:5, D.S. #1
Type - Symbol - Picture of. The believer's salvation. 5:5, D.S. #1

ABUNDANCE
Danger of. Comfort, ease, satisfaction. 6:12-19

ABUSE
How to prevent. 24:1-22

ACCIDENTS
Fact. In a fallen world, **a.** do happen. 19:1-13, Thgt.1

ACCUSED
Justice for. 19:15-21

ADMINISTRATION
Of justice. 16:18-17:1

ADULTERY (See **SEX**)
Causes of. Five categories. 5:18
Duty. Must not commit **a**. 22:22
Judgment of. Law demanded execution. 22:22
Laws governing. 5:16-21, esp. v.18; 22:22
Meaning of. 5:18
Seriousness of. Why God forbids **a**. 5:18
Warning. Must not commit adultery. 5:18

AFFLUENCE
Warning against. Will forget & reject God. 32:15-18

AGNOSTIC (See **ATHEIST**)

ALLEGIANCE
Discussed. Why God demands **a**. 10:12-15
Duty. Must make a pledge to the LORD. 10:12-15

ALTAR
Built for the Dedication Service. 27:1-8

ALTAR OF BURNT OFFERING (See **BURNT OFFERING**)
Type - Symbol of. Christ dying as the substitute sacrifice for us. 27:1-8

ALTARS, FALSE
Duty. Israel. Must destroy all the Asherah poles & idols. 12:2-4

AMALEKITES
Example of. A cruel, savage people. 25:17-19

AMMONITES
Discussed.
  Israel was warned by God not to harass the **A**. 2:17-23
  Were the descendants of Lot. 2:17-23
Judgment of. Excluded from the assembly of worship of God. 23:1-8

AMORITES
Conquered by Israel. 2:24-3:11, Types Chart
Enemy of Israel who inhabited the promised land. 7:1-5

ANAK - ANAKITES
Descendants (the giants) inhabited the promised land. 1:18-39
Question. Who can stand up against the **A**.? 9:1-6

ANATH
Canaanite god. 12:29-32

ANGER
Discussed. Reasons why people get angry & develop feelings against others. 5:17, Thgt.2
Kind of. Justified. 5:17
Of the LORD. Provoked. 9:7-21, esp. vv.19-20
Warning. Is dangerous. 5:17

ANIMALS
Conservation of. Animal life. 22:6-7
Dead. Israel was forbidden to eat any animal found dead. 14:3-21
Edible. 14:3-21
Facts.
  God cares not only for man but also for animals. 22:6-7, Thgt.1

INDEX

God has created animals for man. 22:6-7, Thgt.1
Inedible. 14:3-21
Land. 14:3-21
Laws of. Giving all firstborn animals to the LORD. 15:19-23
List of.
    Clean. 14:3-21
    Unclean. 14:3-21
Warning. Must not mix different animals together when plowing. 22:9-11, Types Chart
Water creatures. 14:3-21

ANIMAL SACRIFICE (See **SACRIFICE, ANIMAL**)
Common requirements. 15:19-23

APHRODITE
Goddess of sex. 5:8-10, pt.3, Thgt.2

APOSTASY
Duty. Must not commit **a**. 32:15-18
Of Israel. 4:15-31; 32:15-18
Result of. Will be rejected & suffer the judgment of God. 32:19-27
Warning. God warns us against **a**., against turning away from the living God. 13:12-18, Thgt.1; 31:14-23, Thgt.1

APPEAL
To obey God. 30:19-20
To obey the covenant. A strong call to love & obey the LORD. 30:11-16

APPOINT - APPOINTMENT
Of kings or rulers. 17:14-20

APPROACH - APPROACHABLE
To God. A mediator needed to approach God for man. 5:26-27

ARK, THE
Contents of. The Ten Commandments. 31:24-29

ART
Second Commandment does not forbid artistic talent. 5:8-10

ASHER, TRIBE OF
Blessings of. Prosperity. 33:24-25
Failure of. Were consumed by their luxury & their wealth. 33:24-25
Prophecy concerning. To be most blessed, happy, & highly favored by the other tribes. 33:24-25

ASHERAH
Canaanite god. 12:29-32

ASHERAH POLES
Duty. Israel. Must destroy all the Asherah poles & idols. 12:2-4

ASSEMBLY
Exclusion from. List of four groups of people. 23:1-8

ASSURANCE
Of what.
    God's guidance. 31:1-6
    God's presence. 31:1-6
    Victory. 20:1-4

ASTARTE
Canaanite god. 12:29-32

ATHEIST
People who think there is no God are wrong. 5:7

ATONING SACRIFICE
Discussed. The sacrifice of the Burnt Offering. 27:1-8, Types Chart

AUTHORITY
Disrespect for. 4:1-43, Intro.

AWE (See **HOLINESS, OF GOD; REVERENCE; FEAR, OF GOD**)

B

BAAL
Canaanite god. 12:29-32

BAAL OF PEOR
Warning. Must not commit the sins of Baal Peor, the sins of immorality & false worship. 4:1-5

BACCHUS
Cloven-footed Greek & Roman god of wine & revelry. 5:8-10, pt.3, Thgt.2

BACKSLIDING
Caused by. 4:9-14

BARRIER
Fact. Separates man from God. 5:23-25

BEFORE ME
Meaning of. 5:7

BEHAVIOR
Kind of. Unnatural. 22:5

BELIEVER - BELIEVERS
Blessings of. Abundance of. Promised. An excess of good things is promised to the obedient person. 28:11-12; 33:13-17, Thgt.1
Chosen. God has chosen us to be His people. 10:12-15
Death of.
    Death of a believer is precious in the sight of God. 34:1-8, Thgt.1
    Preparation for. 32:48-52, Thgt.1
Discussed. Two clear reasons why people must support the ministers of God. 18:1-8
Duty.
    Must acknowledge that the LORD—He & He alone—is God. 4:32-40
    Must be a just people. 16:18-17:1
    Must be courageous and stand fast. 33:22, Thgt.1
    Must be faithful in giving a true tithe. 26:12-15
    Must be faithful to keep our promises to God. 29:10-15, Thgt.1
    Must be prepared to enter the spiritual conquest & rest of the promised land. 1:3
    Must be spiritually prepared. 1:6-4:43, Div.1 Overview
    Must be strong & courageous. 31:1-6; 31:7-8
    Must be wholeheartedly committed to the LORD. 32:44-47, Thgt.1
    Must become a center of service, a center for helping all who surround us. 33:18-19, Thgt.1
    Must control our minds throughout the day. 22:12, Thgt.1
    Must diligently teach God's commandments to our children. 6:6-9
    Must do exactly what you vow or pledge. 23:21-23
    Must fear & serve God alone. 10:20-22
    Must give the first of everything to God, the very best that we have. 15:19-23, Thgt.1
    Must grow in the LORD. 31:30-32:2
    Must have a spirit of discernment between what is allowed & forbidden. 12:20-28
    Must hear the law, learn the law, & obey the law. 5:1
    Must keep close to God. 10:20-22
    Must keep the covenant, God's commandments & write them down as a memorial. 27:1-8
    Must keep our body & spirit clean. 23:9-14
    Must keep ourselves free from defilement. 14:3-21
    Must keep the Ten Commandments. 4:9-14
    Must keep ourselves away from sexual sins. 5:18, Thgt.1
    Must know God's Word: God has given us the Word of God to warn us against sin. 31:24-29
    Must know & acknowledge the only true & living God. 5:7
    Must know that it is better not to make a vow than to make it & not fulfill it. 23:21-23
    Must learn the Law of God. 1:4-5, Thgt.1
    Must learn the lessons of history. 1:6-4:43, Div.1 Overview
    Must learn the Word of God before we can enter the promised land. 1:3
    Must live holy lives, totally set apart to God. 14:1-2, Thgt.1
    Must love God with our whole being. 6:4-5; 11:1-7
    Must never misuse, never take the name of the LORD God in vain. 5:11
    Must never personally use anything that has been consecrated to God. 12:20-28
    Must never put another person in a state of destitution. 24:6, Thgt.1
    Must never use excessive force in any situation. 25:11-12, Thgt.1
    Must not abuse the blood nor misuse the tithe. 12:15-18
    Must not be slow to pay our vows or pledges to God. 23:21-23
    Must not conform to the religious practices of the world. 12:29-32
    Must not fear during warfare—God will be with the believer. 20:1-4
    Must not settle down, be complacent, or at ease before conquering all of the promised land. 3:12-20
    Must not show partiality or favoritism to our children nor to anyone else. 21:15-17, Thgt.1
    Must not turn away from any of God's commandments. 28:14
    Must obey all the commandments & laws of God. 26:16-19
    Must obey every commandment of God. 8:1-20
    Must obey God's law even after reaching the promised land. 4:1-5

INDEX

Must obey the LORD. 28:1-3
Must place the commandments in our heart. 6:6-9
Must obey the LORD God & follow His commandments. 27:9-10
Must present our bodies as a living sacrifice to God. 15:19-23, Thgt.1
Must press on and conquer the enemies of the promised land. 3:12-20, Thgt.1
Must remember the judgment of God. 8:11-20
Must remember the terrible sins that kept the first generation out of the promised land. 1:18-39, Thgt.1
Must seek peace with our neighbors. 20:10-20, Thgt.1
Must seek the place where God's name is honored. 12:5-7
Must show compassion for the needy of this earth, doing all we can to help. 23:19-20, Thgt.1
Must support the ministers of God. 12:19; 18:1-8
Must teach God's Word & commandments to our children & share one's spiritual experiences with them. 4:9-14, esp. v.9
Must teach the truth of salvation & of the commandments to children. 6:20-25, Types Chart
Must thank God for His salvation & blessings. 26:1-11; Thgt.1
Must use God's commandments as a witness. 6:6-9
Enemies of. 7:1-5
Failure of.
   Some fail to experience spiritual conquest and victory. 1:2, Thgt.1
Identified as.
   A treasured possession. 26:16-19
   Holy, a special treasure, a possession of God. 14:1-2; 26:16-19
Life & Walk.
   Being saved does not free us from our responsibility to obey God. 27:11-26, Thgt.1
   Blessings of. 28:6
   Civic duties are the duties of us all. 17:8-13, Thgt.1
   Death of a believer is precious in the sight of God. 34:1-8, Thgt.1
   Experience with the LORD. 4:9-14
   God gave His Word in order to show us how to live. 31:9-13, Thgt.1
   God has given us the Word of God, to warn us against sin. 31:24-29
   God leads us step by step as we march to the promised land of heaven. 9:22-10:11, pt.4
   God promises to give victory to the believer. 33:7, Thgt.1
   God will enable us to conquer all the trials & temptations of life. 16:13-15, Thgt.2
   Remember God's guidance through the wilderness wanderings. 8:2-10
   Temptation must be removed from our lives and homes. 7:17-26, Thgt.2
   The language of warfare is a picture of the believer's spiritual battle against the enemies of this world. 20:1-4, Thgt.1
   Whatever is needed, we must help people. 33:20-21, Thgt.1
Relationship. With God. 5:6

Symbolized by. Israel. 1:1
Title of.
   Treasured possession. 7:6-11
   Holy, a special treasure, a possession of God. 14:1-2; 26:16-19
Warning.
   God warns us against complacency, against seeking worldly comfort, rest, & ease. 3:12-20, Thgt.1
   Must guard against the false prophet & the interpreter of dreams. 13:1-5
   Must never participate in any practice of false worship. 14:1-2, Thgt.1
   Must not become attached to the luxury, pleasures, bright lights of this earth. 33:24-25, Thgt.1
   Must not commit the sins of Baal Peor, the sins of immorality & false worship. 4:1-5
   Must not live lives of hypocrisy. 29:16-19
   Must not look upon our enemies with pity. 7:12-16
   Must not turn to false gods and false worship. 7:12-16
   Must not worship the LORD like the unbelievers of the world. 12:2-4

BENEFIT - BENEFITS
To a righteous society. 12:1-26:19, Div.3 Overview

BENEVOLENCE
Duty. Must be faithful in giving a true tithe. 26:12-15

BENJAMIN, TRIBE OF
Blessing of. Would rest secure & be safe in the LORD. 33:12
Prophecy concerning. Would rest secure & be safe in the LORD. 33:12

BESTIALITY
Judgment of. Curse. 27:11-26, esp. v.21

BEZER
City of Refuge for Reuben. 4:43
History of. 4:41-43, D.S. #1
Location of. 4:41-43, D.S. #1

BIBLE (SEE **WORD OF GOD**)
Duty to.
   Must be preached. 4:44-49, Thgt.1
   Must hear the law, learn the law, & obey the law. 5:1
   Must learn the Word of God before we can enter the promised land. 1:3
   Must read & teach the law to the people of God. 31:9-13
Importance of. Preserving and correct placement. 31:24-29

BIRDS
Clean **b**. Could be eaten. 14:3-21
Unclean **b**. List of. 14:3-21

BLASPHEMY (See **CURSE - CURSING**)

BLESS - BLESSING - BLESSINGS
Abundance of. Promised. An excess of good things is promised to the obedient person. 28:11-12; 33:13-17, Thgt.1
Caused by. Obeying God. 27:11-26
Chart of. Results of obeying God. 28:1-14
Of Benjamin. Would rest secure & be safe in the LORD. 33:12

Of employment. Promised to the obedient person. 28:8
Of Ephraim. 33:13-17
Of fruitfulness. Promised to the obedient person. 28:4-5
Of God.
   Are conditional. 28:1-3
   God's gift of worship. 33:1-5
   God's glorious, majestic presence. 33:1-5
   God's instruction, the law. 33:1-5
   God's kingship, His rule & reign over His people. 33:1-5
   God's love and care. 33:1-5
   God will keep His covenant of love if His people will obey Him. 7:12-16
   God will love and bless His people in a very special way. 7:12-16
   List of seven great blessings. 33:26-29
   Thanking God for His salvation & blessings. 26:1-11
Of Israel.
   God's gift of worship. 33:1-5
   God's glorious, majestic presence. 33:1-5
   God's instruction, the law. 33:1-5
   God's kingship, His rule & reign over His people. 33:1-5
   God's love and care. 33:1-5
Of Issachar. 33:18-19
Of Joseph. 33:13-17
Of leadership. Exaltation. 28:13
Of Levi.
   They served as the teachers of God's law. 33:8-11
   They were responsible for leading the people in their worship of God (including the offering of sacrifices to God). 33:8-11
   They were responsible for revealing the will of God to the people. 33:8-11
   They were to be greatly blessed by God. 33:8-11
Of Manasseh. 33:13-17
Of Reuben. Was to live & not die as a tribe or state of Israel. 33:6
Of spiritual growth. Is promised to the obedient person. 28:9-10
Of victory. Promised to the obedient person. 28:7
Of work. Promised to the obedient person. 28:8
Of Zebulun. 33:18-19
Promised. 28:6
Provision of. Will become the head and not the tail. 28:13
Result of. Obedience. 7:12-16
Source. God. 11:26-32; 27:11-26

BLOOD
Duty.
   Must be able to discern what is allowed & what is forbidden. 12:20-28
   Must not abuse the blood nor misuse the tithe. 12:15-18
Of Christ. True worship never abuses the **b**. of Jesus Christ. 12:15-18, Thgt.1

INDEX

Respect for.
    Must be able to discern what is allowed & what is forbidden. 12:20-28
    True worship never abuses the **b**. of Jesus Christ. 12:15-18, Thgt.1
Type - Picture - Symbol.
    Of Christ's death. 12:15-18
    Of life. 12:20-28

BODY
Mutilation of. 14:1-2

BONDAGE
Laws governing. 15:12-18

BOOK OF THE LAW
Duty. Must be entrusted into the hands of responsible leaders. 31:1-29, Intro.
Location of. To be stored *next* to the Ark, not *in* the Ark. 31:24-29
Preserved. Importance of. 31:24-29

BUILDING
Codes of. Instructions for building safe homes. 22:8
Reason for. Building codes. To prevent accidents & personal liability. 22:8

BURNT OFFERING
Results of. Atonement, reconciliation with God. 27:1-8
Type - Symbol of. Christ's sacrifice (His death) which secured atonement or reconciliation for us. 27:1-8, Types Chart

BUSINESS DEALINGS
Duty.
    Must not overcharge when selling merchandise. 25:13-16
    Must not underpay when buying merchandise. 25:13-16
    Must prevent the wrong of dishonesty in business dealings. 25:13-16
Law governing dishonest business dealings. 25:13-16
Law governing the payment of wages. 25:4
Reasons for. Honesty in business. 25:13-16
Wages of. The person who works deserves to be paid. 25:4

C

CALEB
Inheritance of. In the promised land. 1:18-39, esp.v.36
Testimony of. Believed and followed the LORD. 1:18-39, esp.v.36

CALL - CALLED
Duty. To love & obey God. 30:11-16
Fact. The call to obey God is not unreasonable nor impossible. 30:11-16
Of the covenant. A strong call to love & obey the LORD. 30:11-16
To decision. Must choose life! 30:19-20

CANAAN, LAND OF
Abraham's perspective.
    The assurance of a personal inheritance. 1:8, D.S.#1
    The assurance of conquest & rest, of spiritual victory & spiritual rest. 1:8, D.S.#1
    The assurance of God's own presence, His love, care, provision, & protection. 1:8, D.S.#1
Boundaries of. 1:6-8
Cities of.
    Bezer. City of
        City of Refuge for Reuben. 4:43
        History of. 4:41-43, D.S. #1
        Location of. 4:41-43, D.S. #1
    Golan.
        City of Refuge for the half-tribe of Manasseh. 4:43
        History of. 4:41-43, D.S. #2
        Location of. 4:41-43, D.S. #2
    Ramoth.
        City of Refuge for Gad. 4:43
        History of. 4:41-43, D.S. #3
        Location of. 4:41-43, D.S. #3
Inheritance of. Promised to Israel. 1:6-8

CANAANITES
Destruction of. 7:2, D.S. #1; Dt.20:16-18, D.S. #1
Enemy of Israel who inhabited the promised land. 7:1-5
Execution of. Three specific reasons given to Israel. 20:10-20, esp. v.17-18
Gods of. List. 12:29-32
Judgment of. Israel was used by God as His instrument of justice & judgment against the nations of Canaan. 20:16-18, D.S. #1
Nations of. 7:1-5
Worship of.
    Full of all kinds of abominations, detestable things. 12:29-32
    Places of **C**. worship were to be destroyed. 12:2-4; 33:26-29

CANCELLATION
Of debts. 15:1-6

CANNIBALISM
Caused by. The suffering the enemy would inflict upon Israel. 28:53-57

CAPITOL CRIME
Execution.
    Adultery. 22:22
    Idolatry & false worship. 17:2-7
    Kidnapping. 24:7
    Premarital immorality. 22:13-21
    Rape. 22:25-29
    Seduction of an engaged woman or man. 22:23-24
Penalty of. Hung upon a tree. 21:22-23

CAPTIVITY
Of Israel. History of. 29:22-29, D.S. #1

CASTRATE - CASTRATION
Judgment of. Castrated man. Excluded from the assembly of worship of God. 23:1-8

CEREMONY
Of blessings & cursings. 11:26-32
Of Firstfruit offering. Thanking God for His salvation & blessings. 26:1-11

CHALLENGE
Duty. To remember the goodness of God. 32:7-14

CHARACTER OF GOD
Discussed. Is not an indulgent grandfather type of person who pampers the evil of this world. 20:16-18, D.S. #1

CHARGE
Against Israel. Corruption. 32:5-6
Described.
    To be strong & courageous. 31:1-6; 31:7-8
    To march to the promised land. 1:6-8, Types Chart
    To obey God. 26:16-19; 27:1-26
    To renew the covenant. 27:1-26
Of God.
    Defeat, conquer, totally destroy all enemies of the promised land. 7:1-5
    Given to Joshua. 3:21-22; 31:7-8
    Given to ministers. 31:9-13
    Given to Moses. 6:1-3; 31:14-23
    Given to priests. 31:9-13
Of Moses. Given to Joshua. 3:21-22; 31:7-8

CHASTISEMENT
Caused by. Sin. 3:23-29
Of God. 2:16; 8:2-6; 32:48-52

CHILDREN
Abuse of. 5:16
Behavior of. The stubborn & rebellious son. 21:18-21
Discipline of. The stubborn & rebellious son. 21:18-21
Discussed. The cult of the child within society. 5:16
Duty. Must honor parents. 5:16; 21:18-21, Thgt.1
Duty to. The believer is to diligently teach the commandments to his children. 6:6-9; 11:18-21, Types Chart
Illegitimate. Judgment of. Excluded from the assembly of worship of God. 23:1-8
Judgment of. Not honoring. Curse. 27:11-26, esp. v.16
Question.
    What does God mean by honoring our parents? 5:16, Thgt.1
    What does the Bible say about the creation of man & the fetus or unborn baby in the womb? 5:17, D.S. #1
    What does the medical profession say about the fetus or unborn child in the mother's womb? 5:17, D.S. #1
    When does the unborn child become a human being? 5:17, D.S. #1
Sacrifice of. Warning against. 18:9-14

CHOICE - CHOICES
Essential. Must choose life! 30:19-20
Warning. Know the consequence of your choices. 11:26-32

CHOSEN
By God. 10:12-15

CHRIST, JESUS (See JESUS CHRIST)

CHRISTIAN LIFE (See BELIEVER)

CHURCH
Duty.
    Must keep itself pure. 17:2-7, Thgt.2
    Must not worship as everyone sees fit, but as God dictates. 12:8-14
    Must seek the place where God's name is honored. 12:5-7
Growth of. Caused by. Removal of sin. 2:16, Thgt.1

INDEX

CHURCH DISCIPLINE
Duty.
Must keep itself pure. 17:2-7, Thgt.2
Must keep the worship of God clean, pure by excluding the unclean. 23:1-8

CIRCUMCISION, SPIRITUAL
Duty. To circumcise or cut sin out of your heart. 10:16-19
Question. What does the ritual of circumcision say to believers today? 10:16-19, Thgt.2

CITIES - AREAS
Bezer
City of Refuge for Reuben. 4:43
Location of. 4:41-43, D.S. #1
History of. 4:41-43, D.S. #1
Ebal, Mount.
Altar built for the Dedication Service. 27:1-8
Discussed. Cursings. 11:26-32; 27:11-26
History of. 27:11-26, D.S. #2
Location of. 27:11-26, D.S. #2
Gerizim, Mount. Discussed. Blessings. 11:26-32; 27:11-26
History of. 27:11-26, D.S. #1
Location of. 27:11-26, D.S. #1
Golan.
City of Refuge for the half-tribe of Manasseh. 4:43
History of. 4:41-43, D.S. #2
Location of. 4:41-43, D.S. #2
Kadesh Barnea.
Discussed. Rebellion at Kadesh Barnea. 9:22-10:11
Location of. In the hill country of the Amorites, on the border of the promised land. 1:19-39
Kibroth Hattaavah. Example of disobedience. 9:22-10:11
Of Refuge.
Bezer.
City of Refuge for Reuben. 4:43
Location of. 4:41-43, D.S. #1
History of. 4:41-43, D.S. #1
Golan.
City of Refuge for the half-tribe of Manasseh. 4:43
History of. 4:41-43, D.S. #2
Location of. 4:41-43, D.S. #2
Ramoth.
City of Refuge for Gad. 4:43
History of. 4:41-43, D.S. #3
Location of. 4:41-43, D.S. #3
Palestine. Restoration of Israel. Recent occurrence. 31:30-32:52, Intro.
Paran, Desert Of (See **Deserts**).
Description of. 1:18-39
Pisgah, Mount (See **Pisgah Peak**).
History of. 34:1-8, D.S. #1
Location of. 34:1-8, D.S. #1
Place where Moses climbed to view the promised land. 34:1-8
Promised land, The.
Abraham's perspective.
The assurance of a personal inheritance. 1:8, D.S.#1
The assurance of conquest & rest, of spiritual victory & spiritual rest. 1:8, D.S.#1
The assurance of God's own presence, His love, care, provision, & protection. 1:8, D.S.#1
Barred from.
Moses. 3:23-29; 34:1-8
The first generation. 1:18-39, esp. v.35; 4:15-31, esp.vv.25-28
Boundaries of. 1:6-8
Discussed. On the threshold of. Israel was. 1:2
Duty.
Must be prepared to enter the spiritual conquest & rest of the promised land. 1:3
Must possess. 1:6-8
Enemies of. 7:1-26
How to enter. By obeying God's commandments. 4:1-5
Inheritance of. Promised to Israel. 1:6-8
March to. 1:4-5
Meaning of.
Refers to a heavenly country & a heavenly city. 1:8, D.S.#1
Refers to heaven. 1:8, D.S.#1
Refers to Palestine, the land of Israel. 1:8, D.S.#1
Praise for. The promised land & its wonderful provision. 8:7-10
Preparation to enter. 1:3; 31:1-29
Provision of.
A land that has no scarcity. 8:7-10
A rich deposit of minerals (iron & copper). 8:7-10
An abundance of food. 8:7-10
An overflowing water supply. 8:7-10
Seen by Moses. 34:1-8
Territory of. Extent of boundaries. 11:22-25
Type - Symbol of.
Heaven & of spiritual conquest & rest. 1:2; 1:6-8, Thgt.1; 4:1-5
Trusting God & resting in God. 26:1-11
Ramoth. City of Refuge for Gad. 4:43
City of Refuge for Gad. 4:43
History of. 4:41-43, D.S. #3
Location of. 4:41-43, D.S. #3
Sinai, Mount. Discussed. Sometimes called Mt. Horeb. 1:6-8
Taberah. Place of disobedience. 9:22-10:11
Warning to. Must guard against allowing an entire city or community to seduce you. 13:12-18

CITIES OF REFUGE (See **REFUGE, CITIES OF**)

CITIZEN - CITIZENSHIP
Duty. To honor parents. 5:16

CIVIC DUTIES
Duty. Are the duties of us all. 17:8-13, Thgt.1

CLEANLINESS, SPIRITUAL
Duty.
Must keep our body & spirit clean. 23:9-14
Must keep ourselves free from defilement. 14:3-21

CLEANSING LAWS
Fact. God had more than health in mind when He gave the cleansing laws. 14:3-21
Type - Symbol of. Being spiritually clean & undefiled. 14:3-21, Types Chart

CLEANSING, SPIRITUAL
Necessity of. 21:1-9

CLING
To God. Must hold fast 10:20-22

CLOSENESS
To God. Must hold fast 10:20-22

CLOTHES - CLOTHING
Cross-dressing. 22:5
Distinctive. Our clothing should be a testimony for Christ. 22:12, Thgt.1, Types Chart
Worn during the wilderness wanderings. Did not wear out. 8:2-6

COLLATERAL
Law governing. 24:6

COMFORT
Danger of. Comfort, ease, satisfaction. 6:12-19
Warning. God warns us against seeking worldly **c**. 3:12-20

COMMANDS - COMMANDMENTS
Discussed.
The commandments will teach us to fear the LORD. 6:1-3
The greatest **c**. 6:4-5
Duty.
Must have a spirit of discernment between what is allowed & forbidden. 12:20-28
Must keep, obey God's commandments. 10:12-15
Must keep the covenant, God's commandments & write them down as a memorial. 27:1-8
Must learn the Word of God before we can enter the promised land. 1:3
Must not abuse the blood nor misuse the tithe. 12:15-18
Must not conform to the religious practices of the world. 12:29-32
Must not turn away from any of God's commandments. 28:14
Must not worship as everyone sees fit, but as God dictates. 12:8-14
Must obey the laws & regulations of God. 12:1
Must obey the LORD God & follow His commandments. 27:9-10
Must reject all false worship. 12:2-4
Must seek the place where God's name is honored. 12:5-7
Must support the ministers of God. 12:19
Of Israel. Duty. Must celebrate the three pilgrimage festivals. 16:16-17
Results of keeping. Will not forget God. 8:1

COMMANDMENTS, THE TEN
Basis of. 5:7-15
Breaking of. By Moses. 9:7-21, esp. v.17
Commandment Eight concerns man's property. 5:19
Commandment Five concerns man's parents. 5:16
Commandment Four concerns God's day. 5:12-15
Commandment Nine concerns man's word: forbids lying, speaking falsely. 5:20

INDEX

Commandment One concerns God's being. 5:7
Commandment Seven concerns man's family: forbids adultery. 5:18
Commandment Six concerns man's life: forbids murder. 5:17 Purpose of. to preserve life. 5:17
Commandment Ten concerns man's desires & security: forbids coveting. 5:21
Commandment Three concerns God's name. 5:11
Commandment Two concerns the worship of God. 5:8-10
Discussed.
   Given to man in two dramatic ways. 5:22
   The law—that is, our failure to keep the law—shows how far short we come. 5:26-27, Thgt.1
Nature of. The very expression of God's being. 5:23-25
Placement of. In the Ark. 31:24-29
Purpose of. Four reasons why God gave the Ten Commandments & the Law. 5:22-23
Receiving of. By Moses. 9:7-21
Second copy of. 9:22-10:11, esp. 10:1-5
Source of. God. 5:22-23

COMMISSIONING
Of Joshua. 31:7-8

COMMIT - COMMITMENT (See **DEDICATION**)
Duty.
   Must be wholeheartedly committed to the LORD. 32:44-47, Thgt.1
   Must make a pledge to the LORD. 10:12-15
Purpose of. To establish that the believers were God's people & that He was their God. 29:10-15

COMMUNITY
Duty. Must assume responsibility for one's neighbor. 21:1-9
Warning to. Must guard against allowing an entire city or community to seduce you. 13:12-18

COMPASSION
Duty.
   Must not be hard-hearted or tightfisted against workers. 15:12-18
   Must show compassion for the needy of this earth, doing all we can to help. 23:19-20, Thgt.1
Of God.
   Conditions for. 32:36-43
   Example of. 32:48-52; 34:1-8

COMPLACENCY
Warning.
   God warns us against c. 3:12-20
   Will cause us to forget God. 8:11-20

COMPROMISE - COMPROMISING
Answer to. 6:12-19
Duty not to. 7:1-5

CONCENTRATION
Duty. To protect. 22:12

CONDITIONS
Of blessings. 28:1-3
Of repentance. 30:1-2

CONFESS - CONFESSION
Duty.
   Must be faithful in giving a true tithe. 26:12-15
   Must obey God without reservation. 26:16-19
False c. Incomplete confession. 1:40-46
Kinds of.
   Made during the offering of the firstfruit. 26:1-11
   Made when offering the three-year tithe. 26:12-15
Laws that require special confession & obedience. 26:1-19
Of salvation. Thanking God for His salvation & blessings. 26:1-11

CONFORM
Duty. Must not conform to the religious practices of the world. 12:29-32

CONQUEST
Blessing of. Over all enemies. 33:26-29
Discussed. Assured by God. 1:6-8
Kind of. Spiritual. 1:8, D.S.#1
Strategy for. 20:10-20

CONSEQUENCE - CONSEQUENCES
Warning. Know the consequence of your choices. 11:26-32

CONSERVATION
Of animal life & of food. 22:6-7

CONSTRUCTION
Building codes. 22:8

CONSULTING THE DEAD
Warning against. 18:9-14

CORRUPT - CORRUPTION
Meaning of. 4:15-31, esp. vv.16-19
Of Israel. 32:5-6

COURAGE
Duty.
   Must be courageous and stand fast. 33:22, Thgt.1
   Must be strong & courageous. 31:1-6; 31:7-8
Need of. In defeating the enemies that confront us. 33:22, Thgt.1

COURT
Witnesses in. 19:15-21

COURT, THE HIGH OR SUPREME
Duty. Must wrestle with & grasp difficult legal cases. 17:8-13
Location of. At the sanctuary or Tabernacle & later at the temple after it had been built. 17:8-13
Power of. The verdict or decision of the High Court had to be carried out. 17:8-13

COVENANT
Abraham's perspective.
   The assurance of a personal inheritance. 1:8, D.S.#1
   The assurance of conquest & rest, of spiritual victory & spiritual rest. 1:8, D.S.#1
   The assurance of God's own presence, His love, care, provision, & protection. 1:8, D.S.#1
Appeal of.
   A strong call to love & obey the LORD. 30:11-16
   To obey. 30:19-20
Basis. Five basic reasons why the c. between God & man was needed. 29:2-9
Between God & His people. Two parts: God's part & the people's part. 27:9-10
Conditions of.
   Must obey the LORD, obey Him with their whole heart and soul. 30:1-2
   Must repent, return to the LORD. 30:1-2
   Must sense the need for repentance. 30:1-2
Duty.
   Must be silent & listen to the covenant. 27:9-10
   Must keep the covenant, God's commandments & write them down as a memorial. 27:1-8
   Must obey the LORD God & follow His commandments. 27:9-10
Given to Israel. Promise of restoration. 30:3-10
Judgment for breaking. A terrifying judgment. 29:20-29
Kinds of.
   Abrahamic. 1:6-8
   Mosaic. Applicable to all. 5:2-5
   Of the Ten Commandments. 4:9-14
   Palestinian. 29:1
Mediator of. Moses. 29:1
Mosaic. Parties. 29:1
Promise of. Restoration—forgiveness & acceptance by the LORD. 30:3-10
Purpose of. To establish that the believers were God's people & that He was their God. 29:10-15
Renewing of. Between God & His people. 1:4-5; 27:1-26; 27:9-10; 27:11-26; 29:10-15
Results of.
   Disobeying the covenant. (curses). 27:11-26
   Obeying the covenant. (blessings). 27:11-26
Scope of. Included future generations as well. 29:10-15
Source of. God. 5:2-5
Terms of. To obey God or face the judgment of God. 29:1-29
Warning against. Breaking the covenant. 29:16-19; 30:17-18

COVET - COVETOUSNESS
Duty. Must not covet. 5:21
Facts.
   An inward sin, a sin of the heart & mind. 5:21
   There is a legitimate c. 5:21
Is idolatry. 5:8-10
Law governing. 5:21
Meaning of. 5:21
Warning. Forbidden. 5:8-10

CRAVE - CRAVING
Duty. Must not covet. 5:21

INDEX

CRIME - CRIMINAL
　Execution of. Hung upon a tree. 21:22-23
　Punishment of. Limited. 25:1-3

CRUEL - CRUELTY
　Judgment of. 25:17-19

CURSE - CURSING
　Caused by.
　　Disobeying God. 11:26-32; 27:11-26
　　　Failing to fear & reverence God. 28:58-68
　　　Failing to serve God. 28:47-57
　Chart of. Results of disobeying God. 28:15-68
　Described.
　　The curse of a devastated economy. 28:38-44
　　The curse of becoming plunder for a conquering nation. 28:30-35
　　The curse of being almost annihilated, exterminated—reduced to a very small population. 28:62-63
　　The curse of being continually cursed. 28:16
　　The curse of being defeated by your enemies. 28:25-26
　　The curse of being uprooted and scattered all over the world, among all nations. 4:27; 28:63-68, Types Chart
　　The curse of confusion or panic and frustration in every activity you undertake. 28:20
　　The curse of deadly diseases or plagues that will sweep across entire populations. 28:21
　　The curse of exile, deportation to a foreign nation. 28:36-37
　　The curse of failure. 28:29
　　The curse of fearful plagues, harsh and prolonged disasters, and severe and lingering sicknesses. 28:59-61
　　The curse of inadequate food. 28:17
　　The curse of incurable physical afflictions. 28:27-28
　　The curse of serving your enemies. 28:48-52
　　The curse of suffering untold horror because of your enemy. 28:53-57
　　The curse on all daily activities. 28:19
　　The curse on crops, on all plant life and vegetation. 28:22-24
　　The curse on production or fruitfulness. 28:18
　Judgment of.
　　Christ bore the curse of the law for us. 28:58-68, Thgt.2
　　Every human person is under the curse of God. 27:11-26, Thgt.1
　　For disobeying. 27:1-26
　　God will hold the guilty accountable. 5:11
　Kinds of.
　　Due to disobedience, refusing to listen to God. 28:15-46
　　Due to lack of fear & reverence for God. 28:58-68
　　Due to lack of service, failing to serve God. 28:47-57
　　List. Of twelve curses. 27:11-26, esp. vv.15-26
　Of disobedience. 27:11-26, esp. vv.15-26; 28:15-46
　Of God. Hung upon a tree. 21:22-23
　Results of. Disobeying God. c. for disobedience. 28:15-68
　Source of. God. 27:11-26
　Warning. Must never misuse, never take the name of the LORD God in vain. 5:11
　Way to escape. To obey all the laws & commandments of God. 11:26-32

D

DAGON
　Canaanite god. 12:29-32

DAN, TRIBE OF
　Blessings of. To be courageous & ferocious in military conflicts. 33:22
　Prophetic blessing of. To be courageous & ferocious in military conflicts. 33:22

DEATH
　Blessing of. 32:48-52, Thgt.1
　Caused by.
　　Abortion. 5:17, D.S. #1
　　Assassination. 27:11-26, esp. v.25
　　Murder. 5:17
　　Suicide. 5:17, D.S. #2
　Experience of. 32:48-52, Thgt.1
　Hope of. 32:48-52, Thgt.1
　Kinds of.
　　Eternal. 28:58-68, Thgt.2
　　Physical. 28:58-68, Thgt.2
　　Spiritual. 28:58-68, Thgt.2
　Meaning of. Separation, *not* annihilation, ceasing to exist. 28:58-68, Thgt.2
　Of believer. 32:48-52, Thgt.1; 34:1-8, Thgt.1
　Of family member. Must care for grieving family members. 25:5-10
　Of Moses. 32:48-52; 34:1-12
　Preparation for.
　　Death of believer. 32:48-52, Thgt.1
　　Death of Moses. 32:48-52; 34:1-12

DEBT - DEBTOR
　Discussed. Law of debt release. 15:1-6
　Protection of. A man's livelihood. 24:6
　Release of. 15:1-6
　Results of. Causes all kinds of pressure for people. 15:1-6

DECEPTION
　Duty. Must never tell a lie, never give a false testimony or witness. 5:20

DECISION
　Call to. Must choose life! 30:19-20
　Essential. Must choose life! 30:19-20
　Importance of. To make the right decision & obey God. 11:26-32
　Result of. The unbeliever & the disobedient stand at the crossroads of life. 11:26-32, Thgt.1

DEDICATION - DEDICATE
　Duty.
　　Must dedicate your life anew to God. 16:9-12
　　Must make a pledge to the LORD. 10:12-15
　Of priests or ministers of God. 18:1-8

DEFENSELESS
　Protection of. Foreigner, orphan, & widow. 24:17-18

DEFILE - DEFILEMENT
　Duty. Must keep ourselves free from defilement. 14:3-21

DELIVER - DELIVERANCE
　Discussed. A basis of the Ten Commandments is God's salvation, d., & redemption. 5:6
　Of Israel. From Egyptian slavery. 1:3

DESIRE
　Duty. Must not covet. 5:21

DEUTERONOMY
　Audience. To whom written. Introduction
　Author of. Moses. Introduction
　Date written. Introduction
　Discussed. Recipients of. The Israelites. 1:1
　Fact. Are around 100 quotations or references to the book in the New Testament. Introduction, Special Features, pt.9
　Meaning. Of the word. Introduction, Special Features pt.1
　Message of. Must learn the Word of God before we can enter the promised land. 1:3
　Purpose of.
　　For encouragement. 1:4-5
　　Three distinct purposes for. Introduction
　　To expound the law of God & to renew the people's covenant with God. 1:4-5

DEVIANCY
　Behavior of. Transvestites. God has made man & woman to be male & female. 22:5

DIET (See **FOOD**)

DISABLED
　Abuse of. Judgment of. Curse. 27:11-26, esp. v.18

DISCERN - DISCERNMENT
　Duty. Must have a spirit of discernment between what is allowed & forbidden. 12:20-28
　Lack of. Results. 32:28-31

DISCIPLINE
　Of God. Purpose of. To humble and test Israel. 8:2-6

DISCIPLINE, SPIRITUAL
　Duty. Must keep the worship of God clean, pure by excluding the unclean. 23:1-8

DISEASE
　Protection from. People with infectious d. 24:8-9

DISHONESTY
　Duty. Must prevent the wrong of dishonesty in business dealings. 25:13-16
　Law governing dishonest business dealings. 25:13-16
　Wrong of. In business dealings. 25:13-16

INDEX

DISOBEY - DISOBEDIENCE
Discussed.
  Rebellion at Kadesh Barnea. 9:22-10:11
  Three major examples. 9:22-10:11
Judgment of. Curse. 27:11-26, esp. v.26; 28:15-68
Results of.
  A set of curses for refusing to listen to God. 28:15-46
  A terrifying judgment. 29:20-29
  Disobeying the covenant: curses. 27:11-26
  Will cause the loss of the promised land. 11:8-15
Warning against.
  Continued disobedience & rebellion. 9:22-10:11
  Is a high crime against God. 28:15-46, Thgt.1
  Is an abomination, detestable to God. 28:15-68, Intro.
  Must not live lives of hypocrisy. 29:16-19
  Provoking God to anger & judgment. 9:7-21

DISRESPECT
Of parents. 5:16-21, Introduction

DISTRIBUTION
Of East Jordan land. Settled by. 3:12-20, Types Chart

DIVINATION
Warning against. 18:9-14

DIVORCE - DIVORCED
Fact. God hates divorce, but He loves the divorced person. 24:1-4
Law governing. 24:1-4
Prohibition against. 24:1-4

DOCUMENTARY HYPOTHESIS
Discussed. History of. Introductory section: Author

DOUBT
Answer to. 7:17-26

E

EASE
Danger of. Comfort, ease, satisfaction. 6:12-19
Warning.
  God warns us against seeking worldly e. 3:12-20
  Being at ease. Will cause you to forget God. 8:11-20

EAST JORDAN
Distribution of land. 3:12-20, Types Chart
Settled by. 3:12-20
Territory of. Former inhabitants. 4:44-49

EAT - EATING (See **FOOD**)

EBAL, MOUNT
Altar built for the Dedication Service. 27:1-8
Discussed. Cursings. 11:26-32; 27:11-26
History of. 27:11-26, D.S. #2
Location of. 27:11-26, D.S. #2

EDOM - EDOMITES
Judgment of. Excluded from the assembly of worship of God. 23:1-8

EDUCATION
Duty. To diligently teach the commandments to our children. 6:6-9; 6:20-25; 11:18-21, Types Chart

EGYPT- EGYPTIANS
Judgment of. Excluded from the assembly of worship of God. 23:1-8
Type - Symbol of. The world & its enslavements. 1:3, Types Chart

EL
Canaanite god. 12:29-32

EMPLOYEE
Duty toward.
  Must not be hard-hearted or tightfisted. 15:12-18
  Must not take advantage of the poor & needy worker. 24:14-15
Law governing wages. 24:14-15

EMPLOYMENT
Blessings of. Promised to the obedient person. 28:8
Duty toward. Employee.
  Must not be hard-hearted or tightfisted. 15:12-18
  Must not take advantage of the poor & needy worker. 24:14-15
For the poor. Work must be provided for the poor & underprivileged. 24:19-22
Law governing the payment of wages. 25:4
On the Sabbath. 5:12-15
Protection of.
  A man's livelihood. 24:6
  The poor worker. 24:14-15
Wages of. The person who works deserves to be paid. 25:4
When to work. 5:12-15

ENCOURAGEMENT
Duty. To live a life of victory. 1:4-5
Source of. From God Himself. 31:1-6; 31:7-8

ENEMIES
Character of. Bear the very c. of Sodom & Gomorrah. 32:32-35
Conquest of. Conditional promise. 11:22-25, Thgt.1
Discussed. Why all enemies of the promised land must be completely destroyed. 7:6-1
Judgment of. Against the enemies of God's people. 32:32-35
List of. 1:4-5, Thgt.1; 2:24, 3:11, Thgt.1; 7:1-26, Intro.
Of believers 7:1-5, Types Chart
Of Israel. Seven major enemies. 7:1-5
Of life. 1:4-5, Thgt.1; 2:24- 3:11, Thgt.1; 7:1-26, Intro.
Of the promised land. 7:1-26
Results of. Destroying e. 7:12-16
Type - Symbol of. Israel's enemies. The spiritual enemies that confront the believer. 28:7, Thgt.1
Victory over. 1:4-5; 20:1-4
Warning. Vengeance belongs to God. 32:32-35

ENGAGEMENT, MARITAL
Abuse of. Seducing an engaged woman or man. 22:23-24
Duty. Of engaged men & women. Must keep themselves pure for the marriage. 22:23-24, Thgt.1
Fact. An engaged person in Israelite society was treated as though he or she were married. 22:23-24

ENTICEMENT
Duty. Must not conform to the religious practices of the world. 12:29-32
Warning against.
  Must guard against being seduced by a loved one or close friend. 13:6-11
  Must guard against the false prophet & the interpreter of dreams. 13:1-5

EPHRAIM, TRIBE OF (See **JOSEPH**)
Blessings of. Material prosperity & military strength. 33:13-17
Prophecy concerning. Material prosperity & military strength. 33:13-17

ESAU
Descendants of. Were used by God to defeat & occupy the lands of stronger nations. 2:17-23

EVIL
Judgment of. By God. 20:16-18, D.S. #1
Of nations. 20:16-18, D.S. #1

EXECUTE - EXECUTION
Method used. Hung upon a tree after criminal had died. 21:22-23

EXEMPT - EXEMPTIONS
From military service. Four exemptions. 20:5-9

EXHORTATION
Of believer. 28:1-3

EXODUS
Type - Symbol of. A picture of God's great deliverance from the enslavement of this world. 1:3

F

FAILURE
Of Israel.
  Apostasy. 4:15-31; De.13:12-18, Thgt.1; 32:15-18, 19-27
  Corruption. 32:5-6
  Self-righteousness. 9:1-6
  The Golden Calf. Israel's sin of idolatry and false worship. 9:7-21

FAINTHEARTED
Duty. Must not be fainthearted during warfare—God will be with the believer. 20:1-4

FAITHFUL - FAITHFULNESS
Example of. In giving. 26:12-15
Of God. 2:1-15; 9:1-6

FALSE PROPHETS
Influence of. Are everywhere, both inside & outside the church. 18:20-22, Thgt.1
Warning. Must execute all false prophets. 18:20-22

INDEX

FALSE WORSHIP
  Warning. Must guard against all false gods & false worship. 4:15-31

FAMILY
  Dangers confronting. Must guard against being seduced by a loved one or close friend. 13:6-11
  Failure of. The wrong of refusing to help the wife of a dead brother. 25:5-10
  Importance of. The basic unit of society, the very foundation of society. 5:16
  Success of. God longs for things to go well for man and his family. 5:28-33

FATHER
  Authority of. Are to be honored by their children. 5:16
  Question. What does God mean by honoring our parents? 5:16, Thgt.1

FAVOR
  Of God. God favors His people. 33:23

FAVORITISM
  Discussed. God is impartial and just. 10:16-19

FEAST
  Duty. Must celebrate the three pilgrimage festivals every year. 16:16-17
  Of Passover. 16:1-8, Types Chart
  Of Pentecost (Weeks or Harvest). 16:9-12, Types Chart
  Of Tabernacles. 16:13-15, Types Chart
  Of Unleavened Bread. 16:1-8, Types Chart

FEAR
  Duty.
    Must be strong & courageous. 31:1-6
    Must fear & serve God alone. 10:20-22
    Must not fear during warfare—God will be with the believer. 20:1-4
  How to overcome. 3:21-22; 7:17-26
  Meaning of. 6:1-3; 6:2, D.S. #1
  Of God.
    Israel failed to fear God. 28:58-68
    The commandments will teach you to **f.** the LORD. 6:1-3
  Results of. 1:18-39

FELLOWSHIP OFFERING (See **PEACE OFFERING**)
  Type - Symbol of. Seeking more of the fellowship & peace of God. 27:1-8, Types Chart

FESTIVAL OF WEEKS
  Type - Symbol of. Pentecost. 16:9-12, Types Chart

FESTIVALS
  Duty. Must celebrate the three pilgrimage festivals every year. 16:16-17
  Of Passover. 16:1-8, Types Chart
  Of Pentecost (Weeks or Harvest). 16:9-12, Types Chart
  Of Tabernacles. 16:13-15, Types Chart
  Of Unleavened Bread. 16:1-8, Types Chart

FIRSTBORN
  Inheritance of. Law that protected his rights. 21:15-17
  Law governing. Giving all the firstborn animals to the LORD. 15:19-23, Types Chart

FIRSTFRUITS, FESTIVAL OF
  Instructions for. 26:1-11

FIRSTFRUITS, OFFERING OF
  Reason for. Thanking God for His salvation & blessings. 26:1-11

FOLLOW, TO
  Meaning of. 5:1

FOOD
  Conservation of. 22:6-7
  Duty. Must not eat detestable things, only clean things. 13:3-21
  Kinds of.
    Clean. 14:3-21
    Manna. 8:2-6
    Unclean. 14:3-21
  Protection of. The food supply for the poor & underprivileged. 24:19-22
  Provision of. 28:4-5
  Remember: God's provision of Manna. 8:2-6

FORCE
  Abuse of. The wrong use of force. 25:11-12
  Duty. Must never use excessive force in any situation. 25:11-12, Thgt.1

FOREIGNER, THE
  Law governing. 24:17-18
  Protection of. 24:17-18

FORGET - FORGETTING
  F. God.
    Answer to. 6:12-19; 8:1-20, Types Chart
    Causes of. 8:11-20
    Duty. Must not forget God. 8:11-20
    Result of. 8:11-20
  Warning against. 32:15-18

FORGIVE - FORGIVENESS
  Promise of. Restoration—forgiveness & acceptance by the LORD. 30:3-10

FORNICATION
  Duty. Of young men & women. Must keep themselves sexually pure. 22:13-21
  Warning. To flee **f.**, that is, premarital sex. 22:13-21, Thgt.1

FORTUNE-TELLING (See **OCCULT**)

FOUL LANGUAGE
  Judgment of. God will hold the guilty accountable. 5:11
  Warning. Must never misuse, never take the name of the LORD God in vain. 5:11

FRUITFULNESS
  Source of. God. 28:4-5

FULLNESS
  Blessing of. Spiritual **f.** 33:13-17, Thgt.1

G

GAD, TRIBE OF
  Blessings of.
    To choose & possess the best land. 33:20-21
    To fight alongside the other tribes until victory was secured over the enemies of the promised land. 33:20-21
    To have the military strength of a lion & be victorious. 33:20-21
    To stand as praise to God. 33:20-21
  Prophecy concerning.
    To choose & possess the best land. 33:20-21
    To fight alongside the other tribes until victory was secured over the enemies of the promised land. 33:20-21
    To have the military strength of a lion & be victorious. 33:20-21
    To stand as praise to God. 33:20-21
  Territory of. Ramoth.
    City of Refuge for Gad. 4:43
    History of. 4:41-43, D.S. #3
    Location of. 4:41-43, D.S. #3

GENEROUS - GENEROSITY
  Discussed. Law of **g.** 15:7-11
  Duty. Must be generous to the poor. 15:7-11, Thgt.1

GERIZIM, MOUNT
  Discussed. Blessings. 11:26-32; 27:11-26
  History of. 27:11-26, D.S. #1
  Location of. 27:11-26, D.S. #1

GIANTS
  Discussed. The Rephaites or Zamzummites were giants of the land, a tall race of people. 2:17-23

GIRGASHITES
  Enemy of Israel who inhabited the promised land. 7:1-5

GIVE - GIVING
  Duty.
    Must be generous to the poor. 15:7-11
    Must not be hard-hearted nor tightfisted against God. 15:19-23
  Faithfulness in. The three-year tithe. 26:12-15

GLORY
  Of God. Revealed. 5:22; 5:23-25

GOD
  Blessings of.
    Are conditional. 28:1-3
    God's gift of worship. 33:1-5
    God's glorious, majestic presence. 33:1-5
    God's instruction, the law. 33:1-5
    God's kingship, His rule & reign over His people. 33:1-5
    God's love and care. 33:1-5
    God will keep His covenant of love if His people will obey Him. 7:12-16
    God will love and bless you in a very special way. 7:12-16
    List of seven great blessings. 33:26-29
    Thanking God for His salvation & blessings. 26:1-11
  Character of. Is not an indulgent grandfather type of person who pampers the evil of this world. 20:16-18, D.S. #1
  Chastisement of. Example of. 32:48-52

INDEX

Compassion of God.
    Conditions for. 32:36-43
    Example of. 32:48-52
Discussion. God demands conservation, the preservation of the land of the earth. 20:10-20, Thgt.1
Facts about.
    God hates divorce, but He loves the divorced person. 24:1-4
    God is a just God as well as a God of love. 7:2, D.S. #1
    God is Spirit. 5:8-10
    God is the only living and true God. 6:4-5
    God's knowledge is complete & perfect. 31:14-23, Thgt.1
    God will keep His promises to us. 29:10-15, Thgt.1
    The LORD is Sovereign—He is God over all in heaven and on earth. 4:32-40, esp. 39
    The LORD is the God of communication. 4:32-40
    The LORD is the God of discipline and holiness. 4:32-40, esp. v.36
    The LORD is the God of love and salvation. 4:32-40, esp. v.37
    The LORD is the God of power and might and of miraculous works. 4:32-40
    The LORD is the God who demands obedience. 4:32-40, esp. v.40
    The LORD is the God who gives victory over all enemies and who guides His dear people to the promised land. 4:32-40, esp. v.38
    The LORD is the great Creator of man. 4:32-40, esp. v.32
    The LORD is the only living and true God (Jehovah, Yahweh). 4:32-40, esp. v.35
    There is only one God & one Mediator between God & man—Jesus Christ. 6:4-5
Faithfulness of. Is faithful, never failing to keep His promises. 2:1-15, Thgt.1
Fear of. Meaning of. 6:1-3; 6:2, D.S. #1
Goodness of. 32:7-14
Greatness of.
    Is incomparable. 33:26-29
    Is to be praised. 32:3-4
Jealousy of. God became jealous & angry at Israel's idolatry & false worship. 32:19-27
Judgment of. 20:10-20, Thgt.1
Knowledge of. God's knowledge is complete & perfect. 31:14-23, Thgt.1
Mercy of. 34:1-8
Name of.
    A basis of the Ten Commandments is God's name. 5:6
    Is to be proclaimed. 32:3-4
    Meaning of. 5:6
Nature of. 4:32-40; 5:7; 6:4-5; 10:16-19; 33:26-29
Omnipotence of. 2:17-23
Promises of. (See **PROMISES**)
    The LORD is our Atoning Sacrifice who delivers us from the avenger of death. 4:41-43, Thgt.1
    The LORD is our Hiding Place. 4:41-43, Thgt.1
    The LORD is our Refuge. 4:41-43, Thgt.1
    The LORD is our Shield in protecting us. 4:41-43, Thgt.1
Proof of. 4:32-40
Relationship with man. 5:6
Revelation of. 5:22
Reverence of. 6:2, D.S. #1
Sovereign power of. Over nations. 2:17-23
Title of. Rock. 32:3-4
Warning.
    God is honored by being obeyed. 4:1-43, Introduction
    God must be honored. 4:1-43, Introduction
    God warns us against apostasy, against turning away from Him. 31:14-23, Thgt.1
    God will judge every evil & brutal person on earth. 20:10-20, Thgt.1
    Must never misuse, never take the name of the LORD God in vain. 5:11
Works of. 4:32-40
Wrath of. God aroused His **w.** to know no limits. 32:19-27

GODS, FALSE
Warning. Must not make any idol nor worship or serve any false god. 5:8-10

GOLAN
City of Refuge for the half-tribe of Manasseh. 4:43
History of. 4:41-43, D.S. #2
Location of. 4:41-43, D.S. #2

GOLDEN CALF
Discussed. Israel's sin of idolatry and false worship. 9:7-21

GOMORRAH
Fact. Enemies bear the very character of Sodom & Gomorrah. 32:32-35

GOODNESS
Of God. Is beyond imagination & beyond description. 32:7-14, Thgt.1

GROWTH, SPIRITUAL
Conditional. Is promised to the obedient person. 28:9-10
Duty. Must grow in the LORD. 31:30-32:2

GRUMBLE - GRUMBLING
Results of. 1:18-39

GUIDANCE
Of God. 2:1-15; 9:22-10:11; 11:1-7

GUILT
Kind of. Corporate. 21:1-9

GUILTLESS
Meaning of. 5:11

GULF
Fact. Separates man from God. 5:23-25

H

HADAD
Canaanite god. 12:29-32

HALFHEARTED COMMITMENT
Example of. 3:12-20

HARDNESS OF HEART
Discussed. Remedy against. 15:1-6; 15:7-11
Duty.
    Must not be hard-hearted nor tightfisted against God. 15:19-23
    Must not be hard-hearted or tightfisted against workers. 15:12-18

HARVEST, FESTIVAL OF
Type - Symbol of. Pentecost, of salvation. 16:9-12, Thgt.1, Types Chart

HEALTH
Blessing of. 33:13-17, Thgt.1

HEAR, TO
Meaning of. 5:1

HEART
Duty. To circumcise or cut sin out of your **h.** 10:16-19
Meaning of. 6:4-5
Of God. 5:28-33

HEAVEN
Fact. The promised land of Canaan is a symbol of **h.** 1:8, D.S.#1, Types Chart
Journey to. Must march through this world to the promised land of heaven. 16:13-15, Types Chart

HEAVEN AND EARTH
Appeal to. To hear the words & message of the song of Moses. 31:30-32:2

HEREM PRINCIPLE OR LAW
Discussed. 7:2, D.S. #1

HISTORY
Duty. Must learn the lessons of history. 1:6-4:43, Div.1 Overview

HITTITES
Enemy of Israel who inhabited the promised land. 7:1-5

HIVITES
Enemy of Israel who inhabited the promised land. 7:1-5

HOLD FAST
To God. Must hold fast. 10:20-22

HOLY - HOLINESS
Duty.
    Must keep ourselves free from defilement. 14:3-21
    Must remind ourselves to obey God's commandments & to live **h.** lives. 22:12
Of God. 5:23-25
Of life. 22:12
Position of. 7:6-11

HOME
Witness of. Must be a strong testimony & witness for the LORD. 11:18-21

HOMICIDE
Kinds of.
    Abortion. 5:17, D.S. #1
    Assassination. 27:11-26, esp. v.25
    Murder. 5:17
    Suicide. 5:17, D.S. #2
    Unsolved. 21:1-9

HOMOSEXUAL - HOMOSEXUALITY
Duty. Must not wear the clothes of the other sex. 22:5
Fact. Transvestism sometimes leads to homosexuality. 22:5

INDEX

Warning. Is an abomination, detested by God. 22:5

HONESTY
Duty. Must prevent the wrong of dishonesty in business dealings. 25:13-16
Law governing dishonest business dealings. 25:13-16

HONOR
Meaning of. 5:16
Of believer. 28:1-3
Question. What does God mean by honoring our parents? 5:16, Thgt.1

HOPE
Discussed. One of the most powerful forces on earth. 1:6-2:15, Introduction

HOREB, MOUNT
Meaning of. 1:6-8

HORITES
History of. Were defeated by those who lived in Seir. 2:17-23

HORNET
Type - Symbol of. Some enemy or plague or of God's power. 7:17-26, esp. v.20, Types Chart

HUMAN RIGHTS
Laws governing. 21:1-23

HYGIENE, PERSONAL
Duty. Must keep our body & spirit clean. 23:9-14

HYPOCRISY
Warning against. Must not live lives of h. 29:16-19

I

IDOLS - IDOLATRY
Caused by. False worship. 5:8-10
Creation of. Man's imagination & hands. 5:7, Thgt.1
Destruction of. 7:17-26
Discussed. The Golden Calf. Israel's sin of idolatry and false worship. 9:7-21
Duty.
    Must destroy all the false worship of enemies. 7:1-5
    Must guard against false worship & false gods. 11:16-17
Duty. Israel. Must destroy all the Asherah poles & idols. 12:2-4
Fact. Permeates society. 12:29-32, Thgt.1
Forbidden. Must refuse to follow false gods and false worship. 28:14
Judgment of. Curse. 27:11-26, esp. v.15
Penalty of. Execution. 17:2-7
Results of.
    A terrifying judgment. 29:20-29
    Bears bitter & poisonous fruit (wormwood). 29:16-19
    Dangers of being seduced into false worship. 13:1-18
    Impact upon the next generation and beyond. 5:8-10
    Spiritual adultery. 5:8-10
Warnings against.
    Forbidden. Must have no other gods before the LORD. 5:7
    Must guard against all false gods & false worship. 4:15-31

Must not make any idol nor worship or serve any false god. 5:8-10

IMAGES
Of God. Jesus Christ. 5:8-10, Thgt.2
Of worship.
    Commandment does not forbid artistic talent. 5:8-10
    Must not make any idol nor worship or serve any false god. 5:8-10

IMMORAL - IMMORALITY
Adultery. 22:22
Causes of. Five categories. 5:18
Incest. 22:30
Judgment of. 22:13-21
Premarital immorality. 22:13-21
Rape. 22:25-29
Results of. A person becomes sexually impure in at least three ways. 5:18
Seduction of an engaged woman (or man). 22:23-24
Seriousness of. Why God forbids i. 5:18

INCEST
Judgment of. Curse. 27:11-26, esp. v.20; 27:11-26, esp. v.22; 27:11-26, esp. v.23
Kind of.
    With one's in-laws. 27:11-26, esp. v.23
    With one's parents. 27:11-26, esp. v.20
    With one's siblings. 27:11-26, esp. v.22
Law governing. 22:30
Warning. Must not marry a stepmother. 22:30

INFECTIOUS SKIN DISEASE
Protection from. 24:8-9
Type - Symbol of. The spread of sin. 24:8-9, Thgt.1

INHERITANCE
Of Abraham.
    The assurance of a personal inheritance. 1:8, D.S.#1
    The assurance of conquest & rest, of spiritual victory & spiritual rest. 1:8, D.S.#1
    The assurance of God's own presence, His love, care, provision, & protection. 1:8, D.S.#1
Of firstborn son. Law that protected his rights. 21:15-17
Of Isaac. 1:8, D.S.#1
Of Joshua. 1:8, D.S.#1
Of priests. 18:1-8
Rights of. Firstborn son. 21:15-17

INHUMANE
Judgment of. 25:17-19

INIQUITY
Cup of. 7:2, D.S. #1; 20:16-18, D.S.#1

INSECTS
Israel forbidden to eat any i. that flew. 14:3-21

INTERCESSION
Of Moses.
    It was only the prayer of Moses that kept God from executing Aaron. 9:7-21, esp. v.20
    Three reasons why he fell prostrate before the LORD. 8:7-21, esp. vv.18-20

Result of. It was intercessory prayer that saved God's people. 9:22-10:11, esp. vv.25-29

INTEREST
Charging i. 23:19-20
Duty to. The poor.
    Must be generous to the poor. 15:7-11; 23:19-20
    Must meet the needs of the poor. 15:1-6, Thgt.1

INTERMARRIAGE
Warning. Forbidden. 7:1-5

ISRAEL
Apostasy of. 4:15-31; 32:15-18
Blessings of. God's glorious, majestic presence. 33:1-5
Camp of. Duty of Israel. Must maintain a clean camp. 23:9-14, Types Chart
Cannibalism of. Caused by. The suffering the enemy would inflict upon Israel. 28:53-57
Charge. To be victorious over all the enemies of the promised land. 11:22-25
Defeat of. 1:40-46
Deliverance of. From Egyptian slavery. 1:3
Discussed.
    Preparation to enter the promised land. 1:2
    Was used by God as His instrument of justice & judgment against the nations of Canaan. 20:16-18, D.S. #1
Duty.
    Must be a just people. 16:18-17:1
    Must be spiritually prepared. 1:6-4:43, Div.1 Overview
    Must hear the law, learn the law, & obey the law. 5:1
    Must learn the lessons of history. 1:6-4:43, Div.1 Overview
Enemies of. Seven major enemies. 7:1-5
Failure of.
    Apostasy. 4:15-31; 13:12-18, Thgt.1; 32:15-18, 19-27
    Corruption. 32:5-6
    Self-righteousness. 9:1-6
    The Golden Calf. Israel's sin of idolatry and false worship. 9:7-21
First generation of. Prohibited from ever entering the promised land. 1:18-39, esp.v.35
Government of. A theocracy. 17:2-7
Indictment against. Corruption. 32:5-6
Judges of. 1:9-17
Judgment of.
    All the adults of the first generation had died because of sin & unbelief. 1:3; 1:18-39

INDEX

Will be barred from the promised land for not guarding against false gods & false worship. 4:15-31, esp.vv.25-28
Will be rejected & suffer the judgment of God. 32:19-27
Kings of.
  Appointment of. 17:14-20
  Duties or responsibilities of. 17:14-20
  Prediction of. 17:14-20
Laws of.
  L. dealing with a man hung on a tree. 21:22-23, Types Chart
  L. governing a newly married couple. 24:5
  L. governing abuse of punishment. 25:1-3
  L. governing charging interest. 23:19-20
  L. governing children. 21:18-21
  L. governing clothing. 22:5
  L. governing collateral. 24:6
  L. governing conservation of animals & food. 22:6-7
  L. governing dishonesty in business dealings. 25:13-16
  L. governing divorce. 24:1-4
  L. governing exemptions from military duty. 24:5
  L. governing incest. 22:30
  L. governing infectious skin diseases. 24:8-9
  L. governing leprosy. 24:8-9, Types Chart
  L. governing loan collectors. 24:10-13
  L. governing lost property. 22:1-3
  L. governing man's duty to God. 5:7-15
  L. governing man's duty to others. 5:16-21
  L. governing marriage, divorce, & remarriage. 24:1-4
  L. governing pledges. 23:21-23
  L. governing property rights. 23:24-25
  L. governing prostitution. 23:17-18
  L. governing purity in the military camp. 23:9-14, Types Chart
  L. governing rape. 22:25-29
  L. governing relationships with neighbor. 22:1-3; 22:4
  L. governing remarriage. 24:1-4
  L. governing seven important social issues. 22:1-12
  L. governing several social & religious issues. 23:1-25
  L. governing sexual behavior. 22:13-30
  L. governing some unique issues within families & society. 21:1-23
  L. governing the administration of justice & the appointment of rulers. 16:18-17:20
  L. governing the administration of religion. 18:1-22
  L. governing the conduct of war. 20:1-20, Types Chart
  L. governing the muzzling of an ox while working. 25:4
  L. governing the needy. 20:19-22
  L. governing the payment of wages. 25:4
  L. governing the release of debts. 15:1-6
  L. governing the three pilgrimage festivals of worship. 16:1-17
  L. governing the wife of a dead brother. 25:5-10
  L. governing the wrong of a cruel people. 25:17-19
  L. governing the wrong of excessive force. 25:11-12
  L. governing transvestism. 22:5
  L. governing unsolved murders. 21:1-9
  L. governing vows. 23:21-23
  L. governing wages. 24:14-15
  L. of giving all firstborn animals to the LORD. 15:19-23
  L. of releasing slaves. 15:12-18
  L. that dealt with the stubborn & rebellious son. 21:18-21
  L. that demand generosity & giving. 15:1-23
  L. that demand justice for the defenseless. 19:1-21
  L. that mark the believer as a child of God. 14:1-29
  L. that prevent wrong behavior & that demand justice. 25:1-19
  L. that protect a man's livelihood. 24:6
  L. that protect a newly married couple. 24:5
  L. that protect a person from idolatry. 13:1-18
  L. that protect against kidnapping. 24:7
  L. that protect from loan collectors. 24:10-13
  L. that protect from people with infectious diseases. 24:8
  L. that protect marriage. 24:1-4
  L. that protect relationships within society (how to prevent abuse). 24:1-22
  L. that protect the food supply for the poor & underprivileged. 24:19-22
  L. that protect the poor worker. 24:14-15
  L. that protect female war prisoners. 21:10-14, Types Chart
  L. that protect the inheritance rights of the firstborn son. 21:15-17
  L. that protect justice. 24:16
  L. that protect the defenseless (foreigner, orphan, & widow). 24:17-18
  L. that regulate the worship of God. 12:1-32
  L. that require special confession & obedience. 26:1-19
Leaders of. Were appointed to help Moses. 1:9-17
Messages to. 1:1
Organization of. 1:9-17
Picture of. All believers. 1:1
Promises to. Conditional promise. Victory over enemies. 11:22-25, Thgt.1
Prophecies concerning.
  Asher. 33:24-25
  Benjamin. 33:12
  Dan. 33:22
  Ephraim. 33:13-17
  Gad. 33:20-21
  Issachar. 33:18-19
  Judah. 33:7
  Joseph. 33:13-17
  Levi. 33:8-11
  Manasseh. 33:13-17
  Naphtali. 33:23
  Reuben. 33:6
  Zebulun. 33:18-19
Recipients of the Law. 4:44-49
Rededication of. 29:10-15
Renewal of the Covenant. Purpose of. To establish that the believers were God's people & that He was their God. 29:10-15
Restoration of.
  Conditions of. 30:1-2
  Promise of. Restoration—forgiveness & acceptance by the LORD. 30:3-10
  Recent occurrence. 31:30-32:52, Intro.
Second generation of. 1:2; 1:3; 1:18-39, esp.v.39
Sins of.
  Apostasy. 4:15-31; Dt.13:12-18, Thgt.1; 32:15-18; 32:19-27
  Corruption. 32:5-6
  Self-righteousness. 9:1-6
  The Golden Calf. Israel's sin of idolatry and false worship. 9:7-21
Twelve spies of. 1:18-39
Type - Symbol of. All true believers. 1:1, Types Chart
Unbelief of. 1:18-39; 9:22-10:11
Warfare of.
  Conquest of Amorites. 2:24-3:11, Types Chart
Warning to.
  Must guard against allowing an entire city or community to seduce you. 13:12-18
  Must not become self-righteous. 9:1-6
Wilderness Wanderings of.
  God's guidance. 2:1-15
  Purpose of. 8:2-6

ISSACHAR, TRIBE OF
Blessing of.
  To call people to seek God through worship & sacrifice. 33:18-19
  To grow rich from sea & land trade. 33:18-19
  To rejoice in all their activities. 33:18-19
Prophecy concerning.
  To call people to seek God through worship & sacrifice. 33:18-19
  To grow rich from sea & land trade. 33:18-19
  To rejoice in all their activities. 33:18-19

J

JEALOUS - JEALOUSY
Meaning of. 5:8-10
Of God. God became jealous & angry at Israel's idolatry & false worship. 32:19-27

JEBUSITES
Enemy of Israel who inhabited the promised land. 7:1-5

JEHOVAH
Name of God. 5:6

JESUS CHRIST
Blood of.
  List. Facts concerning. 12:15-18, Thgt.1
  True worship never abuses the blood of Jesus Christ. 12:15-18, Thgt.1
Discussed. The Living Word of God is a far greater gift than even the Written Word of God. 30:11-16, Thgt.1
Mediation of.

INDEX

It is Jesus Christ who stands as the Mediator between God and man: it is He and He alone who reconciles man to God. 5:2-5; 5:26-27, Thgt.1
There is only one God & one Mediator between God & man—Jesus Christ. 6:4-5
Message of. As our great High Priest. 20:1-20, Types Chart
Obedience to.
    To follow Christ is to follow all that He is & represents. 1:4-5, Note 2, Thgt.1
Parallel between Moses and Christ. 34:10-12, Thgt.6
Prophecy concerning. Would be a very special Prophet. 18:15-19
Protection of.
    Our atoning sacrifice. 19:1-13, Thgt.2
    Our hiding place. 19:1-13, Thgt.2
    Our refuge. 19:1-13, Thgt.2
    Our shield in protecting us. 19:1-13, Thgt.2
Sacrifice of. Bore the curse of the law for us. 28:58-68, Thgt.2
Sacrifice of. Died as our substitute sacrifice to secure atonement for us. 27:1-8
Typed - Symbolized - Pictured.
    By the appointed priest: as our great High Priest. 20:1-20, Types Chart
    By the cities of refuge: Christ is our refuge from the storms & threats of life. 19:1-13, Types Chart
    By the sacrifice of the Burnt Offerings. Symbolized Israel's seeking atonement, reconciliation through the substitute sacrifice. 27:1-8, Types Chart
    Christ's death. Hung upon a tree. 21:22-23, Types Chart

JOSEPH
Blessings of. Material prosperity & military strength. 33:13-17
Prophecy concerning. Material prosperity & military strength. 33:13-17

JOSHUA
Charge to. From Moses. 3:21-22; 31:7-8
Leadership of.
    Was eminently qualified to lead the Israelites into the promised land. 34:9
    Was to replace Moses as leader of the people. 1:18-39, esp.v.38
Parallel between Moses & Joshua. Chart 34:1-12, esp. v.9, D.S. #1
Qualifications of.
    Was a leader of strong faith, decision, obedience, & courage (Num.14:6-9). 31:1-6
    Was a military leader (Ex.17:9-16). 31:1-6
    Was a spy (Num.13:1-16). 31:1-6
    Was eminently qualified to lead the Israelites into the promised land. 34:9
    Was personally trained by Moses (Num.11:28; Josh.1:1). 31:1-6

JOURNEYS, WILDERNESS THE (See **WILDERNESS WANDERING**)
Duty. Must march through this world to the promised land of heaven. 16:13-15, Types Chart

JOY
Blessing of. 33:13-17, Thgt.1

JUDAH, TRIBE OF
Blessing of.
    To be heard by God. 33:7
    To be settled as a people in the promised land. 33:7
    To be victorious in defending himself—with the help of God. 33:7
Prophecy concerning. The blessing of Judah. 33:7

JUDGES (See **OFFICERS OF THE LAW**)
Duties of. 1:9-17; 16:18-17:1
Execution. Of lawbreakers. 17:2-7

JUDGMENT
Caused by.
    Breaking the covenant. 29:20-29
    Disobeying God. 11:26-32
    Failing to fear & reverence God. 28:58-68
    Failing to serve God. 28:47-57
    Lacking sense, discernment. 32:28-31
Described.
    As a curse. 28:15-46; 28:47-57; 28:58-68
    As a result of apostasy. 32:19-27
Duty. Must remember the j. of God. 8:11-20
Facts.
    Christ bore the curse of the law for us. 28:58-68, Thgt.2
    Is stored up by God. 32:32-35
    There is to be a day of j. out in the future for every human being. 1:18-39, Thgt.1
Of adultery. Law demanded execution. 22:22
Of God. Will judge every evil & brutal person on earth. 20:10-20, Thgt.1
Of Israel. History of. 29:22-29, D.S. #1
Results of.
    Will be cursed by God. 28:15-46
    Would surely perish & be destroyed. 30:17-18
Safeguards against. Must guard against all false gods & false worship. 4:15-31
Surety of. Against the enemies of God's people. 32:32-35
Warning. Will fall upon any person who lives a hypocritical life. 29:20-29, Thgt.1

JUDICIAL JUDGMENT
Surety of. 25:17-19

JUSTICE
Administration of. 16:18-17:1
Concerning.
    For the accused. 19:15-21
    For the land owner. 19:14
    The unintentional killer (manslaughter). 19:1-13
Duty.
    Must be a just people. 16:18-17:1
    Must be executed fairly. 1:9-17, Thgt.1
    Must execute j. against the major crime of society (idolatry & false worship). 17:2-7
    Must hold each individual responsible for his own behavior. 24:16
    Must never steal. 19:14
    Must wrestle with & grasp difficult legal cases. 17:8-13
Discussion. Difficult legal cases. 17:8-13
Equal. Must prevent the wrong of excessive force. 25:11-12
Execution of. Against the major crime of society (idolatry & false worship). 17:2-7
Facts.
    Is an absolute essential for a strong and healthy society. 25:1-3, Thgt.1
    Is the foundation of society, the tie that binds society together. 16:18-17:20
Laws. (See **LAWS**)
    L. governing personal responsibility. 24:16
    L. that demand justice for the defenseless. 19:1-21
Organization of. 1:9-17
Of God. Toward Moses. 34:1-8
Protection of. 24:16
Safeguards to assure. 17:2-7
Surety of. 25:17-19

K

KADESH BARNEA
Discussed. Rebellion at Kadesh Barnea. 9:22-10:11
Location of. In the hill country of the Amorites, on the border of the promised land. 1:19-39

KEEP (The Sabbath)
Meaning of. 5:12-15

KIBROTH HATTAAVAH
Example of disobedience. 9:22-10:11

KIDNAP - KIDNAPPING
Law governing. 24:7
Protection from. 24:7
Punishment of. Execution. 24:7

KILL - KILLING - KILLER
Discussed.
    An inward act; an act of anger, bitterness, enmity. 5:17
    When the taking of life is justified, understandable, allowed. 5:17
Example of. Abortion. 5:17, D.S. #1
Judgment of. Death, spiritual & eternal. 5:17
Kinds of.
    Abortion. 5:17, D.S. #1
    Hired out. 27:11-26, esp. v.25
    Secret. 27:11-26, esp. v.24
    Suicide. 5:17, D.S. #2
    Unsolved. 21:1-9
Meaning of. 5:17
Salvation of. 5:17
Source of. Twofold source. 5:17
Warning. Must not murder. 5:17

KINGS
Appointment of. 17:14-20
Duty of. 17:14-20
Fact. The only laws dealing with kings in the Pentateuch. 17:14-20
Results of. The king's obedience. 17:14-20

KINSMAN REDEEMER
Duties of. 19:1-13

L

LABOR
Blessings of. Promised to the obedient person. 28:8
Results of. Produces a sense of achievement & success, a sense of fulfillment & satisfaction. 28:8

INDEX

LAND (See **PROMISED LAND, THE**)
Discussed. The need to make a new beginning as we march toward the promised land. 2:16
Distribution of East Jordan. 3:12-20 Settled by. 3:12-20
Strategy. For preserving the land for the public good. 20:10-20, esp. vv.19-20

LAND OWNER
Justice for. 19:14
Wrongs against. 19:14

LAW - LAWS
Assisting a neighbor. 22:4
Basis of. 5:6
Civil.
    Charging interest to a needy brother. 23:19-20
    Release of debts. 15:1-6
Curse of. Jesus Christ bore the curse of the law for us. 28:58-68, Thgt.2
Debt release. 15:1-6
Declared by Moses. Must be preached (God's Word). 4:44-49, Thgt.1
Discussed. The law—that is, our failure to keep the law—shows how far short we come. 5:26-27, Thgt.1
Duty. Man's duty to.
    Must have a spirit of discernment between what is allowed & forbidden. 12:20-28
    Must hear the law, learn the law, & obey the law. 5:1
    Must learn the Law of God. 1:4-5, Thgt.1
    Must not abuse the blood nor misuse the tithe. 12:15-18
    Must not conform to the religious practices of the world. 12:29-32
    Must not worship as everyone sees fit, but as God dictates. 12:8-14
    Must obey all the commandments & laws of God. 26:16-19
    Must obey the laws & regulations of God. 12:1
    Must reject all false worship. 12:2-4
    Must seek the place where God's name is honored. 12:5-7
    Must support the ministers of God. 12:19
Generosity. 15:7-11
Heart of. The Covenant, the Ten Commandments. 5:2-5
Importance of. 4:44-5:6
Kinds of.
    L. dealing with a man hung on a tree. 21:22-23, Types Chart
    L. governing a newly married couple. 24:5
    L. governing abuse of punishment. 25:1-3
    L. governing charging interest. 23:19-20
    L. governing children. 21:18-21
    L. governing clothing. 22:5
    L. governing collateral. 24:6
    L. governing conservation of animals & food. 22:6-7
    L. governing dishonesty in business dealings. 25:13-16
    L. governing divorce. 24:1-4
    L. governing exemptions from military duty. 24:5
    L. governing incest. 22:30
    L. governing infectious skin diseases. 24:8-9
    L. governing leprosy. 24:8-9, Types Chart
    L. governing loan collectors. 24:10-13
    L. governing lost property. 22:1-3
    L. governing man's duty to God. 5:7-15
    L. governing man's duty to others. 5:16-21
    L. governing marriage, divorce, & remarriage. 24:1-4
    L. governing pledges. 23:21-23
    L. governing property rights. 23:24-25
    L. governing prostitution. 23:17-18
    L. governing purity in the military camp. 23:9-14, Types Chart
    L. governing rape. 22:25-29
    L. governing relationships with neighbor. 22:1-3; 22:4
    L. governing remarriage. 24:1-4
    L. governing seven important social issues. 22:1-12
    L. governing several social & religious issues. 23:1-25
    L. governing sexual behavior. 22:13-30
    L. governing some unique issues within families & society. 21:1-23
    L. governing the administration of justice & the appointment of rulers. 16:18-17:20
    L. governing the administration of religion. 18:1-22
    L. governing the conduct of war. 20:1-20, Types Chart
    L. governing the muzzling of an ox while working. 25:4
    L. governing the needy. 20:19-22
    L. governing the payment of wages. 25:4
    L. governing the release of debts. 15:1-6
    L. governing the three pilgrimage festivals of worship. 16:1-17
    L. governing the wife of a dead brother. 25:5-10
    L. governing the wrong of a cruel people. 25:17-19
    L. governing the wrong of excessive force. 25:11-12
    L. governing transvestism. 22:5
    L. governing unsolved murders. 21:1-9
    L. governing vows. 23:21-23
    L. governing wages. 24:14-15
    L. of giving all firstborn animals to the LORD. 15:19-23
    L. dealing with the release of slaves. 15:12-18
    L. dealing with the stubborn & rebellious son. 21:18-21
    L. demanding generosity & giving. 15:1-23
    L. demanding justice for the defenseless. 19:1-21
    L. marking the believer as a child of God. 14:1-29
    L. preventing wrong behavior & that demand justice. 25:1-19
    L. protecting a man's livelihood. 24:6
    L. protecting a newly married couple. 24:5
    L. protecting a person from idolatry. 13:1-18
    L. protecting against kidnapping. 24:7
    L. protecting female war prisoners. 21:10-14, Types Chart
    L. protecting from loan collectors. 24:10-13
    L. protecting from people with infectious diseases. 24:8
    L. protecting justice. 24:16
    L. protecting marriage. 24:1-4
    L. protecting relationships within society (how to prevent abuse). 24:1-22
    L. protecting the defenseless (foreigner, orphan, & widow). 24:17-18
    L. protecting the food supply for the poor & underprivileged. 24:19-22
    L. protecting the inheritance rights of the firstborn son. 21:15-17
    L. protecting the poor worker. 24:14-15
    L. regulating the worship of God. 12:1-32
    L. requiring special confession & obedience. 26:1-19
Meaning of. 1:4-5; 4:1-2, D.S.#1
Nature of. 4:6-8; 5:23-25
Of God.
    Man is not to tamper with God's holy commandments. 4:1-5
    Man is to keep, obey God's commandments. 10:12-15
Protection of. Security for a debt. 24:6
Purpose of. Four reasons why God gave the Ten Commandments & the Law. 5:22-23
Reasons for.
    Was a totally new concept to the world. 12:1-26:19, Div.3 Overview
    Was founded upon God's great love & compassion for people. 12:1–26:19, Div.3 Overview
    Was given by God in order to mold a community of people into law-abiding citizens. 12:1-26:19, Div.3 Overview
    Was given so God's people could live in security & peace. 12:1-26:19, Div.3 Overview
Results of obedience. What happens when you carefully obey God's law. 4:6-8
Source of. God. 5:22
Subject of preaching. Law of God, His testimonies, statutes, & judgments. 4:44-49, Thgt.1

LAWLESSNESS
Warning. Must not murder. 5:17

LEADER - LEADERSHIP
Action of. Washed their hands over the young cow. 21:6, Types Chart
Appointment of. Joshua. 34:9
Blessings of. Exaltation. 28:13
Need for. People will never reach the promised land of heaven without qualified leaders. 1:9-17, Thgt.1
Of Joshua.
    Was eminently qualified to lead the Israelites into the promised land. 34:9
    Was to replace Moses as leader of the people. 1:18-39, esp.v.38
Qualifications of.
    Must be understanding. 1:9-17
    Must be wise. 1:9-17

LEARN, TO
Meaning of. 5:1

INDEX

LEGACY
Of Moses. 34:10-12

LEGAL CASES - LEGAL DISPUTES
Duty. Must wrestle with & grasp difficult legal cases. 17:8-13

Litigation of. Must take legal disputes before a judge. 25:1-3

Punishment.
Law governing the wrong of abusive punishment in legal disputes. 25:1-3

Limits of. 25:1-3

Must prevent the wrong of excessive force. 25:11-12

LEPROSY
Protection from. 24:8-9

Type - Symbol of. The spread of sin. 24:8-9, Thgt.1, Types Chart

LEVI, TRIBE OF
Blessings of.
Served as the teachers of God's law. 33:8-11

Were responsible for leading the people in their worship of God (including the offering of sacrifices to God). 33:8-11

Were responsible for revealing the will of God to the people. 33:8-11

Were to be greatly blessed by God. 33:8-11

Prophetic blessing of.
Served as the teachers of God's law. 33:8-11

Were responsible for leading the people in their worship of God (including the offering of sacrifices to God). 33:8-11

Were responsible for revealing the will of God to the people. 33:8-11

Were to be greatly blessed by God. 33:8-11

LEVITES
Discussed. Their role in shouting out the blessings and curses. 27:11-26

Duty.
To be totally committed to God & His service. 9:22-10:11

To look after the Tabernacle. 9:22-10:11

To stand as a mediator between God and man. 9:22-10:11

LEX TALIONIS
Principle of. 19:15-21; 25:11-12

LIBERTY
Duty to. Escaped slaves.
Must give sanctuary to an escaped slave. 23:15-16
Must not be oppressed. 23:15-16

LIFE
Created order of. God has made man & woman to be male & female. 22:5
Crossroads of. 11:26-32
Discussed. Victorious l. 2:16-3:29, Intro.; 5:28-33; 7:17-26
Fullness of. 5:28-33
Of believer. Blessings of. 28:6
Sanctity of. 21:1-9
Storms of. 4:31-43; 19:1-13

LIFESTYLE
Distinctive. Must live a life of separation. 7:1-5; 22:9-11, Types Chart

LISTEN
Refusing to. Will be cursed by God. 28:15-46

LIVELIHOOD
Protection of. A man's l. 24:6

LOANS
Duty. Must be generous to the poor. 15:7-11; 23:19-20
Law governing. Loan collectors. 24:10-13
Protection from. Loan collectors. 24:10-13
Release of. 15:1-6

LOT
Discussed. The Ammonites were descendants of L. 2:17-23

LOVE
For God. Duty.
Must love God with your whole being. 6:4-5; 11:1-7
Must love & obey God. 30:11-16
Of neighbor. 22:1-3; 22:4

LUST - LUSTING
Duty. Must not covet. 5:21
Source of. Murder. 5:17

LYING
Examples of. There are innumerable ways in which we lie. 5:20
Fact. All men are liars (Ps.116:11). 5:20
Judgment of. Shall be judged by God. 5:20
Kinds of.
Deception. 5:20
Exaggeration & blown up flattery. 5:20
False charges & criticism. 5:20
Rumor or gossip or talebearing. 5:20
Slander. 5:20
Suggestive hints or insinuations. 5:20
Law governing. 5:20
Meaning of. 5:20
Results of. Three terrible effects upon people. 5:20
Source of. Satan. 5:20
Warning. Threatens the very foundation of society. 5:20

M

MAJESTY
Of God. 5:23-25

MAN
Duty. Must take care of the earth. 21:1-9
Needs of. There is only one sovereign Creator who meets the needs of man. 5:7, Thgt.1
Protection of. A man's livelihood. 24:6

MANASSEH, TRIBE OF (See **JOSEPH**)
Blessings of. Material prosperity & military strength. 33:13-17
Prophecy concerning. Material prosperity & military strength. 33:13-17

MANNA
Remember: God's provision of. 8:2-6

MANSLAUGHTER
Justice of. 19:1-13

MARCH
Believer's m. God will give us victory as we m. to the promised land. 3:24–3:11
Discussed. To the promised land. 2:16
Type - Symbol - Picture of. Marching to heaven & of spiritual conquest & rest. 1:6-8, Types Chart

MARRIAGE
Benefits of. Monogamy. 21:15-17
Divorce. God hates divorce but He loves the divorced person. 24:1-4
Duty. Of young men & women. Must keep themselves sexually pure. 22:13-21
Importance of. Is honorable & is to be protected at all costs. 21:10-14, Thgt.1
Levirate m. Duty of. 25:5-10
Protection of.
Law governing. 24:1-4
Newly married couple. 24:5
Remarriage.
Example of a *cheap marriage*. 24:1-4
Prohibition against. 24:1-4
Sanctity of. God demands. 5:18; 22:13-21
Sexual relationships in. Results of. Sexual impurity. A person becomes sexually impure in at least three ways. 5:18

MASSAH
Example of disobedience. 9:22-10:11

MEASURE - MEASURES
Duty. Must prevent the wrong of dishonesty in business dealings. 25:13-16
Law governing dishonest business dealings. 25:13-16

MEDIATOR
Man's need for. Reason why God gave the Ten Commandments to man. 5:26-27
Type - Symbol of.
Moses as the m. of the Covenant. 5:2-5, 29:1; Types Chart

MEDICAL PROFESSION
Question. What does the medical profession say about the fetus or unborn child in the mother's womb? 5:17, D.S. #1

MEDIUMS (See **PSYCHICS**)

MEMORIAL SERVICE
Dedication of Covenant renewal. 27:1-8

INDEX

MEN
  Fact. All men are liars (Ps.116:11). 5:20

MERCY
  Discussed. God is merciful & compassionate. 34:1-8
  Duty. Must show compassion for the needy of this earth, doing all we can to help. 23:19-20, Thgt.1
  Of God. It was intercessory prayer that saved God's people. 9:22-10:11, esp. vv.25-29

MESSAGE
  Duty.
    Must be preached (God's Word). 4:44-49, Thgt.1
    Must grow in the LORD. 31:30-32:2
  Kind of. False. 18:20-22
  Purpose of. Must grow in the LORD. 31:30-32:2
  Test of. Of a false prophet. 18:20-22

MESSENGER
  Of God. Moses. 1:1
  Type - Symbol of.
    The Perfect Messenger of God. 1:1, Types Chart

MILITARY
  Camp of. Duty of Israel. Must maintain a clean camp. 23:9-14, Types Chart
  Discussed. The need for total commitment by all in mobilizing for war. 20:5-9
  Duty. Must protect female war prisoners. 21:10-14, Types Chart
  Exemption from m. service.
    Four exemptions. 20:5-9
    Newly wed groom for a year. 24:5
  Picture of. Purity. in the military camp. Being spiritually clean. 23:9-14, Types Chart
  Strength of. Promised to the tribes of Joseph, Ephraim, & Manasseh. 33:13-17

MIND
  Duty.
    To concentrate. 22:12
    To protect. 22:12

MINISTERS (See **PRIESTS**)
  Blessings of. Will be greatly blessed by God if he is faithful. 33:8-11, Thgt.1
  Called. Chosen to proclaim the Word of God. 1:1
  Charge to. To read & teach the law to the people of God. 31:9-13
  Dedication & support of. 18:1-8
  Discussed.
  Duty.
    To be responsible for leading the people in their worship of God. 33:8-11
    To be responsible for revealing the will of God to the people. 33:8-11
    To care for God's people. 18:15-19
    To read & teach the law to the people of God. 31:9-13
    To serve as the teachers of God's law. 33:8-11
    To warn of the dangers of sin. 31:24-29
  Focus of. The m. must focus totally upon the LORD & his ministry to God's people. 18:1-8
  Support of.
    Believer's must support the ministers of God. 12:19
  Two clear reasons why people must support the m. of God. 18:1-8
  Type - Symbol of. Moses as symbol of Christ & of the minister. 1:1, Types Chart

MINISTRY - MINISTERING
  Duty. Must care for grieving family members. 25:5-10
  Failure in. Failure to serve God. 28:47-57
  Focus of. The priest must focus totally upon the LORD & his ministry to God's people. 18:1-8
  Kinds of.
    To suicidal people & their families. 5:17, D.S. #2
    To the grieving. 25:5-10
    To women with an unwanted pregnancy. 5:17, D.S. #1

MISTREATMENT
  Of foreigners, orphans, & widows. Judgment of. Curse. 27:11-26, esp. v.19

MISUSE (See **VAIN**)
  Meaning of. 5:11

MOAB - MOABITES
  Judgment of. Excluded from the assembly of worship of God. 23:1-8

MONEY
  Charging interest. 23:19-20

MONOGAMY (See **MARRIAGE**)
  Benefits of. 21:15-17

MONOTHEISM
  Meaning of. 6:4-5

MORALITY
  Duty. Of young men & women. Must keep themselves sexually pure. 22:13-21
  Question. What is the basis of m.? 5:7-15, Intro.
  Results of. Sexual impurity. A person becomes sexually impure in at least three ways. 5:18

MOSAIC COVENANT
  Discussed.
    A continuation of the Abrahamic covenant. 5:5, D.S. #1
    The call & promises. 5:5, D.S. #1
  Type - Symbol - Picture of. The believer's life & walk. 5:5, D.S. #1

MOSES
  Authorship of Deuteronomy. Introductory section: Author
  Barred from the promised land. Reasons why. 1:18-39; 3:23-29; 31:1-6; 32:48-52; 34:1-8
  Burden of. The weight of leadership was too heavy for M. to bear all alone. 1:9-17
  Call of. God called Moses.
    To be the founding father. 1:1
    To be the intercessor. 1:1
    To be the leader. 1:1
    To be the liberator. 1:1
  Charge to. By God. 31:14-23
  Charges of.
    To Joshua. 3:21-22; 31:7-8
    To the Levites.
  To preserve the Book of the Law. 31:24-29
  Chastisement of. Barred from the promised land. 1:18-39; 3:23-29; 31:1-6; 32:48-52; 34:1-8
  Comparison of.
    With Christ. 34:10-12, Thgt.6
    With Joshua. Chart. 34:1-12, esp. v.9, D.S. #1
  Death of.
    Death & burial. 34:1-8
    Died at the age of 120 years old. 34:1-8
    Preparation for. 32:48-52
  Discussed.
    A permanent prophet to replace M. (a prediction of Christ.) 18:15-19
    Casting down & breaking the two stone tablets. 9:7-21, Types Chart
    Moses longed to know the LORD personally & intimately. 34:10-12, Thgt.1
    Was the great liberator, prophet, lawgiver, and father of Israel. 34:10-12
  Duty. To warn of the dangers of sin. 31:24-29
  Hope fulfilled. Was able to gaze upon the promised land. 34:1-8
  Intercession of.
    It was intercessory prayer that saved God's people. 9:22-10:1-11, esp. vv.25-29
    It was only the prayer of Moses that kept God from executing Aaron. 9:7-21, esp. v.20
    Three reasons why he fell prostrate before the LORD. 8:7-21, esp. vv.18-20
  Judgment of. Barred from the promised land because of his terrible sin. 1:18-39; 3:23-29; 31:1-6; 32:48-52; 34:1-8
  Last words of. Final message of Moses. 33:26-29
  Legacy of. Three reasons given for his greatness. 34:10-12
  Life - Walk of. Was one of the greatest men in history. 33:1-29, Intro.
  Ministry of.
    Mediator of the covenant. 5:2-5; 29:1, Types Chart
    Messenger of God. 1:1, Types Chart
    Servant of God. 1:1, Types Chart
    Served as God's mediator. 5:2-5, Types Chart
    Was one of the greatest men in history. 33:1-29, Intro.
  Panoramic view of the life of Moses. Practical Bible Helps & Resources
  Parallel between Moses and Christ. 34:10-12, Thgt.6
  Parallel between Moses and Joshua. 34:1-12, D.S.#1
  Prophetic blessing of.
    A message of great assurance & encouragement. 33:1-29
  Replacement of.
    A permanent prophet to replace Moses. 18:15-19
  Sermons of.
    List of subjects. Practical Bible Helps & Resources
  Sin of.
    Lost the privilege of entering into the promised land. 1:18-39; 3:23-29; 31:1-6; 32:48-52; 34:1-8

INDEX

Song of. A strong warning & witness to God's people & to those who reject Him. 31:30-32:52
Titles of.
  Friend of God (Ex.33:11). 33:1-5
  Man of God (De.33:1; Jos.14:6). 33:1-5
  Prophet of God (De.18:15; 34:10). 33:1-5; 34:10-12
  Servant of God (Nu.12:6-8; He.3:5). 33:1-5
Type - Symbol of.
  Christ. As the mediator, Moses was a picture of the coming Savior and Messiah of the world, the LORD Jesus Christ. 5:2-5, esp. v.5; 9:22-10:11, esp. vv.10-11; 29:1, Types Chart
  Christ. 1:1, Types Chart
  Minister. 1:1, Types Chart
Writings of.
  Song of warning & witness. 31:14-23
  Placed under the care of both the political & religious leaders of the nation. 31:9-13

MOTHER
Authority of. Are to be honored by their children. 5:16
Ministry to. Women with an unwanted pregnancy. 5:17, D.S. #1
Question. What does God mean by honoring our parents? 5:16, Thgt.1

MOUNT GERIZIM (See **GERIZIM, MOUNT**)

MOUNT PISGAH (See **PISGAH PEAK**)
History of. 34:1-8, D.S. #1
Location of. 34:1-8, D.S. #1
Place where Moses climbed to view the promised land. 34:1-8

MURDER - MURDERER
Discussed.
  An inward act; an act of anger, bitterness, enmity. 5:17
  When the taking of life is justified, understandable, allowed. 5:17
Example of. Abortion. 5:17, D.S. #1
Judgment of.
  Curse. 27:11-26, esp. v.24; 27:11-26, esp. v.25
  Death, spiritual & eternal. 5:17
Kinds of.
  Abortion. 5:17, D.S. #1
  Hired out. 27:11-26, esp. v.25
  Secret. 27:11-26, esp. v.24
  Suicide. 5:17, D.S. #2
  Unsolved. 21:1-9
Laws governing. 5:16-21, esp. v.17
Meaning of. 5:17
Salvation of. 5:17
Source of. Twofold source. 5:17

N

NAME
Of God. Warning. Must never misuse, never take the name of the LORD God in vain. 5:11

NAPHTALI, TRIBE OF
Blessings of. To be favored by God & filled with the LORD's blessings. 33:23
Prophecy concerning. To be favored by God & filled with the LORD's blessings. 33:23
Territory of. From north of Galilee to the area west and south of Galilee. 33:23

NATION - NATIONS (See **SOCIETY**)
Cup full of iniquity. 20:16-18, D.S. #1
Destruction of. 7:2, D.S. #1
Judgment of. 7:2, D.S. #1
Sin & evil of. 7:2, D.S. #1
Warning to. Must guard against allowing an entire city or community to seduce you. 13:12-18

NEARNESS
To God. Must hold fast. 10:20-22

NECESSITIES
Of life. Provision of. 8:2-6; 8:7-10

NECESSITIES OF LIFE
Abundance of. Promised. An excess of good things is promised to the obedient person. 28:11-12
Blessing of. 28:4-5; 33:13-17, Thgt.1
Source. God. 28:4-5

NEEDS
Of man. 5:28-33

NEEDY, THE
Duty to.
  Must be generous to the poor. 15:7-11; 23:19-20
  Must meet the needs of the poor. 15:1-6, Thgt.1
For the poor. Work must be provided for the poor & underprivileged. 24:19-22
Law governing. 24:17-18

NEIGHBOR
Duty to.
  Must help a n. in a crisis. 22:4
  Must seek peace with our neighbors. 20:10-20, Thgt.1
Example of. Being a good neighbor. 22:1-3; 22:4

NEW AGE MOVEMENT (See **OCCULT**)
Warning against. 18:9-14

NEW BEGINNING
Discussed. Making a fresh start toward the promised land. 2:16

O

OATH - OATHS
Duty. Must take oaths only in God's name. 10:20-22

OBEY - OBEDIENCE
Blessings of.
  Daily activities. 28:6
  Exaltation. 28:13
  Fruitfulness. 28:4-5
  Labor. Promised to the obedient person. 28:8
  Promised. An excess of good things is promised to the obedient person. 28:11-12
  Prosperity. 6:10-11
  Spiritual growth. Is promised to the obedient person. 28:9-10
  Victory over enemies. 28:7
Call to. To love & obey God. 30:11-16
Charge to. Must listen to God's laws & obey His laws. 4:1-5
Discussed.
  Being saved does not free us from our responsibility to obey God. 27:11-26, Thgt.1
  Five strong reasons for obeying God. 7:6-11
  Nine supreme requirements of o. 10:12–11:32
  What happens if all the enemies of the promised land are destroyed. 7:12-16
  What happens when you carefully obey God's law. 4:6-8
Duty.
  Must be careful to keep all the commandments of God. 11:8-15
  Must be faithful in giving a true tithe. 26:12-15
  Must celebrate the three pilgrimage festivals every year. 16:16-17
  Must completely destroy all enemies of the promised land. 7:6-11
  Must have a spirit of discernment between what is allowed & forbidden. 12:20-28
  Must have no other gods before the LORD. 5:7
  Must hear the law, learn the law, & obey the law. 5:1
  Must honor our parents. 5:16
  Must keep the covenant, God's commandments & write them down as a memorial. 27:1-8
  Must keep the Ten Commandments. 4:9-14
  Must learn the Law of God. 1:4-5, Thgt.1
  Must love God with your whole being. 6:4-5; 11:1-7
  Must never commit adultery or sexual immorality. 5:18
  Must never misuse, never take the name of the LORD God in vain. 5:11
  Must never murder a person. 5:17
  Must never personally use anything that had been consecrated to God. 12:20-28
  Must never steal. 5:19
  Must never tell a lie, never give a false testimony or witness. 5:20
  Must not abuse the blood nor misuse the tithe. 12:15-18
  Must not conform to the religious practices of the world. 12:29-32
  Must not make any idol nor worship or serve any false god. 5:8-10
  Must not turn away from any of God's commandments. 28:14

INDEX

Must not worship as we each see fit, but as God dictates. 12:8-14
Must obey every commandment of God. 8:1-20; 10:12-15
Must obey God without reservation. 26:16-19
Must obey the laws & regulations of God. 12:1
Must obey the LORD God & follow His commandments. 27:9-10
Must reject all false worship. 12:2-4
Must seek the place where God's name is honored. 12:5-7
Must support the ministers of God. 12:19
Facts.
  Is an absolute essential to inherit the promised land of God. 4:44-11:32, Div.2 Overview
  The call to obey God is not unreasonable nor impossible. 30:11-16
Laws that require special confession & obedience. 26:1-19
Meaning of. 5:16
On the Sabbath. 5:12-15
Reasons for. Three specific reasons. 26:16-19
Results of.
  There will be blessings for obeying the covenant. 27:11-26
  There will be exaltation. 28:13
  There will be prosperity. 6:1-3; 6:10-11; 12:20-28
  There will be spiritual growth: a direct result of holy living, obedience. 28:9-10, Thgt.1
  There will be a threefold blessing. 28:1-3
  There will be focus. You will not forget God. 8:1
Rewards.
  God will keep His covenant of love if His people will obey Him. 7:12-16
  God will love and bless you in a very special way. 7:12-16
  Of obeying the covenant. 27:11-26
  The promised land will be blessed & cared for by God & made fruitful. 11:8-15
  Will live, prosper, & prolong your days in the promised land of God. 5:28-33
  Will make you strong, assure you of God's very special strength. 11:8-15
Warning.
  Must not murder. 5:17
  The unbeliever & the disobedient stand at the crossroads of life. 11:26-32, Thgt.1

OBSERVE (THE SABBATH)
Meaning of. 5:12-15

OCCULT
Duty.
  Must not follow the detestable of the occult world. 18:9-14
Practices of. 18:9-14
Warning against. 18:9-14

OFFERING - OFFERINGS
Duty. Must be faithful in giving a true tithe. 26:12-15
List of.
  Burnt o. 27:1-8, Types Chart
  Fellowship or Peace O. 27:1-8, Types Chart

Of a young unworked cow whose neck was broken. 21:4, Types Chart
Requirement. Must not be hard-hearted nor tightfisted against God. 15:19-23
What is acceptable & not acceptable. Must not bring money earned by a prostitute into the house of God. 23:17-18

OFFICERS OF THE LAW
Duty.
  Must be fair & just. 16:18-17:1, esp. v.18
  Must follow justice & justice alone. 16:18-17:1, esp. v.20
  Must guard the people against greed & against false approaches to God. 16:18-17:1, esp. ch.17:1
  Must guard the people against idolatry and false worship. 16:18-17:1, esp. v.21
  Must never accept a bribe. 16:18-17:1, esp. v.19
  Must never twist justice nor show partiality. 16:18-17:1, esp. v.19

OG
Bed of. 2:24-3:11, Thgt.1

OMENS
Warning against interpreting. 18:9-14, esp. v.10

ORPHAN
Law governing. 24:17-18
Protection of. 24:17-18

OX
Law governing the muzzling of an ox while working. 25:4
Law governing the payment of wages. 25:4
Warning. Must not muzzle the ox. 25:4

P

PALESTINE
Restoration of Israel. Recent occurrence. 31:30-32:52, Introduction

PALESTINIAN COVENANT
Discussed. 29:1

PARAN, DESERT OF (See **DESERTS**)
Description of. 1:18-39

PARENTS
Abuse of. 5:16
Authority of. Are to be honored by their children. 5:16
Duty.
  Must diligently teach the commandments to their children. 6:6-9; 11:18-21
  Must discipline their children. 21:18-21
  Must teach God's Word & commandments to one's children & share one's spiritual experiences with them. 4:9-14, esp. v.9
  Must teach the truth of salvation & of the commandments to children. 6:20-25, Types Chart
Judgment of. Not honoring. Curse. 27:11-26, esp. v.16
Question. What does God mean by honoring our parents? 5:16, Thgt.1

PARTIALITY (See **EQUAL; JUSTICE**)
Discussed. God is impartial and just. 10:16-19
Duty. Must not show partiality or favoritism to our children nor to anyone else. 21:15-17, Thgt.1
Meaning of. 16:18-17:1

PASSOVER, THE
Duty. Must remember the Passover. 16:1-8, Types Chart
Feast of. 16:1-8, Types Chart
Festival of. 16:1-8, Types Chart
Significance of. Was the most significant event in Israel's history. 16:1-8, Types Chart
Type - Symbol of. Christ the Lamb of God who takes away the sins of the world. 16:1-8, Types Chart

PEACE OFFERING (See **FELLOWSHIP OFFERING**)
Type - Symbol of. Fellowship & peace with God. 27:1-8, Types Chart

PENTECOST (See **HARVEST, FESTIVAL OF**)
Feast of. 16:9-12
Meaning of. Fifty days. 16:9-12
Type - Symbol of. The great harvest of souls and of people giving their lives to God. 16:9-12, Types Chart

PERIZZITES
Enemy of Israel who inhabited the promised land. 7:1-5

PERJURY
Duty.
  Must never be allowed to rule in the courts of the land. 19:15-21
  Must never tell a lie, never give a false testimony or witness. 5:20

PHYLACTERIES
Purpose of. 11:18-21

PILGRIMAGE
Festivals of. Duty. Must celebrate the three pilgrimage festivals every year. 16:16-17
Of the believer. 2:16

PISGAH PEAK (See **MOUNT PISGAH**)
History of. 34:1-8, D.S. #1
Location of. 34:1-8, D.S. #1
Place where Moses climbed to view the promised land. 34:1-8

PLEDGE
Duty.
  Must do exactly what you vow or pledge. 23:21-23
  Must know that it is better not to make a vow than to make it & not fulfill it. 23:21-23
  Must not be slow to pay your vows or pledges to God. 23:21-23
Kinds of. To the LORD. 10:12-15
Meaning of. p. to the LORD. 10:12-15

PLENTY
Danger of. Comfort, ease, satisfaction. 6:12-19

POLYGAMY (See **MARRIAGE**)
Question. Why was p. condoned in this passage? 21:15-17

INDEX

POLYTHEISM
  Meaning of. 6:4-5
  Warning. Man is not to believe in many gods. 5:7

POOR, THE
  Duty to.
    Must be generous to the poor. 15:7-11; 23:19-20
    Must meet the needs of the poor. 15:1-6, Thgt.1; 24:19-22
    Must not take advantage of the poor & needy worker. 24:14-15
  Protection of.
    The food supply for the **p.** & underprivileged. 24:19-22
    The poor worker. 24:14-15
  Respect for. 24:10-13
  Work for. Must be provided for the poor & underprivileged. 24:19-22

POSSESSION
  Treasured covenant. Of God. 7:6-11

POVERTY
  Causes of. Are innumerable. 15:1-23
  Duty.
    Must be generous to the poor. 15:7-11; 23:19-20
    Must meet the needs of the poor. 15:1-6, Thgt.1
    Must not take advantage of the poor & needy worker. 24:14-15

POWER
  Of God. 2:17-23; 7:17-26

PRAISE
  To God. For the promised land & its wonderful provision. 8:7-10

PRAY - PRAYER - PRAYING
  Discussed. God hears prayer. 9:22–10:11, pt. 2, Thgt.1
  How to. 4:6-8
  Kind of. Intercessory. 9:22-10:11

PREACH - PREACHING
  Of Moses. 4:44-49

PREGNANCY
  Question.
    What does the Bible say about the creation of man & the fetus or unborn baby in the womb? 5:17, D.S. #1
    What does the medical profession say about the fetus or unborn child in the mother's womb? 5:17, D.S. #1
    When does the unborn child become a human being? 5:17, D.S. #1

PREMARITAL SEX (See **MARRIAGE**)
  Duty. Of young men & women. Must keep themselves sexually pure. 22:13-21

PREPARATION
  Duty. Must be prepared to enter the spiritual conquest & rest of the promised land. 1:3
  Of Israel. To enter the promised land. 1:3

PRESENCE
  Of God. 4:9-14; 7:17-26; 31:1-6

PRIDE
  Warning against. Will cause you to forget God. 8:11-20

PRIEST (See **MINISTER**)
  Dedication & support of. 18:1-8
  Duty.
    To be responsible for leading the people in their worship of God (including the offering of sacrifices to God). 33:8-11
    To be responsible for leading the people in their worship of God. 33:8-11
    To be responsible for revealing the will of God to the people. 33:8-11
    To care for God's people. 18:15-19
    To read & teach the law to the people of God. 31:9-13
    To serve as the teachers of God's law. 33:8-11

PRISONERS
  Of war. Treatment of female war **p.** 21:10-14, Types Chart

PROFANITY
  Warning. Must never misuse, never take the name of the LORD God in vain. 5:11

PROMISED LAND, THE
  Abraham's perspective.
    The assurance of a personal inheritance. 1:8, D.S.#1
    The assurance of conquest & rest, of spiritual victory & spiritual rest. 1:8, D.S.#1
    The assurance of God's own presence, His love, care, provision, & protection. 1:8, D.S.#1
  Barred from.
    Moses. 1:18-39; 3:23-29; 31:1-6; 32:48-52; 34:1-8
    The first generation. 1:18-39, esp. v.35; 4:15-31, esp.vv.25-28
  Boundaries of. 1:6-8
  Discussed.
    On the threshold of. Israel was. 1:2
  Duty.
    Must be prepared to enter the spiritual conquest & rest of the promised land. 1:3
    Must possess. 1:6-8
  Enemies of. 7:1-26
  How to enter. By obeying God's commandments. 4:1-5
  Inheritance of. Promised to Israel. 1:6-8
  March to. 1:4-5
  Meaning of.
    Refers to a heavenly country & a heavenly city. 1:8, D.S.#1
    Refers to heaven. 1:8, D.S.#1
    Refers to Palestine, the land of Israel. 1:8, D.S.#1
  Praise for. The promised land & its wonderful provision. 8:7-10
  Preparation to enter. 1:3; 31:1-29
  Provision of.
    A land that has no scarcity. 8:7-10
    A rich deposit of minerals (iron & copper). 8:7-10
    An overflowing water supply. 8:7-10
    An abundance of food. 8:7-10
  Seen by Moses. 34:1-8
  Territory of. Extent of boundaries. 11:22-25
  Type - Symbol of.
    Heaven & of spiritual conquest & rest. 1:2; 1:6-8, Thgt.1; 4:1-5, Types Chart

    Trusting God & resting in God. 26:1-11, Types Chart

PROMISES
  Duty. Toward God. Must be faithful to keep our promises to God. 29:10-15, Thgt.1
  Given to Israel. Promise of restoration. 30:3-10
  Of God.
    God has established His covenant with you. 26:16-19
    God has the power to fulfill His promises. 2:17-23
    God is faithful, never failing to keep His **p.** 29:10-15, Thgt.1
  Of greatness & holiness. 26:16-19

PROPERTY (See **LAND**)
  Law governing.
    Must not steal. 5:19; 19:14
    Property rights. 23:24-25
  Protection of. Property rights are to be respected. 23:24-25, Thgt.1; 24:10-13
  Restoration of. Lost **p.** 22:1-3

PROPHECY
  Concerning Apostasy. Israel will be barred from the promised land for not guarding against false gods & false worship. 4:15-31, esp.vv.25-28
  Concerning Israel. Will be barred from the promised land for not guarding against false gods & false worship. 4:15-31, esp.vv.25-28
  Concerning restoration. Hope for those who turn away from idols and return to God. 4:15-31, esp. vv.29-31
  Of Asher. 33:24-25
  Of Benjamin. 33:12
  Of Dan. 33:22
  Of Ephraim. 33:13-17
  Of Gad. 33:20-21
  Of Issachar. 33:18-19
  Of Jesus Christ. 18:15-19
  Of Judah. 33:7
  Of Joseph. 33:13-17
  Of Levi. 33:8-11
  Of Manasseh. 33:13-17
  Of Naphtali. 33:23
  Of Reuben. 33:6
  Of Zebulun. 33:18-19

PROPHET
  Call of. 18:15-19
  Duty of. The special **p.** Threefold work. 18:15-19
  Listed. Moses. 34:10-12

PROPHET, FALSE
  Danger of. Seducing you into false worship. 13:1-5
  Law governing. Must execute all false prophets. 18:20-22

PROSPERITY
  Blessing of.
    An excess of good things is promised to the obedient person. 28:11-12
    Promised to the tribes of Joseph, Ephraim, & Manasseh. 33:13-17
    Provision, supply, and prosperity. 33:26-29
  Danger of. Comfort, ease, satisfaction. 6:12-19

INDEX

Example of. Tribe of Zebulun had a unique opportunity to serve other tribes. 33:18-19, Thgt.1
Source of. Obedience to God. 6:10-11; 8:11-20
Warning against.
    Will cause you to forget God. 8:11-20
    Will forget & reject God. 32:15-18

PROSTITUTE - PROSTITUTION
Fact. God detests **p**. 23:17-18
Influence of. A common practice within every nation. 23:17-18, Thgt.1
Judgment of. Will be judged by God. 23:17-18, Thgt.1
Warning.
    Must not become a **p**. 23:17-18
    Must not bring money earned by a **p**. into the house of God. 23:17-18
    Will be judged by God. 23:17-18, Thgt.1

PROTECT - PROTECTION
Blessing of. The LORD our shield & defender. 33:26-29
Duty. Must prevent the wrong of excessive force. 25:11-12

PROVISION
Blessing of.
    An excess of good things is promised to the obedient person. 28:11-12; 33:13-17, Thgt.1
    Provision, supply, and prosperity. 33:26-29
Of God.
    For the promised land & its wonderful provisions. 8:7-10
    Life's necessities. 8:7-10
Of leadership.
    Provision of. Will become the head and not the tail. 28:13
Source of. God. 8:2-6

PROVOKING GOD
Warning against. Continued disobedience & rebellion. 9:22-10:11

PSYCHICS
Warning against. 18:9-14

PUBLIC SAFETY
Duty. Must be concerned with protecting the safety of visiting neighbors. 22:8
Is a concern of God's. 22:8
Reason for. Building codes. To prevent accidents & personal liability. 22:8

PUNISH - PUNISHMENT (See JUDGMENT)
Law governing the wrong abusive punishment in legal disputes. 25:1-3
Limits of legal. 25:1-3

PURE - PURITY
Blessings of. Spiritual victory & purity. 33:26-29
Duty. Must protect female war prisoners. 21:10-14
Duty. Of young men & women. Must keep themselves sexually pure. 22:13-21
Picture of. **p**. in the military camp. Being spiritually clean. 23:9-14, Types Chart

R

RACE
Question. Is one race of people of more value than another race? 9:1-10:11

RAIN
Blessing of. 28:11-12
Fact. Without **r**. nothing could survive. 28:11-12

RAPE
Judgment of. 22:25-29
Question. What would happen in today's society if a man or woman who raped another person would be executed soon after? 22:25-29, Thgt.1

REBEL - REBELLION
Against God. Incomplete confession. 1:40-46
Law governing. The stubborn & rebellious son. 21:18-21
Of children. The stubborn & rebellious son. 21:18-21
Results of. 1:18-39
Warning against.
    Continued disobedience & rebellion. 9:22-10:11
    Provoking God to anger & judgment. 9:7-21

RECONCILE - RECONCILIATION (See ATONEMENT)
Source of. Christ secured atonement or reconciliation for man. 27:1-8

REDEDICATION
Purpose of. To establish that the believers were God's people & that He was their God. 29:10-15

REFUGE
Blessing of. Refuge & support. 33:26-29
From the storms of life. 4:31-43

REFUGE, CITIES OF
Location of. 4:41-43
Bezer.
    City of Refuge for Reuben. 4:43
    Location of. 4:41-43, D.S. #1
    History of. 4:41-43, D.S. #1
Golan.
    City of Refuge for the half-tribe of Manasseh. 4:43
    History of. 4:41-43, D.S. #2
    Location of. 4:41-43, D.S. #2
Ramoth.
    City of Refuge for Gad. 4:43
    History of. 4:41-43, D.S. #3
    Location of. 4:41-43, D.S. #3
Purpose of. 4:41-43; 19:1-13
Type - Symbol - Picture of. Christ, our refuge from death & from the storms & threats of life. 4:41-43; 19:1-8, Types Chart

REJECTION
Against God.
    A prediction of the future. 32:15-18
    Results of. 28:15-46; 32:19-27

RELATION - RELATIONSHIPS
Kind of. With neighbor. 22:1-3; 22:4

RELEASE
Of debts. 15:1-6

RELIGION
Impact of. Is & always has been one of the dominant forces in the world. 18:1-22

RELIGION, FALSE
Duty.
    Must not bear the marks of false religion. 14:1-2
    Must not conform to the religious practices of the world. 12:29-32
Marks of. The way a person mourns for the dead. 14:1-2

REMARRIAGE
Law governing. 24:1-4
Prohibition against. 24:1-4

REMEMBER - REMEMBRANCE
Duty.
    Must celebrate the three pilgrimage festivals every year. 16:16-17
    Must learn from our past. 11:1-7
Meaning of. 8:2-6

REPENT - REPENTANCE
Conditions of.
    Must obey the LORD, obey Him with our whole heart and soul. 30:1-2
    Must repent, return to the LORD. 30:1-2
    Must sense the need for repentance. 30:1-2
False **r**. Incomplete confession. 1:40-46

REPHAITES
Discussed. Were giants of the land, a tall race of people. 2:17-23
History of. Were defeated by the Ammonites. 2:17-23

RESPECT
For property rights. 24:10-13
For the poor. 24:10-13
Meaning of. 16:18-17:1
Of privacy. 24:10-13

RESPONSE
Rejection of God. 32:15-18

RESPONSIBILITY
Duty. Must never steal. 5:19
Personal. Must hold each individual responsible for his own behavior. 24:16

REST
Warning. God warns us against seeking worldly **r**. 3:12-20

REST, SPIRITUAL
Assurance of. 1:8, D.S.#1

RESTORATION
Hope for those who turn away from idols and return to God. 4:15-31, esp. vv.29-31
Of Israel.
    Conditions of. 30:1-2
    History of. 29:22-29, D.S. #1
    Promise of. 30:3-10
    Recent occurrence. 31:30-32:52, Introduction
Of lost property. 22:1-3
Promise of. Restoration—forgiveness & acceptance by the LORD. 30:3-10

RETURN - RETURNING
To the LORD. Conditions of. 30:1-2

INDEX

REUBEN, TRIBE OF
  Blessing of. Was to live & not die as a tribe or state of Israel. 33:6
  Territory of. Bezer.
    City of Refuge for Reuben. 4:43
    Location of. 4:41-43, D.S. #1
    History of. 4:41-43, D.S. #1
  Type - Symbol - Picture of. God answering prayer. 33:6, Thgt.1
  Weakness of.
    List of five weaknesses. 33:6
    Was unstable as water. 33:6

REVELATION
  Of God's glory. 5:22

REVERENCE
  Lack of. Israel failed to r. God. 28:58-68
  Meaning of. Fear. 6:1-3; 6:2, D.S. #1

RIGHTEOUSNESS
  Meaning. 6:20-25
  Results of. Exalts a nation. 13:12-18, Thgt.1

RIGHTS
  Laws governing human r. 21:1-23
  Of property. Protection of. Property rights are to be respected. 23:24-25, Thgt.1

RITUAL
  Kind of. Cleansing. 21:1-9
  Of blessings & cursings. 11:26-32
  Of the Firstfruit Offering. Thanking God for His salvation & blessings. 26:1-11
  Pagan. Example of. 14:1-2

RITUAL UNCLEANNESS (See **CEREMONIAL UNCLEANNESS**)

ROBBERY
  Discussed. The most serious & damning form of stealing is that of robbing God. 5:19
  How a person robs God. 5:19
  Law governing. Must not steal. 5:19

ROCK
  Title of God. He is the Rock of Ages & the Solid Rock. 32:3-4

RULERS
  Appointment of. 17:14-20
  Duty of. 17:14-20
  Qualifications of. Must be marked with wisdom & integrity. 34:9
  Results of. The ruler's obedience. 17:14-20

S

SABBATH
  Charge. To observe the S. & keep it holy. 5:12-15
  Meaning of. 5:12-15
  Purpose. Two strong reasons why the S. is to be observed & kept holy. 5:12-15

SABBATICAL YEAR
  Discussed. Release of debts. 15:1-6
  Purpose of. 15:1-6

SACRIFICE - SACRIFICES (See **OFFERINGS**)
  Duty. Must never personally use anything that had been consecrated to God. 12:20-28
  Kinds of.
    Animal. 15:19-23, Types Chart
    Burnt Offering. 27:1-8, Types Chart
    Peace or Fellowship Offering. 27:1-8, Types Chart

SAFE - SAFETY
  Blessing of. Perfectly safe from all enemies. 33:26-29

SALVATION
  Blessing of. Made a very distinct people by the LORD. 33:26-29
  Discussed.
    A basis of the Ten Commandments is God's s., deliverance, & redemption. 5:6
    Some people stand on the threshold of receiving Christ, but fail to act. 1:2, Thgt.1
  Duty.
    Must love God with your whole being. 6:4-5; 11:1-7
    Must teach God's commandments. 6:20-25
  Harvest of. Celebrating the feast of Pentecost: power to witness. 16:9-12, Thgt.1, Types Chart
  Man's need for. A mediator needed to approach God for man. 5:26-27
  Source of. God. 9:22-10:11

SANCTUARY
  Discussed. One central s. taught the Israelites several significant lessons. 12:5-7

SATAN
  Source of.
    Lying. 5:20
    Murder. 5:17

SATISFACTION
  Danger of. Comfort, ease, satisfaction. 6:12-19

SAVAGE - SAVAGERY
  Judgment of. 25:17-19

SCRIPTURE - SCRIPTURES (See **WORD OF GOD**)
  Duty to.
    Must be preached. 4:44-49, Thgt.1
    Must hear the law, learn the law, & obey the law. 5:1
    Must learn the Word of God before we can enter the promised land. 1:3
    Must read & teach the law to the people of God. 31:9-13
  Importance of. Preserving and correct placement. 31:24-29

SECRET THINGS
  Discussed. They belong to the LORD. 29:20-29

SECURE - SECURITY
  Blessing of. Perfectly safe from all enemies. 33:26-29
  Discussed. Commandment ten concerns man's security. 5:21
  For debts. Protection of. A man's livelihood. 24:6

SEDUCTION
  Danger of.
    Being seduced by a loved one or close friend. 13:6-11
    Being seduced by an entire city or community. 13:12-18
    Being seduced by a false prophet. 13:1-5
  Discussed.
    Of an engaged woman (or man). 22:23-24
    The seduced person was to take the lead in executing justice. 13:6-11
  Duty. Must not conform to the religious practices of the world. 12:29-32
  Purpose of. To test you, of your love for God. 13:1-5
  Victory over. Three specific things. 13:1-5
  Warning against.
    Must guard against being seduced by a loved one or close friend. 13:6-11
    Must guard against allowing an entire city or community to seduce you. 13:12-18
    Must guard against the false prophet & the interpreter of dreams. 13:1-5

SEED
  Mixing of. Must not mix when planting a field. 22:9-11, Types Chart

SEEK - SEEKING
  Of God. True worship of God. 12:5-7

SELFISHNESS
  Example of. 3:12-20

SELF-RIGHTEOUSNESS
  Discussed. Is a terrible evil. 9:1-6, Thgt.1
  Duty. Must not become self-righteous. 9:1-6
  Results of. Can blind a person & condemn him to be separated forever from God's presence. 9:1-6, Thgt.1
  Warning against. Three strong admonitions. 9:1-6

SELF-SUFFICIENCY
  Warning against. Will cause you to forget God. 8:11-20

SEPARATION, SPIRITUAL
  Duty. Must live a life of s. 7:1-5; 22:9-11; 22:12, Types Chart
  Fact. A great gulf separates man from God. 5:23-25

SERVE - SERVANT
  Call of. Moses. To be the servant of God. 1:1
  Duty. Must fear & serve God alone. 10:20-22

SERVICE
  Discussed. Failure in. 28:47-57

SEX
  Duty. Must protect female war prisoners. 21:10-14, Types Chart
  Illicit S. A person becomes sexually impure in at least three ways. 5:18
  Premarital. Duty. Of young men & women. Must keep themselves sexually pure. 22:13-21

SEXUAL IMMORALITY
  Remedy for. Keeping yourself away from sexual sins. 5:18, Thgt.1
  Results of. A person becomes sexually impure in at least three ways. 5:18

INDEX

SEXUAL PURITY
  Duty. Of young men & women. Must keep themselves sexually pure. 22:13-21
  Lesson on. Treatment of female war prisoners & respect for women. 21:10-14, Types Chart

SIHON
  King of Amorites. Defeated by Israel. 2:24–3:11

SIN - SINS
  Duty. To circumcise or cut sin out of your h. 10:16-19
  Fact. Is universal. 32:5-6, Thgt.1
  Kinds of. (See **TEN COMMANDMENTS**)
    Corruption. 32:5-6
    Coveting. 5:21
    Idolatry & false worship. 9:7-21
    Stealing. 5:19
  Of Israel. (See **TEN COMMANDMENTS**; **ISRAEL**, Sins of)
    Corruption. 32:5-6
    Coveting. 5:21
    Idolatry & false worship. 9:7-21
    Stealing. 5:19
  Remedy for.
    Must acknowledge that the LORD—He & He alone—is God. 4:32-40
    Must be a just people. 16:18-17:1
    Must be courageous and stand fast. 33:22, Thgt.1
    Must be faithful in giving a true tithe. 26:12-15
    Must be faithful to keep our promises to God. 29:10-15, Thgt.1
    Must be prepared spiritually. 1:6-4:43, Div.1 Overview
    Must be prepared to enter the spiritual conquest & rest of the promised land. 1:3
    Must be strong & courageous. 31:1-6; 31:7-8
    Must be wholeheartedly committed to the LORD. 32:44-47, Thgt.1
    Must control our minds throughout the day. 22:12, Thgt.1
    Must diligently teach God's commandments to your children. 6:6-9
    Must do exactly what you vow or pledge. 23:21-23
    Must fear & serve God alone. 10:20-22
    Must give the first of everything to God, the very best that we have. 15:19-23, Thgt.1, Types Chart
    Must grow in the LORD. 31:30-32:2
    Must have a spirit of discernment between what is allowed & forbidden. 12:20-28
    Must hear the law, learn the law, & obey the law. 5:1
    Must keep close to God. 10:20-22
    Must keep the covenant, God's commandments & write them down as a memorial. 27:1-8
    Must keep our body & spirit clean. 23:9-14
    Must keep ourselves free from defilement. 14:3-21
    Must keep the Ten Commandments. 4:9-14
    Must keep yourself away from sexual sins. 5:18, Thgt.1
    Must know & acknowledge the only true & living God. 5:7
    Must know God's Word: God has given us the Word of God, to warn us against sin. 31:24-29
    Must know that it is better not to make a vow than to make it & not fulfill it. 23:21-23
    Must learn the Law of God. 1:4-5, Thgt.1
    Must learn the lessons of history. 1:6-4:43, Div.1 Overview
    Must learn the Word of God before we can enter the promised land. 1:3
    Must live holy lives, totally set apart to God. 14:1-2, Thgt.1
    Must love God with your whole being. 6:4-5; 11:1-7
    Must never misuse, never take the name of the LORD God in vain. 5:11
    Must never personally use anything that had been consecrated to God. 12:20-28
    Must never put another person in a state of destitution. 24:6, Thgt.1
    Must never use excessive force in any situation. 25:11-12, Thgt.1
    Must not abuse the blood nor misuse the tithe. 12:15-18
    Must not be fainthearted during warfare—God will be with the believer. 20:1-4
    Must not be slow to pay your vows or pledges to God. 23:21-23
    Must not conform to the religious practices of the world. 12:29-32
    Must not fear during warfare—God will be with the believer. 20:1-4
    Must not settle down, be complacent, or at ease before conquering all of the promised land. 3:12-20
    Must not show partiality or favoritism to our children nor to anyone else. 21:15-17, Thgt.1
    Must not turn away from any of God's commandments. 28:14
    Must obey all the commandments & laws of God. 26:16-19
    Must obey every commandment of God. 8:1-20
    Must obey God's law even after reaching the promised land. 4:1-5
    Must obey the LORD. 28:1-3
    Must obey the LORD God & follow His commandments. 27:9-10
    Must place the commandments in your heart. 6:6-9
    Must present our bodies as a living sacrifice to God. 15:19-23, Thgt.1, Types Chart
    Must press on and conquer the enemies of the promised land. 3:12-20, Thgt.1
    Must remember the judgment of God. 8:11-20
    Must remember the terrible sins that kept the first generation out of the promised land 1:18-39, Thgt.1
    Must seek peace with our neighbors. 20:10-20, Thgt.1
    Must seek the place where God's name is honored. 12:5-7
    Must show compassion for the needy of this earth, doing all we can to help. 23:19-20, Thgt.1
    Must support the ministers of God. 12:19; 18:1-8
    Must teach God's Word & commandments to one's children & share one's spiritual experiences with them. 4:9-14, esp. v.9
    Must teach the truth of salvation & of the commandments to children. 6:20-25, Types Chart
    Must thank God for His salvation & blessings. 26:1-11; Thgt.1
    Must use God's commandments as a witness. 6:6-9
  Seriousness of. Disrupts our march to the promised land. 2:16, Thgt.1
  Sexual impurity. Results of. A person becomes sexually impure in at least three ways. 5:18
  Warning against. 2:16, Thgt.1

SINAI, MOUNT
  Discussed. Sometimes called Mt. Horeb. 1:6-8

SLAVE - SLAVES - SLAVERY
  Discussed. Law governing the release of slaves. 15:12-18
  Duty to. Escaped slaves.
    Must give sanctuary to an escaped slave. 23:15-16
    Must not be oppressed. 23:15-16
  Hebrew regulations of. 15:12-18, D.S.#1
  History of. 15:12-18, D.S.#1
  Kind of. Escaped. 23:15-16
  Warning. No human being is to be enslaved. 23:15-16, Thgt.1

SOCIETY
  Benefits to a righteous s. 12:1-26:19, Div.3 Overview
  Duty to.
    Must be generous to the poor. 15:7-11; 23:19-20
    Must meet the needs of the poor. 15:1-6, Thgt.1
  Foundations of.
    Fair & equal justice is an absolute essential for a strong and healthy society. 25:1-3, Thgt.1
    The family is the basic unit of society, the very foundation of society. 5:16
    Truth. 5:20
  Laws of. Reasons for. 12:1-26:19, Div.3, Overview
  Solution to problems. 5:7-15
  Warning.
    Lying threatens the very foundation of society. 5:20
    Stealing threatens the very foundation of society. 5:19

SODOM
  Fact. Enemies bear the very character of Sodom & Gomorrah. 32:32-35

SON
  Law governing. The stubborn & rebellious s. 21:18-21

SONG
  Of Moses.
    A strong warning & witness to God's people & to those who reject Him. 31:30-32:52
    Why people needed the s. 31:14-23
    Warning of. 32:44-47

INDEX

Of warning & witness. Of Moses. 31:14-23

SORCERY (See **FORTUNE-TELLING**)
Warning against. 18:9-14

SOUL
Meaning of. 6:4-5

SOUL-WINNING
Harvest of. Celebrating the feast of Pentecost: power to witness. 16:9-12, Thgt.1, Types Chart

SOVEREIGN - SOVEREIGNTY
Of God. In the affairs of nations. 2:17-23

SPEECH
Kinds of. False. Duty. Must never tell a lie, never give a false testimony or witness. 5:20

SPIRITISTS (See **PSYCHICS**)

SPIRITUAL CLEANLINESS
Duty. Must keep ourselves free from defilement. 14:3-21

SPIRITUAL GROWTH
Conditional. Is promised to the obedient person. 28:9-10

SPIRITUAL REST (See **REST, SPIRITUAL**)

SPIRITUAL SEPARATION (See **SEPARATION, SPIRITUAL**)

STEADFASTNESS
To God. Must hold fast. 10:20-22

STEAL - STEALING
Discussed. The most serious & damning form of s. is that of robbing God. 5:19
Duty. Must never steal. 19:14
History of.
  The first recorded sin committed by Israel after entering Canaan. 5:19, Thgt.2
  The first sin committed by the human race. 5:19, Thgt.2
  The first sin to defile the early church. 5:19, Thgt.2
How a person robs God. 5:19
Judgment of. Curse. 27:11-26, esp. v.17
Law governing. 5:19
Source of. A heart problem. 5:19

STEPFATHER
Duty to. Must not marry a step parent. 22:30
Sin against. Incest. 22:30

STEPMOTHER
Duty to. Must not marry a step parent. 22:30
Sin against. Incest. 22:30

STEWARD - STEWARDSHIP
Dedication & support of ministers. 18:1-8
Duty.
  Must be generous to the poor. 15:7-11
  Must not bring money earned by a prostitute into the house of God. 23:17-18
  Must support the ministers of God. 12:19; 18:1-8

STIFF-NECKED
Duty. To circumcise or cut sin out of your heart. 10:16-19
Warning. Do not be. 10:16-19

STORMS
Of life. Deliverance from. 19:1-13

STRATEGY
For conquest. 20:10-20

STRENGTH
Meaning of. 6:4-5

STRONG
Duty. To be strong & courageous. 31:1-6

STUBBORN - STUBBORNNESS
Duty. To circumcise or cut sin out of your heart. 10:16-19
Sin of. The Golden Calf. Israel's sin of idolatry and false worship. 9:7-21
Warning. Do not be. 10:16-19

STUMBLINGBLOCK
Duty. Must not conform to the religious practices of the world. 12:29-32
Warning. Against family being a stumblingblock. 13:6-11

SUICIDE
Form of murder. 5:17, D.S. #2

SUNDAY
Day of worship. Reason why. 5:12-15

SUPPLY
Blessing of. Provision, supply, and prosperity. 33:26-29

SUPPORT
Blessing of. Refuge & support. 33:26-29
Of priests or ministers of God. 18:1-8

SWEARING
Judgment of. God will hold the guilty accountable. 5:11
Warning. Must never misuse, never take the name of the LORD God in vain. 5:11

SYMBOL - SYMBOLIC
List of. Types, Symbols, & Pictures in the book of Deuteronomy. Introductory materials
Of Abraham: All believers. 1:6-8, Thgt.1
Of Abrahamic Covenant: Salvation. 5:5, D.S. #1
Of atonement: Burnt Offering. 27:1-8
Of blood.
  Of Christ's death. 12:15-18
  Of life. 12:20-28
Of Christ:
  Dying as the substitute sacrifice for us. 27:1-8
  His death upon a tree. 21:22-23, Types Chart
  Moses. 1:1, Types Chart
  Our Refuge. 19:1-13, Types Chart
  The Passover Lamb. 16:1-8, Types Chart
Of cleansing laws: being spiritually clean & undefiled. 14:3-21, Types Chart
Of false worship. Duty to. Must destroy. 12:2-4
Of God answering prayer: Symbolized in the tribe of Reuben. 33:6, Thgt.1
Of Heaven: the promised land. 1:6-8, Thgt.1
Of Israel: All believers. 1:1
Of Moses: As mediator, as minister. 1:1; 5:2-5; 9:22-10:11; 29:1
Of one way to God. 12:5-7
Of one worship. 12:5-7
Of Pentecost: Salvation. 16:9-12, Thgt.1, Types Chart
Of purity in the military camp: being spiritually clean. 23:9-14, Types Chart
Of Tabernacles: Marching through this world to the promised land. 16:13-15, Types Chart
Of the believer's spiritual battle: language of warfare. 20:1-4, Thgt.1
Of the fellowship or peace with God: of the Fellowship or Peace Offerings. 27:1-8
Of the spread of sin: Infectious skin diseases. 24:8-9, Thgt.1
Of the Tabernacle: Where God's holy presence was symbolized. 12:5-7
Of the tree: symbolized the crucifixion of Christ. 21:22-23, Types Chart
Of the wilderness wanderings: God saving His people from Egyptian slavery. 32:7-14, Types Chart
Of unleavened bread. 16:1-8, Thgt.1, Types Chart

T

TABERAH
Place of disobedience. 9:22-10:11

TABERNACLE
Type - Symbol of. True worship of God. 12:5-7

TABERNACLES, FEAST OF (See **TABERNACLES, FESTIVAL OF**)
Type - Symbol of. The march through this world to the promised land (heaven). 16:13-15, Types Chart

TABERNACLES, FESTIVAL OF (See **TABERNACLES, FEAST OF**)
Type - Symbol of. The march through this world to the promised land (heaven). 16:13-15, Types Chart

TASSELS
Purpose for. To remind the believer to obey God's commandments & to live a holy life. 22:12

TEACH - TEACHER - TEACHING
Duty. To diligently teach the commandments to our children. 6:6-9; 6:20-25; 11:18-21, Types Chart

TEMPT - TEMPTATION
Duty. Must be removed from our lives and homes. 7:17-26, Thgt.2
Fact. God will enable us to conquer all the trials & temptations of life. 16:13-15, Thgt.2

TEN COMMANDMENTS, THE
Basis of. 5:6; 5:7-15
Discussed.
  Is the heart of the law. 5:2-5
  Is the basis, the very foundation of life. 5:2-5
Duty. Must keep. 4:9-14
Mediator of. Moses. 5:2-5

INDEX

Warning. Do not forget your experience with the LORD nor the Ten Commandments. 4:9-14

TEST - TESTS
Of God. Reason for. To find out if you truly love God. 13:1-5
Purpose of. 18:20-22

TESTIFY - TESTIMONY
Duty.
  Must be a strong **t.** & witness for the LORD. 11:18-21
  Must not bear the marks of false religion. 14:1-2
  Must use God's commandments as a witness. 6:6-9
Kind of.
  A strong. 4:6-8
  False. 5:20
Result of. Having a strong testimony & witness. 11:18-21

TESTING
Of God. Purpose of. To humble and test Israel. 8:2-6

TESTING GOD
Answer to. 6:12-19

THANKS - THANKSGIVING
Duty. Must praise God for the promised land & its wonderful provisions. 8:7-10
To God. For His salvation & blessings. 26:1-11

THEFT - THIEVES
Duty. Must be judged. 19:14
Law governing. Must not steal. 5:19; 19:14

THEOCRACY
Meaning of. 17:2-7; 12:1-26:19, Div.3 Overview

THOUGHTS - THOUGHT LIFE
Duty. To protect. 22:12

THUMMIM
Type - Symbol of. The High Priest seeking God's will for the people. 33:8-11

TIGHTFISTED
Discussed. Remedy against. 15:1-6
Duty.
  Must be generous to the poor. 15:7-11
  Must not be hard-hearted nor tightfisted against God. 15:19-23

TITHE - TITHING
Discernment of. Must never personally use anything that had been consecrated to God. 12:20-28
Duty.
  Must be faithful in giving a true tithe. 26:12-15
  Must not abuse the blood nor misuse the tithe. 12:15-18
  Must support the ministers of God. 12:19
  Must **t.** 14:22-29
How a person robs God. 5:19
Kind of. Three-year **t.** 26:12-15
Seven truths about **t.** 14:22-29

TORAH (See **LAW**)

TONGUE
Duty. Must never tell a lie, never give a false testimony or witness. 5:20

TRANSVESTITE - TRANSVESTISM
Duty. Must not wear the clothes of the other sex. 22:5
Fact. Transvestism sometimes leads to homosexuality. 22:5
Warning. Is an abomination, detested by God. 22:5

TREASURE
Title of. Believers. 7:6-11

TREE
Discussed. Law dealing with a man hung on a tree. 21:22-23
Type - Symbol - Picture of. The crucifixion of Christ. 21:22-23, Types Chart

TRIALS
Fact. God will enable us to conquer all the trials & temptations of life. 16:13-15, Thgt.2

TRIBES OF ISRAEL
Prophecy concerning.
  Asher. 33:24-25
  Benjamin. 33:12
  Dan. 33:22
  Ephraim. 33:13-17
  Gad. 33:20-21
  Issachar. 33:18-19
  Joseph. 33:13-17
  Judah. 33:7
  Levi. 33:8-11
  Manasseh. 33:13-17
  Naphtali. 33:23
  Reuben. 33:6
  Zebulun. 33:18-19

TRIBUNAL, THE CENTRAL
Duty. Must wrestle with & grasp difficult legal cases. 17:8-13
Location of. At the sanctuary or Tabernacle & later at the temple after it had been built. 17:8-13
Power of. The verdict or decision of the High Court had to be carried out. 17:8-13

TRIUMPH
Blessing of. Over all enemies. 2:24–3:11; 33:26-29, Types Chart

TRUTH
Source of. God. 5:20
Standard of. The Holy Word of God. 13:1-5

TWELVE SPIES
Discussed. Sent out by Moses. 1:18-39

U

UNBELIEF
Results of. 1:18-39

UNBELIEVER - UNBELIEVERS
Practices of. Mutilation of the body. 14:1-2

UNBORN, THE
Question.
  What does the Bible say about the creation of man & the fetus or unborn baby in the womb? 5:17, D.S. #1
  What does the medical profession say about the fetus or unborn child in the mother's womb? 5:17, D.S. #1
  When does the unborn child become a human being? 5:17, D.S. #1

UNDEFILED
Duty. Must keep ourselves free from defilement. 14:3-21

UNDERPRIVILEGED
Duty to.
  Must be generous to the poor. 15:7-11; 23:19-20
  Must meet the needs of the poor. 15:1-6, Thgt.1
  Must not take advantage of the poor & needy worker. 24:14-15
Law governing. 24:17-18
Protection of. The food supply for the poor & underprivileged. 24:19-22
Work for. Must be provided for the poor & underprivileged. 24:19-22

UNLEAVENED BREAD, FESTIVAL OF
Type - Symbol of.
  The immediate need & urgency to begin the march to the promised land. 16:1-8, Thgt.2, Types Chart
  The need & urgency for the believer to be freed from the world & its enslavement to sin & death. 16:1-8, Thgt.2, Types Chart

UNINTENTIONAL SIN (See **SIN**)

URIM
Type - Symbol of. The High Priest seeking God's will for the people. 33:8-11

V

VAIN (See **MISUSE**)
Meaning of. 5:11

VENGEANCE
Warning. Vengeance belongs to God. 32:32-35

VICTORIOUS LIFE
Caused by. Obedience. 2:16-3:29, Introduction; 5:28-33
Charge. To be victorious over all the enemies of the promised land. 11:22-25

VICTORY
Assurance of.
  By God. 1:4-5, Thgt.1; 1:6-8; 20:1-4; 33:7, Thgt.1
  By Moses. 3:21-22
  By our obedience. 28:7
Blessing of.
  Over all enemies. 33:26-29
  Promised to the obedient person. 28:7
  Spiritual victory & purity. 33:26-29
Conditions for.
  Must be obedient to God. 28:7
  Must pledge our allegiance to God. 11:22-25, Thgt.1
Discussed. Over enemies. 2:16-3:29, Introduction; 7:17-26
Kind of.

INDEX

Over enemies of life. 1:4-5; 2:24-3:11; 9:1-6, Types Chart
Spiritual. 1:8, D.S.#1; 2:24-3:11, Types Chart
Promised. By God. 11:22-25; 28:7
Source of. God. By the power of. 9:1-6

VIOLENCE
Warning. Must not murder. 5:17

VIRGIN
Duty. Of young men & women. Must keep themselves sexually pure. 22:13-21

VOW - VOWS (See COMMIT - COMMITMENTS)
Duty.
Must do exactly what you vow or pledge. 23:21-23
Must know that it is better not to make a vow than to make it & not fulfill it. 23:21-23
Must not be slow to pay your vows or pledges to God. 23:21-23

VULGARITY
Judgment of. God will hold the guilty accountable. 5:11
Warning. Must never misuse, never take the name of the LORD God in vain. 5:11

W

WAGE - WAGES
Duty toward. The employee.
Must not be hard-hearted or tightfisted. 15:12-18
Must not take advantage of the poor & needy worker. 24:14-15
Law governing the payment of wages. 25:4
Payment of. Within Israelite society. Each day before sunset. 24:14-15

WALK, SPIRITUAL
Of the believer. 28:6

WAR - WARS
Commitment to. Essential in any warfare. 20:5-9, Thgt.1
Inhumane. Judgment of. 25:17-19
Is hell. 20:1-20
Kind of. Holy war. 20:1-4, Thgt.1
Prisoners of. Treatment of female w. prisoners. 21:10-14, Types Chart
Strategy.
For conquering distant enemies. 20:10-20, esp. vv.10-15
For conquering immediate enemies. 20:10-20, esp. vv.16-18
For preserving the land for the public good. 20:10-20, esp. vv.19-20

WARFARE
Discussed.
The language of w. is a picture of the believer's spiritual battle against the enemies of this world. 20:1-4, Thgt.1
The need for total commitment by all in mobilizing for war. 20:5-9

WARFARE, SPIRITUAL
Picture of. Laws that govern the conduct of war. The believer's spiritual warfare against the enemies of this world. 20:1-20, Types Chart

WARN - WARNING
Against breaking the covenant. 29:16-19; 30:17-18
Against continued disobedience & rebellion. 9:22-10:1-11
Against disobedience. 9:7-21
Against enticement. Must guard against allowing an entire city or community to seduce you. 13:12-18
Against false gods. Must guard against all false gods & false worship. 11:16-17; 13:12-18
Against false prophets. Of being seduced by a false prophet. 13:1-5
Against false teachers. Of being seduced by a false prophet. 13:1-5
Against false worship. Must guard against all false gods & false worship. 4:15-31; 11:16-17
Against family being a stumblingblock. 13:6-11
Against forgetting God. 8:11-20
Against hypocrisy. Must not live lives of hypocrisy. 29:16-19
Against idolatry. Must guard against all false gods & false worship. 4:15-31; 17:2-7
Against occult practices. 18:9-14
Against provoking God. To anger & judgment. 9:7-21
Against self-righteousness. 9:1-6
Against sin. 3:23-29
Described as. 4:9-14
Discussed. Sin disrupts our march to the promised land. 2:16, Thgt.1
Duty.
Must guard against all false gods & false worship. 4:15-31
Must not let your experiences with the LORD nor the Ten Commandments slip from your heart. 4:9-14
Must never misuse, never take the name of the LORD God in vain. 5:11
Message of. Of the song & the law. 32:44-47
Of God. 32:3-4
Of judgment. God chastises the believer who sins, no matter who he is. 3:23-29, Thgt.1

WEEKS, FEAST OF (See HARVEST, FESTIVAL OF)
Type - Symbol of. Pentecost, of salvation. 16:9-12, Thgt.1, Types Chart

WEEP - WEEPING
Reasons for. Because of Israel's defeat, not because of their disobedience. 1:40-46

WEIGHTS
Duty. Must prevent the wrong of dishonesty in business dealings. 25:13-16
Law governing dishonest business dealings. 25:13-16

WIDOW
Law governing. 24:17-18
Protection of. 24:17-18

WILDERNESS WANDERINGS, THE
Deliverance through. 2:1-15

Duty.
Must march through this world to the promised land of heaven. 16:13-15
Must remember God's guidance through the wilderness wanderings. 8:2-10
Purpose of. To humble and test Israel. 8:2-6
Type - Symbol of. God saving His people from the slavery of Egypt. 32:7-14, Types Chart

WITCHCRAFT (See FORTUNE-TELLING)

WITNESS - WITNESSES - WITNESSING
Duty.
Must be a strong testimony & witness for the LORD. 11:18-21
Must not bear the marks of false religion. 14:1-2
Must use God's commandments as a witness. 6:6-9
Heaven & earth. Appeal to. To hear the words & message of the song of Moses. 31:30-32:2
In court. Must not commit perjury. 19:15-21
Instructions for. Three basic, essential steps. 11:18-21
Result of.
Celebrating the feast of Pentecost: power to witness. 16:9-12, Thgt.1, Types Chart
Having a strong testimony & witness. 11:18-21

WOMEN
Ministry to. Women with an unwanted pregnancy. 5:17, D.S. #1
Respect for. Female war prisoners. 21:10-14, Types Chart
Treatment of. Female war prisoners. 21:10-14, Types Chart

WORD OF GOD
Abuse of. Must not abuse. 4:1-5
Adding to. Must not add to or take away from. 4:1-5
Discussed.
God gave His Word in order to show us how to live. 31:9-13, Thgt.1
God gave us the Word of God to warn us against sin. 31:24-29
The Living Word of God is a far greater gift than even the Written Word of God. 30:11-16, Thgt.1
Duty.
Must be preached. 4:44-49, Thgt.1
Must hear the law, learn the law, & obey the law. 5:1
Must learn the Word of God before we can enter the promised land. 1:3
Must read & teach the law to the people of God. 31:9-13
Importance of. Preserving and correct placement. 31:24-29
Standard of truth. 13:1-5

492

INDEX

WORK - WORKERS - WORKING
Blessings of. Promised to the obedient person. 28:8
Duty toward.
  Must not be hard-hearted or tightfisted. 15:12-18
  Must not take advantage of the poor & needy worker. 24:14-15
For the poor. Work must be provided for the poor & underprivileged. 24:19-22
Law governing the payment of wages. 25:4
On the Sabbath. 5:12-15
Payment of. The person who works deserves to be paid. 25:4
Protection of.
  A man's livelihood. 24:6
  The poor worker. 24:14-15
Results of. Produces a sense of achievement & success, a sense of fulfillment & satisfaction. 28:8
Wages of. The person who works deserves to be paid. 25:4
When to w. 5:12-15

WORKS OF GOD
Among Israel. Five basic reasons why the covenant between God & man was needed. 29:2-9

WORLDLINESS (See **CORRUPTION**)
Duty. Must not conform to the religious practices of the world. 12:29-32
Warning. Scripture warns against w. 33:24-25

WORSHIP
Center. Duty to. Must seek the place where God's name is honored. 12:5-7
Discussed. Is shaped & determined by God, not man. 27:1-8
Duties. True w.
  Must have a spirit of discernment between what is allowed & forbidden. 12:20-28
  Must keep the worship of God clean, pure by excluding the unclean. 23:1-8
  Must not abuse the blood nor misuse the tithe. 12:15-18
  Must not conform to the religious practices of the world. 12:29-32
  Must not worship as we each see fit, but as God dictates. 12:8-14
  Must obey the laws & regulations of God. 12:1
  Must reject all false worship. 12:2-4
  Must seek the place where God's name is honored. 12:5-7
  Must support the ministers of God. 12:19
Images of.
Must not worship God through physical, visible objects. 5:8-10
Must not make any idol nor worship or serve any false god. 5:8-10
Laws that regulate the worship of God. 12:1-32
List. Of those people excluded from the assembly of worship. 23:1-8
Meaning of. Two meanings of. 12:1
On the Sabbath. 5:12-15
Picture of. True worship. 12:1-32
Seeking. True w. of God. 12:5-7
Type - Symbol of. The Tabernacle, the place where God's holy presence was symbolized. 12:5-7
Warning.
  Must guard against all false gods & false worship. 4:15-31
  Must not make any idol nor worship or serve any false god. 5:8-10

WORSHIP, FALSE (See **FALSE WORSHIPPERS**)
Danger of.
  Being seduced by a loved one or close friend. 13:6-11
  Being seduced by an entire city or community. 13:12-18
  Being seduced by a false prophet. 13:1-5
Discussed. The Golden Calf. Israel's sin of idolatry and false worship. 9:7-21
Duty.
  Must destroy all the false worship of enemies. 7:1-5
  Must guard against false worship & false gods. 11:16-17
  Must reject all false worship. 12:2-4
Fact. Permeates society. 12:29-32, Thgt.1
Forbidden. Must refuse to follow false gods and false worship. 28:14
Result of.
  A terrifying judgment. 29:20-29
  Bears bitter & poisonous fruit (wormwood). 29:16-19
  Dangers of being seduced into false worship. 13:1-18
Warning.
  Must guard against all false gods & false worship. 4:15-31; 11:16-17; 17:2-7
  Must guard against being seduced by a loved one or close friend. 13:6-11
  Must guard against the false prophet & the interpreter of dreams. 13:1-5
  Must not conform to the religious practices of the world. 12:29-32
  Must not make any idol nor worship or serve any false god. 5:8-10

WORSHIP SERVICE
Dedication of Covenant Memorial. 27:1-8

WORSHIP, TRUE
Duty.
  Must have a spirit of discernment between what is allowed & forbidden. 12:20-28
  Must keep the worship of God clean, pure by excluding the unclean. 23:1-8
  Must not abuse the blood nor misuse the tithe. 12:15-18
  Must not conform to the religious practices of the world. 12:29-32
  Must not worship as we each see fit, but as God dictates. 12:8-14
  Must obey the laws & regulations of God. 12:1
  Must reject all false worship. 12:2-4
  Must seek the place where God's name is honored. 12:5-7
  Must support the ministers of God. 12:19
List. Of examples. 12:8-14, Thgt.1

WRATH
Of God. God aroused His w. to know no limits. 32:19-27

WRITINGS
Of Moses. Song of warning & witness. 31:14-23
Of the Book of the Law. Preserving and correct placement. 31:24-29

Z

ZAMZUMMITES
Discussed. Were giants of the land, a tall race of people. 2:17-23
History of. Were defeated by the Ammonites. 2:17-23

ZEBULUN, TRIBE OF
Blessing of.
  To call people to seek God through worship & sacrifice. 33:18-19
  To grow rich from sea & land trade. 33:18-19
  To rejoice in all their activities. 33:18-19
Example of. Had a unique opportunity to serve other tribes. 33:18-19, Thgt.1
Prophecy concerning.
  To call people to seek God through worship & sacrifice. 33:18-19
  To grow rich from sea & land trade. 33:18-19
  To rejoice in all their activities. 33:18-19

OUTLINE BIBLE RESOURCES

This material, like similar works, has come from imperfect man and is thus susceptible to human error. We are nevertheless grateful to God for both calling us and empowering us through His Holy Spirit to undertake this task. Because of His goodness and grace, *The Preacher's Outline & Sermon Bible*® New Testament and Old Testament volumes are now complete.

The Minister's Personal Handbook, The Believer's Personal Handbook, and other helpful **Outline Bible Resources** are available in printed form as well as releasing electronically on various software programs.

God has given the strength and stamina to bring us this far. Our confidence is that as we keep our eyes on Him and remain grounded in the undeniable truths of the Word, we will continue to produce other helpful Outline Bible Resources for God's dear servants to use in their Bible Study and discipleship.

We offer this material, first, to Him in whose Name we labor and serve and for whose glory it has been produced, and, second, to everyone everywhere who preaches and teaches the Word.

Our daily prayer is that each volume will lead thousands, millions, yes, even billions, into a better understanding of the Holy Scriptures and a fuller knowledge of Jesus Christ the Incarnate Word, of whom the Scriptures so faithfully testify.

You will be pleased to know that Leadership Ministries Worldwide partners with Christian organizations, printers, and mission groups around the world to make Outline Bible Resources available and affordable in many countries and foreign languages. It is our goal that *every* leader around the world, both clergy and lay, will be able to understand God's Holy Word and to present God's message with more clarity, authority, and understanding—all beyond his or her own power.

LEADERSHIP MINISTRIES WORLDWIDE
PO Box 21310 • Chattanooga, TN 37424-0310
423) 855-2181 • FAX (423) 855-8616
info@outlinebible.org
www.outlinebible.org - FREE Download materials

7/16

LEADERSHIP MINISTRIES WORLDWIDE

Publishers of Outline Bible Resources

- **THE PREACHER'S OUTLINE & SERMON BIBLE® (POSB)** • KJV – NIV

NEW TESTAMENT

Matthew 1 (chapters 1–15)
Matthew 2 (chapters 16–28)
Mark
Luke
John
Acts
Romans

1 & 2 Corinthians
Galatians, Ephesians, Philippians, Colossians
1 & 2 Thessalonians, 1 & 2 Timothy, Titus, Philemon
Hebrews, James
1 & 2 Peter, 1, 2, & 3 John, Jude
Revelation
Master Outline & Subject Index

OLD TESTAMENT

Genesis 1 (chapters 1–11)
Genesis 2 (chapters 12–50)
Exodus 1 (chapters 1–18)
Exodus 2 (chapters 19–40)
Leviticus
Numbers
Deuteronomy
Joshua
Judges, Ruth
1 Samuel
2 Samuel

1 Kings
2 Kings
1 Chronicles
2 Chronicles
Ezra, Nehemiah, Esther
Job
Psalms 1 (chapters 1-41)
Psalms 2 (chapters 42-106)
Psalms 3 (chapters 107-150)
Proverbs
Ecclesiastes, Song of Solomon

Isaiah 1 (chapters 1-35)
Isaiah 2 (chapters 36-66)
Jeremiah 1 (chapters 1-29)
Jeremiah 2 (chapters 30-52), Lamentations
Ezekiel
Daniel, Hosea
Joel, Amos, Obadiah, Jonah, Micah, Nahum
Habakkuk, Zephaniah, Haggai, Zechariah, Malachi

Print versions of all Outline Bible Resources are available in various forms.

- **The Preacher's Outline & Sermon Bible New Testament — 3 Vol. Hardcover • KJV – NIV**
- ***What the Bible Says to the Believer* — The Believer's Personal Handbook**
  11 Chs. – Over 500 Subjects, 300 Promises, & 400 Verses Expounded - Italian Imitation Leather or Paperback
- ***What the Bible Says to the Minister* — The Minister's Personal Handbook**
  12 Chs. - 127 Subjects - 400 Verses Expounded - Italian Imitation Leather or Paperback
- **Practical Word Studies In the New Testament** — 2 Vol. Hardcover Set
- **The Teacher's Outline & Study Bible™ - Various New Testament Books**
  Complete 30 - 45 minute lessons – with illustrations and discussion questions
- **Practical Illustrations — Companion to the POSB**
  Arranged by topic and Scripture reference
- **What the Bible Says About Series – Various Subjects**
- **OBR on various digital platforms**
  See current digital providers on our website at www.outlinebible.org
- **Non-English Translations of various books**
  See our website for more information or contact our office

— Contact LMW for quantity orders and information —

LEADERSHIP MINISTRIES WORLDWIDE or Your Local Christian Bookstore
PO Box 21310 • Chattanooga, TN 37424-0310
(423) 855-2181 (9am – 5pm Eastern) • FAX (423) 855-8616
E-mail - info@outlinebible.org • Order online at www.outlinebible.org

LEADERSHIP MINISTRIES WORLDWIDE

PURPOSE STATEMENT

LEADERSHIP MINISTRIES WORLDWIDE exists to equip ministers, teachers, and laymen in their understanding, preaching, and teaching of God's Word by publishing and distributing worldwide ***The Preacher's Outline & Sermon Bible®*** and related **Outline Bible Resources**; to reach & disciple men, women, boys and girls for Jesus Christ.

MISSION STATEMENT

1. To make the Bible so understandable – its truth so clear and plain – that men and women everywhere, whether teacher or student, preacher or hearer, can grasp its message and receive Jesus Christ as Savior, and…

2. To place the Bible in the hands of all who will preach and teach God's Holy Word, verse by verse, precept by precept, regardless of the individual's ability to purchase it.

The **Outline Bible Resources** have been given to LMW for printing and distribution worldwide at/below cost, by those who remain anonymous. One fact, however, is as true today as it was in the time of Christ:

THE GOSPEL IS FREE, BUT THE COST OF TAKING IT IS NOT

LMW depends on the generous gifts of believers with a heart for Him and a love for the lost. They help pay for the printing, translating, and distributing of **Outline Bible Resources** into the hands of God's servants worldwide, who will present the Gospel message with clarity, authority, and understanding beyond their own.

LMW was incorporated in the state of Tennessee in July 1992 and received IRS 501 (c)(3) non-profit status in March 1994. LMW is an international, nondenominational mission organization. All proceeds from USA sales, along with donations from donor partners, go directly to underwrite translation and distribution projects of **Outline Bible Resources** to preachers, church and lay leaders, and Bible students around the world.

www.ingramcontent.com/pod-product-compliance
Lightning Source LLC
Chambersburg PA
CBHW080802020526
44114CB00046B/2706